NATIONAL UNDERWRITER

a division of ALM Global, LLC

2023 SOCIAL SECURITY & MEDICARE FACTS

S0-AXJ-368

Michael D. Thomas, J.D., Author
Marc Kiner, CPA and Jim Blair, Contributing Authors

2023 Social Security & Medicare Facts is a one-stop guide for attorneys, CPAs, and retirement and financial planning professionals to advise on tax and policy changes affecting Social Security and Medicare. Organized in a unique and convenient Q&A format, this book helps professionals find exactly what they're looking for quickly and easily to solve clients' important planning issues in a timely manner.

With 1015 questions & answers, this trusted title focuses comprehensively covers all aspects of Social Security & Medicare, including:

- How Social Security retirement and disability benefits are determined
- Effects of other types of income on Social Security benefits
- How to incorporate Social Security and Medicare benefits into planning techniques
- Social Security filing and tax requirements
- Explanations of Medicare coverage details
- Filing and timing requirements for Medicare coverage
- Integration of Medicare Advantage plans
- Medicare claims and appeals process
- Medigap insurance coverage

The 2023 edition has been fully revised, featuring:

- Updated questions & answers on changes related to the CARES Act
- Effect of the Inflation Reduction Act on Medicare Part D and Part D Drug Costs
- Effect of the American Rescue Plan (ARP) Act on Social Security Economic Impact Payments
- Updated eligibility rules for Home Health Care
- Expanded coverage of Part B services

- Expanded coverage of Durable Medical Equipment coverage

- Effect of the new changes in the Stark Law on Medicare Billing

- Coverage of the Program for All-Inclusive Care for the Elderly (PACE)

- New coverage of effect of loss of citizenship/permanent resident alien status on Social Security and ability of non-resident aliens to collect

- Enhanced coverage of the impact of divorce and remarriage on Social Security eligibility and benefits

- Effect of COVID financial assistance on Social Security income

- Expanded coverage of the Government Pension Offset (GPO) and the Windfall Elimination Provision (WEP)

- Expanded coverage of methods for curing overpayments from Social Security and SSDI

- Expanded coverage of non-covered items and services by Medicare

- Changes in coverages under Medicare Advantage, Medicare gap policies and Medicare appeals

- Expanded coverage of disability benefits for Social Security, military, government, and railroad workers

- Changes in railroad worker coverage and the differences from Social Security

- Expanded coverage of Medicare appeals process

- Additional coverage of military retirement including expansion of coverage of the new blended retirement program, military disability pay, and coverage for National Guard and Reservists, including the effect of the CARES Act on the TSP program

- Additional coverage of changes in Survivor Benefit Plan – Dependency Indemnity Compensation

- 2023 inflation-adjusted numbers for Social Security and COLA increases

Authored by retirement planning and estate planning experts, *2023 Social Security & Medicare Facts* is the practical, comprehensive reference you can rely on.

Related titles also available:

- *Telemedicine Facts*

- *Healthcare Reform Facts*

- *Health Savings Accounts Facts*

- *The Tools & Techniques of Trust Planning*

- *The Tools & Techniques of Estate Planning for Modern Families*

- *Tax Facts on Insurance & Employee Benefits*

- *Tax Facts on Investments*

- *Tax Facts on Individuals & Small Business*

- *The Tools & Techniques of Employee Benefit & Retirement Planning*

- *Field Guide to Estate Planning, Business Planning & Employee Benefits*

For customer service questions or to place orders for any of our products, please call 1-800-543-0874 or email CustomerService@nuco.com.

2023
SOCIAL SECURITY & MEDICARE FACTS

- Retirement, Spousal, Survivor, and Disability Benefits
- Qualifying, Calculating and Filing for Benefits
- Medicare and Medicare Advantage • Taxation of Social Security Benefits • Government Pension Offset/Windfall Elimination Provision • Loss and Reduction of Benefits • Delayed Retirement Credits • Medicare Supplement Plans • Military and Veterans Benefits • Government Retirement Benefits • Railroad Retirement • Medicaid • Case Studies and Benefit Maximization • COVID-19/Coronavirus • Impact of Telemedicine • PACE Program

Michael D. Thomas, J.D., Author
Marc Kiner, CPA, Contributing Author
Jim Blair, Contributing Author

This publication is designed to provide accurate and authoritative information in regard to the subject matter covered. It is sold with the understanding that the publisher is not engaged in rendering legal, accounting or other professional service. If legal advice or other expert assistance is required, the services of a competent professional person should be sought.— *From a Declaration of Principles jointly adopted by a Committee of the American Bar Association and a Committee of Publishers and Associations.*

Circular 230 Notice – The content in this publication is not intended or written to be used, and it cannot be used, for the purposes of avoiding U.S. tax penalties.

ISBN 978-1-954096-84-4

Copyright © 2019, 2020, 2021, 2022, 2023

The National Underwriter Company
a division of ALM Global, LLC
4157 Olympic Blvd., Suite 225
Erlanger, KY 41018

All rights reserved.

No part of this publication may be reproduced, stored in a retrieval system, or transmitted, in any form or by any means, electronic, mechanical, photocopying, recording, or otherwise, without prior written permission of the publisher.

Printed in U.S.A.

The National Underwriter Company publishes the following Social Security/Medicare publications:

Social Security & Medicare Facts
Social Security Planner
Medicare Planner

ABOUT THE NATIONAL UNDERWRITER COMPANY
a division of ALM Global, LLC

For over 125 years, The National Underwriter Company, *a division of ALM Global, LLC* has been the first in line with the targeted tax, insurance, and financial planning information you need to make critical business decisions. Boasting nearly a century of expert experience, our reputable editors are dedicated to putting accurate and relevant information right at your fingertips. With *Tax Facts, FC&S® Expert Coverage Interpretation, Tools & Techniques, Field Guide, Insurance Coverage Law Center, Property & Casualty Coverage Guides* and other resources available in print, eBook, or online, you can be assured that as the industry evolves National Underwriter will be at the forefront with the thorough and easy-to-use resources you rely on for success.

Update Service Notification

This National Underwriter Company publication is regularly updated to include coverage of developments and changes that affect the content. If you did not purchase this publication directly from The National Underwriter Company, *a division of ALM Global, LLC* and you want to receive these important updates sent on a 30-day review basis and billed separately, please contact us at (800) 543-0874. Or you can mail your request with your name, company, address, and the title of the book to:

The National Underwriter Company
a division of ALM Global, LLC
4157 Olympic Boulevard
Suite 225
Erlanger, KY 41018

If you purchased this publication from The National Underwriter Company, *a division of ALM Global, LLC,* directly, you have already been registered for the update service.

Contact Information

To order any National Underwriter Company title, please

- call 1-800-543-0874, 8-6 ET Monday – Thursday and 8 to 5 ET Friday

- online bookstore at www.nationalunderwriter.com, or

- mail to Orders Department, The National Underwriter Company, *a division of ALM Global, LLC*, 4157 Olympic Blvd., Ste. 225, Erlanger, KY 41018

ACKNOWLEDGEMENTS

I would like to take this opportunity to extend my gratitude to the editorial and production staff, especially Susan Grusser, and Daniele Tralongo, of National Underwriter/ALM Global, LLC – without their efforts, this book would not be possible. As always, I appreciate the patience of my family who supported my efforts to create and complete this volume.

DEDICATION

I once again dedicate this book firstly to the memory of my parents, Angeline Buccigrossi Thomas and Donald A. Thomas, through whose hard work and sacrifice I was provided the education to be able to undertake the task of creating this book. Additionally, I dedicate this work to my family – my wife, Rita, who has heard me speaking *ad nauseum* about Social Security and Medicare for years (while awake and occasionally asleep), and my children, Caitlin, and Caleb, who inspire me. I would also like to dedicate this book to my friend Audrey, whose questions about Medicare and Social Security have provided additional topics as well as underscoring in my mind that the understanding of these benefits by both caregivers and administrators is critical to ensuring both proper care and positive outcomes for beneficiaries.

Special thanks go out to the civil servants who tirelessly and effectively administer Social Security and Medicare benefits for all of us.

Michael D. Thomas
October 2022

PREFACE TO 2023 SOCIAL SECURITY AND MEDICARE FACTS

The 2023 edition of *Social Security and Medicare Facts* is designed to provide you with all the information needed to help your clients make the most of their Social Security and Medicare benefits. Our goal is to supply you with an up-to=date hands-on reference tool administering both the basic information about Social Security, Medicare, and Medicaid, as well as providing answers to the more complex and confusing aspects and issues associated with these programs.

For the 2023 edition, we have expanded our coverage of these topics by updating information on planning techniques to help your clients maximize their Social Security benefits as well as changes related to the Inflation Reduction Act, the American Rescue Plan Act (ARP) and the CARES Act. Also, questions have been added and updated on telehealth and telemedicine when it is available. We have enhanced and updated information affecting retirement and disability benefits including spousal, parent, survivor, child, and those for the widowed. Additionally we have updated eligibility rules for Home Health and Home Care services, expanded our coverage of Part B services and coverage of Durable Medical Equipment (DME). We continue to cover the continuing effect of the sweeping changes wrought by the 2015 Bi-Partisan Budget Act continuing to affect individuals in the use of "restricted application" to maximize their retirement benefits. In addition, there are updated sections covering how benefits can be reduced or lost though the Windfall Elimination Provision and the Government Pension Offset, loss of citizenship, as well as the effects of divorce and remarriage. There is expanded coverage on important topics such as delayed retirement credits, self-employment income, and additional and updated materials regarding reduction of benefits because of the effect of "excess" earnings. We have also broadened coverage of Social Security and Medicare appeals processes. We have updated the Case Studies to illustrate dozens of examples of how certain actions will affect the amount that your clients collect – or do not collect – from Social Security during their retirement years.

In addition to reviewing the existing questions, we have added dozens of new questions expanding our coverage of nearly every topic as well as updating benefits amounts and costs to 2023 values. State taxation of Social Security benefits have been updated and expanded. We also expanded our coverage of Medicare, Medicare Advantage, Medigap policies, and Medicaid, including the Medicaid expansion under the Affordable Care Act as well as a new section discussing Program for All-Inclusive Care for the Elderly (PACE), Our coverage of benefits relating to military pensions, government pensions and railroad retirement was expanded, as well. Additionally, the effects of the significant changes to the Stark Law on Medicare billing are discussed.

Whether your clients work in the private sector, the government (federal, state, or local), the railroad industry, or the military, this book has information to help them to effectively plan for understanding, collecting, and maximizing their retirement, disability, and survivor benefits. As an advisor, you can use these reference tools to help present your clients with the knowledge necessary to know what to expect in retirement, what their survivors can expect in benefits, and what is available if they should unexpectedly become disabled.

I want to thank my contributing authors, Marc Kiner and Jim Blair who have again updated the Case Studies and are truly experts in how individuals can assure themselves of gaining maximum advantage of their Social Security benefits. In addition, Marc and Jim have added "challenge questions" in Case Studies portion as well as questions and answer that they have received from their own clients. My thanks also extend to everyone at National Underwriter Company/ALM Global, LLC who have worked diligently to ensure that this 2023 edition, especially Danielle Tralongo and Susan Gruesser whose efforts have ensured that this book remains a high-quality project.

Michael D. Thomas
October 2022

ABOUT THE AUTHOR
Michael D. Thomas, J.D.

Michael D. Thomas is an author and consultant and has served as the Manager of Online Product Development and as a Senior Editor with the National Underwriter Company, a division of ALM Global, LLC. In addition, Mike has served in Compliance and Policy Management for CareSource, a major commercial healthcare insurance company and provider of Medicare and Medicaid services, as a consultant to the State of Ohio Department of Medicaid and as a writer for "The Digital Broker Podcast," which focuses on insurance technology and operations. Mike currently works with a California healthcare provider, being responsible for Legal and Regulatory Compliance. In addition to authoring *2023 Healthcare Reform Facts*, Mike has also authored *2023 Social Security & Medicare Facts, 2022 Telemedicine Facts* and has been responsible for the editorial process and development of other healthcare and insurance publications including *Advisor's Guide to Long Term Care 2nd Edition, Social Security & Medicare Facts, ERISA Facts*, and *Health Savings Accounts Facts* for The National Underwriter Company as well as designing, implementing, and managing the *NUPro Healthcare Reform* online service. Mike has also authored numerous articles on healthcare reform, Social Security, Medicare, and Insurance issues. He has developed, hosted, and taught webinars on Healthcare Reform and Social Security, including *"The Affordable Care Act and the Employer Mandate," "The Affordable Care Act and the Cadillac Tax – Use the Delay for Your Advantage!", "How to Successfully Navigate the Latest Changes to the Affordable Care Act"*, and *"The Impact of Social Security on Retirement Plans"*.

Prior to joining National Underwriter/ALM Global, LLC, Mike spent over twenty-five years with LexisNexis®, where he was responsible for the editorial content and new product development of new online and traditional legal products, including *Health Law, Insurance Law, Social Security Law, Labor & Employment Law, Family Law*, as well as other legal research tools. In addition, he worked as a Field Agent for Knights of Columbus Insurance specializing in life, health, disability income, long-term care insurance as well as annuity sales.

Mike has a *Bachelor of Arts* from Tufts University and a *Juris Doctorate* from the University of Dayton.

ABOUT THE CONTRIBUTING AUTHORS

Marc Kiner is the President of Premier Social Security Consulting, LLC, and has thirty years' experience in public accounting. Marc's primary areas of service are to privately-held businesses and to individuals. He consults with clients on a variety of complex tax and business issues. Marc obtained his Bachelor of Science degree in Accounting and Finance and a master's degree from the University of Cincinnati. He is licensed to practice as a CPA in the State of Ohio.

Jim Blair is the lead Social Security consultant at Premier Social Security Consulting, LLC. A former Social Security Administrator, Operations Supervisor and a District Manager, Mr. Blair has **over thirty-five years' experience** in helping individuals manage their Social Security benefits, retirement, survivors, disability, and health insurance.

SUMMARY TABLE OF CONTENTS

LIST OF QUESTIONS
PART I: SOCIAL SECURITY
UNDERSTANDING AND PLANNING FOR SOCIAL SECURITY

21. What makes an individual eligible for the status of "qualified alien"?

22. What enables a "qualified alien" to be considered eligible for SSI benefits?

23. How are Social Security numbers verified?

24. How long does it take to get a Social Security number and card for a newborn baby?

25. How are Social Security numbers assigned?

26. How can a person check on his Social Security earnings record and receive an estimate of future Social Security benefits?

27. What will happen to Social Security benefit payments when the Trust Fund becomes insolvent?

28. Where and how does a person apply for Social Security benefits?

29. Where and how does a person apply for Social Security benefits if they live overseas?

30. How can beneficiaries determine if they can receive Social Security benefits outside the United States?

31. Which government agency issues a beneficiary's Social Security payment?

32. When does a Social Security beneficiary receive a monthly direct deposit?

33. To whom is a benefit payment made payable and how are benefits received?

34. If a husband and wife are both receiving monthly benefits, do they receive one or two monthly payments?

35. If several children are entitled to benefits, will each child receive a separate payment?

36. Can a power of attorney be granted for the purpose of collecting and managing payments?

37. Can Social Security benefits be assigned?

38. Can Social Security benefits be attached for the beneficiary's debts?

39. Are Social Security benefits subject to federal taxes?

40. What happens when a Social Security overpayment is made to a Social Security beneficiary by mistake?

41. What are the options for repaying overpayments of Social Security or Supplemental Security Income?

42. Can individuals request a copy of a deceased individual's Social Security number application?

RETIREMENT AND DISABILITY BENEFITS

90. Can a person become entitled to disability benefits after becoming entitled to some other type of Social Security benefit?

91. Will a disabled person lose benefits by refusing to accept rehabilitation services?

92. What are the special rules for disability benefits when alcoholism or drug addiction is involved?

93. What happens when a person works above the Substantial Gainful Activity the first time?

94. When do a person's disability benefits end?

95. Are benefits payable to the family of a disabled worker?

96. If an individual is already collecting a disability benefit, can they suspend their benefits at Full Retirement Age and earn delayed retirement credits?

Same-Sex Marriages

97. Are same-sex couples eligible for the same Social Security benefits as opposite-sex couples?

98. Does a person qualify for a benefit as a spouse (or surviving spouse) if in a civil union, a domestic partnership, or other non-marital legal relationship?

99. Does the Supreme Court case legalizing same-sex marriage affect Medicare?

100. How can someone in a same-sex marriage be sure as to which benefits that he or she is eligible?

101. Must an individual that is receiving Social Security benefits tell the Social Security Administration that they are in a civil union or other non-marital legal relationship?

102. Can same-sex partners with a child put both of their names on a Social Security number record?

103. Will Social Security adjust the Income Related Monthly Adjustment Amounts for an individual who filed a tax return as "single" but has now amended it to "married" for prior years in a same-sex marriage?

104. Should couples in a same-sex marriage or civil union or other non-marital legal relationship inform Social Security if one or the other are receiving Social Security benefits or Supplemental Security Income (SSI)?

105. Must an individual in a same-sex marriage tell Social Security of the marriage?

106. Once the Internal Revenue Service (IRS) recognizes a same-sex marriage and allows an individual to file as "married filing jointly", can that individual have their Income-Related Monthly Adjustment Amounts (IRMAA) removed?

107. Will the Social Security Administration recognize a same-sex marriage that was celebrated in a foreign country?

108. What is a Non-Marital Legal Relationship (NMLR)?

109. What is the process to recognize same-sex marriages?

Spouse's Benefit

110. Is the spouse of a retired or disabled worker entitled to benefits?

111. What is meant by having a child "in care"?

112. Is the divorced spouse of a retired or disabled worker entitled to a spouse's benefits?

113. How does if effect the spousal benefit if the divorced spouse of a retired or disabled worker continues to work?

114. What is the amount of a spouse's benefit?

115. What is the amount of a divorced spouse's benefit?

116. What was the impact of the 2015 Bi-Partisan Budget Act on divorced spouses and their ability to collect?

117. Must a spouse be dependent upon the worker for support to be eligible for a spouse's benefits?

118. May a spouse lose benefits if the worker works or if the spouse works?

119. When does a spouse's benefit end?

120. Will a spouse's benefit be reduced if the spouse is receiving a government pension?

121. In the event of several marriages, which one will the Social Security Administration consider to be valid?

Child's Benefits (Child of Retired or Disabled Worker)

122. Is a child of a retired or disabled parent entitled to Social Security benefits?

123. Can a child who has been married be considered unmarried?

124. When may a child's benefits not be payable?

125. Who is considered a "child" of a retired or disabled worker for benefit purposes?

126. Must a child be dependent upon the worker to qualify for child's benefits?

127. Is a child considered to be dependent upon his father or mother regardless of actual dependency?

Survivor's Benefits

Mother's or Father's Benefit

149. What are the differences between a mother's or father's benefit and a widow's or widower's benefit?

150. Is a mother's or father's benefit payable regardless of the surviving spouse's need?

151. Can a surviving spouse lose some or all of the benefits by working?

152. If the only child in a surviving spouse's care loses benefits by working, will this cause the child's mother or father to lose benefits?

153. Must a surviving spouse file an application for a mother's or father's benefit?

154. When do a mother's or father's benefits begin?

155. When do a mother's or father's benefits end?

156. Will a mother's or father's benefit be reduced if he or she is receiving a government pension?

157. Will a mother's or father's benefits stop when the youngest child (or only child) reaches age sixteen?

158. Does a mother or father continue to receive benefits until the youngest child (or only child) is age twenty-two if the child is attending school?

159. What documentation is needed to apply for mother or father's benefits?

160. What information will be asked of individuals applying for mother or father's benefits?

Child's Benefit (Child of Deceased Worker)

161. Is a child of a deceased worker entitled to Social Security benefits?

162. How are posthumously conceived children treated under Social Security Survivor benefits?

163. How does one become re-entitled to a child's benefit?

164. Must a parent be fully insured at death to qualify the child for a child's benefits?

165. Must a child have been dependent upon the deceased parent to be eligible for a child's benefit?

166. Under what circumstances is a child considered dependent upon a grandparent, step-grandparent, great-grandparent, or step-great-grandparent?

167. Under what circumstances is a child considered dependent upon a stepfather or stepmother?

168. Can a child receive benefits based on a deceased parent's Social Security account, even though the other parent is still living and supporting the child?

169. Is a child age eighteen or over entitled to benefits if attending school?

Widow(er)'s Benefit

Lump-Sum Death Payment

210. What is the amount of the Social Security lump-sum death payment?

211. Is the lump-sum death benefit payable only if the worker was fully insured at death?

212. Must an application be made for the lump-sum death benefit?

213. What documentation and information is needed to apply for the lump-sum death benefit?

Prisoners

214. Can imprisoned individuals get Social Security or SSI payments?

215. How does the No Social Security Benefits for Prisoners Act of 2009 affect prisoners?

216. Which individuals with criminal histories are barred from serving as Representative Payees?

217. What are the pre-release procedures for Social Security or SSI payments?

218. Will benefits start again if the court reverses a conviction?

219. Can benefits be collected by someone who is on home monitoring and must wear an ankle bracelet or other monitoring device?

220. Can benefits be collected by someone who has been transferred from a prison to a halfway house or "residential reentry center" under control of the Department of Corrections?

221. Can benefits be collected by someone who is under civil commitment?

222. If someone is arrested while on parole or probation, will their benefits stop?

COVERAGE

Qualification

223. How does someone become qualified for retirement, survivor, and disability benefits under Social Security?

224. How does someone obtain a quarter of coverage as an employee?

225. How does someone obtain a quarter of coverage as a self-employed person?

226. What calendar quarters cannot be counted as quarters of coverage even though the earnings requirement has been met?

227. How do the requirements of the Social Security Protection Act of 2004 (SSPA) affect insured status?

228. Who is an "alien worker" under the SSPA?

Totalization Agreements

229. How does work performed in a foreign country get taken into consideration for determining insured status?

230. What is a "totalization agreement" as related to social security?

231. With which countries does the United States have totalization agreements?

232. What is the "territoriality rule" as related to totalization agreements?

233. What about self-employed individuals?

234. What about workers exempt from social security taxes?

Fully Insured

235. How does a person become fully insured?

236. Were there other ways of becoming fully insured?

237. Must a person be fully insured to qualify for retirement benefits?

238. How do you determine the number of quarters of coverage needed for a person to be fully insured for retirement benefits?

239. Can a person be fully insured for retirement benefits even though not working in covered employment for many years?

240. Can a person become fully insured after retirement age?

241. How do you determine the number of quarters of coverage needed for a person to be fully insured at death?

242. When is someone deemed to be fully insured?

243. How many credits are necessary to be deemed fully insured?

243.01. When is a deceased World War II vet deemed fully insured?

Currently Insured

244. What benefits are payable if a person is only currently insured at death?

245. When is a person currently insured?

Insured Status for Disability Benefits

246. What insured status requirements must be met to qualify a person for disability benefits?

Computing Benefits

247. In general, how are Social Security benefits determined?

FILING FOR BENEFITS

General Information

248. What procedure should be followed to determine if a person is eligible for Social Security benefits?

249. At what point should the survivors of a deceased worker file for survivor's benefits?

250. When should an application for disability benefits be filed?

251. When should a person file an application for the lump-sum death payment?

Proof Required

252. What proofs are required before survivors' and retirement benefits can be paid?

253. What are acceptable proofs of death?

253.01. Does a Find of Death by a military service prove death?

254. What are the best forms of proof of age and family relationship?

Right to Appeal

255. Is there a review procedure available if a person is disappointed with the Social Security Administration's initial determination regarding benefits?

256. Is there a right to representation on appeal?

257. How can a person appeal the reconsideration determination?

258. How is a hearing request made and how long will it take from the request to the actual hearing?

259. How long are the average delays in Social Security Hearing offices?

260. What will a hearing cost?

261. If an individual disagrees with the hearing decision, may they ask for a review?

262. May a person file a civil action in the United States District Court?

263. Are there situations where the Social Security Administration may not recover an overpayment to a beneficiary?

Disability

Transitional Guarantee Benefit Method

Minimum and Maximum Single Benefits
Increase in Benefits

Reduction in Benefits

Recomputation of Benefits

Disability Freeze

Calculating the Exact Benefit Amount

299. In calculating the exact amount of each monthly benefit, how must the figures be rounded?

Government Pension Offset and Windfall Elimination Provision

300. What is the Government Pension Offset?

301. Who does the Government Pension Offset (GPO) affect?

302. Does the Government Pension Offset reduce an individual's Social Security benefit from their own work?

303. Does the Government Pension Offset affect a disability benefit?

304. Can the GPO reduce a dependent or survivor benefit to zero?

305. Does ineligibility for a dependent or survivor benefit affect Medicare eligibility?

306. If an individual has a government pension from a non-Social Security military reserve pension, is it subject to the GPO?

307. What happens to an individual that retires from non-Social Security employment and begins to draw a government pension and then begins work in a Social Security eligible position?

308. What happens to an individual that takes a government pension from non-Social Security employment as a lump sum?

309. Can both the Government Pension Offset and the Windfall Elimination Provision reduce Social Security benefits?

310. What was the rationale for the GPO?

311. What is an example of a partial offset?

312. What is a government pension?

313. Does the GPO have exceptions?

314. What was the Congressional intent in establishing survivor and disability benefits?

315. Is an individual eligible for both a survivor benefit and a benefit based on their own work record?

316. What is the Windfall Elimination Provision (WEP)?

317. What is the rationale for the Windfall Elimination Provision (WEP)?

318. What is the argument that WEP is unfair?

MAXIMIZATION OF BENEFITS

Year of Retirement

340. If age 62 is the computation age, is there any advantage to waiting until Full Retirement Age (FRA) to collect benefits?

341. Can a person obtain higher retirement benefits by working past full retirement age?

342. Can the retirement age at which unreduced benefits are available ever be increased?

343. How are a beneficiary's benefits figured when he is entitled to a reduced retirement benefit and a larger spouse's benefit simultaneously?

344. What were the advantages and disadvantages of using file and suspend?

345. How did a "restricted application" differ from "file and suspend"?

346. Could both spouses have used "file and suspend" at the same time?

347. Was it possible to file and suspend and file a restricted application?

348. Could both husband and wife file a restricted application for the other's spousal benefit?

349. Could you file and suspend at sixty-two to allow a nonworking spouse who is in ill health to collect one-half of benefit?

350. After filing a restricted application, does one have to wait until reaching age 70 to begin their own benefit?

351. Is it safe to assume that a single person could only use the File and Suspend strategy but not the restricted application?

352. If a spouse filed and suspended by April 29, 2016 and delayed collecting until age 70, would the other spouse get an amount equal to half of the income based on the Delayed Retirement Credits or based on the Full Retirement Age (FRA) benefit?

353. If a person dies after filing and suspending but before receiving benefits can the widow collect that lump sum?

354. If a husband filed and suspended and the wife took spousal benefits at age 62, would the wife get a stepped-up spousal benefit if the husband died at age 72 after delaying his benefit until age 70?

355. What is the best strategy in a situation where the husband is age 66, with an income of $150,000 per year, and the wife is age 68, with an income of $50,000 per year?

356. What option might one use if there is a significant difference in ages between spouses, for example, if the husband is 12 years older than wife?

357. What are the limitations of the "do-over" as an option?

LOSS OF BENEFITS BECAUSE OF "EXCESS" EARNINGS

Retirement Test

358. Can a person lose some or all Social Security benefits by working?

359. What are the components of the "Earnings Test" or "Retirement Test"?

360. What are the general rules for loss of benefits because of excess earnings?

361. What is the monthly exempt amount?

362. How are "excess" earnings charged against benefits?

363. Can a person who is receiving dependent's or survivor's benefits lose benefits by working?

364. If a widow's benefits are withheld because of work, will this necessarily reduce the total amount of benefits payable to the family?

365. Which beneficiaries are not subjected to the Earnings Test?

366. What is the benefit amount when the monthly earnings test applies?

367. How is the loss of benefits figured for the year in which the worker reaches full retirement age?

368. What kinds of income will not count under the Earnings Test and will not cause loss of benefits?

369. Which earnings will count under the Earnings Test and potentially cause loss of benefits?

370. How does the Annual Earnings Test work?

371. How are total earnings computed?

372. Are earnings counted even if the earner was not entitled to benefits for the entire year?

373. Are earnings counted when the earner reaches Full Retirement Age (FRA)?

374. What is meant by "substantial services" in self-employment?

375. Must a Social Security beneficiary report earnings to the Social Security Administration?

376. How are a life insurance agent's first-year and renewal commissions treated for purposes of the retirement test?

377. What is the Foreign Work Test?

TAXATION OF SOCIAL SECURITY BENEFITS

SOCIAL SECURITY TAXES

WAGES AND SELF-EMPLOYMENT INCOME

460. What is the effect if the employee and the spouse or divorced spouse are both railroad employees?

Railroad Retirement Benefits

461. Can the collection of Social Security benefits result in an overpayment of a railroad retirement annuity account?

462. Why is a railroad retirement annuity reduced when a Social Security benefit is also payable?

463. Are there any exceptions to the railroad annuity reduction for Social Security benefits?

464. What is the effect of workers' compensation or disability benefits on railroad retirement?

465. How do dual benefit restrictions apply when both spouses are railroad employees?

466. How does the Tier I pension reduction affect spousal or widow/widower benefits?

467. Are there benefits other than Social Security that will require dual benefit reductions?

468. Can additional earning result in railroad retirement overpayments?

469. How do earnings after retiring affect disability annuities?

470. What effect does railroad work have on the annuity?

471. How does railroad retirement benefits compare to Social Security benefits?

472. Are benefits for recent retirees on the average larger than in prior years?

473. Must retiring railroad employees give up their rights to railroad jobs?

474. Can railroad retirement annuities be garnished or subject to division in property settlements?

475. What events can affect payments to beneficiaries such as spouses, divorced spouses, and widow(er)s?

476. How does leaving railroad work though accepting a buyout affect future entitlement to an annuity under the Railroad Retirement Act?

477. Can Federal, State, or local government pension result in dual benefit reductions in an employee's railroad retirement annuity?

478. Can workers' compensation or public disability benefits affect railroad retirement benefits?

479. Why is a railroad retirement annuity reduced when a Social Security benefit is also payable?

480. Does the Railroad Retirement Board allow for representative payees as does Social Security?

Unemployment and Sickness Benefits

Applying for Railroad Benefits

Disability Benefits

501. Can an individual collect a disability annuity while working?

502. Does working for a railroad labor organization affect the ability to qualify for disability coverage?

503. In order to qualify for a disability, must the applicant give up employment rights?

Survivor Benefits

504. What survivor benefits are payable under the Railroad Retirement Act?

505. How much are monthly survivor benefits under railroad retirement and Social Security?

506. What if service requirements are not met for disability?

507. Are children and other dependents eligible for survivor benefits?

508. What happens to survivors with dual benefits?

509. Are there work and earnings limitations for those receiving survivor annuities?

510. Can survivors' annuities be offset by receipt of other benefits?

511. When do survivor benefits end?

512. What lump-sum death benefits are payable?

513. What reporting should be done when a railroad annuitant dies?

514. How does the public service pension reduction apply to spouse or widow(er)s' benefits?

515. What dual benefit restrictions apply when both parties in a marriage are railroad employees entitled to railroad retirement annuities?

516. How are dual benefits paid to persons entitled to both railroad retirement and Social Security benefits?

Railroad Retirement Taxes

517. What are the railroad retirement tax rates for employees and employers?

518. How do railroad retirement and Social Security payroll taxes compare?

Appeal Process

519. Can an annuitant contest a decision regarding overpayment?

520. How does a person initiate a review of an unfavorable decision on a claim and what are the time limits?

521. What are the second and third stages of the appeals process and time limits?

535. How are those that remain in the "High-3" legacy retirement plan affected?

536. Are members of the United States Public Health Service Commissioned Corps (USPHS) or the National Oceanic and Atmospheric Administration Commissioned (NOAA) Officer Corps affected by the implementation of the BRS?

537. Which is the better plan for individuals to select?

538. Does prior military service under the 2.5 percent legacy system remain as the calculator if someone opts for the BRS system?

539. Does the BRS change the ability to participate in the Survivor Benefit Plan?

540. Does the BRS affect Veteran Affairs disability compensation?

541. What was the REDUX pension plan?

542. Is CSB/REDUX still available to service members?

543. When did service members need to make a choice about BRS?

544. Did it make any difference if someone opted into BRS at the start of 2018 or at the end?

545. If an individual mistakenly opted into the Blended Retirement System, can they change their choice?

546. Did the service member's spouse need to concur with the member's decision to opt into the BRS?

547. Were cadets and midshipmen at the service academies or in Reserve Officer Training Program (ROTC) given a choice between the BRS and the legacy retirement program?

548. Does participation in the BRS affect a service member's ability to participate in the Survivor benefit plan?

549. Can a new service member get a waiver to join the High-3 legacy retirement system?

550. If an individual had a break in service, can they still opt into the Blended Retirement System?

551. What is the Thrift Saving Plan (TSP) and what is the Federal Retirement Thrift Investment Board (FRTIB)?

552. How does the Thrift Saving Plan figure into the BRS?

553. Does the money in the TSP belong to the service member?

554. How much does the Department of Defense (DOD) contribute to the TSP?

555. What effect did the CARES Act have on TSP participants?

556. If a service member is part of the BRS and retires after twenty years, will they still get an annuity?

557. What are the ramifications for the service members remaining in the legacy (High-3) retirement system?

558. Are the retirement proceeds under the BRS subject to division of assets in a divorce?

559. When does an individual begin collecting retirement pay?

560. Does the BRS plan offer a lump sum option?

561. If a service member dies before age sixty-seven, must the lump sum be repaid?

562. Is a service member that serves less than twenty years eligible for a lump sum distribution?

563. Can a service member roll over their lump sum distribution to the TSP?

564. Can a service member take the lump sum payout over several years to minimize the tax liability?

565. What is continuation pay?

566. Who is eligible for continuation pay and how is it calculated?

567. Can continuation pay be deposited into the Thrift Savings Plan (TSP)?

568. How are the eight to twelve years of service calculated for continuation pay?

569. Will a service member be eligible for other bonuses, such as a reenlistment bonus, if they receive continuation pay?

570. Can continuation pay be collected more than one time?

571. Can the service obligation for continuation pay and other bonuses, such as a reenlistment bonus, be served concurrently?

572. Can someone receive continuation pay while in active duty and then complete their obligation in another service or component?

573. If a service member accepts continuation pay for continued service and does not complete the commitment, must the continuation pay be refunded to the government in whole or in part?

574. Is continuation pay part of the service member's retirement package?

575. What is the Survivor Benefit Plan?

576. Who is eligible to receive Survivor Benefit Plan benefits?

577. What is the amount of the Survivor Benefit Plan annuity?

Veterans

Dependency and Indemnity Compensation

Disability Benefits – Service-Connected

Death Benefits – Service-Connected

PART II: MEDICARE

INTRODUCTION

MEDICARE AND COVID-19
Medicare Coverage

1021. Does Medicare cover lab tests for coronavirus/COVID-19?

1022. Does Medicare cover COVID-19 antibody or serology tests?

1023. Does Medicare cover hospitalization for COVID-19?

1024. Will Medicare cover the cost of COVID-19 vaccines?

1025. Does Medicare Advantage (Part C) cover COVID-19 costs?

1026. Are COVID-19 services available through telehealth?

1027. What other changes has Medicare implemented due to COVID-19?

MEDICARE AND TELEMEDICINE
Coverage

1028. What are telemedicine/telehealth/remote services as related to Medicare?

1029. How has Medicare expanded access to telehealth services?

1030. How do the Section 1135 Waivers expand telehealth?

1031. What types of telehealth services are covered under Medicare?

1032. What are Medicare telehealth visits?

1033. What is a Medicare virtual check-In?

1034. What are Medicare e-visits?

1035. How does HIPAA relate to Telehealth?

PART A: HOSPITAL INSURANCE
Eligibility Rules - Generally

1036. Who is eligible for benefits under Part A (Hospital Insurance)?

1037. What are the special eligibility rules for persons with End-Stage Renal Disease (ESRD)?

Eligibility Rules for Government Employees

1038. What are the special eligibility rules for government employees?

1052. How does a person apply for QMB or SLMB assistance?

Inpatient Hospital Services

1053. Specifically, what inpatient hospital services are paid for under Part A (Hospital Insurance)?

1054. Are inpatient hospital benefits provided for care in a psychiatric hospital?

1055. What special provisions apply to care in Religious Nonmedical Health Care Institutions (RNHCI)?

1056. How does an institution qualify as a Religious Nonmedical Health Care Institutions (RNHCI)?

1057. Can patients choose their own hospitals?

1058. How is it certified that hospitalization is required?

1059. What must a hospital do to qualify for Medicare payments?

Hospice Care

1060. What is hospice care?

1061. How is hospice care covered under Part A (Hospital Insurance)?

1062. What is not covered under Part A (Hospital Insurance) in regard to hospice?

1063. What is the hospice benefit period?

1064. What does the patient pay for hospice care?

1065. How is respite care covered?

1066. Can hospice care be stopped?

Skilled Nursing Facility (SNF) Care

1067. What is a qualified skilled nursing facility?

1068. Does Part A (Hospital Insurance) pay for custodial care in a skilled nursing facility?

1069. Do most nursing home residents qualify for Part A (Hospital Insurance) coverage?

1070. Under what circumstances does a patient qualify for skilled nursing facility benefits under Part A (Hospital Insurance)?

1071. What items and services generally are (and are not) covered under Part A (Hospital Insurance) when provided in a participating skilled nursing facility?

1072. What provisions are made under Part A (Hospital Insurance) for care in a skilled nursing facility?

Benefits

1133. Is alcohol misuse/abuse screening and counseling covered under Medicare Part B (Medical Insurance)?

1134. Is aortic aneurysm (AAA) screening covered under Medicare Part B (Medical Insurance)?

1135. Are Sexually Transmitted Infection (STI) screenings and counseling covered under Medicare Part B (Medical Insurance)?

1136. Does Medicare Part B (Medical Insurance) cover bone mass measurements (bone density)?

1137. Does Medicare Part B (Medical Insurance) cover cardiovascular disease risk reduction and behavior therapy?

1138. Does Medicare Part B (Medical Insurance) cover lung cancer screening?

1139. Does Medicare Part B (Medical Insurance) cover medical nutrition therapy?

1140. Are flu shots covered under Medicare Plan B?

1141. Are cervical and vaginal screenings covered under Medicare Plan B?

1142. What is the "Welcome to Medicare" visit and the annual yearly screenings?

1143. Does Medicare Part B covers Hepatitis B shots?

1144. Does Medicare Part B covers pneumococcal shots?

1145. Under what conditions is an injectable drug for postmenopausal osteoporosis covered by Part B (Medical Insurance)?

1146. When are eyeglasses covered under Part B (Medical Insurance)?

1147. Under what circumstances are the services of nurse practitioners and clinical nurse specialists covered under Part B (Medical Insurance)?

1148. When are organ transplants covered under Part B (Medical Insurance)?

1149. Are prescription drugs used in immunosuppressive therapy covered under Part B (Medical Insurance)?

1150. Are ambulatory surgical services covered under Part B (Medical Insurance)?

1151. When are rural health clinic (RHC) services covered by Part B (Medical Insurance)?

1152. Does Medicare Part B (Medical Insurance) reimburse for telehealth services in rural areas?

1153. Does Medicare Part B (Medical Insurance) reimburse Continuous Positive Airway Pressure (CPAP) therapy?

Medicare Coverage of Blood

Private Contracts

PART C: MEDICARE ADVANTAGE

Definition

Eligibility, Election, and Enrollment

Benefits and Beneficiary Protections

Prescription Drug Marketing Rules

Trusts

Estate Recoveries

Discrimination

Managed Care

INTRODUCTION TO THE 2023 EDITION

Social Security & Medicare Facts provides the reader with a description of Social Security, Medicare, benefits for federal government employees, benefits for service members and veterans, and benefits for workers covered under the Railroad Retirement System.

Social Security is administered by the Social Security Administration and provides Old Age, Survivors, and Disability benefits. Medicare provides hospital and medical insurance for the aged and disabled and is administered by the Centers for Medicare & Medicaid Services.

HISTORY

In June 1934, President Roosevelt created the Committee on Economic Security (CES), composed of five top-level cabinet positions (Labor, Justice, Treasury, Agriculture, and Federal Emergency Relief Administration), and tasked them with creating an economic security bill. Led by the first woman to hold a U.S. cabinet post, Secretary of Labor Frances Perkins, the CES drafted the Social Security Act aimed at giving people economic security throughout their lives. The bill included an old-age pension program, unemployment insurance funded by employers, health insurance for people in financial need, financial assistance for widows with children and for the disabled.

After much Congressional debate, the Social Security Act was signed into law on August 14, 1935, by President Franklin D. Roosevelt. Originally the Social Security Act of 1935 was named the "Economic Security Act", but the title was changed during the Congressional debate. The original program created a social insurance program that was created to pay retirees some income after the age of sixty-five. Registration of employers and workers began in November 1936, through the United States Post Office to begin allowing workers to acquire credits beginning in January 1937. A man named John David Sweeney, Jr. from New Rochelle, NY was the first person to be assigned a Social Security account but the honor of the lowest Social Security number "001-01-0001" went to Grace Dorothy Owen of New Hampshire. By July 1937, The Social Security Board had issued over 30 million SS cards. FICA contributions began in January 1937. The Social Security Administration reports that since the inception of the program, over $8.9 trillion dollars has been paid into the Trust Fund and more than $7.6 trillion has been paid out.

UNDERSTANDING AND PLANNING FOR SOCIAL SECURITY

1. What is the Social Security Act?

The Social Security Act has established numerous programs that provide supplemental income for insured individuals and their families in the event of disability, when they retire, or at death. This supplemental income acts as a safety net – especially in old age – and keeps an estimated 22 million elderly Americans out of poverty.

Congress passed the Social Security Act and President Franklin D. Roosevelt signed the measure into law on August 14, 1935 and the retirement benefits program went into effect on January 1, 1937. The law has been amended many times since its original enactment.

There have been many changes in Social Security and the United States since 1935. In 1935, the life expectancy was only age sixty, while in 2022, it is 77.0 years[1]. Therefore, in 1935, most people would not have lived long enough to collect Social Security retirement benefits. Today, many retirees are concerned that they will outlive their retirement savings.

In 1935, Social Security was designed to supplement a retiree's retirement income. Today, Social Security provides about 40 percent of the average retiree's income. This statistic worries many analysts who contend that workers rely too much on Social Security and should save more.

In 1949, the worker/retiree ratio was about 160:1. By 2013 (the latest figures available through Social Security), it had fallen to 2.8:1.[2] As of 2021, it is estimated at 2.7:1[3] and is expected to fall to 2.3:1 by 2035.[4] This is due in part to the continuing retirement of baby boomers, as well as the increase in life expectancy. When the program began, Social Security paid out about $35 million in benefits annually. Today, it pays out over $1 trillion annually.[5] It is projected that by 2030, the ratio will be down to 2.3:1 and by 2100 is projected to be down to 1.9:1.

Finally, in 1935, the poverty rate for seniors exceeded 50 percent. As measured in 2020, the poverty rate for seniors was approximately 9.4 percent nationwide.[6] Across the nation, the highest level of senior poverty is 13.3 percent in New Mexico, and lowest in New Hampshire at 5.5 percent.[7]

Nearly 90 percent of Americans over the age of sixty-five receive some Social Security income, and approximately 35 percent of that same group relies almost entirely on Social Security payments alone. With longer life expectancy and the recent issues with the economy, it has become increasingly important to understand and plan for Social Security benefits. With a thorough understanding of the program and useful strategies for applying for and receiving Social Security, most recipients can increase the amount of benefits they would receive if they simply apply for Social Security at Full Retirement Age (FRA), also referred to as Normal Retirement Age.

Notes

1. https://www.cdc.gov/nchs/data/nvsr/nvsr71/nvsr71-02.pdf
2. https://www.ssa.gov/history/ratios.html (last accessed August 27, 2022).
3. https://www.federalbudgetinpictures.com/social-security-recipient-worker-ratio/ (Last accessed August 27, 2022).
4. https://www.ssa.gov/news/press/factsheets/basicfact-alt.pdf (last accessed August 27, 2022).
5. https://www.ssa.gov/news/press/factsheets/basicfact-alt.pdf (last accessed August 27, 2022).
6. https://www.kff.org/medicare/issue-brief/how-many-seniors-live-in-poverty/ (last accessed August 27, 2022).
7. U.S. Census Bureau, American Community Survey, 2018.

2. What are the stated purposes of Social Security?

The basic purposes of the Social Security Act are to establish programs that will:

- provide for the material needs of individuals and families;

- protect aged and disabled persons against the expenses of illnesses that may otherwise use up their savings;

- keep families together; and

- give children the chance to grow up healthy and secure.

From the original legislation:

- "An act to provide for the general welfare by establishing a system of Federal old-age benefits, and by enabling the several States to make more adequate provision for aged persons, blind persons, dependent and crippled children, maternal and child welfare, public health, and the administration of their unemployment compensation laws; to establish a Social Security Board; to raise revenue; and for other purposes."[1]

Note

1. The Social Security Act (H.R. 7260, August 14, 1935).

3. What programs are covered by the Social Security Act?

The original Social Security Act (1935) and the current version of the Act, as amended, encompass several social welfare and social insurance programs.

The following programs are covered by the Social Security Act:

- Social Security

    o Retirement insurance

    o Survivors insurance

    o Disability insurance

- Medicare

    - Hospital and medical insurance for the aged, disabled, and those with end-stage renal disease

    - Prescription drug benefits

    - Extra help with Medicare Prescription Drug costs

- Unemployment insurance

- Black lung benefits

- Supplemental Security Income (SSI)

- Special Veterans benefits

- Public assistance and welfare services, including:

    - Aid to needy families with children

    - Medical assistance

    - Maternal and child health services

    - Child-support enforcement

    - Family and child welfare services

    - Food stamps

    - Energy assistance

The Federal Old-Age (Retirement), Survivors, and Disability Insurance program (OASDI) is the main program that people think of when they think of the term "Social Security". You will also hear this program referred to as the Old-Age, Survivor, Disability, and Health Insurance (OASDHI) program, as well as the Retirement, Survivor, Disability, and Health Insurance (RSDHI) program. This program covers workers and their dependents.[1]

Note

1. 42 U.S.C. sec. 402.

4. Who is covered by Social Security?

Most workers are covered by Social Security and if they work long enough (and accrue enough credits) will be entitled to retirement benefits and/or disability.

An individual is NOT covered if they were:

- Workers with too few Social Security credits

- Certain divorced spouses

- Certain non-citizens

- A Federal civilian employee who was hired before 1984. There is an exception for anyone that changed to the Federal Employee Retirement System during the 1987 transition period (see Q 558). The Federal civilian employees not covered by Social Security are instead covered under the Civil Service Retirement System (see Q 586). However, all Federal civilian employees are covered under the Medicare Part A hospital insurance program.

- Individuals covered under the Railroad Retirement System, which is governed by the Railroad Retirement Act (see Q 441).

- Employees of a state or local government entity that is not part of their employer's retirement system and not covered by a voluntary State/Federal Social Security agreement.

- Certain farm workers, workers of a family business, or domestic workers.

5. In general, who can receive Social Security?

Who Can Receive Social Security Benefits

- A disabled insured worker under the age of 65.

- A retired insured worker at age 62 or over.

- The spouse of a retired or disabled worker entitled to benefits who:

  o   is age 62 or over; OR

  o   has in care a child under age 16 (or over age 16 and disabled), who is entitled to benefits on the worker's Social Security record.

- The divorced spouse of a retired or disabled worker entitled to benefits if age 62 or over and married to the worker for at least 10 years.

- The divorced spouse of a fully insured worker who has not yet filed a claim for benefits if both are age 62 or over, were married for at least 10 years, and have been finally divorced for at least two continuous years.

- The dependent, unmarried child of a retired or disabled worker entitled to benefits, or of a deceased insured worker if the child is:

  o   under age 18; OR

  o   under age 19 and a full-time elementary or secondary school student; OR

- ○   aged 18 or over but under a disability that began before age 22.

- The surviving spouse (including a surviving divorced spouse) of a deceased insured worker if the widow(er) is age 60 or over.

- The disabled surviving spouse (including a surviving divorced spouse in some cases) of a deceased insured worker, if the widow(er) is age 50 to 59 and becomes disabled within a specified period.

- The surviving spouse (including a surviving divorced spouse) of a deceased insured worker, regardless of age, if caring for an entitled child of the deceased who is either under age 16 or disabled before age 22.

- The dependent parents of a deceased insured worker at age 62 or over.

In addition to monthly survivor benefits, a lump-sum death payment is payable upon the death of an insured worker.

For explanation of these benefits and eligibility requirements, see RETIREMENT AND DISABILITY BENEFITS, Q 43 to Q 222.

6. What do the phrases "Normal Retirement Age" (NRA) and "Full Retirement Age" (FRA) mean?

Normal Retirement Age and Full Retirement Age

For many years, "Normal Retirement Age" (NRA) meant the age at which someone was eligible for benefits that were not reduced for taking early benefits (see Q 291 and Q 342). But recently, this phrase has come to mean the age when many people "normally" apply for benefits among planners and the general public, which is often when they are generally first eligible— at age sixty-two. According to the Social Security Administration, 34.3 percent of people begin collecting Social Security benefits at age sixty-two, when they first become eligible. For those that do not begin collecting at age sixty-two, the following is the breakout of the age that people begin collecting:

- Age sixty-three: 6.3 percent

- Age sixty-four: 6.4 percent

- Age sixty-five: 10.3 percent

- Age sixty-six: 18.1 percent

- Ages sixty-seven to sixty-nine: 3.9 percent

- Age seventy: 3.7 percent

- The remaining 17 percent of Social Security is collected by those under sixty-five who qualify for disability.

As a result of this shift in language, a new phrase has developed among planners and the public to describe the age when unreduced benefits may be received – "Full Retirement Age" (FRA). As may seem obvious, FRA refers to the age at which a person qualifies for full Social Security benefits. This age is now determined by a person's year of birth and for those born during 1960 or later it is age sixty-seven. The prevailing definition by the Social Security Administration (SSA) at their website is that the normal retirement age (NRA) is the age at which retirement benefits are equal to the "primary insurance amount," (unreduced benefits), although the SSA still uses both phrases to describe when unreduced benefits may be taken.

For the 2023 edition of *Social Security & Medicare Facts*, the phrase "Normal Retirement Age" is used in the place of the phrase "Full Retirement Age" to describe the age at which unreduced benefits may be taken. Below is listed how the Normal Retirement Age varies by year of birth.[1]

NORMAL RETIREMENT AGE	
Year of birth	Age
1937 and prior	65
1938	65 and 2 months
1939	65 and 4 months
1940	65 and 6 months
1941	65 and 8 months
1942	65 and 10 months
1943-54	66
1955	66 and 2 months
1956	66 and 4 months
1957	66 and 6 months
1958	66 and 8 months
1959	66 and 10 months
1960 and later	67

Notes:
1. Persons born on January 1 of any year should refer to the normal retirement age for the previous year.
2. For the purpose of determining benefit reductions for early retirement, widows, and widowers whose entitlement is based on having attained age 60 should add two years to the year of birth shown in the table.

Note

1. Normal Retirement Age, https://www.ssa.gov/oact/progdata/nra.html (last accessed August 27, 2022).

7. Does Social Security accept donations for the solvency of the trust fund?

The Social Security trust funds have a combined balance of $2.852 trillion dollars as of June 2022, down from $2.908 trillion in 2021.[1] The Social Security Administration does accept voluntary donations to the trust fund. If inclined, donations can be made to extend the fund's solvency. Visit the Social Security website area dealing with donations[2] for additional information.

Voluntary donations can be made via check or money order or by will. Voluntary donations are deductible on Schedule A as a casualty or theft loss.

Since 2011 the program has received the following donations:

2011	$1,000,000
2012	$1,000
2013	0
2014	$5,000
2015	0
2016	0
2017	0
2018	0
2019	0
2020	0
2021	0
2022	0

Notes

1. Summary: Actuarial Status of the Social Security Trust Funds https://www.ssa.gov/policy/trust-funds-summary.html (last accessed August 27, 2022).
2. https://www.ssa.gov/agency/donations.html (last accessed August 27, 2022).

8. Are same-sex couples treated any differently than other married couples?

No. The Social Security Administration now recognizes same-sex marriages in all states and some marital legal relationships such as civil unions and domestic partnerships for the purposes of determining entitlement to Social Security, Medicare, and Supplemental Security Income. The SSA also recognizes same-sex marriages and some non-marital legal relationships entered into in foreign jurisdictions as well.[1] Social Security is now processing retirement, surviving spouse, and lump-sum death payment claims for same-sex couples in nonmarital legal relationships and paying benefits where they are due. In addition, the Social Security Administration considers same-sex marriage when determining SSI eligibility and benefit amounts.

On June 26, 2015, the United States Supreme Court issued a decision in *Obergefell v. Hodges*,[2] holding that same-sex couples have a constitutional right to marry in all states. This decision enables same-sex couples to be married in one state and have their marriage recognized by all other states. As a direct result of this decision, all same-sex couples will be recognized as being married for the purposes of determining their entitlement to Social Security benefits and as well as Supplemental Security Income (SSI) payments. The Social Security Administration recommends that someone who is the spouse, divorced spouse, or surviving spouse of a same-sex marriage or other legal same-sex relationship to immediately apply for benefits. Immediate applying will preserve the filing date, which can affect benefits.

This had been a developing area of law. In June 2013, the Supreme Court ruling in *United States v. Windsor*[3] had established that same sex couples who were married in a jurisdiction where same-sex marriages are recognized were eligible for spousal benefits, such as the spousal survivor benefit, the spousal retirement benefit, and the lump sum death benefit. At that time, the Social Security Administration reviewed its own policies regarding same-sex marriage after the Supreme Court decision and concluded that same-sex couples who are legally married in one state remain married for federal tax purposes even if they reside in a state that does not recognize their marriage.[4] Of course, the *Obergefell* case made that issue moot.

Notes

1. SSA Publication No. 05-10014, June 2022, What Same-Sex Couples Need to Know, https://www.ssa.gov/pubs/EN-05-10014.pdf (last accessed August 27, 2022).
2. 576 U.S 473, 135 S. Ct. 2587, 192 L.Ed.2d 609 (2015).
3. 570 U.S. 744, 133 S. Ct. 2675, 186 L.Ed. 808 (2013).
4. Rev. Rul. 2013-17.

9. Increasingly, the government has experienced the threat of, or actual shutdowns of services. What happens to Social Security benefits during government shutdowns?

The threat of a government shutdown has been and continues to be a highly charged political issue that emerges frequently due to stop-gap funding efforts. Funding is often through short-term spending bills. To date, the policy during a government shutdown or the threat of a government shutdown has been to ensure that benefit payments continue without interruption. Although payments continue without interruption, some services provided at regional offices are curtailed. When a government shutdown is anticipated, see the Social Security Administration website (www.ssa.gov) for announcements of curtailment of services. In the past, Social Security disability and SSI hearings were held, but new hearings were not scheduled. Additionally, new claims were not processed and new Social Security cards were not issued during a shutdown.

Office closings are specifically addressed at http://www.ssa.gov/agency/emergency/.

10. What federal agency administers the Social Security or OASDI program?

The Social Security Administration

The central office is located in Baltimore, Maryland. The administrative offices and computer operations are housed at this location.

The Social Security Administration is an independent agency in the executive branch of the federal government. It is required to administer the retirement, survivors, and disability program under the Social Security and the Supplemental Security Income (SSI) programs. The commissioner of the Social Security Administration is appointed by the President and approved by the Senate and serves a term of six years.

In recent years, the Social Security has increasingly provided services through its website at www.ssa.gov. Many of the services that were traditionally carried out through local Social Security offices or through the mail can now be done online at http://www.ssa.gov/onlineservices/. These services allow a person to apply for benefits, get a *Social Security Statement*, appeal a decision, find out about qualifying for benefits, estimate future benefits, and do other activities related to the management of benefits.

Alternatively, the local Social Security office is the place where a person can apply for a Social Security number, check on an earnings record, apply for Social Security benefits, black lung benefits, SSI, and Hospital Insurance (Medicare Part A) protection, enroll in Medical Insurance (Medicare Part B), receive assistance in applying for food stamps, and get full information about individual and family rights and obligations under the law. Also, a person can call the Social Security Administration's toll-free telephone number, 1-800-772-1213, to receive these services. This toll-free telephone number is available from 7:00 a.m. to 7:00 p.m. any business day. From a touch-tone phone, recorded information and services are available twenty-four hours a day, including weekends and holidays. People who are hearing impaired may call 1-800-325-0778 between 7:00 a.m. and 7:00 p.m. Monday through Friday.

Regular visits to outlying areas are made by the Social Security office staff to serve people who live at a distance from the city or town in which the office is located. These visits that are made to locations are called contact stations. A schedule of these visits may be obtained from the nearest Social Security office. If because of illness or disability, an SSA representative can make a visit to a person's home if they are unable to reach an office or a contact station.

Social Security Administration regional offices are located in Atlanta, Boston, Chicago, Dallas, Denver, Kansas City, New York, Philadelphia, San Francisco, and Seattle. There are 1,230 local Social Security field offices, 164 local hearing offices, and thirty-seven tele-service centers throughout the United States, Puerto Rico, the Virgin Islands, Guam, and American Samoa that deal directly with the public. Each region also has a number of teleservice centers located primarily in metropolitan areas. These offices handle telephone inquiries and refer callers appropriately. To find a local office, visit the Social Security Administration website at https://www.ssa.gov/locator/.

The Office of Hearings and Appeals administers the nationwide hearings and appeals program for the Social Security Administration. Administrative law judges, located in or traveling to major cities throughout the United States, hold hearings and issue decisions when a claimant or organization has appealed a determination affecting rights to benefits or participation in programs under the Social Security Act. The Appeals Council, located in Falls Church, Virginia, may review hearing decisions as the last administrative decisional level. (See FILING FOR BENEFITS, Q 248 to Q 267.)

The Social Security Administration maintains program service centers in Birmingham, AL; Chicago, IL: Kansas City, MO; New York, NY; Philadelphia, PA; and Richmond, CA. These offices, in addition to the Office of International Operations and the Office of Disability Operations located in Baltimore, MD, are the locations which house and service the records of individuals collecting benefits.

The Office of Central Operations maintains records of an individual's earnings and prepares benefit computations. These offices are located in Salinas, CA and Wilkes-Barre, PA. Data processing operations occur at the Office of Systems in Baltimore.

11. Where can I get forms related to Social Security and disability?

The Social Security Administration provides many, though not all, of its forms online at https://www.ssa.gov/forms/. Increasingly, the Social Security Administration encourages people to go online to download, fill out, and submit forms. All forms are free, but the SSA cautions that not all forms are listed on the website – however, as of August 2022, there were 165 forms listed. These forms, however, can still be obtained from the local Social Security Office during regular business hours.

For a list of Forms available, see Appendix M.

12. How does a person obtain a Social Security number?

By filling out Form SS-5[1] (Application for a Social Security Card) and submitting evidence of age, identity, and citizenship or alien status.

Parents applying for a Social Security number for their children under age seven will need to furnish only a birth record if no other record of age or identity has been established for the child.

Applicants eighteen and older must apply in person at a Social Security office. Applicants will need to provide two documents proving age, identity, and U.S. citizenship (or lawful employment-authorized immigrant status). Other documents may be required for noncitizens that are lawfully in the United State without Department of Homeland Security employment-authorization.

A Social Security number is needed not only for Social Security purposes, but also for income tax purposes. The Internal Revenue Service uses this number as a Taxpayer Identification Number (TIN) for processing tax returns and controlling the interest and dividend reports of banks and other financial institutions. Failure to put a valid Social Security number on a tax return may mean a delay or reduction in any refund claimed.

A Social Security number is also needed by persons age one or older who are claimed as dependents on someone's federal income tax return. All income tax returns claiming dependents (whether taxpayer's children or others) one year old or older must show the dependent's Social Security number. Failure to include a dependent's Social Security number on a tax return could result in the Internal Revenue Service, disallowing related items such as the personal exemption, child tax credit, child care credit, or earned income credit.

A person must have a Social Security number in order to receive Social Security benefits. Those lacking a Social Security number are required to apply for one. Beneficiaries on the Social Security rolls prior to May 10, 1989 are not required to have a Social Security number. However, as a practical matter, Social Security numbers are also commonly used by many nongovernmental entities, such as health care providers or banks, for tracking and security purposes.

Foreign-born applicants of any age must submit evidence of United States citizenship or alien status.

Form SS-5 can be obtained from any local Social Security office or online from the Social Security Administration's website. Forms must be either mailed to or presented to a local Social Security office. The SS-5 online can now be filled out online (but not electronically submitted).

Some businesses advertise that they can provide Social Security cards or name changes for a fee. There is no need to use such a business. Getting a Social Security number is free through the Social Security Administration.[2]

Notes

1. See Form SS https://www.ssa.gov/forms/ss-5.pdf (last accessed August 27, 2022).
2. See www.ssa.gov/ssnumber (last accessed August 27, 2022).

13. What do you do if you need a replacement Social Security card or need to make changes?

If the Social Security card is lost, a person can apply for a duplicate card by filling out another Form SS-5[1] and showing a driver's license, voter registration card, school identification card, or other official proof of identity. The new card will have the same number as the one that was lost. There is no charge for a lost Social Security card.

You can use a Social Security account to request a replacement Social Security card *online* if you:

- Are a U.S. citizen aged eighteen years or older with a U.S. mailing address;

- Are not requesting a name change or any other change to your card; and

- Have a driver's license or a state-issued identification card from one of the following states: AK, AZ, AR, CA, CO, CT, DE (driver license only), DC, FL, GA, HI, ID, IL, IN, IA, KS, KY, ME, MD, MA, MS, MI, MO, MT, NC, NE, ND, NJ, NM, NY, OH, PA, RI, SC, SD, TN, TX, UT, VA, VT, WA, WI (driver license only), and WY.

- Online service is not available using the following state identifications: AL, MN, NV, NH, OK, OR, WV, American Samoa, Guam, Northern Mariana Islands, Puerto Rico, or U.S. Virgin Islands.

It is necessary to have an online account called a "my Social Security" account which can be created at this website: https://secure.ssa.gov/RIL/SiView.action.

There is a limit on the number of replacement Social Security Cards. An individual can request **three** per year and is limited to **ten** in a lifetime. Changes in legal name or changes to a restrictive legend (validity to work notation, etc.) do not count for the lifetime ten or three annual cards. This service is also not yet available if your driver's license or identification card was issued by a U.S. territory (such as American Samoa, Guam, Northern Mariana Islands, Puerto Rico, or the U.S. Virgin Islands).

Note

1. https://www.ssa.gov/ssnumber/ (last accessed August 27, 2022).

14. How can you change or correct your name or other information on a Social Security card?

If a person wishes to correct or update the identifying information given on the original application for a Social Security number, a new Form SS-5 must be submitted. The applicant will need to submit documents supporting whatever changes need to be made. A change in name (for example, upon marriage) should always be reported.

An individual changing their name because of marriage, divorce, court order, or any other reason must inform Social Security to get an updated corrected card. A corrected card cannot be applied for online. The same applies to the I-766 card, Employment Authorization Document (EAD), from the U.S. Citizenship and Immigration Services (USCIS).

Corrected Card

To get a corrected Social Security card, an individual must show required documents that prove identity and/or citizenship.

Replacement Card

U.S. citizens applying for a replacement SSN card, that mail application to the local office, may use original or certified copies of secondary proofs of identity such as:

- A marriage document showing name and either date of birth or age (only when submitted to support the application for a name change)

- A U.S. government employee identification card

- A non-government employee identity card/badge card showing name and either a photograph or date of birth

- A health insurance card or U.S. Medicaid card showing name and one of the following:

  ○ Date of birth

  ○ A photograph

- A school identity card

- A school record or transcript (for the **current** school year) showing name and one of the following:

  o Date of birth

  o A photograph

- A life insurance policy showing name and age or date of birth

NOTE: U.S. Citizens applying for a replacement SSN card are not required to submit original primary evidence (e.g., driver's license, state ID, U.S. passport), for mailed applications.

15. If someone is a victim of identity theft, can they get a new Social Security number?

Perhaps. The Social Security Administration MAY issue a new Social Security number if someone is using an individual's number and it cannot be stopped. The Social Security Administration offers advice regarding identity theft as related to an SSN in their publication "Identity Theft and Your Social Security Number"[1]

If an individual has done all they can to fix the problems resulting from misuse of their Social Security number, and someone is still using their number, SSA may assign a new number.

The SSA will issue a new Social Security number if:

- More than one person is using the same number

- A victim of identity theft continues to be impacted by the original number

- Situations of harassment, abuse, or life endangerment

- Religious or cultural objections to certain numbers in the original number

  o This requires written documentation from a religious group with which the number holder has an established relationship.

When Social Security assigns a new numbers, they cross-reference the new number with the original to ensure that the person receives credit for all earnings under both.

A person cannot get a new Social Security number:

- if the Social Security card is lost or stolen, but there is no evidence that someone is using the number;

- to avoid the consequences of filing for bankruptcy; or

- if the person intends to avoid the law or legal responsibility.

1. https://www.ssa.gov/pubs/EN-05-10064.pdf , Jun. 2, 2018 edition (last accessed August 27, 2022).

16. Can individuals that are not U.S. citizens get a Social Security number?

Generally not. Only temporary workers and those in non-immigrant visa status who are authorized to work in the United States by the Department of Homeland Security (DHS) can get a Social Security number if they are not a U.S. citizen. Further guidance is available at *Social Security for Noncitizens*, Publication 10096.[1]

If a person is an immigrant, they can apply in two ways:

- Apply in their home country before coming to the United States when filing an application for an immigrant visa with the U.S. Department of State. In almost all cases, applying for an SSN and card with an immigrant visa application eliminates the need to visit a Social Security office in the United States.[2]

- For those lawfully present in the United States, they must contact the local Social Security office.

If a person is a nonimmigrant, they can apply two ways, depending on visa status:

- If lawfully present in the United States and plan to apply for work authorization or lawful permanent resident status from DHS, U.S. Citizenship, and Immigration Services (USCIS), one can apply for a SSN or replacement card. This can be done on the same USCIS application Form I-765 (Application for Employment Authorization), or via Form I-485 (Application for Lawful Permanent Residency or to Adjust Status).[3]

- If lawfully present in the United States and visa status allows the person to work, then they must contact the local Social Security office to apply.

Notes

1. EN-05-10096 - Social Security Numbers for Noncitizens (September 2021) (ssa.gov) (last accessed August 27, 2022).
2. www.ssa.gov/ssnvisa (Last accessed August 27, 2022)
3. https://www.ssa.gov/ssnvisa/ebe.html (Last accessed August 27, 2022)

17. What types of Social Security cards are issued?

There are three kinds of Social Security cards.

1. **Basic:** The first type of Social Security card is the basic one. It lists name and Social Security number and allows work without restriction. These cards are issued to

   a. U.S. citizens, and

   b. noncitizens to whom the Department of Homeland Security (DHS, the agency that oversees immigration) has given permission to live and work in the United States permanently. These include green card holders as well as refugees and people granted political asylum.

2. **Work Only:** The second type of card carries the words *"VALID FOR WORK ONLY WITH DHS AUTHORIZATION"*. It is issued to people who have permission to live and work here only for temporary periods.

3. **Non-Work:** The third type has the words *"NOT VALID FOR EMPLOYMENT"*. This type is issued to noncitizens who do not have work permission but need a Social Security number for other reasons, such as to apply for government benefits or services.

18. What documents are required to get a Social Security number?

Regardless of whether the applicant is an American citizen or a foreigner, the following information needs to be provided to Social Security in order to apply:

- **Evidence of age:** Usually, a birth certificate will suffice. Other proof of age consists of a record of birth from a U.S. hospital, a U.S. passport, or an adoption record.

- **Evidence of identity:** Documents must show legal name and, preferably, include a photograph and physical description such as height, weight, hair, and eye color. The document must be a U.S. driver's license, a U.S. state-issued nondriver identity card, or a U.S. passport. For non-citizens, Social Security will need current immigration documents and a foreign passport.

- **Evidence of U.S. citizenship:** These documents include a U.S. birth certificate, a U.S. passport, a certificate of naturalization, or a consular report of birth.

- **Evidence of immigration status:** For non-citizens, the documents issued by DHS showing immigration status and authorization to work in the United States.

All documents must be originals or certified copies from the agency that issued the document. Photocopies or notarized copies are not accepted.

19. Can individuals with Deferred Action Status and employment authorization get a Social Security number?

Probably. If the U.S. Citizenship and Immigration Services grants an individual Deferred Action status and employment authorization, they may be eligible for a Social Security number. This directly affects individuals with Deferred Action for Childhood Arrivals (DACA) status.

If the U.S. Citizenship and Immigration Services (USCIS) approves the request on the Form I-765 for Deferred Action for Childhood Arrivals and the application to work in the United States, the individual may be eligible for a Social Security number. Through a program called Enumeration Beyond Entry (EBE), an applicant no longer needs to wait to get an I-766

Employment Authorization Card. Through the EBE program, the application for a Social Security Number and an I-766 can be submitted together.

Social Security must interview the individual in person so they can complete and sign the application. The applicant must bring papers proving they have permission to work in the United States, as well as their immigration status, age, and identity.

The applicant needs to bring the following ORIGINALS or CERTIFIED COPIES of the following:

1.   Form I-766 Employment Authorization Card (EAD, work permit), and

2.   Foreign birth certificate (if in possession of the applicant or available within ten business days). If not available, Social Security might accept:

    o   Foreign passport;

    o   U.S. military record; or

    o   Religious record showing age or date of birth.

In the alternative that the above items in #2 are unavailable within ten (10) business days, Social Security might accept:

- U.S. driver's license;

- U.S. state-issued identification card; or

- School record (issued five or more years ago) showing age or date of birth.

Note

1. https://secure.ssa.gov/poms.nsf/lnx/0110205700 (last accessed August 27, 2022).

20. Under what circumstances can a non-citizen be eligible for SSI?

A non-citizen (also called an "alien" for immigration purposes) may be eligible for Supplemental Security Income (SSI) if he or she meets the requirements of the laws for non–citizens that went into effect on August 22, 1996. In general, beginning August 22, 1996, in order to be potentially eligible for SSI most non-citizens must:

1.   be in a **qualified alien** category (see Q 21); and

2.   meet a condition that allows qualified aliens to get SSI (see Q 22).

Note that a non-citizen must also meet all of the other rules for SSI eligibility, including the limits on income and resources.

21. What makes an individual eligible for the status of "qualified alien"?

There are seven categories of qualified aliens. An individual is a qualified alien if the Department of Homeland Security (DHS) finds that they meet the qualifications for one of these categories:

1. **Lawfully Admitted for Permanent Residence (LAPR)** in the U.S., which includes "Amerasian immigrant" as defined in P.L. 100-202, with a class of admission AM-1 through AM-8;

2. Granted **conditional entry under Section 203(a)(7)** of the Immigration and Nationality Act (INA) as in effect before April 1, 1980;

3. **Paroled into the U.S.** under Section 212(d)(5) of the INA for a period of at least one year;

4. **Refugee** admitted to the U.S. under Section 207 of the INA;

5. **Granted asylum** under Section 208 of the INA;

6. **Deportation is being withheld** under Section 243(h) of the INA, as in effect before April 1, 1997; or removal is being withheld under Section 241(b)(3) of the INA;

7. *A* **"Cuban and Haitian entrant"** as defined in Section 501(e) of the Refugee Education Assistance Act of 1980 or in a status that is to be treated as a "Cuban/Haitian entrant" for SSI purposes.

In addition, an individual can be a "deemed qualified alien" if, under certain circumstances, they, their parent, or their child were subjected to battery or extreme cruelty by a family member while in the United States.

22. What enables a "qualified alien" to be considered eligible for SSI benefits?

An individual meeting one of the "qualified alien" categories listed in Q 21 might make the person eligible for SSI if they also meet one of two conditions.

First, someone who was receiving SSI and lawfully residing in the U.S. on August 22, 1996, is eligible.

Second, a Lawfully Admitted for Permanent Residence (LAPR) with forty qualifying quarters of work may be eligible with certain conditions:

•   Work done by a spouse or parent may also count toward the forty quarters of work, but only for getting SSI.

- Quarters of work earned after December 31, 1996, cannot be counted if the individual, spouse, or parent who worked received certain benefits from the United States government, based on limited income and resources during that period.

  - NOTE: Individuals entering the U.S. after August 22, 1996 may not be eligible for SSI during the first five years as an LAPR if with forty qualifying quarters of coverage.

- Currently on active duty in the U.S. Armed Forces or an honorably discharged veteran and the discharge is not because of alien status. This condition may also apply if the spouse, widow(er), or dependent child of certain U.S. military personnel.

- Lawfully residing in the U.S. on August 22, 1996, **and** are blind or disabled.

- An individual may receive SSI for a maximum of seven years from the date DHS granted them immigration status in one of the following categories, and the status was granted within seven years of filing for SSI:

  - A refugee under Section 207 of the INA

  - An alien whose deportation was withheld under Section 243(h) of the INA or whose removal is withheld under Section 241(b)(3) of the INA

  - Asylee under Section 208 of the INA

  - "Cuban or Haitian entrant" Section 501(e) of the Refugee Education Assistance Act of 1980 or in a status that is to be treated as a "Cuban/ Haitian entrant" for SSI purposes; or

  - "Amerasian immigrant" pursuant to P.L. 100-202, with a class of admission of AM-1 through AM-8

For purposes of SSI eligibility, individuals are **not** considered qualified aliens if they were admitted to the U.S. under the provisions of the Victims of Trafficking and Violence Protection Act of 2000. Their eligibility is subject to the proper certification in such status by the U.S. Department of Health and Human Services and possession of a valid "T" non-immigrant visa. Once the alien obtains proper certification and is in possession of a "T" non-immigrant visa, he or she becomes potentially eligible for SSI.

Certain categories of noncitizens may be eligible for SSI and not subject to the August 26, 1996 law. Included here are:

1. American Indians born in Canada who were admitted to the United States under Section 289 of the Immigration and Nationality Act

2. Noncitizen members of a federal recognized Indian tribe under section 4(e) of the Indian Self-Determination and Education Assistance Act

3. Victims of severe forms of human trafficking

a. A person may be eligible for SSI under certain circumstances if the Department of Health and Human Services' Office of Refugee Resettlement and the Department of Homeland Security determines the person meets requirements of the Trafficking Victims Protection Act of 2000.

4. Special eligibility for nationals of Iraq or Afghanistan

a. If someone is an Iraqi or Afghan national who was admitted to the U.S. as a special immigrant, they may qualify for seven years of SSI benefits if having served as a translator/interpreter for the U.S. Armed Forces in Iraq or Afghanistan or worked for the U.S. government in Iraq

b. If someone is an Afghan humanitarian parolee or Afghan Non-Special Immigrant Parolee, they may qualify for SSI until March 31, 2023, or until the end of the parole period, whichever is later

5. Special eligibility for Ukrainian resettlement is also offered as of July 2022

Note

1. http://www.acf.hhs.gov/programs/orr/

23. How are Social Security numbers verified?

Employers, organizations, or third-party submitters can verify Social Security numbers for wage reporting purposes only. Social Security offers the following options to verify Social Security numbers:

1. **The Social Security Verification Service (SSNVS)** – This free online service allows registered users to verify that the names and Social Security numbers of hired employees match Social Security's records.

    ○ One option allows verification of up to ten names and SSNs (per screen) online and receive immediate results. This option is ideal to verify new hires.

    ○ Another option allows overnight upload of files of up to 250,000 names and SSNs and usually receive results the next government business day. This option is ideal to verify an entire payroll database, or if hiring a large number of workers at a time.

2. **The Consent Based Social Security Number Verification Service** – This fee-based Social Security number verification service is available to enrolled private companies, as well as state and local government agencies, to provide instant automated verification and can handle large volume requests.

Note

1. https://www.ssa.gov/employer/ssnv.htm (last accessed August 27, 2022).

24. How long does it take to get a Social Security number and card for a newborn baby?

Times vary, but generally the card will be mailed within an average of two weeks of the infant's birth. In some instances, it may take as long as a month.

25. How are Social Security numbers assigned?

Current Method

On June 25, 2011, the Social Security Administration changed the method in which Social Security numbers are issued to a process referred to as "randomization". This new method was developed to help protect the integrity of the SSN and to extend the longevity of the nine-digit SSN.

The SSA began assigning the nine-digit SSN in 1936 to track workers' earnings over the course of their lifetimes in order to pay benefits. The SSN has always been comprised of the three-digit area number, followed by the two-digit group number, and ending with the four-digit serial number. Since 1972, the area number reflected the state, as determined by the ZIP code in the mailing address of the application.

There are approximately 420 million numbers available for assignment. The previous assignment process limited the number of SSNs available for issuance to individuals by each state.

SSN randomization affected the SSN assignment process in the following ways:

- It eliminated the geographical significance of the first three digits of the SSN, referred to as the area number, by no longer allocating the area numbers for assignment to individuals in specific states.

- It eliminated the significance of the highest group number and, as a result, the High Group List is frozen in time and can only be used to see the area and group numbers SSA issued prior to the randomization implementation date.

- Previously unassigned area numbers were introduced for assignment excluding area numbers 000, 666 and 900-999.

Historical Background

Originally, the nine-digit SSN is composed of three parts:

- The first set of three digits is called the **Area Number**

- The second set of two digits is called the **Group Number**

- The final set of four digits is the **Serial Number**

Area Number

The Area Number was assigned by the geographical region. Prior to 1972, cards were issued in local Social Security offices around the country and the Area Number represented the State in which the card was issued. This did not necessarily have to be the State where the applicant lived, since a person could apply for their card in any Social Security office. Since 1972, when SSA began assigning SSNs and issuing cards centrally from Baltimore, the area number assigned has been based on the ZIP code in the mailing address provided on the application for the original Social Security card. The applicant's mailing address does not have to be the same as their place of residence. Thus, the Area Number does not necessarily represent the State of residence of the applicant, either prior to 1972 or since.

Generally, numbers were assigned beginning in the northeast and moving westward. Therefore, people on the east coast have the lowest numbers and those on the west coast have the highest numbers.

Note: One should not make too much of the "geographical code." It is not meant to be any kind of useable geographical information. The numbering scheme was designed in 1936 (before computers) to make it easier for SSA to store the applications in the SSA files in Baltimore since the files were organized by regions as well as alphabetically. It was really just a bookkeeping device.

Group Number

Within each area, the group number (middle two digits) range from 01 to 99 but were not assigned in consecutive order. For administrative reasons, group numbers issued first consisted of the odd numbers from 01 through 09 and then even numbers from 10 through 98, within each area number allocated to a state. After all numbers in group 98 of a particular area were issued, the even Groups 02 through 08 were used, followed by odd Groups 11 through 99.

Group numbers are assigned as follows:
ODD - 01, 03, 05, 07, 09------EVEN - 10 to 98
EVEN - 02, 04, 06, 08------ODD - 11 to 99

Serial Number

Within each group, the serial numbers (last four digits) run consecutively from 0001 through 9999.

---

26. How can a person check on his Social Security earnings record and receive an estimate of future Social Security benefits?

The Social Security Statement containing both an estimate of benefits and a record of earnings is available either online or by the mail. To access the statement online, a person must create a *"my Social Security"* account at www.ssa.gov/myaccount/. This account also allows a person to manage personal information such as changing an address or the way in which a direct deposit is received.

To receive the statement by mail, a person should fill out Form SSA-7004 (Request for Social Security Statement). The form is available at the Social Security Administrations website at www.ssa.gov, at any Social Security office, or by calling the Social Security Administration's toll-free number, 1-800-772-1213. A statement of total wages and self-employment income credited to the earnings record and an estimate of current Social Security disability and survivor benefits and future Social Security retirement benefits will be mailed to the individual.

If all earnings have not been credited, the individual should contact a Social Security office and ask how to correct the records. The time limit for correcting an earnings record is set by law. An earnings record can be corrected at any time up to three years, three months, and fifteen days after the year in which the wages were paid or the self-employment income was derived. "Year" means calendar year for wages and taxable year for self-employment income. An individual's earnings record can be corrected after this time limit for a number of reasons, including to correct an entry established through fraud; to correct a mechanical, clerical, or other obvious error; or to correct errors in crediting earnings to the wrong person or to the wrong period.

The Social Security Administration must provide individuals age twenty-five or older who have a Social Security number and have wages or net self-employment income with a Social Security account statement upon request. These statements must show:

- the individual's earnings;

- an estimate of the individual's contributions to the Social Security program (including a separate estimate for Medicare Part A Hospital Insurance); and

- an estimate of the individual's current disability and survivor benefits as well as future benefits at retirement (including spouse and other family member benefits) and a description of Medicare benefits.

Earnings and benefit estimates statements are automatically mailed on an annual basis to all persons age twenty-five or over who are not yet receiving benefits.

These earnings and benefit estimates statements contain the following information:

- The individual's Social Security taxed earnings as shown by Social Security Administration records as of the date selected to receive a statement.

- An estimate of the Social Security and Medicare Part A Hospital Insurance taxes paid on the individual's earnings.

- The number of credits (i.e., quarters of coverage, not exceeding forty) that the individual has for both Social Security and Medicare Hospital Insurance purposes, and the number the individual needs to be eligible for Social Security benefits and also for Medicare Hospital Insurance coverage.

- A statement as to whether the individual meets the credit (quarters of coverage) requirements for each type of Social Security benefit, as well as whether the individual is eligible for Medicare Hospital Insurance coverage.

- Estimates of the monthly retirement, disability, dependents', and survivors' insurance benefits potentially payable on the individual's record if he meets the credits (quarters of coverage) requirements. If the individual is age fifty or older, the estimates will include the retirement insurance benefits he could receive at age sixty-two (or his current age if he is already over age sixty-two), at full retirement age (currently age sixty-six to sixty-seven, depending on year of birth) or at the individual's current age if he is already over full retirement age, and at age seventy. If the individual is under age fifty, the Social Security Administration may provide a general description, rather than estimates, of the benefits that are available upon retirement.

- A description of the coverage provided under the Medicare program.

- A reminder of the right to request a correction in an earnings record.

- A remark that an annually updated statement is available upon request.

Note

1. *See* Request for Social Security Statement at https://www.ssa.gov/hlp/global/hlp-statement-7004.htm (last accessed August 27, 2022).

27. What will happen to Social Security benefit payments when the Trust Fund becomes insolvent?

Social Security and disability benefits are financed through the payroll tax. In 2021, the revenue collected by this tax went to pay out benefits that were due. The payroll tax was insufficient to pay out all benefits, so the balance was made up by interest payments due on government bonds held in the Social Security trust funds.

Over the eighty-two years of Social Security, the program has brought in approximately $23.8 trillion and paid out $19.5 trillion, with an asset reserve of $3.0 trillion as of June 30, 2019. The asset reserves have grown by $48 billion since 1986. The Bipartisan Budget Act of 2015, effective in November 2015, was supposed to postpone the exhaustion of the Social Security Disability Trust Fund from 2016 to 2032 by temporarily reallocating some of the payroll tax from the Old Age and Survivors Insurance Trust Fund to the Disability Insurance Trust Fund.

The Trustees are now estimating that the DI Fund should remain solvent until 2057, eight years less than last year's report. Much of this decline is blamed on the lessening of revenue due to the COVID-19 pandemic and its effect on the economy. After depletion in 2057, coverage would need to be lessened to 91 percent of current benefits.

The Trustees project that the combined fund asset reserves of OASI and DI Trust Funds, at the beginning of each year will exceed that year's projected cost through 2029. The Trustees project that the combined trust funds will be depleted in 2034, a year earlier than projected in the 2020 report. Social Security's total income is projected to exceed its total cost through 2022, as it has since 1982. The 2018 surplus of total income relative to cost was $34.4 billion. However, when interest income is excluded, Social Security's cost is projected to exceed its non-interest income throughout the projection period, as it has since 2010. It is projected that annual non-interest deficit will average approximately $51 billion between 2017 and 2020 and begin to rise dramatically after that as the number of beneficiaries continue to grow at a faster and faster rate. After 2021, the Trustees project that interest income and redemption of trust fund asset reserves from the US Treasury's General Fund will offset Social Security's annual deficits until 2033 (a year less than last year's estimate). In 2035, the OASDI reserves will be depleted, with estimated payments from Social Security taxes being sufficient to cover about 76 percent of scheduled benefits through the end of the projection period in 2091. At that point, the reserves will be exhausted according to the intermediate assumptions of the Office of the Chief Actuary in the Social Security Administration and other funding sources will be necessary.

The Trustees current projections indicate that annual costs of Social Security benefits as a share of taxable earnings will increase from 13.7 percent in 2016 to roughly 17.0 percent in 2038. This percentage will begin to decline slightly until 2051 and then begin to increase. The Trustees also compare program costs to Gross Domestic Product, noting that Social Security costs constituted 5.0 percent of GDP during 2016 with an anticipated increase to 6.1 percent by 2037, and then decline to 5.9 percent by 2050, after which the costs measured against GDP will increase back to 6.1 percent by 2091.

Note

1. The 2021 Annual Report of the Board of Trustees of the Federal Old-Age and Survivors Insurance and Federal Disability Insurance Trust Funds, https://www.ssa.gov/oact/TR/2021/index.html (last accessed September 7, 2022).

28. Where and how does a person apply for Social Security benefits?

A person can apply for Social Security benefits in a number of ways:

- online at www.ssa.gov,

- by mail,

- by telephone (at 1-800-772-1213), or

- by visiting one of the 1,230 Social Security field offices. In person services were resumed beginning on April 7, 2022.

The SSA still encourages people to go online first, call for help, and if necessary to come in— schedule appointment in advance.

The online application is the most efficient way to apply for benefits, and increasingly the Social Security Administration is encouraging people to apply using this method. The Social Security Administration estimates that completing the application online will take only ten to thirty minutes.

29. Where and how does a person apply for Social Security benefits if they live overseas?

Someone who does not live in the United States should consult the Social Security Administration's website resource on International Programs and Resources at www.ssa.gov/international for general information. The Office of International Operations (OIP) provides online instructions for how to apply for benefits if living overseas at www.ssa.gov/foreign/index.html. A person may also contact a U.S. embassy or consulate for information.

If the claimant lives overseas, the SSI payments are handled based on the following:

- Blind or Disabled Child of Military Parent(s) stationed overseas: this type of claim is handled by the Social Security office in Cumberland, Maryland.

- Students overseas temporarily: this type of claim is handled by ANY Social Security office.

- Any other claimant living overseas: this claim is handled by the Office of International Operations of the Office of Disability and International Operations (ODIO).

Outside of the United States is defined as being physically outside the fifty states, the District of Columbia, Puerto Rico, the U.S. Virgin Islands, Guam, the Northern Mariana Islands, and American Samoa. There is a tool at the Social Security website to help beneficiaries determine if they can receive Social Security benefits outside the United States.[1]

Note

1. https://www.ssa.gov/international/payments_outsideUS.html (last accessed August 27, 2022).

30. How can beneficiaries determine if they can receive Social Security benefits outside the United States?

The Payments Abroad Screening Tool will enable someone to learn if they can receive benefits outside the United States.[1] The Non-Resident Alien Tax Screening Tool will enable an individual to learn if nonresident alien tax should be withheld for their benefits.[2]

The U.S. Internal Revenue Code (IRC) requires the Social Security Administration (SSA) to withhold nonresident alien tax from certain Social Security monthly benefits. A nonresident alien receiving retirement, disability, or survivors benefits will result in SSA withholding a 30 percent flat tax from 85 percent of those benefits unless they qualify for a tax treaty benefit.

This results in a withholding of 25.5 percent of a person's monthly benefit amount. SSA acts as the withholding agent for the Internal Revenue Service (IRS) and applies their laws and definitions in withholding this tax.

The Windfall Elimination Provision Tool will enable an individual to learn if a foreign pension will reduce a U.S. Social Security benefit.[3]

Notes

1. https://www.ssa.gov/international/payments_outsideUS.html (last accessed August 27, 2022).
2. https://www.ssa.gov/international/AlienTax.html (last accessed August 27, 2022).
3. https://www.ssa.gov/international/wep_intro.html (last accessed August 27, 2022).

31. Which government agency issues a beneficiary's Social Security payment?

Social Security benefit payments are issued and electronic deposits are made by the Treasury Department – not by program service centers. However, questions about a missing direct deposit should be directed to a Social Security office or by calling 1-800-772-1213 between 7:00 a.m. and 7:00 p.m. Monday through Friday.

On March 1, 2013, the government required that all beneficiaries for Social Security or Supplemental Security Income receive payments electronically. Prior to that, a person could have received a check through the mail. The electronic payment must be made either through a direct deposit to a bank account or to a Direct Express® Debit MasterCard® card. The Direct Express® Debit MasterCard® is a prepaid debit card payment option for those who do not have a bank account.[1] There are fees for some transactions and services such as ATM withdrawals, cash at Walmart Service Centers, monthly paper statements, funds transfer, card replacements, and international transactions.

In some limited circumstances, a person can still seek a waiver and receive a check by using FS Form 1201W. The Treasury Department provides the following exception:[2]

- Check recipients living in remote areas without sufficient banking infrastructure may apply for a waiver, as well as check recipients for whom electronic payments would impose a hardship due to a mental impairment. Automatic waivers are granted to people born on or before May 1, 1921, and people who qualify for this waiver do not need to submit an application.

- For more information or to request a waiver, call 855-290-1545. You may also print and fill out a waiver form and return it to the address on the form.

Notes

1. Social Security: Get Your Payments Electronically https://www.ssa.gov/pubs/EN-05-10073.pdf, July 2022 edition (last accessed August 30, 2022).
2. See http://www.ssa.gov/deposit/EFT%20Waiver%20Form.pdf (last accessed August 30, 2022).

32. When does a Social Security beneficiary receive a monthly direct deposit?

For persons who started receiving benefits on or before May 1, 1997, Social Security benefits are direct deposited into the specified account on the third day of the month following the month for which the payment is due. For example, payments for January are delivered on February 3rd.

If the third day of the month falls on a weekend or federal holiday, deposits are made on the first day preceding the third of the month that is not a Saturday, Sunday, or federal holiday. For example, if the third is a Saturday or Sunday, deposits are made on the preceding Friday.

Persons who began receiving Social Security benefits after May 1, 1997, will be paid on a different monthly schedule than that described above. The payment day will be selected based on the day of the month on which the insured individual was born.

- Insured individuals born on the first through the tenth of the month will be paid on the second Wednesday of each month.

- Insured individuals born on the eleventh through the twentieth of the month will be paid on the third Wednesday of each month.

- Insured individuals born after the twentieth of the month will be paid on the fourth Wednesday of each month.

- New beneficiaries living in foreign countries will have deposits made on the third day of the month. Note, however, that deposits cannot be made in some countries. See the International Programs section of the Social Security Administration's website at www.socialsecurity.gov/international/payments.html for more information.

If a direct deposit is not made, then report the nonreceipt by calling 1-800-772-1213 (TTY 1-800-325-0778) between 7:00 a.m. and 7:00 p.m., Monday through Friday. The following information will be needed to report the nonreceipt:

(1)   The Social Security claim number on which the benefit is being paid

(2)   The period of payment covered by the missing deposit

(3)   The name and account number of the bank where the deposit was to be made

A change in the direct deposit account to which benefits are deposited should be reported promptly to the Social Security Administration through your online *my Social Security* account, by telephone, or in writing, signed by the payee. Promptly reporting a change of in the bank account will avoid having the deposits going to an incorrect or old account.

33. To whom is a benefit payment made payable and how are benefits received?

Payment is made through direct deposit to a beneficiary's account with a financial institution, or to a representative payee if the beneficiary is incapable of managing finances.

All beneficiaries with accounts in financial institutions will have their benefit checks deposited directly into those accounts instead of mailed to their homes. A financial institution may be a bank, trust company, savings, loan association, or a federal or state-chartered credit union. The beneficiary continues to be responsible for notifying the Social Security Administration of any changes that affect eligibility to receive benefits. Beneficiaries without accounts in financial institutions will receive a payment to a Direct Express® Debit MasterCard®. The Direct Express® Debit MasterCard® is a prepaid debit card payment option for those who do not have a bank account.

A minor child (a child under eighteen years of age) is ordinarily considered incapable of managing benefit payments, and a representative payee (usually a parent, close relative, or legal guardian) will be selected to receive payments on the child's behalf.

However, payment will be made directly to a child over eighteen, or to a child under eighteen if there is no indication that the child is immature or unstable and it appears to be in the minor's best interest to make direct payment.

Also, if alcoholism or drug addiction is a contributing factor in determining that an individual is entitled to disability benefits, the benefits must be paid through a representative payee.

For a beneficiary outside the United States, direct deposit may be available into a bank or financial institution in the country where they live.

34. If a husband and wife are both receiving monthly benefits, do they receive one or two monthly payments?

If a husband and wife have both worked, they will each be paid their own Social Security benefit by direct deposit to their designated bank account.

However, monthly benefits payable to a husband and wife who are entitled on the same Social Security record and are living at the same address are usually combined in one payment.

35. If several children are entitled to benefits, will each child receive a separate payment?

No. Social Security benefit payments for minor children in one family unit are usually combined into one payment. Where the children customarily reside in different households, separate payments will be issued to each family group.

36. Can a power of attorney be granted for the purpose of collecting and managing payments?

Yes. If payments are to be deposited in an account at a United States financial institution, completion of **SF-1199A (Direct Deposit Sign-Up Form)** is required. This form can be obtained on the Social Security Administration's website.[1] If payments are to be directed to a foreign financial institution, Standard Form 233 (Power of Attorney by Individual to a Bank for the collection of checks drawn on the Treasury of the United States) must be completed.[2]

Notes

1. https://www.irs.gov/pub/irs-utl/sf-1199-a_dirdeposit.pdf (Direct Deposit Sign-Up Form) (last accessed August 31, 2022).
2. https://fiscal.treasury.gov/files/check-claims/form_233.pdf (Power of Attorney) (last accessed August 31, 2022).

37. Can Social Security benefits be assigned?

No. The provision in the Social Security Act (Section 207)[1] prohibiting assignment of benefits or subjecting them to the operations of bankruptcy laws may not be superseded by another law unless the other law does so by express reference to Section 207. Some bankruptcy courts have considered Social Security benefits listed by the debtor to be income for purposes of bankruptcy proceedings and have ordered the Social Security Administration to send all or part of a debtor's benefit payment to the trustee in bankruptcy. Such orders are not appropriate.

The following exceptions to assignment have been allowed:

1.   **Garnishment of benefit payments for child support or alimony:** Under Section 659 of the Act,[2] garnishment of benefit payments for the purpose of collecting amounts owed for child support or alimony is permitted.

2.   **Garnishment of benefit payments for victim restitution:** Garnishment of benefit payments to recover court-ordered victim restitution is permitted under 18 USC secs. 3613(a), 3663, 3663A, and 3664.

3.   **Levy for unpaid federal taxes:** The IRS can place a levy on benefit payments to recover unpaid federal taxes under 26 USC secs. 6331 and 6334.

Notes

1.   42 USC sec. 407.
2.   42 USC sec. 659.

38. Can Social Security benefits be attached for the beneficiary's debts?

Benefits are not subject to levy, garnishment, or attachment, except in very restricted circumstances, such as by court order for the collection of child support or alimony, or by the Internal Revenue Service for unpaid federal taxes.

- Enforcement of child support and alimony obligations under Section 459 of the Social Security Act.[1]

- Collection of civil penalties under the Mandatory Victim Restitution Act.[2]

- Under a Notice of Levy to collect overdue federal taxes under Section 6334(c) of the Internal Revenue Code.

- Collection via the Federal Payment Levy Program to collect overdue federal taxes by levying up to 15 percent of each monthly payment until the debt is paid under Section 1024 of the Taxpayer Relief Act of 1997.[3]

- Nontax debt owed to an agency under the Debt Collection Improvement Act of 1996.[4]

A U.S. District Court reaffirmed the right of the Internal Revenue Service to seize Social Security benefits to collect overdue taxes. The plaintiff owed the IRS over $100,000. The IRS sent a notice of levy to the Social Security Administration, garnishing the plaintiff's entire Social Security benefit for one month and approximately half of his benefit for each month thereafter. The plaintiff sought reimbursement of the benefit garnished by the IRS and a judgment declaring future benefits exempt from collection. The court ruled that Social Security benefits are subject to levy by the IRS, and that the IRS may garnish the plaintiff's Social Security benefits until his federal income taxes and assessed penalties are paid.[5]

Notes

1. 42 U.S.C. sec. 659.
2. 18 U.S.C. sec. 3613.
3. Public Law 105-34.
4. Public Law 104-134.
5. *Leining v. U.S.*, 97-1 USTC ¶50,254 (D. Conn. 1996).

39. Are Social Security benefits subject to federal taxes?

Up to one-half of the Social Security benefits received by taxpayers whose incomes exceed certain base amounts are subject to income taxation.[1]

The base amounts are $32,000 for married taxpayers filing jointly, $25,000 for unmarried taxpayers, and zero for married taxpayers filing separately who did not live apart for the entire taxable year.[2]

There is an additional tier of taxation based upon a base amount of $44,000 for married taxpayers filing jointly, $34,000 for unmarried taxpayers, and zero for married taxpayers filing separately who did not live apart for the entire taxable year.[3]

The maximum percentage of Social Security benefits subject to income tax increases to 85 percent under this second tier of taxation.[4] (The rules listed in the paragraph above continue to apply to taxpayers not meeting these thresholds.)

After the end of the year, Form SSA-1099 (Social Security Benefit Statement)[5] is sent to each beneficiary showing the amount of benefits received. A worksheet (IRS Notice 703)[6] is enclosed for figuring whether any portion of the Social Security benefits received is subject to income tax.

For a detailed explanation of taxation of benefits, see TAXATION OF SOCIAL SECURITY BENEFITS, Q 387 to Q 396.

Notes

1. IRC sec. 86.
2. IRC sec. 86(c)(1).
3. IRC sec. 86(c)(2).
4. IRC sec. 86(a)(2).
5. http://www.irs.gov/pub/irs-pdf/p915.pdf (last accessed August 31, 2022).
6. IRS Notice 703 (2014), http://www.irs.gov/pub/irs-prior/n703--2014.pdf (last accessed August 31, 2022).

40. What happens when a Social Security overpayment is made to a Social Security beneficiary by mistake?

An overpayment made to a beneficiary is normally recovered from a beneficiary by withholding future payments until the overpayment is paid back.[1] If a beneficiary receives an overpayment, he should contact the Social Security Administration directly as soon as possible to make the SSA aware of the overpayment. If a beneficiary received a notice of overpayment and believes the notice is incorrect, then he should file Form SSA-561, **Request for Reconsideration,** which is available on the Social Security Administration's website.[2]

Notes

1. See http://www.ssa.gov/pubs/EN-05-10098.pdf (last accessed August 31, 2022).
2. See http://www.socialsecurity.gov/forms/ssa-561.html (last accessed August 31, 2022).

41. What are the options for repaying overpayments of Social Security or Supplemental Security Income?

A number of options for repaying exist, including:

- **If receiving Social Security benefits**, SSA will withhold the full amount of benefit each month, unless a lesser withholding amount is approved.

  ○ Full withholding would start 30 days after notification of the overpayment.

- **If receiving Supplemental Security Income (SSI),** generally SSA withholds 10 percent of the maximum federal benefit rate each month.

  ○ The individual may ask that SSA take less from the benefit each month.

  ○ The individual may ask to pay back the overpayment at a rate greater than 10 percent.

  ○ SSN starts deducting money from SSI payments no earlier than 60 days after notification of the overpayment.

- **If no longer receiving SSI, but the individual receives Social Security**, they can pay back the SSI overpayment by having up to 10 percent of the monthly Social Security benefit withheld.

- **If not receiving benefits**, the individual should do one of the following:

  - Access to pay by credit card, debit card, or bank account.[1]

  - There is an online payment system which is available to enable people to repay the overage.

  - Send a check to SSA for the entire amount of the overpayment within 30 days.

  - Contact SSA to set up a plan to pay back the amount in monthly installments.

The SSA can recover the overpayment from a person's federal income tax refund or from their wages. SSA can also recover overpayments from future SSI or Social Security benefits. Additionally, the Social Security Administration reports the delinquency to credit bureaus.

Note

1. www.pay.gov/public/form/start/834689469 . (Last accessed August 31, 2022)

42. Can individuals request a copy of a deceased individual's Social Security number application?

Social Security can provide information about a Social Security number record, but will charge a fee when an individual asks for information for a purpose that does not directly relate to the administration of a Social Security program, such as genealogy research. The fee depends upon the format of the information, and whether or not the Social Security number is known.[1]

Social Security can send you a photocopy of an original *Application for a Social Security Card* (Form SS-5) or a computer extract of information from the form. Social Security has recorded information from the original SS5s onto computer record and can furnish computer extracts instead of photocopies. Processing is limited to individuals who died before 1936 or born after 1865 unless a Social Security number is provided. The current fee in 2023 is $21.00 for a photocopy and $20.00 for a computer extract.

Note

1. Request for Deceased Individual's Social Security Record, https://secure.ssa.gov/apps9/eFOIA-FEWeb/internet/main.jsp (last accessed August 31, 2022) or Form SSA-711 https://www.ssa.gov/forms/ssa-711.pdf (last accessed August 31, 2022).

RETIREMENT AND DISABILITY BENEFITS

43. What Social Security benefits are available for retired or disabled workers and their families?

There are different types of benefits available for workers and their dependents. The following benefits are available for workers and their families while the worker is still alive:

- A monthly Retirement benefit for a retired worker

- A monthly Disability benefit for a disabled worker

- A monthly Spouse's benefit for a retired or disabled worker's spouse if:

    (1) at least sixty-two years old; or

    (2) caring for at least one child (under age sixteen, or over age sixteen and disabled [if disability began before age twenty-two]) of the retired or disabled worker

- A monthly Child's benefit for a retired or disabled worker's child if the child is:

    (1) under age eighteen;

    (2) age eighteen and a full-time high school or elementary school student; or

    (3) age eighteen or over and disabled, if the disability began before age twenty-two

44. How has COVID-19 affected dealing with Social Security?

In-Office Appointments

Local Social Security offices are offering more in-person appointments and have resumed in-person service for people without an appointment. As they expand in-person service, they encourage the public to continue to go online, call for help, and schedule appointments in advance.

Individuals Needing Help with Benefits

Generally, in-person appointment will be scheduled only in limited, critical situations. Limited, critical situations exist when a person:

- Is without food or shelter, including utilities, or is without medical care or coverage and needs to apply for or reinstate benefits.

- Currently receives benefits and has an urgent need for payment to meet expenses for food, shelter, or medical treatment, and cannot receive the payment electronically.

Help is Needed with a Social Security Number

SSA is prioritizing requests for in-person SSN services for:

- Individuals aged 12 or older applying for their first SSN card

- Individuals who need to update or correct their SSN information (such as your name, date of birth, or citizenship) to obtain income, resources, or medical care or coverage, or other services or benefits (for example filing a tax return, applying for housing, or seeking an Economic Impact Payment).

Overpayments

Waivers can be requested for overpayments incurred during COVID-19. If an overpayment was not the recipient's fault and they need to request a waiver of the overpayment debt, certain debts may qualify for a streamlined waiver decision if:

- The overpayment debt happened between March 1 and September 30, 2020 because Social Security did not process an action due to the COVID-19 pandemic; and

- SSA identified the debt by December 31, 2020.

Hearings and Appeals

- **Failing to file a timely appeal:** SSA will mail the individual a notice requesting a written explanation for the untimely filing. This notice will give an opportunity to explain the inability to file the hearing request on time. Although Form HA-L61 identifies a shorter timeframe for a response, SSA will provide 30 days from the date on the request before we will issue a dismissal, to account for potential mail delivery and processing delays.

- **Failure to appear at appeal:** SSA will mail a "Request to Show Cause for Failure to Appear" form, allowing an opportunity to explain why the individual did not appear for a telephone hearing. Although the Form HA-L90 identifies a shorter timeframe for a response, SSA will provide 30 days from the date on the request before issuing a dismissal, to account for potential mail delivery and processing delays.

---

45. What effect does COVID-19 financial assistance have on SSI eligibility or payments?

The following forms of income do not count against SSI eligibility or payments:

- Economic Impact Payments (EIP)

- State Stimulus Payments (*some exclusions may apply*)

- Unemployment Assistance (also includes regular unemployment)

- Paycheck Protection Program (PPP): Loan Forgiveness to Employers and Self-Employed Individuals

- Economic Injury Disaster Loan (EIDL) Program: Loans/Grants to Employers and Self-Employed Individuals /Grants

- Coronavirus Food Assistance Program: Direct Payments to Farmers and Ranchers

- COVID-19 Veteran Rapid Retraining Assistance Program

- COVID-19 Funeral Assistance

- Emergency Rental Assistance Fund

- Emergency Assistance for Rural Housing/Rural Rental Assistance

- Homeowner Assistance Fund

- Housing Assistance and Supportive Services Programs for Native Americans

- Tribal Payments from the Coronavirus Relief Fund and the Coronavirus State and Local Fiscal Recovery Funds

- Supporting Foster Youth and Families

- Higher Education Emergency Relief Fund

- Emergency Assistance to Children and Families through the Pandemic Emergency Assistance Fund

- Farm Loan Assistance for Socially Disadvantaged Farmers and Ranchers

- USDA Assistance and Support for Socially Disadvantaged Farmers, Ranchers, Forest Land Owners and Operators, and Groups

46. What is the date that benefits are paid?

Benefits are paid based on the recipient's birthdate. See schedule below:

Date of Birth	Benefit Paid
1 - 10	2nd Wednesday (following month)
11 - 20	3rd Wednesday (following month)
21 - 31	4th Wednesday (following month)

If the payment date falls on a weekend, then the benefit will be paid on the previous Friday. If the payment date falls on a holiday, the benefit will be paid the business day previous to the holiday. Social Security benefits are paid a month in arrears. Recipients must survive the entire previous month to earn a check in the current month.

Example: if John passes away on June 29, either he will not receive a July benefit or, if the Social Security benefit is deposited in July, it will be reversed. His estate will keep the June benefit as it was based on surviving all of May.

Retirement Benefits

47. In general, what requirements must be met to qualify a person for retirement benefits?

An individual is entitled to a retirement benefit if he or she:

(1)   is fully insured;

(2)   is at least age sixty-two throughout the first month of entitlement; and

(3)   has filed an application for retirement benefits.[1]

Note

1. 42 U.S.C. sec. 402(a).

48. Must a person be fully insured to qualify for retirement benefits?

Generally, yes. However, in the past, a small monthly benefit was payable to some men who reached age seventy-two before 1972 (born before 1900) and some women who reached age seventy-two (born before 1899) before 1970.[1] Obviously, none of those are alive today.

Note

1. 42 U.S.C. sec. 428.

49. What is the earliest age at which a person can start to receive retirement benefits?

Age sixty-two.

A retired worker who is fully insured can elect to start receiving a reduced benefit at any time between ages sixty-two[1] and Full Retirement Age (FRA) (which is gradually increasing from sixty-five to sixty-seven; see Q 6 and subsequent explanation) when he or she would receive the full benefit rate. A person is not required to be completely retired to receive retirement benefits. A person is considered "retired" if the retirement test is met. (See LOSS OF BENEFITS BECAUSE OF "EXCESS" EARNINGS, Q 358 to Q 386.)

The retirement age when unreduced benefits are available (previously age sixty-five) increased by two months per year for workers reaching age sixty-two in 2000 through 2005. It is age sixty-six for workers reaching age sixty-two in 2006 through 2016. It will increase again by two months per year for workers reaching age sixty-two in 2017 through 2022. Finally, the retirement age will be age sixty-seven for workers reaching age sixty-two after 2022 (i.e., reaching age sixty-seven in 2027).[2] See Q 291 for more detailed information about the increase in the full retirement age.

The Full Retirement Age (FRA) for spouse's benefits (also previously age sixty-five) moves upward in exactly the same way as that for workers. The Full Retirement Age for widow(er)'s benefits also rises, but in a slightly different manner (beginning for widow(er)s who attain age sixty in 2000 and reaching a full retirement age of sixty-seven in 2029).

Reduced benefits will continue to be available at age sixty-two, but the reduction factors are revised so that there is a further reduction of up to a maximum of 30 percent for workers entitled at age sixty-two after the retirement age is increased to age sixty-seven (rather than only 20 percent for entitlement at age sixty-two under previous law). See Q 293.

Notes

1. 42 U.S.C. sec. 402(a)(2).
2. 42 U.S.C. sec. 416.

---

50. Must a person file an application for retirement benefits?

Yes. Retirement benefits are not automatic. An application MUST be filed in order to collect. A person can file an application within three months before the first month in which he becomes entitled to benefits. The earliest date for filing would be three months before the month of attaining age sixty-two.

As evidence of age, a claimant must ordinarily submit one or more of the following:

- Birth certificate

- Church record of birth or baptism

- Census Bureau notification of registration of birth

- Hospital birth record

- Physician's birth record

- Family Bible

- Naturalization record

- Immigration record

- Military record

- Passport

- School record

- Vaccination record

- Insurance policy

- Labor union or fraternal record

- Marriage record

- Other evidence of probative value

Note that if a public or religious record was not made before the claimant was age five, they must produce at least two other documents that prove age, such as a:

- birth certificate recorded after age five;

- school record;

- State census record;

- vaccination record;

- insurance policy;

- hospital admission record, etc.

Preference is given to the oldest documents.

If a person is receiving Social Security disability benefits for the month before the month he reaches full retirement age, no application is required; the disability benefit ends and the retirement benefit begins automatically. For an explanation of how to file for benefits, see FILING FOR BENEFITS, Q 248 to Q 267.

51. What is the amount of a retirement benefit?

A retirement benefit that starts at Full Retirement Age (FRA) (see Q 49) equals the worker's Primary Insurance Amount (PIA).[1]

A worker who elects to have benefits start before Full Retirement Age will receive a monthly benefit equal to only a percentage of the PIA. The PIA will be reduced by:

- 5/9 of 1 percent for each of the **first thirty-six months** the worker is under FRA when payments commence;

- and by 5/12 of 1 percent for each such month **in excess of thirty-six**.[2] (See Table 10 for reduced retirement benefits.)

As a general rule, a person taking reduced retirement benefits before FRA will continue to receive a reduced rate after normal retirement age.

An individual can obtain higher retirement benefits by working past FRA to the age of seventy. (See Q 343.)

Notes

1. 20 CFR §404.201.
2. https://www.ssa.gov/oact/quickcalc/earlyretire.html (last accessed September 8, 2022).

52. What is the financial effect of early retirement?

This table illustrates the financial effect of early retirement for both a retired worker and his/her spouse, assuming a $1,000 primary insurance amount. With this primary insurance amount and both the primary and spouse retiring at their respective full retirement ages, the primary would receive $1,000 per month and his/her spouse would receive $500 per month. The table shows that retirement at age 62 results in substantial reductions in monthly benefits. Very few people actually begin receiving a benefit at exactly age 62 because a person must be 62 throughout the first month of retirement. Most early retirees begin at age 62 and 1 month.

PRIMARY AND SPOUSAL BENEFITS AT AGE 62 (BENEFITS BASED ON A $1,000 PRIMARY INSURANCE AMOUNT)						
Year of birth [1]	Normal (or full) retirement age	Number of reduction months [2]	Primary		Spouse	
			Amount	Percent reduction [3]	Amount	Percent reduction [4]
1937 or earlier	65	36	$800	20.00%	$375	25.00%
1938	65 and 2 months	38	791	20.83%	370	25.83%
1939	65 and 4 months	40	783	21.67%	366	26.67%
1940	65 and 6 months	42	775	22.50%	362	27.50%
1941	65 and 8 months	44	766	23.33%	358	28.33%
1942	65 and 10 months	46	758	24.17%	354	29.17%
1943-1954	66	48	750	25.00%	350	30.00%
1955	66 and 2 months	50	741	25.83%	345	30.83%
1956	66 and 4 months	52	733	26.67%	341	31.67%
1957	66 and 6 months	54	725	27.50%	337	32.50%
1958	66 and 8 months	56	716	28.33%	333	33.33%
1959	66 and 10 months	58	708	29.17%	329	34.17%
1960 and later	67	60	700	30.00%	325	35.00%

Notes

1. If birthday is January 1, use the prior year of birth.
2. Applies only if born on the second of the month; otherwise, the number of reduction months is one less than the number shown.

3. Reduction applied to primary insurance amount ($1,000 in this example). The percentage reduction is 5/9 of 1 percent per month for the first 36 months and 5/12 of 1 percent for each additional month.

4. Reduction applied to $500, which is 50 percent of the primary insurance amount in this example. The percentage reduction is 25/36 of 1 percent per month for the first thirty-six months and 5/12 of 1% for each additional month.

53. What is the first month for which a retired person receives a retirement benefit?

A monthly benefit is available to a retired worker when he reaches age sixty-two, provided he is fully insured.

Workers and their spouses (including divorced spouses) do not receive retirement benefits for a month unless they meet the requirements for entitlement throughout the month. The major effect of this provision is to postpone, in the vast majority of cases, entitlement to retirement benefits for persons who claim benefits in the month in which they reach age sixty-two to the next month. Only in the case of a person who attains age sixty-two on the first or second day of a month can benefits be paid for the month of attainment of age sixty-two. Note that a person attains his age on the day preceding the anniversary of his birth. For example, if an individual was born on May 2, 1961, he is considered sixty-two years old on May 1, 2023.

Most entitlement requirements (other than the entitlement of the worker) affecting young spouses or children of retired or disabled workers are deemed to have occurred as of the first of the month in which they occurred. However, in the case of a child who is born in or after the first month of entitlement of a retired or disabled worker, benefits are not payable for the month of birth (unless born on the first day of the month).

Retroactive benefits are usually prohibited if permanently reduced benefits (as compared with what would be payable for the month the application is filed) would occur in the initial month of eligibility. However, retroactive benefits may be applied for if:

(1) with respect to widow(er)'s benefits, the application is for benefits for the month of death of the worker, if filed for in the next month; and

(2) retroactive benefits for any month before attaining age sixty are applied for by a disabled widow(er) or disabled surviving divorced spouse.

54. Can a person receive retirement benefits regardless of the amount of his wealth or the amount of his retirement income?

Yes, a person is entitled to retirement benefits regardless of how wealthy he is. Also, the amount of retirement income a person receives (e.g., dividends, interest, rents, etc.) is immaterial. A person is subject to loss of benefits only because of excess earnings arising from his personal services (earned income).

See Q 55 and also see LOSS OF BENEFITS BECAUSE OF "EXCESS" EARNINGS, Q 358 to Q 386.

55. Can a person lose retirement benefits by working?

Yes, a person can lose some or all monthly benefits if he or she is under the Full Retirement Age ("FRA," see Q 49) for all of 2021 and his or her earnings for the year exceed $19,560[1]. A person may lose benefits if he or she reaches full retirement age in 2022 and if he or she earns over $51,960, but only those earnings earned before the month he or she reaches FRA count towards the $51,960 limit. The amount of loss depends on the amount of earnings in excess of these earnings limits. In no case will a person lose benefits for earnings earned after reaching FRA. For the initial year of retirement of a person who is under the Full Retirement Age for all of 2021, the monthly earnings limit is $1,630.

For purposes of this test, "earnings" include not only earnings in covered employment, but also earnings in noncovered employment in the United States. As to noncovered employment outside the United States, benefits are lost for any month before reaching FRA when so employed for more than forty-five hours, regardless of the amount of earnings. It should be noted that benefits are not truly "lost" as benefits at full retirement age will be increased to account for benefits withheld due to later earnings.

The dollar exempt amounts mentioned above will be increased automatically after 2021 as wage levels rise.

See LOSS OF BENEFITS BECAUSE OF "EXCESS" EARNINGS, Q 358 through Q 386.

See Q 293 for a discussion of the increase in the Full Retirement Age.

Note

1. *See* 42 U.S.C. 403.

56. Do unemployment benefits affect Social Security benefits?

Social Security does not count unemployment benefits as earnings. They do not affect retirement benefits.

In the past, a number of states would use formulas to offset Social Security if an individual filed for unemployment. As of 2023, only Minnesota uses an offset formula for reducing unemployment benefits, and even this formula is somewhat limited.

57. When do retirement benefits end?

Retirement benefits end at the worker's death. No retirement benefit is paid for the month of death regardless of the date of death, even if the worker dies on the last day of the month. With benefits being directly deposited, the Social Security Administration will reach into the account and withdrawal the last month's deposit upon receipt of the individual's death certificate.

Disability Benefits

58. In general, what requirements must be met to qualify a person for disability benefits?

A worker is entitled to disability benefits if he:

(1)   is insured for disability benefits;

(2)   has not attained retirement age;

(3)   has been disabled for twelve months, or is expected to be disabled for at least twelve months, or has a disability that is expected to result in death;

(4)   has filed an application for disability benefits; and

(5)   has completed a five-month waiting period or is exempted from this requirement.[1]

Determinations of disability are generally made by Disability Determination Services (DDS), which are agencies of each individual state. The Social Security Administration makes disability insurance determinations for persons living outside the United States (and for a few other applicants whose cases are specifically excluded from the federal-state regulations). Disability claims and supporting evidence are sent to the DDS located in the state where the claimant resides. The evaluation team makes every reasonable effort to obtain medical evidence from the claimant's treating sources. This team is composed of a medical consultant and a lay disability evaluation specialist, and is responsible for making the disability determination.

The Social Security Administration's Office of Program and Integrity Reviews may reverse a DDS finding that no disability exists, or, on the basis of evidence in the folder, reverse an allowance of disability.

The claimant may request a reconsideration of the claim and submit new evidence, if available. A reconsideration determination as to disability is generally handled by the DDS that made the original determination, and is reviewed by a special group in the Office of Disability Operations. In a further appealed case, an administrative law judge or the Appeals Council of the Office of Hearings and Appeals may issue an independent decision.

The Social Security Administration uses a multistep process to determine whether someone is eligible for disability benefits. These steps are as follows:

Step 1: Is the individual engaging in substantial gainful activity? If yes, benefits are denied. If the individual was working and their earnings average more than $1,630 in 2022, they generally cannot be considered disabled. If no, continue to Step 2.

Step 2: Does the individual have a severe medically determinable physical or mental impairment? The individual's condition must significantly limit ability to do basic work such as lifting, standing, walking, sitting, and remembering for at least twelve months. If not, benefits are denied. If yes, continue to Step 3.

Step 3: Does the individual have an impairment included in the Listing of Disabling Conditions? If yes, benefits are allowed. If no, continue to Step 4.

Step 4: Does the impairment prevent the individual from doing past relevant work (such as the work they did previously)? If the individual is able to do work that was done in the past, then benefits are denied. If not, continue to Step 5.

Step 5: Does the impairment prevent the individual from doing any other work? Can the person not do other work because of the impairment? If yes, benefits are allowed, if no, benefits are denied. Social Security will consider medical conditions and age, education, past work experience, and any transferable skills. If the individual cannot do other work, Social Security will decide if there is a disability. If the person can do other work, SSA will decide that the person does not have a qualifying disability.

The Social Security Administration (SSA) issued a final rule on March 20, 2015 that changed several of the Social Security Regulations related to EVIDENCE in Social Security Disability Insurance ("SSDI") and Supplemental Security Income ("SSI") disability claims. These changes require that someone applying for disability benefits is now required to inform or submit **all** evidence to SSA **regardless of whether it helps establish disability**. This is a big change from the prior Social Security Regulations that only requires that only "material" evidence be submitted to SSA that shows you are disabled. The changes to the Social Security Regulations were effective April 20, 2015. However, since the changes provide a continuing obligation to disclose information or evidence to SSA, any decisions not made prior to April 20, 2015 will be impacted as pending claims.

In the Regulations that were in effect until April 19, 2015, sections 404.900 and 416.1400 included text indicating that "you may present any information you feel is helpful to your case," and sections 404.1512 and 416.912 stated that an individual is only required to bring attention to everything that shows SSA that the individual is disabled.

Under the revised Regulations, sections 404.900 and 416.1400 remove the sentences that indicate that an individual may present any information they feel is helpful, and sections 404.1512 and 416.912 now indicate that an individual must inform SSA or submit to SSA all evidence that they are aware of that relates to whether they are disabled. This means that where in the past a person applying for benefits only had to give evidence that helped prove they are disabled, they will now also be required to provide information or submit evidence that shows they are not disabled.[2]

Summary of Rule Changes

- Must submit ALL evidence "relates" to a disability claim. This includes favorable *and* unfavorable evidence, even if not "material".

- Exceptions to privileged communications: Confidential communications between claimant and attorney or non-attorney representative are protected unless waived:

  - Factual information is not covered

  - Oral communication with a medical personnel IS covered as well as notes taken

  - Work product can be withheld

- The duty is to submit "ALL" evidence received in "entirety". There is an exception for exact "same" evidence which was "previously submitted" or if agency instructs "otherwise".

- There is a duty to inform about evidence NOT submitted – "ALL" evidence is not LITERAL. For example, there is no duty to take notes, identify people with knowledge, provide information about adverse witnesses.

- The duty to submit and inform is a continuing one. See Q 578 for additional information on disability claims.

Notes

1. 42 U.S.C. sec. 423.
2. *See* Submission of Evidence in Disability Claims, https://www.federalregister.gov/articles/2015/03/20/2015-05921/submission-of-evidence-in-disability-claims (last accessed August 25, 2022).

59. What insured status is required for disability benefits?

Generally, a person is insured for disability benefits if he:

1. is fully insured (least one QC for each calendar year after the person turned 21 and the earliest of the following: the year they turn 62, the year before they die, or the year before they became disabled); and

2. is disability insured-has worked under Social Security for at least five of the ten years (twenty-out-of-forty quarters) just before becoming disabled.

The minimum number of quarters is six and the maximum is forty.

EXCEPTION:

To be eligible for disability benefits, an individual must meet a **recent work test** and a **duration work test**.

The number of credits necessary to meet the recent work test depends the person's age. The rules are as follows:

- **Before age 24** – The person may qualify if they have 6 credits earned in the 3-year period ending when the disability starts.

- **Age 24 to 31** – In general, the person may qualify if they have credit for working half the time between age 21 and the time your disability began. As a general example, if the person develops a disability at age 27, they would need 3 years of work (12 credits) out of the past 6 years (between ages 21 and 27).

- **Age 31 or older** – In general, they must have at least 20 credits in the 10-year period immediately before the disability began.

The following table shows how many years of work credits a person needs to meet the duration of work test based on the age when the disability began. This table only provides an estimate of how many work credits are needed, but does not cover all situations. If the person is statutorily blind, they must only meet the duration of work test. When statutory blindness is involved, there is not a recent work test requirement.

If the person develops a disability	Years of work needed
Before age 28	1.5 years of work
Age 30	2 years
Age 34	3 years
Age 38	4 years
Age 42	5 years
Age 44	5.5 years
Age 46	6 years
Age 48	6.5 years
Age 50	7 years
Age 52	7.5 years
Age 54	8 years
Age 56	8.5 years
Age 58	9 years
Age 60	9.5 years

60. How disabled must a person be to qualify for disability benefits?

Disability is defined as the inability to engage in any substantial gainful activity by reason of any medically determinable physical or mental impairment, which can be expected to result in death or that has lasted or can be expected to last for a continuous period of no less than twelve months.[1] A person must be not only unable to do his previous work but cannot (considering age, education, and work experience) engage in any other kind of substantial work that exists in the national economy. It is immaterial whether such work exists in the immediate area, or whether a specific job vacancy exists, or whether the worker would be hired if he applied for work.

The worker's impairment or impairments must be the primary reason for his or her inability to engage in substantial gainful activity, although age, education, and work experience are also taken into consideration in determining the worker's ability to do work other than previous work.

The term "substantial gainful activity" is used to describe a level of work activity that is both substantial and gainful. Substantial work activity involves the performance of significant physical or mental duties, or a combination of both, which are productive in nature. Gainful work activity is activity for remuneration or profit, whether or not a profit is realized. For work activity to be substantial, it need not necessarily be performed on a full-time basis; work activity performed on a part-time basis may also be substantial.

Illegal activities can constitute substantial gainful activity. For example, tax fraud is an illegal activity that can be both substantial and gainful because of the possibility of significant mental activity and potential gain involved.

Impairments related to the commission of a felony for which the individual is subsequently convicted or related to confinement in a correctional facility for conviction of a felony, may not be used to establish a disability for Social Security benefits.

Note

1. 42 U.S.C. sec. 423(d).

61. What is a medically determinable impairment?

Disability is defined as "an impairment that results from anatomical, physiological, or psychological abnormalities that can be shown by medically acceptable clinical and laboratory diagnostic techniques."[1] The medical evidence must establish that an individual has a physical or mental impairment; a statement about the individual's symptoms is not enough without confirmation by clinical or laboratory findings.

Physiological impairments are conditions that cause physical harm, such as muscular issues, cancer, bone issues, diseases, HIV, COVID-19, heart disease, etc. Psychological impairments are those conditions causing harm to someone's mental health, such as depression, anxiety, etc.

The SSA needs to see medical evidence of a physiological or psychological impairment that reveals signs, symptoms, and laboratory findings to consider someone for disability benefits. Disability claims examiners want to see a medical record with solid medical evidence documenting the condition.

Types of Impairments

The severity of the illness or condition must meet or be equivalent to the criteria, or requirements, of a particular medical condition

- Disabilities are referred to as The Listings or "The Blue Book," and are discussed in Q 68 and Q 69

- Disabilities are categorized by body system (i.e., cardiovascular, musculoskeletal, mental)

- Separate disabilities are listed for adults and children

- Disabilities are updated to reflect advancements in treatment, prognosis, and recovery

Note

1. https://secure.ssa.gov/poms.nsf/lnx/0425205005 (last accessed August 22, 2022).

62. How is a disability evaluated and documented?

Disability evaluations are based solely on medical evidence under both the Title II and Title XVI programs. The claimant is responsible for providing medical evidence showing an impairment(s) and the severity of the impairment(s).

The Social Security Administration (SSA), with the claimant's permission, will help the claimant get medical evidence from his or her own medical sources who have evaluated, examined, or treated the claimant for his or her impairment(s). SSA will also request copies of medical evidence from hospitals, clinics, or other health facilities when appropriate.

The evaluation process is designed to provide physicians and other health professionals with an understanding of the disability programs administered by the Social Security Administration. It explains how each program works, and the kinds of information a health professional can furnish to help ensure sound and prompt determinations and decisions on disability claims.

The diagnosis must be documented in medical records, laboratory reports, or other clinical findings of an Acceptable Medical Source (AMS).

The AMS may be a:

- Doctor (incudes M.D./D.O./Ph.D./E.D./Psy.D)

- Advanced Practice Registered Nurse (APRN), which includes Certified Nurse Midwife, Nurse Practitioner, Certified Registered Nurse Anesthetist, and Clinical Nurse Specialist

- Physician Assistant

- Audiologist

63. What is the procedure in a disability evaluation?

The evaluation is essentially a three-step process as detailed below:

Step One: Establishment of Existence of an impairment

By law, SSA needs specific medical evidence to establish that a claimant has an impairment. SSA regulations require "objective medical evidence" from an "acceptable medical source" to establish that a claimant has a medically determinable impairment. The regulations define these terms.

Step Two: Determination of Severity

Once the existence of an impairment is established, SSA considers all evidence from all medical and nonmedical sources to assess the extent to which a claimant's impairment(s) affects his or her ability to function in a work setting; or in the case of a child, the ability to function compared to that of children the same age who do not have impairments. Nonmedical sources include, but are not limited to the claimant, educational personnel, public and private social welfare agency personnel, family members, caregivers, friends, neighbors, employers, and clergy.

Step Three: Consultative Examinations

If the evidence provided by the claimant's own medical sources is inadequate to determine if he or she is disabled, additional medical information may be sought by recontacting the medical source for additional information or clarification, or by arranging for a consultative examination (CE). A claimant's own medical source(s) is the preferred source to perform the needed examination or test, and SSA will pay the authorized fee for the CE. However, SSA may use an independent medical source other than the claimant's own medical source(s) to conduct the CE in several situations, such as:

- the claimant's own medical source(s) prefers not to perform the examination;

- the claimant's own medical source(s) does not have the equipment to provide the specific data needed;

- there are conflicts or inconsistencies in the file that cannot be resolved by going back to the claimant's own medical source(s);

- the claimant prefers another source and has good reason for doing so;

- SSA knows from prior experience that the claimant's own medical source(s) may not be a productive source; or

- the claimant's own medical source(s) is not qualified, as is defined by regulation.

In developing evidence of the effects of symptoms on a claimant's ability to function, SSA investigates all avenues presented that relate to the complaints. These include evidence about:

- the claimant's daily activities;

- the location, duration, frequency, and intensity of the pain or other symptom;

- precipitating and aggravating factors;

- the type, dosage, effectiveness, and side effects of any medication;

- treatments, other than medications, for the relief of pain or other symptoms;

- any measures the claimant uses or has used to relieve pain or other symptoms; and

- other factors concerning the claimant's functional limitations due to pain or other symptoms.

In assessing the claimant's pain or other symptoms, SSA considers all of the above-mentioned factors. It is important that medical sources address these factors in the reports they provide.

64. What are the responsibilities of the claimant in the process of disability determination?

A claimant must inform SSA about or submit all evidence known to him or her that relates to whether or not he or she is blind or disabled. This duty is ongoing and requires the claimant to disclose any additional related evidence about which he or she becomes aware throughout the administrative review process. This includes identifying and informing SSA of his or her medical sources; providing any evidence already in his or her possession that is not contained in other medical records; cooperating with case development requests; attending consultative examinations.

The evidence must be complete and detailed enough for SSA to determine:

- the nature and severity of the claimant's impairment(s),

- how long the claimant has experienced the impairment(s), and

- whether the claimant can still do work-related physical and mental activities with the impairment(s).

If the claimant is not the applicant, a proper applicant is legally responsible to meet the claimant's obligations for case development.

65. What are the guidelines used in a Consultative Evaluation?

If the evidence provided by the claimant's own medical sources is inadequate to determine if he or she is disabled, additional medical information may be sought by recontacting the treating source for additional information or clarification, or by arranging for a Consultative Evaluation (CE).

The treating source is the preferred source of purchased examinations when the treating source is qualified, equipped and willing to perform the additional examination or tests for the fee schedule payment, and generally furnishes complete and timely reports. Even if only a supplemental test is required, the treating source is ordinarily the preferred source for this service. SSA's rules provide for using an independent source (other than the treating source) for a CE or diagnostic study if:

- the treating source prefers not to perform the examination;

- there are conflicts or inconsistencies in the file that cannot be resolved by going back to the treating source;

- the claimant prefers another source and has a good reason for doing so; or

- prior experience indicates that the treating source may not be a productive source.

The type of examination and/or test(s) purchased depends upon the specific additional evidence needed for adjudication. If an ancillary test (e.g., X-ray, PFS, or EKG) will furnish the additional evidence needed for adjudication, the DDS will not request or authorize a more comprehensive examination. If the examination indicates that additional testing may be warranted, the medical source must contact the DDS for approval before performing such testing.

Fees for CEs are set by each state and may vary from state to state. Each state agency is responsible for comprehensive oversight management of its CE program.

Social Security is committed to providing fair and equitable service to the American public, regardless of an individual's inability to communicate effectively in English. Social Security recognizes that using qualified interpreters efficiently facilitates the Agency's processes, deters fraud, and assures that individuals with limited English proficiency (LEP) are not disadvantaged. Therefore, the DDS will provide an interpreter free of charge, to any individual requesting language assistance, or when it is evident that such assistance is necessary to ensure that the individual is not disadvantaged. Individuals have the option of using their own interpreter, such as a family member, friend, or third party, providing the interpreter meets the Agency's criteria for interpreters. A qualified interpreter is an individual or vendor who is able to read, write, and speak fluently in English and the language or dialect of the individual needing language assistance, and who meets the following criteria:

- provides an accurate interpretation of questions and responses by both the individual being interviewed and the CE provider (i.e., does not self-initiate follow-up questions or infer facts or dates not provided by the individual or the CE provider);

- demonstrates familiarity with basic terminology used in the disability determination process, including medical and social welfare terminology when necessary;

- agrees to comply with Social Security's disclosure and confidentiality of information requirements; and

- has no personal stake in the outcome of the case that would create a conflict of interest. An individual who is a potential or actual claimant or beneficiary on the same record as the individual needing language assistance can act as an interpreter, providing that there is no other conflict of interest.

66. How is a Consultative Examination Source selected?

The DDS purchases consultative examinations only from qualified medical sources. The medical source may be the individual's own physician or psychologist, or another source. In the case of a child, the medical source may be a pediatrician.

By "qualified," it is meant that the medical source must be currently licensed in the state and have the training and experience to perform the type of examination or test we request. Also, the medical source must not be barred from participation in SSA programs. The medical source must also have the equipment required to provide an adequate assessment and record of the existence and level of severity of the individual's alleged impairments.

Medical sources who perform CEs must have a good understanding of SSA's disability programs and their evidence requirements. The medical source chosen may use support staff to help perform the consultative examination. Any such support staff (e.g., X-ray technician, nurse, etc.) must meet appropriate licensing or certification requirements of the state.

Generally, medical sources are selected based on appointment availability, distance from a claimant's home, and ability to perform specific examinations and tests.

67. What is contained within the Consultative Examination Report?

A complete Consultative Examination report will involve all the elements of a standard examination in the applicable medical specialty and should include the following elements:

- The claimant's SSS or other non-SSN case identifier and a physical description of the claimant

- The claimant's major or chief complaint(s)

- A detailed description, within the area of specialty of the examination, of the history of the major complaint(s)

- A description, and disposition, of pertinent "positive" and "negative" detailed findings based on the history, examination, and laboratory tests related to the major complaint(s), and any other abnormalities or lack thereof reported or found during examination or laboratory testing

- Results of laboratory and other tests (for example, X-rays) performed according to the requirements stated in the Listing of Impairments (see Part III of this guide)

- The diagnosis and prognosis for the claimant's impairment(s)

- In claims for adults, a statement about what a claimant can still do despite his or her impairment(s) and whether the claimant has one or more impairment-related limitations or restrictions in the following abilities:

  o The ability to perform physical demands of work activities, such as sitting, standing, walking, lifting, carrying, pushing, pulling, or other physical functions (including manipulative or postural functions, such as reaching, handling, stooping, or crouching)

  o The ability to perform mental demands of work activities, such as understanding; remembering; maintaining concentration, persistence, or pace; carrying out instructions; or responding appropriately to supervision, co-workers, or work pressures in a work setting

  o The ability to perform other demands of work, such as seeing, hearing, or using other senses

  o The ability to adapt to environmental conditions, such as temperature extremes or fumes

- In claims for children under age 18, a statement about the child's impairment-related limitations and restrictions (as compared to children his or her age who do not have impairments) in:

  o acquiring and using information;

  o attending and completing tasks;

  o interacting and relating with others;

  o moving about and manipulating objects;

  o caring for yourself; and

  o health and physical well-being.

The consultant's consideration, and some explanation or comment on, the claimant's major complaint(s) and any other abnormalities found during the history and examination or reported from the laboratory tests. The history, examination, evaluation of laboratory test results, and the conclusions will represent the information provided by the consultant who signs the report. The CE report must:

- Provide evidence that serves as an adequate basis for disability decision making in terms of the impairment it assesses.

- Be internally consistent. Are all the diseases, impairments, and complaints described in the history adequately assessed and reported in the clinical findings?

- Do the conclusions correlate the medical history, the clinical examination and laboratory tests, and explain all abnormalities?

- Be consistent with the other information available within the specialty of the examination requested.

- Did the report fail to mention an important or relevant complaint within that specialty that is noted in other evidence in the file (e.g., blindness in one eye, amputations, pain, alcoholism, depression)?

- Be adequate as compared to the standards set out in the course of a medical education.

- Be properly signed.

Signature Requirements

All CE reports must be personally reviewed and signed by the medical source who actually performed the examination. The medical source doing the examination or testing is solely responsible for the report contents and for the conclusions, explanations, or comments provided. The source's signature on a report annotated "not proofed" or "dictated but not read" is not acceptable. A rubber stamp signature or signature entered by another person, such as a nurse or secretary, is not acceptable.

68. How are adult disabilities classified?

The following sections detail the classification of impairments in adults age eighteen and over and that may apply to the evaluation of impairments in children under age eighteen if the disease processes have a similar effect on adults and younger children. Greater detail of each disability classification is found in "The Blue Book":[1]

- Musculoskeletal Systems

- Special Senses and Speech

- Respiratory Disorders

- Cardiovascular system

- Digestive system

- Genitourinary disorders

- Hematological disorders

- Skin disorders

- Endocrine disorder

- Congenital disorders that affect multiple body systems

- Neurological disorders

- Mental disorders

- Cancer (Malignant Neoplastic Diseases)

- Immune System disorders

Note

1. https://www.ssa.gov/disability/professionals/bluebook/AdultListings.htm (last accessed August 22, 2022).

69. How are childhood disabilities classified?

The following sections detail the classification of impairments in children under the age of eighteen. Greater detail of classifications of disabilities can be found in "The Blue Book"[1]

- Low Weight Birth and Failure to Thrive

- Musculoskeletal System

- Special Senses and Speech

- Respiratory Disorders

- Cardiovascular system

- Digestive system

- Genitourinary disorders

- Hematological disorders

- Skin disorders

- Endocrine disorders

- Congenital disorders that affect multiple body systems

- Neurological disorders

- Mental disorders

- Cancer (Malignant Neoplastic Diseases)

- Immune System disorders

Note

1. https://www.ssa.gov/disability/professionals/bluebook/ChildhoodListings.htm (last accessed August 22, 2022).

70. What is a compassionate allowance?

Compassionate allowances allow expediting of Social Security Disability Insurance (SSDI) and Supplemental Security Income (SSI) applications for people whose medical conditions are so severe that their conditions obviously meet Social Security's definition of disability. Compassionate allowances are a way to quickly identify diseases and other medical conditions that, by definition, meet Social Security's standards for disability benefits.

These conditions primarily include certain cancers, adult brain disorders, and a number of rare disorders that affect children. The Compassionate Allowance List (CAL) helps reduce waiting time to reach a disability determination for individuals with the most serious disabilities.

The Compassionate Allowances program identifies claims where the applicant's disease or condition clearly meets Social Security's statutory standard for disability. The SSA can easily identify potential compassionate allowances to quickly make decisions. The Social Security Administration (SSA) uses the same rules to evaluate CAL conditions when evaluating either Social Security Disability Insurance (SSDI) or Supplemental Security Income (SSI) programs.

71. Which illnesses currently qualify for Compassionate Allowances?

Compassionate Allowances (CALs) are a way to quickly identify diseases and other medical conditions that, by definition, meet Social Security's standards for disability benefits. These conditions primarily include certain cancers, adult brain disorders, and a number of rare disorders that affect children. The CAL initiative helps us reduce waiting time to reach a disability determination for individuals with the most serious disabilities.

The Compassionate Allowances program identifies claims where the applicant's disease or condition clearly meets Social Security's statutory standard for disability. By incorporating cutting-edge technology, the agency can easily identify potential Compassionate Allowances to quickly make decisions. Social Security Administration (SSA) uses the same rules to evaluate CAL conditions when evaluating both Social Security Disability Insurance (SSDI) or Supplemental Security Income (SSI) programs.

The Social Security Administration will accept conditions for consideration at their website.[1]

Acute Leukemia

Adrenal Cancer - with distant metastases or inoperable, unresectable or recurrent

Adult Non-Hodgkin Lymphoma

Adult Onset Huntington Disease

Aicardi-Goutieres Syndrome

Alexander Disease (ALX) - Neonatal and Infantile

Allan-Herndon-Dudley Syndrome

Alobar Holoprosencephaly

Alpers Disease

Alpha Mannosidosis - Type II and III

ALS/Parkinsonism Dementia Complex

Alstrom Syndrome

Alveolar Soft Part Sarcoma

Amegakaryocytic Thrombocytopenia

Amyotrophic Lateral Sclerosis (ALS)

Anaplastic Adrenal Cancer - Adult with distant metastases or inoperable, unresectable or recurrent

Angelman Syndrome

Angioimmunoblastic T-Cell Lymphoma (New)

Angiosarcoma
Aortic Atresia
Aplastic Anemia
Astrocytoma - Grade III and IV
Ataxia Telangiectasia
Atypical Teratoid/Rhabdoid Tumor
Batten Disease
Beta Thalassemia Major
Bilateral Optic Atrophy- Infantile
Bilateral Retinoblastoma
Bladder Cancer - with distant metastases or inoperable or unresectable
Blastic Plasmacytoid Dendritic Cell Neoplasm (New)
Breast Cancer - with distant metastases or inoperable or unresectable
Canavan Disease (CD)
CACH--Vanishing White Matter Disease- Infantile and Childhood Onset Forms
Carcinoma of Unknown Primary Site
Cardiac Amyloidosis- AL Type
Caudal Regression Syndrome - Types III and IV
CDKL5 Deficiency Disorder
Cerebro Oculo Facio Skeletal (COFS) Syndrome
Cerebrotendinous Xanthomatosis
Charlevoix-Saguenay Spastic Ataxia
Child Lymphoblastic Lymphoma
Child Lymphoma
Child Neuroblastoma - with distant metastases or recurrent
Chondrosarcoma - with multimodal therapy
Choroid Plexus Carcinoma
Chronic Idiopathic Intestinal Pseudo Obstruction
Chronic Myelogenous Leukemia (CML) - Blast Phase
CIC-rearranged Sarcoma
Coffin-Lowry Syndrome
Congenital Lymphedema
Congenital Myotonic Dystrophy
Congenital Zika Syndrome
Cornelia de Lange Syndrome - Classic Form
Corticobasal Degeneration
Creutzfeldt-Jakob Disease (CJD) – Adult

Cri du Chat Syndrome
Degos Disease - Systemic
DeSanctis Cacchione Syndrome
Desmoplastic Mesothelioma
Desmoplastic Small Round Cell Tumors
Dravet Syndrome
Duchenne Muscular Dystrophy- Adult
Early-Onset Alzheimer's Disease
Edwards Syndrome (Trisomy 18)
Eisenmenger Syndrome
Endometrial Stromal Sarcoma
Endomyocardial Fibrosis
Ependymoblastoma (Child Brain Cancer)
Erdheim Chester Disease
Esophageal Cancer
Esthesioneuroblastoma
Ewing Sarcoma
Farber Disease (FD) – Infantile
Fatal Familial Insomnia
Fibrodysplasia Ossificans Progressiva
Fibrolamellar Cancer
Follicular Dendritic Cell Sarcoma - metastatic or recurrent
Friedreichs Ataxia (FRDA)
Frontotemporal Dementia (FTD), Picks Disease - Type A – Adult
Fryns Syndrome
Fucosidosis - Type 1
Fukuyama Congenital Muscular Dystrophy
Fulminant Giant Cell Myocarditis
Galactosialidosis - Early and Late Infantile Types
Gallbladder Cancer
Gaucher Disease (GD) - Type 2
Gerstmann-Straussler-Scheinker Disease (New)
Giant Axonal Neuropathy
Glioblastoma Multiforme (Brain Cancer)
Glioma Grade III and IV
Glutaric Acidemia - Type II
GM1 Gangliosidosis - Infantile and Juvenile Forms
Head and Neck Cancers - with distant metastasis or inoperable or unresectable
Heart Transplant Graft Failure

Heart Transplant Wait List - 1A/1B
Hemophagocytic Lymphohistiocytosis (HLH) - Familial Type
Hepatoblastoma
Hepatopulmonary Syndrome
Hepatorenal Syndrome
Histiocytosis Syndromes
Hoyeraal-Hreidarsson Syndrome
Hutchinson-Gilford Progeria Syndrome
Hydranencephaly
Hypocomplementemic Urticarial Vasculitis Syndrome
Hypophosphatasia Perinatal (Lethal) and Infantile Onset Types
Hypoplastic Left Heart Syndrome
I Cell Disease
Idiopathic Pulmonary Fibrosis
Infantile Free Sialic Acid Storage Disease
Infantile Neuroaxonal Dystrophy (INAD)
Infantile Neuronal Ceroid Lipofuscinoses
Inflammatory Breast Cancer (IBC)
Intracranial Hemangiopericytoma
Jervell and Lange-Nielsen Syndrome
Joubert Syndrome
Junctional Epidermolysis Bullosa - Lethal Type
Juvenile Onset Huntington Disease
Kidney Cancer - inoperable or unresectable
Kleefstra Syndrome
Krabbe Disease (KD) – Infantile
Kufs Disease - Type A and B
Large Intestine Cancer - with distant metastasis or inoperable, unresectable or recurrent
Late Infantile Neuronal Ceroid Lipofuscinoses
Leigh's Disease
Leiomyosarcoma
Leptomeningeal Carcinomatosis
Lesch-Nyhan Syndrome (LNS)
Lewy Body Dementia
Liposarcoma - metastatic or recurrent
Lissencephaly
Liver Cancer
Lowe Syndrome
Lymphomatoid Granulomatosis - Grade III

Malignant Brain Stem Gliomas – Childhood
Malignant Ectomesenchymoma
Malignant Gastrointestinal Stromal Tumor
Malignant Germ Cell Tumor
Malignant Multiple Sclerosis
Malignant Renal Rhabdoid Tumor
Mantle Cell Lymphoma (MCL)
Maple Syrup Urine Disease
Marshall-Smith Syndrome
Mastocytosis - Type IV
MECP2 Duplication Syndrome
Medulloblastoma - with metastases
Megacystis Microcolon Intestinal Hypoperistalsis Syndrome
Megalencephaly Capillary Malformation Syndrome
Menkes Disease - Classic or Infantile Onset Form
Merkel Cell Carcinoma - with metastases
Merosin Deficient Congenital Muscular Dystrophy
Metachromatic Leukodystrophy (MLD) - Late Infantile
Microvillus Inclusion Disease – Child (New)
Mitral Valve Atresia
Mixed Dementias
Mowat-Wilson Syndrome (New)
MPS I, formerly known as Hurler Syndrome
MPS II, formerly known as Hunter Syndrome
MPS III, formerly known as Sanfilippo Syndrome
Mucosal Malignant Melanoma
Multicentric Castleman Disease
Multiple System Atrophy
Myelodysplastic Syndrome with Excess Blasts (New)
Myoclonic Epilepsy with Ragged Red Fibers Syndrome
Neonatal Adrenoleukodystrophy
Nephrogenic Systemic Fibrosis
Neurodegeneration with Brain Iron Accumulation - Types 1 and 2
NFU-1 Mitochondrial Disease
Nicolaides-Baraister Syndrome

Niemann-Pick Disease (NPD) - Type A

Niemann-Pick Disease-Type C

Nonketotic Hyperglycinemia

Non-Small Cell Lung Cancer

Nut Carcinoma (New)

Obliterative Bronchiolitis

Ohtahara Syndrome

Oligodendroglioma Brain Cancer- Grade III

Ornithine Transcarbamylase (OTC) Deficiency

Orthochromatic Leukodystrophy with Pigmented Glia

Osteogenesis Imperfecta (OI) - Type II

Osteosarcoma, formerly known as Bone Cancer - with distant metastases or inoperable or unresectable

Ovarian Cancer – with distant metastases or inoperable or unresectable

Pallister-Killian Syndrome

Pancreatic Cancer

Paraneoplastic Pemphigus

Patau Syndrome (Trisomy 13)

Pearson Syndrome

Pelizaeus-Merzbacher Disease-Classic Form

Pelizaeus-Merzbacher Disease-Connatal Form

Pericardial Mesothelioma

Peripheral Nerve Cancer - metastatic or recurrent

Peritoneal Mesothelioma

Peritoneal Mucinous Carcinomatosis

Perry Syndrome

Pfeiffer Syndrome - Types II and III (New)

Phelan-McDermid Syndrome

Pitt Hopkins Syndrome

Pleural Mesothelioma

Pompe Disease – Infantile

Pontocerebellar Hypoplasia (New)

Posterior Cortical Atrophy (New)

Primary Central Nervous System Lymphoma

Primary Effusion Lymphoma

Primary Peritoneal Cancer

Primary Progressive Aphasia

Progressive Bulbar Palsy

Progressive Multifocal Leukoencephalopathy

Progressive Supranuclear Palsy

Prostate Cancer - Hormone Refractory Disease – or with visceral metastases

Pulmonary Atresia

Pulmonary Kaposi Sarcoma

Refractory Hodgkin Lymphoma

Renal Amyloidosis - AL Type (New)

Renpenning Syndrome

Retinopathy of Prematurity - Stage V

Rett (RTT) Syndrome

Revesz Syndrome

Rhabdomyosarcoma

Rhizomelic Chondrodysplasia Punctata

Richter Syndrome

Roberts Syndrome

Rubinstein-Taybi Syndrome

Salivary Cancers

Sandhoff Disease

Sarcomatoid Mesothelioma (New)

Schindler Disease - Type 1

SCN8A Related Epilepsy with Encephalopathy

Seckel Syndrome

Secondary Adenocarcinoma of the Brain

Severe Combined Immunodeficiency - Childhood

Single Ventricle

Sinonasal Cancer

Sjogren-Larsson Syndrome

Skin Malignant Melanoma with Metastases

Small Cell Cancer (Large Intestine, Prostate or Thymus)

Small Cell Cancer of the Female Genital Tract

Small Cell Lung Cancer

Small Intestine Cancer - with distant metastases or inoperable, unresectable or recurrent

Smith Lemli Opitz Syndrome

Soft Tissue Sarcoma - with distant metastases or recurrent

Spinal Muscular Atrophy (SMA) - Types 0 and 1

Spinal Nerve Root Cancer-metastatic or recurrent

Spinocerebellar Ataxia

Stiff Person Syndrome

Stomach Cancer - with distant metastases or inoperable, unresectable or recurrent

Subacute Sclerosing Panencephalitis

Superficial Siderosis of the Central Nervous System

SYNGAP1-related NSID

Tabes Dorsalis

Tay Sachs Disease - Infantile Type

Taybi-Linder Syndrome

Tetrasomy 18p

Thanatophoric Dysplasia - Type 1

Thyroid Cancer

Transplant Coronary Artery Vasculopathy

Tricuspid Atresia

Ullrich Congenital Muscular Dystrophy

Ureter Cancer - with distant metastases or inoperable, unresectable or recurrent

Usher Syndrome - Type I

Ventricular Assist Device Recipient - Left, Right, or Biventricular

Walker Warburg Syndrome

Wolf-Hirschhorn Syndrome

Wolman Disease

X-Linked Lymphoproliferative Disease

Xeroderma Pigmentosum

Zellweger Syndrome

X-Linked Myotubular Myopathy

Note

1. https://www.ssa.gov/compassionateallowances/submit_potential_cal.html (last accessed August 22, 2022).

72. Can a child qualify for disability benefits?

A child under age eighteen will be considered disabled if he or she has a "medically determinable" physical or mental impairment or combination of impairments that causes marked and severe functional limitations, and that can be expected to cause death or that has lasted or can be expected to last for a continuous period of not less than twelve months.[1]

Note

1. https://www.ssa.gov/OP_Home/cfr20/404/404-1529.htm (Last accessed August 22, 2022).

73. What disability benefits are available for Wounded Warriors?

Social Security pays disability benefits through the Social Security disability insurance program or through the Supplemental Security Income (SSI) program to military members or veterans who meet Social Security's definition of disability. If a military member or veteran sustained an illness, injury, or wound while on active duty status on or after October 1, 2001, they will receive expedited processing of their disability claim, regardless of how or where the disability occurred. Benefits available through Social Security are different than those from the Department of Veterans Affairs and require a separate application.

Social Security pays disability benefits through two programs:

(1)   the Social Security disability insurance program, which pays benefits to the beneficiary and certain members of their family if insured (worked enough quarters and paid Social Security taxes; and

(2)   the Supplemental Security Income (SSI) program, which pays benefits based on financial need.

The member must be:

- unable to do substantial work because of medical condition(s); and

- the medical condition(s) must have lasted, or be expected to last, at least one year or to result in death.

The SSA also considers how long someone worked, and whether or not he or she has paid Social Security taxes. The years worked to qualify for these benefits vary by age. More information is available at the Disability Benefits for Wounded Warriors page.[1]

Note

1. https://www.ssa.gov/people/veterans/ww.html#1. (Last access August 22, 2022).

74. Does blindness qualify a person for disability benefits?

A special definition of "disability" is provided for an individual age fifty-five or over who is blind. Such an individual is disabled for the purpose of disability benefits, if he is unable to engage in substantial gainful activity requiring skills or abilities comparable to those of any gainful activity in which he has previously engaged with some regularity and over a substantial period of time.

A person who is not statutorily blind and is earning (in 2022) more than $1,470 a month (net of impairment-related work expenses) is ordinarily considered to be engaging in substantial gainful activity. This represents an increase of $120 from the 2022 level of $1,350 per month.

The Social Security Act has established a higher substantial gainful activity amount for statutorily blind individuals. The monthly substantial gainful activity amount for blind individuals is $2,460 in 2023, up from $2,260 in 2022. Also, under SSDI, this condition has to have lasted or be expected to last at least twelve months. There is no duration requirement for blindness under SSI.

Blindness, for Social Security purposes, means either central visual acuity of 20/200 or less in the better eye with the use of a correcting lens, or a limitation in the fields of vision such that the widest diameter of the visual field subtends an angle of twenty degrees or less. However, no benefits will be payable for any month in which the individual engages in substantial gainful activity.

75. At what age can a person receive disability benefits?

At any age under the full retirement age (see Q 49).[1] If a person is receiving disability benefits when reaching full retirement age, the disability benefit automatically ends and the retirement benefit begins. It should be noted that children can collect disability benefits.

Note

1. 42 U.S.C. sec. 423(a)(1)(B).

76. Is there a waiting period for disability benefits?

Yes, there is a full five-month waiting period.[1] Generally, benefits will start with the sixth full month of disability. However, if an application is not made until later, benefits are payable retroactively for up to twelve months, beginning with the first month after the waiting period.

Ordinarily, no benefits are payable for the first five full months of disability. Under some circumstances, however, where the person has had a prior period of disability, benefits will begin with the first full month of disability.

Benefits will begin with the first full month of disability in two situations:

Reinstated Benefits

(1) the new disability arises within five years after the previous one ended; and

(2) the new disability is expected to last for at least twelve months, or to result in death.

Dependent Benefits

The benefits are for the child of a disabled worker.

Note

1. 42 U.S.C. sec. 423(c)(2).

77. When must an application for disability benefits be filed?

An application for disability benefits may be filed before the first month for which the person can be entitled to benefits. An application filed before the first month in which the applicant satisfies the requirements for disability benefits is valid only if the applicant satisfies the requirements at some time before a final decision on his application is made. If the applicant is found to satisfy the requirements, the application is deemed to have been filed in the first month in which he satisfied the requirements. An application for disability benefits may be made retroactively effective for as many as twelve months before the one in which the application is filed. For an explanation of how to file for benefits, see FILING FOR BENEFITS, Q 248 to Q 263.

Social Security disability benefits may be reinstated without a new disability application if, during the fifteen-month period following a trial work period, a person who has not recovered medically no longer engages in substantially gainful activity. (See Q 94.)

78. What is the process used to determine disability?

Ordinarily, disability claims are initially processed through a local Social Security field offices and State agencies (referred to as Disability Determination Services, or DDSs). Subsequent appeals of unfavorable determinations may be decided in the DDSs or by an Administrative law judge in the SSA's Office of Disability Adjudication and Review (ODAR).

Representations in SSA field offices will take applications which may be online, in person, by telephone, or by mail.

Application and forms provide information about the application, and related forms ask for a description of the claimant's impairment(s), treatment sources, and other information that relates to the alleged disability such as names, addresses, and telephone numbers of medical sources.

The field office will verify the NONMEDICAL eligibility requirement including age, employment, marital status, residency, citizenship, income, and resources, as well as living arrangements. The field office then sends the case to a DDS for determination of disability.

Disability Determination Services (DDSs) are state agencies fully funded by the Federal Government. Responsibilities include developing the medical evidence and coming to an initial determination regarding whether the claimant is disabled or blind. Claimant's medical sources are contacted. If they are not sufficient, the DDS may request a Consultative Examination (CE) to get additional information.

A DDS makes a disability determination through an adjudicative team consisting of a medical or psychological consultant and a disability examiner. The case might be referred to a state vocational rehabilitation agency if appropriate. After a decision, the case is returned to the field office.

If the claimant is found to be disabled, the field office will complete the paperwork and begin paying benefits. If the claimant is found to not be disabled, the file is retained pending any appeal. Appeals are handled in a similar fashion to the initial claim (other than a different DDS adjudicative team does the review and reconsideration).

Claimants who are denied disability benefits can request a hearing before an Administrative Law Judge (ALJ) in the Office of Disability Adjudication and Review (ODAR). Additional evidence can be submitted and the ALJ will decide.

---

79. What is the amount of a disability benefit?

The amount of a disabled worker's benefit generally equals his Primary Insurance Amount (PIA), determined as if the worker were at Full Retirement Age (FRA) and eligible for retirement benefits in the first month of his waiting period.[1]

However, the formula for determining a disabled worker's Average Indexed Monthly Earnings (AIME) and PIA differs from the formula used for a retiring worker. (See Primary Insurance Amount, Q 271 to Q 282.) There are also different limits on the amount of family benefits that can be paid to a disabled worker and his family. (See Maximum Family Benefits, Q 283 to Q 286.)

Disability benefits may be reduced before the worker attains Full Retirement Age (FRA) (see Q 49) to fully or partially offset a workers' compensation benefit or disability benefit under a federal, state, or local public law. This reduction will be made only if the total benefits payable to the worker (and dependents) under both programs exceed either 80 percent of his "average current earnings" before the onset of disability, or the family's total Social Security benefit, whichever is higher.

"Average current earnings" is defined as the highest of:

(1)   the "average monthly wage" used for computing primary insurance amounts for some beneficiaries, even though not used for this particular one; or

(2)   the average monthly earnings from covered employment during the highest five consecutive years after 1950; or

(3)   the average monthly earnings based on the one calendar year of highest earnings from covered employment during a period consisting of the year in which disability began and the five preceding years.

Note that the "highest earnings" in items (2) and (3) are determined without considering the maximum taxable earnings base.

Different factors are used in determining whether there is an offset and the amount of the offset. The factors used are determined by the date the worker first became disabled and the date the worker first became entitled to benefits. For workers who first became disabled after February 1981, and who first became entitled to disability benefits after August 1981, benefits paid as workers' compensation and received under a federal, state, or local public program will be considered in determining the amount of the offset.

Specifically excluded are all VA disability benefits, needs-based benefits, federal benefits based on employment covered for Social Security purposes, and state and local benefits based on covered state and local employment. Private pension or insurance benefits will also not be considered in determining the amount of the offset. The offset of benefits will continue until the worker reaches full retirement age.

For a worker disabled and receiving benefits prior to the above dates, only benefits paid as workers' compensation are considered in determining the amount of the offset. The offset of benefits stops when the worker reaches age sixty-two (rather than full retirement age).

The amount of the reduction is the amount by which Social Security benefits plus workers' compensation, and, where applicable, public disability benefits exceeds 80 percent of the average current earnings. The combined payments after the reduction will never be less than the total Social Security benefits were before the reduction. However, the amount of Social Security benefits can fluctuate based on the decrease or increase in the amount of workers' compensation. In addition, the amount of the reduction is adjusted periodically to take into account increases in national earnings levels (as applied to the initially-determined average current earnings), but this adjustment will never decrease the amount of benefits payable on the worker's earnings record.

When a state workers' compensation law, and, where applicable, a federal, state, or local public disability benefit law or plan generally provides for periodic payments, but permits a lump-sum settlement either in the form of a commutation or compromise agreement that discharges the liability of the insurer or the employer, such settlement is a substitute for periodic payments and is subject to the offset provisions. In this situation, the lump sum is prorated to reflect, as accurately as possible, the monthly rate that would have been paid had the lump sum award not been made. Medical and legal expenses incurred by the worker in connection with the workers' compensation/public disability benefit claim may be excluded from computing the offset.

In Oregon, when prorating a lump-sum award or settlement made under Oregon workers' compensation law for a permanent disability, the Social Security Administration will treat the lump sum as a substitute for periodic payments and will calculate the offset rate on a monthly basis by dividing the lump sum by the number of months between the date of the award and the date the worker reaches age sixty-five. However, if a workers' compensation award expressly establishes an offset rate under the Oregon statutory scheme, the Social Security Administration will prorate the lump-sum award according to that expressly stated offset rate.[2]

Workers' compensation payments for loss of bodily function, in addition to wage loss, can be used to offset Social Security disability insurance benefits. In a New Hampshire case, the claimant applied for, and was found entitled to, Social Security disability benefits. However, these benefits were offset because he also received New Hampshire workers' compensation payments, including a permanent impairment lump-sum award. After unsuccessfully appealing his case through administrative channels, the claimant appealed to the district court, claiming that the portion of his lump-sum settlement representing compensation for permanent impairment was not subject to offset. The district court held that permanent impairment payments under workers' compensation were to compensate an individual for loss of bodily function (not loss of wages), and thus could not be used to offset Social Security disability benefits.

The U.S. Court of Appeals for the First Circuit reversed the decision of the district court, holding that, although permanent impairment awards may be paid regardless of any actual loss of wages, the awards were never intended to be a departure from, or an exception to, the wage-loss principle. Permanent impairment benefits under New Hampshire workers' compensation law are for compensable disability under a state workers' compensation law and, therefore, are subject to offset against Social Security disability benefits.[3]

Notes

1. 42 U.S.C. sec. 423(a)(2).
2. Social Security Acquiescence Ruling 95-2(9) https://www.ssa.gov/OP_Home/rulings/ar/09/AR95-02-ar-09.html (last accessed August 22, 2022.
3. *Davidson v. Sullivan*, 942 F.2d 90, 34 Soc. Sec. Rep. Serv. 389 (1st Cir. 1991).

80. Is a person entitled to disability benefits regardless of wealth?

Yes, benefits are not payable on a "needs" basis. If a person meets the requirements for entitlement, disability benefits are payable regardless of wealth or assets.

It should be noted that Social Security disability (SSDI) and SSI disability are two separate disability benefit programs administered by the Social Security Administration. Individuals who apply for Social Security disability are able to do so because their record of work activity has allowed them to become insured which entitles them for SSDI benefits. Since this is an earned benefit, SSDI is this type of benefit, a person's assets have nothing to do with their eligibility to collect SSDI. SSI disability is a different program, being "needs-based" where a person's resources ARE taken into consideration.

81. Can a disabled person receive disability benefits even though his spouse is employed?

Yes, if the person is entitled to benefits based on his own earnings record. Entitlement to benefits as a worker is entirely independent of a spouse's employment.

82. Can a disabled person return to work while getting Social Security benefits?

Yes. Social Security allows what is referred to as a "trial work period" to see if an individual is able to return to work. Trial work periods can last up to nine months. A disability benefits recipient has nine months of trial work period in each period of sixty months.

83. What is the trial work period?

A trial work period is provided as an incentive for personal rehabilitation efforts for disabled workers, disabled widow(er)s and childhood disability beneficiaries who are still disabled but return to work. It allows them to perform services in as many as nine months (within a sixty-consecutive-month period if nine months of services were not completed before January 1992) without affecting their right to benefits during the trial work period, if their impairment does not improve during this period. (Because benefits will continue for the month the disability is determined to have ceased and the two months after that, benefits may be paid for at least twelve months during which the individual works.) The idea behind the trial work period is that if someone's medical condition has improved to the point that they think they might be able to make a living, they can go to work and earn money for that nine-month period of time without jeopardizing their Social Security Disability payments. The ability to participate in the program is dependent on reporting to the Social Security Administration work activity, income, and expenses.

A person is generally entitled to a trial work period if receiving disability insurance benefits, child's benefits based on disability, or widow(er)'s or surviving divorced spouse's benefits based on disability. Even after the end of the trial work period, a person can still receive disability benefits for any month in which they do not make more than the substantial gainful activity (SGA) amount. A person will lose disability benefits if they make more than the maximum SGA.

The trial work period begins with the month in which the person becomes entitled to:

(1)   disability insurance benefits;

(2)   child's benefits based on disability; or

(3)   widow(er)'s or surviving divorced spouse's benefits based on disability.

It cannot begin before the month in which the person files an application for benefits.

The trial work period ends with the close of whichever of the following calendar months is earlier:

(1) The ninth month (whether or not the months have been consecutive) in which the person has performed services if that ninth month is prior to January 1992.

(2) The ninth month (whether or not the months have been consecutive and whether or not the previous eight months of services were prior to January 1992) in which the person has performed services within a rolling sixty-month period if that ninth month is after December 1991.

(3) The month in which new evidence, other than evidence relating to any work the person did during the trial work period, shows that the person is not disabled, even though the person has not worked a full nine months. The Social Security Administration may find that the disability has ended at any time during the trial work period if the medical or other evidence shows that the person is no longer disabled.

A person is not entitled to a trial work period if:

(1) the person is entitled to a period of disability but not to disability insurance benefits, child's benefits based on disability, or widow(er)'s or surviving divorced spouse's benefits based on disability; or

(2) the person performs work demonstrating the ability to engage in substantial gainful activity during any required waiting period for benefits; or

(3) the person performs work demonstrating the ability to engage in substantial gainful activity within twelve months of the onset of the impairment(s) that prevented him from performing substantial gainful activity and before the date of the decision awarding him disability benefits; or

(4) the person performs work demonstrating the ability to engage in substantial gainful activity at any time after the onset of the impairment(s) that prevented him from engaging in substantial gainful activity but before the month he files his application for disability benefits.

84. What amount of earnings trigger a trial work period?

During a trial work period, a beneficiary receiving Social Security disability benefits may test his or her ability to work and still be considered disabled. The SSA does not consider services performed during the trial work period as showing that the disability has ended until services have been performed in at least nine months (not necessarily consecutive) in a rolling sixty-month period.

During 2021, any month in which earnings exceeded $940 was considered a month of services for an individual's trial work period. In 2022, this monthly amount increased to $970 and will be $1,050 for 2023.

AMOUNT OF MONTHLY EARNINGS THAT INITIATE A TRIAL WORK PERIOD	
Year	Monthly earnings
1978 and before	$50
1979 through 1989	75
1990 through 2000	200
2001	530
2002	560
2003	570
2004	580
2005	590
2006	620
2007	640
2008	670
2009	700
2010	720
2011	720
2012	720
2013	750
2014	770
2015	780
2016	810
2017	840
2018	850
2019	880
2020	910
2021	940
2022	970
2023	1,050

85. What is the trigger amount of income which indicates a person is engaged in Substantial Gainful Activity?

To be eligible for disability benefits, a person must be unable to engage in substantial gainful activity (SGA). A person who is earning more than a certain monthly amount (net of impairment-related work expenses) is ordinarily considered to be engaging in SGA. The amount of monthly earnings considered as SGA depends on the nature of a person's disability. The Social Security Act specifies a higher SGA amount for statutorily blind individuals; Federal regulations specify a lower SGA amount for non-blind individuals. The amount is set annually based on the national average wage index.

Amounts for 2021

The monthly SGA amount for statutorily blind individuals for 2023 is $1,470. For non-blind individuals, the monthly SGA amount for 2023 is $2,460. SGA for the blind does not apply to Supplemental Security Income (SSI) benefits, while SGA for the non-blind disabled applies to Social Security and SSI benefits. See historical series of SGA amounts below.

HISTORICAL SGA AMOUNTS		
Year	Blind	Non-blind
1975	$200	$200
1976	230	230
1977	240	240
1978	334	260
1979	375	280
1980	417	300
1981	459	300
1982	500	300
1983	550	300
1984	580	300
1985	610	300
1986	650	300
1987	680	300
1988	700	300
1989	740	300
1990	780	500
1991	810	500
1992	850	500
1993	880	500
1994	930	500
1995	940	500
1996	960	500
1997	1,000	500
1998	1,050	500
1999	1,110	700[a]

HISTORICAL SGA AMOUNTS		
Year	Blind	Non-blind
2000	1,170	700
2001	1,240	740
2002	1,300	780
2003	1,330	800
2004	1,350	810
2005	1,380	830
2006	1,450	860
2007	1,500	900
2008	1,570	940
2009	1,640	980
2010	1,640	1,000
2011	1,640	1,000
2012	1,690	1,010
2013	1,740	1,040
2014	1,800	1,070
2015	1,820	1,090
2016	1,820	1,130
2017	1,950	1,170
2018	1,970	1,180
2019	2,040	1,220
2020	2,110	1,260
2021	2,190	1,310
2022	2,260	1,350
2023	2,460	1.470

86. What is the re-entitlement period or Extended Period of Eligibility (EPE)?

The re-entitlement period, or Extended Period of Eligibility, is an additional period after nine months of trial work during which a person may continue to test their ability to work if they have a disabling impairment. The EPE begins the month after the Trial Work Period (TWP) ends, even if the person is not working that month. The first thirty-six months of the EPE is the re-entitlement period. A person will not be paid benefits for any month after the second month following the month disability ceased due to substantial gainful activity in this period in which they did substantial gainful activity. A person will be paid benefits for months in which they did not do substantial gainful activity.

If anyone else is receiving monthly benefits based on a disabled person's earnings record, that individual will not be paid benefits for any month for which the disabled person cannot be paid benefits during the re-entitlement period. If a disabled person's benefits are stopped because he or she does substantial gainful activity, the benefits may be started again without a new application and a new determination of disability if the person discontinues doing substantial gainful activity during this period. In determining, for re-entitlement benefit purposes, whether a person does substantial gainful activity in a month, the Social Security Administration considers only work in or earnings for that month. It does not consider the average amount of work or earnings over a period of months. (See Q 94.)

87. How does the Extended Period of Eligibility (EPE) work?

During the thirty-six-month re-entitlement period, an individual gets benefits for all months their earnings or work activities are below the substantial gainful activity (SGA) level as long as they continue to have a disabling impairment. SSA suspends cash benefits for months earnings are over the SGA level. If earnings fall below the SGA level in the re-entitlement period, SSA can start the individual's benefits again.

Once an individual works above SGA in the EPE, they will no longer meet the requirements for disability due to work and their disability ceases. SSA will pay benefits for the month the disability ceased and for the following two months. This is referred to as "the grace period". If earnings fall below SGA again and the person is still in the thirty-six-month re-entitlement period, SSA can restart their benefits without a new application.

88. What is the Vocational Reimbursement Program?

Social Security administers a program called the Vocational Rehabilitation Reimbursement Program to assist beneficiaries with disabilities to be able to work. Under this program, Social Security pays State vocational rehabilitation agencies for services provided to beneficiaries with disabilities if the services result in the person's achieving work at a specified amount of earnings. Although the primary focus of the vocational rehabilitation program is to help people with disabilities work, SSA also pays for vocational rehabilitation services if the individual continues with a program after it is determined that the person's disability ceased because of medical recovery. These services must result in the individual's return to work for at least nine continuous months at the substantial gainful activity (SGA) level.

89. Can an individual continue to receive benefits after the Extended Period of Eligibility (EPE) ends?

Yes, if the individual is not working above Substantial Gainful Activity (SGA) and is eligible for a benefit payment for the thirty-seventh month of the EPE, they will continue to receive benefits until they work:

- a month at the SGA level, or

- medically recover.

90. Can a person become entitled to disability benefits after becoming entitled to some other type of Social Security benefit?

Yes. For example, a person who is receiving a reduced retirement benefit before Full Retirement Age (FRA) can become entitled to disability benefits. However, the disability benefit is actuarially reduced for the months that the person has already received retirement benefits.

91. Will a disabled person lose benefits by refusing to accept rehabilitation services?

Yes, a person will lose the disabled worker's benefit by refusing without good cause to accept vocational rehabilitation services.

Good cause for refusing vocational rehabilitation services exists if, for example, the person is a member of any recognized church or religious sect that teaches reliance solely upon prayer or spiritual means for the treatment of any impairment, and refusal to accept vocational rehabilitation services is based solely on adherence to these teachings.[1]

Note

1. See SSR 64-13: SECTION 222(b). -- DISABILITY -- DEDUCTION FOR REFUSAL TO ACCEPT VOCATIONAL REHABILITATION SERVICES https://www.socialsecurity.gov/OP_Home/rulings/di/02/SSR64-13-di-02.html (last accessed August 22, 2022) and SSR 78-24: DISABILITY --- REFUSAL TO ACCEPT VOCATIONAL REHABILITATION SERVICES https://www.socialsecurity.gov/OP_Home/rulings/di/02/SSR78-24-di-02.html (last accessed August 22, 2022).

92. What are the special rules for disability benefits when alcoholism or drug addiction is involved?

An individual is not considered disabled if alcoholism or drug addiction is a contributing factor material to the Social Security Administration's determination that the individual is disabled.

Since 1996, a claimant cannot get Social Security disability insurance (SSDI) or SSI benefits for alcoholism or drug addiction alone. Disability benefits for damage caused by alcohol or drug abuse, such as liver damage, emotional problems, cardiovascular disease, or cancer ARE available, with a caveat – the claimant must no longer have a drinking problem or be abusing drugs unless the condition is so severe that the damage is not reversible. However, if the SSA determines that illness of a claimant would go away if they stopped the abuse of alcohol or drugs, the SSA can deny the claim. Social Security does not consider substance abuse to be disabling until it causes irreversible medical conditions. Social Security agrees that some medical and mental conditions from abuse cannot be reversed merely by abstaining from continuing the abuse. Most chronic substance abusers have irreversible medical or mental problems because of the changes in their body from the abuse.

Social Security no longer has a specific list of items used to qualify for drug addiction.

Up until 2017, there was a listing for substance addiction disorders that could be used to determine if the claimant had suffered specific changes in behaviors or physical health due to regular abuse of any prescription or illegal drugs affecting the central nervous system. However, a claimant can still qualify for disability benefits by meeting the criteria for the following conditions:

- brain damage (neurocognitive disorder)/organic brain syndrome

- liver damage

- pancreatitis

- gastritis

- peripheral neuropathy

- seizures

- anxiety disorders

- major clinical depression/depression syndrome

- personality disorder

A beneficiary who qualifies for disability benefits on a basis other than alcoholism or drug addiction, but is determined by the Social Security Administration to have an alcohol or drug addiction and to be incapable of managing the disability benefits, must have the disability benefit paid to a representative payee. The Social Security Administration must notify the beneficiary that benefits are being deposited to a representative payee because of alcoholism or drug addiction. In addition, the Social Security Administration must refer these individuals to the appropriate state agency administering the state plan for substance abuse treatment services.

The Social Security Administration determines whether drug addiction or alcoholism is a contributing factor material to the determination of disability by evaluating which physical and mental limitations would remain if the disabled person stopped using drugs or alcohol. If the Social Security Administration determines that the disabled person's remaining limitations are not disabling, the Social Security Administration will find that drug addiction or alcoholism is a contributing factor material to the determination of disability and deny disability benefits.[1]

Note

1. http://www.ssa.gov/OP_Home/cfr20/416/416-0935.htm (last accessed August 22, 2022).

93. What happens when a person works above the Substantial Gainful Activity the first time?

The first time that someone works above Substantial Gainful Activity (SGA) in the Extended Period of Eligibility (EPE), Social Security will decide that they no longer meet the requirements for disability due to work, and say that the disability "ceased". SSN will pay benefits for the month the disability ceased and the following two months ("the grace period"). If earnings fall below SGA and the person is still in the thirty-six-month re-entitlement period, SSN can restart their benefits without a new application.

94. When do a person's disability benefits end?

The last month of entitlement to a disabled worker's benefit generally is whichever of the following occurs earliest:

- the second month after the month in which the disability ceases;

- the month before the month the worker attains Full Retirement Age (at which time benefits are automatically converted to retirement benefits); or

- the month before the month in which the worker dies.

However, there are certain conditions under which benefits may continue or re-entitlement to benefits may be established after disability ceases:

1. *Benefits for persons in vocational rehabilitation programs.* Benefits for disabled and blind workers participating in a vocational rehabilitation program may continue until completion of the program, or for a specified period of time in certain situations where disability ceases prior to completion of the program. This provision applies only to disabled individuals who have medically recovered, who began the vocational rehabilitation program before disability ceased, and for whom the Social Security Administration has determined that continued participation in the vocational rehabilitation program would increase the likelihood of permanent removal from the disability benefit rolls.[1]

2. *Extended period of eligibility for re-entitlement to benefits following trial work period.* Individuals who continue to have a disabling impairment receive an extended period of eligibility immediately following the completion of a nine-month trial work period. If disability ceased because of work activity and earnings subsequently fall below the level considered substantial gainful activity within a specified period, benefits may be reinstated without the need for a new application and disability determination. This re-entitlement period to disability benefits is thirty-six months. Benefits for the family of the worker are suspended during this period if the worker's benefits are suspended.[2]

    Example 1. A disabled person completes the trial work period in December 2019. He is then working at the substantial gainful activity level and continues to do so throughout the thirty-six months following completion of his trial work period and thereafter. The disabled person's termination month is January 2022, which is the thirty-seventh month – that is, the first month in which the disabled person performed substantial gainful activity after the thirty-sixth month following his trial work period.

    Example 2. A disabled person completes the trial work period in December 2019, but she is not able to work at the substantial gainful activity level until March 2023, three months after the last month of his re-entitlement period. The disabled person's termination month is June 2022 – that is, the third month after the earliest month he or she performed substantial gainful activity.

The Social Security Administration may use a "medical improvement standard" to terminate disability benefits. Benefits can be terminated only if one of the following conditions applies:

- There is substantial evidence that there has been medical improvement in the individual's impairment or combination of impairments (other than medical improvement which is not related to the person's ability to work), and the individual is able to engage in substantial gainful activity (see Q 60).

- There is substantial evidence demonstrating that, although there is no medical improvement, the person has benefited from advances in medical or vocational therapy or technology related to the ability to work, and the person is now able to perform substantial gainful activity.

- There is substantial evidence that, although there is no medical improvement, the person has benefited from vocational therapy, and the beneficiary can now perform substantial gainful activity.

- There is substantial evidence that, based on new or improved diagnostic techniques or evaluations, the person's impairment or combination of impairments is not as disabling as it was considered to be at the time of the prior determination, and therefore the individual is able to perform substantial gainful activity.

- There is substantial evidence, either in the file at the original determination or newly obtained, showing that the prior determination was in error.

- There is substantial evidence that the original decision was obtained by fraud.

- The individual is engaging in substantial gainful activity and fails without good cause to cooperate in the review or follow prescribed treatment or cannot be located.

Notes

1. See Vocational Rehabilitation Cost Reimbursement Program, http://www.ssa.gov/work/vocational_rehab.html (last accessed September 19, 2021).
2. See DI 13010.210 Extended Period of Eligibility (EPE) – Overview, https://secure.ssa.gov/poms.nsf/lnx/0413010210 (last accessed September 20, 2021) and 20 C.F.R. 404.1592a.

95. Are benefits payable to the family of a disabled worker?

Yes.

See SPOUSE'S BENEFIT and CHILD'S BENEFIT, immediately following.

96. If an individual is already collecting a disability benefit, can they suspend their benefits at Full Retirement Age and earn delayed retirement credits?

Yes. They can suspend at Full Retirement Age (FRA) to earn Delayed Retirement Credits. The beneficiary needs to realize, however, that any benefits being paid off their record to any other individuals will also be suspended.

Same-Sex Marriages

97. Are same-sex couples eligible for the same Social Security benefits as opposite-sex couples?

Yes. The Social Security Administration fully recognizes same-sex marriages in all states and some marital legal relationships such as civil unions and domestic partnerships for the purposes of determining entitlement to Social Security, Medicare and Supplemental Security Income. The SSA is also recognizing same-sex marriages and some nonmartial legal relationships entered into in foreign jurisdictions as well.[1] Social Security is now processing retirement, surviving spouse, and lump-sum death payment claims for same-sex couples in nonmarital legal relationships and paying benefits where they are due. In addition, the Social Security Administration considers same-sex marriage when determining SSI eligibility and benefit amounts.

More surviving same-sex partners now can qualify for Social Security survivors' benefits. People who were in a same-sex relationship with a partner who passed away may qualify for Social Security survivors' benefits based on their partner's record. Qualifications for survivors' benefits are possible if one of the following requirements are met:

1.   The survivor and deceased partner would have been married at the time of the partner's death if state laws hadn't prevented the marriage.

2.   The survivor and deceased partner would have been married longer if not for unconstitutional state laws that prevented marriage.

Historical Background

On June 26, 2015, the United States Supreme Court issued a decision in *Obergefell v. Hodges*,[2] holding that same-sex couples have a constitutional right to marry in all states. This decision enables same-sex couples to be married in one state and have their marriage recognized by all other states. As a direct result of this decision, all same-sex marriages (including some foreign same-sex marriages) and some nonmarital legal relationships (such as some civil unions and domestic partnerships), will be recognized as being married for the purposes of determining their entitlement to Social Security benefits and as well as Supplemental Security Income (SSI) payments (see Q 108). The Social Security Administration recommends that someone who is the spouse, divorced spouse, or surviving spouse or a same-sex marriage or other legal same-sex relationship to immediately apply for benefits. Immediate applying will preserve the filing date, which can affect benefits.

This had been a changing area of law. In June 2013, the Supreme Court ruling in *United States v. Windsor*,[3] had established that same sex couples who were married in a jurisdiction where same-sex marriages are recognized were eligible for spousal benefits, such as the spousal survivor benefit, the spousal retirement benefit, and the lump sum death benefit. At that time, the Social Security Administration reviewed its own policies regarding same-sex marriage after the Supreme Court decision, and concluded that same-sex couples who are legally married in one state remain married for federal tax purposes even if they reside in a state that does not recognize their marriage.[4]

Notes

1. SSA Publication No. 05-10014, June 2022, What Same-Sex Couples Need to Know, https://www.ssa.gov/pubs/EN-05-10014.pdf (last accessed August 25, 2022).
2. 576 U.S. 644, 135 S. Ct. 2587, 192 L. Ed.2d 609 (2015).
3. 570 U.S. 744, 133 S. Ct. 2675, 186 L. Ed. 808 (2013).
4. Rev. Rul. 2013-17, https://www.irs.gov/pub/irs-drop/rr-13-17.pdf (last accessed August 25, 2022).

98. Does a person qualify for a benefit as a spouse (or surviving spouse) if in a civil union, a domestic partnership, or other non-marital legal relationship?

Very likely. Social Security is now processing some retirement, surviving spouse, and lump-sum death payment claims for same-sex couples in non-marital legal relationships (such as some civil unions and domestic partnerships) and paying benefits where they are due. The best action would be to apply immediately for benefits, which will protect the filer against loss of any potential benefits.

99. Does the Supreme Court case legalizing same-sex marriage affect Medicare?

Yes. Medicare is managed by the Centers for Medicare & Medicare Services (CMS). The Social Security Administration works with CMS by determining eligibility for and enrolling people in Medicare.

In light of the Supreme Court's rulings that legitimized same-sex marriage in all states, there were changes to Medicare rules for same-sex spouses. Spouses in same-sex marriages now fully qualify for the following based on a same-sex spouse's work history:

- Premium-free Part A

- Social Security Retirement benefits

- End-Stage Renal Disease Medicare

In addition,

- Same-sex spouses can delay Medicare Part B enrollment without penalty while they are covered by insurance based on their spouse's current work (job-based insurance).

- Same-sex spouses is able to use a spouse's job-based insurance as primary coverage to Medicare, even after becoming eligible for Medicare.

- A same-sex spouse is eligible for a Part B Special Enrollment Period if they are or were covered by a spouse's job-based insurance.

- There may be changes to Part B and Part D Premiums.

100. How can someone in a same-sex marriage be sure as to which benefits that he or she is eligible?

The best way is simply to apply immediately and get a determination. In addition, it will preserve the filing date that is used to determine the start date of benefits.

101. Must an individual that is receiving Social Security benefits tell the Social Security Administration that they are in a civil union or other non-marital legal relationship?

Yes. An individual's status in a civil union or other non-marital legal relationship may affect their entitlement to benefits.

Non-traditional marital relationships, like civil unions and domestic partnerships, differ in types of qualification of benefits by state. All same-sex marriages are legal and qualify for benefits at the federal level, but be mindful that this is specific to marriage. At the federal level, the Social Security Administration (SSA) recognizes some legal non-marital relationships, like civil unions, for the purposes of receiving retirement, surviving spouse, and lump-sum death payments benefits – but not all.

Civil unions and domestic partnerships are not recognized by every state, which requires an individual to check state laws in each circumstance.

SSA advice is that an application be tendered as soon as possible for benefits, even if the applicant(s) are unsure of eligibility status. The questionable cases are investigated, which takes time. Applying sooner rather than later will also help ensure loss of future benefits.

Five states allow for civil unions: Colorado, Hawaii, Illinois, Vermont, and New Jersey.

California, District of Columbia, Maine, Nevada, Oregon, Washington, and Wisconsin allow for domestic partnerships, while Hawaii allows for a similar relationship known as "reciprocal beneficiaries".

Following the passage of same sex marriage laws, five states — Connecticut, Delaware, New Hampshire, Rhode Island, and Vermont — have converted all civil unions into marriages.

102. Can same-sex partners with a child put both of their names on a Social Security number record?

Yes. Regardless of the gender of either partner, SSA can place both parents' names on the child's Social Security number record. Both parents need to provide proof of being the legal parents of the child. The following documents (provided by both parents) will provide proof of legal parentage.

- Original or amended birth certificate

- The final adoption decree

- Court determination of paternity (also referred to as a court order of parentage)

All documents must be originals or certified copies from the issuing agency. Photocopies or notarized copies are not acceptable.

103. Will Social Security adjust the Income Related Monthly Adjustment Amounts for an individual who filed a tax return as "single" but has now amended it to "married" for prior years in a same-sex marriage?

Yes. If an amended return is filed and it changes the income counted to determine the IRMAA, Social Security will change it. The filer will need to provide:

- the amended return; and

- the acknowledgment receipt from the Internal Revenue Service.

Social Security will update the records as necessary.

104. Should couples in a same-sex marriage or civil union or other non-marital legal relationship inform Social Security if one or the other are receiving Social Security benefits or Supplemental Security Income (SSI)?

A same-sex marriage, civil union, or other non-marital legal relationship may affect entitlement to benefits. Individuals in a civil union or other non-marital legal relationship need to report this status to the Social Security Administration. The Social Security Administration now recognizes same-sex marriages in all states and foreign jurisdictions, as well as some nonmarital legal relationships such as civil unions and domestic partnerships, including those established in foreign jurisdictions for purposes of determining entitlement to Social Security benefits, Medicare, and SSI.

In the case of separation, divorce, or annulment, as well as becoming a parent, this information must be reported as well as it can affect eligibility and or payment amounts.

In addition, a spouse's income and resources may affect SSI eligibility or the payment amount.

105. Must an individual in a same-sex marriage tell Social Security of the marriage?

Yes. An individual must inform the Social Security Administration of their status as married, separated, or divorced, or if a marriage has been annulled. This information could affect SSI eligibility or payment amount.

106. Once the Internal Revenue Service (IRS) recognizes a same-sex marriage and allows an individual to file as "married filing jointly," can that individual have their Income-Related Monthly Adjustment Amounts (IRMAA) removed?

Yes. Any life-changing event, such as marriage, can create eligibility for a new determination. The individual must provide proof of marriage and estimated income for the tax year. If a tax return is amended and it changes the income used to determine the income-related monthly adjustment amounts, this information needs to be provided, including the amended return and the receipt of acknowledgement from the IRS.

107. Will the Social Security Administration recognize a same-sex marriage that was celebrated in a foreign country?

Yes. The SSA is now recognizing foreign same-sex marriages and some foreign marriages for purposes of determining entitlement to benefits. The best way to be certain if the foreign same-sex marriage will be recognized is to apply.

108. What is a Non-Marital Legal Relationship (NMLR)?

Social Security uses the term "NMLR" to describe a variety of legal relationships for two individuals who are not considered married, but are provided with some (or all) rights that could be associated with a marriage. Examples of NMLRs include but are not limited to the following:

- Civil unions

- Domestic partnerships

- Designated beneficiary

- Reciprocal beneficiary[1].

The Social Security Act authorizes the SSA to consider the claimant to be the social security number holder's spouse for benefit purposes when the state of the number holder's domicile would allow the claimant to inherit a spouse's share of the number holder's personal property should the number holder die without leaving a will. Under these circumstances, SSA will treat the couple's NMLR as a marital relationship for Title II and Medicare benefit purposes.[2]

Notes

1. https://health.hawaii.gov/vitalrecords/reciprocal-beneficiary-relationships/#:~:text=A%20reciprocal%20beneficiary%20relationship%20is,to%20 another%20reciprocal%20beneficiary%20relationship. (Last accessed August 26, 2022).
2. https://secure.ssa.gov/apps10/poms.nsf/lnx/0200210004 (last accessed August 26, 2022).

109. What is the process to recognize same-sex marriages?

Marriage Within the United States

Social Security will recognize a valid same-sex marriage as of the date of the marriage, including during periods when the individuals' state of domicile did not recognize same-sex marriages.

The SSA looks at state law to decide if an individual is married. They may decide individuals are married if:

- There was a ceremony while the state of residence allowed same-sex marriage.

- There wasn't a legal marriage ceremony under state law, but individuals lived like they were married and told people they were married.

- There was a marriage ceremony before the state of residence allowed same-sex marriage.

Marriage Outside The United States

In the instance of the same-sex marriage or NMLR celebrated in a foreign jurisdiction (other than a U.S. state, the District of Columbia, the U.S. Virgin Islands, Puerto Rico, Guam, American Samoa, or the Northern Mariana Islands), the SSA says it "recognize[s] same-sex marriages and some non-marital legal relationships established in foreign jurisdictions for purposes of determining entitlement to Social Security benefits, Medicare entitlement, and SSI".[1] In the cases of foreign marriage, the SSA will look at factors including:

- Prior non-marital legal relationships (NMLR)

- Existence of a foreign ceremonial marriage – proof of marriage is required

- Existence of a foreign non-ceremonial marriage, such as a common-law marriage, deemed marriage, NMLR, etc.

    o SSA must address if the non-ceremonial marriage, deemed marriage, or NMLR was permitted in the foreign jurisdiction and recognized by the state of the NH's domicile (or the District of Columbia if domicile is in a foreign jurisdiction) to convey spousal inheritance rights.

- If a marriage occurred in a country listed in the table below:

Foreign Jurisdiction	Date Same-Sex Marriages Were Permitted
American Samoa	6/26/2015
Argentina	7/21/2010
Australia	1/9/2018
Austria	1/1/2019

Foreign Jurisdiction	Date Same-Sex Marriages Were Permitted
Belgium	6/1/2003
Brazil	5/14/2013
Canada - Alberta, Prince Edward Island, Northwest Territories, Nunavut	7/20/2005
Canada - British Columbia	7/8/2003
Canada — Manitoba	9/16/2004
Canada - Newfoundland and Labrador	12/21/2004
Canada - New Brunswick	7/4/2005
Canada - Nova Scotia	9/24/2004
Canada — Ontario	6/10/2003
Canada — Saskatchewan	11/5/2004
Canada — Quebec	3/19/2004
Canada —Yukon	7/14/2004
England	3/13/2014
France	5/17/2013
Guam	6/9/2015
Ireland	11/16/2015
Netherlands	4/1/2001
Norway	1/1/2009
Puerto Rico	6/26/2015
South Africa	11/30/2006
Spain[1]	7/2/2005
Sweden	5/1/2009
U.S. Virgin Islands	6/26/2015
1. For marriages between a Spanish citizen and a non-Spanish national contracted between July 2, 2005 and October 26, 2005, it is necessary to refer the case for a legal opinion.	

Note

1. https://secure.ssa.gov/apps10/poms.nsf/lnx/0200210006 (last accessed September 19, 2022).

Spouse's Benefit

110. Is the spouse of a retired or disabled worker entitled to benefits?

Yes, an individual is entitled to spouse's benefits on a worker's Social Security record if:[1]

- the worker is entitled to retirement or disability benefits;

- the individual has filed an application for spouse's benefits;

- the spouse is not entitled to a retirement or disability benefit based on a primary insurance amount equal to or larger than one-half of the worker's primary insurance amount; and

- the spouse is either age sixty-two or over, or has in their care a child under age sixteen, or disabled, who is entitled to benefits on the worker's Social Security record.

The spouse of a worker must also meet at least one of the following conditions:

(1) The spouse must have been married to the worker for at least one year just before filing an application for benefits.

(2) The spouse must be the natural mother or father of the worker's biological child.

(3) The spouse was entitled or potentially entitled to spouse's, widow(er)'s, parent's, or childhood disability benefits in the month before the month of marriage to the worker.

(4) The spouse was entitled or potentially entitled to a widow(er)'s, parent's, or child's (over eighteen) annuity under the Railroad Retirement Act in the month before the month of marriage to the worker.

A spouse is "potentially entitled" if he or she meets all of the requirements for entitlement other than the filing of an application and attaining the required age.

Note

1. 42 U.S.C. sec. 402(b), 402(c).

---

111. What is meant by having a child "in care"?

Having a child in care is a basic requirement for spouse's benefits when the spouse is under age sixty-two and for mother's and father's benefits (see Q 144 to Q 158).[1]

"In care" means that the mother or father:

(1) exercises parental control and responsibility for the welfare and care of a child under age sixteen or mentally incompetent child aged sixteen or over; or

(2) performs personal services for a disabled but mentally competent child aged sixteen or over.

The mother or father may exercise parental control and responsibility or perform personal services alone or together.

A claimant for mother's/father's, surviving divorced mother's/father's, or spouse's (under age sixty-two) benefits must have in-care an entitled child of the wage earner. To receive an unreduced benefit, a spouse age sixty-two to full retirement age (FRA) must have a child of the wage earner in their care.

The in-care child must meet **all** of the following:[2]

- be entitled to a child's insurance benefit,

- meet the conditions for entitlement,

  - For mother's/father's or spouse's (age sixty-two to FRA) benefits, the child may be entitled on any earnings record.

  - For surviving divorced mother's/father's and spouse's benefits (under age sixty-two), the child must be entitled on the wage earner's earning record.)

- meet the relationship requirements to be considered a child of the deceased NH; and

- be under age sixteen (age eighteen prior to September 1981), or be disabled.

- Child-in-care also applies when the child was entitled to childhood disability benefits (CDB) prior to age twenty-two termination and became re-entitled to a new period of disability as a CDB after age twenty-two.

A mother/father must have in-care an entitled child of the wage earner when:[3]

- he or she files an application for benefits;

- he or she seeks entitlement within the retroactive period; or

- converting a spouse's benefit to a mother's/father's benefit.

Notes

1. 42 U.S.C. sec. 402(b)(1)(B), 402(c)(1)(B).
2. RS 00208.005 Child-in-care benefits, SSA - POMS: RS 00208.005 - Child-in-Care Benefits - 02/24/2017 (last accessed August 26, 2022).
3. *Id.*

112. Is the divorced spouse of a retired or disabled worker entitled to a spouse's benefits?

The spouse is entitled to a divorced spouse's benefit on the worker's Social Security record if:[1]

(1)   the worker is entitled to retirement or disability benefits;

(2)   the spouse has filed an application for divorced spouse's benefits;

(3)   the spouse is not entitled to a retirement or disability benefit based on a primary insurance amount that equals or exceeds one-half the worker's primary insurance amount;

(4)   the spouse is age sixty-two or over;

(5)   the spouse is not married; and

(6)   the spouse was married to the worker for at least ten years before the date the divorce became final.

A divorced spouse who is age sixty-two or over and who has been divorced for at least two years is able to receive benefits based on the earnings of a former spouse who is eligible for retirement benefits, regardless of whether the former spouse has retired or applied for benefits. This two-year waiting period for independent entitlement to divorced spouse's benefits is waived if the worker was entitled to benefits prior to the divorce. A spouse whose divorce took place after the couple had begun to receive retirement benefits, and whose former spouse (the worker) returned to work after the divorce (thus causing a suspension of benefits), will not lose benefits on which he or she had come to depend.

Note

1. 42 U.S.C. sec. 402(b)(1), 402(c)(1); https://secure.ssa.gov/apps10/poms.nsf/lnx/0300202005 (last accessed August 26, 2022).

113. How does if effect the spousal benefit if the divorced spouse of a retired or disabled worker continues to work?

If the ex-spouse continues to work while receiving benefits, the same earnings limits apply to them as apply to their ex. If the ex-spouse is eligible for benefits and is also working, they can use the Social Security retirement earnings test calculator to see how those earnings would affect those benefit payments.

If the ex-spouse will also receive a pension based on work not covered by Social Security, such as government work, their Social Security may be affected.

The amount of benefits a divorced spouse gets has no effect on the amount of benefits a person or their current spouse may receive.

114. What is the amount of a spouse's benefit?

If the spouse of a retired or disabled worker is caring for the worker's child under age sixteen or disabled child, the monthly benefit equals half of the worker's PIA, regardless of his age.[1] If the spouse is not caring for a child, monthly benefits starting at full retirement age likewise equal half of the worker's PIA; but if the spouse chooses to start receiving benefits at or after age sixty-two, but before full retirement age, the benefit is reduced. (See Table 10 for spouse's reduced benefits.)

If the spouse chooses to receive, and is paid, a reduced spouse's benefit for months before full retirement age, the spouse is not entitled to the full spouse's benefit rate upon reaching full retirement age. A reduced benefit rate is payable for as long as the spouse remains entitled to spouse's benefits. (But see Q 299, Recomputation of Benefits.)

A spouse will not always receive a spouse's full benefit; under the following circumstances a spouse will receive a smaller amount:

(1)   If the total amount of monthly benefits payable on the worker's Social Security account exceeds the Maximum Family Benefit, all benefits (except the worker's benefit) will be reduced proportionately to bring the total within the family maximum limit. (See BENEFIT COMPUTATION, Q 268 to Q 326.)

(2)   If a spouse who is not caring for a child elects to start receiving a spouse's benefit at age sixty-two (or at any time between age sixty-two and full retirement age), the benefit will be reduced by 25/36 of 1 percent for each of the first thirty-six months that the spouse is under full retirement age when benefits commence, and by 5/12 of 1 percent for each such month in excess of thirty-six months.

(3)   If the spouse is entitled to a retirement or disability benefit that is smaller than the spouse's benefit rate, the spouse will receive a spouse's benefit equal to only the difference between the retirement or disability benefit and the full spouse's benefit rate.

(4)   The amount of a spouse's monthly benefit is usually reduced if the spouse receives a pension based on his or her own work for a federal, state, or local government that is not covered by Social Security on the last day of such employment. However, the Social Security Protection Act of 2004 generally requires that a person work in a situation covered by Social Security for five years to be exempt from this Government Pension Offset (GPO). See Q 120 for more information on the GPO.

If a spouse is entitled to a retirement or disability benefit that is larger than the spouse's benefit rate, he or she will receive only the retirement or disability benefit.

Note

1.   42 U.S.C. sec. 402(b)(2), 402(c)(2).

115. What is the amount of a divorced spouse's benefit?

The amount of a divorced spouse's benefit is the same as a current spouse's benefit amount.[1] As a general rule, it will equal half of the beneficiary's former spouse's PIA and will be reduced if he or she elects to start receiving benefits before Full Retirement Age. However, a divorced spouse's benefit is paid independently of other family benefits. In other words, it will not be subject to reduction because of the family maximum limit and will not be considered in figuring the maximum limit for the former spouse's family.

Note

1. 42 U.S.C. sec. 402(b)(2), 402(c)(2).

116. What was the impact of the 2015 Bi-Partisan Budget Act on divorced spouses and their ability to collect?

The Bi-Partisan Budget Act DOES impact divorced individuals. Individuals divorced for greater than two years are considered an **Independently Entitled Divorced Spouse** and can collect a benefit from an ex-spouse even if the ex-spouse is not receiving any benefit. If divorced for two years or fewer, the ex-spouse must be receiving a retirement or disability benefit or have filed and suspended benefits by April 29, 2016 for the other ex-spouse to collect.

FIRST CHANGE: Timing of Multiple Benefits ("Deemed Filing")

Prior to change, some spouses received spousal benefits at full retirement age, while letting the retirement benefits based on their earnings record grow by delaying to file for benefits.

Under the changes of the 2015 Act, if an individual was eligible for benefits both as a retired worker and as a spouse (even as a divorced spouse) in the first month they want their benefits to begin and they turned 62 before January 2, 2016, they will receive the higher of the two benefits. If they **were not yet full retirement age**, they have to apply for both benefits (known as deemed filing).

If an individual turned 62 **on or after** January 2, 2016 and was eligible for benefits both as a retired worker and as a spouse (or even as a divorced spouse) in the first month they want their benefits to begin, then deemed filing applies **at age 62 and extends to full retirement age and beyond**. In addition, deemed filing may occur in any month after becoming entitled to retirement benefits.

Deemed filing operates in a matter that when the person files for either their retirement or their spouse's benefit, they are required or "deemed" to file for the other benefit as well. The Bipartisan Budget Act extends deemed filing rules to apply at full retirement age and beyond.

The rationale for the change was that historically, if spousal benefits were higher than their own retirement benefit, they received a combination of benefits equaling the higher benefit. They intent of the law is to preserve the fairness of the incentives to delay, but it means that a person cannot receive one type of benefit while at the same time earning a bonus for delaying the other benefit.

There are exceptions. Deemed filing applies to retirement benefits, not survivor's benefits. If and individual is a widow or widower, they may start their survivor benefit independently of retirement benefit.

Deemed filing also does not apply if the beneficiary receives spouse's benefits and is entitled to disability, or if receiving spousal benefits because of caring for the retired worker's child.

SECOND CHANGE: Voluntary Suspension
("File and Suspend" or "Claim and Suspend")

Prior to Change

- A worker at full retirement age or older applied for retirement benefits and then voluntarily suspended payment of their retirement benefits.

- The worker's voluntary suspension permitted a spousal benefit to be paid to their spouse while the worker was not collecting retirement benefits.

- The worker would then restart their retirement benefits later, for example at age 70, with an increase for every month retirement benefits were suspended.

Changes of the 2015 Act

For requests submitted on or after April 30, 2016:

- A person can still voluntarily suspend benefit payments at full retirement age to earn higher benefits for delaying.

- During a voluntary suspension, other benefits payable on their record, such as benefits to their spouse, are also suspended.

- If a person has suspended their benefits, they cannot continue receiving other benefits (such as spousal benefits) on another person's record.

The exceptions to this rule is that a divorced spouse can continue receiving a divorced spousal benefit even if their ex-spouse voluntarily suspends his or her retirement benefit.

The Rationale for change was to make is fair to delay payments for the workers spouse, and dependents if the worker has not retired or is in suspense. Couples can no longer simultaneously receive a benefit and get a bonus for delaying filing.

The Social Security Administration provided guidance during 2016 when a benefit is being paid to an ex-spouse as the other ex is either receiving a retirement or disability benefit and they have not divorced for greater than two years. This situation, if the ex-spouse from whose account is being drawn decides to suspend benefits, then spousal benefit payable to the ex-spouse will continue.

117. Must a spouse be dependent upon the worker for support to be eligible for a spouse's benefits?

No, a spouse is entitled to benefits if the worker is receiving benefits and the spouse is otherwise qualified. A spouse need not be dependent upon the worker and may be independently wealthy.

118. May a spouse lose benefits if the worker works or if the spouse works?

Yes, a spouse can lose some or all of his or her monthly benefits if the worker is under the full retirement age for the entire year and earnings exceed $21,240 in 2023.[1] A spouse may also lose benefits in the year the worker reaches full retirement age if the worker earns over $51,960 in 2022 and $56,520 in 2023, but only earnings earned before the month the worker reaches full retirement age count towards the $56,520 limit. Similarly, if the spouse is under full retirement age for the entire year and has earnings of over $21,240 (or earnings of over $56,520 in the year that full retirement age is attained), some or all benefits can be lost. (See LOSS OF BENEFITS BECAUSE OF "EXCESS" EARNINGS, Q 358 to Q 386.) See Q 293 for a discussion of the increase in the full retirement age.

When both the worker and the spouse have earnings in excess of the earnings limitation:

(1)   50 percent of the worker's "excess" earnings are charged against the total monthly family benefits if the worker is under the full retirement age, and 33⅓ percent in the year the worker is to reach the full retirement age; and then

(2)   the spouse's "excess" earnings are charged against his or her own benefits in the same manner, depending upon the age of the spouse, but only to the extent that those benefits have not already been charged with the worker's excess earnings.

Example. Mr. Smith, age sixty-two on January 1, 2022, is entitled to a monthly retirement benefit of $346, and his wife, also age sixty-two on January 1, 2022, is entitled to a monthly spouse's benefit of $162. Mr. Smith had earnings that were $4,064 in excess of the earnings limitation. His wife had earnings that were $1,620 in excess of the earnings limitation. Mr. Smith's earnings are charged against the total monthly family benefit of $508 ($346 + $162), so neither Mr. Smith nor his wife receives payments for January through April (50 percent of $4,064 = $2,032, and 4 × $508 = $2,032). The wife's excess earnings are charged only against her own benefit of $162. As her benefits for January through April were charged with the worker's excess earnings, the charging of her own earnings cannot begin until May; she thus receives no benefits for May through September (50 percent of $1,620 = $810, and 5 × $162 = $810).

Exception. The excess earnings of the worker do not cause deductions from the benefits of an entitled divorced spouse who has been divorced from the worker at least two years or whose former spouse was entitled to benefits before the divorce.

Note

1. See 42 U.S.C. sec. 403(b)(1).

119. When does a spouse's benefit end?

A spouse's benefits end when:

(1)   the spouse dies;

(2)   the worker dies (in this case, the spouse will be entitled to widow(er)'s, mother's, or father's benefits);

(3)   the worker's entitlement to disability benefits ends and he or she is not entitled to retirement benefits (unless the divorced spouse meets the requirements for an independently entitled divorced spouse);

(4)   the spouse is under age sixty-two and there is no longer a child of the worker under sixteen or disabled who is entitled to child's benefits;

(5)   the spouse becomes entitled to retirement or disability benefits and his or her PIA is equal to or larger than one-half of the worker's PIA;

(6)   the spouse and the worker are divorced before the spouse reaches age sixty-two and before the spouse and worker had been married for ten years; or

(7)   the divorced spouse marries someone other than the worker. However, the divorced spouse's benefit will not be terminated by marriage to an individual entitled to widow(er)'s, mother's, father's, or parent's monthly benefits, or to an individual age eighteen or over who is entitled to childhood disability benefits.

A spouse is not entitled to a spouse's benefit for the month in which any of the above events occurs. The last payment will be the payment for the preceding month.

---

120. Will a spouse's benefit be reduced if the spouse is receiving a government pension?

Social Security benefits payable to spouses—including surviving spouses and divorced spouses—are reduced (but not below zero) by two-thirds of the amount of any governmental (federal, state, or local) retirement benefit payable to the spouse based on his or her own earnings in employment not covered by Social Security, if that person's last day of employment was not covered by Social Security (but see below for Social Security Protection Act (SSPA) of 2004). Thus, for the affected group, the spouse's benefit is reduced two dollars for every three dollars of the government pension.[1] For example, if the monthly civil service pension is $600, then two-thirds or $400 will be used to offset benefits.

The Social Security Protection Act of 2004 (SSPA 2004) requires a person to work in covered employment for the last sixty months (instead of one day) of employment to be exempt from the Government Pension Offset (GPO). This change will not apply to someone whose last day of government service was before July 1, 2004. Also, the required sixty months will be reduced for each month of government service that was covered by Social Security before the enactment of SSPA 2004. These reduced months of service must be performed after enactment.

This offset against Social Security benefits did not apply prior to December 1977, or if the individual:

(1)   met all the requirements for entitlement to Social Security benefits that existed and were applied in January 1977; and

(2)   received or was eligible to receive a government pension between December 1977 and December 1982.

In addition, it does not apply to those first eligible to receive a government pension prior to July 1983 if they also meet the one-half support test.

Generally, federal workers hired before 1984 are part of the Civil Service Retirement System (CSRS) and are not covered by Social Security. Most Federal workers hired after 1983 are covered by the Federal Employees' Retirement System Act of 1986 (FERS), which includes coverage by Social Security. The FERS law provided that employees covered by the CSRS could—from July 1, 1987 to December 31, 1987—make a one-time election to join FERS (and thereby obtain Social Security coverage). Thus, a CSRS employee who switched to FERS during this period immediately became exempt from the government pension offset. Also, an employee who elected FERS on or before December 31, 1987 is exempt from the government pension offset, even if that person retired from government service before his FERS coverage became effective.

However, federal employees who elected to become covered under FERS during any election period which may occur on or after January 1, 1988 are exempt from the government pension offset only if they have five or more years of federal employment covered by Social Security after January 1, 1988. This rule also applies to certain legislative branch employees who first become covered under FERS on or after January 1, 1988.

Pensions based wholly on service performed as a member of a uniformed service, whether on active or inactive duty, are excluded from the offset.

The GPO reduces the spousal or widow/widower benefit by two-thirds of the monthly non-covered pension and can partially or fully offset an individual's spousal or widow(er) benefit, depending on the amount of the non-covered pension. During 2020, the GPO applied to 716,662 beneficiaries which constitutes 11.5 percent of the 6.25 million spousal or widowed beneficiaries.[2]

Notes

1. Social Security Publication No. 05-10007, https://www.socialsecurity.gov/pubs/EN-05-10007.pdf Current through May 2019 (last accessed August 26, 2022).
2. https://www.ssa.gov/policy/docs/program-explainers/government-pension-offset.html (last accessed August 26, 2022).

121. In the event of several marriages, which one will the Social Security Administration consider to be valid?

Generally, the most recent (latest in time) marriage will be the one considered to be valid unless there is direct evidence of its invalidity, such as bigamy or a court order dissolving or invalidating the marriage.

Child's Benefits
(Child of Retired or Disabled Worker)

122. Is a child of a retired or disabled parent entitled to Social Security benefits?

Yes, if:

(1)   the parent is entitled to retirement or disability benefits;

(2)   the child is (or was) dependent upon the parent (but see Q 126 to Q 129);

(3)   the child is under age eighteen, or between the ages of eighteen and nineteen and a full-time elementary or high school student, or eighteen or over and under a disability that began before age twenty-two;

(4)   the child is unmarried (but see Q 135); and (5) an application for the child's benefit has been filed.[1]

A **grandchild or step-grandchild** is considered the child of the worker in the following certain circumstances:

(1)   The grandchild's natural or adoptive parents are deceased or disabled: (1) at the time the worker became entitled to retirement or disability benefits or died, or (2) at the beginning of the worker's period of disability, which continued until the worker became entitled to disability or retirement benefits.

(2)   The grandchild was legally adopted by the worker's surviving spouse in an adoption decreed by a court, and the grandchild's natural or adopting parent or stepparent was not living in the same household and making regular contributions to the child's support at the time the insured worker died.

The grandchild or step-grandchild also must be dependent on the insured. (See Q 126.)

An **illegitimate child** is eligible for child's benefits if the worker:

(1)   has acknowledged in writing that the child is his or her son or daughter;

(2)   has been decreed by a court to be the father or mother of the child;

(3)   has been ordered by a court to contribute to the support of the child because the child is his or her son or daughter; or

(4)   has been shown to be the child's father or mother by other satisfactory evidence and was living with the child or contributing to the child's support when the child's application is filed (in life cases) or when the worker died (in survivor cases).

Note

1. https://secure.ssa.gov/apps10/poms.nsf/lnx/0300203001 (last access September 19, 2022).

123. Can a child who has been married be considered unmarried?

Yes. A child who has been married is considered unmarried at the time of filing an application for initial entitlement to child's benefits if:

- at that time, the marriage has been terminated by annulment, divorce, or death; or

- the marriage was void (including putative marriages in all states except Louisiana).

A "void marriage" is a marriage that is legally nonexistent from the beginning under State law. The parties to a void marriage are considered never to have been validly married.

The essential basis of a "putative marriage" is a good faith belief in the existence of a valid marriage at its inception and continuous good faith belief during the marriage (or until the number holder dies in case of death).

If the child's marriage was a putative marriage in Louisiana, there can be no entitlement for months before the termination of the putative relationship by acquisition of knowledge of the defect in the marriage. A putative marriage in any other state that recognizes such marriages does not bar entitlement to child's insurance benefits.

Where a child is considered "unmarried" because the marriage has been dissolved, the child cannot become entitled to benefits for months in the retroactive period before the marriage was terminated.

124. When may a child's benefits not be payable?

A child's benefit may not be payable in the following situations:

- A monthly benefit would not be payable to the number holder because of his or her deportation, and the child is an alien residing outside the U.S.

- The child is an alien who has been outside the U.S. for more than six months. The number holder or child receives a court sentence to lose certain benefit rights after conviction for an offense involving espionage, sabotage, treason, sedition, or subversive activities.

- The number holder or child is a former or current Federal employee and commits an offense against national security.

- The number holder or claimant has a tax exemption as a member of a religious sect or minister.

- The number holder is a disability insurance benefit beneficiary and is entitled to a worker's compensation (WC) benefit that causes disability offset. (Partial child's benefits may be payable depending upon the amount of the WC payments.)

- The adult child entitled as a childhood disability beneficiary (CDB) engages in substantial gainful activity (SGA) and is in their extended period of eligibility (EPE).

- The adult child, age 55 or over, is entitled as a CDB based on the special blindness provision and engages in SGA.

- The child, age 13 or older or CDB, has an unsatisfied Federal, State, or international law enforcement warrant for more than 30 continuous days for crimes or attempted crimes of escape from custody (offense code 4901), flight to avoid prosecution or confinement (offense code 4902), and flight-escape (offense code 4999).

- The child, age 13 or older or CDB, is violating a condition of probation or parole imposed under Federal or State law for more than 30 continuous days.

- The child's confinement exists based on a sentence of more than 30 continuous days in a correctional institution due to the conviction for a criminal offense. These provisions apply for children entitled to Social Security benefits beginning with April 1, 2000.

- The child does not have a Social Security number and the child or his or her parent, guardian, or person acting on child's behalf refuses to apply for one.

Note: This is effective with dates of entitlement of June 1989 or later.[1]

Note

1. https://secure.ssa.gov/apps10/poms.nsf/lnx/0300203030 . (Last accessed August 26, 2022).

125. Who is considered a "child" of a retired or disabled worker for benefit purposes?

The term "child" includes the worker's:

(1)   legitimate child, or any child who would have the right under applicable state law to inherit intestate personal property from the worker as a child;

(2)   stepchild, under certain circumstances;

(3)   legally adopted child;

(4)   illegitimate child, under certain circumstances (see Q 122); and

(5)   grandchild or step-grandchild, under certain circumstances (see Q 122).

A stepchild-stepparent relationship arises when the worker marries the child's natural parent or marries the child's adopting parent after the adoption. Death of the stepparent does not end the relationship. If the stepparent and the child's natural parent are divorced, the stepparent-stepchild relationship ends. However, in either case, there is no termination of a stepchild's existing established entitlement to child's benefits as a child of a stepparent. A stepchild must have been a stepchild of the parent on whose Social Security record the claim for benefits is filed for at least one year before the day the child's application is filed (if the parent is alive).

126. Must a child be dependent upon the worker to qualify for child's benefits?

Yes. A child must be dependent upon the worker to qualify for benefits on the worker's Social Security record. The factors that determine whether a child is dependent upon a worker vary, depending upon whether the worker is the natural parent (see Q 127), the legally adopting parent, the stepparent (see Q 128), or the grandparent (see below).

DEPENDENCY TEST: To be dependent on the worker, a grandchild or step-grandchild must have:

(1)   begun living with the worker before the grandchild became eighteen years old; and

(2)   lived with the worker in the United States and received at least one-half support for the worker.

SUPPORT TEST: The support test is met if the worker provides at least one-half of the support:

(1)   for the year before the month the worker became entitled to retirement or disability benefits or died; or

(2)   if the worker had a period of disability that lasted until he or she became entitled to benefits or died, for the year immediately before the month in which the period of disability began.

127. Is a child considered to be dependent upon his father or mother regardless of actual dependency?

Yes, a child is deemed to be dependent upon his parent (father or mother). The fact that the parent and child are not living together, or one of the parents is not contributing to the child's support, is not a factor unless the child has been adopted by another person.

128. Under what circumstances is a child considered to be dependent upon a stepparent?

The child is considered dependent upon a stepparent if the stepparent is contributing at least one-half of the child's support, or if the child is living with the stepparent.

129. Can a child receive benefits based on one parent's Social Security account even though the other parent is working and furnishing support?

Yes. A good example would be where the child is entitled to benefits due to the death of his or her mother who was a covered worker. The fact that the child's father was supporting him or her would not matter.

130. When is a child a full-time elementary or secondary school student?

A child may be eligible for child's benefits if she is a full-time elementary or secondary school student.[1]

A child is a full-time elementary or secondary school student if she attends a school that provides elementary or secondary education as determined under the law of the state or other jurisdiction in which it is located. Participation in the following programs also meets the requirements:

(1)   *Home Schooling.* The child is instructed in elementary or secondary education at home in accordance with a home-schooling law of the state or other jurisdiction in which the child resides. Students in these types of situations include a wide range of individuals. For example, home-schooling students may be in that situation for religious reasons or because the parents do not agree with the local school curriculum.

(2)   *Independent Study.* The child is in an independent study elementary or secondary education program in accordance with state law or other jurisdiction in which he or she resides, which is administered by the local school or school district jurisdiction. Students in independent study programs may include those individuals who cannot take advantage of the traditional school setting, such as hard-to-keep-in-school students (unable to adjust or delinquents), single mothers, or expectant mothers.

A child must be in full-time attendance in a day or evening course of at least thirteen weeks duration and must be carrying a subject load which is considered full-time for day students under the institution's standards and practices. If a child is in a home-schooling program, the child must be carrying a subject load that is considered full-time for day students under standards and practices set by the state or other jurisdiction in which the child resides.

To be considered in full-time attendance, a child's scheduled attendance must be at the rate of at least twenty hours per week. If a child is in an independent study program, the number of hours spent in school attendance are determined by combining the number of hours of attendance at a school facility with the agreed-upon number of hours spent in independent study.

A child may still be considered in full-time attendance if the scheduled rate of attendance is below twenty hours per week if the Social Security Administration finds that:

(1)   the school attended does not schedule at least twenty hours per week and going to that particular school is the child's only reasonable alternative; or

(2)   the child's medical condition prevents him or her from having scheduled attendance of at least twenty hours per week. To prove that a child's medical condition
prevents scheduling twenty hours per week, the Social Security Administration
may request that the child provide appropriate medical evidence or a statement
from the school.

A child enrolled solely in correspondence courses is not a full-time elementary or secondary
school student. The student is not being paid by an employer who has requested that the student
attend the school. In addition, the student must be in grade twelve or below.

Benefits paid to students age eighteen who attend elementary or secondary schools on a
full-time basis end with the last month they are full-time students or, if earlier, the month before
the month they become age nineteen.

Note

1. 20 C.F.R. sec. 404.367. See also 20 C.F.R. sec. 216.74.

---

131. Is the disabled child of a retired or disabled worker entitled to benefits past age twenty-two?

Yes, if the disability began before the child reached age twenty-two and continued
until the filing date of the application. The definition of "disability" is the same as for a worker
applying for disability benefits in that the disability has lasted twelve months, is expected to
last twelve months, or is expected to result in death, and the impairment, or the treatment for
the impairment, causes the person to be unable to perform substantial work. (See also Q 60).

---

132. What is the amount of the benefit for a retired or disabled worker's child?

The child of a retired or disabled worker is entitled to a monthly benefit equal to 50 percent
of his parent's PIA. Usually, this is an amount equal to one-half of the worker's benefit, but if
the worker has elected to receive a reduced retirement benefit before full retirement age (see
Q 49), the child's benefit will be based on one-half of his parent's PIA, not on one-half of the
reduced benefit. If the worker receives a larger benefit than the PIA due to delayed retirement
beyond full retirement age, the child's benefit is still only 50 percent of the PIA.

Although a child's full benefit is equal to one-half his parent's PIA, in many cases the benefit
actually paid to a child will be smaller because of the "family maximum" limit. Thus, if the total
amount of benefits based on the parent's Social Security account exceeds the family maximum,
all benefits (except the worker's benefit) will be reduced to bring the total within the family
maximum. (See Q 283, Maximum Family Benefits and Table 11.)

Note that the benefit for a retired or disabled worker's child is less than the benefit for a
deceased worker's child. The child of a deceased worker is entitled to a benefit equal to 75 percent
of his deceased parent's PIA (see Q 161, Child's Benefit, Child of Deceased Worker).

---

133. Can a child lose his benefits by working?

Yes, a child can lose some or all of his benefits if he or she works and earns over $19,560 in 2022 or $21,240 in 2023. A child's benefit is subject to deductions due to work by:

- the child, unless the child is age 18 or over and under a disability that began before age 22;

- the number holder on whose earnings record the child's benefits are paid; and

- a number holder to whom a disabled child age 18 or over is married.

See LOSS OF BENEFITS BECAUSE OF "EXCESS" EARNINGS, Q 358 to Q 386.

134. If the retired or disabled parent loses benefits, will the child lose benefits also?

Yes. The child's benefits are directly linked to the parent's benefits. For example, if a disabled worker loses his benefits because he refuses to accept rehabilitation services, his child's benefits will also be discontinued. Or, if the disabled worker recovers and is no longer entitled to benefits, the child's benefits will also end.

135. Will a child lose his or her benefits if he or she marries?

Yes, with one exception: a disabled child aged eighteen or over will not lose his or her benefits because of marriage to another disabled child aged eighteen or over who is receiving child's benefits, or because of marriage to a person entitled to retirement, widow(er)'s, mother's, father's, parent's, disability, or spouse's benefits. However, reference the prior question Q 123 which addresses situations where a previously married child can be deemed "unmarried".

136. When does a child's benefit end?

A child's benefits end when:

(1)   the child dies;

(2)   the child marries (but not if the child is a disabled child over eighteen and the child marries another Social Security beneficiary);

(3)   the child's parent is no longer entitled to disability benefits, unless entitlement ended because the insured parent became entitled to retirement benefits or died; or

(4)   the child reaches age eighteen and is neither under a disability nor a full-time student. Benefits for full-time elementary or secondary school students end when the child reaches age nineteen. Entitlement to childhood disability benefits ends when

the child over age eighteen ceases to be under a disability, which began before age twenty-two, unless the child is age eighteen to nineteen and a full-time elementary or secondary school student.

The beneficiary is not entitled to child's insurance benefits for the month in which any of the above events occur, except that a disabled child's benefits will end with the second month following the month in which the child ceases to be under a disability.

Also, if the benefits of a stepchild are based on the wages or self-employment income of a stepparent who is subsequently divorced from the child's natural parent, the stepchild's benefit ends the month after the month in which the divorce becomes final.

A child's benefit may also end if the child is missing. In 1993, the Social Security Administration suspended benefits for a child who disappeared mysteriously and was missing for five years. Further payment of benefits was suspended until the beneficiary's whereabouts and continuing eligibility for benefits were determined.[1]

Note

1. Social Security Ruling SSR 93-3. https://www.ssa.gov/OP_Home/rulings/oasi/09/SSR93-03-oasi-09.html (last accessed August 26, 2022).

137. If a child is neither disabled nor a full-time elementary or secondary student, when does the child's benefit end?

When the child reaches age eighteen, unless the child legally marries before then. The last benefit is the benefit for the month preceding the month when the child reaches age eighteen.

138. Who files the application for a child's benefits?

If the child is at least age eighteen and physically and mentally competent, the child must file the application form. Otherwise, an application may be filed on the child's behalf by a legal guardian or by the person (e.g., parent or relative) who is caring for the child (see FILING FOR BENEFITS, Q 248 to Q 267). The Form SSA-4-BK[1], Application for Child's Insurance Benefits, can be used for this purpose or can be completed by visiting the local SSA office or by telephone at 1-800-772-1213.

Note

1. Application for Child's Insurance Benefits (ssa.gov).

139. What is needed to apply for child's benefits?

Social Security may ask for the applicant to provide specific documents to determine if a child is eligible for benefits, such as:

- An application for child's benefits on an SSA-4-BK[1] or an electronic equivalent needs to be filed;

- The child's birth certificate or other proof of birth or adoption;

- Proof of the worker's marriage to the child's natural or adoptive parent if the child is the worker's stepchild;

- Proof of the child's U.S. citizenship or lawful alien status if the child was not born in the United States;

- W-2 form(s) and/or self-employment tax returns if the child had earnings last year; or

- If the worker is deceased, proof of the worker's death and U.S. military discharge paper(s).

Note

1. https://www.ssa.gov/forms/ssa-4.pdf (January 2017) (last accessed August 22, 2022).

140. What is needed to apply for disability benefits for an adult child?

If applying for disability benefits for an adult child disabled before age twenty-two, it is necessary to complete two forms that describe the child's medical condition and authorize disclosure of relevant information:

1. Adult Disability Report (Form SSA-3368-BK *Disability Report - Adult*);[1] and

2. Authorization to Disclose Information to the Social Security Administration (Form SSA-827)[2]

Social Security may also ask for documents to determine eligibility for benefits for having the child in their care:

- Caregiver's birth certificate or other proof of birth;

- Proof of marriage if they are or were married to the worker; and

- Proof of U.S. citizenship or lawful alien status, if not born in the United States.

Notes

1. https://www.ssa.gov/forms/ss3368-bk.pdf (effective November 2020) (last accessed August 26, 2022).
2. https://www.ssa.gov/forms/ssa-827.pdf (effective March 2020) (last accessed August 26, 2022).

141. Can a child receive their own benefits?

It depends. Ordinarily, a representative payee, such as a parent or relative, will be appointed to receive the child's benefits. However, if the child is over age eighteen and competent, payment will be made directly to the child. Also, if the child is under eighteen, away from home (e.g., in the Army), and is deemed mature enough to handle the benefit, payment may be made directly to the child.

141.01. What is a representative payee?

The Social Security Administration has a Representative Payee Program that helps provides benefit payment management for Social Security beneficiaries who are incapable of managing their Social Security or Supplemental Security Income (SSI) payments. SSA will appoint a suitable representative payee who will manage the payments on behalf of the beneficiaries.

A representative payee generally may not collect a fee for services provided to the beneficiary; although there are certain exceptions, a payee may not collect a fee for services provided to the beneficiary unless Social Security allows it, or the payee is the legal guardian authorized by a court to charge a guardian fee.

141.02. Who can serve as a representative payee?

Generally, Social Security will look to the beneficiary's family or friends to serve as payees. When friends or family members are not able to serve as payees, SSA will look to qualified organizations to fill the role.

The beneficiary is also given the option to advance designate up to three individuals who could serve as payee for you if the need arises.

The law requires representative payees to use the benefits in the beneficiary's best interest. If a payee misuses benefits, they must repay the misused funds. A payee who's convicted of misusing funds may be fined and imprisoned. The appointment as a representative payee is to manage Social Security and SSI funds only. A payee has no legal authority to manage non-Social Security income or medical matters. A representative payee, however, may need to help a beneficiary get medical services or treatment.

141.03. Are representative payees subject to audit?

Yes, possibly. Representative payees may receive an annual Representative Payee Report to account for the benefit payments received. The following payees are no longer required to complete the annual report since the law was changed.

- Natural or adoptive parents of a minor child beneficiary who primarily reside in the same household as the child;

- Legal guardians of a minor child beneficiary who primarily reside in the same household as the child;

- Natural or adoptive parents of a disabled adult beneficiary who primarily reside in the same household with the beneficiary; and

- A spouse of a beneficiary.

All payees, including the exempted ones above, are responsible for keeping records of how the payments are spent or saved, and making all records available for review if requested by SSA.

The SSA sends an annual Representative Payee Report to the payees who are required to complete the report. Payees who are under 18 must complete the paper version. Individual payees who are 18 or older can complete it online by logging in to their SSA account[1].

The Treasury Department requires all federal benefit payments to be made using a form of electronic payment and recommends that benefits are maintained in a checking or savings account to protect against loss or theft. Additionally, the payee must not comingle the beneficiary's funds with their own or other funds. Any money left over after meeting the beneficiary's day-to-day and personal needs must be saved.

The checking or savings account title must show the beneficiary's ownership of the funds and show the payee as the financial agent. Neither the payee, nor another third party, can have any ownership of the account. The beneficiary must never have direct access to the account. Any account title (under state law) that shows beneficiary ownership of the account with the payee as the financial agent is acceptable.

Exception: A common checking account for all family members living in the same household who receive benefits may show a parent or spouse as the owner of the account. Children's savings, however, must be in separate savings accounts for each child, showing the child as the account owner.

Organization Accounts

Sometimes, nursing homes or other organizations place funds for several beneficiaries in a single checking or savings account known as a "collective account". This is generally acceptable, but special rules apply to these accounts:

- Account titles must show the funds belong to the beneficiaries and not the representative payee.

- The account must be separate from the organization's operating account.

- Any interest earned belongs to the beneficiaries.

- There must be proper procedures to document credits and debits with clear and current records of each beneficiary's share.

- The organization must make the account and supporting records available to us when we ask for them.

- The organization must obtain approval from SSA before establishing the account.

Note

1. my Social Security | SSA (Last accessed August 27, 2022).

Survivor's Benefits

142. What benefits are payable to the survivors of a deceased insured worker?

The surviving family members of a deceased worker may be entitled to benefits under certain circumstances:

(1) **Mother's or Father's benefit:** a monthly benefit for widow(er), regardless of age, who is caring for at least one child, under sixteen or disabled before age 22, of the deceased worker) – see Q 144 to Q 158.

(2) **Child's benefit:** a monthly benefit for each child who is (1) under age 18, (2) over age 18 and disabled before age 22, or (3) under age 19 and attending a full-time elementary or high school – see Q 161 to Q 178.

(3) **Widow(er)'s benefit:** a monthly benefit for widow(er), or surviving divorced widow(er), age 60 or older) – see Q 181 to Q 197.

(4) **Disabled Widow(er)'s benefit:** a monthly benefit for a disabled widow(er), age 50 to 60 – see Q 198.

(5) **Parent's benefit:** a monthly benefit for parent age 62 or older who was dependent upon deceased worker for support – see Q 200 to Q 209.

(6) **Lump sum death payment:** see Q 210 to Q 212.

(7) **Parent's monthly benefit:** The decedent must have been providing at least half of parent's support and parent was not be eligible to receive a retirement benefit that is higher than the benefit Social Security could pay on decedent's record. Generally, parents also must not have married after decedent's death; however, there are some exceptions. In addition to a natural parent, stepparents or adoptive parents may receive benefits if they became the parent before decedent was 16.

(8) **A surviving divorced spouse** could get the same benefits as a widow or widower if that marriage lasted ten years or more. If surviving divorced spouse qualifies for retirement benefits on their own record, they can switch to their own retirement benefit as early as age 62. Benefits paid to a surviving divorced spouse won't affect the benefit amounts the other survivors will receive based on the worker's earnings record.

If the surviving divorced spouse remarries after they reach age 60 (age 50 if disabled), the remarriage will not affect their eligibility for survivors benefits.

If the former spouse is caring for decedent's child who is under age 16 or disabled and gets benefits on that record, they will not have to meet the length-of-marriage rule. The child must be decedent's natural or legally adopted child. However, if they qualify for benefits as a surviving divorced mother or father who is caring for the child, their benefits may affect the amount of benefits the decedent's other survivors will receive based on the earnings record.

143. How is the survivor benefit calculated if the spouse had not filed for Social Security before they died?

The calculation depends on if the spouse passed away before or after reaching Full Retirement Age.

If the spouse passed away **before** Full Retirement Age, the survivor benefit is based on what the deceased would have received as a retirement benefit at Full Retirement Age. If the spouse passed away **after** Full Retirement Age, the survivor benefit is based on what the deceased would have received on the date of their death.

Mother's or Father's Benefit

144. Is the surviving spouse of an insured worker entitled to a monthly mother's or father's benefit at any age?

Yes, if caring for a child of the deceased worker under age 16 or disabled before age 22. Otherwise, a surviving spouse is not eligible for benefits until age 60 (age 50 if disabled). A mother/father is the widow(er) of a deceased social security number holder, who has in-care an entitled child of the deceased.[1]

The surviving spouse of a fully or currently insured worker is entitled to a mother's or father's benefit at any age if:

(1) he or she is caring for a child of the deceased worker under age 16 or disabled before age 22 who is entitled to a child's benefit on the deceased worker's account;

(2) he or she is not married;

(3) he or she is not entitled to widow(er)'s benefits;

(4) he or she is not entitled to a retirement benefit based on his or her own work record that is equal to or larger than the amount of the unadjusted mother's or father's benefit; and

(5) he or she has filed an application for benefits.

One of the following requirements must also be met:

(1) the surviving spouse was married to the deceased worker for at least nine months before the worker died (see exception below);

(2) the surviving spouse is the biological parent of the worker's child;

(3)   the surviving spouse legally adopted the worker's child during their marriage and before the child reached age 18;

(4)   the surviving spouse was married to the worker when they both legally adopted a child under age 18;

(5)   the worker legally adopted the surviving spouse's child during their marriage and before the child reached age 18; or

(6)   the surviving spouse was entitled or potentially entitled to spouse's, widow(er)'s, father's, mother's, parent's, or childhood disability benefits in the month before the month the surviving spouse married the deceased worker.

A surviving spouse is "potentially entitled" if he or she meets all requirements for entitlement, other than the filing of an application and attainment of the required age.

Note

1. https://secure.ssa.gov/apps10/poms.nsf/lnx/0300208001 (last accessed August 27, 2022).

145. Is there an exception to the rule that the surviving spouse be married for at least nine months?

Yes. There is an exception to the requirement that the surviving spouse be married to the deceased worker for at least nine months before the worker died. The reason for this rule is to avoid having someone marry a person who is clearly not likely to live nine months— where the marriage was clearly to gain the deceased's social security benefits.

The rule is waived if:

- the worker's death was accidental;

- the worker's death occurred in the line of duty while a member of a uniformed service[1] serving on active duty; or

- if the surviving spouse who was married to the worker at the time of death was previously married to and divorced from the worker and the previous marriage had lasted nine months.[2]

The worker's death is defined as accidental[3] only if the worker received bodily injuries solely through violent, external, and accidental means and, as a direct result of the bodily injuries and independent of all other causes, died within three months after the day the injuries were received. The exception does not apply if, at the time of the marriage, the worker could not reasonably have been expected to live for nine months.

Notes

1. 20 CFR § 404.1330 Who is a member of an uniformed service.
2. Section 404.1 Social Security Handbook, What are the exceptions to the nine-month duration-of-marriage requirement? https://www.ssa.gov/OP_Home/handbook/handbook.04/handbook-0404.html (last accessed August 28, 2022).

3. Section 404.2, Social Security Handbook, When is a death considered "accidental"? https://www.ssa.gov/OP_Home/handbook/handbook.04/ handbook-0404.html (section 404.2) (last accessed August 28, 2022).

146. Can a divorced spouse qualify for a survivor's benefit?

Yes, a person is entitled to mother's or father's benefits as a surviving divorced spouse of a worker who died fully or currently insured if he or she:

(1)   is the parent of the worker's child, was married to the worker when either of them adopted the other's child, or when both of them adopted a child and the child was then under eighteen;

(2)   filed an application for these benefits;

(3)   is not married (final divorce);

(4)   is not entitled to a widow(er)'s benefits, or to a retirement benefit that is equal to or larger than the mother's or father's full benefit; and

(5)   has in care the worker's child who is entitled to child's benefits based on the worker's earnings record. The child must be under age sixteen or disabled.

There is no ten-year marriage duration requirement for surviving divorced mother/father benefits. Incomplete divorces, such as limited divorces from bed and board or preliminary divorces (decree nisi or interlocutory), do not count. Annulments are not "divorces" as they nullify a marriage and establish that a marriage never existed.

147. Must a worker be fully insured at death to qualify for the mother's or father's benefit?

No. The mother's or father's benefit is payable if the worker was either fully or currently insured.

See Q 241 to Q 245.

148. What is the amount of a mother's or father's benefit?

The amount of a mother's or father's benefit is equal to 75 percent of the deceased spouse's Primary Insurance Amount (PIA). However, because of the "family maximum" limit, the monthly benefit actually received by the surviving spouse may be less. If the total benefits payable on one worker's Social Security account exceeds the family maximum, all benefits are reduced proportionately to bring the total within the family maximum. (See Maximum Family Benefits, Q 283). A surviving divorced mother's or father's benefit is the same amount. However, benefits paid to a divorced mother or father will not be reduced because of the limit on total family benefits, and such benefits are not counted in figuring the total benefits payable to others on the basis of the deceased worker's account.

If the surviving spouse is entitled to a smaller retirement or disability benefit based on his own earnings record, he will receive the benefit based on his own account and will receive as a mother's or father's benefit only the difference between the mother's or father's benefit rate and the other benefit rate.

149. What are the differences between a mother's or father's benefit and a widow's or widower's benefit?

Mother or Father's Benefit

A mother's or father's benefit is payable to a surviving spouse (widow/widower) at any age, but he or she must be caring for at least one child under age sixteen or a disabled child of the deceased spouse.

A surviving spouse will qualify for a mother's or father's benefit if the deceased spouse was either fully or currently insured at death. However, a surviving spouse will not qualify for a widow's or widower's benefit unless the deceased spouse was fully insured at death.

A full mother's or father's benefit is equal to only 75 percent of the deceased spouse's PIA. A full widow's or widower's benefit (at the Full Retirement Age, see Q 49) is equal to 100 percent of the deceased spouse's PIA.

Widow or Widower's Benefit

A widow's or widower's benefit is not payable until the surviving spouse reaches age sixty unless the surviving spouse is disabled, in which case benefits may begin at age fifty.

150. Is a mother's or father's benefit payable regardless of the surviving spouse's need?

Yes, if the surviving spouse meets the necessary qualifications (see Q 144), he or she will receive benefits regardless of wealth or income. This is an earned benefit, not a need-based one.

151. Can a surviving spouse lose some or all of the benefits by working?

Yes, in 2023 by earning over $21,240 a year ($19,560 a year in 2022) if under the full retirement age (see Q 49) for the entire year. In the year the surviving spouse reaches full retirement age, benefits may be lost by earning over $56,520 ($51,960 in 2022). However, only earnings earned before the month the surviving spouse reaches full retirement age count toward the $56,520 limit. The loss of benefits by a surviving spouse will not cause the children to lose their benefits.

See LOSS OF BENEFITS BECAUSE OF "EXCESS" EARNINGS, Q 358 to Q 386.

152. If the only child in a surviving spouse's care loses benefits by working, will this cause the child's mother or father to lose benefits?

No.

See LOSS OF BENEFITS BECAUSE OF "EXCESS" EARNINGS, Q 358 to Q 386.

153. Must a surviving spouse file an application for a mother's or father's benefit?

Yes, unless receiving a spouse's benefit before the worker's death. The application should be filed within six months after the worker's death, because no more than six month's benefits will be paid retroactively. Applications filed greater that six months after the worker's death will still be processed, though the six-month retroactive limit will apply. However, if COVID-19 issues prevented filing, it is worth filing an appeal to attempt to get the entire amount. When filing an appeal request, the SSA suggests including include a statement explaining the delay in the appeal, noting that they extend good cause for late filing in many situations.[1]

Note

1. https://www.ssa.gov/coronavirus/faqs/?c=hearings-and-appeals. (Last accessed August 30, 2022).

154. When do a mother's or father's benefits begin?

If a surviving spouse qualifies, benefits will begin with a payment for the month in which his or her spouse died (see Q 153).

155. When do a mother's or father's benefits end?

Mother's or father's benefits end when:

(1)   there is no longer a child of the deceased under age 16 or disabled in the parent's care;

(2)   in the case of a surviving divorced father or mother, no natural or legally adopted child of the surviving spouse under age 16 or disabled is entitled to a child's benefit on the deceased worker's earnings record;

(3)   the surviving spouse becomes entitled to a widow(er)'s benefit;

(4)   the surviving spouse dies;

(5)   the surviving spouse becomes entitled to retirement benefits in an amount equal to or greater than three-fourths of the deceased spouse's PIA; or

(6)   the surviving spouse marries. However, if the surviving spouse marries a person entitled to retirement, disability, divorced spouse's, widow(er)'s, father's, mother's,

parent's, or childhood disability benefits, the marriage has no effect on entitlement (unless marriage is to a child under age 18 or a full-time student under the age 19, in which case both benefits terminate).[1]

If the subsequent marriage ends, the surviving spouse may be re-entitled to mother's or father's benefits on the prior deceased spouse's (or former spouse's) earnings record, beginning with the month the subsequent marriage ends.

The surviving spouse can receive no further benefits until he or she becomes entitled to a widow(er)'s benefit at age 60 (or a disabled widow's or widower's benefits at age 50). The period during which the surviving spouse is entitled to no benefits is known as the black-out period. The fact that a child's benefits will continue after age 16 does not entitle the child's mother or father to a continuation of benefits.

Note

1. https://secure.ssa.gov/apps10/poms.nsf/lnx/0300208030 (effective August 7, 2018) (last accessed August 30, 2022).

156. Will a mother's or father's benefit be reduced if he or she is receiving a government pension?

Social Security benefits payable to spouses—including surviving spouses and divorced spouses—are reduced (but not below zero) by two-thirds of the amount of any governmental (federal, state, or local) retirement benefit payable to the spouse based on his or her own earnings in employment not covered by Social Security if that person's last day of employment is not covered by Social Security. Thus, for the affected group, the spouse's benefit is reduced two dollars for every three dollars of the government pension. However, the Social Security Protection Act of 2004 generally requires that a person work in covered employment for five years (instead of one day) to be exempt from this Government Pension Offset (GPO). See Q 120 and Q 195 for more information on the GPO.

This offset against Social Security benefits does not apply if the individual:

(1)   met all the requirements for entitlement to Social Security benefits that existed and were applied in January 1977; and

(2)   received or was eligible to receive a government pension between December 1977 and December 1982.

Pensions based entirely on service performed as a member of a uniformed service, whether on active or inactive duty, are excluded from the offset.

157. Will a mother's or father's benefits stop when the youngest child (or only child) reaches age sixteen?

Yes (unless the child is disabled and was disabled before age twenty-two), and he or she will not become eligible for widow(er)'s benefits until age sixty. The time when a surviving spouse is not entitled to any Social Security benefits is commonly called the **black-out period**. But if the surviving spouse is caring for a disabled child whose disability began before age twenty-two, mother's or father's benefits will not stop so long as the child continues to be disabled and entitled to a child's benefits. If the surviving spouse is disabled, he or she may qualify for a disabled widow(er)'s benefit at age fifty. (See Q 197.)

158. Does a mother or father continue to receive benefits until the youngest child (or only child) is age twenty-two if the child is attending school?

No. A mother's or father's benefits are payable only so long as the child in his or her care is under age sixteen or disabled. See Q 130.

159. What documentation is needed to apply for mother or father's benefits?

The following documentation may be requested by the Social Security Administration in order to determine eligibility for benefits for a child that is in care.

- Proof of the worker's death

- Applicant's birth certificate or other proof of birth

- Proof of U.S. citizenship or lawful alien status if applicant was not born in the United States

    - Most normal documentation is accepted of most applicants born in the U.S. Applicants who are U.S. citizens born outside of the country should provide:

        - U.S. consular report of birth

            o   U.S. passport

            o   Certificate of Naturalization

            o   Certificate of Citizenship

- U.S. military discharge paper(s)

- W-2 form(s) and/or self-employment tax returns for last year

- Proof of marriage

- Final divorce decree if applying as a surviving divorced mother or father

- Child's birth certificate or other proof of birth

- Applicants who are not U.S. citizens need to produce their Department of Homeland Security (DHS) documents, including form I-551 (Permanent Resident Card, with 9-digit

Alien Registration Number (A-Number)). In addition, the applicant should produce their DHS form I-94, Admission-Departure Record.[1]

Note

1. Form I-94 Arrival/Departure Record, Information for Completing USCIS Forms, https://www.uscis.gov/I-94information (last accessed August 30, 2022).

160. What information will be asked of individuals applying for mother or father's benefits?

- Name and Social Security number of applicant

- Deceased worker's name, date of birth, gender, and Social Security number

- Deceased worker's date of death and place of death

- Applicant's name at birth (if different) and any other names used

- Date and place of birth (City, State, and/or foreign country)

- Whether a public or religious record was made of applicant's birth before age five

- Applicant's citizenship status

- Any other Social Security number(s) used

- Whether applicant or anyone else has ever filed for Social Security benefits, Medicare, or Supplemental Security Income on behalf of the applicant

- Whether the deceased worker ever filed for Social Security benefits, Medicare, or Supplemental Security Income

- Whether applicant or the deceased worker were ever in the active military service before 1968 or ever worked for the railroad industry

- Whether applicant became unable to work because of illnesses, injuries, or conditions at any time within the past fourteen months

- Whether the deceased worker was disabled at the time of death

- Whether the deceased worker has a surviving parent who was dependent on the worker for one-half of his or her support at the time of the worker's death

- Whether applicant or the deceased worker have earned Social Security credits under another country's Social Security system

- Whether the deceased worker was a civilian employee of the Federal Government in January 1983

- Whether applicant qualified for or expects to receive a pension or annuity based on employment with the Federal government of the United States or one of its States or local subdivisions

- Names, dates of birth (or age), and Social Security numbers (if known) of former spouses or and the deceased worker's former spouses

- Dates and locations of applicant's marriages, and for marriages that have ended, how, when, and where they ended

- Dates of the deceased worker's marriages and how, when, and where they ended

- Names of the deceased worker's children under 18, 18 to 19 and attending secondary school, or disabled before age 22

- Names and Social Security numbers of the deceased worker's unmarried children under sixteen or sixteen and older and disabled before age 22 in applicant's care and the months the child lived with applicant

- Whether the deceased worker had earnings (and the amount) last year or this year

- Amount of applicant's earnings for current, prior, and last years

- Whether applicant and the deceased worker were living together at the time of death

- If applicant is within three months of age 65, a decision needs to be made on whether to enroll in Medicare Part B (Medical Insurance)

Form SSA-5-BK- *Application for Mother's or Father's Insurance Benefits* is available on the Social Security Administration website and can be pre-filled for printing there.[1]

Note

1. https://www.ssa.gov/forms/ssa-5-bk.pdf (last Accessed August 30, 2022).

Child's Benefit
(Child of Deceased Worker)

161. Is a child of a deceased worker entitled to Social Security benefits?

If a worker dies either fully or currently insured, each child who meets the relationship requirements is entitled to a child's benefit if:

(1)   under age eighteen, or over age eighteen and disabled by a disability that began before age twenty-two, or under age nineteen and a full-time elementary or secondary school student;

(2)   not married;

(3)   dependent upon the deceased parent; and

(4)   an application has been filed for benefits.

162. How are posthumously conceived children treated under Social Security Survivor benefits?

Controlling law on this subject is found in *Astrue v. Capato ex rel. B. N. C.,*[1] a 2012 U.S. Supreme Court decision. The decision has created a complicated situation in defining "children" under the Social Security Act. In *Astrue,* the Court held that children conceived after a parent's death are not entitled to Social Security Survivors benefits if the laws in the state where the parent's will was signed do not allow it. In addition, a claimant is considered "the child" of an insured individual if the claimant could inherit the insured individual's intestate personal property under the law of the state in which the insured individual was domiciled when he died.

A claimant may be eligible for children's insurance benefits based on the earnings record of a deceased insured individual under the Social Security Act, if the claimant is the insured individual's "child".[2] In addition, the claimant must be dependent upon the insured. Dependency is determined based on the relationship of the child to the insured.[3]

The Social Security Administration has used state inheritance laws as the deciding factor if a person was a "child" under the Social Security Act, and therefore eligible for survivors benefits, since the 1940s. However, there is no consensus among the 50 states as to how to classify posthumously conceived children, or how to determine legal paternity. Since there is a lack of consensus among the states, the eligibility of survivors' benefits actually varies from state to state, even though Social Security is a federal benefit because of the reliance on state inheritance laws. The hodgepodge of state laws and regulations allows for posthumously conceived children to be denied benefits that to which natural born children of a decedent would be entitled.

The best possible solution is likely a Congressional amendment to the Social Security Act, which would include posthumously conceived children in the definition of a child and would create a uniform system in which all posthumously conceived children would be held to the same standards to qualify for survivors' benefits. At this writing, there has been no action in this regard.

Notes

1. 566 U.S. 541, 132 S. Ct. 2021 (2012).
2. Social Security Act § 202(d)(1); 20 C.F.R. § 404.350(a)(1); Program Operations Manual System (POMS) GN 00306.002A, B; POMS RS 00203.001A.1.b.; POMS PR-22-034 (2022) (Last accessed August 30, 2022).
3. See 20 C.F.R. § 404.360 (Last accessed August 30, 2022).

163. How does one become re-entitled to a child's benefit?

Definition of re-entitlement- Re-entitlement to child's benefits is a subsequent award for an auxiliary or surviving child:[1]

- who was previously entitled on the same Social Security Number (SSN);

- whose prior benefits were correctly terminated; and

- whose break in entitlement on that SSN was for at least one month.

If entitlement to a child's benefits has ended, one may be re-entitled on the same earnings record if the child has not married and if they apply for re-entitlement. The re-entitlement may begin with:

- the first month in which the child qualifies as a full-time student;

- the first month in which the child is disabled, if disability began before age 22; or

- the first month the child is under a disability that began before the end of the eighty-fourth month following the month in which benefits had ended, because an earlier disability had ended.

With respect to benefits payable for months beginning October 2004, the child can be re-entitled to childhood disability benefits anytime if the prior entitlement terminated because disability ceased due to the performance of substantial gainful activity and the other requirements for re-entitlement were met. The eighty-four-month time limit continues to apply if the previous entitlement to childhood disability benefits terminated because of medical improvement.

Note

1. https://secure.ssa.gov/apps10/poms.nsf/lnx/0300203015; 20 C.F.R. sec. 404.351 (last accessed August 30, 2022).

164. Must a parent be fully insured at death to qualify the child for a child's benefits?

No, the child is eligible for benefits on the parent's Social Security account if the parent was either fully or currently insured at death.

See Q 241 to Q 245.

165. Must a child have been dependent upon the deceased parent to be eligible for a child's benefit?

Yes, the child must have been dependent upon the deceased worker.

The factors that determine whether a child is dependent upon a worker vary, depending upon whether the worker is the natural parent, the legally adopting parent, the stepparent, or the grandparent.

A child is "deemed" dependent upon the worker if the child has not been legally adopted by someone other than the worker and:

(1)   is the legitimate child of the worker;

(2)   an illegitimate child who would have the right under applicable state law to inherit intestate property from the worker as a child;

(3)   the child of a void or voidable marriage;

(4)   the child of an invalid ceremonial marriage; or

(5)   the legally adopted child of the worker adopted prior to the worker's death.

166. Under what circumstances is a child considered dependent upon a grandparent, step-grandparent, great-grandparent, or step-great-grandparent?

A child is dependent upon a grandparent, step-grandparent, great-grandparent, or step-great-grandparent if the child:

(1)   began living with the worker before he or she reached age eighteen; and

(2)   lived with the worker in the United States and received at least one-half support from the worker.

The support test is met if the worker provides one-half of the support:

(1)   for the year before the month the worker died; or

(2)   if the worker had a period of disability that lasted until he or she became entitled to benefits, for the year immediately before the month in which the period of disability began.[1]

Note

1. https://www.ssa.gov/OP_Home/cfr20/404/404-0364.htm (as amended July 17, 2008) (last accessed August 30, 2022).

167. Under what circumstances is a child considered dependent upon a stepfather or stepmother?

The child is considered dependent upon a stepfather or stepmother if the stepfather or stepmother is contributing at least one-half of the child's support. The child is not required to live with the stepfather or stepmother.

A stepchild must have been the stepchild of the insured worker for at least nine months immediately preceding the day the worker died, unless the worker and the child's natural or adopting parent were previously married, divorced, and then remarried at the time of the worker's death, and the nine-month-duration-of-relationship requirement was met at the time of the divorce. If the death of the worker was accidental or occurred in the line of duty while a member of a uniformed service serving on active duty, the nine-month requirement may be considered satisfied, unless at the time of the marriage, the worker could not have been expected to live for nine months. A child who was not legally adopted by the worker will nevertheless be treated as a legally adopted child if the child was living in the worker's home or receiving at least one-half of his support from the worker at the time of the worker's death, and the child is adopted by the worker's surviving spouse after the worker's death (but only if adoption proceedings were instituted by the worker before his death or adoption by the surviving spouse occurs within two years after the worker's death). However, such a child will not be treated as the worker's legally adopted child if at the time of the worker's death he was receiving regular contributions toward his support from someone other than the worker or the worker's spouse or a public or private welfare organization.

A child is eligible for benefits based on his parent's Social Security earnings record, even if the child was supported by a stepparent when the parent died.

168. Can a child receive benefits based on a deceased parent's Social Security account, even though the other parent is still living and supporting the child?

Yes. Benefits are available to any children for whom the deceased worker provided at least half of the child's support. This includes children who did not live with the deceased parent, stepchildren, grandchildren, and adopted children.

The deceased parent must have earned at least six credits within three years of their death for their child to receive monthly survivors' benefits. The child must be under age 18, or up to age 19 and still attending high school.

Benefits end once the child reaches the maximum age unless he or she is disabled. In these cases, benefits continue for the duration of the child's life, or until the SSA determines the child is no longer disabled.

169. Is a child age eighteen or over entitled to benefits if attending school?

In general, the children of retired, deceased, or disabled beneficiaries who remain full-time students at age eighteen are entitled to benefits until they reach age nineteen or complete their secondary (grade 12 or below) education, whichever occurs first.[1]

Benefits paid to a student age eighteen who attends elementary or secondary schools on a full-time basis end with the last month that the student is a full-time student or, if earlier, the month before the month the student becomes age nineteen.

A child is a full-time elementary or secondary school student if he or she attends a school that provides elementary or secondary education, as determined under the law of the state or other jurisdiction in which it is located. Participation in one of the following programs also meets the following requirements:

(1)   The child is instructed in elementary or secondary education at home in accordance with a home-schooling law of the state or other jurisdiction in which the child

resides. Students in these types of situations include a wide range of individuals. For example, home-schooling students may be in that situation for religious reasons or because the parents do not agree with the local school curriculum.

(2) The child is in an alternate school, independent study elementary, or secondary education program in accordance with state law or other jurisdiction in which she resides, which is administered by the local school or school district jurisdiction. Students in independent study programs may include those individuals who cannot take advantage of the traditional school setting, such as hard-to-keep-in-school students (unable to adjust or delinquents), single mothers, or expectant mothers.

A child must be in full-time attendance in a day or evening course of at least thirteen weeks duration and must be carrying a subject load that is considered full-time for day students under the institution's standards and practices. If a child is in a home-schooling program, the child must be carrying a subject load that is considered full-time for day students under standards and practices set by the state or other jurisdiction in which the child resides.

To be considered in full-time attendance, a child's scheduled attendance must be at the rate of at least twenty hours per week. If a child is in an independent study program, the number of hours spent in school attendance are determined by combining the number of hours of attendance at a school facility with the agreed-upon number of hours spent in independent study.

A child may still be considered in full-time attendance if the scheduled rate of attendance is below twenty hours per week if the Social Security Administration finds that:

(1) the school attended does not schedule at least twenty hours per week, and going to that particular school is the child's only reasonable alternative; or

(2) the child's medical condition prevents him or her from having scheduled attendance of at least twenty hours per week. To prove that a child's medical condition prevents scheduling twenty hours per week, the Social Security Administration may request that the child provide appropriate medical evidence or a statement from the school.

A child enrolled solely in correspondence courses is not a full-time elementary or secondary school student. A child does not qualify as a student if being paid by an employer to attend school. Students in General Education Development (GED) programs may qualify for benefits if they are in full-time attendance.

Note

1. 20 C.F.R. sec. 404.367, https://www.ssa.gov/OP_Home/cfr20/404/404-0367.htm (last accessed August 30, 2022).

170. When do student benefits stop?

In general, benefits stop the month before the month in which the student attains age nineteen or the first month in which the student is not a full-time student, whichever is earlier. (Benefits can also continue if the student qualifies for disability payments).

Benefits may also stop if the student marries, stops attending school, attendance is reduced below full-time, schools are changed, an employer pays the student to attend school, or the student is convicted of a crime.

Benefits continue during the summer, even if the student is not attending school, as long as:

- the break is shorter than four months;

- the student was in full-time attendance immediately before this break; and

- the student intends to return to elementary or secondary school immediately after the break. If the student turns nineteen however, during a month when not attending school, the last month that will be paid is the month before turning age nineteen.

In the case of a student who does not graduate on schedule, they must complete a new SSA-1372-BK *Advance Notice of Termination of a Child's Benefits.*[1]

Note

1. https://www.ssa.gov/forms/ssa-1372.pdf (last accessed August 30, 2022).

171. When must a student report information to the Social Security Administration?

A student must inform SSA if they:

- marry;

- stop attending school;

- reduce attendance below full-time;

- are paid by an employer to attend school;

- change schools;

- are convicted of a crime;

- move or change mailing address; or

- change their estimated earnings from work.

Reports are completed by using Form SSA-1383 *Student Reporting Form.*[1]

Note that the Form SSA-1383 has been updated in July 2022 and continues a warning/ admonishment that failure to report could result in loss of benefits and potential responsibility to repay benefits paid. The notice also cautions that conceal or failure to disclose a reporting event with intent to obtain benefits fraudulently can result in fines and/or imprisonment.[2]

Notes

1. https://www.ssa.gov/forms/ssa-1383.pdf (Issued July 2022) (last accessed August 30, 2022).
2. Section 208 of the Social Security Act.

172. Will the Social Security Administration pay benefits to college students?

No. At one time, SSA did pay benefits to college students, but the law changed in 1981. Benefits are paid only to students taking courses at twelfth grade or below.[1] This is because they are over the age limit set by the Social Security Administration.

However, certain college students can receive Social Security benefits as a child under the Social Security Disability Insurance (SSDI) program or as an adult from the Supplemental Security Income (SSI) program.

Note

1. Social Security Administration, Frequently Asked Questions – Students, Question 8, https://www.ssa.gov/schoolofficials/faqs_students.htm (last accessed August 30, 2022).

173. What is the amount of the monthly benefit for a child of a deceased worker?

The surviving child's benefit is equal to 75 percent of the deceased parent's primary insurance amount. However, because of the "family maximum" limit, the monthly benefit actually received by the child may be less. The family maximum payment is determined as part of every Social Security benefit computation. It can be from 150 to 180 percent of the parent's full benefit amount. If the total amount payable in benefits based on one worker's Social Security account exceeds the "family maximum," all benefits are reduced proportionately to bring the total within the "family maximum" (see Maximum Family Benefits, Q 283 to Q 286).

A child entitled to benefits based on more than one worker's record will receive the benefit based on the record that provides the highest amount, if the payment does not reduce the benefits of any other individual who is entitled to benefits based on the same earnings record.

174. Will a child lose benefits if the child works or the child's parent works?

The child can lose part or all of his benefits if he earns over $19,560 in 2021 or $21,240 in 2023. However, none of the child's benefits will be lost because his surviving parent works. Also, the child's work will not affect the parent's benefits.

See LOSS OF BENEFITS BECAUSE OF "EXCESS" EARNINGS, Q 358 to Q 386.

175. If a child is entitled to benefits on more than one person's Social Security account, will the child receive both benefits?

No, the child will receive only **one** benefit, but it will always be the **higher** one as to which he or she is entitled. (But see Q 297.) In no circumstances will an individual receive more than one benefit under Social Security but is always entitled to the **larger** one.

176. When does a child's benefit begin?

Ordinarily, the first benefit is payable for the month in which the parent died. However, unless the child was receiving benefits before the parent's death, an application should be filed within six months after death. Benefits will be paid retroactively for up to, but not more than, six months. If an application was not filed within six months of death because of COVID-19 issues, an applicant should contact the local SSA office or could potentially appeal a decision not to pay benefits retroactively for more than six months. In the case of not filing because of COVID-19, the SSA recommends including an explanation within the appeal, as they have been willing to be flexible in this regard.

177. When does a child's benefit end?

A child's benefit ends:

(1)   at death;

(2)   at age eighteen (age nineteen if a full-time elementary or secondary school student);

(3)   when disability ceases if benefits are received only because the child was disabled before age twenty-two (but further benefits may be available if disability occurs again within seven years after childhood disability benefits terminate); or

(4)   when married. However, marriage of a disabled child age eighteen or over to another Social Security beneficiary over age eighteen (other than to a person receiving child's benefits under age eighteen or age eighteen as a full-time elementary or secondary school student) will ordinarily not terminate the child's benefits.

The benefits of a childhood disability beneficiary, regardless of sex, continue after the child's spouse is no longer eligible for benefits as a childhood disability beneficiary or disabled worker beneficiary.

The child is not entitled to a payment for the month in which any of the foregoing events occur, but benefits will be continued through the second month after the month that a disabled child's disability ceases.

A child's benefit may end if the child is missing. In 1993, the Social Security Administration suspended benefits for a child who disappeared mysteriously and was missing for five years.

Further payment of benefits was suspended until the beneficiary's whereabouts and continuing eligibility for benefits could be determined.[1]

Note

1. Social Security Ruling SSR 93-3, https://www.ssa.gov/OP_Home/rulings/oasi/09/SSR93-03-oasi-09.html (last accessed August 30, 2022).

178. Will a child's benefits end if the child marries?

Yes, as a general rule. However, marriage of a disabled child over age eighteen to another Social Security beneficiary over age eighteen will ordinarily not terminate the child's benefits (see Q 177).[1] However, in some instances, a child that was married can be deemed as having been never married.

Note

1. Benefits for Children with Disabilities, February 2021, https://www.ssa.gov/pubs/EN-05-10026.pdf (last accessed September 19, 2022).

179. What documents will be needed to apply for a child's benefits?

- The applicant's birth certificate or other proof of birth or adoption

- The child's birth certificate or other proof of birth or adoption

- The applicant's proof of marriage to the worker

- Proof of U.S. citizenship or lawful alien status, if applicant was not born in the United States

- U.S. military discharge paper(s)

- W-2 forms(s) and/or self-employment tax returns for last year

180. What information will be needed to apply for a child's benefits?

- Applicant's name and Social Security number

- The worker's name and Social Security number

- The date of birth, Social Security number, and relationship to the worker (i.e., legitimate child, adopted child, stepchild, dependent grandchild, other) of each child listed on the application

- The child's citizenship status

- Whether any child seventeen- and one-half years of age or older is a student or is disabled

- If any child is the worker's stepchild, when and where the worker and the child's parent married

- Whether applicant is the child's natural or adoptive parent

- Whether any child has a legal representative (guardian, curator, conservator, etc.) as well as the representative's name, address, telephone number, and an explanation of circumstances which led the court to appoint a legal representative

- Whether any child has been adopted by someone other than the worker

- Whether the children live with applicant and whether they lived with the worker during each of the last thirteen months

     - If no, applicant will need to list each month the child did not live with the worker and for the name and address of the person with whom the child lived and their relationship to the child;

- Whether any child has ever been married and, if so, the dates and locations of the marriages, and how, when, and where they ended

- Whether applicant or anyone else has ever filed for Social Security benefits, Medicare, or Supplemental Security Income on behalf of the child(ren)

- The amount of each child's earnings for this year, last year, and next year

- The dates of adoption for any children adopted by the worker

- If any child is within two months of age sixty-five or older, blind, or disabled, SSA will ask the applicant if they want to file on his or her behalf for Supplemental Security Income;

- Whether applicant has ever been convicted of a felony if applying to be a representative payee

- Whether applicant ever served as a representative payee for someone's Social Security benefits

DECEASED WORKER SITUATION

If the worker is deceased, Social Security will also need the following information:

- The worker's date of birth and his or her name at birth (if different)

- The worker's date of death and the place of death

- The State or foreign country of the worker's fixed permanent residence at the time of death

- Whether the worker was unable to work because of illnesses, injuries, or conditions at any time during the fourteen months before his or her death (and the date he or she became unable to work)

- Whether the worker was in the active military service before 1968 or ever worked for the railroad industry (and dates of service and whether a pension was received)

- Whether the worker earned Social Security credits under another country's Social Security system

- Whether the worker was employed or self-employed in all years from 1978 through last year

- How much the worker earned in the year of death and the year before death

- Whether the worker ever filed for Social Security benefits, Medicare, or Supplemental Security Income

- Whether each child was living with the worker at the time of death

Widow(er)'s Benefit

181. Is the widow(er) of an insured worker entitled to benefits if there are no children in his or her care?

A widow(er) is entitled to a widow(er)'s benefit based on the deceased spouse's earnings if:

(1)   the widow(er) is age sixty or over, or is at least age fifty but not age sixty and is disabled;

(2)   the worker died fully insured;

(3)   the widow(er) is not entitled to a retirement benefit that is equal to or larger than the worker's primary insurance amount;

(4)   the widow(er) has filed an application for widow(er)'s benefits; and

(5)   the widow(er) is not married except under special circumstances discussed below.

In addition, one of the following conditions must be met:

(1)   the widow(er) was married to the deceased worker for at least nine months immediately prior to the worker's death (see exceptions below);

(2)   the widow(er) is the biological mother or father of the worker's child (this requirement is met if a live child was born to the worker and the widow(er), although the child need not still survive);

(3)   the widow(er) legally adopted the worker's child during their marriage and before the child reached age eighteen;

(4)   the widow(er) was married to the worker when they both legally adopted a child under age eighteen;

(5)   the worker legally adopted the widow(er)'s child during their marriage and before the child reached age eighteen; or

(6)   the widow(er) was entitled (or potentially entitled) to spouse's, widow(er)'s, father's (based on the record of a fully insured individual), mother's (based on the record of a fully insured individual), parent's, or childhood disability benefits, or to a widow(er)'s, child's (age eighteen or over) or parent's annuity under the Railroad Retirement Act, in the month before the month the widow(er) married the deceased worker.

A widow(er) is "potentially entitled" if he or she meets all requirements for entitlement, other than filing of an application and attainment of the required age.

The nine-month duration of marriage requirement is waived if the worker's death was accidental or it occurred in the line of duty while a member of a uniformed service serving on active duty, or if the widow(er) who was married to the worker at the time of death, was previously married to and divorced from the worker and the previous marriage had lasted nine months.

The worker's death is "accidental" if he or she received bodily injuries solely through violent, external, and accidental means and, as a direct result, died within three months after the day the injuries were received. The exception to the nine-month duration of marriage requirement does not apply if, at the time of marriage, the worker could not reasonably have been expected to live for nine months.

An application for widow(er)'s benefits is not required if the person was age sixty-five or over and entitled to spouse's benefits for the month immediately preceding the month in which the worker died, or if the person was entitled to mother's or father's benefits for the month immediately preceding the month in which age sixty-five was attained. If an entitled spouse is between ages sixty-two and sixty-five when the worker dies and the spouse is not also entitled to a disability or retirement benefit, the spouse's benefits will automatically be converted to widow(er)'s benefits.

182. Can Social Security payments go to the estates of deceased beneficiaries?

Yes. A deceased beneficiary may have been due a Social Security payment (or a Medicare Premium refund) at the time of death. The Social Security Administration may pay amounts due a deceased beneficiary to a family member or legal representative of the estate.[1]

Payment of Social Security Payment Due

In the case of a Social Security payment due to a deceased beneficiary, the payment may be paid to a family member or a legal representative of the estate in the following order:

•   the surviving spouse who was either living in the same household as the deceased at the time of death or who, for the month of death, was entitled to a monthly benefit on the same record as the deceased;

- children who, for the month of death, were entitled to a monthly benefit on the same record as the deceased;

- parents who, for the month of death, were entitled to a monthly benefit on the same record as the deceased;

- a surviving spouse not qualified under the condition above;

- children not qualified under the condition above;

- parents not qualified under the condition above; or

- the legal representative of the deceased person's estate.

Payment of Medicare Premium Refund Due

A Medicare Premium refund may be issued to the person or organization that paid the beneficiary's premiums. If the beneficiary paid the premiums, refunds may be issued to a family member or the legal representative of the estate in the following order:

- the surviving spouse who was either living in the same household as the deceased at the time of death or who, for the month of death, was entitled to a monthly benefit on the same record as the deceased;

- children who, for the month of death, were entitled to a monthly benefit on the same record as the deceased;

- parents who, for the month of death, were entitled to a monthly benefit on the same record as the deceased;

- a surviving spouse not qualified under the condition above;

- children not qualified under the condition above;

- parents not qualified under the condition above; or

- the legal representative of the deceased person's estate.

- Form SSA-1724[2] *Claim for Amounts Due in the Case of Deceased Beneficiary* is used in the event that a deceased beneficiary is due a Social Security or Medicare Premium refund at the time of death.

Notes

1. https://faq.ssa.gov/en-us/Topic/article/KA-02101 (last accessed August 31, 2022).
2. https://www.ssa.gov/forms/ssa-1724.html (Last accessed August 31, 2022).

183. What is the impact of the 2015 Bi-Partisan Budget Act on the ability of a widow or widower to collect from a deceased spouse?

The Bi-Partisan Budget Act signed into law on November 2, 2015 does not impact surviving spouse benefits as "deemed filing" does NOT apply to widows and widowers. Thus, surviving spouses can receive the survivor's benefit as early as age sixty (or age fifty if disabled) and switch to their own benefits anywhere from age sixty-two through age seventy.

In the alternative, a surviving spouse may begin collecting their own benefit as early as age sixty-two and switch to the survivor's benefit at their Full Retirement Age. The Full Retirement Age for surviving spouses born between 1943 and 1944 is sixty-six and represents the age that a surviving spouse can collect 100 percent of survivor's benefit.

184. Must the worker be fully insured at death to qualify the widow(er) for a widow(er)'s benefit?

Yes, the widow(er) must be fully insured at death to qualify the widow(er) for a widow(er)'s benefit. The widow(er) will not be entitled to a widow(er)'s benefit at age sixty or over if the worker was only currently insured at death (see Q 149, Q 244, and Q 245).

185. Can the divorced spouse of a deceased worker qualify for a widow(er)'s benefit?

Yes. A widow(er) is entitled to surviving divorced spouse's benefits on the worker's Social Security record if:

(1)   the surviving divorced spouse was married to the worker for at least ten years prior to the date the divorce became final;

(2)   the surviving divorced spouse is age sixty or over, or is at least age fifty but not age sixty and is disabled;

(3)   the deceased spouse died fully insured;

(4)   the surviving divorced spouse is not married (but see Q 189 below);

(5)   the surviving divorced spouse is not entitled to a retirement benefit that is equal to or greater than the deceased worker's primary insurance amount (PIA); and

(6)   the surviving divorced spouse has filed an application for widow(er)'s benefits.

A surviving divorced spouse meets the ten-year marriage requirement even if, within the ten-year period, they were divorced, provided they remarried each other no later than the calendar year after the year of the divorce.

186. What are the requirements for a divorced spouse to be able to file for spousal benefits from the former spouse?

These requirements include:

(1)   an application must actually be filed (important because benefits are not AUTO-MATICALLY trigged by death);

(2)   the marriage must have lasted ten years or longer;

(3)   if the divorce was fewer than two years ago, the ex-spouse upon whose record the benefits are being paid must have also filed an application; and

(4)   each party must be at least sixty-two years of age.

187. What is the earliest age at which a widow(er) can receive a widow(er)'s benefit?

A widow(er) can elect to start receiving a reduced widow(er)'s benefit at age sixty[1] (see Q 189). A disabled widow(er) can start receiving benefits at age fifty. If a person receives widow(er)'s benefits and will also qualify for a retirement benefit that's more than their survivors' benefit, they can switch to their own retirement benefit as early as age 62 or as late as age 70.

Note

1.   https://www.ssa.gov/benefits/survivors/survivorchartred.html#:~:text=The%20earliest%20a%20widow%20or,retirement%20age%20as%20a%20survivor (last accessed September 19, 2022)

188. Can a widow(er) start with retirement benefits and switch to survivor benefits or vice versa?

Yes. If a person receives widow(er)'s benefits and also can qualify for a retirement benefit that is more than their survivor's benefit, they can switch to their own retirement benefit.

Example 1: The surviving spouse could begin with reduced survivors benefit as early as age sixty, and then switch to their retirement benefit at any time between age sixty-two and seventy.

Example 2: The surviving spouse may also be able to start with their reduced retirement benefit as early as age sixty-two, and then switch to their survivor's benefit.

189. What is the monthly rate of a widow(er)'s benefit?

The monthly amount someone would get is a percentage of the deceased's basic Social Security benefit. It depends on their age and the type of benefit they would be eligible to receive.

A widow(er) who is eligible for a widow(er)'s benefit may apply for a reduced benefit at any time between sixty and full retirement age or may wait until Full Retirement Age (FRA) to receive a full widow(er)'s benefit.

If the widow(er) is Full Retirement Age or older when benefits commence, the monthly benefit is equal to 100 percent of the deceased worker's PIA (the amount the worker would have been entitled to receive upon retirement at Full Retirement Age), plus any additional amount the deceased worker was entitled to because of delayed retirement credits (the delayed retirement credit is discussed at Q 193 and Q 293). If the worker was actually receiving benefits that began before Full Retirement Age, the widow(er) would be entitled to an amount equal to the reduced benefit the worker would have been receiving had he lived (but not less than 82.5 percent of the PIA).

If the widow(er) chooses to receive, and is paid, a reduced widow(er)'s benefit for months before full retirement age, he or she is not entitled to the widow(er)'s full benefit rate upon reaching full retirement age. A reduced benefit is payable for as long as he or she remains entitled to widow(er)'s benefits.

If the widow(er)'s full retirement age is sixty-five, the widow(er)'s benefit is reduced by 19/40 of 1 percent for each month that the widow(er) is under age sixty-five when the benefits commence. A benefit beginning at age sixty will equal 71.5 percent of the deceased worker's PIA. If the widow(er)'s Full Retirement Age is more than sixty-five, the 71.5 percent at age sixty will remain unchanged, but the reduction factor will be different (based on 71.5 percent at age sixty percent to 99 percent until hitting 100 percent at Full Retirement Age).

The monthly payment amount of a widow(er) who remarries after attaining age sixty is not reduced.

If there are other survivors entitled to benefits based on the deceased worker's earnings record, the widow(er) could receive a smaller benefit because of the family maximum limit. (See Maximum Family Benefits, Q 283 to Q 286, and Table 11.)

If the widow(er) has in care the deceased spouse's child, under sixteen or disabled, who is entitled to child's benefits, for some months while he or she is under sixty-five, his or her widow(er)'s benefits are not reduced for those months below 75 percent of the deceased spouse's PIA.

The surviving divorced spouse's benefit is the same amount as a widow(er)'s benefit. However, it is paid independently of benefits for the former spouse's family. In other words, it is not subject to reduction because of the family maximum limit, and does not affect the family maximum for the former spouse's family.

A widow(er) who files an application for actuarially reduced widow(er)'s benefits in the calendar month following the month his or her spouse died is entitled to one month of retroactive benefit payments.

A disabled widow(er) aged 50 to 59 will collect 71.5 percent.

190. How much will a spouse, aged sixty-four, collect when an older spouse dies at age sixty-nine before filing or receiving benefits?

The spouse is eligible for 100 percent of what the deceased was eligible for in the month of death.

> *Example:* If the Full Retirement Age benefit was $2,000 and the spouse died at age sixty-eight, the deceased spouse would have earned twenty-four percent Delayed Retirement Credits, then the surviving spouse's benefit is based on $2,000 plus 16 percent. However, if the surviving spouse takes the benefit at age sixty-four, it will be reduced because of age.

191. How does remarriage affect a widow(er)'s benefits?

The remarriage of a widow(er) or surviving divorced spouse after age sixty, or the remarriage of a disabled widow(er) or disabled surviving divorced spouse after age fifty and after the date he or she became disabled, will not prevent that individual from becoming entitled to benefits on his or her prior deceased spouse's Social Security record.

A widow(er) or a surviving divorced spouse's remarriage before age sixty will prevent entitlement unless the subsequent marriage ends, whether by death, divorce, or annulment. If the subsequent marriage ends, the widow(er) or surviving divorced spouse may become entitled or re-entitled to benefits on the prior deceased spouse's earnings record beginning with the month the subsequent marriage ends.

A widower is entitled to benefits even when remarriage takes place prior to the death of the former spouse.

There is a distinct advantage in being able to receive the widow(er)'s benefit instead of the spouse's benefit. Part or all of a spouse's benefit could be lost if the new spouse is under full retirement age and loses benefits by working and earning more than the Social Security earnings limit. The widow(er)'s benefit, on the other hand, will be unaffected by the new spouse's work.

192. If a widow(er) is entitled to a retirement benefit and a widow(er)'s benefit, will the widow(er) receive both benefits?

No. The widow(er) will receive the retirement benefit plus the difference if the widow(er)'s benefit is greater. In other words, the widow(er) will receive only the larger benefit. (See also Reduction in Benefits, Q 291 to Q 295.) The Social Security Administration does not allow "double-dipping" in that a beneficiary will always be paid the larger entitled benefit, but not more than one benefit.

However, it is possible to take a widow(er)'s benefit for a period of time (such as starting at age sixty), and then later apply for a full retirement benefit at full retirement age. It is also possible to take a retirement benefit for a period of time (such as starting at age sixty-two), and then later apply for a full widow(er)'s benefit at the full retirement age.

193. How does the Delayed Retirement Credit affect a widow(er)'s benefit?

A widow(er) whose spouse reaches age sixty-five after 2007 receives an increase in benefits equal to 8 percent, for each year (2/3 of 1 percent per month) in which the spouse deferred retirement benefits between age sixty-five and age seventy. Since there are no Delayed Retirement Credits for survivors benefit, it makes little sense to wait past Full Retirement Age to switch to the survivor benefit. Another strategy is to claim a survivor benefit at age 60 and then switch to a worker benefit at age 70.

For spouses' reaching age sixty-five prior to 2008, the increases per year of deferring retirement were as follows:

- Age sixty-five in 2006-2007, 7.5 percent

- Age sixty-five in 2004-2005, 7 percent

- Age sixty-five in 2002-2003, 6.5 percent

- Age sixty-five in 2000-2001, 6 percent

- Age sixty-five in 1998-99, 5.5 percent

- Age sixty-five in 1996-97, 5 percent

- Age sixty-five in 1994-95, 4.5 percent

- Age sixty-five in 1992-93, 4.0 percent

- Age sixty-five in 1990-91, 3.5 percent

- Age sixty-five in 1982-89, 3 percent

- Age sixty-five before 1982, 1 percent

The Delayed Retirement Credit is based on the year of attainment of age sixty-two (not the year of work), and it can be earned only after full retirement age. (See Q 293 for further information.)

A surviving divorced spouse is entitled to the same increase that had been applied to the benefit of the deceased worker or for which the deceased worker was eligible at the time of death.

194. Can a widow(er) lose benefits by working?

Yes. Although benefits are payable regardless of how wealthy the widow(er) is, the widow(er) will lose some or all benefits if she is under the normal retirement age (see Q 49) for the entire year and her earnings exceed $19,560 in 2022 or $21,240 in 2023. In the year the widow(er) reaches normal retirement age, the widow(er) will lose some or all benefits if her earnings exceed

$19,560 in 2022 or $21,240 in 2023. However, only earnings earned before the month that normal retirement age is reached count towards the $51,960 limit in 2022 or $56,520 in 2023.

See LOSS OF BENEFITS BECAUSE OF "EXCESS" EARNINGS, Q 362 to Q 386.

195. Will a widow(er)'s benefits be reduced if the widow(er) is receiving a government pension?

Social Security benefits payable to spouses—including surviving spouses and divorced spouses—are reduced (but not below zero) by two-thirds of the amount of any governmental (federal, state, or local) retirement benefit payable to the spouse based on his or her own earnings in employment not covered by Social Security if that person's last day of employment was not covered by Social Security. Thus, for the affected group, the spouse's benefit is reduced two dollars for every three dollars of the government pension. However, the Social Security Protection Act of 2004 generally requires that a person work in covered employment for five years to be exempt from this Government Pension Offset (GPO). See Q 120 for more information on the GPO.

This offset against Social Security benefits does not apply if the individual:

(1)   met all the requirements for entitlement to Social Security benefits that existed and applied in January 1977; and

(2)   received or was eligible to receive a government pension between December 1977 and December 1982.

Generally, federal workers hired before 1984 are part of the Civil Service Retirement System (CSRS) and are not covered by Social Security. Federal workers hired after 1983 are covered by the Federal Employees' Retirement System Act of 1986 (FERS), which includes Social Security coverage. Legislation provided an opportunity for federal employees covered by CSRS to join FERS in 1987 (and thereby obtain Social Security coverage). Thus, a CSRS employee who switched to FERS during this period immediately became exempt from the government-pension offset.

Federal employees who switch from CSRS to FERS during any election period on or after January 1, 1988, are exempt from the government-pension offset only if they have five or more years of federal employment covered by Social Security beginning January 1, 1988. This rule also applies to certain legislative branch employees who first become covered under FERS on or after January 1, 1988.

Pensions based wholly on service performed as a member of a uniformed service, whether on active or inactive duty, are excluded from the offset.

196. How is the effect of public employee pension income on how Social Security benefits calculated?

There are TWO factors that come into play.

The first factor is the **Windfall Elimination Provision (WEP),** which affects Social Security benefits based upon what you can receive on your own work record because of pensions from a job which did NOT contribute to Social Security. Under the WEP, the Social Security benefit reduction is capped at one-half of the amount of the pension from noncovered employment, which substantially reduces the WEP penalty and prevents the WEP adjustment from falling disproportionately on households in the lowest earnings category. Social Security benefits are based on the worker's average monthly earnings adjusted for inflation. This average is separated into three brackets: The first is 90 percent of the first $1.115 of a person's average wage. With WEP, the 90 percent can be as low at 40 percent. The fact sheets on WEP and GPO from Social Security provide further reference – Publication Numbers 05-10045 (WEP)[1] and 05-10007 (GPO).[2]

Secondly, the **Government Pension Offset (GPO)** reduces Social Security benefits paid to spouses or survivors when the spouse or survivor earned a pension from a government job that was not covered by Social Security. The GPO reduction equals two-thirds of the amount of the pension payment from noncovered government work.

Efforts to repeal the Windfall Elimination Provision and the Government Pension Offset have thus far been unsuccessful. However, there currently are efforts in the legislature to repeal both the GPO and the WEP, namely the following two bills:

H.R. 82, the *Social Security Fairness Act of 2021*, introduced in January 2021, has been referred to the Subcommittee on Social Security, and supported by over 290 co-sponsors. This bill has also been introduced in the Senate without action as well.

H.R. 2337, *Public Servants Protection and Fairness Act of 2021*, introduced in April 2021, intends to modify the WEP with an alternative formula for calculating an individual's Social Security benefit. Supporters argue that this is fairer, as well as politically more realistic, than a full repeal.

Not surprisingly, in today's divisive political climate, neither bill has gained significant traction – but at the time of publication, Congressman Rodney Davis (R-IL) has filed a motion to bring H.R. 82 to the floor for a full floor vote.

Notes

1. See Publication No. 05-10045 Windfall Elimination Provision (2022) http://www.ssa.gov/pubs/EN-05-10045.pdf (last accessed August 31, 2022).
2. See Publication 05-10007 Government Pension Offset (May 2019), https://www.socialsecurity.gov/pubs/EN-05-10007.pdf (last accessed August 31, 2022).

197. When do widow(er)'s benefits end?

Widow(er)'s benefits end when:

(1)   the widow(er) dies; or

(2)   the widow(er) becomes entitled to a retirement benefit which is as large as or larger than the deceased worker's primary insurance amount; or

(3)   the widow(er)'s disability ceases.

If a widow(er)'s disability ceases, the last month of entitlement is the second month after the month in which the disability ceased, except that entitlement continues if the widow(er) becomes age sixty-five on or before the last day of the third month after the disability ends.

Disabled Widow(er)'s Benefit

198. Is a disabled widow(er) entitled to benefits starting before age sixty?

Yes. A disabled widow(er) (or surviving divorced widow(er)) who otherwise qualifies for a widow(er)'s benefit can start receiving a disabled widow(er)'s benefit at any time after attaining age fifty and before attaining age sixty. The monthly benefit will be based on 100 percent of the deceased spouse's PIA but will be reduced by 28.5 percent so that the benefit equals 71.5 percent of the deceased spouse's PIA at age sixty. The monthly benefit remains at 71.5 percent of the deceased spouse's PIA for disabled widow(er)'s between ages fifty and fifty-nine. Once established, the benefit rate remains the same; it will not be increased when the widow(er) reaches age sixty or full retirement age.

Disabled widow(er)'s benefits are payable to a disabled widow(er) or surviving divorced spouse age fifty to fifty-nine if the individual:

(1)   meets the definition of disability for disabled workers,

(2)   became disabled no later than seven years after the month the worker died or seven years after the last month the widow(er) was previously entitled to benefits on the worker's earnings record,

(3)   has been disabled throughout a waiting period of five consecutive full calendar months, except that no waiting period is required if the widow(er) was previously entitled to disabled widow(er)'s benefits, and

(4)   meets the nondisability requirements for a surviving spouse or a surviving divorced spouse.

The first month of entitlement to disabled widow(er)'s benefits is the latest of the following months:

(1)   either the sixth consecutive calendar month of disability, where a waiting period is required, or the first full calendar month of disability, if a waiting period is not required;

(2)   the month the insured spouse died;

(3)   the twelfth month before the month the widow(er) applied for benefits; or

(4)   the month the widow(er) attains age fifty.

Widow(er)s must meet the definition of disability used to determine if workers are entitled to disability benefits. In other words, the widow(er) must be unable to engage in any substantial gainful activity by reason of physical or mental impairment. The impairment must be medically determinable and expected to last for at least twelve months or result in death.

If benefits to a widow(er) who is disabled based on drug addiction or alcoholism are terminated after thirty-six months of benefits, that person cannot become entitled again to widow(er)'s benefits if drug addiction or alcoholism is a contributing factor material to the later determination of disability. See Q 92.

199. How does someone qualify for Disabled Widow(er) Benefits?

The following requirements must be met to qualify for Disabled Widow(er) Benefits (DWB):

1. **Attain the age of 50.** To be eligible for DWB, a widow(er) must have attained age 50, but not yet attained age 60. Benefits to a widow(er) on the basis of disability before the attainment of age fifty even though the impairment may have existed before age 50. If a widow(er) receiving benefits paid to widows(er)s age 60 and older becomes disabled after attaining age 60, and is still within the prescribed period, he or she may file a DWB claim for Medicare entitlement purposes.

2. **Prove spousal relationship to the deceased.** The claimant is considered the widow(er) of the deceased if he or she meets one the required conditions:

   - Spousal relationship established - the parties were legally married, putative spouse, or deemed spouse.

   - Married not less than nine months before death (unless certain exceptions are met).

   - Mother or father of the deceased's child even if the child is deceased.

   - While married to the deceased, legally adopted the deceased's child before the child attained age 18.

   - Legally adopted the child of deceased before the child turned eighteen.

   - Married to the deceased at the same time they adopted a child.

   - The adoption of a child by the claimant within two years after the deceased's death will qualify the claimant if the adoption of a child by the claimant is valid where it took place and the adoption meets all federal requirements of adoption.

- The claimant was entitled or potentially entitled to the following benefits under the Social Security Act in the month before the month he or she married the deceased:

  ○ Spousal benefits

  ○ Widow(er) benefits

  ○ Father or mother benefits

  ○ Parent benefits

  ○ Children's disability benefits

- The claimant was entitled or potentially entitled to a widow(er)'s, child's (age 18 or older), or parent's annuity payment under the Railroad Retirement Act (RRA) in the month before he or she married the deceased.

3. **Prove disability under the Social Security Act.** The disability standard for disabled widow(er)s and surviving divorced spouses, collectively referred to as disabled widow(er) beneficiaries (DWBs), is the same as the disability standard for disabled wage earners effective for benefits payable January 1991 and later.

4. **Be found to be disabled before the end of the prescribed period.** To qualify for disability benefits, a widow(er) (including certain surviving divorced spouses) must be found disabled before the end of a certain prescribed period as defined in the law. The widow(er) may allege a disability onset date that is earlier than the prescribed period; however, the SSA will determine if disability can be established before the prescribed period end date.

5. **File an application and complete the disability report.** An application for DWB is necessary unless an automatic conversion from a spouse's benefit is involved. Complete the SSA-3368 (Disability Report – Adult)[1] to obtain basic information about the claimant's condition, sources of medical evidence, and other information needed to process the claim to completion. Additionally, the claimant must sign medical release forms SSA-827 (Authorization to Disclose Information to the Social Security Administration)[2] so that SSA may obtain medical records from his or her treating sources.

6. **Complete the waiting period.** Payment of DWB is subject to a waiting period of five full consecutive calendar months. The waiting period can begin no earlier than the later of:

   a. The first day of the seventeenth month before the month of filing; or

   b. The first day of the fifth month before the month in which the prescribed period began.

There is no waiting period if the claimant becomes disabled again before age 60, and the new period of disability began within eighty-four months following the month in which prior entitlement to DWB terminated. Benefits begin the first month the claimant is disabled for the entire month.

Notes

1. https://www.ssa.gov/forms/ssa-3368.pdf (October 2015 version) (last accessed August 31, 2022).
2. https://www.ssa.gov/forms/ssa-827.pdf (March 2020 version) (last accessed August 31, 2022).

Parent's Benefits

200. Under what circumstances is a deceased worker's parent entitled to benefits?

The parent of a deceased insured person is entitled to a parent's benefit if:

(1)   the insured person was fully insured at the time of death;

(2)   the parent files an application for parent's benefits;

(3)   the parent has reached age 62;

(4)   the parent is not entitled to a retirement benefit that is equal to or larger than the amount of the unadjusted parent's benefit after any increase to the minimum benefit;

(5)   the parent was receiving at least one-half support from the insured person;

(6)   evidence (documentation) that the support requirement was met has been filed with the Social Security Administration within the appropriate time limit; and

(7)   the parent has not remarried since the insured person's death.

The support requirement must be met at:

(1)   the time that the insured person died; or

(2)   the beginning of a period of disability that was established for the deceased if it continued up until the month in which he or she died.

Evidence of support must be filed within the two-year period:

(1)   after the date of the death of the insured person, if that point is being used; or

(2)   after the month in which the insured person had filed an application to establish a period of disability, if that point is being used. Evidence of support must be filed within the appropriate period, even though the parent may not be eligible for

benefits at that time (e.g., has not reached retirement age). The time limit may be extended for good cause.

The insured provided one-half of a parent's support if:

(1)   the insured made regular contributions for the parent's ordinary living costs;

(2)   the amount of these contributions equaled or exceeded one-half of the parent's ordinary living costs; and

(3)   any income (from sources other than the insured person) for support purposes was one-half or less of the parent's ordinary living costs.

The insured was not providing at least one-half of the parent's support unless the insured had done so for a reasonable period of time. Ordinarily, the Social Security Administration will consider a reasonable period to be the twelve-month period immediately preceding the time when the one-half support requirement must be met.[1] Social Security also cautions that in the case of parent's benefits – the benefits may stop if the parent remarries or becomes entitled to a retirement amount higher than the parent benefit amount. Remember that Social Security always pays the HIGHER benefit, but never two benefits.

Note

1. Parent's Benefits, Publication No. 05-10036 (January 2022 – note that March 2017 is still valid as well), https://www.ssa.gov/pubs/EN-05-10036.pdf (last accessed August 31, 2022).

201. Who is a parent for the purpose of receiving a parent's benefit?

One of the following conditions must be met:

(1)   the parent is a natural parent and would be eligible under the law of the state of the worker's domicile to share in the intestate property of the worker as the worker's father or mother;

(2)   the parent has legally adopted the insured person before the insured person attained age 16; or

(3)   the person claiming benefits became the deceased's stepparent by a marriage entered into before the deceased had attained age 16.

(4)   it is uncertain if a surviving parent of a posthumously conceived child who met the requirements of Q 200 would always be a "parent" in this situation. The state law would control in providing the definition.

It should be noted that "domicile"[1] refers to the true and fixed home (legal domicile) of a person and is the place to which the person intends to return whenever he or she is absent.

Note

1. 20 CFR 404.303 Definitions.

202. What is the amount of a parent's monthly benefit?

A parent's benefit is equal to 82.5 percent of the deceased worker's Primary Insurance Amount (PIA), if there is only one eligible parent. If two parents are entitled to benefits, the benefit for each is 75 percent of the worker's PIA. The full benefit is payable at age sixty-two. However, because of the maximum family limit, the monthly benefit actually received by a parent may be less. If total monthly benefits payable on the basis of one worker's earnings record exceeds the family maximum, all benefits are reduced proportionately, to bring the total within the family maximum.

See Maximum Family Benefits, Q 283 to Q 286.

203. Can a parent receive benefits, even if the worker's widow(er) and children are eligible for benefits?

Yes, but benefits payable to a parent may reduce the benefits payable to the worker's widow(er) and children. See Q 204.)

204. May benefits payable to a parent reduce the benefits payable to the worker's widow(er) and children?

Yes, because the total amount of monthly benefits based on one worker's Social Security account is limited by the maximum family benefit ceiling. If total benefits computed separately exceed this limit, all benefits are reduced proportionately to bring the total within the family maximum. (See Maximum Family Benefits, Q 283 to Q 286.)

205. Is a parent's benefit starting at age 62 smaller than one starting at age sixty-five?

No, the full parent's benefit becomes fully payable (to a father or mother) at age 62, rather than age 65.

206. If a person is entitled to a parent's benefit and a retirement benefit, will he receive both full benefits?

No. If the parent is also eligible for a retired worker's benefit based on his own earnings record, he will receive the retired worker's benefit if it equals or exceeds the parent's benefit. However, he is not compelled to take a reduced retired worker's benefit before Full Retirement Age (see Q 49). He can opt to receive the parent's benefit and then switch to a full retired worker's benefit at Full Retirement Age. The Social Security Administration always pays the higher benefit to which the individual is entitled, but never more than one benefit.

207. Can a person lose a parent's benefit by working?

Yes, a person will lose some or all benefits if the person is under normal retirement age for the entire year and his earnings exceed $19,560 in 2022 or $21,240 in 2023. In the year the person reaches normal retirement age (see Q 55), he will lose some or all benefits if his earnings exceed $51,960 in 2022 or $56,520 in 2023. However, only earnings earned before the month that he or she reaches normal retirement age count toward the $56,520 limit.

See LOSS OF BENEFITS BECAUSE OF "EXCESS" EARNINGS, Q 358 to Q 386.

208. When do a parent's benefits end?

The parent's benefit ends

- when the parent dies, marries (but see Q 209), or

- when the parent becomes entitled to a retirement benefit or disability benefit equal to or larger than the amount of the unadjusted parent's benefit.

209. If a parent remarries after the worker's death, will the parent lose benefits?

Yes, unless the marriage is to a person entitled to monthly Social Security benefits as a divorced spouse, widow(er), mother, father, parent, or a disabled child aged 18 or over.

Blackout Period

209.01. What is the blackout period and how does it work?

Background

When a worker covered by Social Security dies, certain monthly benefits may be available to his or her survivors. These can include:

- **Mother or Father's benefit:** Monthly income paid to a surviving spouse caring for a worker's dependent child either

  o Under the age of 16 OR

  o Disabled before the age of 22

- **Child's benefit:** A monthly income for the dependent child of a deceased. Disabled, or retired worker. To qualify, a child must be:

  o Under age 18, OR

  o Age 18 or 19 and a full time elementary or high school student, OR

       ○   18 or over and disabled before age 22.

- **Widower's benefit:** Monthly retirement income for the surviving spouse or former spouse of a deceased worker

- **Parent's benefit:** Monthly income paid to the surviving dependent parent(s) of a deceased worker.

Illustration of the Social Security Blackout Period

Survivor benefits under Social Security are paid only for limited amounts of time. In a situation where a spouse loses the other spouse and is the surviving spouse left behind to raise a minor child:

Benefits Period

- **Mother or Father's benefit:** Surviving spouse receives a mother or father's benefit until the child reaches the age of 16

- **Child's benefit:** The child receives a child's benefit until reaching the age of 18

- **Widow/Widower's benefit:** The surviving spouse is eligible for a widow/widower's benefit. This can be paid as early as age 60.

Blackout Period

- **No Benefits:** This is the period between when the child reaches age 18 and the survivor begins to collect retirement benefits. No benefits are eligible to be paid during that period until the widow/widower reaches age 60 (widow/widower's benefits), or age 62 (retirement benefits).

Lump-Sum Death Payment

210. What is the amount of the Social Security lump-sum death payment?

A lump-sum death benefit of $255 is paid upon the death of an insured worker, provided he is survived by a spouse who was living in the same household as the deceased at the time of death, or a spouse or dependent child eligible to receive Social Security benefits for the month of death based on his earnings record. In 2020, the Social Security Administration (SSA) paid 914,176 claims for nearly $224 million in lump-sum benefits for 877,943 deaths.[1] The number of claims is higher than the deaths because the $255 was split between multiple individuals. This benefit was established by the Omnibus Budget Reconciliation Act of 1981, which made two changes to lump-sum death benefit:

1.   Previously, if no spouse or child of the deceased worker was eligible for receipt of the lump-sum death benefit, a funeral home or other party who was responsible for the funeral expenses could sometimes claim the benefit. After the 1981 changes, the only people eligible for the lump-sum death benefit are

   a. a spouse who was living with the worker at the time of his/her death, or

   b. a spouse or child who is receiving monthly benefits on the worker's record.

2. The second change in the 1981 law eliminated the minimum benefit guarantee of previous law. To prevent lump-sum death benefits from being lower than $255, the law provides that the provisions of the 1981 OBRA act which eliminated the minimum benefit are not considered when computing the lump-sum death benefit.

   a. Current law provides that the benefit is three times the PIA, or $255, whichever is less. The PIA is computed as if the minimum benefit repeal provision of the 1981 law had never been passed.

Also, the lump-sum death benefit is paid to a spouse when the widow(er) and the deceased customarily lived together as husband and wife in the same residence. While temporary separations do not necessarily preclude the Social Security Administration from considering a couple to be living in the same household, extended separations (including most that last six months or more) generally indicate the couple was not living in the same household.

"Living in the same household" requires a male and female living together as husband and wife in the same residence. The couple may be considered to be living in the same household although one of them is temporarily absent from the residence. An absence is considered temporary if:

(1) it was due to service in the United States Armed Forces;

(2) it was six months or less and neither spouse was outside of the United States during this time, and the absence was due to business, employment, or confinement in a hospital, nursing home, other medical institution, or a penal institution;

(3) it was for an extended separation, regardless of the duration, due to the confinement of either spouse in a hospital, nursing home, or other medical institution, if the evidence indicates that the spouses were separated solely for medical reasons and the spouses otherwise would have resided together;

(4) it was based on other circumstances, and it is shown that the spouses could have expected to live together in the near future.

The lump-sum death payment is paid in the following order of priority:

(1) The widow(er) of the deceased wage earner who was living in the same household as the deceased wage earner (or customarily lived together as husband and wife in the same residence) at the time of death

   a. If there is more than one widow(er), the benefit is divided equally

(2) The widow(er) (excluding a divorced spouse) who is eligible for or entitled to benefits based on the deceased wage earner's record for the month of death

(3)   In the event no spouse exists, children who are eligible for, or entitled to, benefits based on the deceased wage earner's record for the month of death

If no surviving widow(er) or child as defined above survives, no lump sum is payable.

However, if an otherwise eligible widow(er) dies before making application for the lump-sum death payment or before negotiating the benefit check, the legal representative of the estate of the deceased widow(er) may claim the lump-sum payment. Where the legal representative of the estate is a state or political subdivision of a state, the lump-sum death benefit is not payable.

The lump-sum death benefit is not payable to an otherwise ineligible child of the wage earner after the wage earner's widow, who applied for the benefit, died before it could be paid.[2]

No part of the lump-sum benefit is taxable.[3] While the benefit has remained unchanged, the median cost of a funeral in 2021 was $7,848 and was $9,135 if a vault was included.[4]

Legislative attempts have been made to increase the lump sum benefit:

- H.R. 341 proposed expanding eligibility for the benefit to insured workers upon the death of their uninsured spouses.

- The Social Security Death Benefit Increase Act of 2010 (H.R. 6388) would have increased the benefit from $255 to $332.

- The BASIC Act (H.R. 5001) would have increased it to 47 percent of the worker's PIA.

- The Social Security Lump-Sum Death Benefit Improvement and Modernization Act of 2015 (H.R. 1109) proposed an increase of the benefit to $1,000.

- H.R. 5302 and S. 1739 (BASIC Act) proposed to increase the lump-sum death benefit to 50 percent of the worker's PIA.

At the time of publication, none of these proposals have been enacted into law.

It should also be noted that for most deaths, no lump-sum death benefit is paid. In 2020, fewer than 38% of the deaths among insured workers resulted in lump-sum death benefit payments, most likely because for many deaths, there was no eligible family member to receive the death payment.

Notes

1. SSA, Annual Statistical Supplement, 2021, Table 6.D1 https://www.ssa.gov/policy/docs/statcomps/supplement/2021/6d.html#table6.d1 (Latest report available – last accessed August 31, 2022).
2. Social Security Ruling 85-24a, 20 CFR sec. 404.392 (October 1985), https://www.ssa.gov/OP_Home/rulings/oasi/17/SSR85-24-oasi-17.html (last accessed August 31, 2022).
3. See Publication 915, Social Security and Equivalent Railroad Retirement Benefits, https://www.irs.gov/pub/irs-pdf/p915.pdf (last accessed August 31, 2022).
4. National Funeral Directors Association, "Statistics" (last updated July, 2021), https://nfda.org/news/statistics#:~:text=Cost%20of%20a%20Funeral%3A%20The,with%20cremation%20was%20approximately%20%246%2C971 (last accessed August 31, 2022).

211. Is the lump-sum death benefit payable only if the worker was fully insured at death?

No, it is payable if the worker was either fully or merely currently insured.

212. Must an application be made for the lump-sum death benefit?

An application need not be made by the widow(er) if he or she was receiving a spouse's benefit when the insured person died. Otherwise, an application must be filed within two years after the insured person's death unless good cause can be shown why the application was not filed within the two-year period. Examples of "good cause" for the two year extension are found in SSR 61-55.[1]

Generally, good cause will exist if:[2]

- Evidence of illness, mental or physical incapacity, communication difficulties, or other handicaps;

- incorrect or incomplete information furnished the claimant by SSA;

- delays because of efforts by the claimant to secure supporting evidence which the claimant assumed must be submitted at the same time the claim is filed; or

- unusual or unavoidable circumstances under which the individual is not reasonably expected to have been aware of the need to file timely.

For example, the individual's education or environment is such that the claimant is not familiar with filing a claim, does not understand the process, and requires guidance for his or her actions by the technical time-limitation provision.

"Good cause" for failure to file within the prescribed period does not exist when the evidence shows that the individual was informed of the time limitation for filing and failed to file within the specified period through negligence or intent not to file.

Notes

1. SSR 61-55, Good Cause for Extension of 2-Year Limitation for Filing Application for Lump-sum Death Payment – Incomplete Information; Written Statement Considered Application for Benefits, https://www.ssa.gov/OP_Home/rulings/oasi/17/SSR61-55-oasi-17.html (last accessed August 31, 2022).
2. Social Security Administration, Operating Policy for Good Cause and LSDP, https://secure.ssa.gov/apps10/poms.nsf/lnx/0300210030 (last accessed August 31, 2022).

213. What documentation and information is needed to apply for the lump-sum death benefit?

Documents from Applicant to prove eligibility:

- A birth certificate or other proof of birth

- Proof of U.S. citizenship or lawful alien status if applicant was not born in the United States

- U.S. military discharge paper(s) if applicant had military service before 1968

- W-2 forms(s) and/or self-employment tax returns for last year

- A death certificate for the deceased worker

Information Needed:[1]

- Applicant's name and Social Security number

- The deceased worker's name, gender, date of birth, and Social Security number

- The deceased worker's date and place of death

- Whether the deceased worker ever filed for Social Security benefits, Medicare, or Supplemental Security Income (if so, we will also ask for information on whose Social Security record he or she applied)

- Whether the deceased worker was unable to work because of illnesses, injuries, or conditions at any time during the fourteen months before his or her death (if "Yes," when he or she became unable to work)

- Whether the deceased worker was ever in the active military service (if "Yes," dates of his or her service)

- Whether the deceased worker worked for the railroad industry for seven years or more

- Whether the deceased worker earned Social Security credits under another country's social security system

- The names, dates of birth (or age), and Social Security numbers (if known) of any of the deceased worker's former spouses and the dates of the marriages and how and when they ended

- The names of any of the deceased worker's unmarried children under age 18, age 18 to 19 and in elementary or secondary school, or disabled prior to age 22

- The amount of the deceased worker's earnings in the year of death and the preceding year

- Whether the deceased worker had a parent who was dependent on the worker for half of his or her support at the time of the worker's death

- Whether the deceased worker and surviving spouse were living together at the time of death

If applicant is the surviving spouse, SSA will need to know:

- whether applicant has been unable to work because of illnesses, injuries, or conditions at any time within the past fourteen months (if "Yes," when applicant became unable to work);

- whether applicant or anyone else ever filed for Social Security benefits, Medicare or Supplemental Security Income on applicant's behalf; and

- the names, dates of birth (or age), and social security numbers (if known) of any of former spouses and the dates of the marriages and how and when they ended.

If applicant is not the surviving spouse, SSA will also ask for the surviving spouse's name and address.

Note

1. POMS RS 00210.005 Evidence Requirements for the Lump-Sum Death Payment (LSDP) https://secure.ssa.gov/poms.nsf/lnx/0300210005 (Issued May 11, 2022).

Prisoners

214. Can imprisoned individuals get Social Security or SSI payments?

Both Social Security and Supplemental Security Income prohibit payments to most prisoners.

Social Security benefits are suspended if an individual is confined to a jail, prison, or other penal institution for more than thirty continuous days due to a criminal conviction. Social Security WILL continue to pay benefits to a dependent spouse or children as long as they remain eligible.

SSI recipients will have payments stopped after month of imprisonment.

Social Security and SSI benefits can be reinstated with the month of release if the pre-release procedures are followed; however, SSI recipients who are confined twelve consecutive months or longer, must reapply for SSI and again be approved.

215. How does the No Social Security Benefits for Prisoners Act of 2009 affect prisoners?

The Act prohibits payment of any retroactive Title II or Title XVI payments to a current or terminated beneficiary or recipient who is subject to suspension because he or she is:

- a prisoner;

- confined in a public institution based on a court order for a criminal act (CPICO);

- a fugitive felon (FF); or

- in violation of probation or parole (PPV).

When the NSSBP was enacted in 2009, Congressional intent was to prohibit any payments of Social Security benefits to prisoners, even retroactive payments. Therefore, under NSSBP, the SSA will not pay retroactive benefits until the beneficiary is no longer a prisoner, probation or parole violator, or fugitive felon. The law also prohibits paying death underpayments on the record of a deceased beneficiary or recipient to a surviving beneficiary or recipient who is not eligible for monthly benefits or payments based on being a prisoner, confined in a public institution based on a court order for a criminal act, a fugitive felon, or parole violator.

Under the No Social Security Benefits for Prisoners Act, Social Security benefit payments are held until an individual is released from incarceration. The benefits are suspended if an individual is convicted of a criminal offense and sent to jail or prison for more than thirty continuous days. Benefits are not suspended if the person is awaiting trial or pleas or not yet convicted.

Payment will be suspended beginning with the month in which the individual was first incarcerated after being convicted and sentenced. Benefits payments would not be received if the individual was confined by court order and at public expense to an institution because of being found to be incompetent to stand trial or found guilty by reason of insanity or mental disease.

216. Which individuals with criminal histories are barred from serving as Representative Payees?

1. **Fugitive Felons:** Section 103 of the Social Security Protection Act (SSPA) of 2004 provides that, effective April 1, 2005, fugitive felons are prohibited from serving as payees. Based on the settlement agreement reached in the *Martinez et al. v. Astrue* court case, effective April 1, 2009, a person is considered a fugitive felon and cannot serve as payee if he or she has an unsatisfied felony warrant for one of the following three offenses: escape from custody, flight to avoid prosecution, confinement, etc., and flight-escape.

2. **Representative payee fraud:** Individuals convicted of representative payee-related fraud means the person was convicted of fraud directly related to his or her payee duties. These crimes appear on an Office of the Inspector General (OIG) list and appear in the electronic Representative Payee System (eRPS) as a remark. There are NO exceptions to this rule including parents, spouses, grandparents, and guardians with custody.

3. **Selected Felony Convictions:** Section 202 of the Strengthening Protections for Social Security Beneficiaries Act of 2018 bars an individual convicted of any of the following felonies or convicted of attempt or conspiracy in connection with the following felony crimes from serving as a payee:

    a. Human Trafficking

    b. False Imprisonment

    c. Kidnapping

    d. Rape and Sexual Assault

e.   First-Degree Homicide

f.   Robbery

g.   Fraud to obtain access to government assistance

h.   Fraud by scheme

i.   Theft of Government Funds/Property

j.   Abuse or Neglect

k.   Forgery

l.   Identity Theft or Identity Fraud

The above felonies do not bar the following individuals from serving as representative payees if the individual is:

- custodial parent of the minor child for whom the individual applies to serve;

- custodial spouse of the beneficiary for whom the individual applies to serve;

- custodial parent of an adult beneficiary who has a disability which began before the beneficiary attained age 22, for whom the individual applies to serve;

- custodial court appointed guardian of a beneficiary for whom the individual applies to serve;

- custodial grandparent of the minor grandchild for whom the individual applies to serve; parent who was previously payee for his or her minor child who has since turned 18 and continues to be eligible for benefits; or recipient of a presidential or gubernatorial pardon for the conviction.

4.   **Individuals convicted under Sections 208, 811, or 1632(a) of the Social Security Act:** Cannot serve as payee. These violations include: making any false statement or representation about earnings, factors of entitlement to, or payment of benefits and factors in determining disability; concealing knowledge of events affecting entitlement to or payment of benefits; misuse of benefits; Social Security number fraud; and violation of disclosure laws.

217. What are the pre-release procedures for Social Security or SSI payments?

If the institution has a prerelease agreement with the local Social Security office, when the prisoner knows their release date they will need to notify someone at their facility that they want to start SSI payments or Social Security benefits. The institution then will notify Social Security that the individual is likely to meet the requirements for benefits. Social Security will start an application several months before the anticipated release and begin processing the application. Benefits can start as soon as possible after release. The prerelease procedure allows the applicant to apply for Supplemental Nutrition Assistance Program (SNAP) as well as Supplemental Security Income (SSI).

If the institution does not have a prerelease agreement with the local Social Security office, then the prisoner will need to call Social Security at 1-800-772-1213 when they know their anticipated release date. Social Security will set up an appointment with the local Social Security office. Prerelease agreements can be formal or informal, but an application can be filed even if there is no agreement in effect. Social Security works with the institution to

- Determine if the application appears to meet the criteria for SSI and could be released within 30 days of notification of potential SSI eligibility

- Obtain current medical and non-medical evidence needed

- Obtain anticipated release date and any delays that may result in a later release date

- Obtain notification of actual release date

Social Security will process an application if the person is

- In an institution – hospital, nursing home, prison, or jail AND

- Appears to be likely to meet criteria for SSI eligibility when released AND

- Scheduled to be released within several months of the date of application

218. Will benefits start again if the court reverses a conviction?

If an individual is entitled to Retirement, Survivors, or Disability Insurance benefits, SSA can restart benefits if the correctional institution releases the individual and the court reverses all charges of the conviction. The court must also agree not to prosecute again on the same charges. If the court retries on the same charges, it must find the individual not guilty after the new trial.

If an individual is eligible for Supplement Security Income payments and lives in a public institution (jail, prison, detention center, etc.) over a calendar month, SSA cannot start benefits until the institution releases the person.

219. Can benefits be collected by someone who is on home monitoring and must wear an ankle bracelet or other monitoring device?

Yes. A person's benefits can start again once they contact the local Social Security office to report their release from a correctional institution and the change to ankle bracelet monitoring.

220. Can benefits be collected by someone who has been transferred from a prison to a halfway house or "residential reentry center" under control of the Department of Corrections?

No. Social Security will not pay benefits to someone residing in any facility under the authority of the state or federal Department of Corrections. Even though no longer in prison, the person is still under the control and custody of the Department of Corrections or state authority until the court-ordered sentence is completed and the person officially released, or until the Department of Corrections or state authority places the person on parole.

221. Can benefits be collected by someone who is under civil commitment?

No. Social Security will not pay benefits to someone transferred from a jail or prison to a civil mental health center due to being found not guilty due to insanity or similar reason for acquittal. Benefits can be received after being released.

222. If someone is arrested while on parole or probation, will their benefits stop?

- If someone receives Social Security Retirement, Survivors, or Disability benefits, benefits will not stop until a court or parole board cancels the recipient's parole or probation and confines them in a correctional institution for more than 30 consecutive days.

- Supplemental Security Income will be stopped within the first month spent in a correctional institution.

COVERAGE

Qualification

223. How does someone become qualified for retirement, survivor, and disability benefits under Social Security?

By becoming "insured". Most types of benefits are payable if the person is fully insured. Some types of benefits are payable if the person is either fully or currently insured. A special insured status is required for disability benefits (see Q 246).

A person becomes insured by acquiring a certain number of quarters of coverage.

---

224. How does someone obtain a quarter of coverage as an employee?

For 2023, an employee receives one quarter of coverage for each $1.640 ($1,510 in 2022) of earnings up to a maximum of four quarters.[1]

> *Example.* Mrs. Hall works for two months in 2023 and earns $3,940. She is credited with two quarters of coverage for the year because she receives one quarter of coverage for each $1,640 of earnings, up to a maximum of four. In order to receive four quarters of coverage in 2023, Mrs. Hall would have needed earnings totaling $6,560 ($1,640 × 4 = $6,560).

This method of determining quarters of coverage will also be used for years after 2014, but the measure of earnings ($1,640 in 2023) will automatically increase each year to take into account increases in average wages.

However, see Q 226 for quarters that cannot be counted as quarters of coverage, regardless of whether the earnings requirement has been met.

Note

1. *See generally* 20 CFR sec. 404.

---

225. How does someone obtain a quarter of coverage as a self-employed person?

For 2023, a person who is self-employed receives one quarter of coverage for each $1,640 of earnings from self-employment, up to a maximum of four quarters.[1]

Note that earnings from self-employment are gross receipts minus expenses in the business. Therefore, if the business suffers a loss or if profits are low for a particular year, the self-employed person could earn less than four quarters of coverage.

> *Example.* Mr. Smith is self-employed. His gross receipts for the year are $50,000, but his expenses for the year are $48,000. Because his earnings from self-employment are only $2,000 he earns only one quarter of coverage. If Mr. Smith had incurred expenses in excess of $48.360, he would not have earned any quarters of coverage ($50,000 − $48,360 = $1,640).

Note

1. *See generally* 20 CFR sec. 404.

226. What calendar quarters cannot be counted as quarters of coverage even though the earnings requirement has been met?

A calendar quarter cannot be counted as a quarter of coverage if:

- it begins after the calendar quarter in which the person died;

- it has not started yet;

- it is within a period of disability that is excluded in figuring benefit rights (see BENEFIT COMPUTATION, Q 269 to Q 299). (However, the beginning and ending quarters of a prior disability period may be counted as quarters of coverage if the earnings requirement is met in these quarters.)

> *Example.* Mr. Smith dies on June 24, 2023, after having earned $160.200 (the maximum earnings base for 2023). Normally, he would be credited with four quarters of coverage for that year (see Q 224). However, he is credited with only two because the quarters after his death cannot be counted.

227. How do the requirements of the Social Security Protection Act of 2004 (SSPA) affect insured status?

Alien workers, who had Social Security numbers assigned on or after January 1, 2004, must meet ONE of the following additional requirements to become either fully or currently insured and to establish eligibility under Social Security or Medicare.[1] These requirements affect members of the family of the alien worker as well.

(1)   The alien worker must have been issued a Social Security Number for work purposes at any time on or after January 1, 2004; or

(2)   The alien worker must have been admitted to the United States as a nonimmigrant visitor for business (B-1 visa) or as an alien crewman (D-1 or D-2 visa).

Without meeting either of these requirements, the alien worker is not fully insured nor is currently insured, regardless of whether the alien has the required number of Social Security credits. For greater detail on requirements for alien workers, see Additional Requirements for Alien Workers – Social Security Protection Act of 2014.[2]

Notes

1. Social Security Protection Act of 2004, Section 211.
2. Social Security Administration, Program Operations Manual System (POMS), https://secure.ssa.gov/poms.nsf/lnx/0300301102 (last accessed August 31, 2022).

228. Who is an "alien worker" under the SSPA?

An alien worker, as defined by the Social Security Protection Act of 2004, is a worker who is not a citizen of the United States under the sections 301 through 310 of the Immigration and Nationality Act.[1] The SSA prohibits making payments to aliens removed from the United States for smuggling other aliens into the United States.[2]

Notes

1. Social Security Administration, Program Operations Manual System (POMS), https://secure.ssa.gov/poms.nsf/lnx/0300301102 (last accessed August 31, 2022).
2. 70 Fed. Reg. 16409.

Totalization Agreements

229. How does work performed in a foreign country get taken into consideration for determining insured status?

If someone worked under the social security system of a foreign country, those periods of work might be taken into consideration toward meeting Social Security insured status if:

(1) a social security agreement between the United States and the other country (referred to as a totalization agreement) covers the overseas coverage;

(2) the worked has at least six credits under U.S. Social Security;

(3) the worker would not gain insured status without taking the foreign employment into consideration.

If an individual qualifies for coverage because of foreign employment, the amount payable is based on the United State Primary Insurance Amount only, not the foreign earnings.

Unless there is some means of coordinating Social Security coverage, people who work outside their native country may find themselves covered under the systems of two countries simultaneously for the same work. Generally, in this situation, both countries generally require the employer and employee or self-employed person to pay Social Security taxes.

Dual Social Security tax liability is a widespread problem for U.S. multinational companies and their employees because the U.S. Social Security program covers expatriate workers—those coming to the United States and those going abroad—to a greater extent than the programs of most other countries. U.S. Social Security extends to American citizens and U.S. resident aliens employed abroad by American employers without regard to the duration of an employee's foreign assignment, even if the employee has been hired abroad. This frequently results in dual tax liability for the employer and employee. This dual tax liability can also affect U.S. citizens and residents working for foreign affiliates of American companies.

Foreign workers in the United States may also face dual coverage. U.S. law provides compulsory Social Security coverage for services performed in the United States as an employee, regardless of the citizenship or country of residence of the employee or employer, and irrespective of the length of time the employee stays in the United States. Unlike many other countries, the United States generally does not provide coverage exemptions for nonresident alien employees or for employees who have been sent to work within its borders for short periods. For this reason, most foreign workers in the United States are covered under the U.S. program.

Paying dual Social Security contributions is especially costly for companies that offer "tax equalization" arrangements for their expatriate employees. A firm that sends an employee to work in another country often guarantees that the assignment will not result in a reduction of the employee's after-tax income. Employers with tax equalization programs, therefore, typically agree to pay both the employer and employee share of host country Social Security taxes on behalf of their transferred employees.

The intent of U.S. totalization agreements is to eliminate dual Social Security coverage and taxation while maintaining the coverage of as many workers as possible under the system of the country where they are likely to have the greatest attachment, both while working and after retirement. Each agreement seeks to achieve this goal through a set of objective rules.

A misconception about U.S. agreements is that they allow dually-covered workers or their employers to elect the system to which they will contribute. This is not the case. The agreements, moreover, do not change the basic coverage provisions of the participating countries' Social Security laws, such as those that define covered earnings or work. They simply exempt workers from coverage under the system of one country or the other when their work would otherwise be covered under both systems.

Each agreement (except the one with Italy) includes an exception to the territoriality rule designed to minimize disruptions in the coverage careers of workers whose employers send them abroad on temporary assignment. Under this "detached-worker" exception, a person who is temporarily transferred to work for the same employer in another country remains covered only by the country from which he or she has been sent. A U.S. citizen or resident, for example, who is temporarily transferred by an American employer to work in an agreement country continues to be covered under the U.S. program and is exempt from coverage under the system of the host country. The worker and employer pay contributions only to the U.S. program.

The detached-worker rule in U.S. agreements generally applies to employees whose assignments in the host country are expected to last five years or less. The five-year limit on exemptions for detached workers is substantially longer than the limit normally provided in the agreements of other countries.

The detached-worker rule can apply whether the American employer transfers an employee to work in a branch office in the foreign country or in one of its foreign affiliates. However, for U.S. coverage to continue when a transferred employee works for a foreign affiliate, the American employer must have entered into a Section 3121(l) agreement with the U.S. Treasury Department with respect to the foreign affiliate.

Under certain conditions, a worker may be exempted from coverage in an agreement country even if he or she was not assigned there directly from the United States. If, for example, a U.S. company sends an employee from its New York office to work for four years in its Hong Kong office and then reassigns the employee to work for four additional years in its London office, the employee can be exempted from U.K. Social Security coverage under the U.S.-U.K. agreement. The detached worker rule applies in cases like this provided the worker was originally sent from the United States and remained covered under U.S. Social Security for the entire period preceding the assignment in the agreement country.

The agreement with Italy represents a departure from other U.S. agreements in that it does not include a detached-worker rule. As in other agreements, its basic coverage criterion is the territoriality rule. Coverage for expatriate workers, however, is based principally on the worker's nationality. If a U.S. citizen who is employed or self-employed in Italy would be covered by U.S. Social Security absent the agreement, he or she will remain covered under the U.S. program and be exempt from Italian coverage and contributions.

230. What is a "totalization agreement" as related to social security?

Since the late 1970's, the United States has established a network of bilateral Social Security agreements that coordinate the U.S. Social Security program with the comparable programs of other countries. This effect of these agreements is of particular interest to multinational companies and to persons who work abroad during their careers.

International Social Security agreements, often called "totalization agreements," have two main purposes.

(1) Elimination of dual Social Security taxation, which can occur when a worker from one country works in another country and is required to pay Social Security taxes to both countries on the same earnings.

(2) These agreements help fill gaps in benefit protection for workers who have divided their careers between the United States and another country.

Agreements to coordinate Social Security protection across national boundaries have been common in Western Europe for decades. In the next question is a list of agreements currently in place and the date they were put into place. The aim of all U.S. totalization agreements is to eliminate dual Social Security coverage and taxation while maintaining the coverage of as many workers as possible under the system of the country where they are likely to have the greatest attachment, both while working and after retirement.

A general misconception about U.S. agreements is that they allow dually covered workers or their employers to elect the system to which they will contribute. This is not the case. The agreements, moreover, do not change the basic coverage provisions of the participating countries' Social Security laws, such as those that define covered earnings or work. They simply exempt workers from coverage under the system of one country or the other when their work would otherwise be covered under both systems.

231. With which countries does the United States have totalization agreements?

The United States has entered into agreements, called Totalization Agreements, with many nations for the purpose of avoiding double taxation of income with respect to social security taxes. These agreements must be considered when determining whether any alien is subject to the U.S. Social Security/Medicare tax, or whether any U.S. citizen or resident alien is subject to the social security taxes of a foreign country. The following is the list of nations that the United States currently has agreements and the date the agreement went into force:

(1)   A social security agreement between the United States and the other country (referred to as a totalization agreement) covers the overseas coverage

(2)   The worked has at least six credits under United States Social Security

(3)   The worker would not gain insured status without taking the foreign employment into consideration.

If an individual qualifies for coverage because of foreign employment, the amount payable is based on the United States Primary Insurance Amount only, not the foreign earnings.

As of 2020, the countries with agreements in place include:

Countries with Social Security Agreements	
Country	*Entry into Force*
Italy	November 1, 1978
Germany	December 1, 1979
Switzerland	November 1, 1980
Belgium	July 1, 1984
Norway	July 1, 1984
Canada	August 1, 1984
United Kingdom	January 1, 1985
Sweden	January 1, 1987
Spain	April 1, 1988
France	July 1, 1988
Portugal	August 1, 1989
Netherlands	November 1, 1990
Austria	November 1, 1991
Finland	November 1, 1992
Ireland	September 1, 1993
Luxembourg	November 1, 1993
Greece	September 1, 1994

Countries with Social Security Agreements	
South Korea	April 1, 2001
Chile	December 1, 2001
Australia	October 1, 2002
Japan	October 1, 2005
Denmark	October 1, 2008
Czech Republic	January 1, 2009
Poland	March 1, 2009
Slovak Republic	May 1, 2014
Hungary	September 1, 2016
Brazil	October 1, 2018
Uruguay	November 1, 2018
Slovenia	February 1, 2019
Iceland	March 1, 2019

Despite the fact that these agreements are designed to assign Social Security coverage to the country where the worker has the greatest attachment, unusual situations occasionally arise in which strict application of the agreement rules would yield anomalous or inequitable results. For this reason, each agreement includes a provision that permits the authorities in both countries to grant exceptions to the normal rules if both sides agree. An exception might be granted, for example, if the overseas assignment of a U.S. citizen were unexpectedly extended for a few months beyond the 5-year limit under the detached-worker rule (see next question). In this case, the worker could be granted continued U.S. coverage for the additional period.

As a cautionary note, it should be pointed out that the exception provision is invoked infrequently and only in compelling cases. It is not intended to give workers or employers the freedom to routinely elect coverage in conflict with normal agreement rules.

French Contribution Sociale Generalisee (CSG) and Contribution au Remboursement de la Dette Sociate (CRDS)

The United States and the French Republic have memorialized an understanding that the French Contribution Sociale Generalisee (CSG) and Contribution au Remboursement de la Dette Sociate (CRDS) taxes are not social taxes covered by the Agreement on Social Security between the two countries. The IRS will not challenge foreign tax credits for any CSG and/or CRDS payments on the basis that the Agreement on Social Security applies to those taxes.

This change in policy by the IRS means that individuals who paid or accrued taxes, but did not claim them, can file amended returns to claim a foreign tax credit. Since taxpayers have ten years to file a claim for refund of US income taxes, affected individuals can file Form 1040-X to include Form 1116, going back to Tax Year 2013.

The IRS recommends that taxpayers write "French CSG/CRDS Taxes" in red at the top of Forms 1040-X and file them with accompanying Forms 1116 in accordance with the instructions for these forms. U.S. employers may not file for refunds claiming a foreign tax credit for CSG/CRDS withheld or otherwise paid on behalf of their employees.

232. What is the "territoriality rule" as related to totalization agreements?

The provisions for eliminating dual coverage with respect to employed persons are similar in all U.S. agreements. Each one establishes a basic rule that looks to the location of a worker's employment. Under this basic "territoriality" rule, an employee who would otherwise be covered by both the U.S. and a foreign system remains subject exclusively to the coverage laws of the country in which he or she is working.

Detached Worker Rule – Exception to the Territoriality Rule

Each agreement (except the one with Italy) includes an exception to the territoriality rule designed to minimize disruptions in the coverage careers of workers whose employers send them abroad on temporary assignment. Under this "detached-worker" exception, a person who is temporarily transferred to work for the same employer in another country remains covered only by the country from which he or she has been sent. A U.S. citizen or resident, for example, who is temporarily transferred by an American employer to work in an agreement country continues to be covered under the U.S. program and is exempt from coverage under the system of the host country. The worker and employer pay contributions only to the U.S. program.

Five-Year Limit

The detached-worker rule in U.S. agreements generally applies to employees whose assignments in the host country are expected to last five years or less. The five-year limit on exemptions for detached workers is substantially longer than the limit normally provided in the agreements of other countries.

The detached-worker rule can apply whether the American employer transfers an employee to work in a branch office in the foreign country or in one of its foreign affiliates. However, for U.S. coverage to continue when a transferred employee works for a foreign affiliate, the American employer must have entered into a section 3121(l) agreement with the U.S. Treasury Department with respect to the foreign affiliate.

Under certain conditions, a worker may be exempted from coverage in an agreement country even if he or she was not assigned there directly from the United States. If, for example, a U.S. company sends an employee from its New York office to work for four years in its Hong Kong office and then reassigns the employee to work for four additional years in its London office, the employee can be exempted from U.K. Social Security coverage under the U.S.-U.K. agreement. The detached worker rule applies in cases like this provided the worker was originally sent from the United States and remained covered under U.S. Social Security for the entire period preceding the assignment in the agreement country.

Exception to the Exception - Italy

The agreement with Italy represents a departure from other U.S. agreements in that it does not include a detached-worker rule. As in other agreements, its basic coverage criterion is the territoriality rule. Coverage for expatriate workers, however, is based principally on the worker's nationality. If a U.S. citizen who is employed or self-employed in Italy would be covered by U.S. Social Security absent the agreement, he or she will remain covered under the U.S. program and be exempt from Italian coverage and contributions.

Self-Employed Exception to the Territoriality Rule

There are two common exceptions to the Territoriality Rule for self-employed workers- the transferred self-employment rule and the residence rule. An agreement can only contain one of these rules, not both. Thus, agreements assign self-employment coverage based either on transferred work activity or on residence.

1. **Transferred Self-Employment Rule**: The transferred self-employment rule, similar to the detached worker rule, notes that a self-employed worker who temporarily transfers his or her work from one country to another will retain coverage under the laws of the country from which he or she transferred. Like the detached worker rule, this period is considered to be temporary if it is not expected to exceed 5 years from the time the worker transfers his or her self-employment activity to the other country.

2. **Residence Rule**: The residence rule establishes that the laws of the country in which the person resides will cover his or her self-employment activity exclusively, without regard to the duration of that residence.

Other Special Rules

Additional special rules have been established for specialties such as mariners, airline crew, diplomats, government employees, and people whose employers did not transfer them directly from one totalization agreement country to another, but from one totalization country to a third country before a subsequent transfer to the other totalization country.

Totalization partner countries can also mutually agree to special exceptions for individual workers or entire classes of workers, as appropriate.

However, for the United States to agree to a special exception, the following conditions must be established:

- The person is covered in only one country, and

- the person continues coverage in the country with the most economic attachment.

233. What about self-employed individuals?

U.S. Social Security coverage extends to self-employed U.S. citizens and residents whether their work is performed in the United States or another country. As a result, when they work outside the United States, citizens and residents are almost always dually covered, since the host country will normally cover them also.

Most U.S. agreements eliminate dual coverage of self-employment by assigning coverage to the worker's country of residence. For example, under the U.S.-Swedish agreement, a dually covered self-employed U.S. citizen living in Sweden is covered only by the Swedish system and is excluded from U.S. coverage.

Although the agreements with Belgium, France (however note rules affecting French Contribution Sociale Generalisee (CSG) and Contribution au Remboursement de la Dette Sociate (CRDS), Germany, Italy, and Japan do not use the residence rule as the primary determinant of self-employment coverage), each of them includes a provision to ensure that workers are covered and taxed in only one country.

234. What about workers exempt from social security taxes?

Workers who are exempt from U.S. or foreign Social Security taxes under an agreement must document their exemption by obtaining a certificate of coverage from the country that will continue to cover them. For example, a U.S. worker sent on temporary assignment to the United Kingdom would need a certificate of coverage issued by SSA to prove his or her exemption from U.K. Social Security contributions. Conversely, a U.K.-based employee working temporarily in the United States would need a certificate from the U.K. authorities as evidence of the exemption from U.S. Social Security tax.

When SSA issues a certificate certifying U.S. coverage, a copy of the certificate usually must be presented to the appropriate foreign authorities as proof of entitlement to the foreign exemption for the U.S. employee and the employer. When the other country issues a certificate certifying that the employee is covered by the foreign system, the employer can immediately stop withholding and paying U.S. Social Security taxes on the employee's earnings. The certificate should just be retained in the employer's files so it can be produced in the event the Internal Revenue Service ever questions why no taxes are being paid for the employee. A self-employed U.S. citizen or resident must attach a photocopy of the foreign certificate to his U.S. tax return each year as proof of the U.S. exemption from self-employment taxes. In accordance with Revenue Procedure 84-54, the foreign certificate serves as proof of the exemption from U.S. Social Security taxes for the period shown on the certificate.

Employers generally are required to request certificates on behalf of employees they have transferred abroad; self-employed persons request their own certificate.

When requesting a certificate, the request should include:

- the employer's name and address in the United States and the other country;

- the worker's full name, place and date of birth, citizenship, U.S. and foreign Social Security numbers;

- place and date of hiring; and

- the beginning and ending dates of the assignment in the foreign country.

If the employee will be working for a foreign affiliate of the U.S. company, the request should also indicate whether U.S. Social Security coverage has been arranged for the employees of the affiliate under section 3121(l) of the Internal Revenue Code.

Self-employed persons should indicate their country of residence and the nature of their self-employment activity. Note that when requesting certificates under the agreements with France and Japan, the employer (or self-employed person) must also indicate whether the worker and any accompanying family members are covered by health insurance.

Fully Insured

235. How does a person become fully insured?

A person becomes fully insured by acquiring a sufficient number of quarters of coverage to meet either of these two tests:[1]

(1)   A person is fully insured if they have forty quarters of coverage (a total of ten years in covered work). Once a person has acquired forty quarters of coverage, they are fully insured for life ("permanently insured"), even if they spend no further time in covered employment or covered self-employment.

(2)   A person is fully insured if:

(a) they have at least six quarters of coverage; and

(b) have acquired at least as many quarters of coverage as there are years elapsing after 1950 (or, if later, after the year in which the person reaches age twenty-one) and before the year of death, becoming disabled, or reaching (or will reach) age sixty-two, whichever occurs first. (However, if a year, or any part of a year, falls within an established period of disability, that year need not be counted.)

Note that prior to 1975, there is a transition period in effect for men. See Q 238 and Q 241.

The two tests above serve only to determine the number of quarters of coverage needed to be fully insured. It is immaterial when these quarters of coverage were acquired (however, they can be acquired only after 1936). Also, in applying Test Number Two, it is not necessary that the quarters of coverage be acquired during the elapsed period. All quarters of coverage, whether within or outside the elapsed period, are counted to determine whether the person has the required number.

For method of determining fully insured status for retirement benefits, see Q 235 to Q 240. For method of determining fully insured status for survivors' benefits, see Q 241. For method of determining fully insured status for disability benefits, see Q 246.

Note

1. 42 U.S.C. sec. 414.

236. Were there other ways of becoming fully insured?

Yes. Although unlikely that any people living in 2023 would qualify under this rule, a person could in the past, have become fully insured if they were:

    (1)   a male born before January 2, 1911 (needed one credit for each year after 1950 up to the year before the year that occurs first as listed below);

        a.   turned age sixty-five;

        b.   died; or

        c.   became disabled;

    (2)   a male born from January 2, 1911 through January 1, 1913 (needed one credit for each year after 1950 up to the year before the year that occurs first in the list);

        d.   1975;

        e.   year of death; or

        f.   became disabled.

237. Must a person be fully insured to qualify for retirement benefits?

Yes, in addition to all other requirements (see RETIREMENT AND DISABILITY BENEFITS, Q 43 to Q 212), a person must be fully insured.

238. How do you determine the number of quarters of coverage needed for a person to be fully insured for retirement benefits?

To make this determination, count the number of years after 1950 (or, if later, after the year in which the person attained age 21), and before attaining age 62. Do not count any part of a year which was in an established period of disability. Generally, this is the minimum number of quarters of coverage a person will need to be fully insured. However, the person must have at least six quarters of coverage to be fully insured, and a person is fully insured in any event if the person has 40 or more quarters of coverage.[1]

See APPENDIX A, TABLE 2 for minimum numbers of quarters of coverage needed to be fully insured for retirement benefits.

Example 1. Mr. Jones applies for retirement benefits in 2022; he attained age 62 in 2021. He needs 40 quarters of coverage to be fully insured (there are over 40 years between 1980 and 2021, the year he attained age 62).

Example 2. Miss Johnson applies for retirement benefits in 2023, the year she attains age 65. She needs 40 quarters of coverage to be fully insured (there are over 40 years between 1979 and 2020, the year she attained age 62).

Example 3. Mr. Jackson was born in 1961 and will be 62 in 2023. Normally, he would need 40 quarters of coverage to be fully insured for retirement benefits. However, Mr. Jackson had a period of disability lasting from August 1994 to February 1996. Therefore, he would need only thirty-seven quarters of coverage to be fully insured for retirement benefits (the three years, 1994-1996, would not be counted in determining the number of quarters of coverage required).

Note

1. 42 U.S.C. sec. 414.

239. Can a person be fully insured for retirement benefits even though not working in covered employment for many years?

Yes. To be fully insured for retirement benefits, a person needs at least as many quarters of coverage as there are years after 1950 (or, if later, the year of the person's twenty-first birthday) and before the year when the person reaches age 62. However, it is immaterial when these quarters of coverage were acquired.

Example. Mrs. Luck was born in 1958. In 2023 (at age sixty-five), she applied for retirement benefits. She needs 40 quarters of coverage to be fully insured (one quarter of coverage for each year between 1979 and 2020). Mrs. Luck worked in covered employment for ten years (acquiring 40 quarters of coverage) prior to her 35th birthday in 1993. Mrs. Luck is fully insured – she has the required 40 quarters of coverage.

240. Can a person become fully insured after retirement age?

Yes. A person can acquire (or continue to acquire) quarters of coverage after age sixty, sixty-two, or even after Full Retirement Age. There is no age limit to when a person can acquire quarters of coverage, presuming they can continue to work.

241. How do you determine the number of quarters of coverage needed for a person to be fully insured at death?

Count the number of years after 1950 or, if later, after the year in which the person reached age 21 and before the year the person died (but do not count any part of a year of which was in an established period of disability). A person needs at least this many quarters of coverage to be fully insured at death. However, no person can be fully insured with fewer than six quarters of coverage; and a person is fully insured in any event with 40 quarters of coverage.

NOTE: A person born in 1929 reached age 21 in 1950. Consequently, for persons born in 1929 or before, count the years after 1950 and before the year of death. For persons born after 1929, see APPENDIX A, TABLE 4 for year of 21st birthday.

> *Example 1.* Mr. Smith, who was born in 1961, dies in 2023. He is fully insured if he has 40 quarters of coverage (there are 40 years between 1981, the year he reached age 21, and 2023, the year in which he died, so that the maximum of 40 quarters of coverage applies).

> *Example 2.* Mr. Jones, who was born in 1981, dies in 2023. He is fully insured if he has 20 quarters of coverage (there are 20 years between 2002, the year in which he reached age 21, and 2023, the year in which he died).

The above rule applies to persons who die before age 62. If a person dies after reaching age 62, count only the years between 1950 (or the year of attainment of age 21, if later) and age 62.

242. When is someone deemed to be fully insured?

A person is deemed to be fully insured[1] if they are:

(1)   at least fifty-five years old on January 1, 1984;

(2)   an employee of a nonprofit (noncovered) employer on January 1, 1984; and

(3)   the employer did not have a waiver certificate under Internal Revenue Code section 312(k)[2] in effect on January 1, 1984.

Notes

1. Social Security Administration, Social Security Handbook, Section 205.1, https://www.ssa.gov/OP_Home/handbook/handbook.02/handbook-0205.html (last accessed August 31, 2022).
2. IRC sec. 312, https://www.law.cornell.edu/uscode/text/26/312 (last accessed August 31, 2022).

243. How many credits are necessary to be deemed fully insured?

The number of credits[1] necessary for being deemed fully insured depends upon age as of January 1, 1984:

If sixty years old or older on January 1, 1984:	six credits are required
If fifty-nine years old but less than sixty years old on January 1, 1984:	eight credits are required
If fifty-eight years old but less than fifty-nine years old on January 1, 1984	twelve credits are required
If fifty-seven years old but less than fifty-eight years old on January 1, 1984:	sixteen credits are required
If fifty-five years old but less than fifty-seven years old on January 1, 1984:	twenty credits are required

Note

1. https://www.ssa.gov/OP_Home/handbook/handbook.02/handbook-0205.html (Section 205.3). Last accessed August 31, 2022

243.01 When is a deceased World War II vet deemed fully insured?

Certain World War II veterans who separated from active military service before July 27, 1951 and died within three years of their separation are considered to have died fully insured.

A deceased World War II Veteran is fully insured with an average monthly wage of $160 if:

- The veteran died before July 27, 1954; or

- The veteran died within three years after separation (death no later than July 26, 1954) from active military or naval service; and

- The veteran's service was in the World War II period (September 16, 1940 - July 24, 1947).

Note: If a Veterans Affairs pension or a compensation benefit was ever paid, even if terminated, based on the veteran's death, deemed insured status benefits are prohibited.

Currently Insured

244. What benefits are payable if a person is only currently insured at death?

Child's benefits, mother's or father's benefits, and the lump-sum death payment. Benefits for a widow(er) age 60 or over, and benefits for a dependent parent, are payable only if the worker was fully insured at death.

245. When is a person currently insured?

A person is currently insured when having at least six quarters of coverage during the full thirteen-quarter period ending with the calendar quarter in which:

(1)   death occurred; or

(2)   most recently became entitled to disability benefits; or

(3)   became entitled to retirement benefits.[1]

The six quarters of coverage need not be consecutive, but they must be acquired during the thirteen-quarter period. As insured status is based on quarters of coverage, one can work for as little as two months in two different years and be currently insured (calendar quarters, any part of which are in an established prior period of disability, are not counted in figuring the thirteen-quarter period, except that the first and last quarters of the disability period are counted if they are quarters of coverage).

Example. Mrs. Smith, who reached age twenty-one in 2018, dies in February 2023. Mrs. Smith had started to work in covered employment on October 1, 2020 and worked until her death. During that period, she acquired nine quarters of coverage (four in 2021, because her earnings in October-December were at least $5,880; four in 2022, because her earnings in the year were at least $6,040 and one in 2023 because her earnings in January and February were at least $1,640). Mrs. Smith was currently insured at death because she had more than the required six quarters of coverage in the thirteen-calendar-quarter period.

Insured Status for Disability Benefits

246. What insured status requirements must be met to qualify a person for disability benefits?

A person is qualified for disability benefits fully insured (see Q 241) and has at least 20 quarters of coverage during a 40-quarter period ending with the quarter in which the person is determined to be disabled.[1]

In order to meet the 20-out-of-40-quarters requirement, the 20 quarters of coverage need not be consecutive, but they must all be acquired during the 40-quarter period. (A quarter any part of which was included in a prior period of disability is not counted as one of the 40 quarters, unless it was a quarter of coverage and was either the first or last quarter of the period.) Generally speaking, this requirement is met if the person has worked five years in covered employment or covered self-employment out of the last ten years before disability.

Special insured status is needed by individuals who are disabled before age 31 to qualify for disability benefits or to establish a period of disability. The special insured-status requirements are met if, in the quarter that disability is determined to have begun or in a later quarter, a person:

(1)   is disabled before the quarter in which age 31 is attained; and

(2)   has credits in one-half of the quarters, during the period beginning with the quarter after the quarter in which the person attained age 21 and ending with the quarter in which the person became disabled.

The credits must be earned in this period. If the number of elapsing quarters is an odd number, the next lower even number is used, and a minimum of six credits is required. If a person became disabled before the quarter in which age 24 is attained, the person must have six quarters of coverage in the twelve-quarter period ending with the quarter in which the disability began.

A special insured status can apply to disabled individuals over age 31 who had a previous period of disability established prior to the attainment of age 31; had then met, and currently meet, the special insured requirements (as set out above); and who do not currently meet the 20/40 rule or fully insured status requirements.

To qualify for entitlement to disability benefits, fully insured status is required for a person who meets the statutory definition of blindness.

If a disability period is established for a person, the earnings records are frozen, and the period of disability may be excluded in determining insured status when either becoming eligible for retirement benefits or dying. The disability period may also be excluded in figuring the Primary Insurance Amount (PIA) for benefit purposes (see Computing Benefits). The same insured status is required to qualify a person for a disability "freeze," as is required for disability benefits. In 2022, there were 159,249 (82,089 male and 77,160 female) estimated disability insured workers.[2]

Notes

1. 42 U.S.C. sec. 423(c).
2. Social Security Administration, Disability Insured Workers, https://www.ssa.gov/oact/STATS/table4c2DI.html (August 2022 with numbers subject to revision) (last accessed August 31, 2022).

Computing Benefits

247. In general, how are Social Security benefits determined?

Benefits payable under the retirement, survivors, and disability benefits program are almost always based on the insured's Social Security earnings since 1950. (Under some circumstances—where an individual has little or no earnings since 1950—benefits may be computed based on earnings since 1937.)

The wage indexing formula is used to compute benefits if disability, death, or age 62 occurs after 1978. (See Q 272).

If disability, death, or age 62 occurred before 1979, benefits are determined using the simplified old-start benefit computation method. (See Q 269.)

A transition period took place from 1979 through 1983. A worker who became 62, or a worker who died after reaching age 62 during this period, is guaranteed that the method producing the larger benefit will be used.

To be eligible for the guarantee, the worker must:

(1)   have had income credited for one year prior to 1979; and

(2)   must not have been disabled prior to 1979.

The transitional guarantee does not apply to disability computations, even if disability occurs after reaching age 62. It does, however, apply to benefits for survivors if the insured becomes 62, then dies, during the transition period. (See Q 287.)

FILING FOR BENEFITS
General Information

248. What procedure should be followed to determine if a person is eligible for Social Security benefits?

An application must be filed for a person to become entitled to benefits, including Medicare, or to establish a period of disability under the retirement, survivors, and disability programs. The easiest and quickest way for most people to apply for benefits is by filling out an application on the Social Security Administration's website, www.ssa.gov. The process normally takes between ten and thirty minutes.

Alternatively, a person can apply by phone, the mail, or by visiting one of the Social Security Administration's approximately 1,230 field offices.[1]

Since a person age 65 or older who is entitled to monthly benefits under Social Security or Railroad Retirement is automatically entitled to Medicare Part A Hospital Insurance and Part B Medical Insurance, no separate application is required. However, a person who is eligible for monthly Social Security benefits and is at least age 65 may apply for Hospital Insurance and Medical Insurance without applying for Social Security benefits. Also, an application is necessary for persons age 65 or older who have no Social Security coverage or other entitlement, but who wish to file for Hospital Insurance and Medical Insurance, and who are willing to pay the monthly premiums involved.

Prompt filing of an application is generally advantageous, even if the person is still working. Delay may result in fewer payments, since monthly benefits cannot be paid retroactively in some instances and not for more than twelve months (depending on the situation) before the month in which the application is filed.

A person may be entitled to monthly benefits retroactively for months before the month in which he filed an application for benefits. Retirement and survivor claims may be paid for up to six months retroactively, and benefits may be paid in certain cases involving disability up to twelve months retroactively. The claimant is entitled to benefits beginning with the first month in the retroactive period in which all the requirements for entitlement to benefits are met (except for the filing of an application). For example, if a man reaches age 66 in March 2022 and is then fully insured, but does not file an application for retirement benefits until March 2023, he may be entitled retroactively beginning with the month of September 2022.

Retroactive benefits for months prior to attainment of full retirement age are not payable to a retired worker, a spouse, or a widow(er) if this would result in a permanent reduction of the monthly benefit amount. However, there are exceptions to this rule, which permit payment of retroactive benefits even though it causes an actuarial reduction in benefits. This limitation does not apply if the applicant is a surviving spouse or surviving divorced spouse who is under a disability and could be entitled to retroactive benefits for any month before attaining age 60.

A widow(er) or surviving divorced spouse who files an application in the month after the month of the worker's death may be entitled to benefits in the month of his or her death if otherwise eligible in that month.

Regulations issued by the Social Security Administration establish deemed filing dates for applications filed by persons who have received misinformation about eligibility from the Social Security Administration. The Social Security Administration may establish an earlier filing date when there is evidence that the Social Security Administration gave the claimant misinformation, which caused the claimant not to file an application at the appropriate time.

> *Example.* Mr. Smith contacts a Social Security office at age 62 to inquire about applying for retirement benefits. He is told by an employee of the Social Security Administration that he must be age 65 to be eligible for retirement benefits. This information is incorrect and causes Mr. Smith to delay filing an application for retirement benefits for three years. When he reaches age 65, he contacts the Social Security Administration and is told that he could have received reduced retirement benefits at age 62. After filing an application for retirement benefits, Mr. Smith provides information to show that a Social Security Administration employee provided misinformation and requests a deemed filing date based on the misinformation he received when he was age 62.

If the Social Security Administration determines that a person failed to apply for monthly benefits because it gave the person incorrect information about eligibility for such benefits, the Social Security Administration will deem an application for such benefits to have been filed with the Social Security Administration on the later of:

(1)   the date on which the misinformation was provided to the person; or

(2)   the date on which the person met all of the requirements for entitlement to the benefits, other than the requirement for filing an application for benefits.

Preferred evidence that misinformation was given by the Social Security Administration includes a notice, letter, or other document issued by the Social Security Administration and addressed to the claimant, or the Social Security Administration's record of the claimant's letter, phone call, or visit to an office of the Social Security Administration. In the absence of preferred evidence, the Social Security Administration will consider statements by the claimant about misinformation and other evidence. The claimant's statements, however, must be supported by other evidence for the Social Security Administration to find that the claimant was given misinformation.

A person may make a claim for benefits based on misinformation at any time. The claim must be in writing and must contain the information that was provided by the Social Security Administration and why this information resulted in the person not filing an application for Social Security benefits.

A person cannot receive more than one full monthly benefit. If eligible for more than one monthly benefit, the amount payable will be equal to the largest one for which the person is eligible.

Each application form is clearly worded to show its scope as an application for one or more types of benefits. For example, the present applications for entitlement to Medicare Part A

Hospital Insurance protection, or for monthly Social Security benefits, may be applications for all benefits that a claimant may be entitled to on any Social Security earnings record. The scope of any application may, however, be expanded or restricted, as the claimant desires, if appropriate remarks are added in writing prior to adjudication. The Social Security Administration will use the application to make an initial determination regarding the amount of benefits, if any.

Note

1. See https://www.ssa.gov/org/#:~:text=The%20field%20organization%2C%20which%20is,centers%20in%20the%20central%20office (last accessed September 1, 2022).

249. At what point should the survivors of a deceased worker file for survivor's benefits?

An application should be filed immediately in the month of death by or for each person who is entitled to a benefit as a survivor of a deceased worker.

An application for the lump-sum death payment must be filed within the two-year period after the worker's death by the person eligible for the lump sum, unless the eligible person is the widow(er) of the deceased worker and was entitled to spouse's benefits for the month before the month in which the worker died. In the latter case, no application for the lump sum is required.

250. When should an application for disability benefits be filed?

An application for the establishment of a period of disability may be filed before the first day this period can begin. In these circumstances, the application will be effective if the person actually becomes eligible for the benefit, or for the period of disability, at some time before a final decision on the application is made.

When a person applies for monthly disability benefits, he simultaneously applies for a "disability freeze" (see Q 298).

251. When should a person file an application for the lump-sum death payment?

An application for the lump-sum death payment must be filed within a two-year period by the person eligible for the lump sum, unless the eligible person is the widow(er) of the deceased worker and was entitled to spouse's benefits for the month before the month in which the worker died. In the latter case, no application for the lump sum is required.

An application filed after the two-year period will be deemed to have been filed within the two-year period if there is good cause for a failure to file the application in time. Good cause means that the claimant did not file the lump-sum death payment application within the time limit because of:

(1)   circumstances beyond the claimant's control, such as extended illness, communication difficulties, etc.;

(2)   incorrect or incomplete information given the claimant by the Social Security Administration;

(3)   efforts to get the evidence to support the claim, not realizing she could file the application within the time limit and submit the supporting evidence later; or

(4)   unusual or unavoidable circumstances that show that the claimant could not reasonably be expected to have been aware of the need to file the application within a specified period.

It might be possible to file after the two-year period due to issues with COVID-19; however, it will be necessary to assert circumstances establishing good cause to the SSA. The time limit is discussed in the Social Security Handbook.[1]

Good cause is also specifically defined as meaning that the lump-sum death payment application was not filed within the time limit because of:

- Circumstances beyond control, such as extended illness, communication difficulties, etc.;

- Incorrect or incomplete information given to you SSA;

- Efforts to get evidence to support the claim, not realizing the application could within the time limit and submit the supporting evidence later; or

- Unusual or unavoidable circumstances that show that applicant could not reasonably be expected to have been aware of the need to file the application within a specified period.[2]

Good cause is not established if

- Applicant was informed that an application for the lump-sum death payment had to be filed within the initial two-year period; and

- Applicant did not file the application because of neglect, or because you did not then want to claim the lump-sum death payment.[3]

Normally, the two-year filing period ends with the second anniversary of the insured person's death. However, under the conditions set out in the following sections, the filing period may be extended. Also, there are conditions for extending the filing period for members of the U.S. Armed Forces. If the last day of the filing period is a Saturday, Sunday, legal holiday, or other non-work day for Federal employees set by statute or Executive Order, the application may be filed on the next work day.

Notes

1. https://www.ssa.gov/OP_Home/handbook/handbook.15/handbook-1518.html (Last accessed September 1, 2022) and https://www.ssa.gov/OP_Home/handbook/handbook.15/handbook-1517.html (Last accessed September 1, 2022)
2. https://www.ssa.gov/OP_Home/handbook/handbook.15/handbook-1519.html.
3. *Id.*

Proof Required

252. What proofs are required before survivors' and retirement benefits can be paid?

Social Security survivors' and retirement benefits cannot be paid until satisfactory proofs have been furnished. Claimants must prove their identity and that they have met all the requirements to be entitled to the benefits which are being claimed. Evidence usually required to be submitted to the Social Security Administration in claims for monthly benefits is summarized below:

- **Insured person:** evidence of age. If disability is involved, evidence to establish disability.

- **Spouse (62 or over):** evidence of age and marriage.

- **Spouse under 62 (child in care):** evidence of marriage and child in care.

- **Divorced spouse (62 or over):** evidence of age, marriage, and divorce.

- **Child:** evidence of age, parent-child relationship, dependency or support, school attendance (if 18 to 19 years old and not disabled), and death of the worker in survivor claims. If disability is involved, evidence to establish disability.

- **Widow(er) (60 or over, 50 or over if disabled):** evidence of age, marriage, and death of worker. If disability is involved, evidence to establish disability.

- **Surviving divorced spouse:** evidence of age, marriage, divorce, and death of worker. If disability is involved, evidence to establish disability.

- **Widow(er) under 62 or surviving divorced mother or father (child in care):** evidence of marriage, divorce (surviving divorced mother or father only), parent-child relationship, child in care, and death of worker.

- **Parent:** evidence of age, parent-child relationship, dependency or support, and death of worker.

253. What are acceptable proofs of death?

Evidence of death may consist of:[1]

(1)   a certified copy of a public record of death;

(2)   a Statement of Death[2] by a funeral director;

(3)   a statement of death by the attending physician or the superintendent, physician, or intern of the institution where the person died;

(4)   a certified copy of the coroner's report of death or the verdict of the coroner's jury;

(5)   a certified copy of an official report of death or finding of death, made by an agency or department of the United States government that is authorized or required to make such report or finding in the administration of any law of the United States;

(6)   if death occurred outside the United States, an official report of death by a U.S. Consul or other employee of the State Department; or a copy of the public record of death in the foreign country;

(7)   Numident record that shows death data based on an Electronic Death Registration (EDR) report or Numident record that shows a "proven" (POD:P) Date of Death.[3]

Note that obituaries are NOT considered proof of death, but can be used as leads to gain acceptable proof.

If none of the above can be obtained, one can submit statements from two or more persons (preferably not related to the claimant) who saw the body. These statements must be complete and indicate the following:

(1)   why none of the types of evidence above can be obtained;

(2)   the date and place of death;

(3)   the date and place of viewing the body;

(4)   the cause of death, if known;

(5)   the occupation, age, sex, and race of the deceased;

(6)   the relationship of the deceased, if any, to the person making the statements; and

(7)   the basis for identification of the body.

PROVING DEATH IN THE CASE OF A DISAPPEARANCE

In a disappearance case where the body is not recovered, it must be clearly proven that the death of the missing person occurred. All available evidence must be submitted including:

- Statements of persons having knowledge of the situation.

- Letters or notes left by the missing person that have a bearing on the case.

- Results of insurance or police investigations; and

- Complete facts surrounding the person's disappearance.

Recent court cases have held that a claimant had to show only that the missing person had been absent for seven years, and that the Social Security Administration had the burden of proving that the individual was still alive, or an explanation to account for the individual's absence in a manner consistent with continued life.

Social Security Administration regulations conform with the court cases by providing that the presumption of death arises when a claimant establishes that an individual has been absent from his residence and not heard from for seven years. Once the presumption arises, the burden then shifts to the Social Security Administration to rebut the presumption, either by presenting evidence that the missing individual is still alive or by providing an explanation to account for the individual's absence in a manner consistent with continued life rather than death.

The regulations also state that the presumption of death can be rebutted by evidence that establishes that the person is still alive or explains the individual's absence in a manner consistent with continued life. Two examples are provided. In one, evidence in a claim for surviving child's benefits showed that the worker had wages posted in his earnings record in the year following his disappearance. It was established that the wages belonged to the worker and were for work done after he was supposed to have disappeared. The presumption of death is rebutted by evidence (wages belonging to the worker) that the worker is still alive. In a second example, evidence showed that the worker left the family home shortly after a woman, whom he had been seeing, also disappeared. The worker phoned his wife a few days after he left home to tell her he was starting a new life in California. The presumption of death is rebutted in this case, because the evidence explains the worker's absence in a manner consistent with continued life.

No one convicted of the felonious and intentional homicide of the worker can be entitled to benefits on the worker's earnings record. Further, the convicted person is considered not to exist in deciding the rights of other persons to benefits on the worker's record.

Notes

1. Social Security Handbook, Section 1720, Evidence of Death. https://www.ssa.gov/OP_Home/handbook/handbook.17/handbook-1720.html (last accessed September 1, 2022).
2. Form SSA-721, Statement of Death by Funeral Director https://www.ssa.gov/forms/ssa-721.pdf (Effective June 2021) (last accessed September 1, 2022).
3. POMS GN 00304.005 https://secure.ssa.gov/apps10/poms.nsf/lnx/0200304005 (last accessed September 1, 2022).

253.01 Does a Find of Death by a military service prove death?

A presumptive finding of death by the military establishes the FACT of death, but not the DATE of death.

The date of death shown by the military in these cases is a statutory date. It is usually a year and a day from the "missing" date, but may be later or earlier. If there is no evidence to establish a later date, the date the individual was "missing" is used as the date of death.

254. What are the best forms of proof of age and family relationship?

Proof of age is required when age is a factor in determining benefit rights. A public record of birth or a religious record of birth or baptism established or recorded before the individual's fifth birthday must be submitted as proof of age, if available. Where such a document is unavailable, the individual must submit another document or documents that may serve as the basis for a determination of date or birth, provided the evidence is corroborated by other evidence or by information in the records of the Social Security Administration.

Some records that may be submitted are listed below; these records must show the individual's date of birth or age:

(1)   School record

(2)   Census record

(3)   Bible or other family record

(4)   Religious record of confirmation or baptism in youth or early adult life

(5)   Insurance policy

(6)   Marriage record

(7)   Employment record

(8)   Labor union record

(9)   Fraternal organization record

(10)   Military record

(11)   Voting record

(12)   Vaccination record

(13)   Delayed birth certificate

(14)   Birth certificate of child, showing age of parent

(15)   Physician's or midwife's record of birth

(16)   Passport

(17)   Immigration record

(18)   Naturalization record

A person should obtain, and file among his or her valuable papers, the most acceptable form of proof of the ages and relationships of all members of his or her family. This will save time, effort, and money later, when Social Security benefits become payable.

A natural legitimate parent-child relationship may be shown by the child's birth or baptismal certificate if it shows the worker to be the child's parent. If the child is illegitimate, he or she may be considered the worker's child for Social Security purposes if he or she is legitimated, or can inherit the worker's intestate personal property under applicable state law. The evidence required would depend on state law requirements for legitimation or inheritance rights.

The legal adoption of a child may be provided by an amended birth certificate issued as the result of an adoption.

A step-relationship is proved by:

(1)   first proving the relationship between the child and the natural (or adopting) parent; and

(2)   then proving the marriage between the natural (or adopting) parent and the stepparent.

Evidence of full-time school attendance is required if a child age 18 to 19 is not under a disability. Necessary information is obtained from the child and verified by the school or schools involved.

A ceremonial marriage may be proved by:

(1)   a certified copy of the public record of the marriage;

(2)   a certified copy of the religious record of the marriage; or

(3)   the original marriage certificate.

Evidence to prove a common-law marriage in those states that recognize such marriages must, where obtainable, include:

(1)   if the husband and wife are living, a statement from each and a statement from a blood relative of each;

(2)   if either the husband or wife is dead, a statement from the surviving widow or widower and statements from two blood relatives of the decedent; and

(3)   if both a husband and wife are dead, a statement from a blood relative of the husband and from a blood relative of the wife.

Evidence of termination of a marriage may be required if the claimant's right to benefits depends upon the validity of a subsequent marriage or the termination of a prior marriage. The termination of a marriage may be established by:

(1)   a certified copy of the divorce decree;

(2)   a certified copy of the annulment decree;

(3)   a certified copy of the death certificate; or

(4)   if none of the above is available, any other evidence of probative value.

Evidence that a child is in a claimant's care usually consists of:

(1)   statements by the claimant;

(2)   where the claimant and the child are living apart, statements by the person with whom the child is living or by an official of the school which the child is attending, or both; and

(3)   statements of other people who know the facts, if necessary.

Evidence of support includes a statement from the claimant, and whatever other evidence may be necessary to substantiate the claimant's statements concerning support.

Evidence of United States citizenship may be required in certain cases (for instance, to determine coverage status of people working in foreign countries or the applicability of the alien nonpayment provision). The most acceptable evidence is a birth certificate showing birth within the United States. Other acceptable evidence includes:

(1)   Certificate of Naturalization;

(2)   Citizenship Certificate issued by the Immigration and Naturalization Service to United States citizens who derived their citizenship through another person;

(3)   a United States passport issued by the Department of State;

(4)   Consular report of birth issued by the Department of State;

(5)   proof of marriage to a male United States citizen before September 22, 1922;

(6)   a card of identity and registration as a United States citizen, or an official communication from an American Foreign Service post indicating the individual is registered there as a United States citizen; or

(7)   Form I-197 (United States Citizen Identification Card).[1]

Note

1. U.S. Citizen Identification Card, https://www.uscis.gov/i-9-central/133-list-c-documents-establish-employment-authorization (last accessed September 1, 2022).

Right to Appeal

255. Is there a review procedure available if a person is disappointed with the Social Security Administration's initial determination regarding benefits?

There is an administrative review process for a person who is dissatisfied with the Social Security Administration's action concerning a claim for benefits. After the Social Security Administration makes an initial determination, further review may be requested by the person or his representative. The administrative review process consists of several steps (four levels of appeal) that must be requested in writing, usually within specified time periods, and in the following order:

(1)   **Reconsideration:** The person or representative may request that the initial determination be reconsidered. A reconsideration is a complete review and reexamination of the administrative records that results in another determination. This is done by someone that did not participate in the first determination. The appeal is submitted on Form SSA-5610 – *Request for Reconsideration*.[1]

   o   Appeal for reconsideration of a determination about a qualifying disability, the request goes to the Disability Determination Services (DDS) for review.

   o   Appeal about a nonmedical *issue* (such as an overpayment), the reconsideration will be handled a local SSA office or payment center.

(2)   **Administrative Law Judge (ALJ) Hearing:** If there is still disagreement with the reconsidered determination, the person or representative may request a hearing before an Administrative Law Judge of the Office of Hearings and Appeals. The ALJ Hearing is another review by the ALJ of all the evidence who did not take part in the first decision or reconsideration. The appeal is submitted on Form HA-501 *Request for Hearing by Administrative Law Judge*[2]. If requesting a hearing on the denial of a claim for disability benefits, Form SSA-3441 *Disability Report*[3] and Form SSA-827 *Authorization to Disclose Information*[4] to SSA must be submitted as well.

(3)   **Appeals Council Review:** If the person disagrees with the administrative law judge's decision or dismissal, he may request a review by the Appeals Council of the Office of Hearings and Appeals, which has the authority to deny or grant review or dismiss the request for any reason for which the administrative law judge could have dismissed. Also, the Appeals Council may, on its own motion, review an administrative law judge's decision. If the Appeals Council grants a request for review, it will either issue a new decision or return the case to an ALJ for action. The appeal is submitted on form HA-520 *Request for Review of Hearing Decision/Order*.[5]

(4)   **Federal Court Action – United States District Court:** After Appeals Council review (or denial of review), a person who is still dissatisfied may file a civil action in a federal district court.

An initial determination becomes final unless reconsideration is requested within sixty days from the date notice of the initial determination is received by the person or the person's representative. In counting the sixty days, it is presumed that the Notice of Decision is received **five days** after mailing.

Reconsideration is the first step in the administrative review process that is provided if there is dissatisfaction with the initial determination. The request for reconsideration may be made by the claimant, by another person whose benefit rights are affected by the determination, or by the appointed representative of either. The reconsideration must be requested in writing by the person (or the person's representative).

The reconsideration process is an independent reexamination of all evidence on record related to the case by the Social Security Administration. It is based on evidence submitted for the initial determination, plus any additional information that the claimant or representative may submit in connection with the reconsideration. The reconsideration is not limited to the issues raised by the claimant. A reconsideration is made by a member of a different staff from the one that made the initial determination and who is specially trained in the handling of reconsiderations. The claimant receives a personalized notice detailing the basis for the determination in his case.

When a person can demonstrate that he failed to appeal an adverse decision because of reliance on incorrect, incomplete, or misleading information provided by the Social Security Administration, his failure to appeal may not serve as the basis for denial of a second application for any Social Security benefit. This protection applies to both initial denials and reconsiderations. The Social Security Administration is required to include, in all notices of denial, a clear, simple description on the effect of reapplying for benefits rather than filing an appeal.[6]

The Social Security Administration issued a ruling in 1995 on establishing good cause for late filing of a request for administrative review, for a claimant who received an initial or reconsideration determination notice that did not state that filing a new application instead of a request for administrative review could result in the loss of benefits. The Social Security Administration will make a finding of good cause for late filing of a request for administrative review for a claim, if the claimant received an initial or reconsideration determination notice and demonstrates that, as a result of the notice, he did not timely request such review. Notices covered by this ruling include only those dated prior to July 1, 1991, that did not state that filing a new application for benefits instead of a request for review could result in the loss of benefits. If the adjudicator determines that good cause exists, the Social Security Administration will extend the time for requesting administrative review and take the action that would have been appropriate had the claimant filed a timely request for administrative review.[7]

Notes

1. https://www.ssa.gov/forms/ssa-561.pdf (Last accessed September 1, 2022)
2. https://www.ssa.gov/forms/ha-501.pdf (Last accessed September 1, 2022)
3. https://www.ssa.gov/forms/ssa-3441.pdf (Last accessed September 1, 2022)
4. https://www.ssa.gov/forms/ssa-827.pdf (Last accessed September 1, 2022)
5. https://www.ssa.gov/forms/ha-520.pdf (Last Accessed September 1, 2022)
6. Publication 05-10058, Your Right to Question the Decision Made on Your Claim (May 2022 Edition), https://www.ssa.gov/pubs/EN-05-10058.pdf (last accessed September 1, 2022).
7. Social Security Ruling SSR 95-1p, https://www.ssa.gov/OP_Home/rulings/oasi/33/SSR95-01-oasi-33.html (last accessed September 1, 2022).

256. Is there a right to representation on appeal?

An individual may choose to have someone help with an appeal or to represent them. A representative may be a lawyer or other qualified person familiar with the appeal and the Social Security program. SSA will work with a person's representation. A representative can act for the appellant in most Social Security matters and will receive a copy of any decisions made regarding the claim. A representative cannot charge or collect a fee without prior written approval from SSA.[1]

Role of the Representative

- Getting information from the Social Security file

- Helping obtain medical records or information to support a claim

- Representing a person at interviews, conferences, or hearings

- Requesting a reconsideration, a hearing, or an Appeals Council review

- Helping the appellant and witnesses prepare for a hearing and questioning any witnesses

- The representative will also receive a copy of the decision(s) made

Payment of the Representative

- To charge a fee for services, the representative must first file either a fee agreement or a petition asking for approval to charge a fee.

- The representative cannot charge more than the amount SSA authorizes. If the appellant or representative disagrees with the authorized fee, either can ask SSA to reassess the amount.

- If a representative charges or collects a fee without SSA's approval, or charges or collects more than the authorized fee, SSA may suspend or disqualify them from representing anyone before the agency.

Note

1. https://www.ssa.gov/pubs/EN-05-10075.pdf May 2022 (last accessed September 1, 2022).

257. How can a person appeal the reconsideration determination?

A hearing before an Administrative Law Judge may be requested by the person or appointed representative who disagrees with the reconsidered determination, or by a person who can show that the reconsidered determination will harm the person's rights under the Social Security Act.

The person and/or person's representative may appear in person, submit new evidence, examine the evidence used in making the determination under review, give testimony, and present and question witnesses. If a person properly waives the right to an oral hearing, the Administrative Law Judge will ordinarily decide on the basis of the evidence already submitted or otherwise obtained by the person or any other party to the hearing. Often, a hearing by video teleconference can be scheduled faster than an in-person hearing and lessens the likelihood that an individual will need to travel for hearing. The Social Security Administration has 163 hearing offices nationwide and there are satellite hearing offices. Approximately 40 percent of hearings are held in remote locations. There are more than 1,500 administrative law judges and more than 9,300 employees overall in the field organization.

If the claim is about the amount of Part A Hospital Insurance benefits under Medicare, the amount in question must be $100 or more. Carriers review complaints about the amount of Medical Insurance benefits under Medicare.

A person may also be able to use an expedited appeals procedure, if he or she has no dispute with the findings of fact of the reconsideration determination beyond a contention that a section of the applicable statute is unconstitutional. (For further details, see Q 261.)

Notice of time and place of the hearing is sent by the Administrative Law Judge to the parties to the hearing at least twenty days before the date set for the hearing. The hearing is usually held in the area where the person requesting the hearing resides, although the person may be required to travel up to 75 miles or participate in a video conference. (Travel expenses are paid by the government, if travel over 75 miles is required.)

At times, the Administrative Law Judge will examine the evidence and certify a case to the Appeals Council with a recommended decision. (See Q 261.)

258. How is a hearing request made and how long will it take from the request to the actual hearing?

A request for a hearing is made by filling out Form HA-501, "Request for Hearing by Administrative Law Judge,"[1] or by writing a letter to the nearest Social Security office, a presiding officer, or with the Appeals Council. If the hearing request is for disability benefits, then the appeal may be made online.

The request for a hearing must be made within sixty days after the date that the notice of the reconsidered decision is received and must include:

(1)   the name and Social Security number of the individual;

(2)   the reason for disagreeing with the reconsidered or revised determination;

(3)   a statement of additional evidence that will be submitted; and

(4)   the name and address of the individual's representative, if any. The sixty-day time limit can be extended if there is a good reason. Note that the SSA presumes receipt of the notice of decision is five days after mailing.

A beneficiary of disability benefits has the option of having his benefits continued through the hearing stage of appeal if there was a determination of medical improvement (also called medical cessation). But where benefits are adversely affected because of the performance of substantial gainful activity (also called work cessation), benefits may not be continued. If the earlier unfavorable determinations are upheld by the administrative law judge, the benefits that were received during the appeal process are subject to recovery by the Social Security Administration. (If an appeal is made in good faith, recovery may be waived.) Medicare eligibility is also continued, but Medicare benefits are not subject to recovery.

In recent years, the Social Security Administration has come under criticism for its backlog of hearings. In the 2008 fiscal year, the average processing time was 514 days. It had decreased to 415 days by June 2010. Since then, the Social Security Administration has devoted efforts to decrease the processing times. Processing times were reduced to 353 days by the end of 2012, but climbed to 378 for 2013, 437 for 2014, 477 for 2015, 544 for 2016, 602 for 2017, 505 for 2018, 480 for 2019, 393 for 2020 and improved to 327 for 2021. Figures reported on July 29, 2022 show an average backlog of 327 days (down from 393 last year), ranging from 74 days by the National Adjudication Team to 578 days in the Ponce, Puerto Rico office.[2] The Special Review Cadre, handling specialized cases took 769 days in 2020 but did not report days for 2021 or 2022.[3]

Notes

1. Form HA-501 Request for Hearing By Administrative Law Judge https://www.ssa.gov/forms/ha-501.html (last accessed September 1, 2022).
2. Hearing Office Average Processing Time Ranking Report FY 2019 (For Reporting Purposes: 8/25/2020 through 07/25/2022). https://www.ssa.gov/appeals/DataSets/05_Average_Processing_Time_Report.html (last accessed September 1, 2022).
3. https://www.ssa.gov/org/orgOHO.htm. (Last accessed September 1, 2022)

259. How long are the average delays in Social Security Hearing offices?

The following is a list of Office of Disability Adjudication and Review (ODAR) with the average number of days until final disposition of hearing requests. The average shown is combined average of all cases completed in that particular office. This can be helpful estimating time until final disposition.

Rank	Hearing Office	Region	Average Processing Time
1	NATL ADJUDICATION TEAM	12	74
2	TOLEDO OH	5	212
3	AKRON OH	5	216
4	EVANSVILLE	5	217
5	PEORIA	5	230
6	COLUMBIA SC	4	232
7	FORT MYERS FL	4	234
7	MINNEAPOLIS	5	234
9	MADISON	5	238
9	ORLAND PARK	5	238
11	ORLANDO	4	241
12	CINCINNATI	5	242
13	DAYTON	5	248
14	HOUSTON NORTH	6	251
15	VALPARAISO IN	5	254
16	MORGANTOWN	3	256
16	MT PLEASANT MI	5	256

Rank	Hearing Office	Region	Average Processing Time
18	WHITE PLAINS	2	257
19	MILWAUKEE	5	258
20	LANSING	5	259
20	OAK BROOK	5	259
20	ROANOKE	3	259
23	SYRACUSE	2	260
24	CLEVELAND	5	263
24	KINGSPORT	4	263
24	SEVEN FIELDS	3	263
27	FORT WAYNE	5	265
28	LIVONIA MI	5	268
29	CHARLOTTESVILLE	3	270
29	GRAND RAPIDS	5	270
29	LEXINGTON	4	270
32	ALBANY	2	271
32	FRANKLIN TN	4	271
32	JACKSONVILLE	4	271
35	EVANSTON	5	274
36	OMAHA	7	277
37	HARTFORD	1	280
37	SALT LAKE CITY	8	280
39	MANCHESTER	1	281
40	FLORENCE	4	282
40	HARRISBURG	3	282
40	INDIANAPOLIS	5	282
43	FLINT	5	283
43	FT LAUDERDALE	4	283
43	WILKES BARRE	3	283
46	TUPELO	4	284
47	ST PETERSBURG FL OHO	4	285
48	LAS VEGAS	9	286
49	LONG ISLAND	2	287
50	ELKINS PARK	3	288
51	OAK PARK	5	289
52	MIDDLESBORO	4	290
52	NASHVILLE	4	290

Rank	Hearing Office	Region	Average Processing Time
54	JERSEY CITY	2	294
55	CHICAGO	5	295
55	PITTSBURGH	3	295
57	PHILADELPHIA	3	296
58	SPECIAL REVIEW CADRE	12	298
59	DETROIT	5	299
60	ATLANTA NORTH	4	300
60	JACKSON MS OHO	4	300
60	RALEIGH	4	300
63	QUEENS	2	301
64	COVINGTON GA	4	302
64	FARGO	8	302
66	CHARLESTON SC	4	303
67	HATTIESBURG	4	305
68	LOUISVILLE	4	307
68	WASHINGTON	3	307
70	TAMPA OHO	4	309
71	BIRMINGHAM	4	312
71	NEW HAVEN	1	312
73	RICHMOND	3	313
74	COLUMBUS	5	314
75	SPRINGFIELD MO	7	315
76	NEWARK	2	317
77	CHATTANOOGA	4	319
77	KANSAS CITY	7	319
79	MCALESTER	6	320
79	NEW YORK VARICK	2	320
79	PHOENIX DOWNTOWN	9	320
82	PROVIDENCE	1	321
83	SAN BERNARDINO	9	322
84	MONTGOMERY	4	324
85	BILLINGS	8	325
86	DALLAS NORTH OHO	6	326
87	FAYETTEVILLE NC	4	327
87	MOBILE	4	327
89	DENVER	8	329

Rank	Hearing Office	Region	Average Processing Time
90	DOVER	3	331
90	KNOXVILLE	4	331
92	BOSTON	1	332
92	COLORADO SPRINGS	8	332
94	TOPEKA KS	7	333
95	GREENVILLE	4	334
95	PHILADELPHIA EAST	3	334
97	CREVE COEUR	7	335
97	EUGENE	10	335
97	TALLAHASSEE FL OHO	4	335
97	TUCSON	9	335
101	WEST DES MOINES	7	336
102	MEMPHIS	4	337
103	COLUMBIA MO	7	338
104	BALTIMORE	3	339
105	NEW YORK	2	342
106	SPRINGFIELD MA	1	343
107	WICHITA	7	344
108	SAN ANTONIO	6	345
109	LITTLE ROCK	6	346
109	PADUCAH	4	346
111	ALEXANDRIA	6	347
111	SACRAMENTO	9	347
113	FORT WORTH	6	348
114	PORTLAND OR	10	353
115	SAVANNAH	4	354
116	LAWRENCE MA	1	355
117	SOUTH JERSEY	2	357
117	SPOKANE	10	357
119	TULSA OHO	6	359
120	SAN JOSE	9	361
121	CHARLOTTE	4	362
122	ST LOUIS	7	363
123	METAIRIE	6	366
124	HOUSTON WEST	6	367
124	JOHNSTOWN	3	367

Rank	Hearing Office	Region	Average Processing Time
124	NORFOLK	3	367
127	NORWALK	9	369
128	BRONX	2	372
129	TACOMA	10	374
130	MACON	4	377
131	ATLANTA DOWNTOWN	4	378
131	ROCHESTER	2	378
133	SAN FRANCISCO	9	379
133	SAN RAFAEL	9	379
135	MIAMI OHO	4	385
135	SAN DIEGO	9	385
137	OKLAHOMA CITY	6	387
138	FORT SMITH	6	388
139	ALBUQUERQUE	6	390
140	PHOENIX NORTH	9	393
140	SEATTLE	10	393
140	STOCKTON	9	393
143	LONG BEACH	9	394
143	NEW ORLEANS	6	394
145	CHARLESTON WV	3	398
145	ORANGE	9	398
147	GREENSBORO	4	407
148	BUFFALO	2	408
148	RENO	9	408
150	PASADENA	9	421
151	DALLAS DOWNTOWN	6	425
151	LOS ANGELES WEST	9	425
153	OAKLAND	9	428
153	PORTLAND ME	1	428
155	MORENO VALLEY	9	430
156	SANTA BARBARA	9	440
157	HUNTINGTON WV	3	451
158	RIO GRANDE VALLEY TX	6	457
159	LOS ANGELES DOWNTOWN	9	460
160	SHREVEPORT	6	461
161	HONOLULU	9	469

Rank	Hearing Office	Region	Average Processing Time
162	FRESNO	9	543
163	SAN JUAN, PR	2	546
164	PONCE PR	2	578

260. What will a hearing cost?

There is no charge for a hearing. If counsel represents an individual, there will of course be attorney's fees. There are also travel expenses, which are not reimbursed, unless the hearing is held more than 75 miles from the individual's home. If the hearing is more than seventy-five miles from the person's home, there are reimbursed for reasonable travel expenses, however many hearings are now done using remote video.

261. If an individual disagrees with the hearing decision, may they ask for a review?

Yes. A review of the hearing by the Appeals Council of the Office of Hearings and Appeals must be in writing and must be filed within 60 days from the date the person or the person's representative receives notice of the administrative law judge's action.

Within 60 days from the date of the administrative law judge's decision or dismissal, the Appeals Council may on its own initiative decide to review the action that was taken. Notice of this review is mailed to all parties at the last known address.

The Appeals Council will review a hearing decision or dismissal where:

(1)   there appears to be an abuse of discretion by the administrative law judge;

(2)   there is an error of law;

(3)   the presiding officer's action, findings, or conclusions are not supported by substantial evidence; or

(4)   there is a broad policy or procedural issue that may affect the general public interest.

The Appeals Council will notify the person whether it will review the case. If the Appeals Council decides to review the case, the claimant or representative may request an appearance before the Appeals Council for the presentation of oral arguments. If the Appeals Council determines that a significant question of law or policy is presented, or that oral arguments would be beneficial in rendering a proper decision, the appearance will be granted. The claimant may also file written statements in support of his claim. The Appeals Council will notify the claimant of its action in the case.

The Appeals Council may deny or dismiss a party's request for review, or it may grant the request and either issue a decision or remand the case to an administrative law judge. If the

Appeals Council denies a request for review of a decision by an administrative law judge, the administrative law judge's decision becomes a final decision of the Social Security Administration, subject to judicial review (except when judicial review is precluded in certain Medicare cases). If the Appeals Council grants a request for review and issues a decision, that decision also becomes a final decision of the Social Security Administration, subject to judicial review except in certain Medicare cases.

If an administrative law judge makes a decision in favor of a person in a disability case and the Appeals Council does not render a final decision within 110 days, interim disability benefits are provided to the person. (Delays in excess of 20 days caused by or on behalf of the claimant do not count in determining the 110-day period.) These benefits begin with the month before the month in which the 110-day period expires and are not considered overpayments if the final decision is adverse, unless the benefits are fraudulently obtained.

262. May a person file a civil action in the United States District Court?

Yes, a person dissatisfied with the decision of the Appeals Council or denial of the request for review of the Administrative Law Judge's decision by the Appeals Council may bring suit in a federal district court. To file a civil action regarding the amount of Part A Hospital Insurance benefits under Medicare, however, the amount in question must be $1,000 or more. The Social Security Act does not provide for court review of a determination concerning the amount of benefits payable under Medicare Part B Medical Insurance.

The civil action in the court must be filed within 60 days from the date notice of the Appeals Council decision or denial of the request for review is received by the person or appointed representative. This time limit may be extended by the Appeals Council for good reason.

The court may issue a decision on the record or remand for further development. There is no right to court action where the Appeals Council has dismissed a request for review or denied a request for review of an Administrative Law Judge's dismissal.

A person may be able to advance directly from a reconsideration determination to a federal district court by filing a claim contending that the applicable statute of the Social Security Act is unconstitutional. This procedure, known as expedited appeals process, is allowable when:

(1)   the individual has presented a claim at the reconsideration level;

(2)   the only issue is the constitutionality of the statutory requirement;

(3)   the claim is neither invalid or cognizable under a different section of the Social Security Act; and

(4)   the amount in controversy is $1,000 or more.

In order to reach a federal district court after a reconsideration determination, the Social Security Administration must determine that the claim raises a constitutional question and is appropriate for treatment under the expedited appeals procedure. After this is done, the Social

Security Administration and the person must sign an agreement that identifies the constitutional issue involved and explains the final reconsideration determination.

A person must file for expedited judicial review within 60 days after the date of receipt of notice of the reconsideration determination. An extension of time is available if good cause is established for not filing on time.

Should the Social Security Administration determine that a claim is not appropriate for expedited judicial review before a federal district court, its decision is final and not subject to administrative or judicial review. It is required, however, to notify the person filing the claim of its decision, and to treat the person's request as a request for a reconsideration, a hearing, or an Appeals Council review (whichever is appropriate).

The Supreme Court has held that the Social Security Act does not permit a person to have subject-matter jurisdiction to the federal district courts to review a decision of the Social Security Administration, nor to reopen a previously adjudicated claim for Social Security benefits. The Court found that, unless the claim was based on a constitutional challenge, the Act did not authorize judicial review to reopen a final decision on disability benefits after the 60-day limit for a review by civil action had terminated.[1]

Social Security received 17,192 new court cases during fiscal year 2019 (October 2018 - September 2019) 16,448 new court cases during fiscal year 2020 (October 2019 - September 2020) 14,242 during fiscal year 2021 (October 2020 – September 2021) and 12, 757 during fiscal year 2022 (October 2021 – June 2022).

Note

1. *Califano v. Sanders*, 430 U.S. 99 (1977).

263. Are there situations where the Social Security Administration may not recover an overpayment to a beneficiary?

Yes, the Social Security Administration is barred from recovering an overpayment if recovery is "against equity and good conscience". According to the Social Security regulations, recovery of an overpayment is "against equity and good conscience" under three conditions:

(1)   if the beneficiary has changed his or her position for the worse;

(2)   if the beneficiary relinquished a valuable right because of reliance upon a notice that a payment would be made or because of the overpayment itself; or

(3)   if the beneficiary was living in a separate household from the overpaid person or the eligible spouse, and did not receive the overpayment.

The Ninth Circuit Court of Appeals has broadened the definition of "against equity and good conscience".[1] The case involved a former inmate who had been in prison from 1963 to 1985 on a felony conviction, and who had been receiving Social Security disability benefits while in prison. Although the Social Security Act was amended in 1980 to prohibit payment of disability benefits to certain incarcerated felons, he continued to receive benefits until 1982 and was unaware of the change in the law. After learning about the change in the law, the inmate informed the Social Security Administration of his situation. The Social Security Administration requested repayment. The inmate requested a waiver of recovery for the overpayment; a personal conference with a government representative was held in 1984, but no decision was issued at that time. The inmate was released from prison in 1985 and spent his overpayment.

The Ninth Circuit held that requiring the former inmate to repay the overpayment was against equity and good conscience because Congress intended a broad concept of fairness to apply to waiver requests, one that takes into account the facts and circumstances of each case. The court noted that the former inmate had no material goods, no means of transportation, no income, and had only worked in a few temporary jobs. Also, the court pointed to the presence of a psychological impairment as a factor in favor of waiver of recovery of the overpayment.

Social Security regulations address the rights of individuals regarding overpayment and waiver determinations. The rules follow policy established as a result of a series of court decisions. Whenever an initial determination is made that more than the correct amount of payment has been made, and the Social Security Administration seeks adjustment or recovery of the overpayment, the individual involved must be immediately notified.

The notice must include:

(1)   the overpayment amount, and how and when it occurred;

(2)   a request for full, immediate refund, unless the overpayment can be withheld from the next month's benefit;

(3)   the proposed adjustment of benefits if refund is not received within 30 days after the date of the notice and adjustment of benefits is available;

(4)   an explanation of the availability of a different rate of withholding;

(5)   an explanation of the right to request waiver of adjustment or recovery, and the automatic scheduling of a file review and prerecoupment hearing if a request for waiver cannot be approved after initial paper review;

(6)   an explanation of the right to request reconsideration of the fact and/or amount of the overpayment determination;

(7)   instructions about the availability of forms for requesting reconsideration and waiver;

(8)   an explanation that, if the individual does not request waiver or reconsideration within 30 days of the date of the overpayment notice, adjustment or recovery of the overpayment will begin;

(9)   a statement that a Social Security Administration office will help the individual complete and submit forms for appeal or waiver requests; and

(10) a statement that the individual receiving the notice should notify the Social Security Administration promptly if reconsideration, waiver, a lesser rate of withholding, repayment by installments, or cross-program adjustment is wanted.

There can be no adjustment or recovery in any case where an overpayment has been made to an individual who is without fault, if adjustment or recovery would either defeat the purpose of the Social Security Act or be against equity and good conscience.

If an individual requests waiver of adjustment or recovery within 30 days after receiving a notice of overpayment, no action will be taken until after the initial waiver determination is made. If an individual requests waiver of adjustment or recovery more than 30 days after receiving a notice of overpayment, the Social Security Administration will stop any adjustment or recovery actions until after the initial waiver determination is made.

When waiver is requested, the individual should provide the Social Security Administration with information to support the contention that the individual is without fault in causing the overpayment, and that adjustment or recovery would either defeat the purpose of the Social Security Act or be against equity and good conscience. That information, along with supporting documentation, is reviewed to determine if waiver can be approved. If waiver cannot be approved after this review, the individual is notified in writing and given the dates, times, and place of the file review and personal conference. The file review is always scheduled at least five days before the personal conference.

At the file review, the individual and the individual's representative have the right to review the claims file and applicable law and regulations with the decision maker or another Social Security Administration representative who is prepared to answer questions.

At the personal conference, the individual is given the opportunity to:

(1) appear personally, testify, cross-examine any witnesses, and make arguments;

(2) be represented by an attorney or other representative, although the individual must be present at the conference; and

(3) submit documents for consideration by the decision maker.

The decision maker:

(1) explains the provisions of law and regulations applicable to the issue;

(2) briefly summarizes the evidence already on file;

(3) ascertains from the individual whether the information presented is correct and understandable;

(4) allows the individual and the individual's representative to present the individual's case;

(5)   allows each witness to present information and allows the individual and the individual's representative to question each witness;

(6)   ascertains whether there is any further evidence;

(7)   reminds the individual of any evidence promised by the individual that has not been presented;

(8)   allows the individual and the individual's representative to present a proposed summary or closing statement;

(9)   explains that a decision will be made and the individual will be notified in writing; and

(10)   explains repayment options and further appeal rights in the event the decision is adverse to the individual.

The Social Security Administration will issue a written decision, specifying the findings of fact and conclusions in support of the decision to approve or deny waiver and advising of the individual's right to appeal the decision. If waiver is denied, adjustment or recovery of the overpayment begins, even if the individual appeals.

If the individual is dissatisfied with the initial determination, reconsideration is the first step in the administrative review process. If dissatisfied with the reconsidered determination, the individual may request a hearing before an administrative law judge.

Note

1. *Quinlivan v. Sullivan*, 916 F.2d 524 (9th Cir. 1990).

264. When is an individual considered to be "without fault" for getting an overpayment?

An individual is considered to be without fault for an overpayment that did not result due to lack of care and the degree of care of the person receiving payment, including:

- not providing full and accurate information;

- an incorrect statement by the person which he/she knew or should have known was false;

- the person's failure to furnish information which he/she knew or should have known was material;

- the person's acceptance of any payment that he/she knew or should have known was incorrect;

- not complying with annual earning reporting and other reporting requirement; and

- returning payments believed not to be earned.

The individual has the responsibility to show lack of fault, even if the Social Security Administration caused the check to be issued or the deposit to be made.[1]

Note

1. https://secure.ssa.gov/poms.nsf/lnx/0202250005#:~:text=If%20the%20number%20holder%20is,c (last accessed September 1, 2022).

265. What are the factors considered by the Social Security Administration to determine whether a person is "at fault" or "without fault?"

Factors considered include:

- understanding of reporting requirements;

- understanding of obligation to return payments not due or owed;

- actual knowledge of events that should have been reported;

- opportunities to comply with reporting requirements and efforts made to report;

- ability to comply with reporting requirements, including any mental or physical limitations.

266. When is an individual considered to be "at fault" for getting an overpayment?

An individual is considered to be at fault for an overpayment which resulted from:

- willful misstatement;

- obscuring of facts which caused the overpayment, whether directly or indirectly;

- failure to furnish or disclose information which was known to be important or should have been known to be important;

- accepting payments that were known to be incorrect or should have been known to be incorrect.

267. What presumptions exist concerning fault?

Certain presumptions can be made concerning the fault of persons other than the overpaid person:

- If the social security number holder is without fault in causing the overpayment, it will be presumed that any other beneficiary is also without fault if overpaid for the same event.

- If the overpaid person is at fault, a spouse will be presumed at fault if living in the same household and overpaid for the same event.

- If the overpaid person is at fault, a minor or an incompetent adult will be presumed without fault even though living in the same household and overpaid for the same event.

Any of these presumptions can be rebutted by clear and convincing evidence to the contrary.

BENEFIT COMPUTATION

268. What are the various methods of computing the Primary Insurance Amount?

Social Security benefits are based on average lifetime earnings, expressed as the Primary Insurance Amount (PIA). Calculating PIA is complicated because some factors used in the benefit formula change annually.

Currently, the two PIA calculation methods most frequently used are:

1. The **simplified old-start benefit method**: This method is used if age sixty-two, disability, or death occurred prior to 1979. It averages actual (not indexed) earnings and uses a table to calculate the PIA.

2. The **wage indexing method**: This method has been used since 1979 and after. Indexing earnings is a way of adjusting them to reflect changes in wage levels throughout years of employment. This ensures that benefits reflect increases in the standard of living. In general, the wage indexing method calculates PIA by indexing lifetime earnings up to and including the year the person turns fifty-nine. Then, the highest earnings for a specific number of years (usually thirty-five) are averaged and a benefit formula is applied to this figure to calculate the PIA.

Two other benefit computation methods are less frequently used:

1. **"Special minimum" benefit tables** are used sometimes to compute benefits payable to some individuals who have long periods of low earnings and who have at least eleven years of coverage.

2. **Flat-rate benefits** are provided to workers (and to their spouses or surviving spouses) who became age seventy-two before 1969 and who were not insured under the usual requirements.

269. How are benefits computed under the simplified old-start benefit computation method?

The simplified old-start benefit computation[1] method must be used if disability, death, or age sixty-two occurred before 1979.

Step I. Count the number of years elapsed after 1950 (or after year the insured reached age twenty-one, if later) and before (not including) the year of death, disability, or year of attaining age 62 (65 for a worker born before 1911, 64 if born in 1911, 63 if born in 1912).

Step II. Subtract five. (Also subtract any years that fell wholly or partly in a period of disability.) The result is the number of years of earnings (but not less than two) to be used in computing Average Monthly Earnings (AME).

Step III. List earnings for each year starting with 1951 and including the year in which the worker died, or the year prior to disability or application for old-age benefits. Earnings listed cannot exceed the maximum earnings base for that particular year (see Q 274).

Step IV. From this list, select years of highest earnings (same number found in Step I).

Step V. Total the earnings in the selected years and divide by the number of months in those years (drop cents). This is the worker's AME.

A worker's AME are subject to recalculation, if earnings in his year of retirement or year of disability are higher than the lowest year of earnings used in the original calculation. Earnings in the last year are substituted for earnings in the lowest year if this results in higher AIME.

Step VI. Determine the insured's Primary Insurance Amount (PIA).

Note

1. 20 C.F.R. sec. 404.241 (1977) (simplified old-start method).

270. How does the Special Minimum Benefit work?

The special minimum benefit is a special minimum Primary Insurance Amount (PIA) enacted in 1972 to provide adequate benefits to long-term low earners. The first full special minimum PIA in 1973 was $170 per month. Beginning in 1979, its value has increased with price growth and was increased to $804 per month in 2013. Before 1979, the special minimum benefit amounts did not increase when benefit increases occurred. Legislation provided the benefit amounts for January 1973, March 1974, and January 1979. Automatic benefit cost of living increases, first increased the benefits beginning with June 1979.[1] A person with 30 years of coverage in 2020 would qualify for a special minimum PIA of $886.40, $897.90 in 2021, and $950.80 for 2022.

- The number of beneficiaries receiving the special minimum PIA has declined from about 200,000 in the early 1990s to about 32,000 in 2019.

- Fewer new beneficiaries are receiving the price-indexed special minimum PIA because wage growth typically exceeds price growth, thus, their wage-indexed regular PIA is usually higher.

- 2018 was projected as the last year a new beneficiary could theoretically be awarded a special minimum PIA that is higher than his or her regular PIA, but 1998 is the last year it actually happened.

- The value of the regular PIA has held constant while the value of the special minimum PIA has declined relative to the average wage.

- The value of the regular PIA has risen while the value of the special minimum PIA has held constant relative to the poverty threshold.

To be eligible for a special minimum benefit, a person must have at least eleven years of coverage. A person acquires a year of coverage by having a certain minimum amount of earnings in the year.

For persons eligible for benefits before 1979, or for deaths prior to 1979, benefits are determined on the basis of Primary Insurance Amounts (PIAs) given either by tables or, for years prior to 1959, by formulas. In either case, a person's PIA depends on the Average Monthly Wage computed on the basis of that individual's earnings record. (For persons eligible after 1978, benefits are computed using formulas instead of tables.)

Before automatic benefit increases existed, there were years where no benefit increase occurred. If no table became effective in the year you select, the table which provided benefits in that year will be given. There were no cost-of-living adjustments effective December 2009 or December 2010, so the table effective for December 2008 remained the benefit table in effect until December 2011.

Note

1. Social Security Administration, Special Minimum Benefit, https://www.ssa.gov/policy/docs/program-explainers/special-minimum. html#:~:text=DEFINITION%3A%20The%20special%20minimum%20benefit,%24804%20per%20month%20in%202013.

Primary Insurance Amount

271. What is the Primary Insurance Amount (PIA)?

The Primary Insurance Amount (PIA) is the basic unit used to determine the amount of each monthly benefit payable under Social Security. It applies to both the old and new method of computing benefits.

A disabled worker—or a retired worker whose retirement benefits start at normal retirement age—receives monthly benefits equal to the PIA.[1] Retired workers who are fully insured and whose retirement benefits start after full retirement age also receive an additional delayed retirement credit (see Q 293).

Monthly benefits for members of an insured worker's family (dependent's and survivor's benefits) are all figured as percentages of the worker's PIA (see Appendix A, Table 1).

The total amount of monthly benefits payable on a worker's Social Security account is limited by a "maximum family benefit," which is also related to the worker's PIA.

In some instances, monthly benefits will be reduced if the insured elects to receive benefits before a specified age (see Q 343).

The retirement benefit is reduced if the retired worker elects to start receiving a benefit at or after age 62 but before full retirement age. The benefit for the spouse of a retired worker is also reduced if received before full retirement age (see Q 295, Q 343, and Appendix A, Table 10).

The benefit for a widow(er) is reduced if he or she elects to start receiving benefits at or after age 60 but before full retirement age (see Q 296 and Appendix A, Table 11).

Disabled widow(er)'s benefits are payable beginning at age 50 for disability occurring before age 60 and are always reduced from what would have been payable at full retirement age (see Q 198).

The law provides a minimum benefit for insured workers and for survivors of insured workers when the worker had many years of coverage (see Q 288 and Q 289).

Note

1. 42 U.S.C. § 402(a); 20 CFR § 404.201.

"Wage Indexing" Benefit Computation Method

272. In general, how is the PIA computed under the "wage indexing" method?

It is based on "indexed" earnings over a fixed number of years after 1950. (Indexing is a mechanism for expressing prior years' earnings in terms of their current dollar value.) Previous computations used actual earnings and a PIA Table. The "wage indexing" method uses a formula to determine the PIA.

Step I. Index the earnings record

Step II. Determine the Average Indexed Monthly Earnings (AIME)

Step III. Apply the PIA formula to the AIME

273. Who is eligible to use the "wage indexing" benefit computation method?

The "wage indexing" method applies where first eligibility begins after 1978. First eligibility is the earliest of:

(1)   the year of death;

(2)   the year disability begins; or

(3)   the year the insured reaches age sixty-two.

However, if the worker was entitled to a disability benefit before 1979 and that benefit terminated more than twelve months before death, another disability, or age 62, the new method will be used in determining the PIA for the subsequent entitlement. (See Q 282.)

274. What earnings are used in computing a person's Average Indexed Monthly Earnings (AIME)?

The AIME is based on Social Security earnings for years after 1950. This includes wages earned as an employee and/or self-employment income. (For an explanation of the terms wages and self-employment income, see WAGES AND SELF-EMPLOYMENT INCOME, Q 409 to Q 437.)

Only earnings credited to the person's Social Security account can be used and the maximum earnings creditable for specific years are as follows:

$160,200 for 2023	$43,800 for 1987
$147,000 for 2022	$42,000 for 1986
$142,800 for 2021	$37,800 for 1984
$137,700 for 2020	$35,700 for 1983
$132,900 for 2019	$32,400 for 1982
$128,700 for 2018	$29,700 for 1981
$127,200 for 2017	$25,900 for 1980
$118,500 for 2016	$22,900 for 1979
$118,500 for 2015	$17,700 for 1978
$117,000 for 2014	$16,500 for 1977
$113,700 for 2013	$15,300 for 1976
$110,100 for 2012	$14,100 for 1975
$106,800 for 2011	$13,200 for 1974
$106,800 for 2010	$10,800 for 1973
$106,800 for 2009	$9,000 for 1972
$102,000 for 2008	$7,800 for 1971
$97,500 for 2007	$7,800 for 1970
$94,200 for 2006	$7,800 for 1969
$90,000 for 2005	$7,800 for 1968
$87,900 for 2004	$6,600 for 1967
$87,000 for 2003	$6,600 for 1966
$84,900 for 2002	$4,800 for 1965
$80,400 for 2001	$4,800 for 1964
$76,200 for 2000	$4,800 for 1963
$72,600 for 1999	$4,800 for 1962
$68,400 for 1998	$4,800 for 1961
$65,400 for 1997	$4,800 for 1960
$62,700 for 1996	$4,800 for 1959
$61,200 for 1995	$4,200 for 1958

$60,600 for 1994	$4,200 for 1957
$57,600 for 1993	$4,200 for 1956
$55,500 for 1992	$4,200 for 1955
$53,400 for 1991	$3,600 for 1954
$51,300 for 1990	$3,600 for 1953
$48,000 for 1989	$3,600 for 1952
$45,000 for 1988	$3,600 for 1951

275. How is the earnings record indexed for the AIME computation?

The AIME is based on the earnings record after wages have been indexed.[1] Indexing creates an earnings history that more accurately reflects the value of the individual's actual earnings in comparison to the national average wage level at the time of eligibility. Earnings for each year are indexed up to the "indexing year"—the second year before the worker reaches age 62—or dies or becomes disabled before age 62.

Wages are indexed by applying a ratio to the worker's earnings for each year beginning with 1951. The ratio is the "indexing average wage" for the second year before the year of the worker's eligibility for benefits or death, divided by the "indexing average wage" for the year being indexed. Thus, indexed earnings for each year are computed as follows:

$$\text{Worker's Actual Earnings (Up to the Social Security Maximum) for Year to be Indexed} \times \frac{\text{Average Earnings of All Workers in Indexing Year (Second year before Eligibility or Death)}}{\text{Average Earnings of All Workers for Year being Indexed}}$$

Example. Mr. Martin earned $15,000 in 1997 and reached age 62 in 2022. The indexing average wage for 2020 (his "indexing year") was $55,628.20 and the indexing average wage for 1996 was $27,426.00. Indexed earnings for 1997 are computed as follows:

$$\$15,000 \times \frac{\$55,628.20}{\$27,426,00} = \$30,424.52$$

Indexed earnings of $30,424.52 are used in place of actual earnings for 1997 in Mr. Martin's AIME computation.

The indexing formula must be applied to earnings in each year after 1950 – up to, but not including, the "indexing year." Actual earnings are used for the indexing year and all later years.

The list below shows the indexing average wages for each year beginning with 1951. These amounts must be used in 2018 to index earnings from 1951 through the "indexing year."

1964	$4,576.32	1979	$11,479.46	1994	$23,753.53	2009	$40,711.61
1965	$4,658.72	1980	$12,513.46	1995	$24,705.66	2010	$41,673.83
1966	$4,938.36	1981	$13,773.10	1996	$25,913.90	2011	$42,971.61
1967	$5,213.44	1982	$14,531.34	1997	$27,426.00	2012	$44,321.67
1968	$5,571.76	1983	$15,239.24	1998	$28,861.44	2013	$44,888.16

1969	$5,893.76	1984	$16,135.07	1999	$30,469.84	2014	$46,481.52
1970	$6,186.24	1985	$16,822.51	2000	$32,154.82	2015	$48,098.63
1971	$6,497.08	1986	$17,321.82	2001	$32,921.92	2016	$48,642.15
1972	$7,133.80	1987	$18,426.51	2002	$33,252.09	2017	$50,321.89
1973	$7,580.16	1988	$19,334.04	2003	$34,064.95	2018	$52,145.80
1974	$8,030.76	1989	$20,099.55	2004	$35,648.55	2019	$54,099.99
1975	$8,630.92	1990	$21,027.98	2005	$36,952.94	2020	$55,628.60
1976	$9,226.48	1991	$21,811.60	2006	$38,651.41		
1977	$9,779.44	1992	$22,935.42	2007	$40,405.48		
1978	$10,556.03	1993	$23,132.67	2008	$41,334.97		

Each year, before November 1, the Social Security Administration publishes the indexing average wage for the next indexing year. The indexing average wage for 2021—the "indexing year" for those reaching age 62 or dying or becoming disabled before age 62 in 2021—is $60.575.07

It is important to remember that the "indexing year" is related to the year of first eligibility, and not necessarily to the year of entitlement. A person filing for a retirement benefit in 2023 at age 64 is first eligible in 2021 (at age 62) and the earnings record will be indexed based on the indexing year 2019 (two years prior to first eligibility).

Note

1. 20 CFR sec. 404.210.

276. How is the Average Indexed Monthly Earnings (AIME) determined?

Earnings listed in the records of the Social Security Administration—up to the annual wage limitation—are the basis for computing the AIME.

Step I. Count the number of years after 1950 (or after year person reached age 21, if later) and up to (not including) the year of attaining age 62 (or the year of disability or death, if before age 62). The number of years counted is the number of **computation elapsed years.**

Step II. Subtract five from the number of computation elapsed years when computing the AIME for retirement or death benefits. The number remaining (if less than two, use two) is the **number of computation base years** to be used in computing the AIME.

Example 1. An insured worker attained age 62 on December 2, 2021 and filed his application for retirement benefits on January 3, 2022. There are 40 elapsed years, counting the years from age 22 (1981) through 2020. The number of computation years is 35 (40 minus 5).

Example 2. An insured worker died on November 3, 2021, at the age of 59. The widow filed a claim for mother's benefits on November 10, 2021. There are 37 elapsed years beginning with 1984 (age 22) through 2020. There are 32 computation years (37 minus 5).

The number of years to be subtracted for disability benefits is scaled accordingly to the worker's age, under the following schedule:

Worker's Age in year of disability	Number of dropout years
Under 27	0
27 through 31	1
32 through 36	2
37 through 41	3
42 through 46	4
47 and over	5

Example 3. An insured woman attained age 40 in January 2022 and is found entitled to disability benefits. It is determined that her waiting period began on March 1, 2022. The elapsed years run from 2004 (age 22) through 2021 and total 18. Because the woman is 40 years old, there are 15 computation years (18 minus 3).

Step III. List Social Security earnings in the *computation base years*. (See Q 274 for Social Security earnings limits.) Computation base years are years after 1950, up to and including the year of death, or the year before entitlement to retirement or disability benefits. (A person is not entitled to benefits until an application for benefits is filed.)

Notice that the year of death is included as a computation base year, but the year in which an application is made for retirement or disability benefits is not included. However, for benefits payable for the next year after an application is made for retirement or disability benefits, the AIME for retirement or disability benefits will be recomputed, and earnings for this final year substituted for the lowest year if the result is a higher AIME.

Where benefits are estimated for entitlement at some future time, use anticipated earnings (but not over the Social Security maximum) for future computation base years.

Step IV. Index earnings in each computation base year up to, but not including, the "indexing year." (See Q 275 for instructions on how to index earnings.)

Step V. From the list of indexed earnings (and nonindexed earnings for and after the "indexing year"), select years of highest earnings (same number as found in Step II). Selected years need not be in consecutive order.

Step VI. Total indexed and nonindexed earnings for the selected years are divided by the number of months in the number of years found in Step II, dropping cents. This is the person's AIME.

If a person does not have earnings covered by Social Security in as many years as are required to be used as benefit computation years, total earnings must nevertheless be divided by the number of months in the required number of years. In other words, one or more years of zero earnings must be used. (See Q 277.)

AIME for Widow(er)'s Benefits. In computing aged widow(er)'s benefits for the spouse of a worker who died before age 62, the deceased worker's earnings are indexed to wages up to the earliest of:

(1)   two years before the worker would have reached age 62;

(2)   two years before the survivor becomes eligible for aged widow(er)'s benefits; or

(3)   two years before the survivor becomes eligible for disabled widow(er)'s benefits. This computation applies only if it results in a higher benefit than the standard computation above (including applicable cost-of-living adjustments for the deferred period before benefits start). It will provide higher benefits for many widow(er)s whose spouses died before age 62 and will assure that the widow(er)'s initial benefit reflects wage levels prevailing nearer the time that he or she comes on the rolls.

Examples

In each of the three examples provided below, the worker earned at least the Social Security maximum each year. See Q 273 for the Social Security maximum for a particular year.

Example I. Computation of AIME for person entitled to retirement benefits.

Mr. Smith, born in 1959, reaches age 62 on November 1, 2021. On November 1, he retires and applies for retirement benefits. Earnings and months in 35 years must be used in computing his AIME (40 computation elapsed years, 1981-2020, minus 5). Mr. Smith has worked in covered employment and earned at least the Social Security maximum in every year after 1977. Earnings are indexed from 1982-2019. Mr. Smith's earnings in 2020, his "indexing year" and the next two years are not indexed.

Indexed earnings that apply to each example in-whole or in-part are as follows:

1964	$48,753.43	1984	$108,893.33	2004	$114,611.27
1965	$47,891.12	1985	$109,416.18	2005	$113,207.14
1966	$62,121.44	1986	$112,703.16	2006	$113,283.30
1967	$58,843.69	1987	$110,487.04	2007	$112,161.72
1968	$61,515.21	1988	$108,185.79	2008	$114,699.85
1969	$61,515.21	1989	$111,003.13	2009	$121,936.38
1970	$58,606.82	1990	$113,396.63	2010	$119,120.95
1971	$55,802.89	1991	$113,797.85	2011	$115,501.89
1972	$58,641.07	1992	$112,477.75	2012	$115,465.31
1973	$66,225.27	1993	$115,738.28	2013	$117,735.92
1974	$76,400.75	1994	$118,583.64	2014	$117,000.00
1975	$75,935.06	1995	$115,112.40	2015	$118,500.00
1976	$77,078.94	1996	$112,464.40	2016	$118,500.00
1977	$78,424.23	1997	$110,839.77	2017	$127,200.00
1978	$77,938.67	1998	$110,158.60	2018	$128,700.00

1979	$92,724.47	1999	$110,750.77	2019	$132,900.00
1980	$96,206.11	2000	$110,151.19	2020	$137,700.00
1981	$100,231.69	2001	$113,514.47	2021	$142,800.00
1982	$103,638.15	2002	$118,677.68	2022	$147,000.00
1983	$108,889.31	2003	$118,711.23	2023	$160,200

Mr. Smith's highest AIME is obtained by selecting the highest 35 years of the 40 years from 1983 to 2023. His AIME is $9,881.93 ($4,150,411.07 ÷ 420).

His AIME will later be recomputed to include earnings in 2021 and, if this results in a higher AIME, the higher benefit will be paid beginning the following year. Thus, if Mr. Smith earned at least $160,200 in 2023, the recomputation will be based on the highest 35 years of the 41 years from 1984 to 2023, giving him an AIME of $10,886.36 ($4,572,272.75 ÷ 420).

Example II. Computation of AIME for disability benefits.

Mr. Jones, born in February 1975, is disabled as a result of an accident on October 15, 2021. He applies for disability benefits on December 1, 2021. In computing his AIME for disability benefits, 20 benefit computation years must be used (24 years in 1997-2020, less 4). Mr. Jones has worked in covered employment every year since 1993 and in each year (including the year in which he became disabled) was paid at least the maximum Social Security earnings base for that year.

Earnings in 1999-2020 are indexed. Earnings in 2020-2022 are not adjusted because they were paid in and after his "indexing year" (2020).

Mr. Jones' highest AIME is obtained by selecting the highest 20 years of the 24 years from 1997 to 2021. His AIME is $10,915,43 ($2,718,732.04 ÷ 240).

The AIME will be recomputed to include earnings in 2022 and, if this results in a higher AIME, the higher benefit will be paid beginning the following year. If Mr. Jones earned at least $160,200 in 2023, the recomputation will be based on the highest 20 years of the 25 years from 2001 to 2022, giving him an AIME of $11,995.55 ($2,878,932.04 ÷ 240).

Example III. Computation of AIME for person who dies before retirement age.

Mr. Martin dies in November 2023, at age 60 (he was born in February 1962). In computing his AIME, 33 benefit computation years must be used (38 years in 1985-2021, less 5). Mr. Martin has worked in covered employment every year since 1981 and in each year (including the year of death) was paid at least the maximum Social Security earnings base for that year. Earnings in Mr. Martin's computation base years through 2020 are indexed. Actual earnings in 2021-2023 are not adjusted because 2019 is his "indexing year".

Mr. Martin's highest AIME is obtained by selecting the highest 33 years of the 38 years from 1985 to 2023. Mr. Martin's AIME is $10,277.31 ($4,069,814.91 ÷ 396).

277. How are Average Indexed Monthly Earnings (AIME) computed for a self-employed individual whose self-employment came under Social Security after 1951?

The same formula and starting date (1951) are used as in the computation for employees. In many cases, this will mean that years of zero earnings must be used in the AIME contribution.

Example. Dr. Smith, a physician, came under Social Security in 1967. He applies for retirement benefits in 1997 when he reaches age 62. Earnings and months in 35 years must be used in computing his AIME (40 elapsed years, 1957-1996, less 5). Social Security earnings in his elapsed years are at the- maximum creditable amount in 1966-1998.

Although Dr. Smith has covered earnings in only thirty years before 1997, the total earnings for these 30 years must be divided by the number of months in 35 years (420). His AIME is computed by indexing his earnings from 1967-1994, adding actual earnings in 1995 and 1998 to total indexed earnings, and dividing by 420. Thus, his AIME is $3,329 ($1,398,443 ÷ 420).

Recomputation to include Dr. Smith's earnings in 1996 (assuming they are at least $61,200) will give him an AIME of $3,487.

278. An individual is considering early retirement at age 55. If she retires at 55 with NO earned income for the next 7 years, how will this affect her benefits at age 62?

Benefits are based on the highest 35 years of indexed earnings. The effect in this case is generally that the highest earning years are often the last years of employment; therefore, benefits may not be as high as estimated by the Social Security Administration.

279. Do Social Security benefits increase by continuing to work and contributing to social security?

It depends. When benefits are computed, Social Security uses the highest 35 years of indexed earnings. If the current earnings exceed the lowest year used in the computation, the benefits will increase. If the current earnings are lesser than the lowest year used in the computation, then there will be no change, regardless of how many years the individual works.

280. How is the Primary Insurance Amount (PIA) for a person who first becomes eligible in 2023 determined?

The Primary Insurance Amount (PIA) is determined by applying a formula to the person's Average Indexed Monthly Earnings (AIME). Where first eligibility is in calendar year 2023, the PIA is the sum of three separate percentages of portions of the AIME. It is found by taking 90 percent of the first $1,116 or less of the AIME, 32 percent of the AIME in excess of $1,116 and $6,721, and 15 percent of the AIME in excess of $6,721.

If the resulting PIA is not an even multiple of 10 cents, it is rounded to the next lower multiple of 10 cents.

The percentage figures and the dollar figures in the PIA formula will remain constant for computations and re-computations where first eligibility is in 2022, no matter when entitlement is established.

The PIA is subject to cost-of-living increases beginning with the year of first eligibility. (See Q 340.)

Example 1. Mr. Bell, born May 10, 1957, filed an application for retirement benefits on May 1, 2021. His AIME is $8,000. His PIA is calculated as follows:

$$90\% \text{ of } \$1,024 = \$921.60$$
$$32\% \text{ of } \$6,172 = \$1,975.04$$
$$15\% \text{ of } \$804 \quad = \$120.60$$

$$\$921.60 + \$1,975.04 + \$120.60 = \text{PIA of } \$3,017.24$$

Example 2. Mr. Jones, born February 13, 1958, filed an application for retirement benefits on February 10, 2021. His AIME is $600. His PIA is $540 (90 percent of $600 = $540).

Note, however, that the PIA is calculated differently if eligibility begins before 2021. The percentages in the PIA formula remain constant, but the dollar amounts differ each year. The dollar amounts in the formula since 1979 are as follows:

Eligibility Begins	AIME Dollar Amounts
1979	$180 and $1,085
1980	$194 and $1,171
1981	$211 and $1,274
1982	$230 and $1,388
1983	$254 and $1,528
1984	$267 and $1,612
1985	$280 and $1,691
1986	$297 and $1,790
1987	$310 and $1,866
1988	$319 and $1,922
1989	$339 and $2,044
1990	$356 and $2,145
1991	$370 and $2,230
1992	$387 and $2,333
1993	$401 and $2,420
1994	$422 and $2,545
1995	$426 and $2,567
1996	$437 and $2,635
1997	$455 and $2,741

Eligibility Begins	AIME Dollar Amounts
1998	$477 and $2,875
1999	$505 and $3,043
2000	$531 and $3,202
2001	$561 and $3,381
2002	$592 and $3,567
2003	$606 and $3,653
2004	$612 and $3,689
2005	$627 and $3,779
2006	$656 and $3,955
2007	$680 and $4,100
2008	$711 and $4,288
2009	$744 and $4,483
2010	$761 and $4,586
2011	$749 and $4,517
2012	$767 and $4,624
2013	$791 and $4,768
2014	$816 and $4,917
2015	$826 and $4,980
2016	$856 and $5,157
2017	$885 and $5,336
2018	$896 and $5,399
2019	$926 and $5,583
2020	$960 and $5,785
2021	$996 and $6,002
2022	$1.074 and $6,172
2023	$1,115 and $6,721

Example 3. Mr. Smith, born March 12, 1944, filed an application for retirement benefits on August 19, 2009. His AIME was $5,200. As he became eligible for retirement benefits in 2007 (the year he reached age 62), his PIA is calculated as follows:

$$90 \text{ percent of } \$711 \quad = \$639.90$$
$$32 \text{ percent of } \$4,288 \quad = \$1,372.16$$
$$15 \text{ percent of } \$201 \quad = \$30.15$$

$$\$639.90 + \$1,372.16 + \$30.15 = \$2,042.21 = \text{PIA of } \$2,042$$

This amount was subject to increases in December 2009 or 2010, a 3.6 percent increase in December 2011, a 1.7 percent increase in December 2012, a 1.5 percent increase in December 2013, a 1.7 percent increase in December 2014, no increase in December 2015, a 0.3 percent increase in December 2016, and a 2.0 percent increase in 2017, a 2.8 percent increase in 2018, a 1.6 percent increase in 2019, and a 1.3 percent increase in 2020. Thus, his PIA is $2,042 for December 2009, $2,042 for December 2010, $2,077 for December 2011, $2,108 for December 2012, $2,139 for December 2013, $2,176 for December 2014, $2,176 for December 2015, $2,182 for December 2016, $2,226 for 2017, $2,288 for 2018, $2,333 for 2019, $2,469 for 2020 and $2,533 for 2021.

Formula for Workers Receiving a Pension from Work Not Covered by Social Security

If a worker receives a pension from a job not covered by Social Security, and the worker also has enough Social Security credits to be eligible for retirement or disability benefits, a different formula may be used to figure the Social Security benefit. This formula results in a lower benefit. But the worker's pension from the job not covered by Social Security is not affected by this change.

The reason a different formula is used is that Social Security benefits are weighted in favor of low earners (i.e., low earners' benefits represent a higher percentage of their prior earnings than do the benefits of workers with higher earnings). If the benefits of people who work for only a portion of their careers in jobs covered by Social Security were computed as if they had been long-term, low-wage workers, these individuals would receive the advantage of the weighted benefit formula. Instead, a modified formula eliminates this unintended windfall.

The modified formula does not affect survivor benefits. It affects only workers who reach age 62 or become disabled after 1985 and first become eligible after 1985 for a monthly pension based in whole or in part on work not covered by Social Security. A worker is considered eligible to receive a pension if he meets the requirements of the pension, even if he continues to work.

The modified formula does not apply if:

- the worker is a federal worker hired after December 31, 1983;

- the worker was employed on January 1, 1984, by a nonprofit organization that was mandatorily covered under Social Security on that date;

- the worker has 30 or more years of substantial earnings under Social Security;

- the worker's only pension from work not covered by Social Security is based solely on railroad employment;

- the worker's only work not under Social Security was before 1957.

The modified formula is used in figuring the Social Security benefit beginning with the first month for which the worker receives both a Social Security benefit and a pension from work not covered under Social Security.

Social Security benefits are normally based on the worker's AIME. In figuring benefits, the first part of the average earnings is multiplied by 90 percent; the second part is multiplied by

32 percent; and any part of the AIME remaining is multiplied by 15 percent. In the modified benefit formula, the 90 percent used in the first factor is reduced.

Benefits for workers first eligible in 2023 who use the modified formula are determined by taking 40 percent of the first $1,116 of Average Indexed Monthly Earnings; 32 percent of AIME from $1,116 and $6,721; and 15 percent of AIME above $6,721.

The reduction was phased in gradually for workers who reached 62 or became disabled in 1986 through 1989. The phase-in applies as follows:

Year Person Became 62 or Disabled	First Factor
1986	80 percent
1987	70 percent
1988	60 percent
1989	50 percent
1990 or later	40 percent

Workers with 30 or more years of substantial Social Security coverage are not affected by the modified benefit formula. Workers with 21 to 29 years of Social Security coverage (as defined in Q 288) will have the first factor reduced as follows:

Years of Coverage	First Factor
30 or more	90 percent
29	85 percent
28	80 percent
27	75 percent
26	70 percent
25	65 percent
24	60 percent
23	55 percent
22	50 percent
21	45 percent
20 or less	40 percent

In this formula, a worker is credited with a year of coverage if earnings equal or exceed the figures shown for each year in the following chart.

Year	Earnings	Year	Earnings
1937-50	$900	1994	11,250
1951-54	900	1995	11,325
1955-58	1,050	1996	11,625
1959-65	1,200	1997	12,150
1966-67	1,650	1998	12,675
1968-71	1,950	1999	13,425
1972	2,250	2000	14,175
1973	2,700	2001	14,925

Year	Earnings	Year	Earnings
1974	3,300	2002	15,750
1975	3,525	2003	16,125
1976	3,825	2004	16,275
1977	4,125	2005	16,725
1978	4,425	2006	17,475
1979	4,725	2007	18,150
1980	5,100	2008	18,975
1981	5,550	2009	19,800
1982	6,075	2010	19,800
1983	6,675	2011	19,800
1984	7,050	2012	20,475
1985	7,425	2013	21,075
1986	7,875	2014	21,750
1987	8,175	2015	22,050
1988	8,400	2016	22,050
1989	8,925	2017	23,625
1990	9,525	2018	23,850
1991	$9,900	2019	24,675
1992	10,350	2020	25,575
1993	10,725	2021	26,550
		2022	27,300

Numbers for 2023 are not yet available. A guarantee is provided to protect workers with relatively low "noncovered" pensions. It provides that the reduction in the Social Security benefit under the modified formula cannot be more than one-half of that part of the pension attributable to earnings after 1956 not covered by Social Security. Effective for benefits based on applications filed in or after November 1989, the amount of the pension considered when determining the windfall guarantee is the amount payable in the first month of concurrent entitlement to both Social Security and the pension from noncovered employment.

281. How is the Primary Insurance Amount (PIA) determined after 2017?

For individuals who attain age sixty-two or become disabled or die before age 62 in any calendar year after 2017, the PIA will be determined by formulas using the same percentage amounts listed in Q 280 above. However, the bend points (dollar amounts) will be adjusted yearly as average wages rise or fall.

On or before November 1 of each year, the Social Security Administration must publish in the Federal Register the bend points (dollar amounts) that will be used in computing the PIA for those eligible in the year after publication. The bend points for 2022 are $1,042 and $6,172 and the bend points for 2023 are $1,116 and $6,721.

Remember that the bend points used in calculating an individual's PIA are determined from the year the individual first became eligible for the benefits and not necessarily the year first entitled to benefits.

282. How is the PIA computed for an individual who was previously entitled to a disability benefit?

The PIA is not always computed under the "wage indexing" benefit computation method when a worker reaches age 62 or becomes disabled. Other benefit computations may be required if the worker was previously entitled to a disability benefit.

The PIA will be computed or recomputed under the simplified old-start benefit computation method if the individual was entitled to a disability benefit before 1979 and fewer than twelve months have passed between the prior entitlement to the disability benefit and current entitlement to benefits.

If an individual has been entitled to a disability benefit either before or after 1979—but within twelve months of current entitlement to retirement, disability, or death benefits—the PIA is the largest of the following:

(1)   The PIA (including one computed under the simplified old-start benefit computation method) that was used in figuring the individual's previous disability benefit, increased by any cost-of-living or general benefit increases that occurred since the individual was last entitled

(2)   The special minimum PIA (See Q 270)

(3)   A recomputation of the former PIA, to consider earnings after the disability entitlement ended

If an individual's entitlement to a disability benefit ended more than twelve months before his current entitlement to benefits, a new PIA must be computed under the "wage indexing" method. The PIA will be the higher of the recalculated PIA or the individual's PIA during the last month of his former entitlement to disability benefits (without regard to any interim cost-of-living increases).

283. How is the Maximum Family Benefit determined under the wage indexing method in 2023?

The following formula determines the Maximum Family Benefit for those reaching age 62 or dying before age 62 in 2022:

(1)   150 percent of the first $1.425 of PIA; plus

(2)   272 percent of PIA over $1.425 through $2,056; plus

(3)   134 percent of PIA over $2.056 though $2,682; plus

(4)   175 percent of PIA over $2.682.

The result is the family maximum. (The final figure should be rounded to the next lower multiple of $ .10 if not an even multiple of $ .10). The Maximum Family Benefit is subject to cost-of-living increases beginning with the year of first eligibility (see Q 340).

The Maximum Family Benefit is calculated differently if eligibility begins before 2015. The percentages in the Maximum Family Benefit formula remain constant, but the dollar amounts differ each year. The dollar amounts in the formula since 1979 are as follows:

Eligibility Begins	PIA Dollar Amounts
1979	$230, $332, and $433
1980	$248, $358, and $467
1981	$270, $390, and $508
1982	$294, $425, and $554
1983	$324, $468, and $610
1984	$342, $493, and $643
1985	$358, $517, and $675
1986	$379, $548, and $714
1987	$396, $571, and $745
1988	$407, $588, and $767
1989	$433, $626, and $816
1990	$455, $656, and $856
1991	$473, $682, and $890
1992	$495, $714, and $931
1993	$513, $740, and $966
1994	$539, $779, and $1,016
1995	$544, $785, and $1,024
1996	$559, $806, and $1,052
1997	$581, $839, and $1,094
1998	$609, $880, and $1,147
1999	$645, $931, and $1,214
2000	$679, $980, and $1,278
2001	$717, $1,034, and $1,349
2002	$756, $1,092, and $1,424
2003	$774, $1,118, and $1,458
2004	$782, $1,129, and $1,472
2005	$801, $1,156, and $1,508
2006	$838, $1,210, and $1,578
2007	$869, $1,255, and $1,636

Eligibility Begins	PIA Dollar Amounts
2008	$909, $1,312, and $1,711
2009	$950, $1,372, and $1,789
2010	$972, $1,403, and $1,830
2011	$957, $1,382, and $1,803
2012	$980, $1,415, and $1,845
2013	$1,011, $1,459, and $1,903
2014	$1,042, $1,505, and $1,962
2015	$1,056, $1,524, and $1,987
2016	$1,093, $1,578, and $2,058
2017	$1,131, $1,633, and $2,130
2018	$1,145, $1,652, and $2,155
2019	$1,184, $1,708, and $2,228
2020	$1,226, $1,770 and $2,309
2021	$1,272, $1,837 and $2,395
2022	$1,038, $1,889 and $2,463
2023	$1,425, $2,056, and $2,682

Disability

For a disabled worker and family, benefits may not exceed the lesser of 85 percent of the Average Indexed Monthly Earnings (AIME) on which the worker's disability benefit is based, or 150 percent of the disability benefit payable to the worker alone. However, in no case will a family's benefit be reduced below 100 percent of the benefit that would be payable to the worker alone.

This limit on family disability benefits applies to workers who first become entitled to disability benefits after June 30, 1980. A worker who first becomes entitled to disability benefits in the first six months of 1980 will compute the maximum family benefit in the same manner as those who reach age 62 or die in 1980.

> *Example.* Mr. Smith becomes entitled to disability benefits on October 1, 2020. His AIME is $2,000 and he would be eligible to receive $1,136 a month in disability payments on his own. However, Mr. Smith also has a wife and a 10-year-old child. His maximum family benefit is the lesser of 85 percent of his AIME (85 percent × $2,000 = $1,700), or 150 percent of his disability benefit (150 percent × $1,136 = $1,704). As 150 percent of his disability benefit is more than 85 percent of his AIME, his maximum family benefit is $1,700.

284. How is the Maximum Family Benefit determined under the simplified old-start benefit computation method?

Maximum Family Benefits applicable under the law in December 1978 remain in effect for those individuals who attained age 62, became disabled, or died before January 1979. Maximum Family Benefits—based on the worker's Average Monthly Earnings (AME) —are listed in the June 1978 benefit table of the Social Security Administration.

See Table 13. Consumer Price Index increases after June 1978 must be applied to Maximum Family Benefits listed in Table 13.

285. How are individual benefit rates reduced to bring the total amount payable within the family maximum limit?

Adjustment of individual benefit rates because of the family maximum limit is required, whenever the total monthly benefits of all the beneficiaries payable on one Social Security account exceed the family maximum that can be paid on that record for the month. All the benefit rates, except the retirement or disability benefit and benefits payable to a divorced spouse or surviving divorced spouse, must be reduced to bring the total monthly benefits payable within the family maximum. This means that, even though a beneficiary's benefit rate is originally set by law as a percentage of the insured person's PIA, the actual benefit paid may be less when the total monthly benefits payable on one earnings record exceed the family maximum prescribed by law.

The entitlement of a divorced spouse to a spouse's benefit or a surviving divorced spouse's benefit does not result in reducing the benefits of other categories of beneficiaries. Likewise, the entitlement of a legal spouse where a deemed spouse is also entitled will not affect the benefit of other beneficiaries entitled in the month. The other dependents or survivors' benefits are reduced for the maximum, not considering the existence of the divorced spouse, surviving divorced spouse, or the legal spouse. Nor are the benefits of the divorced spouse, surviving divorced spouse, or the legal spouse ever reduced because of the family maximum. (See Q 115 and Q 191.)

Adjustment for the family maximum is made by proportionately reducing all the monthly benefits subject to the family maximum on the Social Security earnings record (except for retired worker's or disabled worker's benefits) to bring the total monthly benefits payable within the limit applicable in the particular case.

The individual reduced benefit rates are figured as follows:

(1) If the insured person is alive, the insured person's benefit is subtracted from the applicable family maximum amount. Any remainder is divided among the other persons entitled to benefits on the insured person's Social Security earnings record.

(2) If the insured worker is dead and all monthly benefits are based on the same percentage (e.g., all are based on 100 percent of the PIA, or all are based on 75 percent), the applicable family maximum is divided equally among all those who are entitled to benefits on the Social Security earnings record.

(3) If the insured person is deceased and some benefits are based on 100 percent, some on 82.5 percent, and some on 75 percent of the PIA, each beneficiary is paid a proportionate share of the applicable family maximum based on that beneficiary's original benefit rate.

This adjustment is made after any deductions that may be applicable. Thus, where: (1) reduction for the family maximum is required, and (2) a benefit payable to someone other than the worker must be withheld, the reapportionment for the maximum is made as if the beneficiary whose benefit must be withheld were not entitled to the amounts withheld.

> *Example 1.* Mr. Edwards dies before age 62 in 2022, leaving a widow aged 35 and two small children. His AIME is $2,500, and his PIA is $1,296. The full benefit for the widow and each child is $972 (75 percent of $1,296). However, the sum of the full benefits is $2,916 (3 × $972), which exceeds $2,192 – the maximum family benefit for a PIA of $1,296. Thus, the benefit actually payable to each beneficiary is $730 (1/3 of $2,192).

When a person is entitled to benefits based on two different earnings records, only the amount of benefits actually paid on a record is considered in determining how much to reduce monthly benefits because of the family maximum. Any amount not paid because of a person's entitlement on another earnings record is not included. The effect of this provision is to permit payment of up to the full maximum benefits to other beneficiaries who are not subject to a deduction or reduction.

> *Example 2.* Mr. Smith, his wife, and two children are entitled to benefits. Mr. Smith's PIA is $1,250 and his family maximum is $2,066. Due to the maximum limit, the monthly benefits for his wife and children must be reduced to $272 each ($816 ÷ 3). Their original rates (50 percent of Mr. Smith's benefit) are $625 each. Mr. Smith's children are also entitled to benefits on their own records. One child is entitled to $390 per month and the other child is entitled to $280 per month. This causes a reduction in the benefit to the first child to $118, and the benefit to the second child to $7.

In computing the total benefits payable on Mr. Smith's record, only the benefits actually paid to the children, or $125, are considered. This allows payment of an additional amount to Mrs. Smith, increasing her benefit to $625.00 (50 percent of her husband's benefit). This is how the calculation works:

(1)   The amount available under the family maximum for the wife and children is $816 $2,066 – $1,250 = 816).

(2)   Subtract the amount that is due the children after a reduction due to entitlement to their own benefits ($125).

(3)   The amount available for Mrs. Smith is $816 ($2,066 – $1,250 = 816).

(4)   The amount payable to Mrs. Smith is $625, which is the lesser of $625 and $691.

286. If one or more members of a family cease to be entitled to benefits, will the benefits of the remaining beneficiaries be increased?

Yes, if their benefits have been reduced because of the family maximum limit.

> *Example.* Mr. Jones dies in 2022, leaving a widow and two children, aged six and twelve, entitled to survivor's benefits. His AIME is $1,800, his PIA is $1,072, and the maximum family benefit is $1,608. As the full benefit for each family member is $804 (75 percent of $1,072), the total of all three benefits exceeds the family maximum of $1,608 (3 × $804 = $2,412). Initially then, each beneficiary receives only $536

(1/3 of $1,608, rounded to the next lowest dollar). Eventually, the older child reaches age eighteen, and his benefits end. The widow and younger child then receive their full benefits (the widow until the child attains age sixteen, and the child until attaining age eighteen or, if enrolled in a full-time elementary or secondary school program, upon attaining age nineteen) because the sum of these two benefits does not exceed the maximum family benefit.

Transitional Guarantee Benefit Method

287. What does the transitional guarantee benefit method work?

To provide a degree of protection for workers nearing retirement when decoupling was implemented, those who reach age 62 after 1978 and before 1984 are guaranteed a retirement benefit no lower than they would have received under the simplified old-start benefit computation method as of December 1978. The benefit computed under this method is known as the transitional guarantee PIA.

Those eligible for retirement benefits in the transition period are eligible for the larger of the PIA under the "wage indexing" benefit computation method or the transitional guarantee method.

The PIA under the transitional guarantee method is based on the June 1978 benefit table (see Table 13). The benefit table will not be subject to future automatic benefit increases, but an individual's retirement benefits will automatically increase beginning with age 62 for cost-of-living adjustments.

To be eligible for the guarantee, an individual must:

(1)   have had income credited for one year prior to 1979; and

(2)   must not have been disabled prior to 1979.

The transitional guarantee does not apply to disability computations, even when the disability begins after age 62. It does apply to survivors of individuals who attain age 62 in the transition period and who die in or after the month they reach age 62.

The transitional guarantee method is basically the same as the simplified old-start benefit computation method, but earnings in the year in which the worker reached age 62 and any year thereafter may not be included in the benefit computation.

Example. Mr. White, born 1917, reaches age 62 on October 7, 1979. He retires one day later and applies for retirement benefits. Earnings and months in 23 years must be used in computing his AME (28 computation elapsed years, 1951-1978, less 5). Mr. White has worked in covered employment and earned at least the Social Security maximum in every year after 1950. Social Security earnings in his computation base years are therefore as follows: $3,600 (1951-1954); $4,200 (1955-1958); $4,800 (1959-1965); $6,600 (1966-1967); $7,800 (1968-1971); $9,900 (1972); $10,800 (1973); $13,200 (1974); $14,100 (1975); $15,300 (1976); $16,500 (1977); $17,700 (1978). Mr. White's highest AIME is obtained by selecting the 23 years 1956-1978. His AME is $678 ($187,200 ÷ 276), and his PIA is $486.10.

The PIA computed above under the transitional guarantee method will be used if it is higher than Mr. White's PIA computed under the "wage indexing" method.

The PIA under the transitional guarantee method is subject to cost-of-living increases beginning with the month applicable for the year of first eligibility. A worker who attains age 62 in 1982 is entitled to a transitional guarantee PIA determined from the PIA Table printed in 1978. The PIA was not affected by cost-of-living benefit increases in 1979, 1980, or 1981, but the June 1982 cost-of-living increase and subsequent increases apply.

Minimum and Maximum Single Benefits
Increase in Benefits

288. Do benefits increase when the cost-of-living increases?

The Social Security Act provides for automatic increases in benefits and in the maximum earnings base (earnings subject to Social Security taxes) due to changing economic conditions.

The automatic increases in benefits are determined by increases in the Consumer Price Index for All Urban Wage Earners and Clerical Workers prepared by the Department of Labor. (But see Q 342) The increases in the maximum earnings base are determined from increases in average nationwide wages if there has been a cost-of-living increase in benefits for the preceding December. (See Q 410).

Benefits have been raised by the following percentages since 1977:

Month/Year	Increase in Benefits
July 1977	5.9%
July 1978	6.5%
July 1979	9.9%
July 1980	14.3%
July 1981	11.2%
July 1982	7.4%
January 1984	3.5%
January 1985	3.5%
January 1986	3.1%
January 1987	1.3%
January 1988	4.2%
January 1989	4.0%
January 1990	4.7%
January 1991	5.4%
January 1992	3.7%
January 1993	3.0%

Month/Year	Increase in Benefits
January 1994	2.6%
January 1995	2.8%
January 1996	2.6%
January 1997	2.9%
January 1998	2.1%
January 1999	1.3%
January 2000	2.5%
January 2001	3.5%
January 2002	2.6%
January 2003	1.4%
January 2004	2.1%
January 2005	2.7%
January 2006	4.1%
January 2007	3.3%
January 2008	2.3%
January 2009	5.8%
January 2010	0.0%
January 2011	0.0%
January 2012	3.6%
January 2013	1.7%
January 2014	1.5%
January 2015	1.7%
January 2016	0.0%
January 2017	0.3%
January 2018	2.0%
January 2019	2.8%
January 2020	1.6%
January 2021	1.3%
January 2022	5.9%
January 2023	N.N%

There can be no cost-of-living computation quarter in any calendar year if, in the year prior to that year, a general benefit increase has been enacted or become effective.

The amount of excess earnings that results in loss of benefits will be increased whenever there is an automatic cost-of-living benefit increase and nationwide average wages have risen (the increase is based on the rise in average wages). (See Q 360).

289. Who is entitled to a cost-of-living benefit increase?

Individuals using the "wage indexing" benefit computation method are entitled to cost-of-living increases, beginning with the year of first eligibility (the year of attaining age 62, or disability or death before age 62). The PIA is calculated for the year of first eligibility and the cost-of-living increases in that year and subsequent years will be added. As long as eligibility exists in any month of the year, the PIA will be increased by the automatic-benefit increase percentage applicable to the check sent in January of the following year.

> *Example.* Mr. Johnson attains age 62 in November 2023 and waits until January 2025 to apply for benefits. The PIA is calculated and will be increased by the automatic cost-of-living benefit increases applicable to December 2023 and December 2024. The resultant PIA will be payable in the benefit paid for January 2025.

The automatic cost-of-living increase provisions in effect in December 1978 continue to apply for those who reached age 62, became disabled, or died before January 1979. A revised benefit table is published each year by the Social Security Administration. (See Table 13.) These revised tables are not applicable to individuals who become eligible for benefits after 1978, except those using the transitional guarantee.

Beneficiaries using the transitional guarantee will also receive cost-of-living increases beginning with the year of first eligibility. (See Q 287).

290. How will the cost-of-living stabilizer affect future cost-of-living benefit increases?

The Social Security Amendments of 1983 include a provision designed to protect the system from the kinds of trust-fund depletions that occur when price increases outpace wage gains. This stabilizer provision goes into effect if reserves in the trust fund providing retirement, disability, and survivor benefits fall below 20 percent of what is needed to provide benefits for a year. When the stabilizer takes effect, automatic cost-of-living benefit increases are based on the lower of the percentage increase in the Consumer Price Index (CPI) or the percentage rise in the nationwide average wage.

Later, if the fund reserves exceed 32 percent of what is estimated to be needed for a year, recipients will be entitled to extra cost-of-living increases, to compensate for losses in inflation protection resulting from having benefit increases tied to wage levels in the past (if this occurred).

Reduction in Benefits

291. When a person elects to start receiving a retirement benefit before full retirement age, how is the benefit reduced?

A fully insured worker can start receiving retirement benefits the month after she reaches age 62 (or the month she reaches age 62 if his or her birthday is on the first or second of the month), or for any month thereafter (see Q 53). However, if the worker elects to start receiving benefits before full retirement age, the benefit is reduced.

In making the reduction, the worker's PIA must first be determined. The PIA is then reduced by 5/9 of 1 percent (1/180) for each of the first 36 months that the worker is under full retirement age when the benefits commence and by 5/12 of 1 percent (1/240) for each such month in excess of 36. (The amount of the reduction, if not an even multiple of 10 cents, is increased to the next higher multiple of 10 cents.) For example, if the worker's PIA is $1,000, and he elects to retire and start receiving benefits 24 months before his full retirement age, his benefit will be reduced by $133.33 (24 × 1/180 × $1,000), giving him a monthly benefit of $866.67. Ordinarily, he will continue to receive the reduced benefit even after full retirement age (but see Recomputation of Benefits, Q 299).

292. If the spouse of a retired worker starts receiving a spouse's benefit before full retirement age, how is the benefit reduced?

First, the spouse's full benefit is determined. This is one-half of the retired worker's PIA. (Where the retired worker is receiving a reduced retirement benefit starting before full retirement age, the spouse's full benefit is computed as 50 percent of the retired worker's PIA, not 50 percent of the reduced benefit.) The spouse's full benefit is then reduced by 25/36 of 1 percent (1/144) for each of the first 36 months that the spouse is under full retirement age when benefits commence and by 5/12 of 1 percent (1/240) for each month in excess of 36. (The amount of the reduction, if not an even multiple of 10 cents, is increased to the next higher multiple of 10 cents.)

For example, suppose that the retired worker's PIA is $1,000, and the spouse's full benefit is $500 (1/2 of $1,000). If the spouse takes the benefit exactly 24 months before his full retirement age, the full benefit will be reduced by $83.33 (24 × 1/144 × $500), giving the spouse a monthly benefit of $416.67 ($500 - $83.33). If a spouse starts receiving benefits for the month 36 months before full retirement age, the benefit under this formula will be 75 percent of the full benefit, or 37.5 percent of the retired worker's PIA. Ordinarily, the spouse will continue to receive the reduced benefit even after normal retirement age (but see Recomputation of Benefits, Q 299). (See also Table 10.)

293. If a widow(er) elects to start receiving a widow(er)'s benefit before full retirement age, how is the benefit reduced?

The widow(er)'s full benefit must first be determined. The full benefit (to which he would be entitled by waiting until full retirement age) is 100 percent of the deceased spouse's PIA. When the full retirement age was 65, this benefit was reduced by 19/40 of 1 percent (19/4000) for each month that the widow(er) was under full retirement age when benefits began.

For example, suppose that the deceased spouse's PIA was $1,000. The widow(er)'s full benefit would have been $1,000. However, if the widow(er) elected to receive benefits starting with the month of his 60th birthday (60 months before age 65), the full widow(er)'s benefit would have been reduced by $285 (60 × 19/4000 × $1,000), resulting in a benefit of $715 ($1,000 − $285). The amount of the reduction, if not an even multiple of 10 cents, is increased to the next higher multiple of 10 cents. A benefit beginning with the month of a widow(er)'s 60th birthday accordingly will equal 71.5 percent of the spouse's PIA.

When the full retirement age is more than 65, the 71.5 percent reduction at age 60 remains unchanged, but the reduction factor will be different (based on 71.5 percent at age 60 and 100 percent at full retirement age). Ordinarily, the widow(er) will continue to receive the reduced benefit, even after full retirement age (but see Recomputation of Benefits, Q 299). (See Table 11 for widow(er)'s reduced benefits.)

If the widow(er)'s deceased spouse started receiving benefits before full retirement age, the widow(er)'s benefit cannot exceed the deceased spouse's reduced benefit or, if larger, 82.5 percent of his PIA.

The benefit of a disabled widow(er) who starts receiving benefits before age 60 is equal to 71.5 percent of his spouse's PIA. (See Q 198.)

294. How do the benefit reduction rules affect a high-earning spouse who dies after reaching Full Retirement Age (FRA) with a surviving spouse who is younger than Full Retirement Age?

The "Reduction Factor" depends upon the year that the widow attains Full Retirement Age (FRA). If the FRA is age sixty-six, the reduction factor is the original benefit multiplied by the number of months that benefits are taken before FRA multiplied by 19 multiplied by .01 divided by 48.

For example: The original benefit is $2,000. The widow takes benefits at age 60 and her FRA is 66. Her Reduction Factor is 72 (the 72 months from age 60 until her FRA of 66). Her benefits will be:

- $2,000 × 72 (the Reduction Factor) × 19 multiplied by .01/48 = $570

- The spouse will receive $1,430 as a result of the Reduction Factor ($2,000 − $570 = $1,430)

295. How are benefits figured if a beneficiary starts receiving a reduced retirement benefit and later becomes entitled to a larger spouse's benefit?

The beneficiary will continue to receive the retirement benefit reduced in the regular manner (see Q 291). When he becomes entitled to the larger spouse's benefit, he will receive, in addition, a partial spouse's benefit. This benefit will be based on the difference between a spouse's full benefit (1/2 of his spouse's PIA) and the beneficiary's PIA. If he becomes entitled to the spouse's benefits at or after full retirement age, the spouse's benefit will equal this difference. If he becomes entitled to the spouse's benefit before full retirement age, this difference must be reduced by 25/36 of 1 percent (1/144) for each of the first 36 months that he is under full retirement age when the spouse's benefits commence, and 5/12 of 1 percent (1/240) for each month in excess of 36.

Recomputation of Benefits

296. Under what circumstances are benefits recomputed?

Automatic recomputation of benefits is provided each year to take account of any earnings a beneficiary might have that would increase his benefit amount. Also, the recomputation takes into account the final year's earnings in the case of retirement and disability benefits. The recomputation for a living beneficiary is effective with January of the year following the one in which the earnings were received. A recomputation affecting survivor's benefits is effective with the month of death.

The "wage indexing" computation method must be used to recompute the PIA for an individual who has earnings after 1978, if the PIA was originally computed (or could have been computed) under this method.

The actual dollar amounts in the records of the Social Security Administration for the year of entitlement and each later year will annually be compared with the earnings in the base years that were used in the last computation. Higher earnings in any year that was not used in the last computation will be substituted for one or more years of lower earnings that were used, and the PIA will be recomputed.

The PIA will be recomputed using the same "bend points" and "indexing year" that applied when current eligibility was established. (See Q 280.) Recomputation must result in a PIA increase of at least one dollar to be effective.

A PIA computed using the transitional guarantee benefit computation method or the simplified old-start benefit computation method—based on eligibility after 1978—cannot be recomputed to include earnings in or after the year of current eligibility.

---

297. If a person is simultaneously entitled to two or more benefits, which benefit will be paid?

As a general rule, Social Security will pay the higher (or highest amount). There are a number of situations where a person may be entitled to more than one Social Security benefit at the same time.

For example, a woman may be entitled to a both a parent's benefit on her deceased child's account and to a spouse's benefit on her husband's account. However, only the HIGHER benefit will be paid, except when one of the benefits is a retirement or disability benefit. The lower benefit cannot be paid, even though the higher benefit is not payable for one or more months. But if the higher benefit is terminated, the lower benefit will be reinstalled automatically.

If a person is entitled to retirement or disability benefits and to a higher benefit, he or she will receive the retirement or disability benefit plus the difference between this benefit and the higher one. Payment, however, may be made in a single check. If one benefit is not payable for one or more months, the other benefit may be payable. For example, if a spouse's benefit is not payable for some months because of the worker's excess earnings, he or she will nevertheless receive a retirement benefit.

A child may be entitled to child's benefits on more than one earnings record, for example, his father's record and his mother's record. A child can receive the benefit based on the PIA that will result in the highest original benefit. However, if the highest original benefit is payable on the lowest PIA, he is paid on this account only if it would not reduce (after the reduction for the family maximum) the benefit of any beneficiary because of his entitlement.

Disability Freeze

298. How does a period of disability affect retirement and survivor's benefits?

A person who has an established period of disability will have his or her earnings record "frozen" during the period of disability. This means that the years of disability need not be included in computing his or her AIME. Otherwise, if the worker died or recovered and returned to work before he or she reached retirement age, the years of zero earnings in his or her period of disability might reduce his or her PIA for retirement or survivors' benefits. In figuring the number of years that must be used in computing the worker's AIME, a year which fell wholly or partly within a period of disability is not counted. However, a year that is partly within a period of disability will be used as a computation base year, if inclusion of earnings for that year will produce a higher AIME.

Calculating the Exact Benefit Amount

299. In calculating the exact amount of each monthly benefit, how must the figures be rounded?

Benefits for members of a worker's family, if not an even multiple of one dollar, are rounded (after deducting the premium for Medical Insurance under Medicare, if any) to the next lower multiple of one dollar. For example, if the PIA of a deceased worker is $1,042.52, a child's survivor benefit is figured as $781.89 (75 percent of $1,042.52). However, this amount will be rounded to $781.00 (the next lower multiple of one dollar).

Government Pension Offset and
Windfall Elimination Provision

300. What is the Government Pension Offset?

The Government Pension Offset (GPO) is a reduction in the Social Security dependent benefits paid to the spouse (including the surviving spouse or, in certain circumstances, divorced spouse) of a Social Security contributor. Some of an employee's spousal Social Security benefit may be offset if the employee has a government pension from work not covered by Social Security.

The offset does not apply to the employee's own Social Security benefit, only the benefit that comes from a spouse's employment. If the Government Pension Offset applies, the spousal Social Security benefit will be reduced by two-thirds of any Federal pension based on employment not covered by Social Security. It applies to a spouse who also receives a federal, state, or local government pension based on the spouse's own earnings for which no Social Security taxes were paid.

Some employees are exempt from the Government Pension Offset. They are employees who are automatically covered by the Federal Employees Retirement System (FERS), Civil Service Retirement System (CSRS) Offset, and those who elected to transfer to the FERS before January 1, 1988, or during the belated transfer period that ended June 30, 1988. Employees who were covered by the CSRS and who elected FERS coverage after June 30, 1988, must have five years of Federal employment covered by Social Security to be exempt from the offset.

301. Who does the Government Pension Offset (GPO) affect?

There are three general criteria:

- **First**, you work or worked for a state or local government in non-SS-covered employment.

- **Second**, you are entitled to a government pension from that employment.

  o SSA deems you to be "entitled to a pension" when you file an application for the pension and a benefit is payable.[1]

- **Third**, you are entitled to a Social Security survivor/dependent benefit from a marriage that lasted ten years or longer.

The GPO reduces Social Security survivor/dependent benefits by two-thirds of the person's public pension. It can cause a total loss of Social Security benefits.

Note

1. Social Security Administration, Program Operations Manual System, https://secure.ssa.gov/poms.nsf/lnx/0202608100 (last accessed September 1, 2022).

302. Does the Government Pension Offset reduce an individual's Social Security benefit from their own work?

No. The GPO affects a person's dependent/survivor benefit only. The Windfall Elimination Provision is the provision that can result in a reduction of the Social Security benefit the individual has earned from Social Security covered employment.

303. Does the Government Pension Offset affect a disability benefit?

Yes. If an individual is entitled to a dependent/survivor benefit based on a spouse's disability, the GPO applies.

304. Can the GPO reduce a dependent or survivor benefit to zero?

Yes. This is referred to as a "total GPO offset".

305. Does ineligibility for a dependent or survivor benefit affect Medicare eligibility?

No. An individual is still eligible for Medicare at age 65 based on a spouse's Social Security covered employment even if the individual is not eligible for it from their own employment.

306. If an individual has a government pension from a non-Social Security military reserve pension, is it subject to the GPO?

No. Congress has specifically exempted that type of service from the GPO.

307. What happens to an individual that retires from non-Social Security employment and begins to draw a government pension and then begins work in a Social Security eligible position?

The SSA will still reduce survivor/dependent benefit by the applicable amount.

308. What happens to an individual that takes a government pension from non-Social Security employment as a lump sum?

The SSA will determine how much the non-Social Security government pension would have been if it were paid monthly and then subsequently reduce the monthly survivor/dependent benefit accordingly.

309. Can both the Government Pension Offset and the Windfall Elimination Provision reduce Social Security benefits?

Yes. The Social Security retirement that was earned as well as dependent/survivor benefit may be reduced if:

- the individual has some Social Security-covered work and non-Social Security-covered work; and

- the individual is or was married.

Example: During Barry's career, he works both in the private sector, where he was covered by Social Security, and for a government agency in a non-Social Security position. Barry's wife spends her entire career in employment covered by Social Security. Barry reaches the age at which he can draw a Social Security benefit. He goes to the local SSA office to apply for his benefits and learns that because of the WEP, Barry's Social Security benefit is reduced unless he had thirty or more years of Social Security coverage. Because of the GPO, Barry's dependent benefit from his wife is either reduced or eliminated. If Barry had not worked in the non-Social Security role for the government agency, the reductions would not have applied.

310. What was the rationale for the GPO?

In 1977, Congress studied the Social Security Act and took note of the dual entitlement rule, which forbids an individual from receiving both a Social Security benefit from his/her own work and a Social Security dependent/survivor benefit. The GPO was enacted in 1977, after the Supreme Court ruled that men were not required to prove that they received at least one-half of their support from their wives in order to qualify for husband's or widower's benefits. (Women were not subject to an explicit dependency test, as they were presumed to be dependent on their husbands.) This ruling made hundreds of thousands of male retirees who worked in non-covered government employment immediately eligible for Social Security benefits as spouses or widowers, adding hundreds of millions of dollars annually to the cost of the program and raising questions about whether these were unnecessary or "windfall" benefits.

To prevent the payment of full Social Security spousal benefits to people receiving a pension from noncovered government employment, Congress created the GPO as part of the Social Security Amendments of 1977 (P.L. 95-216), which provided that 100 percent of the noncovered government pension be subtracted from the Social Security spousal benefit. The dollar-for-dollar reduction implicitly assumed exact equivalency between government pensions and Social Security worker benefits. However, government pensions often combined the elements of a worker's Social Security benefit and a pension intended to supplement Social Security. Although a spouse covered under Social Security may have his or her spousal benefits reduced under the dual entitlement rule, that rule considers only the worker's Social Security benefits and does not count income the worker may have from a private pension.

Congress decided that someone with both a government pension and a survivor/dependent benefit violated the dual entitlement rule. The rationale for this conclusion was reached by equating the government pension with a Social Security retirement benefit. Congress could have just as easily determined that the government pension was analogous to a pension from a private sector employment or Social Security covered work for a state or local government, in which case no dual entitlement would arise, but did not. In response to this criticism, Congress lowered the GPO reduction to two-thirds of the noncovered government pension under the Social Security Amendments of 1983 (P.L. 98-21).

311. What is an example of a partial offset?

Under the GPO, the SSA reduces dependent/survivor benefit by two-thirds of the person's government pension. The GPO lowers the dependent/survivor benefit by $2 for every $3 received from a government pension.

Example: Jake works in non-Social Security-covered employment for a government agency. He will receive a government pension from the job of $1,200 per month. His wife, Caitlin, works in Social Security covered employment. She is entitled to a dependent benefit from his work of $900 per month before the SSA applies the GPO. To calculate the GPO, SSA does the following:

$1,200 is multiplied by two-thirds ($1,200 \times 2/3 = \$800$)

$800 is subtracted from the $900 dependent benefit ($\$900 - \$800 = \$100$)

The result is that Caitlin receives a dependent or survivor benefit of $100 per month. This is called a partial GPO offset.

312. What is a government pension?

It is any periodic or lump sum benefit that is based upon the worker's own non-SS-covered employment for a state or local government (SLG). The government pension is payable because the worker qualifies for either: [1]

- a retirement benefit based on age and length of service; or

- a permanent disability – that is, a condition which is expected to continue throughout their lifetime and precludes return to work. A government pension does not include such payment as:

    o a Social Security retirement or disability benefit;

    o a payment from an optional savings plan, e.g., a 403(b) or 457 plan, which is separate from the retirement plan and yields only the amount the employee paid in (plus interest) rather than an amount calculated based upon certain conditions such as age, earnings and length of service;

    o an early incentive retirement payment, e.g., a bonus paid as an incentive to retire early; or

    o a survivor annuity from a spouse's government pension.

Note

1. Social Security Administration, Programs Operation Manual System, Program for Government Pension Offset, https://secure.ssa.gov/poms. nsf/lnx/0202608100 (last accessed September 1, 2022).

313. Does the GPO have exceptions?

Yes. The GPO does not apply for persons who:

- receive a government pension from state or local government employment that is not based on their own earnings (such as a survivor's annuity from a deceased spouse);

- were eligible for a dependent/survivor benefit before December 1, 1977;

- were eligible to receive a government pension from non-SS-covered employment before December 1, 1982, and met the requirements for a dependent/survivor benefit in effect in January 1977; or

- receive a government pension from non-SS-covered military reserve service.

- Worker was a federal (including Civil Service Offset), state, or local government employee and the government pension is from a job for which they were paid Social Security taxes; and:

  o last day of employment (that pension is based on) is before July 1, 2004; or

  o worker filed for and was entitled to spouses, widows, or widowers benefits before April 1, 2004 (last working day in Social Security covered employment can be at any time); or

  o worked the last five years of a state or local government job in a position covered both by Social Security and the same government pension as the non-Social Security position;

There are other situations for which SSA won't reduce Social Security benefits as a spouse, widow, or widower including:

- Being a federal employee who switched from the Civil Service Retirement System (CSRS) to the Federal Employees' Retirement System (FERS) after December 31, 1987; and

  o Worker's last day of service (that pension is based on) is before July 1, 2004.

  o Worker paid Social Security taxes on earnings for 60 months or more during the period beginning January 1988 and ending with the first month of entitlement to benefits; or

  o Worker filed for and was entitled to spouses, widows, or widowers benefits before April 1, 2004 (a worker may work their last day in Social Security covered employment at any time).

- Received, or were eligible to receive, a government pension before December 1982, and meet all the requirements for Social Security spouse's benefits in effect in January 1977; or

- Received, or were eligible to receive, a federal, state, or local government pension before July 1, 1983, and were receiving one-half support from a spouse.

Note: A Civil Service Offset employee is a federal employee, rehired after December 31, 1983, following a break in service of more than 365 days, with five years of prior CSRS coverage.

314. What was the Congressional intent in establishing survivor and disability benefits?

Congress enacted the survivor benefit as part of the Social Security Act. It recognized that a worker's family requires financial support if the worker dies. Even in cases where the surviving spouse has always worked, the loss of the deceased worker's income reduces the family's total income. Congress realized a few years later that the retirement or disability of a worker also affects household income. While a Social Security benefit may be adequate for the retiree or disabled person to live on, the amount is insufficient, especially when the retired or disabled worker was the family's principal breadwinner. In 1939, therefore, Congress provided a dependent benefit, payable to the spouse and minor children of a retired or disabled worker. There had been much resistance to the introduction of disability benefits. Major concerns then underscore the same operational issues that challenge the program today: the difficulty in determining whether a disabled individual has lost the capacity to work and the concern over managing program costs. Opponents of implementing cash disability payments had legitimate concerns, and Social Security planners recognized this. However, historically, as well as currently, planners believed that problems encountered were surmountable and that the need for disability benefits was so great that the federal government had an obligation to address the issue.

When auxiliary benefits were first established, most households consisted of a single earner— usually the husband—and a wife who cared for children and remained out of the paid workforce. As a result, benefits for nonworking spouses were structured to be relatively generous. A woman who was never employed but is married to a man with high Social Security-covered wages may receive a Social Security spousal benefit that is higher than the retirement benefit received by a single woman, or a divorced woman who was married less than 10 years, who worked a full career in a low-wage job. In recent decades, this household structure has changed in part because women have entered the workforce in increasing numbers. The labor force participation rate of women with children under the age of eighteen increased from 47 percent in 1975 to 70.8 percent in March 2016. As a result, many women now qualify for Social Security benefits based on their own work records. Women are, however, more likely than men to take breaks in employment to care for family members, which can result in fewer years of contributions to Social Security and employer-sponsored pension plans.

Another change since 1939 has been an increase in the number of men and women who remain single or who have divorced. Persons who have never been married, or divorced before 10 years of marriage, do not qualify for Social Security spousal or survivors benefits under current law.

315. Is an individual eligible for both a survivor benefit and a benefit based on their own work record?

No. The Social Security Act does not permit an individual to receive a Social Security benefit from his/her own work and also a survivor/dependent benefit. This "dual entitlement rule" allows an individual to receive only the higher of the two benefits. Beneficiaries who qualify for multiple benefits do not receive both benefits in full.

For example, for a beneficiary eligible for his or her own retired-worker benefits as well as spousal benefits, the spousal benefit is reduced by the amount of the retired-worker benefit. The beneficiary receives a reduced spousal benefit (if not reduced to zero) in addition to his or her retired-worker benefit. This effectively means the beneficiary receives the higher of the two benefit amounts. Because of this, a two-earner household may receive lower total Social Security benefits than a single-earner household with identical total Social Security-covered earnings.

316. What is the Windfall Elimination Provision (WEP)?

The WEP is a penalty imposed on one's own Social Security retirement benefit when one begins to collect a pension from an employer that did not collect FICA taxes during their employment ("non-covered pension"). Typically, these are state and local governments and non-U.S. employers. The WEP reduces the Social Security benefit for retired and disabled workers receiving pensions from non-Social Security covered employment. Congress passed the WEP to prevent workers who receive non-covered pensions from receiving higher Social Security benefits as if they were long-time, low-wage earners.

317. What is the rationale for the Windfall Elimination Provision (WEP)?

SSA uses a formula for computing Social Security benefits that provides individuals with low average lifetime wages a proportionally higher rate of return on their contributions to Social Security than individuals with relatively high average lifetime wages. Those who have spent most of their careers in non-Social Security employment with a state or local government and a minimal amount of time in SS-covered employment will appear to SSA as lower-paid workers. Congress enacted the WEP in the belief that one should not receive a Social Security benefit as a low-paid worker, plus receive a government pension from non-Social Security covered employment.

318. What is the argument that WEP is unfair?

It is argued that the WEP penalizes those who have had two jobs:

- One job that entitles them to a Social Security retirement or disability benefit from work that paid the required Social Security taxes.

- A second job that did not pay Social Security taxes, but instead entitled them to a pension from a separate pension system.

The argument is that these pensions were earned separately and differently from Social Security, yet they are used to reduce the amount of Social Security benefits that a worker receives during retirement. When participation is required by both Social Security and also State and local pensions, the public pension is earned and collected separately.

It should be noted that President Joe Biden, during his campaign, announced his intentions to eliminate the WEP. In light of this intent, currently under consideration is the Social Security Fairness Act (HR 82). This bill intends to eliminate both the Windfall Elimination Provision and the Government Pension Offset. Currently, there are more than 290 cosponsors for the bill. Congressman Rodney Davis (R-IL) obtained more than 290 cosponsors and has filed a motion to force a vote on the bill. This will be the first time this type of bill has made it to the floor of the House of Representatives.

319. What is the argument that Government Pension Offset is unfair?

When it enacted the GPO, it has been argued that Congress ignored the principle that the intent of the dependent and or survivor benefit was to assist a husband or wife who was financially dependent on his or her spouse, especially if that spouse was the primary breadwinner. These two benefits provide additional income to help the financially dependent spouse once the breadwinner retires or is disabled (in which case, the dependent benefit applies) or in a situation where the breadwinner dies and the survivor benefit comes into play.

The argument is that that GPO actually HARMS the financially dependent spouse by reducing the dependent and/or survivor benefit. Studies indicate that most affected by the GPO are women that worked outside the home for a limited time and spend a good period of time at home raising families.

It should be noted that President Joe Biden during his campaign announced his intentions to eliminate the Government Pension Offset. In light of this intent, currently under consideration is the Social Security Fairness Act (HR 82). This bill intends to eliminate both the Windfall Elimination Provision and the Government Pension Offset. Currently, there are more than 290 cosponsors for the bill. Congressman Rodney Davis (R-IL) obtained more than 290 cosponsors and has filed a motion to force a vote on the bill. This will be the first time this type of bill has made it to the floor of the House of Representatives.

320. How many people are affected by the GPO and WEP?

According to federal figures released in December 2021, according to a Congressional Research Service study, approximately 2.0 million Social Security beneficiaries or about 3 percent of all Social Security beneficiaries were affected by the WEP[1] and 723,979 (about 1 percent of all beneficiaries) had their benefits reduced by the GPO[2]. Of those people penalized by the GPO, about 72 percent of all GPO affected beneficiaries had their benefits fully offset and about 28 percent had their benefits partially offset. Of those directly affected by the GPO, 54 percent were spouses and 46 percent were widow(er)s.

About 1.9 million of those affected were retired worker beneficiaries, which was about 4 percent of the entire retired-worker beneficiary population. The remaining affected individuals were disabled-worker beneficiaries and eligible family members of retired- or disabled-worker beneficiaries.[3]

Notes

1. Congressional Research Service, Social Security: The Windfall Elimination Provision (WEP and the Government Pension Offset (GPO)), https://crsreports.congress.gov/product/pdf/IF/IF10203#:~:text=How%20Many%20People%20Are%20Affected,entire%20retired-worker%20 beneficiary%20population (last accessed September 1, 2022).

2. Congressional Research Service, The Government Pension Offset (GPO), https://sgp.fas.org/crs/misc/RL32453.pdf (last accessed September 1, 2022).
3. Congressional Research Service, Social Security: The Windfall Elimination Provision (WEP), https://crsreports.congress.gov/product/pdf/RS/98-35 (last accessed September 1, 2022).

321. If the GPO and WEP offsets were eliminated, what would be the cost to Social Security?

It is estimated that the total cost of repealing of both the Government Pension offset and the Windfall Elimination Program would be approximately 1.9 percent of the total amount of Social Security expenditures each year.

322. How does the WEP work?

The WEP reduces the factor by which average earnings are multiplied to determine Social Security benefits. The amount of reduction depends on when the person retires and how many years of earnings he or she has accumulated. The reduction may be no more than one-half of the government pension to which the person is entitled in the initial month of entitlement to the pension.

323. Who does the WEP affect?

The WEP affects persons who:

- work or worked for a state or local government in non-Social-Security-covered employment;

- are entitled to a government pension from that employment; and

- are also entitled to a Social Security retirement or disability benefit from Social-Security covered work.

Examples include:

- teachers (in 15 states);

- police, firefighters, postal workers, air traffic controllers, federal employees hired before 1983 (CSRS);

- along with some state, county, local and special district workers.

324. In which states are teachers affected by the GPO and WEP?

Teachers are affected in the following states (an asterisk indicates only some school districts are affected):

- Alaska

- California

- Colorado

- Connecticut

- Georgia*

- Illinois

- Kentucky*

- Louisiana

- Maine

- Massachusetts

- Missouri

- Nevada

- Ohio

- Rhode Island

- Texas

- And Washington, D.C.

In addition, state, county, municipal, and special district employees are affected by GPO and WEP in 26 states including California, Colorado, Illinois, Louisiana, Ohio, Texas, and others.

325. What are the exceptions to the WEP?

The WEP does not apply for persons who:

- have thirty or more years of coverage under Social Security;

- those with twenty-one to twenty-nine years of coverage are eligible for a partial exemption; or

- have a government pension from non-SS-covered military reserve service.

326. When do the offsets begin?

The trigger of the offset is the receipt of the pension from non-Social Security covered employment. The offsets will apply when one retires from non-Social Security covered employment and begins drawing the government pension.

MAXIMIZATION OF BENEFITS

327. When is the best time to apply for Social Security retirement benefits, and what are some of the ways of maximizing Social Security Benefits over time?

Many individuals treat deciding which benefits to collect and when to collect as a one-time choice. However, there are a few cases that offer opportunities to switch between different types of benefits over time.

Two strategies, "File and Suspend" and "Restricted Application," were impacted by the 2015 Bi-Partisan Budget Act. Through this Act, Congress included Section 831 titled "Closure of Unintended Loopholes". Section 831 phased out these strategies over time. The benefits of the "file and suspend" strategy, such as the payment of spousal and children benefits while the wage earner's benefits have been suspended, are only available if the application was filed by April 29, 2016. The opportunity to file a restricted application was only available for folks turning age 62 by January 1, 2016.

Before the law changed, an individual who qualified for both individual and spousal and who was at least Full Retirement Age (FRA – also called Normal Retirement Age (NRA)) when filing for benefits was able to choose which benefits to collect. This option allowed him or her to collect spousal benefits (which are highest at FRA) while allowing his or her own benefits to receive Delayed Retirement Credits (DRCs). Unfortunately, the law passed in November 2015 phases out this strategy referred to as Restricted Application. Only individuals turning age 62 by January 1, 2016 (those born by January 1, 1954) can file a Restricted Application at Full Retirement Age. This strategy is still available for some individuals. If the age requirement is met, the individual can then file for his or her own benefits later, potentially as late as age 70, and claim increased individual benefits. The major benefit is the receipt of a spousal benefit from ages 62 through 70. Assuming a spousal benefit of $1,000, if the recipient files a Restricted Application, they will receive $48,000. As a reminder, to collect "spouse only" benefits, the individual cannot have filed for his or her own individual benefits. Therefore, at any given time, only one spouse may be collecting spousal benefits.

Prior to the change in the law, individuals reaching Full Retirement Age had the opportunity to file and suspend, allowing for the payment of spousal and children benefits while the worker's Social Security benefits have been suspended. The wage earner is earning Delayed Retirement Credits while spousal benefits are paid to the spouse and or children.

The Restricted Application and File and Suspend strategies are only available at Full Retirement Age. FRA for folks born between 1943 and 1954 is age 66. These strategies, together and individually, represent the "Coordination of Spousal Benefits". Use of these strategies will greatly increase the total Social Security benefits paid to a married couple.

In addition, an individual who qualifies for both individual and survivor benefits can choose which benefits to collect. This option enables him or her to collect survivor benefits, potentially as early as age 60, while allowing his or her own benefits to increase and potentially receive DRCs. The individual can then switch to his or her own benefits later, potentially as late as age 70, and claim higher individual benefits. On the other hand, the individual could also elect to collect his or her individual benefits early and switch to the survivor benefits later. It is important to note that Deemed Filing does not apply to surviving spouse benefits, thus permitting the opportunity to switch among benefits.

It should be noted that only taxpayers between 68 and 70 can now submit restricted applications, and only if they have not already filed for Social Security benefits.

For working examples of maximization of benefits, see Case Studies Used in Planning for Social Security Maximization.

328. What was the "file and suspend" strategy in regard to applying for Social Security benefits?

The file and suspend strategy was only available for individuals filing and suspending by April 29, 2016. "File and Suspend" (also referred to as "claim and suspend") was a strategy that allowed the primary earner to delay and grow benefits at a guaranteed 8 percent per year while the lower-earning spouse collects a spousal benefit every month. The primary earner could file for benefits, making the spouse eligible to begin collecting the spousal benefit, and the primary earner could then immediately request that the retirement benefit be suspended. The person requests to receive no checks, and that triggers an 8 percent growth per year. The primary earner can then elect to begin drawing Social Security benefits later.

Filing and suspending also allowed an individual to retroactively change his or her mind about suspending and start collecting as if he or she had not suspended. For example, if an individual filed and suspended at age 66 and then decided at age 69 that he or she should have begun collecting at age 66, he or she can retroactively reverse the decision. The SSA will send the individual a lump-sum payment of the benefits he or she would have collected without the suspension and, going forward, will pay monthly benefits based on beginning collection at age 66.

See Case Studies illustrating use of "File and Suspend" planning.

329. What is a "restricted application" strategy for maximizing Social Security benefits?

Another concept in Social Security planning strategy was the Restricted Application. This strategy was used to maximize Social Security benefits for a married couple or for an ex-spouse. One spouse filed a Restricted Application to receive a spousal benefit. While receiving a spousal benefit, the worker will earn Delayed Retirement Credits (DRCs) of 8 percent annually. If we assume that the wife's PIA is $1,250 and that she was eligible to file a restricted application at her Full Retirement Age as she turned age 62 by January 1, 2016. She would have filed a restricted application at her FRA and began to collect a spousal benefit of $1,000 per month. At age 70, she would file for her own benefits and receive a monthly benefit of $1,650 after earning DRCs of 32 percent. In this situation, she not only received $48,000 in spousal benefits, but also her own monthly benefit has grown by 32 percent. A restricted application could be appropriate when husband and wife PIAs are similar or when there is a disparity in earnings.

Another variation of the restricted application was that the lower earner could file an application for retirement benefits. In this instance, the higher earner will file a "restricted application" for spousal benefits on the spouse's earnings record. The higher earner then would delay Social Security to age 70 to get the full 32 percent growth. DRCs of 32 percent were available to individuals with an FRA of age 66. Folks with FRAs between age 66 and 2 months to age 70 would receive decreased DRCs. This allowed the higher earner to collect half of the spouse's retirement benefit until turning age 70 without adversely affecting delayed earnings.

See Case Studies illustrating use of "Restricted Application" planning.

---

330. Were there differences in strategies for maximizing Social Security benefits for a married couple depending upon the earnings history of the couple?

Yes. Depending on whether the members of the couple had a significant difference in earnings or similar earnings, there were different considerations.

Married Couple – Large Difference in Benefits

This collection strategy, often referred to as the Hybrid Approach, tended to work best for couples who were around the same age with one individual entitled to benefits that were more than double those of the other spouse.

This approach entailed the lower earner claiming individual benefits early to start the flow of income and adding adjusted spousal benefits later, with the higher earner deferring, which maximizes benefits as well as potential survivor benefits. The lower earner filed at age 62 and collected individual benefits. When the lower earner reached full retirement age, assuming the higher earner is also at least Full Retirement Age (FRA), the higher earner filed for benefits to allow spousal benefits to be paid but suspended collecting until reaching age 70. Due to Congressional changes, this strategy was only available to individuals that filed and suspended by April 29, 2016.

By filing for benefits when the lower earner reaches FRA, the higher earner enabled the spouse to collect unreduced adjusted spousal (spousal boost) benefits in addition to the lower earner's reduced individual benefits. The higher earner deferring collection to age 70 allowed for the highest possible benefits to be paid not only during the higher earner's lifetime, but also as survivor benefits when the higher earner passes.

Married Couple – Small Difference in Benefits

This collection strategy, sometimes referred to as a "Two High Earners strategy," tended to work best for couples who were entitled to similar benefits.

This approach entailed the lower earner claiming spousal benefits at FRA and switching to individual benefits at age 70, while the higher earner deferred until age 70, maximizing potential survivor benefits. When the lower earner reached FRA, assuming the higher earner was also at least FRA, the higher earner would file for benefits to allow spousal benefits to be paid but suspend collecting until reaching age 70. The April 29, 2016 deadline applied in this situation.

By filing for benefits when the lower earner reaches FRA, the higher earner enables the spouse to collect unreduced spousal benefits. Since the lower earner has attained FRA, the lower earner can choose to collect "spouse only" benefits (which are their highest at FRA) and defer collecting individual benefits until later when benefits have accumulated delayed retirement credits. The collection of a spousal benefit only is referred to as restricting the scope of the Social Security application and is known as filing a Restricted Application. Recent law changes limited the use of the Restricted Application to folks turning age 62 by January 1, 2016. The higher earner deferring collection to age 70 allowed for the highest possible benefits to be paid not only during the higher earner's lifetime, but also as survivor benefits when the higher earner passes.

See Case Studies illustrating situations such as Married Couples with Large Differences in Benefits, Married Couples with Small Differences in Benefits, and Sole Breadwinner.

Other factors include:

- estimated life expectancy of each spouse;

- effect that timing of filing will have on widow's/widower's benefits; and

- effect of Government Pension Offset (GPO) and Windfall Elimination Provision (WEP).

---

331. Is voluntary suspension a possibility for an individual who is laid off from a job due to the economy or the COVID-19/Coronavirus crisis?

Yes. If an individual, who is between age 62 and 67, who had intended to begin his or her Social Security benefits at his or her full retirement age, loses their job due to being laid off or furloughs due to COVID-19, they can begin collecting benefits immediately to help with extra income. Later, assuming they find another job or when the need for the additional income is gone, they can do a voluntary suspension of Social Security benefits and make up for some of the early-filing reduction in benefits.

> *Example:* Bob was born February 21, 1955, so he is age 65 during 2020. His full retirement age is 66 years and 2 months. Assume Bob's FRA benefit is $2,500 a month. If he files now, his monthly benefit is reduced to $2,291. This is a reduction of $209 per month. However, the $2,201 Social Security benefit helps provide relief from his income loss.

Later, when Bob finds a new job and no longer needs his Social Security benefits, he can invoke voluntary suspension. At this point, he will begin earning Delayed Retirement Credits of 2/3 of 1 percent per month (8 percent per year). When he reaches FRA at age 67 years and 2 months, he can ask the Social Security Administration to restart his payments. The delayed retirement credits would add nearly the amount of his reduction in benefits for starting early – assuming he secured a job around the salary he had been making.

CAUTION: An individual that does this at age 65 or older who was paying for Medicare benefits from their Social Security check will now have to pay Medicare quarterly by check. Additionally, if anyone else in the family is collecting Social Security based on his record, those benefits will be suspended by the voluntary suspension as well.

332. Are there any strategies a widow or widower can use to maximize benefits?

Yes. A potential for strategic collection occurs when a widow or widower is entitled to survivor benefits as well as his or her own individual benefits. Since survivor benefits can be collected earlier than other benefits (as young as age 60 or age 50 if disabled) and are highest at Full Benefit Age, a common strategy involves the widow or widower collecting survivor benefits beginning at age 60 while deferring collecting individual benefits until age 70 when they are at their highest. A widow(er) or survivor of a deceased spouse may file a restricted application, even though not at full retirement age or regardless of the date of birth.

Another strategy available to surviving spouses is to collect their own benefit at age 62 and then switch to the surviving spouse benefit at Full Benefit Age.

Collecting survivor benefits early starts the flow of income while allowing the individual to defer collecting his or her own benefits until they are higher.

Surviving spouses have greater latitude regarding structuring of their benefits because Deemed Filing does not apply to surviving spouses. Deemed Filing applies to worker and spousal benefits but NOT to surviving spouses.

See Case Studies for illustrations of strategies that a widow or widower can use.

333. Can both spouses receive retirement benefits?

Yes. If each is entitled to receive benefits based on their own earnings record, each can receive retirement benefits independently of the other's benefits. However, a spouse who is entitled to a retirement benefit AND a spouse's benefit cannot receive both in full. In this situation they would need to choose the one for collection. (For details of how a spouse's benefit is determined, see Q 114.)

See Case Studies for illustrations of situations where married couples have used planning to maximize benefits.

334. What kind of planning can be done regarding when Social Security benefits are started?

People today are much more interested in how they can maximize benefits. In dealing with clients now, it is more than just a question of "When should I take benefits?" Married couples can engage in planning, especially if both have worked and paid into Social Security for most of their careers. Ex-spouses also have claiming options. These planning techniques include taking a spousal benefit for a certain period of time and then switching to a benefit on the worker's own record or a worker filing for benefits, but then electing not to take the benefits so that a spouse can take benefits. Please keep in mind that the use of following strategies listed below are subject to the deadlines identified in the 2015 Bi-Partisan Budget Act.

Among the strategies available for married couples are:

- Both the husband and the wife file for retirement benefits at age 62.

- The wife files for retirement benefits at age 62. The husband files for spousal benefits at age 66 (FRA). The husband files for retirement benefits on his own at age 70.

- The wife takes retirement benefits at age 62. Husband files for retirement benefits at his full retirement age and suspended his benefits by April 29, 2016. The wife files for spousal benefits at this time. The husband reinstates his benefits at age 70. This was called "File & Suspend" (see Q 328).

- The wife takes retirement benefits at her full retirement age the husband takes spousal benefits at his full retirement age. The husband files for retirement benefits at age 70. This is often referred to as "Restricted Application" (see Q 329).

- The wife files for retirement benefits at her full retirement age. The husband files for retirement benefits at his full retirement age and suspended his benefits by April 29, 2016. The wife files for spousal benefits when the husband files at his full retirement age. The husband reinstates his retirement benefits at age 70.

- The husband files for retirement benefits at his full retirement age and suspended his benefits by April 29, 2016. The wife files for spousal benefits at her full retirement age. The husband reinstates his retirement benefits at age 70 and wife files for her own retirement benefits at age 70.

- The wife files for retirement at her full retirement age and suspends benefits by April 29, 2016. The husband files for spousal benefits at his full retirement age. The wife reinstates her retirement benefits at age 70 and the husband files for his own retirement benefits at age 70.

- The husband takes retirement benefits at age 62. The wife files for spousal benefits at her full retirement age; the wife files for her own retirement benefits at age 70. Remember that the wife must have been born on before January 1, 1954, to file a Restricted Application. Of course, if not desiring to file a Restricted Application, wife will be subject to the Deemed Filing rules.

- Recent law changes may encourage the higher wage earner to claim benefits at FRA, to allow the payment of spousal benefits to spouse. Assume that the husband is eligible for $2,000 at FRA. One option is to wait to age 70, thereby maximizing his benefit due to the receipt of Delayed Retirement Credits. His wife has not earned 40 credits and is not eligible to her own Social Security benefits. The wife is only eligible for a spousal benefit. If the husband delays to age 70, then the wife will miss out on four years of spousal benefits. If the husband begins at FRA, then the wife will be eligible for spousal benefits sooner. Thus, the decision by the husband on when he begins his benefits will have a direct impact to the timing of spousal benefits by the wife.

- In the case of a married couple, the husband's PIA is $2,250 and wife's PIA is $1,000. One strategy is for the wife to begin her benefit at age 62. At age 62, the wife will receive $750 per month. The husband waits to age 70 to begin his benefits, thereby receiving the maximum in DRCs. The wife will "step into the shoes" of her husband upon his death as she will be eligible for a survivor's benefit. This strategy makes sense, as the wife will most likely collect as a surviving spouse. In the meantime, she receives her benefit albeit at a reduced amount. If the wife waits to age 70 to begin her benefit, she will receive $1,320. But she will only receive this higher amount until the husband passes away. It might be best for the wife to begin her benefit at age 62. The wife will of course be subject to the Annual Earnings Test. The husband, if born on or before January 1, 1954, can file a Restricted Application.

As Deemed Filing does not apply to surviving spouses but the following strategies are still available for widows or widowers:

- The widow/widower takes the higher benefit at the earliest time; thus, she would take widows/widowers benefits at age 60 or retirement benefits at age 62.

- The widow/widower takes surviving spouse benefits at age 60, then begins benefits on own retirement at full retirement age.

- The widow/widower takes surviving spouse benefits at age 60, then begins benefits on own retirement at age 70.

- The widow/widower takes her own retirement at age 62, and then begins widows/widowers benefits at full benefit age.

See Case Studies which illustrate situational planning resulting in maximization of benefits.

---

335. In a situation where there is a lower earning spouse aged 62 and a higher earning spouse aged 66 – can the lower earning spouse claim benefits at age 62 and then switch to a spousal benefit when the higher earning spouse applies at age 70?

Technically – no. A 62-year-old cannot simply switch to a spousal benefit when the spouse begins to receive. The younger spouse may be eligible for the spousal boost in addition to their own benefit. The spousal boost is equal to 50 percent of the higher earner's PIA, (Primary

Insurance Amount), minus the PIA of the younger lower earning spouse. The spousal boost is added to the younger spouse's own benefit. If the spouse aged 62 took their own benefits prior to FRA, then he or she will never receive 50 percent of spouse's PIA. Once someone takes a reduced benefit on their own work record, it remains reduced. An erroneous misunderstanding is that a wife can begin her benefits at age 62 (reduced by 25 percent) and then switch to 50 percent of husband's PIA when eligible.

See Case Studies for illustration of situations where one spouse has significantly lower earnings than the other spouse.

336. Can you file for spousal benefits only at FRA if your spouse is only 62 and has not filed?

No. You could only file the Restricted Application at Full Retirement Age (FRA) if your spouse is 62 and receiving retirement benefits or receiving disability benefits or filed and suspended by the April 2016 deadline. If receiving disability benefits, the spouse you are collecting from may be under age 62. **The individual must have turned age 62 by January 1, 2016, to file a restricted application at Full Retirement Age**.

See Case Studies illustrating where spousal benefit is claimed and also where the restricted application is used.

337. If a person files for a spousal benefit before age 70 and then begins receiving monthly benefits at age 70, do they get BOTH the spousal amount plus the age seventy monthly benefit?

No, they get the only the HIGHER benefit of the two.

See Case Studies illustrating situations where people filed for spousal benefits.

338. When is the best time to file for Social Security retirement benefits?

The decision on when to apply for Social Security retirement benefits depends on several factors. Taking benefits early (before Full Retirement Age) will result in a permanent reduction of benefits. Taking retirement benefits later can result in a higher benefit amount, but a shorter life may result in collecting lower total benefits. The Social Security Administration provides a benefit on its website which includes several calculators to help a person determine the right time to file for benefits and the effect on benefits of filing early or late.[1]

However, the federal government does allow an individual a "re-do" if he or she decides that the application for retirement benefits was made too early. By filing Form SSA-521,[2] an individual can request that the original application for retirement benefits be withdrawn and a new application date be substituted. The catch is that the individual must pay back all retirement benefits received up to the date of the withdrawal. However, the federal government does not charge a penalty or interest for filing a Form SSA-521 *Request for Withdrawal of Application*, but the individual must have the cash to repay the federal government. Note that a "re-do" can only be done within one year of first filing for benefits.

Another consideration to be considered as to when to take retirement benefits is how much income will be earned in the year for which benefits are applied. Too much earned income can result in a loss of benefits (see Q 358).

Additionally, since Social Security benefits may be subject to income taxation (see Q 387), the individual's income and tax situation should be considered.

A person should access the Social Security Administration's website or contact a Social Security office two or three months before reaching age 62. The website and/or the Social Security office will furnish the information needed to decide whether to file an application for retirement benefits at that time. Because of the rules regarding retroactive benefits, a person should consider filing for benefits on January 1 of the year that he attains full retirement age, which may be older than age 65 (see Q 49).

If a worker does not file an application, he should contact the Social Security office again:

(1)   two or three months before retirement;

(2)   as soon as the worker knows that he will neither earn more than the monthly exempt amount in wages nor render substantial services in self-employment in one or more months of the year, regardless of expected total annual earnings; or

(3)   two or three months before the worker reaches Full Retirement Age (FRA), even if still working.

It may be advantageous to delay filing an application for benefits where:

(1)   the person is under the FRA and wishes to wait and receive an unreduced benefit at FRA, but benefits are not payable because of earnings;

(2)   application at or near retirement may provide higher benefits in the year of retirement; or

(3)   the person would lose benefits payable under some other program.

See the Case Studies for illustration of situations detailing the best time to file for Social Security benefits.

Notes

1. Benefits Planners, https://www.ssa.gov/planners/index.html (last accessed October 21, 2022).
2. Social Security Administration, Form SSA-521, Request for Withdrawal of Application, http://www.ssa.gov/forms/ssa-521.pdf (last accessed October 21, 2022).

339. When should a person file for retirement benefits?

In the past, the Social Security Administration suggested that a person contact a Social Security office within two months of reaching age 62 (or the age in which they wanted to begin collecting retirement benefits.) This suggestion was before the advent of computers and online filing – at this point, the person can file the application in the month they want benefits to begin.

It may be advantageous to delay filing an application for benefits where:

(1)   the person is under the Full Retirement Age (FRA) and wishes to wait and receive an unreduced benefit at FRA;

(2)   the person is at the FRA, but benefits are not payable because of earnings (application at or near retirement may provide higher benefits in the year of retirement); or

(3)   the person would lose benefits payable under some other program.

Year of Retirement

340. If age 62 is the computation age, is there any advantage to waiting until Full Retirement Age (FRA) to collect benefits?

Yes, the full PIA is payable at Full Retirement Age (FRA) (see Q 291), with a reduced amount paid in case of an earlier retirement age. Age 62 is used to determine elapsed years but earnings are counted to full retirement age.

Filing at an early retirement age usually affects the benefit in two ways:

• the PIA usually will be smaller (because fewer years of possibly higher earnings will be used in computing the AIME); and

• the lower PIA will be subject to reduction (5/9 of 1 percent per month for the first 36 months under the full retirement age and 5/12 of 1 percent per month for any additional months under the full retirement age).

See Case Studies for illustrations of advantages of waiting until Full Retirement Age (FRA) or later.

341. Can a person obtain higher retirement benefits by working past full retirement age?

Yes, in two ways.

Increase in Retirement Benefits

First, workers who continue on the job receive an increase in retirement benefits for each year they work between full retirement age and age 70. Note that this is not an increase in the worker's PIA. Other benefits based on the PIA, such as those payable to a spouse or children, are not affected.

This delayed retirement credit is also payable to a worker's surviving spouse receiving a widow(er)'s benefit.

Beginning in 1990, the delayed retirement credit payable to workers who attain age 62 after 1986 and who delay retirement past the full retirement age, the full-benefit age (gradually rising from age 65 to age 67) is gradually increased. The delayed retirement credit is increased by one-half of 1 percent every other year until reaching 8 percent per year in 2009 or later. The higher delayed retirement credits are based on the year of attaining age 62 and are payable only at and after full retirement age.

DELAYED RETIREMENT CREDIT RATES		
Attain Age 62	**Monthly Percentage**	**Yearly Percentage**
1979-1986	1/4 of 1%	3%
1987-1988	7/24 of 1%	3.50%
1989-1990	1/3 of 1%	4%
1991-1992	3/8 of 1%	4.50%
1993-1994	5/12 of 1%	5%
1995-1996	11/24 of 1%	5.50%
1997-1998	1/2 of 1%	6%
1999-2000	13/24 of 1%	6.50%
2001-2002	7/12 of 1%	7%
2003-2004	5/8 of 1%	7.50%
2005 or after	2/3 of 1%	8%

Workers who became age 65 before 1990 (and after 1981) and continued on the job received an increase in retirement benefits usually equal to 3 percent for each year (1/12 of 3 percent for each month) they worked between age 65 and 70. (The factor was only 1 percent for workers who became age 65 before 1982.)

Larger PIA

Second, working past the full retirement age may result in a larger PIA due to higher earnings. The reason: In figuring the earnings to be used in the 35 calculations, the Social Security Administration will compare recent earnings to the lowest earnings level used and, if higher, the recent earnings will replace a lower year resulting in increased benefits.

Assume that Paul, age 62, has paid in the maximum SS tax resulting in the maximum benefit. Paul decides to work from age 62 to age 66. Paul's higher earnings will replace the prior earnings years used in the calculating resulting in a $20 increase to his PIA. Paul would have paid around $28,000 in FICA taxes. Breakeven point is 100 years or age 166. (See Q 276).

See the Case Studies for illustrations of advantages of working past Full Retirement Age (FRA).

342. Can the retirement age at which unreduced benefits are available ever be increased?

Yes, the Social Security Amendments of 1983 increased the full retirement age (the age at which unreduced benefits are available), by two months per year for workers reaching age 62 in 2000-2005 to age 66; maintained age 66 for workers reaching age 62 in 2006-2016; increased by two months a year the retirement age for workers reaching age 62 in 2017-2022; and maintained age 67 for workers reaching age 62 after 2022. It does not change the age of eligibility for Medicare. There has been talk of raising the retirement age again, but thus far, no action has been taken.

The 1983 amendments do not change the availability of reduced benefits at 62 (sixty for widow(er)s), but revise the reduction factors so that there is a further reduction (up to a maximum of 30 percent for workers entitled at age 62 after the full retirement age is increased to age 67, rather than only up to 20 percent for entitlement at age 62 under prior rules). There is no increase in the maximum reduction in the case of widow(er)s, but some increases in the reduction occur at ages over sixty and under full retirement age.

EFFECTS OF RETIREMENT-AGE PROVISION IN SOCIAL SECURITY AMENDMENTS OF 1983*				
Year of Birth	Attainment of Age 62	Full retirement age (Year/Months)	Date of Attainment of Full retirement age[1]	Age-62 Benefit as Percent of PIA[2]
1938	2000	65/2	March 1, 2003	79.2
1939	2001	65/4	May 1, 2004	78.3
1940	2002	65/6	July 1, 2005	77.5
1941	2003	65/8	September 1, 2006	76.7
1942	2004	65/10	November 1, 2007	75.8
1943-1954	2005-2016	66/0	January 1, 2009-2020	75.0
1955	2017	66/2	March 1, 2021	74.2
1956	2018	66/4	May 1, 2022	73.3
1957	2019	66/6	July 1, 2023	72.5
1958	2020	66/8	September 1, 2024	71.7
1959	2021	66/10	November 1, 2025	70.8
1960 and after	2022 and after	67/0	January 1, 2027 and after	70.0

* Full retirement age is for worker and spouse benefits only. Full retirement age for widow(er)s is based on attainment of age 60 in 2000 or later, so that full retirement age is age 67 beginning 2029.

1 Birth date assumed to be January 2 of year (for benefit-entitlement purposes, the Social Security Administration considers a person to reach a given age on the day before the anniversary of his birth, thus, someone born on the 1st of the month is considered to reach a given age on the last day of the previous month). For later months of birth, add number of months elapsing after January up to birth month.

2 Applies present-law reduction factor (5/9 of 1 percent per month) for the first 36 months' receipt of early retirement benefits and new reduction factor of 5/12 of 1 percent per month for additional months.

343. How are a beneficiary's benefits figured when he is entitled to a reduced retirement benefit and a larger spouse's benefit simultaneously?

The beneficiary will receive the retirement benefit, reduced in the regular manner. (See Q 291.) That is, the PIA is reduced by 5/9 of 1 percent (1/180) for each of the first 36 months that he is under Full Retirement Age (FRA) when benefits commence, and 5/12 of 1 percent (1/240) for each month in excess of 36.

The beneficiary will also receive a spouse's benefit based on the difference between the (1/2 of his or her spouse's PIA) and his or her PIA. This spouse's benefit is reduced by 25/36 of 1 percent (1/144) for each of the first 36 months that he is under Full Retirement Age (FRA) when benefits commence, and 5/12 of 1 percent (1/240) for each month in excess of 36. (See Q 295.)

344. What were the advantages and disadvantages of using file and suspend?

Prior to recent changes by Congress, there were two advantages and one disadvantage.

The advantages included:

1)   If an individual filed and suspended, this allowed anyone else eligible on that individual's work record (i.e., spouse or child) to draw their benefits.

2)   You also created a safety net so if at some point before you reach age 70, you can request your benefits all the way back to when you filed (i.e., age 66).

The disadvantage to file and suspend was

1)   A Limitation on having a Health Savings Account (HSA) – if a person filed and suspended, the person would at least have Part A of Medicare. Participating in Medicare precludes a beneficiary from contributing to a Health Savings Account.

The benefits discussed above were only available if an individual filed and suspended by April 29, 2016.

345. How did a "restricted application" differ from "file and suspend"?

"File and Suspend" was the action of filing for benefits on your own work record but suspending payment. Delayed retirement credits are earned and a safety net was created. Prior to recent law changes the main benefit of the strategy was the payment of a spousal benefit while the high-income earner's benefits were suspended. Due to the recent change, auxiliary benefits such as to a spouse or children will also be suspended.

A "restricted application" is filing for spousal benefits. You will still earn Delayed Retirement Credits (DRC) on your own work record but draw benefits as a spouse at the same time.

See Case Studies for illustrations of using "File and Suspend" and for using "Restricted Application".

346. Could both spouses have used "file and suspend" at the same time?

Assuming the April 2016 deadline had been met, both spouses could have filed and suspended at the same time.

Caution – in this situation, it might have been beneficial for one of the spouses to file a restricted application at Full Retirement Age (FRA) if they reached age 62 by January 1, 2016.

347. Was it possible to file and suspend and file a restricted application?

No. It was permitted to do only one. Of course, it was necessary to meet the deadlines outlined in the Bipartisan Budget Act of 2015.

348. Could both husband and wife file a restricted application for the other's spousal benefit?

No. To file a restricted application, the other spouse must have already filed for retirement or disability benefits or filed and suspended by April 29, 2016 on their own work record.

349. Could you file and suspend at sixty-two to allow a nonworking spouse who is in ill health to collect one-half of benefit?

No, you could not file and suspend until Full Retirement Age (FRA). Due to changes in the law, an individual must have filed and suspended by April 29, 2016.

350. After filing a restricted application, does one have to wait until reaching age 70 to begin their own benefit?

No. A person is not locked in until age 70, but can begin benefits at any time.

351. Is it safe to assume that a single person could only use the File and Suspend strategy but not the restricted application?

Yes, unless they have an ex-spouse and were married to them for over ten years. One of the benefits to filing and suspending was the accumulation of a cash reserve. Due to the changes from the 2015 Bipartisan Budget Act, the opportunity to build a cash reserve while benefits have been suspended has been terminated. Thus, the incentives to suspend benefits have been greatly reduced.

See Case Studies for an illustration of individuals with ex-spouses.

352. If a spouse filed and suspended by April 29, 2016 and delayed collecting until age 70, would the other spouse get an amount equal to half of the income based on the Delayed Retirement Credits or based on the Full Retirement Age (FRA) benefit?

The spousal benefit is based on Primary Insurance Amount (PIA). The PIA represents the amount of Social Security benefits at Full Retirement Age (FRA). A current spouse does not receive any advantage of the delayed retirement credits. Of course, the opposite is also true. If the husband took his benefit at age 62 and took the 25 percent reduction, his spouse is still eligible for a spousal benefit based on his PIA at her Full Retirement Age (FRA).

353. If a person dies after filing and suspending but before receiving benefits, can the widow collect that lump sum?

No. Only the person filing the application can request the lump sum benefit. The widow would still get the Delayed Retirement Credits, which results in a higher monthly benefit.

354. If a husband filed and suspended and the wife took spousal benefits at age 62, would the wife get a stepped-up spousal benefit if the husband died at age 72 after delaying his benefit until age 70?

Yes. The spouse taking a reduced benefit, either on their own or as a spouse, does not affect the survivor's benefit. If the surviving spouse is Full Benefit Age when their spouse dies, they will get 100 percent of what the deceased was receiving or was eligible to receive.

355. What is the best strategy in a situation where the husband is age 66, with an income of $150,000 per year, and the wife is age 68, with an income of $50,000 per year?

This depended on the PIA of each and when the husband turned FRA. Assuming that the husband had the higher PIA and turned FRA by May 1, 2016, he should have filed and suspended by the April 29, 2016 deadline allowing the wife to file a restricted application. This would have ensured the maximization of benefits.

See Case Studies for illustrations of couples where one spouse had significantly more income than the other spouse.

356. What option might one use if there is a significant difference in ages between spouses, for example, if the husband is 12 years older than wife?

Normally in this case, the older individual (in this case, the husband) is looking at the same options as a single person; however, unlike the single person, they DO want to maximize survivor benefits. For example, the older spouse takes benefits at age 70 and the younger spouse takes benefits at age 60. This works because based on life expectancies, the younger spouse will collect survivor benefits for many years.

See Case Studies for illustrations of planning where one spouse is significantly older than the other.

357. What are the limitations of the "do-over" as an option?

The "do-over" still exists, with limitations. It must be done within the first year of entitlement and can only be done once. If an individual begins benefits in July, the last day to file Form SSA-521 *Request for Withdrawal of* Application is June 30th of the following year.

In the event that someone regrets submitting an early filing claim, Form SSA-521, officially the "Request for Withdrawal of Application," allows retirees who've recently enrolled in Social Security to undo their claims. As stated above, there are two major conditions to this "do over."

1. There are only 12 months after beginning to receive benefits to file Form SSA-521.[1]

2. One needs to pay back every cent in benefits received to the SSA in order for the claiming benefit to be undone. This includes any money that may have gone to a spouse or child, based on the filer's claim.

If the filer returns what's been paid within twelve months and the SSA processes the application, it'll be as if the claim was never made.

Note

1. Social Security Administration, Request for Withdrawal of Application, https://www.ssa.gov/forms/ssa-521.pdf (last accessed Septermber 1, 2022).

LOSS OF BENEFITS BECAUSE OF "EXCESS" EARNINGS

Retirement Test

358. Can a person lose some or all Social Security benefits by working?

Yes, if the person is under Full Retirement Age (FRA) (see Q 49) for all of 2022 and earns over $21,240; or in the year the person reaches Full Retirement Age he or she earns over $56,520, except that only earnings earned before the month he or she reaches Full Retirement Age count towards the $56,520 limit.[1] An alternative test applies in the initial year of retirement if it produces a more favorable result (see the last "bullet" of Q 360). See Q 295 for a discussion of the Full Retirement Age.

The annual exempt amounts will be increased each year as wage levels rise.

A beneficiary who is older than the Full Retirement Age can earn any amount without losing benefits. Regardless of how much earnings are in the year of attaining Full Retirement Age, no benefits are withheld for the month in which Full Retirement Age is reached, or for any subsequent month. Also, earnings in and after the month in which a person attains Full Retirement Age will not be included in determining total earnings for the year.

The retirement test does not apply to individuals entitled to benefits because of their disability or to beneficiaries outside the United States whose work is not covered by Social Security.

ANNUAL EXEMPT AMOUNTS		
Year	Year Retirement Age Reached	Under Retirement Age
1985	$7,320	$5,400
1986	7,800	5,760
1987	8,160	6,000
1988	8,400	6,120
1989	8,880	6,480
1990	9,360	6,840
1991	9,720	7,080
1992	10,200	7,440
1993	10,560	7,680
1994	11,160	8,040
1995	11,280	8,160
1996	11,520	8,280

ANNUAL EXEMPT AMOUNTS		
Year	Year Retirement Age Reached	Under Retirement Age
1997	13,500	8,640
1998	14,500	9,120
1999	15,500	9,600
2000	17,000	10,080
2001	25,000	10,680
2002	30,000	11,280
2003	30,720	11,520
2004	31,080	11,640
2005	31,800	12,000
2006	33,240	12,480
2007	34,440	12,960
2008	36,120	13,560
2009-2011	37,680	14,160
2012	38,880	14,640
2013	40,080	15,120
2014	41,400	15,480
2015-2016	41,880	15,720
2017	44,880	16,920
2018	45,360	17,040
2019	46,920	17,640
2020	48,600	18,240
2021	50,520	18,960
2022	51,960	19,560
2023	$56,520	$21,240

Note

1. 42 U.S.C. § 403(f).

359. What are the components of the "Earnings Test" or "Retirement Test"?

The "Earnings Test" is also commonly referred to as the "Retirement Test" and is used to:[1]

(1)   measure the extent of a person's retirement;

(2)   determine any amount that needs to be deducted from monthly benefits (if any); and

(3)   measure the work activity of any other individuals entitled to collect from a person's record and the amount due to them.

Note

1. 20 CFR sec 404.430, https://www.law.cornell.edu/cfr/text/20/404.430 (last accessed September 28, 2021).

360. What are the general rules for loss of benefits because of excess earnings?

When the beneficiary is older than the Full Retirement Age (FRA) (see Q 49), no benefits are lost because of his earnings. If he is under the Full Retirement Age, the following rules apply:[1]

- If no more than $56,520 is earned in 2023 by a beneficiary who reaches the Full Retirement Age in 2023, no benefits will be lost for that year.

- If more than $56,520 is earned in 2023 before the month the beneficiary reaches Full Retirement Age, one dollar of benefits will ordinarily be lost for each three dollars of earnings over $56,520.

- If not more than $21,240 is earned in 2023 by a beneficiary who is under the Full Retirement Age for the entire year, no benefits will be lost for that year.

- If more than $21,240 is earned in 2023 by a beneficiary who is under the Full Retirement Age for the entire year, one dollar of benefits will ordinarily be lost for each two dollars of earnings over $21,240.

- No matter how much is earned during 2023, no retirement benefits in the initial year of retirement will be lost for any month in which the beneficiary neither: (1) earns over $1,770 as an employee if retiring in a year prior to the year he reaches Full Retirement Age, nor (2) renders any substantial services in self-employment.

The initial year of retirement is the first year in which he is both entitled to benefits and has a month in which he does not earn over the monthly exempt wage amount (as listed previously) and does not render substantial services in self-employment.

When the monthly earnings test applies, regardless of the amount of annual earnings, the beneficiary gets full benefits for any month in which earnings do not exceed the monthly exempt amount, and the beneficiary does not perform substantial services in self-employment.

The attainment of Full Retirement Age in a year determines which test applies. The Full Retirement Age test applies if the beneficiary attains Full Retirement Age on or before the last day of the taxable year involved. The "under Full Retirement Age" test applies if the beneficiary does not attain Full Retirement Age on or before the last day of the taxable year. See Q 295 for a discussion of the increase in the Full Retirement Age.

Example 1. Dr. James, who reports his earnings on a calendar year basis, reaches Full Retirement Age (sixty-six years old) on June 18, 2022. The under Full Retirement Age test $21,240 for 2023) applies for calendar year 2022, and the Full Retirement Age test $56,520) applies for calendar year 2023. However, none of Dr. James' earnings earned in June through December 2022 count towards the $56,520 limit.

Example 2. Miss Norton, who reports her earnings on the basis of a fiscal year ending June 30, attains Full Retirement Age (66 years old) on September 15, 2023. The under Full Retirement Age test ($56.520) applies for her fiscal year July 1, 2022 through June 30, 2023. The Full Retirement Age test ($56,520) applies for her next fiscal year; however, only earnings earned in July and August, 2023 count towards the $56,520 limit.

Note

1. 42 U.S.C. 403(f).

361. What is the monthly exempt amount?

The monthly exempt amount that applies to earnings from employment is as follows:

(1)   For years 2015 and 2016 –

    (a) Prior to reaching Full Retirement Age: $1,310

    (b) After reaching Full Retirement Age: $3,490

(2)   For 2017 –

    (a) Prior to reaching Full Retirement Age: $1,410

    (b) After reaching Full Retirement Age: $3,740

(3)   For 2018 –

    (a) Prior to reaching Full Retirement Age: $1,420

    (b) After reaching Full Retirement Age: $3,780

(4)   For 2019 –

    (a) Prior to reaching Full Retirement Age: $1,470

    (b) After reaching Full Retirement Age: $3,910

(5)   For 2020 –

    (a) Prior to reaching Full Retirement Age: $1,520

    (b) After reaching Full Retirement Age: $4,050

(6)   For 2021–

    (a) Prior to reaching Full Retirement Age: $1,580

    (b) After reaching Full Retirement Age: $4,210

(7)   For 2022—

    (a) Prior to reaching Full Retirement Age: $1,630

    (b) After reaching Full Retirement Age: $4,330

(8)   For 2023—

    (a) Prior to reaching Full Retirement Age: $1,770

    (b) After reaching Full Retirement Age: $4,710

362. How are "excess" earnings charged against benefits?

In determining the amount of benefits for a given year that will be lost, two factors must be taken into consideration:

(1)   the amount of the person's "excess" earnings for the year; and

(2)   the months in the year that can actually be charged with all or a portion of the excess earnings potentially chargeable in the initial year of retirement.[1]

Both wages earned as employee and net earnings from self-employment are combined for purposes of determining the individual's total earnings for the year. Only "excess earnings" are potentially chargeable against benefits. If a person is under the Full Retirement Age (FRA) for the entire year and earns $21,240 or less (in 2023) for the year, there are no "excess earnings". If earnings for the year are more than $21,240, one-half of the amount over $21,240 is "excess earnings". In the year a person reaches the Full Retirement Age, he or she can earn up to $56.520 (in 2023) before losing benefits. However, only earnings earned before the month the person reaches Full Retirement Age count toward the $56,520 limit. See Q 293 for a discussion of the Full Retirement Age.

Excess earnings are charged against retirement benefits in the following manner. They are charged first against all benefits payable on the worker's account for the first month of the year. If any excess earnings remain, they are charged against all benefits payable for the second month of the year, and so on until all the excess earnings have been charged, or no benefits remain for the year. However, a month cannot be charged with any excess earnings and must be skipped if the individual:

(1)   was not entitled to benefits for that month;

(2)   was over Full Retirement Age in that month;

(3)   in the initial year of retirement, he or she did not earn over $1.770 (using 2023 figures) if he or she retires in a year before the year he or she reaches Full Retirement Age; or

(4)   he or she did not render substantial services as a self-employed person in that month.

If the excess earnings chargeable to a month are less than the benefits payable to the worker and to other persons on his account, the excess is chargeable to each beneficiary in the proportion that the original entitlement rate of each bears to the sum of all their original entitlement rates.

> *Example 1*. Dr. Brown partially retires in January 2023 at the age of sixty-two. Based on his earnings history and the age he starts receiving benefits, his Social Security benefit is $1,200 per month. He practices for three months in 2023 and earns $30,000. The remainder of his initial year of retirement is spent in Florida playing golf. Despite the fact that Dr. Brown has excess earnings in 2023 that would, under the test, cause a benefit loss of $9,480, he will lose only the $3,600 in benefits for the three months during which he performed substantial services in self-employment, because 2023 is his initial year of retirement.

> *Example 2*. Dr. Smith, who partially retired in 2022 at age sixty-two, practices for four months in 2022 and earns $32,000. As 2023 is his second year of retirement, the monthly-earnings test does not apply. His benefit will be reduced by $1 for each $2 of earnings over $21,240. This means that Dr. Smith's benefits in 2022 will be reduced by $10,620 (one-half of the amount in excess of $21,240).

> *Example 3*. Mr. Martin is sixty-six years old and has not retired. He earns $46,000 a year. Mr. Martin receives Social Security retirement benefits of $700 a month. Because he is over the Full Retirement Age, he loses none of his benefits by working.

The annual exempt amount is not prorated in the year of death. In addition, the higher exempt amount applies to persons who die before their date of birth in the year that they otherwise would have attained Full Retirement Age.

Note

1. 20 CFR Part 404, Subpart E.

363. Can a person who is receiving dependent's or survivor's benefits lose benefits by working?

Yes, if the person is under the Full Retirement Age (FRA) for the entire year and earns over $21,240 (in 2023), or in the year the person reaches Full Retirement Age he earns over $56,520. Only earnings earned before the month the person reaches Full Retirement Age count toward the $56,520 limit.[1] The same "retirement test" applies as applies to retirement beneficiaries (see Q 360). However, the excess earnings of a person receiving dependent's or survivor's benefits are not charged against the benefits payable to other dependents or survivors. For example, a child's excess earnings are not chargeable against a mother's benefits. A retirement beneficiary's excess earnings, on the other hand, are chargeable against a dependent's benefits, as those benefits are based on the retirement beneficiary's Social Security account.[1]

Note

1. 42 U.S.C. § 403(f).

364. If a widow's benefits are withheld because of work, will this necessarily reduce the total amount of benefits payable to the family?

No. Where there are several children, all survivor benefits may have to be reduced to come within the maximum family benefit. Even though the mother works and loses her benefits, the maximum may still be payable to the children. In many cases, however, loss of the mother's benefits will reduce the total amount of benefits payable to the family.[1]

Example 1. Mr. Smith dies in 2022, leaving a widow and four small children. His PIA is $900. If it were not for the maximum family limit, the widow and each child would be entitled to a survivor's benefit of $675 (75 percent of $900). However, because the maximum family benefit for a PIA of $900 is $1,250, each beneficiary receives only $250 (one-fifth of $1,250, rounded to the next lower even dollar). Mrs. Smith goes to work and earns an amount sufficient to eliminate her mother's benefits ($1 is withheld for every $2 of excess earnings). Nevertheless, the family still receives $1,250 in benefits, because each child's benefit is raised to $312 (one-fourth of $1,050, rounded to the next lower even dollar).

Example 2. Mr. Jones dies in 2022, leaving a widow and two small children. His PIA is $900, and the maximum family benefit is $1,250. If it were not for the maximum family limit, the widow and each child would be entitled to a monthly benefit of $675 (75 percent of $900). Because of the family maximum limit, however, each receives only $416 (one-third of $1,250, rounded to the next lower even dollar). Mrs. Jones goes to work and earns an amount sufficient to eliminate her widow's benefits. Each child then receives a full benefit of $625.

Note

1. *See* 20 CFR Part 404, Subpart E.

365. Which beneficiaries are not subjected to the Earnings Test?

The "Earnings Test" will not apply if the individual:

(1)   has reached Full Retirement Age (FRA);

(2)   has become eligible to collect benefits based on disability;

(3)   is living outside of the United States AND the work performed is not covered by Social Security; or

(4)   is a divorced spouse of the earner whose month of entitlement is prior to the month of the divorce.

366. What is the benefit amount when the monthly earnings test applies?

When the monthly earnings test applies, the individual will receive fully benefits for any month that they did not:

(1)   exceed the monthly exemption amount; and

(2)   perform substantial services in self-employment.

367. How is the loss of benefits figured for the year in which the worker reaches full retirement age?

In the year in which a person reaches Full Retirement Age (FRA), his earnings in and after the month in which he reaches FRA will not be included in determining his total earnings for the year.[1]

Note

1. 42 U.S.C. 403(f).

368. What kinds of income will not count under the Earnings Test and will not cause loss of benefits?

The following types of income are not counted as "earnings" for purposes of the retirement test:[1]

- Any income from employment earned in or after the month the individual reaches Full Retirement Age (FRA). (Self-employment income earned in the year is not examined as to when earned, but is prorated by months, even though actually earned after Full Retirement Age.) See Q 293 for a discussion of Full Retirement Age.

- Any income from self-employment received in a taxable year after the year the individual becomes entitled to benefits, but not attributable to significant services performed after the first month of entitlement to benefits. This income is excluded from gross income only for purposes of the earnings test.

- Damages, attorneys' fees, interest, or penalties paid under court judgment or by compromise settlement with an employer based on a wage claim. However, back pay recovered in such proceedings counts for the earnings test.

- Payments to secure release of an unexpired contract of employment.

- Certain payments made under a plan or system established for making payments because of the employee's sickness or accident disability, medical or hospitalization expenses, or death.

- Payments from certain trust funds that are exempt from income tax.

- Payments from certain annuity plans that are exempt from income tax.

- Pensions and retirement pay.

- Sick pay, if paid more than six months after the month the employee last worked.

- Payments-in-kind for domestic service in the employer's private home, for agricultural labor, for work not in the course of the employer's trade or business, or the value of meals and lodging furnished under certain conditions.

- Rentals from real estate that cannot be counted in earnings from self-employment because, for instance, the beneficiary did not materially participate in production work on the farm, the beneficiary was not a real estate dealer, etc.

- Interest and dividends from stocks and bonds (unless they are received by a dealer in securities in the course of business).

- Gain or loss from the sale of capital assets, or sale, exchange, or conversion of other property that is not stock in trade or includable in inventory.

- Net operating loss carryovers resulting from self-employment activities.

- Loans received by employees, unless the employees repay the loans by their work.

- Workers' compensation and unemployment compensation benefits.

- Veterans' training pay or allowances.

- Pay for jury duty.

- Prize winnings from contests, hobbies, or prize winnings, unless the person enters contests as a trade or business.

- Payments for length of service awards or achievement awards.

- Tips paid to an employee that are less than twenty dollars a month or are not paid in cash.

- Payments by an employer that are reimbursements specifically for travel expenses of the employee and that are so identified by the employer at the time of payment.

- Payments to an employee as a reimbursement or allowance for moving expenses, if they are not counted as wages for Social Security purposes.

- Royalties received in or after the year in which a person reaches Full Retirement Age, to the extent that they flow from property created by the person's own personal efforts that she copyrighted or patented before the taxable year in which she reached Full Retirement Age.

  - These royalties are excluded from gross income from self-employment only for purposes of the earnings test.

- Retirement payments received by a retired partner from a partnership, provided certain conditions are met.

- Certain payments or series of payments paid by an employer to an employee or any of his or her dependents on or after the employment relationship has terminated because of death, retirement for disability, or retirement for age and paid under a plan established by the employer.

- Payments from Individual Retirement Accounts (IRAs) and Keogh Plans.

In other words, a person can receive almost any amount of investment or passive income without loss of benefits.[2]

Notes

1. 20 CFR Part 404, Subpart E.
2. https://www.ssa.gov/OP_Home/handbook/handbook.18/handbook-1812.html (last accessed September 1, 2022).

369. Which earnings will count under the Earnings Test and potentially cause loss of benefits?

Generally, wages received as an employee and net earnings from self-employment. Bonuses, commissions, fees, and earnings from all types of work, whether or not covered by Social Security, count for the retirement test. For example, earnings from family employment are counted, even though such employment is not covered by Social Security. Earnings above the Social Security "earnings base" are counted. Income as an absentee owner counts as "earnings" for the retirement test.[1] If the person renders substantial services as a self-employed person (even in another business), such income also will count as "earnings" for the taxable year in the initial year of retirement.

Specifically, the following types of earnings count for purposes of the earnings test:

- Wages for employment covered by Social Security

- Cash pay (even if not considered as "wages" under the cash-pay test) for:

    o Agricultural work;

    o Domestic work in a private home, or

    o Service not in the course of the employer's trade or business

- All pay, cash and noncash, for work as a homeworker or for a nonprofit organization whether or not the $100 per year test is met

- Cash tips that equal or exceed $20 a month

- All pay for work not covered by Social Security, if the work is done in the U.S., including pay for:

    o Family employment;

    o Work by students, student nurses, interns, newspaper, and magazine vendors;

    o Work by Federal or State or foreign governments or instrumentalities; or

    o Word covered by the Railroad Retirement Act

- All net earnings from self-employment

- All pay for incentive, suggestion, and outstanding work awards

- All pay for occasional and regular bonuses

- All pay from a "cafeteria" plan if the payments meet the definition of wages and the plan is not a "qualified benefit"

- All pay from a non-qualified deferred compensation plan/system

- All pay by an employer for educational assistance

- All pay from federally sponsored economic and human development programs only if payments are wages

- All pay for non-work periods including idle time, standby, and subject to call related payments

- All pay for prizes, awards, and gratuities only if it is part of the salesperson's wage structure

- All pay from television, radio, and motion picture residuals if the performer was an employee at the time of the original performance[2]

Notes

1. 42 U.S.C. 403(f).
2. Social Security Administration, 1811. What types of income count under the earnings test? https://www.ssa.gov/OP_Home/handbook/handbook.18/handbook-1811.html (last accessed September 1, 2022).

370. How does the Annual Earnings Test work?

If you take Social Security benefits before reaching Full Retirement Age (FRA), and you earn income in excess of the annual earnings limit, your Social Security benefit will be reduced. Only "earned income" applies, NOT investment income. The annual earnings test limits (in 2023) earnings to $21.240. If your earnings exceed $21.240, Social Security will withhold one dollar of benefits for each two dollars that exceeds the earnings test limit.

During the year you reach Full Retirement Age, and up until the month you reach Full Retirement Age, Social Security will deduct one dollar for every three dollars you earn over the annual earnings limit, however you can earn up to (in 2023) $56.520 during the year you reach Full Retirement Age.

Once you reach Full Retirement Age, you are no longer subject to the annual earnings limit; you can earn as much as you like without incurring a reduction in your Social Security benefits. Your social benefits may however still be subject to income taxes.

371. How are total earnings computed?

Earnings, for the taxable year, as computed under the Earnings Test are:

(1)   the sum of wages for services performed during the taxable year; plus

(2)   all net earnings from self-employment for the taxable year; minus

(3)   any net loss from self-employment for the taxable year.

372. Are earnings counted even if the earner was not entitled to benefits for the entire year?

Yes. Earnings for the entire year are counted regardless of when during the year the individual became eligible for benefits.

373. Are earnings counted when the earner reaches Full Retirement Age (FRA)?

No. Earnings are not counted if earned in the month when the individual reaches Full Retirement Age (FRA) or any month thereafter.

374. What is meant by "substantial services" in self-employment?

Whether a self-employed beneficiary is rendering "substantial services" in the initial year of retirement is determined by the actual services rendered in the month. Each month is considered individually in determining if there are substantial services. The test is whether the person can reasonably be considered retired in the month. In applying the test, consideration is given to such factors as:

(1)   the amount of time devoted to the business (including all time spent at the place of business or elsewhere) in any activity related to the business (including the time spent in planning and managing, as well as doing physical work);

(2)   the nature of the services;

(3)   the relationship of the activities performed before retirement to those performed after retirement; and

(4)   other circumstances, such as the amount of capital the beneficiary has invested in the business, the type of business establishment, the presence of a paid manager, partner, or family member who manages the business, and the seasonal nature of the business.[1]

Generally, services of forty-five hours or less in a month are not considered substantial. However, as few as fifteen hours of service a month could be substantial if, for instance, they involved management of a sizeable business or were spent in a highly skilled occupation. Services of fewer than fifteen hours a month are never considered substantial.

There ARE limited instances in which regardless of the time devoted to business, services are not substantial if:

(1)   the person's monthly earnings are readily determinable (e.g. personal service type self-employment involving no significant investment);

(2)   the person's gross earnings, figured on a time basis, for services in a month are equal to or less than the monthly exempt amount; and

(3)   there is no evidence to the contrary.

This exception to the forty-five-hour rule has limited application since in most self-employment, the monthly earnings are not easily determined.

The amount of earnings is not controlling. High earnings do not necessarily mean that substantial services were rendered, nor do low or no earnings mean that they were not rendered.

The Social Security Administration Program Operations Manual System (POMS) provides some illustrative examples of "substantial" and "not substantial":[2]

Services of More Than Forty-Five Hours per Month Not Substantial

Example 1: A minister retires from a large church. He accepts appointment to a small church for monthly income which is equal to or less than the monthly exempt amount (including the value of parsonage he receives). Considering that the earnings do not exceed the monthly exempt amount, it would be reasonable to find that the services are not substantial even though the time he devotes to his ministry exceeds forty-five hours in a calendar month.

Example 2: An individual worked as an employee January through April and became entitled in May. He again works as an employee in November and December and the monthly earnings test applies to these months. He states he was self-employed from June through September and furnishes a contract with a company stating the services, he, as a self-employed individual, was to provide as a grounds keeper. The contract calls for payment on an hourly basis. Development shows the beneficiary was validly self-employed. In each of the months June through September he rendered over forty-five hours of service, but, because of the modest hourly fee paid for his services he earned less than the monthly test amount in each of the months. Based on the contract, his monthly earnings could be readily determined since he was paid an hourly rate and his earnings depended solely on his personal services. He had no significant investment in a "business." Therefore, it was determined that work deductions would not apply for June through September even though he exceeded forty-five hours of service in each of the months.

Services from Fifteen through Forty-five Hours A Month That Are Substantial

The beneficiary devotes fifteen hours or more per month to managing a large business or engages in a highly skilled occupation. In such cases, the services could be considered substantial. In SSR 71-13c, an experienced engineer who, as a member of the board of directors of a loan association, inspected properties for a high fee but worked less than forty-five hours per month. A court determined that the services were substantial.[3]

NOTE: The "substantial services" test is used only for the initial year of retirement. After that, the amount of earnings alone determines whether benefits will be lost.

Notes

1. 20 CFR Part 404, Subpart E.
2. Social Security Administration, RS 02505.065, Meaning of Substantial Services (SS) in Self-Employment (SE), https://secure.ssa.gov/poms. nsf/lnx/0302505065 (last accessed September 26, 2021).
3. *deVilla v. Finch*, (S.D. Ind. 1970), discussed in Social Security Administration, SSR 71-13c, Work Deductions – Substantial Service in Self-Employment – Highly Skilled and Technical Services, https://www.ssa.gov/OP_Home/rulings/oasi/29/SSR71-13-oasi-29.html.

375. Must a Social Security beneficiary report earnings to the Social Security Administration?

No. The Social Security Administration uses earnings information for workers that has been reported by employers on W-2 income tax forms or income reported by the self-employed on their tax forms. For most beneficiaries, the process is totally automated, with the Social Security Administration receiving and processing earnings information reported for tax purposes and using that information to adjust the Social Security benefits payable accordingly.

Benefits will be stopped for the number of months necessary to offset excess earnings. If too much has been withheld, the beneficiary will receive a check for the underpayment. If too little, the overpayment will be withheld from future benefits or must be refunded.

376. How are a life insurance agent's first-year and renewal commissions treated for purposes of the retirement test?

Whether original (first year) and renewal commissions from the sale of life insurance policies are wages or earnings from self-employment depends upon the status of the agent when the sale of the policy was completed. If the agent was an employee when the sale of the policy was consummated, both original and renewal commissions from that policy are wages. If the agent was self-employed when the sale of the policy was completed, both the original and renewal commissions from the policy are earnings from self-employment.[1]

Each insurance company normally furnishes its agents with sufficient information identifying policies on which commission payments are made, amounts of payments that are regular commissions, the commuted value of the renewals, service fees, efficiency income, etc., to enable a beneficiary to figure how much the earnings are for Social Security purposes.

A life insurance agent will receive retirement benefits for the month in which Full Retirement Age (FRA) is reached, and for every month thereafter, regardless of whether still working and regardless of how much is earned.

Moreover, in the initial year of retirement, and regardless of the amount of earnings for the taxable year, benefits will not be lost for any month in which the individual neither:

(1)   earns more than $1,580 (if under Full Retirement Age) as an employee; nor

(2)   renders substantial services in self-employment. See Q 293 for a discussion of the Full Retirement Age.

It is necessary to determine whether the agent was an employee or a self-employed person when the policy was sold. (For status of a life insurance agent as an employee or as a self-employed person under Social Security, see Q 437.) The reason is that, for retirement test purposes, "wages" of an employee are treated as earnings in the year in which they are earned. But net earnings for self-employment are treated as earnings in the year in which they are received.

Original (first-policy-year) commissions are earnings for purposes of the retirement test for the month and year in which an employee-agent completed the sale of the policy. As a rule, an employee-agent is paid the original commission on a policy according to the way the insured person pays the premium. The entire original commission is earnings for the month in which the agent completed the sale of the policy, regardless of whether the commission is received on a monthly, quarterly, semi-annual, or annual basis.

Renewal commissions of an employee-agent are earnings for purposes of the retirement test for the month in which the employee completed the sale of the life insurance policy and are includable in total earnings for the taxable year. They are deferred compensation for services rendered in completing the sale.

All of the renewal commissions that an employee-agent anticipates receiving from a life insurance policy sold while an employee must be reported as earnings for purposes of the retirement test for the month and year in which the original sale of the policy was completed. If the anticipated renewal commissions fail to materialize (thus making incorrect the total annual or monthly earnings), any benefit previously withheld but now due the beneficiary will be paid.

An employee-agent beneficiary must include the following in figuring total earnings for purposes of the retirement test for a taxable year:

- All original commissions on life insurance policies sold during the year.

- All anticipated renewal commissions on life insurance policies sold in the year. If the agent-beneficiary cannot determine the exact amount of anticipated renewals from such policies, as a last resort it should be assumed that they equal the amount of the original commission.

- Insurance service fees, persistency fees, and the like earned during the year.

- All renewal commissions received in the taxable year from policies sold in prior years while self-employed.

- All remuneration classified as earnings from other jobs, trades, or business.

Thus, renewal commissions on business in past years are not "earnings" for retirement test purposes when received by the agent-beneficiary if he was an employee when the policies were sold.

An employee-agent earns commission on a life insurance policy in the month in which the last act required for entitlement to the commission is performed. The acts to be performed before entitlement to commissions are usually set out in the agent's contract with the company, or can be determined from the company's regulations, rules, or practices. The agent should submit a copy of the contract or other evidence if there is any doubt about the last act required.

The month in which the company approves the policy is not the month in which the commission was earned, unless it happens to coincide with the last act required of the agent (for instance, if later in that month the agent forwarded the first premium due on the approved policy and this qualified for the commission). Similarly, the month in which the agent delivered the policy and collected the initial premium is not the month in which the commission was earned if the agent qualified for the commission when the customer signed the policy application.

This same rule applies to converted policies. If the conversion of the life insurance policy resulted in new commissions, the commissions are earned in the month in which the agent performed the last act that qualified for those new commissions. In the latter case, it is immaterial that the conversion was accomplished with the help of another agent through the insistence of the purchaser of the policy; some action (even if it is only the signature) was required of the selling agent in order to be entitled to the new rate of commissions.

If the life insurance agent is a self-employed person when the policy is sold, first-year and renewal commissions are treated as earnings for purposes of Social Security taxes for the taxable year in which they are received. When a policy is sold, there should be reported in the year of sale only the first-year commission received on the policy in that year. Renewal commissions on such a policy will be treated as earnings for purposes of Social Security taxes in the year when received. Renewal commissions received in a year after the year of entitlement to Social Security benefits are not included as earnings for purposes of the retirement test, if they were the result of services rendered in or prior to the initial month of entitlement.

A self-employed agent includes the following in figuring total earnings for a particular taxable year for purposes of the retirement test:

- Original commissions received during the year.

- Renewal commissions received during the year from policies sold while a self-employed agent, if the policies were sold after the initial month of entitlement to Social Security benefits, but not for such policies sold in or before such initial month. Further, there will be excluded all renewal commissions received from policies sold in prior years while an employee. Also excluded will be anticipated renewal commissions on policies sold during the current year while self-employed.

- All net earnings from self-employment derived during the year in the form of insurance service fees, persistency fees, etc.

- All remuneration classified as earnings from other jobs, trades, or businesses.

- Any net loss from other self-employment during the year.

ARE SELF-EMPLOYED EARNINGS SUBJECT TO SOCIAL SECURITY RETIREMENT TEST?	Commissions Received In	
Time of Sale	Year of First Entitlement*	Year After Year of First Entitlement*
Prior to Year of First Entitlement	Yes	No
In Year of First Entitlement		
(1) Sold in months through month of First Entitlement	Yes	No
(2) Sold in months after month of First Entitlement	Yes	Yes
After Year of First Entitlement	Yes	Yes

* Entitlement means (a) being eligible by virtue of age and insured status (i.e., having the required number of quarters of coverage), and (b) having filed a claim for benefits.

The receipt of renewal commissions in the initial year of retirement on policies sold by a self-employed agent will not necessarily result in a loss of benefits, even though they exceed the earnings limit for the taxable year. The reason is that such "self-employment" earnings cannot be charged against benefits for any month in the initial year of retirement in which the agent-beneficiary does not render any substantial services in self-employment. Even large amounts of renewal commissions will not cause loss of any benefits if the agent-beneficiary renders no substantial services in self-employment during the taxable year in which the commissions are received.

Generally, repeat commissions paid on casualty insurance policies (e.g., accident and health) differ from renewal commissions in the life insurance field. This is true even though the repeat commissions are sometimes called "renewal" commissions. Each repeat commission is, in fact, for a policy written for a new and different term.

Ordinarily, the rate of commission on these repeats is the same regardless of how many times the insurance is extended for a new term. In life insurance renewals, on the other hand, there is a limit on the number of years for which renewal commissions are paid on the same life insurance policy. Regardless of the amount of work done by an agent when a casualty insurance policy is extended, the commission paid is for the new term only. It is not additional compensation for the original term of the policy. For these reasons, repeat commissions from accident and health policies are normally earned in the month in which the policy is extended. Thus, they are wages for the month and year if the agent then was an employee. If the agent then was self-employed, they may be included as earnings from self-employment for the year in which they are received.

Note

1. 20 CFR Part 404, Subpart E.

377. What is the Foreign Work Test?

The "foreign work test" is a separate retirement test that applies to beneficiaries who engage in employment (or self-employment) outside of the United States that is not covered by the Social Security system. The foreign work test is based only on the amount of time in which the beneficiary was employed or self-employed and is not based on the amount of earnings or losses by the beneficiary. The intention was to make it unnecessary to convert earnings or losses from non-US currency into specific dollar amounts.

The foreign work test applies to persons living abroad who are being paid Social Security benefits (other than those entitled because of disability), and who work prior to full retirement age in employment or self-employment outside the US that is not covered by the US Social Security system.

The test is based only on the amount of time during which the beneficiary is employed or self-employed, not on the amount of the beneficiary's earnings or losses. The foreign work test was intended to make it unnecessary to convert earnings in a foreign currency into earnings in specific dollar amounts.

Under the foreign work test, your monthly benefit is withheld for each calendar month that you work (or are deemed to have been available to work) for more than 45 hours.

378. When are benefits withheld under the Foreign Work Test?

Under the "foreign work test," monthly benefits are withheld for each calendar month that an individual (or a person entitled to benefits on that individual's work record) works:

- outside of the United States;

- performing work for pay not covered by Social Security;

- for more than forty-five hours.

The test applies only to persons who have not reached Full Retirement Age. Benefits are not withheld for anyone over Full Retirement Age. The test USED to apply to Social Security recipients under the age of 70 but the "Under 70" rule was eliminated by the Senior Citizens Work Act of 2000.

If a benefit holder works and loses benefits for one or more months, it should be noted that family benefits are withheld for those same months. These benefits would include:

- benefits payable to spouse or children based on the earnings record; and

- benefits payable to a spouse on earnings as disabled child, mother, or father.

NOTE: A divorced spouse, divorced at least two years, is not subject to withholding because of the beneficiary's work.

379. What constitutes "work outside of the United States"?

Work outside of the United States is any work that takes place outside of the territorial boundaries of the fifty United States, the District of Columbia, Puerto Rico, the U.S. Virgin Islands, Guam, American Samoa, and the Commonwealth of the Northern Mariana Islands.

NOTE: Self-employment by resident aliens in Puerto Rico, the U.S. Virgin Islands, Guam, American Samoa, and the Commonwealth of the Northern Mariana Islands IS considered to be outside of the United States, unless the nonresident alien is a resident of a State, the District of Columbia, Puerto Rico, the U.S. Virgin Islands, Guam, American Samoa, and the Commonwealth of the Northern Mariana Islands.

The foreign work test does not apply to activity which would, if carried on in the U.S., result only in income which is specifically excepted from coverage such as:

- rentals from real estate;

- capital gains;

- dividends or interest;

- retirement pay to partners who rendered no services; or

- limited partnership income.

380. What is "noncovered work for pay" under the foreign work test?

Noncovered work for pay includes work: [1]

- outside of the United States in a job not covered by Social Security; OR

- being self-employed outside the United States in a trade or business where your income is not subject to the Social Security tax; OR

- being a self-employed owner or part-owner of a trade or business outside the United States not subject to the Social Security tax where the owner or part-owner holds themselves out to work for more than forty-five hours a month, regardless of whether that much work is performed.

In the case of a trade or business that produces only income that would be excluded from net earnings if carried on within the United States, (e.g., dividends, rentals from real estate, etc.) is not "non-covered work for pay". Neither the foreign work test nor the earnings test applies to such income.

Note

1. https://www.ssa.gov/OP_Home/handbook/handbook.18/handbook-1825.html (Last accessed September 28, 2022).

381. Does work performed outside the United States have to be reported?

Yes. If the beneficiary is under Full Retirement Age and receives retirement or disability benefits as a worker, spouse, survivor, or dependent of a worker, a report must be filed with the Social Security Administration if the worker becomes employed for forty-five or more hours per month or becomes self-employed outside of the United States.

Employment must be reported to the nearest United States Embassy or Consulate if outside of the United States. The report must be filed before the receipt of the second month's benefit after work began.

382. What is the penalty for failure to report foreign work?

Penalty deductions may be imposed for failure to report the following:

(a)   For the first time to fail to report: a penalty of one month's benefit is withheld. This is regardless of the number of months worked before reporting.

(b)   For the second time to fail to report: two months benefits can be withheld.

(c)   For the third and subsequent times that there is a failure to report: three additional months benefits can be withheld.

These penalties are in addition to the monthly benefits lost because of the application of the Foreign Work Test.

383. Can benefits be lost by residing overseas?

Yes, in some instances if the Treasury Department is enforcing sanctions or if the Social Security Administration (SSA) has restrictions on ability to pay individuals in certain countries.

Treasury Department Sanctions

The U.S. Department of the Treasury prohibits making payments to persons residing in Cuba or North Korea. If the person is a U.S. citizen residing in Cuba or North Korea, they can get all the payments that SSA withhold once they move to a country where the SSA can send payments.

• Exception for non-citizens: Under the Social Security Act, if they person is not a U.S. citizen, they cannot receive payments for the months they lived in Cuba or North Korea, even if they go to another country and satisfy all other requirements.

Other Treasury Department sanctions could affect payments to persons in other countries.

Social Security Restrictions

Generally, SSA cannot send Social Security payments to persons in Azerbaijan, Belarus, Kazakhstan, Kyrgyzstan, Moldova, Tajikistan, Turkmenistan, Ukraine, and Uzbekistan. However, they can make exceptions for certain eligible persons in these countries. To qualify for an exception, the person must meet and agree to restricted payment conditions.

If the person does not qualify for an exception, SSA will withhold payments until the person leaves the country with Social Security restrictions and go to a country where they can send payments.

384. Can a recipient lose Social Security if they lose permanent resident status ("green card") or if they renounce US citizenship?

An individual that renounces US citizenship is a non-resident alien (NRA) and are governed by NRA rules. The recipient has the responsibility to inform authorities of the change in citizenship and this is also asked the annual questionnaire that Social Security beneficiaries submit.

The place of residence determines if a Non-Resident Alien can continue to collect Social Security. The ability to collect depends on the existence or non-existence of US bilateral agreements, current citizenship, and the country of residence. Depending on agreements in place, it can range from only a minor payment difference to having Social Security payments discontinued after being more than six months outside the US.

If a recipient has not been in the United States at any time during the six calendar months before the first month of entitlement, then to get benefits started they must come to the United States and stay every hour of a full calendar month.

> *Example*: the NRA arrives February 25 – they would need to stay the entire month of March and not leave until April 1.

After the NRA complete the establishment visit for a full calendar month, there are two ways to continue receiving benefits. You can choose one or the other:

- the recipient must spend any part of one day in the United States at least once every 30 days or less; or

- If the NRA does not do one-day visits (or fails to make a visit in a 30-day time period), they must come to the United States and stay every hour of 30 consecutive days. This visit for 30 days must be completed no later than the end of the six-month period that started with their first full calendar month outside the United States.

There are a couple of countries to which Social Security cannot make payments. U.S. citizens can accumulate unpaid payments while in these countries and receive them after departing the country, but NRA's will lose those payments.

Note that dependent's and survivor's benefits may also be affected by change of status from "citizen" to "NRA" of the individuals or the worker concerned.

In any case, the NRA should keep their Social Security card.

385. Can an NRA spouse or child receive survivor benefits or dependent benefits while overseas?

Generally, the spouse of an NRA can receive survivor benefits if they are a citizen of a specific country or resides in a country with which the US has a social security agreement, or he/she has lived in the US for at least five years while the family relationship existed.

386. Are taxes withheld on Social Security and survivors' benefits of NRA spouse of US citizens?

There may be an automatic federal withholding tax of 30 percent on 85 percent (i.e. 25.5 percent of the monthly benefit) of each benefit payment made to an NRA. Some NRA may be exempt from this tax or taxed at a lower rate because of treaties entered into by the U.S. and the other country involved. This is discussed in greater detail in the IRS publication "U.S. Tax Guide for Aliens".[1]

Note

1. https://www.irs.gov/pub/irs-pdf/p519.pdf.

TAXATION OF SOCIAL SECURITY BENEFITS

387. Are Social Security benefits subject to federal income taxation?

Social Security retirement, survivor, and disability benefits may be subject to federal income taxes in some cases. The person who has the legal right to receive the benefits must determine if the benefits are taxable. For example, if a parent and child both receive benefits, but the payment for the child is made to the parent's account, the parent must use only the parent's portion of the benefits in figuring if benefits are taxable. The portion of the benefits that belongs to the child must be added to the child's other income to see if any of those benefits are taxable.

If the only income a person receives is Social Security benefits, the benefits generally are not taxable and the person probably does not need to file a tax return. However, if a person has other income in addition to benefits, it may be necessary to file a return (even if none of the benefits are taxable).

If the total of a person's income plus half of his or her benefits is more than the base amount, some of the benefits are taxable. Included in the person's total income is any tax-exempt interest income, excludable interest from United States savings bonds, and excludable income earned in a foreign country, United States possessions, or Puerto Rico.[1]

Voluntary federal income tax withholding is allowed on Social Security benefits. Recipients may submit a Form W-4V[2] *Voluntary Withholding Request*, if they want federal income tax withheld from their benefits. Beneficiaries are able to choose withholding at 7 percent, 10 percent, 12 percent, or 22 percent of their total benefit payment. Note that the most current version of Form W4-V was updated during February 2018 due to tax law changes.

Notes

1. IRC Sec. 86.
2. Form W-4V, https://www.irs.gov/pub/irs-pdf/fw4v.pdf (last accessed September 2, 2022).

---

388. What are the base amounts?

The base amount is as follows, depending upon a person's filing status:[1]

- $32,000 for married couples filing jointly

- $0 for married couples filing separately and who lived together at any time during the year

- $25,000 for other taxpayers

If a person is married and files a joint return, the person and his spouse must combine their incomes and their Social Security benefits when figuring if any of their combined benefits are taxable. Even if the spouse did not receive any benefits, the person must add the spouse's income to his when figuring if any of his benefits are taxable.

Example. Jim and Julie Smith are filing a joint return for 2022 and both received Social Security benefits during the year. Jim received net benefits of $6,600, while Julie received net benefits of $2,400. Jim also received a taxable pension of $10,000 and interest income of $500. Jim did not have any tax-exempt interest income. Jim and Julie's Social Security benefits are not taxable for 2020 because the sum of their income ($10,500) and one-half of their benefits ($9,000 ÷ 2 = $4,500) is not more than their base amount ($32,000).

Any repayment of Social Security benefits a person made during the year must be subtracted from the gross benefits received. It does not matter whether the repayment was for a benefit the person received in that year or in an earlier year.

Summary

For **individual** filers, income tax may be due on up to 50 percent of benefits if the taxpayer's combined income is between $25,000 and $34,000. Up to 85 percent of benefits may be taxable the combined income exceeds $34,000.

For **joint** filers, income tax may be due on up to 50 percent of benefits if the couple's combined income is between $32,000 and $44,000. Up to 85 percent of benefits may be taxable the combined income exceeds $44,000.

If a married couple files separate returns, the entire benefit is likely to be taxable.

Note

1. IRC Sec. 86(c)(1).

---

389. What portion of Social Security benefits are subject to income taxes?

The amount of benefits to be included in taxable income depends on the person's total income plus half his or her Social Security benefits. The higher the total, the more benefits a person must include in taxable income. Depending upon a person's income, he or she may be required to include either up to 50 percent or up to 85 percent of benefits in income.

50 Percent Taxable

If a person's income plus half of his Social Security benefits is more than the following base amount for his filing status, up to 50 percent of his or her benefits will be included in his or her gross income:[1]

- $32,000 for married couples filing jointly

- $0 for married couples filing separately and who lived together at any time during the year

- $25,000 for all other taxpayers

85 Percent Taxable

If a person's income plus half of his or her Social Security benefits is more than the following adjusted base amount for his or her filing status, up to 85 percent of his or her benefits will be included in his or her gross income:[2]

- $44,000 for married couples filing jointly

- $0 for married couples filing separately and who lived together at any time during the year

- $34,000 for other taxpayers

If a person is married filing separately and lived with his or her spouse at any time during the year, up to 85 percent of his or her benefits will be included in his or her gross income.

Note

1. IRC Sec. 86(c)(1).
2. IRC Sec. 86(c)(2).

390. Why is nontaxable interest income included in a taxpayer's adjusted gross income?

Nontaxable interest income is included in income to limit opportunities for manipulation of tax liability on benefits. Individuals whose incomes consist of different mixes of taxable and nontaxable income are treated the same as individuals whose total income is taxable for federal income tax purposes.

391. Are workers' compensation benefits included in the definition of Social Security benefits for tax purposes?

Yes, and they are also included in the definition of Social Security benefits for tax purposes are workers' compensation benefits, to the extent they cause a reduction in Social Security and Railroad Retirement Tier I disability benefits.[1] This is intended to assure that these social insurance benefits, which are paid in lieu of Social Security payments, are treated similarly for purposes of taxation. For additional details, see Publication 05-10018 *How Workers' Compensation and Other Disability Payments May Affect Your Benefits*.[2]

If a person receives workers' compensation or other public disability benefits, AND Social Security disability benefits, the total amount of these benefits can't exceed 80 percent of your average current earnings before the disability occurred.

Social Security disability benefits, including benefits payable to family members, are added together with workers' compensation and other public disability payments. If the total amount of these benefits exceeds 80 percent of average current earnings, the excess amount is deducted from your Social Security benefit.

The Social Security benefit will be reduced until the month the beneficiary reaches age sixty-five, or the month other benefits stop, whichever comes first. Starting December 19, 2015, due to a change in the law, benefits are continuing to be reduced until the person reaches full retirement age.

Average Current Earnings is calculated by the highest of three computation methods:

- High-1 Average Current Earnings

  o Highest yearly earnings from the year of current onset and the five previous years and divide the yearly total by twelve months and round to the next-lower dollar amount.

- High-5 Average Current Earnings

  o Sum of the five consecutive years after 1950 with the highest unindexed earnings and divided by sixty months and round to the next-lowest dollar amount.

- Average Monthly Wage (AMW)

  o Divide the total unindexed earnings for the computation years (dividend) by number of months in the computation years (divisor) and round to the next-lowest dollar amount.

Notes

1. IRC Sec. 86(d)(3).
2. Social Security Administration, How Workers' Compensation and Other Disability Payments May Affect Your Benefits (December 2021 edition), https://www.ssa.gov/pubs/EN-05-10018.pdf (last accessed September 3, 2022).

392. How are overpayments and lump-sum retroactive benefits taxed?

Special rules are provided for dealing with overpayments and lump-sum retroactive benefit payments.[1] Benefits paid to an individual in any taxable year are reduced by any overpayments repaid during the year. Taxpayers who received a lump-sum payment of retroactive benefits may treat the benefits as wholly payable for the year in which they receive them, or may elect to attribute the benefits to the tax years in which they would have fallen had they been paid timely. No benefits for months before 1984 are taxable, regardless of when they are paid.

> *Example 1.* Ms. Jones is single. In 2022, she applied for Social Security disability benefits but was told she was ineligible to receive them. She appealed the decision and won her appeal. In 2023, she received a lump-sum payment of $6,000, which included $2,000 for 2022. She has two choices. She can use her 2023 income to figure the taxable part of the entire $6,000 payment, or she can use her 2021 income to figure the taxable part of the $2,000 received for 2022. In the latter case, for 2022 she would include only the $4,000 attributable to 2023.

> *Example 2.* Assume that Mr. Jackson receives a $1,000 Social Security benefit in 2022, $400 of which is attributable to 2021. Assume also that the $1,000 benefit would increase Mr. Jackson's 2021 gross income by $500 (i.e., by the full 50 percent), but that the $400 would have increased his 2020 gross income by only $150, and the remaining $600 would have increased his 2020 gross income by $300. He may limit the increase in 2020 gross income to only $450, the sum of the increases in gross income that would have occurred had the $400 been paid in 2019.

Note

1. IRC Secs. 86(d)(2), 86(e).

393. What reporting requirements must be met by the Social Security Administration?

The Commissioner of Social Security must file annual returns with the Secretary of the Treasury setting forth the amounts of benefits paid to each individual in each calendar year, together with the name and address of the individual. The Commissioner of Social Security must also furnish similar information to each beneficiary by January 31 of the year following the benefit payments. The statement will show the total amount of Social Security benefits paid to the beneficiary, the total amount of Social Security benefits repaid by the beneficiary to the Social Security Administration during the calendar year, and the total reductions in benefits to offset workers' compensation benefits received by the beneficiary.

394. Are Social Security benefits subject to income tax withholding?

Voluntary federal income tax withholding on Social Security benefits is allowed. Recipients may submit a Form W-4V[1] *Voluntary Withholding Request* if they want federal income tax withheld from their benefits. Recipients may choose withholding at 7 percent, 10 percent, 12 percent, or 22 percent of their total benefit payment. Withholding is not mandatory.

The following are **not** subject to Voluntary Tax Withholding (VTW):

- Title XVI payments,

- Black Lung payments,

- Lump Sum Death Payments,

- returned check reissuances, or

- benefits due before January 1984.

Beneficiaries can change their minds and file a new Form W-4V to start, stop, or change the withholding.

Note

1. Form W-4V Voluntary Withholding Request https://www.irs.gov/pub/irs-pdf/fw4v.pdf (revised February 2018) (last accessed September 3, 2022).

395. If a recipient of Social Security benefits elects Medical Insurance (Part B) under Medicare and the premiums are deducted from the individual's benefits, is the whole benefit, before the deduction, a Social Security benefit?

Yes, the individual is treated as if he received the whole benefit and later paid separately for the Medical Insurance (Part B) coverage. Both the Commissioner of Social Security and the Railroad Retirement Board will include the entire amount as paid to the individual in the statements they furnish.

396. Which states currently tax Social Security benefits as income?

Significant changes have occurred in the states that tax Social Security benefits. Twelve states currently tax Social Security benefits (one fewer than last year), with particulars detailed below.

- **Colorado:** Benefit income is taxable at a flat rate of 4.55 percent. For individuals between the ages of 55 and 64, up to $20,000 of Social Security benefits can be excluded, along with other retirement income. Individuals sixty-five and older can exclude benefits and other retirement income up to $24,000. In addition, Social Security income not taxed by the federal government is not added back to adjusted gross income for state income tax purposes. Both spouses can take the deduction. Beginning with the 2022 tax year, Colorado taxpayers will be able to deduct all federally taxable Social Security benefits from their state income, part of a tax-code re-write that Colorado enacted during June 2021.

- **Connecticut:** Social Security is exempt for individual taxpayers with federal adjusted gross income of less than $75,000 and for married taxpayers filing jointly with federal AGI of less than $100,000. The Colorado income-tax rate ranges from 3 percent to 6.99 percent

- **Kansas:** Social Security benefits are exempt from Kansas income tax for residents with a federal adjusted gross income of $75,000 or less. Kansas tax rates range from 3.1 percent to 5.7 percent.

- **Minnesota:** Minnesota follows federal rules in determining Social Security tax-ability. Social Security income is taxable, but a married couple filing jointly can subtract $5,290 of their federally taxable Social Security benefits from their state income. The tax break is $4,130 for single and head of household, $2,250 for married separate filers. For those with $80,270 of income (married joint filers) and $62,710 (singles) the tax break to begin to be phased out with it being completely eliminated for those with more than $103,930 of taxable income. (2021 figures – adjusted annually based on annual CP inflation rate).

- **Missouri:** Social Security benefits are not taxed and fully deductible for single taxpayers with adjusted gross income of less than $85,000 and married couples with AGI of less than $100,000 aged sixty-two and older. Taxpayers who exceed those income limits may qualify for a partial exemption on their benefits. Missouri's income-tax rates range from 0 percent to 5.4 percent.

- **Montana:** Social Security benefits are taxable. Montana does not tax Social Security for people with overall incomes of less than $25,000 for a single filer and $32,000 for a couple filing jointly. Residents who make more are liable for tax on their bene-fits, but the state uses a different method and taxes different types of income than the federal government to determine the taxable amount. The state tax form includes a worksheet for calculating the difference[1]. Montana has a tax rate ranging from 1 to 6.9 percent.

- **Nebraska:** A taxpayer may subtract Social Security income included in federal adjusted gross income if the taxpayer's federal adjusted gross income is less than or equal to $59,960 for married couples filing jointly, or $44,460 for all other filers. Above these levels, a portion of Social Security is taxable, but the percentage is set to decline annually as the state eliminates taxation of Social Security benefits. Legislation enacted in 2021 established a timetable to reduce the taxable portion of a beneficiary's Social Security in annual increments through 2030. However, a bill passed by the legislature on April 7, 2022, and subsequently signed by Governor Pete Ricketts' shortened the timetable by five years dropping the taxable share of Nebraskans' Social Security income from 60 percent during 2022 to zero in 2025. Nebraska taxes income at rates of 2.46 percent to 6.84 percent. The top rate is set to decline over the next several years as part of the new tax law.

- **New Mexico:** For the 2021 tax year, Social Security benefits are taxable for residents with incomes of more than $25,000 (individuals) and $32,000 (couples filing jointly). New Mexico allows individuals sixty-five and older with AGIs under $28,500 (single) and $51,000 (married couples) to deduct up to $8,000 in income, which can be applied to benefits. Legislation passed by state lawmakers in February and signed by Gov. Michelle Lujan Grisham in March 2022 eliminates future taxation of benefits for most residents. Beginning in the 2022 tax year, Social Security income is fully deductible for residents with AGIs below $100,000 for an individual and $150,000 for a couple filing jointly. New Mexico taxes income at rates from 1.7 percent to 5.9 percent.

- **North Dakota:** Taxation of Social Security benefits in North Dakota has been repealed.

- **Rhode Island:** For people of Full Retirement Age (FRA), Rhode Island does not tax Social Security benefits for single filers or head of household with up to $86,350 in adjusted gross income and couples filing jointly with up to $107,950 in AGI. (2022 figures – adjusted annually based on annual CP inflation rate). Rhode Island taxes income at rates ranging from 3.75 percent to 5.99 percent.

- **Utah:** Social Security benefits are taxed. Utah uses the federal formula to calculate how much Social Security income is taxable at the state tax rate, which is 4.95 percent, but beginning in 2021, couples reporting income of $50,000 or less and singles making $30,000 or less qualify for a full tax credit on their benefit income. Those earning more can still get a partial break on their benefits, with the tax credit reduced by 25 percent on each dollar above the income thresholds above.

- **Vermont:** Effective in 2022, Social Security benefits are exempt for single filers making an AGI less than $50,000 a year ($65,000 for joint filers). There is a partial exemption for single filers making between $50,000 and $60,000 and for married joint filers between $65,000 and $75,000. This exemption is eliminated for single filers making more than $65,000 and married joint filers making $75,000 or more. For single filers earning $60,000 or more and couples making $75,000 or more, benefits are fully taxed at the state rate, which ranges from 3.35 percent to 8.75 percent.

- **West Virginia:** West Virginia has phased out state income tax on Social Security for many residents. For the 2021 tax year, West Virginians that made $50,000 or less ($100,000 for couples filing jointly) were allowed to exclude up to 65 percent of the benefits they receive from Social Security. Beginning in 2022, 100 percent of Social Security benefits will be free of tax. For people with incomes above those levels, benefits are taxed according to the federal model. West Virginia's income-tax rates range from 3 percent to 6.5 percent.

Thirty-eight states and the District of Columbia do not tax Social Security benefits. The states are:

- Alabama, Alaska, Arizona, Arkansas, California, Delaware, Florida, Georgia, Hawaii, Idaho, Illinois, Indiana, Iowa, Kentucky, Louisiana, Maine, Maryland, Massachusetts, Michigan, Mississippi, Nevada, New Hampshire, New Jersey, New York, North Carolina, Ohio, Oklahoma, Oregon, Pennsylvania, South Carolina, South Dakota, Tennessee, Texas, Virginia, Washington, Wisconsin, and Wyoming as well as the District of Columbia. North Dakota is a new addition to this list.

Note

1. https://mtrevenue.gov/publications/montana-individual-income-tax-return-form-2/. (Last accessed October 21, 2022).

SOCIAL SECURITY TAXES

397. What are the Social Security and Medicare tax rates for employers and employees?

The tax rate is the same for both the employer and the employee. Every employer who employs one or more persons and every employee in covered employment is subject to the tax imposed under the Federal Insurance Contributions Act (FICA).[1]

The tax consists of two taxes: the OASDI tax (the tax for old-age, survivors, and disability insurance) and the Hospital Insurance (HI) tax (for Medicare Part A).

For 2023, the maximum earnings base (the maximum amount of annual earnings subject to the tax) for the OASDI tax is $160,200. There is no maximum earnings base for the HI tax. All wages and self-employment income are subject to the HI tax.

For employees and employers, the rate of the OASDI tax is 6.20 percent, and the rate of the HI tax is 1.45 percent. Thus, the maximum OASDI tax for an employee in 2023 (with maximum earnings of $160,200) is $9,932.40 as an eimployee or $19,864.80 as an independent contractor. The maximum HI tax is unlimited because all wages are subject to the tax.

OASDI TAX ON EMPLOYEES AND EMPLOYERS				
Year	% Rate (OASDI)	Max. Wage Base	Max. Tax (each)	Max. Tax (both)
1986	5.7	$42,000	$2,394.00	$4,788.00
1987	5.7	43,800	2,496.60	4,993.20
1988	6.06	45,000	2,727.00	5,454.00
1989	6.06	48,000	2,908.80	5,817.60
1990	6.2	51,300	3,180.60	6,361.20
1991	6.2	53,400	3,310.80	6,621.60
1992	6.2	55,500	3,441.00	6,882.00
1993	6.2	57,600	3,571.20	7,142.40
1994	6.2	60,600	3,757.20	7,514.40
1995	6.2	61,200	3,794.40	7,588.80
1996	6.2	62,700	3,887.40	7,774.80
1997	6.2	65,400	4,054.80	8,109.60
1998	6.2	68,400	4,240.80	8,481.60
1999	6.2	72,600	4,501.20	9,002.40
2000	6.2	76,200	4,724.40	9,448.80
2001	6.2	80,400	4,984.80	9,969.60

OASDI TAX ON EMPLOYEES AND EMPLOYERS				
Year	% Rate (OASDI)	Max. Wage Base	Max. Tax (each)	Max. Tax (both)
2002	6.2	84,900	5,263.80	10,527.60
2003	6.2	87,000	5,394.00	10,788.00
2004	6.2	87,900	5,449.80	10,899.60
2005	6.2	90,000	5,580.00	11,160.00
2006	6.2	94,200	5,840.40	11,680.80
2007	6.2	97,500	6,045.00	12,090.00
2008	6.2	102,000	6,324.00	12,648.00
2009-2011	6.2	106,800	6,621.60	13,243.20
2012	6.2	110,100	6,826.20	13,652.40
2013	6.2	113,700	7,049.40	14,098.80
2014	6.2	117,000	7,254.00	14,508.00
2015-2016	6.2	118,500	7,347.00	14,694.00
2017	6.2	127,200	7,886.40	15,772.80
2018	6.2	128,700	7,979.40	15,958.80
2019	6.2	132,900	8,239.80	16,479.60
2020	6.2	137,700	8,537.40	17,074.80
2021	6.2	142,800	8,853.60	17,707.20
2022	6.2	147,000	9,114.00	18,288.00
2023	6.2	$160,200	9,932.40	19,864.80

Note: The 1.45 percent Medicare tax applies to all wages.

The OASDI maximum earnings base and maximum tax are subject to automatic adjustment in 2023, and after based on changes in wage levels. For 2023, the 6.2 percent rate applied to the maximum wage base of $160,200 causes a maximum tax of $9,932.40 for each and $19,864.80 for both.

Under the Patient Protection and Affordable Care Act of 2010, new Medicare taxes were imposed starting in 2013. Under the provisions of the new law most taxpayers will continue to pay the 1.45 percent Medicare tax, but single people earning more than $200,000 and married couples earning more than $250,000 will be taxed at an additional 0.9 percent (2.35 percent in total) on the excess over those base amounts. Self-employed persons pay 3.8 percent on earnings over those thresholds.

Employers will collect the extra 0.9 percent on wages exceeding $200,000 just as they would withhold Medicare taxes and remit them to the IRS. However, companies won't be responsible for determining whether a worker's combined income with his or her spouse made them subject to the tax.

Instead, some employees will have to remit additional Medicare taxes when they file income tax returns, and some will get a tax credit for amounts overpaid. Married couples with combined incomes approaching $250,000 will have to keep tabs on both spouses' pay to avoid an unexpected tax bill.

Beginning in 2013, Medicare tax was, for the first time, applied to investment income. A tax of 3.8 percent is imposed on net investment income of single taxpayers with Adjusted Gross Income (AGI) above $200,000 and joint filers with AGI over $250,000.

Net investment income is interest, dividends, royalties, rents, gross income from a trade or business involving passive activities, and net gain from disposition of property (other than property held in a trade or business). Net investment income is reduced by the deductions that are allocable to that income. However, the tax doesn't apply to income in tax-deferred retirement accounts such as 401(k) plans.

Not all earnings are subject to Social Security taxes. A person can be an employee but be exempt from the Social Security tax. An example is an individual hired by a federal agency on a temporary basis as an emergency firefighter to help fight forest fires. The individual performed the service for three months, twelve hours a day, and the federal agency supplied the necessary equipment and gave him directions on a daily basis. The Internal Revenue Service ruled that, although the individual was an employee under common-law rules, he was exempt from Social Security taxes, as the Internal Revenue Code exempts from the definition of employment those services performed for the United States by an individual serving on a temporary basis in case of fire or other emergencies.

Note

1. IRC Secs. 3101, 3111.

398. If an employee works for two employers during the year and more than the maximum tax is paid on his or her wages, will the overpayment be refunded to the employee and his or her employers?

Each employer is required to withhold the employee's tax, and to pay the employer's tax, on wages up to the maximum earnings base for the year. Consequently, if an employee works for more than one employer during the year, the taxes paid may exceed the maximum payable for the year. In this case, the employee is entitled to a refund of his or her overpayment, or the overpayment will be credited to his or her income tax for the year. His or her employers, however, are not entitled to any refund or credit. Each employer is liable for tax on his or her wages, up to the maximum earnings base.

However, a group of corporations concurrently employing an individual will be considered a single employer if one of the group serves as a common paymaster for the entire group. This will result in such corporations having to pay no more in Social Security taxes than a single employer pays.

399. Does an employer receive an income tax deduction for Social Security tax payments?

Yes, the employer's Social Security tax is deductible as a business expense, but only if wages upon which taxes are paid are also deductible.[1]

Note

1. See IRC Sec. 162.

400. Must Social Security taxes be paid on cash tips?

Yes, an employee must pay Social Security taxes on cash tips of twenty dollars ($20) or more a month from one employer. These tips are treated as wages for Social Security and income tax withholding purposes and must be reported. Cash tips of less than twenty dollars ($20) a month are not reported.

The employee is required to report tips to an employer within ten days following the month in which the tips equal or exceed twenty dollars.

The employer must pay the usual employer tax on tips.

The employer must withhold income tax and deduct the employee Social Security and Hospital Insurance (HI) tax on tips reported to him. The withholding is to be made from any wages (other than tips) that are under the employer's control. Employers may deduct the tax due on tips during a calendar quarter on an estimated basis, and adjust the amount deducted from wages paid to the employee either during the calendar quarter or within thirty days thereafter. If these wages are not sufficient to cover the employee tax due, the employee may (but is not required to) furnish the employer with additional funds to cover the tax.

The employee is directly responsible for paying any portion of the employee tax that the employer cannot collect from wages or from funds furnished by the employee. The employer is required to give statements to both the employee and the Internal Revenue Service, showing the difference between the amount of the employee tax due and the amount collected by the employer.

Food or beverage establishments are provided with a business tax credit, equal to the amount of the employer's Social Security tax obligation (7.65 percent) attributable to reported tips in excess of those treated as wages for purposes of satisfying the minimum wage provisions of the Fair Labor Standards Act (FLSA). An employer must pay a Social Security tax on the tip income of employees, and tips can be counted as satisfying one-half of the minimum wage requirement.

The credit also applies to tips received from customers in connection with the delivery or serving of food or beverages, regardless of whether the food or beverages are for consumption on an establishment's premises. The credit is available, even if the employee failed to report the tips.[1]

Note

1. For further information regarding income and employment taxes on tips, see *IRS Publication 531 (Reporting Tip Income)*. https://www.irs.gov/pub/irs-pdf/p531.pdf (most current version is for use in preparing 2021 returns) (last accessed September 3, 2022).

401. How are uncollected Social Security and other taxes collected?

A person must report on their tax return any Social Security and Medicare taxes, or railroad retirement taxes that remained uncollected at the end of 2022. These uncollected taxes will be shown on Form W-2.

Reporting social security, Medicare, Additional Medicare, or railroad retirement taxes on tips not reported to an employer:

- If a person received $20 or more in cash and charge tips in a month from any one job and did not report all of those tips to the employer, they must report the Social Security, Medicare, and Additional Medicare taxes on the unreported tips as additional tax on their return. The individual must use Form 4137, *Social Security and Medicare Tax on Unreported Tip Income*,[1] to figure Social Security and Medicare taxes and/or Form 8959,[2] *Additional Medicare Tax*, to figure Additional Medicare Tax.

Reporting uncollected Social Security, Medicare, Additional Medicare, or railroad retirement taxes on tips reported to an employer:

- A person may have uncollected taxes if their regular pay was not enough for the employer to withhold all the taxes owed and the employee did not give the employer enough money to pay the rest of the taxes.

- If the employer could not collect all of the Social Security and Medicare, and Additional Medicare taxes, or railroad retirement taxes owed on tips reported, the uncollected taxes will be shown in box 12 of Form W-2 (codes A and B). These must be reported as additional tax on the return. Unlike the uncollected portion of the regular (1.45 percent) Medicare tax, uncollected Additional Medicare Tax is not reported on Form W-2.

Notes

1. Form 4137 (2020), https://www.irs.gov/pub/irs-pdf/f4137.pdf (last accessed September 4, 2022).
2. Form 8959 (2020), https://www.irs.gov/pub/irs-pdf/f8959.pdf (last accessed September 4, 2022).

402. How does an individual report Social Security taxes for domestic help?

The threshold amount for Social Security coverage of a domestic worker is $2.600 in 2023 up from $2,400 in 2022. In 2020, it was $2,200 and in 2019 and 2018 it was $2,100, up from the $2,000 it was in 2017 and 2016.[1] This threshold amount is indexed in future years for increases in average wages in the economy. Indexing occurs in $100 increments, rounded down to the nearest $100.

CALCULATION DETAILS		
Amounts in formula	1995 threshold	$1,000
	1994 average wage index	23,753.53
	2020 average wage index (latest reported)	55,628.60
Computation	$1,000 times 55,628.00 divided by 23,753.53 equals $2,341.91, which rounds down to $2,300	

Exempt from Social Security taxes are any wages paid to a worker for domestic services performed in any year during which the worker is under age eighteen, except for workers under age eighteen whose principal occupation is household employment. Being a student is considered to be an occupation for purposes of this test. Thus, for example, the wages of a student who is sixteen years old and also babysits will be exempt from the reporting and payment requirements, regardless of whether the amount of wages paid is above or below the threshold. On the other hand, the wages of a seventeen-year-old single mother, who leaves school and goes to work as a domestic to support her family, will be subject to the reporting and payment requirements.

Employers may satisfy their tax obligations through regular estimated tax payments or increased tax withholding from their own wages. Estimated tax penalties will apply in appropriate circumstances.

> *Example 1.* Assume an employer pays a domestic employee $1,500 in wages for calendar year 2022. Because the amount of these taxes is below the $2,400 threshold, the employer is not subject to reporting.

> *Example 2.* Assume an employer pays a domestic employee $2,900 in wages for calendar year 2022. Because the amount of these wages is above the $2,300 threshold, the employer is subject to reporting.

In addition, wages paid to Election Workers are also reported but at the $2,000 level which was remained the same from 2021.

COVERAGE THRESHOLDS FOR DOMESTIC EMPLOYEES [a] AND ELECTION OFFICIALS/WORKERS					
Year	Domestic Employees	Election Workers	Year	Domestic Employees	Election workers
1994	$1,000	$1,000	2010	$1,700	$1,500
1995	1,000	1,000	2011	1,700	1,500
1996	1,000	1,000	2012	1,800	1,500
1997	1,000	1,000	2013	1,800	1,600
1998	1,100	1,000	2014	1,900	1,600
1999	1,100	1,000	2015	1,900	1,600
2000	1,200	1,100	2016	2,000	1,700
2001	1,300	1,200	2017	2,000	1,800
2002	1,300	1,100	2018	2,100	1,800

COVERAGE THRESHOLDS FOR DOMESTIC EMPLOYEES [a] AND ELECTION OFFICIALS/WORKERS					
Year	Domestic Employees	Election Workers	Year	Domestic Employees	Election workers
2003	1,400	1,200	2019	2,100	1,800
2004	1,400	1,200	2020	2,200	1,900
2005	1,400	1,200	2021	2,300	2,000
2006	1,500	1,300	2022	2,400	2,000
2007	1,500	1,300	2023	2,600	2,200
2008	1,600	1,400			
2009	1,700	1,500			

a. Prior to 1994, the threshold wage amount was $50 per calendar quarter for domestic employee. For 1994 and later, the threshold applies to calendar year wages.

b. The thresholds for election officials & workers apply to calendar year earnings.

Note

1. See IRC Sec. 3121(x) and https://www.ssa.gov/oact/cola/CovThresh.html (Last accessed September 4, 2022).

403. What is the rate of Social Security and Medicare tax for a self-employed person?

The tax on self-employed persons is imposed under the Self-Employment Contributions Act.[1]

The self-employment tax consists of two taxes: the OASDI tax (the tax for old-age, survivors, and disability insurance) and the Hospital Insurance (HI) tax (for Medicare Part A).

For 2023, the maximum earnings base (the maximum amount of net earnings subject to the tax) for the OASDI tax is $160.200/. There is no maximum earnings base for the HI tax. In other words, all earnings from self-employment are subject to the HI tax.

The rate of the OASDI tax is 12.40 percent, and the rate of the HI tax is 2.90 percent. Thus, the maximum OASDI tax for a self-employed person in 2023 (with maximum earnings of $160,200) is $19,864.80. The maximum HI tax for a self-employed person s unlimited, because all self-employment earnings are subject to the tax.

For self-employed taxpayers with income above $200,000 ($250,000 for married filing jointly), the HI tax will be 3.8 percent in tax years 2013 and after.

There is a special federal (and generally following through to state) income tax deduction of 50 percent of the Social Security and Medicare self-employment tax.[2] This income tax deduction is designed to treat the self-employed in much the same manner as employees and employers are treated for Social Security, Medicare, and income tax purposes under present law.

OASDI TAX ON SELF-EMPLOYED PERSONS*			
Year	**% Rates (OASDI)**	**Max. Earnings Base**	**Max. Tax**
1986	11.4	$42,000	$4,788.00
1987	11.4	43,800	4,993.20
1988	12.12	45,000	5,454.00
1989	12.12	48,000	5,817.60
1990	12.4	51,300	6,361.20
1991	12.4	53,400	6,621.60
1992	12.4	55,500	6,882.00
1993	12.4	57,600	7,142.40
1994	12.4	60,600	7,514.40
1995	12.4	61,200	7,588.80
1996	12.4	62,700	7,774.80
1997	12.4	65,400	8,109.60
1998	12.4	68,400	8,481.60
1999	12.4	72,600	9,002.40
2000	12.4	76,200	9,448.80
2001	12.4	80,400	9,969.60
2002	12.4	84,900	10,527.60
2003	12.4	87,000	10,788.00
2004	12.4	87,900	10,899.60
2005	12.4	90,000	11,160.00
2006	12.4	94,200	11,680.80
2007	12.4	97,500	12,090.00
2008	12.4	102,000	12,648.00
2009-2011	12.4	106,800	13,243.20
2012	12.4	110,100	13,652.40
2013	12.4	113,700	14,098.80
2014	12.4	117,000	14,508.00
2015-2016	12.4	118,500	14,694.00
2017	12.4	127,200	15,772.80
2018	12.4	128,700	15,958.80
2019	12.4	132,900	15,479.60
2020	12.4	137,700	17,074.80
2021	12.4	142.800	17,707.20
2022	12.4	147,000	18,288.00
2023	12.4	$160,200	$19,864.80

*There is a special income tax deduction of 50 percent of the self-employment tax.

Note: The 2.90 percent Medicare tax applies to all self-employment earnings.

The OASDI maximum earnings base and maximum tax are subject to automatic adjustment in 2020, and after based on changes in wage levels. The maximum earnings for 2023 is $160,200. The maximum tax at 12.4 percent on $160,200 is $19,864.80.

If a self-employed person reports earnings on a fiscal-year basis, the tax rate to be used is the one that applies to the calendar year in which the fiscal year began.

Notes

1. IRC Sec. 1401.
2. IRC Sec. 164.

404. If a self-employed person also receives wages as an employee, what portion of income is subject to tax as self-employment income?

Only the difference between the maximum earnings base for the year and the wages received as an employee is subject to tax as self-employment income.[1]

> *Example 1.* Mr. Smith, an attorney, is employed as a part-time instructor for a law school, and his salary is $30,000 a year. During 2023, Mr. Smith earned an additional $100,000 from his private practice, which counts as $92,350 for Social Security purposes (i.e., 92.35 percent of $100,000). Only $122,350 of his net earnings from self-employment is subject to the OASDI self-employment tax $160,200 - $30,000). Note, however, that all of Mr. Smith's wages and $92,350 of his self-employment income are subject to the HI self-employment tax, because all wages and self-employment income are subject to the HI tax.

No self-employment tax is due unless net earnings from self-employment are at least $434 for the taxable year ($400/92.35 percent). Nevertheless, in some cases, the amount of income subject to OASDI self-employment tax may be less than $400.

> *Example 2.* Assume the same facts as in Example 1, except that Mr. Smith's salary as a law instructor is $175,000. Mr. Smith's net earnings from self-employment after application of the 92.35 percent factor ($161,612.50) exceed $400, and therefore must be reported. However, only $13,387.50 is subject to the OASDI self-employment tax ($175,000 - $151,612.50), but the entire $175,000 is subject to the HI tax.

Note

1. IRC Sec. 1402(b)(2).

405. Must a Social Security beneficiary who works pay Social Security and Medicare taxes?

Yes, even though receiving Social Security benefits, the beneficiary must pay taxes at the same rate as other individuals. Social Security and Medicare taxes must be paid even if the earnings are too small to increase the Social Security benefits the beneficiary will receive in the future.

> *Example.* Ms. Anderson, age seventy-three, receives $800 a month in Social Security retirement benefits. She also works part-time and earns $4,000 for the year. Ms. Anderson must pay $306 in Social Security and Medicare HI taxes.

406. How does a life insurance agent pay Social Security taxes on first-year and renewal commissions?

If the agent is an employee when the policy is sold, both first-year and renewal commissions are wages at the time they are paid. Consequently, they are subject to the employer-employee tax in the year they are received by him. It does not matter whether, at the time of payment, the agent is an employee or a self-employed person. If the agent is a self-employed individual when the policy is sold, first-year and renewal commissions are treated as net earnings from self-employment in the year they are received[1] (see Social Security Taxes, Q 397 to Q 408).

Renewal commissions paid to the estate (or other beneficiary) of a deceased life insurance agent in a year after death are not subject to the employer-employee tax. Renewal commissions paid to a disabled life insurance agent are not subject to the Social Security tax, if he or she became entitled to disability insurance benefits before the year in which the renewal commission is paid and did not work for the employer during the period for which the payment is made. The renewal commissions of a self-employed agent do not constitute net earnings from self-employment to a widow(er) (they were not derived from a trade or business carried on by the widow(er)).

Note

1. 20 CFR Part 404, Subpart K.

407. Must the self-employment tax be included in a person's estimated tax return?

Yes. Failure to pay self-employment taxes can result in penalty.

408. What is the federal income tax deduction for medical expense insurance premiums?

For those that itemize, payments for insurance premiums paid for policies that cover medical care or for a qualified long-term care insurance policy covering qualified long-term care services can deductible after meeting the 7.5 percent Adjusted Gross Income (AGI) threshold.[1]

However, if one is an employee, they cannot include in medical expenses the portion of premiums treated as paid by the employer. Employer-sponsored premiums paid under a premium conversion plan, cafeteria plan, or any other medical and dental expenses paid by the plan are not deductible unless the premiums are included in box 1 of the employee's W-2.

Note

1. https://www.irs.gov/taxtopics/tc502. (Last accessed September 4, 2022).

WAGES AND SELF-EMPLOYMENT INCOME

409. What earnings are subject to Social Security tax and are counted in computing Social Security benefits?

Earnings that are the wages of an employee or the self-employment income of a self-employed person. However, earnings are counted as "wages" or as "self-employment income" only if they are earned in employment or self-employment covered by the Social Security Act.

---

410. For Social Security purposes, what is meant by the term "wages"?

"Wages" mean pay received by an employee for employment covered by the Social Security Act. The maximum amount of wages subject to the Old-Age, Survivors, and Disability Insurance tax (OASDI) and credited to a worker's Social Security record for any calendar year cannot exceed:

$4,800 paid in any of the years	1959-1965
$6,600 paid in any of the years	1966-1967
$7,800 paid in any of the years	1968-1971
$9,000 paid in the year	1972
$10,800 paid in the year	1973
$13,200 paid in the year	1974
$14,100 paid in the year	1975
$15,300 paid in the year	1976
$16,500 paid in the year	1977
$17,700 paid in the year	1978
$22,900 paid in the year	1979
$25,900 paid in the year	1980
$29,700 paid in the year	1981
$32,400 paid in the year	1982
$35,700 paid in the year	1983
$37,800 paid in the year	1984
$39,600 paid in the year	1985
$42,000 paid in the year	1986
$43,800 paid in the year	1987
$45,000 paid in the year	1988
$48,000 paid in the year	1989
$51,300 paid in the year	1990
$53,400 paid in the year	1991
$55,500 paid in the year	1992

$57,600 paid in the year..	1993
$60,600 paid in the year..	1994
$61,200 paid in the year..	1995
$62,700 paid in the year..	1996
$65,400 paid in the year..	1997
$68,400 paid in the year..	1998
$72,600 paid in the year..	1999
$76,200 paid in the year..	2000
$80,400 paid in the year..	2001
$84,900 paid in the year..	2002
$87,000 paid in the year..	2003
$87,900 paid in the year..	2004
$90,000 paid in the year..	2005
$94,200 paid in the year..	2006
$97,500 paid in the year..	2007
$102,000 paid in the year..	2008
$106,800 paid in any of the years...	2009-2011
$110,100 paid in the year..	2012
$113,700 paid in the year..	2013
$117,000 paid in the year..	2014
$118,500 paid in either of the years..	2015-2016
$127,200 paid in the year..	. 2017
$128,700 paid in the year..	2018
$132,900 paid in the year..	2019
$137,700 paid in the year..	2020
$142,800 paid in the year..	2021
$147,000 paid in the year..	2022
$160,200 paid in the year..	2023

Employees pay the tax on wages up to the base amount from each employer but receive a refund on their income tax returns for the excess of total taxes paid over the tax on the base amount. Each employer pays the tax on wages up to the base amount for all of its employees. In addition to the regular Social Security tax on wages, all wages are subject to the Part A Medicare Hospital Insurance tax (HI).

The maximum earnings base is automatically adjusted each year by the Social Security Administration, if average nationwide (covered and noncovered) total wages have increased.

Note that the maximum amount of wages subject to the OASDI tax is also the maximum amount credited to a worker's record. For example, if an employee is paid $160,200 or less in 2023, the full amount of wages will be subject to OASDI tax and will be credited to the Social Security record for benefit purposes. But if an employee is paid $165,000 in 2023, only $160,200 will be subject to OASDI tax and credited to the Social Security record (but HI taxes will be paid on the entire $165,000). In other words, earnings in excess of the maximum amount for a particular calendar year are not considered wages for Social Security coverage purposes.[1]

A stabilizer provision protects the system from trust-fund depletions that could occur when price increases outpace wage gains. This stabilizer provision goes into effect if reserves in the trust funds providing retirement, disability, and survivor benefits fall below 20 percent of what is needed to meet outgo for a year. When the stabilizer takes effect, automatic cost-of-living benefit increases will be based on the lower of the annual percentage increase in the Consumer Price Index or the annual percentage rise in the nation's average wage.[2]

Later, if the fund reserves exceed 32 percent of what is estimated to be needed for a year, recipients will be entitled to extra cost-of-living increases, to compensate for losses in inflation protection resulting from having benefit increases tied to wage levels.[3]

Notes

1. Social Security Administration, Old Age and Survivor's Insurance, https://www.ssa.gov/OP_Home/rulings/oasi/43/SSR-OASI43toc.html (last accessed September 4, 2022).
2. 42 U.S.C. sec. 415(i)(1)(C).
3. 42 U.S.C. sec. 415(i)(5)(A).

411. Are only payments in cash counted as wages?

No; amounts paid by check, promissory note, or in other media (such as goods, clothing, board or lodging) usually count as wages. In a few cases, however, only cash pay is counted (see Q 427; Domestic and Household Workers, Q 402).

Any fringe benefit that is not specifically excluded from Social Security taxes is wages for Social Security purposes. The amount of wages is the difference between the discount price paid by the employee for the benefit and its fair market value.

The following five categories of fringe benefits are not wages:

(1)   "*De minimis*" fringe (a property or service furnished by the employer that is so small in value that accounting for it would be administratively impractical)

- These include such items as: controlled, occasional employee use of photocopier; occasional snacks, coffee, doughnuts, etc.; occasional tickets for entertainment events; holiday gifts, occasional meal money or transportation expense for working overtime; group-term life insurance for employee spouse or dependent with face value not more than $2,000; flowers, fruit, books, etc., provided under special circumstances; personal use of a cell phone provided by an employer primarily for business purposes. An essential element of a de minimis benefit is that it is occasional or unusual in frequency.

It also must not be a form of disguised compensation. The IRS has ruled previously in a particular case that items with a value exceeding $100 could not be considered de minimis, even under unusual circumstances.

- Cash is generally intended as a wage, and usually provides no administrative burden to account for. Cash therefore cannot be a de minimis fringe benefit. Gift certificates that are redeemable for general merchandise or have a cash equivalent value are not de minimis benefits and are taxable.

- A certificate that allows an employee to receive a specific item of personal property that is minimal in value, provided infrequently, and is administratively impractical to account for, may be excludable as a de minimis benefit, depending on facts and circumstances.

- Achievement Awards: Special rules apply to allow exclusion from employee wages of certain employee achievement awards of tangible personal property given for length of service or safety. These awards cannot be disguised wages; must be awarded as part of a meaningful presentation; and cannot be cash, cash equivalent, vacation, meals, lodging, theater or sports tickets, or securities.

(2)   Gyms and other athletic facilities (the value of an employer-provided on-premises athletic facility)

(3)   No-additional-cost service (any service provided by an employer to the employee for the employee's use)

(4)   Qualified employee discount (employee discount with respect to property or services)

(5)   Working-condition fringe (any employer-provided service or property to the employee, such as a parking space)

Ordinarily, only pay actually received by the employee in a calendar year is counted as wages for that year. However, pay that is "constructively received" during the year is also counted. Wages are constructively received when they have been credited or set apart for the employee without any substantial limitation or restriction on the time or manner of payment and are available to him so that he can get them at any time. A special provision applies to pay under a nonqualified deferred compensation plan that is generally based on payments made after 1983.

412. Are employer payments for group life insurance covered wages?

The cost of group-term life insurance that is includable in the gross income of the employee is considered "wages" subject to Social Security tax.[1] This provision does not apply to coverage of former employees who separated from service before January 1, 1989, to the extent the cost is not for any period the employee was employed by the employer after separation.

The general rule is that the employee may exclude the cost of the first $50,000 of employer-provided group-term life insurance from income. Therefore, generally, only the cost of coverage in excess of $50,000 will be subject to the Social Security tax.[2]

The employer is required to report amounts includable in the wages of current employees for purposes of the Social Security tax on the employees' W-2. Generally, the employer may treat the wages as though paid on any basis, so long as they are treated as paid at least once each year.

The Social Security tax must be paid by the employee if the payment for the group-term life insurance is considered wages and is for periods during which there is no longer an employment relationship between the employer and the employee. The employer is required to state the portion of an employee's wages that consist of payments for group-term life insurance and the amount of the Social Security tax separately.

If there is more than one policy from the same insurer providing coverage to employees, a combined test is generally used to determine whether it is a direct or indirect policy by the employer. However, the regulations provide exceptions that allow the policies to be tested separately if the costs and coverage can be clearly allocated between the two policies.

If coverage is provided by more than one insurer, each policy must be tested separately to determine whether it is carried directly or indirectly by the employer.

The cost of employer-provided group-term life insurance on the life of an employee's spouse or dependent, paid by the employer, is not taxable to the employee if the face amount of the coverage does not exceed $2,000. This coverage is excluded as a de minimis fringe benefit.

Whether a benefit provided is considered de minimis depends on all the facts and circumstances. In some cases, an amount greater than $2,000 of coverage could be considered a de minimis benefit. See Notice 89-110[3] for more information.

Notes

1. IRC Sec. 3121(a)(2).
2. IRC Sec. 79. See also IRS, Group-Term Life Insurance, https://www.irs.gov/government-entities/federal-state-local-governments/group-term-life-insurance (last accessed September 4, 2022).
3 https://www.irs.gov/pub/irs-drop/n-89-110.pdf (last accessed September 4, 2022).

413. Are vacation pay and severance pay wages?

Yes, but the Internal Revenue Service ruled in 1996 that contributions of an employee's forfeitable vacation pay benefit, to a qualified stock purchase plan with a cash or deferred arrangement, are excludable from gross wages for Social Security purposes.

The company involved in the ruling had established a qualified stock-purchase plan with profit-sharing features and cash or deferred arrangements. Company employees were entitled to annual leave based on years of service, and had to use it during the same year or forfeit it. Employees who did not use all of their paid vacation in excess of two weeks could elect to have the equivalent in pay contributed to the qualified plan. The employees could take the vacation time, forfeit the time, or contribute its value to the plan. They did not have the option to receive cash or any other taxable benefit in lieu of the contribution to the plan. Thus, the Internal Revenue Service considered the contribution of vacation pay to be a nonelective employer contribution and excluded from wages for Social Security purposes under IRC Sec. 3121(a)(5)(A).[1]

Note

1. IRS Technical Advice Memoranda 9635002. (November 9, 1995).

414. Are payments on account of sickness or accident disability counted as wages for Social Security purposes?

Yes, generally payments made to, or on behalf of, an employee or an employee's dependents for sickness or disability are considered wages. The following payments, however, are specifically excluded from the definition of wages:

(1)   Any payment that an employer makes to an employee, or on the employee's behalf, on account of the employee's sickness or accident disability, or related medical or hospitalization expenses, if the payment is made more than six consecutive months following the last calendar month in which the employee worked for the employer. Payments made during the six consecutive months are included as wages.

(2)   The exclusion listed in (1) above also applies to any payment made by a third party (such as an insurance company). In addition, if the employee contributed to the employer's sick pay plan that portion of the third-party payments attributable to the employee's contribution is not wages.

(3)   Payments of medical or hospitalization expenses connected with sickness or accident disability are excluded from wages beginning with the first payment, only if made under a plan or system of the employer for medical or hospitalization expenses connected with sickness or accident disability.

(4)   Payments under workers' compensation law are not wages.

For payments to be excluded under a plan or system, the plan must provide for all employees generally or for a class or classes of employees. Some or all of the following features may also be a part of the plan:

- set a definite basis for determining who is eligible, such as length of service, or occupation, or salary classification;

- set definite standards for determining the minimum duration of payments; and

- provide a formula for determining the minimum amount to be paid an eligible employee.

Sick pay that is not paid under a plan or system by the employer is counted as wages for Social Security purposes, if paid before the end of six calendar months after the last month in which the employee worked.[1]

Note

1. Social Security Administration, SSR 72-56, https://www.ssa.gov/OP_Home/rulings/oasi/43/SSR72-56-oasi-43.html (last accessed September 4, 2022).

415. Are payments made under a deferred compensation plan counted as wages?

Yes; generally, under a special timing rule, the "amount deferred" by an employee under a traditional nonqualified deferred compensation plan—whether a salary reduction or supplemental plan, whether a funded or unfunded plan, or whether a private or (eligible or ineligible) Section 457 plan—of an employer covered by the Social Security tax is considered "wages" for Social Security tax purposes at the later of:

(1)   when the services are performed; or

(2)   when the employee's rights to such amount are no longer subject to a substantial risk of forfeiture.[1] Once an amount is treated as wages, it (and any income attributable to it) will not be treated as wages for Social Security tax purposes in any later year.[2]

In general, many employees would prefer to have amounts deferred treated as wages for Social Security purposes at the time the services are performed. At such time, their salaries, in all likelihood, already exceed the Social Security taxable wage base (in 2023, $160,200 for OASDI), and the amounts deferred would thus escape Social Security taxes. (Remember, however, that the HI tax applies to all wages.)

Regulations expressly identify certain plans and benefits that do not provide for the deferral of compensation for Social Security tax purposes: stock options, stock appreciation rights, and other stock value rights; some restricted property received in connection with the performance of services; compensatory time, disability pay, severance pay, and death benefits; certain benefits provided in connection with impending termination (including window benefits); excess (golden) parachute payments; benefits established twelve months before an employee's termination, if indication that benefits were provided in contemplation of termination; benefits established after termination of employment; and compensation paid for current services.[3]

Under the regulations, the manner in which the amount deferred for a period is determined depends upon whether the nonqualified deferred compensation plan is an account balance plan or a nonaccount balance plan. If the plan is an account balance plan, the amount deferred for a period equals the principal amount credited to the employee's account for the period, increased or decreased by any income or loss attributable to the principal amount through the date the principal amount is required to be taken into account as wages for Social Security tax purposes. A plan is an account balance plan only if, under the terms of the plan, a principal amount is credited to an individual account for an employee, the income attributable to each principal account is credited or debited to the individual account, and the benefits payable to the employee are based solely on the balance credited to the individual account.[4]

If the plan is a nonaccount balance plan, the amount deferred for a period equals the present value of the additional future payment or payments to which the employee has obtained a legally binding right under the plan during that period.

Notes

1. IRC Sec. 3121(v)(2)(A).
2. IRC Sec. 3121(v)(2)(B).
3. Treas. Regs. §§31.3121(v)(2)-1(b)(4), 31.3306(r)(2)-1(a).
4. Treas. Regs. §§ 31.3121(v)(2)-1(c)(1), 31.3306(r)(2)-1(a); see also IRS PLR 9417013 (amounts deferred in defined-contribution-type plan with delayed vesting are amounts attributable to employer contributions when such amounts vest).

---

416. Are payments made to or from a qualified pension or annuity plan counted as wages?

No, neither the employer's contribution to the plan nor payments to the employee from the plan are treated as wages. They are not subject to Social Security tax and are not creditable for benefit purposes.

The following payments made to or under a deferred compensation plan are excludable from the definition of wages:

(1)   Payments made from or to qualified pension, profit-sharing, or stock bonus plans if, at the time of payment, the trust is exempt from tax under IRC Sec. 501(a), unless the payment is made to an employee of the trust as remuneration for services rendered as an employee and not as a beneficiary of the trust.[1]

(2)   Payments made under or to an IRC Sec. 403(a) annuity plan.[2]

(3)   Payments made under a Simplified Employee Pension (SEP), other than any contributions made pursuant to a salary reduction agreement described in IRC Sec. 408(k)(6).[3]

(4)   Payments under an annuity contract described in IRC Sec. 403(b), other than a payment for the purchase of the contract that is made by reason of a salary reduction agreement (whether evidenced by a written instrument or otherwise).[4]

(5)   Payments under or to an exempt governmental deferred compensation plan.[5]

(6)   Payments to supplement pension benefits under a plan or trust described above to take into account some or all of the increase in the cost of living since retirement.[6]

(7)   Payments under a cafeteria plan (IRC Sec. 125), if the payment is not treated as wages without regard to the plan and it is reasonable to believe that IRC Sec. 125 would not treat any wages as constructively received.[7]

(8)   Payments under a SIMPLE IRA plan arrangement, other than elective contributions under IRC Sec. 408(p)(2)(A)(i).[8]

(9)   Amounts exempted from Section 457 requirements under Section 457(e)(11)(A)
(ii) (plans paying solely length of service awards to bona fide volunteers (or their
beneficiaries) on account of qualified services performed by such volunteers) and
maintained by an eligible employer.[9]

However, the definition of wages does include certain employer contributions under qualified cash or deferred arrangements that are not included in gross income.[10]

Notes

1. IRC Sec. 3121(a)(5)(A).
2. IRC Sec. 3121(a)(5)(B).
3. IRC Sec. 3121(a)(5)(C).
4. IRC Sec. 3121(a)(5)(D).
5. IRC Sec. 3121(a)(5)(E).
6. IRC Sec. 3121(a)(5)(F).
7. IRC Sec. 3121(a)(5)(G).
8. IRC Sec. 3121(a)(5)(H).
9. IRC Sec. 3121(a)(5)(I).
10. IRC Sec. 3121(v)(1)(A).

417. If a teacher takes a reduction in salary to provide funds for a tax-sheltered annuity, how are his or her wages computed for Social Security purposes?

The salary before the reduction will be treated as wages.[1] In other words, the amount of reduction, although paid to the insurer by the employer, is nevertheless not considered an employer contribution to a retirement fund.

Example: A teacher, whose salary is $66,000, takes a $2,000 salary cut for 2023 so that this amount can be used to purchase a tax-sheltered annuity for his or her benefit. Social Security taxes will still be payable on the full $66,000, and this is the amount that will be credited to the teacher's Social Security account for benefit purposes.

Employer payments from employer funds into such plans are excluded from wages.

Note

1. See IRC Sec. 3121(a)(5)(D); Rev. Rul. 65-208, 1965-2 CB 383.

418. Are cash tips considered wages?

Tips received by an employee in the course of employment by any one employer are wages for Social Security purposes, if the tips total or exceed twenty dollars in a calendar month. This includes all tips received directly from customers, tips from charge customers that are paid by the employer to the employee, and any tips received under a tip-splitting arrangement. Noncash tips, such as passes, tickets, or services, are not counted as wages. Tips are considered received when the employee reports the tips to the employer. If the employee fails to report the tips to the employer, the tips are treated as received when the employee actually received them.

For each calendar month during which an employee receives twenty dollars or more in tips, the employee must give the employer a written statement of cash and charge tips by the tenth day of the month after the month in which the tips are received. IRS Form 4070 *Employee's Report of Tips to Employer*,[1] which is in IRS Publication 1244 Employee's *Daily Record of Tips and Report to Employer*,[2] is available for this purpose.

A club, hotel, or restaurant may require customers to pay a service charge, which is given to the employees. These service charges added to a bill or fixed by the employer that the customer must pay, when paid to an employee, don't constitute a tip but rather constitute non-tip wages. These non-tip wages are subject to social security tax, Medicare tax and federal income tax withholding. In addition, the employer can't use these non-tip wages when computing the credit available to employers under section 45B of the Internal Revenue Code, because these amounts are not considered to be tips.

Common service charges or "auto-gratuities" in service industries include:

- Large party charge (restaurant),

- Bottle service charge (restaurant and night-club),

- Room service charge (hotel and resort),

- Contracted luggage assistance charge (hotel and resort), and

- Mandated delivery charge (pizza or other retail deliveries).

(For method of reporting tips, see SOCIAL SECURITY TAXES, Q 397 to Q 408.)

Q&A 1 of Revenue Ruling 2012-18 provides that the absence of **any** of the following factors creates a doubt as to whether a payment is a tip and indicates that the payment may be a service charge:

- The payment must be made free from compulsion;

- The customer must have the unrestricted right to determine the amount;

- The payment should not be the subject of negotiation or dictated by employer policy; and,

- Generally, the customer has the right to determine who receives the payment.

Notes

1. *See* IRS Form 4070, Employee's Report of Tips to Employer, https://www.irs.gov/pub/irs-prior/f4070--2005.pdf (Revised August 2005) (last accessed September 4, 2022).
2. IRS Publication 1244, Employee's Daily Record of Tips and Report to Employer, https://www.irs.gov/pub/irs-pdf/p1244.pdf (last accessed September 4, 2022).

419. Are noncash tips considered wages?

Noncash tips such as tickets, services, and passes do not count as wages.

NOTE: Establishments that require customers to pay a service charge for use of banquet facilities or dining rooms where the money is given to the employees is NOT considered a cash tip, but part of wages. Some of these include: large party charges, bottle service charges, contracted luggage assistance charges, mandated delivery charges.

420. Do prizes and awards from someone not an employer count as wages?

No. Prizes from someone other than the beneficiary's employer do not count as wages.

421. Do taxes withheld from pay count as a beneficiary's wage?

Yes. However, Social Security taxes paid by the employer from the employer's funds for agricultural work or domestic service performed in a private home DO NOT count as wages.

422. Do expense reimbursements and travel expenses count as wages?

No, not generally. Under a situation where expenses must be verified. In this situation, business expense reimbursements are not considered wages (therefore, not taxable income) if the employer uses an accountable plan. This type of plan has three prongs of accountability that must be met:

- The expense must have been occurred while acting as an employee by performing a service for the employer, and the reimbursement for that expense must not be an amount that would otherwise be to the employee as wages.

- The expense must be substantiated within a reasonable period of time. The IRS defines this as sixty days after the expense is incurred.

- The employee must return any amount that exceeds the actual expense within a reasonable period of time. The IRS defines "reasonable" to be 120 days after the expense was incurred or paid.

    NOTE: Failure for an employee to follow these guidelines will result in the reimbursement becoming classified as taxable income.

However, they CAN count as wages if it is a non-accountable plan or a per diem plan:

(a)   the employer does not require verification of expenses (Non-accountable plan). Business expense reimbursements are considered supplemental wages (therefore, taxable income) if your employer uses a nonaccountable plan. The following indicate a non-accountable plan:

- The employees is not required to substantiate expenses in a timely manner by providing receipts or other documentation;

- The employee is not required to return in a timely manner any overages of business expenses paid by the employer;

- The employer compensated the employee for an amount that was not truly a business expense;

- The employee received a business expense reimbursement that would normally have been included as regular wages; or

(b)   the employer can keep any amount in excess of the verifiable expenses (PER DIEM PLAN).

These types of employee reimbursements are for fixed expenses, such as mileage, meals, and lodging. The federal allowable mileage rate for the remainder of 2022 is 62.5 cents per mile[1], and the U.S. General Services Administration establishes other federal per diem rates, such as lodging and meals. These allowances vary from state to state. It is expected that the rate will rise again at the start of 2023 and be reviewed throughout the year. The rate is subject adjustment and has varied throughout the years at 58.5 cents for 2022[2], 56 cents for 2021[3], 57.5 cents for 2020[4], 58 cents for 2019[5], and 54.5 cents for 2018[6].

Under this situation, an individual must provide their employer with documentation that supports the justification for the business travel and the actual mileage incurred on a business trip. If the per diem exceeds actual expenses, the overage is considered wages and therefore, income that is taxable.

Expenditures must be in advancement of the employer's business – expenses for items of personal use are not business expenses.

Notes

1. Notice 2022-03 https://www.irs.gov/pub/irs-drop/n-22-03.pdf (Last accessed September 29, 2022).
2. IR 2021-251 https://www.irs.gov/newsroom/irs-issues-standard-mileage-rates-for-2022.
3. IR 2020-279 https://www.irs.gov/newsroom/irs-issues-standard-mileage-rates-for-2021.
4. IR 2019-215 https://www.irs.gov/newsroom/irs-issues-standard-mileage-rates-for-2020.
5. IR 2018-251 https://www.irs.gov/newsroom/irs-issues-standard-mileage-rates-for-2019.
6. IR 2017-204 https://www.irs.gov/newsroom/irs-issues-standard-mileage-rates-for-2018.

423. Are payments made to a disabled former employee counted as wages?

No. If the person is a disabled beneficiary, any payments received from the employer after 1972 does count as wages as long as:

(a)   the beneficiary was entitled to disability insurance benefits before the year of which payment was made; AND

(b)   the beneficiary did not work for the employer during the pay period in which the payment was made.

424. Do wages include the portion of an employee's Social Security taxes paid by an employer?

Yes, except for domestic service in the private home of the employer and agricultural labor. However, payments by a state or local employer are wages for Social Security tax purposes, only if the payment is pursuant to a salary reduction agreement (whether evidenced by a written instrument or otherwise). The term "salary reduction agreement" includes any salary reduction arrangement, regardless of whether there is approval or choice of participation by individual employees or whether such approval or choice is mandated by state statute.

425. Are a salesperson's commissions considered to be wages?

Yes, they are wages if the salesperson is an employee (see Social Security Taxes, Q 397 to Q 408). When the commissions are the sole pay and no advances are given, the commissions are wages in the calendar year in which they are paid. However, when advances are made against future commissions, the year in which the advances are paid is the year to which the amount advanced is credited.

426. Under what circumstances are the first-year and renewal commissions of a life insurance agent treated as wages?

If the agent is an employee when the policy is sold, both first-year and renewal commissions are treated as wages when they are paid to him. Thus, the commissions are subject to the employer-employee tax in each year as he receives them (see SOCIAL SECURITY TAXES, Q 397 to Q 408). For retirement-test purposes, however, if the agent is an employee when the policy is sold, both first-year and renewal commissions are treated as "earned" in the month and year in which the policy was sold (see LOSS OF BENEFITS BECAUSE OF "EXCESS" EARNINGS, Q 358 to Q 376).

427. Is the value of meals and lodging furnished by an employer to an employee considered wages for Social Security taxation purposes?

The Supreme Court has held that the value of meals and lodging furnished to an employee for the convenience of the employer is not wages for Social Security coverage and tax purposes.[1]

Such meals must be provided at the employer's place of business. The employee must accept lodging at the employer's place of business in order for the value of the lodging to be excluded from wages.

The Social Security Amendments of 1983 state, however, that the exclusion of income from income tax withholding by the employer does not necessarily affect the treatment of the income for Social Security coverage and taxation purposes in other cases.

303

Note

1. *Rowan Companies, Inc. v. U.S.*, 452 U.S. 247 (1981).

Self-Employment Income

428. What is taxable and creditable self-employment income?

It is that part of an individual's net earnings from self-employment that is subject to Social Security tax and counted for Social Security benefits. In determining what part of a person's net earnings from self-employment is creditable for Social Security purposes, the following rules apply:

- 92.35 percent of all net earnings from self-employment is taxable and creditable self-employment income unless the trade, business, or profession is not covered by the Social Security Act. The 92.35 percent factor has been used only in 1990 and after (when the self-employed first began paying the full employer-employee tax rate).

- The reason that 92.35 percent is used is based on the fact that the FICA tax on wages, the employer is incurring a 7.65% expense on each dollar paid to an employee. This is a real expense to the company.

- If such amount for the taxable year is less than $400, the net earnings are not treated as self-employment income. That is, no Social Security tax is paid on the net earnings, and they are not credited to the person's Social Security account.

- The maximum amount of self-employment income for a taxable year that is subject to the Old-Age, Survivors, and Disability Insurance tax (OASDI) and used to determine benefits cannot exceed:

$160,200	2023
$147,000	2022
$142,800	2021
$137,700	2020
$132,900	2019
$128,700	2018
$127,200	2017
$118,500	2015-2016
$117,000	2014
$113,700	2013
$110,100	2012
$106,800	2009-2011
$102,000	2008

$97,500	2007
$94,200	2006
$90,000	2005
$87,900	2004
$87,000	2003
$84,900	2002
$80,400	2001
$76,200	2000
$72,600	1999
$68,400	1998
$65,400	1997
$62,700	1996
$61,200	1995
$60,600	1994
$57,600	1993
$55,500	1992
$53,400	1991
$51,300	1990
$48,000	1989
$45,000	1988
$43,800	1987
$42,000	1986
$39,600	1985
$37,800	1984
$35,700	1983
$32,400	1982
$29,700	1981
$25,900	1980
$22,900	1979
$17,700	1978
$16,500	1977
$15,300	1976
$14,100	1975
$13,200	1974
$10,800	1973
$9,000	1972
$7,800	1968-1971

| $6,600 | 1966-1967 |
| $4,800 | 1959-1965 |

There is no limit to the amount of self-employment income subject to the (Part A) Medicare Hospital Insurance tax (HI). The HI tax applies to all self-employment income.

Net earnings in excess of the maximum amount for a particular taxable year are not considered self-employment income for Social Security purposes.

429. How is the amount of self-employment income figured if a person has both wages and net earnings from self-employment in the same year?

If a person has both wages (as an employee) and net earnings from self-employment in a taxable year, self-employment income is the difference, if any, between wages and the maximum Social Security earnings base for that year (see Q 428).

> *Example.* Mr. Smith, an attorney, is also employed part-time as an instructor in a law school. In 2023, he draws a salary of $40,000 from the school and also earns $130,000 in private practice, which counts as $156,995 for Social Security purposes (i.e., 92.35 percent of $170,000). His self-employment income for OASDI purposes for 2023 is $130,200 ($160,200 maximum less $30,000 wages). Only $130,000 is subject to self-employment Social Security tax, $30,000 is subject to the employer-employee tax. Note, however, that $92,350 of the $100,000 earned in private practice is subject to the Part A Medicare Hospital Insurance tax for self-employed individuals. In addition, Mr. Smith must pay the Medicare Hospital Insurance tax for employees on the $30,000 he earned as a law school instructor.

430. In general, what constitutes net earnings from self-employment?

Net earnings from self-employment may be the net income from a trade, business, or profession carried on by the individual alone, or it may be his or her distributive share of the ordinary net income of a partnership. In computing net earnings from self-employment, gross income and deductions are, for the most part, the same as for income tax purposes. However, the following differences must be taken into account:

- Rentals from real estate are excluded in determining net earnings from self-employment unless:

    (1) the rentals are received in the course of a trade or business by a real estate dealer; or

    (2) services are rendered primarily for the convenience of the occupants of the premises, as in the case of hotels, motels, etc. (but income from renting property for business or commercial use (such as a store, factory, office space, etc.) is excluded, regardless of the amount of services rendered to the tenant); or

    (3) in the case of farm rentals, the farm landlord materially participates in the management or in the production of farm commodities on land rented to someone else.

- Dividends on stock and interest on bonds do not count for Social Security, unless they are received in the course of business by a dealer in stocks or securities. The term "bond" includes debentures, notes, certificates, and other evidence of indebtedness issued with interest coupons or in registered form by a corporation. Bonds also include government bonds. Other interest received in the course of a trade or business does count for Social Security. For example, interest received by a merchant on accounts or notes receivable are included in computing net earnings from self-employment.

- Partnerships are treated as individuals when it comes to the dividend and interest exclusion. Dividends and interest on securities held for investment are excluded from net earnings of the partners. However, if a partnership is in business as a securities dealer, income on the securities held for resale by the partnership is included as net earnings of the partners.

- Capital gains and losses, and gains and losses from the sale or exchange of property which is not inventory or stock in trade, are excluded in computing net earnings from self-employment.

- Retirement payments received by a retired partner from a partnership, of which the individual is a member or a former member, are excluded from net earnings from self-employment if the following conditions are met:

  (1) The payments are made under a written plan of the partnership that provides for periodic payments because of retirement, to partners generally or to a class or classes of partners, to continue at least until the partner's death

  (2) The partner rendered no services in any business conducted by the partnership (or its successors) during the taxable year of the partnership ending within or with the taxable year in which such payments were received

  (3) At the end of the partnership's taxable year, there is no obligation from the other partners to the retired partner other than for the retirement payments under the plan

  (4) The partner's share in the capital of the partnership has been paid in full by the end of the partnership's taxable year

- No deductions for net operating losses of other years are permitted in determining net earnings from self-employment.

- The following retirement benefits for ministers are not considered earnings from self-employment:

  (1) Retirement benefits received from a church plan after retirement

  (2) The rental value or allowance of a parsonage, including utilities, furnished to the minister after retirement

- Income taxable as "dividends" to shareholders of a Subchapter S corporation (a corporation electing not to be taxed as a corporation) is not considered "net earnings from self-employment".

431. When did Social Security coverage begin for self-employed individuals?

Most became covered beginning in 1951.

Exceptions:

- Farmers, ministers, and some others were not covered until 1955

- Additional groups of professionals were covered after 1955

- Military have been covered since 1957

- Self-employed Medical Doctors (physicians) were covered for taxable years ending on or after December 31, 1965

432. How is self-employment income calculated?

Self-employment income is calculated from "net earnings from self-employment" which is derived from a "trade or business" covered by the law.

An individual is self-employed in the eyes of Social Security if they are:

- a sole proprietor (including an independent contractor)

    o The term "sole proprietor" also includes the member of a single member LLC that's disregarded for federal income tax purposes and a member of a qualified joint venture.

- a partner in a partnership (including a member of a multi-member limited liability company (LLC) that has elected to be treated as a partnership for federal tax purposes)

- otherwise in business for oneself.

Self-employment tax must usually be paid upon net earnings from self-employment of $400 or more. Generally, the amount subject to self-employment tax is 92.35 percent of net earnings from self-employment. Net earnings are calculated by subtracting ordinary and necessary trade or business expenses from the gross income derived from the trade or business. One can be liable for paying self-employment tax even if currently receiving Social Security benefits. The law sets a maximum amount of net earnings subject to the Social Security tax. For 2023 this amount is $160,200 – up from $147,000 in 2022. All net earnings are subject to the Medicare tax.

Optional Methods

For those with a loss or small amount of income from self-employment, it may be of benefit to use one of the two optional methods to compute net earnings from self-employment. Refer to Form 1040, Schedule SE for the "Farm Optional Method" and the "Non-Farm Optional Method,"[1] to review the optional method. An optional method may give credit toward social security coverage or increase the earned income credit or the child and dependent care credit.

Church Employee

An employee of a church or qualified church-controlled organization who elected exemption from social security and Medicare taxes must pay self-employment tax if the church or qualified church-controlled organization paid more than $108.28[2] to the employee, unless they are personally exempt from self-employment tax. For more information on church-related income and self-employment taxes, refer to Publication 517 *Social Security and Other Information for Members of the Clergy and Religious Workers*.[3]

Self-Employment Tax Rate

The law sets the self-employment tax rate as a percentage of net earnings from self-employment. This rate consists of 12.4 percent for social security and 2.9 percent for Medicare taxes.

Additional Medicare Tax

Additional Medicare Tax applies to self-employment income above a threshold. The threshold amounts are $250,000 for a married individual filing a joint return, $125,000 for a married individual filing a separate return, and $200,000 for all others.

Reporting Self-Employment Tax

Compute self-employment tax on Schedule SE. When figuring adjusted gross income on Form 1040, one-half of the self-employment tax can be deducted.

Notes

1. Form 1040 Schedule SE, https://www.irs.gov/pub/irs-pdf/f1040sse.pdf (last accessed September 4, 2022).
2. IRS, Elective FICA Election – Church and Church-Controlled Organizations, https://www.irs.gov/charities-non-profits/churches-religious-organizations/elective-fica-exemption-churches-and-church-controlled-organizations (last accessed September 4, 2022).
3. *Social Security and Other Information for Members of the Clergy and Religious Workers*. https://www.irs.gov/pub/irs-pdf/p517.pdf (Last accessed September 4, 2022).

---

433. Can an illegal activity or a hobby be a trade or business?

<u>Illegal activity</u>: Simply because an activity is illegal does not prevent it from being considered a trade or business. For example, professional gamblers or drug smugglers would be considered self-employed and required to report income and pay self-employment taxes. Of course, the act of reporting may bring the attention of law enforcement to the illegal activities.

<u>Hobbies</u>: Hobbies are generally not considered to be trades or businesses.

In making the distinction between a hobby or business activity, it is necessary to consider all facts and circumstances with respect to the activity. A hobby activity is done mainly for recreation or pleasure. No one factor alone is decisive. One must generally consider these factors in determining whether an activity is a business engaged in making a profit:

- Whether the activity is carried on in a businesslike manner and one maintains complete and accurate books and records.

- Whether the time and effort put into the activity indicate an intent to make it profitable.

- Whether the owner depends on income from the activity for livelihood.

- Whether losses are due to circumstances beyond the owner's control (or are normal in the startup phase of this type of business).

- Whether the owner changes methods of operation in an attempt to improve profitability.

- Whether the owner or advisors have the knowledge needed to carry on the activity as a successful business.

- Whether the owner was successful in making a profit in similar activities in the past.

- Whether the activity makes a profit in some years and how much profit it makes.

- Whether one can expect to make a future profit from the appreciation of the assets used in the activity.

434. What exclusions apply to trades and business for Social Security?

The term "trade or business" does not include the following for Social Security purposes:

- Work as an employee, except newspaper vendors who are age eighteen or older.

- Work by U.S. citizens performing services in the U.S. as employees of a foreign government and, in some circumstances, as employees of an instrumentality wholly owned by a foreign government, or an international organization.

- Employees of a State or political subdivision thereof who are paid solely on a fee basis and whose services are not otherwise covered as employment under a Federal-State coverage agreement.

- Work as an employee or employee representative covered by the Railroad Retirement system.

- Work as a public official (except public officials of a State or political subdivision who are paid solely on a fee basis and whose services are not covered under a Federal-State coverage agreement).

- Self-employment by members of certain religious sects exempt from self-employment taxes.

- Services performed by ordained, commissioned, or licensed ministers if they elected to be exempted from coverage under the Internal Revenue Code, and by members of religious orders who have not taken a vow of poverty.

- Services performed by Christian Science practitioners, if they have elected to be exempted from coverage under the Internal Revenue Code.

- Deemed self-employment income of employees of church or church-controlled organizations that have elected to be exempt from payment of Social Security taxes for its employees.

- Services by a member of a religious order who has taken a vow of poverty when these services are performed in the exercise of the duties required by the order. However, effective October 30, 1972, these services may be covered as employment for the order if the order irrevocably elects coverage for its entire active membership and its lay employees.

435. Can you get an extension for filing an Annual Report of Earnings?

Yes. An extension if possible for a valid reason. A written request must be made before the annual report is due.[1]

Valid reasons include:[2]

- illness or disability (COVID-19 would be an accepted illness in this situation);

- absence or travel from home for a great distance that causes the individual not to have access to records needed;

- inability to get evidence from another source;

- inability of an accountant to compile data required;

- any other situation that has a direct bearing on the obligation to complete the report.

Notes

1. 20 CFR sec. 404.452, https://www.ssa.gov/OP_Home/cfr20/404/404-0452.htm (last accessed September 4, 2022).
2. 20 CFR sec. 404.454, https://www.ssa.gov/OP_Home/cfr20/404/404-0454.htm (last accessed September 4, 2022).

436. Does farm rental income count as net earnings?

Yes, if the property owner or landlord, as part of the rental agreement, materially participates in the production of the crop or livestock. If the property owner or landlord does not materially participate, then the farm rental income is not income for Social Security considerations.

Note: «Landlord» means anyone who has rented to another individual, whether the land is owned or rented by the individual from a third party.

437. How does a self-employed life insurance agent report first-year and renewal commissions?

If the agent is self-employed when the policy is sold, commissions are treated as earnings from self-employment in the year they are paid to the agent. It is immaterial whether the agent is an employee or self-employed when the commissions are received. For retirement-test purposes, renewal commissions paid to a self-employed agent after retirement are not included as earnings after the initial month of retirement if they were the result of services rendered prior to retirement (see Social Security Taxes, Q 397 to Q 408). (For treatment of commissions as "earnings" for "retirement test" purposes, see LOSS OF BENEFITS BECAUSE OF "EXCESS" EARNINGS, Q 358 to Q 376.)

RAILROAD RETIREMENT

Overview of Railroad Retirement

438. What is the Railroad Retirement program?

The Railroad Retirement Board, which administers the Railroad Retirement program, was established in 1935 as an independent agency of the Executive Branch. It provides retirement, survivor, unemployment, and sickness benefits to individuals who have spent a substantial portion of their career in railroad employment, as well as to these workers' families. In the 1930s, amidst concern about the ability of existing pension programs to provide former railroad workers with adequate assistance in old age, Congress established a national Railroad Retirement system.

This system is primarily administered by the Railroad Retirement Board (RRB), which is an independent federal agency charged with providing benefits to eligible employees of the railroad industry and their families. Today, the Railroad Retirement program is closely tied to the Social Security program, and although the Railroad Retirement program and Social Security share a number of common elements, key differences also exist between the two in areas such as funding and benefit structure.

Both RRB and Social Security offer retirement, disability, spousal, and survivor benefits that are generally calculated in the same manner. However, the benefits provided by each program are not identical. For example, RRB offers unique unemployment and sickness benefits, as well as Tier II benefits that resemble private pensions. RRB's benefits are discussed below, but this analysis is not meant to be a comprehensive description of every aspect of Railroad Retirement program benefit structure and calculation methodology. Instead, this section provides a useful overview. For readers interested in greater detail about RRB benefits or programs, the agency offers numerous publications in print and on its Web site.

Railroad Retirement Program

While Railroad Retirement has remained separate from Social Security, the two systems are closely coordinated in regard to earnings credits, benefit payments, and taxes. The two systems are linked financially through a coordination of the portion of Railroad Retirement annuities that is equivalent to Social Security benefits with the social security system. This is designed to place the Social Security trust funds in the same position they would be in if the Social Security program covered railroad service retirement.

Legislation restructured the railroad retirement benefits into the current two tiers to coordinate them more fully with social security benefits. The first tier is based on combined Railroad Retirement and Social Security credits, using Social Security benefit formulas. The second tier is based on only on railroad service tracks with private pensions paid over and above social security benefits in other industries.

Payroll taxes paid by railroad employers and their employees are the primary source of funding for the railroad retirement-survivor benefit programs. Railroad retirement taxes, which have historically been higher than social security taxes, are calculated, like benefit payments, on a two-tier basis. Railroad retirement Tier I payroll taxes are coordinated with social security taxes, so employees and employers pay Tier I taxes at the same rate as social security taxes. In addition, both employees and employers pay Tier II taxes to finance railroad retirement benefit payments beyond social security levels. The ratio of certain asset balances to the sum of benefit payments and administrative expenses determines Tier II tax rates. Revenues in excess of benefit payments are invested with the National Railroad Retirement Investment Trust in both non-governmental asset and government securities. Additional trust fund income comes from revenues from Federal income taxes on railroad retirement benefits, and appropriations from general treasury revenues provided after 1974 as part of a phase-out of certain vested dual benefits.

Unemployment Insurance Program

The railroad unemployment insurance system was also established in the 1930s. While the Social Security Act created state unemployment programs and these programs generally covered railroad workers, railroad businesses which crossed State lines created problems with benefits. In some instances, a state would deny compensation for unemployed railroad workers because their employers had paid unemployment taxes in another state. There were cases where employees appeared to be covered in more than one state, more often than not, however, they qualified in none. Congress enacted the Railroad Unemployment Insurance Act in June 1938 which established a system of benefits for unemployed railroaders, financed by railroad employers and administered by the RRB. Legislation later added sick pay benefits in 1946. Under the Railroad Unemployment Insurance Act, unemployment insurance benefits are paid to railroad workers who are unemployed but "ready, willing, and able to work," and sickness benefits to railroad workers unable to work because of illness or injury. The RRB also operates a placement service to help unemployed railroaders secure employment.

A new unemployment-sickness benefit year begins each July 1, with eligibility generally based on railroad service and earnings in the preceding calendar year. Up to 26 weeks of normal unemployment or sickness benefits are payable to an individual in a benefit year. Additional extended benefits are payable to persons with ten or more years of service.

Taxes on railroad employers under an experience-rating system finance the railroad unemployment-sickness benefits program. The RRB calculates each employer's payroll tax rate annually on the basis of benefit payments to the railroad's employees.

Medicare for Railroad Workers

The Medicare program covers railroad workers just like workers covered under Social Security. Eligible railroad retirement annuitants and social security beneficiaries whose benefits are payable by the RRB are automatically enrolled under both plans, but the annuitant or beneficiary can decline Medicare Part B. Eligible nonretired persons must apply in order to obtain Medicare coverage. The RRB automatically enrolled nearly 21,700 beneficiaries for Medicare during fiscal year 2021. As of the end of that fiscal year, about 459,300 people were enrolled in

Part A, and over 441,600 (96 percent) of them were also enrolled in Part B. Palmetto GBA, a subsidiary of Blue Cross and Blue Shield, processes medical insurance (Part B) claims for railroad retirement Medicare beneficiaries.

During fiscal year 2021, the RRB paid the following benefits:

- RETIREMENT AND SURVIVOR BENEFITS: Nearly $13.2 billion was paid to about 519,000 beneficiaries.

    o Average annuity paid to retired rail employees was $2,985 a month.

    o Average spousal benefits were $1,110 a month.

    o Average widow(er)s benefits were $1,905 a month.

- NET UNEMPLOYMENT BENEFITS: Over $164 million to approximately 41,000 claimants.

    o Maximum biweekly rate for unemployment and sickness benefits was $820 prior to sequestration, which reduced benefits by 5.7 percent for days after September 30, 2020.

    o The Continued Assistance to Rail Workers Act of 2020 exempted these benefits from sequestration beginning January 3, 2021, until 30 days after the termination of the national emergency related to the COVID-19 pandemic.

439. What are Tier I Benefits under Railroad Retirement?

Tier I benefits are designed to take the place of Social Security. Benefits under the two programs are quite similar, although workers who have paid Railroad Retirement taxes will not receive benefits through the Railroad Retirement program.

Workers with fewer than 10 years of service in positions subject to railroad specific taxes, or fewer than 5 years after 1995, are not vested under the Railroad Retirement program and have their accounts transferred into Social Security. All survivor claims with railroad involvement require a determination of jurisdiction. Railroad Retirement has jurisdiction if the deceased worker has been vested and was employed in a railroad industry job covered by Railroad Retirement until retirement or death. If these conditions are not met, Railroad Retirement cedes jurisdiction to the Social Security Administration.

Retirement

Tier I retirement benefits are generally designed to be comparable to Social Security benefits, and employ the same benefit formula, based on the highest 35 years of indexed earnings. Eligibility for retirement benefits through Railroad Retirement occurs when a worker has worked at least 10 years in covered service for the railroad industry, or at least 5 years after 1995. Credit for a month's service is recorded if any time during the month was spent in railroad employment, even as little as one day. As with Social Security, Railroad Retirement benefits are generally first payable at age 62, with the full retirement age ranging from 65 to 67, depending on a recipient's year of birth. Benefit reductions for early retirement between age 62 and the full retirement age for those with less than 30 years of service are the same as those for Social Security. A retirement earnings test also applies to Railroad Retirement benefits prior to the full retirement age and is calculated using the same thresholds and reductions as the Social Security test.

Differences

However, retirement benefits under Railroad Retirement differ from Social Security in two critical ways.

- Early retirement reductions do not apply if the worker has at least 30 years of service in Railroad Retirement-covered employment. In these cases, an individual can begin receiving benefits as early as age 60 with no age-based reduction.

- A supplemental annuity is payable if

    o an employee had at least 25 years of service which began before October 1, 1981, and

    o has a current connection to the railroad.

Eligibility for this annuity begins at age 60 if the employee has at least 30 years of creditable service, and at age 65 if the employee has 25 to 29 years of service. The fixed maximum amount of a supplemental annuity is $43 a month.

Disability Coverage

Railroad Retirement and Social Security both use the same definition of total disability, and the same formula to calculate the disability annuity. The annuity for total and permanent disability is payable under the full retirement age for any employee with at least 10 years of railroad service, or with 5 years of service after 1995 as long as the individual's combined credits for work under Social Security and the Railroad Retirement program meet the eligibility requirements for Social Security disability benefits.

Additionally, the substantial gainful activity (SGA) amount that may disqualify a person from receiving a total disability annuity is the same as the one used in Social Security and is wage-indexed annually.

In addition to the total disability benefit, however, Railroad Retirement offers an occupational disability benefit that does not exist under Social Security. Where "total disability" refers to a limitation that prevents regular employment in ANY job, the occupational disability benefit covers disabilities preventing work in an individual's regular railroad position. In this instance, the occupational disability is payable to disabled workers who cannot perform his or her regular duties, even if they could perform another job. This annuity is payable at any age to workers with at least 20 years of service and a current connection to the railroad industry and to workers between age 60 and the full retirement age with at least 10 years of service and a current connection to the railroad industry. The occupational disability annuity is calculated in the same manner as the total disability annuity.

Spousal Benefits

Tier I benefits are provided to spouses of employees qualifying for Railroad Retirement benefits. These spousal annuities are initially computed to equal half of the worker's unreduced Tier I benefit but can be reduced based on applicable factors such as early collection.

To be eligible based on a current marriage, the marriage generally must be at least one year old, or the couple must have conceived a child and the spouse must cease any employment covered by Railroad Retirement. Spousal payments are subject to the same age and service rules as retirement benefits; however, for spouses of employees with less than 30 years of service, reductions are generally slightly larger than those applied to workers' retirement benefits. Consistent with Social Security, a spouse can also receive benefits at any age if he or she is caring for a child under the age of16 or a child who became disabled prior to age 22. Divorced spouses are eligible for Tier I spousal benefits under the same conditions as those that apply to Social Security.

Survivor Benefits

Tier I survivor benefits are generally computed to match the Social Security benefit that would be received under similar circumstances. For survivors to be eligible for benefits from Railroad Retirement, the deceased employee must have at least 10 years of covered service, or 5 years of covered service after 1995, and had a current connection to the railroad at the time of retirement or death. If these conditions are not met, the credits for work earned in Railroad Retirement-covered employment used in computing survivor benefits are transferred to Social Security.

As with Social Security, Railroad Retirement survivor benefits can be paid to:

- widows/widowers,

- divorced spouses,

- dependent parents, and

- children who are

    o under age 18,

    o 18–19 years old and a full-time student (12th grade or below), or

    o disabled prior to age 22.

    o Dependent grandchildren are also eligible for benefits if both parents are disabled or deceased.

The percentage of the deceased worker's Tier I benefit that survivors can receive varies depending on the type of survivor. The maximum survivor benefit per family under Social Security also applies to Railroad Retirement survivor benefits.

Surviving divorced spouses are eligible to receive benefits if the marriage lasted at least 10 years, up to the Tier I amount. Surviving divorced spouses can also receive a payment for dependent children under age 16, or for a child in their care who became disabled prior to age 22 (in such cases, the length-of-marriage rule does not apply). To be eligible for widow or widower benefits, the recipient must not have remarried, unless the remarriage occurred after age 60, or after age 50 if disabled before the remarriage.

An important difference between Social Security and Railroad Retirement benefits is that children can only receive railroad benefits if the parent is deceased. Under Social Security, children of retired or disabled annuitants can also receive benefits. However, the families of workers covered by the Railroad Retirement program do not receive lower benefits than if they were under Social Security, because Railroad Retirement includes a special minimum guaranty provision. The provision increases the employee's benefit to account for any differences between the total benefits a Railroad Retirement worker's family is receiving and those a family with the same circumstances would receive through Social Security.

Unemployment and Illness

Railroad Retirement also provides recipients with benefits in cases of unemployment or sickness. Analogous benefits do not exist under Social Security, and railroad employers pay an additional tax to cover this benefit.

440. What are Tier II Benefits under Railroad Retirement?

The biggest difference between the benefits that the Railroad Retirement program and Social Security provide is the additional Tier II benefit available for railroad workers. The Tier II benefit is designed to resemble a comparable private defined benefit pension.

Tier II benefits are calculated by computing average monthly earnings up to the annual Tier II taxable maximum for an employee's 60 months of highest earnings. The average monthly earnings figure is then multiplied by seven-tenths of 1 percent, and then again by the number of years spent in railroad employment. Tier II benefits generally have the same age restrictions as those for Tier I. The Tier II benefit is also reduced by 25 percent for dually vested beneficiaries. As with Tier I benefits, Tier II benefits have cost of living adjustments (COLA). Tier II benefits increase annually by 32.5 percent of any increase in the Consumer Price Index for Urban Wage Earners and Clerical Workers, known as the CPI-W.

In addition to workers, Tier II benefits are provided to current spouses and survivors, while divorced spouses can only receive these benefits as part of a property settlement. Tier II spousal benefits are equal to 45 percent of the employee's Tier II benefits, while Tier II survivor benefits vary depending on the type of survivor.

441. Who is eligible for an employee annuity?

The Railroad Retirement Act[1] provides annuities for employees who have reached a specific age and have been credited with a specified number of years of service. The Act also provides annuities for employees who become disabled. The basic requirement for a regular employee retirement annuity is 120 months (10 years) of creditable railroad service (or five years, if the five years are performed after 1995). Service months need not be consecutive and, in some cases, military service may be counted as railroad service.

Benefits are based on months of service and earnings credits. Earnings are creditable up to certain annual maximums on the amount of compensation subject to railroad retirement taxes.

(1) **Annuities based on 10 years of service (or five years in certain cases).** An employee with 10 years of railroad service (or five years, if the five years were performed after 1995), but less than 30 years of service, is eligible for an annuity if he: (a) has attained retirement age, or (b) has attained age 62 (the annuity cannot begin prior to the first full month during which the employee is age 62) but is less than retirement age. Early retirement annuity reductions are applied to annuities awarded before retirement age.

(2) **Annuities based on 30 years of service.** An employee who has been credited with 30 years of railroad service is eligible for a regular annuity based on age and service the first full month he or she is age 60. Early retirement reductions are applied to annuities awarded before age 62.

Starting in the year 2000, the age at which full benefits are payable increases in gradual steps until it reaches age 67. This affects people born in 1938 and later. Reduced annuities will still be payable at age 62, but the maximum reduction will be 30 percent, rather than 20 percent, by the year 2022. Part of an annuity is not reduced beyond 20 percent if the employee had any creditable railroad service before August 12, 1983. These reductions do not affect those who retire at age 62 with 30 years of service.

There are two types of disability annuities for employees who have been credited with at least 10 years of railroad service. An employee may receive an occupational disability at age 60, if he or she has at least 10 years of railroad service, or at any age, if the employee has at least 20 years (240 months) of service, when the employee is permanently disabled for his or her regular railroad occupation. An employee who cannot be considered for a disability annuity based on ability to work in his or her regular railroad occupation may receive a total disability annuity at any age, if he or she is permanently disabled for all regular work and has at least 10 years (120 months) of creditable railroad service.

A five-month waiting period beginning with the month after the month of the onset of disability is required before disability annuity payments can begin.

While an annuity based on disability is not paid until the employee has stopped working for a railroad, employment rights need not be relinquished until the employee attains age 65.

Note

1. 45 U.S.C. sec. 231 et. seq.

442. Who is entitled to a supplemental annuity?

An employee with a "current connection" with the railroad industry at the time of retirement may qualify for a supplemental annuity, in addition to the regular employee annuity. Supplemental annuities are paid from a separate account funded by employer taxes in addition to those assessed for regular annuities. The supplemental annuity is reduced if the employee receives a private pension based on contributions from a railroad employer.

An employee is entitled to a supplemental annuity if he or she:

(1)   has been credited with railroad service in at least one month before October 1, 1981;

(2)   is entitled to the payment of an employee annuity awarded after June 30, 1966;

(3)   has a current connection with the railroad industry when the employee annuity begins (see Q 443);

(4)   has given up the right to return to work, and either;

(5)   is age 65 or older and has completed 25 years of service; or

(6)   is age 60 or older and under age 65, has completed 30 years of service, and is awarded an annuity on or after July 1, 1974.

A supplemental annuity that begins after December 21, 1974 does not affect the payment of the regular employee annuity. The payment of a supplemental annuity does not affect the amount of a spouse or survivor annuity.

443. What is a "current connection" with the railroad industry?

An employee who worked for a railroad in at least twelve of the 30 consecutive months immediately preceding the month his annuity begins will meet the current-connection requirement. If the employee has 12 months' service in an earlier 30-consecutive-month period, he may still meet the current-connection requirement. This alternative generally applies if the employee did not have any regular employment outside the railroad industry after the end of the 30-consecutive-month period that included 12 months of railroad service.

If an employee died before retirement, railroad service in at least 12 of the 30 consecutive months before death will meet the current-connection requirement for the purpose of paying survivor benefits.

However, if an employee does not qualify on this basis, but has 12 months of service in an earlier 30-month period, he or she may still meet the current connection requirement. This alternative generally applies if the employee did not have any regular employment outside the railroad industry after the end of the last 30-month period which included 12 months of railroad service, and before the month the annuity begins or the date of death.

Once a current connection is established at the time the railroad retirement annuity begins, an employee never loses it, no matter what kind of work is performed thereafter.

443.01. Does someone have to have a "current connection" to collect benefits?

A worker must have a current connection in order to receive an occupational disability annuity, or a supplemental annuity. A current connection is **NOT** required for any other type of railroad retirement benefit payable to railroad employees, or to qualify for Medicare coverage.

A current connection is also a factor in determining which agency, the RRB, or the Social Security Administration (SSA), will pay monthly benefits to the survivors of a railroad employee. (As a general rule, where survivor benefits are paid by the RRB because a current connection was maintained, the survivors receive a larger monthly payment than would be payable by SSA.)

444. Can nonrailroad work before retirement break a former railroad employee's current connection?

Full or part-time work for a nonrailroad employer in the interval between the end of the last 30-month period including 12 months of railroad service and the month an employee's annuity begins, or the month of death if earlier, can break a current connection.

A current connection can only be broken if the person works for a nonrailroad employer after leaving railroad service and before the railroad retirement annuity begins. It is important to note that once one establishes a current connection at the time their railroad retirement annuity begins, they never lose it, no matter what work they might perform thereafter.

Self-employment in an unincorporated business will **not** break a current connection. However, if the business is incorporated, self-employment may break a current connection.

The following types of work do not break a Current Connection:

- Work for the following government agencies will not break a Current Connection:
    - Alaska Railroad (as long as it is an entity owned by the State of Alaska);
    - U.S. Department of Transportation;
    - Surface Transportation Board (or its predecessor the Interstate Commerce Commission);
    - Transportation Security Administration;

- National Mediation Board;

- National Transportation Safety Board; or

- Railroad Retirement Board.

- Service for a railroad whose principal operation is in Canada and service by a Canadian citizen in Canada for a railroad whose principal operation is in the United States will neither break nor preserve a current connection

- Self-employment as defined under the Railroad Retirement Act.

- Nonrailroad work after the annuity beginning date.

445. What is non-railroad work and self-employment under the Railroad Retirement Act?

Earnings from nonrailroad employment, including self-employment, may affect an individual's annuity computation. Nonrailroad work is any job that is not in the railroad industry. This includes work for a Canadian railroad that is not covered under the Railroad Retirement Act and work as an elected or appointed public official.

The RRB asks for information regarding a person's nonrailroad work, any government jobs as to which they were employed, and any self-employment to determine whether or not they have a current connection with the railroad industry. Earnings after an individual's annuity start date from any nonrailroad employment or self-employment may also cause work deductions.

If an individual claims self-employment, the RRB determines whether or not they are performing "substantial services" as an independent contractor. The payment of self-employment taxes can serve as evidence of independent contractor status, but is not conclusive. If an individual is working for an incorporated business that that they own, the RRB does not consider that work self-employment. If the individual is self-employed as a consultant, the RRB considers how the self-employment compares to the work that person performed for their former railroad or nonrailroad employer before applying for their annuity. See Form AA-4, *"Self-Employment and Substantial Service Questionnaire,"* which the RRB uses to make that decision.[1]

Note

1. Railroad Retirement Board, Self-Employment and Substantial Service Questionnaire, https://omb.report/icr/201702-3220-003/doc/71524501.pdf (last accessed September 10, 20221).

446. What are the exceptions to the normal methods of determining a current connection?

A current connection can also be maintained, for purposes of supplemental and survivor annuities, but **not** for an occupational disability annuity, if

- the employee completed 25 years of railroad service,

- was involuntarily terminated without fault from his or her last job in the railroad industry, and

- did not thereafter decline an offer to return to work in the same class or craft as his or her most recent railroad service, regardless of the distance to the new position.

Provided that all of these requirements are met, an employee's current connection may not be broken, even if the employee works in regular nonrailroad employment after the thirty-month period and before retirement or death.

This exception to the normal current connection requirement became effective October 1, 1981, but only for employees still living on that date who left the rail industry on or after October 1, 1975, or who were on leave of absence, on furlough, or absent due to injury on October 1, 1975.

447. What are the effects of a buy out on the existence of a current connection?

In cases where an employee has no option to remain in the service of his or her railroad employer, the termination of the employment is considered involuntary, regardless of whether the employee does or does not receive a buy-out.

However, if an employee has the choice of either accepting a position in the same class or craft in the railroad industry or termination with a buy-out, accepting the buy-out is a part of his or her voluntary termination, and the employee would not maintain a current connection under the exception provision.

448. How would acquiring 25 years of railroad service assist an employee in maintaining a current connection?

The current connection requirement is normally met if the employee has railroad service in at least 12 of the last 30 consecutive months before retirement or death. If an employee does not qualify on this basis but has 12 months of service in an earlier 30-month period, he or she may still meet the requirement if the employee does not work outside the railroad industry in the interval following the 30-month period and the employee's retirement, or death if that occurs earlier. Nonrailroad employment in that interval will likely break the employee's current connection.

However, a current connection can be maintained for purposes of supplemental and survivor annuities, but not occupational disability annuities, if the employee completed twenty-five years of railroad service, was involuntarily terminated without fault from his or her last job in the railroad industry, and did not thereafter decline an offer of employment in the same class or craft in the railroad industry, regardless of the distance to the new position. If all of these requirements are met, an employee's current connection may not be broken, even if the employee works in regular nonrailroad employment after the thirty-month period and before retirement or death. This exception to the normal current connection requirements became effective October 1, 1981, but only for employees still living on that date who left the rail industry on or after October 1, 1975, or who were on leave of absence, on furlough, or absent due to injury on October 1, 1975.

449. Would the acceptance of a buyout have any effect on determining if an employee could maintain a current connection under the exception provision?

In cases where an employee has no option to remain in the service of his or her employer, the termination of the employment is considered involuntary, regardless of whether the employee does or does not receive a separation or dismissal allowance.

However, an employee who chooses a separation allowance instead of keeping his or her seniority rights to railroad employment would, for railroad retirement purposes, generally be considered to have voluntarily terminated railroad service and, consequently, would not maintain a current connection under the exception provision.

If the employee had the choice to remain in employer service and voluntarily relinquished job rights prior to accepting the payments, his or her current connection would not be maintained under the exception provision, regardless of which payment option is chosen. Therefore, nonrailroad work after the 30-month period and before retirement, or the employee's death if earlier, could break the employee's current connection. Such an employee could only meet the current connection requirement under the normal procedures.

450. Is it always advantageous to maintain a current connection?

While a current connection is generally advantageous for railroad retirement purposes, the costs of maintaining a current connection could outweigh its value, depending on individual circumstances. There may be other financial or personal factors involved besides railroad retirement eligibility and/or the preservation of a current connection, and these will vary from individual to individual.

451. How are buyout payments treated under the Railroad Retirement and Railroad Unemployment Insurance Acts?

Buyout payments that result from the abolishment of an employee's job are creditable as compensation under the Railroad Retirement and Railroad Unemployment Insurance Acts. While the actual names of these employer payments may vary, the treatment given them by the RRB will depend upon whether the employee relinquished or retained his or her job rights. If the employee relinquishes job rights to obtain the compensation, the RRB considers the payment a separation allowance. This compensation is credited to either the month last worked or, if later, the month in which the employee relinquishes his or her employment relationship. While all compensation subject to Tier I payroll taxes is considered in the computation of a railroad retirement annuity, no additional service months can be credited after the month in which rights are relinquished.

The RRB considers the buyout payment a dismissal allowance, even though the employer might designate the payment a separation allowance, if the employee retains job rights and receives monthly payments credited to the months for which they are allocated under the dismissal allowance agreement. This is true even if the employee relinquishes job rights after the end of the period for which a monthly dismissal allowance was paid. However, supplemental unemployment or sickness benefits paid under an RRB-approved nongovernmental plan by a railroad or third party are not considered compensation for railroad retirement purposes.

452. Does the method of payment affect the employee's current connection under the exception provision?

The employee must always relinquish job rights in order to accept the buy-out, regardless of whether it is paid in a lump sum or in monthly payments. Neither payment option would extend the 30-month period. The determining factor for the exception provision to apply when a buy-out is paid is not the payment option. It is whether or not the employee stopped working involuntarily.

An employee considering accepting a buy-out should also be aware that if he or she relinquishes job rights to accept the buy-out, the compensation cannot be used to credit additional service months beyond the month in which the employee severed his or her employment relation, regardless of whether payment is made in a lump sum or on a periodic basis.

453. How are annuities for spouses of railroad retirees computed?

Regular railroad retirement annuities are computed under a two-tier formula. The spouse annuity formula is based on certain percentages of the employee's Tier I and Tier II amounts.

The Tier I portion of an employee's annuity is based on both railroad retirement credits and any Social Security credits that the employee also earned. Computed using Social Security benefit formulas, an employee's Tier I benefit approximates the Social Security benefit that would be payable if all the employee's work were performed under the Social Security Act.

The Tier II portion of the employee's annuity is based on railroad retirement credits only and may be compared to the retirement benefits paid over and above Social Security benefits to workers in other industries.

The first tier of a spouse annuity, before any applicable reductions, is 50 percent of the railroad employee's unreduced Tier I amount.

The second-tier amount, before any reductions, is 45 percent of the employee's unreduced Tier II amount.

454. How does spousal railroad retirement annuity compare to a Social Security benefit?

The average railroad annuity awarded to spouses during 2021, excluding divorced spouses, was $1,205 a month, while the average monthly Social Security spouse benefit was about $767.

Annuities awarded during 2021 to the spouses of employees who were at or over Full Retirement Age (FRA) and who retired directly from the rail industry with at least 25 years of service averaged $1,425 a month; and the average award to the spouses of employees retiring at age 60 or over with at least thirty years of service was $1,602 a month.

If a retired railroad employee with 30 or more years of service is age 60, the employee's spouse is also eligible for an annuity the first full month the spouse is age 60. The spouse of a worker under Social Security is not eligible for a spouse benefit based on age until both the worker and the spouse are at least age 62. Regardless of age, the spouses of workers under both retirement systems are eligible if the worker is retired and the spouse is caring for a qualifying child.

455. Can a spouse of a Railroad worker collect benefits at an earlier age than a Social Security beneficiary spouse?

If a retired railroad employee with 30 or more years of service is age 60, the employee's spouse is also eligible for an annuity the first full month the spouse is age 60. The spouse of a worker under social security is not eligible for a spouse benefit based on age until both the worker and the spouse are at least age 62. Regardless of age, the spouses of workers under both retirement systems are eligible if the worker is retired and the spouse is caring for a qualifying child.

456. Does Social Security offer benefits not available under Railroad Retirement?

Social Security pay certain benefits that are not available under railroad retirement. Social Security provides children's benefits when an employee is disabled, retired, or deceased, whereas the RRB only pays children's benefits when the employee is deceased.

However, the Railroad Retirement Act provides a special minimum guaranty provision which ensures that railroad families will not receive less in monthly benefits than they would have if railroad earnings were covered by Social Security rather than railroad retirement laws. This provision is intended to cover situations in which one or more members of a family would otherwise be eligible for a type of Social Security benefit that is not provided under the Railroad Retirement Act. Therefore, if a retired worker under the RRB has children who would otherwise be eligible for a benefit under Social Security, the employee's annuity will be increased to reflect what Social Security would cover.

457. When is a spouse eligible for an annuity if caring for a child of the retired employee?

A spouse of an employee receiving an age and service annuity (or a spouse of a disability annuitant who is otherwise eligible for an age and service annuity) is eligible for a spouse annuity at any age if caring for the employee's unmarried child, and the child is under age 18 or a disabled child of any age who became disabled before age 22. This rules mirror the rules for Social Security disability.

458. Can a spouse of a railroad employee in a same-sex marriage file for a railroad retirement spouse annuity?

Yes. On June 26, 2015, the United States Supreme Court held in *Obergefell v. Hodges,*[1] that the Constitution of the United States requires all states, the District of Columbia and the U.S. Insular Areas to recognize that same-sex couples have a fundamental right to marry under the Due Process Clause and the Equal Protection Clause.

Prior to this landmark decision, on June 26, 2013, the Supreme Court in *United States v. Windsor,*[2] found Section 3 of the Defense of Marriage Act (DOMA), which prevented the Federal government from recognizing marriages of same-sex couples, to be unconstitutional. As a result of the *Windsor* decision, the Railroad Retirement Board began accepting applications for benefits from those eligible spouses in same-sex marriages who were validly licensed under State law. At that time, same-sex marriage had been made legal at the state level in 36 states. With the *Obergefell* decision, the Supreme Court extended the requirement that all States license same-sex marriages, and recognize lawfully licensed same-sex marriages performed in all States.

Notes

1. 576 U.S. 644 (2015).
2. 570 U.S. 744 (2013).

459. If a divorced spouse becomes entitled to an annuity, will the affect the monthly rated paid to the retired employee or current spouse?

No. If a divorced spouse becomes entitled to an annuity based on the employee's railroad service, the award of the divorced spouse's benefit would not affect the amount of the employee's annuity, nor would it affect the amount of the railroad retirement annuity that may be payable to the current spouse.

460. What is the effect if the employee and the spouse or divorced spouse are both railroad employees?

If both started railroad employment after 1974, the amount of any spouse or divorced spouse annuity is reduced by the amount of the employee annuity to which the spouse is also entitled. If both the employee and spouse are qualified railroad employees and either had some railroad service before 1975, both can receive separate railroad retirement employee and spouse annuities, without a full dual benefit reduction.

Railroad Retirement Benefits

461. Can the collection of Social Security benefits result in an overpayment of a railroad retirement annuity account?

Yes, in the case of the Tier I portion.

The Tier I portion of a railroad retirement annuity is based on both the railroad retirement and Social Security credits acquired by an employee and figured under Social Security formulas. It approximates what Social Security would pay if railroad work were covered by Social Security. Tier I benefits are, therefore, reduced by the amount of any actual Social Security benefit paid based on nonrailroad employment, to prevent a duplication of benefits based on the same earnings.

The Tier I dual benefit reduction also applies to the annuity of an employee qualified for Social Security benefits on the earnings record of another person, such as a spouse. And, the Tier I portion of a spouse or survivor annuity is reduced for any Social Security entitlement, even if the Social Security benefit is based on the spouse's or survivor's own earnings. These reductions follow principles of Social Security law which limit payment to the higher of any two or more benefits that are payable to an individual at one time.

If a railroad retirement annuitant is also awarded a Social Security benefit, in most cases a combined monthly dual benefit payment will be issued by the Railroad Retirement Board (RRB). The Social Security Administration determines the amount of the Social Security benefit due, and the RRB determines the amount of the railroad retirement annuity due. The Tier I portion of a railroad retirement annuity is reduced by the amount of the Social Security benefit due.

A person should notify the RRB when he or she files for Social Security benefits. If the Social Security Administration begins paying benefits directly to a railroad retirement annuitant without the RRB's knowledge, a Tier I overpayment will occur. This frequently happens when a railroad employee's spouse or widow(er) is awarded Social Security benefits not based on the employee's earnings.

Also, annuitants who are receiving their Social Security benefits directly from the Social Security Administration must notify the RRB if their Social Security benefits are subsequently increased for any reason other than annual cost-of-living increases, such as a recomputation to reflect post-retirement earnings. As such recomputations are usually retroactive, they can result in substantial Tier I overpayments.

While Social Security benefit information is provided to the RRB because of routine information exchanges between the RRB and the Social Security Administration, it will generally not be provided in time to avoid such a benefit overpayment.

462. Why is a railroad retirement annuity reduced when a Social Security benefit is also payable?

The Tier I portion of a railroad retirement annuity is based on both the railroad retirement and Social Security credits acquired by an employee and computed under Social Security formulas. It approximates what Social Security would pay if railroad work were covered by Social Security. Tier I benefits are, therefore, reduced by the amount of any ACTUAL Social Security benefit paid on the basis of nonrailroad employment, in order to prevent a duplication of benefits based on Social Security-covered earnings.

The tenets of Social Security law payment to the higher of any two or more benefits payable to an individual at one time, the Tier I dual benefit reduction applies to an annuity even if the Social Security benefit is based on the earnings record of someone other than the railroad employee, such as a spouse or former spouse. An annuitant is required to advise the RRB if any benefits are received directly from the Social Security Administration or if those benefits increase (other than for a cost-of living increase).

The Tier II portion of a railroad retirement annuity is based on the railroad employee's railroad service and earnings alone and is computed under a separate formula. It is not reduced for entitlement to a Social Security benefit.

463. Are there any exceptions to the railroad annuity reduction for Social Security benefits?

No. There are no exceptions to the railroad retirement annuity reduction for Social Security benefits.

464. What is the effect of workers' compensation or disability benefits on railroad retirement?

If an employee is receiving a railroad retirement disability annuity, Tier I benefits for the employee and spouse may, under certain circumstances, be reduced for receipt of workers' compensation or public disability benefits.

465. How do dual benefit restrictions apply when both spouses are railroad employees?

If both parties began working for the railroad after 1974, the amount of any spouse or divorced spouse annuity is reduced by the amount of the employee annuity to which the spouse or divorced spouse is also entitled.

If either party had some railroad service before 1975, the spouse/divorced spouse Tier I amount is reduced by the amount of the railroad employee Tier I to which the spouse/divorced spouse is entitled. The spouse/divorced spouse Tier I amount cannot be reduced below zero.

The initial reduction is restored in the spouse Tier II amount. Divorced spouses are not entitled to a Tier II component and are not eligible to have the reduction restored.

In survivor cases, if the widow or widower is entitled to a railroad retirement employee annuity and neither the widow or widower nor the deceased employee had any railroad service before 1975, the survivor annuity (Tier I and Tier II) payable to the widow or widower is reduced by the total amount of the widow or widower's own employee annuity.

If a widow or dependent widower is also a railroad employee annuitant, and either the widow or widower or the deceased employee had 120 months of railroad service before 1975, the Tier I reduction may be partially restored in the survivor Tier II amount.

If either the deceased employee or the widow or widower had some railroad service before 1975 but less than 120 months of service, the widow or widower's own employee annuity and the Tier II portion of the survivor annuity would be payable to the widow or widower. The Tier I portion of the survivor annuity would be payable only to the extent that it exceeds the Tier I portion of the widow or widower's own employee annuity.

466. How does the Tier I pension reduction affect spousal or widow/widower benefits?

The Tier I portion of a spouse's or widow's or widower's annuity may be reduced for receipt of any Federal, State, or local government pension separately payable to the spouse or widow or widower based on her or his own earnings. The reduction generally does not apply if the employment on which the public service pension is based was covered under the Social Security Act throughout the last 60 months of public employment. Most military service pensions and payments from the Department of Veterans Affairs will not cause a reduction. Pensions paid by a foreign government or interstate instrumentality will also not cause a reduction. For spouses and widow or widowers subject to a public service pension reduction, the Tier I reduction is equal to two-thirds of the amount of the public service pension.

467. Are there benefits other than Social Security that will require dual benefit reductions?

For employees first eligible for a railroad retirement annuity and a Federal, State, or local government pension after 1985, there may be a reduction in Tier I for receipt of a public pension based, in part or in whole, on employment not covered by Social Security or railroad retirement after 1956. This may also apply to certain other payments not covered by Social Security, such as payments from a non-profit organization or from a foreign government or a foreign employer. However, it does not include military service pensions, payments by the Department of Veterans Affairs, or certain benefits payable by a foreign government because of a totalization agreement between that government and the United States.

The Tier I portion of a spouse's or widow's or widower's annuity may also be reduced for receipt of any Federal, State, or local government pension separately payable to the spouse or widow or widower based on her or his own earnings. The reduction generally does not apply if the employment on which the public pension is based was covered under the Social Security Act throughout the last 60 months of public employment. In addition, most military service pensions and payments from the Department of Veterans Affairs will not cause a reduction. Pensions paid by a foreign government or interstate instrumentality will also not cause a reduction.

If an employee is receiving a disability annuity, Tier I benefits for the employee and spouse may, under certain circumstances, be reduced for receipt of workers' compensation or public disability benefits.

If annuitants become entitled to any of the above payments, they should promptly notify the RRB. If there is any question as to whether a payment requires a reduction in an annuity, an RRB field office should be contacted.

468. Can additional earning result in railroad retirement overpayments?

Unreported post-retirement work and earnings in nonrailroad employment (including self-employment) are a major cause of overpayments in railroad retirement annuities. Like Social Security benefits, railroad retirement Tier I benefits and vested dual benefits paid to employees and spouses, plus Tier I, Tier II, and vested dual benefits paid to survivors, are subject to deductions if post-retirement earnings exceed certain exempt amounts, which increase annually.

These earnings deductions do not apply to those who have attained full Social Security retirement age. Full retirement age for employees and spouses ranges from age 65 for those born before 1938 to age 67 for those born in 1960 or later. Full retirement age for survivor annuitants ranges from age 65 for those born before 1940 to age 67 for those born in 1962 or later.

For those under full retirement age throughout 2023, the exempt earnings amount is $21,240 For beneficiaries attaining full retirement age in 2023, the exempt earnings amount is $56,520 for the months before the month full retirement age is attained. Prior to the calendar year in which full retirement age is attained, the earnings deduction is $1 in benefits for every $2 of earnings over the exempt amount. For those attaining full retirement age during a calendar year, the deduction is $1 for every $3 of earnings over the exempt amount in the months before the month full retirement age is attained.

Annuitants who work after retirement and expect that their earnings for a year will be more than the annual exempt amount must promptly notify the nearest RRB field office and furnish an estimate of their expected earnings. This way, their annuities can be adjusted to take the excess earnings into consideration and prevent an overpayment. Annuitants whose original estimate changes significantly during the year, either upwards or downwards, should also notify the RRB.

Retired employees and spouses, regardless of age, who work for their last pre-retirement nonrailroad employer are also subject to an earnings deduction in their Tier II and railroad retirement supplemental annuity benefits, if applicable, of $1 for every $2 in earnings up to a maximum reduction of 50 percent. This earnings restriction does not change from year to year and does not allow for an exempt amount. Retired employees and spouses should therefore promptly notify the RRB if they return to employment for their last pre-retirement nonrailroad employer, or if the amount of their earnings from such employment changes.

A spousal benefit is subject to reductions not only for the spouse's earnings, but also for the earnings of the employee, regardless of whether the earnings are from service for the last pre-retirement nonrailroad employer or any other post-retirement employment. An annuity paid to a divorced spouse may continue despite the employee's work activity. However, the employee's non-railroad earnings over the annual earnings exempt amount may reduce a divorced spouse benefit.

469. How do earnings after retiring affect disability annuities?

Special restrictions limiting earnings to $1,150 per month during 2023 (up from $1,050 in 2022) exclusive of disability-related work expenses, apply to disabled railroad retirement employee annuitants. In addition, any work performed by a disabled annuitant—whether for pay or not—may be considered an indication of an individual's recovery from disability, regardless of the amount of earnings. Therefore, any earnings by a disability annuitant must be reported promptly to avoid potential overpayments.

These disability work restrictions apply until the disabled employee annuitant attains full retirement age. This transition is effective no earlier than full retirement age even if the annuitant had 30 years of service. These work restrictions apply even if the annuitant has 30 years of railroad service. Also, a disabled employee annuitant who works for his or her last pre-retirement nonrailroad employer would be subject to the additional earnings deduction that applies in these cases.

470. What effect does railroad work have on the annuity?

No railroad retirement annuity is payable for any month in which an employee, spouse, or survivor annuitant performs compensated service for a railroad or railroad union. This includes local lodge compensation for $24.99 or more in a calendar month, and work by a local lodge or division secretary collecting insurance premiums, regardless of the amount of salary.

471. How does railroad retirement benefits compare to Social Security benefits?

The average age annuity being paid by the Railroad Retirement Board (RRB) at the end of fiscal year 2021 to career rail employees was $3,815 a month, and for all retired rail employees the average was $3,045. The average age retirement benefit being paid under Social Security was over $1,550 a month. Spouse benefits averaged $1,110 a month under railroad retirement compared to $775 under Social Security. These averages have increased since fiscal year 2019.

The Railroad Retirement Act also provides supplemental railroad retirement annuities of between $23 and $43 a month, which are payable to employees who retire directly from the rail industry with twenty-five or more years of service.

472. Are benefits for recent retirees on the average larger than in prior years?

Yes, because recent awards are based on higher average earnings. Age annuities awarded to career railroad employees retiring at the end of fiscal year 2021 (last year published) averaged about $4,425 a month, while monthly benefits awarded to workers retiring at full retirement age under Social Security averaged $2,180. If spouse benefits are added, the combined benefits for the employee and spouse would total $6,155 under railroad retirement coverage, compared to $3,270 under Social Security. Adding a supplemental annuity to the railroad family's benefit increases average total benefits for current career rail retirees to over $6,180 a month.

473. Must retiring railroad employees give up their rights to railroad jobs?

It depends.

AGE-BASED RETIREMENT: An employee annuity based on age cannot be paid until the employee stops railroad employment and gives up any rights to return to work for a railroad employer.

DISABILITY-BASED RETIREMENT: While an annuity based on disability is not paid until an employee has stopped working for a railroad, employment rights need not be relinquished until the employee attains full retirement age. For a supplemental annuity to be paid by the RRB, or for an eligible spouse to begin receiving annuity payments, a disabled annuitant under full retirement age must relinquish employment rights.

Regardless of age and/or earnings, no railroad retirement annuity is payable for any month in which a retired or disabled employee annuitant, a spouse annuitant or a survivor annuitant works for an employer covered under the Railroad Retirement Act, including labor organizations. Such work includes service for $25 or more in a calendar month to a local lodge or division of a railway labor organization. Also, work by a local lodge or division secretary collecting insurance premiums, regardless of the amount of salary, is railroad work which must be stopped.

Railroad retirement annuitants may work in nonrailroad employment, but benefits may be reduced if a beneficiary under full retirement age works after retirement and earnings exceed annual exempt amounts. Additional earnings deductions are assessed if a retired or disabled employee annuitant, or a spouse annuitant, works for his or her last pre-retirement nonrailroad employer, regardless of age or the level of earnings.

Other restrictions may also apply to any earnings by disabled employees.

474. Can railroad retirement annuities be garnished or subject to division in property settlements?

Yes, to a certain degree.

Garnishment

Certain percentages of railroad retirement annuity, be it for an employee, a spouse, a divorced spouse, or survivor annuity may be subject to garnishment or other legal action to enforce obligations such as child support or alimony payments.

Also, a court-ordered partition payment may be paid even if the employee is not entitled to an annuity provided that the employee has ten years of railroad service or five years after 1995 and both the employee and former spouse are 62.

Property Settlements/Divisions

Employee Tier II benefits, vested dual benefits, and supplemental annuities ARE subject to court-ordered property settlements in proceedings related to divorce, annulment, or legal separation.

Tier I benefits are not subject to property settlements.

---

475. What events can affect payments to beneficiaries such as spouses, divorced spouses, and widow(er)s?

A spouse or divorced spouse must immediately notify the RRB if the railroad employee upon whose service the annuity is based dies. A spouse must notify the RRB if her or his marriage to the railroad employee ends in divorce or annulment and a widow(er) or divorced spouse must notify the RRB if she or he remarries.

Also, benefits paid to spouses, widow(er)s, and surviving divorced spouses that are based on the beneficiary caring for the employee's unmarried child are normally terminated by the RRB when the child attains age 18 (age 16 for a surviving divorced spouse) or if a disabled child over age 18 (age 16 for a surviving divorced spouse) recovers from the disability. Therefore, the RRB must be notified if the child leaves the beneficiary's care or marries.

Benefits are also payable to an unmarried child aged 18 in full-time attendance at an elementary or secondary school or in approved home schooling until the student attains age 19 or the end of the school term in progress when the student attains age 19. (In most cases where a student attains age 19 during the school term, benefits are limited to the two months following the month age 19 is attained.) These benefits will be terminated earlier if the student marries, graduates, or ceases full-time attendance. Therefore, the RRB must be notified promptly to prevent an overpayment.

---

476. How does leaving railroad work though accepting a buyout affect future entitlement to an annuity under the Railroad Retirement Act?

As long as an employee has acquired at least ten years (120 months) of creditable rail service, or five years (60 months) of creditable service if such service was performed after 1995, he or she would still be eligible for a regular railroad retirement annuity upon reaching retirement age, or, if totally disabled, for an annuity before retirement age, regardless of whether or not a buyout was ever accepted.

However, if a person permanently leaves railroad employment before attaining retirement age, the employee may not be able to meet the requirements for certain other benefits, particularly the current connection requirement for annuities based on occupational, rather than total, disability and for supplemental annuities paid by the RRB to career employees.

In addition, if an employee does not have a current connection, the Social Security Administration, rather than the RRB, would have jurisdiction of any survivor benefits that become payable on the basis of the employee's combined railroad retirement and social security covered earnings. The survivor benefits payable by the RRB are generally greater than those paid by the Social Security Administration.

477. Can Federal, State, or local government pensions result in dual benefit reductions in an employee's railroad retirement annuity?

Yes. Tier I benefits for employees first eligible for a railroad retirement annuity AND a Federal, State, or local government pension after 1985 may be reduced for receipt of a public pension based, in part or in whole, on employment not covered by social security or railroad retirement after 1956.

This may also apply to certain other payments not covered by railroad retirement or social security, such as from a non-profit organization or from a foreign government or a foreign employer. Usually, an employee's Tier I benefit will not be reduced by more than half of his or her pension from noncovered employment. However, if the employee is under age 65 and receiving a disability annuity, the Tier I benefit may be reduced by an added amount if the pension from noncovered employment is a public disability benefit.

Military service pensions, payments by the Department of Veterans Affairs, or certain benefits payable by a foreign government as a result of a totalization agreement between that government and the United States will not cause a reduction.

478. Can workers' compensation or public disability benefits affect railroad retirement benefits?

If an employee is receiving a railroad retirement disability annuity, Tier I benefits for the employee and spouse may, under certain circumstances, be reduced for receipt of workers' compensation or public disability benefits.

479. Why is a railroad retirement annuity reduced when a Social Security benefit is also payable?

The Tier I portion of a railroad retirement annuity is based on both the railroad retirement and social security credits acquired by an employee and computed under social security formulas.

It approximates what social security would pay if railroad work were covered by social security. Tier I benefits are, therefore, reduced by the amount of any actual social security benefit paid on the basis of nonrailroad employment, in order to prevent a duplication of benefits based on social security-covered earnings.

In addition, following principles of social security law which limit payment to the higher of any two or more benefits payable to an individual at one time, the Tier I dual benefit reduction applies to an annuity even if the social security benefit is based on the earnings record of someone other than the railroad employee, such as a spouse or former spouse. An annuitant is required to advise the RRB if any benefits are received directly from the Social Security Administration or if those benefits increase (other than for a cost-of living increase).

The Tier II portion of a railroad retirement annuity is based on the railroad employee's railroad service and earnings alone and is computed under a separate formula. It is not reduced for entitlement to a social security benefit.

There are no exceptions to the railroad retirement annuity reduction for social security benefits.

480. Does the Railroad Retirement Board allow for representative payees as does Social Security?

Yes.

Every annuitant has the right to manage his or her own benefits. However, when physical or mental impairments make a railroad retirement annuitant incapable of properly handling benefit payments, or where the RRB determines that the interests of the annuitant so require, the agency can appoint a representative payee to act on the annuitant's behalf. A representative payee may be either a person or an organization selected by the RRB to receive benefits on behalf of an annuitant.

Differences between Representative Payee and Power of Attorney

This differs from power of attorney, which is a legal process where one person grants another the authority to transact certain business on his or her behalf; but the RRB, like the Social Security Administration, does not recognize power of attorney for purposes of managing benefit payments for a beneficiary. Power of attorney creates an assignment-like situation in that it would give a third-party authority to act on an annuitant's behalf. The RRB Act likewise gives the RRB exclusive jurisdiction in determining whether to appoint a representative payee for an annuitant. If the RRB recognized power of attorney, it would be deferring to a designation made by someone outside of the agency and would, in effect, be relinquishing its responsibility to the annuitant.

Appointment and Duties

Generally, the RRB's local field offices determine the need for a representative payee and interview potential payees. The field office also advises the payee of his or her duties, monitors the payee, investigates any allegations of misuse of funds, and changes the method of payment, or the payee, when appropriate.

The RRB provides 15 days' advance notice to an annuitant of its intent to appoint a representative payee, and the name of the payee, in order to allow the annuitant a period in which to contest the appointment. The Railroad Retirement Act gives the RRB authority to determine whether direct payment of benefits, or payment to a representative payee, will best serve an annuitant's interest. The RRB appoint a representative payee regardless of whether there has been a legal finding of incompetence or commitment and, depending on the circumstances in a particular case, they can select someone other than the individual's legal representative to be the representative payee.

The payee must first consider the annuitant's day-to-day needs. This includes paying for food, shelter, clothing, medical care, and miscellaneous personal needs. Beyond day-to-day needs, railroad retirement benefits may be used for other expenses.

The payee is also responsible for reporting events to the RRB that affect the individual's annuity and is required to account for the funds received on behalf of the annuitant.

In addition, since railroad retirement benefits are subject to federal income tax, a representative payee is responsible for delivering the benefit information statements issued each year by the RRB to the person handling the annuitant's tax matters.

Periodically, the payee will be asked to complete a report which includes questions regarding how much of the railroad retirement benefits available during the year were used for the support of the beneficiary, how much of the benefits were saved, and how the savings were invested. In order to complete the questionnaire correctly, a payee must keep current records of the railroad retirement benefits received and how the benefits were used. The records should be retained for four years.

Unemployment and Sickness Benefits

481. What are the Unemployment and Sickness Benefits for Railroad Employees?

The Railroad Retirement Board (RRB) administers the Railroad Unemployment Insurance Act (RUIA), which provides two kinds of benefits for qualified railroaders: unemployment benefits for those who become unemployed but are ready, willing, and able to work; and sickness benefits for those who are unable to work because of sickness or injury. Sickness benefits are also payable to female rail workers for periods of time when they are unable to work because of health conditions related to pregnancy, miscarriage, or childbirth. A new benefit year begins each July 1.

Eligibility

To qualify for **normal** railroad unemployment or sickness benefits, an employee must have had railroad earnings of at least $4,275.00 in calendar year 2021, counting no more than

$1,710 for any month. Those who were first employed in the rail industry in 2021 must also have at least five months of creditable railroad service in 2021.

Under certain conditions, employees who do not qualify on the basis of their 2021 earnings may still be able to receive benefits in the new benefit year. Employees with at least 10 years of service (120 or more months of service) who received normal benefits in the benefit year ending June 30, 2022, may be eligible for **extended** benefits, and employees with at least 10 years of service (120 or more months of service) might qualify for **accelerated** benefits if they have rail earnings of at least $4,387.50 in 2023, not counting earnings of more than $1,755 a month.

In order to qualify for **extended** unemployment benefits, a claimant must not have voluntarily quit work without good cause and not have voluntarily retired. To qualify for extended sickness benefits, a claimant must not have voluntarily retired and must be under age 65.

To be eligible for accelerated benefits, a claimant must have 14 or more consecutive days of unemployment or sickness; not have voluntarily retired or, if claiming unemployment benefits, quit work without good cause; and, when claiming sickness benefits, be under age 65.

481.01. When is an employee eligible for unemployment or sickness benefits?

If a worker's railroad earnings were at least $4,275 in calendar year 2021 (counting no more than $1,710 for any one month), they qualify for *normal* railroad unemployment or illness benefits in the benefit year that began July 2022. If they first worked in the rail industry in 2021, they must also have at least five months of creditable railroad service in 2021 to be eligible. The Form BA-6 Certificate of Service Months and Compensation is used to determine eligibility.[1]

Under certain conditions, employees who do not qualify on the basis of their 2021 earnings may still be able to receive benefits in the new benefit year. Employees with at least 120 months of service who received normal benefits in the benefit year that ended June 30, 2022, may be eligible for extended benefits. Employees with at least 120 months of service might qualify for accelerated benefits if they have railroad earnings of at least $4,387.50 in 2022, not counting earnings of more than $1,755 in any one month.

Either a claim form or a denial letter will be issued within 10 days of receiving an application. If filing a claim for subsequent biweekly unemployment or sickness benefits, the RRB will certify a payment or release a denial letter within 10 days of the date of receipt of the claim form. If entitled to a payment, the employee's benefits will generally be paid within one week of that decision by direct deposit.

Note

1. BA-6_SAMPLE (rrb.gov) (Last accessed September 6, 2022).

481.02. How long is an employee eligible to collect unemployment or sickness benefits?

Employees can receive normal unemployment or sickness benefits for up to 130 days (26 weeks) in a benefit year. The total amount of each kind of benefit which may be paid in the current benefit year cannot exceed the employee's railroad earnings in calendar year 2021, counting earnings up to $2,209 per month. If normal benefits are exhausted, extended benefits are payable for up to 65 days (during 7 consecutive 14-day claim periods) if the employee has at least 10 years of service (120 or more cumulative service months).

482. How much is payable under the Unemployment and Sickness Benefits for Railroad Employees?

BIWEEKLY BENEFITS

In the benefit year beginning July 2022, nearly all employees will qualify for the maximum daily benefit rate of $85. This benefit will rise to $87 in July 2023. Benefits are generally payable for the number of days of unemployment or sickness over four in a 14-day claim periods, which provides $850 for each two full weeks of unemployment or sickness ($870 beginning July 2023). Sickness benefits payable for the first six months after the month the employee last worked are subject to Tier I railroad retirement payroll taxes, unless benefits are being paid for an on-the-job injury.

Due to a sequestration order under the Budget Control Act of 2011, the RRB reduced unemployment and sickness benefits by 5.7 percent through September 30, 2021. As a result, the total maximum amount payable in a two-week period covering 10 days of unemployment or sickness was $773.26. The maximum amount payable for sickness benefits subject to Tier I payroll taxes of 7.65 percent will be $714.11 over two weeks. Future reductions, should they occur, will be calculated based on applicable law.

In addition, under the CARES Act, the amount of an unemployment benefit was increased by $1,200 per two-week period. This increased amount, which is not subject to sequestration, is applied to any two-week registration periods that began on or after April 1, 2020, through July 31, 2020.

Normal unemployment or sickness benefits are each payable for up to 130 days (26 weeks) in a benefit year. The total amount of each kind of benefit which may be paid in the new benefit year cannot exceed the employee's railroad earnings in calendar year 2020, counting earnings up to $2,138 per month.

If normal benefits are exhausted, extended benefits are payable for up to 65 days (during seven consecutive 14-day claim periods) to employees with at least 10 years of service (120 or more cumulative service months).

Temporary benefits created under the Coronavirus Aid, Relief, and Economic Security Act, Continued Assistance to Rail Workers Act of 2020 (CARWA), and American Rescue Plan

Act of 2021 are not subject to sequestration. Under CARWA, beginning January 3, 2021, all benefits under the RUIA (including normal unemployment and sickness benefits as well as normal extended unemployment and sickness benefits) will be exempt from sequestration until 30 days after the Presidential declaration of a national emergency concerning COVID-19 terminates.)

483. What are the waiting periods for Unemployment and Sickness Benefits for Railroad Employees?

Registration and waiting period

Benefits are normally paid for the number of days of unemployment or sickness over four days in a 14-day registration periods. Initial sickness claims must also begin with four consecutive days of sickness. However, during the first 14-day claim period in a benefit year, benefits are only payable for each day of unemployment or sickness in excess of seven which, in effect, provides a one week waiting period. Separate waiting periods are required for unemployment and sickness benefits. However, only one seven-day waiting period is required during any period of continuing unemployment or sickness, even if that period continues into a subsequent benefit year.

Duration of Benefits

- **Normal benefits** are paid for up to 130 days (26 weeks) in a benefit year. Benefit rights are exhausted when a benefit year ends (normally June 30) or earlier if benefit payments equal base year creditable earnings. Maximum normal benefits payable in the benefit year beginning July 2022 cannot exceed the railroad earnings in base year 2021, counting monthly earnings of up to $2,209. In the benefit year beginning July 2023, monthly earnings up to $2,267 in base year 2022 will be counted.

To qualify for normal unemployment benefits, the person must not have voluntarily quit work without good cause and not have voluntarily retired.

In order to qualify for normal unemployment benefits, the employee must not have voluntarily quit work without good cause and not have voluntarily retired.

- **Extended benefits:** If the work has 10 or more years of service (120 cumulative service months or more) and exhaust their normal unemployment or sickness benefits, they may be eligible to receive extended benefits for up to 65 days (during 7 consecutive 14-day registration periods). Also, if they are not qualified for normal benefits in the current benefit year, but received normal benefits in the previous year, they may still be eligible for extended benefits.

In order to qualify for extended unemployment benefits, the worker must not have voluntarily quit work without good cause and not have voluntarily retired. To qualify for extended sickness benefits, they must not have voluntarily retired and must be under age 65.

- **Accelerated benefits:** If the worker has 10 or more years of service (120 or more cumulative service months) and their earnings do not qualify them for unemployment or sickness benefits in the current benefit year, but will qualify them in the next benefit year, they may be able to receive normal unemployment or sickness benefits before the regular beginning date of the next benefit year. To be eligible for accelerated benefits, they must have 14 or more consecutive days of either unemployment or sickness and not have voluntarily retired, or quit work without good cause if claiming unemployment benefits, and be under age 65 when claiming sickness benefits.

Strikes

If a worker is unemployed because of a strike conducted in accordance with the Railway Labor Act, benefits are not payable for days of unemployment during the first 14 days of the strike, but benefits are payable during subsequent 14-day periods.

If a strike is in violation of the Railway Labor Act, unemployment benefits are not payable to employees participating in the strike. However, employees not among those participating in such an illegal strike, but who are unemployed on account of the strike, may receive benefits after the first two weeks of the strike.

While a benefit year waiting period cannot count toward a strike waiting period, the 14-day strike waiting period may count as the benefit year waiting period if a worker subsequently becomes unemployed for reasons other than a strike later in the benefit year.

---

484. Do earnings in a claim period by an employee affect unemployment benefit eligibility?

If a claimant's earnings for days worked and days of vacation, paid leave, or other leave in a 14-day registration period are more than a certain indexed amount, no benefits are payable for any days of unemployment in that period. The registration period can be used to satisfy the waiting period.

Earnings include pay from railroad and non-railroad work, as well as part-time work and self-employment. Earnings also include pay that an employee would have earned except for failure to mark up or report for duty on time, or because he or she missed a turn in pool service or was otherwise not ready or willing to work. For the 2023 benefit year beginning in July, earnings of $2,267 or more in a claim period will disqualify a claim for unemployment benefits, even if there are more than four days of unemployment claimed. This amount corresponds to the base year monthly compensation amount used in determining eligibility for benefits in each year. An earnings test that applies on the first claim in a benefit year will not prevent the first claim from satisfying the waiting period in a benefit year.

Earnings of $15 or less per day from work which is substantially less than full-time and not inconsistent with the holding of normal full-time employment may be considered subsidiary remuneration and may not prevent payment of any days in a claim. However, a claimant must report all full and part-time work on each claim, regardless of the amount of earnings, so the RRB can determine if the work affects benefits.

485. Do special circumstances affect unemployment benefits?

Yes, some special situations directly affect unemployment benefits.

Employees working in train and engine service cannot collect unemployment benefits for days that they are standing by or laying over for scheduled or regularly assigned runs or they missed a turn in pool service.

Extra-board employees can collect unemployment benefits between jobs only if the miles and hours they actually worked were less than the equivalent of normal full-time work in their class of service during the 14-day claim period. Entitlement to benefits would also depend on the employee's earnings.

Applying for Railroad Benefits

486. How does one apply for railroad annuities?

Applications are filed through the RRB's field offices. There are 54 RRB field offices throughout the country.[1] Applicants may file in person or by telephone and mail. Those filing in person may do so at any RRB office or at one of the office's customer outreach program service locations. Applicants filing by telephone receive the same information and instructions that are provided to those filing in person; forms requiring signatures and other documents are then handled by mail. A toll-free number is available for questions at 1-877-772-5772.

Note

1. https://www.rrb.gov/sites/default/files/2021-09/do_addr.pdf (last accessed September 10, 2022).

487. Can an application be filed prior to a person's actual retirement?

Yes. The RRB accepts annuity applications up to three months in advance of an annuity beginning date, which allows the RRB to complete the processing of most new claims by a person's retirement date. An employee can be in compensated service while filing a disability application, provided that the compensated service is not active service and terminates within 90 days from the date of filing. When an employee files a disability application while still in compensated service, it will be necessary to provide a specific ending date of the compensation. Compensated service includes not only compensation with respect to active service performed by an employee for an employer, but also includes pay for time lost, wage continuation payments, certain employee protection payments, and any other payment for which the employee will receive additional creditable service.

Applicants can contact their local RRB field office to schedule a pre-retirement consultation (by phone or in person) and to confirm their eligibility and learn procedures and documentation required. Railroad employees can also get estimates of their future annuities over the Internet by visiting the RRB's website. To do so, employees must first establish an RRB online account at www.rrb.gov.

488. What documentation is required for apply for an annuity?

- Proof of age.

- Notice of any Social Security benefit award or other Social Security claim determination.

- Information regarding any other Federal, State, or local government pension for which he or she also qualifies, as well as certain other payments not covered by railroad retirement or Social Security, such as from a non-profit organization or from a foreign government or a foreign employer.

- An employee or survivor filing for a disability annuity is required to submit supporting medical information from his or her treating physician, as well as any reports or records from recent hospitalizations.

  - Specialized medical examinations given by a doctor named by the RRB may be required.

- Proof of any military service claimed.

- A spouse, divorced spouse, or widow(er) applying for a railroad retirement annuity must furnish proof of marriage to the employee.

  - A divorced spouse must furnish proof of a final divorce from the employee, as well as proof that any subsequent marriages have terminated.

  - A spouse, divorced spouse, or survivor also qualified to receive a pension from a Federal, State, or local government must submit information regarding that pension.

489. When is a spouse eligible for spouse annuities?

The Railroad Retirement Act provides annuities for the spouse (and divorced spouse) of an employee who is entitled to an employee annuity. A spouse may receive an annuity based on age, or on having a child of the employee in his or her care. A divorced spouse may only receive an annuity based on age. No spouse or divorced spouse annuity may be paid based upon disability.

To be eligible for an annuity, a spouse must:

(1)   be the husband or wife of an employee who is entitled to an annuity; and

(2)   stop working for any railroad employer.

Where the employee has completed 10 years but less than 30 years of railroad service, and has attained age 62, the spouse must be:

(1)   retirement age or older;

(2)   less than retirement age and have in his or her care a disabled child or a minor child (a child under 18 years old if the spouse claimant is a wife or under 16 years old if the spouse claimant is a husband) of the employee; or

(3)   age 62 or older but under retirement age. (In such case, all annuity components are reduced for each month the spouse is under retirement age at the time the annuity begins.)

Where the employee has completed 30 years of railroad service and is age 60 or older, the spouse must be:

(1)   age 60 or older;

(2)   less than age 60 and have in his or her care a disabled or minor child of the employee; or

(3)   age 60 but less than retirement age.

To be eligible for a divorced spouse annuity, the employee annuitant must be at least age 62, must have been married for at least 10 years, and the divorced spouse must:

(1)   be the divorced wife or husband of an employee;

(2)   stop working for a railroad employer;

(3)   not be entitled to a retirement or disability benefit under the Social Security Act, based on a Primary Insurance Amount (PIA) that is equal to or greater than one-half of the employee's Tier I PIA; and either

(4)   have attained retirement age; or

(5)   have attained age 62 but be under retirement age. (The annuity is reduced for each month the spouse is under retirement age at the time the annuity begins.)

The amount of the divorced spouse's annuity is, in effect, equal to what Social Security would pay in the same situation, and therefore less than the amount of the spouse annuity otherwise payable.

490. Can railroad retirees receive benefits at earlier ages than Social Security workers?

Yes. Railroad employees with 30 or more years of creditable service are eligible for regular annuities based on age and service the first full month they are age 60, and railroad employees with less than 30 years of creditable service are eligible for regular annuities based on age and service the first full month they are age 62.

No early retirement reduction applies if a rail employee retires at age 60 or older with 30 years of service and his or her retirement is after 2001, or if the employee retired before 2002 at age 62 or older with 30 years of service.

Early retirement reductions are otherwise applied to annuities awarded before full retirement age, the age at which an employee can receive full benefits with no reduction for early retirement. This ranges from age 65 for those born before 1938 to age 67 for those born in 1960 or later, the same as under Social Security.

Under Social Security, a worker cannot begin receiving retirement benefits based on age until age 62, regardless of how long he or she worked, and Social Security retirement benefits are reduced for retirement prior to full retirement age regardless of years of coverage.

491. How does early retirement reduce the annuity amount versus Full Retirement Age?

The early retirement annuity reductions applied to annuities awarded before full retirement age are increasing. For employees retiring between age 62 and full retirement age with less than 30 years of service, the maximum reduction will be 30 percent by the year 2022. Prior to 2000, the maximum reduction was 20 percent.

Age reductions are applied separately to the Tier I and Tier II components of an annuity. The Tier I reduction is 1/180 for each of the first 36 months the employee is under full retirement age when his or her annuity begins and 1/240 for each additional month (if any). This will result in a gradual increase in the reduction at age 62 to 30 percent for an employee once the age 67 retirement age is in effect.

These same reductions apply to the Tier II component of the annuity. However, if an employee had any creditable railroad service before August 12, 1983, the retirement age for Tier II purposes will remain 65, and the Tier II benefit will not be reduced beyond 20 percent.

The following chart shows how the gradual increase in full retirement age will affect employees.

Employee Retires with Less than 30 Years of Service

Year of Birth*	Full Retirement Age**	Annuity Reduction at Age 62
1937 or earlier	65	20.00%
1938	65 and 2 months	20.833%
1939	65 and 4 months	21.667%
1940	65 and 6 months	22.50%
1941	65 and 8 months	23.333%

Year of Birth*	Full Retirement Age**	Annuity Reduction at Age 62
1942	65 and 10 months	24.167%
1943 through 1954	66	25.00%
1955	66 and 2 months	25.833%
1956	66 and 4 months	26.667%
1957	66 and 6 months	27.50%
1958	66 and 8 months	28.333%
1959	66 and 10 months	29.167%
1960 or later	67	30.00%

* A person attains a given age the day before his or her birthday. Consequently, someone born on January 1 is considered to have attained his or her given age on December 31 of the previous year.

** If an employee has less than 10 years of railroad service and is already entitled to an age-reduced social security benefit, the Tier I reduction is based on the reduction applicable on the beginning date of the social security benefit, even if the employee is already of full retirement age on the beginning date of the railroad retirement annuity.

The following chart shows the effect on spouses if the employee retires with less than 30 years of service.

Spouse Age Reductions

Year of Birth*	Full Retirement Age**	Annuity Reduction at Age 62
1937 or earlier	65	25.00%
1938	65 and 2 months	25.833%
1939	65 and 4 months	26.667%
1940	65 and 6 months	27.50%
1941	65 and 8 months	28.333%
1942	65 and 10 months	29.167%
1943 through 1954	66	30.00%
1955	66 and 2 months	30.833%
1956	66 and 4 months	31.667%
1957	66 and 6 months	32.50%
1958	66 and 8 months	33.333%
1959	66 and 10 months	34.167%
1960 or later	67	35.00%

* A person attains a given age the day before her or his birthday. Consequently, someone born on January 1 is considered to have attained his or her given age on December 31 of the previous year.

** If the employee has less than 10 years of railroad service and the spouse is already entitled to an age-reduced social security benefit, the age reduction in her or his tier I will be based on the age reduction applicable on the beginning date of the spouse's social security benefit, even if the spouse is already of full retirement age on the beginning date of her or his railroad retirement annuity.

492. Can the spouse of a railroad employee receive benefits at earlier ages than Social Security workers?

If a retired railroad employee with 30 or more years of service is age 60, the employee's spouse is also eligible for an annuity the first full month the spouse is age sixty.

Certain early retirement reductions are applied if the employee first became eligible for a 60/30 annuity July 1, 1984 or later, and retired at ages 60 or 61 before 2002. If the employee was awarded a disability annuity, and has attained age 60 and has 30 years of service, the spouse can receive an unreduced annuity the first full month she or he is age 60, and regardless of whether the employee annuity began before or after 2002, as long as the spouse's annuity beginning date is after 2001.

To qualify for a spouse's benefit under Social Security, an applicant must be at least age 62, or any age if caring for a child who is entitled to receive benefits based on the applicant's spouse's record.

493. What benefits does Social Security offer that are not available under railroad retirement?

Social Security does pay certain types of benefits that are not available under railroad retirement. For example, Social Security provides children's benefits when an employee is disabled, retired, or deceased. Under current law, the Railroad Retirement Act only provides children's benefits if the employee is deceased.

However, the Railroad Retirement Act includes a special minimum guaranty provision which ensures that railroad families will not receive less in monthly benefits than they would have if railroad earnings were covered by Social Security rather than railroad retirement laws. This guaranty is intended to cover situations in which one or more members of a family would otherwise be eligible for a type of Social Security benefit that is not provided under the Railroad Retirement Act. Therefore, if a retired rail employee has children who would otherwise be eligible for a benefit under Social Security, the employee's annuity can be increased to reflect what Social Security would pay the family.

494. How do railroad retirement and Social Security lump-sum benefits differ?

Both the railroad retirement and Social Security systems provide a lump-sum death benefit. The railroad retirement lump-sum benefit is generally payable only if survivor annuities are not immediately due upon an employee's death. The Social Security lump-sum benefit may be payable regardless of whether monthly benefits are also due. Both railroad retirement and Social Security provide a lump-sum benefit of $255. However, if a railroad employee completed ten years of creditable railroad service before 1975, the average railroad retirement lump-sum benefit payable is $1,030. Also, if an employee had less than ten years of service, but had at least five years of such service after 1995, he or she would have to have had an insured status under

Social Security law (counting both railroad retirement and Social Security credits) in order for the $255 lump-sum benefit to be payable.

The Social Security lump sum is generally only payable to the widow(er) living with the employee at the time of death. Under railroad retirement, if the employee had ten years of service before 1975 and was not survived by a living-with widow(er), the lump sum may be paid to the funeral home or the payer of the funeral expenses.

Disability Benefits

495. Are disability annuities subject to reduction due to age?

Employee annuities based on disability are not subject to age reductions except for employees with less than ten years of service, but who have five years of service after 1995. Such employees may qualify for a Tier I benefit before retirement age based on total disability, but only if they have a disability insured status (disability freeze) under Social Security rules, counting both railroad retirement and social security-covered earnings. Unlike with a 10-year employee, a Tier II benefit is not payable in these disability cases until the employee attains age 62. The employee's Tier II benefit will be reduced for early retirement in the same manner as the Tier II benefit of an employee who retired at age 62 with less than 30 years of service.

496. What is the difference between total disability provisions and occupational disability provisions?

Total Disability Annuity

This annuity is based on disability for all regular work and is payable at any age to employees with at least 10 years (120 months) of creditable railroad service and, under certain conditions, to employees with 5 to 9 years of creditable railroad service after 1995.

Occupational Disability Annuity

This annuity is based on a disability for the regular railroad occupation and is payable at age 60 if the employee has 10 years (120 months) of railroad service, or at any age if the employee has at least 20 years (240 months) of service. This type of annuity requires a current connection with the railroad industry. The current connection requirement is normally met if the employee worked for a railroad in at least 12 of the 30 months immediately preceding his or her annuity beginning date.

If an employee does not qualify for a current connection but has 12 months of service in an earlier 30-month period, the employee may still meet the current connection requirement. This alternative generally applies if the employee did not have any regular employment outside the railroad industry after the end of the last 30-month period which included 12 months of railroad service, and before the month the annuity begins. Full or part-time work for a nonrailroad employer in the interval between the end of the last 30-month period including 12 months of railroad service, and the month an employee's annuity begins, can break a current connection.

497. When can a disabled employee with five to nine years of service qualify for a railroad retirement disability annuity?

Employees with five to nine years of service may qualify if:

- At least of the five years of service were after 1995

- Disability is total, not occupational disability

- Have a disability insured status under Social Security law

    o   Disability insured status is usually established when an employee has Social Security or railroad retirement earnings credits in 20 calendar quarters in a period of 40 consecutive quarters ending in, or after, the quarter in which the disability began.

Unlike the two-tier annuities payable to a 10-year employee, disability annuities payable to five-year employees are initially limited to a Tier I social security equivalent benefit; Tier II benefit is not payable in these cases until the employee attains age 62. Additionally, the Tier II will be reduced for early retirement in the same manner as the Tier II benefit of an employee who retired on the basis of age, rather than disability, at age 62 with less than 30 years of service.

498. What are the differences in standards for total disability and occupational disability?

Total Disability

An employee is considered to be totally disabled if medical evidence shows a physical and/or mental impairment preventing the performance of **any** regular and gainful work.

Occupational Disability

An employee is considered to be occupationally disabled if a physical or mental impairment prevents the employee from performing the duties of his or her regular railroad occupation, even though the employee may be able to perform other kinds of work.

An employee's regular occupation is generally that particular work he or she has performed for hire in more calendar months, which may or may not be consecutive, than any other work during the last five years; or that work which was performed for hire in at least one-half of all the months, which must be consecutive, in which the employee worked for hire during the last 15 years.

499. Is there a waiting period for railroad retirement disability similar to Social Security disability?

Yes. A five-month waiting period beginning with the month after the month of the disability's onset is required before railroad retirement disability annuity payments can begin. It is unnecessary for the applicant wait until this five-month period is over to file for benefits.

500. What documentation is required to qualify for a RR disability annuity?

Applicants are required to submit medical evidence supporting their claim. Required evidence includes

- dates of hospitalization,

- names and dosages of medication,

- names of doctors, and

- workers' compensation or public disability benefits if applicable.

- Special medical examinations performed by a doctor named by the RRB may also be required.

Evidence generally should not be more than 12 months old.

501. Can an individual collect a disability annuity while working?

Possibly.

Rules for disability benefits are more stringent than those that apply to individuals who have retired on the basis of age and service. The individual cannot earn more than $1.050 in 2022 in any employment or self-employment, exclusive of work-related expenses. Withheld payments will be restored if earnings are less than $12,600 after deduction of disability-related work expenses. Failure to report such earnings could involve a significant penalty charge.

These disability work restrictions cease upon a disabled employee annuitant's attainment of Full Retirement Age. This transition is effective no earlier than full retirement age, even if the annuitant had thirty years of service.

502. Does working for a railroad labor organization affect the ability to qualify for disability coverage?

Payment of disability coverage cannot begin earlier than the day after the employee stops working in compensated service for any railroad employer, including labor organizations. This includes service compensated for more than $24.99 during a calendar month to a local lodge or division of a railway labor organization. Work by a local lodge or division secretary collecting insurance premiums is railroad work which must be stopped regardless of salary.

503. In order to qualify for a disability, must the applicant give up employment rights?

Yes. In order for a supplemental to be paid or for an eligible spouse to begin receiving benefits, a disability annuitant under full retirement age must relinquish employment rights.

Survivor Benefits

504. What survivor benefits are payable under the Railroad Retirement Act?

The Railroad Retirement Act provides annuities for the widow(er), surviving divorced spouse, or remarried widow(er) of an employee. The deceased employee must have completed 10 years of railroad service (or five years of service after 1995) and have had a current connection with the railroad industry at the time of his or her death. A widow(er), surviving divorced spouse, or remarried widow(er) may receive an annuity based on age, on disability, or on having a child of the employee in his or her care.

A widow(er) of an employee who has completed 10 years of railroad service (or five years of service after 1995) and had a current connection with the railroad industry at death is eligible for an annuity if he or she has not remarried, and:

(1)   has attained retirement age;

(2)   is at least 50 but less than 60 years of age and becomes disabled (this results in a reduced annuity);

(3)   is less than retirement age but has in his or her care a child who either is under age 18 (16 with respect to the Tier I component) or is disabled and who is entitled to a child's annuity; or

(4)   is at least 60 years of age but has not attained retirement age. If eligibility is based on (4), all components of the annuity are reduced for each month the widow(er) is age 62 or over but under retirement age when the annuity begins. For each month, the widow(er) is at least 60 but under age 62, all components of the annuity are reduced as if the widow(er) were age 62.

A surviving divorced spouse of an employee who completed 10 years of railroad service (or five years of service after 1995) and had a current connection with the railroad industry at death is eligible for an annuity, if he or she:

(1)   is unmarried;

(2)   was married to the employee for at least 10 years; and

(3)   is not entitled to a Social Security retirement benefit that is equal to or higher than the surviving divorced spouse's annuity before any reduction for age.

In addition, the divorced spouse must meet one of the following requirements:

(1)   have attained retirement age;

(2)   be at least 50 years old but less than retirement age and disabled (this results in a reduced annuity);

(3)   be less than retirement age but have in his or her care a child who either is under age 16 or is disabled and who is entitled to a child's benefit; or

(4)   is at least 60 years of age but has not attained retirement age. In this case, the annuity is reduced for each month the surviving spouse is under retirement age when the annuity begins.

If a surviving divorced spouse marries after attaining age 60 (or age 50 if he or she is a disabled surviving divorced spouse), the marriage is deemed not to have occurred.

A widow(er) of an employee who completed 10 years of railroad service (or five years of service after 1995) and had a current connection with the railroad industry at death is eligible for an annuity as a remarried widow(er), if he or she:

(1)   remarried either after having attained age 60 (after age 50 if disabled) or before age 60 but the marriage terminated; and

(2)   is not entitled to a Social Security retirement benefit that is equal to or higher than the full amount of the remarried widow(er) annuity before any reduction for age.

In addition, the remarried widow(er) must meet one of the following requirements:

(1)   have attained retirement age;

(2)   be at least 50 but less than 60 years of age and disabled (this results in a reduced annuity);

(3)   have not attained retirement age but have in his or her care a child who either is under age 16 or is disabled, and who is entitled to a child's annuity; or

(4)   be at least age 60 but have not attained retirement age. (In this case, the annuity is reduced for each month the remarried widow(er) is under retirement age when the annuity begins.)

If an employee does not qualify on the above basis but has twelve months of service in an earlier 30-month period, he or she may still meet the current connection requirement. This alternative generally applies if the employee did not have any regular employment outside the railroad industry after the end of the last 30-month period, which included twelve months of railroad service, and before the month the annuity begins or the date of death.

Full or part-time work for a nonrailroad employer in the interval between the end of the last 30-month period, including twelve months of railroad service, and the beginning date of an employee's annuity, or the month of death if earlier, can break a current connection.

Self-employment in an unincorporated business will not break a current connection; however, self-employment can break a current connection if the business is incorporated.

Working for certain U.S. Government agencies—Department of Transportation, National Transportation Safety Board, Surface Transportation Board, Transportation Security Administration, National Mediation Board, and Railroad Retirement Board—will not break a current connection. State employment with the Alaska Railroad, so long as that railroad remains an entity of the State of Alaska, will not break a current connection. Also, railroad service in Canada for a Canadian railroad will neither break nor preserve a current connection.

A current connection can also be maintained, for purposes of supplemental and survivor annuities, if the employee completed 25 years of railroad service, was involuntarily terminated without fault from his or her last job in the rail industry, and did not thereafter decline an offer of employment in the same class or craft in the rail industry, regardless of the distance to the new position. Once a current connection is established at the time the railroad retirement annuity begins, an employee never loses it no matter what kind of work is performed thereafter.

505. How much are monthly survivor benefits under railroad retirement and Social Security?

Survivor benefits are generally higher if payable by the RRB rather than social security. At the end of fiscal year 2021, the average annuity being paid to all aged and disabled widow(er)s was $2,420 a month, compared to $1.365 under social security.

Benefits awarded by the RRB in fiscal year 2021 to aged and disabled widow(er)s of railroaders averaged nearly $2,420 a month, compared to approximately $1,365 under social security.

The annuities being paid at the end of fiscal year 2021 to widowed mothers/fathers averaged $2,040 a month and children's annuities averaged $1,235, compared to $11,050 and $920 a month for widowed mothers/fathers and children, respectively, under social security.

Those awarded in fiscal year 2021 averaged $2,090 a month for widowed mothers/fathers and $1,590 a month for children under railroad retirement, compared to $1,045 and $930 for widowed mothers/fathers and children, respectively, under social security.

506. What if service requirements are not met for disability?

If a deceased employee did not have an insured status, jurisdiction of any survivor benefits payable is transferred to the Social Security Administration and survivor benefits are paid by that agency instead of the RRB. Regardless of which agency has jurisdiction, the deceased employee's railroad retirement and Social Security credits will be combined for benefit computation purposes.

507. Are children and other dependents eligible for survivor benefits?

Other survivor annuities are payable to:

- A child under age 18.

- A child age 18 in full-time attendance at an elementary or secondary school, until the student attains age 19 or the end of the school term after the student attains age 19.

- A disabled child over age 18, if the child became totally and permanently disabled before age 22.

- A dependent grandchild meeting any of the requirements described previously for a child, if both the grandchild's parents are deceased or disabled.

- A parent at age 60 who was dependent on the employee for at least half of the parent's support. If the employee was also survived by a widow(er) or child who can qualify for an annuity, the parent's annuity is limited to the amount that Social Security would pay.

In order to be eligible for a child's annuity, the child must be:

(1)   a child of an employee who has completed 10 years of railroad service (or five years of service after 1995) and had a current connection with the railroad industry when he died;

(2)   unmarried at the time the application was filed; and

(3)   dependent upon the employee.

508. What happens to survivors with dual benefits?

Survivor annuities, like retirement annuities, consist of Tier I and Tier II components. Tier I is based on the deceased employee's combined railroad retirement and Social Security credits and is generally equivalent to the amount that would have been payable under Social Security. Tier II amounts are percentages of the deceased employee's Tier I amount.

The Tier I portion is reduced by the amount of any Social Security benefits received by a survivor annuitant, even if the Social Security benefits are based on the survivor's own earnings. This reduction follows the principles of Social Security law under which only the higher of a retirement or survivor benefit is, in effect, payable to a beneficiary. When both railroad retirement annuities and Social Security benefits are payable, the payments are generally combined into a single payment, issued through the Railroad Retirement Board.

The Tier I annuity portion of a widow's or widower's annuity may be reduced for receipt of any federal, state, or local government pension based on the widow(er)'s own earnings. The reduction does not apply if the employment on which the public pension is based was covered under Social Security as of the last day of the individual's employment.

Military service pensions based entirely on active duty before 1957 will cause a reduction. However, payments from the Department of Veterans Affairs will not cause a reduction. For those subject to the government-pension reduction, the Tier I reduction is equal to two-thirds of the amount of the government pension.

If a widow or widower is qualified for a railroad retirement employee annuity as well as a survivor annuity, a special guarantee applies in some cases. If both the widow (or widower) and the deceased employee started railroad employment after 1974, only the railroad retirement employee annuity or the survivor annuity chosen by the annuitant is payable. If either the deceased employee or the survivor annuitant had some service before 1975 but had not completed 120 months of railroad service before 1975, the employee annuity and the Tier II portion of the survivor annuity would be payable to the widow or widower. The Tier I portion of the survivor annuity would be payable, only to the extent that it exceeds the Tier I portion of the employee annuity. If either the deceased employee or the survivor annuitant completed 120 months of railroad service before 1975, the widow or dependent widower would receive both an employee annuity and a survivor annuity, without a full dual-benefit reduction.

509. Are there work and earnings limitations for those receiving survivor annuities?

A survivor annuity is not payable for any month in which the survivor works for a railroad or railroad union.

Survivors who are receiving Social Security benefits have their railroad retirement annuity and Social Security benefit combined for earnings-limitation purposes. The combined annuity and benefits are reduced by one dollar for every two dollars of earnings over $19,560 (in 2022) and $21,240 (in 2023) if the survivor is under the full retirement age. Benefits are reduced by one dollar for every three dollars of earnings over $51,960 (in 2022) and $56,520 (in 2023) in the year an annuitant reaches full retirement age; however, only earnings earned prior to the month the full retirement age is reached count toward the $51,960 limit. The earnings limitation does not apply to annuitants who are older than the full retirement age, starting with the month they reach full retirement age. See Q 293 for a discussion of the full retirement age.

If the annuitant is under the full retirement age in the first year, benefits are payable, if the individual earns more than the annual exempt amount, work deductions apply only if monthly earnings are greater than one-twelfth of the annual exempt amount ($21,240 in 2023).

These earnings restrictions do not apply to disabled widows or widowers under age 60 or to disabled children. However, any work or earnings by a disability annuitant is reviewed to determine whether it indicates recovery from the disability.

510. Can survivors' annuities be offset by receipt of other benefits?

Under the Railroad Retirement Act, the Tier I portion of a survivor annuity is subject to reduction if any Social Security benefits are also payable, even if the Social Security benefit is based on the survivor's own earnings. This reduction follows the principles of Social Security law which, in effect, limit payment to the highest of any two or more benefits payable to an individual at one time.

The Tier I portion of a widow(er)'s annuity may also be reduced for the receipt of any Federal, State, or local government pension based on the widow(er)'s own earnings. The reduction generally does not apply if the employment on which the public pension is based was covered under the Social Security Act throughout the last sixty months of public employment. However, most military service pensions and payments from the Department of Veterans Affairs will not cause a reduction. For those subject to the public pension reduction, the Tier I reduction is equal to two thirds of the amount of the public pension.

511. When do survivor benefits end?

Payment stops upon death, and no annuity is payable for the month of death.

A widow or widower's annuity or surviving divorced spouse's benefit stops if:

(1)   the annuity was based on caring for a child under age 18 (16, for a surviving divorced spouse) or a disabled child and the child is no longer under age 18 (16, for a surviving divorced spouse) or disabled; or

(2)   the annuity was based on disability and the beneficiary recovers from the disability before age 60.

A disability annuity can be reinstated if the disability recurs within seven years. Remarriage will reduce a widow or widower's annuity rate, and, in some cases, prevent payment.

A child's or grandchild's annuity will stop if the child:

(1)   marries;

(2)   reaches age 18; or

(3)   recovers from the disability on which the annuity was based.

If the child is 18 and a full-time elementary or high school student, the annuity stops upon graduation from high school, attainment of age 19, or the end of the first school term after attainment of age 19.

A parent's survivor annuity may stop upon remarriage; in certain cases, a remarried parent is entitled to a Tier I benefit.

512. What lump-sum death benefits are payable?

A lump-sum death benefit is payable to certain survivors of an employee with 10 or more years of railroad service, or less than 10 years if at least five years were after 1995, and a current connection with the railroad industry if there is no survivor immediately eligible for a monthly annuity upon the employee's death.

If the employee did not have 10 years of service before 1975, the lump sum is limited to $255 and is payable only to the widow(er) living in the same household as the employee at the time of the employee's death.

If the employee had less than 10 years of service but had five years after 1995, he or she must have met Social Security's insured status requirements for the lump sum to be payable.

If the employee had 10 years of service before 1975, the lump sum is payable to the living-with widow(er). If there is no such widow(er), the lump sum may be paid to the funeral home or the payer of the funeral expenses. These lump sums averaged $1,030 in fiscal year 2020.

If a widow(er) is eligible for monthly benefits at the time of the employee's death, but the widow(er) had excess earnings deductions which prevented annuity payments or for any other reason did not receive monthly benefits in the twelve-month period beginning with the month of the employee's death totaling at least as much as the lump sum, the difference between the lump-sum benefit and monthly benefits actually paid, if any, is payable in the form of a deferred lump-sum benefit.

The railroad retirement system also provides, under certain conditions, a residual lump-sum death benefit which ensures that a railroad family receives at least as much in benefits as the employee paid in railroad retirement taxes before 1975. This benefit is, in effect, a refund of an employee's pre-1975 railroad retirement taxes, after subtraction of any benefits previously paid on the basis of the employee's service. This benefit is seldom payable.

The average of all types of lump sums paid in 2020 was $933.

513. What reporting should be done when a railroad annuitant dies?

The RRB should be notified immediately upon the death of any retirement or survivor annuitant. Payment of a railroad retirement annuity stops upon an annuitant's death and the annuity is not payable for any day in the month of death. This is true regardless of how late in the month death occurs and there is no provision for prorating such a payment. Any payments received after the annuitant's death must be returned. The sooner the RRB is notified, the less chance there is of payments continuing and an overpayment accruing. The RRB also determines whether any survivor benefits due are payable by the RRB or the Social Security Administration.

514. How does the public service pension reduction apply to spouse or widow(er)s' benefits?

The Tier I portion of a spouse's or widow(er)'s annuity may be reduced for receipt of any Federal, State, or local government pension separately payable to the spouse or widow(er) based on her or his own earnings. The reduction generally does not apply if the employment on which the public service pension is based was covered under the Social Security Act throughout the last 60 months of public employment. Most military service pensions and payments from the Department of Veterans Affairs will not cause a reduction. Pensions paid by a foreign government or interstate instrumentality will also not cause a reduction. For spouses and widow(er)s subject to a public service pension reduction, the Tier I reduction is equal to two-thirds of the amount of the public service pension.

515. What dual benefit restrictions apply when both parties in a marriage are railroad employees entitled to railroad retirement annuities?

If both parties started railroad employment after 1974, the amount of any spouse or divorced spouse annuity is reduced by the amount of the employee annuity to which the spouse or divorced spouse is also entitled.

If either party had some railroad service before 1975, the spouse/divorced spouse Tier I amount is reduced by the amount of the railroad employee Tier I to which the spouse/divorced spouse is entitled. The spouse/divorced spouse Tier I amount cannot be reduced below zero. The initial reduction is restored in the spouse Tier II amount. Divorced spouses are not entitled to a Tier II component and are not eligible to have the reduction restored.

In survivor cases, if the widow(er) is entitled to a railroad retirement employee annuity and neither the widow(er) nor the deceased employee had any railroad service before 1975, the survivor annuity (Tier I and Tier II) payable to the widow(er) is reduced by the total amount of the widow(er)'s own employee annuity.

If a widow or dependent widower is also a railroad employee annuitant, and either the widow(er) or the deceased employee had 120 months of railroad service before 1975, the Tier I reduction may be partially restored in the survivor Tier II amount.

If either the deceased employee or the widow(er) had some railroad service before 1975 but less than 120 months of service, the widow(er)'s own employee annuity and the Tier II portion of the survivor annuity would be payable to the widow(er). The Tier I portion of the survivor annuity would be payable only to the extent that it exceeds the Tier I portion of the widow(er)'s own employee annuity.

516. How are dual benefits paid to persons entitled to both railroad retirement and Social Security benefits?

If a railroad retirement annuitant is also awarded a Social Security benefit, the Social Security Administration determines the amount of the Social Security benefit due, but a combined monthly dual benefit payment should, in most cases, be issued by the RRB after the railroad retirement annuity has been reduced by the amount of the Social Security benefit.

Railroad Retirement Taxes

517. What are the railroad retirement tax rates for employees and employers?

Railroad retirement Tier I taxes are coordinated with Social Security taxes and increase automatically when Social Security taxes rise. Employees and employers pay Tier I taxes that are the same as Social Security taxes. In addition, both employees and employers pay Tier II taxes, to finance railroad retirement benefit payments over and above Social Security levels.

Tier I is the first level of the regular annuity for employees. It is calculated in generally the same way as a Social Security benefit.

Tier II is the second tier of a regular annuity and is computed under a separate formula. Tier II is based on railroad service alone. Tier II benefits are equal to 7/10 of 1 percent of the employee's average monthly earnings, using the Tier II tax base in the sixty months of highest earnings multiplied by the employee's years of service in the rail industry.

The Tier I tax rate for employees and employers is 7.65 percent. In 2023, the Tier II tax rate for employers is 13.1 percent and the Tier II tax rate for employees is 4.9 percent. Tier II taxes are imposed on a maximum of $111,200 (projected) of earnings (in 2023). The Tier II tax rates are adjusted each year based on the amount of assets and expenses of the railroad retirement system.

Tax Rate for Employees and Employers

Employers and Employees each		Tier II tax rate	
Hospital insurance (HI) tax rate	Tier I tax rate including HI tax	Employers	Employees
1.45%	7.65%	13.1% (2023)	4.9% (2023)

*   Medicare Hospital Insurance (HI) tax applies to all annual earnings.

Regular Railroad Retirement Taxes

Tier I	Tax rate	Taxable earnings
Employees	7.65%	$160,200 * (2023)
Employers	7.65%	$160,200 * (2023)
Tier II		
Employees	4.9% (2023)	$111.200 (2023)
Employers	13.1% (2023)	$111, 200 (2023)

Taxes on Someone Earning $160,200 (2023)

	Tier I	Tier II	Total
Employees	$109,200	$5,380.50	$16,596.30
Employers	$11,245.50	$19,257.00	$30,502.50

* Medicare Hospital Insurance (HI) tax applies to all annual earnings.

Railroad employees who also worked for a Social Security-covered employer in the same year may, under certain circumstances, receive a tax credit or refund equivalent to any excess Social Security taxes withheld.

Employees who worked for two or more railroads in a year, or who had Tier I taxes withheld from their Railroad Retirement Board sickness insurance benefits in addition to their railroad earnings, may be eligible for a tax credit or refund of any excess Tier I or Tier II railroad retirement taxes withheld. Such tax credits or refunds may be claimed on an employee's federal income tax return.

518. How do railroad retirement and Social Security payroll taxes compare?

Railroad retirement payroll taxes, like railroad retirement benefits, are calculated on a two-tier basis. Rail employees and employers pay Tier I taxes at the same rate as Social Security taxes, 7.65 percent, consisting of 6.2 percent for retirement on earnings up to $160,200 in 2023, and 1.45 percent for Medicare hospital insurance on all earnings. An additional 0.9 percent in Medicare taxes (2.35 percent in total) will be withheld from employees on earnings above $200,000.

In addition, rail employees and employers both pay Tier II taxes which are used to finance railroad retirement benefit payments over and above Social Security levels.

In 2023, the Tier II tax rate on earnings up to $111,200 (projected) is 4.9 percent for employees and 13.1 percent for employers.

The maximum amount of regular railroad retirement taxes that an employee earning $160,200 can pay in 2023 is $17,753.10, compared to $12,255.30 under social security. For railroad employers, the maximum annual regular retirement taxes on an employee earning $16,596.50 are $30,502.50, compared to $12,255.30 under social security. Employees earning over $160,200 and their employers, will pay more in retirement taxes than the above amounts because the Medicare hospital insurance tax is applied to all earnings.

Appeal Process

519. Can an annuitant contest a decision regarding overpayment?

Annuitants who believe a decision regarding a benefit overpayment is incorrect may ask for reconsideration and/or waiver of the overpayment. If not satisfied with the result of the initial review, the annuitant may appeal to the RRB's Bureau of Hearings and Appeals. Further appeals can be carried to the three-member Board itself, and beyond the Board to Federal courts.

Annuitants are told about these appeal rights any time a decision is made regarding a benefit overpayment.

520. How does a person initiate a review of an unfavorable decision on a claim and what are the time limits?

For all claims under the Railroad Retirement and Railroad Unemployment Insurance Acts, there is a three-stage review and appeals process within the RRB.

Request for Reconsideration

An individual dissatisfied with the initial decision on his or her claim may first request reconsideration from the RRB unit which issued that decision. An individual has 60 days from the date on which notice of the initial decision is mailed to the claimant to file a written request for reconsideration. This step is mandatory before an appeal may be filed with the RRB's Bureau of Hearings and Appeals. The filing date of an appeals is the date upon which it was received in the RRB office. The worker will lose their right to appeal if the appeal is not filed withing the 60-day period, although a hearing officer can waive the timeliness requirement if it is determined that there was good cause for the untimely filing. The appeal is docketed and assigned to a hearings officer who will decide whether or not the appeal is granted. Appeals are generally handled in the order that they are received. The hearing officer undertakes a review of the appeal and determines if additional evidence is required for the decision.

The hearing officer will question the appellant regarding the appeal. Appellant can retain an attorney for representation at any time during the process. Witnesses who have been called to testify are also questioned by the hearing officer and appellant and/or attorney.

After the hearing, the hearing officer issue a decision after consideration of all evidence. The decision is normally issued within 60 days of the hearing. A decision is normally issued within 215 days (7 months) of when the appeal was filed. Favorable decisions are forwarded to an adjudication unit for payment and, if an unfavorable decision is issued, the appellant will be instructed as to how to contest the decision.

In cases involving overpayments under the Railroad Retirement Act, an individual has the right to request waiver of recovery and also a personal conference. For cases involving overpayments under the Railroad Unemployment Insurance Act, if the case involves a benefit overpayment of more than ten times the maximum daily benefit rate, the claimant may request a waiver of recovery. In order for recovery of the overpayment to be deferred while a waiver request is pending, the waiver request must be in writing and filed within 60 days from the date on which notice of the overpayment was mailed to the beneficiary. A request for waiver received after sixty days will be considered but will not defer collection of the overpayment, and any amount of the overpayment recovered prior to the date on which the waiver request is filed will not be subject to waiver.

521. What are the second and third stages of the appeals process and time limits?

If dissatisfied with the reconsideration or waiver decision on a retirement, disability, survivor, unemployment, or sickness claim, a person may appeal to the RRB's Bureau of Hearings and Appeals, which is independent of those units responsible for initial and reconsideration decisions. An appellant has 60 days from the date on which notice of the reconsideration or waiver decision notice is mailed to the claimant to file an appeal. This appeal must be filed using RRB Form HA-1 *Claimant Appeal Under the Railroad Retirement Act or Railroad Unemployment Insurance Act*,[1] which may be obtained online or the agency's field offices. The Bureau of Hearings and Appeals may, if necessary, further investigate the case and obtain reports through the RRB's field representatives, designated medical examiners, and others who may be in a position to furnish information pertinent to the appellant's claim. When the appeal involves a question of fact, the appellant has the right to an oral hearing before a hearings officer. In most cases, video conferencing or phone hearings are held. In cases where an in-person hearing is held, it may be conducted in the RRB office closest to the appellant's home.

If not satisfied with the Bureau of Hearings and Appeals' decision, an appellant may further appeal to the three-member Board, which heads the agency, within 60 days from the date on which notice of the Bureau of Hearings and Appeals' decision is mailed to the appellant. This appeal must be filed using RRB Form HA-1 *Claimant Appeal Under the Railroad Retirement Act or Railroad Unemployment Insurance Act*[2] which, as stated previously, may be obtained online or from the agency's field offices. The three-member Board ordinarily will not accept additional evidence or convene a formal hearing.

Failure to request reconsideration or to file an appeal within the allocated time period will result in forfeiture of further appeal rights, unless there is good cause for the delay. Some examples of good cause include: serious illness; a death or serious illness in the appellant's immediate family; destruction of important or relevant records; failure to be notified of a decision; an unusual or unavoidable circumstance which demonstrated that the appellant could not have known of the need for timely filing or which prevented the appellant from filing in a timely manner; or the claimant thought that his or her representative had requested reconsideration or appeal. If good cause is not established, further appeal is forfeited, except that the appellant may contest the determination that the request for reconsideration or appeal was not filed timely.

Notes

1. https://rrb.gov/sites/default/files/2017-06/HA1%5B1%5D_0.pdf (last accessed September 5, 2022).
2. https://rrb.gov/sites/default/files/2017-06/HA1%5B1%5D_0.pdf (last accessed September 5, 2022).

522. How can someone obtain a waiver of overpayments of retirement, disability, survivor, unemployment, or sickness benefit overpayments?

A person's obligation to repay any erroneous benefit payments may be waived only if the following conditions are met:

1.   The person was not at fault in causing the overpayment; and

2.   Recovery of the overpayment would cause financial hardship to the extent that he or she would not be able to meet ordinary and necessary living expenses, or recovery would be against equity or good conscience. "Against equity or good conscience" is defined in the regulations of the RRB as meaning that the claimant has, by reliance on the payments made to him or her, or on notice that payment would be made, relinquished a significant and valuable right or changed his or her position to his or her substantial detriment.

In cases involving unemployment or sickness benefits, there is an additional requirement that the overpayment must be more than ten times the current maximum daily benefit rate.

Persons requesting waiver may be asked to complete a financial statement on a form provided by the RRB.

523. What is the appeal process beyond the RRB?

Appellants dissatisfied with the three-member Board's final decision may then file a petition with the appropriate U.S. Court of Appeals to review the Board's decision. In cases involving retirement, disability, or survivor claims, the petition for review must be filed within one year after notice of the three-member Board's decision has been mailed to the appellant. In cases involving claims for unemployment or sickness benefits, the petition for review must be filed within ninety days of the Board's decision notice.

There are different time frame to file under the Railroad Retirement Act and the Railroad Unemployment Insurance Act to appeal a decision of the Board. If the Railroad Retirement Board approves the denial of a claim, a further appeal to federal court is available.

- Appeal must be filed within ONE YEAR after the date of the RRB decision for decisions under the Railroad Retirement Act.

- Appeal must be filed within NINETY DAYS after the date of the RRB decision for decisions under the Railroad Unemployment Insurance Act.

Appeals may be filed in the U.S. Court of Appeals for the Circuit where the appellant resides, the U.S. Court of Appeals for the District of Columbia, or the U.S. Court of Appeals for the Seventh Circuit.

3.2.1 What is the appeal process beyond the RRB?

BENEFITS FOR SERVICE MEMBERS AND VETERANS

Military Retirement – Generally

524. In general, who is entitled to military retirement benefits?

Members of the armed forces may retire after a certain period of active service. Monthly retirement pay, up until December 31, 2017, is based on a percentage of base pay of the highest rank held, as well as number of years of service. After 2017, a new plan called Blended Retirement was introduced.

Service members who become disabled while in service may be placed on either temporary or permanent disability retirement, depending on the degree and length of disability, and also on whether they satisfy certain other conditions of eligibility.

Reservists are entitled to receive retirement benefits if they meet certain eligibility requirements.

Members of the uniformed services may also participate in the federal Thrift Savings Plan (see Q 531, Q 666).

---

525. Who is considered a member of a uniformed service?

A member of a uniformed service consists of any of the following:[1]

- An appointed, enlisted, inducted, or retired member of:

  - one of the armed services without a specified component; or

  - a component of the Army, Navy, Air Force, Marine Corps, or Coast Guard, including any of the following Reserve components: Army, Navy, Marine Corps, Air Force, or Coast Guard Reserve, the Reserve Corps of the Public Health Service, the U.S. National Guard, the Air National Guard of the U.S., and, under limited circumstances, the National Guard or Air National Guard of the States or the District of Columbia. (NOTE: A temporary member of the Coast Guard Reserve is not considered a member of a uniformed service.)

- A commissioned officer (including a retired commissioned officer) of the National Oceanic and Atmospheric Administration (NOAA) or the Regular or Reserve Corps of the Public Health Service.

- A member of the Fleet Reserve or Fleet Marine Corps Reserve.

- A midshipman at the U.S. Naval Academy, and a cadet at the U.S. Military, Coast Guard, or Air Force Academy.

- A member of the Reserve Officers' Training Corps and the Naval or Air Force Reserve Officers' Training Corps, when ordered to annual training duty for 14 days or more, and while performing authorized travel to and from that duty.

- In route to or from a place of final acceptance for entry upon active military or naval service, provided that they were:

    o   ordered or directed to proceed to such place; and

    o   have been provisionally accepted for duty, or have been selected for active military, or naval service under the Universal Military Training and Service Act.

Note

1. 20 CFR § 404.1330 - Who is a member of a uniformed service; https://www.law.cornell.edu/cfr/text/20/404.1330. (Last accessed September 10, 2022).

---

526. What does "active duty" and "active duty for training" mean?

The term "active duty" means:

- full-time duty (other than active duty for training) performed by a member of the uniformed services;

- full-time duty (other than for training purposes) as a commissioned officer of the National Oceanic and Atmospheric Administration or its predecessor organization the Coast and Geodetic Survey, or in the Regular or Reserve Corps of the Public Health Service;

- service as a cadet at the United States Military, Air Force, or Coast Guard Academy, or as a midshipman at the United States Naval Academy; and

- authorized travel to or from the duties described above.

The term "active duty for training" means:

- full-time duty performed by a member of a Reserve component of a uniformed service in the active military or naval service of the U.S. for training purposes;

- full-time duty as a commissioned officer of the Reserve Corps of the Public Health Service for training purposes;

- full-time duty as a member of the Army National Guard or Air National Guard of any State;

- annual training duty performed for a period of fourteen days or more as a member of the Reserve Officers' Training Corps, the Naval Reserve Officers' Training Corps, or the Air Force Reserve Officers' Training Corps; and

- authorized travel to and from any duty or service described above.[1]

- This term does not include duty performed as a temporary member of the Coast Guard Reserve.[2]

Notes

1. Duty Periods Defined - 38 CFR § 17.31.
2. 38 USC Section 101(22).

---

527. What are the types of military discharges and what are their effects of benefits?

Honorable Discharge

An honorable discharge is the best possible classification of a discharge from military service that a person can obtain. This is the discharge of a person who has fulfilled obligations efficiently, honorably, and faithfully while meeting or exceeding the conduct and performance standards of the military. This individual is eligible for all veteran (and military) benefits. Some benefits actually require an honorable discharge, including Post 9/11 GI Bill and the Montgomery GI Bill education benefits.

General Discharge Under Honorable Conditions

A general discharge under honorable conditions means that performance was considered satisfactory. As with an honorable discharge, the person is eligible for most veteran (and military) benefits, including disability compensation, education assistance (except for GI bills), survivor pensions, VA health care, and TRICARE's Continued Health Care Benefit Program (military health insurance). However, certain specific benefits, such as GI Bill education benefits, are reserved only for service members who receive an honorable discharge. To receive a General Discharge from the military, there has to be some form of nonjudicial punishment to correct unacceptable military behavior or failure to meet military standards. The discharging officer must give the reason for the discharge in writing, and the military member must sign paperwork stating they understand the reason for their discharge. Veterans with General Discharges cannot apply for VA education benefits.

Other Than Honorable (OTH) Discharge

An OTH discharge means that the individual had some serious departures from the conduct and performance expected of a service member. This is the most severe administrative discharge that can be received. Some examples of when this discharge can be received: security violations, trouble with civilian authorities, drug use, serious misconduct that endangers other members of the military, conviction by a civilian court with a sentence of prison time or use of deliberate force to seriously hurt another person. The person will not be likely to be eligible for any veteran benefits with an OTH discharge, but the Department of Veterans Affairs (VA) will examine the circumstances the OTH discharge to determine eligibility. In most cases, veterans who receive an Other Than Honorable Discharge cannot re-enlist in the Armed Forces or reserves, except under exceedingly rare circumstances.

Bad Conduct Discharge (BCD)

A bad conduct discharge is a punitive discharge that's imposed by court-martial. If a person receives a bad conduct discharge from a special court-martial, the VA will determine whether they are eligible for benefits. A person is not entitled to any veteran or military benefits if they receive a bad conduct discharge from a general court-martial. The Bad Conduct Discharge is only passed on to enlisted military members. A Bad Conduct discharge is often preceded by time in military prison. This type of discharge is often sardonically referred to as the "Big Chicken Dinner" by members of the armed services. Offenses that could result in a BCD include (but are not limited to) drunkenness on duty, DWI/DUI/OVI, adultery, and disorderly conduct. Consequences can include forfeiture of pay, loss of rank, loss of benefits, loss of recognition by the government as a veteran, barred from owning firearms, required disclosure when applying for employment.

Dishonorable Discharge

A dishonorable discharge is the worst type of discharge one can receive. This usually means that the individual committed a serious offense. Examples include fraud, desertion, rape, treason, espionage, sexual assault, or murder. A dishonorable discharge is issued only if the person is convicted at a general court-martial that calls for a dishonorable discharge as part of the sentence. All veteran and military benefits are lost with this discharge. If someone is dishonorably discharged from the military, they are not allowed to own firearms according to US federal law. Military members who receive a dishonorable discharge forfeit all military and veterans' benefits as well as civilian government benefits such as student loans, etc., and may have a difficult time finding work in the civilian sector.

Medical Discharge

A medical discharge may be given to service members who become sick or injured to the point where military service is no longer possible based on a medical evaluation. This process can be lengthy and may or may not be appealed depending on a variety of factors. Military members who receive medical discharges should apply for VA compensation for service-connected medical issues, especially those that resulted in the discharge. If the injury or medical condition is service related or a condition such as traumatic brain injury, combat injuries, PTSD, or chemical exposures, the individual may be eligible for disability benefits.

Entry-Level Separation or Entry-Level Discharge

Individuals that aren't suited for the military may receive an entry-level separation. This type of action occurs within the first 180 days of service and indicates that the individual doesn't belong in the military, but their service isn't considered good or bad. No benefits are earned with this discharge, nor is veteran's status achieved, since benefits generally require serving longer than 180 days, unless the individual suffered an illness or injury as a result of service. This type of military discharge can happen for a variety of reasons (medical, administrative, inability to complete basic training, etc.).

Separation for the Convenience of the Government

A member of the military may be separated "for the convenience of the government" due to budget constraints, force reductions, or circumstances that interfere with the service member's ability to perform their duties, including personal hardships.

Dismissal (Officer Discharge)

Commissioned officers who need to be discharged from the military undergo a different process than non-officers. While it is still a negative discharge, they do not receive a Bad Conduct Discharge or a dishonorable discharge for wrongdoings. Instead, officers can receive a dismissal or officer discharge that relieves them from their service. While the titles are different, an officer discharge carries the same weight as a BCD or dishonorable discharge in terms of the officer's record and their ability to claim veterans benefits later. An officer's discharge can result in a reduced rank set to the last rank the officer completed without issue and an inability to receive benefits. This happens if the officer has been court-martialed.

---

528. What effect does a dishonorable discharge have on noncontributory military service wage credits?

A discharge under dishonorable conditions prohibits the granting of noncontributory military service wage credits for any period of active service to which the discharge applies. The following types of separations are issued under dishonorable conditions:

- A dishonorable discharge

- A bad conduct discharge issued as a result of a sentence by a general court martial

- A discharge for desertion

- In the case of an officer, a resignation accepted "for the good of the service"

- A discharge on the grounds that the person was a conscientious objector who refused to do military duty, to wear the uniform, or otherwise to comply with lawful orders of competent military authority

- A discharge by reason of conviction by a civil court for treason, sabotage, espionage, murder, rape, arson, burglary, robbery, kidnapping, assault with intent to kill, assault with a dangerous weapon, or an attempt to commit any of these crimes

528.01. What effect do various discharges have on veterans' benefits?

The type of discharge can have a significant effect on what benefits are available to a veteran after leaving the service. The specifics are detailed in the chart below:

Type of Discharge

VA BENEFITS	HONORABLE	GENERAL	OTH	BCD SPECIAL COURT MARTIAL	BCD GENERAL COURT MARTIAL	DISHONORABLE
Disability Compensation	Eligible	Eligible	Service review necessary	Service review necessary	Disqualified	Disqualified
Health Care	Eligible	Eligible	Service review necessary	Service review necessary	Disqualified	Disqualified
Dependency and Indemnity Compensation (DIC)	Eligible	Eligible	Service review necessary	Service review necessary	Disqualified	Disqualified
Montgomery GI Bill or Post 9/11 GI Bill	Eligible	Disqualified	Disqualified	Disqualified	Disqualified	Disqualified
Survivor Pension	Eligible	Eligible	Service review necessary	Service review necessary	Disqualified	Disqualified
Burial Benefits	Eligible	Eligible	Service review necessary	Service review necessary	Disqualified	Disqualified
Special Housing	Eligible	Eligible	Service review necessary	Service review necessary	Disqualified	Disqualified
Vocational Rehabilitation	Eligible	Eligible	Service review necessary	Service review necessary	Disqualified	Disqualified
Disabled Automotive	Eligible	Eligible	Service review necessary	Service review necessary	Disqualified	Disqualified
Reenlistment	Eligible	Eligible	Service review necessary	Service review necessary	Disqualified	Disqualified
Veterans' Group Life Insurance (VGLI)	Eligible	Eligible	Eligible	Eligible	Eligible	Eligible
Service-Disabled Veterans Insurance (S-DVI) and Veterans' Mortgage Life Insurance (VMLI)	Eligible	Eligible	Eligible	Eligible	Eligible	Eligible

528.02. Can a discharge be upgraded?

Yes. Each branch has its own discharge review board that can correct military discharges, except for medical discharges or discharges issued by a general court-martial. Some less than honorable discharges be eligible for a second look. Sometimes, there are flaws in these discharge classifications, the most important being that these types of punitive discharges do not consider aggravating factors such as PTSD, traumatic brain injuries, experiencing sexual assault, mental health issues, or other circumstances. Some of these may have led to the outward behavior causing discharge proceedings to begin in the first place. An additional factor is those who were discharged from the military based on their sexual orientation alone under the old "Don't Ask, Don't Tell" anti-gay policies that prevented LGBT service members from serving openly. Over ten thousand service members were expelled under this policy by some estimations.

Discharged veterans, surviving family members, and legal representatives can request a discharge review board review the discharge circumstances.

The applicant must provide a reason for a petition to upgrade a discharge and submit documentation to justify it. Veterans whose discharge was connected to a traumatic brain injury (TBI), military sexual trauma, or a mental health condition like PTSD have a "strong case for a discharge upgrade," according to the VA. Additionally, veterans who were wrongfully discharged for their sexual orientation, gender identity or HIV status under "Don't Ask, Don't Tell" are eligible for all Department of Veterans Affairs benefits and a discharge upgrade.

There is a "Discharge Review Tool" available on the VA Website[1] which asks questions about service and discharge to provide specific instructions for submitting your application. The applicant answers a series of questions to get customized step-by-step instructions on how to apply for a discharge upgrade or correction. If the application is approved and the discharge is upgraded, the applicant will be eligible for the VA benefits earned during the service.

Service Level Discharge Review Boards

Included are links to the discharge review boards for each branch of service:

- Air Force Board of Correction of Military Records

- Army Review Board Agency (ARBA)

- Board for Correction of Military Records of the Coast Guard

- The Board for Correction of Naval Records

Each specific branch of service may impose time restrictions on discharge review applications.

The below list details how to contact each branch of service's discharge review board.

- Air Force Board for Correction of Military Records: usaf.pentagon.saf-mr.mbx. saf-mrbc@mail.mil

- Air Force Discharge Review Board: usaf.pentagon.saf-mr.mbx.saf-mrb@mail.mil

- Army Board for Correction of Military Records: army.arbainquiry@mail.mil

- Army Discharge Review Board: army.arbainquiry@mail.mil

- Navy Board for Correction of Naval Records: BCNR_Application@navy.mil

- Navy Discharge Review Board: NDRB@navy.mil

DOD Level Discharge Board

In early 2021, the Department of Defense announced a DOD-level appeals process for service members who separated after December 20, 2019. Persons who wish to appeal a service-level Review board's decision can appeal to the Discharge Appeal Review Board (DARB). DARB reviews cases for veterans who have exhausted all other avenues to appeal their service review board's decision, according to DOD. This board's decisions are final and cannot be appealed.

The DARB provides "final review of discharge or dismissal characterization upgrade requests when petitioners have exhausted all available administrative remedies." Regulations require that a DARB review of a military discharge must come only AFTER all other lower-level options have been exhausted. DARB is the last stop for review before the matter is considered officially closed.

DARB appeals are never automatic – an applicant will be required to submit the same type of application and supporting information as they did in their lower-level discharge review requests.

Note

1. https://www.va.gov/discharge-upgrade-instructions/ (Last accessed September 11, 2022).

United States Space Force

528.03. How are service personnel that transfer to the Space Force affected?

All members transferring into the Space Force retain their existing grade. Personnel are transferred in the same status (grade, duty, and pay status) they had prior to transfer. There will be no penalty for transferring to the Space Force, and it will not affect time-in-grade or retirement eligibility.

528.04. What grades and ranks will the Space Force have?

At this time, the Space Force has the same grade structure as the other military services (i.e., E-1 to E-9, O-1 to O-10).

The ranks are as follows:

Officer Rank	Enlisted Rank
O1 Second Lieutenant	E1 Specialist 1
O2 First Lieutenant	E2 Specialist 2
O3 Captain	E3 Specialist 3
O4 Major	E4 Specialist 4
O5 Lieutenant Colonel	E5 Sergeant
O6 Colonel	E6 Technical Sergeant
O7 Brigadier General	E7 Master Sergeant
O8 Major General	E8 Senior Master Sergeant
O9 Lieutenant General	E9 Chief Master Sergeant
O10 General	E9 Chief Master Sergeant of the Space Force

528.05. How will joining Space Force affect pay, benefits, and retirement?

There will be no change to base pay and allowances or benefits, including retirement plans and Thrift Savings Plan benefits. All currently issued leave will transfer as well.

If a service member is currently receiving a bonus from their current service, it is up to the losing service to determine if the bonus will be stopped or if any unearned portions already paid will be recouped. In the future, the Space Force will utilize available enlistment and reenlistment bonus authorities as needed to encourage enlistment or reenlistment of sufficient numbers of qualified enlisted personnel in military skills with either demonstrated shortfalls or high training costs. However, no determination has been made at this time.

528.06. Is the Space Force a fully recognized part of the U.S. Military?

The Space Force is an official part of the United States uniformed services, becoming the eighth branch upon being established on December 20, 2019. USSF Headquarters is located in the Pentagon. The Space Force will leverage the Air Force for more than 75 percent of enabling functions to reduce cost and avoid duplication. The Air Force will provide support including logistics, base operating support, IT support, and audit functions.

Additionally, Congress has officially expanded the definition of "veteran" by adding the U.S. Space Force to the law requiring the Veterans Administration to provide benefits and services to Space Force veterans. The legal language defining the Armed Forces as "the United States Army, Navy, Marine Corps, Air Force, and Coast Guard, including their Reserve components" was updated by adding "Space Force" to the list.[1]

§ 3.1 Definitions

(a) *Armed Forces* means the United States Army, Navy, Marine Corps, Air Force, Space Force, and Coast Guard, including their Reserve components.

Note

1. eCFR :: 38 CFR Part 3 -- Adjudication (Last accessed September 12, 2022).

Military Retirement Plans – High-3 and Blended Retirement

529. What retirement benefits are available for those who first became members before August 1, 1986?

An immediate annuity is available to a service member who completes twenty years of service. Until January 1, 2018, no benefits were available to a servicemember who did not complete twenty years of service. However, effective January 1, 2018, a retirement plan was introduced called the Blended Retirement System (BRS). The current retirement system is retained as a legacy system.

The retirement annuity is based in part on the servicemember's retirement "pay base," as well as the date on which the individual became a member of the uniformed service.

High Pay or Final Pay Plan

For those becoming members of a uniformed service for the first time on or before September 7, 1980, the retired pay base equals the servicemember's final monthly basic pay to which he was entitled the day before retirement. This plan is called the "High Pay" plan or "Final Pay" plan.

High-3 Plan

For persons becoming members of a uniformed service for the first time after September 7, 1980, the monthly retired pay base is one 36 of the total amount of the monthly basic pay that the servicemember received for the highest 36 months (whether or not consecutive) of active duty.

In order to compute the monthly retirement benefit, the monthly retired pay base is multiplied by an amount equaling 2.5 percent for each year of service, up to a maximum of 30 years. The benefits range from 50 percent at twenty years of service to 75 percent at 30 or more years of service.

Retired pay is adjusted annually by the increase in the cost of living, as measured by the Consumer Price Index for All Urban Wage Earners and Clerical Workers (CPI).

The uniformed services retirement system is noncontributory. However, the servicemember contributes, while on active duty, to the Social Security system and, thereby, earns eligibility for a Social Security retirement benefit. Members may also contribute to the federal Thrift Savings Plan (see Q 531).

530. What is the "High-3" or "High-36" retirement system for those who became members between August 1, 1986 and December 31, 2017?

Under the Military Retirement Reform Act of 1986, anyone who became a member of a uniformed service on or after August 1, 1986, through December 31, 2017, was subject to a new retirement system.

The average monthly basic pay for the highest three years of pay during service becomes the pay base for servicemembers. This is known as "high-3" or "high-36" (for the average of highest 36 months of pay). The multiplier, or percentage, for each year of service that is multiplied by the pay base remains unchanged at 2.5 percent for each year of service. The maximum number of years creditable toward retirement is 30 – or 75 percent of pay base.

Under this system, where the servicemember has retired and has completed fewer than 30 years of service, the percent reached above is reduced by one percentage point for each year between 30 years and the number of years completed.

This means that a 20-year retiree will receive 40 percent of the pay base (as opposed to 50 percent under the system for those who became servicemembers before August 1, 1986). A 30-year retiree, however, will receive the full 75 percent of the pay base, the same as under the old system.

Years of Service	Multiplier	
	Before 62	After 62
20	40.0	50.0
21	43.5	52.5
22	47.0	55.0
23	50.5	57.5
24	54.0	60.0
25	57.5	62.5
26	61.0	65.0
27	64.5	67.5
28	68.0	70.0
29	71.5	72.5
30	75.0	75.0

Cost-of-living adjustments to retirement benefits are guaranteed in years of inflation. Annual benefit increases will equal the increase in the Consumer Price Index (CPI), less one percentage point. This formula is known as "CPI Minus 1."

There is a one-time recomputation of retirement pay at age 62, in recognition of the fact that at about age 62 military retirement pay becomes the primary source of retirement income for career military personnel. At the point when a retiree reaches age 62, retirement pay is recomputed as if the one percentage point penalty for retirement at less than 30 years of service had not been applied. Additionally, at the same time, the retirement pay is increased to the level it would have reached if cost-of-living adjustments had been made under the full CPI rather than the "CPI Minus 1" formula.

In short, at age 62, the level of military retirement pay is restored to the level at which it would have been under the law for military members who entered the service prior to

August 1, 1986. Note, however, that all cost-of-living adjustments after age 62 are under the "CPI Minus 1" formula. Thus, military retirees will lose 1 percent to inflation each year after age 62.

A servicemember retiring after 30 years of service will receive 75 percent of basic pay both before and after age 62. His retirement pay will be affected only by the change in the cost-of-living adjustment formula.

531. May servicemembers contribute to the Thrift Savings Plan?

Yes. All active duty and Ready Reserve members of the uniformed services can participate in the Thrift Savings Plan (TSP) (see Q 666). The uniformed services include the Army, Navy, Air Force, Marine Corps, Coast Guard, Public Health Service, and the National Oceanic and Atmospheric Administration.

Uniformed service members can contribute up to 100 percent of their base pay. If a member contributes from base pay, he or she can elect to contribute up to 100 percent of any incentive pay, special pay, or bonus pay. Deferred contributions to the TSP generally cannot exceed $22,500 (projected) (in 2023, a projected increase of $2,000 from 2022).[1] Catch-up contributions of up to $6,500 for members over age fifty are also available[2] (see Q 666). The maximum annual addition limit is $61,000.[3] The "catch-up" contribution is separate from the elective deferred and annual addition limits.

The individual service secretaries may designate certain critical specialties as eligible for matching contributions in the same way that contributions are matched for FERS participants. There is no automatic one percent contribution for uniformed service members. Also, unlike many civilian companies, the government generally does not make matching contributions to the Thrift Savings Plan.

Notes

1. IRC Section 402(g).
2. IRC Section 414(v).
3. IRC Section 415(c).

532. How has the military retirement system changed since 2017?

Significantly.

The National Defense Authorization Act (NDAA) for Fiscal Year 2016, created a new military retirement system that went into effect in January 2018.

The Blended Retirement System (BRS) blends a defined benefit annuity with a defined contribution plan, through the Thrift Savings Plan (TSP). Service members who joined after 2006 but before January 1, 2018 had the option of remaining with the existing system or opting into the BRS.

The primary difference between BRS and the legacy "High-3" system is that BRS adjusts the years of service multiplier from 2.5 percent to 2.0 percent for calculating monthly retirement pay. In addition, the BRS includes automatic government contributions of 1 percent of basic pay and government matching contributions of up to an additional 4 percent of basic pay to a service member's TSP account. The law also included a continuation pay provision, which is a direct cash payout (like a bonus), in return for additional obligated service.

533. Why was the Blended Retirement System created?

Prior to the creation of the BRS, 81 percent of service members did not receive a government pension after leaving the service. Under BRS, about 85 percent of service members will receive a government retirement benefit if they serve at least two years, even if they do not qualify for a full retirement. This expansion of government retirement benefits ensures a greater number of service members receive government-provided retirement benefits, which had been previously only available to the 19 percent of active duty individuals and 14 percent of National Guard and Reservists who had served twenty or more years.

534. Who is affected by the implementation of the BRS?

The BRS went into effect on January 1, 2018. New service members, who joined the uniformed services for the first time on or after January 1, 2018, will be enrolled automatically in BRS. All members who were serving as of December 31, 2017 are grandfathered under the legacy retirement system. No member who was serving on, or prior to, December 31, 2017, will be automatically switched to the BRS. Active duty service members who had fewer than 12 years of service as of December 31, 2017, and National Guard and Reserve service members in a paid status, who had accrued fewer than 4,320 retirement points as of December 31, 2017, may choose to opt into the BRS. The opt-in window for BRS was from January 1, 2018, to December 31, 2018.

535. How are those that remain in the "High-3" legacy retirement plan affected?

Nothing changes for those who choose to remain in the legacy retirement system. They can remain in the plan until and through their retirement.

536. Are members of the United States Public Health Service Commissioned Corps (USPHS) or the National Oceanic and Atmospheric Administration Commissioned (NOAA) Officer Corps affected by the implementation of the BRS?

Yes, the Uniformed Services Blended Retirement System impacts all eight of the uniformed services of the United States.

The uniformed services include:

- United States Army

- United States Marine Corps

- United States Navy

- United States Air Force

- United States Space Force

- United States Coast Guard

- United States Public Health Commissioned Corps

- United States Oceanic and Atmospheric Administration Commissioned Officer Corps

537. Which is the better plan for individuals to select?

Everyone should carefully consider the decision. For those members who do not intend to serve a full 20-year career, or think they are unlikely to serve a full 20-year career, the BRS is probably the better choice because it ensures they will receive government contributions toward their retirement. Those who do plan to serve a full 20 years will want to compare their lifetime benefits under both the BRS and the legacy retirement systems to see which is more beneficial.

The Department of Defense offers a number of benefits comparison calculators that can assist in seeing the options and will present the benefits side-by-side. The calculator is designed for use by both active duty and reservists.[1] The calculators include:

- **BRS Comparison Calculator** – This calculator provides a comparison between the Legacy High-3 vs. the Blended Retirement System (BRS).

- **BRS Calculator** – This calculator estimates retirement benefits under the Blended Retirement System (BRS).

- **High-Three Calculator** – This calculator estimates retirement benefits under the Legacy High-3 retirement plan.

- **Final Pay Calculator** – This calculator estimates retirement benefits under the Final Pay retirement plan, for those members who first joined prior to September 8, 1980.

- **Redux Calculator** – This calculator estimates retirement benefits under the REDUX retirement plan for those who opted for the Career Status Bonus at 15 years of service, but are not yet retired.

- **RMC Calculator** – RMC represents a basic level of compensation which every service member receives, directly or indirectly, in-cash or in-kind, and which is common to all military personnel based on their pay grade, years of service, and family size.

- **SCAADL Calculator** - This special monthly compensation is for an eligible catastrophically injured or ill Service member who requires assistance with activities of daily living or who is at a high risk for personal safety and cannot live independently in the community without caregiver support.

To use the calculators, the individual will need to know:

- Pay Entry Base Date: The date that denotes how much of an individual's service is creditable towards longevity for pay purposes

- Estimated life expectancy

- Thrift Savings Plan withdrawal age

- TSP rate of return

- Lump sum payouts

Note

1. https://militarypay.defense.gov/calculators/ (last accessed September 11, 2022).

538. Does prior military service under the 2.5 percent legacy system remain as the calculator if someone opts for the BRS system?

No, opting into the BRS is a complete move into the new retirement system. For example, if the individual had eight years under the legacy retirement system (Final Pay or High-3) and twelve years under BRS, at retirement all twenty years are calculated under the BRS multiplier of 2.0 percent.

539. Does the BRS change the ability to participate in the Survivor Benefit Plan?

No, all service members will still have the option of participating in the Survivor Benefit Plan.

540. Does the BRS affect Veteran Affairs disability compensation?

No, for most members retiring under BRS, there will be no impact to their eligibility to receive VA disability compensation, Combat-Related Special Compensation (CRSC), or Concurrent Retirement and Disability Pay (CRDP). However, if a service member covered by BRS elects the lump-sum option, there may be an impact to his or her ability to receive some or all of his or her VA disability compensation due to the law requiring an offset of the retired pay that has already been received via the lump sum. Regardless, however, those with CRSC-qualifying disabilities will still be able to receive CRSC even if they elect a lump sum. Those qualified for CRDP will be able to receive VA disability compensation and military retired pay without offset.

541. What was the REDUX pension plan?

Retirees who choose the REDUX plan received a $30,000 cash bonus at their fifteen-year mark, in exchange for receiving a retirement multiple based on 2.0 percent of their base pay for each year served. Under this plan, a twenty-year retirement pension is worth 40 percent of the member's base pay. In addition, the annual COLA pay raise is based on CPI – 1. Therefore, if the CPI was 2.0 percent, REDUX retirees would only receive a 1 percent COLA increase.

In general, the REDUX plan is not a good payout for military retirees as seen by the comparison below:

BONUS:

- **High-3:** No bonus;

- **REDUX:** $30,000 Career Status Bonus.

PAYOUT AT TWENTY YEARS:

- **High-3:** 50 percent pay at thirty years, plus 2.5 percent per additional year;

- **REDUX:** 40 percent monthly retirement at twenty years, plus 3.5 percent per additional year.

PAYOUT AT THIRTY YEARS:

- **High-3 & REDUX:** Maximum monthly retirement benefit 75 percent of base pay at thirty years.

- At first glance it appears that at thirty years, the REDUX plan would be better because of the bonus and the 75 percent pay, but the decreased COLA adjustment (reduced by 1 percent) it doesn't take long for the raises to exceed the difference in the Career Retention Bonus (especially when taxes are considered).

542. Is CSB/REDUX still available to service members?

No, authority to elect the Career Status Bonus (CSB)/REDUX ended on December 31, 2017. No CSB is now offered.

543. When did service members need to make a choice about BRS?

Service members who were eligible to opt into BRS had all of calendar year 2018 to make their opt-in decision. The enrollment period went from January 1, 2018 through December 31, 2018. Members of the Army, Navy, or Air Force who wished to remain in the legacy system did not have to do anything. However, Marines needed to affirmatively decline enrollment in the BRS via the Marine Online portal. The United States Space Force did not yet exist and did not have an opportunity to opt into BRS.

544. Did it make any difference if someone opted into BRS at the start of 2018 or at the end?

Yes. Eligible service members could opt into BRS anytime between January 1, 2018 and December 31, 2018. However, those opting into the new retirement system began receiving automatic and applicable matching government contributions effective the first pay period that began on or after the day the member opted into the BRS. Therefore, if waiting until the end of 2018, the contributions were smaller for 2018.

545. If an individual mistakenly opted into the Blended Retirement System, can they change their choice?

No. The decision to opt-in is irrevocable. Following the mandatory training, the opt-in process was a multi-step layered process that required the Service member to consciously opt-in with intent. A member acknowledged no less than three times that he or she was aware and fully understood the decision to opt-in was irrevocable.

The only option is to apply with the Board for Correction of Military/Naval Records[1] for relief for any matter related to pay and benefits and prove a specific error or injustice.

Note

1. https://www.secnav.navy.mil/mra/bcnr/Pages/default.aspx (last accessed September 11, 2022).

546. Did the service member's spouse need to concur with the member's decision to opt into the BRS?

No, although DoD encourages service members to make their opt-in decision in consultation with their spouse, significant other, financial advisor, or other trusted advisor prior to making an opt-in election, the law does not require spousal concurrence with the decision.

547. Were cadets and midshipmen at the service academies or in Reserve Officer Training Program (ROTC) given a choice between the BRS and the legacy retirement program?

Cadets and midshipmen attending a service academy as of December 31, 2017 were grandfathered under the legacy retirement system and had the option to opt into BRS upon commissioning. ROTC cadets and midshipmen had the same option as long as they have signed their "contract" as of December 31, 2017.

Cadets and midshipmen that are grandfathered under the legacy retirement system, upon commissioning (or being placed in a pay status) after 2018, had thirty days to decide to remain in the legacy retirement system or opt into BRS. Each individual service member had a deadline, which was thirty days after their first day of duty following commissioning.

Cadets and midshipmen who entered a service academy and ROTC cadets and midshipmen who sign their "contract" on or after January 1, 2018 are automatically covered by BRS upon commissioning with no option to opt-in.

548. Does participation in the BRS affect a service member's ability to participate in the Survivor benefit plan?

No, service members participating in the BRS still have the option of participating in the Survivor Benefit Plan.

549. Can a new service member get a waiver to join the High-3 legacy retirement system?

No. This option was only available to members who entered the service on, or prior to, December 31, 2017.

550. If an individual had a break in service, can they still opt into the Blended Retirement System?

It depends.

If someone left the military prior to January 1, 2018 and rejoined the service after the opt-in decision year on January 1, 2019 or later, they are offered thirty days to decide whether to stay in the legacy retirement system or to elect the new BRS. They will need to have had fewer than twelve years of service as of December 31, 2017, or, for reservists or National Guard, fewer than 4,320 retirement points as of December 31, 2017. For those who reentered the service during 2018, they had the remaining time in calendar year 2018 or thirty days, whichever is longer, to have decided whether to opt into BRS.

551. What is the Thrift Saving Plan (TSP) and what is the Federal Retirement Thrift Investment Board (FRTIB)?

The TSP is a defined contribution retirement savings and tax-deferred investment plan that offers the same types of savings and tax benefits many private corporations offer their employees under 401(k) or similar plans. The TSP is one of the world's largest defined contribution plans, managing over $500 billion for more than 5 million participants located in every time zone around the world.

The FRTIB[1] is an independent government agency required by law to manage and administer the TSP. The FRTIB is charged with helping Federal employees and members of the Uniformed Services prepare for retirement by providing benefits similar to private sector 401(k) plans. The TSP is considered to be one of the better retirement plans in the world and a model for defined contribution plans. The FRTIB's mission is to administer the TSP in the interest of its participants and beneficiaries.

Note

1. https://www.frtib.gov (Last accessed September 11, 2022).

552. How does the Thrift Saving Plan figure into the BRS?

The BRS includes a defined contribution component through TSP. Uniformed service members who are covered by the BRS are eligible to receive government automatic and matching contributions to their TSP accounts. These government contributions to TSP are portable retirement savings that begin early in a member's career.

All service members who joined on or after January 2018 are automatically enrolled into TSP contributing 3 percent of their basic pay (or Inactive Duty Pay, sometimes referred to as "Drill Pay" in the National Guard and Reserve), DOD will automatically match 1 percent of basic pay starting sixty days after entry. DoD will also match service member contributions up to an additional 4 percent after two years of service.

The maximum government contribution is 5 percent if the service member is contributing 5 percent of their basic pay. Both the DoD automatic 1 percent and the matching contributions continue through the end of the pay period during which the service member attains twenty-six years of service.

NOTE: Currently serving members who opt-in will see automatic and matching contributions the first pay period after opting in – there is no waiting period. Current service members who opted into the new Blended Retirement System between January 1, 2018 and December 31, 2018, received the DOD automatic 1 percent contribution and up to 4 percent additional DoD matching beginning the first pay period after opting in – there was no sixty day/two-year waiting period as there was for new accessions starting January 1, 2018.

553. Does the money in the TSP belong to the service member?

It depends.

Current Service Members

For current service members who opt into BRS, they are immediately vested in their own contributions and any government matching contributions.

However, service members must have at least two years of service in order to be vested in the government's automatic one percent contributions and associated earnings. This does not mean two years from the date they opted-in or started the TSP, but total time in service as measured from their Pay Entry Base Date.

New Service Members

New accessions are immediately vested in their own contributions and earnings. They will begin to receive the government automatic one percent of their basic pay after sixty days in service and must have two years of service in order to be vested in the government's automatic one percent contributions and associated earnings. At the beginning of two years of service, they can begin receiving matching contributions up to an additional 4 percent of their basic pay. Service members are immediately vested in any government matching contributions and earnings at this point.

554. How much does the Department of Defense (DOD) contribute to the TSP?

The following chart identifies the TSP matching component of the Blended Retirement System.

Service Member Contribution	DoD Auto Contribution	DoD Match	Total Percentage
0.00%	1.00%	0.00%	1.00%
1.00%	1.00%	1.00%	3.00%
2.00%	1.00%	2.00%	5.00%
3.00%	1.00%	3.00%	7.00%
4.00%	1.00%	3.50%	8.50%
5.00%	1.00%	4.00%	10.00%

555. What effect did the CARES Act have on TSP participants?

The Coronavirus Aid, Relief, and Economic Security (CARES) Act included several important provisions for TSP participants:

- It waived Required Minimum Distributions (RMDs) for the year 2020 for all TSP participants who would otherwise have been subject to RMDs, including those who would not have been required to receive one until April 1, 2021.

   o This included participants for whom 2020 would have been their first RMD year, even though that distribution would not have been due until April 1, 2021. RMDs were not been waived for 2021.

- It temporarily doubled the maximum amount that COVID-affected TSP participants could borrow from their accounts.

- It allowed COVID-affected TSP participants to suspend TSP loan payments for the year 2020.

- It authorized creation of a special withdrawal type for COVID-affected participants.

- It provided favorable tax treatment for COVID-affected participants who made a withdrawal from their accounts in 2020.

The deadlines for the increased loan maximum, for suspending loan payments, and for taking withdrawals that are covered by the CARES Act have passed.

Update for 2022
Increased Maximum for General Purpose Loans

For participants who meet the criteria of the CARES Act, the total maximum loan amount for a general-purpose loan has been increased from $50,000 to $100,000, and the maximum portion of vested balance increased from 50% to 100%. The increased maximum loan amount is only available through September 22, 2020. **Residential loans are not available under this special program. All other TSP loan eligibility rules still apply.**

If the participant qualifies as an affected individual under the CARES Act, the participant can use the online tool on the TSP website (tsp.gov) to apply for a CARES Act loan. To access the tool, participants must log into My Account and click on "Loans."

The online tool will walk the participant through the loan request by prompting the participant to answer questions. Based upon answers, the tool will generate Form TSP-21-G, *Loan Agreement*, which is a summary of the request with the participant's provided information.

The *Loan Agreement* must be received by the TSP no later than **September 22, 2020. Note:** If a participant alters any of the pre-printed information on the TSP-21-G, the form will not be processed.

556. If a service member is part of the BRS and retires after twenty years, will they still get an annuity?

Yes, for those service members who retire after at least twenty years of service (twenty qualifying years for the National Guard and Reserve), their retirement remains a defined benefit in which the service member will get monthly retirement pay. Under BRS, the service member's monthly retired pay will be calculated with a 2.0 percent multiplier (in lieu of the 2.5 percent under the legacy High-3 system), times the average of the service member's highest thirty-six months of basic pay.

557. What are the ramifications for the service members remaining in the legacy (High-3) retirement system?

For those who remained in the legacy retirement system, nothing about the current retirement plan changes. The individual will still need to complete twenty years of service (or twenty qualifying years of service if they are in the National Guard or Reserve) to receive a military retirement pension.

558. Are the retirement proceeds under the BRS subject to division of assets in a divorce?

Yes, they can be. A member's pension under the BRS is similarly subject to a divorce decree as it is under the legacy retirement plan and subject to state court decisions.

559. When does an individual begin collecting retirement pay?

BRS does not change any of the existing rules about when the military retired pay defined benefit begins. If the individual served at least 20 years on active duty, retired pay will begin on the first day of the first month following retirement. If the individual served at least 20 qualifying years of service in the National Guard or Reserve, eligibility to receive retired pay begins at age 60. This age of eligibility for retired pay may be reduced for members of the National Guard and Reserve who have certain qualifying active duty service performed after 2008.

560. Does the BRS plan offer a lump sum option?

Yes.

The lump sum provision of BRS gives service members choices at retirement. A service member may choose to receive either 25 or 50 percent of the discounted present value of a portion of their future retirement pay, in exchange for reduced monthly retirement pay. Monthly retirement pay returns to the full amount when the service member reaches full Social Security retirement age, which for most is age 67. No such lump sum option exists under the legacy, High-3, military retirement system.

The lump sum disbursement is not mandatory. All active component service members will have a choice to receive their full monthly retired pay upon retirement or to elect a lump sum payment and reduced retired pay. The lump sum payment will be calculated from the date of retirement until the date the member would reach full Social Security retirement age, which for most is 67 years old. At full Social Security retirement age, all service members will receive their full monthly retired pay, regardless of their lump sum payment election.

An individual can receive one lump sum payment or annual equal payments as one per year for up to four years. Monthly retired pay reverts to the full amount at full Social Security age.

If someone takes either 25 or 50 percent in a lump sum, their monthly retired paycheck is reduced to 75 or 50 percent of the full value of the monthly retired pay until they reach full Social Security retirement age.

The lump sum of 25 or 50 percent is discounted to the present value based on an annual DoD discount rate published in June of each year. A lifetime of equal, non-discounted monthly payments may be worth more. For most service members, a guaranteed stream of income for life is likely better than a lump sum.

If an individual chooses the lump sum option, they must notify the servicing personnel office no less than 90 days before retirement. For National Guard and Reserves, no less than

90 days before receipt of monthly retired pay (which is at age 60, or earlier based on creditable active service).

Other Considerations

- Lump sum payments are considered earned income. Depending on the amount, it could put an individual into a higher tax bracket.

- Payments for the Survivor Benefit Plan will still be deducted from remaining monthly retired pay should someone elect the lump sum.

- If a person expects to receive a disability rating from the Department of Veterans Affairs, depending upon the person's rating, disability compensation could be offset.

561. If a service member dies before age sixty-seven, must the lump sum be repaid?

No. Once the lump sum is selected and distributed to the service member, the money belongs to the individual – it will not be recouped in the event of death. However, the remaining annuity will end unless the service member is enrolled in the Survivor Benefit Plan.

562. Is a service member that serves less than twenty years eligible for a lump sum distribution?

No. Lump sum refers to a portion of the monthly retired pay a service member receives upfront after serving twenty or more years (or twenty qualifying years in the National Guard and Reserve). Therefore, the lump sum is only available for those that serve twenty or more years and retire from one of the Uniformed Services.

563. Can a service member roll over their lump sum distribution to the TSP?

No. The service member would not be able to roll over their lump sum payment into another retirement plan. Only an "eligible rollover distribution" can be moved to another retirement plan. In order for a distribution to be eligible to rollover, among other things, it must come from a "qualified trust". The military retirement fund is not a "qualified trust" under the Internal Revenue Code and therefore money that comes from it cannot be rolled over to another retirement plan.

564. Can a service member take the lump sum payout over several years to minimize the tax liability?

The lump sum is considered earned income and is therefore taxable. Service members may choose to receive their lump sum payments in up to four installments over four years to reduce their tax burden.

Continuation Pay

565. What is continuation pay?

BRS includes a continuation pay provision as a method to encourage service members to continue serving in the uniformed services. Continuation pay is a direct cash payout, much like a bonus. It is payable between the completion of eight years of service, but before completion of twelve years of service, as determined and announced by the particular branch. Members receive continuation pay in return for additional obligated service. Active component service members (including Active Guard Reserve (AGR) and Full Time Support (FTS)) enrolled in the BRS will be eligible for a cash incentive of two and one-half to thirteen times their regular monthly basic pay. Reserve Component members will be eligible for one-half to six times their monthly basic pay (as if serving on active duty). Each service will publish guidance related to Continuation Pay rates. The rates for each calendar year will be determined by the retention needs, occupational series, and critically manned career fields of the Military Services and published yearly.

566. Who is eligible for continuation pay and how is it calculated?

All service members, both active duty and reserve who are enrolled in the BRS are eligible for continuation pay.

However, each service branch will determine when and at what rate service members will receive continuation pay. It is offered between years eight and twelve of service and the individual must commit to at least an additional three years of service.

For active duty members, it will be at least 2.5 times monthly base pay and no more than 13 times monthly base pay. For reserve members, it will be at least 0.5 times monthly base pay, based on active duty pay charts, and no more than 6 times monthly base pay. The continuation pay multiplier can vary and be based on factors such as hard-to-fill positions, retention rates and specialty skill, among others. The services continue to work on guidance related to this provision of the plan.

The rates of continuation pay remained the same during 2022 as they were in 2021. It is expected that the standard rates below will be unchanged for 2023 as well:

- Army Active: 2.5x at 12th year of service with an additional obligation of 4 years

- Army Reserve: 4.0x at 11th year of service with additional obligation of 4 years

- Marine Corps Active: 2.5x at 12th year of service with additional obligation of 4 years

- Marine Corps Reserve: 0.5x at 12th year of service with additional obligation of 4 years

- Navy Active: 2.5x at 12th year of service with additional obligation of 4 years

- Navy Reserve: 0.5x at 12th year of service with additional obligation of 4 years

- Air Force Active: 2.5x at 12th year of service with additional obligation of 4 years

- Air Force Reserve: 0.5x at 12th year of service with additional obligation of 4 years

- Coast Guard Active: 2.5x at 12th year of service with additional obligation of 4 years

- Coast Guard Reserve: 0.5x at 12th year of service with additional obligation of 4 years

- NOAA: 2.5x at 12th year of service with additional obligation of 4 years

- USPHS: 2.5x at 10th year of service with additional obligation of 4 years

567. Can continuation pay be deposited into the Thrift Savings Plan (TSP)?

Yes, bonuses (such as continuation pay), as well as incentives and special pay, can all be contributed to the individual's TSP. It is important to note that each year, the IRS determines the maximum amount one can contribute to tax-deferred savings plans like the TSP ($21,500 [anticipated] for calendar year 2023). The annual contribution limit should be kept in mind when deciding how much to contribute to the TSP account from continuation pay. If a person reaches the annual maximum too quickly, they could lose some government matching contributions, because a person will only receive government matching contributions on the first five percent of basic pay contributed each pay period. Reaching the annual limit before the end of the year will result in contributions (and, consequently, government matching contributions) coming to a stop. Contributing some or all of continuation pay to a TSP and going over the IRS limit could result in meeting the IRS limit earlier in the year and losing out on additional government matching contributions.

568. How are the eight to twelve years of service calculated for continuation pay?

Active duty service members and National Guard and Reserve service members in a pay status are eligible for continuation pay when they complete between their eighth to twelfth year of service, which is calculated from that service member's Pay Entry Base Date (PEBD). Continuation pay may be paid at any time during this period, as determined by the Service. PEBD can be affected by broken service, lost time, transfer to/from reserve components, etc.

569. Will a service member be eligible for other bonuses, such as a reenlistment bonus, if they receive continuation pay?

Yes. Continuation pay can be received in conjunction with other bonus if not otherwise prohibited by law.

570. Can continuation pay be collected more than one time?

No. Continuation pay is a one-time payout to a service member, regardless of whether they change service, component, or career specialty.

571. Can the service obligation for continuation pay and other bonuses, such as a reenlistment bonus, be served concurrently?

Yes. The service obligation, because of continuation pay, can be served concurrently.

572. Can someone receive continuation pay while in active duty and then complete their obligation in another service or component?

This depends. Continuation pay is designed to retain the individual in their current occupation, service, and component.

573. If a service member accepts continuation pay for continued service and does not complete the commitment, must the continuation pay be refunded to the government in whole or in part?

It depends. While all situations are unique, continuation pay may be subject to repayment in a prorated amount. The decision as to whether or not to recoup payment is determined by the branch of service.

574. Is continuation pay part of the service member's retirement package?

No. Continuation pay is not part of a service member's retirement benefit, but it is part of the Department of Defense strategy to maintain existing rates of retention of experienced personnel for the All-Volunteer Force. Department of Defense analysis suggests that the reduction in the monthly retired pay may result in fewer members staying for a full career. Providing continuation pay as a retention tool will help encourage these members to stay.

Survivor Annuity

575. What is the Survivor Benefit Plan?

The Survivor Benefit Plan provides survivor monthly benefits for eligible widows, widowers, and dependent children of eligible military personnel. Benefits are essentially the same as those provided federal government employees.

Those eligible to participate in the Survivor Benefit Plan (SBP) must be:

(1)   entitled to retired or retainer pay; or

(2)   eligible for retired pay but for the fact that they are under sixty years of age.

The standard annuity is paid to those entitled to retired or retainer pay. The reserve-component annuity is paid to those who are eligible but under age sixty. If a person entitled to retired or retainer pay is married or has a dependent child, he is automatically covered by the SBP with maximum coverage, unless he elects lesser coverage or declines participation before the first day he becomes eligible for the retired or retainer pay. Unmarried service personnel who have no dependent children can elect a survivor annuity in favor of someone who has an insurable interest in their life. Retired pay is, of course, reduced for Plan participants.

A retiree who has a spouse and a child (or children) at retirement can elect survivor benefits for the spouse only or for the child (or children) only. Absent some election, coverage for both the spouse and child (or children) is automatic. The spouse must concur in:

(1)   an election not to participate in the plan;

(2)   an election to provide the spouse with an annuity at less than the maximum level; and

(3)   an election to provide an annuity for a dependent child but not the spouse.

An election not to participate in the Plan by a person eligible for retired pay is irrevocable unless revoked before the date on which the person first becomes entitled to that pay. An election by a person under age sixty not to participate in the Plan becomes irrevocable if not revoked by the end of the ninety-day period beginning on the date he receives notification that he has completed the required years of service.

576. Who is eligible to receive Survivor Benefit Plan benefits?

The Survivor Benefit Plan provides a monthly annuity payment effective the first day after the death of the retiree. The annuity is paid to one of the following:

- **The eligible surviving widow or widower.** The surviving spouse may remarry after age fifty-five and continue to receive SBP payments for life. If the surviving spouse remarries before age fifty-five, SBP payments will stop, but may be resumed if the marriage later ends due to death or divorce.

- **The surviving dependent children in equal shares** if the eligible widow or widower or eligible former spouse is dead, dies, or otherwise becomes ineligible. The payments for children equal 55 percent of covered retired pay. All eligible children divide this benefit in equal shares. If the SBP election was for spouse (or former spouse) and children, the children receive payments if the spouse is dead or dies, or otherwise becomes ineligible for the annuity.

- **The dependent children in equal shares,** if the retiree elected to provide an annuity for dependent children but not for the spouse or former spouse.

- **The former spouse under certain conditions.** Election of a former spouse precludes coverage of a current spouse and/or children of the current spouse.

The following criteria apply for the purposes of determining eligible beneficiaries:

- A **widow** is the surviving wife of a person who, if not married to the retiree at the time he became eligible for retired pay, was married to him for at least one year immediately before his death or is the mother of issue by that marriage.

- A **widower** is the surviving husband of a retiree who, if not married to the person at the time she became eligible for retired pay, was married to her for at least one year immediately before her death or is the father of issue by that marriage.

- A **former spouse** is the surviving former husband or wife of a person who is eligible to participate in the Plan.

- A **dependent child** is a person who is:

  o   unmarried,

  o   under eighteen years of age; or at least eighteen, but under twenty-two years of age, and pursuing a full-time course of study or training in a high school, vocational school or college; or incapable of self-support because of a mental or physical incapability existing before age eighteen or incurred on or after that birthday, but before age twenty-two, while pursuing such a full-time course of study or training,

  o   the child of a retiring participant, including an adopted child, a stepchild, foster child, or recognized natural child who lived with the retiree in a regular parent-child relationship.

- A **person with an insurable interest** is any person who has a bona fide financial interest in the continued life of the retiree. The insurable interest option is available only if the individual is unmarried with either no dependent children or one dependent child. One may elect insurable interest coverage for that child regardless of the child's age or dependency. Only one individual may be covered under the insurable interest option. People who can be covered include:

  o   Any relative more closely related to the individual than a cousin. This includes relatives such as parents, stepparents, grandparents, grandchildren, aunts, uncles, sisters, brothers, half-sisters, half-brothers, or dependent or nondependent child or stepchild; or

  o   An individual who would be financially affected by the person's death. This must be a natural person (not a company, organization, fraternity, etc.) with a financial interest in the person's life.

The annuity payable to a surviving spouse of the retiree is paid for life, except that if the annuitant remarries before age fifty-five, the remarriage terminates the annuity. If the remarriage is terminated by death, annulment, or divorce, payment of the annuity is resumed upon the termination of the remarriage. Survivor Benefits are subject to Cost-Of-Living Adjustments (COLA).

576.01. What is the effect of the Elimination of the Optional Annuity for Dependent Children?

The Survivor Benefit Plan (SBP) is a vehicle providing ongoing monthly annuity payment to military spouses or dependent children when a military member dies while on active duty, on inactive duty in the line of duty, or after retirement if the retiree purchases coverage.

What is the Optional Annuity for Dependent Children?

When a member of the armed forces dies on the line of duty, the surviving spouse can request to have the Survivor Benefit Plan annuity paid directly to an eligible dependent child or children instead of to the spouse. This program is also referred to as the "Optional Child Annuity".

The option exists because of the requirement that a spouse's SBP payments needed to be reduced by the full amount of the spouse's Dependency and Indemnity Compensation (DIC) payment from the Department of Veterans Affairs (VA). Payments to the surviving child were considered a more favorable option because SBP paid to a child is not required to be offset (reduced) by the amount of the DIC payment.

The Optional Annuity for Dependent Children is only enabled when the service member died on active duty or inactive duty in the line of duty after October 7, 2001. Changes to the Optional Annuity for Dependent Children do not impact the SBP coverage for families of a service member who retired prior to passing away or the SBP coverage for any current living retiree.

Changes Effected in 2023

The National Defense Authorization Act (NDAA) for Fiscal Year 2020 eliminated optional annuity for dependent children will be eliminated as of January 1, 2023, and the SBP monthly annuity payment must revert to the surviving spouse. The surviving spouse also must submit documentation verifying eligibility.

The first SBP monthly payment (the January 2023 benefit) to surviving spouses documented as eligible will be February 1, 2023. The last SBP monthly payment to a child will be the December 2022 benefit that is paid on January 3, 2023 (unless the surviving spouse is documented as deceased or not eligible). The change is part of the law and is not optional. An eligible child cannot continue to receive the SBP annuity, and the spouse cannot choose to have the annuity paid to the child. The surviving spouse cannot refuse the annuity to have it continue to be paid to a surviving child.

Situations Where an Eligible Child can Continue to Collect the SBP Payment in 2023

A.   DFAS receives documentation that there was no surviving spouse at the time of the service member's death.

B.   DFAS receives documentation that the surviving spouse is deceased.

C.   DFAS receives documentation that the surviving spouse remarried prior to age 55.

NOTE: If DFAS does not receive the documentation in the above situations, the annuity will be suspended until documentation is received. The documentation needed for a deceased spouse is a copy of the death certificate with contact information for the person submitting the documentation.

Changes for the Remainder of 2022

A.   CURRENT RECIPIENTS: If a child(ren) are current designated recipients of the Optional Annuity for Dependent Children the SBP payments will continue (as long as they remain eligible) until the SBP-DIC offset is fully eliminated in 2023.

B.   LOSS OF ELIGIBILITY DURING 2022: If a child(ren) lose eligibility because they marry or reach age 18 (or age 22 if a full-time student) prior to January 1, 2023, the annuity will be suspended until January 1, 2023. On January 1, 2023, the annuity will revert to the surviving spouse (if the spouse is eligible and submits documentation).

1.   If the annuity is already suspended because the child or children are no longer eligible, it will continue to be suspended until January 1, 2023. On January 1, 2023, the annuity will revert to the surviving spouse (if the spouse is eligible and submits documentation).

2.   If the annuity is suspended because the child/children are no longer eligible and DFAS does not receive eligibility documentation for the surviving spouse, the annuity will remain suspended until documentation is submitted.

577. What is the amount of the Survivor Benefit Plan annuity?

The amount of a Survivor Benefit Plan annuity payable to a widow, widower, former eligible spouse, or dependent children is based on a figure known as the base amount. The base amount is:

(1)   the amount of monthly retired pay to which a retiree became entitled when first eligible, or later became entitled to by being advanced on the retired list, performing active duty, or being transferred from the temporary disability retired list to the permanent disability retired list; or

(2)   any lesser amount designated by the retiree on or before the first day of eligibility for retired pay, but not less than $300. This is unchanged for 2023.

A retiree who wants maximum survivor benefits for a spouse and children (at the cost of maximum reduction in retirement pay), will designate as the base amount on which survivor benefits are figured the full amount of retired pay. For a lower level of survivor benefits (in exchange for a smaller reduction in retirement pay), a base amount less than full retirement pay will be designated.

The following are categories of dependents and the rules for determining the amount of annuity payable:

(1)   In the case of a standard annuity for a widow, widower, or child, the monthly annuity is an amount equal to 55 percent of the base amount, if the beneficiary is under sixty-two years of age or is a dependent child when becoming entitled to the annuity. If the beneficiary (other than a dependent child) is sixty-two years of age or older when becoming entitled to the annuity, the monthly annuity is an amount equal to 35 percent of the base amount.

(2)   In the case of a standard annuity for an ex-spouse or person with an insurable interest in the annuitant (other than a widow, widower, or dependent child), the monthly annuity payable to the beneficiary is an amount equal to 55 percent of the retired pay of the person who elected to provide the annuity.

(3)   An annuity is also payable to a surviving spouse of a member who dies on active duty after: (a) becoming eligible to receive retired pay, (b) qualifying for retired pay, except that he or she has not applied for or been granted that pay, or (c) completing twenty years of active service but before he or she is eligible to retire as a commissioned officer because he or she has not completed ten years of active commissioned service. An annuity is payable to the dependent child of the servicemember if there is no surviving spouse or if the servicemember's surviving spouse subsequently dies.

If a person receiving an annuity in item (3) in preceding list is under sixty-two or is a dependent child when the servicemember or former servicemember dies, the monthly annuity is an amount equal to 55 percent of the retired pay to which the servicemember or former servicemember would have been entitled if the servicemember or former servicemember had been entitled to that pay based upon his or her years of active service when he or she died.

If a person receiving an annuity in item (3) in the preceding list (other than a dependent child) is sixty-two or older when the servicemember or former servicemember dies, the monthly annuity is an amount equal to 35 percent of the retired pay to which the servicemember or former servicemember would have been entitled if the servicemember or former servicemember had been entitled to that pay based upon his or her years of active service when he or she died.

578. Are Survivor Benefit Plan annuities subject to cost-of-living increases?

Yes, whenever retirees receive a cost-of-living increase in their retired pay, Survivor Benefit Plan annuities are increased at the same time by the same total percent. The percentage is applied to the monthly annuity payable before any reduction is made, in consideration of the annuitant's eligibility for Dependency and Indemnity Compensation or Social Security survivor benefits.

579. How does the remarriage of a surviving spouse affect payments from the Survivor Benefits Plan?

Surviving spouses continue eligibility for SBP until death, as long as they do not remarry before the age of 55. If the annuitant remarries before age 55, annuity payments stop.

If the annuitant's marriage later ends for any reason, even after age 55, the annuity payment will restart from the date the marriage ends, once DFAS is notified.

If DIC payments stop and the spouse's SBP payment was previously reduced or eliminated because of DIC, the full SBP payment may resume.

Spouse annuitants who remarry after age 57 are entitled to receive full SBP and DIC benefits at the same time. This was established of the United States Court of Appeals for the Federal Circuit in 2009. The court, in ruling that the offset violated the Veterans Benefits Act, established that DFAS is not required to offset DIC payments from a monthly SBP annuity if a spouse is entitled to both benefits and has remarried after age 57.[1]

Note

1. *Sharp v. United States*, 580 F.3d 1234 (Fed. Cir. 2009).

580. How does the Survivor Benefit Plan reduce the regular retirement annuity?

The Survivor Benefit Plan reduces the regular retirement annuity according to the following formulas.

Where the individual first becomes a member of the uniformed service before March 1, 1990, the reduction is the lesser of:

(1)   an amount equal to 2.5 percent of the first $725 of the base amount (the "threshold amount") of the annuity subject to the survivor benefit, plus 10 percent of the remainder; or

(2)   an amount equal to 6.5 percent of the base amount of the annuity subject to the survivor benefit.

Where the individual first becomes a member of the uniformed service on or after March 1, 1990, the reduction for the Survivor Benefit Plan is a flat 6.5 percent of the base amount of the annuity.

"Base amount" does not include cost-of-living increases.

581. What is the Special Survivor Indemnity Allowance (SSIA)?

The Special Survivor Indemnity Allowance (SSIA) is a benefit for surviving spouses who receive a Survivor Benefit Plan annuity that is offset by a Dependency and Indemnity Compensation (DIC) payment from the VA.

During 2022, SSIA is paid at up to $346 per month. Eligible survivors will continue to receive the Special Survivors Indemnity Allowance, up to the maximum amount per month, or up to the amount of SBP reduced by DIC (if the amount of the SBP reduction is less than the maximum amount) until December 31, 2022.

SSIA is not used to repay past due SBP premiums. If the spouse annuitant is entitled to SSIA, we will pay the SSIA, even when there are past due premiums.

DIC payments to children do not affect SBP child annuitant payments, so child annuitants are not eligible to receive SSIA.

582. What is the Survivor Benefit Plan – Dependency and Indemnity Compensation Offset?

The National Defense Authorization Act for Fiscal Year 2020 repealed the law requiring an offset of Survivor Benefit Plan (SBP) payments for surviving spouses who are also entitled to Dependency and Indemnity Compensation (DIC) from the Department of Veterans Affairs (VA).

Previous Law

Under the previous law, a surviving spouse who received DIC is subject to a dollar-for-dollar reduction of SBP payments, which can result in SBP being either partially or fully offset.

Impact of Repeal of Offset

The repeal brings the reduction of this offset in phases which began on January 1, 2021, with the complete elimination of the offset on January 1, 2023. During 2020, surviving spouses remained subject to the existing dollar-for-dollar offset of SBP payments by the amount of DIC paid by VA. After January 1, 2021, survivors subject to the "SBP-DIC Offset" will likely see changes in their SBP payments as follows:

- During 2021, SBP will be reduced by no more than two-thirds of the amount of DIC rather than by the entire amount of DIC, even though eligible surviving spouses will continue to receive the full amount of DIC.

- During 2022, SBP will be reduced by no more than one-third of the amount of DIC received.

- In 2023, the SBP-DIC offset will be eliminated in total, so that surviving spouses eligible for both programs will receive both SBP and DIC in full, effective January 1.

This change affects surviving spouses who are, or who will become in the future, eligible for both Survivor Benefit Plan (SBP) payments and Dependency and Indemnity Compensation (DIC) payments, and who were previously subject to a full or partial SBP-DIC offset. Additionally, the offset affect children of service members who died while on active duty or inactive duty, in the line of duty, who are currently receiving SBP payments because the surviving spouse chose the optional child annuity.

It does not impact surviving spouses who receive only SBP but not DIC. Spouses who are in receipt of DIC-only, are not impacted.

583. How are same-sex marriages handled in regard to participation in the SBP?

In regard to same-sex marriage and participation in the SBP, the DoD guidance generally provides that effective June 26, 2013, any person who is married to a same-sex partner may participate in the SBP in the same manner as any other married person. This includes the requirement for spousal concurrence for certain elections. A summary of the guidance is provided below:

- Any claims to SBP spouse coverage for same-sex spouses of eligible participants of the SBP for periods before June 26, 2013 are not valid as the Defense of Marriage Act was still the law and in effect prior to June 26, 2013. As a result, no SBP premiums for such coverage will be charged prior to that date. Further, no SBP annuity payments for such coverage will be paid for deaths occurring before that date.

- Effective from June 26, 2013, a person who becomes eligible to participate under 10 U.S.C. 1448 (a)(1) and is married to a same-sex partner shall have the SBP program applied as for any other married couple under section 10 U.S.C. 1448, including the requirements for spousal consent for less than full annuity coverage of the spouse. Effective June 26, 2015, there is no need to determine if any particular state permits same sex marriage. Any marriage license issued from a state is presumed valid.

- A person who was married to a same-sex partner upon becoming eligible to participate in the plan prior to June 26, 2013, and who had married that same-sex partner before June 26, 2013, shall have one year from June 26, 2013 to make a spouse election under 10 U.S.C. 1448(a)(3). Such person may not participate at less than maximum coverage described in 10 U.S.C. 1448(a)(3) without the concurrence of the person's spouse unless they already had provided an annuity for a dependent child. If an election is not received on or before June 25, 2014, full spousal coverage shall be entered and the member shall be responsible for payment of premiums effective from June 26, 2013.

- A person who is married to a same-sex partner on June 26, 2013 and has insurable interest coverage under the SBP may terminate the insurable interest coverage and elect spouse coverage. This election must be received on or before June 25, 2014.

- A person who was not married upon becoming eligible to participate in the plan, but who married a same-sex partner before June 26, 2013, shall have one year from June 26, 2013, to make a spouse election under 10 U.S.C. 1448(a)(5). The election must be received on or before June 25, 2014, or the person shall be prohibited by law from making such election.

- Generally, a person who is a participant in the plan and is providing coverage under the SBP for a spouse, who later does not have an eligible spouse beneficiary may, under 10 U.S.C. 1448(a)(6), elect not to provide coverage for a new spouse in the event of a remarriage.

- For a person who enters into a same-sex marriage after June 26, 2013, the election to discontinue participation under 10 U.S.C. 1448(a)(6) must be made within one year of the remarriage. If a member does not discontinue participation, then pursuant to 10 U.S.C. 1448(a)(6), spouse coverage will resume effective on the first anniversary of the marriage.

- If the remarriage took place prior to June 26, 2013, the participant has one year from June 26, 2013 to elect out of SBP. If a member does not make such an election within one year of June 26, 2013, then pursuant to section 10 U.S.C. 1448(a)(6), spouse coverage will resume effective no earlier than June 25, 2014.

- Additionally, any such person falling within the parameters of section 10 U.S.C. 1448(g), shall have one year from June 26, 2013, or the date of any marriage subsequent to that date, to elect to increase the level of coverage under 10 U.S.C. 1448(g).

Note: Any person eligible to participate (either already retired and receiving retired pay or in receipt of a twenty-year letter and awaiting pay), who was not married at the time they become eligible to participate and who marries after June 26, 2015, has one year from the date of the marriage to enter a spousal election for SBP purposes.

Disability Retirement

584. When is a servicemember entitled to retire on permanent disability?

Disability retirement is referred to as Chapter 61 retirement, in a reference to Chapter 61 of title 10 United States Code. Members who have been determined to be unfit for duty with a disability rated by the military Service as 3 percent or greater are eligible for disability retirement. A member whose condition is not stable may be placed on the temporary disability retired list (TDRL) for up to five years at which point they must be either discharged, retired, or returned to active duty. Members whose condition has stabilized at a disability rating of 30 percent or higher may be placed on the permanent disability retired list (PDRL).

A servicemember is entitled to retire on permanent disability when the individual has been called or ordered to active duty for a period of more than thirty days (excluding Ready Reserve training duty), and:

(1)   is unfit to perform his duties because of incurring a physical disability while entitled to basic pay;

(2)   the disability is of a permanent and stable nature based on commonly accepted medical principles;

(3)   the disability is not due to intentional or willful neglect, and not incurred during a period of unauthorized absence; and

(4)   one of the following applies: (a) the disability is rated at least 30 percent under the Department of Veterans Affairs disability rating schedule, or (b) the service member has completed at least twenty years of service.

Where the service member has not completed twenty years of service but has a disability of at least 30 percent, as explained in (a) in preceding list, one of the following tests must additionally be satisfied:

(1)   The disability must be incurred in the line of duty.

(2)   The disability must be the proximate result of performing active duty.

(3)   The servicemember must have completed at least eight years of service.

Where the active-duty or inactive training period is thirty days or less, a regular servicemember or reservist is entitled to permanent disability based on injury where the following conditions are met:

(1)   If they are unfit to perform duties because of incurring a physical disability while entitled to basic pay.

(2)   The disability is of a permanent and stable nature based on commonly accepted medical principles.

(3)   The disability is the proximate result of performing active duty or inactive training.

(4)   The disability is not due to intentional misconduct or willful neglect, and not incurred during a period of unauthorized absence.

    (5)   One of the following applies:

        (a) the disability is rated at least 30 percent under the Department of Veterans Affairs disability rating schedule, or

        (b) the servicemember has completed at least twenty years of service.

585. How is disability retirement pay determined?

Disability retirement pay is figured by either of two methods, at the retiree's option, up to a maximum of 75 percent of basic pay:

    (1)   2.5 percent of monthly basic pay multiplied by the number of years of active service, or

    (2)   the percentage rating of disability.

A servicemember who meets the requirements of temporary disability may be placed on temporary disability retirement for up to five years. Retired pay for temporary disability is no less than 50 percent of basic pay. A servicemember will be permanently retired for physical disability if still disabled after five years.

586. How does a Servicemember qualify for Disability Retirement?

A person's disability percentage will be assigned by the Physical Evaluation Board and will determine whether their disability qualifies them for retirement or separation:

- If the person has **less than twenty years of active service** a disability rating of 30 percent or higher will qualify them for retirement, and a disability rating below 30 percent will result in separation.

- If the person has **twenty or more years of active service**, retirement will be recommended regardless of the disability rating.

- If the disability existed before entering the armed forces the person will be recommended for discharge without benefits.

The Branch of Service may place the person on either the Temporary Disability Retired List (TDRL) or the Permanent Disability Retired List (PDRL).

A member of the TDRL or the PDRL is a retired member of the armed forces and is entitled to all rights and privileges of a military retiree, which may include:

- Participation in Survivor Benefit Plans

- Voluntary/involuntary allotments from retired pay

- Disability compensation from the Department of Veterans Affairs

If the person meets additional requirements that person may also qualify for Combat-Related Special Compensation or Concurrent Retirement Disability Pay.

Temporary Disability Retirement List

If a person is found unfit to perform their duties because of a disability that may not be permanent, they may be placed on the Temporary Disability List (TDRL).

Their retired pay will be computed using one of two methods:

- The disability percentage (using a minimum of 50 percent for payment purposes while on the TDRL), referred to as Method A, or

- The person's years of active service, referred to as Method B.

Their pay will be computed based on whichever is more beneficial.

While on the TDRL, a physical examination is required at least once every eighteen months. Failure to report for the physical examination will result in the Branch of Service removing the person from the TDRL list and the retired pay will be suspended until the examination has been completed.

A person who was placed on the TDRL prior to January 1, 2017 may remain on the TDRL for up to five years, providing their condition does not change during that time. **If the person was placed on the TDRL on or after January 1, 2017, they will remain on that list for up to three years providing their condition does not change during that time.** If at any time they are found fit for duty, they may be removed from the TDRL and returned to active duty.

If their disability stabilizes and is rated at 30 percent or greater, the person will be transferred to the Permanent Disability Retired List (PDRL). If their disability stabilizes and is rated at less than 30 percent and they do not have twenty years of service, they will be discharged from the TDRL with severance pay.

Permanent Disability Retired List

If their disability is found to be permanent and is rated at 30 percent or greater, or they have twenty or more years of service, they will be placed on the Permanent Disability Retired List (PDRL).

Their retired pay will be computed using one of two methods.

- Their disability percentage, referred to as Method A.

- Their years of active service, referred to as Method B.

Their pay will be computed based on whichever method is more beneficial.

If a person has been transferred from the TDRL to the PDRL, their retired pay will be recalculated using their most current disability rating.

586.01. How does the Temporary Disability Retired List work?

The Physical Evaluation Board (PEB) places a service-member on the Temporary Disability Retired List (TDRL) instead of medically separating them if they feel that their conditions could improve enough to return the member to active duty within three years.

When someone is on the TDRL, they are effectively medically retired from the military and eligible to receive medical retirement benefits with a minimum 50% rating. They are also eligible to apply for and receive benefits from the VA. The DoD will monitor the person's conditions during this time.

If a person's condition improves enough, the PEB will return someone to full active duty, stopping all veterans' benefits. The TDRL can last for a maximum of five years. If a person's condition improves enough to return to duty during that time, it could end earlier. The person is not forced to return to active duty in this situation, and will not qualify for a medical retirement, but can choose instead to undergo a regular separation/retirement. If, however, the condition has not improved at the end of the five years, the person will officially and fully separated. Exact compensation while on TDRL depends on the disability rating and whether the person has dependents.

The Temporary Disability Retired List (TDRL) is only for service-members with medical conditions that could improve for a return to active duty. The Permanent Disability Retired List (PDRL) is for service-members with medical conditions that are not expected to improve enough to return them to active duty. Those on PDRL are permanently and fully separated from the military.

587. What is Combat-Related Special Compensation (CRSC)?

Combat-Related Special Compensation (CRSC) is a program created by Congress to allow eligible military retirees to receive tax-free monthly VA disability compensation in addition to retired pay.

CRSC is a special compensation for combat-related disabilities. It is non-taxable, and retirees must apply to their branch of service to receive it.

What are the qualifications to be eligible for Combat-Related Special Compensation (CRSC)?

Eligibility includes the following:

- Retired and entitlement to receive military retired pay (regardless of time served on active duty).

- Rating of disability at least 10 percent by the VA.

- Waiver of VA pay from the retired pay – retirement pay reduced by VA disability payments

- Service-connected disabilities that were incurred as a direct result of war or instrumentality of war.

Disabilities include combat-related include injuries incurred as a direct result of:

- armed conflict,

- hazardous duty,

- an instrumentality of war, or

- simulated war (war games or maneuvers).

In addition to monthly CRSC payments, the individual may be eligible for a retroactive payment. DFAS will perform an audit determine whether or not retroactive payments are due.

The retroactive payment date may go back as far as June 1, 2003, but can be limited based on:

- overall CRSC start date as awarded by the Branch of Service

- Purple Heart eligibility

- retirement date

- retirement law (disability or non-disability)

- six-year barring statute

Disability retirees with less than twenty years of service will be automatically limited to a retroactive date of January 1, 2008, as required by legislation passed by Congress effective 2008.

All retroactive pay is limited to six years from the date the VA awarded compensation for each disability.

588. Can National Guard or Reservists receive Combat-Related Special Compensation (CRSC)?

No. Regular Guard and Reservist retirees cannot receive retired pay until age 60. Therefore, even if these veterans are receiving VA disability compensation before age 60, they will not be eligible for CRSC until they turn 60 and start receiving retired pay and VA disability compensation simultaneously.

589. How does one apply for Combat-Related Special Compensation (CRSC)?

CRSC is not automatically applied to eligible veterans. For CRSC, one must apply to their branch of service by submitting DD Form 2860.[1] Veterans should also consider submitting copies of previous VA rating decisions, including the award letters and narrative summaries; copies of DD 214s and DD 215s (discharge paperwork); and official documented evidence that supports how the specific disability being claimed can be linked to one of the combat-related events outlined above. When applying for CRSC, veterans should not submit medical records that are unrelated to the disability being claimed or lay statements.

Each branch of service has a website that explains their eligibility requirements, how to apply, and what documentation is needed. Each site also has downloadable CRSC application forms and the appropriate mailing address for that branch of service.

- **Army:** https://www.hrc.army.mil/content/Apply%20for%20CRSC

- **Navy and Marine Corps:** https://www.secnav.navy.mil/mra/CORB/Pages/CRSCB/default.aspx

- **Air Force and Space Force:** https://www.myairforcebenefits.us.af.mil/Benefit-Library/Federal-Benefits/Combat-Related-Special-Compensation-(CRSC)?serv=25

- **Coast Guard:** https://www.dcms.uscg.mil/Our-Organization/Assistant-Commandant-for-Human-Resources-CG-1/Personnel-Service-Center-PSC/Personnel-Services-Division-PSC-PSD/Disability-Evaluation-Branch-PSC-PSD-MED/

Note

1. https://www.esd.whs.mil/Portals/54/Documents/DD/forms/dd/dd2860.pdf (last accessed September 20, 2022).

590. What is Concurrent Retirement and Disability Pay (CRDP)?

Concurrent Retirement and Disability Pay (CRDP) is a program created by Congress to allow eligible military retirees to receive monthly VA disability compensation in addition to retired pay.

CRDP is a restoration of retired pay for retirees with service-connected disabilities that was lost due to the VA compensation offset prior to January 1, 2004. Through this law, an eligible retiree's retired pay was fully restored. CRDP is taxed in the same manner as retirement pay and is taxable income. No application is required. Eligible retirees receive CRDP automatically.

What are the qualifications to be eligible for Concurrent Retirement and Disability Pay (CRDP)?

Eligibility includes:

- a regular retiree with twenty or more years of active service who has a VA disability rating of 50 percent or greater,

- a reserve retiree with twenty qualifying years of service who has a VA disability rating of 50 percent or greater and who has reached retirement age, or

- retired under Temporary Early Retirement Act (TERA) and have a VA disability rating of 50 percent or greater.

In addition to monthly CRDP payments, a person may be eligible for a retroactive payment. Retroactive payment dates may go as far back as January 1, 2004, but can be limited based on:

- retirement date, or

- when the person first increased to at least 50 percent disability rating.

No CRDP is payable for any month before January 2004.

Individual Unemployability

An individual is eligible for full concurrent receipt of both VA disability compensation and retired pay, if a military retiree who meets all of the above eligibility requirements in addition to **both of the following**:

- rated by the VA as unemployable, generally referred to as Individual Unemployability (IU)

- in receipt of VA disability compensation as a result of IU

Military Retirement – National Guard and Reservists

Reservists' and National Guard Retirement Pay

591. Are Reservists and National Guard members entitled to retirement pay?

To qualify for retirement pay in the Reserves, a person must complete at least 20 years of "satisfactory Federal service" (qualifying years) as a member of the armed forces. One meets this requirement for a year by earning at least 50 retirement points each year. Points are earned for both inactive duty and active duty. The branch of service will advise the reservist of point totals and the number of years of satisfactory federal service he has completed. The last eight qualifying years must have been spent in a Reserve unit. Entitlement to Reserve retirement pay begins at age 60.

The Reserve point system is an element used in computing retirement pay. In totaling points, there is no limit to the number of active points that may be earned in a year, but no more than 60 inactive-duty points may be counted for any one year.

Guard/Reserve members may accumulate a total of 365 points per year (366 in a leap year) from inactive and active duty service (one point for each day of duty). However, for retired pay calculation purposes, members cannot use more than 130 inactive points per year.

592. How is retirement calculated?

Credit can be received for up to 60 inactive points for retirement years that ended before Sep. 23, 1996, up to 75 inactive points for retirement years ending on or after Sep. 23, 1996 and before Oct. 30, 2000, and up to 90 points in the retirement year that includes Oct. 30, 2000 and in any subsequent year of service.

Points from these sources may be added to points earned from active duty and active duty for training for a maximum total of 365 or 366 points per retirement year. Points are credited on the following basis:

- One point for each day of active service (active duty or active duty for training).

- 15 points for each year of membership in a Reserve Component (Guard and Reserve).

- One point for each unit training assembly.

- One point for each day in which a member is in a funeral honors duty status.

- Satisfactory completion of accredited correspondence courses at one point for each three credit hours earned.

Reserve and Guard members with 20 or more years can begin collecting retirement benefits before age 60 if they deploy for war or national emergency for deployment time served after January 28, 2008. With each 90 consecutive days mobilized, members of the Guard and Reserve have their start date for annuities reduced by three months.

593. How has the Retirement System changed for the National Guard and Reservists?

The new military retirement system blends elements of the legacy retirement system with government automatic and matching contributions to a member's Thrift Savings Plan (TSP) – a more modern, 401(k)-style portable defined contribution plan that many civilian government employees enjoy today. Many of the elements of the legacy retirement system remain and both National Guard and Reserve service members should have a familiarity with how it works. The Blended Retirement System does not change when a National Guard or Reserve member is eligible to retire, and National Guard and Reserve service members covered by the Blended Retirement System are still eligible for reduced age retirement if they perform qualifying active service.

594. How is eligibility for the BRS different for National Guard members and Reservists?

Eligibility to opt-in is much broader for the National Guard and Reserve than the active component. Eligibility to opt into BRS is based on retirement points. National Guard and Reserve members who had fewer than 4,320 retirement points as of December 31, 2017, and who were in a pay status, were eligible to opt into BRS, regardless of how many service or qualifying years they had accumulated. Those who served after December 31, 2005 and before December 31, 2005 were required to either opt into the BRS or remain in the legacy retirement system. The

Blended Retirement System "retains the traditional defined benefit annuity, but adjusts the years of service multiplier from 2.5 percent to 2.0 percent for calculating monthly retired pay".

595. Why does the Department of Defense use a retirement point system for National Guard and Reservists?

The different eligibility criteria for National Guard and Reserve members is based on language in the National Defense Authorization Act of 2016 that mandated use of 10 U.S.C. § 12733[1] to compute eligibility for Reserve component members.

Note

1. https://www.law.cornell.edu/uscode/text/10/12733 (last accessed September 20, 2022).

596. Why are 4,320 retirement points required?

For retirement, National Guard and Reserve service is converted to equivalent active service by dividing accumulated retirement points by 360. The military considers a month to constitute 30 days for pay purposes, therefore each day is calculated as 1/30th of a month and 12 months would then equal 360 days. Using this formula, National Guardsmen or Reservists with 4,320 retirement points would have 12 equivalent years of active service.

How are Points Accrued

A year of Guard or Reserve service can earn more than 70 points, including:

- One point for each day of active service;

- One point for each unit training assembly;

- 15 points for participating each year;

- 48 points for monthly drill activities;

- 15 points for annual training which may vary; and

- One point for each day in a funeral honors duty.

- Any extra points earned through continuing education, being mobilized.

These figures are based on a typical year where the Guard or Reserve member serves the normal one weekend each month and two weeks per year of service. An individual may receive far more than 50 points in a year if the unit is active.

597. Does the BRS change how National Guard members and Reservist acquire retirement points?

No. The Blended Retirement System does not change how retirement points are calculated for members of the National Guard and Reserve. Points are still earned by participating in drill, attending annual training, and completing active duty, among other eligible categories. BRS does not affect when a member of the National Guard or Reserve is eligible to retire. Retirement eligibility and timing remains the same as it is under the legacy retirement system. National Guard or Reserve members with 20 or more qualifying years are eligible to receive their monthly retired pay starting at age 60 or earlier based on qualifying active service.

598. Are members of the Individual Ready Reserve (IRR) or Standby Reserve eligible to participate in the BRS?

Yes. Members of the IRR and Standby Reserve are eligible to participate in the BRS. However, they must be receiving pay to enroll in BRS. Therefore, members of the IRR and Standby Reserve who are eligible to enroll in the new system (because they were in the IRR or Standby Reserve as of December 31, 2017), but who did not drill in a paid status or were not on orders during calendar year 2018, were allowed a one-time extension of the enrollment window beyond 2018 if and when they entered a paid status.

599. How long does a member of the Individual Ready Reserve or the Standby Reserve have to opt-in once they are in paid status?

If a member of the IRR and Standby Reserve returned to a pay status in 2018, they had the remainder of 2018 to make an opt-in decision. After 2018, all BRS-eligible members of the IRR and Standby Reserve had thirty days to opt into the Blended Retirement System upon the first time he or she returns to a pay status.

600. How does the process work when a National Guard or Reservist retires under the Blended Retirement System?

The Blended Retirement System does not affect when a member (either active duty, National Guard, or Reserve) is eligible to retire. It remains the same; qualified National Guard and Reserve service members are eligible to receive their retirement pay starting at age sixty or earlier based on qualifying active service.

601. How is Reserve retired pay computed?

Members who accumulate 20 or more years of qualifying service are eligible for reserve retirement when they reach age 60 or, under some circumstances, a younger age. There are two retirement plans currently in effect for qualified retirees of the reserves. These include the Final Pay plan and the High-36 Month Average plan. There is no REDUX retirement plan under reserve retirement.

Final Pay Plan

The retired pay base for a qualified reserve retirement under the Final Pay plan is the monthly basic pay determined at the rates applicable on the day of retirement at the highest grade satisfactorily held during service. This takes into account the rate of pay for the member's pay grade and the years of service taken from the pay table in effect on the date that retired pay begins.

The Final Pay plan uses a multiplier percentage that is 2.5 percent times the years of creditable service. The creditable years of service for a reserve retirement calculation is determined by the sum of all accumulated reserve points divided by 360.

High-36 Plan (High-3 Plan)

The retired pay base for a qualified reserve retirement under the High-36 retirement plan is the total amount of monthly basic pay that the member was entitled during the member's high-36 months divided by 36. This includes months to which the member would have been entitled if the member had served on active duty during the entire period. Most of the times, this will be the average of the 36 months for the member's pay grade and years of service taken from the pay tables in effect for the 36 months immediately preceding the date that retired pay begins.

The High-36 plan uses a multiplier percentage that is 2.5 percent times the years of creditable service. The creditable years of service for a reserve retirement calculation is determined by the sum of all accumulated reserve points divided by 360.

Years of Service

There are three categories for determining years of creditable service that have applicability to the computation of reserve retired pay. One for determining when an individual is entitled to retired pay, one for determining the applicable active duty base pay upon which to compute retired pay, and one for determining the retired pay percentage multiplier. For reserve retirements, these are generally different.

Category One: Years of Service for Retirement Entitlement. This category of years of service includes each one year period in which the person has been credited with at least 50 points, as follows:

- 1 point for each day of active service

- 1 point for each attendance at a drill period

- 1 point for each day of performing funeral honors duty

- 15 points for each year of membership in a reserve component

A member retiring with a Reserve retirement must have 20 years of service.

Category Two: Years of Service for Pay Base. When combined with pay grade, the years of service for pay base determines the active duty pay entitlement by defining the appropriate pay. This category of includes all active duty and all periods of Reserve or National Guard service counted day for day. Reserve retirement pay base is determined as though the reserve member were serving on active duty immediately prior to retirement, thus the years of service continue to accumulate even after the member has entered the retired reserve and continue until they actually begin receiving such pay (usually age 60).

Category Three: Years of Service for Retired Pay Percentage Multiple. The Years of Service for Retirement Percentage Multiple determines the years of service for computing the retired pay multiplier. This category of years of service includes all periods of active service which are counted as one point for each day, plus all points earned through qualifying reserve duty, not exceeding annual limits, divided by 360.

Retirement Age

A member is generally not eligible for Reserve retired pay until they reach age 60. However, any member of the Ready Reserve who is recalled to active duty or, in response to a national emergency, is called to certain active service after January 28, 2008, shall have the age 60 requirement reduced by 3 months for each cumulative period of 90 days so performed in any fiscal year after that date.

602. If someone has a civilian 401(k) or civil service TSP AND a military TSP, can they contribute to both?

Yes, however the TSP and similar civilian retirement plans (e.g.: 401(k)), share the same annual contribution limit ($23,000 for 2023 – projected) under IRS regulations. This means a person cannot contribute more than the IRS elective deferral limit across both accounts in any given calendar year.

Generally, this will not impact active component service members. However, many members of the National Guard and Reserve are either military technicians and have access to both a military TSP and a civil service TSP account or are traditional members of the National Guard and Reserve who have another retirement plan through their civilian employment. As such, service members can make contributions to their TSP accounts and/or a 401(k) or similar retirement account in the same tax year but are subject to a single IRS elective deferral limit.

Service members should be careful not to exceed their annual contribution limit across their retirement accounts. If a service member's contributions reach the IRS elective deferral limit before the last pay date of the year, they will not receive all of the matching contributions to which they would otherwise be entitled.

The only time a service member can exceed the IRS elective deferral limit is when they are deployed to a combat zone or direct support area or contributing catch up contributions.

It is important to note that this annual additional limit includes automatic and matching contributions to the service member's retirement accounts from all sources.

603. Does a National Guard or Reserve member's TSP election percentage carry over when activating or deactivating?

National Guard and Reserve service members will not have to re-elect TSP percentages every time their pay status changes (activating and deactivating), the TSP elections carry-over.

604. Is the lump sum payment available for National Guard and Reserve?

Yes. Like their active duty counterparts, eligible National Guard and Reserve members have the option of electing a lump sum payment upon becoming eligible to begin receiving retired pay at age 60, or earlier with creditable active service, in exchange for a reduced level of monthly retired pay until reaching full Social Security retirement age, which is age 67 for most people. For National Guard and Reserve members, the lump sum election must be made to the component no less than ninety days before receipt of the non-regular retirement pay begins. This is typically at age 60, or earlier based on creditable active service.

605. Do full-time National Guard and Reserve members receive continuation pay at the same rate as active duty counterparts?

Yes. The National Defense Authorization Act of Fiscal Year 2017 clarifies that Active Guard Reserve (AGR) and Full Time Support (FTS) service members are eligible for the same rates of continuation pay as their active component counterparts. FTS and AGR will be eligible for a cash incentive of 2½ to thirteen times their regular monthly basic pay.

606. What are the requirements for National Guard and Reservists to receive continuation pay?

National Guard and Reserve service members must be able to serve their continuation pay obligation in the Select Reserve if they receive continuation pay.

607. How does the Survivor Benefit Plan work for Reservists?

Generally, the Survivor Benefit Plan for Reservists follows the rules for the regular service member's Survivor Benefit Plan. With respect to the amount of reduction in retired pay of the reserve component annuity, the reduction is the lesser of:

(1)   an amount equal to 2.5 percent of the first $750 of the base amount of the annuity subject to the survivor benefit, plus 10 percent of the remainder; or

(2)   an amount equal to 6.5 percent of the base amount of the annuity subject to the survivor benefit.

Veterans

Dependency and Indemnity Compensation

608. What is Dependency and Indemnity Compensation?

Dependency and Indemnity Compensation (DIC) is the benefit program providing monthly payments to a surviving spouse, child, or parent of the veteran due to a service-connected (line-of duty or service-related injury or illness) death that occurs after 1956. (Where the death occurred prior to 1957, certain survivors could have elected to take benefits under DIC.)

Generally, DIC is payable to survivors of service members or reservists who died from:

(1)   disease or injury incurred or aggravated in the line of duty while on active or inactive duty training; or

(2)   a result of a service-connected injury or disease,

(3)   a result of a non-service connected injury or disease, and who were totally disabled from service-connected disabilities for

- at least ten years immediately preceding death, OR

- since the Veteran's release from active duty and for at least five years immediately preceding death, OR

- at least one year immediately preceding death if the Veteran was a former prisoner of war.

(4)   disability compensable under laws administered by the Department of Veterans Affairs.

Veterans and dependents may obtain information on benefits by calling the toll-free number 1-800-827-1000. Callers are automatically connected to the Department of Veterans Affairs regional office serving the area from which their call originates. In addition, Veterans and dependents can contact the Department of Veterans Affairs online at https://www.ebenefits.va.gov/ebenefits/contact or 1-800-983-0987.

609. Who is eligible for DIC benefits?

Dependency and Indemnity Compensation (DIC) are monthly benefits payable to eligible survivors, regardless of the survivor's income or employment status.

Benefits are paid to eligible survivors of:

- Service members who died while on active duty, active duty for training, or inactive duty training;

- Veterans who died as a result of a service-connected injury or disease;

- Veterans who did not die as a result of a service-connected injury or disease, but were totally disabled by a service-connected disability:

    o   For at least ten years before death;

    o   Since their release from active duty and for at least five years before death; or o   For at least one year before death, if they were a former prisoner of war and died after September 30, 1999.

610. How does a surviving spouse show eligibility?

Surviving Spouses may be eligible for DIC benefits if they are a surviving spouse who:

- Married a service member who died on active duty, active duty for training, or inactive duty training;

- Married the deceased veteran before January 1, 1957;

- Married a veteran who died from a service-connected injury or disease, as long as the marriage began within fifteen years of discharge;

- Married the deceased veteran for at least one year; or

- Had a child with the veteran and cohabitated with the veteran until their death.

Note: If they had a child with the veteran but were separated, they must not be at fault for the separation and not be remarried in order to be eligible. If they remarried on or after December 16, 2003 and were at least fifty-seven years old, they may still be eligible.

Surviving Spouses will also need to provide evidence showing that one of these descriptions is true for the Veteran or service member:

- The service member died while on active duty, active duty for training, or inactive-duty training,

- The veteran died from a service-connected illness or injury, or

- The veteran didn't die from a service-connected illness or injury, but was eligible to receive VA compensation for a service-connected disability rated as totally disabling for a certain period of time.

If the Veteran's eligibility was due to a rating of totally disabling, they must have had this rating:

- For at least 10 years before their death,

- Since their release from active duty and for at least 5 years immediately before their death, or

- For at least 1 year before their death if they were a former prisoner of war who died after September 30, 1999.

Note: "Totally disabling" means the Veteran's injuries made it impossible for them to work.[1]

Note

1. https://www.law.cornell.edu/cfr/text/38/3.340 (Last accessed September 20, 2022).

611. How does a surviving child show eligibility?

A surviving child may be able to get compensation if they meet the following conditions.

You'll also need to provide evidence with your claim showing that one of the descriptions below is true for the Veteran or service member. Evidence may include documents like military service records, doctor's reports, and medical test results.

Each of these conditions must be shown

- The child is not married,

- The child is not included on the surviving spouse's compensation, and

- The child is under the age of 18 (or under the age of 23 if attending school).

Note: Adopted children that meet all other eligibility criteria still qualify for compensation.

The child will need to provide evidence that one of these descriptions is true for the Veteran or service member:

- The service member died while on active duty, active duty for training, or inactive-duty training,

- The Veteran died from a service-connected illness or injury, or

- The Veteran didn't die from a service-connected illness or injury, but was eligible to receive VA compensation for a service-connected disability that was rated as totally disabling for a certain period of time.

If the Veteran's eligibility was due to a service-connected disability rated as totally disabling, they must have had this rating:

- For at least 10 years before their death,

- Since their release from active duty and for at least 5 years immediately before their death, or

- For at least 1 year before their death if they were a former prisoner of war who died after September 30, 1999.

Note: "Totally disabling" means the Veteran's injuries make it impossible for them to work.[1]

Note

1. https://www.law.cornell.edu/cfr/text/38/3.340 (Last accessed September 20, 2022).

612. How does a surviving parent show eligibility?

Surviving parent may be eligible if both of the descriptions below are true. The parent will also need to provide evidence with the claim showing that one of the listed descriptions below is true for the veteran or service member.

Both of these must be true:

- The parent is the biological, adoptive, or foster parent of the Veteran or service member, and

- The parent's income is below a certain amount based on the Parent DIC rate table.

Note: A foster parent is defined as someone who served in the role of a parent to the veteran or service member before their last entry into active service.

Evidence will be need to show that one of these descriptions is true for the veteran or service member:

- The service member died from an injury or illness while on active duty or in the line of duty while on active duty for training,

- The service member died from an injury or certain illnesses in the line of duty while on inactive training, or

- The Veteran died from a service-connected illness or injury.

613. How is the amount of the DIC benefit determined?

DIC payments to surviving spouses of veterans whose service-connected deaths occur on or after January 1, 1993 are standardized; there had been a schedule of benefits based on the military rank of the deceased veteran. In 2022, a monthly base rate of $1,437.66 was payable to the surviving spouses of all such veterans. That rate is increased by $306.00 a month, if the veteran was totally disabled due to service-connected disabilities continuously for at least eight years prior to death.

If there is a surviving spouse with one or more children below the age of eighteen of a deceased veteran, the DIC paid monthly to the surviving spouse is increased by $356.16 for each child.

In addition to an annual limitation, the amount of DIC payable monthly to a parent depends upon whether there is only one parent, whether two surviving parents are or are not living together, and whether a parent has remarried and is living with a spouse.

The maximum monthly benefit payable to one parent only is $622. No DIC is payable if the parent's annual income exceeds $14,680. Two parents not living together are entitled to a maximum monthly benefit of $450 each. Again, no DIC is paid to a parent whose annual income exceeds $14,680. Two parents living together (or remarried parents living with spouses, when both parents are alive) are entitled to a maximum monthly benefit of $423 each. No DIC is paid to a parent if total combined annual income exceeds $19,733.

The monthly rate of DIC payable to a parent is increased by $337 if such parent is:

(1)   a patient in a nursing home; or

(2)   helpless or blind, or so nearly helpless and blind as to need or require the regular aid and attendance of another person.

Death Prior to January 1, 1993

For surviving spouses of veterans who died prior to January 1, 1993, monthly payments are made according to the veteran's pay grade at the time of death or under the new formula, whichever provides the highest benefit. (See Appendix C, Table 4, Servicemembers and Veterans Tables, for benefits based on pay grade.)

If the veteran did not die in active service, the pay grade will be determined as of:

(1)   the time of last discharge or release from active duty; or

(2)   the time of discharge or release from any period of active duty for training or inactive duty training, if death results from service-connected disability incurred during such period. The discharge must have been other than dishonorable.

The monthly rate of DIC is increased by $337 if the surviving spouse is:

(1)   a patient in a nursing home; or

(2)   helpless and blind, or so nearly helpless and blind as to need the regular aid and attendance of another person.

The monthly rate of DIC will be increased by $155.53, if the surviving spouse is permanently housebound by reason of disability and does not qualify for the aid and attendance allowance described above.

DIC Benefits for Children

If a child is under age eighteen, and there is no surviving spouse entitled to DIC, DIC is paid in equal shares to the children of the deceased veteran at the following monthly rates:

- one child, $565.84;

- two children, $814.01;

- three children, $1.062.20;

- four children, $1,264.06;

- five children, $1,465.92;

- six children, $1,667.78;

- seven children, $1,869.64;

- eight children, $2,071.50;

- nine children, $2,273.36;

- more than nine children, $2,273.36 plus $201.86 for each child in excess of three.

If a child is eighteen or over, and the child became permanently incapable of self-support while under eighteen and eligible for DIC, the child's DIC is continued past age eighteen and increased by $332 per month. If DIC is payable to a surviving spouse with a child, age eighteen or older, who became permanently incapable of support while under eighteen, the Department of Veterans Affairs will pay an additional sum of $565.84 for such child.

If DIC is payable to a spouse with a child, age eighteen or over and under age twenty-three, who is attending an approved educational institution, DIC is paid to the child, concurrently with the payment of DIC to the spouse, in the amount of $332 per month if in school or $565.84 per month if considered to be helpless.

Disability Benefits – Service-Connected

614. What benefits are available for service-connected disability?

There are three kinds of benefits for a service-connected disability:

(1)   compensation paid by Department of Veterans Affairs;

(2)   severance pay; and

(3)   disability retirement pay.

Disability retirement is discussed in BENEFITS FOR FEDERAL GOVERNMENT EMPLOY-EES, Q 644 to Q 709.

Monthly compensation is paid by the Department of Veterans Affairs without regard to other income, on the basis of average impairments of earning capacity in civilian employment. A person eligible for both disability retirement pay and this compensation may elect which to receive, but cannot receive full benefits from both sources.

The veteran must be disabled by injury or disease incurred in, or aggravated by, active service in the line of duty. Discharge or separation must be other than dishonorable, and the injury cannot have resulted from willful misconduct. Reservists disabled while on active training duty may qualify for compensation.

The monthly compensation amount depends on the veteran's degree of disability. The rates in the subsequent table projected for 2023 assuming an increase of 9.6% percent.

VA Disability Rating: 10% – 20% (No Dependents)	
Percentage	Rate
10%	$167.29
20%	$339.71

VA Disability Rating: 30% – 60% Without Children				
Dependent Status	30%	40%	50%	60%
Veteran Alone	$512.26	$737.91	$1,050.45	$1,330.58
Veteran with Spouse Only	$523.09	$748.71	$1,052.68	$1,327.03
Veteran with Spouse & One Parent	$567.16	$807.83	$1,126.85	$1,416.23
Veteran with Spouse and Two Parents	$611.22	$866.94	$1,201.01	$1,505.44
Veteran with One Parent	$512.34	$733.66	$1,034.41	$1,305.53
Veteran with Two Parents	$556.41	$792.78	$1,108.57	$1,394.74
Additional for A/A spouse	$51.59	$67.71	$85.98	$103.18

VA Disability Rating: 30% – 60% With Children				
Dependent Status	30%	40%	50%	60%
Veteran with Spouse and Child	$565.01	$803.53	$1,121.47	$1,409.70
Veteran with Child Only	$504.82	$723.99	$1,021.52	$1,290.40
Veteran with Spouse, One Parent and Child	$609.07	$862.64	$1,195.63	$1,498.99
Veteran with Spouse, Two Parents and Child	$653.14	$921.75	$1,269.79	$1,588.20
Veteran with One Parent and Child	$548.89	$783.10	$1,095.68	$1,379.69
Veteran with Two Parents and Child	$592.95	$842.22	$1,169.84	$1,468.90
Add for Each Additional Child Under Age 18	$26.87	$36.54	$46.22	$54.81
Each Additional Schoolchild Over Age 18	$89.21	$119.30	$148.32	$178.42
Additional for A/A spouse	$51.59	$67.71	$85.98	$103.18

2023 VA Disability Rates - Veterans Guardian VA Claim Consulting (vetsguardian.com)

VA Disability Rating: 70% – 100% Without Children				
Dependent Status	70%	80%	90%	100%
Veteran Alone	$1,676.63	$1,949.16	$2,190.38	$3,451.94
Veteran with Spouse Only	$1,662.89	$1,930.11	$2,168.89	$3,524.48
Veteran with Spouse and One Parent	$1,767.14	$2,049.42	$2,303.24	$3,673.86
Veteran with Spouse and Two Parents	$1,871.40	$2,168.72	$2,437.59	$3,823.23
Veteran with One Parent	$1,637.09	$1,901.09	$2,136.65	$3,487.72
Veteran with Two Parents	$1,741.35	$2,020.40	$2,270.99	$3,637.10
Additional for A/A spouse	$119.30	$136.50	$153.70	$170.70

VA Disability Rating: 70% – 100% With Children				
Dependent Status	70%	80%	90%	100%
Veteran with Spouse and Child	$1,758.54	$2,039.74	$2,292.49	$3,660.79
Veteran with Child Only	$1,619.90	$1,880.67	$2,114.07	$3,462.82
Veteran with Spouse, One Parent and Child	$1,862.80	$2,159.04	$2,426.84	$3,810.16
Veteran with Spouse, Two Parents and Child	$1,967.05	$2,278.35	$2,561.19	$3,959.54
Veteran with One Parent and Child	$1,724.15	$1,999.97	$2,248.42	$3,612.20
Veteran with Two Parents and Child	$1,828.41	$2,119.28	$2,382.77	$3,761.57
Add for Each Additional Child Under Age 18	$64.49	$73.09	$82.76	$92.49
Each Additional Schoolchild Over Age 18	$208.51	$238.60	$268.70	$298.75
Additional for A/A spouse	$119.30	$136.50	$153.70	$170.70

Rates for each school child are shown separately. They are not included with any other compensation rates. All other entries on this chart reflecting a rate for children show the rate payable for children under 18 or helpless. To find the amount payable to a 70 percent disabled veteran with a spouse and four children, one of whom is over 18 and attending school, take the 70 percent rate for a veteran with a spouse and two children, $1,967.05, and add the rate for two school children, $208.51 x 2 = $417.02. The total amount payable is $2.384.07.

Where the veteran has a spouse who is determined to require A/A, add the figure shown as "additional for A/A spouse" to the amount shown for the proper dependency code. For example, veteran has A/A spouse and two minor children and is 70 percent disabled. Add $119.30, additional for A/A spouse, to the rate for a 70 percent veteran with dependency code 12, $1,967.05. The total amount payable is $2,084.80.

A service-connected disability rating may be increased or decreased in accordance with medical findings of changes in the affected condition. However, once a condition has been rated at or above a particular evaluation for twenty continuous years, the rating is protected by law and may not be changed (unless the rating was established by fraud).

Any veteran entitled to monthly compensation whose disability is rated not less than 30 percent is entitled to additional compensation for dependents. The current rates listed below are based upon 100 percent disability. If the disability rating is at least 30 percent, but less than 100 percent, the amount of dependent benefits will be approximately the same percent of these rates as the percent-of-disability rating.

A child's benefit usually ends at age 18. However, each dependent child between ages 18 and 23 who is attending an approved school is eligible for $281.57 monthly if the veteran is totally disabled, and a proportionate amount if the veteran is partially disabled.

The spouse of a totally disabled veteran is entitled to $3 a month if: (1) a patient in a nursing home; or (2) helpless and blind, or so nearly helpless and blind as to need or require the regular aid and attendance of another person. The spouse of a veteran who is not totally disabled, but at least 30 percent disabled, is entitled to a proportionate monthly benefit.

These dependency allowances are not payable if the service member receives any other allowance for dependents under any other law (with the exception of Social Security benefits). The higher of the two amounts may be elected, but not both. Social Security benefits for total and permanent disability will not be reduced by the amount of any service-connected disability compensation received from the Department of Veterans Affairs.

Service personnel are entitled to disability severance pay when separated from service for physical disability, but are not eligible for disability retirement pay where:

(1)   the rated disability is less than 30 percent; or

(2)   length-of-service credits are insufficient.

Disability severance pay is a lump sum equal to twice the monthly base and longevity pay multiplied by years of service, but not exceeding the amount of two years' basic pay, and is payable by the member's branch of service.

Veterans with a 10 percent disability rating may be entitled to a program of vocational rehabilitation, if the Department of Veterans Affairs finds that the veteran has a "serious employment handicap" and needs rehabilitative services to prepare for, obtain, or retain suitable employment.

Any veteran receiving a pension awarded between January 30, 1985 and December 31, 1995 can apply for a vocational rehabilitation evaluation. If an evaluation shows the veteran can achieve a vocational goal if provided the appropriate rehabilitative services, the Department of Veterans Affairs will help develop a plan of services which can lead to employment. There is no requirement that a pensioner participate in an evaluation or training and, if the veteran elects to enter a rehabilitative program, the pension benefit is protected until the veteran is employed.

The Department of Veterans Affairs makes disability payments based on a presumption that veterans who served in Vietnam were exposed to Agent Orange and other herbicides. The conditions the Department of Veterans Affairs recognizes on this basis are soft-tissue sarcoma, non-Hodgkin's lymphoma, chloracne, Hodgkin's disease, Porphyria Cutanea Tarda (PCT), multiple myeloma (a cancer involving the bone marrow), and respiratory cancers (lung, bronchus, larynx, and trachea). All Department of Veterans Affairs medical centers provide a special examination to assist Vietnam veterans who were exposed to Agent Orange in determining their current health status.

Death Benefits – Service-Connected

615. What other service-connected death benefits are available?
Burial Expense Reimbursement

For veterans who died after September 1, 2001, the Department of Veterans Affairs reimburses survivors up to $2,000 (or more, in the case of a federal employee who dies in the performance of duty) for the burial expenses of a veteran who dies as a result of service-connected disability or disabilities. For deaths before September 11, 2001, the reimbursement is up to $1,500.

VA will pay up to $828 toward burial and funeral expenses for deaths on or after October 1, 2022 (if hospitalized by VA at time of death), or $300 toward burial and funeral expenses (if not hospitalized by VA at time of death), and a $828 plot-interment allowance (if not buried in a national cemetery). For deaths on or after December 1, 2001, but before October 1, 2011, VA will pay up to $300 toward burial and funeral expenses and a $300 plot-interment allowance. For deaths on or after April 1, 1988 but before October 1, 2011, VA will pay $300 toward burial and funeral expenses (for Veterans hospitalized by VA at the time of death).

Disposition of Remains and Burial

When a member of the armed forces dies while on active duty, active or inactive training duty, or while receiving hospital treatment for a service-connected ailment, his or her branch of service will provide for the disposition of his or her remains. Additional costs of transportation of the remains of the deceased may be allowed if the veteran died while hospitalized or residing in a Department of Veterans Affairs facility, or while in transit, at Department of Veterans Affairs' expense, to or from a hospital, domiciliary, or a Department of Veterans Affairs regional office.

Other allowances include burial in a national cemetery, American flag, and transportation from place of death to place of burial. The next of kin is also entitled to a headstone, or a headstone monetary allowance (in the event the veteran purchased a headstone prior to death).

Death Gratuity

A lump sum of $100,000 is paid to the survivors of a servicemember who dies on active duty or active or inactive training duty or a former service member that dies within 120 days after separation from active duty. This death gratuity is paid by the branch of service of the deceased to the spouse, if living; otherwise to any children in equal shares; otherwise to parents, brothers, or sisters, as designated by the deceased.

Government Housing

Dependents of a servicemember may remain in government housing for ninety days without charge after the servicemember's death.

Educational Assistance Program

Survivors and dependents may also be eligible for the survivors' and dependents' educational assistance program. The purpose of this program is:

(1)   to enable children to obtain an education they might not otherwise have had an opportunity to obtain; and

(2)   to enable surviving spouses to prepare to support themselves and their families at a standard of living that the veteran, but for death or disability, could have expected to provide.

Pension, Disability, and Death Benefits
Not Service-Connected

616. When is a veteran eligible for nonservice-connected pension, disability, and death benefits?

Veterans with limited income who are discharged under conditions other than dishonorable may be eligible for:

(1)   an Improved Pension;

(2)   Section 306 pension; or

(3)   old law pension. The old law pension is for veterans who died before July 1, 1960.

The pension-eligible veteran must have:

(1)   had ninety days active service during the Mexican border period, World War I, World War II, the Korean Conflict, or Vietnam Era;

(2)   been discharged because of service-connected disability; or

(3)   at the time of death been receiving (or entitled to receive) compensation or retirement pay based on a service-connected disability incurred during wartime.

617. When is a surviving spouse and dependents eligible for nonservice-connected pension, disability, and death benefits?

A surviving spouse must have lived continuously with the veteran from the time of marriage until the veteran's death, except where there was a separation due to the misconduct of, or caused by, the veteran, without fault on the surviving spouse's part. The surviving spouse's valid remarriage or death permanently terminates the benefit. However, if the remarriage is annulled, or is terminated by death or divorce (unless the divorce was secured by fraud or collusion), the surviving spouse is not barred from receiving benefits.

The surviving spouse must have been married to the veteran:

(1)   for at least one year; or

(2)   for any period, if a child was born either before or after the marriage.

For Vietnam Era veterans, the marriage must have taken place before May 8, 1985.

618. Are children entitled to benefits?

Unmarried children and surviving spouses under eighteen of a deceased veteran may be eligible for a pension. The pension is based on need. Regardless of the income limit, however, benefits will be denied a child or surviving spouse who owns capital which, in the Department of Veterans Affairs' judgment, should be consumed for his or her support.

Unmarried children and surviving spouses over eighteen may qualify for pensions in their own right, if they are:

(1)   permanently incapable of self-support since prior to age eighteen, or

(2)   under twenty-three and attending a Department of Veterans Affairs approved educational institution.

619. What is the amount of the Improved Pension?

Under the "Improved Pension Program," which went into effect on January 1, 1979, the maximum annual rates payable (effective December 1, 2021) are presented in the subsequent tables. Note that 2023 numbers were not available as this 2023 edition went to press.

Veterans and Dependents

Veteran without dependent spouse or child	$13,931
Veteran with one dependent (spouse or child)	$18,243
Veteran in need of regular aid and attendance without dependents	$23,238
Veteran in need of regular aid and attendance with one dependent	$27,549
Veteran permanently housebound without dependents	$17,024
Veteran permanently housebound with one dependent	$21,337
Two veterans married to each other	$18.808
Increase for each additional dependent child	$2,382

Spouse and Dependents

Surviving spouse without dependent children	$9,224
Surviving spouse with one dependent child	$12,072
Surviving spouse in need of regular aid and attendance without dependent child	$14,742
Surviving spouse in need of regular aid and attendance with one dependent child	$17,586
Surviving spouse permanently housebound without dependent child	$11,273
Surviving spouse permanently housebound with one dependent child	$15339
Increase for each additional dependent child	$2,351
Child not in custody of veteran's surviving spouse, or child if no living surviving spouse of the veteran	$2,351

Benefits are generally paid monthly and are reduced by the annual countable income of the claimant and any dependent of the claimant. Generally, all nonpension income is included for this purpose, but income paid for certain educational or medical expenses are excluded from the computation.

In addition, the pension may be denied or discontinued if the claimant's net worth is such that it is reasonable that some portion of the estate be used for his support. Additional pension for a child may be denied if the child's net worth is excessive.

Pensioners must provide income and net worth reports to the Department of Veterans Affairs on an annual basis.

620. What is the Section 306 Pension?

The veteran, surviving spouse, and children who came on the pension rolls on or after July 1, 1960 but prior to January 1, 1979 may continue to receive a pension at the monthly rate in effect as of December 31, 1978. The pension will be paid so long as the veteran remains permanently and totally disabled, there is no charge in dependency, and income does not exceed the adjusted income limitation. The income limitation is Consumer Price Index (CPI)-sensitive. There was a 1.3 percent Cost of Living Adjustment effective December 1, 2020.

Pensions range from $5 to $197 monthly for veterans with no dependents, and up to $222 per month for veterans with dependents. If the annual income of a veteran with no children exceeds $15,845, no pension is paid. Where there is one child and annual income exceeds $21,298, no pension is paid.

A surviving spouse with no minor children may receive up to $139 a month but, if annual income exceeds $15,845, no pension is paid. Where there is one child and annual income exceeds $21,298, no pension is paid.

Where there is no eligible surviving spouse, a child may receive sixty-one dollars a month with twenty-six dollars added for each additional child and the total divided among them. A child is not entitled if the income, not counting his or her own earnings, exceeds $12,956.

621. What is the Old Law Pension?

Eligible veterans, their surviving spouses, and children of certain deceased veterans who died before July 1, 1960, may be entitled to an Old Law pension or death benefit. Where the veteran's surviving spouse or children are claiming Old Law death benefits, it must be shown that the veteran died of causes not due to service. The veteran must have served during World War I, World War II, or the Korean conflict.

These pensions are not payable to a veteran or surviving spouse without children, or to an entitled child, if the claimant receives other income over $15.845 annually, or to a veteran or surviving spouse with child if his or her other income is in excess of $21.298.

Government Life Insurance
Servicemembers' Group Life Insurance

622. Who is eligible to be insured automatically under Servicemembers' Group Life Insurance (SGLI)?

Someone can be eligible for full-time SGLI coverage if meeting at least one of these requirements are true:

- Active-duty member of the Army, Navy, Air Force, Space Force, Marines, or Coast Guard, OR

- Commissioned member of the National Oceanic and Atmospheric Administration (NOAA) or the U.S. Public Health Service (USPHS), OR

- cadet or midshipman of the U.S. military academies, OR

- a member, cadet, or midshipman of the Reserve Officers Training Corps (ROTC) engaged in authorized training and practice cruises, OR

- a member of the Ready Reserve or National Guard, assigned to a unit, and scheduled to perform at least 12 periods of inactive training per year, OR

- a volunteer in an Individual Ready Reserve (IRR) mobilization category.

An individual in a non-pay status with Ready Reserve or National Guard must meet BOTH of these requirements:

- scheduled for 12 periods of inactive training for the year, AND

- drilling for points rather than pay.

623. What is the SGLI Online Enrollment System (SOES)?

SOES is the Servicemembers' Group Life Insurance (SGLI) On-Line Enrollment System. It replaces the paper-based SGLI/Family SGLI (FSGLI) enrollment, maintains elections and beneficiary information, and provides 24/7 self-service access to SGLI information. SGLI provides insurance coverage to eligible members of the active and reserve components. SOES centralizes SGLI/FSGLI data into one authoritative system capable of providing consistent SGLI/FSGLI information to members and their leadership.

Beginning October 1, 2018, Coast Guard and NOAA members began managing their Servicemembers' Group Life Insurance (SGLI) coverage using the SGLI Online Enrollment System (SOES). The Coast Guard and NOAA members join the Army, the Navy, Marines, and Air Force in using the new system. The Navy began using SOES on April 5, 2017 and the Air Force on August 2, 2017. The Space Force is also using the Air Force SOES system.[1]

Note

1. https://www.benefits.va.gov/INSURANCE/SOES.asp.

624. What can Service members do in SOES?

Servicemembers may:

- Increase, reduce or cancel SGLI and FSGLI coverage

- Add a beneficiary or edit SGLI beneficiary information

- View, save, print, or email a SGLI Coverage Certificate

If they don't have access to a computer, Members can complete paper elections using the SGLV 8286 and provide it to their Personnel Office to ensure their wishes are known. When computer access is obtained, go into SOES and make the appropriate elections/updates. They will only be able to submit changes via paper if a computer is not readily available, or if the member is only eligible for part-time coverage, such as Guard or reserve members who are not assigned to a unit, or not scheduled to drill at least twelve times per year. Servicemembers need a Common Access Card (CAC) or a DoD Self-Service (DS) Logon.

Changes to beneficiaries, coverage increases, and restorations of coverage are effective immediately. Reductions to coverage amounts and coverage cancellations are not effective until the first day of the month following the date a member makes his/her request. Until that date passes, the member will continue to see the previous coverage amount.

It should be noted that beneficiaries will need to contact the Casualty Office to make a claim.

625. Can reservists and National Guard members with part-time SGLI also access their coverage online?

No, online access is only available to those with full-time SGLI coverage. This includes:

- Active duty members

- Reserve and Guard members assigned to a unit and scheduled to drill twelve times or more per year

SGLI members with part-time coverage will continue to use the paper SGLV 8286 to make coverage and beneficiary changes.

626. Can service members automatically enroll in Veteran's Group Life Insurance through SOES?

No, SOES is only for SGLI coverage for eligible active-duty and reserve components. Service-members may apply for VGLI using the SGLV 8714 or online at www.benefits.va.gov/insurance/

vgli.asp upon separation. VGLI is lifetime renewable group term insurance for Servicemembers who had SGLI at separation or for up to two years following separation due to total disability. Generally, Servicemembers must apply for VGLI within one year and 120 days of separation. Applications received within 240 days of separation do not require a health questionnaire.

NOTE: Servicemembers who are totally disabled at separation may qualify for the SGLI Disability Extension, free coverage for up to two years from separation, before conversion to VGLI. Servicemembers cannot use SOES to apply for this coverage. Instead, servicemembers who believe they may be eligible should use the SGLV 8715.

627. What is the amount and nature of the coverage?

If eligible, service members are **automatically** issued the maximum SGLI coverage of $400,000. If one qualifies for SGLI, they are **automatically** enrolled and do **not** need to apply for coverage.

Servicemembers can make changes to their SGLI coverage. For example, Servicemembers can decline SGLI coverage, select a lesser amount than maximum coverage, designate beneficiaries, and/or make other changes.

SGLI coverage is available in $50,000 increments up to the maximum of $400,000. Covered members receive 120 days of free coverage from their date of separation. Coverage can be extended for up to two years if the Servicemember is totally disabled at separation. Part-time coverage is also provided to Reserve members who do not qualify for full-time coverage (members covered part-time do not receive 120 days of free coverage).

If the individual is totally disabled at the time of separation (unable to work), they can apply for the SGLI Disability Extension, which provides free coverage for up to two years from the date of separation. At the end of the extension period, the individual automatically become eligible for VGLI, subject to premium payments.

The coverage under SGLI is group-term life insurance evidenced by a certificate issued to the insured and is entirely separate from and in addition to any other government life insurance the insured may have or later acquire. The insurance is underwritten by a pool of commercial insurers, with one acting as the primary insurer and the others participating as reinsurers.

CONTACT INFORMATION IS AS FOLLOWS

General Correspondence:
Department of Veterans Affairs Insurance Center
PO Box 42954
Philadelphia, PA 19101

Death Claims, Waiver of Premium Applications, S-DVI, and VMLI Applications:
Department of Veterans Affairs Insurance Center
PO Box 7208
Philadelphia, PA 19101

Loans and Cash Surrenders:
Department of Veterans Affairs Insurance Center
PO Box 7327
Philadelphia, PA 19101

Premium and Loan/Lien Payments:
US Department of Veterans Affairs
VA Life Insurance Center
PO BOX 4019
Portland, OR 97208-4019

File a new Beneficiary Designation:
Online: Update your beneficiary using Online Policy Access
Mail: Department of Veterans Affairs Insurance Center
PO Box 8638

Office of Servicemembers' Group Life Insurance
Contact the Office of Servicemembers' Group Life Insurance (OSGLI) with questions about Veterans' Group Life Insurance (VGLI) or Claims for Servicemembers' Group Life Insurance (SGLI) and Family SGLI (FSGLI).

Toll-free telephone: 1-800-419-1473

Toll-free fax numbers:
Death and accelerated benefits claims only:
1-877-832-4943
All other fax inquiries:
1-800-236-6142

E-mail:
Death and accelerated benefits claims only: osgli.claims@prudential.com
All other inquiries: osgli.osgli@prudential.com

General Correspondence:
Office of Servicemembers' Group Life Insurance
PO Box 41618
Philadelphia, PA 19176-9913

New VGLI Applications and VGLI Reinstatements:
OSGLI
PO Box 41618
Philadelphia, PA 19176-9913

628. What are the eligibility requirements for SGLI?

A servicemember is automatically insured and eligible under full-time SGLI if they are one of the following:

- Active duty member of the Army, Navy, Air Force, Marines, Space Force, or Coast Guard

- Commissioned member of the National Oceanic and Atmospheric Administration (NOAA) or the U.S. Public Health Service (USPHS)

- Cadet or midshipman of the U.S. military academies

- Member, cadet, or midshipman of the Reserve Officers Training Corps (ROTC) engaged in authorized training and practice cruises

- Member of the Ready Reserve or National Guard and are scheduled to perform at least twelve periods of inactive training per year

- Servicemember who volunteers for a mobilization category in the Individual Ready Reserve (IRR)

629. What are the premium rates for SGLI?

The current basic SGLI premium rate is 6 cents per month per $1,000 of insurance. The premium includes an additional $1.00 per month for Traumatic Injury Protection Insurance (TSGLI). These rates were set effect on July 1, 2019 and have not changed since. This is actually a reduction from prior years where it was 7 cents a month per $1,000 and $28 per month for $400,000. The prior rates are in the second chart below.

SGLI PREMIUM RATES – EFFECTIVE JULY 1, 2019 (CURRENT AS OF SEPTEMBER 25, 2022)			
Coverage Amount	Monthly premium rate	TSGLI Premium	Total Monthly Premium Deduction
400,000	$24.00	$1.00	$25.00
350,000	$21.00	$1.00	$22.00
300,000	$18.00	$1.00	$19.00
250,000	$15.00	$1.00	$16.00
200,000	$12.00	$1.00	$13.00
150,000	$9.00	$1.00	$10.00
100,000	$6.00	$1.00	$7.00
50,000	$3.00	$1.00	$4.00

Note: The SGLI premium rate for members who participate in one-day musters or funeral honors duty is also decreasing from $.25 per $100,000 of coverage to $.20 per $100,000 of coverage.

SGLI PREMIUM RATES – JULY 1, 2014 – JUNE 30, 2019			
Coverage Amount	Monthly premium rate	TSGLI Premium	Total Monthly Premium Deduction
400,000	$28.00	$1.00	$29.00
350,000	$24.50	$1.00	$25.50
300,000	$21.00	$1.00	$22.00
250,000	$17.50	$1.00	$18.50
200,000	$14.00	$1.00	$15.00
150,000	$10.50	$1.00	$11.50
100,000	$7.00	$1.00	$8.00
50,000	$3.50	$1.00	$4.50

630. When is coverage terminated and can the policy be converted?

A servicemember may convert SGLI coverage to Veterans' Group Life Insurance (VGLI) within one year and 120 days from discharge. A servicemember has 120 days following separation to apply for VGLI. The member will be sent a computer printout application, usually within forty-five to sixty days following release from duty. The completed application and the first premium must be sent within 120 days after separation from service. If an application for VGLI is filed after this 120-day period, proof of insurability must be provided, and the application must be submitted within one year after the SGLI terminates. A servicemember is not eligible to apply for VGLI more than one year and 120 days after separation from service.

SGLI may be converted to an individual policy of life insurance with a commercial company that participates in SGLI within 120 days following release from active duty. The policies are issued at a standard premium rate regardless of health. A policy cannot be issued for an amount greater than the prior SGLI coverage.

631. Who pays the cost of SGLI?

The government pays, from a revolving fund in the U.S. Treasury, the administrative expenses of the SGLI program and costs traceable to the extra hazard of duty in the uniformed services. The balance is paid by the insured members. As of 2021[1], a serviceman pays, by deduction, 6¢ per month per $1,000, or $24 per month for $400,000 of insurance. A Ready Reservist (one who is assigned to a unit or position that requires at least twelve periods of inactive-duty training that is creditable for retirement purposes) pays the same rates as those servicemen on active duty. Reservists with part-time coverage pay a premium at an annual rate of $24 per year for $400,000 of coverage. There is an additional $1.00 per month charge for TSGLI (Traumatic Injury Protection Insurance), which increases the cost of coverage for $400,000 to $25.00 per month.[2]

Notes

1. Rates set in 2019 but current through 2023.

2. Servicemembers and Veterans Group Life Insurance Handbook https://benefits.va.gov/INSURANCE/resources_handbook_ins.asp (revised August, 2019) (last accessed September 25, 2022).

632. How does a person designate a beneficiary?

Death proceeds are paid to the beneficiary or beneficiaries designated by the insured in writing or in SOES. Designation of a beneficiary is made using Form SGLV 8721.[1] If no named beneficiary survives, payment is made in the following order of preference:

(1) Surviving spouse

(2) Child or children of the insured and descendants of deceased children by representation

(3) Insured parents or their survivors

(4) Executor or administrator of insured's estate

(5) Insured's other next of kin entitled under laws of the insured's domicile at time of his or her death

An adopted child may qualify for SGLI based on the death of both of his or her natural and adopted parents. But no person who consents to the adoption of a child may be recognized as a parent for SGLI purposes. A child, in other words, cannot claim from more than one father or one mother in an adoption case. An illegitimate child is considered the child of his or her natural mother.

If a person otherwise entitled to payment does not make claim within one year after the insured's death, or if payment to that person is prohibited by federal law, payment may be made in the order of precedence as if the person had not survived the insured, and any such payment is a bar to recovery by any other person.

If a person entitled to benefits does not file a claim for benefits within two years after the insured's death and there is no notice that a claim will be made, the Department of Veterans Affairs may pay the benefit to someone it deems is appropriate. Such payment is a bar to recovery by any other person.

The insured may elect settlement of the proceeds either in a lump sum or in thirty-six equal monthly installments. If no election is made by the insured, the payment will be made in a lump sum.

Note

1. https://www.benefits.va.gov/insurance/forms/SGLV_8721_ed2014-06.pdf (Last accessed September 25, 2022).

633. Does payment TSGLI reduce the amount of SGLI payable at the time of the service member's death?

No. Payment of TSGLI has no impact on the amount of SGLI payable. As an example, if a service member is insured with $400,000 of SGLI coverage and had received a TSGLI payment of $50,000 due to a traumatic injury, that member remains insured for the full $400,000 of SGLI coverage, which will be paid upon the service member's death.

634. Does SGLI cover Reservists and National Guard members?

Yes, in addition to coverage while at drill, Reservists and National Guard members that have been assigned to a unit in which they are scheduled to perform at least twelve periods of inactive duty that is creditable for retirement purposes under Title 10 of the U.S. Code, full-time SGLI coverage is in effect 365 days of the year. They are also covered for 120 days following separation or release from duty. Additionally, members of the Individual Ready Reserve (IRR) who volunteer for an assignment to "mobilization" category under 10 U.S.C. Section 12304(i)(1).[1]

Note

1. 10 U.S. Code section 12304 Selected Reserve and Individual Ready Reserve members; order to active duty other than during war or national emergency https://www.law.cornell.edu/uscode/text/10/12304 (Last accessed September 25, 2022).

635. Does SGLI cover deaths as of the result of a terrorist attack?

Yes, SGLI or VGLI proceeds will be paid if a service member dies in a terrorist attack. There are no exclusions that apply to SGLI or VGLI coverage including the location of the death (which includes "black-zoned" or "no-go" areas). Many life insurance policies specifically exclude deaths for acts of war and terrorism SGLI covers every situation.

635.01. Does SGLI cover deaths as of the result of a suicide?

Yes, SGLI or VGLI proceeds will be paid if a service member dies through suicide.

Veterans' Group Life Insurance

636. Who is eligible for Veterans' Group Life Insurance (VGLI)?

Servicemembers leaving active duty can convert their SGLI to Veterans' Group Life Insurance (VGLI) without medical examination. The day after SGLI coverage ceases for any member on active duty for training, or inactive duty training, the policy is automatically converted to VGLI, subject to timely payment of the initial premium. Reservists performing active duty or inactive duty for training under a call or orders specifying a period of less than thirty-one days, who are injured or disabled, and become uninsurable at standard rates, are eligible for VGLI. Also, members of the Individual Ready Reserve and Inactive National Guard are eligible for SGLI. An application for coverage must be filed by a member of these groups.

All Retired Reserve SGLI policyholders will have their policies automatically exchanged for policies under the VGLI program. Retired reservists may retain lifetime coverage under VGLI, instead of being cut off from coverage at age sixty-one or when receiving retired pay (as is the case with Retired Reserve SGLI).

In addition, VGLI is extended generally to reservists and National Guard members who decide to separate prior to reaching twenty-year retirement.

Veterans, who were granted a service-connected disability but are otherwise in good health, may apply to the Department of Veterans Affairs for up to $10,000 life insurance coverage at standard insurance rates, within two years from the date the Department of Veterans Affairs notifies the veteran that the disability has been rated as service-connected. This applies even if the disability rating is zero percent.

An individual may be eligible for VGLI if they meet at least one of the requirements listed below.

- Applicant had part-time Servicemembers' Group Life Insurance (SGLI) as a member of the National Guard or Reserves, and suffered an injury or disability (damage to your body or mind that makes it hard for you to do everyday tasks, including meaningful work) while on duty—including direct traveling to and from duty—that disqualified the individual for standard premium insurance rates, or

- Had SGLI while in the military and within 1 year and 120 days of being released from an active-duty period of 31 or more days, or

- Are within 1 year and 120 days of retiring or being released from the Ready Reserves or National Guard, or

- Are within 1 year and 120 days of assignment to the Individual Ready Reserves (IRR) of a branch of service, or to the Inactive National Guard (ING). This includes members of the United States Public Health Service Inactive Reserve Corps (IRC), or

- Are within 1 year and 120 days of being put on the Temporary Disability Retirement List (TDRL)

Coverage is extended to Veterans and former service members.

637. What is the amount of Veterans' Group Life Insurance and the enrollment and eligibility periods?

The maximum amount of VGLI is $400,000. No one may carry a combined amount of SGLI and VGLI more than $400,000 at any one time. Also, the amount is limited to an amount equal to or less than the amount of the veteran's terminating SGLI. VGLI is available only in increments of $10,000.

VGLI is a renewable five-year term insurance. It has no cash, loan, paid-up, or extended values, and lapses for nonpayment of premiums (except in the case of a mental incompetent who dies within one year after becoming insured). After leaving the military, one can sign up through VGLI for coverage for the amount purchased through SGLI. Coverage can be increased by $25,000 every five years to a maximum of $400,000. The ability to increase coverage ends at age 60.

ENROLLMENT:

An individual has one year and 120 days from date of separation to apply for VGLI. If the applicant applies for coverage within 240 days of date of separation, they will not need to answer health questions.

ELIGIBILITY:

An individual is eligible to apply for VGLI, if they had SGLI, and are within one year and 120 days of the following events:

- Release from active duty or active duty for training under a call or order to duty that does not specify a period of less than thirty-one days

- Separation, retirement, or release from assignment from the Ready Reserves/ National Guard

- Assignment to the Individual Ready Reserves (IRR) of a branch of service or to the Inactive National Guard (ING). This includes members of the United States Public Health Service Inactive Reserve Corps (IRC)

- Placement on the Temporary Disability Retirement List (TDRL)

They are also eligible to apply for VGLI, if they had part-time SGLI and while performing duty, suffered an injury or disability that rendered them uninsurable at standard premium rates. This includes travel directly to and from duty.

VGLI has a reinstatement period of five years after a policy has lapsed. If an insured does not pay their premium when it is due or within a grace period of sixty days, the VGLI coverage will lapse. If VGLI lapses due to failure to pay the premiums on time, the insured will receive a notification of the lapse and a reinstatement form. An insured may apply to reinstate coverage at any time within five years of the date of the unpaid premium. If they apply for reinstatement within six months from the date of lapse, they need only to provide evidence that they are in the same state of health on the date of reinstatement as they were on the date of lapse. Otherwise, they will need to provide proof of good health.

638. How is the beneficiary designated under Veterans' Group Life Insurance?

VGLI proceeds are paid to the designated beneficiary or beneficiaries when a valid claim is established. If no beneficiary survives, or the insured fails to designate a beneficiary, payment is made in the following order of preference:

(1) Surviving spouse

(2) Child or children of the insured and descendants of deceased children by representation

(3)   Insured's parents or survivor of them

(4)   Executor or administrator of insured's estate

(5)   Insured's other next of kin entitled under laws of the insured's domicile at the time of death

There are no restrictions on beneficiary designations, and the insured may change the designation without the knowledge or consent of the beneficiary. This right cannot be waived or restricted. The Department of Veterans Affairs does not recognize state court divorce decrees that require veterans to keep their ex-spouses as beneficiaries on their Department of Veterans Affairs life insurance policies. The forms required for a change of beneficiary may be obtained from the Office of Servicemembers' Group Life Insurance, any Department of Veterans Affairs office, or by calling the Department of Veterans Affairs Insurance Center at 1-800-419-1473.

Any designation of beneficiary or beneficiaries for SGLI filed with a uniformed service is considered a designation for VGLI, but only for sixty days after the VGLI becomes effective. Where the insured is incompetent at the end of the sixty-day period, the designation made for SGLI may continue in force until the disability is removed, but not for more than five years after the effective date of the insured's VGLI.

The designation of beneficiary or beneficiaries, except for a designation by an incompetent, must be in writing signed by the insured and received by the administrative office to be effective.

No claim for VGLI will be denied because of a failure to file a claim within four years of the insured's death.

If the insured, in the application for VGLI, does not limit the beneficiary's payments, the beneficiary can elect to receive the insurance in a single payment or in thirty-six equal monthly installments.

Payment of benefits under VGLI, made to or on account of a beneficiary, are exempt from taxation and the claims of creditors. The benefits are not liable to attachment, levy, or seizure by or under any legal or equitable process.

639. What are the premium rates for Veterans' Group Life Insurance?

Premium rates depend on age. Premium payment options include the use of automatic payments by deductions from Department of Veterans Affairs benefits or retirement checks, and an option to take a one-month discount for annual payments. New rates were established on April 1, 2021[1] and are in effect at the time of this 2023 edition's printing. Veteran's Group Life Insurance Rates were REDUCED SIGNIFICANTLY during 2021 as indicated below.

VETERANS' GROUP LIFE INSURANCE
MONTHLY PREMIUM RATES
Up to age 54

Amount of Insurance	Age 29 or less	Age 30-34	Age 35-39	Age 40-44	Age 45-49	Age 50-54
$400,000	28.00	36.00	48.00	64.00	84.00	132.00
390,000	27.30	35.10	46.80	62.40	81.90	128.70
380,000	26.60	34.20	45.60	60.80	79.80	125.40
370,000	25.90	33.30	44.40	59.20	77.70	122.10
360,000	25.20	32.40	43.20	57.60	75.60	118.80
350,000	24.50	31.50	42.00	56.00	73.50	115.50
340,000	23.80	30.60	40.80	54.40	71.40	112.20
330,000	23.10	29.70	39.60	52.80	69.30	108.90
320,000	22.40	28.80	38.40	51.20	67.20	105.60
310,000	21.70	27.90	37.20	49.60	65.10	102.30
300,000	21.00	27.00	36.00	48.00	63.00	99.00
290,000	20.30	26.10	34.80	46.40	60.90	95.70
280,000	19.60	25.20	33.60	44.80	58.80	92.40
270,000	18.90	24.30	32.40	43.20	56.70	89.10
260,000	18.20	23.40	31.20	41.60	54.60	85.80
250,000	17.50	22.50	30.00	40.00	52.50	82.50
240,000	16.80	21.60	28.80	38.40	50.40	79.20
230,000	16.10	20.70	27.60	36.80	48.30	75.90
220,000	15.40	19.80	26.40	35.20	46.20	72.60
210,000	14.70	18.90	25.20	33.60	44.10	69.30
200,000	14.00	18.00	24.00	32.00	42.00	66.00
190,000	13.30	17.10	22.80	30.40	39.90	62.70
180,000	12.60	16.20	21.60	28.80	37.80	59.40
170,000	11.90	15.30	20.40	27.20	35.70	56.10
160,000	11.20	14.40	19.20	25.60	33.60	52.80
150,000	10.50	13.50	18.00	24.00	31.50	49.50
140,000	9.80	12.60	16.80	22.40	29.40	46.20
130,000	9.10	11.70	15.60	20.80	27.30	42.90
120,000	8.40	10.80	14.40	19.20	25.20	39.60
110,000	7.70	9.90	13.20	17.60	23.10	36.30
100,000	7.00	9.00	12.00	16.00	21.00	33.00
90,000	6.30	8.10	10.80	14.40	18.90	29.70
80,000	5.60	7.20	9.60	12.80	16.80	26.40

Amount of Insurance	Age 29 or less	Age 30-34	Age 35-39	Age 40-44	Age 45-49	Age 50-54
70,000	4.90	6.30	8.40	11.20	14.70	23.10
60,000	4.20	5.40	7.20	9.60	12.60	19.80
50,000	3.50	4.50	6.00	8.00	10.50	16.50
40,000	2.80	3.60	4.80	6.40	8.40	13.20
30,000	2.10	2.70	3.60	4.80	6.30	9.90
20,000	1.40	1.80	2.40	3.20	4.20	6.60
10,000	0.70	0.90	1.20	1.60	2.10	3.30

VETERANS' GROUP LIFE INSURANCE
MONTHLY PREMIUM RATES
Ages 55 and up

Amount of Insurance	Age 55-59	Age 60-64	Age 65-69	Age 70-74	Age 75 -79	Age 80 and up
$400,000	$240.00	$396.00	$588.00	$904.00	$1,712.00	$1,800.00
390,000	$234.00	$386.10	$573.30	$881.40	$1,669.20	$1,755.00
380,000	$228.00	$376.20	$558.60	$858.80	$1,626.40	$1,710.00
370,000	$222.00	$366.30	$543.90	$836.20	$1,583.60	$1,665.00
360,000	$216.00	$356.40	$529.20	$813.60	$1,540.80	$1,620.00
350,000	$210.00	$346.50	$514.50	$791.00	$1,498.00	$1,575.00
340,000	$204.00	$336.60	$499.80	$768.40	$1,455.20	$1,530.00
330,000	$198.00	$326.70	$485.10	$745.80	$1,412.40	$1,485.00
320,000	$192.00	$316.80	$470.40	$723.20	$1,369.60	$1,440.00
310,000	$186.00	$306.90	$455.70	$700.60	$1,326.80	$1,395.00
300,000	$180.00	$297.00	$441.00	$678.00	$1,284.00	$1,350.00
290,000	$174.00	$287.10	$426.30	$655.40	$1,241.20	$1,305.00
280,000	$168.00	$277.20	$411.60	$632.80	$1,198.40	$1,260.00
270,000	$162.00	$267.30	$396.90	$610.20	$1,155.60	$1,215.00
260,000	$156.00	$257.40	$382.20	$587.60	$1,112.80	$1,170.00
250,000	$150.00	$247.50	$367.50	$565.00	$1,070.00	$1,125.00
240,000	$144.00	$237.60	$352.80	$542.40	$1,027.20	$1,080.00
230,000	$138.00	$227.70	$338.10	$519.80	$984.40	$1,035.00
220,000	$132.00	$217.80	$323.40	$497.20	$941.60	$990.00
210,000	$126.00	$207.90	$308.70	$474.60	$898.80	$945.00
200,000	$120.00	$198.00	$294.00	$452.00	$856.00	$900.00
190,000	$114.00	$188.10	$279.30	$429.40	$813.20	$855.00
180,000	$108.00	$178.20	$264.60	$406.80	$770.40	$810.00

Amount of Insurance	Age 55-59	Age 60-64	Age 65-69	Age 70-74	Age 75 -79	Age 80 and up
170,000	$102.00	$168.30	$249.90	$384.20	$727.60	$765.00
160,000	$96.00	$158.40	$235.20	$361.60	$684.80	$720.00
150,000	$90.00	$148.50	$220.50	$339.00	$642.00	$675.00
140,000	$84.00	$138.60	$205.80	$316.40	$599.20	$630.00
130,000	$78.00	$128.70	$191.10	$293.80	$556.40	$585.00
120,000	$72.00	$118.80	$176.40	$271.20	$513.60	$540.00
110,000	$66.00	$108.90	$161.70	$248.60	$470.80	$495.00
100,000	$60.00	$99.00	$147.00	$226.00	$428.00	$450.00
90,000	$54.00	$89.10	$132.30	$203.40	$385.20	$405.00
80,000	$48.00	$79.20	$117.60	$180.80	$342.40	$360.00
70,000	$42.00	$69.30	$102.90	$158.20	$299.60	$315.00
60,000	$36.00	$59.40	$88.20	$135.60	$256.80	$270.00
50,000	$30.00	$49.50	$73.50	$113.00	$214.00	$225.00
40,000	$24.00	$39.60	$58.80	$90.40	$171.20	$180.00
30,000	$18.00	$29.70	$44.10	$67.80	$128.40	$135.00
20,000	$12.00	$19.80	$29.40	$45.20	$85.60	$90.00
10,000	$6.00	$9.90	$14.70	$22.60	$42.80	$45.00

These premium rates are subject to change, depending on emerging experience.

Note

1. https://www.benefits.va.gov/INSURANCE/docs/VGLI_Rates_04-2021.pdf (New Rates established April 1, 2021). Last accessed September 25, 2022).

640. How is Veterans' Group Life Insurance converted to an individual policy?

VGLI may be converted to an individual policy at any time[1], upon written application for conversion to the participating company selected and payment of the required premiums. The individual policy will be issued without medical examination on a plan currently written by the company.

The process is as follows - the policyholder must:

- Select a company from the listing of participating companies,[2]

- Apply to a local sales office of the company selected,

- Obtain a letter from OSGLI verifying coverage (VGLI Conversion Notice),

- Give a copy of that notice to the agent who takes the application.

Policyholders may convert their coverage to a commercial policy at standard premium rates without having to provide proof of good health. The conversion policy must be a permanent policy, such as a whole life policy.

Other types of policies such as Term, Variable Life, or Universal Life Insurance are not allowed as conversion policies. In addition, supplementary policy benefits such as Accidental Death and Dismemberment or Waiver of Premium for Disability are not considered part of the conversion policy.

On request, the administrative office will furnish a list of life insurance companies participating in the program and companies (not participating in the program) that meet qualifying criteria, terms, and conditions established by the administrator, and that agree to sell insurance to former members in accordance with the rules described.

Notes

1. https://www.benefits.va.gov/INSURANCE/forms/ParticList.htm (Last accessed September 25, 2022).
2. List of participating companies https://www.benefits.va.gov/INSURANCE/resources-forms.asp (last accessed September 25, 2022).

641. Will SGLI or TSGLI pay benefits if an insured dies while wearing privately-owned body armor or helmet?

SGLI claims are paid regardless of body armor or helmet type. Wearing body armor or a helmet is not a requirement for a SGLI or TSGLI claim to be paid.

642. Will SGLI or VGLI pay deny benefits if an insured is not complying with seatbelt or helmet laws and dies in a traffic accident?

SGLI or VGLI claims are paid regardless of whether the member was or was not wearing a seatbelt or, in the case of a motorcycle accident, whether or not a helmet was being worn.

643. Are there limitations of effectiveness of coverage for National Guard or Reservists?

In the case of Reservists or a National Guard member assigned to a unit and scheduled to perform at least twelve periods of inactive duty that is creditable for retirement purposes, full-time SGLI coverage is in effect 365 days of the year. Coverage also extends for 120 days following separation or release from duty.

BENEFITS FOR FEDERAL GOVERNMENT EMPLOYEES

Introduction

644. What are the two retirement systems for federal employees?

There are two retirement systems for federal employees: The **Civil Service Retirement System (CSRS)** and the **Federal Employees' Retirement System (FERS).**

CSRS

The CSRS, created on August 1, 1920, was the only retirement system for federal employees until the FERS became public law in 1986. The Civil Service Retirement System (CSRS) is a defined benefit, contributory retirement system. Employees share in the expense of the annuities to which they become entitled. CSRS covered employees contribute 7, 7 ½, or 8 percent of pay to CSRS and, while they generally pay no Social Security retirement, survivor, and disability (OASDI) tax, they must pay the Medicare tax (currently 1.45 percent of pay). The employing agency matches the employee's CSRS contributions. CSRS employees may increase their earned annuity by contributing up to 10 percent of the basic pay for their creditable service to a voluntary contribution account. Employees may also pay into the Thrift Savings Plan, a plan which offers tax-deferred contributions. CSRS employees may increase their earned annuity by contributing up to 10 percent of the basic pay for their creditable service to a voluntary contribution account. Employees may also contribute a portion of pay to the Thrift Savings Plan (TSP), there is no Government contribution, but the employee contributions are tax-deferred.

FERS

Created a new federal retirement program coordinated with Social Security retirement benefits for federal employees hired after 1983. While federal employees who remain in CSRS are exempt from Social Security taxes, FERS employees are covered under Social Security. FERS also provides a guaranteed basic annuity and a tax-deferred savings plan similar to a Section 401(k) retirement plan.

FERS is a retirement plan that provides three different sources of benefits:

- a Basic Benefit Plan,

- Social Security, and

- the Thrift Savings Plan (TSP).

Two of the three parts of FERS (Social Security and the TSP) are transferrable from federal service to the private sector. The Basic Benefit and Social Security parts of FERS require paying a contribution each pay period. The federal agency withholds the cost of the Basic Benefit and

Social Security from pay as payroll deductions as well as contributing the governmental share. Upon retirement, the retiree receives annuity payments each month until death. The Basic Plan vests members at five years of service. Individuals contribute the difference between 7 percent of their basic pay and the Social Security OASDI tax rate.

The Thrift Savings Plan is a defined contribution plan that shares similarities with 401(k) pension plans. The TSP part of FERS is an account that that is automatically established. Each pay period, there is a deposit made by the federal agency equal to 1 percent of the basic pay for the pay period into the TSP account of which the member is vested after three years. Employees can also make their own contributions to the TSP account which are matched by the agency. Contributions are tax-deferred. The government matches 100 percent of the employee's contribution for the first three percent; 50 percent of the employee's contributions for the next two percent; zero percent of the employee's contributions above five percent. An individual can contribute a maximum of 10 percent of basic pay each pay period subject to Internal Revenue Service restrictions. Individuals are immediately vested in their own contributions, and their contributions (and earnings from all the contributions) are tax deferred.

The Thrift Savings Plan is administered by the Federal Retirement Thrift Investment Board.

Federal Employees' Retirement System

645. Who is covered under the Federal Employees' Retirement System?

The Federal Employees' Retirement System (FERS) is a three-tier retirement system for federal workers who began work with the government after 1983. In addition, a number of federal employees hired before 1984 elected to transfer from the Civil Service Retirement System (CSRS) to FERS during a 1987 transfer period.

The following are excluded from FERS coverage:

- A person not covered by Social Security, including a person covered by full CSRS.

- A person who has served without a break in service of more than 365 days since December 31, 1983, in the position of:

    o   Vice President of the United States;

    o   member of Congress (U.S. House of Representatives and the U.S. Senate);

    o   a senior executive Service or Senior Foreign Service non-career appointee; or

    o   persons appointed by the President or Vice President to positions where the maximum rate of basic pay is at or above the rate for Level V of the Executive Schedule.

- An employee who is rehired after December 31, 1986 who has had a break in service and who, at the time of the last separation from the service, had at least five years of civilian service creditable under CSRS rules, any part of which was covered by CSRS or the Foreign Service Retirement system.

- An employee who has not had a break in service of more than three days ending after December 31, 1986 and who, as of December 31, 1986, had at least five years of creditable civilian service under CSRS rules (even if none of this service was covered by CSRS).

646. What is creditable service under FERS?

Creditable service under FERS usually includes:

- Federal covered service, that is, service in which the individual's pay is subject to FERS retirement deductions, such as service under a career or career conditional appointment

- Unused Sick Leave under FERS can be used to increase an individual's total creditable service for annuity computation purposes only

- Federal service performed before 1989, where an employee's pay is not subject to retirement deductions, such as service under a temporary appointment, as long as a deposit is paid. The following are exceptions to the rule that the service must have been performed before 1989:

  - Part-time, Intermittent, Temporary "PIT" service performed abroad after December 31, 1988 and before May 24, 1998, under a temporary part-time or intermittent appointment pursuant to sections 309 and 311 of the Foreign Service Act of 1980

  - Service performed under the Foreign Service Pension System

  - Service as a Senate Employee Child Care Center worker

  - Service as a volunteer or volunteer leader in the Peace Corps

  - Service as a VISTA volunteer

  - Service before 12/31/1990 with either the Democratic or Republican Senatorial Campaign or National Congressional Committees

  - Service before 12/21/2000 with the Library of Congress Child Development Center

  - Service as a Senior Official

  - Congressional Employees that do no elect program coverage and are subject to the Social Security Amendments of 1983

  - Service performed under a Federal Reserve Bank Plan

- Non-appropriated fund instrumentality (NAF) service under P.L. 107-107 that can be used for title to an annuity under the FERS, but not in the computation

- CSRS refund service that flips to FERS

NOTE ON DEPOSITS: A deposit is the payment for a period of employment when retirement deductions were not withheld from a person's salary. The deposit amount is, generally, 1.3 percent of salary plus interest. The employee is not required to make this type of payment. However, not making the payment will eliminate this service from being used for title or computation purposes.

647. Who is eligible for FERS benefits?

Unreduced retirement benefits are provided at age sixty with twenty or more years of service, at age sixty-two with five or more years of service, and at "minimum retirement age" with thirty years of service. The Minimum Retirement Age (MRA) is currently fifty-seven. FERS uses "the Rule of 80," meaning to be eligible for retirement, the employee must reach eighty years when combining chronological years and years of service.

Eligibility is determined by age and number of years of creditable service. In some cases, the individual must reach Minimum Retirement Age (MRA).

Eligibility information:

If born	Minimum Retirement Age is
Before 1948	55 years
In 1948	55 years and 2 months
In 1949	55 years and 4 months
In 1950	55 years and 6 months
In 1951	55 years and 8 months
In 1952	55 and 10 months
In 1953-1964	56 years
In 1965	56 years and 2 months
In 1966	56 years and 4 months
In 1967	56 years and 6 months
In 1968	56 years and 8 months
In 1969	56 years and 10 months
In 1970 and after	57 years

Beginning in the year 2021, the minimum retirement age again increases by two-month increments until the year 2027. The minimum retirement age for employees with thirty or more years of service is fifty-seven in the year 2027 and after. The minimum retirement age for reduced benefits is also being gradually increased from fifty-five to fifty-seven. An employee must have at least ten years of service to be eligible for reduced retirement benefits. For an employee retiring with less than thirty years of service, a reduction of 5 percent per year for each year under age sixty-two is imposed. Thus, benefits for an employee retiring at age fifty-five are reduced 35 percent.

An employee can leave government employment prior to the date that he is eligible for a retirement benefit and still be eligible for a Basic Annuity at a later date. If the employee has five years of creditable service and does not withdraw contributions when he terminates government service, he may receive a deferred, unreduced annuity when he attains age sixty-two with at least five years of civil service employment; age sixty with at least twenty years of service; or at minimum retirement age (currently age fifty-five) with at least thirty years of service.

An employee is entitled to a Basic Annuity at age fifty with twenty years of service, or at any age after completing twenty-five years of service, if:

(1)   his retirement is involuntary (except by removal by cause for misconduct or delinquency) and he did not decline a reasonable offer for a position which is not lower than two grades below his present position; or

(2)   his retirement is voluntary because his agency is undergoing a major reduction in employees, reorganization, or a transfer of function in which a number of employees are separated or downgraded.

648. What is Early Retirement under FERS?

The early retirement benefit is available in certain involuntary separation cases and in cases of voluntary separations during a major reorganization or reduction in force. To be eligible, an individual must either have twenty years of service and be age fifty or older; or have twenty-five years of service at any age.

The term "involuntary separation" means any separation against the will and without the consent of the employee, other than "for cause" for misconduct or delinquency. The most common cause of an involuntary separation is a reduction in force. Another frequent cause for an involuntary separation is when the location of an office or unit is moved to an area outside the commuting area of the old worksite. Employees who decline reasonable offers of other positions are not eligible for discontinued service annuities. An exception exists if a position was accepted under a "general mobility" agreement where the individual agreed to be subject to geographic reassignment. In this instance, the individual would not be eligible for discontinued service annuity rights if the position was moved outside the commuting area.

A separation would not qualify for discontinued service if an agency

•   makes an individual a reasonable offer and they choose to decline the offer and resign, they will not qualify for discontinued service retirement; or

•   separates the individual by adverse action procedures for not complying with a directed reassignment to a position that is a "reasonable offer".

A reasonable offer is defined as:

- a written offer of another position in the same agency and commuting area for which the individual is qualified, and

- which is no more than two grades or pay levels below the current grade or pay level.

The commuting area is defined as the geographic area that usually constitutes one area for employment purposes. It includes any population center (or two or more neighboring ones) and the surrounding localities in which people live and reasonably can be expected to travel back and forth daily in their usual employment.

649. What is Immediate Retirement under FERS?

An immediate retirement benefit is one that begins within thirty days from the date the individual stops working. A person is entitled to the immediate retirement benefit if they meet one of the following requirements:

- age sixty-two with five years of service (called 62+5)

- age sixty with twenty years of service (called 60+20)

- Minimum Retirement Age and thirty years of service (called MRA+30)

- Minimum Retirement Age and ten years of service (called MRA+10)

If retiring at the MRA with at least ten but less than thirty years of service, the benefit will be reduced by 5 percent per year for each year under age sixty-two, unless the person has at least twenty years of service and the benefit starts when at age sixty or later.

A pension will not get a Cost of Living Adjustment (COLA) until age 62. Additionally, there will be no retroactive COLA increases.

650. What is Deferred Retirement under FERS?

This refers to delayed payment of benefits until the age and service requirements are met for the immediate retirement benefit. Eligibility is based on at least five years of creditable civilian services with benefits being available as follows:

- Aged sixty-two with five years of service

- Minimum Retirement Age and thirty years of service

- Minimum Retirement Age with ten years of service

  - Note that retiring at MRA with at least ten years of service but less than thirty years of service will cause the benefit to be reduced by 5 percent a year for each year until the beneficiary is age sixty-two, unless the individual has twenty years of service and the benefit starts at age sixty or later.

651. What is Disability Retirement under FERS?

Disability Retirement is available at any age as long as the person has at least eighteen months of service. The requirements for disability retirement are:

- One must have become disabled, while employed in a position subject to FERS, because of a disease or injury, for useful and efficient service in their current position.

- The disability must be expected to last at least one year.

- The individual's agency must certify that it is unable to accommodate the individual's disabling medical condition in their present position and that it has considered them for any vacant position in the same agency at the same grade/pay level, within the same commuting area, for which they are qualified for reassignment.

- The individual, their guardian, or other interested person must apply before their separation from service or within one year thereafter. The application must be received by either OPM or their former employing agency within one year of the date of their separation. This time limit can be waived only if the individual were mentally incompetent on the date of separation or within one year of this date.

- The individual must apply for social security disability benefits. Application for disability retirement under FERS requires an application for social security benefits. If the application for social security disability benefits is withdrawn for any reason, OPM will dismiss the FERS disability retirement application upon notification by the Social Security Administration.

- The Office of Personnel Management advises that employees should consider application for disability retirement "only after you have provided your employing agency with complete documentation of your medical condition and your agency has exhausted all reasonable attempts to retain you in a productive capacity, through accommodation or reassignment".[1]

Note

1. https://www.opm.gov (last accessed September 25, 2022).

652. What is the new Phased Retirement benefit?

Phased Retirement is a human resources process that allows full-time employees to work part-time schedules while beginning to draw retirement benefits. Essentially, they "retire" from PART of their job while continuing to execute other parts of their role. This allows managers to better provide unique mentoring opportunities for employees while increasing access to the decades of institutional knowledge and experience that retirees can provide. This is fully voluntary and is not an entitlement and must be approved by the agency. This benefit was developed in 2014 with final regulations issued on August 8, 2014 and federal agencies beginning to use it on November 6, 2014. and has been clarified as below for 2019.

Working Percentage and Official Established Hours for Phased Employment

- The established working percentage for phased retirement is 50 percent, which equates to forty hours per pay period.

- The working percentage of 50 percent is defined as half of the full-time schedule of an eighty-hour per pay period.[1]

- There are no exceptions that allow employees to work less than 50 percent of the full-time schedule.

- Phased employees must commit 20 percent of their new part-time schedule to mentoring activities as outlined in the phased retirement guidelines.

- By regulation, only the Director of the Office of Personnel Management may provide for working percentages other than the currently established working percentage.[2] The Director has not provided for any new working percentages pursuant to her/his authority.

- Agencies do not have the authority to approve a working percentage other than 50 percent.

- The working percentage for a phased retiree may not be changed during the phased retiree's phased retirement period.[3]

- In rare and exceptional circumstances, an authorized agency official may approve an employee in phased retirement status to temporarily perform hours of work in excess of the officially established work schedule of forty hours per pay period as long as certain requirements are met.

Eligibility

When an employee elects and participates in the phased retirement program, their annuity will be calculated as if they were fully retired and then it will be divided in half. The employee will receive 50 percent of their annuity while also receiving 50 percent of their regular pay, since they are continuing to work in a part time role. When they completely retire, OPM will calculate their annuity based on a salary as if they were working full time. In general, this final amount will be more than if the employee fully retired and did not keep working part time. The final annuity amount will be the basis for any other federal retirement benefits, like for survivors or those with a disability.

Participation is voluntary, and requires the mutual agreement of both the employee and the federal agency. Eligibility is limited to employees that have been employed on a full-time basis for the previous three years.

- Under CSRS, the employee must be eligible for immediate retirement with at least 30 years of service at age 55, or with 20 years of service at age 60.

- Under FERS, the employee must be eligible for immediate retirement with at least 30 years of service at MRA (minimum retirement age 55-57 depending upon year of birth), or with 20 years of service at age 60.

Notes

1. 5 CFR para. 831.1702.
2. 5 U.S.C. §§ 8331a(b) and 8412a(b).
3. 5 U.S.C. § 8412a.

652.01. What roles are not eligible for phased retirement?

- Disability candidates, FERS employees retiring under MRA+10 provisions, reemployed annuitants, and individuals who have already served a period of phased retirement and returned to full-time duty (opted out) are all excluded from participation in the phased retirement program.

- Additionally, law enforcement officers, fire fighters, air traffic controllers, nuclear materials couriers, Capitol Police, Supreme Court Police, and some Customs and Border Protection (CBP) officers are subject to mandatory retirement provisions and may also be excluded.

- Individuals working special work schedules that don't allow a recurring part-time schedule are also excluded, including fire fighters covered by 5 USC 5545b and nurses working under 38 USC 7456 or 7456A.

652.02. Can someone opt out of phased retirement?

- To opt out of phased retirement, the employee and approving agency official must complete part 2A of the SF-3116 and send a copy to OPM's point of contact email address: phase-dret@opm.gov.[1]

- Phased retirement is a one-time deal. Once a phased retiree opts out of the program and returns to full time employment, they aren't allowed to take part in phased retirement again.

Note

1. https://www.opm.gov/forms/pdf_fill/sf3116.pdf (Last accessed September 25, 2022).

653. Can military retirement pay be credited under FERS?

Depends. A person cannot receive credit for any military service in a FERS retirement computation, if receiving military retirement pay, unless they were awarded the retirement pay:

- due to a service-connected disability either incurred in combat with an enemy of the United States or caused by an instrumentality of war and incurred in the line of duty during a period of war, or

- under the provisions of Chapter 1223, Title 10, U.S.C. (pertaining to retirement from a reserve component of the Armed Forces).[1]

However, a person can elect to waive the retirement pay and have the military service added to their civilian service in computing the FERS annuity. In addition to waiving the military retirement pay, they MUST pay a deposit for their post 1956 military deposit prior to separating from the agency in order for it to be creditable in the FERS retirement.

Note

1. Retired Pay for Non-Regular Service, https://www.law.cornell.edu/uscode/text/10/subtitle-E/part-II/chapter-1223 (last accessed September 25, 2022).

Basic Annuity

654. What is the Basic Annuity?

Social Security is the **first tier** of benefits. Social Security includes retirement, disability, and survivor benefits, and health insurance benefits under Medicare.

The Basic Annuity is the **second tier** of benefits under FERS.

The FERS annuity is based on a percentage multiplied by

- length of Federal service eligible for FERS retirement

    o this is "creditable Federal service", and

    o an employee must have five years minimum creditable service

- the "High-3" period rate of pay

    o the average annual rate of basic pay of the employee's highest-paid consecutive three years of service

    o the "high-3" period does not have to be the last three years of service – but generally is those years

The FERS annuity begins after one full calendar month after the employee's retirement. Under this system, it is best to retire on the last day of the month.

The Basic Annuity provides retirement, disability, and survivor benefits in addition to those provided by Social Security. The Basic Annuity guarantees a specific monthly retirement payment, based on the employee's age, length of creditable service, and "high-3" years' average salary.

655. How much must an employee contribute to the Basic Annuity?

From the time of the creation of FERS and up through 2012, ALL employees contributed 0.8 percent of his or her basic pay to the Basic Annuity. New Federal workers starting in 2013 contributed 3.1 percent while those hired before 2013 continue to contribute 0.8 percent. The Bipartisan Budget Act of 2013 increased the contribution for those hired after December 31, 2013 to 4.4 percent.

Certain FERS members pay an additional 0.5 percent to the Basic Annuity. These members include firefighters, law enforcement personnel, air traffic controllers, members of Congress, and Congressional employees. Basic pay does not include bonuses, overtime pay, military pay, holiday pay, cash awards, or special allowances given in addition to basic pay. The federal government makes a contribution to the Basic Annuity plan pursuant to a formula.

656. What annuities are available to a retiring employee?

The following annuities are available to a retiring federal employee:

- An annuity, with no survivor benefit

- A lump-sum credit of the employee's contributions (excluding interest), with a reduced annuity

- An annuity to the employee for life, with a survivor annuity payable for the life of the surviving spouse

- A lump-sum credit of the employee's contributions (excluding interest), with a reduced annuity that is further reduced to provide a survivor benefit

- A reduced annuity with a survivor benefit to a person with an insurable interest, provided the employee is in good health

Note, however, that an employee cannot elect against providing survivor benefits to his spouse, unless his spouse consents to the election in writing.

657. What is the amount of the Basic Annuity?

The amount of the Basic Annuity depends on the employee's years of service and highest three-year (high-3) average salary. It also depends on whether an annuity supplement is added into the Basic Annuity formula.

For employees under age sixty-two (or age sixty-two or older with less than twenty years of FERS service), the formula, not including the supplement where applicable, is:

- 1.0 percent × high-3 average salary times length of service.

For employees age sixty-two or older with at least twenty years of FERS service, the formula is:

- 1.1 percent × high-3 average salary times length of service.

(No annuity supplement is payable if the employee is age sixty-two or older.)

For certain employees, including law enforcement officers, firefighters, air traffic controllers, and employees of Congress, the formula is:

- 1.7 percent × high-3 average salary times years of service up to twenty years; plus

- 1.0 percent × high-3 average salary times years of service over twenty years; plus

- the annuity supplement, where applicable.

All periods of creditable service are totaled to determine length of service. Years and months of creditable service (extra days are dropped) are then used in the annuity computation formula.

High-3 average salary is the highest pay obtainable by averaging an employee's rates of basic pay in effect over any three consecutive years of service. The three years need not be continuous, but they must consist of consecutive periods of service. In other words, two or more separate periods of employment that follow each other can be joined to make up the three consecutive years.

> *Example.* Steve James retires at age 65 after 30 years of civil service employment. His High-3 average salary is $31,000 ($60,000 + $61,000 + $62,000 ÷ 3 = $61,000). His FERS benefit is computed as follows:
>
> (1)   1.1 percent × $61,000 = $671
>
> (2) $671 × 30 years of service = $20,130 Basic Annuity.

658. How is the Basic Annuity adjusted for cost-of-living increases?

The Basic Annuity for employees age sixty-two or older is adjusted for cost-of-living increases pursuant to the following schedule:

(1)   Where the change in the Consumer Price Index for All Urban Wage Earners and Clerical Workers (CPI) for the year is less than 2.0 percent, the annuity is increased by the full amount of the CPI increase.

(2)   Where the change in the CPI for the year is at least 2.0 percent, but is not more than 3.0 percent, the annuity is increased by 2.0 percent.

(3)   Where the change in the CPI for the year is more than 3.0 percent, the annuity is increased by the CPI less 1 percent. For example, if the CPI increases 4.5 percent, the Basic Annuity will increase 3.5 percent.

New amounts are rounded down to the whole dollar. Cost of living increases for 2022 were 5.9 percent for CSRS and 4.9 percent for FERS. Cost of living increases for 2023 have not yet been announced but are expected to be substantial. Cost of living increases have been as follows:

The following chart provides a historical perspective of cost-of-living increases

RETIREE COLAs		
Year	CSRS Rate	FERS Rate
2023	TBD	TBD
2022	5.9	4.8
2021	1.3	1.3
2020	1.6	1.6
2019	2.8	2.0
2018	2.0	2.0
2017	0.3	0.3
2016	0	0
2015	1.7	1.7
2014	1.5	1.5
2013	1.7	1.7
2012	3.6	2.6
2011	0	0
2010	0	0
2009	5.8	4.8
2008	2.3	2.0
2007	3.3	2.3
2006	4.1	3.1
2005	2.7	2.0
2004	2.1	2.0
2003	1.4	1.4
2002	2.6	2.0
2001	3.5	2.5
2000	2.4	2.0
1999	1.3	1.3
1998	2.1	2.0
1997	2.9	2.0
1995	2.6	2.0
1994	2.6	2.0
1993	3.0	2.0
1992	3.7	2.7
1991	5.4	4.4
1990	4.7	3.7
1989	4.0	3.0
1988	4.2	-
1987	1.3	-

RETIREE COLAs		
Year	CSRS Rate	FERS Rate
1986	0.0	-
1985	3.5	-
1984	3.9	-
1983	8.7	-
1982	4.4	-
1981	7.7	-
1980	6.0	-

659. What is the Annuity Supplement?

An Annuity Supplement is added to the Basic Annuity as a substitute for Social Security, when the employee is receiving the Basic Annuity and is under age sixty-two. It is equal to the estimated amount of Social Security benefits that the employee would be eligible to receive at age sixty-two based on civil service employment earnings. The supplement ends when the employee first becomes eligible for a Social Security retirement benefit (age sixty-two).

The supplement is payable to:

(1)   employees who retire after the minimum retirement age (currently between ages fifty-six and fifty-seven) with thirty years of service;

(2)   employees who retire at age sixty with twenty years of service; and

(3)   employees who retire involuntarily and have reached minimum retirement age (currently age fifty-six).

The supplement is not subject to cost-of-living increases and is reduced for excess earnings after retirement in much the same way that Social Security benefits are reduced for excess earnings. In 2022, the supplement was reduced by one dollar for every two dollars that the beneficiary earns over $19.560. For 2023, the supplement will be reduced by one dollar for every two dollars earned over $21,240.

Survivor Benefits

660. What survivor benefits are payable under FERS?

The types of benefits payable are:

• Current spouse survivor annuity

• Former spouse annuity that is voluntarily elected or awarded by a court order in divorces granted on or after May 7, 1985

• A one-time lump sum benefit

Under FERS, a basic employee death benefit may be payable to the surviving widow, widower, or former spouse of an employee who dies while employed.

Survivor benefits are paid upon the death of an employee or retired civil service employee. Benefits are paid on a monthly basis or in a lump sum to eligible survivors. The spouse, former spouse, and dependent children of a deceased employee may be entitled to a survivor annuity.

A spouse may be entitled to a "post-retirement survivor benefit". The annuity of a married employee who retires is generally reduced by 10 percent to provide a survivor annuity for the spouse, unless the employee and his or her spouse both waive the survivor annuity. A surviving spouse is entitled to 50 percent of the employee's unreduced annuity increased by cost-of-living benefit adjustments. There is also a 5 percent reduction in the annuity of a married employee who retires and selects a 25 percent survivor annuity.

There is a permanent actuarial reduction in the retiree's annuity in the case of a retiree who marries after retirement and elects a survivor benefit. The reduction may not be more than 25 percent of the retiree's annuity. The reduction is permanent and unaffected by any future termination of the marriage.

The surviving spouse must have been married to the employee for at least nine months or must be the parent of a child of the marriage at the time of death, or the death of the retired employee must have been accidental.

If the survivor is under age sixty and Social Security survivor benefits are not payable, benefits are the lesser of:

(1)   current CSRS survivor benefits; or

(2)   50 percent (25 percent if elected) of accrued annuity plus a Social Security "equivalent". When Social Security survivor benefits are payable, FERS pays 50 percent (25 percent if elected) of the deceased retiree's annuity.

If the employee was unmarried at the time of retirement and then married after retirement, he or she may elect a reduced annuity with a survivor benefit for his or her spouse. Such an election must take place within two years after the marriage.

If the spouse dies before the retired employee, and the retired employee remarries, the new spouse is eligible to receive the same survivor benefits as the former spouse. The retired employee must elect to take a reduced annuity with a survivor benefit for his or her new spouse.

A retired employee and spouse who have elected against a survivor benefit can change their election within eighteen months. The retired employee must pay the full cost of providing the survivor annuity if an election is made during this second election period.

There is also a survivor benefit for the spouse of an employee who dies prior to retirement. The surviving spouse is entitled to the basic employee death benefit, which is a guaranteed amount of around $37,000 for 2022, plus 50 percent of the employee's final salary or, if higher, his or her "high-3" average. In addition, if the deceased employee completed ten or more years of service, the surviving spouse is entitled to an annuity equal to 50 percent of the unreduced annuity the employee would have been entitled to had he or she reached retirement age. Survivor benefits are subject to cost-of-living adjustments. The cost of living increase for 2022 was 5.9 percent for CSRS and 4.9 percent for FERS.

The $37,000 payment, which is indexed to the Consumer Price Index, can be paid in a lump sum or in monthly installments over a three-year period.

The surviving spouse must have been married to the employee for at least nine months or must be the parent of a child of the marriage, or the death of the employee must have been accidental. The deceased employee must also have at least eighteen months of creditable service while subject to FERS.

660.01. What is a full survivor benefit?

If someone retires under the Civil Service Retirement System (CSRS), the maximum survivor benefit payable is 55 percent of the unreduced annual benefit.

If one retires under the Federal Employees Retirement System (FERS), the maximum survivor benefit payable is 50 percent of the unreduced annual benefit.

660.02. What elections can be made for survivor benefits?

An employee can make one of the following elections:

- No survivor benefit

- A partially reduced annuity

- A fully reduced annuity

These elections provide the following benefits to the survivor spouse:

- No survivor benefit

- A full or partial annuity for a spouse

- A full or partial annuity for a former spouse

- A combination of a full or partial annuity for a spouse and for a former spouse

There is an opportunity to increase survivor benefits within 18 months after the annuity begins. However, this election may be more expensive than the one made at retirement.

661. Is the former spouse of a deceased employee entitled to a survivor benefit?

Yes, the former spouse of a deceased employee may be entitled to a survivor benefit if he or she:

(1)   was married to the deceased employee for at least nine months;

(2)   has not remarried prior to age fifty-five; and

(3)   a court order or court-approved property settlement agreement provides for payment of a survivor annuity to the former spouse.

The survivor annuity is payable to a former spouse when:

(1)   the deceased employee has at least eighteen months of creditable service under FERS; or

(2)   the deceased former employee has title to a deferred annuity and has ten years of service.

A former spouse who does not meet the requirements listed above may still be entitled to an annuity if the retiree, at the time of retirement, elected to provide the former spouse with a survivor annuity.

The amount of the survivor annuity for a former spouse is the same as that for a spouse, except that the Guaranteed Amount of approximately $37,000 (for 2022, see Q 660) is not payable unless payment is required under a court order or agreement. The cost of living increase for 2022 is 5.9 percent for CSRS and 4.9 percent for FERS.

662. Is there a survivor benefit for the children of a deceased employee?

Yes. If a retiree or an employee has eighteen months of creditable service under FERS before he or she dies, his or her dependent children are entitled to monthly annuities reduced by the amount of any Social Security survivor benefits they receive.

The annuity begins on the day after the death, and ends on the last day of the month before the one in which the child:

(1)   dies;

(2)   marries;

(3)   reaches age eighteen; or

(4)   if over eighteen, becomes capable of self-support.

The annuity of a child who is a student ends on the last day of the month before the child:

(1)   marries;

(2)   dies;

(3)   ceases to be a student; or

(4)   attains the age of twenty-two. If a student drops out of school or his annuity is terminated, it can be restored if he later returns to school and is still under age twenty-two and unmarried.

Annuity payments restart again if the child's marriage has ended and he or she is still eligible for benefits because of disability or enrollment as a full-time student while under age twenty-two. If a child's marriage ends because of divorce or death, the child's annuity and health benefits coverage is restored, beginning the first day of the month in which dissolution of the marriage occurs.

The amount of the benefit depends on whether the child is eligible to receive Social Security benefits and whether the deceased worker's spouse is still living.

If the retiree or employee is survived by a spouse or the child has a living parent, each eligible child is entitled to receive an annuity in 2022 equal to the lesser of:

(1) $1,730 per month, divided by the number of qualified children; or

(2) $590 per month.

Note that 2023 numbers were not available as this 2023 edition went to press. These figures should be available on the OPM website during March 2023.

If the retiree or employee is not survived by a spouse or the child has no living parent, each eligible child is entitled to receive an annuity in 2022 equal to the lesser of:

(1) $2,140 per month, divided by the number of qualified children; or

(2) $690 per month.

The children's rate where one parent is still alive is about $590 per month for each eligible child or $1,740 per month divided by the number of children if four or more. If there is no surviving parent, the rates are about $690 per month per child or $2,140 divided by the number of children if four or more. The amounts vary slightly in certain situations.

663. Is a person with an insurable interest in a retiree or employee eligible for a survivor benefit?

A retiree or employee can designate that a survivor annuity be paid to a person with an insurable interest in the life of the retiree or employee. The benefit is equal to 50 percent of the retiree's benefit, but is reduced, depending on the difference in the age of the person with the insurable interest and the age of the retiring employee.

If the age difference is thirty years or more, the annuity is reduced 40 percent; if the age difference is twenty-five to twenty-nine years, the reduction is 35 percent; if the age difference is twenty to twenty-four years, the reduction is 30 percent; if the age difference is fifteen to nineteen years, the reduction is 25 percent; if the age difference is ten to fourteen years, the reduction is 20 percent; if the age difference is five to nine years, the reduction is 15 percent; if the age difference is less than five years, the reduction is 10 percent.

664. When is a lump-sum survivor benefit paid?

A lump-sum survivor benefit is payable immediately after the death of an employee if the employee:

(1)   has less than eighteen months of creditable service; or

(2)   leaves no widow, widower, former spouse, or children who are eligible for a survivor annuity.

The lump-sum survivor benefit is the amount paid into the Civil Service Retirement and Disability Fund by the employee. It also includes accrued interest.

The employee, former employee, or annuitant has the right to name the lump-sum survivor benefit beneficiary. If no beneficiary is named, the lump sum is payable to the widow or widower; if there is no widow or widower, it is paid to his living children in equal shares; if no children, it is paid to his parents; if no parents, it is paid to the executor or administrator of his estate; if none of the above, it is paid to the next of kin under the laws of the state where the deceased was domiciled.

Disability Benefits

665. What disability benefits are paid under FERS?

Disability benefits are payable to an employee with eighteen months of creditable service who, because of injury or disease, can no longer perform his job in a useful and efficient manner. The beneficiary is entitled to a benefit equal to 60 percent of his high-3 average pay during the first year of disability, reduced dollar for dollar by any Social Security disability benefit. After the first year, the beneficiary is entitled to 40 percent of his high-3 average pay, reduced by 60 percent of the Social Security disability benefit.

The benefit is further adjusted at age sixty-two to equal the lesser of:

(1)   a retirement benefit computed as if he had worked during his years of disability; or

(2)   the disability benefits he would receive after the benefit is offset by any Social Security disability benefit.

Disability benefits are adjusted after the first year of disability by the increase in the Consumer Price Index for All Urban Wage Earners and Clerical Workers (CPI). Where the change in the CPI for the year is less than 2.0 percent, the benefit is increased by the full amount of the CPI increase. Where the change in the CPI for the year is at least 2.0 percent but is not more than 3.0 percent, the benefit is increased by 2 percent. Where the change in the CPI for the year is more than 3.0 percent, the benefit is increased by the CPI less 1 percent. Periodic medical examinations are required until the beneficiary reaches age sixty.

Thrift Savings Plan

666. What is the Thrift Savings Plan for FERS employees?

The Thrift Savings Plan (TSP) is a tax-deferred retirement savings and investment plan that offers Federal employees and members of the uniformed services, including the Ready Reserve, the same type of savings and tax benefits that many private corporations offer their employees under 401(k) plans. By participating in the TSP, Federal employees have the opportunity to save part of their income for retirement, receive matching agency contributions, and reduce their current taxes. It was established by Congress in the Federal Employees' Retirement System Act of 1986.

The Thrift Plan creates a third tier of benefits under FERS. A thrift plan account is set up automatically for every employee covered under FERS. Members of the uniformed services may also participate in the Plan (see Q 575).

The government contributes 1 percent of pay to an account for each employee, even if the employee declines to contribute to the plan. In addition, the government matches employee contributions as follows:

(1)   Contributions up to the first 3 percent of pay, dollar for dollar

(2)   Contributions that are more than 3 percent but not more than 5 percent of pay, fifty cents per dollar

A FERS employee may contribute up to 100 percent of his or her salary towards the Thrift Plan. However, the maximum amount that a FERS employee can contribute is $22,500 in 2023, up from $20,500 in 2022. Federal employees who are fifty or older are allowed to make additional "catch-up" contributions of $7.500 in 2023, an increase of $500 from 2022. The additional catch-up contribution limit for individuals aged 50 and over is not subject to an annual cost-of-living adjustment and remains $1,000. The total contribution for someone under 50 has increased from $61,000 to $66,000 and from $67,500 to $73,500 for those over age 50.

Contributions, and earnings on contributions, are not subject to federal income taxation until distributed to the employee at retirement. In addition, contributions reduce the employee's gross income for federal income tax purposes. (Contributions are subject to Social Security taxes, however.)

Contributions can be directed by employees to five investment funds:

(1)   Government Securities Investment (G) Fund

(2)   Fixed Income Index Investment (F) Fund

(3)   Common Stock Index Investment (C) Fund

(4)   Small Capitalization Stock Index Investment (S) Fund

(5)   International Stock Index Investment (I) Fund

FERS employees may elect to invest any portion of their current account balances and/or future contributions in the G Fund, F Fund, C Fund, S Fund, or I Fund.

The Thrift Savings Plan also allows participants to invest in five Lifecycle funds. These Lifecycle funds are L 2050, L 2040, L 2030, L 2020, and L Income. These L funds invest their assets in the G, F, C, S, and I funds in different proportions. It is recommended that, if a participant chooses a lifecycle fund, that he or she choose the one closest to when the money will be needed.

Thrift Plan payments may be made in the following manner:

(1)   At retirement or disability, if eligible for a Basic Annuity, the payment may be made as an immediate or deferred annuity, a lump-sum payment, a fixed-term payment, or by transfer to an IRA or other qualified pension plan

(2)   At death, funds in the Thrift Plan are paid to eligible survivors or to beneficiaries as specified by FERS

(3)   At termination of employment, if eligible for a deferred Basic Annuity, the payment may be made as an immediate or deferred annuity, a transfer to an IRA or other qualified pension plan, or over a fixed term after the employee retires with a Basic Annuity

(4)   At termination of employment, if not eligible for a deferred Basic Annuity, the payment must be transferred to an IRA or qualified pension plan

(5)   At age fifty-nine-and-a-half or during a period of financial hardship (see next)

A participant must withdraw his or her account balance in a single payment or begin receiving his or her Thrift Savings Plan account balance in monthly payments (or in the form of a Thrift Savings Plan annuity) by April 1 of the later of:

(1)   the year following the year in which the participant reaches age seventy-and-a-half; or

(2)   the year following the year in which the participant separates from federal service. If the participant does not make an election so that payment can be made by this

deadline, the Federal Retirement Thrift Investment Board must use the Thrift Savings Plan to purchase an annuity for the participant.

A participant who has turned age fifty-nine-and-a-half can withdraw an amount up to his or her vested Thrift Savings Plan account balance before separating from government employment. A participant is allowed only one withdrawal under this provision. In addition, a participant can obtain a withdrawal before separating from government employment on the basis of financial hardship. A financial hardship withdrawal is limited to the amount the participant contributed to the Thrift Savings Plan (plus the earnings attributed to those contributions). There is no limit on the number of such withdrawals. The participant may ask the Thrift Savings Plan to transfer all or a portion of the withdrawal to an IRA or other eligible retirement plan.

A participant can continue to contribute to the Thrift Savings Plan after obtaining an aged-based withdrawal but is not eligible to contribute to the Thrift Savings Plan for a period of six months after obtaining a financial hardship withdrawal. After six months of ineligibility to contribute, the participant can resume Thrift Savings Plan contributions only by making a new Thrift Savings Plan election on Form TSP-1.

The spouse of a FERS participant must consent to an in-service withdrawal and the spouse of a CSRS participant is entitled to notice when the participant applies for an in-service withdrawal.

Federal employees who separate or enter leave-without-pay status to serve in the military may make up contributions to the Thrift Plan missed because of military service. A federal employee would be permitted to contribute an amount equal to what an employee would have been eligible to contribute. The federal government must give such an employee two to four times the length of his military service to make up the Thrift Plan contributions. The government would match employee contributions in the same manner as regular matching contributions under the Thrift Plan.

667. Can a person leave their money in a TSP account after leaving federal service?

Yes, a person can leave their entire account balance in the TSP when they leave federal service if the balance is $200 or more. They will continue to enjoy tax-deferred earnings and low administrative expenses. Once an individual separates, they will no longer be able to make employee contributions. However, a former employee can transfer money into the TSP account from IRAs (although not from Roth IRAs) and eligible employer plans. The account will continue to accrue earnings, and the depositor can continue to change the way money is invested in the TSP investment funds by making interfund transfers.

668. Can members of the Civil Service Retirement System take advantage of the Thrift Plan?

Yes, but the government does not contribute to the employee's plan, no matter how much the employee contributes. The Federal employee may contribute up to 100 percent of annual pay, but the contribution is limited to $22,500 in 2023. This is up from $20,500 from 2022. Additional catch-up contributions of $7,500 are allowed for those who are age fifty or older in 2023.

Civil Service Retirement System

669. Which federal employees are covered under the Civil Service Retirement System?

The Civil Service Retirement System (CSRS) covers employees of the U.S. government and the District of Columbia who were hired before January 1, 1984, unless coverage is specifically excluded by law. Among the exclusions from CSRS coverage are employees who are subject to another federal retirement system. Employees subject to the Federal Employees' Retirement System (FERS) are excluded from participation in CSRS.

CSRS coverage for pre-1984 employees is automatic for all federal employees except those who are employed by Congress. Congressional employees had to elect coverage.

670. Who is eligible for a CSRS retirement annuity?

An employee must meet two requirements in order to be eligible for a CSRS retirement annuity. First, the employee must complete at least five years of civilian service with the government. Second, the employee, unless retiring on account of total disability, must have been employed under the CSRS for at least one year out of the last two years before separation from service.

The total service of an employee or member of Congress is measured in full years and months. Anything less than a full month is not counted. An employee's service is credited from the date of original employment to the date of separation. No credit is allowed for a period of separation from service in excess of three calendar days.

An employee is allowed credit for periods of military service, if performed prior to the date of separation from a civilian position.

671. Who is eligible for a CSRS retirement annuity?

There are five categories of benefits under the Civil Service Retirement System (CSRS). Eligibility is based on age and the number of years of creditable service and any other specific requirements. In addition, the individual must have served in a position subject to CSRS coverage for one of the last two years before retirement. If meeting one of the following sets of requirements, an individual may be eligible for an immediate retirement benefit. An immediate annuity is one that begins within thirty days after the individual's separation.

Optional: If the individual leaves Federal service before they meet the age and service requirements for an immediate retirement benefit, they may be eligible for deferred retirement benefits. To be eligible, the individual must have at least five years of creditable civilian service and be age sixty-two or be sixty years of age and have twenty years of service or be fifty-five years of age and have thirty years of service.

Special/Early Optional: An agency must be undergoing a major reorganization, reduction-in-force, or transfer of function determined by the Office of Personnel Management. An annuity is reduced if the individual is under age fifty-five. To be eligible, the person must be fifty years of age with twenty years of service or of any age with twenty-five years of service.

Special Provision Retirement: The individual can retire under special provisions for air traffic controllers or law enforcement and firefighter personnel, nuclear materials courier, Supreme Court Police and Capitol Police. To be eligible, the person must be fifty years of age with twenty years of service or if an air traffic controller, the person can retire at any age with twenty-five years of service. (Only air traffic controllers can retire at any age with twenty-five years of service as an air traffic controller.)

Discontinued Service: To be eligible, the person must be fifty years of age with twenty years of service or if an air traffic controller, can retire at any age with twenty-five years of service. The separation must be involuntary and not a removal for misconduct or delinquency.

Disability Retirement: To be eligible, the person must have five years of service. Any age is acceptable.

Special Requirements: The person must be disabled for useful and efficient service in their current position and any other vacant position at the same grade or pay level within their commuting area and current agency for which they are qualified. They must have been disabled prior to retirement and the disability should be expected to last for more than one year.

672. How are CSRS benefits paid for?

CSRS benefits are funded by deductions from the basic pay of covered employees, matching contributions from their employing agencies, and by payments from the General Treasury for the balance of the cost of the system. Under the current law, the employee and the employing agency each contribute:

- 8.0 percent of basic pay for Members of Congress

- 7.5 percent of basic pay for Congressional employees, law enforcement officers, and firefighters

- 7.0 percent of basic pay for other employees

The portion of compensation withheld and contributed to the retirement and disability fund is includable in the employee's gross income, in the same taxable year in which it would have been included if it had been paid to the employee directly. No refund is allowed for taxes attributable to mandatory contributions from the employee's salary to the Civil Service Retirement Fund.

673. Who is entitled to an immediate annuity?

An immediate annuity begins no later than one month after separation from service. This includes an annuity for an employee who retires optionally – for age, for disability, or due to involuntary separation from service. It does not include an annuity for a separated employee who is entitled to a deferred retirement annuity at a future date.

An employee who is separated from service is entitled to an annuity:

(1)   at age fifty-five with thirty years of service;

(2)   at age sixty with twenty years of service;

(3)   at age sixty-two with five years of service; or

(4)   at age fifty with twenty years of service as a law enforcement officer or firefighter, or a combination of such service totaling at least twenty years.

An employee whose separation is involuntary, except for removal for cause on charges of misconduct or delinquency, is entitled to a reduced annuity after twenty-five years of service or after age fifty and twenty years of service. However, no annuity is payable if the employee has declined a reasonable offer of another position in the employee's agency for which the employee is qualified, which is not lower than two grades (pay levels) below the employee's grade and which is within the employee's commuting area.

Also entitled to this reduced annuity is an employee who, while serving in a geographic area designated by the Office of Personnel Management, is voluntarily separated during a period in which:

(1)   the agency in which the employee is serving is undergoing a major reorganization, a major reduction in force, or a major transfer of function; and

(2)   a significant percentage of employees serving in this agency will be separated or subject to an immediate reduction in the rate of basic pay.

Such early retirements must be approved by the Office of Personnel Management. The annuities are reduced by 2 percent for each year the employee is under age fifty-five.

674. Are there alternative forms of CSRS retirement annuities?

Yes, an employee may, at the time of retirement, elect the following alternative forms of annuities:

(1)   Payment of an annuity to the employee for life

(2)   Payment of an annuity to the employee for life, with a survivor annuity payable for the life of a surviving spouse

(3) Payment of an annuity to the employee for life, with benefit to a named person having an insurable interest

(4) Election of lump-sum credit option and reduced monthly annuity

675. What is an annuity for life?

The annuitant has a right to receive monthly payments during his or her lifetime unless he or she is convicted of certain offenses against the United States.

Upon the annuitant's death, any accrued annuity that remains unpaid will be paid to:

(1) the deceased annuitant's executor or administrator; or

(2) if there is no executor or administrator, to the decedent's next of kin under state law, after thirty days have passed from the date of death.

676. Can benefits be lost?

There are only a few circumstances in which a federal employee will lose their retirement benefits. Federal employees will forfeit their retirement benefits only if they are convicted of one or more specific federal crimes.[1] These relate to acts against the national security of the United States, including:

- Gathering, transmitting, or losing defense information;

- Espionage;

- Treason;

- Enlisting to serve against the United States;

- Aiding the enemy;

- Disclosure of classified information; and

- Perjury under federal law.

Related statutory sections cover additional crimes that would render a federal employee ineligible for benefits. These include:

- Fleeing the United States to avoid prosecution;

- Refusing to testify before a federal grand jury about involvement with a foreign government or other interference with national security; and

- Falsifying information on an employment application about the employee's previous association with groups advocating for the overthrow of the government.

Note

1. 5 U.S.C. section 8312.

677. What are the features of an annuity with a survivor benefit?

An annuity with survivor benefit entitles the survivor to an annuity equal to 55 percent of the annuity amount prior to reduction for the election of the survivor benefit. An annuity for a married employee will automatically include an annuity for a surviving spouse, unless the employee and spouse waive the spouse's annuity in writing. The written-waiver requirement can be overcome only in instances where the employee's spouse cannot be located or where other exceptional circumstances are present.

Generally, the survivor benefit is paid until the survivor dies or remarries. However, remarriage of a widow or widower who is at least age fifty-five does not terminate the survivor annuity. Where the survivor annuity is terminated because the survivor had remarried prior to reaching age fifty-five, the annuity may be restored if the remarriage is dissolved by death, annulment, or divorce.

Where the spouse properly consents, an employee may elect to reduce that portion of the annuity that is to be treated as a survivor annuity.

The portion of the employee's annuity treated as a survivor annuity will be reduced according to a formula. The reduction is 2.5 percent of the first $3,600 chosen as a base, plus 10 percent of any amount over $3,600. For example, if the employee chooses $4,800 as a base, the reduction in the annual annuity would be 2.5 percent of the first $3,600 ($90 a year), plus 10 percent of the $1,200 balance ($120 a year), making a total reduction of $210 ($90 + $120) a year.

If marriage is terminated after retirement by the divorce, annulment, or death of the spouse named as beneficiary, the retiree may elect to have the annuity recomputed, and payment at the single-life unreduced rate will be made for each full month the employee is not married. Should the employee remarry, he has two years from the date of remarriage to notify the Office of Personnel Management in writing that he wants the annuity reduced again to provide a survivor annuity for the new spouse.

If a retired employee dies, absent a waiver of benefits by the survivor, the surviving spouse will receive 55 percent of the yearly annuity that the deceased employee had earned at the time of death. This earned annuity is computed in the same manner as if the deceased employee had retired, but with no reduction for being under age fifty-five, and no increase for voluntary contributions.

The surviving spouse's annuity begins on the day after the employee's death and terminates on the last day of the month before the surviving spouse dies or remarries before age fifty-five.

678. How does an annuity with benefit to a named person having an insurable interest work?

If the employee is in good health at retirement, he or she may elect an Annuity with Benefit to Named Person Having an Insurable Interest. A disabled dependent relative or former spouse is considered as having an insurable interest. An employee electing this annuity will have their annuity reduced by a percentage amount as follows:

Age of Named Person In Relation to Retiring Employee's Age	Reduction in Annuity of Retiring Employee
Older, same age, or less than 5 years younger	10%
5 but less than 10 years younger	15%
10 but less than 15 years younger	20%
15 but less than 20 years younger	25%
20 but less than 25 years younger	30%
25 but less than 30 years younger	35%
30 or more years younger.................................	40%

Upon the employee's death after retirement, the named beneficiary will receive an annuity equal to 55 percent of the employee's reduced annuity rate. The survivor's annuity begins on the day after the retired employee's death and terminates on the last day of the month before the survivor dies. However, if the person named as having an insurable interest dies before the employee, the employee's annuity will be restored to life rate upon written request.

679. Is there a lump-sum credit option upon retirement under CSRS?

Employees are allowed to receive a payment equal to the value of the contributions they made to the retirement program over their working years. The lump-sum payments option is paid in one payment at first and then in two installments of equal amounts. Workers eligible to voluntarily retire who have a critical or life-threatening illness can receive the lump sum in one payment.

680. How is the reduced annuity computed?

First, determine the amount of the member's contributions into the plan. The member's regular annuity is then calculated. To determine the amount of monthly reduction of the annuity, the computation is as follows:

- LS/PV = monthly reduction in annuity, where LS equals the lump-sum credit and PV equals the present value factor of the annuity

The present value factors of CSRS and FERS appear in the Reduced Annuity Tables, below.

To obtain the amount of the reduced monthly annuity, subtract the monthly reduction figure obtained above from the amount of the regular (unreduced) monthly annuity.

Example. Mr. Edwards, a member of the CSRS, is sixty-four at the time he retires from government service. His contributions to CSRS total $55,000. His present value factor (from the table) is 212.9. Using the formula above, $55,000 ÷ 212.9 = $258.38. Mr. Edwards' monthly annuity would therefore be reduced by $258.38.

Reduced Annuity Tables

CSRS

Present Value Factors

Age at Retirement	Factor	Age at Retirement	Factor
40	351.8	66	199
41	347.1	67	192
42	342.2	68	184.9
43	337.2	69	177.8
44	332.1	70	170.7
45	326.9	71	163.6
46	321.6	72	156.5
47	316.4	73	149.5
48	311.1	74	142.5
49	305.9	75	135.6
50	300.7	76	128.8
51	295.3	77	122.1
52	289.8	78	115.5
53	284.1	79	109
54	278.2	80	102.7
55	272.2	81	96.6
56	266	82	90.6
57	259.7	83	84.9
58	253.3	84	79.4
59	246.8	85	74.1
60	240.2	86	69
61	233.5	87	64.1
62	226.7	88	59.6
63	219.8	89	55.3
64	212.9	90	51.3
65	206	91	47.7

FERS

Present Value
Factors for Most
Employees

Age at Retirement	Factor	Age at Retirement	Factor
40	244.2	66	189.1
41	243.3	67	182.7
42	242.3	68	176.3
43	241.2	69	169.8
44	240.0	70	163.3
45	238.9	71	156.8
46	237.7	72	150.3
47	236.5	73	143.8
48	235.4	74	137.3
49	234.3	75	130.9
50	233.2	76	124.5
51	232.0	77	118.2
52	230.8	78	112.0
53	229.5	79	105.9
54	228.0	80	99.9
55	226.4	81	94.1
56	224.8	82	88.4
57	223.1	83	83.0
58	221.4	84	77.7
59	219.6	85	72.6
60	217.7	86	67.7
61	215.8	87	63.0
62	213.9	88	58.6
63	207.8	89	54.5
64	201.6	90	50.6
65	195.4	91	47.0

Computing the CSRS Annuity

681. How is the amount of the CSRS annuity determined?

The amount of an annuity depends primarily on the employee's length of service and high-3 average pay. These two factors are used in a formula to determine the basic annuity, which may then be reduced or increased for various reasons.

The high-3 average pay is the highest pay obtainable by averaging the rates of basic pay in effect during any three consecutive years of service, with each rate weighted by the time it was in effect. The three years need not be continuous, but they must consist of consecutive periods of service. Thus, two or more separate periods of employment that follow each other may be joined to make up the three consecutive years of service on which the high-3 average pay is based. The pay rates for each period of employment are weighted on an annual basis.

Example. Mr. Smith's final three years of government service included pay rates of:

6 months at $64,500	—	½ year	×	$64,500	=	$32,250
18 months at $65,000	—	1½ years	×	$65,000	=	$97,500
12 months at $65,000	—	1 year	×	$65,000	=	$65,000
					$194,750

Mr. Smith's average pay is computed as:

$$\frac{\$194,750}{3} = \$64,917$$

A three-step formula is used to determine the basic annuity.

- *Step I.* 1.5 percent × Average Pay times number of years of service up to five years, plus

- *Step II.* 1.75 percent × Average Pay times number of years of service over five and up to ten years, plus

- *Step III.* 2 percent × Average Pay times number of years of service over ten.

Note that for employees with over ten years of service, all three steps apply. For those with fewer than ten years of service, only steps I and II apply. For those with fewer than five years of service, only Step I applies.

Example. Mr. Martin retires from civil service employment with thirty years of service. The three consecutive years of service with the highest rates of basic pay were his last three years before retirement.

Rate of pay during 28th year of service	$64,500
Rate of pay during 29th year of service	$65,000
Rate of pay during 30th year of service	$65,500
	$194,750 (total)

$$\frac{\$194,750}{3} = \$64,917$$

The general formula, using Mr. Martin's $64,917 average pay and thirty years of service, is applied as follows:

1.	1.5%	×	$64,917	×	5 years	=	$4,868.78
2.	1.75%	×	$64,917	×	5 years	=	$5,680.24
3.	2%	×	$64,917	×	20 years	=	$25,966.80
					Basic Annuity	=	$36,515.82

The employee's basic annuity may not exceed 80 percent of his average pay. If the formula produces an amount exceeding the 80 percent maximum, it must be reduced to an amount that equals 80 percent of the average pay.

682. What is the special computation for Law Enforcement, Firefighters, and Nuclear Materials Couriers?

If retired under special provisions for firefighters, law enforcement, nuclear material couriers, Supreme Court Police, or Capitol Police:

- First twenty years of CSRS law enforcement officer, firefighter, and/or nuclear material courier service – retiree receives 2.5 percent of high-3 average salary for each year

- Plus, all remaining CSRS service receives 2 percent of high-3 average salary for each year

This is unchanged for 2023.

683. What is the substitute computation method?

A substitute computation method is provided as an alternative for employees with a high-3 of under $5,000. Instead of taking the 1.5 percent, 1.75 percent, and 2 percent of the high-3 average pay, the employee may substitute 1 percent of the high-3 average pay plus $25 for all parts of the general formula.

If the high-3 average pay is between $2,500 and $3,333, substitute the 1 percent plus $25 for the 1.5 percent and 1.75 percent in the first and second parts of the general formula. If the high-3 average pay is between $3,334 and $4,999, substitute the 1 percent plus $25 for the 1.5 percent in the first part of the general formula.

684. How is the benefit determined for disability retirement?

An employee under age sixty who retires on account of total disability will receive no less than the guaranteed minimum annuity, which is the lesser of:

(1)   40 percent of the employee's high-3 average pay; or

(2)   the amount obtained under the general formula, after adding to years of actual service the number of years the employee is under age sixty on the date of separation.

An employee must have completed at least five years of government service in order to be eligible for disability benefits. The provision for a minimum disability annuity does not apply to employees over age sixty. The disability annuity rate for an employee over age sixty is always computed by using actual service in the general formula.

685. Can an employee obtain a larger retirement annuity by making voluntary contributions?

Yes, an employee can obtain a larger retirement annuity by making voluntary contributions, in multiples of twenty-five dollars, to purchase an additional annuity. Total voluntary contributions may not exceed 10 percent of the employee's total basic pay.

Voluntary contributions are interest-bearing. The interest rate is determined at the end of each year by the Treasury Department. Each $100 in the account provides an additional annuity in the amount of seven dollars, plus twenty cents for each full year the employee is over age fifty-five at retirement.

Death Benefits

686. Is there a death benefit under the CSRS?

Death benefits are of two kinds: survivor annuities and lump-sum payments.

Survivor annuities are payable to an employee's surviving spouse and children upon the death of the employee.

A **lump-sum benefit** is payable upon the death of the employee if there is no spouse or dependent children entitled to an annuity or, if one is payable, after the right of the last person entitled thereto has been terminated.

While not formally called a "death benefit," where the employee has retired, annuities are payable to the surviving spouse (unless the spouse had waived survivor benefit entitlement) and, where applicable, payable to a named person with an insurable interest.

Annuity Eligibility Requirements

687. Who is eligible for a survivor annuity?

Employee's Spouse. In order for the surviving spouse to qualify for a survivor annuity:

(1)   the spouse must have been married to the employee for at least nine months before death; or

(2)   the spouse must be the parent of the deceased's child born of the marriage.

These requirements are waived where:

(1)   the employee dies as a result of an accident; or

(2)   the employee had previously married and subsequently divorced the surviving spouse, and the aggregate time married is at least nine months.

Employee's Child. Generally, for a deceased employee's child to qualify for the survivor annuity, the child must be unmarried, under eighteen years of age, and a dependent of the employee. The following rules also apply:

(1)   An adopted child is considered to be the employee's child.

(2)   A stepchild is considered to be the employee's child, even if the child did not live with the deceased employee. An illegitimate child, however, must prove he or she was dependent upon the deceased employee.

(3)   An illegitimate child is considered to be the employee's child, even if the child did not live with the deceased employee. An illegitimate child, however, must prove he or she was dependent upon the deceased employee.

(4)   A child who lived with the employee and for whom the employee had filed an adoption petition is considered to be the employee's child, but only where the surviving spouse did in fact adopt the child following the employee's death.

Notwithstanding the age requirement above, each of the following persons is considered to be a child for purposes of the survivorship annuity:

(1)   An unmarried dependent child, regardless of age, who is incapable of self-support because of a mental or physical disability incurred before age 18.

(2)   An unmarried dependent child between eighteen and twenty-two, who is a student (pursuing a full-time course of study or training in residence in a high school, trade school, college, university, or comparable recognized educational institution).

Benefits for a child end upon marriage. However, annuity payments restart again if the child's marriage has ended and he or she is still eligible for benefits because of disability or enrollment as a full-time student while under age twenty-two. If a child's marriage ends because of divorce or death, the child's annuity and health benefits coverage is restored beginning the first day of the month in which dissolution of the marriage occurs.

Computing the Survivor Annuity

688. How is the survivor annuity computed?

If an employee dies after completing at least eighteen months of civilian service, there is a guaranteed minimum survivor annuity based upon the employee's average pay over the total civilian service.

The annuity, however, is at least 55 percent of the smaller of:

(1)   40 percent of the deceased employee's high-3 average pay; or

(2)   the regular computation obtained after increasing service by the period of time between the date of death and the date the employee would have become age sixty.

This guaranteed minimum does not apply if 55 percent of the employee's earned annuity produces a higher benefit than the guaranteed minimum. Also, since active service cannot be projected beyond age sixty in any case, the guaranteed minimum does not apply where the employee dies after reaching age sixty.

For 2021, where an employee is survived by a spouse and is survived by children who qualify for survivor benefits, each surviving child is entitled to a benefit equal to whichever of the following amounts is the least:

(1)   60 percent of the employee's high-3 average pay, divided by the number of qualified children;

(2) $1.940 per month, divided by the number of qualified children; or

(3) $590 per month. When an employee leaves no surviving spouse, but leaves children who qualify for survivor benefits, each child will be paid the least of:

    (a) 75 percent of the employee's high-3 average pay, divided by the number of qualified children;

    (b) $2,140 per month, divided by the number of qualified children; or

    (c) $690 per month.

Note that 2023 figures were not available at the time on the printing of this 2023 edition.

A child's annuity begins on the day after the employee or annuitant dies and continues until the last day of the month before the child marries, dies, or reaches age eighteen, except in the following cases:

(1)   For a child age eighteen or over who is incapable of self-support because of a disability that began before age eighteen, payments stop at the end of the month before the child becomes capable of self-support, marries, or dies.

(2)   The annuity of a student age eighteen or over stops at the end of the month before the child ceases to be a student, reaches age twenty-two, marries, or dies, whichever occurs first.

Lump-Sum Death Benefit

689. When does the lump-sum death benefit become payable?

The lump-sum death benefit becomes payable to the estate of the proper party where the employee dies:

(1)   without a survivor; or

(2)   with a survivor, but the survivor's right to an annuity terminates before a claim for a survivor annuity has been filed.

The lump-sum benefit consists of the amount paid into the Civil Service Retirement and Disability Fund by the employee, plus any accrued interest.

If all rights to a CSRS annuity cease before the total annuity paid equals the lump-sum credit, the difference between the lump-sum credit and the total annuity paid becomes payable to the estate of the proper party. Thus, if an employee leaves a spouse or children who are eligible for a survivor annuity, a lump-sum death benefit may be payable after all survivors' annuities have been paid. The lump-sum benefit would consist of that portion of the employee's lump-sum credit that has not been exhausted by the annuity payments to survivors.

Annuity Payments

690. How are annuity payments made?

Annuities are paid by monthly check. The Office of Personnel Management (OPM) authorizes the payment, and the Treasury Department issues the check. After the initial check, each regular check is dated the first workday of the month after the month for which the annuity is due. For example, the annuity payment for the month of April will be made by a direct deposit on May 1.

An employee annuity begins on the first day of the month after:

(1)   separation from service; or

(2)   pay ceases and the service and age requirements for entitlement to an annuity are met.

Any other annuity payable begins on the first day of the month after the occurrence of the event on which payment is based.

Disability Retirement

691. When is an annuity payable for disability retirement?

An immediate annuity is payable to an employee for disability retirement when each of the following conditions is met:

(1)   The employee has completed five years of civilian service.

(2)   The employee has become totally disabled for useful and efficient service in the position occupied, or the duties of a similar position at the same grade or level.

A claim for disability retirement must be filed with the Office of Personnel Management before separation from service or within one year thereafter. The one-year requirement may be waived in cases of incompetency.

The annuity payable will be the earned annuity based on the high-3 average salary, the years of actual service, and the three-part formula (see Q 681), but not less than:

(1)   40 percent of the high-3 average salary; or

(2)   the amount computed under the general formula after adding to years of actual service the number of years he is under age sixty on the date of separation.

Unless the disability is permanent in nature, an employee receiving a disability retirement annuity must be medically examined annually until age sixty. The Government pays for the examination.

Upon recovery before reaching age sixty, the annuity is continued temporarily (not to exceed one year) to give the individual an opportunity to find a position. If re-employed in Government service within the year, the annuity stops on re-employment. If the individual is not re-employed, the annuity stops at the expiration of the 180-day period.

Cost-of-Living Adjustments

692. Is there a cost-of-living adjustment to CSRS annuities?

Annuities for retirees and survivors are subject to a cost-of-living adjustment in December of each year. The increases are reflected in the annuity payment received the following month. The percentage of the cost-of-living increase each year is determined by the average price index for the third quarter of each year over the third quarter average of the Consumer Price Index for Urban Wage Earners and Clerical Workers of the previous year.

The cost-of-living increase for 2022 is 5.9 percent, while 2021 was 1.3 percent, 2020 was 1.6 percent, 2019 was 2.8 percent, 2018 was 2.0 percent, 2017 was 0.3 percent, and there was NO cost-of-living (COLA) increase for annuitants in 2016.

Refund of Contributions

693. Is there a refund of contributions if an employee leaves government service?

Yes, an employee who leaves government service or transfers to government work under another retirement system may withdraw his retirement lump-sum credit (contributions plus any interest payable), so long as the employee:

(1)   is separated from the job for at least thirty-one consecutive days;

(2)   is transferred to a position that is not subject to CSRS or FERS and remains in that position for at least thirty-one consecutive days;

(3)   files an application for a refund of retirement deductions;

(4)   is not reemployed in a position subject to CSRS or FERS at the time the application is filed; and

(5)   will not become eligible to receive an annuity within thirty-one days after filing the application.

Life Insurance Benefits

694. In general, what life insurance benefits are available to federal civil service employees?

The Federal Government established the Federal Employees' Group Life Insurance (FEGLI) Program on August 29, 1954. It is the largest group life insurance program in the world, covering over 4 million Federal employees and retirees, as well as many of their family members.

All federal civil service employees—whether CSRS or FERS members—and employees of the District of Columbia are automatically insured under the provisions of a group policy purchased by the U.S. Office of Personnel Management. Most employees are eligible for FEGLI coverage.

FEGLI provides group term life insurance. As such, it does not build up any cash value or paid-up value. It consists of Basic life insurance coverage and three options. In most cases, new Federal employees are automatically covered by Basic life insurance and payroll deduct premiums from the paycheck unless coverage is waived. In addition to the Basic, there are three forms of Optional insurance that can be elected. An individual must have Basic insurance in order to elect any of the options. Unlike Basic, enrollment in Optional insurance is not automatic – the individual must take action to elect the options.

Basic insurance coverage may be declined by written notice only. If coverage has been declined, the employee cannot obtain coverage for at least one year and, then, only if the applicant is in good health. Special rules apply if the employee has experienced a break in service of at least 180 days. Under this exception, all previous waivers of life insurance coverage are canceled, but any of the optional coverages must be affirmatively elected within thirty-one days after the employee's return. Each insured receives a certificate setting forth the group insurance benefits, to whom benefits are payable, to whom claims are submitted, and summarizing the provisions of the policy. The group insurance is underwritten by a large number of private insurance companies and claims are settled by the Office of Federal Employees' Group Life Insurance, P.O. Box 6080, Scranton, PA 18505-6080.

Group insurance includes:

(1)   group-term life coverage without a medical examination; and

(2)   accidental death and dismemberment insurance protection.

The amount of each type of insurance is based on the employee's "basic insurance amount," which is determined by rounding the employee's annual salary to the next higher multiple of $1,000, and adding $2,000. However, in no case may the basic insurance amount be less than $10,000.

The group accidental death and dismemberment insurance provides payment for:

(1)   loss of life or loss of two or more members; and

(2)   loss of one hand or one foot, or for permanent and total loss of sight in one eye.

The accidental death benefit equals the employee's basic insurance amount and is paid in addition to the group life insurance.

An insured individual who is certified by a doctor as terminally ill may elect to receive a lump-sum payment of Basic Insurance. Optional insurance is not available for payment as a Living Benefit. The effective date of a Living Benefit election is the date on which the Living Benefit payment is cashed or deposited. Once an election becomes effective, it cannot be revoked. No further election of Living Benefits can be made. If the insured individual has assigned his or her insurance, he or she cannot elect a Living Benefit; nor can an assignee elect a Living Benefit on behalf of an insured individual. If an individual has elected a Living Benefit, he or she may assign his or her remaining insurance. An individual may elect to receive either a full Living Benefit (all of the Basic Insurance) or a partial Living Benefit (a portion of the Basic Insurance, in a multiple of $1,000). The amount of Basic Insurance elected as a Living Benefit will be reduced by an actuarial amount representing the amount of interest lost to the fund because of the early payment of benefits.

An individual may assign ownership of all life insurance, except Option C (which covers family members). If an individual wishing to make an assignment owns more than one type of coverage, he or she must assign all the insurance; an individual cannot assign only a portion of the coverage. Option C cannot be assigned. If the insurance is assigned to two or more individuals, corporations, or trustees, the insured individual must specify percentage shares (rather than dollar amounts or types of insurance) to go to each assignee.

695. How does an employee designate the beneficiary or beneficiaries?

An employee's designation of beneficiary or beneficiaries is made in a signed and witnessed writing that is received before the employee's death by his employing office. The Designation of Beneficiary (Form SF 2823[1]) needs to be completed.[2] If no beneficiary is designated when the employee dies, payment is made in the following order: to the employee's widow or widower; or, if none, to the child or children of the employee in equal shares and descendants of deceased children by representation; or, if none, to the parents of the employee in equal shares or the entire amount to the surviving parent; or, if none, to the duly appointed executor or administrator of the employee; or, if none, to the next of kin of the employee, under the law of the employee's domicile at the time of death. All forms are available on the website.[3]

Beneficiaries receiving insurance proceeds in excess of $7,500 receive a money market account instead of a check from the government. Beneficiaries entitled to less than $7,500 receive a single check from the government for the full amount of insurance coverage. Insurance proceeds earn interest in the money market account. Beneficiaries receive special checkbooks and can write checks on the money market account for $250, up to the full amount of the insurance payment.

Notes

1. https://www.opm.gov/forms/pdf_fill/sf2823.pdf . (Revised May 2014) (last accessed September 25, 2022).
2. Form SF 2823, https://www.opm.gov/forms/pdf_fill/sf2823.pdf . – Form revised 2014 (last accessed September 25, 2022).
3. https://www.opm.gov/healthcare-insurance (last accessed September 25, 2022).

696. When does insurance coverage cease?

Subject to the exceptions below, an employee's group insurance coverage ceases on the earliest of:

(1)   the date of separation from the service;

(2)   the date on which a period of twelve months of continuous nonpay status ends; or

(3)   the date of any other change in employment that results in the employee's ineligibility for insurance coverage.

In addition, coverage may be terminated at the end of the pay period in which it is determined that periodic pay, after all other deductions, is insufficient to cover the required withholdings (such as court-ordered child support) to a point at which deductions for federal employee group life insurance cannot be made.

An exception to the termination rule occurs where:

(1)   the employee retires on an immediate annuity; or

(2)   the employee becomes entitled to workers' compensation.

An employee who does not want insurance may waive group insurance coverage. In such a case, coverage ceases on the last day of the pay period in which the agency receives the employee's waiver of coverage.

697. What is the Living Benefit Option?

A Living Benefit payment is a lump sum payment to those who are terminally ill and have a documented medical prognosis showing a life expectancy of no more than nine months. The policy owner is eligible to elect a Living Benefit if they are an employee, annuitant, or compensationer and enrolled in the FEGLI Program.

Employees can choose a full or partial (a multiple of $1,000) Living Benefit. Annuitants and compensationers can elect only a full Living Benefit.

A Living Benefit is equal to the Basic Life insurance amount, plus any extra benefit for persons under age forty-five, that would be in effect nine months after the date of the Office of Federal Employees' Group Life Insurance (OFEGLI) receives a completed claim for Living Benefits form. If this option is elected, the individual ceases paying premiums. If a partial living benefit is taken, the agency will adjust the withholdings.

If a person has assigned their life insurance, they cannot elect a Living Benefit.

Living Benefit payments are reduced by a nominal amount (4.9 percent) to make up for lost earnings to the Life Insurance Fund because of the early payment of benefits.

The election of Living Benefits has no effect on the amount of any Optional life insurance. One must continue to pay premiums for any Optional insurance. If a person election a living benefit and does not die within nine months, they do not have to return the money.

The policy owner must contact OFEGLI at 1-800-633-4542 to obtain the form to elect Living Benefits (Form FE-8[1]). This form is not available from human resources office or the Office of Personnel Management (OPM). Note also that there are no electronic versions of the form and agencies cannot order the form.

Note

1. https://www.opm.gov/healthcare-insurance/life-insurance/reference-materials/publications-forms/living-benefits-claim-form/.

698. Can an employee convert to an individual policy?

Yes, if coverage ceases as a result of one of the occurrences described in Q 696 above, the employee may apply for an individual life insurance policy. The employee's coverage cannot exceed the amount for which he was insured at the time of the terminating event. **The conversion excludes the Option C coverage**. (See Q 700.) The insured may convert all or any part of the Basic and Optional coverage. No medical examination is required, although a few questions about health may be asked to see if the insured might qualify for a lower premium. These questions are not mandatory but, if unanswered, the insured may pay a higher premium than necessary.

The employee's request for conversion information must be submitted to the Office of Federal Employee's Group Life Insurance and postmarked within thirty-one days following the date of the terminating event, or within thirty-one days of the date the employee received notice of loss of the group coverage and right to convert, whichever is later. Detailed information concerning how to apply for the policy may be obtained from the Office of Federal Employees' Group Life Insurance, P.O. Box 6080, Scranton, PA 18505-6080 or contacting them by telephone at 1-800-633-4542.

699. What is the cost of basic insurance?

The employee pays two-thirds, by means of salary withholding, of the cost of that amount of group-term life and accidental death and dismemberment that equals his or her basic insurance amount. The cost of the additional group-term life (i.e., that amount in excess of his or her basic insurance amount) is paid entirely by the government. The amount withheld from the bi-weekly pay of an employee is fifteen cents for each $1,000 of his or her basic insurance amount; the amount withheld from the monthly pay of an employee is 32.5 cents for each $1,000 of coverage. The following table shows the amount withheld from pay to meet the employee's share of the cost. The figures reported here were current as published on the opm.gov website as of September 25, 2022 at the rates established in 2016.[1]

INSURANCE WITHHOLDINGS					
Amount of Withholdings Per Pay Period					
Basic Insurance Amount	Biweekly	Monthly	Basic Insurance Amount	Biweekly	Monthly
$18,000	$2.70	$5.85	$80,000	$12.00	$26.00
g19,000	2.85	6.18	81,000	12.15	26.33
20,000	3.00	6.50	82,000	12.30	26.65
21,000	3.15	6.83	83,000	12.45	26.98
22,000	3.30	7.15	84,000	12.60	27.30
23,000	3.45	7.48	85,000	12.75	27.63
24,000	3.60	7.80	86,000	12.90	27.95
25,000	3.75	8.13	87,000	13.05	28.28
26,000	3.90	8.45	88,000	13.20	28.60
27,000	4.05	8.78	89,000	13.35	28.93
28,000	4.20	9.10	90,000	13.50	29.25
29,000	4.35	9.43	91,000	13.65	29.58
30,000	4.50	9.75	92,000	13.80	29.90
31,000	4.65	10.08	93,000	13.95	30.23
32,000	4.80	10.40	94,000	14.10	30.55
33,000	4.95	10.73	95,000	14.25	30.88
34,000	5.10	11.05	96,000	14.40	31.20
35,000	5.25	11.38	97,000	14.55	31.53
36,000	5.40	11.70	98,000	14.70	31.85
37,000	5.55	12.03	99,000	14.85	32.18
38,000	5.70	12.35	100,000	15.00	32.50
39,000	5.85	12.68	101,000	15.15	32.83
40,000	6.00	13.00	102,000	15.30	33.15
41,000	6.15	13.33	103,000	15.45	33.48
42,000	6.30	13.65	104,000	15.60	33.80
43,000	6.45	13.98	105,000	15.75	34.13
44,000	6.60	14.30	106,000	15.90	34.45
45,000	6.75	14.63	107,000	16.05	34.78

INSURANCE WITHHOLDINGS					
Amount of Withholdings Per Pay Period					
Basic Insurance Amount	Biweekly	Monthly	Basic Insurance Amount	Biweekly	Monthly
46,000	6.90	14.95	108,000	16.20	35.10
47,000	7.05	15.28	109,000	16.35	35.43
48,000	7.20	15.60	110,000	16.50	35.75
49,000	7.35	15.93	111,000	16.65	36.08
50,000	7.50	16.25	112,000	16.80	36.40
51,000	7.65	16.58	113,000	16.95	36.73
52,000	7.80	16.90	114,000	17.10	37.05
53,000	7.95	17.23	115,000	17.25	37.38
54,000	8.10	17.55	116,000	17.40	37.70
55,000	8.25	17.88	117,000	17.55	38.03
56,000	8.40	18.20	118,000	17.70	38.35
57,000	8.55	18.53	119,000	17.85	38.68
58,000	8.70	18.85	120,000	18.00	39.00
59,000	8.85	19.18	121,000	18.15	39.33
60,000	9.00	19.50	122,000	18.30	39.65
61,000	9.15	19.83	123,000	18.45	39.98
62,000	9.30	20.15	124,000	18.60	40.30
63,000	9.45	20.48	125,000	18.75	40.63
64,000	9.60	20.80	126,000	18.90	40.95
65,000	9.75	21.13	127,000	19.05	41.28
66,000	9.90	21.45	128,000	19.20	41.60
67,000	10.05	21.78	129,000	19.35	41.93
68,000	10.20	22.10	130,000	19.50	42.25
69,000	10.35	22.43	131,000	19.65	42.58
70,000	10.50	22.75	132,000	19.80	42.90
71,000	10.65	23.08	133,000	19.95	43.23
72,000	10.80	23.40	134,000	20.10	43.55
73,000	10.95	23.73	135,000	20.25	43.88
74,000	11.10	24.05	136,000	20.40	44.20
75,000	11.25	24.38	137,000	20.55	44.53
76,000	11.40	24.70	138,000	20.70	44.85
77,000	11.55	25.03	139,000	20.85	45.18
78,000	11.70	25.35	140,000	21.00	45.50
79,000	11.85	25.68			

Note

1. Office of Personnel Management, "Federal Employees' Group Life Insurance Program (FEGLI) Premium Rates", available online at https://www.opm.gov/retirement-services/publications-forms/benefits-administration-letters/2015/15-203a1.pdf (last accessed September 25, 2022).

700. What optional insurance coverages are available to the civil service employee?

Optional insurance coverages currently available include:

    (1)   optional life insurance (termed Option A – Standard Insurance);

    (2)   additional optional life insurance (Option B – Additional Insurance); and

    (3)   optional life insurance on family members (Option C – Family Coverage).

Beneficiary provisions for optional insurances on the life of the employee are the same as for basic (regular) insurance.[1]

Option A – Standard Insurance

Employees covered under the basic life insurance program can purchase $10,000 of optional group-term life insurance. This coverage includes accidental death and dismemberment.

The premium is paid entirely by the employee through withholding, and the cost is as follows:

	Withholding for $10,000 Insurance	
Age Group	**Biweekly**	**Monthly**
Under age 35	$0.20	$0.43
35 through 39	0.30	0.65
40 through 44	0.40	0.87
45 through 49	0.70	1.52
50 through 54	1.10	2.38
55 through 59	2.00	4.33
60 and over	6.00	13.00

Where Option A insurance has been declined, the employee is eligible to enroll for this coverage only by meeting the two requirements for canceling a waiver of basic life insurance. Neither a retiree nor an employee receiving basic life insurance while receiving workers' compensation can cancel a previous declination of Option A – Standard.

Option B – Additional Optional Insurance

An employee with basic life insurance can purchase Option B—additional optional life insurance on himself—without regard to whether he has purchased Option A insurance. Option B coverage comes in one, two, three, four, or five multiples of an employee's annual pay (after the pay has been rounded to the next higher thousand).

The cost of Option B insurance, like Option A, is paid entirely by the employee through withholdings. The rates per $1,000 of coverage are as follows:

Age Group	Withholding for $1,000 Insurance	
	Biweekly	Monthly
Under age 35	$0.02	$0.043
35 through 39	0.03	0.065
40 through 44	0.04	0.087
45 through 49	0.07	0.152
50 through 54	0.11	0.238
55 through 59	0.20	0.433
60 through 64	0.44	0.953
65 through 69	0.54	1.170
70 through 74	0.96	2.080
75 through 79	1.80	3.900
80 and over	2.64	5.720

Retiring employees or compensationers can elect to continue Option B coverage on an unreduced basis by continuing to pay premiums after age sixty-five. Annuitants and compensationers who elect unreduced Option B can later cancel that election and have the full reduction.

Option C – Family Coverage

Option C—life insurance coverage on the life of spouse and dependents—is available in either one, two, three, four, or five multiples of coverage. One multiple is equal to $5,000 for a spouse and $2,500 for each dependent child. The cost of this insurance is paid entirely by the employee through withholding. The rates for coverage of the spouse and child (or children) are as follows:

Age of Person	Withholding per Multiple	
	Biweekly	Monthly
Under age 35	$0.22	$0.48
35 through 39	0.27	0.59
40 through 44	0.41	0.89
45 through 49	0.59	1.28
50 through 54	0.92	1.99
55 through 59	1.48	3.21
60 through 64	2.70	5.85
65 through 69	3.14	6.80
70 through 74	3.83	8.30
75 through 79	5.26	11.40
80 and over	7.20	15.60

Retiring employees can choose to elect unreduced Option C coverage by continuing to pay premiums after age sixty-five. Annuitants and compensationers who elect unreduced Option C can later cancel that election and have the full reduction.

Foster children are covered under Option C. Dependency of the foster child must be established before the child is approved for coverage under Option C. These figures are current as of September 25, 2022. An easy-to-use calculator is available on the OPM website.[2]

Notes

1. Rates are found at https://www.opm.gov/retirement-services/publications-forms/benefits-administration-letters/2015/15-203a1.pdf (last accessed September 25, 2022).
2. https://www.opm.gov/retirement-services/calculators/fegli-calculator/. (Last accessed October 1, 2022).

701. May a retiring employee continue life insurance coverage?

With respect to basic (regular) life insurance, an employee who retires on an immediate annuity can continue his basic life insurance (excluding accidental death and dismemberment), so long as he satisfies the "five or less than five" rule. This requires that the retiree be insured either: (1) through the five years of service immediately preceding his retirement; or (2) if less than five years, then throughout the period or periods of service during which he was entitled to coverage. An additional requirement for continuing basic insurance is that the employee cannot have converted the policy to an individual life policy.

The retiring employee's basic life options are as follows:

	Election	Monthly Cost Before 65	Monthly Cost After 65
1.	75% REDUCTION — Amount of insurance reduces 2% per month after age 65 to a minimum of 25% of Basic Insurance Amount at retirement.	$.325 per $1,000*	No Cost
2.	50% REDUCTION — Amount of insurance reduces 1% per month after age 65 to a minimum of 50% of Basic Insurance Amount at retirement.	1.035 per $1,000*	$.71 per $1,000*
3.	NO REDUCTION — 100% of Basic Insurance Amount at retirement is retained after age 65.	$2,245 per $1,000*	$1.97 per $1,000*

*of Basic Insurance Amount at retirement

Where the employee chooses the 75 percent Reduction and retired before December 31, 1989, there is no cost to the individual after retirement, regardless of age. If the employee retires after December 31, 1989 and elects the 75 percent Reduction, the life insurance withholdings will be at the same rate to age sixty-five as for active employees, and withholdings will be deducted from his annuity. After the individual reaches age sixty-five, withholding will stop.

Where the employee chooses the 50 percent Reduction or No Reduction, the full cost of the additional protection is deducted from the retiree's monthly annuity payment. The withholdings begin at retirement and continue for life or until the election is canceled or coverage is otherwise discontinued.

Where the employee elected Option A – Standard Insurance, the retiree may continue the insurance so long as it was in force during the "five or less than five" period explained earlier. The cost of the Option A life insurance will be withheld from the annuity until the end of the calendar month in which he attains age sixty-five. After that time, the Option A life insurance will be continued without cost to the retiree.

Option A life insurance, in all cases, is subject to a reduction of 2 percent at the end of each full calendar month following the date on which the employee attains age sixty-five or retires, whichever occurs later. These reductions continue until a minimum (but in no event, less than 25 percent of the amount of Option A life in force before the first reduction) is reached.

An employee who retires on an immediate annuity can continue the amount of Option B – Additional Life Insurance so long as it was in force for the required "five or less than five" period explained above. The full cost of the Option B life that is continued will be withheld from the retiree's annuity until the calendar month in which the retiree attains age sixty-five. Beginning with the end of that calendar month, Option B life insurance will be continued without cost to the retiree. The amount of Option B life insurance is subject to a reduction of 2 percent each month beginning with the second calendar month after the date on which the employee attains age sixty-five or retires, whichever occurs later. These reductions continue for fifty months, at which time the Option B life coverage ends.

Retiring employees or compensationers can elect to continue Option B coverage on an unreduced basis by continuing to pay premiums after age sixty-five. Annuitants and compensationers who elect unreduced Option B can later cancel that election and have the full reduction. Annuitants and compensationers who have Option B coverage on a reduction schedule will be offered the opportunity to elect an unreduced schedule on a prospective basis.

An employee who retires on an immediate annuity may continue his Option C – Family Coverage that was in force during the "five or less than five" period. The full cost of the optional family coverage that is continued will be withheld from the retiree's annuity until the calendar month in which the retiree attains age sixty-five. Beginning with the end of that calendar month, the optional family life coverage will be continued without cost to the retiree. Optional family life coverage that is continued after retirement is subject to the same method of reduction as is the additional optional life insurance (see previous). Thus, coverage of optional family life will end following the expiration of the same fifty months.

Retiring employees can choose to elect unreduced Option C coverage by continuing to pay premiums after age sixty-five. Annuitants and compensationers who elect unreduced Option C can later cancel that election and have the full reduction.

A recipient of federal workers' compensation avoids a termination of federal employee group life insurance so long as he has met the "five or less than five" rule. This rule applies to basic life insurance, as well as any of the optional coverages. No accidental death and dismemberment insurance is available to the workers' compensation recipient.

702. How are State and Local Government employees covered under Social Security and Medicare?

State and local government employees are covered through Social Security and Medicare in one of the following ways:

- The coverage is mandated by law.

- There is a Section 218 agreement between the state and the Social Security Administration (SSA).

703. What is a Section 218 Agreement?

A Section 218 agreement (referring to section 218 of the Social Security Act) is an agreement entered into voluntarily between the state government and the Social Security Administration to provide Social Security coverage, Medicare Hospital Insurance (HI) coverage or both to local and state government employees. Under the agreement, the state decides whether to cover retirement system groups, non-retirement system groups, or both. Section 218 agreements are irrevocable.

All States, including the fifty states, Puerto Rico, the Virgin Islands, and approximately sixty interstate instrumentalities, have a Section 218 Agreement with SSA. These agreements allow the States, if they desire, to provide Social Security and Medicare Hospital Insurance (HI) or Medicare HI-only coverage for public employees.

Section 218 agreements cover positions, not individuals. If the position is covered for Social Security and Medicare under a Section 218 agreement, then any employee filling that position is subject to Social Security and Medicare taxes. Employees covered under a Section 218 agreement have the same coverage and benefit rights as employees in the private sector.

Public employees are brought under a Section 218 agreement in groups known as coverage groups. There are two basic coverage groups: absolute coverage groups and retirement system coverage groups. An absolute coverage group is composed of employees whose positions are not covered under a public retirement system. A retirement system coverage group is composed of employees whose positions are covered under a public retirement system.

A public retirement system may be covered under a Section 218 agreement only after a referendum is held. All States are authorized to use the majority vote referendum process. If a majority of all the eligible members vote in favor of coverage, all current and future employees in positions under the retirement system will be covered.

In addition to the majority vote referendum procedure, certain States and all interstate instrumentalities are authorized to divide a retirement system based on whether the employees in positions under the retirement system want coverage. Under the divided vote referendum, only those employees who vote "yes" and all future employees who become members of the retirement system will be covered. Members who vote "no" are not covered as long as they maintain continuous employment in a position within the same public retirement system coverage group.

704. What types of coverage are provided under a Section 218 agreement?

A Section 218 provides Old-Age, Survivors, Disability, and Hospital Insurance (OASDHI) coverage and protection. Employees have the same Social Security and Medicare Hospital Insurance (HI) coverage and rights that employees in the private sector who are covered for Social Security and Medicare on a mandatory basis.

705. Is Social Security and Medicare Hospital Insurance coverage mandatory or voluntary?

Social Security and Medicare Hospital Insurance became mandatory for state and local government employees after July 2, 1991 – if they meet the following criteria:

- They are not covered under a public retirement system; AND

- They are not covered under a Section 218 agreement unless specifically excluded by law.

Exclusions from Mandatory Social Security and Medicare Coverage

The following situations exclude a person from being covered by mandatory Social Security and Medicare:

- Hiring took place to relieve the individual from unemployment

- Employment consists of services as either a patient or an inmate in a hospital, home, or other institution

- Temporary services performed during an emergency such as a fire, storm, earthquake, snowstorm/blizzard, flood, or other emergency

- Performance of services as an elected official or election worker and pay is less that the threshold amount mandated by Federal law:

1968-1977	Less than $50
1978-1994	Less than $100
1995-1999	Less than $1,000
2000-2001	Less than $1,100
2002-2005	Less than $1,200

2006-2007	Less than $1,300
2008	Less than $1,400
2009-2012	Less than $1,500
2013-2015	Less than $1,600
2016	Less than $1,700
2017-2019	Less than $1,800
2020	Less than $1,900
2021	Less than $2,000
2022	Less than $2,000
2023	Less than $2,000

Note that in some states, poll workers are covered under a Section 218 agreement making the dollar amounts different.[1]

- Performance of services which are compensated solely on a fee basis

- Performance of services at a school where enrolled and regularly attending classes (although some states cover this under a Section 218 agreement)

- Performance of services as a non-resident alien with the below-listed conditions being met:

  o Temporary United States resident

  o Possession of a F1, J1, M1, or Q1 visa

  o Performance of the type of work for which admitted to the United States

Note

1. https://www.ssa.gov/slge/election_workers_chart.htm (Last accessed September 25, 2022).

706. What are the employment coverage thresholds for domestic employees for Social Security and Medicare Hospital Insurance?

For 2023, the domestic employee coverage threshold amount is $2,400. The table below shows the coverage thresholds for domestic employees beginning with 1994.

1994-1997	Less than $1,000
1998-1999	Less than $1,100
2000	Less than $1,200
2001-2002	Less than $1,300
2003-2005	Less than $1,400

2006-2007	Less than $1,500
2008	Less than $1,600
2009-2011	Less than $1,700
2012-2013	Less than $1,800
2014-2015	Less than $1,900
2016-2017	Less than $2,000
2018-2019	Less than $2,100
2020	Less than $2,200
2021	Less than $2,300
2022	Less than $2,400
2023	Less than $2,400

707. What are the definition of terms used in Section 218 Agreements?

Several terms are used when referencing Section 218 Agreements – these include[1]:

- State: For a Section 218 agreement, the term "state" includes all 50 United States, Puerto Rico, the U.S. Virgin Islands, and interstate instrumentalities. It DOES NOT include the District of Columbia, Guam, American Samoa, and the Commonwealth of the Northern Mariana Islands.

- Political Subdivision: For a Section 218 agreement, the term "political subdivision" means the separate legal entity of a state that has governmental powers and functions. This can include cities, counties, towns, townships, villages, school districts, utility service districts, etc.

- Interstate Instrumentality: For a Section 218 agreement, the term "interstate instrumentality" is an independent legal entity, created by two or more states, to carry out some function of government, such as a regional transportation commission or a bridge commission.

- Employee: For a Section 218 agreement, the term "employee" means the definition of employee in Section 210 of the Social Security Act. It can include appointed or elected officials.

- Absolute coverage group – a permanent grouping of employees, e.g. all the employees of a city or town. It is a coverage group for coverage purposes as well as for reporting purposes. When used for coverage purposes, the term also refers to groups of employees whose positions are not under a retirement system; such groups are also referred to as Section 218(b)(5) coverage groups.

- Coverage groups – employee groupings by which employees are covered under a Section 218 Agreement.

Note

1. SSA - POMS: SL 30001.302 - Definition of Terms for Section 218 - 01/02/2018 https://secure.ssa.gov/poms.nsf/lnx/193000130 (last accessed September 25, 2022).

708. What are coverage groups and retirement systems?

Several terms are used when referencing Section 218 Agreements – these include:

- Coverage Groups: A coverage group is a group of state and local governmental employees brought under a Section 218 agreement. The state decides, as defined by state and federal law, which groups to cover and when Social Security coverage begins. There are two kinds of coverage groups – absolute coverage groups and retirement system coverage groups.

  Absolute coverage groups contain employees in positions not covered by a state or local retirement system. Coverage is provided for all of these employees unless specifically excluded. Some employees can be ineligible for inclusion in the retirement system because of numerous factors, including age, service length, date of hire, etc.

- Retirement Systems: A retirement system is any pension, annuity, retirement fund, or similar vehicle or system maintained by a state or local government or instrumentality with the purpose of providing retirement benefits to participating employees. The IRS determines whether retirement systems not covered by Section 219 are exempt from mandatory Social Security and Medicare coverage.

709. Can states divide retirement systems?

Yes, twenty-three states are authorized to divide retirement systems based on the whether employees in positions in that retirement system want Social Security coverage. Under the divided vote referendum, only those employees that vote "YES" and all future employees who become members of the retirement system will be covered. Members who vote "NO" are not covered as long as they maintain continuous employment in a position within the same public retirement system coverage group. More information is available in a Social Security training presentation.[1] There have been no changes between 2022 and 2023.

These states authorized to divide coverage include:

Alaska	New Jersey
California	New Mexico
Connecticut	New York
Florida	North Dakota
Georgia	Pennsylvania
Hawaii	Rhode Island

Illinois	Tennessee
Kentucky	Texas
Louisiana	Vermont
Massachusetts	Wisconsin
Minnesota	Washington
Nevada	

Note

1. https://www.ssa.gov/section218training/documents/Resource_3.pdf (last accessed September 25, 2022).

CASE STUDIES USED IN PLANNING FOR SOCIAL SECURITY MAXIMIZATION

SITUATIONAL SOCIAL SECURITY

By Premier Social Security Consulting and the National Social Security Advisor Certificate Program

The case studies represent Situational Social Security. Each case study represents a different type of client. Advisors must understand the issues and strategies that relate to their unique clients. Situational Social Security represents clients in the following categories:

- Single

- Married Couples with narrow age differences

- Married Couples with wide age differences

- Ex-spouse for one or more ex-spouses

- Surviving spouse with one or more deceased spouse

- Clients eligible to file a Restricted Application

- Clients that filed and suspended by April 29, 2019

- Children

- Full Retirement Age ranging from 66 to 67

- Public Employees

Mr. Kiner and Mr. Blair prepared a list of questions advisors should ask clients depending on the client unique situation. To receive a complimentary copy, please send an e-mail to Marc Kiner at mkiner@mypremierplan.com.

Mr. Kiner and Mr. Blair created the National Social Security Advisor Certificate Program. To learn more about this program, please see the ad in this chapter or contact Marc Kiner at mkiner@mypremierplan.com.

National Social Security Advisor Certificate

Do you or your team have the knowledge and education to be a trusted resource for the 78 million baby boomers maturing into Social Security?

The National Underwriter Company and NSSA® can help!

The National Underwriter Company in partnership with National Social Security Association is offering a limited-time opportunity to earn the National Social Security Advisor (NSSA®) Certificate at a discounted group rate. *Training is also available on an individual basis.*

Your instructors, Marc Kiner, CPA, NSSA® and Jim Blair, NSSA®, are Social Security experts and co-authors of *2023 Social Security and Medicare Facts.*

Marc and Jim will travel to your facility and provide live training and support for your team! *Training is also available in live web-based as well as on-demand formats.*

Earn the National Social Security Advisor Certificate today!

Increasing Advisor Value With National Social Security Advisor Certificate Training

Advisors who earn the NSSA® Certificate will:

- Increase their credibility as a Social Security professional
- Gain confidence in educating others about Social Security
- Be a trusted resource to the millions of baby boomers who have questions about Social Security

Among the topics covered by the NSSA® program:

- Benefit Computations
- Retirement Benefits
- Medicare
- Spousal Elections
- Surviving Spousal Benefits
- Lump Sum Death Payments
- WEP/GPO
- Benefits Taxation
- COLA
- Case Studies
- Situational Social Security
- ...and much more

Contact Marc Kiner at mkiner@mypremierplan.com for your complimentary copy of *Situational Social Security — Questions to ask your clients regardless of their unique situation.*

For more information on providing training and the Certificate program for you or your team of advisors, please contact Marc Kiner, CPA:

mkiner@mypremierplan.com

513-247-0526 (office) • 513-218-8505 (cell)

www.mypremierplan.com

OVERVIEW

As people approach retirement age, a common concern that arises is that they will not have enough money to maintain the lifestyle to which they became accustomed to during their working years. Interest in understanding how Social Security benefits are calculated and established—and how to MAXIMIZE those benefits—is becoming more of an interest to individuals now that postretirement income has been shifted from the employer to the individual. The traditional "Defined Benefit" pension plan established by the employer as a fringe benefit has shifted to the "Defined Contribution" plan, such as 401(k) plans, managed by the individual.

Even with concerns regarding the future of the program, Social Security represents a source of retirement income that most individuals consider a critical and expected component of their retirement plan. Social Security provides workers (who have reached the defined eligibility) —as well as spouses, widows/widowers, and dependent children with an identified and steady monthly income that will increase over time—and in many cases, continue for as long as the individual lives. Although it does not fully replace an individual's earnings, in many cases it serves as a significant portion (or all) of the income of retirees. It is obvious that it is important to think about and analyze when advising an individual on when they should claim benefits under Social Security.

There is a myriad of strategies that can help maximize Social Security benefits for an individual or a couple. These strategies will vary based on the individual situation, the individuals involved, and the goals and desires of the parties. There is no "cookie-cutter" or "one-size-fits-all" situation; for each individual or couple involved, there can be a dozen or more strategies that can be formulated. Which strategy is "best" or correct will vary. One party may wish to maximize monthly income, while another may wish to establish a program to maximize lifetime benefits (the total amount collected from start of benefits to end-of-life).

Many factors will affect strategies:

- Income level over last thirty-five years (determination of Primary Insurance Amount [PIA])

- Income levels of spouse and eligibility for benefits

- Income needs during retirement

- Desire to maximize monthly income versus total benefits collected

- Life expectancy

- Age and Life expectancy of spouse

- Widow/Widower benefits

- Other sources of income: pensions, 401(k), investments

- Application of Earnings Test

- Marital status (Single, Married, Divorced)

- Filing date including:

  o Reduction Factor for early filing

  o Use of Delayed Retirement Credit by waiting to file after Full Retirement Age (FRA)

  o Use of "File and Suspend", Spousal Benefit, "Restricted Application" strategies

- Effect of other provisions such as Public Employee Pensions, Windfall Elimination Provision (WEP) and Government Pension Offset (GPO)

The Case Studies included in this section, developed by Premier Social Security Consulting, LLC and their principals, Marc Kiner and Jim Blair are not designed to be all-inclusive. As stated above, each situation is unique and will require both investigation and analysis. These Case Studies are designed to show you selected situations and some of the various outcomes that will result based on the different choices made. As you will see, the outcomes will vary based on the variance of the various factors detailed above. Please keep in mind that the figures used in the Case Studies are based upon CASH FLOW not PRESENT VALUE. Often, different choices will cause one spouse's benefits to increase while the other spouse's is lessened – but coordination of choices can lead to a higher combined benefit. Depending upon the choices made, the dollar amounts of the money collected over the life of the beneficiary can vary greatly – literally by hundreds of thousands of dollars and often 15, 20, or even close to 30 percent. Winding the confusing and complicated road of Social Security benefits requires both skill and focus. It is necessary to consider all factors—to review all options—to ensure the most favorable and lucrative outcome. For more information on how Premier Social Security Consultants can help you or your clients maximize the amount of Social Security benefits, please see the information in the front of this book.

CASE STUDIES

Case Study #1 Amanda: Divorced woman with two deceased ex-husbands, eligible for Surviving Divorced benefit

Case Study #2 Bob and Lisa: Married couple close in age, one is a high earner and the other has above average earnings

Case Study #3 Brenda: Divorced woman with deceased ex-husband, eligible for Surviving Divorced benefit

Case Study #4 Bruce and Debbie: Married couple with one high earner and other spouse with insufficient credits, approximately same age

Case Study #5 Carl: Widower

Case Study #6 Don and MaryAnn: Married couple three years apart in age, husband is high earner and wife is middle income earner

Case Study #7 Gordon and Cynthia: Married couple three years apart in age, husband is sole breadwinner

Case Study #8 George and Joan: Married couple approximately four years apart in age, husband had significantly more earnings

Case Study #9 Harold and Belinda: Married couple approximately four years apart in age, wife expected to die first, husband made moderately more than wife

Case Study #10 Greg and Alice: Married couple, approximately seven years apart in age, one is a high earner and other is a middle-income earner

Case Study #11 Jeff and Gary: Married same-sex couple, three years apart in age, one spouse with significantly more earnings than the other

Case Study #12 Jose and Kathy: Divorced couple, both now unmarried and past Full Retirement Age

Case Study #13 Larry and Judy: Married couple, one is a high earner with a spouse subject to Windfall Elimination Provision/Government Pension Offset

Case Study #14 Mark and Cindy: Married couple roughly the same age, with husband having significantly higher earnings than wife

Case Study #15 Mike and Leslie: Married couple approximately eleven years apart in age, husband made slightly less than wife

Case Study #16 Mike and Rita: Married couple, approximately a year apart in age, husband made moderately more than wife

Case Study #17 Paul and Kirsten: Married couple four years apart in age, with husband having significantly higher earnings

Case Study #18 Roger and Susan: Husband already at FRA with significantly younger spouse with children

Case Study #19 Sandy: Widow approaching FRA

Case Study #20 Shaun and JoAnn: Married couple, roughly the same age, one spouse is a high earner, the other spouse subject to the Government Pension Offset

Case Study #21 Sherry: Twice divorced woman

Case Study #22 Virginia: Single woman

Case Study #23 Jerry and Lyn: Married couple, Jerry on spouse is high earner, the other is not eligible for benefits

Case Study #24 Tony and Jessie: a married couple 5 years apart in age

Case Study #1

Amanda

Amanda was married to both of her ex-husbands for more than 10 years. Both have passed away and she is now eligible for Surviving Divorced Spouse benefits from either divorced spouse's record or her own retirement benefits. She can file for the survivor benefits at age 60 or later and she can apply on her own work record at any time starting with age 62, 1 month. Her full retirement age is 67. She is currently single. She has options such as filing for either ex-spousal benefit at age 60 or her own after attainment of age 62, 1 month. She can take the higher benefit in the beginning or a lower amount before full retirement (or benefit) age and the higher benefit at a later age. Even though she is eligible on her own work record, she will end up taking only surviving divorced spousal benefits as both are higher than her own. Her own benefit increased for full delayed retirement credits (24%) is not higher than either of the divorced spousal benefit.

Amanda	DOB: November 25, 1963 | Full Retirement Age Benefit: **$1,548 at 67** | Expected Death Age: **87.05**
Surviving Divorced Spouse #1	Full Retirement Age Benefit: **$2,186** at **67**
Surviving Divorced Spouse #2	Full Retirement Age Benefit: **$2,457** at **67**

	Strategy	Amanda
1	Nov, 2023 Amanda files for 71.5% of Surviving Divorced Spouse #1 Benefit ($1,562) at age 60. Nov, 2030 Amanda files for 100% of Surviving Divorced Spouse #2 ($2,457) at age 67.	$733,173
2	Nov, 2023 Amanda files for 71.5% of Surviving Divorced Spouse #2 Benefit ($1,756) at age 60. Nov, 2030 Amanda files for 100% of Surviving Divorced Spouse #1 ($2,186) at age 67.	$683,074
3	Nov, 2030 Amanda files for 100% of Surviving Divorced Spouse #2 ($2,457) at age 67.	$601,965

Case Study #2
Bob and Lisa

Bob and Lisa are a married couple who have no ex-spouses or children eligible for benefits on their earnings record. Bob is a high wage earner and Lisa is an above average wage earner. They are close in age, however, Bob and Lisa's full retirement age are both 67. They have 9 reasonable options. The determination of the best option, however, belongs to Bob and Lisa. Factors to take into consideration are dependent on when they want benefits to begin.

Benefits before full retirement age lowers the monthly benefit amount and this reduction is permanent. Earnings from employment or the net profit from self-employment may increase benefits paid. The importance of survivor benefits (widow or widower benefits) will determine if Bob's benefits are taken at age 62, 1 month, age 70 or somewhere in between.

Bob and Lisa want to make sure they maximize benefits. To maximize benefits, one of them (normally the higher earner) will wait until age 70 to take benefits. This directly effects and maximizes the survivor benefit. Keeping in mind with all options they will want to coordinate benefits to maximize benefits for the household.

Bob	DOB: August 16, 1961 | Full Retirement Age Benefit: **$2,540** at **67** | Expected Death Age: **85**
Lisa	DOB: January 9, 1962 | Full Retirement Age Benefit: **$1,777** at **67** | Expected Death Age: **87.04**

	Strategy	Bob	Lisa	Total
1	Aug, 2031 Bob files for worker benefits ($3,149) at age 70 for 124% of PIA (36 Months Delayed Retirement Credit). Jan, 2032 Lisa files for worker benefits ($2,203) at age 70 for 124.00% of PIA (36 Months Delayed Retirement Credit). Survivor benefit $3,149	$566,820	$489,442	$1,056,262
2	Jan, 2029 Lisa files for worker benefits ($1,777) at age 67 for 100.00% of PIA. Aug, 2031 Bob files for worker benefits ($3,149) at age 70 for 124% of PIA (36 Months Delayed Retirement Credit). Survivor benefit $3,149	$566,820	$478,864	$1,045,684
3	Aug, 2027 Bob files for worker benefits ($2,540) at age 67 for 100.00% of PIA. Jan, 2031 Lisa files for worker benefits ($2,203) at age 70 for 124.00% of PIA (36 Months Delayed Retirement Credit). Survivor benefit $2,540	$538,480	$465,613	$1,004,093

	Strategy	Bob	Lisa	Total
4	Feb, 2023 Lisa files for worker benefits ($1,251) at age 62, 1 months for 70.42% of PIA (59 Months Reduction). Aug, 2030 Bob files for worker benefits ($3,149) at age 70 for 124% of PIA (36 Months Delayed Retirement Credit). Survivor benefit $3,149	$554,224	$442,981	$997,205
5	Aug, 2027 Bob files for worker benefits ($2,540) at age 67 for 100.00% of PIA. Jan, 2028 Lisa files for worker benefits ($1,777) at age 67 for 100.00% of PIA. Survivor benefit $2,540	$538,480	$456,739	$995,219
6	Feb, 2023 Lisa files for worker benefits ($1,251) at age 62, 1 months for 70.42% of PIA (59 Months Reduction). Aug, 2027 Bob files for worker benefits ($2,540) at age 67 for 100.00% of PIA. Survivor benefit $2,540	$538,480	$421,666	$960,146
7	Sep, 2022 Bob files for worker benefits ($1,788) at age 62, 1 months for 70.42% of PIA (59 Months Reduction). Jan, 2031 Lisa files for worker benefits ($2,203) at age 70 for 124.00% of PIA (36 Months Delayed Retirement Credit). Survivor benefit $2,203	$484,548	$453,818	$938,366
8	Sep, 2022 Bob files for worker benefits ($1,788) at age 62, 1 months for 70.42% of PIA (59 Months Reduction). Jan, 2028 Lisa files for worker benefits ($1,777) at age 67 for 100.00% of PIA. Survivor benefit $1,788	$484,548	$430,419	$914,967
9	Sep, 2022 Bob files for worker benefits ($1,788) at age 62, 1 months for 70.42% of PIA (59 Months Reduction). Feb, 2023 Lisa files for worker benefits ($1,251) at age 62, 1 months for 70.42% of PIA (59 Months Reduction). Survivor benefit $1,788	$484,548	$395,346	$879,894

CASE STUDY #3
Brenda

Brenda was married to her ex-husband for more than 10 years. Her ex-spouse has passed away and she is now eligible for Surviving Divorced Spouse benefits or her own retirement benefits. She can file for the survivor benefit at any time now since she is past age 60. She is currently single although since she is past age 60, even if she remarries she is still entitled to Surviving Divorced Spouse benefits. She has options such as filing for the ex-spousal benefit and taking her own at age 70, filing on her own before her full retirement age and staying on those benefits, etc.

Brenda	DOB: May 3, 1960	Full Retirement Age Benefit: **$2,630** at age **67**	Expected Death Age: **87.03**
Surviving Divorced Spouse	Full Retirement Age For Survivor Benefit: **$1,888** at **66** year & **8** months

	Strategy	Brenda
1	Jan 2023 Benda files for survivor benefits ($1,565) at age 62, 8 months for 82.9% of PIA. May 2030 Brenda files for worker benefits ($3,295) at age 70 for 124% of retirement PIA.	$819,785
2	Jan 2027 Brenda files for survivor benefits ($1,888) at age 66, 8 months for 100% of PIA. May 2030 Brenda files for worker benefits ($3,295) at age 70 for 124% of retirement PIA.	$757,585
3	Jan 2023 Benda files for survivor benefits ($1,565) at age 62, 8 months for 82.9% of PIA. May 2027 Brenda files for worker benefits ($2,630) at age 67 for 100% of retirement PIA.	$720,470
4	Jan 2027 Brenda files for survivor benefits ($1,888) at age 66, 8 months for 100% of PIA. May 2027 Brenda files for worker benefits ($2,630) at age 67 for 100% of retirement PIA.	$646,642
5	Jan 2024 Brenda files for worker benefits ($1,928) at age 62, 8 months for 73.333% of PIA (52 Months Reduction).	$568,760

CASE STUDY #4
Bruce and Debbie

Bruce and Debbie are a married couple who have no ex-spouses they are eligible to draw benefits from since they are currently married. They have no children who are eligible for benefits on their earnings record. Bruce is a high earner and Debbie did not earn enough credits to be eligible for Social Security benefits from her own work record. Both have a full retirement age of 67. Factors to take into consideration are dependent on when they want benefits to begin. Debbie cannot begin benefits until Bruce files an application for benefits. Neither can take advantage of the restricted application strategy.

If Bruce takes benefits before his full retirement age, he will not only reduce his own benefit, but also the widows benefit payable to Debbie if she survives him. The importance of that benefit will have a lot to do with the decision Bruce makes when determining his filing date for Social Security.

Bruce	DOB: November 3, 1961 | Full Retirement Age Benefit: **$2,302** at **67** | Expected Death Age: **85**
Debbie	DOB: January 10, 1961 | Full Retirement Age Benefit: **$0** at **67** | Expected Death Age: **87.04**

	Strategy	Bruce	Debbie	Total
1	Nov, 2028 Bruce files for worker benefits ($2,302) at age 67 for 100.00% of PIA. Nov, 2028 Debbie files for 100.00% of spousal benefits ($1,151) at age 67, 10 months. Survivor benefit $2,302	$497,232	$290,052	$787,284
2	Nov, 2031 Bruce files for worker benefits ($2,854) at age 70 for 124.00% of PIA (36 Months Delayed Retirement Credit). Nov, 2031 Debbie files for 100.00% of spousal benefits ($1,151) at age 70, 10 months. Survivor benefit $2,854	$513,720	$258,552	$772,272
3	Dec, 2023 Bruce files for worker benefits ($1,620) at age 62, 1 month for 70.417% of PIA (59 Months Reduction). Jan, 2027 Debbie files for 100.00% of spousal benefits ($1,151) at age 67. Survivor benefit $1,620	$445,500	$289,286	$734,786
4	Dec, 2023 Bruce files for worker benefits ($1,620) at age 62, 1 month for 70.417% of PIA (59 Months Reduction). Dec, 2023 Debbie files for 69.583% (49 Months Reduction) of spousal benefits ($800) at age 62, 11 months. Survivor benefit $1,620	$445,500	$249,160	$694,660

CASE STUDY #5

Carl

Carl's spouse died leaving him eligible for widower benefits. Carl has the option to file for benefits as a widower and switch to his own work record later (no later than age 70) or file on his own work record before his full retirement age and take the survivor benefit at his full benefit age. Note that Carl's full retirement age for retirement benefits is age 66, 4 months and his full benefit age for widower benefits is age 66.

Carl	DOB: June 3, 1961 | Full Retirement Age Benefit: **$2,244** at **67** | Expected Death Age: **85**
Widower	Survivor Benefit: **$1,886**

	Strategy	**Carl**
1	Jan, 2023 Carl files at age 61, 7 months for 78.1% of survivor benefits ($1,472). Jun, 2030 Carl files for worker benefits ($2,782) at age 70 for 124% of PIA (36 Months Delayed Retirement Credit).	$649,432
2	Jan, 2023 Carl files at age 61, 7 months for 78.1% of survivor benefits ($1,472). Jun, 2027 Carl files for worker benefits ($2,244) at age 67 for 100% of PIA.	$580,384
3	Apr, 2028 Carl files at age 66, 10 months for 100.00% of Survivor Benefit ($1,886). Jun, 2031 Carl files for worker benefits ($2,782) at age 70 for 124% of PIA (36 Months Delayed Retirement Credit).	$568,656
4	Jul, 2023 Carl files for worker benefits ($1,617) at age 62, 1 month for 72.083% of PIA (55 Months Reduction). Apr, 2028 Carl files at age 66, 10 months for 100.00% of Survivor Benefit ($1,886).	$502,779
5	Apr, 2027 Carl files for 100.00% of Survivor Benefits ($1,886) at age 66, 10 months. Jun, 2027 Carl files for worker benefits ($2,303) at age 67 for 102.67% of PIA (4 Months Delayed Retirement Credit).	$488,476
6	Jan, 2023 Carl files at age 61, 7 months for 78.1% of survivor benefits ($1,472). Jul, 2023 Carl files for worker benefits ($1,580) at age 62, 1 month for 70.417% of PIA (59 Months Reduction).	$443,332

CASE STUDY #6
Don and MaryAnn

Carl's spouse died leaving him eligible for widower benefits. Carl has the option to file for benefits as a widower and switch to his own work record later (no later than age 70) or file on his own work record before his full retirement age and take the survivor benefit at his full benefit age. Note that Carl's full retirement age for retirement benefits is age 66, 4 months and his full benefit age for widower benefits is age 66.

Carl	DOB: June 3, 1961 | Full Retirement Age Benefit: **$2,244** at **67** | Expected Death Age: **85**
Widower	Survivor Benefit: **$1,886**

	Strategy	**Carl**
1	Jan, 2023 Carl files at age 61, 7 months for 78.1% of survivor benefits ($1,472). Jun, 2030 Carl files for worker benefits ($2,782) at age 70 for 124% of PIA (36 Months Delayed Retirement Credit).	$649,432
2	Jan, 2023 Carl files at age 61, 7 months for 78.1% of survivor benefits ($1,472). Jun, 2027 Carl files for worker benefits ($2,244) at age 67 for 100% of PIA.	$580,384
3	Apr, 2028 Carl files at age 66, 10 months for 100.00% of Survivor Benefit ($1,886). Jun, 2031 Carl files for worker benefits ($2,782) at age 70 for 124% of PIA (36 Months Delayed Retirement Credit).	$568,656
4	Jul, 2023 Carl files for worker benefits ($1,617) at age 62, 1 month for 72.083% of PIA (55 Months Reduction). Apr, 2028 Carl files at age 66, 10 months for 100.00% of Survivor Benefit ($1,886).	$502,779
5	Apr, 2027 Carl files for 100.00% of Survivor Benefits ($1,886) at age 66, 10 months. Jun, 2027 Carl files for worker benefits ($2,303) at age 67 for 102.67% of PIA (4 Months Delayed Retirement Credit).	$488,476
6	Jan, 2023 Carl files at age 61, 7 months for 78.1% of survivor benefits ($1,472). Jul, 2023 Carl files for worker benefits ($1,580) at age 62, 1 month for 70.417% of PIA (59 Months Reduction).	$443,332

CASE STUDY #7
Gordon and Cynthia

Gordon and Cynthia, a married couple three years apart in age. The husband, Gordon, was the sole breadwinner. Cynthia has no retirement benefit of her own. Gordon will reach full retirement age (FRA) at age sixty-six and six months, while Cynthia's FRA is sixty-seven. Gordon does not have the claim and suspend strategy available. If he waits to file beyond his FRA Cynthia must also wait to file. Cynthia is expected to survive Gordon by approximately six and one half years.

Gordon	DOB: January 13, 1957 | Full Retirement Age Benefit: **$2,338** at **66** year & **6** months | Expected Death Age: **84.06**
Cynthia	DOB: December 5, 1960 | Full Retirement Age Benefit: **$0** at age **67** | Expected Death Age: **87.04**

	Strategy	Gordon	Cynthia	Total
1	Jan, 2027 Gordon files for worker benefits ($2,992) at age 70 for 128% of PIA (42 Months Delayed Retirement Credit). Dec, 2027 Cynthia files for 100.00% of spousal benefits ($1,169) at age 67. Survivor benefit $2,992	$520,608	$432,899	$953,507
2	Jan, 2027 Gordon files for worker benefits ($2,992) at age 70 for 128% of PIA (42 Months Delayed Retirement Credit). Jan, 2027 Cynthia files for 92.361% (11 Months Reduction) of spousal benefits ($1,079) at age 66, 1 month. Survivor benefit $2,992	$520,608	$430,098	$950,706
3	July, 2023 Gordon files for worker benefits ($2,338) at age 66, 6 months for 100.00% of PIA. Dec, 2027 Cynthia files for 100.00% of spousal benefits ($1,169) at age 67. Survivor benefit $2,338	$505,008	$379,925	$884,933
4	Jan, 2023 Gordon files for worker benefits ($2,260) at age 66 for 96.667% of PIA (6 Months Reduction). Dec, 2027 Cynthia files for 100.00% of spousal benefits ($1,169) at age 67. Survivor benefit $2,260	$501,720	$373,607	$875,327

	Strategy	Gordon	Cynthia	Total
5	July, 2023 Gordon files for worker benefits ($2,338) at age 66, 6 months for 100.00% of PIA. July, 2023 Cynthia files for 67.917% (53 Months Reduction) of spousal benefits ($793) at age 62, 7 months. Survivor benefit $2,338	$505,008	$360,666	$865,674
6	Jan, 2023 Gordon files for worker benefits ($2,260) at age 66 for 96.667% of PIA (6 Months Reduction). Jan, 2023 Cynthia files for 65.417% (59 Months Reduction) of spousal benefits ($764) at age 62, 1 months. Survivor benefit $2,260	$501,720	$352,668	$854,388

CASE STUDY #8
George and Joan

George and Joan, a married couple four years apart in age. George will reach full retirement age (FRA) at age sixty-six and 4 months and Joan at age sixty-seven. The husband, George, had significantly more income than the wife, Joan. Joan is expected to survive George by approximately six and a half years.

George	DOB: October 14, 1957 | Full Retirement Age Benefit: **$2,647** at **66** year & **6** months | Expected Death Age: **84.06**
Joan	DOB: September 7, 1961 | Full Retirement Age Benefit: **$724** at **67** | Expected Death Age: **87.04**

	Strategy	George	Joan	Total
1	Oct 2027 George files for worker benefits ($3,388) at age 70 for 128% of PIA (42 Months Delayed Retirement Credit). Sep 2028 Joan files for worker benefits ($724) at age 67 for 100.00% of PIA. Sep 2028 Joan files for 100.00% of spousal benefits ($599) at age 67. Survivor benefit $3,388	$589,512	$490,077	$1,079,589
2	Oct 2023 Joan files for worker benefits ($509) at age 62, 1 month for 70.417% of PIA (59 Months Reduction). Oct 2027 George files for worker benefits ($3,388) at age 70 for 128% of PIA (42 Months Delayed Retirement Credit). Oct 2027 Joan files for 92.361% (11 Months Reduction) of spousal benefits ($553) at age 66, 1 month. Survivor benefit $3,388	$589,512	$483,648	$1,073,160
3	April 2024 George files for worker benefits ($2,647) at age 66, 6 months for 100.00% of PIA. Sept 2028 Joan files for worker benefits ($724) at age 67 for 100.00% of PIA. Sept 2028 Joan files for 100.00% of spousal benefits ($599) at age 67. Survivor benefit $2,647	$571,752	$430,056	$1,001,808

	Strategy	George	Joan	Total
4	Oct, 2023 Joan files for worker benefits ($509) at age 62, 1 month for 70.417% of PIA (59 Months Reduction). April 2024 George files for worker benefits ($2,647) at age 66, 6 months for 100.00% of PIA. April 2024 Joan files for 67.917% (53 Months Reduction) of spousal benefits ($406) at age 62, 7 months. Survivor benefit $2,647	$571,752	$415,610	$987,362
5	Jan 2023 George files for worker benefits ($2,455) at age 65, 3 months for 92.778% of PIA (13 Months Reduction). Sept 2028 Joan files for worker benefits ($724) at age 67 for 100.00% of PIA. Sept 2028 Joan files for 100.00% of spousal benefits ($599) at age 67. Survivor benefit $2,455	$567,105	$414,504	$981,609
6	Jan 2023 George files for worker benefits ($2,455) at age 65, 3 months for 92.778% of PIA (13 Months Reduction). Oct 2023 Joan files for worker benefits ($509) at age 62, 1 month for 70.417% of PIA (59 Months Reduction). Oct 2023 Joan files for 65.417% (59 Months Reduction) of spousal benefits ($391) at age 62, 1 month. Survivor benefit $2,455	$567,105	$398,655	$965,760

CASE STUDY #9
Harold and Belinda

Harold and Belinda, a married couple four years apart in age. Harold will reach full retirement age (FRA) at age sixty-six and six months. Belinda reached FRA at age sixty-six. The husband, Harold, made moderately more than his wife, Belinda. Although Belinda is expected to live to age eighty-seven and two months, she is expected to die approximately 1 1/2 years before Harold.

Harold	DOB: June 10, 1957 | Full Retirement Age Benefit: **$2,331** at **66** year & **6** months | Expected Death Age: **84.05**
Belinda	DOB: April 3, 1953 | Full Retirement Age Benefit: **$1,738** at **66** Year & **0** months | Expected Death Age: **87.02**

	<u>Strategy</u>	<u>Harold</u>	<u>Belinda</u>	<u>Total</u>
1	April, 2023 Belinda files for worker benefits ($2,294) at age 70 for 132.00% of PIA (48 Months Delayed Retirement Credit). June, 2027 Harold files for worker benefits ($2,983) at age 70 for 128.00% of PIA (42 Months Delayed Retirement Credit). Survivor benefit $2,983	$516,059	$472,564	$988,623
2	July, 2022 Belinda files for worker benefits ($2,120) at age 69, 3 months for 122% of PIA (33 Months Delayed Retirement Credit). Jan, 2023 benefit increases to $2,189 to 126% of PIA (39 Delayed Retirement Credits). June, 2027 Harold files for worker benefits ($2,983) at age 70 for 128.00% of PIA (42 Months Delayed Retirement Credit). Survivor benefit $2,983	$516,059	$470,221	$986,280
3	April, 2023 Belinda files for worker benefits ($2,294) at age 70 for 132.00% of PIA (48 Months Delayed Retirement Credit). Dec, 2023 Harold files for worker benefits ($2,331) at age 66, 6 months for 100.00% of PIA. Survivor benefit $2,331	$501,165	$472,564	$973,729

	Strategy	Harold	Belinda	Total
4	Jan, 2023 Harold files for worker benefits ($2,188) at age 65, 7 months for 93.889% of PIA (11 Months Reduction). Jan, 2023 Belinda files a restricted application at age 69, 9 months for 100% of spousal benefit ($1,165). April, 2023 Belinda files for worker benefits ($2,294) at age 70 for 132.00% of PIA (48 Months Delayed Retirement Credit). Survivor benefit $2,294	$496,290	$476,059	$972,349
5	July, 2022 Belinda files for worker benefits ($2,120) at age 69, 3 months for 122% of PIA (33 Months Delayed Retirement Credit). Jan, 2023 benefit increases to $2,189 to 126% of PIA (39 Delayed Retirement Credits). Dec, 2023 Harold files for worker benefits ($2,331) at age 66, 6 months for 100.00% of PIA. Survivor benefit $2,331	$501,165	$470,221	$971,386
6	July, 2022 Belinda files for worker benefits ($2,120) at age 69, 3 months for 122% of PIA (33 Months Delayed Retirement Credit). Jan, 2023 benefit increases to $2,189 to 126% of PIA (39 Delayed Retirement Credits). Jan, 2023 Harold files for worker benefits ($2,188) at age 65, 7 months for 93.889% of PIA (11 Months Reduction). Survivor benefit $2,188	$494,488	$470,221	$964,709

CASE STUDY #10
Greg and Alice

Greg and Alice are a married couple. Greg is a high earner and Alice is a middle-income earner. There is over 7 year's difference in their ages. He should consider waiting beyond his full retirement age to take his benefit to increase the survivor benefit to Alice. Based on normal life expectancies, Alice will receive widow's benefits sooner and longer than a surviving spouse who was similar in age to their spouse. Alice will, however, have various filing options available to her. She should keep in mind that if she survives Greg before filing for any benefits she will need to reconsider her options to include widow's benefits.

Greg	DOB: August 29, 1961 | Full Retirement Age Benefit: **$2,153** at **67** | Expected Death Age: **85**
Alice	DOB: January 11, 1969 | Full Retirement Age Benefit: **$1,449** at **67** | Expected Death Age: **87.08**

	Strategy	**Greg**	**Alice**	**Total**
1	Feb, 2031 Alice files for worker benefits ($1,020) at age 62, 1 month for 70.417% of PIA (59 Months Reduction). Aug, 2031 Greg files for worker benefits ($2,669) at age 70 for 124.00% of PIA (36 Months Delayed Retirement Credit). Survivor benefit $2,669	$480,420	$512,669	$993,089
2	Aug, 2031 Greg files for worker benefits ($2,669) at age 70 for 124.00% of PIA (36 Months Delayed Retirement Credit). Jan, 2036 Alice files for worker benefits ($1,449) at age 67 for 100.00% of PIA. Survivor benefit $2,669	$480,420	$506,972	$987,392
3	Aug, 2031 Greg files for worker benefits ($2,669) at age 70 for 124.00% of PIA (36 Months Delayed Retirement Credit). Jan, 2039 Alice files for worker benefits ($1,796) at age 70 for 124.00% of PIA (36 Months Delayed Retirement Credit). Survivor benefit $2,669	$480,420	$486,385	$966,805
4	Aug, 2028 Greg files for worker benefits ($2,153) at age 67 for 100.00% of PIA. Feb, 2031 Alice files for worker benefits ($1,020) at age 62, 1 month for 70.42% of PIA (59 Months Reduction). Survivor benefit $2,153	$465,048	$450,233	$915,281

	Strategy	Greg	Alice	Total
5	Aug, 2028 Greg files for worker benefits ($2,153) at age 67 for 100.00% of PIA. Jan, 2036 Alice files for worker benefits ($1,449) at age 67 for 100.00% of PIA. Survivor benefit $2,153	$465,048	$444,536	$909,584
6	Aug, 2028 Greg files for worker benefits ($2,153) at age 67 for 100.00% of PIA. Jan, 2039 Alice files for worker benefits ($1,796) at age 70 for 124.00% of PIA (36 Months Delayed Retirement Credit). Survivor benefit $2,153	$465,048	$423,949	$888,997
7	Sep, 2023 Greg files for worker benefits ($1,516) at age 62, 1 month for 70.417% of PIA (59 Months Reduction). Jan, 2039 Alice files for worker benefits ($1,796) at age 70 for 124.00% of PIA (36 Months Delayed Retirement Credit). Survivor benefit $1,796	$416,900	$380,752	$797,652
8	Sep, 2023 Greg files for worker benefits ($1,516) at age 62, 1 month for 70.42% of PIA (59 Months Reduction). Feb, 2031 Alice files for worker benefits ($1,020) at age 62, 1 month for 70.42% of PIA (59 Months Reduction). Survivor benefit $1,516	$416,900	$373,156	$790,056
9	Sep, 2023 Greg files for worker benefits ($1,516) at age 62, 1 month for 70.42% of PIA (59 Months Reduction). Jan, 2036 Alice files for worker benefits ($1,449) at age 67 for 100.00% of PIA. Survivor benefit $1,516	$416,900	$367,459	$784,359

CASE STUDY #11
Jeff and Gary

Jeff and Gary are a married couple. With the ruling on same sex marriages by the Supreme Court, Jeff and Gary were married and eligible for the same benefits as any other married couple. All of the same requirements must be met for eligibility before benefits can be paid. Restricted Application strategies are available for Jeff. Both have their own earnings and can file independently of each other; however, they can also coordinate spousal benefits to maximize the benefits paid to them over their lifetimes. To maximize benefits, Jeff will wait until age 70 to file for benefits which will increase his monthly benefit payment and also maximize the surviving spousal benefit payable to Gary should he survive Jeff. Jeff was born on the 1st day of the month. Social Security regulations say you attain the age of your birthday the day before your birthday. Jeff attains age 70 in December 2023.

Jeff	DOB: January 1, 1954 | Full Retirement Age Benefit: **$2,568** at **66** year & **0** months | Expected Death Age: **85**
Gary	DOB: August 25, 1957 | Full Retirement Age Benefit: **$1,146** at **66** year & **6** months | Expected Death Age: **84.06**

	Strategy	**Jeff**	**Gary**	**Total**
1	Jan, 2023 Gary files for worker benefits ($1,063) at age 65, 5 months for 92.778% of PIA (13 Months Reduction). Jan, 2023 Jeff files a restricted application at age 69, 1 month for 100% of spousal benefit ($573). Dec, 2023 Jeff files for worker benefits ($3,389) at age 70 for 132.00% of PIA (48 Months Delayed Retirement Credit). Dec, 2023 Gary files for 100.00% of spousal benefits ($138) at age 67, 4 months. Survivor benefit $3,389	$616,323	$356,655	$972,978
2	Dec, 2023 Jeff files for worker benefits ($3,389) at age 70 for 132.00% of PIA (49 Months Delayed Retirement Credit). Feb, 2024 Gary files for worker benefits ($1,146) at age 66, 6 months for 100.00% of PIA. Feb, 2024 Gary files for 100.00% of spousal benefits ($138) at age 67, 4 months. Survivor benefit $3,389	$610,020	$357,334	$967,354

	Strategy	Jeff	Gary	Total
3	Jul, 2022 Jeff files for worker benefits ($2,996) at age 68, 7 months for 116.67% of PIA (25 Month Delayed Retirement Credit). Jan, 2023 benefit increases to $3,098 for 120.67% of PIA (31 Months Delayed Retirement Credit). Feb, 2024 Gary files for worker benefits ($1,146) at age 66, 6 months for 100.00% of PIA. Feb, 2024 Gary files for 100.00% of spousal benefits ($138) at age 66, 4 months. Survivor benefit $3,098	$609,694	$346,276	$955,970
4	Jul, 2022 Jeff files for worker benefits ($2,996) at age 68, 7 months for 116.67% of PIA (25 Month Delayed Retirement Credit). Jan, 2023 benefit increases to $3,098 for 120.67% of PIA (31 Months Delayed Retirement Credit). Jan, 2023 Gary files for worker benefits ($1,063) at age 65, 5 months for 92.778% of PIA (13 Months Reduction). Jan, 2023 Gary files for 90.972% of spousal benefits ($125) at age 65, 5 months. Survivor benefit $3,098	$609,694	$344,632	$954,326
5	Dec, 2023 Jeff files for worker benefits ($3,389) at age 70 for 132.00% of PIA (48 Months Delayed Retirement Credit). Aug, 2027 Gary files for worker benefits ($1,466) at age 70 for 128% of PIA (42 Months Delayed Retirement Credit). Survivor benefit $3,389	$610,020	$328,158	$938,178
6	Jul, 2022 Jeff files for worker benefits ($2,996) at age 68, 7 months for 116.67% of PIA (25 Month Delayed Retirement Credit). Jan, 2023 benefit increases to $3,098 for 120.67% of PIA (31 Months Delayed Retirement Credit). Aug, 2027 Gary files for worker benefits ($1,466) at age 70 for 128% of PIA (42 Months Delayed Retirement Credit). Survivor benefit $3,098	$609,694	$317,100	$926,794

CASE STUDY #12
Jose and Kathy

Jose and Kathy are a divorced couple. They were married for over 10 years and have been divorced for over 2 years. They are both are single. They each have their own earnings and are eligible for a benefit from their own work record. Both are past their full retirement age and have filing options independent of the other. They are able to elect benefits 6 months retroactive from when they determined their options. Kathy is eligible for benefits from Jose's record as a divorced spouse regardless of the filing status of Jose. Kathy files for benefits in January 2022. Note the loss in benefits if Kathy does not take advantage of the restricted application while waiting until age 70 to take her own benefit.

Kathy	DOB: July 16, 1953 | Full Retirement Age Benefit: **$1,002** at **66** year & **0** months | Expected Death Age: **87.04**
Jose	DOB: April 11, 1953 | Full Retirement Age Benefit: **$2,270** at **66** year & **0** months | Expected Death Age: **85.02**

	Strategy	Kathy
1	July, 2022 Kathy files a 'restricted application' at age 69 for 100.00% of ex-spousal benefits ($1,135). Jul, 2023 Kathy files for worker benefits ($1,322) at age 70 for 132.00% of PIA (48 Months Delayed Retirement Credit). Surviving Divorced Spouse benefit $2,270	$316,088
2	July, 2022 Kathy files for worker benefits ($1,202) at age 69 for 120% of PIA (30 Months Delayed Retirement Age). Jan, 2023 benefit increases to $1,242 for 124% of PIA (36 Months Delayed Retirement Credit). Surviving Divorced Spouse benefit $2,270	$302,812
3	Jul, 2023 Kathy files for worker benefits ($1,322) at age 70 for 132.00% of PIA (48 Months Delayed Retirement Credit). Widows benefit $2,270	$302,468

CASE STUDY #13
Larry and Judy

Larry is a high earner. Judy worked most of her career in employment that was not covered by Social Security and is eligible for a pension from that work. She also has some work under Social Security covered employment and has earned her 40 credits. Judy's own benefit based from her own Social Security covered work will be reduced due to the Windfall Elimination Provision (WEP). Before the WEP offset, Judy's Social Security benefit would be $571 per month at her full retirement age. WEP reduces this benefit to $254. Her non-covered pension also affects her spousal and potential survivor benefit. These benefits are reduced due to the Government Pension Offset (GPO) by 2/3rds of the amount of her non-covered pension. Her non-covered pension is $1,476 and therefore her spousal and potential survivor benefits are reduced $984. Judy will be full retirement age in June 2022.

Larry	DOB: December 23, 1953 | Full Retirement Age Benefit: **$2,589** at **66** year & **0** months | Expected Death Age: **87.03**
Judy	DOB: February 25, 1957 | Full Retirement Age Benefit: **$254** at **66** year & **6** months | Expected Death Age: **87**

	Strategy	Larry	Judy	Total
1	Jan, 2023 Judy files for worker benefits ($244) at age 65, 11 months for 96.1% of PIA (7 Months Reduction). Jan, 2023 Larry files a restricted application at age 69, 1 month for 100% of spousal benefit ($127). Dec, 2023 Larry files for worker benefits ($3,417) at age 70 for 132.00% of PIA (48 Months Delayed Retirement Credit). Dec, 2023 Judy files for 100.00% of spousal benefits ($56) at age 66, 10 months. Survivor benefit $2,433	$616,457	$207,640	$824,097
2	Aug, 2023 Judy files for worker benefits ($254) at age 66, 6 months for 100.00% of PIA. Aug, 2023 Larry files a restricted application at age 69, 8 months for 100% of spousal benefit ($127) Dec, 2023 Larry files for worker benefits ($3,417) at age 70 for 132.00% of PIA (48 Months Delayed Retirement Credit). Dec, 2023 Judy files for 100.00% of spousal benefits ($56) at age 66, 10 months. Survivor benefit $2,433	$615,568	$207,662	$823,230

	Strategy	Larry	Judy	Total
3	Dec, 2023 Larry files for worker benefits ($3,417) at age 70 for 132.00% of PIA (48 Months Delayed Retirement Credit). Feb, 2027 Judy files for worker benefits ($325) at age 70 for 128% of PIA (42 Months Delayed Retirement Credit). Survivor benefit $2,433	$615,060	$196,996	$812,056
4	July, 2022 Larry files for worker benefits ($3,020) at age 68, 7 months for 116.67% of PIA (25 Month Delayed Retirement Credit). Jan, 2023 benefit increases to $3,124 for 120.67% of PIA (31 Months Delayed Retirement Credit). Aug, 2023 Judy files for worker benefits ($254) at age 66, 4 months for 100.00% of PIA. Aug, 2023 Judy files for 100.00% of spousal benefits ($56) at age 66, 4 months. Survivor benefit $2,140	$614,804	$189,720	$804,524
5	July, 2022 Larry files for worker benefits ($3,020) at age 68, 7 months for 116.67% of PIA (25 Month Delayed Retirement Credit). Jan, 2023 benefit increases to $3,124 for 120.67% of PIA (31 Months Delayed Retirement Credit). Jan, 2023 Judy files for worker benefits ($244) at age 65, 11 months for 96.1% of PIA (7 Months Reduction). Jan, 2023 Judy files for 95.139% of spousal benefits ($53) at age 65, 11 Months. Survivor benefit $2,140	$614,804	$189,407	$804,211
6	July, 2022 Larry files for worker benefits ($3,020) at age 68, 7 months for 116.67% of PIA (25 Month Delayed Retirement Credit). Jan, 2023 benefit increases to $3,124 for 120.67% of PIA (31 Months Delayed Retirement Credit). Feb, 2025 Judy files for worker benefits ($328) at age 70 for 128% of PIA (42 Months Delayed Retirement Credit). Survivor benefit $2,140	$614,804	$178,830	$793,634

CASE STUDY #14
Mark and Cindy

Mark and Cindy, a married couple less than a year apart in age. The couple both born at the latter end of the Baby Boom, will reach full retirement age (FRA) later than those born a decade earlier. Mark and Cindy will each achieve FRA at age sixty-seven. The husband, Mark, had significantly more income than the wife, Cindy. Cindy is expected to survive Mark by approximately three years.

Mark	DOB: September 4, 1961 | Full Retirement Age Benefit: **$2,543** at age **67** | Expected Death Age: **85**
Cindy	DOB: July 18, 1962 | Full Retirement Age Benefit: **$1,292** at age **67** | Expected Death Age: **87.04**

	Strategy	Mark	Cindy	Total
1	Sep, 2031 Mark files for worker benefits ($3,153) at age 70 for 124% of PIA (36 Months Delayed Retirement Credit). July, 2032 Cindy files for worker benefits ($1,602) at age 70 for 124.00% of PIA (36 Months Delayed Retirement Credit). Survivor benefit $3,153	$567,540	$392,154	$959,694
2	Jul, 2029 Cindy files for worker benefits ($1,292) at age 67 for 100.00% of PIA. Sep, 2031 Mark files for worker benefits ($3,153) at age 70 for 124% of PIA (36 Months Delayed Retirement Credit). Survivor benefit $3,153	$567,540	$385,966	$953,506
3	Aug, 2024 Cindy files for worker benefits ($909) at age 62, 1 month for 70.417% of PIA (59 Months Reduction). Sep, 2031 Mark files for worker benefits ($3,153) at age 70 for 124% of PIA (36 Months Delayed Retirement Credit). Survivor benefit $3,153	$567,540	$360,699	$928,239
4	Sept, 2028 Mark files for worker benefits ($2,543) at age 67 months for 100.00% of PIA. Jul, 2032 Cindy files for worker benefits ($1,602) at age 70 for 124.00% of PIA (36 Months Delayed Retirement Credit). Survivor benefit $2,543	$549,288	$368,974	$918,262

	Strategy	Mark	Cindy	Total
5	Sept, 2028 Mark files for worker benefits ($2,543) at age 67 months for 100.00% of PIA. Jul, 2029 Cindy files for worker benefits ($1,292) at age 67 for 100.00% of PIA. Survivor benefit $2,543	$549,288	$362,786	$912,074
6	Aug, 2024 Cindy files for worker benefits ($909) at age 62, 1 month for 70.417% of PIA (59 Months Reduction). Sept, 2028 Mark files for worker benefits ($2,543) at age 67 months for 100.00% of PIA. Survivor benefit $2,543	$549,288	$337,519	$886,807
7	Oct, 2023 Mark files for worker benefits ($1,790) at age 62, 1 month for 70.417% of PIA (59 Months Reduction). Jul, 2032 Cindy files for worker benefits ($1,602) at age 70 for 124.00% of PIA (36 Months Delayed Retirement Credit). Survivor benefit $1,790	$492,250	$340,360	$832,610
8	Oct, 2023 Mark files for worker benefits ($1,790) at age 62, 1 month for 70.417% of PIA (59 Months Reduction). Jul, 2029 Cindy files for worker benefits ($1,292) at age 67 for 100.00% of PIA. Survivor benefit $1,790	$492,250	$334,172	$826,422
9	Oct, 2023 Mark files for worker benefits ($1,790) at age 62, 1 month for 70.417% of PIA (59 Months Reduction). Aug, 2024 Cindy files for worker benefits ($909) at age 62, 1 month for 70.42% of PIA (59 Months Reduction). Survivor benefit $1,790	$492,250	$308,905	$801,155

CASE STUDY #15
Mike and Leslie

Mike and Leslie, a married couple almost 11 years apart in age. The age difference results in their full retirement ages being a year apart. Mike reaches full retirement age (FRA) at age sixty-six and six months. Leslie reaches FRA at age sixty-seven. The husband, Mike, made slightly less than his wife, Leslie. Leslie is expected to survive Mike by approximately twelve years.

Mike	DOB: March 16, 1957 | Full Retirement Age Benefit: **$2,023** at **66** year & 6 months | Expected Death Age: **84.06**
Leslie	DOB: November 12, 1967 | Full Retirement Age Benefit: **$2,198** at age **67** | Expected Death Age: **87.07**

	Strategy	Mike	Leslie	Total
1	Mar, 2027 Mike files for worker benefits ($2,589) at age 70 for 128% of PIA (42 Months Delayed Retirement Credit). Dec, 2029 Leslie files for worker benefits ($1,547) at age 62, 1 month for 70.417% of PIA (59 Months Reduction). Survivor benefit $2,589	$450,486	$645,312	$1,095,798
2	Mar, 2027 Mike files for worker benefits ($2,589) at age 70 for 128% of PIA (42 Months Delayed Retirement Credit). Dec, 2034 Leslie files for worker benefits ($2,198) at age 67 for 100% of PIA. Survivor benefit $2,589	$450,486	$607,421	$1,057,907
3	Mar, 2027 Mike files for worker benefits ($2,589) at age 70 for 128% of PIA (42 Months Delayed Retirement Credit). Nov, 2037 Leslie files for worker benefits ($2,725) at age 70 for 124.00% of PIA (36 Months Delayed Retirement Credit). Survivor benefit $2,725	$450,486	$574,975	$1,025,461
4	Sept, 2023 Mike files for worker benefits ($2,023) at age 66, 6 months for 100.00% of PIA. Nov, 2037 Leslie files for worker benefits ($2,725) at age 70 for 124.00% of PIA (36 Months Delayed Retirement Credit). Survivor benefit $2,725	$436,968	$574,975	$1,011,943

	Strategy	Mike	Leslie	Total
5	Jan, 2023 Mike files for worker benefits ($1,933) at age 65, 10 months for 95.556% of PIA (8 Months Reduction). Nov, 2037 Leslie files for worker benefits ($2,725) at age 70 for 124.00% of PIA (36 Months Delayed Retirement Credit). Survivor benefit $2,725	$432,992	$574,975	$1,007,967
6	Sept, 2023 Mike files for worker benefits ($2,023) at age 66, 6 months for 100.00% of PIA. Dec, 2029 Leslie files for worker benefits ($1,547) at age 62, 1 month for 70.417% of PIA (59 Months Reduction). Survivor benefit $2,023	$436,968	$551,922	$988,890
7	Sept, 2023 Mike files for worker benefits ($2,023) at age 66, 6 months for 100.00% of PIA. Nov, 2034 Leslie files for worker benefits ($2,198) at age 67 for 100.00% of PIA. Survivor benefit $2,198	$436,968	$542,906	$979,874
8	Jan, 2023 Mike files for worker benefits ($1,933) at age 65, 10 months for 95.556% of PIA (8 Months Reduction). Nov, 2034 Leslie files for worker benefits ($2,198) at age 67 for 100.00% of PIA. Survivor benefit $1,955	$432,992	$542,906	$975,898
9	Jan, 2023 Mike files for worker benefits ($1,933) at age 65, 10 months for 95.556% of PIA (8 Months Reduction). Dec, 2029 Leslie files for worker benefits ($1,547) at age 62, 1 month for 70.417% of PIA (59 Months Reduction). Survivor benefit $1.955	$432,992	$537,072	$970,064

CASE STUDY #16
Mike and Rita

Mike and Rita, a married couple where the wife is about 3 years older than the husband. Mike will reach full retirement age at sixty-six and four months. Rita reached full retirement age at sixty-six years of age. She is eligible to file the restricted application for spousal benefits on Mike's work record when he applies for his retirement benefit. Since both are past full retirement, they can elect be begin benefits six months retroactively. The husband, Mike, had moderately more income than the wife, Rita. Despite being a few years older, Rita is expected to survive Mike by approximately six months.

Mike	DOB: March 10, 1956 | Full Retirement Age Benefit: **$2,482** at **66** year & 4 months | Expected Death Age: **84.05**
Rita	DOB: December 25, 1953 | Full Retirement Age Benefit: **$1,788** at **66** year & 0 months | Expected Death Age: **87.03**

	Strategy	Mike	Rita	Total
1	Dec 2023 Rita files for worker benefit ($2,360) at age 70 for 132% of PIA (48 Months Delayed Retirement Credit). March 2026 Mike files for worker benefit ($3,209) at age 70 for 129.33% of PIA (44 Months Delayed Retirement Credit). Survivor benefit $3,209	$555,157	494,463	$1,049,620
2	July 2022 Mike files for worker benefit ($2,482) at age 66, 4 months for 100% of PIA. July 2022 Rita files a restricted application for spousal benefit ($1,241). Dec 2023 Rita files for worker benefit ($2,360) at age 70 for 132% of PIA (48 Months Delayed Retirement Credit). Survivor benefit $2,482	$538,594	$510,471	$1,049,065
3	July 2022 Rita files for worker benefit ($2,086) at age 68, 7 months for 116.67% of PIA (25 Months Delayed Retirement Credit). January 2023 benefit increases to $2,157 to include DRC's earned in 2022 for 120.67% of PIA (31 Months Delayed Retirement Credit). March 2026 Mike files for worker benefit ($3,209) at age 70 for 129.33% of PIA (44 Months Delayed Retirement Credit). Survivor benefit $3,209	$555,157	$490,106	$1,045,263

	Strategy	Mike	Rita	Total
4	July 2022 Mike files for worker benefit ($2,482) at age 66, 4 months for 100% of PIA. July 2022 Rita files for worker benefit ($2,086) at age 68, 7 months for 116.67% of PIA (25 Months Delayed Retirement Credit). January 2023 benefit increases to $2,157 to include DRC's earned in 2022 for 120.67% of PIA (31 Months Delayed Retirement Credit). Survivor benefit $2,482	$538,594	$485,017	$1,023,611

CASE STUDY #17
Paul and Kirsten

Paul and Kirsten, a married couple five years apart in age. Paul will reach Full Retirement Age at age sixty-six and 4 months. Kirsten will reach Full Retirement Age at age sixty-seven. The husband, Paul, had significantly more income than the wife, Kirsten. Kirsten is expected to survive Paul by approximately six plus years.

Paul	DOB: December 4, 1956 | Full Retirement Age Benefit: **$2,418** at **66** year & 4 months | Expected Death Age: **84.05**
Kirsten	DOB: December 9, 1961 | Full Retirement Age Benefit: **$1,182** at age **67** | Expected Death Age: **87.04**

	Strategy	Paul	Kirsten	Total
1	Dec, 2026 Paul files for worker benefits ($3,127) at age 70 for 129.33% of PIA (44 Months Delayed Retirement Credit). Dec, 2028 Kirsten files for worker benefits ($1,182) at age 67 for 100.00% of PIA. Dec, 2028 Kirsten files for 100.00% of spousal benefits ($27) at age 67. Survivor benefit $3,127	$540,971	$477,206	$1,018,177
2	Jan, 2024 Kirsten files for worker benefits ($832) at age 62, 1 month for 70.42% of PIA (59 Months Reduction). Dec, 2026 Paul files for worker benefits ($3,127) at age 70 for 129.33% of PIA (44 Months Delayed Retirement Credit). Dec, 2026 Kirsten files for 83.33% (24 Months Reduction) of spousal benefits ($22) at age 65. Survivor benefit $3,127	$540,971	$473,927	$1,014,898
3	Dec, 2026 Paul files for worker benefits ($3,127) at age 70 for 129.33% of PIA (44 Months Delayed Retirement Credit). Dec, 2031 Kirsten files for worker benefits ($1,465) at age 70 for 124.00% of PIA (36 Months Delayed Retirement Credit). Survivor benefit $3,127	$540,971	$462,610	$1,003,581
4	Apr, 2023 Paul files for worker benefits ($2,418) at age 66, 4 months for 100.00% of PIA. Dec, 2028 Kirsten files for worker benefits ($1,182) at age 67 for 100.00% of PIA. Dec, 2028 Kirsten files for 100.00% of spousal benefits ($27) at age 67. Survivor benefit $2,418	$524,706	$409,851	$934,557

	Strategy	Paul	Kirsten	Total
5	Apr, 2023 Paul files for worker benefits ($2,418) at age 66, 4 months for 100.00% of PIA. Jan, 2024 Kirsten files for worker benefits ($832) at age 62, 1 month for 70.42% of PIA (59 Months Reduction). Jan, 2024 Kirsten files for 65.42% (59 Months Reduction) of spousal benefits ($17) at age 62, 1 month. Survivor benefit $2,418	$524,706	$406,302	$931,008
6	Jan, 2023 Paul files for worker benefits ($2,377) at age 66, 1 months for 98.33% of PIA (3 Months Reduction). Dec, 2028 Kirsten files for worker benefits ($1,182) at age 67 for 100.00% of PIA. Dec, 2028 Kirsten files for 100.00% of spousal benefits ($27) at age 67. Survivor benefit $2,377	$522,940	$405,956	$928,896
7	Jan, 2023 Paul files for worker benefits ($2,377) at age 66, 1 months for 98.33% of PIA (3 Months Reduction). Jan, 2024 Kirsten files for worker benefits ($832) at age 62, 1 month for 70.42% of PIA (59 Months Reduction). Jan, 2024 Kirsten files for 65.42% (59 Months Reduction) of spousal benefits ($17) at age 62, 1 month. Survivor benefit $2,377	$522,940	$402,407	$925,347
8	Apr, 2023 Paul files for worker benefits ($2,418) at age 66, 4 months for 100.00% of PIA. Dec, 2031 Kirsten files for worker benefits ($1,465) at age 70 for 124.00% of PIA (36 Months Delayed Retirement Credit). Survivor benefit $2,418	$524,706	$395,255	$919,961
9	Jan, 2023 Paul files for worker benefits ($2,377) at age 66, 1 months for 98.33% of PIA (3 Months Reduction). Dec, 2031 Kirsten files for worker benefits ($1,465) at age 70 for 124.00% of PIA (36 Months Delayed Retirement Credit). Survivor benefit $2,377	$522,940	$391,360	$914,300

CASE STUDY #18
Roger and Susan

Roger is working but will reach full retirement age in April 2025. Susan is younger and will not reach age 62 until 2029. Roger and Susan have two children. One is almost age 18 and the other is age 16. Roger needs to file for retirement benefits so the children can receive benefits until they reach age 18 or if still in high school, until age 19 or they graduate whichever comes first. If Roger does nothing, the children lose all benefits and those benefits are never recovered. However, by taking benefits prior to age 70, the survivor benefit for Susan will be less.

Roger	DOB: August 28, 1958 | Full Retirement Age Benefit: **$2,278** at **66** year & **8 months** | Expected Death Age: **84.07**
Susan	DOB: June 21, 1967 | Full Retirement Age Benefit: **$1,209** at age **67** | Expected Death Age: **87.07**

	Strategy	Roger	Susan	Sophia Allison	Total
1	Aug, 2028 Roger files for worker benefits ($2,885) at age 70 for 126.67% of PIA (40 Months Delayed Retirement Credit). Jul, 2029 Susan files for worker benefits ($851) at age 62, 1 month for 70.417% of PIA. Widows benefit $2,885	$504,875	$549,234		$1,054,109
2	Aug, 2028 Roger files for worker benefits ($2,885) at age 70 for 126.67% of PIA (40 Months Delayed Retirement Credit). Jun, 2034 Susan files for worker benefits ($1,209) at age 67 for 100.00% of PIA. Widows benefit $2,885	$504,875	$536,615		$1,041,490
3	Aug, 2028 Roger files for worker benefits ($2,885) at age 70 for 126.67% of PIA (40 Months Delayed Retirement Credit). Jun, 2037 Susan files for worker benefits ($1,499) at age 70 for 124.00% of PIA. Widows benefit $2,885	$504,875	$513,101		$1,017,976
4	April, 2025 Roger files for worker benefits ($2,278) at age 66, 8 months for 100.00% of PIA. Jul, 2026 Susan files for worker benefits ($851) at age 62, 1 month for 70.42% of PIA (59 Months Reduction). Widows benefit $2,278	$489,770	$463,040		$952,810

	Strategy	Roger	Susan	Sophia Allison	Total
5	April, 2025 Roger files for worker benefits ($2,278) at age 66, 8 months for 100.00% of PIA. Jun, 2031 Susan files for worker benefits ($1,209) at age 67 for 100.00% of PIA. Widows benefit $2,278	$489,770	$450,421		$940,191
6	April, 2025 Roger files for worker benefits ($2,278) at age 66, 8 months for 100.00% of PIA. Jun, 2034 Susan files for worker benefits ($1,499) at age 70 for 124.00% of PIA. Widows benefit $2,278	$489,770	$426,907		$916,677
7	Jan, 2023 Roger files for worker benefits ($1,936) at age 64, 5 months for 85% of PIA. (27 Months Reduction). Jan, 2023 Sophia files for child's benefits ($892). Benefit increases to $1,139 March 2023. Benefits end October 2024 at age 18 Jan, 2023 Allison files for child's benefits ($892). Benefits end March 2023 at age 18. Jul, 2029 Susan files for worker benefits ($851) at age 62, 1 month for 70.417% of PIA (59 Months Reduction). Widows benefit $1,936	$447,216	$414,476	$11,390	$873,082
8	Jan, 2023 Roger files for worker benefits ($1,936) at age 64, 5 months for 85% of PIA. (27 Months Reduction). Jan, 2023 Sophia files for child's benefits ($892). Benefit increases to $1,139 March 2023. Benefits end October 2024 at age 18 Jan, 2023 Allison files for child's benefits ($892). Benefits end March 2023 at age 18. Jun, 2034 Susan files for worker benefits ($1,209) at age 67 for 100.00% of PIA. Widows benefit $2,278	$447,216	$401,857	$11,390	$860,463
9	Jan, 2023 Roger files for worker benefits ($1,936) at age 64, 5 months for 85% of PIA. (27 Months Reduction). Jan, 2023 Sophia files for child's benefits ($892). Benefit increases to $1,139 March 2023. Benefits end October 2024 at age 18 Jan, 2023 Allison files for child's benefits ($892). Benefits end March 2023 at age 18. Jun, 2034 Susan files for worker benefits ($1,499) at age 70 for 124.00% of PIA. Widows benefit $2,278	$447,216	$378,343	$11,390	$836,949

CASE STUDY #19
Sandy

Sandy is a widow approaching full retirement age and must decide if she will take benefits from her own work record prior to full retirement age and widows at full retirement age or take widows benefits prior to full retirement age. Benefits on her own work record will not exceed the widow's benefit even if she waits until age 70. Sandy's full retirement age for her retirement benefit is age 66, 8 months. Her full benefit age for widows' benefits is age 66, 4 months.

Sandy	DOB: October 31, 1958 | Full Retirement Age Benefit: $1,425 at 66 year & 8 months | Expected Death Age: 87.02
	SS Survivor Benefit at full benefit age: $2,599 at 66 year & 4 Months

	Strategy	Lifetime Benefit
1	Jan, 2023 Sandy files for worker benefits ($1,195) at age 64, 3 months for 83.889% of PIA (29 Months Reduction). Feb, 2025 Sandy files for 100.00% of Survivor Benefit at age 66, 4 months ($2,599).	$679,625
2	Feb, 2025 Sandy files for 100% of survivor benefits ($2,599) at age 66, 4 months.	$649,750
3	Jan, 2023 Sandy files for 90.6% (25 Months Reduction) of survivor benefits ($2,354) at age 64, 3 months.	$647,350

CASE STUDY #20
Shaun and JoAnn

Married couple about 4 months apart in age. Shaun is a high earner. JoAnn has work under both Social Security covered earnings and as a public employee covered under the Public Employees Retirement System. The PERS pension is $440 per month. This pension from work not covered by Social Security will not only reduce her own Social Security benefit, but also any spousal or survivor benefit she may be entitled to receive. Since her non-covered pension is low, the effect is lessened.

Shaun	DOB: May 8, 1961 | Full Retirement Age Benefit: **$2,510** at age **67** | Expected Death Age: **85**
JoAnn	DOB: January 30, 1961 | Full Retirement Age Benefit: **$790** at age **67** | Expected Death Age: **87.04**

	Strategy	Shaun	JoAnn	Total
1	Jan, 2028 JoAnn files for worker benefits ($790) at age 67 for 100.00% of PIA. May, 2028 Shaun files for worker benefits ($2,510) at age 67 for 100.00% of PIA. May, 2028 JoAnn files for 100.00% of spousal benefits ($245) at age 67, 4 months. Widow benefit $2,290	$542,160	$281,680	$823,840
2	Jan, 2028 JoAnn files for worker benefits ($790) at age 67 for 100.00% of PIA. May, 2031 Shaun files for worker benefits ($3,112) at age 70 for 124.00% of PIA (36 Months Delayed Retirement Credit). May, 2031 JoAnn files for 100.00% of spousal benefits ($245) at age 70, 4 months. Widow benefit $2,892	$560,160	$287,308	$847,468
3	Feb, 2023 JoAnn files for worker benefits ($556) at age 62, 1 month for 70.417% of PIA (59 Months Reduction). May, 2031 Shaun files for worker benefits ($3,112) at age 70 for 124.00% of PIA (36 Months Delayed Retirement Credit). May, 2031 JoAnn files for 100.00% of spousal benefits ($245) at age 70, 4 months. Widow benefit $2,892	$560,160	$268,632	$828,792

	Strategy	Shaun	JoAnn	Total
4	Feb, 2023 JoAnn files for worker benefits ($556) at age 62, 1 month for 70.417% of PIA (59 Months Reduction). May, 2028 Shaun files for worker benefits ($2,510) at age 67 for 100.00% of PIA. May, 2028 JoAnn files for 100.00% of spousal benefits ($245) at age 67, 4 months. Widow benefit $2,290	$542,160	$263,004	$805,164
5	Jun, 2023 Shaun files for worker benefits ($1,767) at age 62, 1 month for 70.417% of PIA (59 Months Reduction). Jan, 2028 JoAnn files for worker benefits ($790) at age 67 for 100.00% of PIA. Jan, 2028 JoAnn files for 100.00% of spousal benefits ($245) at age 67. Widow benefit $1,547	$485,925	$264,828	$750,753
6	Feb, 2023 JoAnn files for worker benefits ($556) at age 62, 1 month for 70.417% of PIA (59 Months Reduction). Jun, 2023 Shaun files for worker benefits ($1,767) at age 62, 1 month for 70.417% of PIA (59 Months Reduction). Jun, 2023 JoAnn files for 67.08% (55 Months Reduction) of spousal benefits ($164) at age 62, 5 months. Widow benefit $1,547	$485,925	$237,352	$723,277

CASE STUDY #21
Sherry

Sherry does not have enough credits to be eligible for Social Security benefits based on her own work record. She was married to Charles and Shaun for over 10 years each and has been divorced for over 2 years from each. Regardless of the filing status of her ex-spouses, once they and Sherry are at least age 62, Sherry can file for ex-spousal benefits as an independently entitled divorced spouse. She is eligible first on her 1st husband's record and later eligible on her 2nd husband's record. Due to deemed filing rules, if Sherry takes benefits from Charles' record prior to becoming eligible for benefits on Shaun's record, she must file on Shaun's record in her first month of eligibility or June 2022. Based on expected life expectancies, Sherry is expected to outlive Charles but not Shaun. Survivor benefits are based on Charles' work record. Statistically Sherry is not expected to outlive Shaun but if she does she would be eligible for a survivor benefit based on his work record.

Sherry	DOB: May 13, 1958 | Full Retirement Age Benefit: **$0** at **66** year & **8** months | Expected Death Age: **87.01**
Charles x-spouse #1	DOB: November 28, 1956 | Full Retirement Age Benefit: **$1,875** at **66** year & **4** months | Expected Death Age: **84.05**
Shaun x-spouse #2	DOB: May 28, 1962 | Full Retirement Age Benefit: **$2,250** at **67** | Expected Death Age: **85**

	Strategy	Sherry
1	Jan, 2023 Sherry files an Independently Entitled Divorced Spouse application at age 64, 8 months for 83.333% of spousal benefit on the record of ex-spouse #1, Charles ($781). Jun, 2024 Sherry files an Independently Entitled Divorced Spouse application at age 66, 1 month for 94.444% of spousal benefit on the record of ex-spouse #2, Shaun ($1,062). Survivor benefit $1,875	$338,426
2	Jan, 2025 Sherry files an Independently Entitled Divorced Spouse application at age 66, 8 months for 100.00% of spousal benefit on the record of ex-spouse #2, Shaun ($1,125). Survivor benefit $1,875	$330,000

CASE STUDY #22
Virginia

Virginia is a single individual. She is not eligible for benefits from any other individual's work record. Her options are limited to filing for benefits on her own work record at some point between ages 62, 1 month and 70. If she delays benefits past her full retirement age, she will earn delayed retirement credits but should consider the fact that when she dies the benefit ends.

Virginia	DOB: September 28, 1961	Full Retirement Age Benefit: **$2,024** at **67**	Expected Death Age: **87.04**

	Strategy	Virginia
1	Sep, 2031 Virginia files for worker benefits ($2,509) at age 70 for 124% of PIA (36 Months Delayed Retirement Credit).	$521,872
2	Sept, 2028 Virginia files for worker benefits ($2,024) at age 67 for 100.00% of PIA.	$493,856
3	Oct, 2023 Virginia files for worker benefits ($1,425) at age 62, 1 months for 70.417% of PIA (59 Months Reduction).	$431,775

CASE STUDY #23
Jerry and Lyn

Jerry is a high earner. Lyn has no earnings under Social Security and is not eligible for a benefit from her own record. She must wait for Jerry to file for benefits before she can file for spousal benefits. If Jerry delays filing past Lyn attaining age 65 she will be able to enroll in Medicare only and receive Part A, Hospital Insurance premium free because Jerry will be past age 62 when she attains age 65.

Jerry	DOB: December 14, 1960 | Full Retirement Age Benefit: **$3,017** at age **67** | Expected Death Age: **85**
Lyn	DOB: November 5, 1957 | Full Retirement Age Benefit: **$0** at **66** year & **6** months | Expected Death Age: **87.01**

	<u>Strategy</u>	<u>Jerry</u>	<u>Lyn</u>	<u>Total</u>
1	Dec, 2027 Jerry files for worker benefits ($3,017) at age 67 for 100.00% of PIA. Dec, 2027 Lyn files for 100.00% of spousal benefits ($1,508) at age 70, 1 month. Survivor benefit $3,017	$651,672	$307,632	$959,304
2	Jan, 2023 Jerry files for worker benefits ($2,124) at age 62, 1 month for 70.417% of PIA (59 Months Reduction). May, 2024 Lyn files for 100.00% of spousal benefits ($1,508) at age 66, 6 months. Survivor benefit $2,124	$584,100	$372,476	$956,576
3	Jan, 2023 Jerry files for worker benefits ($2,124) at age 62, 1 month for 70.417% of PIA (59 Months Reduction). Jan, 2023 Lyn files for 88.889% (16 Months Reduction) of spousal benefits ($1,340) at age 65, 2 months. Survivor benefit $2,124	$584,100	$352,420	$936,520
4	Dec, 2030 Jerry files for worker benefits ($3,741) at age 70 for 124% of PIA (36 Months Delayed Retirement Credit). Dec, 2030 Lyn files for 100.00% of spousal benefits ($1,508) at age 73, 1 months. Survivor benefit $3,741	$673,380	$253,344	$926,724

CASE STUDY #24
Tony and Jessie

Tony and Jessie, a married couple 5 years apart in age. Tony reached his full retirement age (FRA) at age sixty-six and has decided not to begin benefits until at least age sixty-six and eleven months or January of the following year. Jessie will reach her FRA at age sixty-six and 8 months. Jessie is expected to survive Tony by more than 7 years.

Tony	DOB: February 14, 1953 | Full Retirement Age Benefit: **$2,592** at **66** year & **0** months | Expected Death Age: **85.03**
Jessie	DOB: February 2, 1958 | Full Retirement Age Benefit: **$1,578** at **66** year & **8** months | Expected Death Age: **87.01**

	Strategy	Tony	Jessie	Total
1	Jan, 2023 Jessie files for worker benefits ($1,393) at age 64, 11 months for 88.333% of PIA (21 Months Reduction). Jan, 2023 Tony files a restricted application for spousal benefit ($789). Feb, 2023 Tony files for worker benefits ($3,421) at age 70 for 132.00% of PIA (48 Months Delayed Retirement Credit). Survivor benefit $3,421	$632,355	$522,638	$1,154,993
2	Feb, 2023 Tony files for worker benefits ($3,421) at age 70 for 132.00% of PIA (48 Months Delayed Retirement Credit). Oct, 2024 Jessie files for worker benefits ($1,578) at age 66, 8 months for 100.00% of PIA. Survivor benefit $3,421	$626,043	$524,835	$1,150,878
3	July, 2022 Tony files for worker benefits ($3,195) at age 69, 4 months for 123.3% of PIA (35 Months Delayed Retirement Credit). Jan, 2023 benefit increases to $3,299 for 127.3% of PIA (41 Delayed Retirement Credits). Oct, 2024 Jessie files for worker benefits ($1,578) at age 66, 8 months for 100.00% of PIA. Survivor benefit $3,299	$629,485	$515,685	$1,145,170
4	Feb, 2023 Tony files for worker benefits ($3,421) at age 70 for 132.00% of PIA (48 Months Delayed Retirement Credit). Feb, 2028 Jessie files for worker benefits ($1,998) at age 70 for 126.67% of PIA (40 Months Delayed Retirement Credit). Survivor benefit $3,421	$626,043	$516,315	$1,142,358

	Strategy	Tony	Jessie	Total
5	July, 2022 Tony files for worker benefits ($3,195) at age 69, 4 months for 123.3% of PIA (35 Months Delayed Retirement Credit). Jan, 2023 benefit increases to $3,299 for 127.3% of PIA (41 Delayed Retirement Credits). Feb, 2028 Jessie files for worker benefits ($1,998) at age 70 for 126.67% of PIA (40 Months Delayed Retirement Credit). Survivor benefit $3,299	$629,485	$507,165	$1,136,650
6	July, 2022 Tony files for worker benefits ($3,195) at age 69, 4 months for 123.3% of PIA (35 Months Delayed Retirement Credit). Jan, 2023 benefit increases to $3,299 for 127.3% of PIA (41 Delayed Retirement Credits). Jan, 2023 Jessie files for worker benefits ($1,393) at age 64, 11 months for 88.333% of PIA (21 Months Reduction). Survivor benefit $3,299	$629,485	$505,130	$1,134,615

INTRODUCTION

1001. In general, what benefits are provided under Part B (Medical Insurance)?

Part B (Medical Insurance), which is a voluntary program that must be elected by an eligible Medicare beneficiary, generally provides coverage of the following benefit costs (subject in most cases to a 20 percent copayment requirement in addition to an annual deductible):

- Physicians' services, whether furnished in a hospital, clinic, office, home, or elsewhere.

- A one-time initial wellness physical ("Welcome to Medicare Visit") within twelve months of enrolling in Part B (Medical Insurance), plus a yearly wellness visit to develop or update a personalized plan based on an individual health profile.

- Various screening tests (including tests for breast cancer, cardiovascular disease, colorectal cancer, diabetes, glaucoma, HIV, obesity, prostate cancer, and sexually transmitted infections, as well as annual pap smears and pelvic exams), plus in some cases self-management training, counseling, and supplies. Most screening tests do not require cost-sharing.

- Certain preventive measures (including annual flu shot, pneumococcal vaccine, and Hepatitis B vaccine for certain beneficiaries; generally, no cost-sharing).

- Pulmonary rehabilitation services for individuals with certain levels of chronic obstructive pulmonary disease.

- Home health care visits, if not covered under Part A (Hospital Insurance) (subject to special rules, including in most cases no cost-sharing other than for durable medical equipment).

- Outpatient medical and surgical services, supplies, and outpatient hospital services for the diagnosis or treatment of an illness or injury.

- Laboratory services (generally no cost-sharing), and X-Rays, MRIs, CT scans, EKGs, and certain other diagnostic tests.

- Outpatient physical therapy, speech language pathology, and occupational therapy services (subject to specific rules and limits; some services to inpatients may be covered depending on the circumstances).

- Rural health clinic services and federally qualified health center services.

- Prosthetic and orthotic devices (subject to various limits), including replacement of such devices; and surgical dressings and casts.

- Home dialysis supplies and equipment, self-care home dialysis support services, institutional dialysis and supplies, and kidney disease education services (subject to various limits).

- Certain chiropractic and podiatric services (subject to various restrictions).

- Rental or purchase of durable medical equipment, such as walkers.

- Ambulance services, under certain circumstances such as ground ambulance transportation when traveling in another vehicle could endanger health, and medically necessary services are need from a hospital, critical access hospital or skilled nursing facility.

  o Medicare may pay for emergency ambulance transportation in an airplane or helicopter if the patient needs immediate and rapid transport that ground transportation can't provide.

  o In some cases, Medicare may pay for limited, medically necessary, non-emergency ambulance transportation there is a written order from a doctor stating that the transportation is medically necessary.

- Eyeglasses (or contact lenses) following cataract surgery (subject to various limits).

- Durable medical equipment, when ordered by a doctor.

- Lung, heart, kidney, pancreas, intestine, and liver transplants, under certain circumstances, and immunosuppressive drugs after a transplant.

- Outpatient mental health services (subject in some cases to additional copayment requirements).

Part B generally covers two broad types of services –

- Medically Necessary Services: services and supplies needed to diagnose or treat a medical issue and meet accepted medical standards.

- Preventive Services: Medical care to either detect illness at an early stage or prevent illness such as inoculation or vaccination. This type of treatment is generally covered without cost, presuming that the services are from a health care provider that accepts Medicare assignment.

For a detailed explanation of these benefits, see Q 1089 through Q 1162.

1002. What federal agency administers Medicare?

The Centers for Medicare & Medicaid Services (CMS), whose central office is at 7500 Security Boulevard, Woodlawn, Maryland 21244 (near Baltimore), directs the Medicare program as well as the federal portion of the Medicaid program, the State Children's Health Insurance Program (SCHIP), and the new Health Insurance Marketplace under the Patient Protection and Affordable Care Act (PPACA). Before 2001, CMS was called the Health Care Financing Administration (HCFA). The Social Security Administration processes Medicare applications and claims, but it does not set Medicare policy. CMS sets the standards that health care providers such as hospitals, skilled nursing facilities, home health agencies, and hospices must meet in order to be certified as qualified providers of services. It also establishes the reimbursement rates for all Medicare-covered services.

1003. Are same-sex couples eligible to receive spousal Medicare benefits?

Yes. The Social Security Administration now recognizes same-sex marriages in all states and some marital legal relationships such as civil unions and domestic partnerships for the purposes of determining entitlement to Social Security, Medicare and Supplemental Security Income. The SSA is also recognizing same-sex marriages and some nonmartial legal relationships entered into in foreign jurisdictions as well.[1] Social Security now processing some retirement, surviving spouse, and lump-sum death payment claims for same-sex couples in nonmarital legal relationships and paying benefits where they are due. In addition, the Social Security Administration considers same-sex marriage when determining SSI eligibility and benefit amounts.

On June 26, 2015, the United States Supreme Court issued a decision in *Obergefell v. Hodges*,[2] holding that same-sex couples have a constitutional right to marry in all states. This decision enables same-sex couples to be married in one state and have their marriage recognized by all other states. As a direct result of this decision, same-sex couples are recognized as married for the purposes of determining their entitlement to Social Security benefits and as well as Supplemental Security Income (SSI) payments. The Social Security Administration recommends that someone who is the spouse, divorced spouse, or surviving spouse of a same-sex marriage or other legal same-sex relationship to immediately apply for benefits. Immediate applying will preserve the filing date, which can affect benefits.

This was a rapidly developing area of the law. In June 2013, the Supreme Court ruling in *United States v. Windsor*,[3] established that same sex couples who were married in a jurisdiction where same-sex marriages are recognized were eligible for spousal benefits, such as the spousal survivor benefit, the spousal retirement benefit, and the lump sum death benefit. At that time, the Social Security Administration reviewed its own policies regarding same-sex marriage after the Supreme Court decision, and concluded that same-sex couples who are legally married in one state remain married for federal tax purposes even if they reside in a state that does not recognize their marriage.[4]

Notes

1. SSA Publication No. 05-10014, June 2022, What Same-Sex Couples Need to Know, https://www.ssa.gov/pubs/EN-05-10014.pdf (last accessed October 2, 2022).
2. 576 U.S. 644, 135 S. Ct. 2587, 192 L. Ed.2d 609 (2015).
3. 570 U.S. 744, 133 S. Ct. 2675, 186 L. Ed.2d 808 (2013).
4. Rev. Rul. 2013-17.

1004. Who can provide services or supplies under Medicare?

A wide array of health care organizations and medical professionals can offer services or supplies to Medicare beneficiaries. All such providers must meet any licensing requirements applicable under state or local law. Certain types of institutional providers must meet additional

Medicare certification requirements and sign participation agreements with CMS before payments will be made for their services. Such providers include:

- hospitals.

- Skilled Nursing Facilities (SNFs).

- home health agencies.

- hospice programs.

- certain outpatient rehabilitation facilities.

- certain diagnostic laboratories.

- certain organizations providing outpatient physical therapy and speech pathology services.

- certain facilities providing kidney dialysis or transplant services.

- rural health clinics.

Medicare provider participation agreements include numerous rules that participating providers must agree to follow, many of which relate to how much such providers can charge Medicare beneficiaries. Other rules, however, mandate cooperation with quality improvement organizations and state health agency and accrediting organizations. Different rules apply to different types of Medicare providers. For example, hospitals are subject to additional requirements, such as compliance with the Emergency Medical Treatment and Active Labor Act (EMTALA), which prohibits refusing to treat certain indigent patients who need emergency care. Despite these rules, a nonparticipating hospital may still be paid by Medicare in case of emergency treatment provided to a Medicare beneficiary, assuming the nonparticipating hospital is the closest one available to handle the emergency.

In addition to the specified types of providers who must satisfy certification requirements and sign participation agreements to receive payment, other types of providers—such as physicians and certain suppliers—are encouraged to sign participation agreements primarily governing how they are paid. For physicians and suppliers, whether they are participating or nonparticipating does not affect their eligibility to be paid by Medicare; only the mechanisms for payment vary.

1005. In general, what benefits are provided under the Part A (Hospital Insurance) program?

The program, which automatically covers eligible persons, generally provides the following benefits:

- The cost of Inpatient Hospital Care for up to ninety days in each benefit period (also known as a "spell of illness").

- ○ Note that "spell of illness" refers to a period on CONSECTUTIVE days.

- ○ For 2023, the patient paid a deductible amount of $1,600 for the first sixty days plus $400 a day for each day). There were also sixty nonrenewable lifetime reserve days (days 91 to 150) with coinsurance of $800 in 2023. For 2023, the patient pays a deductible amount of $1,600 for the first 60 days plus $400 a day for each day. There were also 60 nonrenewable lifetime reserve days (days 91 to 150) with coinsurance of $800 in 2023.

- ○ The cost of Post-Hospital Skilled Nursing Facility Care for up to one-hundred days in each benefit period.

- ○ For 2023, the patient paid $200 after the first 20 days.

- ○ For 2023, the patient will pay $200.00 after the first 20 days.

- ○ Note that the first 20 days following a three-day inpatient hospital stay have a $0 (zero) deductible.

- The cost of Home Health Service Visits (subject to a limit of one-hundred post-institutional home health service visits in a spell of illness for Medicare beneficiaries enrolled in Parts A and B) made under a plan of treatment established by a physician. Additional coverage for home health care services that do not meet the Part A coverage criteria may be available under Part B (Medical Insurance). (See Q 1009.)

- The cost of Hospice Care for terminally ill patients.

For a detailed explanation of these benefits, see Q 1036 through Q 1083.

1006. In general, what benefits are provided under Part B (Medical Insurance)?

Part B (Hospital Insurance), which is a voluntary program that must be elected by an eligible Medicare beneficiary, generally provides coverage of the following benefit costs (subject in most cases to a 20 percent copayment requirement in addition to an annual deductible):

- Physicians' services, whether furnished in a hospital, clinic, office, home, or elsewhere.

- A one-time initial wellness physical ("Welcome to Medicare Visit") within twelve months of enrolling in Part B (Medical Insurance), plus a yearly wellness visit to develop or update a personalized plan based on individual health profile.

- Various screening tests (including tests for breast cancer, cardiovascular disease, colorectal cancer, diabetes, glaucoma, HIV, obesity, prostate cancer, and sexually transmitted infections, as well as annual pap smears and pelvic exams), plus in some cases self-management training, counseling, and supplies. Most screening tests do not require cost-sharing.

- Certain preventive measures (including annual flu shot, pneumococcal vaccine, and Hepatitis B vaccine for certain beneficiaries; generally, no cost-sharing).

- Pulmonary rehabilitation services for individuals with certain levels of chronic obstructive pulmonary disease.

- Home health care visits, if not covered under Part A (Hospital Insurance) (subject to special rules, including in most cases no cost-sharing other than for durable medical equipment).

- Outpatient medical and surgical services, supplies, and outpatient hospital services for the diagnosis or treatment of an illness or injury.

- Laboratory services (generally no cost-sharing), and X-Rays, MRIs, CT scans, EKGs and certain other diagnostic tests.

- Outpatient physical therapy, speech language pathology, and occupational therapy services (subject to specific rules and limits; some services to inpatients may be covered depending on the circumstances).

- Rural health clinic services and federally qualified health center services.

- Prosthetic and orthotic devices (subject to various limits), including replacement of such devices, as well as surgical dressings and casts.

- Home dialysis supplies and equipment, self-care home dialysis support services, institutional dialysis and supplies, and kidney disease education services (subject to various limits).

- Certain chiropractic and podiatric services (subject to various restrictions).

- Rental or purchase of durable medical equipment, such as walkers.

- Ambulance services, under certain circumstances.

- Eyeglasses (or contact lenses) following cataract surgery (subject to various limits).

- Lung, heart, kidney, pancreas, intestine, and liver transplants, under certain circumstances, and immunosuppressive drugs after a transplant.

- Outpatient mental health services (subject in some cases to additional copayment requirements).

Part B generally covers two broad types of services –

- Medically Necessary Services: services and supplies needed to treat a medical issue and meet accepted medical standards.

- Preventive Services: Medical care to either detect illness at an early stage or prevent illness such as inoculation or vaccination. This type of treatment is generally covered without cost.

For a detailed explanation of these benefits, see Q 1089 through Q 1162.

1007. In general, what benefits are provided under Part C (Medicare Advantage)?

Part C (Medicare Advantage) is a voluntary program that must be elected by an eligible Medicare beneficiary. Medicare Advantage Plans are offered by private companies that contract with Medicare to provide a person with all their Part A and Part B benefits. Medicare Advantage Plans include Health Maintenance Organizations (HMOs), Preferred Provider Organizations (PPOs), Private Fee-for-Service Plans (PFFS), Special Needs Plans (SNPs), and Medicare Medical Savings Account Plans (MSAs). Most Medicare Advantage Plans offer prescription drug coverage.

Part C (Medicare Advantage), generally provides coverage of the following benefit costs:

- Choice of primary care physician based on the type of plan selected. For example, In HMO Plans, a primary care physician, hospital choice, and services generally must be chosen from those in the plan's network (except emergency care, out-of-area urgent care, or out-of-area dialysis).

- Prescription drug costs are covered in most plans. For some PFFS plans, a person may need to join a Medicare Prescription Drug Plan to get coverage.

- In order to see a specialist, a person with a Medicare Advantage HMO or SNP plan will generally need to get a referral. Those who have Part C PPO or PFFS plans will generally not need a referral in order to see a specialist.

- Pulmonary rehabilitation services for individuals with certain levels of chronic obstructive pulmonary disease.

- Often coverages such as vision, dental, and hearing are provided.

Out of pocket costs in a Medicare Advantage Plan (Part C) depend on:

- Whether the plan charges a monthly premium.

- Whether the plan pays any of the monthly Medicare Part B (Medical Insurance) premium (which must be paid for).

- Whether the plan has a yearly deductible or any additional deductibles.

- How much must be paid for each visit or service (copayment or coinsurance). Example: the plan may charge a copayment, such $10 or $20 for each occurrence of a doctor visit. These amounts can be different than those under Original Medicare.

- The type of health care services needed and how often used.

- Whether the doctor or supplier visited accepts assignment (if in a PPO, PFFS, or MSA plan and coverage is obtained out-of-network).

- Whether plan rules such as using network providers is followed.

- Whether extra benefits needed are charged for.

- The plan's yearly limit on out-of-pocket costs for all medical services.

- Whether Medicaid or state help is part of the coverage.

- A new development established in 2021 and continuing through 2022 and 2023 is that Medicare Advantage plans are available for people with ESRD.

For a detailed explanation of these benefits, see Q 1178 through Q 1192.

1008. In general, what benefits are provided under Part D (Prescription Drug Insurance)?

Prescription drug coverage is available to everyone covered by Medicare. A person must join a plan, run by an insurance company or other private company approved by Medicare, in order to receive Medicare drug coverage. Each plan can vary in cost and in the drugs that may be covered. Not all drugs are covered by Part D. Further explanation is offered in the Part D section of this book.

- Part D (Prescription Drug Plan) plans are sometimes called PDPs which add drug coverage to Original Medicare, some Medicare Cost Plans, some Medicare Private Fee-for-Service (PFFS) Plans, and Medicare Medical Savings Account (MSA) Plans.

- Each Medicare Prescription Drug Plan has its own list of covered drugs (called a formulary). Many Medicare drug plans place drugs into different "tiers" on their formularies. Drugs in each tier have a different cost.

- Plans generally divide coverage into up to five tiers:

    o Tier 1: "Preferred Generics" – often with no co-pay or costs ranging from $0-$5.

    o Tier 2: covering most generics – low co-pay with a median of $5 but ranging from $1 to $19.

    o Tier 3: brand name prescription drugs on a preferred list with a median of $42 but ranging from $30 to $47.

      o   Tier 4: brand name non-prescription drugs that are not on a preferred list – higher copayment. These drugs are on a percentage basis, averaging between 30 and 40 percent of cost.

      o   Tier 5: a specialty tier with high cost prescription drugs and a high copayment.

- There are rules to understand in enrolling in a specific Part D (Prescription Drug Plan), as enrolling in this type of plan may preclude the use of Part C (Medicare Advantage) prescription drug coverage.

For a detailed explanation of these rules and benefits, see Q 1203 through Q 1210.

1009. What is the difference between home health care coverage under Part A (Hospital Insurance) and Part B (Medical Insurance)?

Medicare coverage of home health services unassociated with a hospital or skilled nursing facility stay has been gradually transferred from Part A to Part B. For most beneficiaries, Medicare Part A continues to cover the first one-hundred visits in a spell of illness following a three-day (seventy-two continuous hours) hospital stay or a Skilled Nursing Facility (SNF) stay. For persons with Part A coverage only, the post institutional and 100-visit limitations do not apply.

Under Part B (Medical Insurance), home health care coverage does not require a preceding institutional stay, nor does it have a one-hundred-visit limit, but coverage is nonetheless subject to various restrictions. If a patient exhausts Part A coverage for home health care, Medicare benefits may still be available for the care under Part B. Other than the Part B coinsurance required for durable medical equipment, if applicable, there is no copayment requirement for home health care coverage.

1010. Is there any overall limit to the benefits a person can receive under Medicare?

While Medicare contains many limits on individual benefits, including financial cost-sharing obligations for beneficiaries, and provides no coverage in certain circumstances, the program imposes no single overall limit on the amount of benefits any individual person may receive. In general, there's no upper dollar limit on Medicare benefits. As long as the person is using medical services that Medicare covers—and provided that they're medically necessary—they can continue to use as many as needed, regardless of how much they cost, in any given year or over the rest of the person's lifetime.

Under Part A (Hospital Insurance), benefits begin anew in each benefit period (although lifetime reserve days for inpatient hospital care are limited to sixty total), but inpatient care in a psychiatric hospital is subject to a lifetime limit of 190 days[1]. Part B (Medical Insurance) generally does not impose dollar limits. In addition, there are limits on Skilled Nursing Facility (SNF) benefits as well as therapy services.

Medicare may limit benefit payments for services for which other third-party insurance programs (e.g., workers' compensation, automobile or liability insurance, and employer health plans) may ultimately be liable. Such limits arise under Medicare's Coordination of Benefits and Secondary Payer programs.

Note

1. 42 CFR 409,62 https://www.law.cornell.edu/cfr/text/42/409.62 (Last accessed October 2, 2022).

1011. When do Medicare benefits become available?

Medicare benefits generally become available at the beginning of the month in which an individual reaches age 65, presuming that the individual has enrolled in Medicare in the month before their 65th birthday. Enrolling after turning 65 generally causes benefits to begin the month after they turn 65. This is known as the Initial Enrollment Period (IEP).

An individual whose birthday falls on the first day of a month is treated as having reached age sixty-five on the last day of the month immediately preceding his or her birthday. Assuming an individual is otherwise eligible for Medicare, benefits become available at age sixty-five even if the individual is still working. Individuals who qualify for Medicare on the basis of disability—other than those who are disabled due to Lou Gehrig's disease (Amyotrophic Lateral Sclerosis)—must be continuously disabled for twenty-four months before they will be able to receive Medicare benefits. There is no waiting period for Medicare benefits when eligibility is based on disability due to Lou Gehrig's disease or on end-stage renal disease.

1012. What is the purpose of a Medicare card?

A Medicare card is issued after a person becomes eligible for Medicare benefits. The card shows the person's coverage (Part A – Hospital Insurance, Part B – Medical Insurance, or both) and the effective date of each type of coverage. The card also shows the person's Medicare claim number. The claim number usually has nine digits (similar to a Social Security number, but not the same number) and one or two letters. On some cards, there will be another number after the letter. When a husband and wife both have Medicare, each receives a separate card and claim number. Each spouse must use the exact name and claim number shown on his or her card.

Important points to remember include:

- A covered person should always show his Medicare card when receiving services that Medicare covers in whole or in part.

- A covered person should always write his entire Medicare claim number (including any letters) on all checks for Medicare premium payments, all claims, and any correspondence about Medicare. Also, the covered person should have his Medicare card available when making a telephone inquiry relating to Medicare.

- A covered person should carry his Medicare card whenever away from home.

- If a Medicare card is lost, a replacement card should be requested immediately through the Medicare Replacement Card section of the Social Security Administration's website (mymedicare.gov)[1]. A replacement card may also be requested by going to a Social Security office or calling Social Security at 1-800-772-1213. Social Security can provide temporary proof of Medicare coverage until a replacement card arrives (in approximately four weeks from the date of a request).

- A covered person should use his Medicare card only after the effective date(s) shown on the card.

- Medicare cards made of metal or plastic, which are sold by some manufacturers, are not a substitute for the officially issued Medicare card.

- No one should ever permit another individual to use his Medicare card or Medicare number.

Note

1. https://faq.ssa.gov/en-us/Topic/article/KA-01735 (last accessed October 2, 2022).

1013. What care is not covered under Part A (Hospital Insurance) and Part B (Medical Insurance)?

Medicare Parts A (Hospital Insurance) and Part B (Medical Insurance) contain a number of specific exclusions. These include the following:

Services "Not Reasonable and Necessary"

Medicare does not pay for services that are not reasonable and necessary for the diagnosis or treatment of an illness or injury. These services include:

- drugs or devices that have not been approved by the Food and Drug Administration (FDA),

- medical procedures and services performed using drugs or devices not approved by FDA, and

- services, including drugs or devices, not considered safe and effective because they are experimental or investigational.

If a doctor places an individual in a hospital or skilled nursing facility (SNF) when the kind of care the individual needs could be provided elsewhere, the individual's stay will not be considered reasonable and necessary, and Medicare will not pay for it. If an individual stays in a hospital or skilled nursing facility longer than necessary, Medicare payments will end when inpatient care is no longer reasonable or necessary.

If a doctor (or other practitioner) comes to treat a person or that person visits the doctor for treatment more often than is medically necessary, Medicare will not pay for the "extra" visits.

Exclusions

In addition, Medicare does not pay for:

- most outpatient prescription drugs (except under Medicare Part D)

- routine or annual physical exams (other than the Welcome to Medicare initial visit and annual wellness visits introduced by the Patient Protection and Affordable Care Act (PPACA)

- most dental care and dentures

- routine foot care

- vision care including routine eye care and eye exams relating to prescription glasses

- hearing aids and exams for fitting them

- personal comfort items

- acupuncture

- massage therapy

- cosmetic surgery

- concierge care (also known as "retainer-based services" or "boutique" or "direct care")

Custodial Care (Long-Term Care)

Medicare also does not cover custodial care when that is the only kind of care the patient needs. Care is considered custodial when it is primarily for the purpose of helping with the activities of daily living (ADLs) or meeting personal needs and could be provided safely and reasonably by persons without professional skills or training. Much of the care provided in nursing homes to people with chronic long-term illnesses or disabilities is considered custodial care.

> *Example*: Custodial care includes help in walking, getting in and out of bed, bathing, dressing, eating, and taking medicine. Even if an individual is in a participating hospital or skilled nursing facility or the individual is receiving care from a participating home health agency, Medicare does not cover the stay if the patient needs only custodial care.

There are exceptions to the custodial care restrictions in the case of hospice care.

Service Providers Who Are Not Covered

Medicare will not pay for services performed by immediate relatives or members of a patient's household. Nor will Medicare pay for services paid for by another government program. Medicare will not pay for any item or service with regard to which there is no legal obligation to pay (for the beneficiary or anyone else), such as free health-related services (e.g., vaccinations) provided at community events. In certain cases, such as health care covered by workers' compensation or an employer-based health plan for an active employee, Medicare acts as the secondary payer, paying to the extent of Medicare's coverage limits but only after another source of insurance pays and then only to the extent the primary payer did not cover the item or service.

Health Care Outside of the United States

Medicare generally does not pay for any health services provided outside the United States, but there are exceptions for emergencies and for inpatient hospital care where the foreign hospital is closer to an individual's residence than a comparable U.S. hospital and is equipped to handle the needed care.

Waiver of Liability

Under Medicare law, a person will not be held responsible for payment of the cost of certain health care services for which the person was denied Medicare payment if the person did not know or could not reasonably be expected to know that the services were not covered by Medicare. This provision is often referred to as a "Waiver of Liability". The waiver provision applies only when the care was denied because it was one of the following:

(1)   custodial care,

(2)   not reasonable or necessary under Medicare program standards for diagnosis or treatment,

(3)   for home health services, the patient was not homebound or not receiving skilled nursing care on an intermittent basis, or

(4)   the only reason for the denial is that, in error, the patient was placed in a skilled nursing facility bed that was not approved by Medicare.

The limitation of liability provision also does not apply to Part B (Medical Insurance) services provided by a nonparticipating physician or supplier who did not accept assignment of the claim. However, in certain situations Medicare will protect the patient from paying for services provided by a nonparticipating physician on a nonassigned basis that are denied as "not reasonable and necessary". If a physician knows or should know that Medicare will not pay for a particular service as "not reasonable and necessary," the physician must give the patient written notice—before performing the service—of the reasons why the physician believes Medicare will not pay. The physician must get the patient's written agreement to pay for the services. If the patient does not receive this notice, the patient is not required to pay for the service. If the patient pays for the service, but did not receive a notice, the patient may be entitled to a refund.

1014. What are the rules regarding self-referrals?

Doctors cannot make self-referrals for certain designated health services. Designated health services (DHS) include:

(1)   clinical laboratory services;

(2)   physical therapy services;

(3)   occupational therapy services;

(4)   radiology services and certain other imaging services, including MRI, CAT scans, and ultrasound services;

(5)   radiation therapy services and supplies;

(6)   durable medical equipment and supplies;

(7)   parenteral and enteral nutrients, equipment, and supplies;

(8)   prosthetics, orthotics, and prosthetic devices, and supplies;

(9)   home health services;

(10)   outpatient prescription drugs;

(11)   inpatient and outpatient hospital services; and

(12)   outpatient speech-language pathology services.

Section 1877 of the Social Security Act (the Act),[1] also known as the physician self-referral law and commonly referred to as the "Stark Law":

> The law prohibits a doctor who has a financial relationship with an entity from referring Medicare patients to that entity to receive a designated health service. The prohibition also applies if a doctor's immediate family member has a financial relationship with the entity. A financial relationship can exist as an ownership or investment interest in or a compensation arrangement with an entity. The law is triggered by the mere fact that a financial relationship exists; it does not matter what the doctor intends when making a referral.

> An entity cannot bill Medicare, Medicaid, the beneficiary, or anyone else for a designated health service furnished to a Medicare patient under a prohibited referral. If a person collects any amount for services billed in violation of the law, a refund must be made.

> A person can be subject to a civil money penalty or exclusion from Medicare if that person:

> (1)   presents or causes to be presented a claim to Medicare or bill to any individual, third-party payer, or other entity for any designated health service the person knows or should know was furnished as the result of a prohibited referral; or

> (2)   fails to make a timely refund.

The law does establish several specific exceptions and grants the Secretary the authority to create regulatory exceptions for financial relationships that do not pose a risk of program or patient abuse.

Note that that modifications to some parts of Stark were made in 2021 and 2022 (See Q 1015).

Note

1. 42 U.S.C. 1395nn,. https://www.law.cornell.edu/uscode/text/42/1395nn (last accessed October 2, 2022).

1015. What are the changes to the Stark Law rule for referrals?

There were significant changes made to Stark by the Final Rule "Medicare Program: Modernizing and Clarifying the Physician Self-Referral Regulations". The changes are detailed below were made in 2021 and 2022

Value-Based Adjustments

The changes to the Stark Law allow for exceptions based on formal collaboration between parties if the purpose is "value-based". CMS defines "values-based" as including

- coordination of care

- improving care, or

- reducing the costs of care.

The original Stark laws, were largely based on "fee-for-service" practice models. The changes address Value-Based Care business models and allow providers more flexibility. The amount of regulation decreases with the amount of financial risk the provider is taking. By encouraging a move to value-based arrangements (VBAs), CMS is trying to move the focus of the healthcare system more towards patient outcomes and rewarding cost savings to the system.

The changes create three new exceptions to allow more value-based activities. The three exceptions include:

- **Full Financial Risk Exception** - applies if the value-based enterprise is at full financial risk (or is contractually obligated to be at full financial risk within the 12 months following the commencement of the value-based arrangement) for the entire duration of the arrangement,

- **Meaningful Downside Financial Risk Exception** - applies if the physician is at meaningful downside financial risk for failure to achieve the value-based purpose(s) of the value-based enterprise for the entire duration of the arrangement; and

- **Value-Based Arrangement Exception** - applies to any value-based arrangement that satisfies the applicable requirements, regardless of the level of risk.

Physician Remuneration Limits

The changes include a new compensation exemption that allows for up to $5,000 between DHS entities and physicians in a calendar year. The payment exceptions can cover items such as professional services, staffing, equipment rental, and office space. Payments can be accepted without the agreement first being in writing.

Cyber Security Exceptions

The changes allow the donation of technology and services for that are necessary and used primarily for the protection of patient data and to enhance cybersecurity are exempted from the standard Stark Law rule. These new rules allow the equipment and services to be entirely donated. There is no requirement that physicians share in the cost.

Clarity and Definition of Terms

The changes contain clarification for terms used in the Stark Law and intend to ease the reporting process, so doctors have less of an administrative burden.

- **Fair Market Value.** The Final Rule clarifies the definition of "fair market value" by dividing the definition into three parts:

    (1) a general definition,

    (2) a definition relating to the rental of equipment, and

    (3) a definition relating to the rental of office space.

The Final Rule eliminates the statement that a rental payment does not factor in intended use if it considers costs incurred by the lessor in developing or upgrading the property or maintaining the property or its improvements. In the Preamble to the final rule, CMS explained that fair market value may not always align with published physician salary surveys.

- **Commercial Reasonableness.** The Final Rule added the definition of "commercially reasonable" (this is referred to in many of the exceptions).

    - An arrangement is "commercially reasonable" if it furthers a legitimate business purpose of the parties to the arrangement and is sensible, considering the characteristics of the parties, including their size, type, scope, and specialty. Such an arrangement may be commercially reasonable even if it does not result in profit for one or more of the parties.

- Amendments to Compensation Terms.

    - Amendments to physician compensation terms at permitted at any time (including during the first year) if certain requirements are met:

○   Period of Disallowance.

○   Rules establishing the determination of the period of disallowance (the time period during which a physician may not make prohibited referral) have been eliminated.

○   The period of disallowance "should begin on the date when a financial relationship fails to satisfy all the requirements of any applicable exception and end on the date that the financial relationship ends or satisfies all the requirements of an applicable exception remains true".

○   The period of disallowance is made on a case-by-case basis.

- Group Practice Requirements.

   ○   The main change is a "deeming" provision relating to the distribution of profits from Designated Health Services (DHS) that are directly attributable to a physician's participation in a value-based enterprise. It does not directly consider the volume or value of the physician's referrals which allows physicians in a group practice using value-based arrangements to be compensated

   ○   Confirming that profit allocations and productivity bonuses may indirectly consider the volume or value of referrals.

   ○   The change revises the definition of "overall profits" to mean the profits derived from all DHS of any component of the group that consists of five or more physicians.

   ○   Clarifying that profits from all of the group's DHS (or from at least five physicians in the group) must be aggregated and THEN distributed. A group practice cannot distribute profits from DHS on a service-by-service basis (also known as "split pooling").

   ○   The change deletes the reference to Medicaid from the provision deeming certain methods for distributing profit shares to be permissible. Revenues derived from DHS can be distributed based on the distribution methodology used for revenue attributed to services that are not Medicare DHS and will not be considered DHS if they were payable by Medicare.

   ○   Harmonizing the requirements for paying productivity bonuses with the provisions addressing the distribution of overall profits.

- Electronic Health Records ("EHR") Exception. The Final Rule eliminates the December 31, 2021 sunset provision, making the exception permanent. The rule also specifies that cybersecurity software and services may be donated under the exception (subject to the cost-sharing requirement).

1016. What are Quality Improvement Organizations?

The QIO Program is one the largest federal programs dedicated to improving health quality for Medicare beneficiaries. The QIO program is part HHS Services' National Quality Strategy which is intended to provide better care and better health at lower cost. By law, the mission of the QIO Program is to improve the effectiveness, efficiency, economy, and quality of services delivered to Medicare beneficiaries. Based on this statutory charge, and CMS's program experience, CMS identifies the core functions of the QIO Program as:

- Improving quality of care for beneficiaries and families

- Maximizing learning and collaboration for improving care

- Supporting the spread of and sustaining of new practices and models of care

- Protecting the integrity of the Medicare Trust Fund by ensuring that Medicare pays only for services and goods that are reasonable and necessary and that are provided in the most appropriate setting; and

- Protecting beneficiaries by expeditiously addressing individual complaints, such as beneficiary complaints; provider-based notice appeals; violations of the Emergency Medical Treatment and Labor Act (EMTALA); and other related responsibilities as articulated in QIO-related law.

Quality Improvement Organizations (QIOs), previously known as Peer Review Organizations, are groups of practicing doctors, health quality experts, clinicians, consumers, and other health care professionals who are paid by the federal government to review and improve the care given to Medicare patients. Generally, QIOs are private, not-for-profit organizations.

In August 2014, CMS reorganized the structure of the QIO program. The reorganization separated review of Medicare Beneficiary Quality of Care and appeals from Quality Improvement work carried out in provider and community settings.

There are two types of QIOs that work under the direction of the Centers for Medicare & Medicaid Services in support of the QIO Program:

Beneficiary and Family Centered Care (BFCC)-QIOs

Two Beneficiary and Family Centered Qualify Improvement Organizations (BFCC-QIOs) are Livanta and KEPRO. They address quality of care concerns and appeals. They serve all fifty states and three territories, which are grouped into five regions.

BFCC-QIOs help Medicare beneficiaries exercise their right to high-quality health care. They manage all beneficiary complaints and quality of care reviews to ensure consistency in the review process while taking into consideration local factors important to beneficiaries and their families. They also handle cases in which beneficiaries want to appeal a healthcare provider's decision to discharge them from the hospital or discontinue other types of services. While BFCC-QIOs are the primary point of contact for Medicare beneficiaries and their families, quality of care complaints can also be made by calling 1-800-MEDICARE.

Quality Innovation Network (QIN)-QIOs

Fourteen Quality Innovation Network – Quality Improvement Organizations (QIN-QIOs) work with providers, stakeholders, and Medicare beneficiaries to improve health care quality for selected health conditions.

- QIN-QIOS serve regions of two to six states each.

- QIN-QIOs focus on four major goals:

    o Promoting effective prevention and treatment of chronic disease by promoting safe care that is patient and family-centered reliable and accessible

    o Making care safer and reducing harm caused in the delivery of care

    o Promoting effective communication and coordination of care

    o Making care more affordable

QIOs also decide whether care meets the standards of quality generally accepted by the medical profession. QIOs have the authority to deny payments if care is not medically necessary or not delivered in the most appropriate setting.

QIOs investigate individual patient complaints about the quality of care and respond to:

(1) requests for review of notices of noncoverage issued by hospitals to beneficiaries; and

(2) requests for reconsideration of QIO decisions by beneficiaries, physicians, and hospitals.

The QIO will tell the patient in writing if the service received was not covered by Medicare.

If a patient is admitted to a Medicare-participating hospital, the patient will receive *An Important Message from Medicare About Your Rights*,[1] which explains the patient's rights as a hospital patient and provides the name, address and phone number of the QIO in the patient's state.

If a patient believes he has been improperly refused admission to a hospital, forced to leave a hospital too soon, or denied coverage of a medical procedure or treatment, the patient should ask for a written explanation of the decision. This written notice must fully explain how the patient can appeal the decision, and it must give the patient the name, address, and phone number of the QIO where an appeal or request for review can be submitted.

If a patient disagrees with the decision of a QIO, the patient can appeal by requesting reconsideration. Then, if the patient disagrees with the QIO's reconsideration decision and the amount in question is $200 or more, the patient can request a hearing by an Administrative Law Judge. Cases involving $2,000 or more can eventually be appealed to a federal court. QIOs also provide alternate dispute resolution options.

Different appeal procedures apply to issues involving other types of Part A (Hospital Insurance) coverage such as skilled nursing facility, home health, or hospice care.

For a detailed explanation of the appeals process, see Q 1212 through Q 1229.

QIO Program Transformation

CMS redesigned its QIO Program to further enhance the quality of services for Medicare beneficiaries. The new program structure maximizes learning and collaboration in improving care, enhances flexibility, supports the spread of effective new practices and models of care, helps achieve the priorities of the National Quality Strategy and the goals of the CMS Quality Strategy, and delivers program value to beneficiaries, patients, and taxpayers.

The QIO Program changes include separating case review from quality improvement, extending the contract period of performance from three to five years, removing requirements to restrict QIO activity to a single entity in each state/territory, and opening contractor consideration to a broad range of entities to perform the work.

Now, one group of QIOs (BFCC-QIOs) addresses quality of care concerns and appeals, while another group (QIN-QIOs) works with providers, stakeholders, and Medicare beneficiaries to improve the quality of health care for targeted health conditions. QIOs will have new skills for transforming practices, employing lean methodologies, assisting Medicare providers with their transition to the Quality Payment Program, and developing innovative approaches to quality improvement. CMS is required to publish a Report to Congress every fiscal year that outlines the administration, cost, and impact of the QIO Program. The latest report can be found at the CMS website.[2]

Notes

1. https://www.cms.gov/Medicare/Quality-Initiatives-Patient-Assessment-Instruments/QualityImprovementOrgs (last accessed Oct. 9, 2021).
2. https://www.cms.gov/files/document/cms-financial-report-fiscal-year-2021.pdf (last accessed October 2, 2022).

1017. How is Medicare and Medicaid fraud combatted?

A key component of the Office of the Inspector General's mission is to detect and root out fraud in Federal health care programs, including Medicare and Medicaid.

OIG's mission to curb fraud includes:

- Conducting criminal, civil, and administrative investigations of fraud and misconduct related to HHS programs, operations, and beneficiaries.

- Using state-of-the-art tools and technology in investigations and audits around the country.

- Imposing program exclusions and civil monetary penalties on health care providers because of criminal conduct such as fraud or other wrongdoing;

- Negotiating global settlements in cases arising under the civil False Claims Act, developing and monitoring corporate integrity agreements, and developing compliance program guidance.

Medicaid Fraud Control Units (MFCUs)

Medicaid Fraud Control Units (MFCUs) investigate and prosecute Medicaid provider fraud as well as patient abuse or neglect in health care facilities and board and care facilities. MFCUs operate in all states, the District of Columbia, Puerto Rico, and the U.S. Virgin Islands. The MFCUs, usually a part of the State Attorney General's office, employ teams of investigators, attorneys, and auditors who operate separately and distinctly from the State Medicaid agency.

Medicare Fraud Strike Force Teams

Medicare Fraud Strike Force Teams harness data analytics and work with Federal, State, and local law enforcement entities to prevent and combat health care fraud, waste, and abuse. First established in March 2007, Strike Force teams currently operate in the following areas: Miami, Florida; Los Angeles, California; Detroit, Michigan; Houston, Texas; Brooklyn, New York; Baton Rouge and New Orleans, Louisiana; Tampa and Orlando, Florida; Chicago, Illinois; Dallas, Texas; Washington, D.C.; Newark, New Jersey/Philadelphia, Pennsylvania (established in August 2018); and the Appalachian Regional Strike Force was established in October 2018 to combat illegal opioid prescriptions. Additionally, the New England Prescription Opioid (NEPO) Strike Force was created in June 2022. These teams have resulted in over 2,400 criminal actions and 3,200 indictments during 2021 alone.

1018. When should a person use the Medicare fraud and abuse hotline?

If a person has reason to believe that a doctor, hospital, or other provider of health care services is performing unnecessary or inappropriate services, or is billing Medicare for services not received, the person should report this information to Medicare at 1-800-MEDICARE (1-800-633-4227). The person reporting alleged fraud and abuse should be prepared to communicate details of the transactions raising questions, including:

(1) the exact nature of the suspected wrongdoing including the service or item being questioned and the reason Medicare shouldn't have paid;

(2) the date it occurred;

(3) the name and address of the party involved;

(4) the payment amount approved and paid by Medicare;

(5) the date on the MSN;

(6) name and Medicare number of the person reporting; and

(7)   any other information that is helpful.

If an individual reports information that serves as the basis for the collection of $100 or more, CMS may pay a portion of the amount collected to the individual (up to a maximum of $1,000). Specific requirements include:

(1)   The allegation must be specific – not general.

(2)   The suspected fraud must be confirmed as potential fraud by the Program Safeguard Contractor, the Zone Program Integrity Contractor, or the Medicare Drug Integrity Contractor and formally referred as part of a case to the Office of the Inspector General.

(3)   The individual reporting cannot be an "excluded individual" (such as being a participant in the fraud or part of another reward program).

(4)   The individual or organization isn't already under investigation by law enforcement.

(5)   The report leads to the recovery of at least $100 in Medicare money.

The incentive reward can't exceed 10 percent of the overpayments recovered in the case or $1,000, whichever is less. If multiple individuals qualify for a reward, the reward is shared among them. In addition, there are also whistleblower awards available that can be substantially larger.

A person can also report the fraud to the Office of the Inspector General of the Department of Health and Human Services.[1]

Note

1. https://oig.hhs.gov/fraud/ (Last accessed October 2, 2022).

1019. Should a person receive Medicare benefits through the original fee-for-service Medicare Parts A and B (Hospital Insurance and Medical Insurance) or through a Medicare Advantage plan?

A person living in an area serviced by a Medicare Advantage plan has a choice between traditional Medicare Parts A and B or a Medicare Advantage plan. If a person chooses Parts A and B, that beneficiary can go to almost any doctor, hospital, or other health care provider the beneficiary prefers. Generally, a fee is charged each time a service is used, Medicare pays its share of the bill, and the patient is responsible for paying the balance. Beneficiaries may purchase a private Medicare Supplemental Insurance (Medigap) policy to cover or help defray the patient's share of charges not covered by Medicare. See Q 1212 through Q 1229 on Medigap insurance.

Medicare Advantage plans in general cover the same core benefits as original Medicare Parts A and B, but may also include other coverage, including prescription drug coverage. Because Medicare Advantage plans are structured to be more inclusive, beneficiaries covered by Medicare Advantage do not need to purchase a separate Medigap plan (and are usually prohibited from doing so). Medicare Advantage plans are provided through private insurers, and the exact terms of the plans—including beneficiary cost-sharing obligations—are established by the private insurers, subject to approval by CMS. Medicare Advantage plans may also charge additional premiums (in addition to the Medicare Part B premium) to reflect the additional benefits offered. Most types of Medicare Advantage plans contain managed care features that attempt to control costs by limiting the providers to which a beneficiary may go for care (or imposing higher cost-sharing requirements if a beneficiary obtains services from an out-of-network provider).

An individual who elects a Medicare Advantage plan one year can always return to traditional Medicare Parts A and B (Hospital and Medical Insurance) in a different year. Also, regardless of whether a person chooses Parts A and B (Hospital and Medical Insurance) Medicare or a Medicare Advantage plan, the individual retains all Medicare protections and appeal rights. See Q 1148 through Q 1188 for a detailed description of Medicare Advantage.

On October 3, 2019, then-President Donald J. Trump issued an Executive Order[1] entitled "Protecting and Improving Medicare for Our Nation's Seniors". This order is designed to encourage further participation in Medicare Advantage (Part C) over "traditional Medicare" (Parts A and B). More on this order can be found at Q 1162.

Note

1. Executive Order 13890, *Protecting and Improving Medicare for Our Nation's Seniors*, 84 Fed. Reg. 53,573 (Oct. 3, 2019), https://www.federalregister. gov/documents/2019/10/08/2019-22073/protecting-and-improving-medicare-for-our-nations-seniors. (Last accessed October 2, 2022).

1020. What is the Medicare Plan Finder Tool?

CMS announced in August 2019 that they were rolling out a new Medicare Plan Finder for the first time in over ten years. The new tool includes a great number of improvements and automation. In order to help drive the user to the correct plan it offers helpful questions as you enter the application to steer the user to the proper plans. The changes are part of the Trump Administration's eMedicare initiative.[1]

The updated Medicare Plan Finder[2] intends to provide the user with a personalized experience through a mobile friendly and easy-to-read design that will help them learn about different options and select coverage that best meets their health needs. The new Plan Finder walks users through the Medicare Advantage and Part D enrollment process and allows people to view and compare many of the supplemental benefits that Medicare Advantage plans offer. The Plan Finder has been updated for 2023.

The redesigned Medicare Plan Finder features fewer text-heavy pages, an online live chat feature with a representative and the ability for enrollees to consult their actual prescription drug histories while comparing plans.

The redesigned Medicare Plan Finder intends to make it easier for beneficiaries to see these changes and to:

- Compare pricing between Original Medicare, Medicare prescription drug plans, Medicare Advantage plans, and Medicare Supplement Insurance (Medigap) policies

- Compare coverage options on their smartphones and tablets

- Compare up to three drug plans or three Medicare Advantage plans side-by-side

- Get plan costs and benefits, including which Medicare Advantage plans offer extra benefits

- Build a personal drug list and find Medicare Part D prescription drug coverage that best meets their needs

Medicare's Plan Finder is the most popular spot on the agency's website. In recent years, though, it has come under criticism as other websites offered sleeker user experiences and more comprehensive search results. This included Healthcare.gov, the site used by individuals seeking insurance outside of a workplace.

On the negative side, Medicare beneficiaries and even the counselors around the country who help enrollees navigate Medicare's plans and choices have told government auditors that the current plan finder is difficult to understand and use and adding to the confusion, it was rolled out right before open enrollment.

Other new tools launched under the initiative that seeks to deliver personalized and customized information that Medicare beneficiaries prefer include:

- The "What's Covered" app that tells people what's covered and what's not in Original Medicare.

- A price transparency tool that lets consumers compare Medicare payments and copayments of certain procedures performed in both hospital outpatient departments and ambulatory surgical centers.

- Interactive online decision support to help people better understand and evaluate their Medicare coverage options and costs between Original Medicare and Medicare Advantage.

- An online service that lets people quickly see how different coverage choices will affect their estimated out-of-pocket costs.

- Webchat option in Medicare Plan Finder helps people get on-the-spot support.

- Easy-to-use surveys across Medicare.gov so consumers can continue to offer feedback about their online experiences.

Notes

1. https://www.medicare.gov/blog/emedicare-another-step-to-strengthening-medicare.
2. https://www.medicare.gov/plan-compare/#/?lang=en&year=2023. (Medicare Plan Finder).

1020.01. How Does the Medicare Plan Finder Tool Work?

The tool will link you to https://www.medicare.gov/plan-compare/#/?lang=en&year=2023 to give you options search for plans. The user will be invited to select a calendar year (either 2022 or 2023) and enter a Zip Code.

Additionally, the user must search for one of the following

- Medicare Advantage plans OR Part D plans OR Part D plans PLUS Medigap coverage OR Medigap Coverage only OR More information

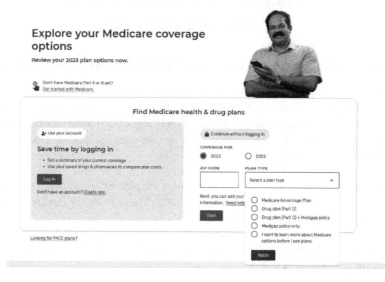

If the user is looking for

- Medicare Advantage OR Part D plans OR Part D plans PLUS Medigap coverage

The following questions will be asked[1]

Help with your costs

Do you get help with your costs from one of these programs?

- ◯ Medicaid
- ◯ Supplemental Security Income
- ◯ Medicare Savings Program
- ◯ Extra Help from Social Security
- ◯ I'm not sure
- ◯ I don't get help from any of these programs

After answering, the user will be presented with the decision of whether they want to see drug costs when comparing plans. If so, they will need to enter each drug of interest.

After selecting "NEXT" – the user will be presented with appropriate plan choices.

Note

1. Note: If the person gets "Extra Help from Social Security, they will be asked an extra step – whether they get partial help or the full amount.

MEDICARE AND COVID-19
Medicare Coverage

1021. Does Medicare cover lab tests for coronavirus/COVID-19?

Yes. Medicare covers all laboratory testing for COVID-19. The Medicare subscriber pays no out-of-pocket costs. Medicare Part B (Medical Insurance) covers a test to see if you have COVID-19. The patient pays nothing for this test when gotten from a laboratory, pharmacy, doctor, or hospital, and when Medicare covers this test in your local area. This coverage continues until the COVID-19 public health emergency ends.

Medicare also covers some tests for related respiratory conditions to aid diagnosis of COVID-19 done together with the COVID-19 tests. These tests are covered regardless of locations, including some "parking lot" test sites.

Medicare now covers up to eight over the counter COVID-19 tests each calendar month, at no cost to subscribers.

Medicare Part B (Medical Insurance) will cover these tests if the individual has Part B. Medicare will not cover over the counter COVID-19 tests if the individual only has Medicare Part A (Hospital Insurance) coverage but may be able to get free tests through other programs or insurance coverage you may have.

Medicare Advantage Plan subscribers will not get this benefit through their plan but will get it like as if were not enrolled in the plan. Medicare Advantage Plans cannot charge copayments, deductibles, or coinsurance for clinical lab tests to detect or diagnose COVID-19.

Medicare also covers COVID-19 anti-body tests, COVID-19 monoclonal antibody tests, COVID-19 monoclonal antibody treatments, and COVID-19 vaccines.

1022. Does Medicare cover COVID-19 antibody or serology tests?

Yes. Medicare covers all medically necessary COVID-19 antibody or serology tests if the patient was diagnosed with a known current or known prior COVID-19 infection or suspected current or suspected past COVID-19 infection.

Medicare also covers COVID-19 antibody tests and COVID-19 monoclonal antibody treatments as necessary. Monoclonal antibody treatments are covered as necessary if the following conditions are met:

- If the person tests positive for COVID-19

- If the person has a "mild to moderate" case of COVID-19

- If the person is at high risk of progressing to a severe case of COVID-19 or a high risk of hospitalization

Medicare Advantage plans are not permitted to charge copayments, deductibles, or coinsurance for clinical lab tests to detect or diagnose COVID-19.

1023. Does Medicare cover hospitalization for COVID-19?

Yes. Medicare covers all medically necessary hospitalizations. This includes if the patient is diagnosed with COVID-19 and might otherwise have been discharged from the hospital after an inpatient stay, but instead need to stay in the hospital under quarantine. The patient will still pay for any hospital deductibles, copays, or coinsurances that apply.

Medicare-covered hospital services include:

- Semi-private rooms

- Meals

- General nursing

- Drugs as part of your inpatient treatment (including methadone to treat an opioid use disorder)

- Other hospital services and supplies

Inpatient hospital care includes care received in:

- Acute care hospitals

- Critical access hospitals

- Inpatient rehabilitation facilities

- Inpatient psychiatric facilities

- Long-term care hospitals

- Inpatient care as part of a qualifying clinical research study

If covered by Part B, it generally covers 80 percent of the Medicare-approved amount for doctor's services received while hospitalized.

Medicare doesn't cover:

- Private-duty nursing

- Private room (unless medically necessary)

- Separate charges for television or phone in the room

- Personal care items (like razors or slipper socks)

1024. Will Medicare cover the cost of COVID-19 vaccines?

Yes.

Medicare covers the COVID-19 vaccine at no cost.

Medicare also currently covers a Pfizer COVID-19 vaccine booster shot if the individual is 65 and older as well as for certain individuals deemed at high risk, at least 6 months after completing a second dose of the Pfizer COVID-19 vaccine series. There are CDC recommendations defining who should get booster shots.[1]

For individuals who are immunocompromised (such as people at risk for infection and people who have had organ transplants), Medicare covers an additional "booster" dose of the COVID-19 vaccine at no cost. At the time of publication, Medicare was recommending that vaccines not be "mixed" – meaning staying with the company that provided the first dose(s), but as of time of publication, discussion was underway as to whether the vaccines could be mixed. Individuals should obviously get qualified medical advice on inoculations.

For individuals with disabilities or who are unable to get to a vaccination location, Medicare covers the costs of a health care professional to provide the COVID-19 vaccine at the person's home at no cost for the medicine or the administration of the vaccines. It can be provided by the person's regular doctor or another healthcare professional.

Note

1. https://www.cdc.gov/media/releases/2021/p0924-booster-recommendations-.html (dated September 24, 2021). (Last accessed October 2, 2022).

1025. Does Medicare Advantage (Part C) cover COVID-19 costs?

Yes. Medicare Advantage Plans are another way to get Medicare Part A and Part B coverage. Medicare Advantage Plans, sometimes called "Part C" or "MA Plans," are offered by Medicare-approved private companies that must follow rules set by Medicare. The Medicare subscriber that has a Medicare Advantage Plan also has access to the COVID-19 benefits described in this section. Medicare allows these plans to waive cost-sharing for COVID-19 lab tests. Many plans offer additional telehealth benefits and expanded benefits, like meal delivery or medical transport services. Medicare Advantage plans are not permitted to charge copayments, deductibles, or coinsurance for clinical lab tests to detect or diagnose COVID-19.

1026. Are COVID-19 services available through telehealth?

Yes. Medicare has expanded its coverage of telehealth services to respond to the current Public Health Emergency. These services expand the current telehealth covered services to enable access from more places (including the patient's home), with a wider range of communication tools (including smartphones), to interact with a range of providers (like doctors, nurse practitioners, clinical psychologists, licensed clinical social workers, physical therapists, occupational therapists, and speech language pathologists).

During this time, Medicare subscribers will be able to receive a specific set of services through telehealth including evaluation and management visits (common office visits), mental health counseling and preventive health screenings without a copayment under Original Medicare. This will help ensure doctor visits from home without having to go to a doctor's office or hospital, which puts people at risk of exposure to COVID-19.

- **Virtual Check-In:** The patient may be able to communicate with your doctors or certain other practitioners without necessarily going to the doctor's office in person for a full visit. Medicare pays for virtual check-ins which are brief, virtual services with a physician or certain practitioners where the communication isn't related to a medical visit within the previous seven days and doesn't lead to a medical visit within the next 24 hours (or soonest appointment available).

- **Consent:** The patient needs to consent verbally to using virtual check-ins and the doctor must document that consent in the medical record before using this service. The patient pays the usual Medicare coinsurance and deductible for these services.

- **Online Patient Portals:** Medicare also pays for the patient to communicate with doctors using online patient portals without going to the doctor's office. Like the virtual check-ins, the patient must initiate these individual communications.

- **Smart Phone Or Audio-Only:** Since some people don't have access to interactive audio-video technology needed for Medicare telehealth services, or choose not to use it even if offered by their practitioner, Medicare is allowing people to use an audio-only phone.

- **Full Visits:** The patient may use communication technology to have full visits with doctors.

- **Rural Health Clinics and Federally Qualified Health Clinics:** The patient can have remote visits with rural health clinics and federally qualified health clinics. Medicare pays for many medical visits through this telehealth benefit.

1027. What other changes has Medicare implemented due to COVID-19?

Medicare has implemented several procedures including:

- Medicare Advantage Plans and Prescription Drug Plans may waive or relax prior authorization requirements during the emergency.

- Taking aggressive actions and exercising regulatory flexibilities to help healthcare providers and Medicare health plans.

- Hospitals can now provide hospital services in other healthcare facilities and sites that aren't currently considered part of a healthcare facility. This includes off-site screenings. Medicare covers medically necessary care in these facilities and sites.

- Waiving certain requirements for Skilled Nursing Facility (SNF) care.

- Establishing new codes to allow providers to correctly bill for services related to diagnosis and treatment of the illness.

- Instructing nursing homes and hospitals to review their infection control procedures, which they are always required to maintain.

MEDICARE AND TELEMEDICINE
Coverage

1028. What are telemedicine/telehealth/remote services as related to Medicare?

Telehealth, telemedicine, and remote services generally refer to the exchange of medical information from one site to another through electronic communication to improve a patient's health. Innovative uses of this kind of technology in the provision of healthcare is increasing.

With the emergence of the virus causing the disease COVID-19, there is an urgency to expand the use of technology to help people who need routine care, and keep vulnerable beneficiaries and beneficiaries with mild symptoms in their homes while maintaining access to the care they need. Limiting community spread of the virus, as well as limiting the exposure to other patients and staff members will slow viral spread.

1029. How has Medicare expanded access to telehealth services?

Centers for Medicare & Medicaid Services (CMS) has broadened access to Medicare telehealth services so that beneficiaries can receive a wider range of services from their doctors without having to travel to a healthcare facility. These policy changes build on the regulatory flexibilities granted under the President Trump's emergency declaration.

CMS is expanding this benefit on a temporary and emergency basis under the 1135 waiver authority and Coronavirus Preparedness and Response Supplemental Appropriations Act. The benefits are part of the broader effort by CMS to ensure that all Americans, particularly those at high-risk of complications from the virus that causes the disease COVID-19 are aware of easy-to-use, accessible benefits that can help keep them healthy while helping to contain the community spread of this virus.

1030. How do the Section 1135 Waivers expand telehealth?

Under the section 1135 waiver, Medicare can pay for office, hospital, and other visits furnished via telehealth across the country - including in patient's places of residence starting March 6, 2020. A range of providers, such as doctors, nurse practitioners, clinical psychologists, and licensed clinical social workers, can offer telehealth to their patients. Additionally, the HHS Office of Inspector General (OIG) is providing flexibility for healthcare providers to reduce or waive cost-sharing for telehealth visits paid by federal healthcare programs.

Prior to the waiver, Medicare could only pay for telehealth on a limited basis: when the person receiving the service was in a designated rural area and when they left their home and go to a clinic, hospital, or certain other types of medical facilities for the service.

Virtual Check-Ins: In 2019, Medicare started making payment for brief communications or "virtual check-ins," which are short patient-initiated communications with a healthcare practitioner. Medicare Part B separately pays clinicians for e-visits, which are non-face-to-face patient-initiated communications through an online patient portal.

Medicare beneficiaries will be able to receive a specific set of services through telehealth including:

- evaluation and management visits (common office visits);

- mental health counseling; and

- preventive health screenings.

This will help ensure Medicare beneficiaries, who are at a higher risk for COVID-19, are able to visit with their doctor from their home, without having to go to a doctor's office or hospital which puts themselves and others at risk.

1031. What types of telehealth services are covered under Medicare?

There are three main types of virtual services physicians and other professionals can provide to Medicare beneficiaries:

- Medicare telehealth visits;

- These replace office appointments, hospital visits, psychotherapy, consultations, and other in-person services. These require audio-visual communication capability

- Virtual check-ins; and

  - Allows an individual to briefly speak to a provider using a phone, secure text messages, email, or a patient portal. The patient must verbally consent to virtual check-ins. This consent must be documented in the medical record and will allow up to a year of virtual visits to be covered. The communication may not be related to a medical visit within the last seven days and must not lead to a medical visit within the next 24 hours.

- e-visits.

  - Allows an individual to speak to a provider through an online patient portal. The individual must be an established patient and must also ask the provider about starting e-visits.

    - These visits need to be "patient-initiated" to be covered.

    - These visits may be for services for appointments with doctors, nurse practitioners, and physician assistants.

    - These visits also may happen with physical therapists, occupational therapists, and speech language pathologists. Under certain circumstances, the individual may have covered e-visits with licensed clinical social workers and clinical psychologists.

The services provided include:

- Wellness visits

- Urgent care

- Office visits

- Consultations

- Prescriptions for medications

- Preventive health screenings

- Mental health counseling

- Substance use disorder treatment

- Monthly end-stage renal disease visits for home dialysis

1032. What are Medicare telehealth visits?

Currently, Medicare patients may use telecommunication technology for office, hospital visits, and other services (telehealth visits) that generally occur in-person.

The provider must use an interactive audio and video telecommunications system that permits real-time communication between the distant site and the patient at home. Distant site practitioners who can furnish and get payment for covered telehealth services (subject to state law) can include:

- physicians,

- nurse practitioners,

- physician assistants,

- nurse midwives,

- certified nurse anesthetists,

- clinical psychologists,

- physical therapists,

- occupational therapists,

- speech language pathologists,

- licensed clinical social workers (in some circumstances),

- registered dietitians, and

- nutrition professionals.

HHS is discouraging travel by patients when possible, to physicians' offices, clinics, hospitals, or other health care facilities where they could risk their own or others' exposure to further illness. To the extent the waiver (section 1135(g)(3)) requires that the patient have a prior established relationship with a practitioner, HHS will not conduct audits to ensure that such a prior relationship existed for claims submitted during this public health emergency.

These visits are considered the same as in-person visits and are paid at the same rate. Medicare will make payment for professional services furnished to beneficiaries in all areas of the country in all settings. For the duration of the emergency, Medicare will pay for Medicare telehealth services in any healthcare facility or the patient's home. The HHS Office of Inspector General is providing flexibility for healthcare providers to reduce or waive cost-sharing for tele-health visits paid by federal healthcare programs.

1033. What is a Medicare virtual check-In?

In all areas (not just rural), established Medicare patients may have a brief communication service from their home with practitioners via several communication technology modalities including:

- Phone

- Audio visit

- Secure text messages

- Email

- Use of a patient portal

These virtual services will be initiated by the patient; however, practitioners may need to educate beneficiaries on the availability of the service prior to patient initiation.

Medicare pays for these "virtual check-ins" (or brief communication technology-based service) for patients to communicate with their doctors and avoid unnecessary trips to the doctor's office. These virtual check-ins are for patients with an established (or existing) relationship with a physician or certain practitioners where the communication is not related to a medical visit within the previous seven days and does not lead to a medical visit within the next 24 hours (or soonest appointment available). The patient must verbally consent to receive virtual check-in services.

The Medicare coinsurance and deductible would generally apply to these services.

Doctors and certain practitioners may bill for virtual check in services furnished through several communication technology modalities, such as telephone (HCPCS code G2012). The practitioner may respond to the patient's concern by telephone, audio/video, secure text messaging, email, or use of a patient portal. Standard Part B cost sharing applies to both.

In addition, separate from these virtual check-in services, captured video or images (store and forward) can be sent to a physician (HCPCS code G2010). This includes interpretation with follow-up with the patient within 24 business hours.

1034. What are Medicare e-visits?

E-visits can occur in all types of locations including the patient's home, and in all areas (not just rural), established Medicare patients may have non-face-to-face patient-initiated communications with their doctors without going to the doctor's office by using online patient portals.

Established relationship: These services can only be reported when the billing practice has an established relationship with the patient. The patient must generate the initial inquiry and communications can occur over a seven-day period.

Billing: The services may be billed using CPT codes 99421-99423 and HCPCS codes G2061-G2063, as applicable. The patient must verbally consent to receive virtual check-in services. The Medicare coinsurance and deductible would apply to these services.

Patient Portal: Medicare Part B also pays for E-visits or patient-initiated online evaluation and management conducted via a patient portal. Practitioners who may independently bill Medicare for evaluation and management visits (for instance, physicians and nurse practitioners) can bill the following codes:

- 99421: Online digital evaluation and management service, for an established patient, for up to seven days, cumulative time during the seven days; 5–10 minutes.

- 99422: Online digital evaluation and management service, for an established patient, for up to seven days cumulative time during the seven days; 11– 20 minutes.

- 99423: Online digital evaluation and management service, for an established patient, for up to seven days, cumulative time during the seven days; 21 or more minutes.

Clinicians who may not independently bill for evaluation and management visits (for example – physical therapists, occupational therapists, speech language pathologists, clinical psychologists) can also provide these e-visits and bill the following codes:

- G2061: Qualified non-physician healthcare professional online assessment and management, for an established patient, for up to seven days, cumulative time during the seven days; 5–10 minutes.

- G2062: Qualified non-physician healthcare professional online assessment and management service, for an established patient, for up to seven days, cumulative time during the seven days; 11–20 minutes.

- G2063: Qualified non-physician qualified healthcare professional assessment and management service, for an established patient, for up to seven days, cumulative time during the seven days; 21 or more minutes.

1035. How does HIPAA relate to Telehealth?

The HHS Office for Civil Rights (OCR) exercises enforcement discretion and waives penalties for Health Insurance Portability and Accountability Act (HIPAA) violations against health care providers that serve patients in good faith through everyday communications technologies, such as FaceTime or Skype, during the COVID-19 nationwide public health emergency.

Telehealth services may be provided through audio, text messaging, or video communication technology, including videoconferencing software. Medicare and Medicaid can impose restrictions on the types of technologies that can be used, but these do not limit the scope of the HIPAA Notification of Enforcement Discretion regarding COVID-19 and remote telehealth communications.

It is expected that health care providers will usually conduct telehealth in private settings, such as a doctor in a clinic or office connecting to a patient who is at home or at another clinic. Providers should always use private locations and patients should not receive telehealth services in public or semi-public settings, absent patient consent or exigent circumstances. If telehealth cannot be provided in a private setting, covered health care providers should continue to implement reasonable HIPAA safeguards to limit incidental uses or disclosures of protected health information (PHI). Reasonable precautions could include using lowered voice, abstaining from the use of speakerphones, or recommending that the patient move to a reasonable distance from others when discussing PHI.

PART A:
HOSPITAL INSURANCE
Eligibility Rules - Generally

1036. Who is eligible for benefits under Part A (Hospital Insurance)?

All persons aged 65 or older, a U.S. citizen, or permanent legal resident of at least five years in a row and who are entitled to monthly Social Security cash benefits (or would be entitled except that an application for cash benefits has not been filed), or monthly cash benefits under Railroad Retirement programs (whether retired or not), are eligible for Medicare Part A benefits. An individual may be eligible for Social Security or Railroad Retirement program benefits based on the individual's own work record or as the current or surviving spouse of someone eligible for such benefits. Such individuals are eligible for Part A (Hospital Insurance) benefits if they are at least sixty-five years old. For example, a woman aged sixty-five or over who is entitled to a spouse's or widow's Social Security benefit is eligible for benefits under Part A.

Persons aged 65 and over can receive Medicare benefits even if they continue to work. Enrollment in the program while working will not affect the amount of future Social Security benefits.

Certain Social Security or Railroad Retirement disability beneficiaries are eligible for Medicare Parts A and B after entitlement to disability benefits for twenty-four months or more. Eligible categories of disability beneficiaries include disabled workers at any age, disabled widows and widowers at least age fifty but not yet age sixty-five, beneficiaries aged eighteen or older who receive benefits because of disability beginning before age twenty-two and disabled qualified Railroad Retirement annuitants. Medicare coverage is automatic. No application is required.

A person who becomes re-entitled to disability benefits within five years after the end of a previous period of entitlement (within seven years in the case of disabled widows or widowers and disabled children) is automatically eligible for Medicare coverage without the need to wait another twenty-four months. In addition, in most cases, an individual covered by Medicare on the basis of disability, but who loses disability benefits for some reason, will again be eligible for Medicare coverage without needing to meet the twenty-four-month waiting period requirement, if the current impairment is the same as (or directly related to) that in the previous period of disability.

Medicare coverage will continue if the individual returns to work during a nine-month trial period and for up to fifteen additional months (a total of twenty-four months).

Individuals with ALS (Amyotrophic Lateral Sclerosis, also known as Lou Gehrig's disease) are eligible for Medicare Part A (Hospital Insurance) the first month they are eligible for Social Security or Railroad Retirement disability benefits. The normal twenty-four month waiting period does not apply.

Medicare Part A also covers individuals with End-Stage Renal Disease (ESRD) who are not yet age sixty-five but who are either currently or fully insured for, or are entitled to, Social Security or Railroad Retirement benefits. Spouses or dependent children of eligible individuals may also be covered if the spouse or dependent child has ESRD.

1037. What are the special eligibility rules for persons with End-Stage Renal Disease (ESRD)?

End-Stage Renal Disease (ESRD) is a situation where a person's kidneys are ceasing to function on a permanent basis leading to the necessity of long-term dialysis or a kidney transplant to maintain life. Individuals in this situation may become entitled to Medicare based on the ESRD diagnosis. Benefits because of ESRD are for all covered services, not only those related to the kidney failure condition. Insured workers (and their spouses and dependents) with ESRD who require renal dialysis, or a kidney transplant are deemed disabled for Medicare coverage purposes even if they are working.

To be eligible for ESRD Medicare, one must be under age sixty-five and diagnosed with ESRD by a doctor. Additionally, the person must have enough work history to qualify for Social Security Disability Insurance (SSDI) or Social Security retirement benefits, or enough railroad work history to qualify for Railroad Retirement benefits or railroad disability annuity. An individual can also qualify through the work history of your spouse or parent.

Coverage can begin with the first day of the third month after the month dialysis treatments begin. This three-month waiting period is waived if the individual participates in a self-care dialysis training course during the waiting period.

Medicare coverage for an ESRD patient who is a candidate for a kidney transplant begins with the month in which the patient is hospitalized for the transplant, if the transplant occurs during the three-month period beginning with that month. If a transplant is delayed more than two months following the initial month of hospitalization for a transplant, coverage is effective on the first day of the second month before the month of transplant.

Coverage is also provided under Medicare for the self-administration of erythropoietin for home renal dialysis patients.

For some individuals who have Medicare solely on the basis of their end-stage renal disease, Medicare is the secondary payer if the person with ESRD has Group Health Plan (GHP) coverage either directly or through a family member for a coordination period of thirty months regardless of the number of employees and regardless of whether coverage is based on current employment status. During this period, if an employer plan pays less than the provider's charges, Medicare may supplement the plan's payments (see Q 1039). Medicare is secondary to GHP coverage provided through the Consolidated Omnibus Budget Reconciliation Act (COBRA), or a retirement plan. Medicare is secondary during the coordination period even if the employer policy or plan contains a provision stating that its benefits are secondary to Medicare. The GHP may not differentiate in the benefits it provides to individuals who have ESRD. Specifically, GHPs are prohibited from terminating coverage, imposing benefit limitations, or charging higher premiums on the basis of the existence of the individuals ESRD.

START OF COVERAGE

When the beneficiary first enrolls in Medicare based on ESRD, Medicare coverage can start at different times based on the situation:

1. **Fourth Month of Dialysis:** On the fourth month of dialysis when the beneficiary participates in dialysis treatment in a dialysis facility.

2. **First Month of Dialysis:** Medicare coverage can start as early as the first month of dialysis if:

    o   The beneficiary takes part in a home dialysis training program in a Medicare-approved training facility to learn how to do self-dialysis treatment at home;

    o   The beneficiary begins home dialysis training before the third month of dialysis; and

    o   The beneficiary expects to finish home dialysis training and give self-dialysis treatments.

3. **Admission for Kidney Transplant:** Medicare coverage can start the month the beneficiary is admitted to a Medicare-approved hospital for kidney transplant or for health care services that are needed before the transplant if the transplant takes place in the same month or within the two following months.

4. **Delay in Kidney Transplant:** Medicare coverage can start two months before the month of the transplant if the transplant is delayed more than two months after the beneficiary is admitted to the hospital for that transplant or for health care services that are needed before the transplant.

END OF COVERAGE

1. If the beneficiary has Medicare only because of ESRD, Medicare coverage will end when one of the following conditions is met:

    •   12 months after the month the beneficiary stops dialysis treatments, or

    •   36 months after the month the beneficiary had a kidney transplant.

There is a separate thirty-month coordination period each time the beneficiary enrolls in Medicare based on kidney failure. For example, if the beneficiary gets a kidney transplant that continues to work for 36 months, Medicare coverage will end. If after thirty-six months the beneficiary enrolls in Medicare again because they start dialysis or get another transplant, the Medicare coverage will start right away. There will be no three-month waiting period before Medicare begins to pay.

NOTE: ESRD patients can now be part of Medicare Advantage plans. For 2023, CMS is finalizing its revised risk adjustment model for payment to Medicare organizations and other programs including Medicare-Medicaid Plans (MMPs) which use the Medicare Advantage risk adjustment models for enrollees with ESRD so as to improve the prediction of costs for these enrollees. The revised model is calibrated on more recent data, using CMS's current approach to identify risk adjustment eligible diagnoses from encounter data records. It also incorporates clinical updates and revised segmentation, which accounts for the differential cost patterns of dual-eligible beneficiaries.

Eligibility Rules for Government Employees

1038. What are the special eligibility rules for government employees?

In general, federal employees began paying the Hospital Insurance (HI) portion of Social Security taxes in 1983 and thus became eligible for Medicare. A transitional provision provides credit for retroactive hospital quarters of coverage for federal employees who were employed before 1983 and also on January 1, 1983. Certain categories of federal employees are not covered, however, including inmates in federal penal institutions, certain interns, and certain temporary employees.

State and local government employees hired after March 31, 1986, generally also pay HI taxes and are covered under Medicare. A person who was performing substantial and regular service for a state or local government before April 1, 1986 is not covered, provided he was a bona fide employee on March 31, 1986, and the employment relationship was not entered into in order to meet the requirements for exemptions from coverage.

State or local government employees who were employed before April 1, 1986, but whose employment terminated after March 31, 1986, are covered under Medicare if they are later rehired. Certain individuals are not automatically covered under Medicare even if employed by a state or local government, including those employed:

(1)   to relieve them of unemployment;

(2)   in a hospital, home, or institution where they are inmates or patients;

(3)   on a temporary basis because of an emergency such as a storm, earthquake, flood, fire, or snow;

(4)   as interns, student nurses, or other student employees of District of Columbia government hospitals, unless the individuals are medical or dental interns or medical or dental residents in training.

State governments may voluntarily enter into agreements called Section 218 Agreements to extend Medicare coverage to employees not covered under the rules above.

1038.01. What are Section 218 Agreements?

In 1950, Congress enacted Section 218 of the Social Security Act. This allowed Social Security coverage to be extended to State and local government employees who were not covered by an alternative retirement system. This coverage can be made available state request, enabled by an agreement signed by the state and the Social Security Administration (SSA).

These agreements are referred to as Section 218 Agreements, Federal-State agreements, modifications, or voluntary agreements (because the coverage is voluntarily requested by the State). Amendments were made to the Act in 1954, which allows state and local workers who were members of a retirement system (except police officers or fire fighters) to also be covered under section 218 Agreements, provided coverage was authorized by the state and approved through a voluntary coverage referendum.

A Section 218 Agreement is a document signed by the individual state and the SSA extending Social Security and Medicare or Medicare-only coverage on a voluntary basis to the state and local employees of that state. Each state has an agreement with SSA. When a state wants to cover additional State or local government employees enact a modification to the original agreement. Nearly all states continue, to this day, to extend coverage through modifications.

The Commonwealths of Puerto Rico and the Virgin Islands also have Section 218 Agreements with SSA. Additionally, interstate organizations can also enter into Section 218 Agreements.

A state Social Security Administrator is required to be designated to ensure coverage for state employees[1]. The administrator is charged with administering all aspects coverage, including interpretation of provisions, and insuring proper application of Social Security coverage to state and political subdivision employees.

Note

1. 20 C.F.R. §404.1204.

1038.02. Are there differences in Social Security taxes for government employees and private sector employees?

Not anymore.

When the Social Security Act was first modified by Section 218, there were two separate tax processes for private and government employees. Private employees contributing to the Social Security tax paid "FICA" taxes and government employees did not pay FICA taxes, but submitted "contributions" to the Social Security program. The SSA was designated to administer its tax collection provisions in a similar fashion that the IRS administered FICA tax provisions. Social Security considered each state to be liable for payment of the Social Security contributions on covered employees, including local governments, because the Section 218 Agreement for Social Security coverage was between the State and SSA, not SSA and the employer. Therefore, while each private employer sent FICA taxes directly to the IRS, government employers with employees covered under a Section 218 Agreement sent Social Security "contributions" directly to the state administrator. The state Administrator then paid the Social Security contributions directly to an SSA account at the Federal Reserve Bank. This separate Social Security tax process for private and public employers existed for almost 40 years.

In 1987, the law was changed, making taxes due pursuant to Section 218 Agreements considered to be FICA taxes. Public employers became responsible for withholding and remitting FICA taxes in the same manner as private employers, and IRS assumed oversight authority.

1038.03. Which states have a Section 218 Agreement?

All states (by definition includes the 50 U.S. states, Puerto Rico, the Virgin Islands, and approximately 60 interstate instrumentalities) have a Section 218 Agreement with SSA. These agreements allow the states, if they desire, to provide either Social Security and Medicare Hospital Insurance (HI) or Medicare HI-only coverage for public employees.

- NOTE: An "interstate instrumentality" is an independent legal entity organized by two or more states to carry out one or more governmental functions, i.e., police power, taxing power, and/or power of eminent domain. For purposes of a Section 218 Agreement, an interstate instrumentality has the status of a State.

- NOTE: A state does not include the District of Columbia, Guam, American Samoa, or the Commonwealth of the Northern Mariana Islands.

When a State enters into a Section 218 Agreement with the SSA, employees of the State and its political subdivisions are brought under the agreement in groups known as "coverage groups."

There are two types of coverage groups:

- non-retirement systems, and

  o An example of a non-retirement system coverage group would be employees of a municipality who are not members of a public retirement system.

- retirement system coverage groups.

  o An example of a retirement system coverage group would be teachers in a city who are members of the Teachers Retirement System.

1038.04. Can a state terminate a Section 218 Agreement?

No. Before 1983, a state could terminate Social Security coverage for employees covered under the state's Section 218 Agreement. The 1983 Social Security Amendments rescinded this provision of the Act and prohibited States from terminating coverage beginning April 20, 1983.

1038.05. Who is covered under a Section 218 agreement?

By law, a section 218 agreement covers positions, not individuals. If the position is included in a Section 218 Agreement, then any employee filling that position is subject to Social Security and Medicare taxes. Employees covered under a Section 218 Agreement have the same coverage and benefit rights as employees in the private sector.

Coverage Groups

Public employees are brought under a Section 218 Agreement in one of two different kinds of coverage groups.

- Absolute coverage groups

    o An absolute coverage group is composed of employees whose positions are not covered under a public retirement system.

- Retirement system coverage groups

    o A retirement system coverage group is composed of employees whose positions are covered under a public retirement system.

    o In the case of a public retirement system, coverage can only occur under a Section 218 Agreement after a referendum is held.

    ♦ Majority Vote Referendum:

        ▪ A majority vote referendum process is utilized and if a majority of all the eligible members vote in favor of coverage, all current and future employees in positions under the retirement system will be covered. All states are authorized to use this process if desired.

    ♦ Divided Vote Referendum:

        ▪ Certain States and all interstate instrumentalities are authorized to divide a retirement system based on whether the employees in positions under the retirement system want coverage.

        ▪ Under the divided vote referendum, only those employees who vote "yes" and all future employees who become members of the retirement system will be covered.

        ▪ Members who vote "no" are not covered as long as they maintain continuous employment in a position within the same public retirement system coverage group.

Under the Act, certain employee services are mandatorily excluded from Social Security coverage under a Section 218 Agreement. In addition, certain services and positions may, if requested by the State, be excluded from Social Security coverage under the State's Section 218 Agreement (optional exclusions). The services that a State may optionally exclude are limited to those listed as optional exclusions in Section 218 of the Act.

Qualifications

1039. When is Medicare considered a secondary payer?

There are limitations on Medicare payments for services covered under group health plans. Medicare is secondary payer, under specified conditions, for services covered under any of the following:

- Group health plans of employers that employ at least twenty employees and that cover Medicare beneficiaries aged sixty-five or older who are covered under the plan by virtue of an individual's current employment status with an employer or the current employment status of a spouse of any age.

- Group health plans (without regard to the number of individuals employed and irrespective of current employment status) that cover individuals who have end-stage renal disease. Generally, group health plans are always primary payers throughout the first thirty months of end-stage renal disease based on Medicare eligibility or entitlement.

- Large group health plans (that is, plans of employers that employ at least 100 employees) that cover Medicare beneficiaries who are under age sixty-five, entitled to Medicare based on disability, and covered under the employer plan by virtue of the individual's or a family member's current employment status with an employer.

A "group health plan" means any arrangement made by one or more employers or employee organizations to provide health care directly or through other methods such as insurance or reimbursement, to current or former employees, the employer, others associated or formerly associated with the employer in a business relationship, or their families, that:

(1)   is of, or contributed to by, one or more employers or employee organizations.

(2)   involves more than one employer or employee organization and provides for common administration: and

(3)   provides substantially the same benefits or the same benefit options to all those enrolled under the arrangement.

Group health plans include self-insured plans, plans of governmental entities (federal, state, and local), and employee organization plans (union plans, employee health and welfare funds, or other employee organization plans). Group health plans also include employee-pay-all plans, which are plans under the auspices of one or more employers or employee organizations, but which receive no financial contributions from them. Not included in the definition of group health plans are plans that are unavailable to employees, for example, a plan only for self-employed persons.

A large group health plan means a group health plan that covers employees of either:

- a single employer or employee organization that employed at least 100 full-time or part-time employees on 50 percent or more of its regular business days during the previous calendar year; or

- two or more employers, or employee organizations, at least one of which employed at least 100 full-time or part-time employees on 50 percent or more of its regular business days during the previous calendar year.

An employer or insurer is prohibited from offering Medicare beneficiaries financial or other benefits as incentives not to enroll in, or to terminate enrollment in, a group health plan that is, or would be, primary to Medicare. The prohibition precludes offering to Medicare beneficiaries an alternative to the employer primary plan (for example, coverage of prescription drugs) unless the beneficiary has primary coverage other than Medicare. An example would be primary coverage through an employee's own or a spouse's employer.

Other prohibited actions by group health plans or large group health plans include, but are not limited to, the following:

- Failure to pay primary benefits as required

- Offering coverage that is secondary to Medicare to individuals entitled to Medicare

- Terminating coverage because the individual has become entitled to Medicare, except as permitted under certain COBRA continuation coverage provisions

- In the case of a large group health plan, denying or terminating coverage because an individual is entitled to Medicare based on disability without denying or terminating coverage for similarly situated individuals who are not entitled to Medicare based on disability

- Imposing limitations on benefits for a Medicare-entitled individual that do not apply to others enrolled in the plan, such as providing less comprehensive health care coverage, excluding benefits, reducing benefits, charging higher deductibles or coinsurance, providing for lower annual or lifetime benefit limits, or more restrictive pre-existing illness limitations

- Charging a Medicare-entitled individual higher premiums

- Requiring a Medicare-entitled individual to wait longer for coverage to begin

- Paying providers and suppliers no more than the Medicare payment rate for services furnished to a Medicare beneficiary but making payments at a higher rate for the same services to an enrollee who is not entitled to Medicare

- Providing misleading or incomplete information that would have the effect of inducing a Medicare entitled individual to reject the employer plan, thereby making Medicare the primary payer. An example of this would be informing the beneficiary of the right to accept or reject the employer plan but failing to inform the individual that, if he rejects the plan, the plan will not be permitted to provide or pay for secondary benefits

- Including in its health insurance cards, claims forms, or brochures distributed to beneficiaries, providers, and suppliers, instructions to bill Medicare first for services furnished to Medicare beneficiaries without stipulating that such action may be taken only when Medicare is the primary payer

- Refusing to enroll an individual for whom Medicare would be secondary payer, when enrollment is available to similarly situated individuals for whom Medicare would not be secondary payer

If a group health plan or large group health plan makes benefit distinctions among various categories of individuals (distinctions unrelated to the fact that the individual is disabled), the group health plan or large group health plan may make the same distinctions among the same categories of individuals entitled to Medicare whose plan coverage is based on current employment status. For example, if a group health plan or large group health plan does not offer coverage to employees who have worked less than one year and who are not entitled to Medicare based on disability or age, the group health plan or large group health plan is not required to offer coverage to employees who have worked less than one year and who *are* entitled to Medicare based on disability or age.

A group health plan or large group health plan may pay benefits secondary to Medicare for an aged or disabled beneficiary who has current employment status if the plan coverage is COBRA continuation coverage because of reduced hours of work. Medicare is primary payer for this beneficiary because, although he has current employment status, the group health plan coverage is by virtue of the COBRA law rather than by virtue of the current employment status.

Aged Beneficiaries and Spouses

Medicare benefits are secondary to benefits payable by a group health plan for services furnished during any month in which the individual is age sixty-five or older, eligible for Medicare Part A, and meets one of the following conditions:

(1)   The individual is covered under a group health plan of an employer that has at least twenty employees (including a multiemployer plan in which at least one of the participating employers meets that condition), and coverage under the plan is by virtue of the individual's current employment status. If the employer has fewer than twenty employees, Medicare is the primary payer.

(2)   The individual is the aged spouse (including a divorced or common-law spouse) of an individual (of any age) who is covered under a group health plan by virtue of the individual's current employment status.

Disabled Beneficiaries

Medicare benefits are secondary to benefits payable by a large group health plan for services furnished during any month in which the individual:

(1)   is entitled to Medicare Part A benefits based on disability;

(2)   is covered under a large group health plan; and

(3)   has large group health plan coverage by virtue of her own or a family member's current employment status.

Medicare becomes primary if the services are:

(1)   furnished to Medicare beneficiaries who have declined to enroll in the group health plan.

(2)   not covered under the plan for the disabled individual or similarly situated individuals.

(3)   covered under the plan but not available to particular disabled individuals because they have exhausted their benefits under the plan.

(4)   furnished to individuals whose COBRA continuation coverage has been terminated because of the individual's Medicare entitlement; or

(5)   covered under COBRA continuation coverage notwithstanding the individual's Medicare entitlement.

End-Stage Renal Disease

A group health plan may not consider that an individual is eligible for or entitled to Medicare benefits based on end-stage renal disease. An individual who has end-stage renal disease but who has not filed an application for entitlement to Medicare on that basis is eligible for Medicare based on end-stage renal disease. A group health plan may not differentiate in the benefits it provides between individuals who have end-stage renal disease and others enrolled in the plan, based on the existence of end-stage renal disease, or in any other manner.

Generally, Medicare is secondary payer during the first thirty months of end-stage renal disease-based eligibility or entitlement. Medicare becomes primary after the thirtieth month of end-stage renal disease-based eligibility or entitlement.

Examples of group health plan actions that constitute differentiation in plan benefits (and that may constitute "taking into account" Medicare eligibility or entitlement) include:

• terminating coverage of the individuals with end-stage renal disease, when there is no basis for such termination unrelated to end-stage renal disease that would result in termination for individuals who do not have end-stage renal disease.

- imposing on persons who have end-stage renal disease, but not on others enrolled in the plan, benefit limitations such as less comprehensive health plan coverage, reductions in benefits, exclusions of benefits, a higher deductible or coinsurance, a longer waiting period, a lower annual or lifetime benefit limit, or more restrictive pre-existing illness limitations.

- charging individuals with end-stage renal disease higher premiums.

- paying providers and suppliers less for services furnished to individuals who have end-stage renal disease, such as paying 80 percent of the Medicare rate for renal dialysis.

- failure to cover routine maintenance dialysis or kidney transplants when a plan covers other dialysis services or other organ transplants.

Other Secondary Payer Rules

An employee may reject the employer's plan and retain Medicare as the primary payer, but regulations prevent employers from offering a health plan or option designed to induce the employee to reject the employer's plan and retain Medicare as primary payer.

For persons who are not eligible for Social Security or Railroad Retirement benefits, see Q 1040.

Medicare is also the secondary payer:

(1)   when medical care can be paid for under no-fault insurance or liability insurance (including automobile insurance).

(2)   if the individual is entitled to veterans' benefits.

(3)   if the individual is entitled to black lung benefits; or

(4)   if the individual is covered by workers' compensation.

Although Medicare is sometimes the secondary payer when liability insurance is available, Medicare may make a conditional payment if it receives a claim for services covered by liability insurance. In these cases, Medicare recovers its conditional payment from the settlement amount when the liability settlement is reached.

A third-party payer must give notice to Medicare if it learns that Medicare has made a primary payment in a situation where the third-party payer made or should have made the primary payment. A third-party payer is considered to learn that Medicare has made a primary payment when the third-party payer receives information that Medicare had made a primary payment, or when it receives information sufficient to draw the conclusion that Medicare has made a primary payment.

> *Example 1.* The third-party payer has received a copy of an Explanation of Medicare Benefits form, and the form shows that Medicare has made a primary payment for services for which the third party has made, or ought to have made, primary payment.

Example 2. A beneficiary for whom Medicare should be secondary payer states in correspondence provided to the third-party payer that Medicare has made primary payment for a given item or service for which the beneficiary has primary coverage under the third-party payer's plan.

Example 3. A beneficiary who is eligible for Medicare files a claim for primary payment with a third-party payer, the claim is denied, the beneficiary appeals, and the denial is reversed. (The third-party payer should assume that Medicare made a conditional primary payment in the interim.)

The Centers for Medicare & Medicaid Services must mail questionnaires to individuals before they become entitled to benefits under Part A (Hospital Insurance) or enroll in Part B (Medical Insurance) to determine whether they are covered under a primary plan. Payments will not be denied for covered services solely on the grounds that a beneficiary's questionnaire fails to note the existence of other health plan coverage.

Providers and suppliers are required to complete information on claim forms regarding potential coverage under other plans. Civil monetary penalties are established for an entity that knowingly, willfully, and repeatedly fails to complete a claim form with accurate information.

Contractors are required to submit annually a report to the Centers for Medicare & Medicaid Services regarding steps taken to recover mistaken payments.

1040. Can a person aged sixty-five or over qualify for Part A (Hospital Insurance) benefits without qualifying for Social Security or Railroad Retirement benefits?

Certain individuals aged sixty-five or over and otherwise ineligible for Part A (Hospital Insurance) may enroll voluntarily and pay a monthly premium if they also enroll in Part B (Medical Insurance) (See Q 1084). Any such person must also be a resident of the United States and also either a U.S. citizen or an alien lawfully admitted for permanent residence status (who has continuously resided in the United States for at least five years immediately before applying for Medicare benefits). Generally, people don't pay a monthly premium for Part A, but if actually purchasing it with less than 30 credits, it can cost up to $506 per month in 2023 ($499 in 2022). With between 30 and 39 credits, the cost is $278 in 2023, up from $274 in 2022.

1041. Is there any way that an individual not automatically eligible for Part A (Hospital Insurance) can be enrolled?

Yes, provided the individual:

(1)   has attained age sixty-five;

(2)   is enrolled in Part B (Medical Insurance) (see Q 1084 through Q 1160);

(3)   is a resident of the United States and is either:

(a) a citizen; or

(b) an alien lawfully admitted for permanent residence who has resided in the United States continuously during the five years immediately preceding the month in which he applies for enrollment; and

(4)   is not otherwise entitled to Part A (Hospital Insurance) benefits.

Certain disabled individuals under age sixty-five may also be able to obtain Part A (Hospital Insurance) coverage by paying monthly premiums. This category of eligibility applies to someone who previously qualified for Medicare coverage on the basis of disability and continues to be disabled, but whose income exceeds the level allowed under Social Security for payment of disability income benefits to disabled persons and thus loses eligibility for Medicare benefits under the normal disability provisions.

Certain government employees who otherwise do not qualify for automatic Part A (Hospital Insurance) may also be able to enroll for Part A coverage by paying a premium.

For individuals who voluntarily enroll in Part A (Hospital Insurance) by paying a premium, the premium is $506 a month in 2023, an increase of $7 from 2022 (but see paragraph below for premium reduction exception). This premium amount increases by up to 10 percent for those who must pay a premium surcharge for late enrollment. (See Q 1086.)

The Part A (Hospital Insurance) premium is reduced – by more than half (to $278 a month in 2023 and $274 for 2022) – for individuals with credits for thirty or more quarters paid into the Social Security system (and certain current, surviving, and divorced spouses of such individuals). Those with fewer than thirty credits will be charged the full monthly rate of $506 for 2023 and $499 for 2022. The reduced premium amount increases by up to 10 percent for those who must pay a premium surcharge for late enrollment (See Q 1086).

An individual who qualifies for the reduction is an individual who:

(1)   has thirty or more quarters of coverage;

(2)   has been married for at least the previous one-year period to a worker who has thirty or more quarters of coverage;

(3)   had been married to a worker who had thirty or more quarters of coverage for a period of at least one year before the death of the worker;

(4)   is divorced from, after at least ten years of marriage to, a worker who had thirty or more quarters of coverage at the time the divorce became final; or

(5)   is divorced from, after at least ten years of marriage to, a worker who subsequently died and who had thirty or more quarters of coverage at the time the divorce became final.

Administration

1042. How do the Centers for Medicare & Medicaid Services (CMS) administer Part A (Hospital Insurance)?

The Centers for Medicare & Medicaid Services (CMS) enters into agreements with state agencies and with private insurance companies (such as Blue Cross and other health insurance organizations) to administer Part A (Hospital Insurance). A Medicare Administrative Contractor (MAS) is a private health care insurer that has been awarded a geographic jurisdiction to process Medicare Part A and Part B medical claims or Durable Medical Equipment (DME) claims for Medicare Fee-For-Service (FFS) beneficiaries.

State agencies survey institutions to determine whether they meet the conditions for participation as a hospital, skilled nursing facility, home health agency, or hospice. They also help the institutions meet the conditions for participation.

Private insurance organizations contracting with CMS determine the amount of Part A (Hospital Insurance) benefits payable to hospitals, skilled nursing facilities, hospices, and home health agencies; pay Part A benefits to such providers out of funds advanced by the federal government; help the providers establish and maintain necessary financial records; serve as a channel of communication of information relating to Part A (Hospital Insurance); and audit records of hospitals, skilled nursing facilities, hospices, and home health agencies, as necessary, to insure that payment of Part A benefits is proper.

The private insurance organizations that contract with CMS to administer Part A are now called Medicare Administrative Contractors (MACs), but previously were referred to as fiscal intermediaries. Each provider of services can nominate a MAC to work with or can deal directly with the CMS. MACs are reimbursed for their reasonable costs of administration.

Most skilled nursing facilities and home health agencies must submit cost reports to MACs in a standardized electronic format. Hospitals have been required to submit cost reports in electronic format for a number of years. No payments are made to a provider unless it has furnished the information needed to determine the amount of payments due the provider. In general, providers submit this information through cost reports that cover a twelve-month period. A provider may request a delay or waiver of the electronic submission requirement by submitting a written request with supporting documentation to its MAC no later than thirty days after the end of its cost reporting period.

MACs perform many activities including:

- processing Medicare FFS claims;

- making and accounting for Medicare FFS payments;

- enrolling providers in the Medicare FFS program;

- handling provider reimbursement services and audit institutional provider cost reports;

- handling redetermination requests (1st stage appeals process);

- responding to provider inquiries;

- educating providers about Medicare FFS billing requirements;

- establishing Local Coverage Determinations (LCD's);

- reviewing medical records for selected claims;

- coordinating with CMS and other FFS contractors.

1043. What is the Prospective Payment System?

Section 1886(d) of the Social Security Act established a system of payment for the operating costs of acute care hospital inpatient stays under Medicare Part A based on prospectively set and predetermined fixed rates. Medicare pays for most inpatient hospital care under this Prospective Payment System (PPS), called more precisely the Inpatient Prospective Payment System (IPPS). Under Medicare's PPS, hospitals are paid a predetermined rate/fixed amount per discharge for inpatient services furnished to Medicare beneficiaries. The payment amount for a particular service is derived based on the classification system of that service (for example, diagnosis-related groups for inpatient hospital services). CMS uses separate PPSs for reimbursement to acute inpatient hospitals, home health agencies, hospice, hospital outpatient, inpatient psychiatric facilities, inpatient rehabilitation facilities, long-term care hospitals, and skilled nursing facilities.

Under the IPPS, each case is categorized into predetermined rates based on payment categories called Diagnosis-Related Groups (DRGs). Each DRG has a payment weight assigned to it, based on the average resources used to treat Medicare patients in that DRG. In some cases, Medicare payment will be more than the hospital's cost; in other cases, the payment will be less than the hospital's costs. In special cases, where costs for necessary care are unusually high or the length of stay is unusually long, the hospital receives additional payment.

The base payment rate is divided into a labor-related and nonlabor share. The labor-related share is adjusted by the wage index applicable to the area where the hospital is located, and if the hospital is in Alaska or Hawaii, the nonlabor share is adjusted by a cost-of-living adjustment factor. This base payment rate is multiplied by the DRG relative weight assigned to it.

If a hospital treats a high-percentage of low-income patients, it receives a percentage add-on payment applied to the DRG-adjusted base payment rate. This add-on, known as the Disproportionate Share Hospital (DSH) adjustment, provides for a percentage increase in Medicare payment for hospitals that qualify under either of two statutory formulas designed to identify hospitals that serve a disproportionate share of low-income patients. For qualifying hospitals, the amount of this adjustment may vary based on the outcome of the statutory calculation.

Also, if the hospital is an approved teaching hospital, it receives a percentage add-on payment for each case paid through IPPS. This add-on, known as the Indirect Medical Education (IME) adjustment, varies depending on the ratio of residents-to-beds under the IPPS for operating costs, and according to the ratio of residents-to-average daily census under the IPPS for capital costs.

Finally, for particular cases that are unusually costly, known as outlier cases, the IPPS payment is increased. This additional payment is designed to protect the hospital from large financial losses due to unusually expensive cases. Any outlier payment due is added to the DRG-adjusted base payment rate, plus any DSH or IME adjustments.

Reimbursement for inpatient hospital services is based on uniform sums for hundreds of DRGs (varying between rural and urban facilities). All other services are reimbursed on a reasonable cost basis.

Health Maintenance Organizations (HMOs) are covered by special reimbursement provisions to reward them financially because of what is believed to be their more favorable operating experience.

The PPS does not change the coverage available to a beneficiary under Part A (Hospital Insurance). For example, the PPS does not determine the length of a stay in the hospital or the extent of care a patient should receive but is likely a factor that providers consider when providing covered care. The law requires participating hospitals to accept Medicare payments as payment in full, and those hospitals are prohibited from billing a Medicare patient for anything other than the applicable deductible and coinsurance amounts, plus any amounts due for noncovered items or services such as television, telephone, or private duty nurses. Providers are limited by these Medicare payment rules even when the cost of a patient's care greatly exceeds the payment the hospital will receive from Medicare.

Despite the requirement to provide care for as long as it is medically necessary, the PPS provides hospitals with a possible incentive to refuse to admit patients for medical procedures that might not be reimbursed by Medicare. Hospitals also have an incentive to treat and discharge patients within or in less than the time frame established by the reimbursement rate for a particular DRG.

The CMS contracts with Quality Improvement Organizations (QIOs) in each state to conduct preadmission, continued stay, and retrospective reviews of the services delivered by a hospital. The reviews determine whether such services are reasonable and necessary. The QIO is also responsible for ensuring that the cost control incentives of the PPS do not adversely affect patients' access to hospitals or the quality of hospital care.

If the hospital, without consulting the QIO, recommends against admitting a patient, review of this decision may be obtained by the patient by writing the QIO in the patient's state. If the

QIO participated in the preadmission denial of the patient, then a reconsideration of that denial may be requested by the patient.

For a detailed explanation of the appeal process, see Q 1230 through Q 1247.

1044. What is the background and common features of a Medicare PPS?

The PPS is designed to encourage providers to deliver efficient and effective patient care while avoiding over utilization of services. The PPS concept is similar to the HMO idea where the HMO receives a capitation or flat dollar amount (i.e., monthly premiums) and is responsible for providing whatever services are needed by the patient. This creates incentive for providers to create utilization management to allow diagnosis and treatment of the patient as efficiently as possible. In contrast, conventional fee-for-service payment systems may create an incentive to add unnecessary treatment sessions for which the need can be easily justified in the medical record. Some common features of the Medicare PPS include:

- Prepayment amounts cover defined periods of time or service (per diem, per stay, sixty-day episodes, etc.)

- Amount of payment is based on a unique assessment classification of each patient.

- Medicare PPS applies only to Part A inpatients (except for HMOs and home health agencies)

- Patients who stay as inpatients can exhaust the Part A benefit and become a Part B case. These cases are no longer paid under PPS. Part B payments for evaluation and treatment visits are determined by the Medicare Physician Fee Schedule

1045. What are some examples of Prospective Payment Systems in use?

The following are summaries of Medicare Part A prospective payment systems for six provider settings:

Provider Setting	Classification System	Summary Description
Inpatient acute care hospital	Diagnosis-Related Groups (DRGs)	Primary diagnosis determines assignment to one of 535 DRGs
		The DRG payment rate is adjusted based on age, sex, secondary diagnosis and major procedures performed. DRG payment is per stay.
		Additional payment (outlier) made only if length of stay far exceeds the norm
Inpatient rehabilitation hospital or distinct unit	Case-Mix Groups (CMGs)	Patient Assessment Instrument (PAI) determines assignment of patient to one of 95 Case-Mix Groups (CMGs). CMG determines payment rate per stay

Provider Setting	Classification System	Summary Description
		Rehabilitation Impairment Categories (RICs) are based on diagnosis; CMGs are based on RIC, patient's motor and cognition scores and age. Discharge assessment incorporates comorbidities
		PAI includes comprehension, expression, and swallowing
Skilled Nursing Facility	Resource Utilization Groups, Third Version (RUG-III)	Fifty-eight groups
		Each beneficiary assigned a per diem payment based on Minimum Data Set (MDS) comprehensive assessment
		A specified minimum number of minutes per week is established for each rehabilitation RUG based on MDS score and rehabilitation team estimates
Home Health Agency	Home Health Resource Groups (HHRGs)	Eighty HHRGs
		The Outcome & Assessment Information Set (OASIS) determines the HHRG and is completed for each 60-period
		A predetermined base payment for each 60-day episode of care is adjusted according to patient's HHRG
		No limit to number of 60-day episodes
		Payment is adjusted if patient's condition significantly changes
Hospice	Each day of care is classified into one of four levels of care	Per diem rate for each of four levels of care:
		Routine home care
		Continuous home care
		Inpatient respite care
		General inpatient care
		Geographic wage adjustments determine the only variation in payment rates within each level

1046. Is Part A (Hospital Insurance) a compulsory program?

Yes, in the sense that every person who works in employment or self-employment covered by the Social Security Act, or in employment covered by the Railroad Retirement Act, must pay the Part A (Hospital Insurance) tax, the system is compulsory. An employee working in covered employment does not have the ability to choose not to pay the Hospital Insurance (HI) tax that funds Part A. Coverage under Part A (Hospital Insurance) for eligible individuals is automatic, but an individual could choose to pay his medical expenses out-of-pocket and not take advantage of the benefits available under Part A. See Q 1036 for eligibility.

Financing Part A (Hospital Insurance)

1047. How is Part A (Hospital Insurance) financed?

Medicare Part A (Hospital Insurance) is financed by a separate Hospital Insurance (HI) tax imposed upon employers, employees, and the self-employed.[1] The tax must be paid by every individual, regardless of age, who is subject to the regular Social Security tax or to the Railroad Retirement tax.

It must also be paid by all federal employees and by all state and local government employees:

(1)   hired after March 1986; or

(2)   not covered by a state retirement system in conjunction with their employment (beginning July 2, 1991).

Unlike the Social Security tax which applies to earnings up to $160,200, the Hospital Insurance (HI) tax applies to ALL earnings. The rates of the HI tax are 1.45 percent each for employees and employers, and 2.9 percent for self-employed persons. There is an additional Hospital Insurance tax of 0.9 percent on earned income exceeding $200,000 for individuals and $250,000 for married couples filing jointly. In addition, there is a Medicare tax applied to investment income. This 3.8 percent tax is imposed on Net Investment Income of single taxpayers with adjusted gross income above $200,000 and joint filers with AGI over $250,000.[2]

There is a special federal (and generally following through to state) income tax deduction of 50 percent of the OASDI/Hospital Insurance self-employment tax. This income tax deduction, which is available regardless of whether or not the taxpayer itemizes deductions, is designed to treat the self-employed in much the same manner as employees and employers are treated for Social Security and income tax purposes.

Net Investment Income – Strategy to Reduce Tax

The following are strategies to reduce the tax on net investment income:

- Sell securities in a loss position that are held in a taxable account to offset earlier gains from such accounts.

- Instead of giving cash, give appreciated securities to charity. That way, the gains will not be included on the tax return, but the client still has a charitable deduction.

- If possible, have the client become more active in business activities in which they have invested, such as those conducted through partnerships and S corporations. Try to convert them from passive status to nonpassive status, because income and gains from nonpassive business activities do not count as investment income and are therefore exempt from the 3.8 percent tax. The surest way to make an activity nonpassive is to spend over 500 hours a year in it. In some cases, however, it can take only 100 hours or even less.

- If possible, defer gains subject to the 3.8 percent tax by spreading them out with an installment sale (the sales proceeds are received over several years) or a Section 1031 like-kind exchanges. Investment real estate is the best candidate for these strategies.

- The purchase of permanent life insurance can also help manage net investment income. Withdrawals up to an owner's investment in the contract, as well as policy loans, are not included in income.

Notes

1. See 26 U.S.C. sec. 1401(b), 3101(b) and 26 U.S. C. sec. 310(b).
2. 26 U.S.C. sec. 1411.

Benefits

1048. In general, what benefits are provided under Part A (Hospital Insurance)?

Part A (Hospital Insurance) provides the following main types of benefits:

(1) **Inpatient hospital care** for up to ninety days in each "benefit period" (also known as a "spell of illness"). The patient pays a deductible of $1,600 in 2023 for the first sixty days and coinsurance of $400 a day for each additional day up to a maximum of thirty days. In addition, each person has a nonrenewable lifetime "reserve" of sixty additional hospital days with coinsurance of $800 a day.

(2) **Posthospital extended care in a skilled nursing facility** for up to 100 days in each "benefit period". The patient pays nothing for the first twenty days in 2023. After twenty days, the patient pays coinsurance of $194.50 a day in 2022 and $200.00 a day in 2023 for each additional day up to the maximum of 100 days (including the twenty days at no charge).

(3) The first 100 **posthospital home health service** visits following a hospital or skilled nursing facility stay. The services must be made under a plan of treatment established by a physician. There is no charge for home health care visits under Part A, except that there is 20 percent cost-sharing payable by the patient for durable medical equipment (other than the purchase of certain used items). The 100-visit

and post-institutional care limits apply only to Medicare beneficiaries enrolled in both Parts A and B.

(4) **Hospice care** for terminally ill patients. Hospice providers offer comprehensive services that benefit both the patient and their family members.

Qualified Medicare Beneficiaries

1049. When will a state pay Medicare costs for a person who is elderly or disabled with low income?

Federal law requires state Medicaid programs to pay Medicare costs for certain elderly and disabled persons with low incomes and very limited resources.

There are two programs to help people pay their Medicare expenses.

Qualified Medicare Beneficiary (QMB) Program

The QMB program is for persons with limited resources (assets) whose incomes are at or below the national poverty level. If an individual is a QMB, the program covers the cost of Medicare premiums, coinsurance, and deductibles that Medicare beneficiaries normally pay out of their own pockets. QMBs do not pay:

- Medicare's Part A hospital deductible;

- the Part A daily coinsurance charges for extended hospital and skilled nursing facility stays;

- the Part B (Medical Insurance) premium, which was $170.10 for new enrollees for 2022 was increased to $164.90 for 2023. Existing beneficiaries of Part B will be protected by the "hold harmless" clause (see Q 1089);

- the annual Part B deductible of $231 for 2022 and $226 for 2023; or

- the 20 percent coinsurance for services covered by Medicare Part B, depending on which doctor the patient goes to.

QMBs remain responsible for paying for medical supplies and services not covered by Medicare, such as routine physicals, dental care, hearing aids, and eyeglasses.

Specified Low-Income Medicare Beneficiary (SLMB) Program

While the QMB programs helps people whose income is at or below the national poverty level, the SLMB program is for persons whose incomes are slightly higher than the poverty level, but not more than 20 percent higher (in other words, up to 120 percent of the federal poverty level). Individuals attempting to qualify for assistance under the SLMB program must satisfy the same asset limits as under the QMB program. SLMBs do not pay the monthly Part B premium, but otherwise remain responsible for Medicare's deductibles and coinsurance, as well as for charges for health care services and medical supplies not covered by Medicare.

Qualifying Individual (QI) Program

Application must be made every year for QI benefits which are granted on a first-come, first-served basis, with priority given to people who received QI benefits the previous year. QI benefits are not granted to those that qualify for Medicaid). This program helps pay for Medicare Part B only.

Qualified Disabled and Working Individuals (QDWI) Program

This program helps pay for Medicare Part A. Any individual can qualify if meeting any of the following criteria:

- Working but disabled and under age sixty-five

- Lost premium-free Part A when returned to work

- Not getting medical assistance from the state

- Meet income and resource requirements from the state

If an individual meets QMB, SLMB, or QI requirements, they automatically qualify for Extra Help to pay for Medicare prescription drug coverage.

1050. How does a person qualify for assistance under the QMB program?

The rules vary from state to state but generally, to qualify for assistance under the QMB program, a person must meet the following requirements:

(1)   The person must be entitled to Part A (Hospital Insurance). If the person does not have Part A or does not know whether he or she is entitled to Part A, the individual should check with any Social Security Administration office or call 1-800-772-1213.

(2)   The person's financial resources, such as bank accounts, stocks, and bonds, cannot exceed specified limits ($8,4,00 for an individual; $12,600 for a married couple through 2022). Some things—the home you live in, one automobile, burial plots, home furnishings, personal jewelry, and life insurance—usually do not count as resources.

(3)   The person's income must be at or below specified monthly limits ($1,153 per month for an individual, $1,546 per month for a couple, through 2022). The income limits are higher in Alaska and Hawaii. Income includes, but is not limited to, Social Security benefits, pensions, and wages. Interest payments and dividends can also count as income.

(4)   Specified Low-Income Medicare Beneficiary (SLMB) who are limited to Part B premiums have income limits of $1,379 per month for an individual or $1,851 for a couple. Qualifying Individuals (QI) have income limits of $1,549 per month for an individual or $2,080 for a couple. Qualified Disabled and Working Individuals (QDWI) have income limits of $4,615 per month for an individual or $6,189 for a couple.

Qualified Medicare Beneficiary (QMB) Program: If a person qualifies for the QMB Program, they are assisted in paying Part A and Part B premiums, deductibles, coinsurance, and copayments. To qualify for QMB, they must be eligible for Medicare Part A, and have an income not exceeding 100 percent of the federal poverty level (FPL) + $20 (amount of the monthly SSI income disregard). This will be effective the first month following the month QMB eligibility is approved. Eligibility can't be retroactive.

Specified Low-Income Medicare Beneficiary (SLMB) Program: To qualify for the SLMB Program, a person must be eligible for Medicare Part A and have an income that is at least 100 percent, but doesn't exceed 120 percent of the FPL + $20 (amount of the monthly SSI income disregard). If qualifying for SLMB, they get help paying for your Part B premium.

Qualified Individual (QI) Program: To qualify for the QI Program, they must be eligible for Medicare Part A, and have an income not exceeding 135 percent of the FPL + $20 (amount of the monthly SSI income disregard).

Qualified Disabled and Working Individual (QDWI) Program: To qualify for QDWI, a person must be entitled to Medicare Part A because of a loss of disability-based Part A due to earnings exceeding Substantial Gainful Activity; have an income not higher than 200 percent of the FPL and resources not exceeding twice the maximum for SSI ($4,000 for an individual, $6,000 for married couple in 2022); and not be otherwise eligible for Medicaid. If qualified, they get help paying the Part A premium. If their income is between 150 percent and 200 percent of the FPL, the state can ask the individual to pay a part of your Medicare Part A premium.

1051. What if a person's income is slightly higher than the poverty level?

If a person does not qualify for QMB assistance because his income is too high, he may be able to get help under the Specified Low-Income Beneficiary (SLMB) program. To qualify for SLMB assistance, a person must meet the following requirements:

(1)   The person must be entitled to Hospital Insurance (Part A). If the person does not have Part A or does not know whether he is entitled to Part A, check with any Social Security Administration office or call 1-800-772-1213.

(2)   A person's financial resources, such as bank accounts, stocks, and bonds, cannot exceed $8,400 for one person or $12,600 for a couple through 2022. The following usually do not count as resources: the home you live in, one automobile, burial plots, home furnishings, personal jewelry, and life insurance.

(3)   A person's income cannot exceed the national poverty level by more than 20 percent (in other words, up to 120 percent of the federal poverty level). This means
the SLMB income limits through 2020 are $1,379 monthly for an individual and
$1,861 monthly for a couple.

1052. How does a person apply for QMB or SLMB assistance?

A person with Part A (Hospital Insurance) must file an application for Medicare assistance
programs at a state, county, or local Medicaid office. The following criteria will need to be met:

- Eligible for, or signed up for Medicare Part A.

- Income for 2022 at, or below, 120 percent of Federal Poverty Level.

- Limited financial resources as defined by law.

Inpatient Hospital Services

1053. Specifically, what inpatient hospital services are paid for under Part A (Hospital Insurance)?

Subject to a deductible and coinsurance, Medicare Part A (Hospital Insurance) pays for
inpatient hospital service for up to ninety days in each "benefit period" (also called a "spell of
illness"). Medicare will also pay (except for a coinsurance amount) for sixty additional hospital
days over each person's lifetime (called the "lifetime reserve" days).

Medicare pays for hospital care if the patient meets the following four conditions:

(1)   a physician prescribes inpatient hospital care for treatment of an illness or
injury;

(2)   the patient requires the kind of care that can be provided only as an inpatient in a
hospital;

(3)   the hospital is participating in Medicare (except in certain emergency situations);
and

(4)   the utilization review committee of the hospital, a Quality Improvement Organization (QIO), or the applicable Medicare Administrative Contractor (MAC) does
not disapprove of the stay.

The patient must pay a deductible of $1,556 in 2022 and $1,600 in 2023 for the first sixty
days in each benefit period. If the stay is longer than sixty days during a benefit period, coinsurance of $389 in 2022 and $400 in 2023 must be paid for each additional day up to a maximum
of thirty days.

Thus, a 90-day stay in 2022 would cost the patient $13,227 and $13,600 in 2023. After ninety days, the patient pays the full bill unless the lifetime reserve of sixty days is drawn upon. The patient must pay coinsurance of $778 in 2022 and $800 for 2023 for each of the sixty additional lifetime reserve days.

The coinsurance amounts are based on those in effect when services are furnished, rather than on those in effect at the beginning of the beneficiary's benefit period.

A "benefit period" is a way of measuring the patient's use of services under Part A (Hospital Insurance). A new ninety-day benefit period starts with each new spell of illness, beginning with the day a patient begins receiving inpatient hospital care. A benefit period ends when the patient has been out of a hospital or other facility primarily providing skilled nursing or rehabilitative services for sixty days in a row (including the day of discharge). After one benefit period has ended, another one will start whenever the patient again receives inpatient hospital care.

There is no limit to the number of ninety-day benefit periods a person can have in a lifetime (except in the case of hospitalization in a psychiatric hospital for mental illness), but the lifetime reserve of sixty days is not renewable. Also, special limited benefit periods apply to hospice care (See Q 1063).

> *Example 1.* Mr. Smith enters the hospital on February 5. He is discharged on February 15. He has used ten days of his first benefit period. Mr. Smith is not hospitalized again until August 20. Since more than sixty days have elapsed between his hospital stays, he begins a new benefit period in August. Part A (Hospital Insurance) will again pay for up to sixty days of inpatient hospital coverage, subject to Mr. Smith's payment of the deductible, and another thirty days subject to Mr. Smith's payment of coinsurance.

> *Example 2.* Mr. Jones enters the hospital on September 14. He is discharged on September 24. He also has used ten days of his first benefit period. He is then readmitted to the hospital on October 20. Because fewer than sixty days have elapsed between hospital stays, Mr. Jones remains in the same benefit period and will not be required to pay another hospital deductible when he re-enters the hospital on October 20. This means that the first day of his second admission is counted as the eleventh day of hospital care in that benefit period. Mr. Jones will not begin a new benefit period until he has been out of the hospital (and has not received any skilled care in a skilled nursing facility) for sixty consecutive days.

"Lifetime reserve" days include an extra sixty hospital days a patient can use if the patient has a lengthy illness and needs to stay in the hospital for more than ninety days. A patient has only sixty reserve days in a lifetime. For example, if a patient uses eight reserve days in that individual's first hospital stay covered under Medicare Part A, he or she will have only fifty-two reserve days left to use during subsequent hospital stays, whether or not such stays fall within new benefit periods. A patient can decide when and whether to use lifetime reserve days.

If a patient does not want to use lifetime reserve days, the patient must tell the hospital in writing, either at the time of admission or at any time up to ninety days after discharge. If a patient uses reserve days and then decides that he or she did not want to use them, the patient must request approval from the hospital to have the lifetime reserve days restored. A patient must pay the full hospital costs for any day after the first ninety days in a benefit period if the patient is not using lifetime reserve days to offset the costs after the ninety days. During 2023, Part A (Hospital Insurance) paid for all covered services except $778 in 2022 and $800 in 2023 for each reserve day the patient uses.

Medicare beneficiaries have the right to receive all the hospital care that is necessary for the proper diagnosis and treatment of their illness or injury. Under federal law, a beneficiary's discharge date must be determined solely by medical needs, not by the Diagnosis-Related Group (DRG) or Medicare payments. Beneficiaries have the right to be fully informed about decisions affecting their Medicare coverage and payment for their hospital stay and for any posthospital services. They also have the right to request a review by a Quality Improvement Organization (QIO) of any written notice of noncoverage they receive from the hospital stating that Medicare will no longer pay for their hospital care. QIOs are usually groups of physicians who are paid by the federal government to review medical necessity, appropriateness and quality of hospital treatment furnished to Medicare patients (See Q 1043).

The following inpatient services are covered by Part A (Hospital Insurance):

- **Bed and board in a semiprivate room** (two to four beds) or a ward (five or more beds). Part A (Hospital Insurance) will pay the cost of a private room only if it is required for medical reasons (e.g., the patient needs isolation for medical reasons or needs immediate hospitalization and no other accommodations are available). If the patient requests a private room, Part A will pay the cost of semiprivate accommodations; the patient must pay the extra charge for the private room. The patient or family must be told the amount of this extra charge when a private room is requested. Normally, Medicare patients are assigned to semiprivate rooms. Ward assignments are made only under extraordinary circumstances.

- **All meals,** including special diets.

- **Nursing services** provided by or under the supervision of licensed nursing personnel (other than the services of a private duty nurse or attendant).

- Services of the hospital's **medical social workers**.

- Use of regular hospital **equipment, supplies, and appliances**, such as oxygen tents, wheelchairs, crutches, casts, surgical dressings, splints, and hospital "admission packs" (toilet articles) when routinely furnished by the hospital to all patients. Certain equipment, supplies, and appliances used by the patient in the hospital continue to be covered after the patient has been discharged. Examples include a cardiac pacemaker and an artificial limb.

- **Drugs and biologicals** ordinarily furnished by the hospital. A limited supply of drugs needed for use outside the hospital is also covered, but only if medically necessary in order to facilitate the patient's departure from the hospital and the supply is necessary until the patient can obtain a continuing supply. Drugs and biologicals that the hospital obtains for the patient from a private source (community pharmacy) are covered when the hospital is responsible for making payment to the supplier.

- **Diagnostic or therapeutic items and services** ordinarily furnished by the hospital or by others (including clinical psychologists, as defined by the Centers for Medicare & Medicaid Services), under arrangements made with the hospital.

- **Operating and recovery room costs,** including hospital costs for anesthesia services.

- Services of **interns and residents in training** under an approved teaching program.

- **Blood transfusions,** after the first three pints. Part A (Hospital Insurance) helps pay for blood (whole blood or units of packed red blood cells), blood components, and the cost of blood processing and administration. If the patient receives blood as an inpatient of a hospital or skilled nursing facility, Part A will pay for these blood costs, except for any non replacement fees charged for the first three pints of whole blood or units of packed red cells per calendar year. The non replacement fee is the amount that some hospitals and skilled nursing facilities charge for blood that is not replaced. The patient is responsible for the non replacement fees for the first three pints or units of blood furnished by a hospital or skilled nursing facility. If the patient is charged no replacement fees, the patient has the option of either paying the fees or having the blood replaced. If the patient chooses to have the blood replaced, the patient can either replace the blood personally or arrange to have another person or an organization replace it. A hospital or skilled nursing facility cannot charge a patient for any of the first three pints of blood that the patient replaces or arranges to replace. If the patient has already paid for or replaced blood under Part B (Medical Insurance) of Medicare during the calendar year, the patient does not have to meet those costs again under Part A.

- **X-rays** and other radiology services, including radiation therapy, billed by the hospital.

- **Lab tests.**

- **Respiratory or inhalation therapy.**

- **Independent clinical laboratory services** under arrangement with the hospital.

- **Alcohol detoxification and rehabilitation services** when furnished as inpatient hospital services. Alcohol detoxification and rehabilitation services may also be covered under Part B (Medical Insurance) when furnished as physician services.

- **Dental services** when the patient requires hospitalization because of the severity of the dental procedure or because of the patient's underlying medical condition and clinical status.

- Cost of **special care units,** such as an intensive care unit, coronary care unit, etc.

- **Rehabilitation services,** such as physical therapy, occupational therapy, and speech pathology services.

- **Appliances** (such as pacemakers, colostomy fittings, and artificial limbs) that are permanently installed while the patient is in the hospital.

- **Lung and heart-lung transplants** (see Q 1148 for additional information on this coverage and what benefits are covered Part A and Part B.)

Part A (Hospital Insurance) does not pay for:

- Services of physicians and surgeons, including the services of pathologists, radiologists, anesthesiologists, and physiatrists. (Part A [Hospital Insurance] also does not pay for the services of a resident physician or intern other than those provided by an intern or resident in training under an approved teaching program.)

- Services of a private duty nurse or attendant, unless the patient's condition requires such services, and the nurse or attendant is a bona fide employee of the hospital.

- Personal convenience (comfort) items supplied at the patient's request, such as television rental, radio rental, or telephone.

- The first three pints of whole blood (or packed red blood cells) received in a calendar year.

- Supplies, appliances, and equipment for use outside the hospital, unless continued use is required (e.g., a pacemaker).

1054. Are inpatient hospital benefits provided for care in a psychiatric hospital?

Yes, but benefits for psychiatric hospital care are subject to a lifetime limit of 190 days. Furthermore, if the patient is already in a mental hospital when he becomes eligible for Medicare, the time spent there in the 150-day period before becoming eligible will be counted against the maximum of 150 days available in such cases (including any later period of such hospitalization when he has not been out of a mental hospital for at least sixty consecutive days between hospitalizations). This latter limitation does not apply to inpatient service in a general hospital for care other than psychiatric care.

1055. What special provisions apply to care in Religious Nonmedical Health Care Institutions (RNHCI)?

A Religious Nonmedical Health Care Institution (RNHCI) is an institution that provides nonmedical nursing items and services to Medicare beneficiaries who choose to rely solely upon a religious method of healing and who feel that acceptance of medical services would be inconsistent with their religious beliefs. In general, these institutions can participate in Medicare as hospitals, and the regular coverages and exclusions relating to inpatient hospital care will apply. Thus, the patient paid a $1,556 deductible in 2022 and $1,600 in 2023 for the first sixty days, and coinsurance of $389 a day in 2022 and $400 in 2023 for the next 30 days (plus $778 per day in 2022 and $800 in 2023 for the sixty lifetime reserve days). A RNHCI may also be paid as a skilled nursing facility, but extended care benefits will be paid for only thirty days in a calendar year (instead of the usual 100 days), and the patient must pay the coinsurance amount $194.50 in 2022 and $200.00 in 2023 for each day of service (instead of only for each day after the twentieth day).

In RNHCIs, religious beliefs prohibit conventional and unconventional medical care. If the beneficiary qualifies for hospital or skilled nursing facility care, Medicare will only cover the inpatient non-religious, non-medical items and services. Examples include room and board, or any items or services that don't require a doctor's order or prescription like un-medicated wound dressings or use of a simple walker. The cost of religious services is a personal financial responsibility. The beneficiary is responsible for applicable Part A deductible/coinsurance costs.

A federal district court ruled in 1996 that certain Christian Science facilities were not eligible for Medicare and Medicaid payments. In response to the ruling, Congress deleted any references to Christian Science sanatoriums in the Social Security Act and replaced them with the term "religious nonmedical health care institutions". RNHCI are subject to detailed eligibility criteria to protect the health and safety of patients and to special limits on the total amount of reimbursement available through Medicare.

1056. How does an institution qualify as a Religious Nonmedical Health Care Institutions (RNHCI)?

To qualify as a Medicare or Medicaid RNHCI, an institution must meet all ten of the following requirements:

1.   Qualifies as a 501(c)(3) under the Internal Revenue Code;

2.   Is lawfully operated under all applicable Federal, State, and local laws and regulations;

3.   Furnishes only nonmedical nursing items and services to beneficiaries who choose to rely solely upon a religious method of healing, and for whom the acceptance of medical services would be inconsistent with their religious beliefs. (NOTE: Religious components of the healing are not covered);

4.   Furnishes nonmedical items and services exclusively through nonmedical nursing personnel who are experienced in caring for the physical needs of nonmedical patients. For example, caring for the physical needs such as assistance with activities of daily living, assistance in moving/positioning/ambulation, nutritional needs, and comfort/support measures;

5.   Furnishes nonmedical items and services to inpatients on a twenty-four-hour basis;

6.   Does not furnish, on the basis of religious beliefs, through its personnel or otherwise, medical items and services (including any medical screening, examination, diagnosis, prognosis, treatment, or the administration of drugs) for its patients;

7.   Is not owned by, under common ownership with, or has an ownership interest of 5 percent or more in, a provider of medical treatment or services and is not affiliated with a provider of medical treatment or services or with an individual who has an ownership interest of 5 percent or more in a provider of medical treatment or services (permissible affiliations are described in §403.739(c));

8.   Has in effect a utilization review plan that meets the requirements of §403.720(a)(8);

9.   Provides information CMS may require to implement §1821 of the Act, including information relating to quality of care and coverage determinations; and

10. Meets other requirements CMS finds necessary in the interest of the health and safety of the patients who receive services in the institution.

For Part A coverage, these conditions must be met:

- The RNHCI is currently certified to participate in Medicare.

- The RNHCI Utilization Review Committee agrees that the beneficiary would require hospital or skilled nursing facility care if the beneficiary was not in the RNHCI.

- The RNHCI has a written election on file with Medicare stating the beneficiary's need for RNHCI care is based on both eligibility and religious beliefs. The election must also state that if the beneficiary decides to accept standard medical care, the election must be canceled and the beneficiary may have to wait one to five years to be eligible for a new election to get RNHCI services.

1057. Can patients choose their own hospitals?

Except for certain emergency cases, Medicare will make payments only to "qualified" hospitals, skilled nursing facilities, home health agencies, and hospices.

Medicare generally does not pay for hospital or medical services outside the United States (Puerto Rico, the U.S. Virgin Islands, Guam, American Samoa, and the Northern Mariana Islands are considered part of the United States.)

Medicare will pay for both emergency and nonemergency inpatient hospital care in a foreign hospital if the foreign hospital is closer to, or substantially more accessible than, the nearest U.S. hospital (that is adequately equipped and available to handle the patient's care) to the patient's U.S. residence. Medicare also authorizes payment for emergency care in a Canadian hospital when the emergency occurred in transit between Alaska and another U.S. state without unreasonable delay and by the most direct route. Necessary physicians' services in connection with Mexican or Canadian hospitalization that qualifies for Medicare coverage are also authorized under Medicare. If a person receives emergency treatment in a Canadian or Mexican hospital or lives near a Canadian or Mexican hospital, he should have the hospital help him contact a Medicare administrative contractor.

1058. How is it certified that hospitalization is required?

CMS requires that all inpatient hospital admissions have an initial "certification" that states, among other details, that the hospitalization is reasonable and necessary and expected to last at least two "midnights". CMS provided a transition period for compliance through 2013.

In October 2013, CMS adjusted the definition of inpatient to include "the two-midnight rule". In order to qualify for inpatient, the admitting physician should expect the beneficiary to require hospital care spanning at least two midnights, rather than the previous twenty-four-hour benchmark, regardless of the severity of illness or risk of adverse outcome. There are exceptions and exemptions to the two-midnight rule.

Under the two-midnight rule, most expected overnight hospitalizations should be outpatients, even if they are more than twenty-four hours in length, and any medically necessary outpatient hospitalization should be "converted" to inpatient if and when it is clear that a second midnight of hospitalization is medically necessary.

Under current general rules, inpatient services should be ordered under the following three situations:[1]

1. It is expected that the beneficiary will require hospital care spanning at least two midnights. The clock begins when patient starts receiving care, the two-midnight stay must be medically necessary, and the need must be appropriate;

2. A service on Medicare's inpatient-only list is being provided; or

3. It is expected that the beneficiary will require hospital care for less than two midnights, but inpatient services are nevertheless appropriate.

In December 2020, CMS amended the two-midnight rule to recognize, as it had done prior to October 2013 and January 2015, that some hospitalizations, based on physician judgment, would be appropriate for inpatient without an expectation of a hospitalization that spans at least two midnights. This includes situations where the expectation of the physician is based on such complex medical factors as patient history and comorbidities, the severity of signs and symptoms, current medical needs, and the risk of an adverse event. The factors that lead to a particular clinical expectation must be documented in the medical record in order to be granted consideration.

It should also be noted that if an unforeseen circumstance, such as a beneficiary's death or transfer, results in a shorter beneficiary stay than the physician's expectation of at least two midnights, the patient may be considered to be appropriately treated on an inpatient basis, and payment for an inpatient hospital stay may be made under Medicare Part A.

Note

1. 42 CFR sec. 412.3 Admissions, https://www.ecfr.gov/current/title-42/chapter-IV/subchapter-B/part-412/subpart-A/section-412.3 (Current through November 16, 2021).

1059. What must a hospital do to qualify for Medicare payments?

Generally, a hospital must meet certain standards and enter into a Medicare participation agreement in order to be paid by Medicare. However, Medicare may pay nonparticipating hospitals in certain emergency cases.

Hospice Care

1060. What is hospice care?

Hospice care is an approach to treatment that recognizes that the impending death of an individual warrants a change in focus from curative care to palliative care (relief of pain and other uncomfortable symptoms). The goal of hospice care is to help terminally ill individuals continue life with minimal disruption to normal activities. A hospice uses an interdisciplinary approach to deliver medical, social, psychological, emotional, and spiritual services through the use of a broad spectrum of professional and other caregivers, with the goal of making the individual as physically and emotionally comfortable as possible. Counseling and respite services are available to the family of the hospice patient. Hospice programs consider both the patient and the family as a unit of care.

Medicare Part A (Hospital Insurance) provides coverage for hospice care for terminally ill Medicare beneficiaries who elect to receive care from a participating hospice.

A hospice is an organization that is primarily engaged in providing pain relief, symptom management, and supportive services to terminally ill people.

1061. How is hospice care covered under Part A (Hospital Insurance)?

Under the Part A (Hospital Insurance) hospice benefit, Medicare pays for hospice services every day and also permits a hospice to provide appropriate custodial care, including homemaker services and counseling. Hospice care under Medicare includes both home care and inpatient care, when needed, and a variety of services not otherwise covered under Medicare (such as custodial care).

Medicare payments to a hospice are based on one of four prospectively determined rates for each day in which a qualified Medicare beneficiary is under the care of the hospice. The four rate categories are **routine home care, continuous home care, inpatient respite care,** and **general inpatient care**. Payment rates are adjusted to reflect local differences in area wage levels.

Hospice care is covered under Part A (Hospital Insurance) when the beneficiary:

    (1)   is eligible for Part A benefits;

(2)   is certified by a physician as terminally ill (i.e., have a life expectancy of six months or less); and

(3)   files a statement electing to waive all other Medicare coverage for hospice care from hospice programs other than the one chosen and elects not to receive other services related to treatment of the terminal condition (the beneficiary can later revoke the election).

The following are covered hospice services:

- Doctor/physician care

- Nursing care provided by or under the supervision of a registered professional nurse.

- Medical supplies

- Hospice aide and homemaker services

- Medical social services provided by a social worker under a physician's direction.

- Counseling (including dietary counseling) with respect to care of the terminally ill patient and adjustment to the patient's approaching death.

- Short-term inpatient care (including both respite care and procedures necessary for pain control and acute and chronic symptom management) provided in a participating hospice, hospital, or skilled nursing facility. The respite care may be provided only on an intermittent, nonroutine, and occasional basis and may not be provided consecutively over longer than five days.

- Durable medical equipment, appliances, and supplies.

- Services of a home health aide and homemaker services.

- Prescription drugs, including outpatient drugs for pain relief and symptom management.

- Physical therapy, occupational therapy, and speech-language pathology services to control symptoms or to enable the patient to maintain activities of daily living and basic functional skills.

- Dietary and nutritional counseling.

- Grief and loss counseling for both patient and family.

- Short-term respite care.

- Any other Medicare-covered services recommended by the hospice team.

Services of a home health aide, homemaker services, and nursing care provided by or under the supervision of a registered professional nurse, may be provided on a twenty-four-hour, continuous basis only during periods of crisis and only as necessary to maintain the terminally ill patient at home.

The definition of hospice care also includes any other item or service which is specified in the patient's plan of care and for which Medicare may pay.

A "hospice program" for Medicare purposes is a public agency or private organization that is primarily engaged in providing the care and services listed above and makes the services available (as needed) on a twenty-four-hour basis. A hospice program also provides bereavement counseling for the immediate family of the terminally ill patient. The care and services must be provided in the patient's home, on an outpatient basis, and on a short-term inpatient basis. The nursing, physician, counseling, and medical social service benefits must be provided directly on a routine basis. The remaining hospice benefits may be provided through arrangements with other hospice programs (provided the agency or organization maintains professional management responsibility for all services).

The Centers for Medicare & Medicaid Services (CMS) may waive certain service requirements for hospices not located in urbanized areas that can demonstrate that they have been unable, despite diligent efforts, to recruit appropriate personnel. For these hospices, CMS may waive the provision requiring physical or occupational therapy or speech-language pathology services and dietary counseling.

A hospice program must have an interdisciplinary group of personnel (at least one physician, one registered nurse, one social worker, and one pastoral or other counselor) to establish the policies of the program and provide the required care and services. The group must maintain central clinical records on all patients, utilize volunteers, and is required to continue hospice care for any patient who is unable to pay for such care.

1062. What is not covered under Part A (Hospital Insurance) in regard to hospice?

Medicare won't cover any of these procedures once the hospice benefit starts:

- Treatment intended to cure a terminal illness and/or related conditions. A hospice patient always has the right to stop hospice coverage to pursue a cure.

- Prescription drugs to address the illness rather than for symptom control or pain relief.

- Care from any hospice provider that wasn't set up by the hospice medical team. All care for the terminal illness must be given by or arranged by the hospice team. A patient can still see their regular doctor or nurse practitioner if they have chosen him or her to be the attending medical professional who helps supervise the hospice care.

- Room and board. Medicare doesn't cover room and board if you get hospice care in your home or if living in a nursing home or a hospice inpatient facility. If the hospice team determines that short-term inpatient or respite care services is needed, Medicare will cover the stay in the facility although there may be a small copayment for the respite stay.

- Hospital outpatient care (such as emergency room visits), hospital inpatient care, or ambulance transportation, unless arranged by the hospice team or unrelated to the terminal illness and related conditions.

1063. What is the hospice benefit period?

The benefit period consists of:

- two 90-day periods, followed by

- an unlimited number of 60-day periods.

At the beginning of the first ninety-day hospice benefit period, both the beneficiary's attending physician (if any) and the medical director or physician member of the hospice interdisciplinary team must certify in writing that the beneficiary is terminally ill. Terminally ill is defined as having a life expectancy of six months or less. The medical director or physician member of the hospice interdisciplinary team must recertify that the beneficiary is terminally ill at the beginning of all successive benefit periods. An individual can change their hospice provider once during each benefit period. If health improves, or the illness goes into remission, hospice care can end.

1064. What does the patient pay for hospice care?

There are no deductibles under the hospice benefit. The beneficiary does not pay for Medicare-covered services for the terminal illness, except for small coinsurance amounts for outpatient drugs and inpatient respite care. For outpatient prescription drugs, the patient is responsible for about 5 percent of the cost of drugs or five dollars, whichever is less. For inpatient respite care, the patient pays 5 percent of the amount paid by Medicare for a respite care day, but the total of all coinsurance for respite care may not exceed the Medicare Part A inpatient hospital deductible for the year in which the hospice period began.

1065. How is respite care covered?

Respite care as an inpatient in a hospice (to give a period of relief to the family providing home care for the patient) is limited to no more than five days in a row. Respite care requires coinsurance in the amount of 5 percent of the amount that Medicare pays for the respite care.

The total respite care coinsurance amount may not exceed the inpatient hospital deductible for the year in which the hospice period began.

1066. Can hospice care be stopped?

If the patient's health improves or the illness goes into remission, hospice care may no longer be necessary. The patient can always stop hospice care at any time. If they choose to stop hospice care, they'll be asked to sign a form that includes the date the care will end.

A patient shouldn't be asked to sign any forms about stopping hospice care at the time of starting hospice. Stopping hospice care is a choice only the patient can make, and they shouldn't sign or date any forms until the actual date that they want hospice care to stop.

If the patient was in a Medicare Advantage Plan when starting hospice, they can stay in that plan by continuing to pay the plan's premiums. If they stop hospice care, they are still a member of the plan and can get Medicare coverage from the plan after stopping hospice care. If the patient wasn't in a Medicare Advantage Plan when starting hospice care, and they decide to stop hospice care, they can continue in Original Medicare.

If eligible, one can go back to hospice care at any time.

Skilled Nursing Facility (SNF) Care

1067. What is a qualified skilled nursing facility?

For purposes of Medicare Part A (Hospital Insurance), a skilled nursing facility is a specially qualified facility that specializes in skilled care. It has the staff and equipment to provide skilled nursing care or skilled rehabilitative services and other related health services.

A skilled nursing facility may be a skilled nursing home, a distinct part of an institution such as a ward or wing of a hospital, or a section of a facility another part of which is an old-age home. Not all nursing homes will qualify; those which offer only custodial care are excluded. The facility must be primarily engaged in providing skilled nursing care or rehabilitation services for injured, disabled, or sick persons. Skilled nursing care means care that can be performed only by, or under the supervision of, licensed nursing personnel. Skilled rehabilitation services may include such services as physical therapy performed by, or under the supervision of, a professional therapist. Skilled nursing care and skilled rehabilitation services must be needed and received on a daily basis (at least five days a week) or the patient is not eligible for Medicare coverage.

At least one registered nurse must be employed full-time, and adequate nursing service (which may include services by practical nurses) must be provided at all times. Every patient must be under the supervision of a physician, and a physician must always be available for emergency care. Generally, the facility must be certified by the state and meet all state licensing requirements. The facility also must have a written agreement with a hospital that is participating in the Medicare program for the transfer of patients.

Medicare also requires that qualified skilled nursing facilities provide patients with the following rights:

(1)   equal access and admission;

(2)   notice of rights and services;

(3)   transfer and discharge rights;

(4)   the right to pretransfer and predischarge notice;

(5)   access and visitation rights;

(6)   rights relating to the protection of resident funds; and

(7)   certain other specified rights.

An institution which is primarily for the care and treatment of mental diseases or tuberculosis is not a skilled nursing facility.

Many nursing homes in the United States do not qualify as "skilled nursing facilities" for purposes of Medicare and are not certified to provide services reimbursed by Medicare. In some facilities, only certain portions participate in Medicare.

1068. Does Part A (Hospital Insurance) pay for custodial care in a skilled nursing facility?

No. Medicare does not pay for custodial care when that is the **only** kind of care needed.

CUSTODIAL CARE: Care is considered custodial when it is primarily for the purpose of helping the patient with Activities of Daily Living (ADL) or meeting personal needs and could be provided safely and reasonably by people without professional skills or training.

For example, custodial care includes help in walking, getting in and out of bed, personal hygiene and grooming/bathing, dressing, toileting, eating, and taking medicine.

1069. Do most nursing home residents qualify for Part A (Hospital Insurance) coverage?

No. Most residents of nursing homes will not qualify for Medicare coverage, because Medicare coverage is restricted to patients in need of skilled nursing and rehabilitative services on a daily basis. Many nursing home residents are in need primarily of custodial care, which is not covered by Medicare.

The initial determination of Medicare coverage is made by the nursing home, but the nursing home cannot charge the patient for care provided before it notifies the patient in writing that it believes Medicare will not pay for the care. The patient may not challenge the nursing home's noncoverage determination until a claim has been submitted to and denied by the Medicare intermediary. The patient does have the right to require a nursing home to submit its claim to the Medicare intermediary so that the intermediary can determine if the nursing home was correct in denying coverage.

1070. Under what circumstances does a patient qualify for skilled nursing facility benefits under Part A (Hospital Insurance)?

In order to qualify for skilled nursing facility (SNF) benefits under Part A (Hospital Insurance), the patient generally must meet all of these five conditions:

(1)   DAILY SKILLED CARE REQUIRED: A doctor has decided that a patient's condition requires daily skilled nursing or skilled rehabilitative services which, as a practical matter, can only be provided in a skilled nursing facility.

(2)   QUALIFYING IN-PATIENT HOSPITAL STAY: The patient has been in a hospital at least three days in a row (not counting the day of discharge) before being admitted to a participating skilled nursing facility.

(3)   TIMELY ADMISSION TO THE SNF: The patient is admitted to the skilled nursing facility within a short time (generally within thirty days) after leaving the hospital.

(4)   QUALIFIED MEDICAL CONDITION: The patient's care in the skilled nursing facility is for a condition that was treated in the hospital, or for a condition that arose while receiving care in the skilled nursing facility for a condition which was treated in the hospital.

(5)   CERTIFICATION OF MEDICAL NEED: A medical professional certifies that the patient needs, and receives, skilled nursing or skilled rehabilitation services (posthospital extended care) on a daily basis.

If a patient leaves a skilled nursing facility and is readmitted within thirty days, the patient does not need to have a new three-day stay in a hospital for care to be covered.

Except for a coinsurance amount payable by the patient after the first twenty days, Part A (Hospital Insurance) will pay the reasonable cost of post-hospital care in a skilled nursing facility for up to 100 days in a benefit period.

Note that during COVID-19, some individuals can get renewed SNF coverage without having to start a new benefit period. Additionally, individuals who cannot stay in their own homes during COVID-19 can get SNF care without a qualifying hospital stay.

1071. What items and services generally are (and are not) covered under Part A (Hospital Insurance) when provided in a participating skilled nursing facility?

The following items and services are covered when provided in a participating skilled nursing facility:

- Bed and board in a semiprivate room (two to four beds in a room) unless the patient's condition requires isolation or no semiprivate rooms are available.

- Nursing care provided by, or under the supervision of, a registered nurse (but not private-duty nursing).

- Drugs, biologicals, supplies (such as splints and casts), appliances (such as wheelchairs), and equipment for use in the facility.

- Medical social services, including the assessment of the patient's medical and nursing requirements, the patient's financial resources, home situation, and the community services available to him. Such services may also include the assessment of the social and emotional factors related to the patient's illness, and the patient's need for care, response to treatment, and adjustment to care in the skilled nursing facility. Appropriate action to obtain case work services to assist in resolving problems in these areas is covered by Medicare.

- Medical services of interns and residents in training under an approved teaching program of a hospital.

- Other diagnostic or therapeutic services provided by a hospital with which the facility has a transfer agreement.

- Ambulance transportation (when other transportation endangers health) to the nearest supplier of needed services that aren't available at the SNF

- Rehabilitation services, such as physical, occupational, and speech therapy, furnished by the skilled nursing facility, or by others under arrangements made by the skilled nursing facility.

- All meals, including special diets furnished by the facility.

- Blood transfusions, other than the first three pints of blood.

- Dietary counseling.

- Such other health services as are generally provided by a skilled nursing facility.

The following services are not covered even if provided by the skilled nursing facility:

- Personal convenience (comfort) items that the patient requests, such as a television, radio, or telephone

- Private duty nurses or attendants

- Any extra charges for a private room, unless it is determined to be medically necessary

- Custodial care, including assistance with the Activities of Daily Living (i.e., walking, getting in and out of bed, bathing, dressing, and feeding), special diets, and supervision of medication that can usually be self-administered, when that is the only care required by the patient

- Physician's services provided to a patient while the patient is in a skilled nursing facility are covered by Part B (Medical Insurance), not Part A (Hospital Insurance)

1072. What provisions are made under Part A (Hospital Insurance) for care in a skilled nursing facility?

Federal regulations include the following services for skilled rehabilitation and nursing care:

(1)   Insertion and sterile irrigation and replacement of catheters;

(2)   Application of dressing involving prescription medications and aseptic techniques;

(3)   Treatment of extensive bed sores or other widespread skin disorders;

(4)   Therapeutic exercises or activities supervised or performed by a qualified occupational or physical therapist;

(5)   Training to restore a patient's ability to walk; and

(6)   Range of motion exercises that are part of a physical therapist's active treatment to restore a patient's mobility.

A number of services involving the development, management, and evaluation of a patient care plan may qualify as skilled services. These services are "skilled" if the patient's condition requires the services to be provided or supervised by a professional to meet the patient's needs, promote recovery, and ensure the patient's medical safety. For example, a patient with a history of diabetes and heart problems, who is recovering from a broken arm, may require skin care, medication, a special diet, an exercise program to preserve muscle tone, and observation to detect signs of deterioration or complications. Although none of these required services necessarily falls within the definition of "skilled" on its own, the combination, provided by a professional, may be considered "skilled".

To qualify for skilled nursing facility reimbursement, skilled physical therapy must be:

(1)   specifically related to a physician's active treatment plan;

(2)   of a complexity, or involving a condition, that requires a physical therapist;

(3)   necessary to establish a safe maintenance program or provided where the patient's condition will improve within a predictable time; and

(4)   of the necessary frequency and duration.

1073. How much does the patient pay for skilled nursing facility care?

The patient pays nothing for the first twenty days of covered services in each spell of illness. After twenty days, coinsurance is payable for each additional day, up to a maximum of eighty days for days twenty-one through one hundred. For a patient in a skilled nursing facility, the coinsurance is $194.50 in 2022 and $200.00 in 2023.

Thus, a one-hundred-day stay in a skilled nursing facility during 2023 will cost the patient $16,000 (up $440 from the 2022 cost of $15,560).

There is no lifetime limit on the amount of skilled nursing facility care provided under Part A (Hospital Insurance). Except for the coinsurance (which must be paid after the first twenty days in each spell of illness), Medicare will cover the cost of one hundred days' post-hospital care in each benefit period, regardless of how many benefit periods the person may have. After one hundred days of coverage, the patient must pay the full cost of skilled nursing facility care.

Skilled nursing facilities cannot require a patient to pay a deposit or other payment as a condition of admission to the facility unless it is clear that services are not covered under Medicare.

1074. How is care in a Skilled Nursing Facility covered after 100 days?

Medicare covers up to one hundred days of care in a skilled nursing facility (SNF) each benefit period. If a patient needs more than one hundred days of SNF care in a benefit period, they will need to pay out of pocket. If care is ending because the patient is running out of days, the facility is not required to provide written notice, although most will usually notify either the patient or family that they are approaching "private responsibility" for care. It is still important that the patient or a caregiver keep track of how many days have been spent in the SNF to avoid unexpected costs after Medicare coverage ends.

Remember that eligibility can begin again for Medicare coverage of SNF care, once the patient has been out of a hospital or SNF for sixty days in a row. They will then be eligible for a new benefit period, including one hundred new days of SNF care, after a three-day qualifying inpatient stay.

If the patient is receiving medically necessary physical, occupational, or speech therapy, Medicare may continue to cover those skilled therapy services even when they have used up their SNF days in a benefit period – but Medicare will not pay for room and board. A patient may qualify for therapy at home through Medicare's Home Health Care benefit, or receive therapy as an outpatient while living at home.

If the patient has long-term care insurance, it may cover a SNF stay after Medicare coverage ends. If the individual's income and assets are low, they could be eligible for Medicaid to cover their care.

1075. When can payment be made for skilled nursing care under Part A (Hospital Insurance)?

Subject to the patient's coinsurance obligation after the first twenty days, Medicare Part A (Hospital Insurance) will be made for skilled nursing care only if the following conditions are met:

(1)   The beneficiary files a written request for payment (another person may sign the request if it is impracticable for the patient to sign).

(2)   A physician certifies that the patient needs skilled nursing care on an inpatient basis. Recertification is required for extended stays. Part A (Hospital Insurance) will not pay for a person's stay if the individual needs skilled nursing or rehabilitation services only occasionally, such as once or twice a week, or if a person does not need to be in a skilled nursing facility to obtain skilled rehabilitation services. Part A (Hospital Insurance) also generally will not pay for a person's continued stay in a skilled nursing facility if the rehabilitation services are no longer improving his or her condition and could be carried out by someone other than a physical therapist or physical therapist assistant.

(3)   The facility is "participating" under Medicare law.

See Q 1070 for more information on skilled nursing care.

Home Health Care

1076. When are post-institutional home health services covered under Part A (Hospital Insurance)?

If a person needs post-institutional skilled health care in his or her home for the treatment of an illness or injury, Medicare pays for covered home health services furnished by a participating home health agency. In general, Part A (Hospital Insurance) covers the cost of 100 (one hundred) home health visits made on an "intermittent" basis during a home health spell of illness under a plan of treatment established by a physician. However, patients may be eligible for additional home health benefits under Part B (see Q 1117).

A "home health agency" is a public agency or private organization that:

(1)   is primarily engaged in providing skilled nursing services and other therapeutic services;

(2)   has policies, established by a group of professional personnel, including one or more physicians and one or more registered professional nurses, to govern the services which it provides, and provides for supervision of its services by a physician or registered professional nurse;

(3)   maintains clinical records on all patients;

(4)   is licensed pursuant to applicable state and local law;

(5)   has in effect an overall plan and budget;

(6)   meets additional requirements and conditions of participation as the Centers for Medicare & Medicaid Services (CMS) finds necessary in the interest of the health and safety of individuals who are furnished services by the home health agency;

(7)   meets additional requirements as specified by CMS for the effective and efficient operation of the program.

A "home health agency" does not include any agency or organization that is primarily for the care and treatment of mental diseases.

A number of rules and procedures have been established to stop fraud and abuse, including regulations requiring all home health agencies serving Medicare to obtain surety bonds. Agencies must be bonded and must provide quality care to at least ten patients before applying to provide care to Medicare patients. At least seven of the ten patients must be receiving active care at the time the agency applies to participate in Medicare.

1077. What conditions must be met for Part A (Hospital Insurance) to cover home health visits?

In general, Part A (Hospital Insurance) pays for the first 100 home health visits in a "home health spell of illness" only if all six of the following conditions are met:

(1)   The care is post-institutional home health services

(2)   The care includes intermittent skilled nursing care, physical therapy, or speech therapy

(3)   The person is confined at home and a doctor must certify that the patient is homebound

(4)   The person is under the care of a physician who determines the need for home health care and sets up a home health plan for the person

(5)   The home health agency providing services participates in Medicare

(6)   The services are provided on a visiting basis in the person's home or, if it is neces-
        sary to use equipment that cannot be readily made available in the home, on an
        outpatient basis in a hospital, skilled nursing facility, or licensed rehabilitation center

The term "post-institutional home health services" means home health services furnished
to an individual:

(1)   After discharge from a hospital or rural primary care hospital in which the
        individual was an inpatient for at least three consecutive days before discharge.
        Home health services must be initiated within fourteen days after the date of
        discharge.

(2)   After discharge from a skilled nursing facility in which the individual was provided
        posthospital extended care services covered by Medicare. Home health services
        must be initiated within fourteen days after the date of discharge.

The term "home health spell of illness" means a period of consecutive days

(1)   beginning with the first day a person is furnished post-institutional home health
        services (in a month in which the person is entitled to benefits under Part A) and

(2)   ending with the close of the first period of sixty consecutive days thereafter for
        which the person is neither an inpatient in a hospital or skilled nursing facility nor
        provided home health services.

"Part-time or intermittent services" is defined as skilled nursing and home health services
(combined) furnished any number of days per week, for less than eight hours per day and twenty-
eight or fewer hours per week (or, subject to review on a case-by-case basis as to the need for
care, less than eight hours each day and thirty-five or fewer hours per week). Home benefit
doesn't apply if more than part-time or intermittent skilled nursing is required, although home
health care is allowed if the patient is getting adult day care.

"Intermittent" is defined as skilled nursing care provided on fewer than seven days
each week, or less than eight hours each day (combined) for twenty-one days or less (with
extensions in exceptional circumstances when the need for additional care is finite and
predictable).

A physician must certify that the patient is under a physician's care, under a plan of care
established and periodically reviewed no less frequently than every two months by a doctor,
confined to the home, and in need of skilled nursing care on an intermittent basis or physical
or speech therapy, or has a continued need for occupational therapy when eligibility for home
health services has been established (because of a prior need for intermittent skilled nursing
care, speech therapy, or physical therapy in the current or prior certification period).

Home health aides, whether employed directly by a home health agency or made available through contract with another entity, must successfully complete a training and competency evaluation program or competency evaluation program approved by CMS.

Generally, a physician may not set up a home health care plan for a patient with any agency in which the physician has a significant ownership interest or a significant financial or contractual relationship. However, a physician who has a financial interest in an agency which is a sole community health agency may carry out certification and plan of care functions for patients served by that agency.

1078. What post-institutional home health services are covered under Part A (Hospital Insurance)?

In general, the following post-institutional home health services are covered under Part A (Hospital Insurance):

- Part-time or intermittent skilled nursing care (See Q 1077)

- Physical therapy

  o   Physical therapy includes gait training and supervision of and training for exercises to regain movement and strength in a body area

- Speech therapy

  o   Speech-language pathology services include exercises to regain and strengthen speech and language skills

- Medical social services

- Continuing occupational therapy services

If a person needs part-time or intermittent skilled nursing care, physical therapy, or speech therapy, Medicare also pays for:

- Part-time or intermittent services of home health aides (coupled with other skilled services). Covered services include, but are not limited to –

  o   personal care;

  o   simple dressing changes that do not require the skills of a licensed nurse;

  o   assistance with medications that are ordinarily self-administered and that do not require a licensed nurse;

  o   assistance with activities supportive of skilled therapy services; and

  o   routine care of prosthetic devices.

- Medical social services.

- Medical supplies for use at home, including catheters, catheter supplies, ostomy bags, and ostomy care supplies.

- Injectable osteoporosis drugs for women.

- Durable medical equipment, including iron lungs, oxygen tents, hospital beds, and wheelchairs (subject to a 20 percent coinsurance as described below).

- Occupational therapy.

  - Occupational therapy helps regain the ability to do usual daily activities, such as eating and putting on clothes.

The patient generally pays nothing under Part A (Hospital Insurance) for the first 100 home health visits; Medicare pays the full approved cost of all covered home health visits. The patient may be charged, however, for any services or costs that Medicare does not cover. Also, if a patient needs durable medical equipment, the patient is responsible for a 20 percent coinsurance payment for the equipment. The home health agency will submit claims for payment. The patient does not submit bills to Medicare.

Both Part A (Hospital Insurance) and Part B (Medical Insurance) cover home health visits, but for beneficiaries covered by both Parts A and B, Part A pays for the first 100 visits following a hospital or skilled nursing facility stay while Part B pays for home health services without regard to a preceding hospital or skilled nursing facility stay.

Medicare does not cover home care services furnished primarily to assist people in meeting personal, family, and domestic needs. These noncovered services include general household services such as laundry, meal preparation, shopping, or assisting in bathing, dressing, or other personal needs.

Home health services generally not covered by Medicare also include:

- twenty-four-hour-a-day nursing care at home;

- drugs and biologicals;

- Custodial or personal care that is help with Activities of Daily Living (ADL) – such as bathing, dressing, transferring, toileting) – when this is the ONLY care needed

- blood transfusions;

- meals delivered to the home;

- homemaker services (such as shopping, cleaning, laundry, etc.); and

- venipuncture (drawing of blood for the purpose of obtaining a blood sample), if venipuncture is the only skilled service needed by the beneficiary.

Although a patient in general must be "confined" to home to be eligible for home health care benefits, payment will be made for services furnished at a hospital, skilled nursing facility, or rehabilitation center, if the patient's condition requires the use of equipment that ordinarily cannot be taken to the patient's home. Medicare usually will not pay the patient's transportation costs.

A patient is considered "confined to the home" if he or she has a condition, due to illness or injury, that restricts the ability to leave home except with the assistance of another person or the aid of a supportive device (such as crutches, a cane, a wheelchair, or a walker), or if the patient has a condition such that leaving home is medically unsafe. Although a patient does not have to be bedridden to be considered "confined to the home," the condition should be such that there exists a normal inability to leave home, that leaving home requires a considerable and taxing effort, and that absences from home are infrequent or of relatively short duration, or are attributable to the need to receive medical treatment.

For these purposes, "infrequent" means an average of five or fewer absences per calendar month, excluding absences to receive medical treatment that cannot be furnished in the home. "Short duration" means an average of three or fewer hours per absence from the home within a calendar month, excluding absences to receive medical treatment that cannot be furnished in the home.

Absences for medical treatment must be:

(1)   based on and in conformance with a physician's order;

(2)   by or under the supervision of a licensed health professional; and

(3)   for the purpose of diagnosis or treatment of an illness or injury.

Examples of patients qualifying as homebound include:

(1)   a person paralyzed from a stroke who is confined to a wheelchair and who requires crutches in order to walk;

(2)   a person who is blind or senile and requires the assistance of another person in leaving his or her residence;

(3)   a person who has lost the use of upper extremities and is unable to open doors, use stairways, etc., and, therefore, requires the assistance of another person to leave his or her residence; and

(4)   a person with a psychiatric problem if the person's illness is manifested in part by a refusal to leave his or her home environment or is of such a nature that it would not be considered safe for the patient to leave home unattended, even if the patient has no physical limitations.

1079. How does Medicare pay the costs of home health services?

The Centers for Medicare & Medicaid Services (CMS) have established a prospective payment system for all costs of home health services. In defining a payment amount under a prospective payment system, CMS considers an appropriate unit of service and the number, type, and duration of visits provided within that unit of service. CMS also considers potential changes in the mix of services provided within a unit and their cost. The general design of a unit of service is to provide for continued access to quality services. All bills for service must be submitted by the home health agency for payment and not by any other person or entity.

Prospective payment amounts are intended to be standardized in a manner that eliminates the effect of variations in relative case mix and wage levels among different home health agencies in a budget-neutral manner. Under the system, CMS may recognize regional differences or differences based upon whether the services or agencies are in an urbanized area. The standard prospective payment amount (or amounts) is adjusted for each fiscal year.

General Information

1080. Does Part A (Hospital Insurance) pay the cost of outpatient hospital services?

No. Outpatient diagnostic and treatment services are covered under Part B (Medical Insurance), not Part A (Hospital Insurance). (See Q 1084 through Q 1163.)

1081. Does a person need to be in financial need to receive Part A (Hospital Insurance) benefits?

No. Medicare benefits are not subject to any means testing and there is no specific dollar limit on coverage.

1082. Will the deductible and coinsurance amounts paid by patients for Part A (Hospital Insurance) remain the same in future years?

No. The $1,556 initial deductible in 2022 and $1,600 in 2023 for Part A inpatient hospital care is based on the 1966-68 figure of forty dollars and on increases in average per diem inpatient hospital cost since 1966 (with some legislative adjustments).

Further adjustments have been made since 1987 based on increases in average national hospital costs. The daily coinsurance amounts for inpatient hospital care are based on a percentage of the deductible. Thus, the daily coinsurance for inpatient hospital care for the sixty-first through ninetieth days in a benefit period is one-fourth of the initial deductible $398 in 2022 and $400 in 2023). The coinsurance for each lifetime reserve day (a total of sixty in a lifetime), used after the ninetieth inpatient hospital stay day is half of the inpatient care deductible $778 in 2022 and $800 in 2023). The daily coinsurance for posthospital extended care in a skilled nursing facility after the first twenty days of such care (up to the maximum of 100 days, including the first twenty) is one-eighth of the inpatient hospital stay deductible (thus, $194.50 in 2022 and $200.00 in 2023).

HISTORY OF MEDICARE PART A DEDUCTIBLE

1998: $ 764	2011: $1,132
1999: $ 768	2012: $1,156
2000: $ 776	2013: $1,184
2001: $ 792	2014: $1.214
2002: $ 812	2015: $1,260
2003: $ 840	2016: $1,288
2004: $ 876	2017: $1,316
2005: $ 912	2018: $1,340
2006: $ 952	2019: $1,364
2007: $ 992	2020: $1,408
2008: $1,024	2021: $1,484
2009: $1,068	2022: $1,556
2010: $1.100	2023: $1,600

1083. What is Medicare's position regarding treatment of a patient with a living will or durable power of attorney for health care?

Medicare requires that all hospitals, skilled nursing facilities, nursing facilities, providers of home health care or personal care services, hospices, and prepaid health plans to provide a Medicare patient with written information concerning rights under state law to make decisions concerning medical care, including the right to accept or refuse medical or surgical treatment and the right to formulate—at the patient's option—advance directives. The regulations do not apply to providers of outpatient hospital services.

The term "advance directive" is defined as a written instrument, such as a living will or durable power of attorney for health care, recognized under state law, relating to the provision of health care when the individual is incapacitated. No individual is required to execute an advance directive. A health care proxy (durable power of attorney) is a document that names a trusted individual to make health decisions. A living will is a document which identifies which treatment the patient wants if life is threatened, including decisions such as dialysis and ventilators, DNR (Do Not Resuscitate) orders, feeding tubes, and organ donation.

The provider must:

(1)   inform the individual, in writing, of state laws regarding advance directives;

(2)   inform the individual, in writing, of the policies of the provider regarding the implementation of advance directives, including (if permitted under state law) a

clear and precise explanation of any objection a provider may have, on the basis of conscience, to honoring an individual's directive;

(3)   document in the individual's medical record whether or not the individual has executed an advance directive;

(4)   educate staff on issues concerning advance directives; and

(5)   provide for community education on issues concerning advance directives.

Written information on advance directives must be provided to an individual upon each admission to a medical facility and each time an individual comes under the care of a home health agency, personal care provider, or hospice. For example: if a person is admitted as an inpatient to a hospital and then to a nursing home, both the hospital and the nursing home are required to provide information on advance directives to the individual. If the patient is incapacitated at the time of admission and is unable to receive information or articulate whether or not an advance directive has been executed, the facility may give advance directive information to the patient's family or surrogate.

All patients are generally entitled to the medically necessary care ordered by a physician and that a provider, under normal procedures, would be required to furnish; providers cannot delay or withhold such care because the individual has not executed an advance directive or the provider is waiting for an advance directive to be executed. However, once a provider receives documentation that an advance directive has been executed, the directive takes precedence over the facility's normal procedures, to the extent required by state law.

A health care provider is not required to implement an advance directive if, as a matter of conscience, the provider cannot implement an advance directive and state law allows any health care provider to conscientiously object. The provider must inform individuals that complaints concerning noncompliance with the advance directive requirements may be filed with the state survey and certification agency.

PART B: MEDICAL INSURANCE

Eligibility

1084. Who is eligible for Part B (Medical Insurance) benefits?

Anyone who is eligible for Part A (Hospital Insurance), whether automatically or through payment of Part A premiums (including disabled individuals who lose entitlement to automatic Part A benefits but may still enroll by paying premiums), may enroll in Part B (Medical Insurance).

Even if a person does not qualify for Part A benefits, that person may enroll in Part B (Medical Insurance) as long as he is at least age sixty-five, a U.S. resident and either

(1) a U.S. citizen or

(2) an alien lawfully admitted for permanent residence who has resided in the United States continuously during the five years immediately prior to the month in which he applies for enrollment in Part B.

NOTE: It should be remembered that participation in Part B is voluntary – however, an individual will pay higher rates if they join Part B later than age 65 (unless covered by creditable healthcare insurance) at age 65.

See Q 1036 for eligibility rules for Part A (Hospital Insurance).

1085. How does a person enroll in Part B (Medical Insurance)?

Individuals who are receiving Social Security and Railroad Retirement benefits are enrolled automatically in Part B (Medical Insurance) when they become entitled to Part A (Hospital Insurance). They may, however, elect not to be covered by Part B (Medical Insurance) by signing a form sent to them by the Social Security Administration. Others may enroll online through the Social Security Administration's website (www.ssa.gov) or at the nearest Social Security office. An individual who already has Part A coverage and wants to add Part B coverage may also call 1-800-772-1213.

The initial enrollment period for Part B (Medical Insurance) is a period of seven full calendar months, the beginning and end of which is determined for each person by the day on which he is first eligible to enroll. The initial enrollment period begins on the first day of the third month before the month a person first becomes eligible to enroll and ends with the close of the last day of the third month following the month a person first becomes eligible to enroll. For example, if the person's sixty-fifth birthday is April 10, 2023, that person's initial enrollment period begins January 1, 2023 and ends July 31, 2023.

If a person decides not to enroll during the initial enrollment period, that individual may enroll later during a general enrollment period. There is a general enrollment period from January 1 through March 31 of each year, with such enrollment effective the following July 1. Under certain circumstances, a person who does not enroll during his initial enrollment period may be able to enroll during a special enrollment period (See Q 1086). The special enrollment period is a period provided by statute to enable certain individuals to enroll in Medicare without waiting for the general enrollment period.

In order to obtain coverage at the earliest possible date, a person must enroll before the beginning of the month in which he reaches age sixty-five. For a person who enrolls during the initial enrollment period, the effective date of coverage is as follows:

(1)   If the person enrolls before the month in which age sixty-five is reached, coverage will commence the first day of the month in which age sixty-five is reached.

(2)   If the person enrolls during the month in which age sixty-five is reached, coverage will commence the first day of the following month.

(3)   If the person enrolls in the month after the month in which age sixty-five is reached, coverage will commence the first day of the second month after the month of enrollment.

(4)   If the person enrolls more than one month (but at least within three months) after the month in which age sixty-five is reached, coverage will commence the first day of the third month following the month of enrollment.

An eight-month special enrollment period is provided if Medicare has been the secondary payer of benefits for individuals aged sixty-five and older who are covered under an employer group health plan because of current employment. The special enrollment period generally begins with the month after the month in which coverage under the private plan ends. Coverage under Part B (Medical Insurance) will begin with the first day of the month after the month in which coverage under the private plan ends if the individual enrolls in that month or with the first day of the month after the month of enrollment if the individual enrolls during the balance of the special enrollment period (See Q 1086).

1086. What if a person declines to enroll during the Part B (Medical Insurance) initial enrollment period?

Anyone who is eligible but fails to enroll in Part B (Medical Insurance) during the initial enrollment period may enroll during a general enrollment period. There are general enrollment periods each year from January 1st through March 31st. Coverage begins the following July 1st.

The Part B premium will be higher for a person who fails to enroll within twelve months, or who drops out of the plan and later re-enrolls. **The monthly premium will be increased by 10 percent for each full twelve months during which such an individual could have been, but was not, enrolled.**

If a person declines to enroll (or terminates enrollment) at a time when Medicare is secondary payer to an employer group health plan covering that person, the months in which the individual is covered under the employer group health plan (based on current employment) will not be counted as months during which the individual could have been but was not enrolled in Part B (Medical Insurance) for the purpose of determining if the premium amount should be increased above the basic rate. Individuals to whom this applies may later enroll during a "special enrollment period". The special enrollment period lasts for eight months after the earlier of the termination of the individual's group health plan coverage or termination of employment.

In general, individuals must meet the following conditions to enroll during a special enrollment period:

(1)   They must be eligible for Part B (Medical Insurance) on the basis of age or disability, but not on the basis of end-stage renal disease.

(2)   When first eligible for Part B (Medical Insurance coverage), they must be covered under a group health plan on the basis of current employment status of the individual or the individual's spouse.

(3)   For all months thereafter, they must maintain coverage under a group health plan. (Generally, if an individual fails to enroll in Part B [Medical Insurance] during any available special enrollment period, that individual is not entitled to any additional special enrollment periods. But if an individual fails to enroll during a special enrollment period because coverage under the same or a different group health plan was restored before the end of that particular special enrollment period, that failure to enroll does not preclude additional special enrollment periods.)

1087. Is there a special enrollment period for disabled workers who lose benefits under a group health plan?

Yes. Certain disabled beneficiaries are eligible for a special enrollment period and waiver of the Part B premium surcharge.

These individuals are disabled beneficiaries:

(1)   who were enrolled in an employment-based group health plan (by reason of current or former employment or the current or former employment of a family member) at the time of initially becoming eligible for Medicare;

(2)   who elected not to enroll in Part B during their initial enrollment period; and

(3)   whose continuous enrollment under the group health plan is involuntarily terminated at a time when the enrollment is by reason of the individual's former employment (or the former employment of a family member).

The special enrollment period begins on the first day of the month that includes the date of the involuntary termination and continues for six months.

1088. How does a person terminate or cancel coverage under Part B (Medical Insurance)?

A person's Part B (Medical Insurance) coverage continues until the individual's enrollment is terminated. A beneficiary may terminate coverage by filing a notice (Form CMS-1763)[1] that he no longer wishes to participate in the program or by not paying the monthly premium. However, Social Security insists that because of the seriousness of this decision, that you have a personal interview to discuss the matter. It can be in person or over the telephone.

The termination of coverage takes effect at the close of the month following the month in which a notice is filed. A grace period, however, is provided before coverage is terminated for not paying premiums. The grace period in which overdue premiums can be paid and coverage continued generally runs for three months from the month for which the unpaid premium was due, but may be extended an additional three months in certain cases where the Centers for Medicare & Medicaid Services (CMS) determines that there was good cause for failure to pay the overdue premiums within the initial three-month grace period.

A termination notice filed by a person enrolled in Part B (Medical Insurance) before the first day of the month in which Part B coverage is scheduled to begin will terminate coverage on the first day of the month in which coverage would otherwise have been effective. If a termination notice is filed in or after the month in which Part B coverage is effective, the coverage is terminated at the close of the month following the month in which the notice is filed.

In the case of a person entitled to Part A (Hospital Insurance) based on twenty-four or more months of disability, rather than on having attained age sixty-five, Part B (Medical Insurance) generally ends at the close of the last month for which the individual is entitled to Part A benefits.

Note

1. https://www.cms.gov/Regulations-and-Guidance/Legislation/PaperworkReductionActof1995/PRA-Listing-Items/CMS-1763 Dated 02/05/2021 Expiration Date TBD (last accessed October 3, 2022).

Financing Part B (Medical Insurance)

1089. How is Part B (Medical Insurance) financed?

Medical Insurance is voluntary and is financed through premiums paid by people who enroll and through funds from the federal government. Monthly premiums are in addition to the deductible and coinsurance amounts that must be paid by beneficiaries.

Most persons enrolled in 2023 pay a standard monthly premium of $164.90 per month. The basic Part B (Medical Insurance) premium is set to cover approximately 25 percent of program costs each year. The federal government pays the remaining cost from general revenues. In September-October of each year, the CMS announce the premium rate for the twelve-month period starting the following January.

Single persons with annual incomes over $97,000 (as indexed in 2022) and married couples with incomes over $194,000 (as indexed in 2022) pay a higher percentage of the cost of Part B (Medical Insurance).

These higher income beneficiaries will pay monthly premiums as follows during 2023:

1. Beneficiaries who file an individual tax return with 2021 income levels:

    o   Greater than $97,000 and less than or equal to $123,000: $230.80

    o   Greater than $123,000 and less than or equal to $153,000: $329.70

    o   Greater than $153,000 and less than or equal to $183,000: $428.60

    o   Greater than $183,000 and less than or equal to $500,000: $527.50

    o   Greater than $500,000: $560.50

2. Beneficiaries who file a joint tax return with 2021 income levels:

    o   Greater than $194,000 and less than or equal to $246,000: $230.80

    o   Greater than $246,000 and less than or equal to $306,000: $329.70

    o   Greater than $306,000 and less than or equal to $366,000: $428.60

    o   Greater than $366,000 and less than or equal to $750,000: $527.50

    o   Greater than $750,000: $560.50

3. Beneficiaries who are married and lived with their spouse at any time during the year, but file a separate tax return from their spouse in 2021:

    o   Less than/equal to $97,000: $164.90

    o   Greater than $97,000 and less than or equal to $403,000: $527.50

    o   Greater than $403,000: $560.50

The premium rate for a person who enrolls after his initial enrollment period (when he is first eligible for Part B coverage), or who re-enrolls after terminating Part B coverage, will be increased by up to 10 percent for each full twelve months the person stayed out of the program. Special enrollment periods apply to certain individuals with employer group health plan coverage, and they are not subject to the late enrollment penalty as long as they enroll during such a special enrollment period. See Q 1086 for more detail on the special enrollment period.

Historical Costs of Part B

Basic Monthly Premium
Part B (Medical Insurance)

Year	Monthly Premium
1994	41.10
1995	46.10
1996	42.50
1997	43.80
1998	43.80
1999	45.50
2000	45.50
2001	50.00
2002	54.00
2003	58.70
2004	66.60
2005	78.20
2006	88.50
2007	93.50
2008	96.40
2009	96.40
2010	110.50
2011	115.40
2012	99.90
2013-2015	104.90
2016	121.80 or 104.90
2017	134.00 or 109.00
2018	134.00 or 109.00
2019	135.50[1]
2020	144.60
2021	148.50
2022	158.50
2023	164.90

Income-Adjusted Monthly Premium
Part B (Medical Insurance in 2023)

Single Taxpayer	Married Taxpayers Filing Jointly	Total Premium
Not greater than $97,000	Not greater than $194,000	$164.90
$971,001 - $123,000	$194,001 - $246,000	$230.80
$123,001 - $153,000	$246,001 - $306,000	$329.70
$153,001 - $183,000	$306,001 - $366,000	$428.60
$183,001 - $500,000	$366,001 - $750,000	$527.50
More than $500,000	More than $750,000	$560.50
	Married Taxpayers Separately	**Total Premium**
	Not greater than $97,000	$164.90
	$97,001 - $403,000	$527.50
	$403,001 and greater	$560.50

Beginning with 2023, some Medicare enrollees who are greater than thirty-six (36) months past a kidney transplant AND no longer eligible for FULL Medicare coverage, are able to continue Part B coverage of immunosuppressive drugs by paying a premium. The premiums begin at $97.10 per month and are further explained in the next question.

Note

1. Some subject to the "hold harmless" provision may pay slightly less.

1089.01. Is Part B available for those under age 65?

Yes. Beginning in 2023, certain Medicare enrollees that are no longer eligible for full Medicare because they are under age 65 and more than 36 months past a kidney transplant, can elect to continue Part B coverage for immunosuppressive drugs only. During 2023, the coverage begins at $97.10 per month

Part B Immunosuppressive Drug Coverage Only			
Beneficiaries who file individual tax returns with modified adjusted gross income:	Beneficiaries who file joint tax returns with modified adjusted gross income:	Income-Related Monthly Adjustment Amount	Total Monthly Premium Amount
Less than or equal to $97,000	Less than or equal to $194,000	$0.00	$97.10
Greater than $97,000 and less than or equal to $123,000	Greater than $194,000 and less than or equal to $246,000	$64.70	$161.80

Greater than $123,000 and less than or equal to $153,000	Greater than $246,000 and less than or equal to $306,000	$161.80	$258.90
Greater than $153,000 and less than or equal to $183,000	Greater than $306,000 and less than or equal to $366,000	$258.90	$356.00
Greater than $183,000 and less than $500,000	Greater than $366,000 and less than $750,000	$356.00	$453.10
Greater than or equal to $500,000	Greater than or equal to $750,000	$388.40	$485.50

Premiums for beneficiaries with Part B coverage for immunosuppressive drugs only who are married and filed a separate return (but lived with their spouse for part of the year) are listed below:

Part B Immunosuppressive Drug Coverage Only		
Beneficiaries who are married and lived with their spouses at any time during the year, but who file separate tax returns from their spouses, with modified adjusted gross income:	Income-Related Monthly Adjustment Amount	Total Monthly Premium Amount
Less than or equal to $97,000	$0.00	$97.10
Greater than $97,000 and less than $403,000	$356.00	$453.10
Greater than or equal to $403,000	$388.40	$485.50

1090. How is Income determined for purposes of setting a person's Part B (Hospital Insurance) Premium?

If the person's Modified Adjusted Gross Income (MAGI) is above the thresholds discussed in Q 1089, then additional Part B premiums are required. Modified Adjusted Gross Income is Adjusted Gross Income (AGI) plus tax exempt interest income.

To determine the 2023 income-related monthly adjustment amounts, Medicare uses the most recent Federal tax return that the IRS provides. This information is from a tax return filed in 2022 for tax year 2021. Sometimes, the IRS only provides information from a return filed in 2021 for tax year 2020. If Medicare uses the 2020 tax year data, and the taxpayer filed a return for tax year 2021 or did not need to file a tax return for tax year 2021, the taxpayer can contact Medicare and records will be updated.

If a person's income has gone down due to any of the following situations and the change makes a difference in the income level Medicare considers, the taxpayer should contact Medicare to explain the latest information, and Medicare may need a new decision about your income-related monthly adjustment amount:

- The taxpayer married, divorced, or became widowed

- The taxpayer or spouse stopped working or reduced work hours

- The taxpayer or spouse lost income-producing property due to a disaster or other event beyond the taxpayer's control

- The taxpayer or spouse experienced a scheduled cessation, termination, or reorganization of an employer's pension plan

- The taxpayer or spouse received a settlement from an employer or former employer because of the employer's closure, bankruptcy, or reorganization

If any of these apply, Medicare needs to see documentation verifying the event and the reduction in income. The documentation provided should relate to the event and may include a death certificate, a letter from an employer about retirement, or something similar. If a taxpayer filed a Federal income tax return for the year in question, a signed copy needs to be shown to Medicare.

If the taxpayer disagrees with the decision regarding the income-related monthly adjustment amounts, there is a right to appeal. The taxpayer may request an appeal in writing by completing a *Request for Reconsideration* (Form SSA-561-U2)[1] or by contacting the local Social Security office. Appeal forms can be found on the Social Security website (www.socialsecurity.gov/online). Forms can also be requested by calling 1-800-772-1213. Taxpayers do not need to file an appeal if they are requesting a new decision because one of the events listed took place which caused income to decrease or if it can be shown that information used was wrong.

Avoiding Higher Part B Premiums

An individual can reduce their Part B premium in a few ways:

- **Understand the timing.** There is a two-year lag for the extra premiums: This year's income will appear on a client's 2022 tax return, which will be filed in 2023. Medicare uses those numbers to set Part B premiums for 2023.

- **Take Action.** Continually take losses in taxable accounts. Each year, an individual can deduct $3,000 of net capital losses. Any excess losses can be carried over to future years. There is no time limit for using them.

Another idea is to convert a traditional IRA to a Roth IRA. An individual can start a conversion at any age. This increases income in the current tax year but lowers it in future years as withdrawals from Roth IRAs are tax-free in most cases.

After a conversion, a person can recharacterize (reverse) some or all of the conversion back to a traditional IRA, until October 15 of the following year. By then, a calculation can be made to determine how much can be converted without moving into a higher tax bracket. And after age sixty-three, recharacterizations can involve fine-tuning to keep an individual below the Part B premium thresholds.

Also, the purchase of permanent life insurance can also help manage Part B premiums. Distributions from permanent life insurance are received income-tax free up to an individual's basis in the contract. After that, policy loans, which are not taxable, can be taken from the policy.

If a person's situation changes, he or she might be able to reduce the Part B premium. Certain situations provide grounds to appeal, including getting married, divorced, or being widowed. If a person or their spouse stops working or cuts work hours, an appeal can be made for the excess Part B premium.

Note

1. *Request for Reconsideration* (Form SSA-561-U2), https://www.ssa.gov/forms/ssa-561.pdf (last accessed October 4, 2022).

1091. What assistance is available for those who cannot afford Medicare costs?

An elderly or disabled person with a low income who is eligible for Medicare may be able to have some or all Medicare expenses paid by their state. Federal law requires state Medicaid programs to pay Medicare costs for certain elderly and disabled persons with low incomes and very limited assets.

There are four programs to help people pay their Medicare expenses:

(1)   the Qualified Medicare Beneficiary (QMB) program

(2)   the Specified Low-Income Medicare Beneficiary (SLMB) program; and

(3)   the Qualifying Individual (QI) program

(4)   the Qualified Disabled and Working Individuals (QDWI) program

Note that to qualify for these programs, one must qualify for Part A.

QMB Program

The QMB program is for a person with limited resources whose income is at or below the national poverty level. It covers the cost of Medicare Part A (Hospital Insurance) premiums, coinsurance, and deductibles that a Medicare beneficiary normally pays out of his own pocket. The QMB program also pays the basic Part B (Medical Insurance) premium, which is $170.10 in 2022 and $164.90 in 2023 for most individuals (see Q 1089).

SLMB Program

While the QMB program helps those whose income is at or below the national poverty level, the SLMB program is for a person whose income is slightly higher than the poverty level, but not more than 20 percent higher. The program pays the Part B (Medical Insurance) premiums $170.10 in 2022 and $164.90 in 2023 see Q 1089) for a person qualifying under the SLMB program, but not any of the Part A or Part B deductibles and coinsurance. SLMBs also remain responsible for charges for health care services and medical supplies not covered by Medicare.

QI Program

The QI program assists individuals and married couples whose income is more than 20 percent greater than the Federal poverty level, but not more than 38 percent greater, by paying the full monthly Part B (Medical Insurance) premium each month. As with SLMBs, persons covered under the QI program remain responsible for Medicare's deductibles and coinsurance and for charges for health care services and medical supplies not covered by Medicare.

QDWI Program

The QDWI program assists individuals with the cost of the Part A premium. An individual can qualify by meeting any of the following criteria:

- a working disabled person under 65;

- lost their premium-free Part A upon return to work;

- not getting medical assistance from the state; and

- meeting the income and resource limits required by the particular state;

See Q 1050 and Q 1052 for more details on eligibility for the QMB and SLMB programs.

1092. What are the Income and Resource limits for the Qualified Medicare Beneficiary (QMB) program?

For 2022, the income and resource limitations are:

- Individual monthly income limit: $1,153

- Married couple monthly income limit: $1,546

- Individual resource limit: $8,400

- Married couple resource limit: $12,600

Those that qualify for this program automatically qualify for extra assistance for Medicare Prescription Drug coverage (Part D). Note that the above income limits are subject to change for 2023.

1093. What are the Income and Resource limits for the Specified Low-Income Medicare Beneficiary (SLMB) program?

For 2022, the income and resource limitations are:

- Individual monthly income limit: $1,379

- Married couple monthly income limit: $1,851

- Individual resource limit: $8,400

- Married couple resource limit: $12,600

Those that qualify for this program automatically qualify for extra assistance for Medicare Prescription Drug coverage (Part D). Note that these income limits are subject to change for 2023.

1094. What are the Income and Resource limits for the Qualifying Individual (QI) program?

For 2023, the income and resource limitations are:

- Individual monthly income limit: $1,549

- Married couple monthly income limit: $2,080

- Individual resource limit: $8,400

- Married couple resource limit: $12,600

Note: Individuals must apply every year for the QI program and assistance is granted on a first-come, first-serve basis. Priority is given to QI recipients of the prior year. QI is not available for those that qualify for Medicaid. These income and resource limits are subject to change during 2023.

Those that qualify for this program automatically qualify for extra assistance for Medicare Prescription Drug coverage (Part D).

1095. What are the Income and Resource limits for the Qualifying Disabled and Working Individuals (QDWI) program?

For 2022, the income and resource limitations are:

- Individual monthly income limit: $4,339 (unchanged)

- Married couple monthly income limit: $5,833 (unchanged)

- Individual resource limit: $4,000 (unchanged)

- Married couple resource limit: $6,000 (unchanged)

1096. How are premiums paid under Part B (Medical Insurance)?

Most persons covered by Part B (Medical Insurance) have the premiums deducted from their Social Security, Railroad Retirement, or federal civil service retirement benefit payments. Persons who are not receiving any of these government benefits pay the premiums directly to the government.

Direct payment of premiums is usually made on a quarterly basis with a grace period, determined by the Centers for Medicare & Medicaid Services (CMS), of up to ninety days.

Public assistance agencies may enroll, and pay premiums for, certain public assistance recipients (usually recipients of public assistance under the Supplemental Security Income program). States must pay premiums for specified low-income persons (See Q 1091).

If a person's Social Security or Railroad Retirement benefits are suspended because of excess earnings, and benefits will not be resumed until the next taxable year, the person will be billed directly for overdue Medicare premiums. If Social Security or Railroad Retirement benefits will be resumed before the close of the taxable year, overdue premiums are deducted from the Social Security or Railroad Retirement cash benefits when they resume.

Premiums must be paid for the entire month of death even though coverage ends on the day of death.

1097. How are "approved charges" for covered medical services determined under Part B (Medical Insurance)?

There are three major elements that determine how much Medicare Part B pays for physician services:

(1)   A fee schedule for the payment of physician services

    a.   The Physician Fee Schedule look up tool can be found at the CMS website [1]

(2)   A method to control the rates of increase in Medicare expenditures for physicians' services

(3)   Limits on the amounts that nonparticipating physicians can charge beneficiaries

Payments under the fee schedule must be based on national uniform Relative Value Units (RVUs) based on the resources used in furnishing a service. National RVUs must be established for physician work, practice expense, and malpractice expense.

Prior to the creation of RVUs, Medicare paid for services using "UCR" – Usual, Customary, and Reasonable rates. The Medicare fee schedule was created in 1989 and about 7,000 distinct services listed in what is called the Current Procedural Terminology owned by the AMA. Each service in the fee schedule is scored under the (RBRVS) (Resource Based Relative Value Scale) to set the payment amount.

The Medicare Physician Fee Schedule Payment Rate Formula is calculated as follows:

Payment = Physician Work RVU × Work GPCI + Practice Expense RVU × Practice Expense GPCI + Malpractice RVU × Malpractice GPCI = Conversion Factor

The formula consists of three RVUs – **physician work** (51 percent), **practice expense** (45 percent), and **malpractice expense** (4 percent). These RVUs are multiplied by "geographic practice cost indices" (GCPI) and adjusted to account for different regional wages and costs. These percentages are revisited and adjusted on a yearly basis. Annual updates to the physician work, practice expense and professional liability insurance relative values are based on recommendations from the AMA/Specialty Society Relative Value Scale Update Committee (RUC), which was formed in 1991 to make recommendations to CMS on the relative values to be assigned to new or revised codes in the Current Procedural Terminology (CPT®) code book. The relative values in the RBRVS were originally developed to correspond to the approximately 10,000 CPT procedure codes. The RBRVS is updated annually to reflect new and revised CPT codes.

Relative Value Units

Physician Work: The factors used to determine this component includes the time it takes to perform the services, the technical skill and physical effort required, the required mental effort and judgment and stress due to the potential risk to the patient. The physician work relative values are updated each year to account for changes in medical practice and CMS reviews the entire scale at least every five years.

Practice Expense: These values are based on a formula using average Medicare-approved charges from 1991 (the year before the RBRVS was implemented) and the proportion of each specialty's revenues attributable to practice expenses. In January 1999, CMS began a transition to resource-based practice expense relative values for each CPT code, which differ based on the site of service.

Professional Liability Insurance/Malpractice: On January 1, 2000, CMS implemented the PLI relative value units. With this implementation and the final transition of the resource-based practice expense relative units on January 1, 2002, all components of the RBRVS became resource-based.

Adjustments in RVUs because of changes resulting from a review of those RVUs may not cause total physician fee schedule payments to differ by more than $20 million from what they would have been had the adjustments not been made. If this amount is exceeded, the Centers for Medicare & Medicaid Services (CMS) must make an adjustment to the conversion factor to preserve budget neutrality. Congress also has the power to override the statutory formula and often does exactly that. Geographic Practice Cost Indices (GPCIs).

Each of the three RVUs are adjusted to account for geographic variations in the costs of practicing medicine in different areas within the country. These adjustments are called GPCIs, and each kind of RVU component has a corresponding GPCI adjustment. CMS is required to review and, if necessary, adjust the Geographic Practice Cost Indices (GPCIs) at least every three years. CMS also must phase in the adjustment over two years and implement only one-half of any adjustment if more than one year has elapsed since the last GPCI revision.

Conversion Factor (CF)

To determine the payment rate for a particular service, the sum of the geographically adjusted RVUs is multiplied by a CF in dollars. The statute specifies the formula by which the CF is updated on an annual basis.

Payment Rates

National and local payment rates are found in the Physician Fee Schedule Search Tool.[2]

Notes

1. How to use the MPFS Look Up Tool https://www.cms.gov/files/document/physician-fee-schedule-guide.pdf (Last accessed October 10, 2022)
2. https://www.cms.gov/apps/physician-fee-schedule/overview.aspx, updated October 1, 2022 (last accessed October 10, 2022).

1098. How are Part B (Medical Insurance) payments made?

Part B (Medical Insurance) payments are made in two ways. Payment can be made directly to the doctor, supplier, or other health care provider. This is the assignment method of payment. Payment can also be made directly to the patient, who then pays the provider.

Under the assignment method, the health care provider agrees to accept the amount approved by the Medicare Administrative Contractor (MAC) as total payment for Medicare-covered services.

The assignment method can save the patient time and money. The health care provider sends the claim to Medicare. Medicare pays the health care provider 80 percent of the Medicare-approved charge, after subtracting any part of the annual deductible the patient has not paid. The health care provider can charge the patient only for the part of the annual deductible the patient has not met and for the Part B coinsurance, which is generally the remaining 20 percent of the approved amount. Of course, a provider also can charge the patient for any services that Medicare does not cover.

If a health care provider does not accept assignment, the provider is considered "nonparticipating," and Medicare pays the patient 80 percent of the approved charge, after subtracting any part of the annual deductible the patient has not paid. The health care provider can bill the patient for the provider's actual charge, even if it is more than the charge approved by the MAC.

Doctors, suppliers, and other providers of Part B (Medical Insurance) services are in most cases required to submit Medicare claims for a patient, even if the providers do not take assignment. Claims are submitted on a form called a CMS-1500,[1] requesting that Part B (Medical Insurance) payment be made for a patient's covered services. The provider completes the form and the patient signs it before it is sent to the proper MAC. Generally, the provider must submit a claim within one year of providing the service or may be subject to certain penalties. A patient should notify the MAC in the patient's area if a Medicare provider refuses to submit a claim to Medicare and the patient believes the services may be covered by Medicare.

If a patient is enrolled in a health care organization such as an HMO, a claim will seldom need to be submitted. Medicare generally pays an HMO a set amount, and the HMO provides medical care for its members. Doctors, suppliers, and other providers of Part B (Medical Insurance) services bill the HMO directly for reimbursement at contractually-agreed rates.

Utilizing a doctor who accepts assignment under Medicare may make a substantial difference in a patient's out-of-pocket costs.

> *Example.* Jane Smith has surgery after meeting the annual deductible for 2023 Part B (Medical Insurance). Dr. Ralph Jones, who is not a participating physician and does not limit his charges to the Medicare fee schedule, bills Ms. Smith $1,200 for the surgery. The Medicare fee schedule sets the charge for this surgery at $1,100. Medicare will pay $880 (80 percent of the Medicare fee), and Ms. Smith must pay the remaining $320 of the $1,200 fee.

> If Dr. Jones had been a participating physician under Medicare, Ms. Smith would have had to pay only $220 (20 percent of the approved charge of $1,100 that Medicare does not pay).

If a physician does not accept the assignment method, the physician must refund all amounts collected from Medicare beneficiaries on claims for services that are deemed not medically necessary. The MAC will send a notice to the beneficiary and physician advising them of the basis for denial, the right of appeal, and the requirement of a refund.

Even though a doctor does not accept assignment, for most covered services there are limits on the amount a nonparticipating provider can actually charge a Medicare beneficiary. In general, the most a doctor can charge is 115 percent of what Medicare approves. The 115 percent limit also applies to fees for physical and occupational therapy services, suppliers, injections, and other services billable under the physician fee schedule.

Physicians must give written notice prior to elective surgery for which the fee is $500 or more. The notice must state the physician's estimated actual charge, the estimated Medicare-approved charge, the excess of the actual charge over the approved charge, and the applicable coinsurance amount. This requirement applies to nonemergency surgical procedures only. (Emergency surgery is surgery performed under conditions and circumstances which afford no alternatives to the physician or the patient and, if delayed, could result in death or permanent impairment of health.) If the physician fails to make this fee disclosure, and the surgery was nonemergency surgery, the physician must refund amounts collected in excess of the Medicare-approved Part B (Medical Insurance) charge. The physician is subject to sanctions if the physician knowingly and willfully fails to comply with this refund requirement.

Note

1. Form CMS-1500 (updated July 1, 2021), https://www.cms.gov/Medicare/CMS-Forms/CMS-Forms/CMS-Forms-Items/CMS1188854 (last accessed October 10, 2022).

1099. How can a person find out if a doctor accepts assignment of all Medicare claims?

Doctors and suppliers sign agreements in advance to accept assignment on all Medicare claims. They are given the opportunity to sign participation agreements each year.

Medicare beneficiaries may use the Physician Compare tool available on the CMS website[1] to find participating physicians. A listing of all Medicare approved suppliers can also be found on the CMS website.[2] The names and addresses of Medicare-participating doctors and suppliers are also listed by geographic area in the *Medicare-Participating Physician Directory3* and the *Medicare-Participating Supplier Directory*.[4] Both directories are available in Social Security offices, from Medicare Administrative Contractors, in state and area offices of the Administration on Aging, at most hospitals, and at www.medicare.gov. Medicare beneficiaries may also call 1-800-MEDI-CARE (1-800-633-4227) to locate physicians and suppliers.

Medicare-participating doctors and suppliers may display emblems or certificates that show they accept assignment on all Medicare claims.

Notes

1. https://www.medicare.gov/care-compare/?providerType=Physician&redirect=true (last accessed October 10, 2022).
2. https://www.medicare.gov/medical-equipment-suppliers (last accessed October 10, 2022).
3. https://www.medicare.gov/forms-help-and-resources/find-doctors-hospitals-and-facilities/quality-care-finder.htmll (last accessed October 10, 2022).
4. https://www.medicare.gov/supplierdirectory/search.html *Medicare-Participating Supplier Directory* (last accessed October 10, 2022).

1100. What are Medicare providers and Medicare suppliers?

The term "provider" generally means a hospital, a rural primary care hospital, a skilled nursing facility, a comprehensive outpatient rehabilitative facility, a home health agency, a PACE facility, or a hospice that has in effect an agreement to participate in Medicare. A clinic, rehabilitation agency, or a public health agency that has a similar agreement to furnish outpatient physical therapy or speech pathology services, or a community mental health center with a similar agreement to furnish partial hospitalization services, is also considered a provider.[1]

In general, "suppliers" are individuals or entities—other than doctors or health care facilities—that furnish equipment or services covered by Part B (Medical Insurance). For example, ambulance firms, independent laboratories, and entities that rent or sell medical equipment are considered suppliers.

There are different definitions of the term supplier and specific regulations governing different types of suppliers. Durable Medical Equipment, Prosthetics, Orthotics, and Supplies (DMEPOS) encompass the types of items included in the definition of "medical equipment and supplies." A "DMEPOS supplier" refers to all individuals or organizations that furnish these items. This can include a physician or Medicare Part A (Hospital Insurance) provider. A DMEPOS supplier must meet Medicare DMEPOS standards in order to obtain a supplier number. Those individuals or entities that do not furnish DMEPOS items but only furnish other types of health care services, such as physician's services or nurse practitioner services, are not subject to these standards. A supplier number is also not necessary before Medicare payment can be made with respect to medical equipment and supplies furnished incident to a physician's service.

For Medicare purposes, DMEPOS suppliers either accept or do not accept assignment. If a DMEPOS supplier accepts assignment, it agrees to accept the Medicare-approved amount as payment in full for the covered item. Such suppliers are referred to as "participating suppliers". Participating DMEPOS suppliers are listed in directories available to Medicare beneficiaries and receive Medicare Part B payment directly from the Medicare program. Nonparticipating DMEPOS suppliers may accept assignment on a case-by-case basis; for claims on which they accept assignment, they receive payment directly from Medicare. If a beneficiary receives a service from a nonparticipating DMEPOS supplier on a nonassigned basis, however, payment is made to the beneficiary (who in turn pays the DMEPOS supplier).

Medicare suppliers are required to meet a number of standards, including the following:

(1)   Complying with all applicable state and federal license and regulatory requirements

(2)   Maintaining a physical facility on an appropriate site

(3)   Having proof of appropriate liability insurance

(4)   Delivering Medicare-covered items to Medicare beneficiaries

(5)   Honoring all warranties

(6)   Maintaining and repairing items rented to beneficiaries

(7)   Accepting returns of substandard or unsuitable items from beneficiaries

Note

1. https://www.cms.gov/Medicare/Provider-Enrollment-and-Certification/MedicareProviderSupEnroll/index.html?redirect=/MedicareProvid-erSupEnroll (last accessed October 10, 2022).

1101. What portion of the cost must be borne by the patient?

The patient pays an annual deductible each year under Part B (medical Insurance). For 2023, the deductible is $226, up from $219 in 2022, which means that the patient pays for the first $226 of covered expenses incurred during the calendar year. After the deductible is met, the patient pays 20 percent of approved charges, and Medicare pay 80 percent. There is no cost-sharing from certain Part B services and supplies, including most home health services, pneumococcal vaccine, flu shots, the costs for second opinions for certain surgical procedures when Medicare requires these opinions, and certain outpatient clinical laboratory tests.

1102. How does a patient find out how much Medicare will pay on a claim?

After the doctor, provider, or supplier send in a Part B (medical Insurance) claim, Medicare sends the patient a notice call *Explanation of Your Medicare Part B Benefits*[1] to explain the decision on the claim.

This notice shoes what charges were made and what Medicare approved. It shows what the coinsurance is and what Medicare is paying. If the annual deductible has not been met, that is also shown. The notice also gives the address and telephone number of the Medicare Administrative Contractor.

Note

1. Your Medicare Benefits https://www.medicare.gov/Pubs/pdf/10116-Your-Medicare-Benefits.pdf Revised January 2022 (Last accessed October 10, 2022).

Benefits

1103. What doctors' services are covered under Part B (Medical Insurance)?

Under Part B (Medical Insurance), Medicare usually pays 80 percent of the approved charges for doctors' services and other services that are covered under Part B after the patient pays an annual deductible. Part B helps pay for covered services received from the doctor in the doctor's office, in a hospital, in a skilled nursing facility, in the patient's home, or any other location. Doctors' fees and services covered by Part B include:

- **Doctors' services** are covered wherever furnished in the United States. This includes the cost of house calls, office visits, and doctors' services in a hospital or other institution. Such services include the fees of physicians, surgeons, pathologists, radiologists, anesthesiologists, physiatrists, and osteopaths. Patients should check their benefits as more and more remote services/telemedicine visits are covered.

- Services from certain **specially qualified practitioners** who are not physicians but are approved by Medicare, including certified registered nurse anesthetists, certified nurse midwifes, clinical psychologists, clinical social workers (other than in a hospital), physician assistants, and nurse practitioners and clinical nurse specialists in collaboration with a physician. Patients should check their benefits as more and more remote services/telemedicine visits are covered.

- Services of **clinical psychologists** are covered if they would otherwise be covered when furnished by a physician (or as an incident to a physician's services). Patients should check their benefits as more and more remote services/telemedicine visits are covered.

- Services by **licensed chiropractors** for manual manipulation of the spine to correct a subluxation. Part B does not otherwise pay for any other diagnostic or therapeutic services, including X-rays, furnished by a chiropractor. Medicare pays for manual manipulation of the spine to correct a subluxation without requiring an X-ray (which previously was required) to prove that the subluxation exists.

- Fees of **podiatrists** are covered, including fees for the treatment of plantar warts, but not for routine foot care. Examples of common problems covered by Part B include ingrown toenails, hammer toe deformities, bunion deformities, and heel spurs. Routine foot care not covered by Part B includes cutting or removal of corns and calluses, trimming of nails, and other hygienic care. Part B does help pay for some routine foot care if the patient is being treated by a medical doctor for a medical condition affecting the patient's legs or feet (such as diabetes or peripheral vascular disease) which requires that a podiatrist or doctor of medicine or osteopathy perform the routine care.

Medicare helps pay for therapeutic shoes and shoe inserts for people who have severe diabetic foot disease. The doctor who treats the diabetes must certify the patient's need for therapeutic shoes. The shoes and inserts must be prescribed by a podiatrist and furnished by a podiatrist, orthotist, prosthetist, or pedorthist. Medicare helps pay for one pair of therapeutic shoes per calendar year and for inserts. Shoe modifications may be substituted for inserts. The fitting of shoes or inserts is included in the Medicare payment for the shoes.

- The cost of diagnosis and treatment **of eye and ear ailments** is covered. Also covered is an **optometrist's treatment of aphakia**. Patients should check their benefits as more and more remote services/telemedicine visits are covered.

- **Plastic surgery** for purely cosmetic reasons is excluded; but plastic surgery for repair of an accidental injury, an impaired limb, or a malformed part of the body is covered.

- **Radiological or pathological services** furnished by a physician to a hospital inpatient are covered. Patients should check their benefits as more and more remote services/telemedicine visits are covered.

Part B also covers:

(1)   medical and surgical services, including anesthesia;

(2)   diagnostic tests and procedures that are part of the patient's treatment;

(3)   radiology and pathology services by doctors while the patient is a hospital inpatient or outpatient;

(4)   treatment of mental illness, (Medicare payments are limited);

(5)   X-rays;

(6)   services of the doctor's office nurse;

(7)   drugs and biologicals that cannot be self-administered;

(8)   transfusions of blood and blood components;

(9)   medical supplies; and

(10)   physical/occupational therapy and speech-language pathology services.

(11)   clinical research studies

(12)   an increasing number of telemedicine/telehealth remote treatments – especially in dermatology, psychiatry/mental health, cardiology, primary care, gynecology, endocrinology, and other specialties.

Part B does not cover:

(1)   most routine physical examinations (the "Welcome to Medicare" initial screening and subsequent annual updates are generally not considered the same as a routine physical), and tests directly related to such examinations (except some Pap smears and mammograms);

(2)   most routine foot care and dental care;

(3)   examinations for prescribing or fitting eyeglasses or hearing aids and most eyeglasses and hearing aids;

(4)   immunizations (except annual flu shots, pneumococcal pneumonia vaccinations, or immunizations required because of an injury or immediate risk of infection, and hepatitis B for certain persons at risk);

(5)   cosmetic surgery, unless it is needed because of accidental injury or to improve the function of a malformed part of the body;

(6)   most prescription drugs;

(7)   custodial care at home or in a nursing home; and

(8)   orthopedic shoes.

Charges imposed by an immediate relative (e.g., a doctor who is the son/daughter or brother/sister of the patient) are not covered.

Doctors cannot make self-referrals for certain designated health services.

Designated health services include any of the following items or services:

(1)   Clinical laboratory services

(2)   Physical therapy services

(3)   Occupational therapy services

(4)   Radiology services, including MRI, CAT scans, and ultrasound services

(5)   Radiation therapy services and supplies

(6)   Durable medical equipment and supplies

(7)   Parenteral and enteral nutrients, equipment, and supplies

(8)   Prosthetics, orthotics, and prosthetic devices and supplies

(9)   Home health services

(10)   Outpatient prescription drugs

(11)   Inpatient and outpatient hospital services

The law prohibits a doctor who has a financial relationship with an entity from referring Medicare patients to that entity to receive a designated health service. The prohibition also applies if a doctor's immediate family member has a financial relationship with an entity. A financial relationship can exist as an ownership or investment interest in, or a compensation arrangement with, an entity. The law is triggered by the mere fact that a financial relationship exists; it does not matter what the doctor intends when making a referral. An entity cannot bill Medicare, Medicaid, the beneficiary, or anyone else for a designated health service furnished to a Medicare patient under a prohibited referral.

The law prohibits Medicare payments for designated health services in violation of the law. If a person collects any amount for services billed in violation of the law, a refund must be made. A person can be subject to a civil money penalty or exclusion from Medicare if that person:

(1)   presents or causes to be presented a claim to Medicare or bill to any individual, third-party payer, or other entity for any designated health service the person knows or should know was furnished as a result of a prohibited referral; or

(2)   fails to make a timely refund.

1104. What outpatient hospital services are covered under Part B (Medical Insurance)?

Part B (Medical Insurance) helps pay for covered services a patient receives as an outpatient from a participating hospital for diagnosis or treatment of an illness or injury. Under certain conditions, Part B helps pay for emergency outpatient care the patient receives from a nonparticipating hospital. The patient must meet the annual Part B (Medical Insurance) deductible before Medicare will begin paying for outpatient hospital charges and then pay a 20 percent copayment.

Major outpatient hospital services covered by Part B include:

(1)   services in an emergency room or outpatient clinic, including same-day surgery;

(2)   laboratory tests billed by the hospital;

(3)   mental health care in a partial hospitalization psychiatric program, if a physician certifies that inpatient treatment would be required without it;

(4)   X-rays and other radiology services billed by the hospital;

(5)   medical supplies such as splints and casts;

(6)   drugs and biologicals that cannot be self-administered (Generally, Part B doesn't cover prescription and over-the-counter drugs one gets in an outpatient setting, sometimes called "self-administered drugs." Also, for safety reasons, many hospitals have policies that don't allow patients to bring prescription or other drugs from home);

(7)   blood transfusions furnished to the patient as an outpatient (after the first three pints);

(8)   preventative and screening services; and

(9)   an increasing number of remote practice / telemedicine visits are covered by Medicare.

Outpatient hospital services not covered by Part B (Medical Insurance) include:

(1)   most routine physical examinations and tests that are directly related to the examinations;

(2)   eye or ear examinations to prescribe or fit eyeglasses or hearing aids;

(3)   most immunizations;

(4)   most prescription drugs;

(5)   most routine foot care; and

(6)   most dental care.

1105. When are outpatient physical therapy and speech-language pathology services covered under Part B (Medical Insurance)?

Outpatient physical therapy and speech-language pathology services are covered if received as part of a patient's treatment in a doctor's office or as an outpatient of a participating hospital, skilled nursing facility, or home health agency, or approved clinic, rehabilitative agency, or public health agency. Services must be furnished under a plan established by a physician or therapist providing the services. A physician is required to review periodically all plans of care. The patient should inquire if remote medicine/telehealth services are available.

A podiatrist (when acting within the scope of his or her practice) is a physician for purposes of establishing a plan for outpatient physical therapy. Dentists and podiatrists are also within the definition of physicians for the purpose of outpatient ambulatory surgery in a physician's office.

1106. Are partial hospitalization services connected to mental health services covered?

Yes. Partial hospitalization services (sometimes called day treatments) related to treatment of mental illness are items and services prescribed by a physician and provided in a program under the supervision of a physician pursuant to an individualized written plan of treatment.

The program must be furnished by a hospital to its outpatients or by a community mental health center and must be in a distinct and organized intensive ambulatory treatment service offering less than twenty-four-hour daily care.

Covered items and services include the following:

- individual and group therapy with physicians or psychologists (or other mental health professionals to the extent authorized by state law);

- occupational therapy requiring the skills of a qualified occupational therapist;

- services of social workers, trained psychiatric nurses, and other staff trained to work with psychiatric patients;

- drugs and biologicals furnished for therapeutic purposes (which cannot be self-administered);

- individualized activity therapies that are not primarily recreational or diversionary;

- family counseling, the primary purpose of which is treatment of the individual's condition;

- patient training and education, to the extent the training and educational activities are closely and clearly related to the individual's care and treatment;

- diagnostic services; and

- other necessary items and services (but not including meals and transportation).

- More and more services of this nature have been approved for remote medicine/telehealth.

Medicare doesn't cover:

- meals;

- transportation to or from mental health care services;

- support groups that bring people together to talk and socialize (this is different from group psychotherapy, which is covered); or

- testing or training for job skills that isn't part of one's mental health treatment.

1107. Are certified nurse-midwife services covered under Part B (Medical Insurance)?

Yes. A certified nurse-midwife is a registered professional nurse who meets the following requirements:

(1)   Is currently licensed to practice in the state as a nurse-midwife in the state where services are performed (assuming the state requires such licensure)

(2)   Has completed a program of study and clinical experience for nurse-midwives that is accredited by an accrediting body approved by the U.S. Department of Education

(3)   Is certified as a nurse-midwife by the American College of Nurse-Midwives or the American College of Nurse-Midwives Certification Council

CNMs in most states are required to

- possess a minimum of a graduate degree, such as a M.S. in Nursing or a Doctor of Nursing Practice.

- pass the NCLEX examination to become a registered nurse.

- pass the American Midwifery Certification Board exams.

- hold an active RN license in the state in which they practice.

- keep up to date on latest medical knowledge as pertains to their field.

Certified nurse-midwife services are services furnished by a certified nurse-midwife and such services and supplies as are incident to nurse-midwife service. The service must be authorized under state law.

The definition of nurse-midwife services includes coverage of services outside the maternity cycle.

The amount paid by Part B (Medical Insurance) for such services is based upon a fee schedule and generally is covered to the same extent such services would be covered if performed by a physician. (Medicare will pay 80 percent of the lesser of the actual charge or 100 percent of the physician fee schedule charge for the service.) Payment is made by assignment only, however.

1108. Is dental work covered under Part B (Medical Insurance)?

Yes, but only in some specific instances. Part B (Medical Insurance) helps pay for services of a dentist in certain cases when the medical problem is more extensive than the teeth or structures directly supporting the teeth. Dental work for jaw or facial bone surgery, whether required because of accident or disease, is covered. If a patient needs to be hospitalized because of the severity of a dental procedure, Part A (Hospital Insurance) may pay for the patient's inpatient hospital stay even if the dental care itself is not covered by Medicare.

Keep in mind that Part B (Medical Insurance) generally does not pay for routine dental care, such as the treatment, cleaning, procedures, filling, removal, or replacement of teeth or other dental devices; root canal therapy; surgery for impacted teeth; or other surgical procedures involving the teeth or structures directly supporting the teeth.

1109. What medical equipment is covered under Part B (Medical Insurance)?

Part B (Medical Insurance) covers a wide array of medical equipment, including: surgical dressings, splints, casts, and other devices for reduction of fractures and dislocations; rental or purchase of durable medical equipment, such as iron lungs, oxygen tents, hospital beds, and wheelchairs, for use in the patient's home; prosthetic devices, such as artificial heart valves or synthetic arteries, designed to replace part or all of an internal organ (but not false teeth, hearing aids, or eyeglasses); colostomy or ileostomy bags and certain related supplies; breast prostheses (including a surgical brassiere) after a mastectomy; braces for arm, leg, back, or neck; and artificial limbs and eyes. Orthopedic shoes are not covered unless they are part of leg braces and the cost is included in the orthopedist's charge. Adhesive tape, antiseptics, and other common first-aid supplies are also not included.

Durable medical equipment is equipment that can be used again by other patients, must primarily serve a medical purpose, must not be useful to people who are not sick or injured, and must be appropriate for use in the patient's home. Part B (Medical Insurance) pays for different kinds of durable medical equipment in different ways: some equipment must be rented, other equipment must be purchased, and for some equipment the patient may choose rental or purchase. A doctor should prescribe medical equipment for the patient.

Medicare covers medically necessary Durable Medical Equipment (DME) that your doctor prescribes for use in your home. Only your doctor can prescribe medical equipment. Depending on the equipment, the patient may need to rent the equipment, buy the equipment or have a choice whether to rent or buy. DME meets these criteria:

- Durable (can withstand repeated use);

- Used for a medical reason;

- Not usually useful to someone who isn't sick or injured;

- Used in the patient's home;

- Has an expected lifetime of at least three years.

Suppliers of medical equipment and supplies (durable medical equipment, prosthetic devices, orthotics and prosthetics, surgical dressings, home dialysis supplies and equipment, immuno-suppressive drugs, therapeutic shoes for diabetics, oral cancer drugs, and self-administered erythropoietin) are not reimbursed by Medicare for these items unless they have a Medicare supplier number. A supplier cannot obtain a supplier number unless the supplier meets uniform national standards.

The standards require suppliers to:

(1)   comply with all applicable state and federal licensure and regulatory requirements;

(2)   maintain a physical facility;

(3)   have proof of appropriate liability insurance; and

(4)   meet other requirements established by the Centers for Medicare & Medicaid Services.

The requirement for suppliers to obtain a supplier number does not apply to medical equipment and supplies furnished as incident to a physician's service.

1110. Is ambulance service covered by Part B (Medical Insurance)?

Yes. Part B (Medical Insurance) helps pay for the "reasonable costs" of medically necessary ambulance transportation, including air ambulances, but only if the patient's condition does not permit the use of other methods of transportation and the ambulance, equipment and personnel meet Medicare requirements. Part B (Medical Insurance) can help pay for ambulance transportation from the scene of an accident to a hospital, from a patient's home to a hospital or skilled nursing facility, between hospitals and skilled nursing facilities, critical access hospital, or from a hospital or skilled nursing facility to the patient's home. Also, if the patient is an inpatient in a hospital or skilled nursing facility that cannot provide a medically necessary service, Part B can help pay for round-trip ambulance transportation to the nearest appropriate facility. Medicare does not pay for ambulance use from a patient's home to a doctor's office.

Some individuals may be affected by a Medicare demonstration program if:

- They have repetitive, scheduled, non-emergency ambulance transportation for three or more round trips in a ten-day period or at least once a week for three weeks or more

- The transportation is from an ambulance company based in one of these states:

  o   Arkansas

- ○ Colorado
- ○ Delaware
- ○ District of Columbia
- ○ Louisiana
- ○ Maryland
- ○ Mississippi
- ○ New Mexico
- ○ New Jersey
- ○ North Carolina
- ○ Oklahoma
- ○ Pennsylvania
- ○ South Carolina
- ○ Texas
- ○ Virginia
- ○ West Virginia

Under this demonstration, the ambulance company may send a request for prior authorization to Medicare before the fourth round trip in a thirty-day period. They'll do this so everyone will know earlier in the process if Medicare is likely to cover the services.

If prior authorization request isn't approved and the person continues getting these services, Medicare will deny the claim and the ambulance company may bill the patient for all charges. Either the patient or the ambulance service can request prior authorization. If prior authorization request isn't approved and services continue, Medicare will deny the claim and the ambulance company may bill the patient for all charges.

In some cases, Medicare may cover non-emergency ambulance transportation when these apply:

- End-Stage Renal Disease (ESRD)
- Need for dialysis
- Need ambulance transportation to or from a dialysis facility

Part B (Medical Insurance) usually helps pay for ambulance transportation only in the patient's local area. However, if there are no local facilities equipped to provide the care the patient needs, Part B will help pay for necessary ambulance transportation to the closest facility outside the patient's local area that can provide the necessary care. If the patient chooses to go to another institution that is farther away, Medicare payment will be based on the reasonable charge for transportation to the closest facility.

Necessary ambulance services in connection with a covered inpatient stay in a Canadian or Mexican hospital may also be covered by Part B.

Medicare pays for use of an air ambulance only in extremely urgent emergency situations. If a patient could have been moved by land ambulance without serious danger to life or health, Medicare pays only the land ambulance rate. The patient is responsible for the difference between the air ambulance rate and the land ambulance rate. Medicare MAY pay for emergency ambulance transportation in an airplane or helicopter if the health condition requires immediate and rapid ambulance transportation that ground transportation can't provide, and one of these applies:

- The pickup location can't be easily reached by ground transportation.

- Long distances or other obstacles, like heavy traffic, could stop from getting to care quickly if traveled by ground ambulance.

Coverage during Covid-19

During the COVID-19 public health emergency, CMS has expanded the list of Medicare-covered destinations to include all destinations that are equipped to treat the condition of the patient consistent with EMS protocols established by state and/or local laws where the services will be furnished. Approved alternative destinations may include, but are not limited to:

- Any location that is an alternative site determined to be part of a hospital, critical access hospital or skilled nursing facility;

- Community mental health centers;

- Federal qualified health clinic;

- Rural health clinics;

- Physicians' offices;

- Urgent care facilities;

- Ambulatory surgery centers;

- Any location furnishing dialysis services outside of an end-stage renal disease (ESRD) facility when an ESRD facility is not available; and

- The beneficiary's home.

This destination expansion applies to emergency and non-emergency ground ambulance transports of beneficiaries from any point of origin during the public health emergency for COVID-19. This list of covered alternative destinations during the pandemic applies to all types of ambulance services in the U.S. that bill Medicare.

Ordinarily, Medicare would only reimburse for transports to "covered destinations" such as hospitals, critical access hospitals and skilled nursing facilities. The expanded list recognizes the increased use of healthcare resources and also acknowledges that patients may be appropriately treated at a non-hospital or other destinations due to the overcrowding seen in hospital emergency rooms. Section 9832 of the American Rescue Plan of 2021 has included the expansion of ambulance services during the COVID-19 pandemic.[1]

Note

1. https://www.cms.gov/files/document/covid-waiver-medicare-ground-ambulance-services-treatment-place.pdf.

1111. How much will Medicare Part B (Medical Insurance) pay for outpatient treatment of mental illness?

Part B (Medical Insurance) helps pay the cost of outpatient mental health services a patient receives from physicians, clinical psychologists, clinical social workers, and other non-physician practitioners. Prior to 2014, when treatment was furnished on an outpatient basis, mental health treatment services were subject to a payment limitation called the "outpatient mental health limitation". Under this limitation, Part B paid a lower percentage for mental health services than for other services. Beginning in 2014, however, Part B (Medical Insurance) began to pay 80 percent of approved charges for outpatient mental health services just as for most other Part B services. Additionally, coverage of these services is increasingly available via telemedicine.

Partial hospitalization (sometimes called day treatment) is a program of outpatient mental health care. Partial hospitalization services mean a distinct and organized intensive ambulatory treatment program that offers less than twenty-four-hour daily care and furnishes mental health care services. Under certain conditions, Part B (Medical Insurance) helps pay for these programs when provided by hospital outpatient departments or by community mental health centers.

The Centers for Medicare & Medicaid Services (CMS) define community mental health centers as any entity that:

(1)   provides outpatient services, including specialized outpatient services for children, the elderly, individuals who are chronically mentally ill, and residents of its mental health service area who have been discharged from inpatient treatment at a mental health facility;

(2)   provides twenty-four-hour-a-day emergency care services;

(3)   provides day treatment or other partial hospitalization services, or psychosocial rehabilitation services;

(4)   provides screening for patients being considered for admission to state mental health facilities;

(5)   provides consultation and education services; and

(6)   meets applicable licensing or certification requirements for community mental health centers in the state in which it is located.

1112. What mental health services does Medicare Part B cover?

Medicare Part B (Medical Insurance) covers mental health services and visits with these types of health professionals: Psychiatrist or other doctors, Clinical psychologists, Clinical social workers, Clinical nurse specialist, Nurse practitioners, and Physician assistants. Medicare only covers these visits, often called counseling or therapy, when they're provided by a health care provider who accepts assignment. Many of these services are available through telemedicine.

Part B covers outpatient mental health services, including services that are usually provided outside a hospital, like in these settings: A doctor's or other health care provider's office, a hospital outpatient department, a community mental health center.

Part B also covers outpatient mental health services for treatment of inappropriate alcohol and drug use.

Part B helps pay for these covered outpatient services:

- One depression screening per year which must be done in a primary care doctor's office or primary care clinic that can provide follow-up treatment and referrals

- Individual and group psychotherapy with doctors or certain other licensed professionals

- Family counseling – if intended to help the Medicare patient

- Testing to find out if the subscriber is getting the services needed and if current treatment is helping

- Psychiatric evaluation

- Medication management

- Certain prescription drugs that aren't usually "self-administered"

- Diagnostic tests

- Partial hospitalization

- A one-time "Welcome to Medicare" visit. This visit includes a review of potential risk factors for depression

- A yearly "wellness" visit

- Additionally, outpatient mental health services for substance abuse is covered under Part B

1113. When is the cost of vaccines covered?

Medicare Part B provides preventive coverage certain vaccinations including;

- Influenza: once per flu season (covers vaccine and administration)

- Pneumococcal: once per lifetime with high-risk booster after 5 years)

- Hepatitis B: for persons at intermediate- to high-risk (when administered in a hospital or renal dialysis facility

Other immunizations are covered under Medicare Part B only if they are directly related to the treatment of an injury or direct exposure (such as anti-rabies treatment, tetanus antitoxin, or booster vaccine, botulin antitoxin, antivenin, or immune globulin).

Neither the annual deductible nor the Part B (Medical Insurance) 20 percent coinsurance applies to flu and pneumonia vaccines. If the provider giving the patient the shot accepts assignment (i.e., accepts the Medicare payment as payment in full), there will be no cost to the patient. If the provider does not accept assignment, the patient may have to pay charges in addition to the Medicare-approved amount. Any health care professional complying with the Medicare rules can give a patient a flu shot or the pneumonia vaccine.

As discussed earlier, the COVID-19 testing and vaccinations are covered.

Coverage of other vaccines provided as a preventive service may be covered under a patient's Part D coverage.

1114. Is the cost of antigens covered under Part B (Medical Insurance)?

Under certain circumstances, Part B (Medical Insurance) helps pay for antigens prepared for a patient by a physician, but only if the physician preparing the antigens also has examined the patient and developed the plan of treatment and dosage.

1115. When are organ transplants covered under Part B (Medical Insurance)?

Part B (Medical Insurance) provides coverage for liver transplants for adult Medicare beneficiaries depending on the medical reason for the transplant. Generally, Part B covers transplants for end-stage liver disease unrelated to malignancies. Effective in 2012, Medicare Administrative Contractors also became authorized to cover liver transplants in cases involving specified types of malignancies.

In addition, Part A covers the transplant of the following organs at Medicare-certified facilities: Heart, lung, kidney (in-patient services, kidney registry fee, related lab tests, cost of finding the kidney, costs of care for the donor, blood), pancreas (coupled with ESRD and kidney transplant), intestine, liver.

Part A also covers some stem cell transplants under certain conditions. Part B covers corneal transplants, under some conditions. Stem cell and corneal transplants are not limited to Medicare-approved transplant centers.

1116. Can Part B (Medical Insurance) help pay for outpatient services at a comprehensive outpatient rehabilitation facility?

Under certain circumstances, Part B (Medical Insurance) helps pay for outpatient services received from a Medicare-participating Comprehensive Outpatient Rehabilitation Facility (CORF).

Outpatient services must be performed by a doctor or other qualified professional. Covered services include physicians' services; physical, speech, occupation, and respiratory therapies; counseling; and other related services. A CORF patient must be referred by a physician who certifies that there is a need for skilled rehabilitation services and creates (and periodically reviews) a plan of treatment for the patient.

Until 2019, CORF services were generally subject to a special prospective payment system and to an annual limit applicable to all kinds of outpatient rehabilitation services (often referred to as the "therapy cap"). However, on February 9, 2018, President Trump signed into law the Bipartisan Budget Act of 2018 (BBA of 2018) (Public Law 115-123). This new law includes two provisions related to Medicare payment for outpatient therapy services including physical therapy (PT), speech-language pathology (SLP), and occupational therapy (OT) services:

- Section 50202 of the BBA of 2018 repeals application of the Medicare outpatient therapy caps and its exceptions process while adding limitations to ensure appropriate therapy.

- Section 53107 of the BBA of 2018 relates to the payment of OT and PT services furnished by an assistant.

The new law, through section 50202 of the BBA of 2018, preserves the former therapy cap amounts as thresholds above which claims must include confirmation that services are medically necessary as justified by appropriate documentation in the medical record. Just as with the incurred expenses for the therapy cap amounts, there is one amount for PT and SLP services combined and a separate amount for OT services. For 2021 the cap is:

- $2,150 for PT and SLP services combined, and

- $22,150 for OT services.

The new law also retains the targeted medical review (MR) process, but at a lower threshold amount of $3,000. From CY 2018 (and each calendar year until 2028 at which time it is indexed annually by the MEI), the MR threshold is $3,000 for PT and SLP services and $3,000 for OT services. The targeted MR process means that not all claims exceeding the MR threshold amount are subject to review as they once were.

1117. Are home health services covered under Part B (Medical Insurance)?

For Medicare beneficiaries who have both Part A (Hospital Insurance) and Part B (Medical Insurance) coverage, home health services not directly related to hospital or skilled nursing facility stays are now covered and paid for by Part B (Medical Insurance).

Part A (Hospital Insurance) covers up to 100 post institutional home health care visits for beneficiaries with both Parts A and B. Home health services covered by Part B (Medical Insurance) tend to be for chronic conditions and are different from home care services needed for convalescence and rehabilitation following a hospital stay. If a Medicare beneficiary continues to need home health care following exhaustion of Part A coverage, however, Part B also covers such care. Medicare pays for the costs of part-time skilled care with no coinsurance requirement and for 80 percent of the cost of durable medical equipment when supplied by a certified home health agency.

1117.01. What are the eligibility requirements for Home Health Care?

A Medicare recipient is eligible for Home Health Care if:

- They are under the care of a doctor and getting services under a plan of care that has been established and reviewed regularly by a doctor or other approved medical provider.

- A doctor certifies the need of at least one of the following:

  - Intermittent skilled nursing care (other than drawing blood)

  - Physical therapy

  - Speech-language pathology services

  - Continued occupational therapy

- The home health agency providing care is Medicare-certified

- A doctor certifies that the recipient is homebound. Qualifications include:

  - Trouble leaving home without help (like using a cane, wheelchair, walker, or crutches; special transportation; or help from another person) because of an illness or injury, or leaving home isn't recommended because of the recipient's medical condition.

- The recipient is normally unable to leave home but requires a major effort to do so.

  - The recipient may leave home for medical treatment or short, infrequent absences for non-medical reasons, like an occasional trip to the barber, a walk around the block or a drive, or attendance at a family reunion, funeral, graduation or other infrequent or unique event.

  - The recipient can still get home health care if attending adult day care or religious services.

- As part of certification of eligibility, a doctor, or approved health care professional must document that they've had a face-to-face encounter with the recipient within required timeframes and that the encounter was related to the reason requiring home health care.

- If a recipient needs more than "intermittent" skilled nursing care, they will not qualify for home health services.

  - Medicare defines "intermittent" as skilled nursing care that's needed:

    - Fewer than 7 days each week.

    - Daily for less than 8 hours each day for up to 21 days. In some cases, Medicare may extend the three week limit if the doctor can predict when the need for daily skilled nursing care will end. If expected to need full-time skilled nursing care over an extended period of time, the recipient would not generally qualify for home health benefits.

1118. Are independent clinical laboratory services covered under Part B (Medical Insurance)?

Part B (Medical Insurance) pays the full approved fee for covered clinical diagnostic tests provided by certain independent laboratories (or laboratories in physicians' offices) that are participating in Medicare. Such laboratories must be licensed in accordance with applicable state and local law (or otherwise approved for such licensure) and must also meet certain requirements specified in the Clinical Laboratory Improvement Amendments of 1988. In order to be paid by Medicare for approved charges, such laboratories must accept assignment for the tests and not bill the patient for the tests.

1119. Does Medicare Part B (Medical Insurance) reimburse for clinical research studies?

Possibly. Clinical research studies test how well different types of medical care work and if they are safe. Medicare covers some costs, like office visits and tests, in qualifying clinical research studies. The patient may pay 20 percent of the Medicare approved amount, and the Part B deductible may apply.

Benefits may include:

- Access to specialized health care

- Access to new drugs and treatments before they become widely available

- Health professionals who monitor a recipient's health care closely for any side effects

- Making an important contribution to research that may help others with the same illness

Risks may include:

- Side effects of new drugs and treatments

- Being treated with drugs and procedures that are either not effective, or less effective, than current approaches

- Not benefiting from a drug or treatment that may benefit others, or being in the placebo group

- Significant time commitment and frequent trips to the study site

Medicare Advantage Plans

Medicare Advantage Plans, or other Medicare health plan, afford the same coverage for clinical research studies as a person in Original Medicare. If the recipient joins certain covered clinical research studies, Medicare will pay for covered services as if in Original Medicare. The Medicare Advantage health plan cannot keep someone from joining a clinical research study.

1120. Are screening pap smears and pelvic exams covered by Part B (Medical Insurance)?

Generally, a screening pap smear and pelvic exam (including a clinical breast exam) are covered every twenty-four months for all women for cervical and vaginal cancer screenings.

Annual coverage is provided for women:

(1)   at high risk for cervical or vaginal cancer; or

(2)   of childbearing age who have had a pap smear during the preceding three years indicating the presence of cervical or vaginal cancer or other abnormality.

The Part B deductible is waived for screening pap smears and pelvic exams. Pelvic exams are paid under the physician fee schedule as are Pap test specimen collection, and breast exams.

1121. What items does Medicare NOT cover?

1. Medically unreasonable and unnecessary services and supplies to diagnose and treat a patient's condition

2. Noncovered items and services

    o   **Custodial Care** (such as long-term care services & supports) - Medicare Fee-for-Service doesn't cover custodial care in the patient's home or an institution. Custodial care is personal care that requires no trained medical or paramedical personnel continuing attention and serves to help an individual in the activities of daily living. There are some exceptions.

    o   Items & Services Furnished Outside the United States

        ▪   Medicare doesn't cover most items and services delivered outside the United States (U.S.) including when the patient purchased the item in the U.S. or purchased the item from an American firm. Medicare won't pay for a medical service sub-contracted to another provider or supplier outside the U.S.

        ▪   Medicare doesn't pay for provider professional services outside the U.S., except for certain limited services.

    o   Items & Services Required as a Result of War

        ▪   Medicare doesn't cover items and services required because of war or an act of war that occur after the effective date of the patient's current entitlement.

    o   Personal Comfort Items & Services

        ▪   Home safety items, such as grab bars in the bathroom, stair lifts or elevators, bathtub lifts or seats, medical emergency alert systems, etc.

        ▪   Medicare coverage is available for a few items it deems medically reasonable if a doctor prescribes them such as seat lifts or trapeze bars.

        ▪   Medicare doesn't cover personal comfort items because these items don't meaningfully contribute to treating a patient's illness or injury or the functioning of a malformed body member.

        ▪   Exceptions - Medicare may cover certain basic personal resident services in a SNF or general psychiatric hospital when they can't perform them for themselves.

    o   Routine Physical Checkups and examinations; Eye Examinations for prescription glasses, Eyeglasses & Lenses; Hearing Aids, Examinations and fittings; Chiropractor Services; & Certain Immunizations

- ○ Cosmetic Surgery (with some exceptions)

- ○ Items & Services Furnished by the Patient's Immediate Relatives & Members of the Patient's Household

- ○ Massage therapy

- ○ Medicare doesn't pay for items and services furnished by the patient's immediate relatives and members of the patient's household since these items and services are ordinarily furnished at no charge because of their relationship

- ○ Concierge care (also called concierge medicine, retainer-based medicine, boutique medicine, platinum practice, or direct care)

- ○ Dental Services

    - ▪ Medicare doesn't cover items and services for the care, treatment, filling, removal, or replacement of teeth or the structures directly supporting the teeth, such as preparing the mouth for dentures, or removing diseased teeth in an infected jaw

- ○ Inpatient Hospital or SNF Services Not Delivered Directly or Under Arrangement by the Provider Medicare normally excludes coverage for non-physician services to Part A or Part B hospital inpatients unless those services are provided either directly by the hospital/SNF or under an arrangement that the hospital/SNF makes with an outside source

- ○ Certain Foot Care Services & Supportive Devices for the Feet such as toenail clipping or the removal of corns and calluses

    - ▪ Exception: if the patient has foot problems caused by conditions such as diabetes, cancer, multiple sclerosis, chronic kidney disease, malnutrition or inflammation of the veins related to blood clots. (Medicare coverage is provided only if the doctor or podiatrist provides evidence that foot care is medically necessary.)

- ○ Investigational Devices Medicare may cover Category B devices if considered medically reasonable and necessary and they meet all other Medicare coverage requirements.

3. Services & Supplies Denied as Bundled or Included in the Basic Allowance of Another Service

4. Items & Services Reimbursable by Other Organizations or Furnished Without Charge A. Services Reimbursable Under the Medicare Secondary Payer Program

    - ○ Services Reimbursable Under the Medicare Secondary Payer Program

    ○   Items & Services Authorized or Paid by a Government Entity Medicare normally doesn't pay for these items and services authorized or paid by a government entity.

    ○   Items & Services the Patient, Another Individual, or an Organization Has No Legal Obligation to Pay for or Furnish Items

    ○   Defective Equipment or Medical Devices Covered Under

1122. Are breast cancer screening and diagnostic mammography covered by Part B (Medical Insurance)?

Yes. Screening mammography and diagnostic mammography are both covered.

"Screening mammography" is defined as a radiologic procedure furnished to a woman without signs or symptoms of breast disease, for the purpose of early detection of breast cancer, and includes a physician's interpretation of the results of the procedure.

"Diagnostic mammography" means a radiologic procedure furnished to a man or woman with signs or symptoms of breast disease, or a personal history of breast cancer or a personal history of biopsy-proven benign breast disease and includes a physician's interpretation of the results of the procedure.

Medicare covers an annual screening (eleven full months must have passed since the last screening) mammogram for all women aged forty and over. Women with Part B between ages thirty-five and thirty-nine can get one baseline mammogram.

Diagnostic mammogram is available whenever medically necessary. The Part B deductible for screening mammography is waived.

1123. Are prostate screening tests covered under Part B (Medical Insurance)?

Annual prostate cancer screening for men aged fifty and older is covered.

Covered procedures include (once every twelve months):

    (1)   digital rectal exam; and

    (2)   Prostate-Specific Antigen (PSA) blood test.

No Part B deductible or coinsurance is required for the screening PSA blood test, but Part B deductible and coinsurance is required regarding the rectal exam. Payment to providers for the PSA blood test will be made under the clinical laboratory fee schedule, and other services will be paid under the physician fee schedule.

1124. How is colorectal screening covered under Part B (Medical Insurance)?

Covered colorectal screening procedures include several types of colorectal cancer screening tests to help find precancerous growths or find cancer early. The following tests are included:

(1) **Screening Fecal Occult Blood Test**: A fecal occult blood test every twelve months for persons aged fifty and over. (Covered at 100 percent of Medicare-approved amount)

(2) **Screening Flexible Sigmoidoscopy**: Flexible sigmoidoscopy for persons aged fifty and over, to be done once every four years. (Covered at 100 percent of Medicare-approved amount)

(3) **Screening Colonoscopy**: A screening colonoscopy for persons at high risk for colorectal cancer, to be done once every twenty-four months (every ten years for all others – or forty-eight months after a previous flexible sigmoidoscopy). (Covered at 100 percent of Medicare-approved amount). There is no minimum age for this coverage.

- If the doctor or other qualified health care provider accepts assignment, there is no charge for this test. However, if a polyp or other tissue is found and removed during the colonoscopy, the beneficiary pays 15% of the Medicare-Approved Amount for the doctors' services. In a hospital outpatient setting, the beneficiary also pays the hospital a 15% coinsurance. The Part B deductible does not apply.

(4) **Screening Barium Enema**: A screening barium enema for persons aged fifty and over, to be done every forty-eight months for those deemed not at high risk and every twenty-four months for others. The Part B deductible is waived for these exams, but Part B co-insurance is increased to 25 percent for a patient for both flexible sigmoidoscopies and colonoscopies. Payment for screening colonoscopies is made only when the procedures are performed in a hospital.

(5) **Multitarget stool DNA Test (Cologuard)**: Medicare covers this test at 100 percent of Medicare-approved amount once every thirty-six months for people that meet ALL of the below conditions:

- Aged 50 to 85

- Show no signs or symptoms of colorectal disease including, but not limited to:

    o   lower gastrointestinal pain

    o   blood in stool

    o   positive guaiac fecal occult blood test or fecal immunochemical test

      ○   average risk for developing colorectal cancer, meaning

      ○   no personal history of adenomatous polyps, colorectal cancer, inflammatory bowel disease, including Crohn's Disease and ulcerative colitis

      ○   no family history of colorectal cancers or adenomatous polyps, familial adenomatous polyposis, or hereditary nonpolyposis colorectal cancer.

Costs in Original Medicare

- For barium enemas, cost is twenty percent of the Medicare-approved amount for the doctor's services. In a hospital outpatient setting, a copayment is incurred.

- In 2023, there is no charge for a multi-target stool DNA test (like Cologuard) if the doctor accepts assignment.

- If a screening colonoscopy or screening flexible sigmoidoscopy results in the biopsy or removal of a lesion or growth during the same visit, the procedure is considered diagnostic and coinsurance and/or a copayment charge will incur, but the Part B deductible doesn't apply.

- There is no charge for the screening fecal occult blood test. This screening test is covered with a referral from your doctor, physician assistant, nurse practitioner, or clinical nurse specialist.

- There is no charge for the screening colonoscopy or screening flexible sigmoidoscopy, if the doctor accepts assignment.

1125. Are diabetes self-management services covered under Part B Medical Insurance?

Services furnished in nonhospital-based programs for diabetes outpatient self-management training are covered under Part B (Medical Insurance). Medicare will cover up to ten hours of initial diabetes self-management training. This includes tips for eating healthy, being active, monitoring blood sugar, taking medication, and reducing risks. Services must be provided by a certified provider, and the physician (or other qualified health care professional) managing the patient's condition must certify that the services are needed under a comprehensive plan of care. Certified providers for these services include physicians as well as hospital outpatient facilities and dialysis facilities.

This may also include up to two hours of follow-up training each year. Generally, follow up must be in a group setting of two to twenty people, lasting for at least thirty minutes, occur in the calendar year after the initial training, and be ordered by a doctor as part of the plan of care.

Coverage includes certain types of home blood glucose monitors, testing strips, lancets, and self-management training. Medicare also covers certain medical nutrition therapy (nutritional assessment, one-on-one counseling, and therapy services) services for individuals with diabetes or renal disease, but only if they have not separately received diabetes outpatient self-management training within a specified period and are not receiving maintenance dialysis.

1126. Are diabetes screenings covered under Part B (Medical Insurance)?

Part B covers lab tests in the event that the following risk factors exist:

- High blood pressure (hypertension)

- History of abnormal cholesterol and triglyceride levels (dyslipidemia)

- Obesity

- History of high blood sugar (glucose)

Part B also covers these tests if two or more of these apply:

- Age sixty-five or older

- Overweight

- Family history of diabetes (parents, brothers, sisters)

- History of gestational diabetes (diabetes during pregnancy), or delivery of a baby weighing more than nine pounds

Medicare Part B covers blood glucose (blood sugar) laboratory test screenings (with or without a carbohydrate challenge) if the doctor determines risk for developing diabetes. A person is eligible for up to 2 screenings each year.

1127. Are glaucoma tests covered under Part B (Medical Insurance)?

Medicare Part B covers a glaucoma test once every twelve months for people at high risk for glaucoma. The screening must be done or supervised by an eye doctor who's legally allowed to do this test.

Costs include:

- Twenty percent of Medicare-Approved amount after meeting Part B Deductible; and

- a copayment if done in a hospital outpatient setting.

Anyone with Part B who is at high risk for glaucoma is covered. The definition of high risk includes:

- diabetes;

- family history of glaucoma;

- African-American aged fifty or older; and

- Hispanic-American aged sixty-five or older.

1128. Is screening for depression and behavioral health issues covered under Part B (Medical Insurance)?

Yes, Medicare Part B covers one depression screening per year. It must be done in a primary care setting (like a doctor's office) that can provide follow-up treatment and/or referrals, if needed. There is no charge for this screening.

The Psychiatric Collaborative Care Model[1] is a set of integrated behavioral health services that includes care management support for a behavioral health condition. This care management support may include:

- Care planning for behavioral health conditions

- Ongoing assessment of condition

- Medication support

- Counseling

- Other treatment that the provider recommends

Note

1. https://www.cms.gov/Outreach-and-Education/Medicare-Learning-Network-MLN/MLNProducts/Downloads/BehavioralHealthIntegration. pdf (Issued February 2022).

1129. Is screening for Hepatitis C covered under Part B (Medical Insurance)?

Medicare Part B covers one Hepatitis C screening test. Medicare also covers yearly repeat screening for certain people at high risk. Medicare covers 100 percent of Medicare-Approved amount when provided by approved provider.

People with Medicare who meet one of these conditions are eligible:

- Those at high risk because they have a current or past history of illicit injection drug use

- Those who had a blood transfusion before 1992

- Those born between 1945 and 1965

1130. Is screening for HIV covered under Part B (Medical Insurance)?

Medicare Part B covers HIV (Human Immunodeficiency Virus) screenings. HIV is the virus that can lead to AIDS (Acquired Immunodeficiency Syndrome). Medicare covers this test once every twelve months for people who meet the guidelines below. Medicare also covers this screening up to three times during a pregnancy. There is no cost if the doctor or qualified health care provider accepts assignment.

People with Part B are covered if they are:

- younger than 15 and older than 65, and are at increased risk for the virus;

- between 15 and 65, and ask for the test; and

- pregnant at the time of testing.

1131. Is obesity screening and counseling covered under Medicare Part B (Medical Insurance)?

Medicare covers obesity screenings and behavioral counseling sessions to help in weight loss. This counseling may be covered if provided in a primary care setting (like a doctor's office), where it can be coordinated with other care and a personalized prevention plan. Persons with a Body Mass Index (BMI) of thirty or greater are covered. There is no cost if the doctor or provider accepts assignment.

1132. Is tobacco (smoking) cessation and counseling covered under Medicare Part B (Medical Insurance)?

Medicare Part B covers up to eight visits in a twelve-month period. These visits must be provided by a qualified doctor or other Medicare-recognized practitioner. If the provider accepts assignment, there is no charge for the sessions.

1133. Is alcohol misuse/abuse screening and counseling covered under Medicare Part B (Medical Insurance)?

Medicare Part B covers this screening once per year. Eligible persons include:

- Adults with Part B (including pregnant women) who use alcohol, but don't meet the medical criteria for alcohol dependency.

- If the primary care doctor determines misuse of alcohol, four brief face-to-face counseling sessions per year are available (if you're competent and alert during counseling). A qualified primary care doctor or other primary care practitioner must provide the counseling in a primary care setting (like a doctor's office).

1134. Is aortic aneurysm (AAA) screening covered under Medicare Part B (Medical Insurance)?

Medicare Part B covers a one-time abdominal aortic aneurysm ultrasound. A referral for it from a doctor is necessary. Eligible parties include those considered at risk, including:

- those with a family history of abdominal aortic aneurysms;

- a man aged sixty-five to seventy-five who has smoked at least one hundred cigarettes during his lifetime.

- Medicare only covers the AAA ultrasound once in a lifetime. If a provider suggests a second AAA ultrasound, Medicare may deny coverage.

1135. Are Sexually Transmitted Infection (STI) screenings and counseling covered under Medicare Part B (Medical Insurance)?

Medicare Part B covers Sexually Transmitted Infection (STI) screenings for chlamydia, gonorrhea, syphilis, and/or Hepatitis B once every twelve months or at certain times during pregnancy. Medicare also covers up to two individual twenty to thirty minute, face-to-face, high-intensity behavioral counseling sessions each year for sexually active adults at increased risk for STIs.

Eligible individuals include:

- people with Part B who are pregnant and certain people who are at increased risk for an STI when the tests are ordered by a primary care doctor or other primary care practitioner;

- sexually active adults who are at an increased risk for STIs are also eligible for behavioral counseling sessions.

1136. Does Medicare Part B (Medical Insurance) cover bone mass measurements (bone density)?

Part B (Medical Insurance) covers procedures to identify bone mass, detect bone loss, or determine bone quality, including a physician's interpretation of the results.

Persons qualifying for these procedures include:

- estrogen-deficient women at risk for osteoporosis;

- individuals with vertebral abnormalities, osteopenia, or possible osteoporosis which are shown on an x-ray;

- individuals diagnosed with primary hyperparathyroidism;

- persons receiving long-term glucocorticoid steroid therapy for more than three months; and

- individuals being monitored to assess the response to, or efficacy of, an approved osteoporosis drug.

The Part B deductible is waived for these tests. Medicare covers this test once every twenty-four months, or more often if medically necessary. It is only covered when ordered by a doctor or other qualified medical provider. Medicare will also cover follow-up measurements and/or more frequent screening if a doctor prescribes them.

1137. Does Medicare Part B (Medical Insurance) cover cardiovascular disease risk reduction and behavior therapy?

Yes. A cardiovascular disease risk reduction visit is covered that includes:

- Encouraging aspirin use when benefits outweigh risks

- Screening for high blood pressure

- Counseling to promote a healthy diet

Medicare also covers cardiovascular disease screenings that check cholesterol and other blood fat (lipid) levels. High levels of cholesterol can increase for heart disease and stroke. These screenings will identify high cholesterol. Medicare covers these tests every five years to test cholesterol, lipid, lipoprotein, and triglyceride levels.

1138. Does Medicare Part B (Medical Insurance) cover lung cancer screening?

Medicare covers an annual lung cancer screening with Low Dose Computed Tomography (LDCT) for people with Medicare who meet these criteria:

- Age fifty-five though age seventy-seven.

- Asymptomatic of lung cancer.

- Either a current smoker or have quit smoking within the last fifteen years.

- Have a tobacco smoking history of at least twenty "pack years" (an average of one pack a day for twenty years). This is a change from the previous standard of thirty pack years.

- Have a written order from their physician or qualified non-physician practitioner.

- Before the first lung cancer screening, the patient needs to schedule an appointment with their doctor to discuss the benefits and risks of lung cancer screening and decide if the test is right.

    ○   The service is furnished by an appropriate radiology imaging center and a reading radiologist that meet Medicare standards.

1139. Does Medicare Part B (Medical Insurance) cover medical nutrition therapy?

Medicare may cover medical nutrition therapy for those that have diabetes or kidney disease, or have had a kidney transplant in the last 36 months, and the doctor refers this service.

These services can be given by a registered dietitian or Medicare-approved nutrition professional, and include a nutritional assessment and counseling to help manage diabetes or kidney disease.

Individuals covered included those who have ANY of these issues:

- Diabetes

- Renal disease (people who have kidney disease, but aren't on dialysis)

- Have had a kidney transplant within the last three years and doctor refer the patient for this service

Medicare covers three hours of one-on-one counseling services the first year, and two hours each year after that. If conditions, treatment, or diagnosis changes, a doctor's referral can enable more hours of treatment.

A doctor must prescribe these services and renew the referral yearly if continuing treatment is needed into another calendar year.

1140. Are flu shots covered under Medicare Plan B?

Yes. Medicare Part B (Medical Insurance) covers one flu shot per flu season at no cost.

1141. Are cervical and vaginal screenings covered under Medicare Plan B?

Medicare Part B (Medical Insurance) covers Pap tests and pelvic exams to check for cervical and vaginal cancer. As part of the exam, Part B also covers a clinical breast exam to check for breast cancer.

Part B covers these screening tests once every twenty-four months for all women, and once every twelve months if

    (1)   the patient is at high risk for cervical or vaginal cancer or

    (2)   the patient is of childbearing age and have had an abnormal Pap test in the past thirty-six months.

Part B also covers Human Papillomavirus (HPV) tests (when received with a Pap test) once every five years if aged thirty to sixty-five without HPV symptoms.

What's covered:

- the lab Pap test

- the lab HPV with Pap test

- the Pap test specimen collection

- the pelvic and breast exams

1142. What is the "Welcome to Medicare" visit and the annual yearly screenings?

A **"Welcome to Medicare" preventive visit:** A person can get this visit only within the first twelve months having Part B. This visit includes a review of medical and social history related to health and education and counseling about preventive services, including these:

- Certain screenings, flu and pneumococcal shots, and referrals for other care, if needed

- Height, weight, and blood pressure measurements

- A calculation of body mass index

- A simple vision test

- A review of potential risk for depression and level of safety

- An offer to talk about creating advance directives

- A written plan as to which screenings, shots, and other preventive services are needed

This visit is covered one time. One does not need to have this visit to be covered for yearly "Wellness" visits.

Yearly "Wellness" visits: This visit is to develop or update a personalized prevention help plan. This plan is designed to help prevent disease and disability based on current health and risk factors. A questionnaire, called a "Health Risk Assessment," is completed as part of this visit. It can also include:

- A review of medical and family history.

- Developing or updating a list of current providers and prescriptions.

- Height, weight, blood pressure, and other routine measurements.

- Detection of any cognitive impairment.

- Personalized health advice.

- A list of risk factors and treatment options.

- A screening schedule (like a checklist) for appropriate preventive services.

A new coverage added during 2022 and subsequent years for an individual with a current prescription for opioids where the provider can review potential risk factors for opioid use disorder, evaluate the severity of pain and current treatment plan, provide information on non-opioid treatment options, and may refer the individual to a specialist, if appropriate. The provider will also review potential risk factors for substance use disorder (including alcohol and tobacco use) and refer the person for treatment, if needed.

An additional new coverage is for the medical provider to perform a cognitive assessment to look for signs of dementia, including Alzheimer's disease. If the provider thinks the individual has cognitive impairment, Medicare covers a separate visit to do a more thorough review of cognitive function and check for conditions like dementia, depression, anxiety, or delirium.

1143. Does Medicare Part B covers Hepatitis B shots?

Yes. People with Part B at medium or high risk for Hepatitis B are covered. The risk for Hepatitis B increases if one of these applies:

- hemophilia

- end-stage renal disease (ESRD)

- diabetes

- living with someone who has Hepatitis B

- employed as a health care worker and have frequent contact with blood or bodily fluids

Other factors may also increase risk for Hepatitis B.

1144. Does Medicare Part B covers pneumococcal shots?

Yes. Medicare Part B covers pneumococcal shots to help prevent pneumococcal infections (like certain types of pneumonia). Medicare now covers both a single dose vaccination as well as a two-shot vaccination. The vaccinations protect against different strains of the bacteria. If opting for the two-shot, Medicare covers the first shot at any time, and also covers a different second shot if it's given one year (or later) after the first shot. The doctor or provider will advise whether a person needs one or both of the two-shot series of pneumococcal shots.

1145. Under what conditions is an injectable drug for postmenopausal osteoporosis covered by Part B (Medical Insurance)?

The cost of an injectable drug provided by a home health agency to a patient for the treatment of a bone fracture related to postmenopausal osteoporosis is covered under the following conditions:

(1)   the patient's attending physician certifies that the patient has suffered a bone fracture related to postmenopausal osteoporosis and is unable to learn the skills needed to self-administer (or is physically or mentally incapable of administering) the drug; and

(2)   the patient is confined to the patient's home (in such a way as meets the requirements for Medicare coverage of home health services).

1146. When are eyeglasses covered under Part B (Medical Insurance)?

Generally, Medicare Part B does not generally pay for eyeglasses or contact lenses.

Part B (Medical Insurance) will pay for one pair of conventional eyeglasses (standard frames) or conventional contact lenses if necessary, after cataract surgery with insertion of an intraocular lens.

Part B (Medical Insurance) will also pay for cataract spectacles, cataract contact lenses, or intraocular lenses that replace the natural lens of the eye after cataract surgery.

Medicare Part B does not pay for routine eye exams or eyeglasses. The beneficiary pays 20 percent of the Medicare-approved amount for one pair of eyeglasses or one set of contact lenses after each cataract surgery with an intraocular lens. Medicare will only pay for contact lenses or eyeglasses from a supplier enrolled in Medicare, no matter who submits the claim. The beneficiary must pay additional costs of upgraded frames and also 100 percent of non-covered services. The Part B deductible applies.

1147. Under what circumstances are the services of nurse practitioners and clinical nurse specialists covered under Part B (Medical Insurance)?

The services of nurse practitioners and clinical nurse specialists are covered when the services performed are those authorized under state law and regulations, provided there is no facility or other provider charges paid in connection with the service. Also, a clinical nurse specialist must be a registered nurse licensed to practice in the state who holds a master's degree in a defined clinical area of nursing and from an accredited educational institution.

1148. When are organ transplants covered under Part B (Medical Insurance)?

Medicare covers doctors' services associated with heart, lung, kidney, pancreas, intestine, and liver organ transplants.

Additionally Part B will sometimes cover bone marrow and cornea transplants.

Part B also covers immunosuppressive drugs (if Medicare paid for the organ transplant). The patient must have Part A at the time of transplant and have Part B at the time of being pre-scribed immunosuppressive drugs.

If the patient only has Medicare because of End-Stage Renal Disease (ESRD), Medicare coverage—and immunosuppressive drug coverage—will end 36 months after a kidney transplant.

BEGINNING JANUARY 2023 – Medicare has implemented a new benefit to help pay for immunosuppressive drugs after thirty-six months, if the patient has no other health coverage. It should be noted that the new benefit is coverage solely for immunosuppressive drugs in this particular instance and covers no other items of services.

COVERAGE

- 20% of the Medicare-Approved Amount for doctor's services after meeting the Part B deductible

- Various costs for transplant facility charges.

- Nothing is paid to the living donor for a kidney transplant.

- No costs for Medicare-certified laboratory tests.

1149. What are the conditions for coverage of prescription drugs used in immunosuppressive therapy covered under Part B (Medical Insurance)?

Payment may be made for prescription drugs used in immunosuppressive therapy that have been approved for marketing by the Food and Drug Administration and that meet one of the following conditions:

(1)   The approved labeling includes the indication for preventing or treating the rejec-tion of a transplanted organ or tissue.

(2)   The approved labeling includes the indication for use in conjunction with immu-nosuppressive drugs to prevent or treat rejection of a transplanted organ or tissue.

(3)   The drugs have been determined by a Medicare Administrative Contractor to be reasonable and necessary for the specific purpose of preventing or treating the rejection of a patient's transplanted organ or tissue, or for use in conjunction with immunosuppressive drugs for the purpose of preventing or treating the rejection of a patient's transplanted organ or tissue.

Coverage under Part B (Medical Insurance) is generally available only for prescription drugs used in immunosuppressive therapy, furnished to an individual who receives an organ or tissue transplant for which Medicare payment is made.

Such drugs are covered regardless of whether they can be self-administered.

1150. Are ambulatory surgical services covered under Part B (Medical Insurance)?

An ambulatory surgical center is a facility that provides surgical services that do not require a hospital stay (outpatient). Part B (Medical Insurance) will pay for the use of an ambulatory surgical center for certain approved surgical procedures, generally those that do not pose a significant risk to the patient's health if performed in an outpatient setting (and that do not typically require an overnight hospital stay). The center must have an agreement to participate in the Medicare program. Medicare also helps pay for physician and anesthesia services that are provided in connection with the procedure. In most cases, the person is released within 24 hours.

1151. When are rural health clinic (RHC) services covered by Part B (Medical Insurance)?

Part B (Medical Insurance) helps pay for services of physicians, nurse practitioners, physician assistants, nurse midwives, visiting nurses (under certain circumstances), clinical psychologists, and clinical social workers furnished by a rural health clinic. Part B (Medical Insurance) also helps pay for certain laboratory tests in these clinics. The patient is responsible for the annual Part B (Medical Insurance) deductible plus 20 percent of the Medicare-approved charge for the clinic services.

Rural health clinics must meet requirements concerning where they are located. There are approximately 4,500 certified rural health clinics in the US as of 2022, which is a decline of 300 clinics since 2020. They must be in areas where there are insufficient numbers of needed health care practitioners (not just primary care physicians). Clinics that no longer meet the shortage area requirements will be permitted to retain their designation only if the Centers for Medicare & Medicaid Services (CMS) determines that such clinics are essential to the delivery of primary care services that would otherwise be unavailable in the area. The only states with no RHCs are Alaska, Connecticut, Delaware, New Jersey, Rhode Island, and the District of Columbia.

The following services are available:

- Physician services

- Nurse practitioner, physician assistant, certified nurse-midwife, clinical psychologist, and clinical social worker services

- Certain care management services

- Certain laboratory services on site

- Certain virtual communication services (see next question)

- Drugs covered by Medicare Part B that are integral to the services the RHC provides

- Immunization services including flu, pneumonia, hepatitis B, and COVID-19 shots

- Services and supplies that are integral to the services provided the RHC's health care professionals' services

- Arrangements with one or more hospitals to provide necessary medical services not available through the RHC

- Visiting nurse services to homebound Medicare beneficiaries (in areas Medicare certifies there is a shortage of home health agencies)

1152. Does Medicare Part B (Medical Insurance) reimburse for telehealth services in rural areas?

Part B (Medical Insurance) payments are made for professional consultation via telecommunications systems with a health care provider furnishing a service for which Medicare payment would be made for a beneficiary residing in a rural county that was designated as a health professional shortage area (and in certain other nonurban areas). Especially during the COVID-19 pandemic, the approval of telehealth has been greatly expanded.

Payments for telehealth services are generally equal to what Medicare would have paid for the services if delivered other than through telecommunications.

Part B covers certain services, like office visits and consultations that are provided:

- Using an interactive two-way telecommunications system (with real-time audio and video)

- By a doctor or certain other health care provider who isn't at your location

In some rural areas, these services are covered under certain conditions and only if you're located at one of these places:

- A doctor's office

- A hospital

- A critical access hospital

- A rural health clinic

- A federally qualified health center

- A hospital-based or critical access hospital-based dialysis facility

- A skilled nursing facility

- A community mental health center

1153. Does Medicare Part B (Medical Insurance) reimburse Continuous Positive Airway Pressure (CPAP) therapy?

Medicare covers a three-month trial of CPAP therapy with a diagnosis of obstructive sleep apnea. Medicare may cover it longer if the patient meets with the doctor in person, and the doctor documents that the CPAP therapy is helping. The patient pays 20 percent of the Medicare-approved amount for rental of the machine and purchase of related accessories (like masks and tubing), and the Part B deductible applies. Medicare pays the supplier to rent the machine for thirteen months the patient has been using it without interruption. After renting the machine for thirteen months, the patient owns it.

Note: Medicare may cover rental or a replacement CPAP machine and/or CPAP accessories under certain requirements such as if the person had a CPAP machine before you got Medicare.

1154. Does Medicare Part B (Medical Insurance) cover blood-based bio-marker tests?

Yes. Blood-based biomarker tests are covered. This coverage began in 2022.

Medicare covers this lab test in certain cases (if available), once every 3 years. To be eligible an individual must meet each of these conditions:

- The person is between 50-85

- The person shows no symptoms of colorectal disease

- The person is at average risk for developing colorectal cancer (you pay nothing for the test if your doctor or other qualified health care provider accepts assignment)

1155. Does Medicare Part B (Medical Insurance) reimburse implantable automatic defibrillators?

Medicare covers these devices for some people diagnosed with heart failure. Medicare Part A will cover if the surgery is hospital inpatient. If the surgery takes place in an outpatient setting, Medicare Part B covers the procedure, and the patient pays 20 percent of the Medicare-approved amount for the doctor's services.

1156. Does Medicare Part B (Medical Insurance) reimburse prosthetic or orthotic items?

Yes. Medicare covers prosthetic devices needed to replace a body part of function when ordered by a Medicare-enrolled doctor or provider:

- arm, leg, back, and neck braces; artificial eyes;

- breast prostheses (including surgical bra);

- conventional eyeglasses or contact lenses (one pair of either) after a cataract operation;

- surgically implanted prosthetic devices such as cochlear implants;

- urological supplies;

- artificial limbs (and their replacement parts); and

- prosthetic devices needed to replace an internal body organ or function of the organ (including ostomy supplies, parenteral and enteral nutrition therapy, and some types of breast prostheses after a mastectomy) when ordered by a doctor or other health care provider enrolled in Medicare.

1157. Does Medicare Part B (Medical Insurance) reimburse for pulmonary rehabilitation?

Medicare covers a comprehensive pulmonary rehabilitation program for moderate to very severe chronic obstructive pulmonary disease (COPD) and have a referral from the doctor treating this chronic respiratory disease. This coverage includes doctors' services, outpatient coverage, medical supplies, as well as preventive services. See also Q 1153 referencing CPAP therapy. Medicare also covers pulmonary rehabilitation if you've had confirmed or suspected COVID-19 and experience persistent symptoms that include respiratory dysfunction for at least 4 weeks.

1158. Does Part B (Medical Insurance) help pay for Federally Qualified Health Center services (FQHC)?

Federally qualified health centers are located in both rural and urban areas, and any Medicare beneficiary may seek services at them. As part of the "federally qualified health center benefit," Part B (Medical Insurance) helps pay for the following outpatient services:

(1)   Physician/doctor services

(2)   Services and supplies furnished as incident to a physician's professional services

(3)   Nurse practitioner or physician assistant services

(4)   Services and supplies furnished as incident to a nurse practitioner or physician assistant services

(5)   Clinical psychologist and clinical social worker services

(6)   Services and supplies furnished as incident to a clinical psychologist or clinical social worker services

(7)   Visiting nurse services

(8)   Nurse-midwife services

(9)   Preventive primary services

(10)   Outpatient chare

Preventive primary services include medical social services, nutritional assessment and referral, preventive health education, children's eye and ear examinations, prenatal and postpartum screening, immunizations, voluntary family planning services, and other services outlined in the recommendations of the U.S. Preventive Services Task Force for patients age sixty-five and older. Preventive services do not include eyeglasses, hearing aids, group or mass information programs or health education classes, or preventive dental services. Preventive services covered under special provisions of Medicare, such as screening mammography, may be provided by a federally qualified health center only if the center meets the special provisions that govern those benefits.

A Medicare beneficiary does not have to pay the Part B (Medical Insurance) annual deductible for services provided under the federally qualified health center benefit. A beneficiary remains responsible for 20 percent of the Medicare-approved charge for the clinic. Federally qualified health centers often provide services in addition to those specified under the Medicare federally qualified health center benefit. Examples of these services are X-rays and equipment like crutches and canes. As long as the center meets Medicare requirements to provide these services, Part B (Medical Insurance) can help pay for them. The patient is responsible for any unmet part of the patient's annual Part B (Medical Insurance) deductible plus 20 percent of the Medicare-approved charge for the service.

1158.01. What are the most common Durable Medical Equipment devices that Medicare Part B covers?

Medicare Part B covers the following as Durable Medical Equipment if a doctor prescribes for use in the home

- Air fluidized beds and other support surfaces

- Blood sugar monitors

- Blood sugar test strips

- Braces for arms, legs, back, and neck when medically necessary

- Canes and Crutches (However, Medicare does NOT cover white canes for the blind)

- Continuous glucose monitors

- Continuous passive motion (CPM) machines – covered for up to 21 days

- Commode chairs

- Hospital beds

- Humidifiers if medically necessary such as oxygen humidifiers used with CPAP or oxygen equipment

- Infusion pumps and supplies

- Nebulizers and associated medications

- Orthopedic shoes if a necessary part of a leg brace

- Oxygen equipment if prescribed by a doctor

- Patient lifts

- Suction pumps

- Traction equipment

- Walkers and rollators

- Wheelchairs and scooters

    o These require a face-to-face examination and written prescription from a doctor or other provider before power wheelchairs are covered

1158.02. Does Part B cover travel outside of the United States?

Medicare Part B generally does not cover healthcare outside of the United States, with some exceptions.

Part B may pay for services on board a ship within the territorial waters adjoining the land areas of the U.S. However, Medicare won't pay for health care services when a ship is more than 6 hours away from a U.S. port.

Medicare may pay for inpatient hospital, doctor, and ambulance services in a foreign country in these rare cases:

- The patient is in U.S. when a medical emergency occurs, and the foreign hospital is closer than the nearest U.S. hospital that can treat the medical condition.

- The patient is through Canada without unreasonable delay by the most direct route between Alaska and another U.S state when a medical emergency occurs, and the Canadian hospital is closer than the nearest U.S. hospital that can treat the emergency.

- The patient lives in the U.S. and the foreign hospital is closer to the patient's home than the nearest U.S. hospital that can treat the medical condition, regardless of whether an emergency exists.

1158.03. Does Part B cover Acupuncture?

Part B covers up to 12 acupuncture visits in 90 days for chronic low back pain and an additional 8 sessions if improvement is shown and the patient's doctor certifies this. There are a maximum of 20 acupuncture treatments in a 12-month period.

1159. What other benefits are provided under Part B (Medical Insurance)?

Additional benefits include the following:

- The cost of **blood clotting factors and supplies** related to their administration for hemophilia patients who are able to use them to control bleeding without medical or other supervision. The number of clotting factors necessary to have on hand for a specific period is determined for each patient individually.

- **Outpatient radiation therapy** given under the supervision of a doctor.

- **Oral anti-nausea drugs used as part of an anticancer chemotherapeutic regimen.** The drug must be administered by a physician (or prescribed by a physician) for use immediately before, at, or within forty-eight hours after, the time of administration of the chemotherapeutic agent and used as a full replacement for the antiemetic therapy which would otherwise be administered intravenously.

- **Portable diagnostic X-ray services** received by a patient at home or at other locations if they are ordered by a doctor and if they are provided by a Medicare-approved supplier.

- Under certain circumstances, **liver and kidney transplants** in a Medicare-approved facility.

- The drug **Epoetin alfa** when used to treat Medicare beneficiaries with anemia related to chronic kidney failure or related to use of AZT in HIV-positive beneficiaries or for other uses that a Medicare Administrative Contractor finds medically appropriate. The Epoetin alfa must be administered incident to the services of a doctor in the office or in a hospital outpatient department. Part B (Medical Insurance) also helps pay for Epoetin alfa that is self-administered by home dialysis patients or administered by their caregivers.

- **Oral cancer drugs** if they are the same chemical entity as those administered intravenously and covered prior to 1994. In addition, off-label anticancer drugs are covered in some cases.

- **Cardiac rehabilitation** is covered if it is a comprehensive program that includes exercise, education, and counseling. Patients must meet certain conditions and have a doctor's referral. Also covered are intensive cardiac rehabilitation programs that are typically more rigorous or more intense than cardiac rehabilitation programs.

1160. What services are covered under Part B (Medical Insurance) with no cost-sharing obligation?

The number of services covered by Part B (Medical Insurance) without any cost-sharing obligations for patients—in other words, subject to neither the Part B deductible nor coinsurance—has expanded in recent years.

Such services include:

(1)   the cost of second opinions for certain surgical procedures when Medicare requires a second opinion,

(2)   the cost of home health services (but a 20 percent coinsurance charge applies for durable medical equipment, except for the purchase of certain used items),

(3)   the cost of a flu shot and pneumococcal vaccine,

(4)   certain outpatient clinical diagnostic laboratory tests, and

(5)   a screening PSA test for prostate cancer.

Medicare Coverage of Blood

1161. Does Medicare help pay for blood?

Both Part A (Hospital Insurance) and Part B (Medical Insurance) can help pay for blood (whole blood or units of packed red blood cells), blood components, and the cost of blood processing and administration. Hospitals usually charge for blood processing and handling for each unit of blood you get, whether the blood is donated or purchased.

In most cases, the hospital gets blood from a blood bank at no charge. If a patient receives blood as an inpatient of a hospital or skilled nursing facility, Part A (Hospital Insurance) will pay all of the blood costs, except for a deductible charged for the first three pints of whole blood or units of packed red cells in each benefit period. The deductible is the charge that some hospitals and skilled nursing facilities make for blood which is not replaced.

The patient is responsible for the deductible for the first three pints or units of blood furnished by a hospital or skilled nursing facility in a calendar year. If the patient is charged a deductible, the patient has the option of either paying the deductible or having the blood replaced, usually through donation. A hospital or skilled nursing facility cannot charge a patient for any of the first three pints of blood the patient replaces. Any blood deductible satisfied under Part B (Medical Insurance) will reduce the blood deductible requirements under Part A (Hospital Insurance).

Part B (Medical Insurance) can help pay for blood and blood components received as an outpatient or as part of other covered services, except for a deductible charged for the first three pints or units received in each calendar year. After the patient has met the annual deductible,

Part B (Medical Insurance) pays 80 percent of the approved charge for blood starting with the fourth pint in a calendar year.

Private Contracts

1162. Can physicians enter into private contracts with Medicare beneficiaries?

Yes, physicians or practitioners can sign private contracts with Medicare beneficiaries for whom no claim is to be submitted to Medicare and for which the physician or practitioner receives no reimbursement from Medicare, on a per person basis, or from an organization that receives reimbursement under Medicare for the item or service. Services provided under private contracts are not covered under Medicare.

A private contract is not valid unless it:

(1) is written and signed by the beneficiary before any item or service is provided pursuant to the contract;

(2) is entered into when the beneficiary is not facing an emergency or urgent health care situation; and

(3) contains specific items listed below.

Among other provisions, the contract must clearly indicate to the beneficiary that by signing the contract the beneficiary:

(1) agrees not to submit a claim to Medicare even if the items or services would otherwise by covered;

(2) agrees to be responsible, through insurance or otherwise, for payment of the items and services and understands that no reimbursement will be provided under Medicare;

(3) acknowledges that no limits will apply to amounts that could be charged for the items and services;

(4) acknowledges that Medigap plans do not make payments for these items and services because Medicare does not make payment; and

(5) acknowledges that the beneficiary has a right to have the items and services provided by other physicians or practitioners for whom payment would be made under Medicare.

Private contracts are not valid unless the physician files an affidavit with the Medicare Administrative Contractor (MAC) for the area in which the physician practices not later than ten days after the first contract to which the affidavit applies is entered into. The affidavit must identify the physician or practitioner, be signed by the physician or practitioner, and provide that—except for emergency services—the physician or practitioner will not submit any claim to Medicare for any item or service provided to any beneficiary for two years beginning on the date the affidavit is signed.

If the physician or practitioner knowingly and willfully submits a claim to Medicare for any item or service furnished to a beneficiary (except emergency services) during the two-year period:

(1)   the physician or practitioner will no longer be allowed to furnish services under private contracts for the remainder of the two-year period; and

(2)   no Medicare payment will be made for any item or service furnished by the physician or practitioner during the remainder of the two-year period.

1163. What is the effect of physicians entering into private contracts with Medicare patients?

Under current law, physicians are paid under a fee schedule in Medicare, with limits on the amount they can balance bill beneficiaries per service, unless they choose to "opt out" of Medicare and "privately contract" with all of their Medicare patients. In recent years, some lawmakers have proposed to broaden the conditions under which doctors and other practitioners can privately contract with Medicare patients for the price of their services.

Under current law, physicians and practitioners have three options for charging their patients in traditional Medicare. These include register with Medicare as:

1.   **Participating providers** (96 percent) - These providers accept Medicare's standard fee. Participating providers accept Medicare's fee-schedule amount as payment-in-full for all Medicare covered services. Patients are charged Medicare's standard amounts and do not face higher out-of-pocket liability than the regular 20-percent coinsurance on most services. Participating providers may collect their applicable fees directly from Medicare.

2.   **Nonparticipating providers** (3.3 percent) - These providers send a balance bill. Non-participating providers may choose—on a service-by-service basis—to charge Medicare patients higher fees than participating providers, up to a maximum limit—115 percent of a reduced fee-schedule amount. When doing so, Medicare patients are fully responsible for this added amount (balance billing) in addition to applicable coinsurance. When engaging in balance billing, non-participating providers bill their Medicare patients directly, rather than Medicare, for the full charge; their patient may then seek reimbursement from Medicare for its portion.

3.   **Opt-out providers** who privately contracts with all of his or her Medicare patients for payment (0.7 percent) - These providers enter into a private contractual relationship with the patient. Opt-out providers with private contracts may charge

their Medicare patients any fee they determine is appropriate for their services, as agreed upon in their contract. When doctors and Medicare patients enter into these private contracts, Medicare does not cover or reimburse the doctor or patient for any services provided by opt-out providers, which means that Medicare patients are responsible for the entire cost of any services they receive from them. Most that have done this are psychiatrists and dentist. Doctors in concierge practice who typically charge an annual membership fee are not required to opt-out of Medicare, but if they do not, they are subject to Medicare's coverage and billing requirements.

Patient Protections Currently in Place for Opting-Out Physicians

- Prior to providing any service to Medicare patients, doctors must inform their Medicare patients in writing that they have "opted out" of Medicare and that Medicare will not reimburse for their services.

- Medicare patients must sign a document noting their understanding and their right to seek care from a doctor or other practitioner who has not opted-out of Medicare.

- Doctors are prohibited from entering into private contracts with beneficiaries who are in the midst of experiencing an urgent or emergent health care event or who qualify for Medicaid.

- Doctors who have decided to opt out of Medicare to do so for all of their Medicare patients and for all of the services they provide to them; they cannot choose which patients and which services apply.

- A two-year minimum time period for opting out was also established to ensure that beneficiaries can make knowledgeable choices when selecting their physicians, rather than be subject to frequent changes.

In recent years, some lawmakers have proposed to broaden the conditions under which doctors and other practitioners can privately contract with Medicare patients for the price of their services. First, they would allow physicians to contract more selectively, on a patient-by-patient and service-by-service basis, rather than be required to privately contract with all of their Medicare patients for all services. Second, they would allow Medicare patients and physicians to seek reimbursement from Medicare for an amount equal to what Medicare would normally pay for that service under the physician fee schedule. There are pros and cons for these proposals.

PROS INCLUDE:

- lifting restrictions on private contracting would provide a way for physicians to receive higher payments for the services they provide, and compensating them for relatively low fees allowed by Medicare.

- lifting restrictions could potentially increase the overall number of doctors and other providers willing to accept Medicare patients because they could charge higher fees to some of their Medicare patients, without having to opt-out of Medicare and turn away all other Medicare patients.

- Lifting restrictions could potentially reduce beneficiary out-of-pocket costs because patients entering into private contracts would be able to seek reimbursement from Medicare for at least a portion of their doctor's charges (or allow their doctors to collect this portion directly from Medicare).

CONS INCLUDE:

- Potentially higher costs for more Medicare beneficiaries.

- Expansion of private contracting could cause loss of access to affordable services, rather than gain it, particularly for less common physician specialties.

PART C:
MEDICARE ADVANTAGE

Definition

1164. What is Medicare Advantage?

Medicare Advantage is a type of Medicare health plan offered by private companies that contract with Medicare to provide the Part A and Part B benefits. If enrolled in a Medicare Advantage Plan, most Medicare services are covered through the plan and aren't paid for under Original Medicare. Most Medicare Advantage Plans offer prescription drug coverage. Medicare Advantage was formerly known as Medicare+Choice permits contracts between the Centers for Medicare & Medicaid Services (CMS) and a variety of different private managed care and fee-for-service entities.

Most Medicare beneficiaries may choose to receive benefits either through the original Medicare fee-for-service program (hospital insurance under Medicare Part A and medical insurance under Medicare Part B). Medicare Advantage Plans cover all Medicare services and may even offer extra coverage including prescription drugs, dental coverage, and vision. Each plan can charge different out-of-pocket costs and have different rules of getting service. Medicare Advantage Plans are sometimes called "Part C" or "MA Plans". These are an "all in one" alternative to Original Medicare. They are offered by private companies approved by Medicare. By joining a Medicare Advantage Plan, one still actually has Medicare coverage. These "bundled" plans include Medicare Part A (Hospital Insurance) and Medicare Part B (Medical Insurance), and usually Medicare prescription drug (Part D).

Main types of Medicare Advantage plans include private fee-for-service plans which reimburse providers on a fee-for-service basis and coordinated care plans, including HMOs, PPOs, PSOs, HMO Point of Service (HMOPOS), and medical savings accounts.

The most common types of Medicare Advantage Plans include Health Maintenance Organization (HMO) plans, Preferred Provider Organization (PPO) plans, Private Fee-For-Service (PFFS) plans, and special needs plans.

Out of pocket costs can vary and depend on:

- whether the plan charges a monthly premium;

- whether the plan pays any or all of the monthly Part B premium;

- whether the plan has a yearly deductible or any additional deductibles;

- how much is paid for each visit or service (copay or coinsurance) – which CAN be different than under original Medicare;

- the type of health care services used;

- whether one goes to a doctor who accepts assignment and follow the plans rules such as using network providers;

- any charges for extra benefits;

- the plan's yearly limit on out-of-pocket costs for all medical services; and

- whether Medicaid is part of the coverage.

1165. Who can join a Medicare Advantage plan?

A person can generally join a Medicare Health Maintenance Organization (HMO), Preferred Provider Organization (PPO), Private Fee-For-Service (PFFS) or Medical Savings Account (MSA) type plan as long as the following conditions are met:

- They live in the service area of the plan you want to join. The plan can provide more information about its service area. If a person lives in another state for part of the year, they should check to see if the plan will cover there.

- They have Medicare Part A and Part B.

- They are a U.S. citizen or lawfully present in the United States.

- Beginning in 2021 individuals diagnosed with End-Stage Renal Disease (ESRD) can join Medicare Advantage Plans as well as Original Medicare.

1166. What happens if plans leave Medicare and Medicare Advantage?

At the end of the year, plans can decide to leave the Medicare Program, although in recent years, very few plans have left.

Generally, a person will be automatically returned to original Medicare if they don't choose to join another Medicare Advantage Plan. Subscribers will also have the right to buy a Medigap policy. No matter what choice is made, the individual is still in the Medicare Program and will get all Medicare-covered services. If returning to original Medicare and prescription drug coverage is desired, Part D will have to be purchased if prescription drug coverage is desired.

1167. How much do Medicare Advantage (Part C) plans cost?

The out of pocket charges for a Medicare Advantage plan depend on several factors:

- Whether the plan charges a monthly premium. (Many Medicare Advantage plans do not.)

- Whether the plan pays any of the monthly Part B premium.

- Whether the plan has a yearly deductible or any additional deductibles.

- How much the copay is for each visit or service?

- The type of health care services needed and how often they are used.

- Whether the doctor or supplied who accepts assignment if the subscriber is in a PPO, PPFFS, or MSA plan or if the subscriber goes out of network.

- Whether the subscriber follows the plan's rules or decides to use out of network health providers.

- Extra benefits and the plan charges for those benefits.

- The plan's yearly limit on out-of-pocket costs for all medical services.

- Whether you have Medicaid or get help from the state.

1168. What is a Health Maintenance Organization (HMO)?

A Medicare HMO is a type of managed care plan that provides to its enrolled Medicare beneficiary members, either directly or through arrangement with others, at least all the Medicare-covered services that are available to Medicare beneficiaries who are not enrolled in the HMO and who reside in the geographic area serviced by the HMO. Some HMOs also provide services not covered by Medicare, either free to the Medicare enrollee (that is, funded out of the payment Medicare makes to the HMO) or for an additional charge to the enrollee. HMOs typically charge a set monthly premium and nominal copayments for services instead of Medicare's coinsurance and deductibles.

Each HMO has its own network of hospitals, skilled nursing facilities, home health agencies, doctors, and other professionals. Depending on how the plan is organized, services are usually provided either at one or more centrally located health facilities or in the private practice offices of the doctors and other health care professionals who are part of the HMO. A beneficiary generally must receive all covered care through the HMO or from health care professionals referred to by the plan. In most cases, prescription drugs are covered in the HMO.

Most HMOs allow an enrollee to select a primary care doctor from those who are part of the HMO. If the beneficiary does not make a selection, a primary care physician will be assigned. If your primary doctor leaves the plan, the beneficiary will need to select another physician from within the plan. The primary care doctor is responsible for managing the beneficiary's medical care, including admitting the beneficiary to a hospital or referring the beneficiary to specialists. The beneficiary is allowed to change his or her primary care doctor as long as another primary care doctor affiliated with the HMO is selected. In most cases, the referral from the primary care doctor to the specialist is required, although certain services, such as mammograms don't require a referral.

Before enrolling in an HMO, the beneficiary should find out whether the plan has a "risk" or a "cost" contract with Medicare. There is an important difference:

- **Risk Plans**. These plans have "lock-in" requirements. This means that the beneficiary generally is locked into receiving all covered care through the HMO or through referrals by the plan. In most cases, if the beneficiary receives services that are not authorized by the HMO, neither the plan nor Medicare will pay. he only exceptions recognized by all Medicare-contracting plans are for emergency services, which the beneficiary may receive anywhere in the United States, and for services the beneficiary urgently needs when temporarily out of the HMO's service area. Additionally, out-of-area dialysis is covered as well.

- **Cost Plans**. These plans do not have lock-in requirements. If a beneficiary enrolls in a cost plan, the beneficiary can either go to health care providers affiliated with the HMO or go outside the plan. If a beneficiary goes outside the plan, the plan probably will not pay, but Medicare will. Medicare will pay its share of charges it approves. The beneficiary will be responsible for Medicare's coinsurance, deductibles, and other charges, just as if receiving care under the regular Medicare program.

1169. What is a Medicare Advantage Private Fee-For-Service (PFFS) plan?

A Medicare PFFS plan is a type of Medicare Advantage Plan (Part C) offered by a private insurance company. PFFS plans aren't the same as Original Medicare or Medigap. The plan determines how much it will pay doctors, other health care providers, and hospitals, and how much you must pay when you get care.

A Medicare Advantage Private Fee-For-Service (PFFS) plan is defined as

- a plan offered by a private insurance company that reimburses doctors, hospitals, and other providers on a fee-for-service basis,

- does not place them at risk,

- does not vary payment rates based on utilization,

- varies provider payment rates only based on the specialty or location of the provider or to increase utilization of certain preventive or screening services,

- Does not permit the use of prior authorization or notification, and

- does not restrict which doctor or hospital the member can use.

In this type of plan, it is not necessary for the member to select a primary care physician or to get referrals to see specialists. PFFS plans can offer full or partial networks of providers, or, in certain cases, they may not use a network of providers at all. No matter what kind of network a PFFS plan provides, its enrollees can see any provider who is eligible to receive payment from Medicare and agrees to accept the plan's terms and conditions of payment.

Subject to some limits and review by the Centers for Medicare & Medicaid Services (CMS), the private insurance company, not CMS, decides how much to reimburse for services received by the beneficiary. The beneficiary pays the Part B premium ($164.90 for new beneficiaries in 2023), any additional monthly premium the private fee-for-service plan charges, and any deductible or coinsurance required by the plan, including any copayment required per visit or service.

1170. What is a Medicare Advantage Provider-Sponsored Organization (PSO)?

For purposes of Medicare Advantage, PSOs are a type of managed care consisting of a group of doctors and hospitals who have created a network plan. Subscribers generally must stay within the plan to receive coverage. They are public or private entities established by or organized by a health care provider (such as a hospital) or a group or network of affiliated health care providers (such as a geriatric unit of a hospital) that provide a substantial proportion of health care items and services directly through that provider or group. Affiliated providers share, directly or indirectly, substantial financial risk and have at least a majority financial interest in the PSO.

This type of plan is not available in all parts of the United States but has experienced rapid growth in the past several years, especially as CMS has been encouraging a shift away from fee-for-service to value-based care. Another term used is "provider-led health plan". In 2014, there were 107 plans of this type in the United States. As of 2020, the number had increased to 320 with over 41 million participants. States showing the biggest increases of this type of plan include Utah (35 percent), Wisconsin (31 percent), New Mexico (30 percent), and Oregon (28 percent).

1171. What is a Preferred Provider Organization (PPO) Plan?

A Medicare PPO Plan is a type of Medicare Advantage Plan offered by a private insurance company. In a PPO Plan, the member pays less when using doctors, hospitals, and other health care providers that belong to the plan's network. In the alternative, the member pays more if they use doctors, hospitals, and providers outside of the network. Generally, a member does not have to choose a primary physician.

In most cases, the member can get health care from any doctor, health care provider, or hospital with the PPO plan at lower co-pays. In addition, members can usually go to health care providers outside of the plan at an additional cost. Generally, a person doesn't need to choose a primary care physician, nor do they generally need to obtain referrals for specialists. In most cases, prescription drugs are covered.

1172. What is a Medicare Advantage Religious Fraternal Benefit (RFB) plan?

A Religious Fraternal Benefit (RFB) plan must restrict enrollment to members of the church, convention, or group with which the society is affiliated and may be approved to offer any MA plan type (e.g., HMO, PPO, PFFS).[1] The requirement for membership can be met by any documentation establishing membership issued by the church, or by using the church's records of membership. An individual must also meet all the other requirements to elect an MA plan.[2]

These plans must meet Medicare financial solvency requirements, and Medicare may adjust payment amounts to these plans to take into account the actuarial characteristics and experience of plan enrollees. In addition to meeting Medicare requirements, any RFB plan must also satisfy certain provisions of the Internal Revenue Code and qualify as a tax-exempt organization in accordance with the Code.

An RFB society is an organization that is described in Section 501(c)(8) of the Internal Revenue Code of 1986, is exempt from taxation under Section 501(a) of that code and is affiliated with, carries out the tenets of, and shares a religious bond with, a church or convention or association of churches or an affiliated group of churches.

Notes

1. 42 CFR sec. 422.57.
2. Medicare Managed Care Manual (revised August 12, 2020), https://www.cms.gov/files/document/cy2021-ma-enrollment-and-disenrollment-guidance.pdf (last accessed October 16, 2022).

1173. What is a Medicare Special Needs (SNP) plan?

Medicare Special Needs Plans (SNPs) are types of Medicare Advantage Plan (like an HMO or PPO). Membership is limited to individuals with specific diseases or characteristics, and customize their benefits, choice of providers, and drug formularies to best meet the specific needs of the groups they serve. Medicare SNPs typically have specialists in the diseases or conditions that affect their members.

A plan must limit membership to these groups:

(1)   people who live in certain institutions (like a nursing home) or who require nursing care at home, or

(2)   people who are eligible for both Medicare and Medicaid (referred to as "dual eligible"), or

(3)   people who have specific severe chronic or disabling conditions (like diabetes, End-Stage Renal Disease (ESRD), HIV/AIDS, chronic heart failure, or dementia).

Plans may further limit membership. You can join a SNP at any time. An SNP provides benefits targeted to its members' special needs, including care coordination services.

Generally, a member of an SNP must get care and services from doctors or hospitals in the Medicare SNP network (except emergency or urgent care, such as care for a sudden illness or injury that needs immediate medical care, or if you have End-Stage Renal Disease (ESRD) and need out-of-area dialysis).

All SNPs MUST provide Medicare prescription drug (Part D) coverage. Medicare SNPs often coverage extra services tailed to the special group served, such as extra hospital days, etc. Medicare SNPs may not be available in all parts of the country.

In most cases, SNPs will require a member to have a primary care doctor, or the plan may require the individual to have a care coordinator to help with health care. Generally, a referral to see a specialist in a SNP is required. Certain services, such as yearly screening for mammograms, pap smears, and pelvic exams don't require a referral.

1174. Who can join a Medicare Special Needs (SNP) plan?

Membership in a SNP is limited by the very nature of the plan. A plan must limit membership to:

(1)   persons who live in certain institutions (such as a nursing home) or who live in the community but require nursing care at home; or

(2)   persons who are eligible for both Medicare and Medicaid; or

(3)   persons who have specific chronic or disabling conditions (like diabetes, End-Stage Renal Disease (ESRD), HIV/AIDS, chronic heart failure, or dementia).

In order to join, one must have Medicare Part A and Part B, live in the plan's service area, and meet the eligibility requirements (see Q 1175).

Additional requirements include: All SNPs must provide Medicare drug coverage (Part D). In most cases, SNPs may require the individual to have a primary care doctor, or the plan may require care coordinator to help with health care. Participants generally need a referral to see a specialist.

1175. What kinds of Medicare Special Needs (SNP) plans and eligibility requirements are there?

Membership in a SNP is limited by the very nature of the plan. A plan must limit membership to:

1.   **Institutional SNP (I-SNP)** – include people who live in certain institutions (such as a nursing home) or who require nursing care at home. Institutional Special Needs Plans are SNPs that restrict enrollment to MA eligible individuals who, for 90 days or longer, have had or are expected to need the level of services provided in:

a.   a long-term care (LTC) skilled nursing facility (SNF),

b.   a LTC nursing facility (NF),

    c.   a SNF/NF, an intermediate care facility for individuals with intellectual disabilities (ICF/IDD), or

    d.   an inpatient psychiatric facility.

A complete list of acceptable types of institutions can be found in the Medicare Advantage Enrollment and Disenrollment Guidance.[1]

2.   **Dual-Eligible SNP or "Dual-Eligible" (D-SNP)** – people who are eligible for both Medicare and Medicaid. The Medicaid eligibility categories encompass all categories of Medicaid eligibility including:

    a.   Full Medicaid (only);

    b.   Qualified Medicare Beneficiary without other Medicaid (QMB Only);

    c.   QMB Plus;

    d.   Specified Low-Income Medicare Beneficiary without other Medicaid (SLMB Only);

    e.   SLMB Plus;

    f.   Qualifying Individual (QI); and

    g.   Qualified Disabled and Working Individual (QDWI)

(3)   **Chronic Condition SNP (C-SNP)** – people who have specific chronic or disabling conditions (like diabetes, End-Stage Renal Disease (ESRD), HIV/AIDS, chronic heart failure, or dementia). One or more of the following chronic conditions must exist:

    a.   Chronic alcohol and/or other drug dependence;

    b.   Autoimmune disorders limited to:

        i.   Polyarteritis nodosa

        ii.   Polymyalgia rheumatica

        iii. Polymyositis

        iv. Rheumatoid arthritis

        v.   Systemic lupus erythematosus

    c.   Cancer (excluding pre-cancer conditions or in situ status);

d. Cardiovascular disorders limited to:

    i. Cardiac arrhythmias

    ii. Coronary artery disease

    iii. Peripheral vascular disease

    iv. Chronic venous thromboemolic disorder

e. Chronic heart failure;

f. Dementia;

g. Diabetes mellitus;

h. End-stage liver disease;

i. End-Stage Renal Disease (ESRD) requiring dialysis (any mode of dialysis);

j. Severe hematologic disorders limited to:

    i. Apastic aneima

    ii. Hemophilia

    iii. Immune thrombocytopenic purpura

    iv. Myelodysplatic syndrome

    v. Sickle-cell disease (excluding sickle-cell trait)

k. HIV/AIDS

l. Chronic lung disorders limited to:

    i. Asthma

    ii. Chronic bronchitis

    iii. Emphysema

    iv. Pulmonary fibrosis

    v. Pulmonary hypertension

m. Chronic and disabling mental health conditions limited to:

    vi. Bipolar disorders

        vii.   Major depressive disorders

        viii.   Paranoid disorder

        ix.   Schizophrenia

        x.   Schizoaffective disorder

   n.   Neurologic disorders limited to:

        i.   Amyotrophic lateral sclerosis (ALS)

        ii.   Epilepsy

        iii.   Extensive paralysis (i.e., hemiplegia, quadriplegia, paraplegia, monoplegia)

        iv.   Huntington's disease

        v.   Multiple sclerosis

        vi.   Parkinson's disease

        vii.   Polyneuropathy

        viii.   Spinal stenosis

        ix.   Stroke-related neurologic deficit

   o.   Stroke

4.   **Institutional-Equivalent SNP (I-SNP)** – people who live in an assisted living facility and receive the same level of care as in a Skilled Nursing Facility (SNP)

An I-SNP can enroll Medicare Advantage eligible individuals who live within the community in the community, but require an institutional level of care (LOC), if the following two conditions are met:

1.   A determination of institutional LOC that is based on the use of a state assessment tool. The assessment tool used for persons living in the community must be the same as that used for individuals residing in an institution. In states and territories without a specific tool, I-SNPs must use the same LOC determination methodology used in the respective state or territory in which the I-SNP is authorized to enroll eligible individuals.

2.   The I-SNP must arrange to have the LOC assessment administered by an independent, impartial party (i.e., an entity other than the respective I-SNP) with the requisite professional knowledge to identify accurately the institutional LOC needs. Importantly, the I-SNP cannot own or control the entity.

This list, while specific, is meant for "classifying" the eligibility for benefits only. CMS may periodically re-evaluate these chronic conditions.

Note

1. https://www.cms.gov/Medicare/Eligibility-and-Enrollment/MedicareMangCareEligEnrol (last accessed October 16, 2022).

1176. What is a Medicare MSA Plan?

There are consumer-directed Medicare Advantage Plans, called a Medicare MSA Plans. These plans are similar to Health Savings Account Plans available outside of Medicare. You can choose your health care services and providers.

Medicare MSA Plans combine a high-deductible insurance plan with a medical savings account that you can use to pay for your health care costs. These plans have two parts:

1. **High-deductible health plan:** The first part is a special type of high-deductible Medicare Advantage Plan (Part C) . The plan will only begin to cover your costs once you meet a high yearly deductible, which varies by plan.

2. **Medical Savings Account (MSA):** The second part is a special type of savings account. The Medicare MSA Plan deposits money into your account. You can use money from this savings account to pay your health care costs before you meet the deductible. Medicare MSA plans do not cover Medicare Part D prescription drugs.

1177. How does a Medicare MSA Plan work?

An individual selects and joins a high-deductible Medicare MSA Plan. The individual then sets up an MSA with a bank the plan selects. Medicare gives the plan an amount of money each year for health care coverage. The plan deposits some money into the account.

The insured can use the money in your account to pay health care costs, including health care costs that are not covered by Medicare. When using account money for Medicare-covered Part A and Part B services, it counts towards the plan's deductible. If a person uses all the money in the account and has additional health care costs, they will have to pay for Medicare-covered services out-of-pocket until reaching the plan's deductible.

During the time the person is paying out-of-pocket for services before the deductible is met, doctors and other providers can't charge more than the Medicare-approved amount. After reaching the deductible, the plan will cover Medicare-covered services. Money remaining in the account at the end of the year stays in the account and may be used for health care costs in future years.

If funds are used from the account, the owner must include IRS Form 8853[1] with their tax return with information on how the account money was used.

Note

1. Archer MSAs and Long-Term Care Insurance Contracts, Form 8853, https://www.irs.gov/pub/irs-pdf/f8853.pdf. (last accessed October 16, 2022).

Eligibility, Election, and Enrollment

1178. What is the enrollment/disenrollment process for Medicare Advantage?

Beneficiaries entitled to Part A (Hospital Insurance) and enrolled in Part B (Medical Insurance) are eligible to enroll in any Medicare Advantage plan that serves the geographic area in which they reside, except beneficiaries with end-stage renal disease (although beneficiaries who develop end-stage renal disease may remain in the plan if already enrolled) and beneficiaries receiving inpatient hospice care. Part B only enrollees are ineligible.

The Centers for Medicare & Medicaid Services (CMS) have established procedures for enrollment and disenrollment in Medicare Advantage options. Newly eligible enrollees who do not choose a Medicare Advantage plan are deemed to have chosen the original Medicare fee-for-service option (in other words, Medicare Parts A and B). Individuals generally remain enrolled in the Medicare option of their choice unless and until they choose another plan. CMS retains the power to implement "passive enrollment" in cases where a Medicare Advantage plan terminates, or CMS determines that remaining in the Medicare Advantage plan poses a risk to the members. Under passive enrollment, CMS treats beneficiaries as enrolled in whatever plan CMS chooses unless the beneficiaries affirmatively elect otherwise.

Process options for joining a Medicare Advantage Plan:

- Use Medicare's Plan Finder.[1] (Open enrollment is October 15 to December 7, 2022)

- Visit the plan's website to see online sign up is possible.

- Fill out a paper enrollment form. Contact the plan to get an enrollment form, fill it out, and return it to the plan. All plans must offer this option.

- Call the plan you want to join. Get your plan's contact information from a Medicare Plan Finder mentioned above with a personalized search (under General Search), or search by plan name.

- Call Medicare at 1-800-MEDICARE (1-800-633-4227).

Note

1. https://www.medicare.gov/plan-compare/#/?lang=en (last accessed October 16, 2022).

1179. Can someone with End Stage Renal Disease opt for Medicare Advantage?

Yes. This has been permitted for the past two years.

End Stage Renal Disease (ESRD), also known as Stage 5 of Chronic Kidney Disease (CKD), occurs when an individual's kidneys cease to function. Unless and until the person can get a kidney transplant, people with ESRD undergo dialysis several times per week. According to the CDC, over 37 million people have CKD[1], over 520,000 people were treated for ESRD through renal dialysis, with an additional 220,000 who received a kidney transplant. Chronic Kidney Disease is most common in persons over age 65 (38%) and is slightly more common in women than men. It is also more common in non-Hispanic Black adults than in non-Hispanic White adults or non-Hispanic Asian adults.

Chart [2]

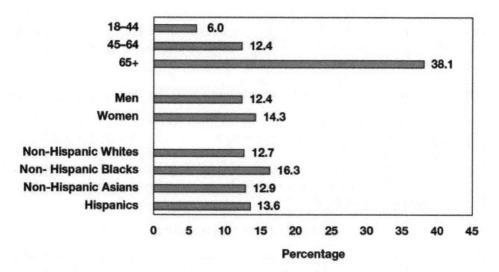

Most beneficiaries with ESRD receive coverage through Traditional Fee-for-Service Medicare although some could enroll in Medicare Advantage under limited circumstances. Medicare beneficiaries who developed ESRD while enrolled in a Medicare Advantage plan could retain their coverage. Currently 130,000 people with ESRD, or 25 percent of the total population on Medicare, have coverage through an MA plan. MA enrollment by individuals with ESRD is expected to accelerate beginning in 2021, when a provision of the *21st Century Cures Act (Cures Act)* lifts the current enrollment restrictions.

Changes

As mandated by Congress, under the *21st Century Cures Act*, beginning January 1, 2021, all ESRD beneficiaries now have the option to enroll in Medicare Advantage, even after diagnosis. Medicare Advantage is advantageous to beneficiaries due to its annual out-of-pocket limit for consumers, supplemental benefits, and ability to coordinate care. CMS estimates that an additional 83,000 people with ESRD will enroll in MA by 2026, which represents an increase of 63 percent.

CMS issued several pieces of regulatory guidance impacted by this change in the rules around MA enrollment for beneficiaries with ESRD:

- the annual MA Advance Notice, which lays out the policies governing plan payment for 2021;

- separate MA bidding instructions for 2021; and

- a Rule that would make policy and technical changes to the MA and Part D programs for 2021-2022.

Additionally, the Cures Act requires that traditional Medicare cover the cost of kidney acquisition for transplant.

In a separate rule on MA and policy changes for 2021-2022 and after issued by CMS, the agency increased plans' ability to reduce dialysis costs by allowing more flexibility to manage dialysis provider networks. These changes included:

- providing medically necessary dialysis services (such as for home health);

- allowing network adequacy exceptions in cases where home dialysis is widely available; and

- customizing network adequacy standards for dialysis facilities. Increasing plan flexibility to design dialysis facility networks, including policies that support the expansion of home dialysis.

Out-of-Pocket Spending

Unlike traditional Medicare, MA plans must cap their enrollees' annual out-of-pocket spending. In addition, MA plans are subject to limits on cost-sharing for certain individual services. CMS has partially increased the maximum annual limit plans set for total beneficiary out-of-pocket spending as well as cost-sharing for certain inpatient hospital services.

Cost Issues

Medicare Advantage plans are paid a capitated, per-beneficiary amount based on traditional fee-for-service Medicare spending at the county level while payment for ESRD patients is set at the state level. In response to rules proposed by CMS for those with ESRD to enroll in Medicare Advantage, proposals were advanced to have county-based rates for ESRD to take into account regional cost differences within a state to allow for more accurate payment.

However, CMS did not make this change and finalized the rule using the statewide methodology. It is expected that pricing changes will have to be worked out over the next several years as data is compiled. In light of this, beginning in 2022 and after, CMS began a phase-in of spending patterns by individuals with ESRD into these calculations until their costs are fully reflected in the annual out-of-pocket and service-level cost-sharing limits.

The 2022 MA contract year was the first time that individuals with end-stage renal disease (ESRD) were able to enroll in a plan. ESRD is generally a very expensive condition to manage. The average beneficiary with ESRD cost over $86,000[3] based on 2015 through 2017 claims data compared to $10,182 per beneficiary without the condition. Of that amount, nearly $30,000 (35%) was for outpatient dialysis, $28,000 (32%) was for inpatient hospital care, and $15,000 (17%) was for physician services. The beneficiary needed to cover approximately $13,000 (15%) of the total cost. Another report showed that costs for members with ESRD exceeded MA benchmarks in nearly half of metropolitan area.[4]

Notes

1. https://www.cdc.gov/kidneydisease/publications-resources/ckd-national-facts.html#:~:text=CKD%20Is%20Common%20Among%20US%20 Adults&text=More%20than%201%20in%207,are%20estimated%20to%20have%20CKD.&text=As%20many%20as%209%20in,not%20 know%20they%20have%20CKD.
2. Chronic Kidney Disease in the United States, 2021 (cdc.gov).
3. https://www.healthmanagement.com/wp-content/uploads/Health-Management-Associates-ESRD-and-Medicare-Advantage-White-Paper. pdf (Last accessed October 16, 2022).
4. https://avalere.com/insights/medicare-advantage-plans-may-be-paid-below-actual-esrd-patients-costs-in-large-metropolitan-areas-in-2021. (Last accessed October 16, 2022).

1180. What are the enrollment periods for Medicare Advantage plans?

Beneficiaries can choose a Medicare Advantage plan at initial Medicare eligibility or during one of the enrollment periods described below.

Medicare Open Enrollment Period

The annual coordinated open enrollment period runs from October 15 through December 7 of each year. Enrollments currently are effective the following January 1. Beneficiaries may:

- Switch from Medicare Advantage to Original Medicare or vice versa.

- Switch from one Medicare Advantage plan to another.

- Switch from one Part D prescription plan to another.

- Join a Medicare Part D plan. (Late-enrollment penalty might apply.)

- Drop Part D coverage altogether. (Re-enrolling in a later year will include a late-enrollment penalty if the person did not maintain other creditable drug coverage.)

Medicare Advantage Open Enrollment Period

The Medicare Advantage Disenrollment Period (January 1 – February 14 in prior years) has been replaced with a different arrangement. Starting in 2019 and subsequent years, a new Medicare Advantage Open Enrollment Period runs from January 1 through March 31 each year. If a person is enrolled in a Medicare Advantage plan, they have a one-time opportunity to:

- Switch to a different Medicare Advantage plan.

- Drop Medicare Advantage plan and return to Original Medicare, Part A and Part B.

- Sign up for a stand-alone Medicare Part D Prescription Drug Plan (if returning to Original Medicare). Most Medicare Advantage plans include prescription drug coverage already. Usually one can't enroll in a stand-alone Medicare Prescription Drug plan if already in a Medicare Advantage plan, but there are some situations where it is allowed.

- Drop your stand-alone Medicare Part D Prescription Drug Plan.

Special election periods are available in which a beneficiary can disenroll if the Medicare Advantage plan in which that beneficiary was enrolled terminates, the beneficiary moves out of the plan's service area, the beneficiary demonstrates that the plan has violated its contract or misrepresented the plan in marketing, or any other conditions specified by the Centers for Medicare & Medicaid Services (CMS).

Newly eligible beneficiaries who elect a Medicare Advantage option may also disenroll into original Medicare fee-for-service program [Part A (Hospital Insurance) and Part B (Medical Insurance)] any time during the first twelve months of their enrollment.

Medicare Advantage plans must accept all beneficiaries on a first-come, first-served basis, subject to capacity limits.

Plans may disenroll beneficiaries only for cause (i.e., failure to pay premiums or disruptive behavior) or plan termination in a beneficiary's geographic area. Beneficiaries terminated for cause are enrolled in the original Medicare fee-for-service program. Others may have a special election period.

1181. How is enrollment information provided to Medicare beneficiaries?

At least fifteen days before the required October coordinated election period (see Q 1192), the Centers for Medicare & Medicaid Services (CMS) must mail to each beneficiary general information on Medicare and comparative information on Medicare Advantage plans available in their area. A new development begun in 2019 and continuing in 2022 is that Medicare Advantage insurance companies can send beneficiaries certain documents electronically, instead of by mail. For example, plans must send you an *Evidence of Coverage* document every year. Now, the plan can email it to you instead of mailing it.

General information includes information on covered benefits, cost sharing, and balance billing liability under the original fee-for-service program [Medicare Part A (Hospital Insurance) and Part B (Medical Insurance)]; election procedures; grievance and appeals rights; and information on Medigap insurance and Medicare SELECT.

Comparative information includes extensive information on benefits and beneficiary liability, premiums, service areas, quality and performance, and supplemental benefits. A sophisticated search engine is available at www.medicare.gov to assist beneficiaries in deciding between Medicare Advantage and traditional Medicare Parts A and Parts B and in locating a Medicare Advantage plan in a beneficiary's area. Beneficiaries may also call CMS at 1-800-772-1213.

Benefits and Beneficiary Protections

1182. What basic benefits are provided by Medicare Advantage plans?

All Medicare Advantage plans are required to provide at least the same benefits available under traditional Medicare Part A (Hospital Insurance) and Part B (Medical Insurance), except for the Part A hospice benefit. If a beneficiary requires hospice services, those benefits are provided through Part A (Hospital Insurance).

Medicare Advantage plans may also offer mandatory and optional supplemental benefits, subject to approval by the Centers for Medicare & Medicaid Services (CMS). Mandatory supplemental benefits must be approved unless CMS determines that offering such benefits would substantially discourage enrollment in the Medicare Advantage plan. Medicare Advantage plans may also offer optional supplemental benefits. Optional supplemental benefits are benefits—such as vision, dental and wellness care—that a beneficiary chooses to add to his or her Medicare Advantage plan coverage. Beneficiaries who enroll in Medicare Advantage plans offering either mandatory or optional supplemental benefits (or both) pay the cost of such benefits through additional premiums or cost-sharing obligations such as copayments or coinsurance.

1183. What are the new Supplemental Benefits announced for Medicare Advantage plans?

With recent legislative changes, there are new categories of Supplemental Benefits. As a result of these various policy changes, beginning in 2020, there are three different categories of supplemental benefits:

1. **Standard**—offered to all enrollees, must be health-related, and targeted to all beneficiaries. Supplemental benefits mandatory or optional, and are uniform across all beneficiaries. Benefits must:

    a. not be covered by original Medicare;

    b. must be primarily health-related (new, more flexible definition); and

    c. MA plan must incur a non-zero direct medical cost.

    These plans generally include Visual, Dental, Hearing, Fitness, Over the counter coverage, and limited additional services such as rides to appointments, meals following inpatient stays, and home-based palliative care.

2.   **Targeted**—offered only to qualifying enrollees with a diagnosed medical condition, must be health-related, and targeted to a specific health status or disease state. Benefits are mandatory, and must have the ability to be tailored to similarly situated beneficiaries. Benefits must:

   a.   not be covered by original Medicare;

   b.   must be primarily health-related (new, more flexible definition); and

   c.   MA plan must incur a non-zero direct medical cost.

   These plans generally include all Standard (traditional) coverage, expanded additional services including more generous meal benefits, additional rides; new services including adult day care, community based services, caregiver support.

3.   **Chronic**—offered only to qualifying enrollees with a chronic illness, does not have to be health-related, targeted to chronically ill beneficiaries as defined in statute. Benefit must have:

   a.   a reasonable expectation of improving or maintaining enrollee health or overall function; and

   b.   an ability to tailor to an individual beneficiaries' specific medical condition and needs.

   These plans generally include therapies, pest control, food and produce, meals, non-medical transportation, structural home modifications, service dog support, social needs benefits, transitional/temporary supports, indoor air quality equipment, and services. See table below.

NON-MEDICAL SUPPLEMENTAL BENEFITS

Number of Plans Offering Benefits (Percentage of Total Plans by Year)

BENEFIT	2020	2021	2022
Food and Produce	101 (2%)	345 (7%)	763 (14%)
Meals (beyond limited basis)	71 (2%)	371 (7%)	403 (14%)
Pest Control	118 (3%)	208 (5%)	326 (8%)
Transportation for Non-Medical Needs	88 (2%)	177 (4%)	375 (7%)
Indoor Air Quality Equipment and Services	52 (1%)	140 (3%)	166 (3%)
Social Needs Benefits	23 (1%)	211 (4%)	244 (5%)
Complementary Therapies	1 (< 1%)	0 (0%)	123 (2%)
Services Supporting Self-Direction	20 (< 1%)	96 (2%)	151 (3%)
Structural Home Modifications	44 (1%)	42 (1%)	57 (1%)
General Supports for Living	67 (2%)	250 (3%)	338 (6%)
Other Non-Primarily Health Related Benefit	51 (1%)	191 (4%)	359 (7%)

1184. What are the most popular Supplemental Benefits in Medicare Advantage plans?

The most popular benefits are probably not surprising and include:

- Eye Examinations and/or glasses and contacts (offered by 99 percent of MA plans)

- Hearing Examinations and/or hearing aids (offered by 98 percent of MA plans)

- Fitness benefits (offered by 98 percent of MA plans)

- Telehealth (offered by 98 percent of MA plans)

- Dental coverage (offered by 96 percent of MA plans)

- Over the counter benefits (offered by 94 percent of MA plans)

- Remote access technologies (offered by 72 percent of MA plans)

- Meal benefits (offered by 71 percent of MA plans)

- Acupuncture (offered by 45 percent of MA plans)

- Transportation (offered by 39 percent of MA plans)

- In Home Support Services (offered by 12 percent of MA plans)

- Bathroom Safety Devices (offered by 9 percent of MA plans)

- Telemonitoring Services (offered by 4 percent of MA plans)

As of 2022, there were 3,834 plans, an eight percent increase from 2021 – the number of plans offering supplemental benefits has steadily increased for every year since 2016. Some benefits have gained less traction, such as acupuncturists, therapeutic massage, telemonitoring, world-wide coverage, and chiropractors (beyond existing Medicare-covered chiropractic services), or safety-related benefits including bathroom/home safety devices.

1185. What standards must Medicare Advantage plans meet for protection of beneficiaries?

In general, Medicare Advantage plans must offer similar protections to Medicare beneficiaries enrolled in traditional Medicare Part A (Hospital Insurance) and Part B (Medical Insurance), including disclosure, access, quality of care, grievance and appeals procedures, confidentiality, and information on advance directives.

1186. What are the rules regarding nondiscrimination for Medicare Advantage plans?

Medicare Advantage plans cannot screen potential enrollees based on their health status, nor can a Medicare Advantage plan discriminate with respect to participation, payment, or indemnification against any provider acting within the scope of the provider's license or certification. Medicare Advantage plans may, however, selectively contract with providers based on a provider's willingness to accept the provisions of the Medicare Advantage plan's contract.

1187. What are the rules regarding disclosure to enrollees?

A Medicare Advantage plan must provide in a clear, accurate, and standardized form, certain plan information to each enrollee, including the following information about the plan:

- service area;

- benefits;

- number;

- mix and distribution of providers;

- out-of-area coverage;

- emergency coverage;

- supplemental benefits;

- prior authorization rules;

- appeals and grievance procedures;

- quality assurance program; and

- disenrollment procedures.

Upon request, enrollees must be provided comparative information, information on the plan's utilization control mechanisms, information on the number of grievances and appeals, and compensation arrangements.

1188. What are the access-to-services requirements for Medicare Advantage plans?

Medicare Advantage plans are permitted to select the providers who may furnish benefits to enrollees, as long as benefits are available and accessible to all enrollees with reasonable promptness and assured continuity, twenty-four hours a day, seven days a week.

The plan must also cover services provided other than through the organization for:

(1)   nonemergency services needed immediately because of an unforeseen illness or injury, if it was not reasonable to obtain the services through the plan;

(2)   renal dialysis services for enrollees who are temporarily out of the plan's service
       area; and

(3)   maintenance or post stabilization care after an emergency condition has been sta-
       bilized, subject to guidelines established by the Centers for Medicare & Medicaid
       Services (CMS).

Medicare Advantage plans are required to pay for emergency services without regard to prior authorization or whether the provider has a contractual relationship with the plan. An emergency medical condition is defined using a "prudent layperson" standard (including condi-tions that may be manifested by "severe pain").

Private fee-for-service plans must demonstrate that the plan includes a sufficient number and range of providers willing to furnish services. This requirement is presumed to have been met if the plan has established payment rates that are not less than payment rates under Medicare, and/or has contracts or agreements with a sufficient number and range of providers.

1189. Is there a quality assurance program for Medicare Advantage plans?

All Medicare Advantage plans must have an internal quality assurance program. There are numerous requirements for internal quality assurance programs, including that such programs include chronic care improvement plans, conduct certain types of quality improvement projects, and encourage contracted providers to participate in various government quality improvement initiatives.

Medicare Advantage plans are deemed to have satisfied certain of the Medicare quality assur-ance requirements by receiving accreditation (and having periodic review and re-accreditation) from a private organization approved by the Centers for Medicare & Medicaid Services (CMS). CMS may also deem Medicare Advantage plans—generally, organizations with good track records—to have satisfied certain of the quality assurance program requirements. The Quality Improvement program requirements for MA organizations for 2023 are described in 42 CFR § 422.152 "Quality Improvement Program".[1]

A change for 2019 and subsequent years is that CMS longer mandates that Medicare Advan-tage plans complete Quality Improvement Project (QIP) requirements. CMS found that Quality Improvement (QI) requirements already include the QIP activities.

Note

1. See also: https://www.cms.gov/files/document/cms-ma-ccip-resource-document-updated-2020.pdf 2020 Update (latest available) – Last accessed October 16, 2022.

1190. How are grievances handled by Medicare Advantage plans?

Medicare Advantage plans must maintain meaningful procedures for hearing and resolving grievances. Medicare Advantage plans also must have a procedure for making determinations regarding whether an enrollee is entitled to receive services and the amount the individual is required to pay for such services. Determinations must be made on a timely basis. The explanation of a plan's determination must be in writing and must explain the reasons for the denial in understandable language and describe the reconsideration and appeals processes. The period for reconsiderations will be specified by the Centers for Medicare & Medicaid Services (CMS) but must not be greater than sixty days after the request by the enrollee. Reconsiderations of coverage determinations to deny coverage based on lack of medical necessity must be made by a physician with expertise in the field of medicine that relates to the condition necessitating treatment.

Plans are required to have an expedited review process in cases where the normal time frame for making a determination or reconsideration could seriously jeopardize the life or health of the enrollee or the enrollee's ability to regain maximum function. Either the beneficiary or the physician can request an expedited review. Requests for expedited reviews made by physicians (even those not affiliated with the organization) must be granted by the plan. Expedited determinations and reconsiderations must be made within time periods specified by CMS, but not later than seventy-two hours after the request for expedited review, or such longer period as CMS may permit in specified cases.

CMS is required to contract with an independent, outside entity to review and resolve plan reconsiderations not favorable to the beneficiary. If the independent review is unfavorable to the beneficiary, the beneficiary has the right to the same appeals process (e.g., Administrative Law Judge, judicial review) as under existing HMO procedures.

1191. Are there special rules covering provider participation?

Yes, a Medicare Advantage plan must establish procedures relating to participation of physicians in the plan, such as notice of rules of participation, written notice of adverse participation decisions, and an appeals process. Medicare Advantage plans must consult with participating physicians regarding medical policy, quality, and medical management procedures.

Plans are prohibited from restricting health care professionals from advising their patients about the patient's health status or treatment options.

A provider, health professional, or other entity is treated as having a contract with a private fee-for-service plan if the provider, health professional, or other entity provides services that are covered under a private fee-for-service plan, and before providing those services, was informed of the individual's enrollment, and either was informed of the terms and conditions of payment for the services under the private fee-for-service plan or was given a reasonable opportunity to obtain information concerning the terms and conditions. A major change for 2019 was that certain providers were no longer be required to meet enrollment requirements.

In addition, CMS, beginning 2019, lifted certain restrictions on the types of Medicare Advantage plans that insurance companies can offer. Under the prior restrictions, a company couldn't offer multiple plans within the same county if the plans appeared too similar to one another.

1192. Are there billing limits under Medicare Advantage?

Noncontracting physicians and other entities must accept as payment in full the amount that would have been paid under Medicare Advantage or a Medicare fee-for-service plan. Noncontracting providers must also accept, as payment in full, the amount that would have been paid under traditional Medicare.

Contracting physicians, providers, and other entities of private fee-for-service plans must accept as payment in full an amount not to exceed (including any deductibles, coinsurance, copayments, or balance billing permitted under the plan) an amount equal to 115 percent (the "limiting charge") of the plan's payment rate. Plans must establish procedures to carry out this requirement. If a plan does not establish and enforce its procedures, the plan is subject to sanctions.

Private fee-for-service plans must provide enrollees with an explanation of benefits that includes a clear statement regarding enrollee liability, including any balance billing. The plan must also provide that the hospital gives enrollees prior notice before they receive inpatient services and certain other services, when the amount of balance billing could be substantial. The notice must include a good faith estimate of the likely amount of balance billing based upon the presenting conditions of the enrollee.

Premiums

1193. How do Medicare Advantage plans submit proposed premiums?

All Medicare Advantage plans must submit to the Centers for Medicare & Medicaid Services (CMS) information on enrollment capacity.

- **Managed care plans** must submit Adjusted Community Rate (ACR) proposals for basic and supplemental benefits, the plan's premium for the basic and supplemental benefits, a description of the plan's proposed cost-sharing requirements, the actuarial value of cost sharing for basic and supplemental benefits, and a description of any additional benefits and the value of these benefits.

- **Private fee-for-service plans** must submit ACRs for basic and additional benefits, the premium for the basic and additional benefits, a description of the plan's proposed cost-sharing requirements and the actuarial value of the cost sharing, a description of additional benefits and the actuarial value of these benefits, and the supplemental premium.

In general, the CMS must review ACRs, premiums, and the actuarial values and approve or disapprove these rates, amounts, and values. CMS does not review premiums of private fee-for-service plans.

Organizations cannot contract to enroll Medicare beneficiaries under the Medicare Advantage program until they have met standards published by the CMS.

1194. What other Medicare Advantage premium rules should a member know about?

- A Medicare Advantage plan can terminate ("disenroll") an enrollee for failure to pay premiums, but only under specified conditions.

  o Any monthly basic and supplementary beneficiary premiums are not paid on a timely basis, subject to the grace period for late payment established under 42 CFR section 422.74 which includes:

    ♦ Alerting the individual of the delinquency.

    ♦ Providing the individual with a grace period, that is, an opportunity to pay past due premiums in full. The length of the grace period must -

      (1)   Be at least 2 months; and

      (2)   Begin on the first day of the month for which the premium is unpaid or the first day of the month following the date on which premium payment is requested, whichever is later.

  o (C) Advising the individual that failure to pay the premiums by the end of the grace period will result in termination of MA coverage.

- A Medicare Advantage organization cannot offer cash or other monetary rebates as an inducement for enrollment or otherwise.

- Premiums cannot vary among plan enrollees in the same Medicare Advantage plan.

- No state can impose a premium tax or similar tax on premiums of Medicare Advantage plans or the offering of these plans.

- For 2021 and beyond, CMS is allowing certain Medicare Advantage plans to charge different annual deductibles for beneficiaries that meet certain medical criteria.

- CMS is allowing Medicare Advantage plans to seamlessly renew coverage for beneficiaries automatically year by year.

Contracts with Medicare Advantage Organizations

1195. How does a plan become part of the Medicare Advantage program?

A Medicare Advantage plan must generally be organized and licensed under state law as a risk-bearing entity to offer health insurance or health benefits coverage.

New regional Preferred Provider Organizations (PPOs) are also eligible for temporary waiver-of-state-licensure requirements. This is intended to facilitate the introduction of these multistate plans. The Centers for Medicare & Medicaid Services (CMS) has indicated that it will grant these waivers only in cases where the organization is licensed in one state and has submitted applications in the other states. The length of the waiver will typically be for less than one year but will depend on how long states take to process applications.

A plan cannot receive payment from Medicare unless it has a contract with CMS. The contract period is for one year and may be automatically renewed in the absence of notice by either party of intention to terminate.

CMS can terminate a contract under the following circumstances:

(1)   the organization has failed to substantially carry out the contract;

(2)   the organization was carrying out the contract in a manner substantially inconsistent with the efficient and effective administration of the Medicare Advantage program; or

(3)   the organization no longer substantially meets Medicare Advantage conditions. CMS generally may not contract with a plan that has been terminated within the last five years.

Medicare Advantage plans must provide prompt payment to noncontracting providers and to enrollees in the case of private fee-for-service plans. If CMS determines (after notice of an opportunity for a hearing) that a plan has failed to pay providers or enrollees promptly, CMS can provide for direct payment. In these cases, CMS will reduce Medicare Advantage payments accordingly.

CMS may impose sanctions under the following circumstances if a plan:

(1)   fails to provide medically necessary services required under law or the contract, and the failure adversely affects or has the substantial likelihood of adversely affecting the enrollee;

(2)   imposes premiums more than the premium permitted;

(3)   acts to expel or refuses to reenroll an individual in violation of the Medicare Advantage requirements;

(4)   engages in practices that effectively deny or discourage enrollment;

(5)   misrepresents or falsifies information to CMS or to others;

(6)   violates rules regarding physician participation;

(7)   employs or contracts with individuals who are excluded from participation in Medicare; or

(8)   performs any other actions that are grounds for termination and, in the case of private fee-for-service plans, does not enforce balance billing limits. The remedies

may include civil money penalties, suspension of enrollment, or suspension of payment.

Medicare Advantage plans must assume full financial risk for the provision of Medicare services, except those plans can:

(1) obtain insurance or make other arrangements for costs more than amounts periodically determined by CMS;

(2) obtain insurance or plan for services needing to be provided other than through the plan;

(3) obtain insurance or make other arrangements for not more than 90 percent of the amount by which its fiscal year costs exceeded 115 percent of its income for the year; or

(4) plan with providers or health institutions to assume all or part of the risk on a prospective basis for the provision of basic services.

1196. What are the minimum enrollment requirements for Medicare Advantage?

Medicare Advantage plans must meet minimum enrollment requirements unless they qualify for a waiver:

- At least 5,000 individuals (or 1,500 if the organization is a PSO) need to be enrolled for the purpose of receiving health benefits from the organization; or

- At least 1,500 individuals (or 500 if the organization is a PSO) are enrolled for purposes of receiving health benefits from the organization and the organization primarily serves individual residing outside of the urbanized areas (rural).[1]

Minimum Enrollment Waiver

CMS may waive the minimum enrollment requirement for the first three years of the contract. To receive a waiver, a contract applicant must demonstrate satisfaction that it is capable of administering and managing an MA contract and is able to manage the level of risk required under the contract during the first three years of the contract. Factors that CMS takes into consideration in making this evaluation include the extent to which:

- The contract applicant management and providers have previous experience in managing and providing health care services under a risk-based payment arrangement to at least as many individuals as the applicable minimum enrollment; OR

- The contract applicant has the financial ability to bear financial risk under an MA contract; and

- The contract applicant is able to establish a marketing and enrollment process that allows it to meet the applicable enrollment requirement before completion of the third contract year.

Note

1. 42 C.F.R. § 422.514, "Enrollment Requirements," https://www.law.cornell.edu/cfr/text/42/422.514 (current through June 2, 2020).

Medigap Insurance Program

1197.What rules apply regarding Medigap insurance and Medicare Advantage plans?

As a general matter, a Medigap insurance policy cannot be sold or issued to a Medicare beneficiary or an individual with the knowledge that the policy duplicates health benefits to which the individual is already entitled under Medicare, including under a Medicare Advantage plan. Medigap policies can't work with Medicare Advantage Plans. If a person has a Medigap policy and joins a Medicare Advantage Plan (Part C), they will want to drop the Medigap policy. The Medigap policy can't be used to pay Medicare Advantage Plan copayments, deductibles, and premiums.

A Medicare Advantage plan is not considered a Medigap insurance policy. Medigap insurance policies supplement original fee-for-service Medicare coverage (Medicare Part A (Hospital Insurance) and Part B (Medical Insurance). As an alternative to original Medicare Parts A and B, Medicare Advantage plans offer at a minimum the same basic coverage as traditional fee-for-service Medicare. Medicare Advantage plans may also offer additional benefits, subject to payment of additional premiums by enrollees (if the Medicare Advantage plan so requires). The additional benefits often duplicate what would otherwise be available through a private Medigap policy. See Q 1212 through Q 1229 for more information on Medigap insurance.

If a person has a Medicare Advantage Plan, it's illegal for anyone to sell them a Medigap policy unless they're switching back to Original Medicare. If a person wants to switch to Original Medicare and buy a Medigap policy, they may need to contact their Medicare Advantage Plan to see if they can disenroll. If someone joins a Medicare Advantage Plan for the first time and isn't happy with the plan, they have special rights under federal law to buy a Medigap policy if they return to Original Medicare within twelve months of joining.

1198. What are the special rules regarding Medigap protections (Guaranteed Issue Rights) under the Medicare Advantage program?

If an individual described below seeks to enroll in a Medigap policy within sixty-three days of the events described next, the issuer may not:

(1)   deny or condition the issuance of a Medigap policy that is offered or available,

(2)   discriminate in the pricing (can't charge someone more for a policy) of a policy because of health status, claims experience, receipt of health care, or medical condition; and

(3)   impose a preexisting condition exclusion (must cover all preexisting conditions).

See Q 1212 through Q 1229 for more information about Medigap insurance.

There is guaranteed issuance of Medigap Plans A, B, K, or L for:

(1)   Individuals enrolled under an employee welfare benefit plan that provides benefits supplementing Medicare if the plan terminates or ceases to provide all benefits.

(2)   Persons enrolled with a Medicare Advantage organization who discontinue under circumstances permitting disenrollment other than during an annual election period. These include:

   (a) the termination of the entity's certification,

   (b) the individual moves outside the entity's service area, or

   (c) the individual elects to terminate due to cause.

(3)   Persons enrolled with a risk or cost contract HMO, a similar organization operating under a demonstration project authority, a health care prepayment plan, or a Medicare SELECT policy, if enrollment ceases under the same circumstances that permit discontinuance of a Medicare Advantage election. In the case of a SELECT policy, there must also be no applicable provision in state law for continuation of the coverage.

(4)   Individuals enrolled under a Medigap policy, if enrollment ceases because of the bankruptcy or insolvency of the issuer, or because of other involuntary termination of coverage (and there is no provision under applicable state law for the continuation of coverage), or the issuer violated or misrepresented a provision of the policy.

Note that new Medigap Plan C or Plan F policies are no longer be able to be sold beginning in 2020 due to Congress passing the MACRA law stating that new Medigap plans will no longer be allowed to cover the Part B deductible after January 1, 2020.

There is guaranteed issuance of Medigap Plans A, B, K, L, or the Medigap insurance policy that the individual most recently previously enrolled in, if the individual:

(1)   was enrolled under a Medigap policy;

(2)   subsequently terminates enrollment and enrolls with a Medicare Advantage organization, a risk or cost contract HMO, a similar organization operating under a demonstration project authority, or a Medicare SELECT policy; and

(3)   terminates the Medicare Advantage enrollment within twelve months, but only if the individual was never previously enrolled with a Medicare Advantage organization.

There is guaranteed issuance of any Medigap plan to an individual who, upon first becoming eligible for Medicare at age sixty-five, enrolled in a Medicare Advantage plan and disenrolled from the plan within twelve months of the effective date of enrollment.

Medicare Advantage Marketing Rules

1199. What are the rules about the marketing of Medicare Advantage plans?

Significant restrictions apply to marketing of Medicare Advantage plans to Medicare beneficiaries. These restrictions include:

- Prohibiting "cold calls" and other unsolicited contact. This prohibition includes door-to-door sales and unsolicited telephone calls. The rules do not prohibit plan mailings, but the final regulations prohibit calling to confirm that the beneficiary received the mailing. Agents may call in response to specific requests by beneficiaries to be contacted.

- Visit sales prospects in their homes, nursing homes, etc. without express permission.

- Ask for personal or financial information if they call a prospect.

- Provide gifts worth more than $15 to encourage enrollment.

- Compare their plan to another by name in advertising materials.

- Sell life insurance or other non-health products at the same appointment (cross-selling).

- Using the term "Medicare-endorsed" or suggest the plan is a preferred Medicare plan.

- Imply they are calling on behalf of Medicare.

- Prohibiting sales activities at educational events. Events designed to provide the public with objective information about Medicare must be free of any marketing materials or enrollment information for a specific plan or organization. Plans and agents may hold sales events that are clearly labeled as such, but they may not be disguised as educational events.

- Prohibiting plans and agents from providing meals at Medicare sales meetings. Light refreshments and "snacks" are permissible.

- Prohibiting sales activities in settings where individuals receive health care services. This rule permits marketing in common areas such as waiting rooms but prohibits marketing in treatment rooms. Plans may arrange meetings with residents in long-term care facilities as with any other private residence.

- Prohibiting the marketing of any nonhealth insurance product (such as life insurance or annuities) during a Medicare marketing or sales meeting.

Agents are also required to document that, prior to making an appointment, beneficiaries agree to the scope of products to be discussed at the meeting. Appointments made in person require written documentation; appointments made over the phone require recorded documentation. At a meeting in an agent's office or on the phone, additional products may not be discussed unless the beneficiary requests the information. In a meeting at a beneficiary's home, an agent may not discuss any product not within the originally-identified scope of the meeting. They must schedule a separate appointment at least forty-eight hours later.

Marketing materials must include:

All Medicare Advantage plans must give a complete description of plan rules to potential members in an enrollment kit that includes:

- Any network requirements

- Specifics on the plan's coverage and costs

- Eligibility requirements

- Instructions on how to file an appeal or grievance

- Written notice advising potential enrollees that costs can change year to year

- Instructions and forms on how to enroll

- Cover letter with the plan's customer service phone number along with the number to contact Medicare

- Information on how to apply for Extra Help

- Plan ratings information

- Translated marketing materials in any non-English language that is the primary language of at least 5 percent of the individuals in a plan's benefit package (PBP) service area, available on their websites and in hard-copy upon request

- Upon enrollment, a pharmacy and provider directory

If an individual decides to enroll in a Medicare Advantage plan, the plan must provide a Summary of Benefits, which details coverage and costs under the plan. The plan must also provide the member with a handbook and Evidence of Coverage (EOC), which explains the plan's coverage. Plans must send this EOC to new members no later than January of that plan year.

They must also provide a pharmacy and provider directory upon enrollment, and every three years thereafter.

1200. What are the pros and cons of Medicare Advantage plans?

<u>**Upsides:**</u>

- Some insurance companies offer zero-dollar premiums for the Medicare Advantage plan.

- Medicare Advantage may save members money – lower cost sharing, copayments, etc. (out of pocket can be lower than traditional Medicare). The maximum out of pocket costs for Medicare Advantage for 2021 and 2022 were $7,550 (not including prescriptions). The 2023 has been set at $8,300. Most MA plans set limits **under** the maximum.

- Medicare Advantage plan availability can depend on the county and state.

- Medicare Advantage plans help coordinate plans among health care providers.

- Medicare Advantage might cover benefits beyond the coverage of Part A and Part B.

- Vision, hearing, and/or dental coverage might be offered.

- Each plan has a maximum out-of-pocket limit on health care costs for the year.

- Once limit is met – no cost for covered services.

- Can be convenient to have all coverage in one plan (one-stop shopping).

- Most—although not all—Medicare Advantage plans offer prescription coverage which is only available in Medicare through Part D.

<u>**Downsides:**</u>

- Since Medicare Advantage plans are run through private insurance companies, there are often differences in rules from company to company.

- Specifics of each plan depend on decisions of the insurance company.

- Some may require higher out-of-pocket costs than with Original Medicare.

- Plan premiums, benefits, and copayments may change each year.

- Limitations of choice: the insurance company may mandate strict rules for coverage for certain services or health products, such as referrals to see specialists.

- Subscribers may have to change doctors or hospitals to one within the Medicare Advantage plan's network for coverage or pay a higher cost.

- Medicare Advantage plans have annual contracts with Medicare and can choose not to renew their contract for the following year.

- Each Medicare Advantage plan can have a different out of pocket limit, and that amount may change each year.

- Most require copays/coinsurance.

- Certain drugs may not be covered – formulary can change at any time.

- Preferred health providers may not be in network.

- Difficult to compare plans.

- "Rationing" of care if shortages of medical personnel.

- Sometimes no nationwide coverage.

- There are over 6,000 plans—members need to do their research—some plans might not be financially stable (as shown by the collapse of Physicians United in Florida).

1201. What are the biggest changes in Medicare Advantage plans during 2022?

- Effective payment growth rate is higher

  ○ CMS is estimating that the effective payment growth rate for 2022 will be 4,88 percent in the final rule, resulting in a 8.05 percent increase in revenue. This is a good sign for Medicare Advantage organizations, indicating that CMS is not expecting a significant cost rebound after the major drop due to deferred or foregone care.

- A new risk score methodology has been finalized

  ○ Although payment growth will be higher than expected in 2023, this revenue increase may be offset for some payers due to changes in the risk adjustment factor (RAF) score calculation. In 2023, the RAF score will be 100 percent based on data from the Encounter Data System (EDS) and fee-for-service claims rather than a mix of encounter data and Risk Adjustment Processing System (RAPS) data.

- Telehealth expansion at record levels

  ○ 2022 continued record setting year for use of telehealth by Medicare beneficiaries. Over four-fifths of Medicare beneficiaries with a regular provider reported access to telehealth appointments.[1] It is expected that telehealth will continue to grow. Over 80 percent of Medicare beneficiaries have high-speed internet access and this rate is likely to increase given that 82 percent of seniors also report that they have high-speed Internet access and 91 percent of Medicare Advantage subscribers have had positive telehealth experiences.[2]

- ESRD Coverage Available in 2022

  o The 2022 MA contract year was the first time individuals with end-stage renal disease (ESRD) will be allowed to enroll in a plan.

Notes

1. https://www.cms.gov/files/document/medicare-current-beneficiary-survey-summer-2020-covid-19-data-snapshot.pdf.
2. https://bettermedicarealliance.org/wp-content/uploads/2020/06/BMA-Memo-CT-D23.pdf.

1202. What things should one remember about Medicare Advantage?

- It is still within the Medicare program.

- Participants still have Medicare protections and rights. Part A and Part B coverage is still provided through the plan. Beneficiaries still get complete Part A and Part B coverage through the plan. Plans may offer some extra benefits that Original Medicare doesn't cover such as vision, hearing, and dental services.

- Out of pocket costs may be lower in a Medicare Advantage Plan.

- Beneficiaries cannot buy and don't need Medigap coverage.

- One can only join a plan at Medicare Advantage Open Enrollment period, Medicare Open Enrollment periods, and Initial Enrollment periods. Usually, one is enrolled in a plan for a year.

- One can join a Medicare Advantage Plan even with pre-existing condition(s).

- One can check with the plan before getting a service to find out if it's covered and what the costs may be.

- Following plan rules can keep costs lower.

- Using doctors and other health care providers, facilities, or suppliers that belong to the network can result in covered services lower costs. In most cases, this applies to Medicare Advantage HMOs and PPOs.

- Providers can join or leave a network anytime during the year. A plan can also change the providers in the network anytime during the year. If this happens, a person may need to choose a new provider.

- If a subscriber joins clinical research studies, some costs may be covered by the plan.

- Medicare Advantage Plans can't charge more than Original Medicare for certain services like chemotherapy, dialysis, and skilled nursing facility care.

- Medicare Advantage Plans have a yearly limit on out-of-pocket costs for medical services. Once the limit is reached, there is no cost for covered services. Each plan can have a different limit, and the limit can change each year.

- If the plan decides to stop participating in Medicare, a subscriber will have to join another Medicare Health Plan or return to Original Medicare.

- One can only be in one Medicare Advantage Plan at a time.

PART D:
PRESCRIPTION DRUG INSURANCE

1203. What is Medicare Part D?

Medicare Part D is the prescription drug insurance program added to Medicare by the Medicare Prescription Drug, Improvement, and Modernization Act of 2003 (MMA).

Part D is a voluntary program of health insurance that covers a portion of outpatient prescription drug costs not generally covered by other Medicare programs, especially traditional Medicare Part A (Hospital Insurance) and Part B (Medical Insurance). Part D prescription drug plans are offered only through private insurance companies. Medicare beneficiaries wishing to enroll in a Part D plan may stay with original Medicare Parts A and B and enroll in a stand-alone Part D prescription drug insurance plan, or they may choose a Medicare Advantage plan that includes Part D prescription drug benefits as part of the Medicare Advantage plan's comprehensive benefit package. Part D prescription drug insurance is partially financed through premiums paid by participants, whether for stand-alone Part D plans or as part of a Medicare Advantage plan.

1204. How is Medicare Prescription Drug coverage obtained?

Medicare prescription drug coverage is an optional benefit offered to everyone who has Medicare. If someone decides not to get Medicare drug coverage when first eligible, they will likely pay a late enrollment penalty if joining later, unless they have creditable drug coverage or receive extra help. If penalized, they will likely pay this penalty for as long as they have Medicare prescription drug coverage.

There are two ways to obtain Medicare Prescription Drug Coverage:

1. **Medicare Prescription Drug Plans** (Part D). These plans (sometimes called "PDPs") add drug coverage to Original Medicare, some Medicare Cost Plans, some Medicare Private Fee-for-Service (PFFS) Plans, and Medicare Medical Savings Account (MSA) Plans.

2. **Medicare Advantage Plans** (Part C, like an HMO or PPO) or other Medicare health plan that offers Medicare prescription drug coverage. You get all of your Medicare Part A (Hospital Insurance) and Medicare Part B (Medical Insurance) coverage, and prescription drug coverage (Part D), through these plans. Medicare Advantage Plans with prescription drug coverage are sometimes called "MA-PDs". You must have Part A and Part B to join a Medicare Advantage Plan.

1205. What is the late enrollment fee for Medicare Part D?

The cost of the late enrollment penalty depends on how long you went without Part D or creditable prescription drug coverage.

Medicare calculates the penalty by multiplying 1 percent of the "national base beneficiary premium" ($33.59 in 2019, $32.74 in 2020, $33.06 in 2021, $33.37 in 2022, and $32.74 in 2023) times the number of full, uncovered months the individual didn't have Part D or creditable coverage. The monthly premium is rounded to the nearest $0.10 and added to the monthly Part D premium.

The national base beneficiary premium may increase each year, so the penalty amount may also increase each year.

1206. When did Medicare Part D become effective?

Medicare Part D (Prescription Drug Insurance) became effective January 1, 2006, with initial enrollment for the first year beginning November 15, 2005, and running for six months.

1207. Who is eligible for Medicare Part D?

Any Medicare beneficiary who is entitled to Medicare Part A or enrolled in Part B is eligible to participate in Part D (Prescription Drug Insurance).

1208. What does the Part D (Prescription Drug Insurance) cost?

Generally, Part D (Prescription Drug Insurance) plans require beneficiaries to pay monthly premiums, meet an annual deductible, and pay coinsurance. Because Part D plans are offered only through private insurance plans, the premiums, deductibles, and coinsurance vary from plan to plan. Premiums may be paid separately for a stand-alone Part D plan or as part of the monthly premium for a comprehensive Medicare Advantage plan.

Beneficiaries who choose not to enroll in Part D during their initial enrollment period may face a late enrollment penalty if they later choose to enroll in a Part D plan. The late enrollment penalty is the greater of "an amount that [the CMS] determines is actuarially sound for each uncovered month" or "1 percent of the base beneficiary premium" (the national average premium for the year of late enrollment) per month. The late enrollment penalty is calculated by multiplying 1 percent of the "national base beneficiary premium" ($32.42 in 2014, $33.13 in 2015, $34.10 in 2016, $35.63 in 2017, $35.02 in 2018, $33.59 in 2019, $32.74 in 2020, $33.06 in 2021, $33.38 in 2022, and $33.74 in 2023) times the number of full, uncovered months you were eligible but didn't join a Medicare Prescription Drug Plan and went without other creditable prescription drug coverage. The final amount is rounded to the nearest ten cents and added to your monthly premium. For example, for a beneficiary enrolling late in 2023, the penalty is approximately 34 cents per full month in which the beneficiary was eligible to enroll in a Part D plan but failed to do so.

Beneficiaries who have other sources of prescription drug coverage (such as through a former employer) may be able to maintain that coverage and delay enrollment in a Part D plan without incurring a penalty in the future. As long as a beneficiary maintains coverage that qualifies as "creditable coverage" (meaning generally that the coverage is at least as valuable—at least actuarially equivalent—as the standard Part D prescription drug package specified by Medicare), the beneficiary will not be subject to late enrollment penalties if he later enrolls in a Part D plan. Failure to maintain creditable prescription drug coverage for a period of sixty-three days or longer may subject an individual to a late enrollment penalty.

Entities (such as a former employer) offering prescription drug coverage to Part D eligible individuals must disclose to those individuals whether the coverage they provide is creditable coverage as defined by CMS. These entities must also inform CMS of the status of this coverage. See Q 1227.

1209. What benefits does Part D (Prescription Drug Insurance) provide?

Medicare establishes a standard prescription drug benefit under Part D (Prescription Drug Insurance). Participants with incomes below 135 percent, and between 135 percent and 150 percent, of the federal poverty guidelines will have lower cost-sharing requirements than under the standard benefit.

The Part D standard drug benefit in 2023 is projected to be:

Prescription Drug Expenses	Beneficiary Costs	Medicare Pays
First $80	100% (up to $80)	Nothing
$80 to $4,640	25%	75%
$4,660 to $10.516.25	25% (up to $7,400)	75%
Above $10,516.25	Up to 5% (based on income)	95% or more

In the "Coverage Gap" ($4,660 to $7,400), a Medicare beneficiary may have to pay for 25 percent of either brand name drugs or generic drugs. Once a Medicare beneficiary has paid $7,400 out-of-pocket, the beneficiary is out of the Coverage Gap.

Beneficiaries with incomes below 135 percent of the federal poverty guidelines have no cost-sharing obligation for prescription drug expenses above $10,516.25. Beneficiaries with incomes between 135 percent and 150 percent of the federal poverty guidelines have $3.75 and $9.24 co-pays for generic and name-brand prescriptions. Those with incomes above 150 percent of the federal poverty level have 5 percent copays.

For 2023, 135 percent of the federal poverty guidelines is $18,346.50 for a single person and $24,718.50 for a married couple; 150 percent of the federal poverty guidelines is $20,835 for a single person and $27,465 for a married couple.

Part D plans are available only through private insurance companies. Those insurers may offer prescription drug plans that vary from the Part D standard benefit as long as the plans:

    (1)   provide coverage, the actuarial value of which is at least equal to the actuarial value of the standard prescription drug coverage;

(2)   offer access to negotiated prices; and

(3)   are approved by the CMS.

Part D plans may also provide supplemental prescription drug coverage that offers cost-sharing reductions and optional drugs. A plan may charge a supplemental premium for the supplemental coverage. However, insurers offering Part D plans with supplemental coverage in an area must also offer a prescription drug plan in the area that provides only basic coverage for no additional supplemental premium. Basic coverage is either the statutorily defined standard benefit or the actuarial equivalent of such standard benefit without any supplemental benefits.

The monthly Medicare Part D base premium is set to pay 25.5 percent of the cost of standard coverage, based on bids submitted annually by Part D plans. The CMS releases the Medicare Part D base premium in early August each year. Actual premiums are based on this set premium, but can vary greatly by plans and regions. Beneficiaries with higher incomes must pay a premium adjustment based on their income. This premium adjustment is called the Income-Related Monthly Adjustment Amount (IRMAA), and is automatically deducted from the Social Security benefit.

Costs for 2023

Beneficiaries who file individual tax returns with income that is:	Beneficiaries who file joint tax returns with income that is:	Medicare Part D Income Related Monthly Adjustment Amount*
		2023
Less than or equal to $97,000	Less than or equal to $194,000	$0.00
Greater than $97,000 and less than or equal to $123,000	Greater than $194,000 than or equal to $246,000	$12.20
Greater than $123,000 and less than or equal to $153,000	Greater than $246,000 and less than or equal to $306,000	$ 31.50
Greater than $183,000 and less than or equal to $500,000	Greater than $306,000 and less than or equal to $366,000	$ 50.70
Greater than $183,000 and less than or equal to $500,000	Greater than $366,000 and less than or equal to $750,000	$ 70.00
Greater than or equal to $500,000	Greater than or equal to $750,000	$ 76.40

Costs for 2022

Beneficiaries who file individual tax returns with income that is:	Beneficiaries who file joint tax returns with income that is:	Medicare Part D Income Related Monthly Adjustment Amount*
		2022
Less than or equal to $91,000	Less than or equal to $182,000	Plan premium
Greater than $88,000 and less than or equal to $114,000	Greater than $182,000 than or equal to $228,000	$12.50 plus plan premium
Greater than $114,000 and less than or equal to $142,000	Greater than $228,000 and less than or equal to $284,000	$ 32.10 plus plan premium
Greater than $142,000 and less than or equal to $170,000	Greater than $284,000 and less than or equal to $340,000	$ 51.50 plus plan premium
Greater than $170,000 and less than or equal to $500,000	Greater than $340,000 and less than or equal to $750,000	$ 71.30 plus plan premium
Greater than $500,000	Greater than $750,000	$ 77.90 plus plan premium

Costs for 2021

Beneficiaries who file individual tax returns with income that is:	Beneficiaries who file joint tax returns with income that is:	Medicare Part D Income Related Monthly Adjustment Amount*
Less than or equal to $88,000	Less than or equal to $176,000	Plan premium
Greater than $88,000 and less than or equal to $111,000	Greater than $176,000 than or equal to $222,000	$12.30 plus plan premium
Greater than $111,000 and less than or equal to $138,000	Greater than $222,000 and less than or equal to $276,000	$31.80 plus plan premium

Beneficiaries who file individual tax returns with income that is:	Beneficiaries who file joint tax returns with income that is:	Medicare Part D Income Related Monthly Adjustment Amount*
Greater than $138,000 and less than or equal to $165,000	Greater than $276,000 and less than or equal to $330,000	$51.20 plus plan premium
Greater than $165,000 and less than or equal to $500,000	Greater than $330,000 and less than or equal to $750,000	$70.70 plus plan premium
Greater than $500,000	Greater than $750,000	$77.10 plus plan premium

Cost for 2020

Beneficiaries who file individual tax returns with income that is:	Beneficiaries who file joint tax returns with income that is:	Medicare Part D Income Related Monthly Adjustment Amount*
Less than or equal to $87,000	Less than or equal to $174,000	$0.00
Greater than $87,000 and less than or equal to $109,000	Greater than $174,000 than or equal to $218,000	$12.20 plus plan premium
Greater than $107,000 and less than or equal to $133,500	Greater than $214,000 and less than or equal to $267,000	$31.50 plus plan premium
Greater than $133,500 and less than or equal to $160,000	Greater than $272,000 and less than or equal to $326,000	$50.70 plus plan premium
Greater than $160,000 and less than or equal to $500,000	Greater than $326,000 and less than or equal to $750,000	$70.00 plus plan premium
Greater than $500,000	Greater than $750,000	$76.40 plus plan premium

Costs for 2019

Beneficiaries who file individual tax returns with income that is:	Beneficiaries who file joint tax returns with income that is:	Medicare Part D Income Related Monthly Adjustment Amount* (plus plan premium)
Less than or equal to $85,000	Less than or equal to $170,000	$0.00
Greater than $85,000 and less than or equal to $107,000	Greater than 170,000 than or equal to $214,000	$12.40
Greater than $107,000 and less than or equal to $133,500	Greater than $214,000 and less than or equal to $267,000	$31.90
Greater than $133,500 and less than or equal to $160,000	Greater than $267,000 and less than or equal to $320,000	$51.40
Greater than $160,000 and less than or equal to $500,000	9 $320,000 and less than or equal to $750,000	$70.90
Greater than $500,000	Greater than $750,000	$77.40

Costs for 2018

Beneficiaries who file individual tax returns with income that is:	Beneficiaries who file joint tax returns with income that is:	Medicare Part D Income Related Monthly Adjustment Amount* (plus plan premium)
Less than or equal to $85,000	Less than or equal to $170,000	$0.00
Greater than $85,000 and less than or equal to $107,000	Greater than 170,000 than or equal to $214,000	$13.00
Greater than $107,000 and less than or equal to $133,500	Greater than $214,000 and less than or equal to $267,000	$33.60

Beneficiaries who file individual tax returns with income that is:	Beneficiaries who file joint tax returns with income that is:	Medicare Part D Income Related Monthly Adjustment Amount* (plus plan premium)
Greater than $133,500 and less than or equal to $160,000	Greater than $267,000 and less than or equal to $320,000	$54.20
Greater than $160,000	Greater than $320,000	$74.80

Costs for 2014 through 2017

Beneficiaries who file individual tax returns with income that is:	Beneficiaries who file joint tax returns with income that is:	Medicare Part D Income Related Monthly Adjustment Amount*			
		2017	2016	2015	2014
Less than or equal to $85,000	Less than or equal to $170,000	$0.00	$0.00	$0.00	$0.00
Greater than $85,000 and less than or equal to $107,000	Greater than $170,000 and less than or equal to $214,000	$13.30	$12.70	$12.30	$12.10
Greater than $107,000 and less than or equal to $160,000	Greater than $214,000 and less than or equal to $320,000	$34.20	$32.80	$31.80	$31.10
Greater than $160,000 and less than or equal to $214,000	Greater than $320,000 and less than or equal to $428,000	$55.20	$52.80	$51.30	$50.20
Greater than $214,000	Greater than $428,000	$76.20	$72.90	$70.80	$69.30

The Patient Protection and Affordable Care Act (PPACA) includes benefits to make Medicare prescription drug coverage (Part D) more affordable for beneficiaries. This is done through providing coverage through a coverage gap (also called the "donut hole") in Medicare prescription drug coverage.

The PPACA coverage provides the following:

- A discount on covered brand-name drugs when a person buys the drug at a pharmacy or orders the drugs through the mail

- Some coverage for generic and brand-name drugs

- Additional savings on brand-name and generic drugs during the coverage gap over the next several years until it is closed in 2020

- The coverage gap closes by maintaining the 50 percent discount the manufacturers offer and increasing what Medicare drug plans cover

1210. What notice must an employer who maintains a prescription drug plan provide to Medicare-eligible individuals?

Employers and plan sponsors who offer prescription drug coverage to individuals eligible for Medicare Part D (Prescription Drug Insurance) must advise those individuals whether the offered coverage is "creditable". Eligible individuals who do not enroll in Part D when first available, but who enroll later, have to pay higher premiums permanently, unless they have creditable prescription drug coverage. (See Q 1227.)

To determine that coverage is creditable, a sponsor need only determine that total expected paid claims for Medicare beneficiaries under the sponsor's plan will be at least equal to the total expected paid claims for the same beneficiaries under the defined standard prescription drug coverage under Part D. The determination of creditable-coverage status for disclosure purposes does not require attestation by a qualified actuary (unless the employer or union is applying for the retiree drug subsidy available under the MMA).

To assist sponsors in making the determination that coverage is creditable, the Centers for Medicare & Medicaid Studies (CMS) issued guidance with example "safe harbor" benefit designs. A plan design will automatically be deemed creditable if it includes:

1. coverage for brand and generic prescriptions;

2. reasonable access to retail providers and, optionally, for mail order coverage;

3. benefits payments designed to pay on average at least 60 percent of participants' prescription drug expenses; and

4. at least one of the following:

    a. an annual prescription drug benefit maximum of at least $25,000;

    b. an actuarial expectation that the plan will pay benefits of at least $2,000 per Medicare-eligible individual; or

    c. for plans that cover both medical expenses and prescription drugs, an annual deductible of no more than $250, an annual benefit maximum of at least $25,000, and a lifetime maximum of at least $1,000,000.

Under the CMS guidance, once a sponsor determines whether coverage is creditable, the sponsor must provide notice to all Part D-eligible individuals covered by or applying for the plan, including Part D-eligible dependents. In lieu of determining who is Part D-eligible, an employer sponsor may provide notice to all active employees, along with an explanation of why the notice is being provided.

The required notice to beneficiaries must, at a minimum:

1. contain a statement that the employer has determined that the coverage is creditable (or not creditable);

2. explain the meaning of creditable coverage;

3. explain why creditable coverage is important, and caution that higher Part D premiums could result if there is a break in creditable coverage of sixty-three days or more before enrolling in a Part D plan; and

4. if coverage is not creditable, explain that an individual may generally enroll in Part D only from November 15 through December 31 of each year.

CMS recommends that sponsors also provide the following clarifications in their notices:

• An explanation of a beneficiary's rights to a notice, i.e., the times when a beneficiary can expect to receive a notice and the times that a beneficiary can request a copy of the notice.

• An explanation of the plan provisions that affect beneficiaries when they (or their dependents) are Medicare Part D-eligible. These options may include, for example:

    ○ that they can retain their existing coverage and choose not to enroll in a Part D plan; or

    ○ that they can enroll in a Part D plan as a supplement to, or in lieu of, the other coverage;

    ○ if their existing prescription drug coverage is under a Medigap policy, that they cannot have both their existing prescription drug coverage and Part D coverage and that, if they enroll in Part D coverage, they should inform their Medigap insurer of that fact and the Medigap insurer must remove the prescription drug coverage from the Medigap policy and adjust the premium, as of the date the Part D coverage starts.

• Whether the covered individuals and/or their covered dependents will still be eligible to receive all of their current health coverage if they or their dependents enroll in a Medicare Part D prescription drug plan.

• A clarification of the circumstances (if any) under which the individual could re-enroll in employment-based prescription drug coverage if the individual drops the current coverage and enrolls in Medicare prescription drug coverage. (For Medigap insurers, this would be a clarification that the individual cannot get his prescription drug coverage back under such circumstances.)

- Information on how to get extra help paying for a Medicare prescription drug plan including the contact information for the Social Security Administration (SSA).

Sponsors must also disclose to CMS whether the coverage is creditable. The disclosure must be made to CMS on an annual basis, and upon any change that affects whether the coverage is creditable. CMS has posted guidance on the timing and format of the required disclosure and a model Disclosure to CMS form on the CMS website at www.cms.hhs.gov/creditablecoverage.

1210.01. What is the effect of the Inflation Reduction Act on Medicare Part D and Part B Drug Prices?

The Inflation Reduction Act was signed into law by President Biden signed into law in August 2022 will result in Medicare enrollees will also seeing lower costs for insulin and vaccines beginning in 2023.

Starting in 2023, all people with Medicare who take insulin covered by their prescription drug plan or through a traditional pump covered under Original Medicare will pay no more than $35 in cost-sharing for a month's supply of each covered insulin product. People with Medicare also will not pay a deductible with respect to each covered insulin product.

Additionally, people with Medicare drug coverage will pay nothing out-of-pocket for adult vaccines recommended by the Advisory Committee on Immunization Practices (ACIP), including the shingles vaccine and Tetanus-Diphtheria-Whooping Cough vaccine.

The act also enables

- Price negotiation with on drug prices in Medicare

- A yearly cap ($2,000 in 2025) on out-of-pocket prescription drug costs in Medicare

October 1 is the start of the first 12-month period for which drug manufacturers will be required to pay rebates to Medicare if their prices for certain Part D drugs increase faster than the rate of inflation over the 12-month period. The Part D inflation rebates for the 12-month periods beginning October 1, 2022, and October 1, 2023, must be invoiced by December 31, 2025.

Starting January 1, 2023, people enrolled in a Medicare prescription drug plan will not pay more than $35 for a month's supply of each insulin that they take and is covered by their Medicare prescription drug plan and dispensed at a pharmacy or through a mail-order pharmacy. Also, Part D deductibles will not apply to the covered insulin product.

Starting July 1, 2023, people with Traditional Medicare who take insulin through a traditional pump will not pay more than $35 for a month's supply of insulin, and the deductible will not apply to the insulin. This will apply to people using pumps covered through the durable medical equipment benefit under Part B.

Starting January 1, 2023, adult vaccines recommended by the Advisory Committee on Immunization Practices (ACIP), including the shingles vaccine, will be available to people with Medicare Part D at no cost to them.

Timeline of Implementation

2022

Medicare Part B qualifying biosimilars

- Starting October 1, Medicare will temporarily pay an add-on fee of 8% instead of 6% for qualifying biosimilars. This increase will encourage competition, lower costs for prescription drugs, and improve patient access to biosimilars.

Medicare Part D drug rebates

- October 1 is the start of the first 12-month period for which drug manufacturers will be required to pay rebates to Medicare if their prices for certain Part D drugs increase faster than the rate of inflation over the 12-month period. The Part D inflation rebates for the 12-month periods beginning October 1, 2022, and October 1, 2023, must be invoiced by December 31, 2025.

2023

Insulin Cost-sharing

- Starting January 1, people enrolled in a Medicare prescription drug plan will not pay more than $35 for a month's supply of each insulin that they take and is covered by their Medicare prescription drug plan and dispensed at a pharmacy or through a mail-order pharmacy. Also, Part D deductibles will not apply to the covered insulin product.

- Starting July 1, people with Traditional Medicare who take insulin through a traditional pump will not pay more than $35 for a month's supply of insulin, and the deductible will not apply to the insulin. This will apply to people using pumps covered through the durable medical equipment benefit under Part B.

Vaccine Cost-sharing

- Starting January 1, adult vaccines recommended by the Advisory Committee on Immunization Practices (ACIP), including the shingles vaccine, will be available to people with Medicare Part D at no cost to them.

Medicare Part B Drug Rebates

- January 1 is the start of the first quarter for which drug manufacturers will be required to pay rebates to Medicare if prices for certain Part B drugs increase faster than the rate of inflation. The Part B inflation rebates for quarters in 2023 and 2024 must be invoiced by September 30, 2025. Coinsurance for Part B drugs.

Coinsurance for Part B Drugs

- Starting April 1, people with Traditional Medicare may pay a lower coinsurance for some Part B drugs if the drug's price increased faster than the rate of inflation in a benchmark quarter.

Medicare Part D drugs selected for the Drug Price Negotiation Program

- By September 1, CMS will announce the first 10 Medicare Part D drugs selected for the Drug Price Negotiation Program. Maximum fair prices negotiated for these first 10 Part D drugs will go into effect in 2026.

Coverage of ACIP-recommended vaccines

- Beginning October 1, most adults with coverage from Medicaid and CHIP will be guaranteed coverage of vaccines recommended by the Advisory Committee on Immunization Practices (ACIP) at no cost to them.

2024

Catastrophic phase of the Medicare prescription drug benefit

- Starting January 1, people with Medicare prescription drug coverage who fall into the catastrophic phase of the prescription drug benefit will not have to pay any coinsurance or co-payments during that phase for covered Medicare prescription drugs.

Part D premium stabilization

- The law provides for a mechanism beginning January 1, 2024, for the average premium increase across most Part D plans to be limited to 6% over the previous year. This protection continues through 2029. The law also provides for a mechanism to stabilize plan premiums in 2030 and subsequent years.

Low-Income Subsidy Program

- Individuals with Medicare Part D who have low incomes will benefit from expanded financial help with prescription drug cost-sharing and premiums. The low-income subsidy program (LIS or "Extra Help") under Medicare Part D will be fully available to certain people with Medicare with limited resources who earn less than 150% of the federal poverty level starting in 2024.

Cap on Part B payment for new biosimilars

- Starting July 1, there will be a cap on the Part B payment amount for new biosimilars when average sales price data is not available.

Drug Price Negotiation Program

- By September 1, CMS will publish the maximum fair prices negotiated for the first 10 Medicare Part D drugs selected for negotiation. Maximum fair prices for these first ten drugs will go into effect in 2026.

2025

Out-of-pocket limit in Part D

- People with Medicare Part D will not pay more than $2,000 out-of-pocket for prescription drugs and will have the option to pay out-of-pocket Part D costs in monthly amounts spread over the year.

Manufacturer Discount Program

- The Manufacturer Discount Program in Medicare Part D will replace the Medicare coverage gap discount program. The new Manufacturer Discount Program will require manufacturer discounts for applicable drugs both in the initial coverage phase and in the catastrophic phase.

Government reinsurance

- Government reinsurance in the catastrophic phase of Part D will decrease from 80% to 20% for brand-name drugs, biologicals, and biosimilars and will decrease from 80% to 40% for generics.

Drug Price Negotiation Program

- By February 1, CMS will announce 15 more Medicare Part D drugs for negotiation.

- By November 30, CMS will publish the maximum fair prices for the 15 Medicare Part D drugs selected for negotiation earlier in the year. Maximum fair prices for these drugs will go into effect in 2027.

2026

Additional drugs selected for the Drug Price Negotiation Program

- Maximum fair prices for the first 10 Medicare Part D drugs selected for negotiation will go into effect. This is the first year that people with Medicare will start to benefit from Medicare negotiating prices with drug companies.

- By February 1, CMS will announce 15 more Medicare Part B or Part D drugs for price negotiation.

- By November 30, CMS will publish the maximum fair prices for the 15 Part B or Part D drugs selected for negotiation earlier in the year. Maximum fair prices for these drugs will go into effect in 2028.

Government reinsurance with respect to Selected Drugs in their Applicability Period

- Beginning in 2026, government reinsurance in the catastrophic phase of Part D will be 40% for Medicare Part D drugs selected for negotiation in their applicability period.

2027

Additional drugs selected for the Drug Price Negotiation Program

- Maximum fair prices for the 15 Medicare Part D drugs selected for negotiation in 2025 will go into effect. This is in addition to the 10 Part D drugs whose maximum fair prices became effective in 2026.

- By February 1, CMS will announce 20 more Part B or Part D drugs for negotiation.

- By November 30, CMS will publish the maximum fair prices for the 20 Part B or Part D drugs selected for negotiation earlier in the year. Maximum fair prices for these drugs will go into effect in 2029.

2028

Additional drugs selected for the Drug Price Negotiation Program

- Maximum fair prices for the 15 Medicare Part B or Part D drugs selected for negotiation in 2026 will go into effect. This is in addition to the Part D drugs whose maximum fair prices became effective in 2026 or 2027.

- By February 1, CMS will announce 20 more Part B or Part D drugs for negotiation.

- By November 30, CMS will publish the maximum fair prices for the 20 Part B or Part D drugs selected for negotiation earlier in the year. Maximum fair prices for these drugs will go into effect in 2030.

2029

Additional drugs selected for the Drug Price Negotiation Program

- Maximum fair prices for the 20 Medicare Part B or Part D drugs selected for negotiation in 2027 will go into effect. This is in addition to the drugs whose maximum fair prices became effective in 2026, 2027, or 2028.

- By February 1, CMS will announce 20 more Part B or Part D drugs for negotiation.

- By November 30, CMS will publish the maximum fair prices for the 20 Part B or Part D drugs selected for negotiation earlier in the year. Maximum fair prices for these drugs will go into effect in 2031.

Prescription Drug Marketing Rules

1211. What are the rules about the marketing of Medicare Part D (Prescription Drug Insurance) plans?

There are significant restrictions regarding the marketing of Medicare Part D plans:

- The rules broadly prohibit "cold calls" and other unsolicited contact. This prohibition includes door-to-door sales and unsolicited telephone calls. The rules do not prohibit plan mailings, but the final regulations prohibit calling to confirm that the beneficiary received the mailing. Agents may call in response to specific requests by beneficiaries to be contacted. Agents may not approach beneficiaries in a hallway or parking lot to attempt to sell coverage.

- The rules prohibit sales activities at educational events. Events designed to provide the public with objective information about Medicare must be free of any marketing materials or enrollment information for a specific plan or organization. Plans and agents may hold sales events that are clearly labeled as such, but they may not be disguised as educational events.

- The rules prohibit plans and agents from providing meals at Medicare sales meetings. The Centers for Medicare & Medicaid Services (CMS) has not yet defined the terms, but light refreshments and "snacks" are permissible.

- Rules prohibit offering gift cards of any amount or money or offer gifts worth more than $15.

- The rules prohibit sales activities in settings where individuals receive healthcare services. This rule permits marketing in common areas such as waiting rooms, but prohibits marketing in treatment rooms. Plans may arrange meetings with residents in long-term care facilities as with any other private residence.

- The rules prohibit marketing any nonhealth insurance product (such as life insurance or annuities) during a Medicare marketing or sales meeting (cross-selling).

- Rules prohibit enrolling a person without their permission or lying to a person to get their permission.

The rules also require agents to document that, prior to making an appointment, beneficiaries agree to the scope of products to be discussed at the meeting. Appointments made in person require written documentation; appointments made over the phone require recorded documentation. At a meeting in an agent's office or on the phone, additional products may not be discussed unless the beneficiary requests the information. In a meeting at a beneficiary's home, an agent may not discuss any product not within the originally-identified scope of the meeting. They must schedule a separate appointment at least forty-eight hours later.

The same marketing restrictions apply to both Medicare Advantage and Medicare Part D prescription drug plans.

MEDIGAP INSURANCE

1212. What is Medigap Insurance?

"Medigap" insurance is a term referring to Medicare Supplement Insurance policies. Medigap is supplemental health insurance that you buy from a private company to pay health care costs not covered by Original Medicare. Medigap policies don't cover long-term care, dental care, vision care, hearing aids, eyeglasses, and private-duty nursing. Most plans do not cover prescription drugs. Medicare provides basic protection against the cost of health care, but it does not pay all medical expenses. The federal government does not sell or service insurance, but regulates the coverage offered by Medigap insurance. Many Medicare beneficiaries enrolled in Part A (Hospital Insurance) and Part B (Medical Insurance) also maintain Medigap policies to cover costs not paid for by Parts A and B.

Medigap insurance is a private insurance policy designed to help pay deductibles and/or coinsurance incurred by beneficiaries who are enrolled in original Medicare Part A (Hospital Insurance) and Part B (Medical Insurance). A Medigap policy may also pay for certain items or services generally not covered by Medicare at all, such as medical expenses incurred during foreign travel. Medigap policies coordinate only with original Medicare Parts A and B, not with Medicare Advantage plans. By law, a Medicare beneficiary cannot be sold a Medigap plan that duplicates benefits otherwise available to that beneficiary under Medicare, including through a Medicare Advantage plan.

1213. Is there an open enrollment period for Medigap policies?

Yes, an open enrollment period for selecting Medigap policies guarantees that, for **six months immediately following the effective date of enrolling in both Medicare Part A and Medicare Part B** (Medical Insurance), a person aged sixty-five or older cannot be denied Medigap insurance or charged higher premiums because of health problems.

Guaranteed Coverage

No matter how a person enrolls in Part B (Medical Insurance)—whether by automatic notification or through an initial, special or general enrollment period—a person is covered by the guarantees if both of the following are true:

- The person is age sixty-five or older and is enrolled in Medicare for the first time, based on age rather than disability

- The person applies for Medigap insurance within six months of enrollment in Part B (Medical Insurance)

Pre-Existing Conditions

In some cases, however, even when a person buys a Medigap policy during his open enrollment period, the policy may still exclude coverage for "pre-existing conditions" during the first six months the policy is in effect. Pre-existing conditions are conditions that were either diagnosed or treated during the six-month period immediately before the Medigap policy became effective. During this protected period, Medigap policies must shorten any pre-existing condition waiting period by the number of months you had prior creditable coverage. (See Q 1231 for exceptions to this rule.)

Once the Medigap open enrollment period ends, a person may not be able to buy the policy of his or her choice. He or she may have to accept whatever Medigap policy an insurance company is willing to sell him or her.

In the case of individuals enrolled in Medicare Part B prior to age sixty-five, Medigap insurers are required to offer coverage, regardless of medical history, for a six-month period when the individual reaches age sixty-five. Insurers are prohibited from discriminating in the price of policies for an individual based on that person's medical or health status.

Also, although Medigap policies are standardized, premiums can vary widely. Insurers can reject an applicant who applies for a Medigap policy after the open enrollment period.

Once issued, all Medigap policies are guaranteed renewable. This means that they continue in force if the premium is paid.

1214. Does a Medicaid recipient need Medigap insurance?

Low-income people who are eligible for Medicaid usually do NOT need additional insurance. Medicaid generally covers almost all the health care needs of a beneficiary that are not paid for by Medicare, in addition to covering long-term nursing home care. If a person purchases Medigap insurance and later becomes eligible for Medicaid, that individual may ask that Medigap insurance benefits and premiums be suspended for up to two years while the individual is covered by Medicaid. If the person becomes ineligible for Medicaid benefits during the two years, the Medigap policy is automatically reinstated as of the date of Medicaid termination and on terms at least as favorable as those in effect at the time of initial suspension, provided the person gives proper notice and begins paying premiums again.

1215. Are there federal standards for Medigap policies?

Yes, Congress established federal standards for Medigap policies in 1990 and again in 2010. Most states have adopted regulations limiting the sale of Medigap insurance to no more than ten standard policies. One of the ten is a basic policy offering a "core package" of benefits.

These standardized plans are identified as follows: A, B, C, D, F, G, K, L, M, and N. (Plans E, H, I, and J have not been sold since June 1, 2010, although beneficiaries who had purchased such policies before that date are able to maintain their coverage. Plans M and N became available June 1, 2010.) Plan A is the core package. Plans B, C, D, F, G, M, and N each have a different combination of benefits, but they all include the core package. Plans K and L do not include the core benefit package; they instead offer catastrophic coverage. The basic Plan A policy, offering the core package of benefits, is available in all states. The availability of other plans varies from state to state.

Insurance companies selling Medigap policies are required to make Plan A available. If they offer any other Medigap policy, they must also offer either Plan C or Plan F to individuals who are not new to Medicare and either Plan D or Plan G to individuals who are new to Medicare. Not all types of Medigap policies may be available in every state.

Plans D and G effective on or after June 1, 2010, have different benefits than Plans D or G bought before June 1, 2010.

Plans E, H, I, and J are no longer sold, but, if someone already had one, they can generally keep it.

Starting January 1, 2020, Medigap plans sold to people new to Medicare won't be allowed to cover the Part B deductible. Because of this, Plans C and F are no longer available to people who are new to Medicare on or after January 1, 2020.

- If the purchaser already has either of these two plans (or the high deductible version of Plan F) or is covered by one of these plans prior to January 1, 2020, they will be able to keep the plan. If they were eligible for Medicare before January 1, 2020 but not yet enrolled, they may be able to buy one of these plans.

- People new to Medicare are those who turn 65 on or after January 1, 2020, and those who first become eligible for Medicare benefits due to age, disability or ESRD on or after January 1, 2020.

The core package of benefits which all policies (except Plans K and L) must contain includes:

- Part A (Hospital Insurance) coinsurance for the sixty-first through ninetieth day of inpatient hospitalization in any Medicare benefit period;

- Part A (Hospital Insurance) coinsurance for the sixty lifetime reserve days that can be used for an inpatient hospitalization that lasts more than ninety days;

- Part A (Hospital Insurance) expenses for an extra 365 days in the hospital;

- Part A (Hospital Insurance) and Part B (Medical Insurance) deductible for the cost of the first three pints of blood;

- Part B (Medical Insurance) coinsurance (20 percent of allowable charges in most cases); and

- Part A (Hospital Insurance) hospice coinsurance, if any.

1216. What else should be known about Medigap policies?

When dealing with Medigap coverage, there are some other rules that apply that should be known including:

- **Requirement of Medicare coverage**: Enrollment in Medicare Part A and Part B are required to have a Medigap policy.

- **Medicare Advantage**: A subscriber to a Medicare Advantage Plan can apply for a Medigap policy but must leave the Medicare Advantage Plan before the Medigap policy begins. A Medicare Advantage policy is different than a Medigap policy.

- **Separate premiums**: Premiums paid to the private insurance company for the Medigap policy is in addition to the monthly Part B premium paid to Medicare.

- **One policy per person**: A Medigap policies covers one person. Spousal coverage in Medigap coverage requires a separate policy.

- **Insurance providers**: Many insurance companies are licensed in each state to sell Medigap coverage.

- **Guaranteed renewability**: All standardized Medigap policies guaranteed renewable regardless of health and cannot be cancelled as long as the premiums are paid.

- **Prescription drug coverage**: Medigap policies sold after January 1, 2006 cannot include prescription drug coverage. Prescription drug coverage is available under Medicare Part D. (Some policies in the past sold prescription drug coverage).

- **Not Compatible with MSAs**: It's illegal for anyone to sell someone a Medigap policy if they have a Medicare Medical Savings Account (MSA) plan.

The following insurance plans should not be confused with Medigap coverage as they are different types of insurance:

- Medicare Advantage Plans (like an HMO, PPO, or Private Fee-for-Service Plan)

- Medicare Prescription Drug Plans

- Medicaid

- Employer or union plans, including the Federal Employees Health Benefits Program (FEHBP)

- TRICARE

- Veterans' benefits

- Long-term care insurance policies

- Indian Health Service, Tribal, and Urban Indian Health plans

1217. How are Medigap policies priced?

Medigap plans are priced based on a number of factors.

Community-rated (also called "no-age rated"): Generally the same premium is charged to everyone who has the Medigap policy, regardless of age or gender.

- Your premium isn't based on your age. Premiums may go up because of inflation and other factors but not because of your age.

Issue-age-rated (also called "entry age-rated"): The premium is based on the age you are when you buy (are "issued") the Medigap policy.

- Premiums are lower for people who buy at a younger age and won't change as you get older. Premiums may go up because of inflation and other factors but not because of your age.

Attained-age-rated: The premium is based on your current age (the age you've "attained"), so your premium goes up as you get older.

- Premiums are low for younger buyers but go up as you get older. They may be the least expensive at first, but they can eventually become the most expensive. Premiums may also go up because of inflation and other factors.

The cost of Medigap policies can vary widely. There can be big differences in the premiums that different insurance companies charge for exactly the same coverage.

The cost of the Medigap policy may also depend on whether the insurance company:

- **Offers discounts** (like discounts for women, non-smokers, or people who are married; discounts for paying yearly; discounts for paying premiums using electronic funds transfer; or discounts for multiple policies).

- **Uses medical underwriting**, or applies a different premium when one doesn't have a guaranteed issue right or is not in a Medigap Open Enrollment Period.

- **Sells Medicare SELECT policies** that may require use of certain providers. With type of Medigap policy, the premium may be less.

- **Offers a "high-deductible option"** for Plan F.

  - **Plan F with a high deductible option,** requires paying the first $2,700 of deductibles, copayments, and coinsurance (in 2023) for covered services not paid by Medicare before the Medigap policy pays anything. There is also a separate deductible ($250 per year) for foreign travel emergency services. The high deductible version of Plan F is only available to those who were Medicare eligible before January 1, 2020.

- **Offers a "high-deductible option"** for Plan G.

      ○   **Plan F with a high deductible option,** requires paying the first $2,700 of deductibles, copayments, and coinsurance (in 2023) for covered services not paid by Medicare before the Medigap policy pays anything. There is also a separate deductible ($250 per year) for foreign travel emergency services. The high deductible version of Plan G is only available to those who were Medicare eligible after January 1, 2020.

- **Medigap Plan J** purchased before January 1, 2006, and if it still covers prescription drugs, there is a separate deductible ($250 per year) for prescription drugs covered by the Medigap policy. Before June 1, 2010, Medigap Plan J could also be sold with a high deductible.

- **Plan J with a high deductible option,** requires one to pay a $2,700 deductible (in 2023) before the policy pays anything for medical benefits.

1218. Do Medigap policies cover medical expenses outside of the United States?

Yes, some Medigap policies offer additional coverage for expenses for health care services or supplies that are incurred outside the United States. Specifically, standard Medigap Plans C, D, E, F, G, H, I, J, M, and N provide foreign travel emergency health care coverage traveling outside the United States. (Plans E, H, I, and J are no longer sold, but if purchased before June 1, 2010, they were able to be retained.)

Medigap Plans C, D, E, F, G, H, I, J, M, and N each pay 80 percent of the billed charges for certain medically necessary emergency care charges outside the United States after meeting a $250 deductible for the year. These policies cover foreign travel emergency care if it begins during the first sixty days of a trip, and if Medicare doesn't otherwise cover the care. Foreign travel emergency coverage with Medigap policies has a lifetime limit of $50,000.

1219. What additional benefits can be offered in the standard Medigap plans?

The following additional benefits above the basic core benefits can be covered:

- The entire Part A (Hospital Insurance) deductible payable for each new spell of illness requiring inpatient hospitalization

- The Part A (Hospital Insurance) coinsurance for days twenty-one through day one-hundred of skilled nursing home care

- The annual Part B (Medical Insurance) deductible

- 80 percent of the "balance billing" paid by Part B (Medical Insurance) beneficiaries whose doctors do not accept assignment; 100 percent of other Part B (Medical Insurance) excess charges billed to beneficiaries

- 80 percent of the Medicare-eligible costs of medically necessary emergency care when the insured is traveling outside the United States

- "Innovative benefits" that are appropriate, cost-effective, and consistent with the goal of simplifying Medigap insurance – with prior approval by the state insurance commissioner

Certain policies sold before 2006 also offered limited coverage of outpatient prescription drug costs. Beneficiaries who purchased those policies before implementation of the Part D (Prescription Drug Insurance) benefit could maintain the policies, but no new policies with such benefits have been allowed after the introduction of Part D. Part D coverage in general is more generous than that available through old Medigap policies.

1220. What benefits are provided in each of the standard Medigap policies and the high deductible Medigap policies?

The Medigap policies offer the following benefits:

Basic Medigap Policy

Policy A is the basic core benefit package which includes:

(1)   Medicare Part A coinsurance and hospital costs up to an additional 365 days after Medicare benefits are exhausted;

(2)   Medicare Part B coinsurance or copayment;

(3)   First three pints of blood; and

(4)   Medicare Part A hospice coinsurance or copayment.

Policies with Additional Coverages

Policy B includes:

(1)   the basic core benefit package (see Policy A above); and

(2)   payment of the Part A (Hospital Insurance) deductible payable for each new benefit period.

Policy C includes (no longer able to be sold in 2020 or later to new purchasers):

(1)   the basic core benefit package (see Policy A above);

(2)   the Part A (Hospital Insurance) deductible;

(3)   the Part A coinsurance for care in a skilled nursing home (days 21-100);

(4)   the Part B (Medical Insurance) deductible; and

(5)   coverage of foreign travel emergencies up to 80 percent.

Policy D includes:

(1)   the basic core benefit package (see Policy A above);

(2)   the Part A (Hospital Insurance) deductible;

(3)   the Part A coinsurance for care in a skilled nursing home (days 21-100); and

(4)   coverage of foreign travel emergencies up to 80 percent.

Policy F includes:

(1)   the basic core benefit package (see Policy A above);

(2)   the Part A (Hospital Insurance) deductible;

(3)   the Part A coinsurance for care in a skilled nursing home (days twenty-one-100);

(4)   the Part B (Medical Insurance) deductible;

(5)   coverage of foreign travel emergencies up to 80 percent; and

(6)   100 percent coverage of excess provider charges under Part B (Medical Insurance).

In addition, there is a policy that is the same as Policy F (called the High Deductible Plan F) but with a $2,490 deductible in 2022 and a $2,700 deductible in 2023. This deductible is increased $210 from 2022. This high-deductible policy covers 100 percent of covered out-of-pocket expenses once the deductible has been satisfied in a year. It requires the beneficiary of the policy to pay annual out-of-pocket expenses (other than premiums) in the amount of $2,700 before the policy begins payment of benefits. The deductible increases by the percentage increase in the Consumer Price Index for all urban consumers for the twelve-month period ending with August of the preceding year.

Policy G includes:

(1)   the basic core benefit package (see Policy A above);

(2)   the Part A (Hospital Insurance) deductible;

(3)   the Part A coinsurance for care in a skilled nursing home (days 21-100);

(4)   coverage of foreign travel emergencies up to 80 percent; and

(5)   100 percent coverage of excess provider charges under Part B (Medical Insurance). Plan G offers a high deductible option starting on January 1, 2020. It will not cover

the Part B deductible, but the Part B deductible will count towards fulfilling the Plan G high deductible.

Medigap Innovative G or G Extra:

(1) Plan G Extra (offered in California)

- ○ Offers the same coverage as Plan G PLUS

- ○ Over the Counter (OTC) items benefits: including coverage for eligible OTC health and wellness products such as cold and allergy medicines, first-aid supplies, pain relievers, and more.

- ○ Physician consultation benefits: available by phone or video via computer or mobile app.

- ○ Hearing aid benefits: including an annual hearing test and savings on Vista brand mid-level and premium-level hearing aids.

- ○ Vision benefits: including coverage for the cost of eye exams, frames, eyeglass or contact lenses that are not traditionally covered by Original Medicare.

(2) Plan Innovative G: (offered in California and Nevada)

- ○ Offers the same coverage as Plan G PLUS

- ○ Routine Hearing Exam: one hearing exam every 12 months

- ○ Hearing Aid(s): includes fitting evaluation; hearing aid cost shares are based on technology level*:

  Level 1 – $0
  Level 2 – $700
  Level 3 – $1,125
  Level 4 – $1,580

- ○ Routine Eye Exam: one vision exam every 12 months

- ○ Eyewear: up to $250 allowance for frame and lens package once every 24 months or contact lens once every 12 months

- ○ Chiropractic/Acupuncture ($0 copay/ 20 visits combined)

- ○ Silver & Fit: exercise and healthy aging program which provides either a no-cost membership at a local participating Silver&Fit fitness facility, or membership in the Silver&Fit Home Fitness Program for members who are unable to participate in a fitness facility or prefer to work out at home.

(3)   Plan High-G (High Deductible

In addition, there is a policy that is the same as Policy G (called the Plan High G) but with a $2,700 deductible in 2023. This is a replacement for the High-F plan no longer sold to new purchasers. This deductible is increased $210 from 2022. This high-deductible policy covers 100 percent of covered out-of-pocket expenses once the deductible has been satisfied in a year. It requires the beneficiary of the policy to pay annual out-of-pocket expenses (other than premiums) in the amount of $2,700 before the policy begins payment of benefits. The deductible increases by the percentage increase in the Consumer Price Index for all urban consumers for the twelve-month period ending with August of the preceding year.

Policies without Core Benefits – Catastrophic Plans

Beginning in 2006, two more standard plans became available. These two plans do not include the entire core benefit package.

Policy K includes:

(1)   Medicare Part A coinsurance and hospital costs up to an additional 365 days after Medicare benefits are exhausted;

(2)   coverage of 50 percent of Part B coinsurance, blood costs under Parts A and B, Part A hospice coinsurance, and Part A skilled nursing facility coinsurance;

(3)   coverage of 100 percent of Part A hospital inpatient coinsurance and 365 extra lifetime days of coverage of inpatient hospital services;

(4)   50 percent of the Part A deductible; and

(5)   a limit on annual out-of-pocket spending under Part A and Part B to $6,940 in 2023.

Policy L includes:

(1)   Medicare Part A coinsurance and hospital costs up to an additional 365 days after Medicare benefits are exhausted;

(2)   coverage of 75 percent the Part B coinsurance, blood costs under Parts A and B, Part A hospice coinsurance, and Part A skilled nursing facility coinsurance;

(3)   coverage of 100 percent of the Part A hospital inpatient coinsurance and 365 extra lifetime days of coverage of inpatient hospital services;

(4)   75 percent of the Part A deductible; and

(5)   a limit on annual out-of-pocket spending under Part A and Part B to $3,470 in 2023.

Policies Added In 2010

Effective June 1, 2010, two new plans became available (both of which include the basic core benefit package):

- **Policy M** is a duplicate of Policy D, but with 50 percent coinsurance on the Part A deductible.

- **Policy N** is a duplicate Policy D with the Part B coinsurance being paid at 100 percent, minus a $20 copayment per physician visit and a $50 copayment per emergency room visit (unless the beneficiary was admitted to the hospital).

Policies Discontinued for Sale after June 1, 2010 But Still In Effect

The following plans are no longer available for purchase effective June 1, 2010 (but if an individual already had or bought one of these plans before June 1, 2010, that individual could keep that plan):

Policy E includes:

(1)   the basic core benefit package;

(2)   the Part A (Hospital Insurance) deductible;

(3)   the Part A coinsurance for care in a skilled nursing home (days twenty-one-one-hundred);

(4)   coverage of foreign travel emergencies; and

(5)   coverage of preventive screening and care.

Policy H includes:

(1)   the basic core benefit package;

(2)   the Part A (Hospital Insurance) deductible;

(3)   the Part A coinsurance for care in a skilled nursing home (days twenty-one-one-hundred);

(4)   coverage of foreign travel emergencies; and

(5)   coverage of 50 percent of the cost of outpatient prescription drugs after payment of a $250 deductible, up to a maximum benefit of $1,250. (See the paragraph below regarding prescription drug coverage.)

Policy I includes:

(1)   the basic core benefit package;

(2)   the Part A (Hospital Insurance) deductible;

(3)   the Part A coinsurance for care in a skilled nursing home (days twenty-one-one-hundred);

(4)   coverage of foreign travel emergencies;

(5)   at-home recovery assistance;

(6)   100 percent of excess charges under Part B (Medical Insurance); and

(7)   50 percent of the cost of outpatient prescription drugs after payment of a $250 deductible, up to a maximum benefit of $1,250. (See the paragraph below regarding prescription drug coverage.)

Policy J includes:

(1)   the basic core benefit package;

(2)   the Part A (Hospital Insurance) deductible;

(3)   the Part A coinsurance for care in a skilled nursing home (days twenty-one-one-hundred);

(4)   the Part B (Medical Insurance) annual deductible;

(5)   coverage of foreign travel emergencies;

(6)   at-home recovery assistance;

(7)   100 percent of excess charges under Part B;

(8)   preventive screening and care; and

(9)   50 percent of the cost of outpatient prescription drugs after payment of a $250 deductible, up to a maximum benefit of $3,000. (See the paragraph below regarding prescription drug coverage.)

There is also a policy that is the same as Policy J but with a $2,700 deductible. This high-deductible policy covers 100 percent of covered out-of-pocket expenses (in 2023) once the deductible has been satisfied in a year. This deductible increased $210 from 2022. It requires the beneficiary of the policy to pay annual out-of-pocket expenses (other than premiums) in the amount of $2,700 before the policy begins payment of benefits.

As of January 1, 2006, beneficiaries who held standard policies H, I, or J could choose between enrolling in Part D or maintaining their prescription drug coverage under their Medigap policies. Beneficiaries who chose to enroll in Part D could keep their existing plan H, I, or J, minus the prescription drug benefit, or could purchase a new Medigap policy. As of January 1, 2006, plans H, I, and J could be sold, but without the prescription drug benefit.

Medigap Coverage in Massachusetts, Minnesota and Wisconsin

Medigap plan choices in Massachusetts, Minnesota, and Wisconsin are different because these states already required standardized Medigap policies prior to 1992.

Medigap Benefits	Comparison of Coverage of Medigap Plans									
	A	B	C	D	F n1	G	K	L	M	N
Part A coinsurance and hospital costs up to an additional 365 days after Medicare benefits are used up	Yes	Yes	Yes	Yes	Yes	Yes	Yes	Yes	Yes	Yes
Part B coinsurance or copayment	Yes	Yes	Yes	Yes	Yes	Yes	50%	75%	Yes	Yes n3
Blood (first 3 pints)	Yes	Yes	Yes	Yes	Yes	Yes	50%	75%	Yes	Yes
Part A hospice care coinsurance or copayment	Yes	Yes	Yes	Yes	Yes	Yes	50%	75%	Yes	Yes
Skilled nursing facility care coinsurance	No	No	Yes	Yes	Yes	Yes	50%	75%	Yes	Yes
Part A deductible	No	Yes	Yes	Yes	Yes	Yes	50%	75%	50%	Yes
Part B deductible	No	No	Yes	No	Yes	No	No	No	No	No
Part B excess charge	No	No	No	No	Yes	Yes	No	No	No	No
Foreign travel exchange (up to plan limits)	No	No	80%	80%	80%	80%	No	No	80%	80%
Out of Pocket Limit n2	NA	NA	NA	NA	NA	NA	$6,940	$3,470	NA	NA

Note 1: Plan F also offers a high-deductible plan. If you choose this option, this means you must pay for Medicare-covered costs up to the deductible amount of $2,700 in 2023 before the Medigap plan pays anything.

Note 2: After meeting the out-of-pocket yearly limit and your yearly Part B deductible, the Medigap plan pays 100 percent of covered services for the rest of the calendar year.

Note 3: Plan N pays 100 percent of the Part B coinsurance, except for a copayment of up to $20 for some office visits and up to a $50 copayment for emergency room visits that don't result in inpatient admission.

1221. What are the most popular Medigap policies?

Ranked by sales, clearly Policy Plan F is the most popular, followed by Plans G, N, and C, according to Boomer Benefits in 2021.[1] Percentages do not include discontinued Plans E, H, and I, nor are sales figures for waiver states of Massachusetts, Wisconsin, and Minnesota included.

Sales	Plan	Percentage
1	F	49%
2	G	22%
3	N	10%
4	C	5%
5	B	2%
6	D	1%
7	A	1%
8	K	1%
9	L	< 0.50%
10	M	{ 0.50%

Note

1. What Are the Most Popular Medicare Supplement Plans? | MedicareSupplement.com | MedicareSupplement.com

1222. Has Medicare Supplement Plan F been eliminated?

Yes. The Medicare Access and CHIP Reauthorization Act of 2015 (MACRA) passed by Congress and signed into law on April 16, 2015 changed the law on various aspects of health care, including some Medicare Supplement plans. The new law states that on or after January 1, 2020, a Medicare Supplement policy that provides coverage of the Part B deductible may not be sold or issued to a newly eligible Medicare beneficiary. Anyone whose birthday is December 31, 1954 (turning sixty-five on December 31, 2019) will be the last group able to enroll in Medicare Supplement Plan F.

After January 1, 2020, individuals are not able to enroll in Medicare Supplement Plan C, one of the closest alternatives to Plan F, either, since it also covers the Part B deductible. Those who already have Plan F, can keep it. The law only affects new enrollees.

1223. What effect does MACRA have on Medigap plans?

Section 401 of the Medicare Access and CHIP Reauthorization Act (MACRA)[1] mandates that effective on January 1, 2020, all newly eligible Medicare beneficiaries cannot sign up for a Medigap plan that covers the Medicare Part B deductible, currently $233 in 2022 and $226 in 2023. Medicare beneficiaries that have those plans already will be exempted and can keep the plans.

The law eliminated two of the ten plans – Plan C and Plan F, two of the most popular Medigap policies. These policies provide first-dollar coverage for EVERY doctor and hospital visit. As of 2015, more than two-thirds (7.5 million) of the 11.8 million Medigap customers had either Plan C or Plan F. It should be noted that there was a 28 percent increase in signups for Plan G, which increased from 697,000 to 895,000 in one year. Those in favor of the elimination of the first-dollar coverage argue that beneficiaries have no incentive to question their care, since they have no additional cost and that health care providers are not incented to manage the amount of care provided. Others argue that it could cause seniors to limit seeing care due to unaffordable costs.

MACRA could be part of the cause of more seniors purchasing Medicare Advantage when becoming eligible. Those that choose Medicare Advantage and later decide to switch to original Medicare and want to purchase a Medigap policy may find themselves locked out – Medigap insurers can deny policies based on underwriting health status as they only have to sell the Medigap plans when seniors enroll in Medicare at age sixty-five or within a year of using a Medicare Advantage plan.

Note

1. https://www.gpo.gov/fdsys/pkg/BILLS-114hr2enr/pdf/BILLS-114hr2enr.pdf (last accessed Nov. 9, 2020).

1224. What are Medicare SELECT policies?

The difference between Medicare SELECT and regular Medigap insurance is that a Medicare SELECT policy may (except in emergencies) limit Medigap benefits to items and services provided by certain selected health care providers (including hospitals) or may pay only partial benefits when a patient gets health care from other health care providers.

Insurers, including some HMOs, offer Medicare SELECT in the same way they offer standard Medigap insurance. The policies are required to meet certain federal standards and are regulated by the states in which they are approved. A person is able to choose from among the available Medigap policies in the state, but the premiums charged for Medicare SELECT policies are generally lower than premiums for comparable Medigap policies that do not have Medicare SELECT's managed care feature. Medicare SELECT can be any of the standardized Medigap plans. These policies generally cost less than other Medigap policies. However, if you don't use a Medicare SELECT hospital or doctor for non-emergency services, you'll have to pay some or all of what Medicare doesn't pay. Medicare will pay its share of approved charges no matter which hospital or doctor you choose.

State insurance departments have information about Medicare SELECT policies that have been approved for sale in their states.

1225. Should a person purchase the most comprehensive Medigap policy if he can afford the premiums?

Not necessarily. A person must determine which benefits he is likely to need before purchasing a Medigap policy. Often, a person does not need the most comprehensive policy.

For example, Policy A is the least expensive policy and offers the basic core package of benefits. Policy G might be considered if a person uses nonparticipating doctors – those who charge more than the amount approved by Medicare; however, excess charges are limited to 115 percent of what Medicare pays (see Q 1098). If the doctors charge no more than the amount approved by Medicare, less expensive policies such as Policy D may be appropriate. Policy D also includes important benefits not covered by Policy A, such as coverage of custodial care at home following an illness or injury and the cost of coinsurance for skilled nursing home care.

1226. What Medigap insurance protections are there for those enrolled in the Medicare Advantage program?

Medicare Advantage expands the types of health plans that can contract with Medicare to enroll beneficiaries.

A person who currently has a Medigap policy may enroll in a Medicare Advantage plan and can keep the Medigap policy after enrollment. Keeping the Medigap policy may give a person time to determine whether to stay in the Medicare Advantage plan or return to the original Medicare plan with Medigap insurance. However, expenses paid for by the Medicare Advantage plan will not be reimbursed by the Medigap insurer. Eventually the person should drop Medigap coverage if satisfied with the Medicare Advantage plan.

A person already enrolled in a Medicare Advantage plan cannot buy Medigap insurance but may have the right to purchase a Medigap policy by returning to the original fee-for-service Medicare program (Parts A and B). To be guaranteed the right to buy Medigap insurance, the person must have enrolled in the Medicare Advantage plan at age sixty-five, must terminate enrollment in the Medicare Advantage plan within twelve months of entry into that plan, and must not have had any previous enrollment in a Medicare managed care plan.

If a Medicare Advantage plan terminates coverage because it leaves the Medicare program, plan enrollees have certain rights to new coverage, but these are time-limited. The Medicare Advantage plan is required to provide information to assist making a decision about enrolling in another Medicare Advantage plan or switching to original Medicare Parts A and B with a Medigap policy to supplement the coverage. In general, most individuals with Medicare have the right to guaranteed issue of any Medigap policies designated A, B, or C that are offered to new enrollees by issuers in the state.

This right applies to individuals by virtue of the involuntary termination of their coverage. However, certain Medicare beneficiaries in terminating Medicare Advantage plans may have another basis for entitlement to guaranteed issue of a Medigap policy. If a person had been enrolled in the Medicare Advantage plan for fewer than twelve months, was never enrolled in any other Medicare HMO, and had a previous Medigap policy, that person may return to the former Medigap policy if the previous Medigap insurance company still sells the policy in the state.

If that coverage is not available under the previous Medigap policy, the individual may purchase Medigap polices A or B from any insurer that sells these policies in the state.

The insurance company selling the policy may not:

(1)   deny or condition the sale of the policy;

(2)   discriminate in the pricing of the policy because of health status, prior history of claims experience, receipt of health care for a medical condition; or

(3)   impose an exclusion for any pre-existing condition.

But the individual has only sixty-three days after coverage ends to select a Medigap insurer. Also, if the individual moves outside the Medicare Advantage plan's service area, that person has sixty-three days to select a Medigap insurer.

An individual is guaranteed issuance of any Medigap policy if:

(1)   at least sixty-five years old;

(2)   eligible for Medicare;

(3)   enrolled in a Medicare Advantage plan; and

(4)   disenrolled from that plan within twelve months of the effective date of enrollment.

See Q 1164 through Q 1202 for a complete description of Medicare Advantage (Part C).

1227. Are there rules for selling Medigap insurance?

Yes, both state and federal laws govern sales of Medigap insurance. Companies or agents selling Medigap insurance must avoid certain illegal practices.

It is unlawful to sell or issue to an individual entitled to benefits under Part A (Hospital Insurance) or enrolled under Part B (Medical Insurance):

(1)   a health insurance policy with knowledge that the policy duplicates health benefits the individual is otherwise entitled to under Medicare or Medicaid;

(2)   a Medigap policy with knowledge that the individual is entitled to benefits under another Medigap policy; or

(3)   a health insurance policy, other than a Medigap policy, with knowledge that the policy duplicates health benefits to which the individual is otherwise entitled.

Penalties do not apply, however, to the sale or issuance of a policy or plan that duplicates health benefits to which the individual is otherwise entitled if, under the policy or plan, all benefits are fully payable directly to or on behalf of the individual without regard to other health benefit coverage of the individual. In addition, for the penalty to be waived in the case of the sale or issuance of a policy or plan that duplicates benefits under Medicare or Medicaid, the application for the policy must include a statement, prominently displayed, disclosing the extent to which benefits payable under the policy or plan duplicate Medicare benefits.

The National Association of Insurance Commissioners (NAIC) has identified ten separate types of health insurance policies that must provide an individualized statement of the extent to which the policy duplicates Medicare. These policies include the following:

- Policies that provide benefits for expenses incurred for an accidental injury only

- Policies that provide benefits for specified limited services

- Policies that reimburse expenses incurred for specified disease or other specific impairments (including cancer policies, specified disease policies, and other policies that limit reimbursement to named medical conditions)

- Policies that pay fixed dollar amounts for specified disease or other specified impairments (including cancer, specified disease policies, and other policies that pay a scheduled benefit or specified payment based on diagnosis of the conditions named in the policy)

- Indemnity policies and other policies that pay a fixed dollar amount per day, excluding long-term care policies

- Policies that provide benefits for both expenses incurred and fixed indemnity

- Long-term care policies providing both nursing home and noninstitutional coverage

- Long-term care policies primarily providing nursing home benefits only

- Home care policies

- Other health insurance policies not specifically identified above

Certain policies are **not** required to carry a disclosure statement:

(1) Policies that do not duplicate Medicare benefits, even incidentally

(2) Life insurance policies that contain long-term care riders or accelerated death benefits

(3) Disability insurance policies

(4) Property and casualty policies

(5) Employer and union group health plans

(6) Managed-care organizations with Medicare contracts

(7) Health Care Prepayment Plans (HCPPs) that provide some or all Medicare Part B benefits under an agreement with the Centers for Medicare & Medicaid Services

Policies offering only long-term care nursing home care, home health care, community-based care, or any combination of the three, are allowed to coordinate benefits with Medicare and are not considered duplicative, provided the coordination is disclosed.

An insurer is subject to civil money and criminal penalties for failing to provide the appropriate disclosure statement. Federal criminal and civil penalties (fines) may also be imposed against any insurance company or agent that knowingly:

- sells a health insurance policy that duplicates a person's Medicare or Medicaid coverage, or any private health insurance coverage the person may have;

- tells a person that they are employees or agents of the Medicare program or of any government agency;

- makes a false statement that a policy meets legal standards for certification when it does not;

- sells a person a Medigap policy that is not one of the ten approved standard policies (after the new standards have been put in place in the person's state);

- denies a person that individual's Medigap open enrollment period by refusing to issue the person a policy, placing conditions on the policy, or discriminating in the price of a policy because of the person's health status, claims experience, receipt of health care, or the person's medical condition; or

- uses the United States mail in a state for advertising or delivering health insurance policies to supplement Medicare if the policies have not been approved for sale in that state.

The sale of a Medigap policy to a Medicaid beneficiary generally is prohibited, but there is no prohibition on sale of policies to low-income Medicare beneficiaries for whom Medicaid pays only the Part B (Medical Insurance) premiums although it is usually unnecessary and unwise for a low-income Medicare beneficiary to purchase a MediGap policy.

1228. What are guaranteed issue rights?

Guaranteed issue rights are rights in certain situations when insurance companies must offer a person certain Medigap policies when they aren't in a Medigap Open Enrollment Period. In these situations, an insurance company must:

- Sell the person a Medigap policy

- Cover all pre-existing health conditions

- Cannot charge more for a Medigap policy regardless of past or present health problems

If living in Massachusetts, Minnesota, or Wisconsin, a person may have guaranteed issue rights to buy a Medigap policy, but the Medigap policies are different.

In most cases, guaranteed issue rights exist when a person has certain types of other health care coverage that changes in some way, like when losing the other health care coverage. In other cases, a person has a "trial right" to try a Medicare Advantage Plan and still buy a Medigap policy if they change their mind.

1229. What should a consumer be aware of when shopping for Medigap insurance?

The Centers for Medicare & Medicaid Services (CMS) offers the following suggestions when shopping for Medigap insurance:

(1)   **Review the plans.** The benefits in each of the standardized Medigap policies are the same no matter which insurance company sells it. Review the plans and choose the benefits needed most.

(2)   **Shop carefully before purchasing.** Although each of the standardized Medigap policies is the same no matter which insurance company sells it, the costs may be very different. Companies use different ways to price Medigap policies. Companies also differ in customer service. Call different insurance companies and compare cost and service before purchasing.

(3)   **Don't buy more than one Medigap policy at a time.** It is illegal for an insurance company to sell a person a second Medigap policy unless they are told in writing that first Medigap policy will be cancelled when the second Medigap policy goes into effect. Anyone who tries to sell a Medigap policy when a person already has one should be reported.

(4)   *Check for pre-existing conditions* **exclusions.** Before purchasing a Medigap policy, a consumer should find out whether it has a waiting period before it fully covers any pre-existing conditions. If the person has a health problem that was diagnosed or treated during the six months immediately before the Medigap policy starts, the policy might not cover the costs right away for care related to that health problem. Medigap policies must cover pre-existing conditions after the policy has been in effect for six months. Some insurance companies may have shorter waiting periods before covering a pre-existing condition. Other insurance companies may not have any waiting period. If a policy is purchased during the Medigap open-enrollment period, the insurance company must shorten the waiting period for pre-existing conditions by the amount of previous health coverage.

(5)   **Be careful of switching from one Medigap policy to another.** A consumer should only switch policies to get different benefits, better service, or a better price. However, a policy that does not meet the person's needs should not be kept simply because the person has had it for a long time. If deciding to buy a new Medigap policy, the company must count the time the person had the same benefits under the first policy towards the pre-existing conditions waiting period. However, a waiting period may be necessary for pre-existing conditions for new benefits that covered under the first policy. A statement must be signed

that says that the first policy will be canceled. The first policy should not be canceled until the consumer is sure that he wants to keep the new policy. A person has thirty days to decide if he wants to keep the new policy. This is called the free-look period.

(6) **Make sure to get a policy within thirty days**. A consumer should get his policy within thirty days. If the person does not, he should call the company and ask them to put in writing why the policy was delayed. If sixty days go by without an answer, he should call his State Insurance Department.

(7) **Watch out for illegal marketing practices**. It is illegal for an insurance company or agent to pressure a person into buying a Medigap policy, or lie or mislead a person to get him to switch from one company or policy to another. False advertising is also illegal. Another type of illegal advertising involves mailing cards to people who may want to buy insurance. If a person fills out and returns the card enclosed in the mailing, the card may be sold to an insurance agent who will try to sell him a policy.

(8) **Neither the state nor federal government sells or services Medigap policies**. State Insurance Departments approve Medigap policies sold by private insurance companies. This means that the company and Medigap policy meet requirements of state law. Do not believe statements that Medigap insurance is a government-sponsored program. It is illegal for anyone to tell a person that they are from the government and try to sell him a Medigap policy. If this happens, that person should be reported to their State Insurance Department. It is also illegal for a company or agent to claim that a Medigap policy has been approved for sale in any state in which it has not been.

(9) **Find out if the insurance company is licensed.** An insurance company must meet certain standards in order to sell policies in a state. A person should check with his State Insurance Department to make sure that the insurance company with whom he is doing business is licensed in his state. This is for the consumer's protection. Insurance agents must also be licensed by the state and the state may require them to carry proof that they are licensed. The proof will show their name and the name of the companies they represent. Do not buy a policy from any insurance agent that cannot prove that he is licensed. A business card is not a license.

(10) **Start looking early so as not to be rushed.** Do not be pressured into buying a Medigap policy. Good sales people will not rush a person. Keep in mind that if a consumer is within his six-month Medigap open enrollment period or in a situation where he has a guaranteed right to buy a Medigap policy, there are time limits to follow. Buying the Medigap policy of choice may be harder after the Medigap open-enrollment or special-protection period ends. This will be especially true if a pre-existing health condition exists. If a consumer is not sure whether a Medigap

policy is what is needed, the salesperson should be asked to explain it to him with a friend or family member present.

(11) **Keep agents' and/or companies' names, addresses, and telephone numbers.** Write down the agents' and/or companies' names, addresses, and telephone numbers, or ask for a business card with this information.

(12) **If deciding to buy, fill out the application carefully.** Do not believe an insurance agent who says that medical history on an application is not important. Some companies ask for detailed medical information. Consumers must answer the medical questions even if they are applying during a Medigap open-enrollment period or are in a situation where they have the right to buy a Medigap policy. During these two times, the company cannot use answers to turn consumers down or use this information to decide how much to charge for a Medigap policy. However, if a consumer leaves out any of the medical information they ask for, the company could refuse coverage for a period of time for any medical condition that was not reported. The company also could deny a claim or cancel a Medigap policy if a consumer sends in a bill for care of a health problem that was not reported.

(13) **Beware of nonstandardized plans.** It is illegal for anyone to sell a policy and call it a Medigap policy if it does not match the standardized Medigap policies sold in that state. A doctor may offer a "retainer agreement" that says he can provide certain non-Medicare-covered services and not charge the Medicare coinsurance and deductible amounts. This type of agreement may be illegal. If a doctor refuses to see a person as a Medicare patient unless that person pays him a yearly fee and signs a "retainer agreement," the person should call 1-800-MEDICARE.

(14) **Look for an outline of coverage.** A clearly worded summary of a Medigap policy must be given to each consumer. Read it carefully.

(15) **Do not pay cash.** Pay by check, money order, or bank draft payable to the insurance company, not to the agent or anyone else. Get a receipt with the insurance company's name, address, and telephone number for records.

CMS publishes a consumer-directed manual called "Choosing a Medigap Policy: A Guide to Health Insurance for People with Medicare".[1]

Note

1. Choosing a Medigap Policy: A Guide to Health Insurance for People with Medicare https://www.medicare.gov/sites/default/files/2022-03/02110-medigap-guide-health-insurance.pdf (Revised March 2022)

HOW TO SUBMIT CLAIMS AND APPEALS

Claims Procedure

1230. How does Medicare pay for Part A (Hospital Insurance) services?

Part A (Hospital Insurance) helps pay for covered services received in a hospital or skilled nursing facility or from a home health agency or hospice program. Hospitals, skilled nursing facilities, home health agencies, and hospices are called "providers" under Part A. Providers submit their claims directly to Medicare. The patient cannot submit claims for services. The provider will charge the patient for any part of the Part A (Hospital Insurance) deductible he has not met and any coinsurance he owes. Providers cannot require the patient to make a deposit before being admitted for inpatient care that is or may be covered under Part A.

Intermediaries process claims submitted on the patient's behalf by hospitals, skilled nursing facilities, home health agencies, hospices, and certain other providers of services. When the Medicare intermediary pays a claim, the patient gets a *Notice of Medicare Benefit*. This notice is not a bill.

1231. How does a person submit Part B (Medical Insurance) claims?

Doctors, suppliers, and other providers of Part B (Medical Insurance) services are in most cases required to submit Medicare claims for the patient even if they do not take assignment. They must submit the claims by December 31 of the following year for services furnished during the first nine months of the year. Claims must be submitted by December 31 of the second following year for services furnished during the last three months of the year. A patient should notify the Medicare Administrative Contractor (MAC) for their area if the doctor or supplier refuses to submit a Part B (Medical Insurance) claim and the patient believes the services may be covered by Medicare.

The doctor or supplier must submit a form, called a CMS-1500,[1] requesting that a Part B (Medical Insurance) payment be made for the patient's covered services, whether or not assignment is taken. The doctor or supplier completes form CMS-1500. The patient must sign the form before the doctor or supplier sends it to the proper Medicare carrier. If a patient's claim is for the rental or purchase of durable medical equipment, a doctor's prescription or certificate of medical necessity must be included with the claim.

In general, if the patient is enrolled in a coordinated care plan (such as an HMO), a claim will seldom need to be submitted on the patient's behalf. Medicare pays the HMO a set amount and the HMO provides the patient's medical care. Physicians, suppliers, and other providers of Part B (Medical Insurance) services bill the HMO to receive payment for their services at a contractually-agreed rate.

After the doctor, provider, or supplier sends in a Part B claim, Medicare will send the patient a notice called *Explanation of Your Medicare Part B Benefits*[2] to tell the patient the decision on the claim. The notice gives the address and toll-free number for contacting the MAC if needed.

Payment can be made directly to the doctor or supplier. This is the **assignment method.** The doctor or supplier is prohibited from charging the patient anything above the 20 percent coinsurance amount and the amount of the patient's deductible, if the deductible has not been paid. Medicare pays the doctor or supplier 80 percent of the approved charge. If a provider does not accept assignment, the MAC still pays 80 percent of the approved charge, but directly to the patient who then pays the provider. The MAC will withhold from the payment any amount of the deductible not yet paid.

Notes

1. CMS-1500 https://www.cms.gov/Medicare/CMS-Forms/CMS-Forms/CMS-Forms-Items/CMS1188854.html (last accessed October 17, 2022).
2. Explanation of Benefits, https://www.medicare.gov/forms-help-resources/mail-you-get-about-medicare/explanation-of-benefits-eob (last accessed October 17, 2022).

1232. What must an itemized bill contain?

The itemized bill must show:

(1)   the date the patient received the services;

(2)   the place where the patient received the services;

(3)   a description of the services;

(4)   the charge for each service;

(5)   the doctor or supplier who provided the services; and

(6)   the patient's name and health insurance claim number, including the letter at the end of the number.

If the bill does not contain all this information, payment may be delayed. It is also helpful if the nature of the patient's illness (diagnosis) is shown on the bill.

A doctor or supplier submitting a claim for the rental or purchase of durable medical equipment should include the bill from the prescription. The prescription must show the equipment needed, the medical reason for the need, and estimate how long the equipment will be medically necessary.

Before Medicare pays any charge for Part B (Medical Insurance) services or supplies, a beneficiary's record must show that the individual has satisfied the applicable Part B deductible for that year. Once a beneficiary has satisfied the deductible, physicians, other health care professionals, or supplies should send in future bills for covered services as soon as possible so that Medicare payment can be made promptly. If all medical bills for the year amount to less than the deductible, Part B (Medical Insurance) cannot pay any part of a person's bills for the year.

1233. What happens if the patient dies with payments due?

Part A (Hospital Insurance) payments due from Medicare will be paid directly to the hospital, skilled nursing facility, home health agency, or hospice that provided covered services.

Special rules apply for services covered under Part B (Medical Insurance). If a bill was paid by the patient or with funds from the patient's estate, payment will be made either to the estate representative or to a surviving member of the patient's immediate family. If someone other than the patient paid the bill, payment may be made to that person. If the bill has not been paid and the doctor or supplier does not accept assignment, Part B (Medical Insurance) payment can be made to the person who has a legal obligation to pay the bill for the deceased patient. This person can claim Part B (Medical Insurance) payment either before or after paying the bill.

1234. Is there a time limit for submitting a Medicare claim?

Yes. In general, providers must file claims within one calendar year from the date of the covered service. In extremely limited circumstances (such as the delay being due to an error by Medicare or a beneficiary's retroactive Medicare entitlement), Medicare may waive the one-year time limit.

1235. Where does a physician or supplier send Part B (Medical Insurance) claims?

See *Appendix G* for the names and addresses of the Medicare Administrative Contractors (MACs) selected to handle Part B (Medical Insurance) claims in each state.

CMS relies on a network of MACs to serve as the primary operational contact between the Medicare FFS program and the health care providers enrolled in the program.

1236. What is a Medicare Administrative Contractor and what does it do?

A Medicare Administrative Contractor (MAC) is a private health care insurer that has been awarded a geographic jurisdiction to process Medicare Part A and Part B (A/B) medical claims or Durable Medical Equipment (DME) claims for Medicare Fee-For-Service (FFS) beneficiaries. CMS relies on a network of MACs to serve as the primary operational contact between the Medicare FFS program and the health care providers enrolled in the program. MACs are multi-state, regional contractors responsible for administering both Medicare Part A and Medicare Part B claims. MACs perform many activities including:

- Process Medicare FFS claims

- Make and account for Medicare FFS payments

- Enroll providers in the Medicare FFS program

- Handle provider reimbursement services and audit institutional provider cost reports

- Handle redetermination requests (1st stage appeals process)

- Respond to provider inquiries

- Educate providers about Medicare FFS billing requirements

- Establish local coverage determinations (LCD's)

- Review medical records for selected claims

- Coordinate with CMS and other FFS contractors

1237. Must Medicare claims be paid in a prompt manner?

Medicare Administrative Contractors (MACs),[1] previously known called "carriers" for Part B (Medical Insurance) and "intermediaries" for Part A (Hospital Insurance), must pay Medicare claims promptly. Not less than 95 percent of "clean claim" payments must be issued, mailed, or otherwise transmitted within specified time limits. A clean claim is a claim that has no defect or impropriety or particular circumstance requiring special treatment that prevents timely payment from being made. The deadline for payment of a clean claim is thirty calendar days.

If payment is not issued, mailed, or otherwise transmitted within thirty calendar days on a clean claim, interest must be paid for the period beginning on the day after the required payment date and ending on the date on which payment is made.

MACs are prohibited from issuing, mailing, or otherwise transmitting payment for any electronic claims within thirteen days after claim receipt. This prohibition on paying claims is expanded to twenty-six days for claims not submitted electronically.

Note

1. What is a MAC https://www.cms.gov/Medicare/Medicare-Contracting/Medicare-Administrative-Contractors/What-is-a-MAC.html (last accessed October 17, 2022).

Appeals Procedure

1238. What are the five levels of the Medicare appeal process?

Level One: Redetermination by the Company That Handles Medicare Claims

- Complete *Redetermination Request*[1] and send to Medicare contractor as listed

- Further details are provided in subsequent questions for Original Medicare, Medicare Advantage, and Part D appeals

Level Two: Reconsideration by Qualified Independent Contractor

- Complete *Redetermination Request*[2] and send to QIC

Level Three: Administrative Law Judge (ALJ) Hearing

- Send request to Office of Medicare Hearings and Appeal (OMHA) Central Operations and complete a Request for an Administrative Law Judge (ALJ) Hearing or Review of Dismissal[3]

- Must meet dollar amount

Level Four: Medicare Appeals Council Review

- Send request to Medicare Appeals Council including a Request for Review of an Administrative Law Judge (ALJ) Medicare Decision/Dismissal Form[4]

- Must meet dollar amount

Level Five: Federal District Court

- File lawsuit in U.S. District Court

- Must meet dollar amount

Notes

1. https://www.cms.gov/Medicare/CMS-Forms/CMS-Forms/downloads/CMS20027.pdf.
2. https://www.cms.gov/Medicare/CMS-Forms/CMS-Forms/downloads/cms20033.pdf.
3. https://www.hhs.gov/sites/default/files/OMHA-100.pdf.
4. https://www.hhs.gov/sites/default/files/dab101.pdf.

1238.01 How is the process started when appealing from Original Medicare?

- With Original Medicare, the first step of appeal is looking at "Medicare Summary Notice"[1] (MSN). Appeals must be filed by the date in the MSN. If the deadline is missed, an appeal can be filed by showing good cause.

- Fill out a "Redetermination Request" form[2] and send it to the company that manages claims for Medicare. Their address is listed in the "Appeals Information" section of the MSN.

- Or send a written request to company that manages claims for Medicare to the address on the MSN.

- Include this information in the written request:

  o The beneficiary's name, address, and the Medicare Number on their Medicare Care

  o Circle the items and/or services disagreed with on the MSN. Or list the specific items and/or services for which a redetermination is requested, and the dates of service.

  o An explanation of why the items and/or services should be covered.

o   The name of an appointed representative if one has been appointed.

o   Any other information.

Generally, a decision is made by the Medicare Administrative Contractor within 60 days after they get the request. If Medicare will cover the item(s) or service(s), it will be listed on the next MSN.

Notes

1. "Medicare Summary Notice" (MSN) | Medicare
2. https://www.cms.gov/Medicare/CMS-Forms/CMS-Forms/downloads/CMS20027.pdf

1238.02 How is the process started when appealing from Medicare Advantage?

- With a Medicare Advantage plan, start the appeal process through the plan. Follow the directions in the plan's initial denial notice and plan materials.

- The Beneficiary, representative, or doctor must ask for an appeal from the plan within 60 days from the date of the coverage determination. If the deadline is missed, a reason for filing late must be provided.

- Include this information in the written request:

  o   Name, address, and the Medicare Number on the Medicare Card

  o   The items or services for which reconsideration is requested, the dates of service, and the reason(s) appealing.

  o   The name of representative and proof of representation if a representative was appointed.

  o   Any other information that may help.

- If the health of the beneficiary could be seriously harmed by waiting the standard 14 days for a decision, a fast or "expedited" decision can be requested. The plan must give its decision within 72 hours if it determines, or the doctor tells the plan, that waiting for a standard decision may seriously jeopardize the beneficiary's life, health, or ability to regain maximum function.

  How long the plan has to respond to the request depends on the type of request:

  - Expedited (fast) request—72 hours

  - Standard service request—30 calendar days

  - Payment request—60 calendar days

1238.03 How is the process started when appealing from a Part D Plan?

- With a separate Medicare drug plan, start the appeal process through the plan.

- If asking to get paid back for drugs already bought, the beneficiary or prescriber must make the standard request in writing. One can send a letter or send them a completed Model Coverage Determination Request form[1].

- If asking for a prescription not yet received, the beneficiary or prescriber can ask the plan for a coverage determination or an exception. To ask for a coverage determination or exception, you can do one of these:

    o   Send a completed Model Coverage Determination Request form or a letter or call the plan.

    o   If requesting an exception, the prescriber must provide a statement explaining the medical reason why the exception should be approved.

- If the beneficiary has not received the prescription yet, they or the prescriber can ask for an expedited (fast) request. The request will be expedited if the plan determines, or the prescriber tells the plan, that waiting for a standard decision may seriously jeopardize the beneficiary's life, health, or ability to regain maximum function.

    How long your plan has to respond to the request depends on the type of request:

    - Expedited (fast) request—24 hours

    - Standard service request—72 hours

    - Payment request—14 calendar days

Note

1. Coverage Determinations | CMS

1239. Does a beneficiary have the right to appeal a decision made on a claim?

Yes, if a Medicare beneficiary disagrees with a decision on the amount Medicare will pay on a claim or whether services received are covered by Medicare, the person has the right to ask for a review of the decision. The notice from Medicare tells the patient the decision made on the claim and what steps to take to appeal the decision. If a person needs more information about the right to appeal, he or she should contact the local Social Security office, the Medicare Administrative Contractor (MAC) that processed the initial claim, or the Quality Improvement Organization (QIO) in the beneficiary's state.

See Appendix H for a list of Quality Improvement Organizations.

1240. Does a beneficiary have the right to appeal a decision made on a claim?

A Quality Improvement Organization (QIO) is a group of health quality experts, clinicians, and consumers organized to improve the quality of care delivered to people with Medicare.

There are two types of QIOs that work under the direction of the Centers for Medicare & Medicaid Services in support of the QIO Program:

1.   **Beneficiary and Family Centered Care (BFCC)-QIOs**

   BFCC-QIOs help Medicare beneficiaries exercise their right to high-quality health care. They manage all beneficiary complaints and quality of care reviews to ensure consistency in the review process while taking into consideration local factors important to beneficiaries and their families. They also handle cases in which beneficiaries want to appeal a health care provider's decision to discharge them from the hospital or discontinue other types of services. They also use the Immediate Advocacy Process to address complaints quickly. They also provide Health Care Navigation services. Two designated BFCC-QIOs serve all fifty states and three territories, which are grouped into five regions.

2.   **Quality Innovation Network (QIN)-QIOs**

   The QIO Program's fourteen Quality Innovation Network-QIOs (QIN-QIOs) bring Medicare beneficiaries, providers, and communities together in data-driven initiatives that increase patient safety, make communities healthier, better coordinate post-hospital care, and improve clinical quality. By serving regions of two to six states each, QIN-QIOs can help best practices for better care spread more quickly, while still accommodating local conditions and cultural factors.

1241. How does a person appeal a Part B (Medical Insurance) claim?

After the doctor or supplier or other provider submits the claim for payment to the appropriate Medicare Administrator Contractor (MAC), Medicare will send a notice of the decision made on the claim. If the patient disagrees with the decision, he or she can ask the MAC that handled the claim to review it. The patient has six months from the date of the decision to ask the MAC to review it. If the patient disagrees with the MAC's written explanation of its review decision and the amount remaining in question is $100 or more, the patient has six months from the date of the review decision to request a hearing before a hearing officer. The patient may combine claims that have been reviewed or reopened, so long as all claims combined are at the proper level of appeal and the appeal for each claim combined is filed on time.

If a person disagrees with the hearing officer's decision and the amount in question is $500 or more, the person has sixty days from the date he or she receives the decision to request a hearing before an Administrative Law Judge. Cases involving $1,000 or more can eventually be appealed to a federal court.

To determine whether an individual meets the minimum amount in controversy needed for a MAC hearing ($100) or administrative law judge hearing ($500), the following rules apply:

(1) The amount in controversy is computed as the actual amount charged the patient for the items and services in question, less any amount for which payment has been made by the MAC and less any deductible and coinsurance amounts applicable in the particular case.

(2) A single patient may aggregate claims from two or more physicians/suppliers to meet the $100 or $500 thresholds. A single physician/supplier may aggregate claims from two or more patients to meet the $100 or $500 threshold levels of appeal.

(3) Two or more claims may be aggregated by an individual patient to meet the amount in controversy for a MAC hearing, only if the claims have previously been reviewed and a request for hearing has been made within six months after the date of the review determination(s).

(4) Two or more claims may be aggregated by an individual patient for an administrative law judge hearing, only if the claims have previously been decided by a MAC hearing officer and a request for an administrative law judge hearing has been made within sixty days after receipt of the MAC hearing officer's decision(s).

(5) When requesting a carrier hearing or an administrative law judge hearing, the appellant must specify in the appeal request the specific claims to be aggregated.

Two or more patients may aggregate their claims together to meet the minimum amount in controversy needed for an administrative law judge hearing ($500).

The determination as to whether the amount in controversy is $100 or more is made by the MAC hearing officer. The determination as to whether the amount in controversy is $500 or more is made by the administrative law judge.

When a civil action is filed by either an individual patient or two or more patients, the Centers for Medicare & Medicaid Services may assert that the aggregation principles may be applied to determine the amount in controversy for judicial review ($1,000). Additional information is available at the CMS website.[1]

Note

1. https://www.medicare.gov/claims-and-appeals / (last accessed Oct. 21, 2020).

1242. How does a person request a review by the Medicare Administrative Contractor that handled the claim?

A reconsideration request must be made in writing and filed at a Social Security Administration or the Centers for Medicare & Medicaid Services office, or in the case of a qualified Railroad Retirement beneficiary, filed at a Railroad Retirement Board office. The request must be filed within six months of receipt of the notice of the initial determination, unless an extension of time for filing the request is granted.

The parties to a reconsideration determination are entitled to written notice specifying the reasons for the decision and advising them of their right to a hearing if the amount in question is $100 or more.

Subsequent review steps include:[1]

- **STEP ONE:** Redetermination by a Medicare Administrative Contractor (MAC). An initial determination decision is communicated on the beneficiary's Medicare Summary Notice (MSN), and on the provider's, physician's and supplier's Remittance Advice (RA). The appellant (the individual filing the appeal) has 120 days from the date of receipt of the initial claim determination to file a redetermination request. The notice of initial determination is presumed to be received five calendar days after the date of the notice, unless there is evidence to the contrary.

- **STEP TWO:** Reconsideration by a Qualified Independent Contractor (QIC). The appellant (the individual filing the appeal) has 180 days from the date of receipt of the redetermination decision to file a reconsideration request. The redetermination decision can be communicated through a Medicare Redetermination Notice (MRN), a Medicare Summary Notice (MSN), or a Remittance Advice (RA). The redetermination decision is presumed to be received five days after the date on the notice unless there is evidence to the contrary.

- **STEP THREE:** Administrative Law Judge (ALJ) Hearing or Review by Office of Medicare Hearings and Appeals (OMHA). Any party that is dissatisfied with the Qualified Independent Contractor's (QIC's) reconsideration decision may request a hearing before an Administrative Law Judge (ALJ), or a review of the administrative record by an attorney adjudicator within the Office of Medicare Hearings and Appeals (OMHA). If the adjudication period for the QIC to complete its reconsideration has elapsed and the QIC is unable to complete the reconsideration by the deadline (with allowance for extensions), the appellant party has the opportunity to escalate the appeal to an ALJ or attorney adjudicator.

- A request for an ALJ hearing must be filed with OMHA within sixty days of receipt of the reconsideration decision. The date of receipt of the reconsideration decision is presumed to be five days after the date of the decision notice, unless there is evidence to the contrary. Appellants must send notice of the ALJ hearing request to all other parties who were sent a copy of the QIC's reconsideration, and include evidence of notification with the request for hearing or review.[2]

- ○ In order to request a hearing by an ALJ, the amount remaining in controversy must meet the threshold requirement. This amount is recalculated each year and may change. For calendar year 2023, the amount in controversy is $1,850.[3]

- ○ **STEP FOUR:** Review by the Medicare Appeals Council (Council). Any party that is dissatisfied with OMHA's decision or dismissal may request a review by the Medicare Appeals Council (the Council). If OMHA's adjudication period has elapsed without an Administrative Law Judge (ALJ) or attorney adjudicator issuing a decision or dismissal on the request for hearing, the appellant party has the opportunity to escalate the appeal to the Council.

A request for Council review must be filed with the Council, a component of the Department of Health & Human Services, Departmental Appeals Board, within sixty days of receipt of the notice of OMHA's decision or dismissal. The notice of OMHA's decision or dismissal is presumed to be received five days after the date of the notice, unless there is evidence to the contrary. The appellant must also send a copy of the request for review to the other parties who received notice of the ALJ or attorney adjudicator decision or dismissal.

There is no requirement regarding the amount of money in controversy for Council review. Refer to the OMHA decision or dismissal for details regarding the procedures to follow when filing a request for Council review. Instructions for filing a request (including where to send the request) can also be found on the Council webpage.[4] The request for review must be made in writing and must specify the parts of the decision or action that the party disagrees with, why they disagree.

- • **STEP FIVE:** Judicial review in U.S. District Court. Any party that is dissatisfied with the Medicare Appeals Council's (the Council) decision may request review in Federal court. If the adjudication period for the Council to complete its review has elapsed and the Council is unable to issue a decision, dismissal, or remand the case to OMHA, the appellant party has the opportunity to escalate the appeal to Federal court.

    A party may file an action in a Federal district court within 60 calendar days after the date it receives notice of the Council's decision. The notice of the Council's decision is presumed to be received five days after the date on the notice, unless there is evidence to the contrary.

    In order to request judicial review in Federal court, the amount remaining in controversy must meet the threshold requirement. This amount is recalculated each year and may change. For calendar year 2022, the amount in controversy rises to $1,760.

- • For more detail in the actual process of appeal, see Q 1238 and Q1239

Notes

1. https://www.federalregister.gov/documents/2021/09/30/2021-21288/medicare-program-medicare-appeals-adjustment-to-the-amount-in-controversy-threshold-amounts-for. (Last accessed October 17, 2022)
2. For details see 42 CFR § 405.1014.
3. Federal Register :: Medicare Program; Medicare Appeals; Adjustment to the Amount in Controversy Threshold Amounts for Calendar Year 2023
4. https://www.hhs.gov/about/agencies/dab/different-appeals-at-dab/appeals-to-council/index.html.

1243. How does a person request a hearing with a Medicare Administrative Contractor hearing officer?

An individual who is dissatisfied with a reconsideration determination is entitled to a hearing if the amount in controversy is $180 or more. The request for a hearing must be made in writing and filed at a Social Security Administration or the Centers for Medicare & Medicaid Services office or, in the case of a qualified Railroad Retirement beneficiary, at a Railroad Retirement Board office. The hearing request must be filed within six months after the date of an individual's receipt of notice of the reconsidered determination unless the deadline is extended.

1244. How does a person appeal a Part A (Hospital Insurance) decision made by a Quality Improvement Organization (QIO)?

Quality Improvement Organizations (QIOs) make decisions on the need for hospital care. Whenever a patient is admitted to a Medicare-participating hospital, the patient is given *An Important Message from Medicare*, which describes the individual's appeal rights as a hospital patient and supplies the name, address, and phone number of the QIO in his or her state. The hospital is also required to provide the patient with *How to Request a Review of the Notice of Noncoverage*, which includes a general statement about the posthospital services to which the patient is entitled.

To determine whether a patient meets the minimum amount in controversy needed for a hearing ($100), the following rules apply:

(1)   The amount in controversy is computed as the actual amount charged the patient for the items and services in question, less any amount for which payment has been made by the intermediary and less any deductible and coinsurance amounts applicable in the particular case.

(2)   A single patient may aggregate claims from two or more providers to meet the $180 hearing threshold and a single provider may aggregate claims for services provided to one or more patients to meet the $180 hearing threshold.

(3)   Two or more claims may be aggregated by an individual patient only if the claims have previously been reconsidered and a request for hearing has been made within sixty days after receipt of the reconsideration determination.

(4)   When requesting a hearing, the appellant must specify in the appeal request the specific claims to be aggregated.

Also, two or more patients may aggregate their claims together to meet the minimum amount in controversy needed for a hearing ($180).

The determination as to whether the amount in controversy is $180 or more is made by the administrative law judge.

If a hospital, without consulting the QIO, recommends against admission to the hospital, review of this decision by the QIO may be obtained by writing to the QIO and requesting a review. If the QIO participated in the preadmission denial, a reconsideration of the denial can be requested. If an expedited request for review is made within three working days of the denial, the QIO has three working days to respond.

The appeals process for determinations of noncoverage after a patient is admitted to the hospital is similar to the process for preadmission denials. The hospital cannot charge the patient for the cost of an additional stay unless:

(1)   the hospital or its utilization review committee determines that hospital care is no longer necessary, or the QIO states in writing that hospital care is unnecessary, and

(2)   the patient receives written notice that charges will be made beginning the third day after receipt of the notice and the decision may be appealed by following procedures specified in the notice.

The hospital must have either the agreement of the physician or the QIO before giving a patient written notice of noncoverage. If the physician, but not the QIO, agrees with the hospital, the patient may make a telephone request to the QIO for review, with a simultaneous written confirmation to the QIO of the request for review. If the patient makes this request prior to noon of the day following receipt of notice of noncoverage, the patient cannot be liable for hospital charges until noon of the working day after receipt of the QIO's decision. The QIO must determine, within one full working day of the request (and receipt of pertinent information and/or records from the hospital), the appropriateness of the hospital's decision that the beneficiary no longer requires inpatient hospital care.

If the patient does not appeal, he or she will be liable for all hospital charges beginning the third day after receipt of the hospital's notice.

If the QIO, rather than the physician, agrees with the hospital's initial notice of noncoverage, the patient can request that the QIO reconsider its decision. If the QIO upholds its initial decision, the patient is liable for all charges beginning the third day after receipt of the hospital's notice of noncoverage.

The patient should request that the QIO review the hospital's notice of noncoverage as soon as possible. If the patient requests a review while in the hospital or within three days of notice of noncoverage, the QIO must render its decision within three working days.

The patient may request a review by the QIO at any time within sixty days after receipt of the hospital's noncoverage determination. The QIO will have thirty days to issue a decision (unless the request was made within three days of receipt of the noncoverage determination or while the patient was hospitalized).

If the HMO, rather than the hospital, makes the determination of noncoverage, the patient may request an immediate QIO review of the determination.

For the immediate QIO review process, the following rules apply:

(1)   the patient or authorized representative must submit the request for immediate review to the QIO that has an agreement with the hospital in writing or by telephone by noon of the first working day after receipt of the written notice of the determination that the hospital stay is no longer necessary;

(2)   on the date it receives the patient's request, the QIO must notify the HMO that a request for immediate review has been filed;

(3)   the HMO must supply any information that the QIO requires to conduct its review by the close of business of the first full working day immediately following the day the enrollee submits the request for review;

(4)   in response to a request from the HMO, the hospital must submit medical records to the QIO by close of business of the first full working day immediately following the day the HMO makes its request;

(5)   the QIO must solicit views of the patient who requested the immediate QIO review; and

(6)   the QIO must make a determination and notify the patient, the hospital, and the HMO by close of business of the first working day after it receives the information from the hospital, the HMO, or both.

The HMO continues to be financially responsible for the costs of the hospital stay until noon of the calendar day following the day the QIO notifies the patient of its review determination. But the hospital may not charge the HMO if it was the hospital (acting on behalf of the patient) that filed the request for an immediate QIO review, and the QIO upholds the noncoverage determination made by the HMO.

The patient may appeal a QIO reconsideration decision to an Administrative Law Judge within sixty days, provided the amount of the controversy is at least $200. Cases involving $2,000 or more can eventually be appealed to a federal court.

1245. How does a person appeal all other Part A (Hospital Insurance) claims?

Appeals of decisions on all other services (generally, those not relating to inpatient hospitalization) covered under Part A (Hospital Insurance) (skilled nursing facility care, home health care, hospice services, and some inpatient hospital matters not handled by QIOs) are handled by the Medicare Administrative Contractors (MACs). If a patient disagrees with the MAC's initial decision, the patient may request reconsideration. The request may be submitted directly to the MAC or through a Social Security office. Any Social Security office will help the patient request reconsideration.

If a patient disagrees with the MAC's reconsideration decision and the amount in question is $180 or more, the patient has sixty days from the date he or she receives the reconsideration decision to request a hearing by an administrative law judge. Cases involving $2,000 or more can eventually be appealed to a federal court.

1246. How does a person appeal a decision made by a Health Maintenance Organization (HMO)?

If a person has Medicare coverage through an HMO, decisions about coverage and payment for services will usually be made by the HMO. When the HMO decides to deny payment for Medicare-covered services or refuses to provide Medicare-covered supplies requested by the patient, the patient will be given a *Notice of Initial Determination*. The HMO is also required to provide a full, written explanation of the patient's appeal rights.

If a patient believes that the decision of the HMO was not correct, the patient has the right to ask for reconsideration. The patient must file a request for reconsideration within sixty days after the patient receives the *Notice of Initial Determination*. The request for reconsideration may be mailed or delivered to the HMO or to a Social Security office.

The HMO must reconsider its initial determination to deny payments or services. If the HMO does not rule fully in the patient's favor, the HMO must send the patient's reconsideration request and its reconsideration determination to the Centers for Medicare & Medicaid Services (CMS) for a review and determination.

A patient may not proceed to the next level of administrative review until the HMO issues its decision or refers the matter to CMS.

An HMO must act on the patient's reconsideration request within sixty calendar days from the date of receipt of the request. If the reconsideration determination made by the HMO is entirely favorable to the patient, the HMO must notify the patient within the sixty-calendar-day period. If the HMO cannot make a decision that is fully favorable to the patient, the organization must submit the case file to CMS within the sixty-calendar-day period.

For good cause, CMS may allow exceptions to the sixty-day limit. "Good cause" is defined as unusual circumstances (such as natural disasters) which make it difficult or impossible for the patient to provide necessary information in a timely way. Failure of the HMO to provide the patient with a reconsideration determination within the sixty-day limit or to obtain a good-cause extension constitutes an adverse determination.

If the patient disagrees with the decision of CMS and the amount in question is $180 or more, the patient has sixty days from receipt of the decision to request a hearing before an administrative law judge. The amount in question can include any combination of Part A (Hospital Insurance) and Part B (Medical Insurance) services. Cases involving $2,000 or more can eventually be appealed to a federal court.

The rules regarding an immediate QIO review of a determination of noncoverage of inpatient hospital care by an HMO or hospital are discussed at Q 1244.

1247. What happens if an organization providing items or services to a person under Medicare ceases to continue providing those items or services?

An organization must provide assurances to the Centers for Medicare & Medicaid Services (CMS) that, in the event it ceases to provide items or services, the organization will provide or arrange for supplemental coverage of benefits related to a pre-existing condition. This coverage must be provided to individuals enrolled with the organization who receive Medicare benefits and must continue for the lesser of six months or the duration of the contract period.

MEDICAID

Overview

1248. What is Medicaid?

Medicaid (Title XIX of the *Social Security Act*) is a federal-state matching entitlement program that pays for medical assistance for certain vulnerable and needy individuals and families with low incomes and resources. The program became law in 1965 as a jointly funded cooperative venture between the federal and state governments to assist states in supplying medical assistance to eligible needy persons. Medicaid is the largest program funding medical and health-related services for America's most at-risk people. Medicaid coverage includes the District of Columbia, as well as U.S. Territories.

The Medicaid program is jointly financed by the federal and state governments and administered by the states. Within federal rules, each state establishes its own standards of eligibility, chooses eligible groups, types and ranges of services, payment levels for most services, and administrative and operating procedures. The nature and scope of a state's Medicaid program is described in the state plan that the state submits to the Centers for Medicare & Medicaid Services (CMS) for approval. The plan is amended whenever necessary to reflect changes in federal or state law, changes in policy, or court decisions. Persons eligible for Medicaid in one state may not be eligible for Medicaid in another, depending on standards set.

Federal responsibility for the Medicaid program lies with the CMS in the Department of Health and Human Services (HHS). Beginning in 2014, the Affordable Care Act expanded eligibility for Medicaid to all individuals under the age of sixty-five in households with income up to 138 percent of the Federal Poverty Level. This expansion would arguably eliminate any need to be in a designated group or the need to clear an "asset test". However, in 2012, the United States Supreme Court ruled that the expansion of eligibility was optional to each state – thus, some states have implemented the expansion, which others have not.

States are required to provide certain basic medical assistance services to eligible recipients. These mandatory Medicaid services include inpatient and outpatient hospital care, health screening, diagnosis and treatment to children, family planning, physician services and nursing facility services to individuals over age twenty-one. States may also elect to cover any of over thirty specified optional services, which include prescription drugs, clinic services, personal care services, and services provided in intermediate care facilities for the mentally retarded.

To qualify for Medicaid, applicants must have both incomes and assets below certain limits, which vary from state to state.

Within broad national guidelines established by federal statutes, regulations, and policies, each of the states:

    (1)   establishes its own eligibility standards;

(2) determines the type, amount, duration, and scope of services;

(3) sets the rate of payment for services; and

(4) administers its own program.

Medicaid policies for eligibility and services are complex and vary considerably even among similar-sized and/or adjacent states. Thus, a person who is eligible for Medicaid in one state might not be eligible in another state; and the services provided by one state may differ considerably in amount, duration, or scope from the services provided in a similar or neighboring state. In addition, Medicaid eligibility and/or services within a state can change during the year.

Medicaid serves as a supplement to health insurance coverage provided by Medicare. Medicaid pays for extended nursing home care for elderly people who cannot afford to pay for it themselves. For those who qualify, Medicaid pays Medicare premiums, as well as Medicare coinsurance and deductibles. It may even pay the full cost of some services not covered by Medicare.

1249. What populations does Medicaid cover?

Medicaid focuses on three primary populations in the United States

1. Low-Income Individuals and Families including:

    a. Pregnant women

    b. Children

    c. Families

2. Disabled Individuals

    a. HIV/AIDs

    b. Mental Illnesses

    c. Children with illnesses

3. Elderly

    a. Dual-eligible population – Medicare-eligible

    b. Nursing home residents with financial need

    c. Community waiver participants

1250. What portion of Medicaid expenses are paid by the federal government?

The federal government pays a portion of the medical assistance expenditures under each state's Medicaid program, known as the Federal Medical Assistance Percentage (FMAP). The FMAP is determined annually by the Secretary of Health and Human Services using a formula that compares the state's average per capita income level with the national income average.[1] States with a higher per capita income level are reimbursed a smaller share of their costs. By law, the FMAP cannot be lower than 50 percent nor higher than 83 percent.

The federal government shares in each state's expenditures for the administration of the Medicaid program. Most administrative costs are matched at 50 percent for all states, with higher rates for certain activities (such as development of mechanized claims processing systems). The Medicaid statute does provide for higher matching rates for certain functions and activities.

Federal payments to states for medical assistance have no set limit (cap); rather, the federal government matches (at FMAP rates) state expenditures for the mandatory services plus the optional services that the individual state decides to cover for eligible recipients, and matches (at the appropriate administrative rate) necessary and proper administrative costs. Listed below is the breakout of Federal and State spending dollars and percentages for Fiscal Year 2021 (the latest figures available).

FEDERAL/STATE SHARE OF MEDICAID SPENDING BY PERCENTAGE AND DOLLARS					
Location	Federal	% Federal	State	% State	Total
United States	$504,591,789,784	69.30%	$223,680,902,387	30.70%	$728,272,692,171
Alabama	$5,305,265,224	79.60%	$1,360,866,656	20.40%	$6,666,131,880
Alaska	$1,648,476,016	75.90%	$523,035,342	24.10%	$2,171,511,358
Arizona	$14,277,244,292	81.20%	$3,311,374,000	18.80%	$17,588,618,292
Arkansas	$5,845,658,215	81.50%	$1,325,306,570	18.50%	$7,170,964,785
California	$71,450,349,509	65.20%	$38,105,817,112	34.80%	$109,556,166,621
Colorado	$6,990,614,767	64.80%	$3,796,392,860	35.20%	$10,787,007,627
Connecticut	$6,062,053,380	64.80%	$3,288,530,802	35.20%	$9,350,584,182
Delaware	$1,673,573,096	69.10%	$748,823,017	30.90%	$2,422,396,113
District of Columbia	$2,668,696,730	79.50%	$689,105,501	20.50%	$3,357,802,231
Florida	$19,438,900,710	69.10%	$8,692,612,545	30.90%	$28,131,513,255
Georgia	$9,042,286,115	73.60%	$3,240,231,258	26.40%	$12,282,517,373
Hawaii	$1,942,769,716	68.60%	$890,915,814	31.40%	$2,833,685,530
Idaho	$2,310,555,588	79.60%	$591,135,136	20.40%	$2,901,690,724
Illinois	$17,491,166,058	65.00%	$9,427,991,645	35.00%	$26,919,157,703

FEDERAL/STATE SHARE OF MEDICAID SPENDING BY PERCENTAGE AND DOLLARS

Location	Federal	% Federal	State	% State	Total
Indiana	$13,020,715,055	77.90%	$3,699,279,427	22.10%	$16,719,994,482
Iowa	$4,370,420,406	72.90%	$1,628,376,598	27.10%	$5,998,797,004
Kansas	$2,706,874,924	66.20%	$1,384,255,921	33.80%	$4,091,130,845
Kentucky	$11,922,773,939	82.20%	$2,581,133,264	17.80%	$14,503,907,203
Louisiana	$10,564,583,347	78.80%	$2,836,172,991	21.20%	$13,400,756,338
Maine	$2,509,471,129	72.60%	$946,017,022	27.40%	$3,455,488,151
Maryland	$8,719,675,366	64.70%	$4,747,014,239	35.30%	$13,466,689,605
Massachusetts	$12,391,568,647	61.70%	$7,690,331,446	38.30%	$20,081,900,093
Michigan	$15,768,118,783	75.60%	$5,084,703,437	24.40%	$20,852,822,220
Minnesota	$9,262,590,498	61.90%	$5,703,038,643	38.10%	$14,965,629,141
Mississippi	$4,867,668,834	84.50%	$890,222,017	15.50%	$5,757,890,851
Missouri	$8,333,237,062	72.40%	$3,181,593,449	27.60%	$11,514,830,511
Montana	$1,767,921,517	81.00%	$415,126,262	19.00%	$2,183,047,779
Nebraska	$2,033,285,559	66.30%	$1,031,967,010	33.70%	$3,065,252,569
Nevada	$3,660,525,482	76.90%	$1,100,083,550	23.10%	$4,760,609,032
New Hampshire	$1,511,602,423	63.10%	$882,382,824	36.90%	$2,393,985,247
New Jersey	$12,390,325,108	64.70%	$6,747,314,258	35.30%	$19,137,639,366
New Mexico	$5,759,563,972	83.60%	$1,129,551,799	16.40%	$6,889,115,771
New York	$47,995,427,686	63.60%	$27,418,548,930	36.40%	$75,413,976,616
North Carolina	$12,436,092,910	73.70%	$4,443,000,837	26.30%	$16,879,093,747
North Dakota	$947,678,053	68.70%	$431,113,780	31.30%	$1,378,791,833
Ohio	$20,518,642,808	74.20%	$7,125,210,299	25.80%	$27,643,853,107
Oklahoma	$4,556,383,119	78.00%	$1,285,931,190	22.00%	$5,842,314,309
Oregon	$8,535,107,966	75.90%	$2,716,219,517	24.10%	$11,251,327,483
Pennsylvania	$23,932,008,524	64.00%	$13,455,814,394	36.00%	$37,387,822,918
Rhode Island	$2,032,213,285	67.30%	$986,352,143	32.70%	$3,018,565,428
South Carolina	$5,566,386,578	76.80%	$1,677,083,636	23.20%	$7,243,470,214
South Dakota	$700,955,705	69.70%	$304,250,958	30.30%	$1,005,206,663
Tennessee	$8,086,158,135	72.50%	$3,073,743,096	27.50%	$11,159,901,231
Texas	$31,234,938,733	68.00%	$14,691,233,047	32.00%	$45,926,171,780
Utah	$2,770,444,255	77.90%	$786,951,963	22.10%	$3,557,396,218

FEDERAL/STATE SHARE OF MEDICAID SPENDING BY PERCENTAGE AND DOLLARS					
Location	Federal	% Federal	State	% State	Total
Vermont	$1,128,538,413	67.40%	$544,901,610	32.60%	$1,673,440,023
Virginia	$10,497,415,709	65.80%	$5,466,345,321	34.20%	$15,963,761,030
Washington	$14,962,345,395	68.30%	$6,951,510,487	31.70%	$21,913,855,882
West Virginia	$3,871,901,502	83.40%	$772,748,263	16.60%	$4,644,649,765
Wisconsin	$6,750,140,570	65.00%	$3,640,860,734	35.00%	$10,391,001,304
Wyoming	$360,478,971	60.20%	$238,379,767	39.80%	$598,858,738

Note

1. Section 2015(b) of the Social Security Act.

1251. Why does Medicaid offer different benefits in every state?

Medicaid is a joint federal-state program. It provides medical assistance to eligible needy persons. Unlike Medicare, it is an entitlement program based on income and asset guidelines.

The federal contribution is approximately 50 percent. (For exact breakout percentages, see Q 1250). The states pay the remaining costs, and they are given wide discretion about whom to cover and what benefits to provide. States can also obtain Section 1115 waivers to test and implement approaches that differ from what is required by federal statute but that the Secretary of HHS determines advance program objectives. There is a single state agency in charge of the program in each state, but many states have the program administered by county and city governments.

Medicaid entitlement is based on two principles:

- Any American meeting Medicaid eligibility requirements are guaranteed coverage, and

- States are guaranteed federal matching dollars without a cap for qualified services provided to eligible enrollees.

  o This matching rate is determined by a formula that provides a match of at least 50 percent and provides a higher federal match rate for poorer states.

Medicaid Eligibility

1252. What major groups are states required to cover?

States have some discretion in determining who their Medicaid programs will cover and the financial criteria for Medicaid eligibility. To be eligible for federal funds, states are required to provide Medicaid coverage for most individuals who receive federally assisted income maintenance payments, as well as for related groups not receiving cash payments. As part of the Patient Protection and Affordable Care Act (PPACA), Medicaid eligibility has been expanded to include more low-income adults. As previously stated, states do have some discretion in determining who their Medicaid programs cover, and as a result some states will not be expanding their Medicaid coverage to include the additional low-income adults who would otherwise be eligible under the PPACA (see Q 1256).

Examples of the mandatory Medicaid eligibility groups (called Mandatory Categorically Needy) include the following for which federally matching funds are supplied:[1]

- Individuals with limited income and have children and who meet the requirements of Aid to Families with Dependent Children (AFDC) that were in effect in their states on July 16, 1996.

- Supplemental Security Income (SSI) recipients (or in states using more restrictive criteria – aged, blind, disabled, and institutionalized individuals).

- Infants born to Medicaid-eligible pregnant women. Medicaid eligibility must continue throughout the first year of life, so long as the infant remains in the mother's household and she remains eligible (or would be eligible if she were still pregnant).

- Children under the age of six whose family income is at or below 133 percent of the FPL. As of 2023, the Federal Poverty Level for a family of four is $27,750 making 133 percent to be $36,907.50. (The minimum mandatory income level for infants in certain states may be higher than 133 percent, if as of certain dates the states had established a higher percentage for covering these groups.) States are required to extend Medicaid eligibility until age nineteen to all children in families with incomes at or below the federal poverty level.

- Pregnant women whose family income is under 133 percent of FPL. (The minimum mandatory income level for pregnant women certain states may be higher than 133 percent, if as of certain dates the states had established a higher percentage for covering these groups.) Services to pregnant women is limited to those related to pregnancy, complications of pregnancy, delivery and postpartum care. Once eligibility is established, pregnant women remain eligible for Medicaid through the end of the calendar month ending sixty days after the end of the pregnancy, regardless of any change in family income. States are not required to have a resource test for these poverty-level related groups. However, any resource test imposed can be no more restrictive than that of the AFDC program for infants and children and the SSI program for pregnant women.

- Infants born to Medicaid-eligible women, for the first year of life.

- Recipients of adoption assistance, foster care, and guardianship care under the Social Security Act.

- Supplemental Security Income (SSI) recipients in most states – or the aged, blind, and disabled in states using more restrictive Medicaid eligibility standards that pre-date SSI.

- Certain Medicare beneficiaries. (See Q 1277.)

- All children under age nineteen, in families at or below the FPL. In 2023, the FPL is $27,750 for a family of four and is $34,690 in Alaska and $31,920 in Hawaii.[2]

- Special protected groups who lose cash assistance because of the cash programs' rules, but who may keep Medicaid for a period of time. Examples are: persons who lose AFDC or SSI payments due to earnings from work or increased Social Security benefits; and two-parent, unemployed families whose AFDC cash assistance time is limited by the state and who are provided a full twelve months of Medicaid coverage following termination of cash assistance.

- Recipients of adoption or foster care assistance under Title IV-E of the Social Security Act.

Certain qualified aliens, including certain permanent residents, certain persons claiming asylum, certain refugees, certain aliens whose deportation has been withheld, and certain veterans and their spouses and dependents, are covered under Medicaid. (Persons claiming asylum, refugees, and deportees are only required to be covered by Medicaid for the first five years of their status in those categories.)

Notes

1. 42 U.S.C. § 1396a.
2. https://www.federalregister.gov/documents/2022/01/21/2022-01166/annual-update-of-the-hhs-poverty-guide;omes.

1253. What are Supplemental Security Income states (SSI States)?

Generally, the Social Security Act requires states to provide Medicaid benefits automatically to those receiving categorical welfare assistance. However, the Section 209(b) provision allows states to provide Medicaid benefits only to those persons who would have qualified for Medicaid on January 1, 1972, without adjustment for medical inflation rates. In most states, the Medicaid program includes ALL SSI recipients. These states are called "SSI States".

Other states, however, cover only those persons who are age sixty-five, disabled, or blind and meet the Section 209(b) means test, which is more restrictive than the SSI means test. These states are called "Section 209(b) states". Section 209(b) states include: Connecticut, Hawaii, Illinois, Minnesota, Missouri, New Hampshire, North Dakota, and Virginia. These eight states have elected to define disability more narrowly than the federal definition for SSI entitlement. Indiana was a Section 209(b) state but converted to automatic enrollment in 2014. The current chart is based on 2019 figures, the latest available.

State or Area	Total	Category		Age			SSI Recipients Also Receiving OASDI
		Aged	Blind and Disabled	Under 18	18–64	65 or Older	
All areas	8,076,867	1,166,666	6,910,201	1,132,080	4,646,559	2,298,228	2,682,082
Alabama	160,187	7,880	152,307	20,923	109,967	29,297	57,460
Alaska	12,471	1,781	10,690	1,171	7,865	3,435	4,293
Arizona	119,532	17,790	101,742	16,913	69,229	33,390	39,526
Arkansas	104,312	4,746	99,566	24,335	64,922	15,055	34,512
California	1,222,078	352,968	869,110	98,943	539,745	583,390	488,100
Colorado	72,761	10,899	61,862	8,473	44,707	19,581	23,784
Connecticut	66,783	7,293	59,490	8,568	41,185	17,030	20,774
Delaware	17,059	1,301	15,758	3,323	10,644	3,092	4,792
District of Columbia	25,521	2,172	23,349	3,691	16,053	5,777	6,819
Florida	576,861	145,520	431,341	97,114	263,907	215,840	186,475
Georgia	259,199	25,989	233,210	42,070	158,161	58,968	84,657
Hawaii	22,694	5,316	17,378	1,214	12,454	9,026	8,678
Idaho	31,007	1,757	29,250	4,990	21,295	4,722	10,137
Illinois	264,282	30,643	233,639	34,704	160,567	69,011	75,074
Indiana	127,800	5,887	121,913	21,720	88,781	17,299	38,447
Iowa	51,633	3,206	48,427	8,202	35,368	8,063	17,621
Kansas	47,365	2,894	44,471	8,388	31,374	7,603	15,502
Kentucky	171,487	9,131	162,356	24,396	114,044	33,047	57,623
Louisiana	173,485	10,882	162,603	31,887	107,518	34,080	56,711
Maine	36,599	1,747	34,852	3,877	26,792	5,930	14,034
Maryland	121,691	15,374	106,317	18,972	74,075	28,644	32,365
Massachusetts	182,701	24,812	157,889	21,273	106,438	54,990	54,619
Michigan	270,396	19,589	250,807	34,956	182,442	52,998	83,188
Minnesota	93,151	11,260	81,891	12,216	56,818	24,117	26,350
Mississippi	115,638	7,572	108,066	18,562	73,473	23,603	42,056
Missouri	136,094	6,918	129,176	19,391	95,134	21,569	45,332
Montana	17,677	1,426	16,251	2,134	11,921	3,622	6,718
Nebraska	28,692	2,430	26,262	3,873	19,547	5,272	9,979
Nevada	56,627	14,749	41,878	9,422	31,084	16,121	17,488

TOTAL SSI BENEFICIARIES BY STATE						
		Category		Age		SSI
State or Area	**Total**	**Aged**	**Blind and Disabled**	**Under 18**	**18–64**	**65 or Older**	**Recipients Also Receiving OASDI**
New Hampshire	18,328	830	17,498	2,124	13,868	2,336	5,830
New Jersey	178,009	36,758	141,251	23,910	92,597	61,502	57,097
New Mexico	62,064	8,082	53,982	7,611	36,548	17,905	23,968
New York	621,220	116,229	504,991	80,443	308,448	232,329	197,742
North Carolina	228,518	17,189	211,329	35,198	147,806	45,514	77,922
North Dakota	8,301	613	7,688	1,148	5,592	1,561	2,982
Ohio	307,783	16,890	290,893	43,510	210,523	53,750	87,703
Oklahoma	96,804	6,162	90,642	15,318	65,190	16,296	31,593
Oregon	88,912	9,737	79,175	10,363	57,716	20,833	28,954
Pennsylvania	354,037	24,899	329,138	59,725	220,528	73,784	101,066
Rhode Island	32,552	3,338	29,214	3,701	20,861	7,990	11,024
South Carolina	114,706	7,669	107,037	17,540	74,078	23,088	38,797
South Dakota	14,438	1,520	12,918	2,223	8,980	3,235	4,891
Tennessee	174,588	10,801	163,787	21,946	119,321	33,321	59,398
Texas	644,093	103,499	540,594	127,990	332,007	184,096	220,144
Utah	31,730	2,841	28,889	5,060	20,908	5,762	8,993
Vermont	15,009	912	14,097	1,356	10,962	2,691	6,128
Virginia	155,582	17,568	138,014	22,070	97,954	35,558	48,690
Washington	148,731	17,678	131,053	16,308	93,503	38,920	42,134
West Virginia	70,844	2,294	68,550	7,174	50,954	12,716	23,129
Wisconsin	116,794	6,724	110,070	20,513	77,113	19,168	38,022
Wyoming	6,995	348	6,647	898	5,017	1,080	2,531
Northern Mariana Islands	1,046	153	893	250	575	221	230

Supplemental Security Income (SSI) is a federal entitlement program that provides cash assistance to low-income aged, blind, and disabled individuals. Individuals receiving SSI benefits are eligible for Medicaid coverage in all states except "Section 209(b)" states, which have opted to use their more restrictive 1972 criteria in determining Medicaid eligibility for SSI recipients. Section 209(b) of the 1972 amendments to the Social Security Act allowed states the option of continuing to use their own eligibility criteria in determining Medicaid eligibility for the elderly and disabled rather than extending Medicaid coverage to all of those individuals who qualify for SSI benefits.

As of October 2022, eight states (Connecticut, Hawaii, Illinois, Minnesota, Missouri, New Hampshire, North Dakota, Oklahoma, and Virginia) had elected the "209(b)" option to apply their 1972 eligibility criteria to aged or disabled individuals receiving SSI benefits for purposes of determining Medicaid eligibility.

1254. Does Medicaid pay a beneficiary's Medicare premiums and deductibles?

Medicaid pays the deductibles, coinsurance and premiums for Medicare Part A and B for low income persons. These individuals are called "Qualified Medicare Beneficiaries" or QMB's. Approximately 7.9 million people (approximately 12 percent of Medicare recipients) are in the QMB program.

1255. Do states have the option of providing additional Medicaid coverage?

Yes, states have the option of providing Medicaid coverage for "Optional Categorically Needy" groups (as opposed to the Mandatory Categorically Needy described in Q 1252). These optional groups share characteristics of the mandatory groups, but the eligibility criteria are somewhat more liberally defined. Examples of the optional groups that states may cover as Optional Categorically Needy (and for which they will receive federal matching funds) under the Medicaid program include the following:

- Infants up to age one and pregnant women not covered under the mandatory rules whose family income is below 185 percent of the Federal Poverty Level (FPL) (the percentage is set by each state).

- Certain aged, blind, or disabled adults who have incomes above those requiring mandatory coverage, but below the Federal Poverty Level (FPL).

- Children under age twenty-one who meet what were the AFDC income and resource requirements in effect in their state on July 16, 1996 (even though they do not meet the mandatory eligibility requirements).

- Certain working-and-disabled persons with family income less than 250 percent of the Federal Poverty Level (FPL) who would qualify for SSI if they were not working.

- Children under age nineteen, or a younger age specified by the state, in households with incomes at or below 100 percent of the Federal Poverty Level (FPL). States may provide a full, continuous twelve months of eligibility for such children.

- Institutionalized individuals with incomes and resources below specified limits. The amount is set by each state – up to 300 percent of the SSI federal benefits rate.

- Persons who would be eligible if institutionalized but are receiving care under home and community-based services waivers.

- Aged, blind, or disabled recipients of state supplementary income payments.

- Tuberculosis-infected persons who would be financially eligible for Medicaid at the SSI income level (only for TB-related ambulatory services and TB drugs).

- Individuals in HMOs Guaranteed Eligibility.

- Individuals receiving Hospice Care.

- "Optional targeted low-income children" included in the CHIP program.

- Certain uninsured or low-income women needing treatment or screened for breast or cervical cancer through a program administered through the Centers for Disease Control and Prevention.

- Individuals age nineteen through sixty-four at or below 133 percent of the Federal Poverty Level (FPL).

- "Medically needy" persons (described below).

The option to have a "medically needy" program allows states to extend Medicaid eligibility to additional qualified persons who may have too much income to qualify under the Mandatory or Optional Categorically Needy groups. This option allows them to "spend down" to Medicaid eligibility by incurring medical and/or remedial care expenses to offset their excess income, thereby reducing it to a level below the maximum allowed by that state's Medicaid plan. States may also allow families to establish eligibility as medically needy by paying monthly premiums to the state in an amount equal to the difference between family income (reduced by unpaid expenses, if any, incurred for medical care in previous months) and the income eligibility standard.

Eligibility for the Medically Needy program does not need to be as extensive as the Categorically Needy programs. But states that elect to include the medically needy under their plans are required to include certain children under age eighteen and pregnant women who, except for income and resources, would be eligible as categorically needy. They may choose to provide coverage to other medically needy persons: aged, blind, and/or disabled persons; certain relatives of children deprived of parental support and care; and certain other financially eligible children up to age twenty-one. As of October 2022, the following states offer medically needy programs to the blind, aged, and disabled individuals: AR, CA, CT, DC, FL, GA, HI, IL, IA, KS, KY, LA, ME, MD, MA, MI, MN, MT, NE, NH, NJ, NY, NC, ND, OK, OR, PA, RI, TN, UT, VT, VA, WA, WV, WI, and the Northern Mariana Islands.

States can expand Medicaid eligibility for children under the State Children's Health Insurance Program. To be eligible for federal funds, states must submit to, and obtain approval from, the Secretary for Health and Human Services for a State Child Health Plan. States that elect to use the child health assistance funds to expand Medicaid eligibility and meet conditions for participating in the program are eligible to receive an enhanced Medicaid match for "optional targeted low-income children". Coverage may start retroactive to any or all of the three months prior to application if the person would have been eligible during the retroactive period. Coverage stops at the end of the month in which a person's circumstances change. Most states have additional "states only" programs to provide medical assistance to specified poor persons who do not qualify for Medicaid. Federal funds are not provided for state-only programs.

Medicaid does not provide health care services for all poor persons. To be eligible for Medicaid, a person must belong to one of the designated groups listed above, as well as meet income and assets/resources tests. Even under the broadest provisions of federal law (except for a few emergency services for certain persons), the Medicaid program does not provide health care services, even for very poor persons, unless they are under age twenty-one, pregnant, aged, blind, disabled, or in certain AFDC-type families. The Patient Protection and Affordable Care Act (PPACA) did expand the eligibility for coverage under Medicaid; however, there are still states that have chosen not to include those who would be covered under this expansion. For more complete coverage of the PPACA expansion see Q 1252 and Q 1256.

1256. What effect does the Patient Protection and Affordable Care Act (PPACA) have on Medicaid eligibility?

Under the PPACA, Medicaid is set to expand its eligibility for coverage to include persons with income levels at or below 133 percent of the federal poverty level. In 2024, a standard 5 percent income disregard applies to most individuals, effectively increasing the eligibility level to 138 percent of the poverty level. For the first three years of Medicaid expansion, the federal government will pay for the additional cost. Beginning in 2020, the federal government will coverage 90 percent of the cost of Medicaid Expansion. Currently, 39 states have adopted Medicaid Expansion.

States Adopting Medicaid Expansion

Alaska	Minnesota
Arizona	Montana
Arkansas	Nebraska
California	Nevada
Colorado	New Hampshire
Connecticut	New Jersey
Delaware	New Mexico
District of Columbia	New York
Hawaii	North Dakota
Idaho	Ohio
Illinois	Oklahoma

Indiana	Oregon
Iowa	Pennsylvania
Kentucky	Rhode Island
Louisiana	Utah
Maine	Virginia
Maryland	Vermont
Massachusetts	Washington
Michigan	West Virginia
Missouri	

[1] Coverage under the Medicaid expansion became effective January 1, 2014 in all states that have adopted the Medicaid expansion except for the following: Michigan (4/1/2014), New Hampshire (8/15/2014), Pennsylvania (1/1/2015), Indiana (2/1/2015), Alaska (9/1/2015), Montana (1/1/2016), Louisiana (7/1/2016), Virginia (1/1/2019), Maine (1/10/2019 with coverage retroactive to 7/2/2018), and Idaho, Nebraska, and Utah (to be determined).

[2] Arizona, Arkansas, Indiana, Iowa, Michigan, Montana, New Hampshire, New Mexico, and Ohio have approved Section 1115 waivers to operate their Medicaid expansion programs in ways not otherwise allowed under federal law. Arkansas continues to operate its expansion program through a waiver, however, the waiver provisions related to the work requirement and reduction of retroactive eligibility were set aside by court on March 27, 2019.

[3] Enrollment in Medicaid coverage under expansion began on November 1, 2019, and coverage for these enrollees began on January 1, 2020. The state is still working with CMS to secure approvals of four waivers that it submitted at direction from the April legislation.

[4] On November 5, 2019, Democratic Attorney General Andy Beshear defeated incumbent Republican Matt Bevin in Kentucky's gubernatorial race. On December 16, 2019, Beshear signed an executive order rescinding the Kentucky HEALTH waiver. CMS subsequently removed the terminated provisions from the demonstration approval.

[5] Maine implemented expansion on January 10, 2019. Maine adopted the Medicaid expansion through a ballot initiative in November 2017. After former Governor LePage delayed implementation of the expansion for months, new Governor Mills signed an executive order on her first day in office (January 3, 2019) directing the Maine Department of Health and Human Services to begin expansion implementation and provide coverage to those eligible retroactive to July 2018. CMS approved the state's plan retroactive to July 2, 2018 on April 3, 2019.

[6] On April 18, 2019, the Montana Legislature passed a bill (which was signed by Governor Bullock on May 9, 2019) to continue the state's expansion program with significant changes until 2025. This action came after Montana voters voted down a measure on the November 2018 ballot that would have extended the Medicaid expansion beyond the June 30, 2019 sunset date and raised taxes on tobacco products to finance the expansion. The approved bill directs the state to seek federal waiver authority to make several changes to the existing expansion program, including adding a work requirement as a condition of eligibility and increasing the premiums required of many beneficiaries. Per the legislation, the state submitted a Section 1115 waiver proposal with these changes to CMS on August 30, 2019 and the request is pending.

[7] Enrollment in Medicaid coverage under expansion in Nebraska began on August 1, 2020, and coverage for these enrollees began on October 1, 2020. Nebraska voters had approved a Medicaid expansion ballot measure in November 2018 and the state submitted a state plan amendment (SPA) for the expansion on April 1, 2019. The SPA delayed Medicaid expansion implementation until October 1, 2020 to allow time for the state to seek a Section 1115 waiver to implement expansion with program elements that differ from what is allowed under federal law. On December 12, 2019, the state submitted this waiver to CMS for review. On April 10, 2020, the Nebraska Department of Health and Human Services announced that CMS would not finish approval of this waiver ahead of the planned implementation date; expansion was implemented on October 1 without the program elements from this waiver.

[8] On December 23, 2019, CMS approved the Fallback Plan waiver's request to expand Medicaid eligibility to 138% FPL, effective January 1, 2020. CMS also approved several other requests from this waiver, including work requirements for the newly-expanded adult Medicaid population, but did not approve the request to cap enrollment. CMS is continuing to review numerous other provisions in the Fallback Plan waiver.

[9] The Virginia General Assembly approved Medicaid expansion as part of its FY 2019-2020 budget on May 30, 2018; Governor Northam signed the budget into law on June 7, 2018. Expansion coverage became effective under state plan amendment (SPA) authority on January 1, 2019 after enrollment began on November 1, 2018.

The following states are currently implementing Medicaid expansion:

- Missouri: Missouri began implementing expansion by accepting applications on August 10, 2021, and the state began applications until October 1, 2021. Coverage will be available retroactive to July 1, 2021, consistent with an order of the Missouri Supreme Court.[1] Missouri voters approved a ballot measure on August 4, 2020, that added Medicaid expansion to the state's constitution.

- Oklahoma: Enrollment in Medicaid coverage under expansion in Oklahoma began on June 1, 2021, with coverage for these enrollees beginning on July 1, 2021. Oklahoma voters approved a ballot measure on June 30, 2020 which adds Medicaid expansion to the state's Constitution. The amendment requires the Oklahoma Health Care Authority to submit a SPA and other necessary documents to CMS within 90 days of the ballot measure's approval, and for expansion coverage to begin no later than July 1, 2021. Language in the approved measure prohibits the imposition of any additional burdens or restrictions on eligibility or enrollment for the expansion population.

The Supreme Court has ruled that states may "opt-out" of the Medicaid expansion.

Currently, the following states have not adopted the Medicaid expansion:

Alabama	South Dakota
Florida	Tennessee
Georgia	Texas
Kansas	Wisconsin[1]
Mississippi	Wyoming
North Carolina	
South Carolina	
[1] Covers adults up to 100 percent of FPL in Medicaid but did not adopt expansion.	

If all states were to participate in this expansion, it is estimated that it would add fifteen million people to the Medicaid program. This expansion would continue to increase Medicaid participation to twenty-six million by 2020. From 2014 to 2016, the federal government covered 100 percent of the cost of Medicaid Expansion. From 2020 forward, the federal government will cover 90 percent.

The Kaiser Family Foundation provides a map indicating Medicaid expansion.[2]

Notes

1. https://www.courts.mo.gov/file.jsp?id=178955.
2. https://www.kff.org/medicaid/issue-brief/status-of-state-medicaid-expansion-decisions-interactive-map/ (last accessed Oct. 13, 2021).

1257. Must someone live in a state for a period of time before being eligible for Medicaid?

States must provide Medicaid for eligible residents. States cannot place length of stay residency requirements.

To qualify for Medicaid, applicants generally must be a resident of the state in which they are applying. Applicants who are adults (defined as age 21 or over) are generally considered residents of the state in which they are living or intend to reside. Individuals who are age 21 or over are also state residents when an individual has entered with a job commitment or seeking employment (whether they are currently employed or not). Children under age 21 are generally residents of the state in which the parent or caretaker is a resident, if the child is living with them, or in which the child resides.

States have flexibility to define the term "intent to reside". However, they may not deny Medicaid eligibility because the individual has not resided in the state for a minimum specified time or lacks a fixed address. States may accept attestation that an individual is a state resident without requiring additional documentation. States also have the flexibility to extend Medicaid eligibility to individuals who are not residents of the state (non-residents) through their State Plan.

Medicaid Services

1258. What basic services must be offered by Medicaid?

The Social Security Act requires that a state Medicaid program must offer medical assistance for certain basic services to most categorically needy populations. These services generally include the following:[1]

Mandatory Benefits

- Inpatient hospital services

- Outpatient hospital services

- Prenatal care and pregnancy related services including sixty days postpartum services

- Vaccines for children

- Physician services

- Nursing facility services for persons aged twenty-one or older

- Family planning services and supplies

- Rural health clinic services

- Home health care for persons eligible for skilled nursing services

- Laboratory and x-ray services

- Pediatric and family nurse-practitioner services

- Nurse-midwife services

- Federally-Qualified Health-Center (FQHC) services, and ambulatory services of an FQHC that would be available in other settings

- Early and Periodic Screening, Diagnostic, and Treatment (EPSDT) services for children under age twenty-one

If a state chooses to include the medically needy population, the state plan must provide, as a minimum, the following services:

- Prenatal care and delivery services for pregnant women

- Ambulatory services to individuals under age eighteen and individuals entitled to institutional services

- Home health services to individuals entitled to nursing facility services

Optional Services

States may also receive federal matching funds for providing certain optional services. The most common optional Medicaid services include the following:

- Home health care services (eligibility does not depend on a need or discharge from a skilled nursing facility)

- Diagnostic services

- Clinic services

- Intermediate-care facilities for the intellectually disabled

- Inpatient psychiatric services for individuals under age 21

- Health homes for those with chronic conditions

- Prescribed drugs and prosthetic devices

- Optometrist services and eyeglasses

- Dental care

- Dentures

- Prosthetics

- Chiropractic services

- Personal care

- Hearing aids

- TB related services

- Nursing facility services for children under age twenty-one

- Transportation services

- Rehabilitation and physical therapy services

- Occupational therapy

- Podiatry services

- Hospice

- Case management

- Home and community-based care to certain persons with chronic impairments (this one is an option with an approved waiver)

States can use waivers to test new or existing ways to deliver and pay for health care services in Medicaid and the Children's Health Insurance Program (CHIP). Some of the items in the previous list as optional services would be included via these waivers. There are four primary types of waivers:

- Waivers for program flexibility to test new or existing approaches to financing and delivering Medicaid and CHIP

- Waivers to provide services through managed care delivery systems or otherwise limit people's choice of providers

- Waivers to provide long-term care services in home and community settings rather than institutional settings

- Simultaneously implementing two types of waivers to provide a continuum of services to the elderly and people with disabilities, as long as all Federal requirements for both programs are met.

Note

1. 42 U.S.C. § 1396d.

1259. Is AIDS covered under Medicaid?

Yes. Medicaid is the largest single payer of direct medical services for persons with AIDS.

States must provide the full range of Medicaid services covered in the state plan to eligible persons with HIV disease. States may also provide optional services that are often appropriate for people with HIV / AIDS (such as targeted case management, preventive services, and hospice care). All states cover FDA-approved prescribed drugs.

While Medicaid provides a range of health care services to people with AIDS and HIV, one of the most important is prescription drugs, an optional Medicaid benefit that all states have chosen to provide to their Medicaid populations. Under the Patient Protection and Affordable Care Act (PPACA), Medicaid eligibility expanded in 2014 to include many people with HIV who are not currently covered by the program. However, this coverage is still dependent on the state approving the Medicaid expansion plan. Many states have chosen to opt out of the expansion or have not yet made a final decision about the expansion (see Q 1256). Individuals should contact their state Medicaid agency for state-specific criteria.

1260. Is COVID-19 testing and vaccination covered under Medicaid?

Yes.

Section 9811 of the American Rescue Plan of 2021 established a new mandatory Medicaid benefit mandating that all Medicaid beneficiaries must receive coverage of COVID-19 vaccines and their administration, without cost-sharing, including beneficiaries enrolled in most groups with limited benefits. Additionally, section 9811 of the ARP established a temporary Medicaid FMAP of 100 percent for amounts expended by a state for medical assistance for the vaccine and its administration. The increased FMAP will apply beginning April 1, 2021 and will end on the last day of the first quarter that begins one year after the last day of the COVID-19 emergency period. This new coverage requirement began on the date of enactment of the ARP (March 11, 2021) and will end on the last day of the first calendar quarter that begins one year after the last day of the COVID-19 emergency period.

Section 9821 of the ARP added a similar mandatory benefit requiring coverage of COVID-19 vaccines and their administration, without cost-sharing, for all CHIP enrollees, during the same ARP coverage period that applies in Medicaid. Section 9821 of the ARP also provides a temporary 100 percent CHIP EFMAP for state expenditures for vaccines and their administration during the same time.

CMS has interpreted the American Rescue Plan to require state Medicaid and CHIP programs to cover a broad array of COVID-19 testing, including all types of U.S. Food & Drug Administration (FDA)-authorized COVID-19 tests, without cost-sharing obligations, for a period that begins March 11, 2021, and extends beyond the end of the COVID-19 public health emergency. In meeting these ARP requirements, states must continue to apply normal third-party liability rules and may continue to apply utilization management techniques.

States are required to cover both diagnostic and screening tests for COVID-19 (which includes their administration), consistent with the Centers for Disease Control and Prevention (CDC) definitions of diagnostic and screening testing for COVID-19 and its recommendations for who should receive diagnostic and screening tests for COVID-19. CMS aligned its interpretation of these ARP amendments with applicable CDC recommendations because the CDC recommendations provide a national reference point for who should be tested during the COVID-19 pandemic and evolve as science evolves.

CMS interprets the ARP amendments to require states to cover, without cost sharing, all diagnostic and screening testing that would be consistent with the CDC recommendations including coverage of screening testing to return to school or work or to meet travel requirements. All types of FDA-authorized COVID-19 tests must be covered under CMS's interpretation of the ARP COVID-19 testing coverage requirements, including "point of care" or "home" tests that have been provided to a Medicaid or CHIP beneficiary by a qualified Medicaid or CHIP provider of COVID-19 tests.

Schools can be Medicaid providers of COVID-19 screening testing covered under the ARP.

1261. Does Medicaid pay a beneficiary's Medicare premiums and deductibles?

Medicaid pays the deductibles, coinsurance and premiums for Medicare Part A and B for low income persons. These individuals are called "Qualified Medicare Beneficiaries" or QMBs. Approximately 7.9 million (about 12 percent) of Medicare recipients are in the QMB program.

1262. What is the difference in coverage between "SSI States" and "Section 209 States"?

State benefits vary depending on the options they have elected.

"SSI states": cover everyone who qualifies for the Supplemental Security Income program (aged, blind and disabled). These states cannot have rules that are more restrictive than the federal government rules for SSI.

"Section 209(b) states": adopt requirements that are more restrictive than the federal SSI rules. These states are Connecticut, Hawaii, Illinois, Minnesota, Missouri, New Hampshire, North Dakota, Virginia.

"Categorically Needy Persons": States may also optionally cover "categorically needy persons". These persons qualify for assistance such as SSI, but are not receiving it (for example, because they live in an institution). States may use a higher income standard, up to three times the SSI benefit amount for an individual living at home. If states do not also adopt the "medically needy standard" described below, they would be considered "Income Cap states." "Income cap states" are AL, AK, CO, DE, ID, MS, NE, NM, SC SD, and WY. CT under a waiver allows spend down for institutionalized care and has an income cap for home care.

"Medically Needy Persons": States may optionally cover "medically needy persons." These are persons who would qualify for Medicaid categorically, but are "over income." These individuals can "spend down" to the Medicaid level by deducting "incurred" medical expenses.

The following states have "medically needy" programs: AR, CA, CT, FL, GA, HI, IL, IA, KS, KY, LA, ME, MD, MA, MI, MN, MT, NH, NJ, NY, NC, ND, PA, RI, TN, UT, VT, VA, WA, WV, and WI (also DC and the Northern Mariana Islands). CT under a waiver allows spend down for institutionalized care and has an income cap for home care.

Some states allow a "spend down" but do not permit nursing home costs to be included. These are AZ, IA, OK and OR. (TX does not include the aged in the spend down program).

1263. Does Medicaid provide behavioral health benefits?

Medicaid is the single largest payer for mental health services in the United States and is increasingly playing a larger role in the reimbursement of substance use disorder services. Individuals with a behavioral health disorder also utilize significant health care services. Behavioral health issues resulted in nearly 12 million visits made to U.S. hospital emergency departments in 2007 and involved individuals with a mental disorder, substance abuse problem, or both. Congress enacted several laws designed to improve access to mental health and substance use disorder services under health insurance or benefit plans that provide medical/surgical benefits. The most recent law, the Mental Health Parity and Addiction Equity Act (MHPAEA), impacts the millions of Medicaid beneficiaries participating in Managed Care Organizations, State alternative benefit plans (as described in Section 1937 of the Social Security Act) and the Children's Health Insurance Program.

The Centers for Medicaid and CHIP Services (CMCS) has identified the following as priorities for the next several years:

- Effective benefit design for mental health services for children, youth, and their families

- Effective benefit design for substance use disorder services

- Mental Health Parity and Addiction Equity Act (MHPAEA) application to Medicaid programs

1264. Does Medicaid provide dental coverage?

Dental health is an important part of people's overall health. States are required to provide dental benefits to children covered by Medicaid and the Children's Health Insurance Program (CHIP), but states choose whether to provide dental benefits for adults.

Children

Medicaid covers dental services for all child enrollees as part of a comprehensive set of benefits, referred to as the Early and Periodic Screening, Diagnostic, and Treatment benefit (EPDST). While oral screenings may be part of a physical exam, they do not substitute for a dental examination performed by a dentist. A referral to a dentist is required for every child in accordance with the periodicity schedule set by a state.

Dental services for children must minimally include:

- Relief of pain and infections

- Restoration of teeth

- Maintenance of dental health

The EPSDT benefit requires that all services must be provided if determined medically necessary. The individual states determine medical necessity. If a condition requiring treatment is discovered during a screening, the state must provide the necessary services to treat that condition, whether or not such services are included in a state's Medicaid plan.

Each state is required to develop a dental periodicity schedule in consultation with recognized dental organizations involved in child health care. Dental services may not be limited to emergency services for children entitled to EPSDT.

Dental services must be provided at intervals that meet reasonable standards of dental practice, and at such other intervals, as indicated by medical necessity, to determine the existence of a suspected illness or condition. States must consult with recognized dental organizations involved in child health care to establish those intervals. A referral to a dentist is required for every child in accordance with each State's periodicity schedule and at other intervals as medically necessary. The periodicity schedule for other EPSDT services may not govern the schedule for dental services.

Children in CHIP

States that provide CHIP coverage to children through a Medicaid expansion program are required to provide the EPSDT benefit. Dental coverage in separate CHIP programs is required to include coverage for dental services "necessary to prevent disease and promote oral health, restore oral structures to health and function, and treat emergency conditions". For more information see CHIP Dental Care Goals.

States with a separate CHIP program may choose from two options for providing dental coverage:

- a package of dental benefits that meets the CHIP requirements, or a benchmark dental benefit package.

- The benchmark dental package must be substantially equal to the (1) the most popular federal employee dental plan for dependents, (2) the most popular plan selected for dependents in the state's employee dental plan, or (3) dental coverage offered through the most popular commercial insurer in the state.

States are also required to post a listing of all participating Medicaid and CHIP dental providers and benefit packages on InsureKidsNow.gov.

Adult Dental Benefits

States have flexibility to determine what dental benefits are provided to adult Medicaid enrollees. While most states provide at least emergency dental services for adults, less than half of the states currently provide comprehensive dental care. There are no minimum requirements for adult dental coverage.

1265. Does Medicaid provide prevention services?

Yes. Medicaid and the Children's Health Insurance Program (CHIP) promote prevention by providing access to preventive health care services.

Preventive health care services include immunizations, screenings for common chronic and infectious diseases and cancers, clinical and behavioral interventions to manage chronic disease and reduce associated risks, and counseling to support healthy living and self-management of chronic disease. Prevention initiatives include the following:

- **Tobacco Cessation:** Smoking causes disease and reduces the overall health of smokers. Tobacco use treatment is one of the most cost-effective clinical preventive services. Medicaid programs may cover a wide range of benefits, including counseling, quitlines, and pharmacotherapy to help beneficiaries quit smoking. States are required to cover tobacco cessation services for pregnant women.

- **Developmental and Behavioral Screening of Young Children:** Periodic developmental and behavioral screening during early childhood can identify possible delays in growth and development, when steps to address deficits can be most effective. These screenings are required for children enrolled in Medicaid, and are also covered for children enrolled in CHIP.

- **EPDST:** The EPSDT benefit includes screening, vision services, dental services, hearing services, and other services necessary to correct or improve health conditions discovered through screenings.

- **Immunizations:** Medicaid facilitates access to vaccines and vaccine administration for children, adolescents and adults.

- **Maternal and Child Health:** Prenatal, postpartum, and neonatal care can affect the long-term health of both mother and child. In July 2014, CMS announced a new initiative to improve maternal and infant health outcomes. This initiative is designed to improve the rate and content of postpartum visits in Medicaid and CHIP, and to increase access and use of effective methods of contraception among women in Medicaid and CHIP.

- **Obesity:** Medicaid and CHIP provide access to screenings and interventions to reduce obesity and promote healthy eating and physical activity

- **Oral Health:** States are required to provide dental benefits to children covered by Medicaid and CHIP, but states choose whether to provide dental benefits for adults.

1266. What is the Early and Periodic Screening, Diagnostic, and Treatment (EPSDT) benefit?

The Early and Periodic Screening, Diagnostic, and Treatment (EPSDT) benefit provides comprehensive and preventive health care services for children under age twenty-one who are enrolled in Medicaid. EPSDT is key to ensuring that children and adolescents receive appropriate preventive, dental, mental health, and developmental, and specialty services. The mission of the program is as follows:

- **Early:** Assessing and identifying problems early;

- **Periodic:** Checking children's health at periodic, age-appropriate intervals;

- **Screening:** Providing physical, mental, developmental, dental, hearing, vision, and other screening tests to detect potential problems;

- **Diagnostic:** Performing diagnostic tests to follow up when a risk is identified; and

- **Treatment:** Control, correct or reduce health problems found.

States are required to provide comprehensive services and furnish all Medicaid coverable, appropriate, and medically necessary services needed to correct and ameliorate health conditions, based on certain federal guidelines. EPSDT is made up of the following screening, diagnostic, and treatment services.

Screening Services

- Comprehensive health and developmental history

- Comprehensive unclothed physical exam

- Appropriate immunizations (according to the Advisory Committee on Immunization Practices)

- Laboratory tests (including lead toxicity screening

- Health Education (anticipatory guidance including child development, healthy lifestyles, and accident and disease prevention)

Vision Services

At a minimum, diagnosis and treatment for defects in vision, including eyeglasses. Vision services must be provided according to a distinct periodicity schedule developed by the state and at other intervals as medically necessary.

Dental Services

At a minimum, dental services include relief of pain and infections, restoration of teeth, and maintenance of dental health. Dental services may not be limited to emergency services. Each state is required to develop a dental periodicity schedule in consultation with recognized dental organizations involved in child health.

Hearing Services

At a minimum, hearing services include diagnosis and treatment for defects in hearing, including hearing aids.

Other Services

States are required to provide any additional health care services that are coverable under the Federal Medicaid program and found to be medically necessary to treat, correct, or reduce illnesses and conditions discovered regardless of whether the service is covered in a state's Medicaid plan. It is the responsibility of states to determine medical necessity on a case-by-case basis.

Diagnostic Services

When a screening examination indicates the need for further evaluation of an individual's health, diagnostic services must be provided. Necessary referrals should be made without delay and there should be follow-up to ensure the enrollee receives a complete diagnostic evaluation. States should develop quality assurance procedures to assure that comprehensive care is provided.

Treatment

Necessary health care services must be made available for treatment of all physical and mental illnesses or conditions discovered by any screening and diagnostic procedures.

State Guidelines

State Medicaid agencies are required to:

- Inform all Medicaid-eligible individuals under age twenty-one that EPSDT services are available and of the need for age-appropriate immunizations;

- Provide or arrange for the provision of screening services for all children;

- Arrange (directly or through referral) for corrective treatment as determined by child health screenings; and

- Report EPSDT performance information annually.

Developmental and Behavioral Screening

Periodic developmental and behavioral screening during early childhood is essential to identify possible delays in growth and development, when steps to address deficits can be most effective. These screenings are required for children enrolled in Medicaid and are also covered for children enrolled in CHIP.

1267. What is the Alternative Benefit Plan Coverage?

States have the option to provide alternative benefits specifically tailored to meet the needs of certain Medicaid population groups, target residents in certain areas of the state, or provide services through specific delivery systems instead of following the traditional Medicaid benefit plan.

A final rule,[1] published on July 15, 2013, made major changes in the Medicaid Benchmark Requirements. Key Requirements of the Rule Include:

- The term 1937 Medicaid Benchmark or Benchmark Equivalent Plan has been retitled to Alternative Benefit Plans.

- Alternative Benefit Plans (ABP) must cover the 10 Essential Health Benefits (EHB) as described in section 1302(b) of the Affordable Care Act whether the state uses an ABP for Medicaid expansion or coverage of any other groups of individuals.

- Individuals in the new adult VIII eligibility group will receive benefits through an ABP.

- Efforts are underway to try to extend alternative benefits for continuous coverage for twelve months of postpartum to reduce infant mortality rates.

Note

1. https://www.federalregister.gov/documents/2013/07/15/2013-16271/medicaid-and-childrens-health-insurance-programs-essential-health-benefits-in-alternative-benefit#h-14 (last accessed October 17, 2022).

PACE (Program of All-Inclusive Care for the Elderly)

1268. What is the PACE Program?

Program of All-Inclusive Care for the Elderly (PACE) is a Medicare and Medicaid program designed to meet the health care needs of persons in their community instead of going to a nursing home or other care facility. PACE provides comprehensive medical and social services to certain frail, elderly people (referred to as "participants") that still live in their homes in the community. Most of the participants who are in PACE are dually eligible for both Medicare and Medicaid.

PACE provides a team of health care professionals working with the participant and their family to ensure that coordinated care is provided. In most cases, the care is personalized within a small group of people. Within a PACE program, a participant generally will be required to use a PACE-preferred doctor.

PACE benefits include, but are not limited to, all Medicaid and Medicare covered services:

- Adult day care

- Dentistry

- Emergency services

- Home care

- Hospital care

- Laboratory/x-ray services

- Meals

- Medical specialty services

- Nursing home care

- Nutritional counseling

- Occupational therapy

- Physical therapy

- Prescription drugs

- Primary care (including doctor & nursing services)

- Recreational therapy

- Social services

- Social work counseling

- Transportation

PACE also includes all other services determined necessary by the health professionals' team to improve and maintain an individual's health. PACE programs provide services primarily in an adult day health center and are supplemented by in-home and referral services in accordance with the enrollee's needs.

Since comprehensive care is provided to PACE participants, individuals who need end-of-life care will receive the appropriate medical, pharmaceutical, and psychosocial services. If the individual wants to elect the hospice benefit, they must voluntarily disenroll from the PACE program.

1269. How does PACE work?

PACE covers all Medicare- and Medicaid-covered care and services, and other services that the PACE team of health care professionals decides are necessary to improve and maintain your health. This includes drugs, as well as any other medically necessary care, like doctor or health care provider visits, transportation, home care, hospital visits, and even nursing home stays when necessary. If the participant has Medicaid, they won't pay a monthly premium for the long-term care part of the PACE benefits. If the participant has Medicare but not Medicaid, they will be charged a monthly premium to cover the longterm care portion of the PACE benefit and a premium for Medicare drug coverage (Part D).

PACE has no deductibles or copayments for any drug, service, or care approved by the PACE team of health care professionals.

Some of the more unique services of PACE include the following.

Home Services, Community Activities, and PACE Center Programs

PACE organizations provide care and services in the PACE center, the home and in the community. PACE participants get their care from staff employed by the PACE organization in the PACE center. PACE centers must meet state and federal safety requirements. Programs include adult day programs, primary care from physicians and nurses, activities, and occupational and physical therapy facilities. Also, PACE organizations have contracts with many specialists and other providers in the community to ensure needed care.

Preventive Care

Preventive care is covered and encouraged. PACE organizations are intended to help an individual remain in the community for as long as possible.

Transportation

PACE provides medical transportation PACE organizations provide all medically necessary transportation to the PACE center for activities or medical appointments. Participants may also be able to get transportation to some medical appointments in the community.

1270. Who can get PACE?

An individual can have either Medicare or Medicaid, or both, to join PACE. PACE is only available in the states that offer PACE under Medicaid. There are currently 148 programs operating in 32 states[1]. There are 62,189 participants in the program as of September 2022.

To qualify for PACE, an individual must:

- Be 55 or older

- Live in the service area of a PACE organization

- Need a nursing home-level of care (as certified by your state)

- Be able to live safely in the community with help from PACE

Note

1. National Pace Association report, October 2022.

1271. What does PACE cost?

The costs for PACE depends on an individual financial resources. Medicaid-eligible participants will not incur a monthly premium for the long-term care portion of the PACE benefit. Individuals that don't qualify for Medicaid but have Medicare, will be charged for

- A monthly premium to cover the long-term care portion of the PACE benefit

- A premium for Medicare Part D drugs

If a person doesn't have Medicare or Medicaid, they can pay for PACE privately. Most PACE participants are dual-eligibes – Medicare and Medicaid-eligible.

PACE providers receive monthly Medicare and Medicaid capitation payments for each enrollee. Medicare enrollees who are not eligible for Medicaid pay monthly premiums equal to the Medicaid capitation amount, but no deductibles, coinsurance, or any other type of Medicare or Medicaid cost-sharing.

1272. How are PACE services managed?

A team of professional and paraprofessional staff, referred to as an Interdisciplinary Team assesses an enrollee's needs, develops care plans, and delivers all services (including acute care services and when necessary, nursing facility services).

Minimally, the team is composed of a:

- Dietician

- Driver

- Home care liaison

- Nurse

- Occupational therapist

- PACE center supervisor

- Personal care attendants

- Physical therapist

- Primary care physician

- Recreational therapist or activity coordinator

- Social worker

The interdisciplinary team meets to ensure that the comprehensive medical and social needs of each participant are met. Teams typically meet daily to discuss the status of participants.

1273. How are PACE organizations structured?

A PACE organization is an entity that is primarily engaged in providing PACE health care services. To qualify for PACE, organizations must have:

- A governing board that includes community representation

- A physical site to provide adult day services

- A defined service area (identified by county or ZIP code)

- The ability to provide the complete service package regardless of frequency or duration of services

- Safeguards against conflict of interest

- Demonstrated fiscal soundness

1274. How does an individual join a PACE program?

Enrollment in the PACE program is voluntary. If an individual meets the eligibility requirements and elects to join PACE, then an enrollment agreement is signed. Enrollment continues as long as desired by the individual, regardless of change in health status, until voluntary or involuntary disenrollment.

Payment under Medicaid

1275. How are providers of health care services paid under Medicaid?

Medicaid operates as a vendor payment program, with states paying providers directly. Providers participating in Medicaid must accept Medicaid payment rates as payment in full. States may pay for Medicaid services through various prepayment arrangements, such as Health Maintenance Organizations (HMOs). Within federally imposed upper limits and specific restrictions, each state generally has broad discretion in determining the payment methodology and payment rate for services. Generally, payment rates must be sufficient to enlist enough providers so that covered services are available, at least to the extent that comparable care and services are available to the general population within that geographic area. States must make additional payments to qualified hospitals that provide inpatient services to a disproportionate number of Medicaid recipients and/or to other low-income persons under what is known as the Disproportionate Share Hospital (DSH) adjustment. These payments are limited.

The federal government pays a portion of the medical assistance expenditures under each state's Medicaid program, known as the Federal Medical Assistance Percentage (FMAP). The FMAP is determined annually by a formula that compares the state's average per capita income level with the national income average. States with a higher per capita income level are reimbursed a smaller share of their costs. By law, the FMAP cannot be lower than 50 percent nor higher than 83 percent. In FY 20, the FMAPs varied from a low of 50 percent in ten states to 76.98 percent in Mississippi and averaged 59.7 percent overall. For children covered through the CHIP (formerly SCHIP) program, the Federal government pays states a higher or "enhanced" FMAP, which averaged 72.67 percent in FY 2020.

FEDERAL MEDICAL ASSISTANCE PERCENTAGES AND ENHANCED FEDERAL MEDICAL ASSISTANCE PERCENTAGES
Effective October 1, 2021–September 30, 2022

	Federal Medical Assistance Percentages	Enhanced Federal Medical Assistance Percentages
Alabama	78.57%	85.00%
Alaska	56.20%	69.34%
Arizona	76.21%	83.35%
Arkansas	77.82%	84.47%
California	56.20%	69.34%
Colorado	56.20%	69.34%
Connecticut	56.20%	69.34%
Delaware	63.92%	74.74%
District of Columbia	76.20%	83.34%
Florida	67.23%	77.06%
Georgia	73.05%	81.14%
Hawaii	59.84%	71.89%
Idaho	76.41%	83.49%
Illinois	57.29%	70.10%
Indiana	72.50%	80.75%
Iowa	68.34%	77.84%
Kansas	66.36%	76.45%
Kentucky	78.95%	85.00%
Louisiana	74.22%	81.95%
Maine	70.20%	79.14%
Maryland	56.20%	69.34%
Massachusetts	56.20%	69.34%
Michigan	71.68%	80.18%
Minnesota	56.71%	69.70%
Mississippi	84.51%	85.00%
Missouri	72.56%	80.79%
Montana	71.10%	79.77%
Nebraska	64.00%	74.80%
Nevada	68.79%	78.15%
New Hampshire	56.20%	69.34%
New Jersey	56.20%	69.34%
New Mexico	79.91%	85.00%

FEDERAL MEDICAL ASSISTANCE PERCENTAGES AND
ENHANCED FEDERAL MEDICAL ASSISTANCE PERCENTAGES
Effective October 1, 2021–September 30, 2022

	Federal Medical Assistance Percentages	Enhanced Federal Medical Assistance Percentages
New York	56.20%	69.34%
North Carolina	73.85%	81.70%
North Dakota	59.79%	71.85%
Ohio	70.30%	79.21%
Oklahoma	74.51%	82.16%
Oregon	66.42%	76.49%
Pennsylvania	58.88%	71.22%
Rhode Island	61.08%	72.76%
South Carolina	76.95%	83.87%
South Dakota	64.89%	75.42%
Tennessee	72.56%	80.79%
Texas	67.00%	76.90%
Utah	73.03%	81.12%
Vermont	62.67%	73.87%
Virginia	56.20%	69.34%
Washington	56.20%	69.34%
West Virginia	80.88%	85.00%
Wisconsin	66.08%	76.26%
Wyoming	56.20%	69.34%
American Samoa	61.20%	72.84%
Guam	61.20%	72.84%
Northern Mariana Islands	61.20%	72.84%
Puerto Rico	61.20%	72.84%
U.S. Virgin Islands	61.20%	72.84%

1276. What is the amount and duration of Medicaid services?

Within broad federal guidelines, states determine the duration and number of services offered under their Medicaid programs. They may limit, for example, the number of days of hospital care or the number of physician visits covered. But some restrictions apply: Limits must result in a sufficient level of services to reasonably achieve the purpose of the benefits. Limits on required (nonoptional) benefits may not discriminate among beneficiaries based on medical diagnosis or condition.

In general, states are required to provide Medicaid coverage for comparable amounts, duration, and scope of services to all Categorically Needy and Categorically Related eligible persons.

There are two important exceptions:

(1)   Medically necessary health care services identified under the Early and Periodic Screening, Diagnostic, and Treatment (EPSDT) program for eligible children that are within the scope of mandatory or optional services under federal law must be covered, even if those services are not included as part of the covered services in that state's plan (i.e., only these specific children might receive that specific service).

(2)   States may require "waivers" to pay for otherwise-uncovered Home and Community-Based Services (HCBS) for Medicaid-eligible persons who might otherwise be institutionalized (i.e., only persons so designated might receive HCBS).

States have few limitations on the services that may be covered under these waivers, as long as the services are cost-effective (except that, other than as a part of respite care, they may not provide room and board for recipients). With certain exceptions, a state's Medicaid plan must allow recipients to have freedom of choice among participating providers of health care.

1277. How does Medicaid help with Medicare coverage for the needy, elderly, and disabled?

Persons who are eligible for Medicare and whose income and assets fall below specified limits may also receive help from Medicaid. For persons who are eligible for full Medicaid coverage, the Medicare health care coverage is supplemented by services that are available under their state's Medicaid program. For example, depending on the state, supplies and services such as eyeglasses, hearing aids, and nursing facility care beyond the 100-day noncustodial-care limit covered by Medicare, may be provided by the Medicaid program. However, if a person is a Medicare beneficiary, payments for any services covered by Medicare are made by Medicare before any payments are made by the Medicaid program; Medicaid is always "payor of last resort". Individuals who are covered by Medicare and who also have full Medicaid coverage are often referred to as "dual eligibles".

In addition, there are four groups of Medicare beneficiaries who may not be fully eligible for Medicaid, but who do receive some help through their state Medicaid program. Most of the Medicare beneficiaries helped by Medicaid are those identified as:

(1)   Qualified Medicare Beneficiaries (QMBs)

(2)   Specified Low-Income Medicare Beneficiaries (SLMBs)

(3)   Qualified Individual (QI)

(4)   Qualified Disabled Working Individual (QDWI)

Qualified Medicare Beneficiary Program (QMB)

- Eligibility Criteria:

    - Must be eligible for Medicare Part A (even if not enrolled)

    - Income must be at or below 100 percent of the Federal Poverty Level (FPL)

    - Less than or equal to three times Supplemental Security Income (SSI) resource limit – this is adjusted annually in reference to the Consumer Price Index

- Coverage:

    - Medicaid pays the individuals Part A and Part B premiums

    - Medicare coinsurance and deductibles – subject to limits imposed by the state

Specified Low Income Beneficiary Program (SLMB)

- Eligibility Criteria:

    - Must be enrolled in Medicare Part A

    - Income must be greater than or equal to 100 percent of the Federal Poverty Level (FPL) but not more than 120 percent of FPL

    - Less than or equal to three times Supplemental Security Income (SSI) resources limit – this is adjusted annually in reference to the Consumer Price Index

- Coverage:

    - Medicaid pays the individuals Part B premiums

Qualified Individual (QI) Program

- Eligibility Criteria:

    - Must be enrolled in Medicare Part A

    - Income must be greater or equal to 120 percent of the Federal Poverty Level (FPL) but not more than 135 percent of FPL

    - Less than or equal to three times Supplemental Security Income (SSI) resource limit – this is adjusted annually in reference to the Consumer Price Index

    - Applications approved on "first-come, first-serve" basis until appropriation runs out

    - Cannot qualify for QI if on Medicaid

- Coverage:

    - Medicaid pays the individuals Part B premiums

Qualified Disabled Working Individual (QDWI) Program

- Eligibility Criteria:

  - Medicare Part A benefits have been lost due to individual's return to work

  - Income must be less than or equal to 200 percent of Federal Poverty Level (FPL)

  - Less than or equal to two times Supplemental Security Income (SSI) resource limit – this is adjusted annually in reference to the Consumer Price Index

- Coverage:

  - Medicaid pays the individuals Part B premiums

  - Selection by states is on a first-come, first-served basis

Long-Term Care

1278. Does Medicaid provide coverage for long-term care?

Yes. Medicaid provides long-term care coverage for eligible people age twenty-one and older in certain settings and as long as the individuals satisfy applicable resource and income limits. Long-term care coverage under Medicaid generally covers nursing home services for all eligible people and covers home and community-based services for people who would need to be in a nursing home if they did not receive the home care services. Most long-term care services assist people with Activities of Daily Living (ADLs), such as dressing, bathing, and using the bathroom. Long-term care can be provided at home, in the community, or in a facility. For purposes of Medicaid eligibility and payment, long-term care services are those provided to an individual who requires a level of care equivalent to that received in a nursing facility.

In most states, Medicaid will also cover services that will help a person remain in his home, such as personal care services, case management, and help with laundry and cleaning. Medicaid will not pay for rent, mortgage, utilities, or food.

Medicaid does not cover assisted living – in most states. This would be the in-between stage before a nursing home, but when an individual is past independent living. This stage can be quite expensive and can last for quite a long time, so preparing in advance is important.

As with all Medicaid programs, eligibility for long-term care services will vary from state to state. Long-term care services that may be available to a person in one state may not be available in another state. For example, some states cover assisted living services, while others do not. An individual should contact their state Medicaid office to find out specific eligibility for that state.

State LTC Partnership Program

1279. What is the Long-Term Care Partnership Program?

The Long-Term Care Partnership Program is a joint federal-state policy initiative to promote the purchase of private long-term care insurance. The Partnership Program is intended to expand access to private long-term care insurance policy to pay for long term care services.

Once an individual purchases a Partnership policy and uses some or all of the policy benefits, the amount of the policy benefits used will be disregarded for purposes of calculating eligibility for Medicaid. This means that they are able to keep their assets up to the amount of the policy benefits that were paid under their policy or coverage.

For example, in a state that chooses to participate in the Long-Term Care Partnership Program, once someone has used part or all of their maximum lifetime benefit (MLB), their assets would be protected up to the amount paid under the policy. They would not need to spend those assets before qualifying for that state's Medicaid program.

The following states have approved Long-Term Care Partnership Insurance for sale:[1]

STATE	EFFECTIVE DATE	RECIPROCITY
Alabama	3/1/2009	Yes
Alaska	Not Filed	---
Arizona	7/1/2008	Yes
Arkansas	7/1/2008	Yes
California	Original Partnership	No
Colorado	1/1/2008	Yes
Connecticut	Original Partnership	Yes
Delaware	11/1/2011	Yes
District of Columbia	Not Filed	---
Florida	1/1/2007	Yes
Georgia	1/1/2007	Yes
Hawaii	Pending	---
Idaho	11/1/2006	Yes
Illinois	Pending	---
Indiana	Original Partnership	Yes
Iowa	1/1/2010	Yes
Kansas	4/1/2007	Yes
Kentucky	6/16/2008	Yes
Louisiana	10/1/2009	Yes
Maine	7/1/2009	Yes
Maryland	1/1/2009	Yes
Massachusetts	Proposed	---
Michigan	Work stopped	---

STATE	EFFECTIVE DATE	RECIPROCITY
Minnesota	7/1/2006	Yes
Mississippi	Not Filed	---
Missouri	8/1/2008	Yes
Montana	7/1/2009	Yes
Nebraska	7/1/2006	Yes
Nevada	1/1/2007	Yes
New Hampshire	2/16/2010	Yes
New Jersey	7/1/2008	Yes
New Mexico	Not Filed	---
New York	Original Partnership	Yes
North Carolina	3/7/2011	Yes
North Dakota	1/1/2007	Yes
Ohio	9/10/2007	Yes
Oklahoma	7/1/2008	Yes
Oregon	1/1/2008	Yes
Pennsylvania	9/15/2007	Yes
Rhode Island	7/1/2008	Yes
South Carolina	1/1/2009	Yes
South Dakota	7/1/2007	Yes
Tennessee	10/1/2008	Yes
Texas	3/1/2008	Yes
Utah	Not Filed	---
Vermont	Not Filed	---
Virginia	9/1/2007	Yes
Washington	1/1/2012	Yes
West Virginia	17/01/2010	Yes
Wisconsin	1/1/2009	Yes
Wyoming	6/29/2009	Yes

Note

1. https://www.aaltci.org/long-term-care-insurance/learning-center/long-term-care-insurance-partnership-plans.php#explain. (Last accessed October 17, 2022).

1280. What is a "qualified state long-term care insurance partnership?"

A qualified state long-term care insurance partnership is a state Medicaid plan amendment that provides for the disregard of assets or resources in an amount equal to the insurance benefit payments made to or on behalf of an individual who is a beneficiary under a qualifying Long-Term Care (LTC) insurance policy.

A qualifying LTC partnership policy must meet the following requirements:

1. The policy covers an insured who was a resident of the state when coverage first became effective under the policy.

2.   The policy is a tax qualified LTC insurance policy issued not earlier than the effective date of the state LTC partnership program.

3.   The policy must meet the standards contained in the 2000 NAIC Model LTC Policy Act and Regulations.

4.   The policy must contain the following inflation protection provisions:

a.   Buyers younger than age sixty-one – compound annual inflation protection

b.   Buyers ages sixty-one to seventy-five –some level of inflation protection

c.   Buyers age seventy-six or older – no inflation protection required

5.   Agents selling the policy must receive appropriate training and demonstrate understanding of the policy.

6.   The issuer of the policy must provide regular reports with information on policy benefits, claims, underwriting, terminations, and other information deemed appropriate.

7.   The policy must not be subject to any state insurance mandates not applicable to all LTC insurance policies sold in the state.

Standards do exist (under the Deficit Reduction Act of 2005 (DRA)) for the uniform reciprocal recognition of LTC partnership policies, under which benefits paid by such policies will be treated the same by all states with qualified state LTC insurance partnerships. A state with a LTC insurance partnership is subject to the standards unless the state formally elects to be exempt from such standards.

Exempt Income and Resources

1281. Are certain income and resources exempt from the financial eligibility standards that govern Medicaid eligibility?

A single individual will not qualify for Medicaid in most states unless he has less than $2,000 in countable assets (although it may be higher in some states).

In determining whether applicants for Medicaid meet asset criteria, certain assets are considered "countable" and other assets are considered "exempt". Exempt assets include the following:

•   The cash value of permanent life insurance policies up to $2,500 of face value, and all life insurance policies with no cash value (term insurance).

•   Household furnishings (furniture, paintings, appliances, etc.), which are exempt only while used in the applicant's home.

- Burial funds up to $1,500 (reduced by the face value of any cash-value life insurance policies otherwise exempted and any amounts held in an irrevocable burial fund trust). There is no dollar limit if the burial plan is irrevocable.

- Property used in a trade or business.

- Burial space (grave site, crypt, mausoleum, urn, grave marker).

- One automobile of any value:

    (1) for a married couple where one spouse is institutionalized;

    (2) if equipped for a handicapped person;

    (3) if used to obtain medical treatment; or

    (4) if used for employment.

- This exemption is limited to $4,500 in all other cases.

- Up to $636,000 of equity in a home provided it is the person's principal place of residence. This includes the land on which the home sits and any adjoining property. States may choose to increase this amount up to $906,000.

- Property owned with one or more other individuals, if the other owners use the property as the principal place of residence and would be forced to move if the property were sold.

- Personal effects, including clothing, photographs, jewelry, etc.

The home is treated as a resource after the individual has been institutionalized for six months, unless the individual's spouse or minor, disabled, or blind child continues to reside in the home, or it can be shown that the individual may be able to leave the institution and return home.

Exempt assets lose that status upon the death of the Medicaid recipient. Therefore, the state may claim reimbursement from the recipient's estate. Medicaid authorities are sometimes granted a lien against the home, collectible after the death of the recipient (or the death of certain relatives living in the home) to compensate for Medicaid benefits paid to the homeowner.

Medicaid applicants must also meet income tests that vary by state. It is important to note that rules do differ quite significantly from state-to-state. In some of the states, there is no upper income limit for persons in nursing homes. The remaining states have "income caps" in determining eligibility for nursing home coverage. If a person has income below the private cost of nursing home care in one of the states where there is no upper income limit, he meets Medicaid's income test. For example, if a person has monthly income of $2,500 and the private cost of nursing home care is $3,000 (and he has less than $2,000 in countable assets), he or she will qualify for Medicaid. He will be required to pay all of his income, except for a small "personal needs allowance," to the nursing home and Medicaid pays the balance of the bill.

Federal law requires states with "income caps" to set those caps no higher than 300 percent of the Federal SSI benefit level ($914 in 2023). Thus, the "income cap" can be no greater than $2,742 in 2023 for a single person. The maximum SSI benefit level is $1,371 for an eligible individual with an eligible spouse, and $458 for an essential person. Not all of the states using income caps set their cap at the maximum allowable level (300 percent of the SSI benefit level). For example, if a person's monthly income is $1,550 in a state that sets its cap at $1,500, he does not qualify for Medicaid.

Spousal Impoverishment

1282. Are there guidelines regarding the amount of income the community spouse of a nursing home resident can maintain?

The expense of nursing home care can rapidly deplete the lifetime savings of elderly couples. Because of this there are specially mandated Medicaid eligibility rules for couples when one-member needs nursing home care. The rules protect income and resources for the other member of the couple. Under these rules, a healthy spouse is not required to give up all of his income or property simply for the spouse in need of nursing care to be eligible through Medicaid. This set of rules, called "spousal protections" allow the spouse of a nursing home resident to keep enough income and assets to live a life outside the nursing home. As with all Medicaid programs, there is great variation among states' spousal protections rules, but the basic guidelines are the same in every state.

Under the rules, certain income, assets, and the couple's home are protected. The following guidelines remain true for all states:

- **Protected Income.** The income of the spouse of the long-term care patient is protected as well as some of the long-term care patient's income if it is needed to financially support the spouse. The money that a spouse may keep and that is exempt from the Medicaid eligibility calculation is called the Minimum Monthly Maintenance Needs Allowance (MMMNA). The MMMNA varies from state to state, but the federal government sets a minimum and a maximum periodically that is tied to poverty guidelines. For 2022, the minimum is $2,288.75 and the maximum is $3,435. This income is disregarded by the state Medicaid agency in evaluating whether the needy spouse is financially eligible for Medicaid.

- **Protected Assets.** The spouse of the long-term care patient is allowed to keep one-half of the couple's combined marital assets subject to state set minimum and maximum allowable amounts (within federal guidelines). The state will measure the resources of the spouse applying for Medicaid on the date that the spouse began a hospital or nursing home stay that lasted at least thirty days. The amount of resources that the healthy spouse, called the "community spouse" is allowed to keep is called the Community Spouse Resource Allowance (CSRA). The CSRA varies by state (within a federally established minimum and maximum CSRA).

If a spouse living in the community needs more income than the MMMNA or more resources than the CSRA, the spouse can seek a court order allowing a variation from the state agency's standard.

- **Protection of Home.** Federal Medicaid rules protect a Medicaid recipient's home and property, which is an important protection for the community spouse. If a Medicaid recipient expresses intent to return to the home, the first $636,000 in equity is excluded as a resource when calculating whether the needy spouse is eligible for Medicaid. Some states choose to raise the equity limit to $906,000. States do have discretion about when they will disregard the value of a home in calculating eligibility; many states require that the recipient must be likely to return to the home, not just that the recipient intends to return to the home.

2023 guidelines will be issued during December of 2022.

1283. What are the resource eligibility requirements that apply to a community spouse?

The spousal impoverishment provisions apply where the member of the couple who is in a nursing facility or medical institution is expected to remain there for at least thirty days. When the couple applies for Medicaid, an assessment of their resources is conducted. The couple's resources are combined and exemptions for the home, household goods, automobile, and burial funds are taken into account (See Q 1281 and Q 1282). The result is the spousal resource amount. The spousal resource amount is the state's minimum resource standard ($27,950 – figures are not yet available for 2023, or the spousal share, which is equal to one-half of the couple's combined resources (not to exceed the maximum permitted by the state ($137,400 in 2022). Some states have a maximum resource limit under the federally set standard of $137,400. For instance, as of 2018, South Carolina limits their maximum resource allowance to $66,480, and Illinois sets their limit at $109,560. Not all resources are counted, which means they are exempt and are not calculated and included in the resource allowance.

In order to determine whether the spouse residing in a medical facility is eligible for Medicaid, a determination of the couple's total countable resources must be made. All resources held by both spouses are considered to be available to the spouse in the medical facility, except for the Protected Resource Amount (PRA). This PRA is the greatest of:

- the spousal resource amount;

- the state spousal resource standard, which is the amount that the state has determined will be protected for the community spouse;

- an amount transferred to the community spouse for her/his support as directed by a court order;

- an amount designated by a state hearing officer to raise the community spouse's protected resources up to the minimum monthly maintenance needs standard (150 percent of the federal poverty level for a household of two).

The remainder becomes attributable to the spouse that is residing in a medical institution as countable resources. If the amount of resources is below the state's resource standard, the individual is eligible for Medicaid. Once resource eligibility is determined, resources of the community spouse are not attributed to the spouse in the medical facility.

1284. What are the income eligibility requirements for Community Spouses?

The community spouse's income is not considered available to the spouse who is in the medical facility, and the two individuals are not considered a couple for these purposes. The state must use the income eligibility standards for one person rather than two. Therefore, the standard income eligibility process for Medicaid is used (See Q 1281 to Q 1283).

1285. What is the process for the post-eligibility treatment of income for Community Spouses?

This process is followed after an individual in a nursing facility/medical institution is determined to be eligible for Medicaid. The post-eligibility process is used to determine how much the spouse in the medical facility must contribute toward the cost of nursing facility/institutional care. The process also determines how much of the income of the spouse who is in the medical facility is actually protected for use by the community spouse.

Deductions are made from the total income of the spouse who is residing in the medical facility in the following order:

- A personal needs allowance of at least thirty dollars

- The community spouse's monthly income allowance—between $2,288.75 and $3.435(in 2022)—as long as the income is actually made available to the spouse

- A family monthly income allowance

- An amount for medical expenses incurred by the spouse who is in the medical facility

The sum of these deductions subtracted from the income of the individual who is in the medical facility will result in the amount the individual must contribute to the cost of care.

1286. What Medicaid planning strategies can spouses use to help with eligibility?

As explained in preceding questions Medicaid will pay for nursing home care only for those who are eligible. While some safe-guards and asset protections remain in place for the community spouse, many people feel that these do not do enough to protect their assets. Since Medicaid will pay for nursing home care only for those with limited assets and will penalize those who give away assets to qualify for Medicaid, people have long used other strategies in to circumvent the rules penalizing gifts of assets. Some of the more popular strategies used for making gifts while avoiding a transfer penalty are listed here. However, take note that new rules have made these strategies either completely ineffective or very difficult.

- **"Half a Loaf" Strategy.** At one time, this strategy was one of the most commonly used gifting strategies. A senior who anticipated needing long-term care would gift half of his assets to those of his choosing (preserving "half a loaf") and use the rest to pay for Medicaid during the penalty period. Using the half a loaf strategy, people often made gifts to family members on a monthly or bimonthly basis, based on state law. Now that the transfer penalty does not begin to run until a person applies for Medicaid and all of the other qualifications are met for Medicaid, periodic gifting is no longer effective.

- **Annuities.** An annuity is when a person pays a lump sum of cash in exchange for a series of guaranteed future payments during that person's lifetime. The strategy of purchasing an annuity to qualify for Medicaid still works for married couples, but there has been refinement in the law causing most of the older methods to be ineffective. The key to using this strategy successfully is to convert an asset into a stream of monthly income for the spouse who does not need long-term care. This works because only the income of the applicant is considered toward eligibility; income of the community spouse is excluded. Purchasing an annuity turns an excess asset into income, so the asset is transparent for Medicaid purposes. The annuity payments must be completed before the end of the community spouse's life expectancy. This rule prevents the likelihood that there would be annuity payments left for the heirs after the community spouse's death.

1287. Can a spouse refuse to support a spouse who has entered a nursing home, causing Medicaid to pay for the nursing home?

Theoretically, husbands and wives have an equal duty to support one another. In many instances, the spouse with more income and assets gets sick and enters a nursing home first. However, it is perfectly possible that the sick spouse will have very limited personal income and resources. In that case, the question becomes, what is the obligation of the healthy, more affluent, community spouse?

Perhaps surprisingly, Federal Medicaid law generally takes a "just say no" position. State Medicaid agencies are not allowed to deny Medicaid benefits to patients on the grounds that their wealthier spouses refuse to support them or let any of their own income or resources be used. However, part of the Medicaid application process is an agreement to assign support rights to the Medicaid agency. The Medicaid agency then has a legal right to sue the community spouse for nonsupport. Whether this is a meaningful threat to individual community spouses depends on the local policy. Some Medicaid agencies are very active in this matter, but most bring few nonsupport suits.

Community spouses who want to preserve their own financial position, but who do not want to engage in outright "spousal refusal" can enter into an agreement with the state Medicaid agency. Usually, offering 25 percent of the difference between the community spouse's actual income and the monthly maintenance allowance will be acceptable. Note that Medicaid benefits can be denied to the spouse of a healthy person who refuses to provide information about his financial situation, so make sure that potential community spouses provide disclosure, even if they want to make a spousal refusal.

1288. Are adult children responsible for the medical bills of their parents?

No. In determining Medicaid eligibility of an adult, federal law does not permit states to use the income or resources of non-spouses. States cannot collect reimbursement from these relatives.

Twenty-seven state have laws making adult children responsible for support of indigent parents. This however would apply for costs not covered by Medicaid. These states include Alaska, Arkansas, California, Connecticut, Delaware, Georgia, Idaho, Indiana, Iowa, Kentucky, Louisiana, Maryland, Massachusetts, Mississippi, Montana, Nevada, New Hampshire, New Jersey, North Carolina, North Dakota, Ohio, Oregon, Pennsylvania, Rhode Island, South Dakota, Tennessee, Utah, Vermont, Virginia, and West Virginia.

1289. Is divorce a viable planning strategy for Medicaid purposes?

Generally, no. Medicaid rules favor married couples. Medicaid-motivated divorce (as distinct from couples who are genuinely unhappy, or where one partner wants to remarry) is usually inadvisable.

When a couple divorces, either their property is community property, which is equally divided between them, or it is marital property which must be "equitably" divided. There are many factors in equitable distribution, but the needs of the parties are considered more important than who owned the property originally, or who contributed the funds used to purchase it. Therefore, it is possible that a large percentage of the couple's property will be distributed to the sick spouse, with resulting negative consequences for Medicaid planning.

Also, divorce courts have the power to order spousal support, depending on the relative needs of the spouses. A person who needs extensive long-term care is incapable of self-support, so it is possible that the divorce court will order the healthy, and wealthier, spouse to provide income to the sick spouse.

Capacity is also a problem. Legal capacity is required to sue or be sued, and a person suffering from Alzheimer's disease, or some other type of dementia may lack such capacity. If a guardian has already been appointed, the guardian may be able to handle the divorce. On the other hand, some states have taken the position that divorce litigation is so inherently personal that a guardian cannot take part in it. In those states, a demented person's marriage is effectively permanent, because there is no way to dissolve it by divorce.

Medicaid Transfer Rules

1290. Can a person transfer property to meet the eligibility requirements for Medicaid?

Transfers of property for less than fair market value prior to applying for Medicaid benefits can result in a denial of benefits. States' rules will vary significantly from state to state; however, states may delay eligibility for Medicaid benefits for a period of time whenever it is determined that a person institutionalized in a medical institution or nursing facility has disposed of resources for less than fair market value within sixty months before application for Medicaid benefits. A transfer is an outright gift, or an exchange for something worth less than the full value of the transferred property.

Certain transfers can be made within sixty months of the application without loss of Medicaid eligibility.

The family home may be transferred to:

(1)   the community spouse (noninstitutionalized spouse);

(2)   a child who is under age twenty-one, blind, or permanently and totally disabled;

(3)   an adult son or daughter residing in the home and providing care that delayed the person's need for care in a medical institution or nursing facility for at least two years;

(4)   a trust created solely for the benefit of disabled children of the applicant;

(5)   certain trusts created for a disabled child or grandchild under age sixty-five; and

(6)   a sibling who has an ownership interest in the house and who has been living in the home for at least one year immediately before the person's admission for care.

Also, eligibility is unaffected if the transferor can prove that the intent of the transfer was to dispose of the resources either at fair market value or for other valuable consideration, or the exclusive purpose of the transfer was not to qualify for Medicaid. States can also grant eligibility where denial would amount to undue hardship.

All transfers of jointly owned property to others are deemed to the Medicaid applicant. This penalty applies when the action taken by a co-owner reduces or eliminates the Medicaid applicant's ownership or control of the asset.

Two ways to transfer assets to family members without disqualifying for Medicaid benefits are:

(1)   by transferring the assets to family members more than sixty months before the person applies for Medicaid benefits; and

(2)   if the applicant is already in a nursing home or about to go into one, by retaining enough assets to pay for sixty months of care, transferring the balance, and not applying for Medicaid until sixty months after the date on which the last asset transfer is completed.

Any planning for Medicaid eligibility should be done with a clear understanding of all the present rules on the federal level and for the state in which the person(s) resides. These rules vary significantly from state to state and change frequently. Additionally, it should be noted that there is the threat of criminal penalty for any lawyer or adviser assisting clients with Medicaid planning.

1291. How is the penalty period determined after an improper transfer of assets?

The penalty period of ineligibility for an improper transfer—see Q 1290—begins on the later of the first day of the month of the transfer or "the date on which the individual is eligible for medical assistance under the State plan...based on an approved application for such care but for the application of the penalty period". The penalty lasts for the number of months equal to the total value of transferred property divided by the average cost of nursing home care to a private patient in the state or community of the applicant (the average private-pay rate). All transfers made in the sixty months prior to the application date are aggregated in determining the length of the penalty period. There is no limit to the length of the penalty period.

For example, a Medicaid applicant who improperly transfers a house worth $900,000 in a state with an average cost of nursing home care of $12,000 a month will be penalized with 75 months of ineligibility for Medicaid ($900,000 ÷ $12,000 = 75). But if a person gives away a house worth $900,000 and then waits more than sixty months to apply for Medicaid, he or she does not have to report the transfer and will not incur the period of ineligibility.

The rules have been made more restrictive in recent years and mean that common gifting strategies involving "half a loaf" or consecutive monthly transfers no longer work. (See Q 1286.)

If both spouses enter a nursing home at or near the same time, states are required to apportion the penalty between the spouses so that only one penalty applies. For example, an improper transfer of $170,000 in a state with a nursing home cost of $8,500 will cause each spouse to be ineligible for ten months ($170,000 ÷ $8,500 = 20 ÷ 2 = 10).

A Medicaid applicant cannot have a portion of the transferred property returned to eliminate the transfer penalty. All assets transferred for less than fair market value must be returned in order to eliminate some or all of the penalty period.

Each state has procedures for waiver of the transfer penalty when the transfer penalty results in undue hardship.

1292. What are the rules under Medicaid regarding the purchase of annuities?

Under the *Deficit Reduction Act of 2005* (DRA), purchasing an annuity by or on behalf of an applicant is considered an improper transfer of assets (see Q 1286, Q 1290, and Q 1291) unless the annuity meets certain requirements.

The purchase of an annuity will not be treated as an improper transfer of assets if the:

1.   state is named as the primary remainder beneficiary for at least the total amount of medical assistance paid by Medicaid on behalf of the applicant

2.   state is named as the secondary beneficiary after the community spouse or minor or disabled child

3.   annuity is purchased inside, or with proceeds from, a retirement account (IRA, Roth IRA, SEP-IRA, etc.)

Any annuity purchased on behalf of a Medicaid applicant must be irrevocable, nonassignable, actuarially sound, and provide for payments in equal amounts during the term of the annuity, with no deferral and no balloon payments.

Annuities purchased prior to February 8, 2006 (the effective date of the DRA) are governed by state-specific provisions. At a minimum, pre-DRA annuities must be actuarially sound (meaning they do not pay out over a time period exceeding the life expectancy of the Medicaid applicant).

Trusts

1293. Can a trust be used to shelter a Medicaid applicant's assets?

There are considerable limits on the use of trusts to shelter a Medicaid applicant's assets. Trust assets created or funded by a Medicaid applicant or by his spouse are considered available to the applicant to the extent the applicant derives any benefit from the trust.

If an institutionalized person or spouse (or, at the option of a state, a noninstitutionalized person or spouse) disposes of trust assets for less than fair market value on or after the look-back date for trusts, the person is ineligible for Medicaid for the following time period:

- For an institutionalized person, the number of months of ineligibility is equal to the total of all assets transferred on or after the look-back date divided by the average monthly cost to a private patient of nursing facility services in the state at the time of application. Ineligibility begins on the first day of the first month during or after which assets have been transferred for less than fair market value.

- For a noninstitutionalized person, the number of months of ineligibility may not be greater than a number equal to the total value of all assets transferred on or after the look-back date, divided by the average monthly cost to a private patient of nursing facility services in the state at the time of application. Ineligibility begins on the first day of the first month during or after which assets have been transferred for less than fair market value.

The look-back period in the case of payments from a trust or portions of a trust that are treated as assets disposed of is sixty months before:

(1)   the first date on which an institutionalized person is both institutionalized and has applied for Medicaid; or

(2)   the first date on which a noninstitutionalized person applies for Medicaid or, if later, the date on which the individual disposes of assets for less than fair market value.

An individual is considered to have established a trust if assets of the individual were used to form all or part of the corpus of the trust and any of the following individuals established the trust other than by will:

- The individual

- The individual's spouse

- A person, including a court or administrative body, with legal authority to act in place of or on behalf of the individual or the individual's spouse

- A person, including any court or administrative body, acting at the direction or upon the request of the individual or the individual's spouse

In the case of a revocable trust:

(1)   the corpus of the trust is considered a resource available to the individual;

(2)   payments from the trust to or for the benefit of the individual are considered income of the individual; and

(3)   any other payments from the trust are considered assets disposed of by the individual.

Assets are defined as all income and resources of the individual and the individual's spouse, including any income or resources which the individual or the individual's spouse is entitled to but does not receive because of action:

(1)   by the individual or the individual's spouse;

(2)   by a person, including a court or administrative body, with legal authority to act in place of or on behalf of the individual or the individual's spouse; or

(3)   by any person, including any court or administrative body, acting at the direction or upon the request of the individual or the individual's spouse.

In the case of an irrevocable trust:

- If there are any circumstances under which payment from the trust could be made to or for the benefit of the individual, the portion of the corpus from which, or the income on the corpus from which, payment to the individual could be made is considered resources available to the individual, and payments from that portion of the corpus or income:

  - to or from the benefit of the individual, is considered income of the individual, and

  - for any other purpose, is considered a transfer of assets by the individual (see preceding definition of "asset").

- Any portion of the trust from which, or any income on the corpus from which, no payment could under any circumstances be made to the individual, is considered, as of the date of establishment of the trust (or, if later, the date on which payment to the individual was foreclosed), to be assets disposed of by the individual and the value of the trust is determined by including the amount of any payments made from such portion of the trust after that date.

A trust includes any legal instrument or device that is similar to a trust but includes an annuity only to such extent and in such manner as the Department of Health and Human Services specifies.

1294. Are there exceptions to the trust rules under Medicaid?

Yes. There are three exceptions. The following trusts are exempt from the Medicaid trust rules:

1. A trust established by a parent, grandparent, guardian, or court for the benefit of an individual who is disabled and under age sixty-five, using the individual's own funds.

2. A trust composed only of pension, Social Security, and other income of the individual, in states which make individuals eligible for institutional care under a special-income level, but do not cover institutional care for the medically needy.

3. A trust established by a disabled individual, parent, grandparent, guardian, or court for the disabled individual, using the individual's own funds, where the trust is made up of pooled funds and managed by a nonprofit organization for the sole benefit of each individual included in the trust.

In all of the above instances, the trust must provide that the state receives any funds, up to the amount of Medicaid benefits paid on behalf of the individual, remaining in the trust when the individual dies.

A trust will not be counted as available to an individual where the state determines that counting the trust would work an undue hardship.

1295. What is a Special Needs Trust (SNT)?

A Special Needs Trust (SNT) is a specialized legal document designed to benefit an individual who is disabled. A SNT is most often a stand-alone document, but it can also be created as part of someone's (such as the disabled person's parent) will. SNTs have been in use for many years, and were given an "official" legal status by Congress in 1993.

An SNT enables a disabled person, or an individual with a chronic or acquired illness, to have held in trust, for his or her benefit, an unlimited amount of assets. In a properly-drafted SNT, those assets are not considered countable assets for purposes of qualification for certain governmental benefits.

These benefits may include Supplemental Security Income (SSI), Medicaid, vocational rehabilitation, subsidized housing, and other benefits based upon need. For purposes of a SNT, an individual is considered impoverished if his or her personal assets are less than $2,000.

An SNT provides for supplemental and extra care over and above that which the government provides.

An SNT must be irrevocable. A properly-drafted SNT will include provisions for trust termination or dissolution under certain circumstances, and will include explicit directions for amendment when necessary.

An SNT can be used for supplemental and extra care over and above what the government provides. A properly-drafted SNT will work on a sliding scale; in the event that the government provides for 100 percent of the disabled beneficiary's needs the trust will provide nothing. If there are no governmental benefits available, the trust can provide 100 percent of what is needed.

A properly-drafted trust will address the issue concerning paybacks to Medicaid or other government sources. The law requires that repayment language must be included in all SNTs, whether repayment is required or not.

A SNT that is funded by parents or other third-party sources will not be required to pay back Medicaid. An SNT that is funded by a personal injury settlement that is properly court-ordered into the SNT will not be required to pay back Medicaid. The only assets within an SNT that are subject to the repayment obligation are those assets which originally belonged to the disabled individual that are transferred into the trust. This type of trust is a first-party trust because the money is considered to be the beneficiary's money as opposed to money that has been gifted.

Examples of assets which would belong to the disabled individual in the first place include earnings from a job, savings, certain Social Security back payments, and personal injury recoveries which are not court-ordered into the SNT.

1296. What are the three different types of Special Needs Trusts (SNT)?

There are three types of Special Needs Trusts (SNT):

(1)   a family-type trust,

(2)   a pooled trust, and

(3)   a court-ordered trust.

These trusts are described in the subsequent questions.

1297. What is a family-type Special Needs Trust (SNT)?

The most commonly used SNT is a family-type trust, which is set up by the parents. The parents provide the money for the trust, often by will, and sometimes by purchasing life insurance payable to the trust.

In most cases, the parents write a will giving money or a house to the disabled son or daughter. After the beneficiary has died, anything left over goes to other family members. The left-over is called the "remainder".

Some parents place their property in a "living" or "inter vivos" trust, and provide in the trust that the disabled son or daughter is the beneficiary. With that type of trust, there is no need to wait for the parents to die. The trust becomes effective immediately. This is a good idea for families where aunts, uncles, and grandparents might want to leave money for the trust. Anyone can give money to the trust, either by writing a check or writing a will.

The key to a family-type SNT is that the money cannot be used for housing, food, or clothing. Those are considered basic needs under the Medicaid laws. If the disabled person is receiving free housing, food, or clothing from someone else, including a family member or a trust, then the government benefits will be reduced or eliminated.

The trust can be used to purchase a home, and perhaps rent it to the disabled person. The trust can pay for repairs, utilities and taxes for a home; it can purchase furnishings for the home. It can pay for vacations, summer camp, or trips. It can buy bowling shoes or other sporting equipment. It can pay for medical costs not otherwise covered by Medicaid, such as vitamins. It can pay for funeral and burial costs. It can pay for a lot of things, but it does not have to pay for anything unless the trustee thinks it is a good idea.

The parents generally serve as trustee as long as they are alive. When they die, a successor trustee must be ready to take over. Some parents choose a bank to serve as trustee, but banks are expensive and do not keep track of the disabled person's individual needs. A responsible family member is usually a better choice, if one can be found.

1298. What is a pooled Special Needs Trust (SNT)?

This type of trust is commonly referred to as a (d)(4)(C) trust, after the code section that authorized it. Anyone can put money into a pooled trust, including parents, grandparents, or even the individual with a disability. The pooled trust has no age restrictions.

There are four major requirements to establish a Pooled Trust:

- The trust must be established and managed through a nonprofit association.

- The trust must maintain separated accounts for beneficiary, but can pool the funds for management and investment.

- Each trust account must be established SOLELY for the benefit of an individual who meets the definition of being "disabled" under the law. The Pooled SNT must be established either by the disabled individual, their parent, their grandparent, their legal guardian or the court.

- Any funds remaining at the death of the beneficiary must be retained by the pooled trust to help or used to reimburse Medicaid.

The cash is kept in a bank, but the nonprofit owns all the deeds to houses and other real estate, as trustee. Banks do not want to own real estate in trust because they are afraid of environmental problems.

A pooled trust can purchase a home for the beneficiary and rent it to him. Before the pooled trust is set up, the parents and other family members explain what they want the trust to pay for, and who should be consulted about these matters. The list of available pooled trusts around the country changes often.[1]

Note

1. *See, e.g.,* https://specialneedsanswers.com/pooled-trust (last accessed October 17, 2022).

1299. What is a court-ordered Special Needs Trust (SNT)?

A court-ordered trust, also called a Type "A" special needs trust, is used only for special circumstances, such as where the person with a disability has inherited money, or received a court settlement.

Because the disabled person actually owns the money, the funds cannot be put into the usual Special Needs Trust such as parents usually set up.

The "A" comes from the last letter of the federal statute, 42 U.S.C. § 1396p(d)(4)(A).

Only certain people are allowed to set up this type of trust:

- One or both of the disabled person's parent

- The disabled person's grandparent(s)

- The legal guardian of the disabled person

- A court of competent jurisdiction

To qualify, the disabled person must be under sixty-five years old and meet the disability standards of Social Security. Someone who is not disabled enough to qualify for Social Security cannot have this type of trust.

The trust must specify that after the disabled person has died, anything left over will pay back the state for whatever medical assistance the government provided to the individual after the trust was set up. As a practical matter, that means that any unspent money will go to the government. It is unlikely that after Medicaid is paid back, anything will be left over.

1300. Should a Special Needs Trust (SNT) be set up during the grantor's life or as part of the grantor's will?

Generally, it is better to set up a Special Needs Trust (SNT) during the lifetime of the grantor. The advantage is that if other family members or friends of the disabled beneficiary wish to provide for the disabled beneficiary they may contribute to the already existing SNT. Another advantage is that if a person is chosen to be a successor trustee this person can gain experience as a trustee by acting as a co-trustee. Also, a trust created during the grantor's lifetime can be a "standby" trust that remains unfunded until the death of the grantor. Then the will or another trust of the grantor can simply add funds as a "pour-over" to the SNT at the grantor's death.

Another reason to create an SNT during the grantor's lifetime is that life insurance policies and retirement accounts can name the SNT as beneficiary of these policies or accounts more easily.

1301. What do Special Needs Trusts (SNT) currently stand?

A number of states are imposing restrictions on distributions from SNTs. Most of these restrictions have been on self-settled trusts. But some states are also restricting third-party trust distributions.

There have been numerous court cases challenging these state-imposed restrictions. Decisions have been made which have both upheld the restrictions and struck them down. Because of these different results, it is very important for individuals to seek legal advice when setting up SNTs.

One new development in the area of Special Needs Trusts is the Special Needs Trust Fairness and Medicaid Improvement Act. It was approved by the House and Senate and on December 20, 2016, President Obama signed into law the Special Needs Trust Fairness Act as part of the 21st Century Cures Act. The new act allows individuals who are mentally capable to independently establish their own special needs trusts (also known as self-settled special needs trusts).

Estate Recoveries

1302. Can a state recover nursing home and long-term care Medicaid expenses from the estate of a deceased Medicaid recipient?

States are required to recover the costs of nursing facility and other long-term care services furnished to a Medicaid beneficiary from the estate of the beneficiary (if aged fifty-five or older) unless undue hardship would result. The estate may include any real or personal property or other assets in which the beneficiary had any legal title or interest at the time of death, including the home. Different estate recovery provisions apply to individuals who purchase specified long-term care insurance policies in designated states. States have the option to recover payments for all other Medicaid services provided to these individuals, except Medicare cost-sharing paid on behalf of Medicare Savings Program beneficiaries.

Under certain conditions, money remaining in a trust after a Medicaid enrollee has passed away may be used to reimburse Medicaid. States may not recover from the estate of a deceased Medicaid enrollee who is survived by a spouse, child under age twenty-one, or blind or disabled child of any age. States are also required to establish procedures for waiving estate recovery when recovery would cause an undue hardship.

States may impose liens for Medicaid benefits incorrectly paid pursuant to a court judgment. States may also impose liens on real property during the lifetime of a Medicaid enrollee who is permanently institutionalized, except when one of the following individuals resides in the home: the spouse, child under age twenty-one, blind, or disabled child of any age, or sibling who has an equity interest in the home. The states must remove the lien when the Medicaid enrollee is discharged from the facility and returns home.

According to the Centers for Medicare & Medicaid Services (CMS), "undue hardship" might exist when the estate subject to recovery is the sole income-producing asset of the survivors and the income is limited or is a homestead of modest value.

It is possible that a state may conclude that an undue hardship does not exist if the individual created the hardship by resorting to estate planning methods under which the individual divested assets in order to avoid estate recovery. A state may adopt a rebuttable presumption that, if the individual obtained estate planning advice from legal counsel and followed this advice, the resulting financial situation would not qualify for an undue-hardship waiver.

The estate-recovery rules apply only to the estates of Medicaid beneficiaries dying on or after October 1, 1993, only to benefits paid on or after that date, and only for costs for a Medicaid recipient who was age fifty-five or older at the time the costs were incurred. Recovery of Medicaid costs cannot take place while the surviving spouse lives.

1303. Can Medicaid impose a lien on a recipient's property?

Yes. Medicaid may impose a lien on a recipient's property under certain limited circumstances but not all states do.

The lien does not allow one's home to be sold without existing debt paid first. The Tax Equity and Fiscal Responsibility Act (TEFRA) gave states the option to use liens to prevent Medicaid beneficiaries from transferring their home to a loved one shortly before they die to avoid estate recovery.

If a Medicaid recipient were to transfer the home, the transfer would be a violation of Medicaid's look-back rule, invoking the penalty period for disqualification. The family would have to pay out-of-pocket for long term care costs during the disqualification. However, a lien prevents the Medicaid recipient from transferring the residence.

Generally, a lien is filed by the state when the Medicaid recipient is institutionalized, and it is not expected to return home. If the individual does return home, the lien is removed. A lien is also removed if the home is sold and Medicaid is reimbursed. Selling the home while the recipient is still living will most likely cause the individual to be ineligible for long term care Medicaid due to having excess assets. The home is exempt from Medicaid's asset limit prior to sale, but if it is sold, it turns an exempt asset into a countable asset. In some states, a lien may be removed following the death of the Medicaid recipient, while in other states, Medicaid will collect on the lien following the death of the recipient.

A lien cannot be put on a Medicaid recipient's home in the following situations:

- A spouse is currently living in the home.

- A child under 21 years old is currently living in the home.

- A disabled or blind child is currently living in the home.

- A brother or sister is living in the home who has an equity interest in it and they had lived in the home a minimum of one year before the Medicaid recipient moved to a nursing home.

Some states may put a lien on the home following a Medicaid recipient's death. This is done when there is a survivor, such as a spouse, still occupying the home. This is done so that the state can collect repayment following the death of the survivor. However, the lien may be lifted if the survivor wishes to sell the home.

1304. What is the Medicaid Estate Recovery Program (MERP)?

MERP is a program that a state Medicaid agency seeks reimbursement of all long term care costs for which it paid for a Medicaid beneficiary. These costs can include nursing home care, home and community-based services to prevent premature institutionalization, as well as hospital costs, and prescription drug costs related to the care.

Estate assets can consist of cash, bank accounts, stocks, bonds, annuities, funds in a trust, vehicles, and of course, the home. Since the home is generally exempt from Medicaid's asset limit while the Medicaid recipient is still living, the home is often the largest asset and the target of Medicaid estate recovery. Life insurance policies are usually safe from estate recovery if a beneficiary is named other than one's estate.

It is a requirement under the 1993 Omnibus Budget Reconciliation Act (OBRA) for all states have a Medicaid estate recovery program and to seek recapture of long-term care costs for persons who are 55 years of age or older. An exception exists for persons under 55 who were permanently institutionalized, such as in a nursing home.

The specifics of each state's estate recovery program varies from state to state. Some states try to recover costs for other Medicaid services outside of long-term care while others focus only on long-term care costs. Funds that are collected are deposited into the state's Medicaid program and are used to pay for Medicaid services for other beneficiaries.

With MERP, all states are required to seek recovery from the deceased's Medicaid recipient's probate estate, but not all assets go through probate, Assets that go through probate include ones that are strictly in the deceased's name, or if jointly owned, are ones that are "tenants in common". It is important to note that probate laws differ for each state. States also have the option to attempt to expand their recovery from assets that do not go through probate.

Discrimination

1305. Does federal law require that Medicaid patients be admitted to any (and all) nursing homes?

There is no requirement that nursing homes participate in Medicaid. Nursing homes receive reimbursement for Medicaid patients, but it is usually much lower than the rates nursing homes charge private-pay patients (those who use their own funds, insurance benefits, or a combination of the two). Most nursing homes participate in Medicaid, but the level of participation can vary. A nursing home can make all beds Medicaid beds, or it can have some Medicaid beds and some private-pay beds.

If a patient in a nursing home starts out paying privately, uses up all excess resources, and becomes eligible for Medicaid, the nursing home is prohibited by federal law from evicting the patient because the method of payment has changed from private payment to Medicaid. The patient can be evicted if he cannot pay the nursing home and is also ineligible for Medicaid.

The nursing home contract defines the rights and responsibilities of the nursing home and patient. There are limitations on certain contract provisions that affect Medicaid patients:

(1)   A nursing home contract may not force the patient to give up the right to receive Medicare or Medicaid. A nursing home must counsel patients about the availability of these benefits.

(2)   A nursing home contract may not force a relative or friend of the patient to guarantee payments in order to get the patient into the nursing home. A nursing home can require a person in charge of a potential resident's funds to commit those funds to the payment of nursing home bills.

(3)   A nursing home cannot require a person or a person's family to pay more than the Medicaid rate in order to have a Medicaid-eligible person admitted to the nursing home.

Managed Care

1306. How has managed care changed the original Medicaid program?

A significant change to the original Medicaid program is the managed-care concept. Under managed-care systems, Health Maintenance Organizations (HMOs), Prepaid Health Plans (PHPs), or comparable entities agree to provide a specific set of services to Medicaid enrollees in return for fixed periodic payments for each enrollee. Managed-care programs seek to enhance access to quality care in a cost-effective manner. However, there are complexities in this, and waivers of certain parts of the Social Security Act are required. These waivers provide states with greater flexibility in the design and implementation of their Medicaid programs.

Section 1915(b) of the Social Security Act allows states to develop innovative health care delivery or reimbursement systems. Section 1115 of the Social Security Act allows statewide health care reform demonstrations for testing various methods of covering uninsured populations, and testing new delivery systems, without increasing costs.

Medicaid managed-care programs are growing rapidly and several states have converted their entire Medicaid programs into managed care. Over 17.6 million Medicaid recipients are enrolled in Medicaid managed-care programs, which is more than 50 percent of all Medicaid enrollees.

States can restrict choice by offering a choice between at least two managed-care organizations or Primary Care Case Managers (PCCMs), or at least one plan and one PCCM. States must permit individuals to change their enrollment for cause at any time, without cause within ninety days of notification of enrollment, and without cause, at least every twelve months thereafter.

States may provide up to six months minimum enrollment that covers all managed-care entities.

There is protection for Medicaid beneficiaries in managed care, including:

(1)   assuring coverage of emergency services;

(2)   protection of enrollee-provider communications;

(3)   grievance procedures;

(4)   demonstration of adequate capacity and services;

(5)   protecting enrollees against liability for payment; and

(6)   antidiscrimination.

APPENDIX A

SOCIAL SECURITY TABLES

TABLE 1—BENEFITS AS PERCENTAGE OF PIA

RETIREMENT BENEFIT
      Starting at Normal Retirement Age (NRA)
      (gradually rising from 65 to 67) .... PIA
      Starting age 62 or above (but below NRA) .... PIA reduced

DISABILITY BENEFIT .... PIA

SPOUSE'S BENEFIT (husband or wife of retired or disabled worker)
      Caring for child (under 16 or disabled) .... 50% of PIA
      Starting at NRA (gradually rising from 65 to 67) .... 50% of PIA
      Starting age 62 or above (but below NRA) .... 50% of PIA reduced

CHILD'S BENEFIT
      Child of retired or disabled worker .... 50% of PIA
      Child of deceased worker .... 75% of PIA

MOTHER'S OR FATHER'S BENEFIT (widow(er) caring for child
      under 16 or disabled) .... 75% of PIA

WIDOW(ER)'S BENEFIT (widow(er) not caring for child)
      Starting at NRA (gradually rising from 65 to 67) .... 100% of PIA
      Starting age 60 or above (but below NRA) .... 100% of PIA reduced

DISABLED WIDOW(ER)'S BENEFIT
      Starting age 50-60 .... 71½% of PIA

PARENT'S BENEFIT (dependent parent of deceased worker)
      One dependent parent .... 82½% of PIA
      Two dependent parents .... 75% of PIA (each)

TABLE 2 QUARTERS OF COVERAGE REQUIRED TO BE FULLY INSURED FOR RETIREMENT BENEFITS		
Birth Year	Men	Women
1892 or earlier	6	6
1893	7	6
1894	8	6
1895	9	6
1896	10	7
1897	11	8
1898	12	9
1899	13	10
1900	14	11
1901	15	12
1902	16	13
1903	17	14
1904	18	15
1905	19	16
1906	20	17
1907	21	18
1908	22	19
1909	23	20
1910	24	21
1911	24	22
1912	24	23
1913	24	24
1914	25	25
1915	26	26
1916	27	27
1917	28	28
1918	29	29
1919	30	30
1920	31	31
1921	32	32
1922	33	33
1923	34	34
1924	35	35
1925	36	36
1926	37	37
1927	38	38
1928	39	39
1929 or after	40	40

TABLE 3 MINIMUM NUMBER OF QUARTERS OF COVERAGE NEEDED TO BE FULLY INSURED AT DEATH		
Birth Year	2022	2023
1958 or before	40	40
1960	39	40
1961	38	39
1962	37	38
1963	36	37
1964	35	36
1965	34	35
1966	33	34
1967	32	33
1968	31	32
1969	30	31
1970	29	30
1971	28	29
1972	27	28
1973	26	27
1974	25	26
1975	24	25
1976	23	24
1977	22	23
1978	21	22
1979	20	21
1980	19	20
1981	18	19
1982	17	18
1983	16	17
1984	15	16
1985	14	15
1986	13	14

	TABLE 4		
	YEARS IN WHICH PERSON REACHES		
	AGE 21		
	Year Person Reaches		Year Person Reaches
Birth Year	Age 21	Birth Year	Age 21
1941	1962	1977	1998
1942	1963	1978	1999
1943	1964	1979	2000
1944	1965	1980	2001
1945	1966	1981	2002
1946	1967	1982	2003
1947	1968	1983	2004
1948	1969	1984	2005
1949	1970	1985	2006
1950	1971	1986	2007
1951	1972	1987	2008
1952	1973	1988	2009
1953	1974	1989	2010
1954	1975	1990	2011
1955	1976	1991	2012
1956	1977	1992	2013
1957	1978	1993	2014
1958	1979	1994	2015
1959	1980	1995	2016
1960	1981	1996	2017
1961	1982	1997	2018
1962	1983	1998	2019
1963	1984	1999	2020
1964	1985	2000	2021
1965	1986	2001	2022
1966	1987	2002	2023
1967	1988	2003	2024
1968	1989	2004	2025
1969	1990	2005	2026
1970	1991	2006	2027
1971	1992	2007	2028
1972	1993	2008	2029
1973	1994	2009	2030
1974	1995	2010	2031
1975	1996	2011	2032
1976	1997	2012	2033

TABLE 5
NUMBER OF YEARS EARNINGS THAT MUST BE
USED IN COMPUTING RETIREMENT BENEFITS
(less if person had an established period of disability)

Birth Year	Computation Age	Year of Computation	Number of Years	Number of Divisor Months
1915	62	1977	21	252
1916	62	1978	22	264
1917	62	1979	23	276
1918	62	1980	24	288
1919	62	1981	25	300
1920	62	1982	26	312
1921	62	1983	27	324
1922	62	1984	28	336
1923	62	1985	29	348
1924	62	1986	30	360
1925	62	1987	31	372
1926	62	1988	32	384
1927	62	1989	33	396
1928	62	1990	34	408
1929	62	1991	35	420
1930 or later	62	1992 or later	35	420

TABLE 6—INSURED STATUS NEEDED FOR SOCIAL SECURITY BENEFITS

The worker must be FULLY insured to provide monthly benefits for:

... Retired worker (at age 62 or over)

... Spouse of retired worker (at age 62 or over)

... Spouse of retired worker (at any age if caring for a child)

... Child of retired worker

... Widow(er) of worker (at age 60 or over)

... Disabled widow(er) of worker (at age 50 or over)

... Dependent parent of deceased worker

The worker may be either FULLY or CURRENTLY insured to provide monthly benefits for:

... Child of deceased worker

... Widow(er) of worker (at any age if caring for child)

A disabled worker must be FULLY insured and (a) if disability began at or after age 31, must have worked in covered employment five (5) out of the last ten (10) years, or (b) if disability began before age 31, must have worked in covered employment one-half of the quarters between age 21 and onset of disability (but not less than 6), to provide benefits for:

... Disabled worker (at any age)

... Child of disabled worker

... Spouse of disabled worker (at age 62 or over)

... Spouse of disabled worker (at any age if caring for a child)

A worker who is either FULLY or CURRENTLY insured qualified for the lump-sum death benefit if he is survived by (1) a spouse who was living with him at the time of his death, or (2) a dependent child or spouse eligible to receive social security benefits based on his earnings record.

TABLE 7—MAXIMUM AIME FOR RETIREMENT, SURVIVOR, AND DISABILITY BENEFITS*
(for workers earning $160,200 or more in 2023)

Year of Birth	Normal Retirement Age	Death in 2023	Disability in 2023	Year of Birth	Normal Retirement Age	Death in 2023	Disability in 2023
1961	11,557	11,184	10,981	1980	12,250	11,899	11,575
1962	11,650	11,286	11,067	1981	12,274	11,923	11,597
1963	11,735	11,376	11,149	1982	12,296	11,941	11,615
1964	11,803	11,523	11,215	1983	12,315	11,944	11,635
1965	11,862	11,590	11,271	1984	12,336	11,999	11,655
1966	11,901	11,659	11,308	1985	12,354	12,036	11,672
1967	11,936	11,709	11,342	1986	12,330	11,970	11,650
1968	11,968	11,762	11,370	1987	12,362	11,961	11,681
1969	12,005	11,781	11,407	1988	12,386	11,994	11,702
1970	12,006	11,800	11,408	1989	12,394	12,023	11,708
1971	12,092	11,817	11,490	1990	12,396	12,090	11,715
1972	12,119	11,841	11,515	1991	12,401	12,122	11,715
1973	12,147	11,859	11,542	1992	12,401	12,295	11,715
1974	12,177	11,873	11,569	1993	12,401	12,294	11,715
1975	12,206	11,895	11,596	1994	12,401	12,388	11,715
1976	12,224	11,907	11,614	1995	12,401	12,388	11,715
1977	12,252	11,943	11,641	1996	12,401	12,388	11,715
1978	12,272	12,020	11,660	1997	12,401	12,388	11,715
1979	12,297	11,974	11,685	1998	12,401	12,388	11,715

* Normal Retirement Age for unreduced benefits (PIA) increases by two months a year for workers reaching age 62 in 2001-2006; maintains age 66 for workers reaching age 62 in 2007-2017; increases by two months a year for workers reaching age 62 in 2017-2023; and maintains age 67 for workers reaching age 62 after 2023.
* AIME calculations assume that the worker earned the Social Security maximum earnings base in all years up to and including, respectively, the year before normal retirement ($160,200 is used for 2023 and later years), the year of death, and the year before disability.

TABLE 8—AIME FOR WORKERS EARNING $7,000-$62,200 IN 2023*

Current Annual Earnings							
Year Born	AIME	$7,000-16,200	$16,200-25,400	$25,400-34,600	$34,600-43,800	$43,800-53,000	$53,000-62,200
1961	Retirement	850	1,525	2,195	2,859	2,859	4,198
	Death	811	1,450	2,090	2,724	2,724	3,996
	Disability	794	1,429	2,057	2,676	2,676	3,927
1962-1966	Retirement	885	1,584	2,281	2,970	2,970	4,361
	Death	814	1,461	2,102	2,737	2,737	4,019
	Disability	801	1,434	2,064	2,685	2,685	3,945
1967-1971	Retirement	946	1,695	2,440	3,178	3,178	4,665
	Death	832	1,498	2,149	2,797	2,797	4,107
	Disability	814	1,461	2,102	2,737	2,737	4,019
1972-1976	Retirement	1,023	1,841	2,655	3,453	3,453	5,069
	Death	868	1,563	2,252	2,931	2,931	4,301
	Disability	845	1,526	2,194	2,860	2,860	4,199
1977-1981	Retirement	1,073	1,933	2,783	3,626	3,626	5,322
	Death	910	1,640	2,364	3,075	3,075	4,517
	Disability	878	1,581	2,282	2,968	2,968	4,357
1982-1986	Retirement	1,117	2,010	2,896	3,773	3,773	5,538
	Death	954	1,719	2,474	3,220	3,220	4,726
	Disability	909	1,640	2,362	3,075	3,075	4,512
1987-1991	Retirement	1,141	2,059	2,962	3,858	3,858	5,661
	Death	1,033	1,831	2,632	3,430	3,430	5,034
	Disability	947	1,706	2,453	3,193	3,193	4,692
1992-1996	Retirement	1,150	2,069	2,976	3,876	3,876	5,692
	Death	1,120	2,009	2,892	3,765	3,765	5,534
	Disability	996	1,790	2,576	3,354	3,354	4,924

* AIMEs are approximate and based on the assumption that the worker has had 6% pay raises each year through 2023. AIME calculations for retirement assume that the worker's current earnings stay the same until Normal Retirement Age. Match AIMEs with AIMEs closest to them in Tables 10, 11, and 12 to determine benefits.

TABLE 9—AIME FOR WORKERS EARNING $62,200-$160.200 IN 2023*

Year Born	AIME	$62,200-71,400	$71,400-80,600	$80,600-89,800	$89,800-99,000	$99,000-108,200	$108,200-160,200
				Current Annual Earnings			
1961	Retirement	4,849	5,551	6,219	6,841	7,494	8,145
	Death	4,616	5,287	5,924	6,510	7,120	7,732
	Disability	4,540	5,197	5,823	6,397	6,992	7,595
1962-1966	Retirement	5,038	5,769	6,468	7,146	7,838	8,526
	Death	4,645	5,318	5,960	6,588	7,226	7,851
	Disability	4,558	5,220	5,851	6,464	7,095	7,702
1967-1971	Retirement	5,390	6,170	6,919	7,642	8,389	9,135
	Death	4,749	5,436	6,093	6,734	7,390	8,045
	Disability	4,644	5,318	5,960	6,586	7,230	7,869
1972-1976	Retirement	5,859	6,708	7,521	8,313	9,118	9,930
	Death	4,971	5,692	6,383	7,053	7,738	8,423
	Disability	4,848	5,552	6,224	6,878	7,550	8,218
1977-1981	Retirement	6,151	7,041	7,892	8,722	9,571	10,418
	Death	5,218	5,974	6,694	7,400	8,117	8,841
	Disability	5,035	5,766	6,464	7,143	7,837	8,533
1982-1986	Retirement	6,398	7,330	8,213	9,075	9,959	10,845
	Death	5,464	6,259	7,015	7,753	8,507	9,259
	Disability	5,213	5,970	6,690	7,396	8,113	8,834
1987-1991	Retirement	6,543	7,492	8,399	9,281	10,185	11,090
	Death	5,814	6,662	7,467	8,251	9,053	9,856
	Disability	5,418	6,204	6,955	7,686	8,432	9,182
1992-1996	Retirement	6,576	7,528	8,439	9,329	10,235	11,143
	Death	6,389	7,319	8,202	9,061	9,942	10,827
	Disability	5,690	6,513	7,302	8,073	8,856	9,641

* AIMEs are approximate and based on the assumption that the worker has had 6% pay raises each year through 2023. AIME calculations for retirement assume that the worker's current earnings stay the same until Normal Retirement Age. Match AIMEs with AIMEs closest to them in Tables 10, 11, and 12 to determine benefits.

TABLE 10—WORKER'S AND SPOUSE'S RETIREMENT BENEFITS*

Average Indexed Monthly Earnings	Worker FRA (PIA)	Spouse FRA	Total FRA Benefit	Worker FRA - 3**	Spouse FRA - 3	Total FRA - 3 Benefit	Worker FRA and Spouse FRA-3
$9,700	3,196	1,598	4,794	2,557	1,278	3,835	4,475
$9,675	3,192	1,596	4,788	2,554	1,277	3,830	4,469
$9,650	3,189	1,594	4,783	2,551	1,276	3,827	4,464
$9,625	3,185	1,592	4,777	2,548	1,274	3,822	4,459
$9,600	3,181	1,590	4,771	2,545	1,272	3,817	4,453
$9,575	3,177	1,588	4,765	2,541	1,271	3,812	4,447
$9,550	3,173	1,587	4,760	2,539	1,269	3,808	4,443
$9,525	3,169	1,585	4,754	2,535	1,268	3,803	4,437
$9,500	3,165	1,583	4,748	2,532	1,266	3,798	4,431
$9,475	3,161	1,581	4,742	2,529	1,264	3,793	4,425
$9,450	3,158	1,579	4,737	2,526	1,263	3,790	4,421
$9,425	3,154	1,577	4,731	2,523	1,262	3,785	4,415
$9,400	3,150	1,575	4,725	2,520	1,260	3,780	4,410
$9,375	3,146	1,573	4,718	2,516	1,258	3,775	4,404
$9,350	3,142	1,571	4,714	2,514	1,257	3,771	4,399
$9,325	3,138	1,569	4,708	2,511	1,255	3,766	4,394
$9,300	3,134	1,567	4,701	2,507	1,254	3,761	4,388
$9,275	3,130	1,565	4,695	2,504	1,252	3,756	4,382
$9,250	3,127	1,564	4,691	2,502	1,251	3,752	4,378
$9,225	3,123	1,561	4,684	2,498	1,249	3,747	4,372
$9,200	3,119	1,559	4,678	2,495	1,248	3,743	4,366
$9,175	3,115	1,557	4,672	2,492	1,246	3,738	4,361
$9,150	3,112	1,556	4,667	2,489	1,245	3,734	4,356
$9,125	3,107	1,554	4,661	2,486	1,243	3,729	4,350
$9,100	3,103	1,552	4,655	2,483	1,241	3,724	4,345
$9,075	3,099	1,550	4,649	2,479	1,240	3,719	4,339
$9,050	3,096	1,548	4,644	2,477	1,238	3,715	4,335
$9,025	3,092	1,546	4,638	2,474	1,237	3,710	4,329
$9,000	3,088	1,544	4,632	2,470	1,235	3,705	4,323
$8,975	3,084	1,542	4,626	2,467	1,233	3,700	4,317
$8,950	3,081	1,540	4,621	2,465	1,232	3,697	4,313
$8,925	3,077	1,538	4,615	2,461	1,231	3,692	4,307
$8,900	3,072	1,536	4,609	2,458	1,229	3,687	4,301
$8,875	3,068	1,534	4,602	2,455	1,227	3,682	4,296
$8,850	3,065	1,533	4,598	2,452	1,226	3,678	4,291
$8,825	3,061	1,531	4,592	2,449	1,224	3,673	4,285
$8,800	3,057	1,528	4,585	2,446	1,223	3,668	4,280
$8,775	3,053	1,526	4,579	2,442	1,221	3,663	4,274
$8,750	3,050	1,525	4,575	2,440	1,220	3,660	4,270
$8,725	3,046	1,523	4,568	2,436	1,218	3,655	4,264
$8,700	3,041	1,521	4,562	2,433	1,217	3,650	4,258
$8,675	3,037	1,519	4,556	2,430	1,215	3,645	4,252
$8,650	3,034	1,517	4,551	2,427	1,214	3,641	4,248
$8,625	3,030	1,515	4,545	2,424	1,212	3,636	4,242
$8,600	3,026	1,513	4,539	2,421	1,210	3,631	4,236
$8,575	3,022	1,511	4,533	2,417	1,209	3,626	4,231
$8,550	3,019	1,509	4,528	2,415	1,208	3,623	4,226
$8,525	3,015	1,507	4,522	2,412	1,206	3,618	4,221
$8,500	3,011	1,505	4,516	2,408	1,204	3,613	4,215
$8,475	3,006	1,503	4,510	2,405	1,203	3,608	4,209

TABLE 10—WORKER'S AND SPOUSE'S RETIREMENT BENEFITS* (CONT'D)

Average Indexed Monthly Earnings	Worker FRA (PIA)	Spouse FRA	Total FRA Benefit	Worker FRA - 3**	Spouse FRA - 3	Total FRA - 3 Benefit	Worker FRA and Spouse FRA-3
$8,450	3,003	1,502	4,505	2,403	1,201	3,604	4,205
$8,425	2,999	1,500	4,499	2,399	1,200	3,599	4,199
$8,400	2,995	1,498	4,493	2,396	1,198	3,594	4,193
$8,375	2,991	1,495	4,486	2,393	1,196	3,589	4,187
$8,350	2,988	1,494	4,482	2,390	1,195	3,585	4,183
$8,325	2,984	1,492	4,476	2,387	1,193	3,580	4,177
$8,300	2,980	1,490	4,469	2,384	1,192	3,576	4,171
$8,275	2,975	1,488	4,463	2,380	1,190	3,571	4,166
$8,250	2,972	1,486	4,459	2,378	1,189	3,567	4,161
$8,225	2,968	1,484	4,452	2,375	1,187	3,562	4,156
$8,200	2,964	1,482	4,446	2,371	1,186	3,557	4,150
$8,175	2,960	1,480	4,440	2,368	1,184	3,552	4,144
$8,150	2,957	1,478	4,435	2,366	1,183	3,548	4,140
$8,125	2,953	1,476	4,429	2,362	1,181	3,543	4,134
$8,100	2,949	1,474	4,423	2,359	1,179	3,538	4,128
$8,075	2,945	1,472	4,417	2,356	1,178	3,533	4,122
$8,050	2,941	1,471	4,412	2,353	1,177	3,530	4,118
$8,025	2,937	1,469	4,406	2,350	1,175	3,525	4,112
$8,000	2,933	1,467	4,400	2,347	1,173	3,520	4,106
$7,975	2,929	1,465	4,394	2,343	1,172	3,515	4,101
$7,950	2,926	1,463	4,389	2,341	1,170	3,511	4,096
$7,925	2,922	1,461	4,383	2,337	1,169	3,506	4,091
$7,900	2,918	1,459	4,377	2,334	1,167	3,501	4,085
$7,875	2,914	1,457	4,370	2,331	1,165	3,496	4,079
$7,850	2,911	1,455	4,366	2,328	1,164	3,493	4,075
$7,825	2,906	1,453	4,360	2,325	1,163	3,488	4,069
$7,800	2,902	1,451	4,353	2,322	1,161	3,483	4,063
$7,775	2,898	1,449	4,347	2,319	1,159	3,478	4,057
$7,750	2,895	1,448	4,343	2,316	1,158	3,474	4,053
$7,725	2,891	1,445	4,336	2,313	1,156	3,469	4,047
$7,700	2,887	1,443	4,330	2,309	1,155	3,464	4,042
$7,675	2,883	1,441	4,324	2,306	1,153	3,459	4,036
$7,650	2,880	1,440	4,319	2,304	1,152	3,455	4,031
$7,625	2,875	1,438	4,313	2,300	1,150	3,451	4,026
$7,600	2,871	1,436	4,307	2,297	1,149	3,446	4,020
$7,575	2,867	1,434	4,301	2,294	1,147	3,441	4,014
$7,550	2,864	1,432	4,296	2,291	1,146	3,437	4,010
$7,525	2,860	1,430	4,290	2,288	1,144	3,432	4,004
$7,500	2,856	1,428	4,284	2,285	1,142	3,427	3,998
$7,475	2,852	1,426	4,278	2,281	1,141	3,422	3,992
$7,450	2,849	1,424	4,273	2,279	1,139	3,418	3,988
$7,425	2,845	1,422	4,267	2,276	1,138	3,413	3,982
$7,400	2,840	1,420	4,261	2,272	1,136	3,408	3,977
$7,375	2,836	1,418	4,254	2,269	1,135	3,404	3,971
$7,350	2,833	1,417	4,250	2,267	1,133	3,400	3,966
$7,325	2,829	1,415	4,244	2,263	1,132	3,395	3,961
$7,300	2,825	1,412	4,237	2,260	1,130	3,390	3,955
$7,275	2,821	1,410	4,231	2,257	1,128	3,385	3,949
$7,250	2,818	1,409	4,227	2,254	1,127	3,381	3,945
$7,225	2,814	1,407	4,220	2,251	1,125	3,376	3,939

TABLE 10—WORKER'S AND SPOUSE'S RETIREMENT BENEFITS* (CONT'D)

Average Indexed Monthly Earnings	Worker FRA (PIA)	Spouse FRA	Total FRA Benefit	Worker FRA - 3**	Spouse FRA - 3	Total FRA - 3 Benefit	Worker FRA and Spouse FRA-3
$7,200	2,809	1,405	4,214	2,248	1,124	3,371	3,933
$7,175	2,805	1,403	4,208	2,244	1,122	3,366	3,927
$7,150	2,802	1,401	4,203	2,242	1,121	3,363	3,923
$7,125	2,798	1,399	4,197	2,239	1,119	3,358	3,917
$7,100	2,794	1,397	4,191	2,235	1,118	3,353	3,912
$7,075	2,790	1,395	4,185	2,232	1,116	3,348	3,906
$7,050	2,787	1,393	4,180	2,229	1,115	3,344	3,902
$7,025	2,783	1,391	4,174	2,226	1,113	3,339	3,896
$7,000	2,779	1,389	4,168	2,223	1,111	3,334	3,890
$6,975	2,774	1,387	4,162	2,220	1,110	3,329	3,884
$6,950	2,771	1,386	4,157	2,217	1,109	3,326	3,880
$6,925	2,767	1,384	4,151	2,214	1,107	3,321	3,874
$6,900	2,763	1,382	4,145	2,210	1,105	3,316	3,868
$6,875	2,759	1,379	4,138	2,207	1,104	3,311	3,863
$6,850	2,756	1,378	4,134	2,205	1,102	3,307	3,858
$6,825	2,752	1,376	4,128	2,201	1,101	3,302	3,852
$6,800	2,748	1,374	4,121	2,198	1,099	3,297	3,847
$6,775	2,743	1,372	4,115	2,195	1,097	3,292	3,841
$6,750	2,740	1,370	4,111	2,192	1,096	3,288	3,837
$6,725	2,736	1,368	4,104	2,189	1,095	3,284	3,831
$6,700	2,732	1,366	4,098	2,186	1,093	3,279	3,825
$6,675	2,728	1,364	4,092	2,182	1,091	3,274	3,819
$6,650	2,725	1,362	4,087	2,180	1,090	3,270	3,815
$6,625	2,721	1,360	4,081	2,177	1,088	3,265	3,809
$6,600	2,717	1,358	4,075	2,173	1,087	3,260	3,803
$6,575	2,713	1,356	4,069	2,170	1,085	3,255	3,798
$6,550	2,709	1,355	4,064	2,168	1,084	3,251	3,793
$6,525	2,705	1,353	4,058	2,164	1,082	3,246	3,787
$6,500	2,701	1,351	4,052	2,161	1,080	3,241	3,782
$6,475	2,697	1,349	4,046	2,158	1,079	3,237	3,776
$6,450	2,694	1,347	4,041	2,155	1,078	3,233	3,772
$6,425	2,690	1,345	4,035	2,152	1,076	3,228	3,766
$6,400	2,686	1,343	4,029	2,149	1,074	3,223	3,760
$6,375	2,682	1,341	4,022	2,145	1,073	3,218	3,754
$6,350	2,679	1,339	4,018	2,143	1,071	3,214	3,750
$6,325	2,674	1,337	4,012	2,140	1,070	3,209	3,744
$6,300	2,670	1,335	4,005	2,136	1,068	3,204	3,738
$6,275	2,666	1,333	3,999	2,133	1,066	3,199	3,733
$6,250	2,663	1,332	3,995	2,130	1,065	3,196	3,728
$6,225	2,659	1,329	3,988	2,127	1,064	3,191	3,723
$6,200	2,655	1,327	3,982	2,124	1,062	3,186	3,717
$6,175	2,651	1,325	3,976	2,121	1,060	3,181	3,711
$6,150	2,642	1,321	3,964	2,114	1,057	3,171	3,699
$6,125	2,634	1,317	3,951	2,107	1,054	3,161	3,688
$6,100	2,626	1,313	3,939	2,101	1,050	3,151	3,676
$6,075	2,618	1,309	3,927	2,094	1,047	3,141	3,665
$6,050	2,609	1,305	3,914	2,088	1,044	3,131	3,653
$6,025	2,601	1,301	3,902	2,081	1,040	3,121	3,642
$6,000	2,593	1,296	3,889	2,074	1,037	3,112	3,630
$5,975	2,585	1,292	3,877	2,068	1,034	3,102	3,619

TABLE 10—WORKER'S AND SPOUSE'S RETIREMENT BENEFITS* (CONT'D)

Average Indexed Monthly Earnings	Worker FRA (PIA)	Spouse FRA	Total FRA Benefit	Worker FRA - 3**	Spouse FRA - 3	Total FRA - 3 Benefit	Worker FRA and Spouse FRA-3
$5,950	2,576	1,288	3,865	2,061	1,031	3,092	3,607
$5,925	2,568	1,284	3,852	2,055	1,027	3,082	3,596
$5,900	2,560	1,280	3,840	2,048	1,024	3,072	3,584
$5,875	2,552	1,276	3,828	2,041	1,021	3,062	3,572
$5,850	2,543	1,272	3,815	2,035	1,017	3,052	3,561
$5,825	2,535	1,268	3,803	2,028	1,014	3,042	3,549
$5,800	2,527	1,263	3,790	2,022	1,011	3,032	3,538
$5,775	2,519	1,259	3,778	2,015	1,007	3,022	3,526
$5,750	2,510	1,255	3,766	2,008	1,004	3,013	3,515
$5,725	2,502	1,251	3,753	2,002	1,001	3,003	3,503
$5,700	2,494	1,247	3,741	1,995	998	2,993	3,492
$5,675	2,486	1,243	3,729	1,989	994	2,983	3,480
$5,650	2,477	1,239	3,716	1,982	991	2,973	3,468
$5,625	2,469	1,235	3,704	1,975	988	2,963	3,457
$5,600	2,461	1,230	3,691	1,969	984	2,953	3,445
$5,575	2,453	1,226	3,679	1,962	981	2,943	3,434
$5,550	2,445	1,222	3,667	1,956	978	2,933	3,422
$5,525	2,436	1,218	3,654	1,949	975	2,924	3,411
$5,500	2,428	1,214	3,642	1,942	971	2,914	3,399
$5,475	2,420	1,210	3,630	1,936	968	2,904	3,388
$5,450	2,412	1,206	3,617	1,929	965	2,894	3,376
$5,425	2,403	1,202	3,605	1,923	961	2,884	3,365
$5,400	2,395	1,198	3,593	1,916	958	2,874	3,353
$5,375	2,387	1,193	3,580	1,909	955	2,864	3,341
$5,350	2,379	1,189	3,568	1,903	951	2,854	3,330
$5,325	2,370	1,185	3,555	1,896	948	2,844	3,318
$5,300	2,362	1,181	3,543	1,890	945	2,834	3,307
$5,275	2,354	1,177	3,531	1,883	942	2,825	3,295
$5,250	2,346	1,173	3,518	1,876	938	2,815	3,284
$5,225	2,337	1,169	3,506	1,870	935	2,805	3,272
$5,200	2,329	1,165	3,494	1,863	932	2,795	3,261
$5,175	2,321	1,160	3,481	1,857	928	2,785	3,249
$5,150	2,313	1,156	3,469	1,850	925	2,775	3,238
$5,125	2,304	1,152	3,456	1,843	922	2,765	3,226
$5,100	2,296	1,148	3,444	1,837	918	2,755	3,214
$5,075	2,288	1,144	3,432	1,830	915	2,745	3,203
$5,050	2,280	1,140	3,419	1,824	912	2,735	3,191
$5,025	2,271	1,136	3,407	1,817	909	2,726	3,180
$5,000	2,263	1,132	3,395	1,810	905	2,716	3,168
$4,975	2,255	1,127	3,382	1,804	902	2,706	3,157
$4,950	2,247	1,123	3,370	1,797	899	2,696	3,145
$4,925	2,238	1,119	3,357	1,791	895	2,686	3,134
$4,900	2,230	1,115	3,345	1,784	892	2,676	3,122
$4,875	2,222	1,111	3,333	1,777	889	2,666	3,111
$4,850	2,214	1,107	3,320	1,771	885	2,656	3,099
$4,825	2,205	1,103	3,308	1,764	882	2,646	3,087
$4,800	2,197	1,099	3,296	1,758	879	2,636	3,076
$4,775	2,189	1,094	3,283	1,751	876	2,627	3,064
$4,750	2,181	1,090	3,271	1,744	872	2,617	3,053
$4,725	2,172	1,086	3,258	1,738	869	2,607	3,041

TABLE 10—WORKER'S AND SPOUSE'S RETIREMENT BENEFITS* (CONT'D)

Average Indexed Monthly Earnings	Worker FRA (PIA)	Spouse FRA	Total FRA Benefit	Worker FRA - 3**	Spouse FRA - 3	Total FRA - 3 Benefit	Worker FRA and Spouse FRA-3
$4,700	2,164	1,082	3,246	1,731	866	2,597	3,030
$4,675	2,156	1,078	3,234	1,725	862	2,587	3,018
$4,650	2,148	1,074	3,221	1,718	859	2,577	3,007
$4,625	2,139	1,070	3,209	1,711	856	2,567	2,995
$4,600	2,131	1,066	3,197	1,705	852	2,557	2,984
$4,575	2,123	1,061	3,184	1,698	849	2,547	2,972
$4,550	2,115	1,057	3,172	1,692	846	2,537	2,960
$4,525	2,106	1,053	3,159	1,685	843	2,528	2,949
$4,500	2,098	1,049	3,147	1,678	839	2,518	2,937
$4,475	2,090	1,045	3,135	1,672	836	2,508	2,926
$4,450	2,082	1,041	3,122	1,665	833	2,498	2,914
$4,425	2,073	1,037	3,110	1,659	829	2,488	2,903
$4,400	2,065	1,033	3,098	1,652	826	2,478	2,891
$4,375	2,057	1,028	3,085	1,645	823	2,468	2,880
$4,350	2,049	1,024	3,073	1,639	819	2,458	2,868
$4,325	2,040	1,020	3,061	1,632	816	2,448	2,856
$4,300	2,032	1,016	3,048	1,626	813	2,439	2,845
$4,275	2,024	1,012	3,036	1,619	810	2,429	2,833
$4,250	2,016	1,008	3,023	1,612	806	2,419	2,822
$4,225	2,007	1,004	3,011	1,606	803	2,409	2,810
$4,200	1,999	1,000	2,999	1,599	800	2,399	2,799
$4,175	1,991	995	2,986	1,593	796	2,389	2,787
$4,150	1,983	991	2,974	1,586	793	2,379	2,776
$4,125	1,974	987	2,962	1,579	790	2,369	2,764
$4,100	1,966	983	2,949	1,573	786	2,359	2,753
$4,075	1,958	979	2,937	1,566	783	2,349	2,741
$4,050	1,950	975	2,924	1,560	780	2,340	2,729
$4,025	1,941	971	2,912	1,553	777	2,330	2,718
$4,000	1,933	967	2,900	1,547	773	2,320	2,706
$3,975	1,925	962	2,887	1,540	770	2,310	2,695
$3,950	1,917	958	2,875	1,533	767	2,300	2,683
$3,925	1,908	954	2,863	1,527	763	2,290	2,672
$3,900	1,900	950	2,850	1,520	760	2,280	2,660
$3,875	1,892	946	2,838	1,514	757	2,270	2,649
$3,850	1,884	942	2,825	1,507	753	2,260	2,637
$3,825	1,875	938	2,813	1,500	750	2,250	2,626
$3,800	1,867	934	2,801	1,494	747	2,241	2,614
$3,775	1,859	929	2,788	1,487	744	2,231	2,602
$3,750	1,851	925	2,776	1,481	740	2,221	2,591
$3,725	1,842	921	2,764	1,474	737	2,211	2,579
$3,700	1,834	917	2,751	1,467	734	2,201	2,568
$3,675	1,826	913	2,739	1,461	730	2,191	2,556
$3,650	1,818	909	2,726	1,454	727	2,181	2,545
$3,625	1,809	905	2,714	1,448	724	2,171	2,533
$3,600	1,801	901	2,702	1,441	720	2,161	2,522
$3,575	1,793	896	2,689	1,434	717	2,151	2,510
$3,550	1,785	892	2,677	1,428	714	2,142	2,499
$3,525	1,776	888	2,665	1,421	711	2,132	2,487
$3,500	1,768	884	2,652	1,415	707	2,122	2,475
$3,475	1,760	880	2,640	1,408	704	2,112	2,464

TABLE 10—WORKER'S AND SPOUSE'S RETIREMENT BENEFITS* (CONT'D)

Average Indexed Monthly Earnings	Worker FRA (PIA)	Spouse FRA	Total FRA Benefit	Worker FRA - 3**	Spouse FRA - 3	Total FRA - 3 Benefit	Worker FRA and Spouse FRA-3
$3,450	1,752	876	2,628	1,401	701	2,102	2,452
$3,425	1,743	872	2,615	1,395	697	2,092	2,441
$3,400	1,735	868	2,603	1,388	694	2,082	2,429
$3,375	1,727	863	2,590	1,382	691	2,072	2,418
$3,350	1,719	859	2,578	1,375	687	2,062	2,406
$3,325	1,710	855	2,566	1,368	684	2,053	2,395
$3,300	1,702	851	2,553	1,362	681	2,043	2,383
$3,275	1,694	847	2,541	1,355	678	2,033	2,372
$3,250	1,686	843	2,529	1,349	674	2,023	2,360
$3,225	1,677	839	2,516	1,342	671	2,013	2,348
$3,200	1,669	835	2,504	1,335	668	2,003	2,337
$3,175	1,661	830	2,491	1,329	664	1,993	2,325
$3,150	1,653	826	2,479	1,322	661	1,983	2,314
$3,125	1,644	822	2,467	1,316	658	1,973	2,302
$3,100	1,636	818	2,454	1,309	654	1,963	2,291
$3,075	1,628	814	2,442	1,302	651	1,954	2,279
$3,050	1,620	810	2,430	1,296	648	1,944	2,268
$3,025	1,611	806	2,417	1,289	645	1,934	2,256
$3,000	1,603	802	2,405	1,283	641	1,924	2,244
$2,975	1,595	797	2,392	1,276	638	1,914	2,233
$2,950	1,587	793	2,380	1,269	635	1,904	2,221
$2,925	1,578	789	2,368	1,263	631	1,894	2,210
$2,900	1,570	785	2,355	1,256	628	1,884	2,198
$2,875	1,562	781	2,343	1,250	625	1,874	2,187
$2,850	1,554	777	2,331	1,243	621	1,864	2,175
$2,825	1,545	773	2,318	1,236	618	1,855	2,164
$2,800	1,537	769	2,306	1,230	615	1,845	2,152
$2,775	1,529	764	2,293	1,223	612	1,835	2,141
$2,750	1,521	760	2,281	1,217	608	1,825	2,129
$2,725	1,512	756	2,269	1,210	605	1,815	2,117
$2,700	1,504	752	2,256	1,203	602	1,805	2,106
$2,675	1,496	748	2,244	1,197	598	1,795	2,094
$2,650	1,488	744	2,232	1,190	595	1,785	2,083
$2,625	1,479	740	2,219	1,184	592	1,775	2,071
$2,600	1,471	736	2,207	1,177	588	1,765	2,060
$2,575	1,463	731	2,194	1,170	585	1,756	2,048
$2,550	1,455	727	2,182	1,164	582	1,746	2,037
$2,525	1,446	723	2,170	1,157	579	1,736	2,025
$2,500	1,438	719	2,157	1,151	575	1,726	2,014
$2,475	1,430	715	2,145	1,144	572	1,716	2,002
$2,450	1,422	711	2,133	1,137	569	1,706	1,990
$2,425	1,414	707	2,120	1,131	565	1,696	1,979
$2,400	1,405	703	2,108	1,124	562	1,686	1,967
$2,375	1,397	699	2,096	1,118	559	1,676	1,956
$2,350	1,389	694	2,083	1,111	556	1,667	1,944
$2,325	1,381	690	2,071	1,104	552	1,657	1,933
$2,300	1,372	686	2,058	1,098	549	1,647	1,921
$2,275	1,364	682	2,046	1,091	546	1,637	1,910
$2,250	1,356	678	2,034	1,085	542	1,627	1,898
$2,225	1,348	674	2,021	1,078	539	1,617	1,887

TABLE 10—WORKER'S AND SPOUSE'S RETIREMENT BENEFITS* (CONT'D)

Average Indexed Monthly Earnings	Worker FRA (PIA)	Spouse FRA	Total FRA Benefit	Worker FRA - 3**	Spouse FRA - 3	Total FRA - 3 Benefit	Worker FRA and Spouse FRA-3
$2,200	1,339	670	2,009	1,071	536	1,607	1,875
$2,175	1,331	666	1,997	1,065	532	1,597	1,863
$2,150	1,323	661	1,984	1,058	529	1,587	1,852
$2,125	1,315	657	1,972	1,052	526	1,577	1,840
$2,100	1,306	653	1,959	1,045	523	1,568	1,829
$2,075	1,298	649	1,947	1,038	519	1,558	1,817
$2,050	1,290	645	1,935	1,032	516	1,548	1,806
$2,025	1,282	641	1,922	1,025	513	1,538	1,794
$2,000	1,273	637	1,910	1,019	509	1,528	1,783
$1,975	1,265	633	1,898	1,012	506	1,518	1,771
$1,950	1,257	628	1,885	1,005	503	1,508	1,760
$1,925	1,249	624	1,873	999	499	1,498	1,748
$1,900	1,240	620	1,860	992	496	1,488	1,736
$1,875	1,232	616	1,848	986	493	1,478	1,725
$1,850	1,224	612	1,836	979	490	1,469	1,713
$1,825	1,216	608	1,823	972	486	1,459	1,702
$1,800	1,207	604	1,811	966	483	1,449	1,690
$1,775	1,199	600	1,799	959	480	1,439	1,679
$1,750	1,191	595	1,786	953	476	1,429	1,667
$1,725	1,183	591	1,774	946	473	1,419	1,656
$1,700	1,174	587	1,761	939	470	1,409	1,644
$1,675	1,166	583	1,749	933	466	1,399	1,632
$1,650	1,158	579	1,737	926	463	1,389	1,621
$1,625	1,150	575	1,724	920	460	1,379	1,609
$1,600	1,141	571	1,712	913	457	1,370	1,598
$1,575	1,133	567	1,700	906	453	1,360	1,586
$1,550	1,125	562	1,687	900	450	1,350	1,575
$1,525	1,117	558	1,675	893	447	1,340	1,563
$1,500	1,108	554	1,662	887	443	1,330	1,552
$1,475	1,100	550	1,650	880	440	1,320	1,540
$1,450	1,092	546	1,638	873	437	1,310	1,529
$1,425	1,084	542	1,625	867	433	1,300	1,517
$1,400	1,075	538	1,613	860	430	1,290	1,505
$1,375	1,067	534	1,601	854	427	1,281	1,494
$1,350	1,059	529	1,588	847	424	1,271	1,482
$1,325	1,051	525	1,576	840	420	1,261	1,471
$1,300	1,042	521	1,564	834	417	1,251	1,459
$1,275	1,034	517	1,551	827	414	1,241	1,448
$1,250	1,026	513	1,539	821	410	1,231	1,436
$1,225	1,018	509	1,526	814	407	1,221	1,425
$1,200	1,009	505	1,514	807	404	1,211	1,413
$1,175	1,001	501	1,502	801	400	1,201	1,402
$1,150	993	496	1,489	794	397	1,191	1,390
$1,125	985	492	1,477	788	394	1,182	1,378
$1,100	976	488	1,465	781	391	1,172	1,367
$1,075	968	484	1,452	774	387	1,162	1,355
$1,050	960	480	1,440	768	384	1,152	1,344
$1,025	952	476	1,427	761	381	1,142	1,332
$1,000	928	464	1,392	742	371	1,113	1,299
$975	905	453	1,358	724	362	1,086	1,267

TABLE 10—WORKER'S AND SPOUSE'S RETIREMENT BENEFITS* (CONT'D)

Average Indexed Monthly Earnings	Worker FRA (PIA)	Spouse FRA	Total FRA Benefit	Worker FRA - 3**	Spouse FRA - 3	Total FRA - 3 Benefit	Worker FRA and Spouse FRA-3
$950	882	441	1,322	705	353	1,058	1,234
$925	859	429	1,288	687	344	1,031	1,202
$900	835	418	1,253	668	334	1,002	1,169
$875	812	406	1,219	650	325	975	1,137
$850	789	394	1,183	631	315	946	1,104
$825	766	383	1,149	613	306	919	1,072
$800	742	371	1,113	594	297	891	1,039

* The retirement age when unreduced benefits are available will be increased to age 67 in gradual steps starting in the year 2000. If you were born in 1943-1954, your retirement age for full benefits is 66. If you were born in 1955-1959, your retirement age for full benefits is your 66th birthday plus two months for every year you were born after 1954. If you were born in 1960 and after, your retirement age for full benefits is 67.

** Benefits listed are 80% of the corresponding PIA, but age 62 benefits are reduced further if worker is born in 1938 or after. Ex: Benefits is 75% of PIA for workers born in 1943-1954 and 70% of PIA for workers born in 1960 and after.

TABLE 11—SURVIVOR'S BENEFITS

Average Indexed Monthly Earnings	Worker's PIA	Surviving Spouse & 1 Child; or 2 Children	Surviving Spouse & 2 Children; or 3 Children	One Child (No Mother)	Widow or Widower Age 60	Widow or Widower FRA	Each of Two Parents	Sole Parent	Maximum Family Benefits
$9,700	3,196	4,794	5,593	2,397	2,285	3,196	3,196	2,637	5,593
$9,675	3,192	4,788	5,586	2,394	2,282	3,192	3,192	2,633	5,586
$9,650	3,189	4,784	5,581	2,392	2,280	3,189	3,189	2,631	5,581
$9,625	3,185	4,778	5,574	2,389	2,277	3,185	3,185	2,628	5,574
$9,600	3,181	4,772	5,567	2,386	2,274	3,181	3,181	2,624	5,567
$9,575	3,177	4,766	5,560	2,383	2,272	3,177	3,177	2,621	5,560
$9,550	3,173	4,760	5,553	2,380	2,269	3,173	3,173	2,618	5,553
$9,525	3,169	4,754	5,546	2,377	2,266	3,169	3,169	2,614	5,546
$9,500	3,165	4,748	5,539	2,374	2,263	3,165	3,165	2,611	5,539
$9,475	3,161	4,742	5,532	2,371	2,260	3,161	3,161	2,608	5,532
$9,450	3,158	4,737	5,527	2,369	2,258	3,158	3,158	2,605	5,527
$9,425	3,154	4,731	5,520	2,366	2,255	3,154	3,154	2,602	5,520
$9,400	3,150	4,725	5,513	2,363	2,252	3,150	3,150	2,599	5,513
$9,375	3,146	4,719	5,506	2,360	2,249	3,146	3,146	2,595	5,506
$9,350	3,142	4,713	5,499	2,357	2,247	3,142	3,142	2,592	5,499
$9,325	3,138	4,707	5,492	2,354	2,244	3,138	3,138	2,589	5,492
$9,300	3,134	4,701	5,485	2,351	2,241	3,134	3,134	2,586	5,485
$9,275	3,130	4,695	5,478	2,348	2,238	3,130	3,130	2,582	5,478
$9,250	3,127	4,691	5,472	2,345	2,236	3,127	3,127	2,580	5,472
$9,225	3,123	4,685	5,465	2,342	2,233	3,123	3,123	2,576	5,465
$9,200	3,119	4,679	5,458	2,339	2,230	3,119	3,119	2,573	5,458
$9,175	3,115	4,673	5,451	2,336	2,227	3,115	3,115	2,570	5,451
$9,150	3,112	4,668	5,446	2,334	2,225	3,112	3,112	2,567	5,446
$9,125	3,107	4,661	5,437	2,330	2,222	3,107	3,107	2,563	5,437
$9,100	3,103	4,655	5,430	2,327	2,219	3,103	3,103	2,560	5,430
$9,075	3,099	4,649	5,423	2,324	2,216	3,099	3,099	2,557	5,423
$9,050	3,096	4,644	5,418	2,322	2,214	3,096	3,096	2,554	5,418
$9,025	3,092	4,638	5,411	2,319	2,211	3,092	3,092	2,551	5,411
$9,000	3,088	4,632	5,404	2,316	2,208	3,088	3,088	2,548	5,404
$8,975	3,084	4,626	5,397	2,313	2,205	3,084	3,084	2,544	5,397
$8,950	3,081	4,622	5,392	2,311	2,203	3,081	3,081	2,542	5,392
$8,925	3,077	4,616	5,385	2,308	2,200	3,077	3,077	2,539	5,385
$8,900	3,072	4,608	5,376	2,304	2,196	3,072	3,072	2,534	5,376
$8,875	3,068	4,602	5,369	2,301	2,194	3,068	3,068	2,531	5,369
$8,850	3,065	4,598	5,364	2,299	2,191	3,065	3,065	2,529	5,364
$8,825	3,061	4,592	5,357	2,296	2,189	3,061	3,061	2,525	5,357
$8,800	3,057	4,586	5,350	2,293	2,186	3,057	3,057	2,522	5,350
$8,775	3,053	4,580	5,343	2,290	2,183	3,053	3,053	2,519	5,343
$8,750	3,050	4,575	5,338	2,288	2,181	3,050	3,050	2,516	5,338
$8,725	3,046	4,569	5,331	2,285	2,178	3,046	3,046	2,513	5,331
$8,700	3,041	4,562	5,322	2,281	2,174	3,041	3,041	2,509	5,322
$8,675	3,037	4,556	5,315	2,278	2,171	3,037	3,037	2,506	5,315
$8,650	3,034	4,551	5,310	2,276	2,169	3,034	3,034	2,503	5,310
$8,625	3,030	4,545	5,303	2,273	2,166	3,030	3,030	2,500	5,303
$8,600	3,026	4,539	5,296	2,270	2,164	3,026	3,026	2,496	5,296
$8,575	3,022	4,533	5,289	2,267	2,161	3,022	3,022	2,493	5,289
$8,550	3,019	4,529	5,283	2,264	2,159	3,019	3,019	2,491	5,283
$8,525	3,015	4,523	5,276	2,261	2,156	3,015	3,015	2,487	5,276
$8,500	3,011	4,517	5,269	2,258	2,153	3,011	3,011	2,484	5,269
$8,475	3,006	4,509	5,261	2,255	2,149	3,006	3,006	2,480	5,261

TABLE 11—SURVIVOR'S BENEFITS (CONT'D)

Average Indexed Monthly Earnings	Worker's PIA	Surviving Spouse & 1 Child; or 2 Children	Surviving Spouse & 2 Children; or 3 Children	One Child (No Mother)	Widow or Widower Age 60	Widow or Widower FRA	Each of Two Parents	Sole Parent	Maximum Family Benefits
$8,450	3,003	4,505	5,255	2,252	2,147	3,003	3,003	2,477	5,255
$8,425	2,999	4,499	5,248	2,249	2,144	2,999	2,999	2,474	5,248
$8,400	2,995	4,493	5,241	2,246	2,141	2,995	2,995	2,471	5,241
$8,375	2,991	4,487	5,234	2,243	2,139	2,991	2,991	2,468	5,234
$8,350	2,988	4,482	5,229	2,241	2,136	2,988	2,988	2,465	5,229
$8,325	2,984	4,476	5,222	2,238	2,134	2,984	2,984	2,462	5,222
$8,300	2,980	4,470	5,215	2,235	2,131	2,980	2,980	2,459	5,215
$8,275	2,975	4,463	5,206	2,231	2,127	2,975	2,975	2,454	5,206
$8,250	2,972	4,458	5,201	2,229	2,125	2,972	2,972	2,452	5,201
$8,225	2,968	4,452	5,194	2,226	2,122	2,968	2,968	2,449	5,194
$8,200	2,964	4,446	5,187	2,223	2,119	2,964	2,964	2,445	5,187
$8,175	2,960	4,440	5,180	2,220	2,116	2,960	2,960	2,442	5,180
$8,150	2,957	4,436	5,175	2,218	2,114	2,957	2,957	2,440	5,175
$8,125	2,953	4,430	5,168	2,215	2,111	2,953	2,953	2,436	5,168
$8,100	2,949	4,424	5,161	2,212	2,109	2,949	2,949	2,433	5,161
$8,075	2,945	4,418	5,154	2,209	2,106	2,945	2,945	2,430	5,154
$8,050	2,941	4,412	5,147	2,206	2,103	2,941	2,941	2,426	5,147
$8,025	2,937	4,406	5,140	2,203	2,100	2,937	2,937	2,423	5,140
$8,000	2,933	4,400	5,133	2,200	2,097	2,933	2,933	2,420	5,133
$7,975	2,929	4,394	5,126	2,197	2,094	2,929	2,929	2,416	5,126
$7,950	2,926	4,389	5,121	2,195	2,092	2,926	2,926	2,414	5,121
$7,925	2,922	4,383	5,114	2,192	2,089	2,922	2,922	2,411	5,114
$7,900	2,918	4,377	5,107	2,189	2,086	2,918	2,918	2,407	5,107
$7,875	2,914	4,371	5,100	2,186	2,084	2,914	2,914	2,404	5,100
$7,850	2,911	4,367	5,094	2,183	2,081	2,911	2,911	2,402	5,094
$7,825	2,906	4,359	5,086	2,180	2,078	2,906	2,906	2,397	5,086
$7,800	2,902	4,353	5,079	2,177	2,075	2,902	2,902	2,394	5,079
$7,775	2,898	4,347	5,072	2,174	2,072	2,898	2,898	2,391	5,072
$7,750	2,895	4,343	5,066	2,171	2,070	2,895	2,895	2,388	5,066
$7,725	2,891	4,337	5,059	2,168	2,067	2,891	2,891	2,385	5,059
$7,700	2,887	4,331	5,052	2,165	2,064	2,887	2,887	2,382	5,052
$7,675	2,883	4,325	5,045	2,162	2,061	2,883	2,883	2,378	5,045
$7,650	2,880	4,320	5,040	2,160	2,059	2,880	2,880	2,376	5,040
$7,625	2,875	4,313	5,031	2,156	2,056	2,875	2,875	2,372	5,031
$7,600	2,871	4,307	5,024	2,153	2,053	2,871	2,871	2,369	5,024
$7,575	2,867	4,301	5,017	2,150	2,050	2,867	2,867	2,365	5,017
$7,550	2,864	4,296	5,012	2,148	2,048	2,864	2,864	2,363	5,012
$7,525	2,860	4,290	5,005	2,145	2,045	2,860	2,860	2,360	5,005
$7,500	2,856	4,284	4,998	2,142	2,042	2,856	2,856	2,356	4,998
$7,475	2,852	4,278	4,991	2,139	2,039	2,852	2,852	2,353	4,991
$7,450	2,849	4,274	4,986	2,137	2,037	2,849	2,849	2,350	4,986
$7,425	2,845	4,268	4,979	2,134	2,034	2,845	2,845	2,347	4,979
$7,400	2,840	4,260	4,970	2,130	2,031	2,840	2,840	2,343	4,970
$7,375	2,836	4,254	4,963	2,127	2,028	2,836	2,836	2,340	4,963
$7,350	2,833	4,250	4,958	2,125	2,026	2,833	2,833	2,337	4,958
$7,325	2,829	4,244	4,951	2,122	2,023	2,829	2,829	2,334	4,951
$7,300	2,825	4,238	4,944	2,119	2,020	2,825	2,825	2,331	4,944
$7,275	2,821	4,232	4,937	2,116	2,017	2,821	2,821	2,327	4,937
$7,250	2,818	4,227	4,932	2,114	2,015	2,818	2,818	2,325	4,932
$7,225	2,814	4,221	4,925	2,111	2,012	2,814	2,814	2,322	4,925

TABLE 11—SURVIVOR'S BENEFITS (CONT'D)

Average Indexed Monthly Earnings	Worker's PIA	Surviving Spouse & 1 Child; or 2 Children	Surviving Spouse & 2 Children; or 3 Children	One Child (No Mother)	Widow or Widower Age 60	Widow or Widower FRA	Each of Two Parents	Sole Parent	Maximum Family Benefits
$7,200	2,809	4,214	4,916	2,107	2,008	2,809	2,809	2,317	4,916
$7,175	2,805	4,208	4,909	2,104	2,006	2,805	2,805	2,314	4,909
$7,150	2,802	4,203	4,904	2,102	2,003	2,802	2,802	2,312	4,904
$7,125	2,798	4,197	4,897	2,099	2,001	2,798	2,798	2,308	4,897
$7,100	2,794	4,191	4,890	2,096	1,998	2,794	2,794	2,305	4,890
$7,075	2,790	4,185	4,883	2,093	1,995	2,790	2,790	2,302	4,883
$7,050	2,787	4,181	4,877	2,090	1,993	2,787	2,787	2,299	4,877
$7,025	2,783	4,175	4,870	2,087	1,990	2,783	2,783	2,296	4,870
$7,000	2,779	4,169	4,863	2,084	1,987	2,779	2,779	2,293	4,863
$6,975	2,774	4,161	4,855	2,081	1,983	2,774	2,774	2,289	4,855
$6,950	2,771	4,157	4,849	2,078	1,981	2,771	2,771	2,286	4,849
$6,925	2,767	4,151	4,842	2,075	1,978	2,767	2,767	2,283	4,842
$6,900	2,763	4,145	4,835	2,072	1,976	2,763	2,763	2,279	4,835
$6,875	2,759	4,139	4,828	2,069	1,973	2,759	2,759	2,276	4,828
$6,850	2,756	4,134	4,823	2,067	1,971	2,756	2,756	2,274	4,823
$6,825	2,752	4,128	4,816	2,064	1,968	2,752	2,752	2,270	4,816
$6,800	2,748	4,122	4,809	2,061	1,965	2,748	2,748	2,267	4,809
$6,775	2,743	4,115	4,800	2,057	1,961	2,743	2,743	2,263	4,800
$6,750	2,740	4,110	4,795	2,055	1,959	2,740	2,740	2,261	4,795
$6,725	2,736	4,104	4,788	2,052	1,956	2,736	2,736	2,257	4,788
$6,700	2,732	4,098	4,781	2,049	1,953	2,732	2,732	2,254	4,781
$6,675	2,728	4,092	4,774	2,046	1,951	2,728	2,728	2,251	4,774
$6,650	2,725	4,088	4,769	2,044	1,948	2,725	2,725	2,248	4,769
$6,625	2,721	4,082	4,762	2,041	1,946	2,721	2,721	2,245	4,762
$6,600	2,717	4,076	4,755	2,038	1,943	2,717	2,717	2,242	4,755
$6,575	2,713	4,070	4,748	2,035	1,940	2,713	2,713	2,238	4,748
$6,550	2,709	4,064	4,741	2,032	1,937	2,709	2,709	2,235	4,741
$6,525	2,705	4,058	4,734	2,029	1,934	2,705	2,705	2,232	4,734
$6,500	2,701	4,052	4,727	2,026	1,931	2,701	2,701	2,228	4,727
$6,475	2,697	4,046	4,720	2,023	1,928	2,697	2,697	2,225	4,720
$6,450	2,694	4,041	4,715	2,021	1,926	2,694	2,694	2,223	4,715
$6,425	2,690	4,035	4,708	2,018	1,923	2,690	2,690	2,219	4,708
$6,400	2,686	4,029	4,701	2,015	1,920	2,686	2,686	2,216	4,701
$6,375	2,682	4,023	4,694	2,012	1,918	2,682	2,682	2,213	4,694
$6,350	2,679	4,019	4,688	2,009	1,915	2,679	2,679	2,210	4,688
$6,325	2,674	4,011	4,680	2,006	1,912	2,674	2,674	2,206	4,680
$6,300	2,670	4,005	4,673	2,003	1,909	2,670	2,670	2,203	4,673
$6,275	2,666	3,999	4,666	2,000	1,906	2,666	2,666	2,199	4,666
$6,250	2,663	3,995	4,660	1,997	1,904	2,663	2,663	2,197	4,660
$6,225	2,659	3,989	4,653	1,994	1,901	2,659	2,659	2,194	4,653
$6,200	2,655	3,983	4,646	1,991	1,898	2,655	2,655	2,190	4,646
$6,175	2,651	3,977	4,639	1,988	1,895	2,651	2,651	2,187	4,639
$6,150	2,642	3,963	4,624	1,982	1,889	2,642	2,642	2,180	4,624
$6,125	2,634	3,951	4,610	1,976	1,883	2,634	2,634	2,173	4,610
$6,100	2,626	3,939	4,596	1,970	1,878	2,626	2,626	2,166	4,596
$6,075	2,618	3,927	4,582	1,964	1,872	2,618	2,618	2,160	4,582
$6,050	2,609	3,914	4,566	1,957	1,865	2,609	2,609	2,152	4,566
$6,025	2,601	3,902	4,552	1,951	1,860	2,601	2,601	2,146	4,552
$6,000	2,593	3,890	4,538	1,945	1,854	2,593	2,593	2,139	4,538
$5,975	2,585	3,878	4,524	1,939	1,848	2,585	2,585	2,133	4,524

TABLE 11—SURVIVOR'S BENEFITS (CONT'D)

Average Indexed Monthly Earnings	Worker's PIA	Surviving Spouse & 1 Child; or 2 Children	Surviving Spouse & 2 Children; or 3 Children	One Child (No Mother)	Widow or Widower Age 60	Widow or Widower FRA	Each of Two Parents	Sole Parent	Maximum Family Benefits
$5,950	2,576	3,864	4,508	1,932	1,842	2,576	2,576	2,125	4,508
$5,925	2,568	3,852	4,494	1,926	1,836	2,568	2,568	2,119	4,494
$5,900	2,560	3,840	4,480	1,920	1,830	2,560	2,560	2,112	4,480
$5,875	2,552	3,828	4,466	1,914	1,825	2,552	2,552	2,105	4,466
$5,850	2,543	3,815	4,450	1,907	1,818	2,543	2,543	2,098	4,450
$5,825	2,535	3,803	4,436	1,901	1,813	2,535	2,535	2,091	4,436
$5,800	2,527	3,791	4,422	1,895	1,807	2,527	2,527	2,085	4,422
$5,775	2,519	3,779	4,408	1,889	1,801	2,519	2,519	2,078	4,408
$5,750	2,510	3,765	4,393	1,883	1,795	2,510	2,510	2,071	4,393
$5,725	2,502	3,753	4,379	1,877	1,789	2,502	2,502	2,064	4,379
$5,700	2,494	3,741	4,365	1,871	1,783	2,494	2,494	2,058	4,365
$5,675	2,486	3,729	4,351	1,865	1,777	2,486	2,486	2,051	4,351
$5,650	2,477	3,716	4,335	1,858	1,771	2,477	2,477	2,044	4,335
$5,625	2,469	3,704	4,321	1,852	1,765	2,469	2,469	2,037	4,321
$5,600	2,461	3,692	4,307	1,846	1,760	2,461	2,461	2,030	4,307
$5,575	2,453	3,680	4,293	1,840	1,754	2,453	2,453	2,024	4,293
$5,550	2,445	3,668	4,279	1,834	1,748	2,445	2,445	2,017	4,279
$5,525	2,436	3,654	4,263	1,827	1,742	2,436	2,436	2,010	4,263
$5,500	2,428	3,642	4,249	1,821	1,736	2,428	2,428	2,003	4,249
$5,475	2,420	3,630	4,235	1,815	1,730	2,420	2,420	1,997	4,235
$5,450	2,412	3,618	4,221	1,809	1,725	2,412	2,412	1,990	4,221
$5,425	2,403	3,605	4,205	1,802	1,718	2,403	2,403	1,982	4,205
$5,400	2,395	3,593	4,191	1,796	1,712	2,395	2,395	1,976	4,191
$5,375	2,387	3,581	4,177	1,790	1,707	2,387	2,387	1,969	4,177
$5,350	2,379	3,569	4,163	1,784	1,701	2,379	2,379	1,963	4,163
$5,325	2,370	3,555	4,148	1,778	1,695	2,370	2,370	1,955	4,148
$5,300	2,362	3,543	4,134	1,772	1,689	2,362	2,362	1,949	4,134
$5,275	2,354	3,531	4,120	1,766	1,683	2,354	2,354	1,942	4,120
$5,250	2,346	3,519	4,106	1,760	1,677	2,346	2,346	1,935	4,106
$5,225	2,337	3,506	4,090	1,753	1,671	2,337	2,337	1,928	4,090
$5,200	2,329	3,494	4,076	1,747	1,665	2,329	2,329	1,921	4,076
$5,175	2,321	3,482	4,062	1,741	1,660	2,321	2,321	1,915	4,062
$5,150	2,313	3,470	4,048	1,735	1,654	2,313	2,313	1,908	4,048
$5,125	2,304	3,456	4,032	1,728	1,647	2,304	2,304	1,901	4,032
$5,100	2,296	3,444	4,018	1,722	1,642	2,296	2,296	1,894	4,018
$5,075	2,288	3,432	4,004	1,716	1,636	2,288	2,288	1,888	4,004
$5,050	2,280	3,420	3,990	1,710	1,630	2,280	2,280	1,881	3,990
$5,025	2,271	3,407	3,974	1,703	1,624	2,271	2,271	1,874	3,974
$5,000	2,263	3,395	3,960	1,697	1,618	2,263	2,263	1,867	3,960
$4,975	2,255	3,383	3,946	1,691	1,612	2,255	2,255	1,860	3,946
$4,950	2,247	3,371	3,932	1,685	1,607	2,247	2,247	1,854	3,932
$4,925	2,238	3,357	3,917	1,679	1,600	2,238	2,238	1,846	3,917
$4,900	2,230	3,345	3,903	1,673	1,594	2,230	2,230	1,840	3,903
$4,875	2,222	3,333	3,889	1,667	1,589	2,222	2,222	1,833	3,889
$4,850	2,214	3,321	3,875	1,661	1,583	2,214	2,214	1,827	3,875
$4,825	2,205	3,308	3,859	1,654	1,577	2,205	2,205	1,819	3,859
$4,800	2,197	3,296	3,845	1,648	1,571	2,197	2,197	1,813	3,845
$4,775	2,189	3,284	3,831	1,642	1,565	2,189	2,189	1,806	3,831
$4,750	2,181	3,272	3,817	1,636	1,559	2,181	2,181	1,799	3,817
$4,725	2,172	3,258	3,801	1,629	1,553	2,172	2,172	1,792	3,801

TABLE 11—SURVIVOR'S BENEFITS (CONT'D)

Average Indexed Monthly Earnings	Worker's PIA	Surviving Spouse & 1 Child; or 2 Children	Surviving Spouse & 2 Children; or 3 Children	One Child (No Mother)	Widow or Widower Age 60	Widow or Widower FRA	Each of Two Parents	Sole Parent	Maximum Family Benefits
$4,700	2,164	3,246	3,787	1,623	1,547	2,164	2,164	1,785	3,787
$4,675	2,156	3,234	3,773	1,617	1,542	2,156	2,156	1,779	3,773
$4,650	2,148	3,222	3,759	1,611	1,536	2,148	2,148	1,772	3,759
$4,625	2,139	3,209	3,743	1,604	1,529	2,139	2,139	1,765	3,743
$4,600	2,131	3,197	3,729	1,598	1,524	2,131	2,131	1,758	3,729
$4,575	2,123	3,185	3,715	1,592	1,518	2,123	2,123	1,751	3,715
$4,550	2,115	3,173	3,701	1,586	1,512	2,115	2,115	1,745	3,701
$4,525	2,106	3,159	3,686	1,580	1,506	2,106	2,106	1,737	3,686
$4,500	2,098	3,147	3,672	1,574	1,500	2,098	2,098	1,731	3,672
$4,475	2,090	3,135	3,658	1,568	1,494	2,090	2,090	1,724	3,658
$4,450	2,082	3,123	3,644	1,562	1,489	2,082	2,082	1,718	3,644
$4,425	2,073	3,110	3,628	1,555	1,482	2,073	2,073	1,710	3,628
$4,400	2,065	3,098	3,614	1,549	1,476	2,065	2,065	1,704	3,614
$4,375	2,057	3,086	3,600	1,543	1,471	2,057	2,057	1,697	3,600
$4,350	2,049	3,074	3,586	1,537	1,465	2,049	2,049	1,690	3,586
$4,325	2,040	3,060	3,570	1,530	1,459	2,040	2,040	1,683	3,570
$4,300	2,032	3,048	3,556	1,524	1,453	2,032	2,032	1,676	3,556
$4,275	2,024	3,036	3,542	1,518	1,447	2,024	2,024	1,670	3,542
$4,250	2,016	3,024	3,528	1,512	1,441	2,016	2,016	1,663	3,528
$4,225	2,007	3,011	3,512	1,505	1,435	2,007	2,007	1,656	3,512
$4,200	1,999	2,999	3,498	1,499	1,429	1,999	1,999	1,649	3,498
$4,175	1,991	2,987	3,484	1,493	1,424	1,991	1,991	1,643	3,484
$4,150	1,983	2,975	3,470	1,487	1,418	1,983	1,983	1,636	3,470
$4,125	1,974	2,961	3,455	1,481	1,411	1,974	1,974	1,629	3,455
$4,100	1,966	2,949	3,441	1,475	1,406	1,966	1,966	1,622	3,441
$4,075	1,958	2,937	3,427	1,469	1,400	1,958	1,958	1,615	3,427
$4,050	1,950	2,925	3,413	1,463	1,394	1,950	1,950	1,609	3,413
$4,025	1,941	2,912	3,397	1,456	1,388	1,941	1,941	1,601	3,397
$4,000	1,933	2,900	3,383	1,450	1,382	1,933	1,933	1,595	3,383
$3,975	1,925	2,888	3,369	1,444	1,376	1,925	1,925	1,588	3,369
$3,950	1,917	2,876	3,355	1,438	1,371	1,917	1,917	1,582	3,355
$3,925	1,908	2,862	3,339	1,431	1,364	1,908	1,908	1,574	3,339
$3,900	1,900	2,850	3,325	1,425	1,359	1,900	1,900	1,568	3,325
$3,875	1,892	2,838	3,311	1,419	1,353	1,892	1,892	1,561	3,311
$3,850	1,884	2,826	3,297	1,413	1,347	1,884	1,884	1,554	3,297
$3,825	1,875	2,813	3,281	1,406	1,341	1,875	1,875	1,547	3,281
$3,800	1,867	2,801	3,267	1,400	1,335	1,867	1,867	1,540	3,267
$3,775	1,859	2,789	3,253	1,394	1,329	1,859	1,859	1,534	3,253
$3,750	1,851	2,777	3,239	1,388	1,323	1,851	1,851	1,527	3,239
$3,725	1,842	2,763	3,224	1,382	1,317	1,842	1,842	1,520	3,224
$3,700	1,834	2,751	3,210	1,376	1,311	1,834	1,834	1,513	3,210
$3,675	1,826	2,739	3,196	1,370	1,306	1,826	1,826	1,506	3,196
$3,650	1,818	2,727	3,182	1,364	1,300	1,818	1,818	1,500	3,182
$3,625	1,809	2,714	3,166	1,357	1,293	1,809	1,809	1,492	3,166
$3,600	1,801	2,702	3,152	1,351	1,288	1,801	1,801	1,486	3,152
$3,575	1,793	2,690	3,138	1,345	1,282	1,793	1,793	1,479	3,138
$3,550	1,785	2,678	3,124	1,339	1,276	1,785	1,785	1,473	3,124
$3,525	1,776	2,664	3,108	1,332	1,270	1,776	1,776	1,465	3,108
$3,500	1,768	2,652	3,094	1,326	1,264	1,768	1,768	1,459	3,094
$3,475	1,760	2,640	3,080	1,320	1,258	1,760	1,760	1,452	3,080

TABLE 11—SURVIVOR'S BENEFITS (CONT'D)

Average Indexed Monthly Earnings	Worker's PIA	Surviving Spouse & 1 Child; or 2 Children	Surviving Spouse & 2 Children; or 3 Children	One Child (No Mother)	Widow or Widower Age 60	Widow or Widower FRA	Each of Two Parents	Sole Parent	Maximum Family Benefits
$3,450	1,752	2,628	3,066	1,314	1,253	1,752	1,752	1,445	3,066
$3,425	1,743	2,615	3,050	1,307	1,246	1,743	1,743	1,438	3,050
$3,400	1,735	2,603	3,036	1,301	1,241	1,735	1,735	1,431	3,036
$3,375	1,727	2,591	3,022	1,295	1,235	1,727	1,727	1,425	3,022
$3,350	1,719	2,579	3,008	1,289	1,229	1,719	1,719	1,418	3,008
$3,325	1,710	2,565	2,993	1,283	1,223	1,710	1,710	1,411	2,993
$3,300	1,702	2,553	2,979	1,277	1,217	1,702	1,702	1,404	2,979
$3,275	1,694	2,541	2,965	1,271	1,211	1,694	1,694	1,398	2,965
$3,250	1,686	2,529	2,951	1,265	1,205	1,686	1,686	1,391	2,951
$3,225	1,677	2,516	2,935	1,258	1,199	1,677	1,677	1,384	2,935
$3,200	1,669	2,504	2,921	1,252	1,193	1,669	1,669	1,377	2,921
$3,175	1,661	2,492	2,907	1,246	1,188	1,661	1,661	1,370	2,907
$3,150	1,653	2,480	2,893	1,240	1,182	1,653	1,653	1,364	2,893
$3,125	1,644	2,466	2,877	1,233	1,175	1,644	1,644	1,356	2,877
$3,100	1,636	2,454	2,863	1,227	1,170	1,636	1,636	1,350	2,863
$3,075	1,628	2,442	2,849	1,221	1,164	1,628	1,628	1,343	2,849
$3,050	1,620	2,430	2,835	1,215	1,158	1,620	1,620	1,337	2,835
$3,025	1,611	2,417	2,819	1,208	1,152	1,611	1,611	1,329	2,819
$3,000	1,603	2,405	2,805	1,202	1,146	1,603	1,603	1,322	2,805
$2,975	1,595	2,393	2,791	1,196	1,140	1,595	1,595	1,316	2,791
$2,950	1,587	2,381	2,777	1,190	1,135	1,587	1,587	1,309	2,777
$2,925	1,578	2,367	2,762	1,184	1,128	1,578	1,578	1,302	2,762
$2,900	1,570	2,355	2,748	1,178	1,123	1,570	1,570	1,295	2,748
$2,875	1,562	2,343	2,734	1,172	1,117	1,562	1,562	1,289	2,734
$2,850	1,554	2,331	2,720	1,166	1,111	1,554	1,554	1,282	2,720
$2,825	1,545	2,318	2,704	1,159	1,105	1,545	1,545	1,275	2,704
$2,800	1,537	2,306	2,690	1,153	1,099	1,537	1,537	1,268	2,690
$2,775	1,529	2,294	2,676	1,147	1,093	1,529	1,529	1,261	2,676
$2,750	1,521	2,282	2,662	1,141	1,088	1,521	1,521	1,255	2,662
$2,725	1,512	2,268	2,646	1,134	1,081	1,512	1,512	1,247	2,646
$2,700	1,504	2,256	2,632	1,128	1,075	1,504	1,504	1,241	2,632
$2,675	1,496	2,244	2,618	1,122	1,070	1,496	1,496	1,234	2,618
$2,650	1,488	2,232	2,604	1,116	1,064	1,488	1,488	1,228	2,604
$2,625	1,479	2,219	2,588	1,109	1,057	1,479	1,479	1,220	2,588
$2,600	1,471	2,207	2,574	1,103	1,052	1,471	1,471	1,214	2,574
$2,575	1,463	2,195	2,560	1,097	1,046	1,463	1,463	1,207	2,560
$2,550	1,455	2,183	2,546	1,091	1,040	1,455	1,455	1,200	2,546
$2,525	1,446	2,169	2,531	1,085	1,034	1,446	1,446	1,193	2,531
$2,500	1,438	2,157	2,517	1,079	1,028	1,438	1,438	1,186	2,517
$2,475	1,430	2,145	2,503	1,073	1,022	1,430	1,430	1,180	2,503
$2,450	1,422	2,133	2,489	1,067	1,017	1,422	1,422	1,173	2,489
$2,425	1,414	2,121	2,475	1,061	1,011	1,414	1,414	1,167	2,475
$2,400	1,405	2,108	2,459	1,054	1,005	1,405	1,405	1,159	2,459
$2,375	1,397	2,096	2,445	1,048	999	1,397	1,397	1,153	2,445
$2,350	1,389	2,084	2,431	1,042	993	1,389	1,389	1,146	2,431
$2,325	1,381	2,072	2,417	1,036	987	1,381	1,381	1,139	2,417
$2,300	1,372	2,058	2,401	1,029	981	1,372	1,372	1,132	2,401
$2,275	1,364	2,046	2,387	1,023	975	1,364	1,364	1,125	2,387
$2,250	1,356	2,034	2,373	1,017	970	1,356	1,356	1,119	2,373
$2,225	1,348	2,022	2,359	1,011	964	1,348	1,348	1,112	2,359

TABLE 11—SURVIVOR'S BENEFITS (CONT'D)

Average Indexed Monthly Earnings	Worker's PIA	Surviving Spouse & 1 Child; or 2 Children	Surviving Spouse & 2 Children; or 3 Children	One Child (No Mother)	Widow or Widower Age 60	Widow or Widower FRA	Each of Two Parents	Sole Parent	Maximum Family Benefits
$2,200	1,339	2,009	2,343	1,004	957	1,339	1,339	1,105	2,343
$2,175	1,331	1,997	2,329	998	952	1,331	1,331	1,098	2,329
$2,150	1,323	1,985	2,315	992	946	1,323	1,323	1,091	2,315
$2,125	1,315	1,973	2,301	986	940	1,315	1,315	1,085	2,301
$2,100	1,306	1,959	2,286	980	934	1,306	1,306	1,077	2,286
$2,075	1,298	1,947	2,272	974	928	1,298	1,298	1,071	2,272
$2,050	1,290	1,935	2,258	968	922	1,290	1,290	1,064	2,258
$2,025	1,282	1,923	2,244	962	917	1,282	1,282	1,058	2,244
$2,000	1,273	1,910	2,228	955	910	1,273	1,273	1,050	2,228
$1,975	1,265	1,898	2,214	949	904	1,265	1,265	1,044	2,214
$1,950	1,257	1,886	2,200	943	899	1,257	1,257	1,037	2,200
$1,925	1,249	1,874	2,186	937	893	1,249	1,249	1,030	2,186
$1,900	1,240	1,860	2,170	930	887	1,240	1,240	1,023	2,170
$1,875	1,232	1,848	2,156	924	881	1,232	1,232	1,016	2,156
$1,850	1,224	1,836	2,142	918	875	1,224	1,224	1,010	2,142
$1,825	1,216	1,824	2,128	912	869	1,216	1,216	1,003	2,128
$1,800	1,207	1,811	2,112	905	863	1,207	1,207	996	2,112
$1,775	1,199	1,799	2,098	899	857	1,199	1,199	989	2,098
$1,750	1,191	1,787	2,084	893	852	1,191	1,191	983	2,084
$1,725	1,183	1,775	2,070	887	846	1,183	1,183	976	2,070
$1,700	1,174	1,761	2,055	881	839	1,174	1,174	969	2,055
$1,675	1,166	1,749	2,041	875	834	1,166	1,166	962	2,041
$1,650	1,158	1,737	2,027	869	828	1,158	1,158	955	2,027
$1,625	1,150	1,725	2,013	863	822	1,150	1,150	949	2,013
$1,600	1,141	1,712	1,997	856	816	1,141	1,141	941	1,997
$1,575	1,133	1,700	1,983	850	810	1,133	1,133	935	1,983
$1,550	1,125	1,688	1,969	844	804	1,125	1,125	928	1,969
$1,525	1,117	1,676	1,955	838	799	1,117	1,117	922	1,955
$1,500	1,108	1,662	1,939	831	792	1,108	1,108	914	1,939
$1,475	1,100	1,650	1,925	825	787	1,100	1,100	908	1,925
$1,450	1,092	1,638	1,911	819	781	1,092	1,092	901	1,911
$1,425	1,084	1,626	1,897	813	775	1,084	1,084	894	1,897
$1,400	1,075	1,613	1,881	806	769	1,075	1,075	887	1,881
$1,375	1,067	1,601	1,867	800	763	1,067	1,067	880	1,867
$1,350	1,059	1,589	1,853	794	757	1,059	1,059	874	1,853
$1,325	1,051	1,577	1,839	788	751	1,051	1,051	867	1,839
$1,300	1,042	1,563	1,824	782	745	1,042	1,042	860	1,824
$1,275	1,034	1,551	1,810	776	739	1,034	1,034	853	1,810
$1,250	1,026	1,539	1,796	770	734	1,026	1,026	846	1,796
$1,225	1,018	1,527	1,782	764	728	1,018	1,018	840	1,782
$1,200	1,009	1,514	1,766	757	721	1,009	1,009	832	1,766
$1,175	1,001	1,502	1,752	751	716	1,001	1,001	826	1,752
$1,150	993	1,490	1,738	745	710	993	993	819	1,738
$1,125	985	1,478	1,724	739	704	985	985	813	1,724
$1,100	976	1,464	1,708	732	698	976	976	805	1,708
$1,075	968	1,452	1,694	726	692	968	968	799	1,694
$1,050	960	1,440	1,680	720	686	960	960	792	1,680
$1,025	952	1,428	1,666	714	681	952	952	785	1,666
$1,000	928	1,392	1,624	696	664	928	928	766	1,624
$975	905	1,358	1,584	679	647	905	905	747	1,584

TABLE 11—SURVIVOR'S BENEFITS (CONT'D)

Average Indexed Monthly Earnings	Worker's PIA	Surviving Spouse & 1 Child; or 2 Children	Surviving Spouse & 2 Children; or 3 Children	One Child (No Mother)	Widow or Widower Age 60	Widow or Widower FRA	Each of Two Parents	Sole Parent	Maximum Family Benefits
$950	882	1,323	1,544	662	631	882	882	728	1,544
$925	859	1,289	1,503	644	614	859	859	709	1,503
$900	835	1,253	1,461	626	597	835	835	689	1,461
$875	812	1,218	1,421	609	581	812	812	670	1,421
$850	789	1,184	1,381	592	564	789	789	651	1,381
$825	766	1,149	1,341	575	548	766	766	632	1,341
$800	742	1,113	1,299	557	531	742	742	612	1,299

TABLE 12—DISABILITY BENEFITS

Average Indexed Monthly Earnings	Disabled Worker	Disabled Worker Spouse and Children	One Child (No Spouse)	Spouse FRA-3
$9,700	3,196	4,794	1,598	1,199
$9,675	3,192	4,788	1,596	1,197
$9,650	3,189	4,784	1,595	1,196
$9,625	3,185	4,778	1,593	1,194
$9,600	3,181	4,772	1,591	1,193
$9,575	3,177	4,766	1,589	1,191
$9,550	3,173	4,760	1,587	1,190
$9,525	3,169	4,754	1,585	1,188
$9,500	3,165	4,748	1,583	1,187
$9,475	3,161	4,742	1,581	1,185
$9,450	3,158	4,737	1,579	1,184
$9,425	3,154	4,731	1,577	1,183
$9,400	3,150	4,725	1,575	1,181
$9,375	3,146	4,719	1,573	1,180
$9,350	3,142	4,713	1,571	1,178
$9,325	3,138	4,707	1,569	1,177
$9,300	3,134	4,701	1,567	1,175
$9,275	3,130	4,695	1,565	1,174
$9,250	3,127	4,691	1,564	1,173
$9,225	3,123	4,685	1,562	1,171
$9,200	3,119	4,679	1,560	1,170
$9,175	3,115	4,673	1,558	1,168
$9,150	3,112	4,668	1,556	1,167
$9,125	3,107	4,661	1,554	1,165
$9,100	3,103	4,655	1,552	1,164
$9,075	3,099	4,649	1,550	1,162
$9,050	3,096	4,644	1,548	1,161
$9,025	3,092	4,638	1,546	1,160
$9,000	3,088	4,632	1,544	1,158
$8,975	3,084	4,626	1,542	1,157
$8,950	3,081	4,622	1,541	1,155
$8,925	3,077	4,616	1,539	1,154
$8,900	3,072	4,608	1,536	1,152
$8,875	3,068	4,602	1,534	1,151
$8,850	3,065	4,598	1,533	1,149
$8,825	3,061	4,592	1,531	1,148
$8,800	3,057	4,586	1,529	1,146
$8,775	3,053	4,580	1,527	1,145
$8,750	3,050	4,575	1,525	1,144
$8,725	3,046	4,569	1,523	1,142
$8,700	3,041	4,562	1,521	1,140
$8,675	3,037	4,556	1,519	1,139
$8,650	3,034	4,551	1,517	1,138
$8,625	3,030	4,545	1,515	1,136
$8,600	3,026	4,539	1,513	1,135
$8,575	3,022	4,533	1,511	1,133

TABLE 12—DISABILITY BENEFITS (CONT'D)

Average Indexed Monthly Earnings	Disabled Worker	Disabled Worker Spouse and Children	One Child (No Spouse)	Spouse FRA-3
$8,550	3,019	4,529	1,510	1,132
$8,525	3,015	4,523	1,508	1,131
$8,500	3,011	4,517	1,506	1,129
$8,475	3,006	4,509	1,503	1,127
$8,450	3,003	4,505	1,502	1,126
$8,425	2,999	4,499	1,500	1,125
$8,400	2,995	4,493	1,498	1,123
$8,375	2,991	4,487	1,496	1,122
$8,350	2,988	4,482	1,494	1,121
$8,325	2,984	4,476	1,492	1,119
$8,300	2,980	4,470	1,490	1,118
$8,275	2,975	4,463	1,488	1,116
$8,250	2,972	4,458	1,486	1,115
$8,225	2,968	4,452	1,484	1,113
$8,200	2,964	4,446	1,482	1,112
$8,175	2,960	4,440	1,480	1,110
$8,150	2,957	4,436	1,479	1,109
$8,125	2,953	4,430	1,477	1,107
$8,100	2,949	4,424	1,475	1,106
$8,075	2,945	4,418	1,473	1,104
$8,050	2,941	4,412	1,471	1,103
$8,025	2,937	4,406	1,469	1,101
$8,000	2,933	4,400	1,467	1,100
$7,975	2,929	4,394	1,465	1,098
$7,950	2,926	4,389	1,463	1,097
$7,925	2,922	4,383	1,461	1,096
$7,900	2,918	4,377	1,459	1,094
$7,875	2,914	4,371	1,457	1,093
$7,850	2,911	4,367	1,456	1,092
$7,825	2,906	4,359	1,453	1,090
$7,800	2,902	4,353	1,451	1,088
$7,775	2,898	4,347	1,449	1,087
$7,750	2,895	4,343	1,448	1,086
$7,725	2,891	4,337	1,446	1,084
$7,700	2,887	4,331	1,444	1,083
$7,675	2,883	4,325	1,442	1,081
$7,650	2,880	4,320	1,440	1,080
$7,625	2,875	4,313	1,438	1,078
$7,600	2,871	4,307	1,436	1,077
$7,575	2,867	4,301	1,434	1,075
$7,550	2,864	4,296	1,432	1,074
$7,525	2,860	4,290	1,430	1,073
$7,500	2,856	4,284	1,428	1,071
$7,475	2,852	4,278	1,426	1,070
$7,450	2,849	4,274	1,425	1,068
$7,425	2,845	4,268	1,423	1,067

TABLE 12—DISABILITY BENEFITS (CONT'D)

Average Indexed Monthly Earnings	Disabled Worker	Disabled Worker Spouse and Children	One Child (No Spouse)	Spouse FRA-3
$7,400	2,840	4,260	1,420	1,065
$7,375	2,836	4,254	1,418	1,064
$7,350	2,833	4,250	1,417	1,062
$7,325	2,829	4,244	1,415	1,061
$7,300	2,825	4,238	1,413	1,059
$7,275	2,821	4,232	1,411	1,058
$7,250	2,818	4,227	1,409	1,057
$7,225	2,814	4,221	1,407	1,055
$7,200	2,809	4,214	1,405	1,053
$7,175	2,805	4,208	1,403	1,052
$7,150	2,802	4,203	1,401	1,051
$7,125	2,798	4,197	1,399	1,049
$7,100	2,794	4,191	1,397	1,048
$7,075	2,790	4,185	1,395	1,046
$7,050	2,787	4,181	1,394	1,045
$7,025	2,783	4,175	1,392	1,044
$7,000	2,779	4,169	1,390	1,042
$6,975	2,774	4,161	1,387	1,040
$6,950	2,771	4,157	1,386	1,039
$6,925	2,767	4,151	1,384	1,038
$6,900	2,763	4,145	1,382	1,036
$6,875	2,759	4,139	1,380	1,035
$6,850	2,756	4,134	1,378	1,034
$6,825	2,752	4,128	1,376	1,032
$6,800	2,748	4,122	1,374	1,031
$6,775	2,743	4,115	1,372	1,029
$6,750	2,740	4,110	1,370	1,028
$6,725	2,736	4,104	1,368	1,026
$6,700	2,732	4,098	1,366	1,025
$6,675	2,728	4,092	1,364	1,023
$6,650	2,725	4,088	1,363	1,022
$6,625	2,721	4,082	1,361	1,020
$6,600	2,717	4,076	1,359	1,019
$6,575	2,713	4,070	1,357	1,017
$6,550	2,709	4,064	1,355	1,016
$6,525	2,705	4,058	1,353	1,014
$6,500	2,701	4,052	1,351	1,013
$6,475	2,697	4,046	1,349	1,011
$6,450	2,694	4,041	1,347	1,010
$6,425	2,690	4,035	1,345	1,009
$6,400	2,686	4,029	1,343	1,007
$6,375	2,682	4,023	1,341	1,006
$6,350	2,679	4,019	1,340	1,005
$6,325	2,674	4,011	1,337	1,003
$6,300	2,670	4,005	1,335	1,001
$6,275	2,666	3,999	1,333	1,000

TABLE 12—DISABILITY BENEFITS (CONT'D)

Average Indexed Monthly Earnings	Disabled Worker	Disabled Worker Spouse and Children	One Child (No Spouse)	Spouse FRA-3
$6,250	2,663	3,995	1,332	999
$6,225	2,659	3,989	1,330	997
$6,200	2,655	3,983	1,328	996
$6,175	2,651	3,977	1,326	994
$6,150	2,642	3,963	1,321	991
$6,125	2,634	3,951	1,317	988
$6,100	2,626	3,939	1,313	985
$6,075	2,618	3,927	1,309	982
$6,050	2,609	3,914	1,305	978
$6,025	2,601	3,902	1,301	975
$6,000	2,593	3,890	1,297	972
$5,975	2,585	3,878	1,293	969
$5,950	2,576	3,864	1,288	966
$5,925	2,568	3,852	1,284	963
$5,900	2,560	3,840	1,280	960
$5,875	2,552	3,828	1,276	957
$5,850	2,543	3,815	1,272	954
$5,825	2,535	3,803	1,268	951
$5,800	2,527	3,791	1,264	948
$5,775	2,519	3,779	1,260	945
$5,750	2,510	3,765	1,255	941
$5,725	2,502	3,753	1,251	938
$5,700	2,494	3,741	1,247	935
$5,675	2,486	3,729	1,243	932
$5,650	2,477	3,716	1,239	929
$5,625	2,469	3,704	1,235	926
$5,600	2,461	3,692	1,231	923
$5,575	2,453	3,680	1,227	920
$5,550	2,445	3,668	1,223	917
$5,525	2,436	3,654	1,218	914
$5,500	2,428	3,642	1,214	911
$5,475	2,420	3,630	1,210	908
$5,450	2,412	3,618	1,206	905
$5,425	2,403	3,605	1,202	901
$5,400	2,395	3,593	1,198	898
$5,375	2,387	3,581	1,194	895
$5,350	2,379	3,569	1,190	892
$5,325	2,370	3,555	1,185	889
$5,300	2,362	3,543	1,181	886
$5,275	2,354	3,531	1,177	883
$5,250	2,346	3,519	1,173	880
$5,225	2,337	3,506	1,169	876
$5,200	2,329	3,494	1,165	873
$5,175	2,321	3,482	1,161	870
$5,150	2,313	3,470	1,157	867
$5,125	2,304	3,456	1,152	864

TABLE 12—DISABILITY BENEFITS (CONT'D)

Average Indexed Monthly Earnings	Disabled Worker	Disabled Worker Spouse and Children	One Child (No Spouse)	Spouse FRA-3
$5,100	2,296	3,444	1,148	861
$5,075	2,288	3,432	1,144	858
$5,050	2,280	3,420	1,140	855
$5,025	2,271	3,407	1,136	852
$5,000	2,263	3,395	1,132	849
$4,975	2,255	3,383	1,128	846
$4,950	2,247	3,371	1,124	843
$4,925	2,238	3,357	1,119	839
$4,900	2,230	3,345	1,115	836
$4,875	2,222	3,333	1,111	833
$4,850	2,214	3,321	1,107	830
$4,825	2,205	3,308	1,103	827
$4,800	2,197	3,296	1,099	824
$4,775	2,189	3,284	1,095	821
$4,750	2,181	3,272	1,091	818
$4,725	2,172	3,258	1,086	815
$4,700	2,164	3,246	1,082	812
$4,675	2,156	3,234	1,078	809
$4,650	2,148	3,222	1,074	806
$4,625	2,139	3,209	1,070	802
$4,600	2,131	3,197	1,066	799
$4,575	2,123	3,185	1,062	796
$4,550	2,115	3,173	1,058	793
$4,525	2,106	3,159	1,053	790
$4,500	2,098	3,147	1,049	787
$4,475	2,090	3,135	1,045	784
$4,450	2,082	3,123	1,041	781
$4,425	2,073	3,110	1,037	777
$4,400	2,065	3,098	1,033	774
$4,375	2,057	3,086	1,029	771
$4,350	2,049	3,074	1,025	768
$4,325	2,040	3,060	1,020	765
$4,300	2,032	3,048	1,016	762
$4,275	2,024	3,036	1,012	759
$4,250	2,016	3,024	1,008	756
$4,225	2,007	3,011	1,004	753
$4,200	1,999	2,999	1,000	750
$4,175	1,991	2,987	996	747
$4,150	1,983	2,975	992	744
$4,125	1,974	2,961	987	740
$4,100	1,966	2,949	983	737
$4,075	1,958	2,937	979	734
$4,050	1,950	2,925	975	731
$4,025	1,941	2,912	971	728
$4,000	1,933	2,900	967	725
$3,975	1,925	2,888	963	722

TABLE 12—DISABILITY BENEFITS (CONT'D)

Average Indexed Monthly Earnings	Disabled Worker	Disabled Worker Spouse and Children	One Child (No Spouse)	Spouse FRA-3
$3,950	1,917	2,876	959	719
$3,925	1,908	2,862	954	716
$3,900	1,900	2,850	950	713
$3,875	1,892	2,838	946	710
$3,850	1,884	2,826	942	707
$3,825	1,875	2,813	938	703
$3,800	1,867	2,801	934	700
$3,775	1,859	2,789	930	697
$3,750	1,851	2,777	926	694
$3,725	1,842	2,763	921	691
$3,700	1,834	2,751	917	688
$3,675	1,826	2,739	913	685
$3,650	1,818	2,727	909	682
$3,625	1,809	2,714	905	678
$3,600	1,801	2,702	901	675
$3,575	1,793	2,690	897	672
$3,550	1,785	2,678	893	669
$3,525	1,776	2,664	888	666
$3,500	1,768	2,652	884	663
$3,475	1,760	2,640	880	660
$3,450	1,752	2,628	876	657
$3,425	1,743	2,615	872	654
$3,400	1,735	2,603	868	651
$3,375	1,727	2,591	864	648
$3,350	1,719	2,579	860	645
$3,325	1,710	2,565	855	641
$3,300	1,702	2,553	851	638
$3,275	1,694	2,541	847	635
$3,250	1,686	2,529	843	632
$3,225	1,677	2,516	839	629
$3,200	1,669	2,504	835	626
$3,175	1,661	2,492	831	623
$3,150	1,653	2,480	827	620
$3,125	1,644	2,466	822	617
$3,100	1,636	2,454	818	614
$3,075	1,628	2,442	814	611
$3,050	1,620	2,430	810	608
$3,025	1,611	2,417	806	604
$3,000	1,603	2,405	802	601
$2,975	1,595	2,393	798	598
$2,950	1,587	2,381	794	595
$2,925	1,578	2,367	789	592
$2,900	1,570	2,355	785	589
$2,875	1,562	2,343	781	586
$2,850	1,554	2,331	777	583
$2,825	1,545	2,318	773	579

TABLE 12—DISABILITY BENEFITS (CONT'D)

Average Indexed Monthly Earnings	Disabled Worker	Disabled Worker Spouse and Children	One Child (No Spouse)	Spouse FRA-3
$2,800	1,537	2,306	769	576
$2,775	1,529	2,294	765	573
$2,750	1,521	2,282	761	570
$2,725	1,512	2,268	756	567
$2,700	1,504	2,256	752	564
$2,675	1,496	2,244	748	561
$2,650	1,488	2,232	744	558
$2,625	1,479	2,219	740	555
$2,600	1,471	2,207	736	552
$2,575	1,463	2,195	732	549
$2,550	1,455	2,183	728	546
$2,525	1,446	2,169	723	542
$2,500	1,438	2,157	719	539
$2,475	1,430	2,145	715	536
$2,450	1,422	2,133	711	533
$2,425	1,414	2,121	707	530
$2,400	1,405	2,108	703	527
$2,375	1,397	2,096	699	524
$2,350	1,389	2,084	695	521
$2,325	1,381	2,072	691	518
$2,300	1,372	2,058	686	515
$2,275	1,364	2,046	682	512
$2,250	1,356	2,034	678	509
$2,225	1,348	2,022	674	506
$2,200	1,339	2,009	670	502
$2,175	1,331	1,997	666	499
$2,150	1,323	1,985	662	496
$2,125	1,315	1,973	658	493
$2,100	1,306	1,959	653	490
$2,075	1,298	1,947	649	487
$2,050	1,290	1,935	645	484
$2,025	1,282	1,923	641	481
$2,000	1,273	1,910	637	477
$1,975	1,265	1,898	633	474
$1,950	1,257	1,886	629	471
$1,925	1,249	1,874	625	468
$1,900	1,240	1,860	620	465
$1,875	1,232	1,848	616	462
$1,850	1,224	1,836	612	459
$1,825	1,216	1,824	608	456
$1,800	1,207	1,811	604	453
$1,775	1,199	1,799	600	450
$1,750	1,191	1,787	596	447
$1,725	1,183	1,775	592	444
$1,700	1,174	1,761	587	440
$1,675	1,166	1,749	583	437

TABLE 12—DISABILITY BENEFITS (CONT'D)

Average Indexed Monthly Earnings	Disabled Worker	Disabled Worker Spouse and Children	One Child (No Spouse)	Spouse FRA-3
$1,650	1,158	1,737	579	434
$1,625	1,150	1,725	575	431
$1,600	1,141	1,712	571	428
$1,575	1,133	1,700	567	425
$1,550	1,125	1,688	563	422
$1,525	1,117	1,676	559	419
$1,500	1,108	1,662	554	416
$1,475	1,100	1,650	550	413
$1,450	1,092	1,638	546	410
$1,425	1,084	1,626	542	407
$1,400	1,075	1,613	538	403
$1,375	1,067	1,601	534	400
$1,350	1,059	1,589	530	397
$1,325	1,051	1,577	526	394
$1,300	1,042	1,563	521	391
$1,275	1,034	1,551	517	388
$1,250	1,026	1,539	513	385
$1,225	1,018	1,527	509	382
$1,200	1,009	1,514	505	378
$1,175	1,001	1,502	501	375
$1,150	993	1,490	497	372
$1,125	985	1,478	493	369
$1,100	976	1,464	488	366
$1,075	968	1,452	484	363
$1,050	960	1,440	480	360
$1,025	952	1,428	476	357
$1,000	928	1,392	464	348
$975	905	1,358	453	339
$950	882	1,323	441	331
$925	859	1,289	430	322
$900	835	1,253	418	313
$875	812	1,218	406	305
$850	789	1,184	395	296
$825	766	1,149	383	287
$800	742	1,113	371	278

APPENDIX B

FEDERAL EMPLOYEE TABLES

TABLE 1—GENERAL PAY SCHEDULE FOR FEDERAL GOVERNMENT WORKERS EFFECTIVE IN JANUARY 2023

These are projected numbers based on President Biden's intent to increase base pay by 4.1%

Step	Step 1	Step 2	Step 3	Step 4	Step 5	Step 6	Step 7	Step 8	Step 9	Step 10
GS-1	20,999	21,704	22,401	23,097	23,794	24,202	24,893	25,589	25,617	26,269
GS-2	23,612	24,174	24,956	25,617	25,906	26,668	27,430	28,192	28,954	29,716
GS-3	25,764	26,623	27,481	28,340	29,199	30,058	30,917	31,775	32,634	33,493
GS-4	28,921	29,885	30,849	31,813	32,777	33,741	34,705	35,669	36,633	37,597
GS-5	32,357	33,436	34,514	35,593	36,671	37,750	38,828	39,907	40,985	42,064
GS-6	36,070	37,272	38,474	39,677	40,879	42,081	43,284	44,486	45,688	46,891
GS-7	40,082	41,417	42,753	44,088	45,424	46,760	48,095	49,431	50,766	52,102
GS-8	44,389	45,869	47,348	48,827	50,306	51,786	53,265	54,744	56,223	57,703
GS-9	49,028	50,662	52,297	53,931	55,565	57,200	58,834	60,469	62,103	63,737
GS-10	53,990	55,790	57,590	59,390	61,190	62,990	64,790	66,590	68,390	70,189
GS-11	59,319	61,296	63,273	65,250	67,227	69,204	71,180	73,157	75,134	77,111
GS-12	71,099	73,470	75,840	78,210	80,581	82,951	85,321	87,692	90,062	92,432
GS-13	84,546	87,364	90,182	93,000	95,818	98,636	101,454	104,272	107,090	109,908
GS-14	99,908	103,238	106,568	109,898	113,229	116,559	119,889	123,219	126,549	129,879
GS-15	117,518	121,436	125,353	129,270	133,188	137,105	141,022	144,939	148,857	152,774

LOCALITY PAY ADJUSTMENTS

Combined national and locality pay adjustments for 54 locations in 2022 are listed below. Percentages for 2023 were not yet official at the time of printing but are expected to increase by 0.5 percent.

Albany, New York	18.68%	Kansas City, Missouri	17.67%
Albuquerque, New Mexico	17.14%	Laredo, Texas	19.85%
Atlanta, Georgia	22.63%	Las Vegas, Nevada	18.25%
Austin, Texas	18.80%	Los Angeles, California	33.61%
Birmingham, Alabama	16.81%	Miami, Florida	23.80%
Boston, Massachusetts	30.09%	Milwaukee, Wisconsin	21.32%
Buffalo, New York	20.78%	Minneapolis, Minnesota	25.49%
Burlington, Vermont	17.62%	New York City, New York	35.06%
Charlotte, North Carolina	18.06%	Omaha, Nebraska	16.93%
Chicago, Illinois	29.18%	Palm Bay, Florida	17.01%
Cincinnati, Ohio	20.94%	Philadelphia, Pennsylvania	26.95%
Cleveland, Ohio	21.25%	Phoenix, Arizona	20.84%
Colorado Springs, Colorado	18.42%	Pittsburgh, Pennsylvania	19.90%
Columbus, Ohio	20.69%	Portland, Oregon	24.34%
Corpus Christi, Texas	16.82%	Raleigh, North Carolina	20.94%
Dallas, Texas	25.68%	Rest of U.S.,	16.20%
Davenport, Iowa	17.58%	Richmond, Virginia	20.64%
Dayton, Ohio	19.93%	Sacramento, California	27.30%
Denver, Colorado	28.10%	San Antonio, Texas	17.39%
Des Moines, Iowa	16.52%	San Diego, California	30.87%
Detroit, Michigan	27.86%	San Francisco, California	42.74%
Harrisburg, Pennsylvania	17.90%	Seattle, Washington	28.28%
Hartford, Connecticut	30.20%	Saint Louis, Missouri	18.35%
Houston, Texas	33.96%	Alaska, Alaska	30.42%
Huntsville, Alabama	20.45%	Hawaii, Hawaii	20.40%
Indianapolis, Indiana	17.26%	Tucson, Arizona	17.77%
Kansas City, Missouri	17.67%	Virginia Beach, Virginia	17.18%
Laredo, Texas	19.85%	Washington DC	31.53%

TABLE 2—BASIC MONTHLY RETIREMENT
ANNUITY FOR CSRS EMPLOYEES

High-3 Annual Salary	Years of Service							
	5	10	15	20	25	30	35	40
$15,000	105	226	364	503	640	780	911	1049
16,000	112	242	391	537	683	831	972	1119
17,000	118	256	413	570	726	883	1032	1188
18,000	126	272	438	605	768	936	1093	1258
19,000	133	286	462	636	811	988	1153	1328
20,000	140	301	487	671	856	1039	1213	1398
21,000	146	317	512	705	896	1091	1275	1467
22,000	153	331	535	739	940	1143	1336	1538
23,000	160	347	560	771	983	1195	1397	1607
24,000	166	362	585	805	1025	1248	1457	1677
25,000	174	377	609	838	1069	1299	1518	1747
26,000	183	393	638	873	1110	1351	1578	1817
27,000	189	408	659	906	1153	1403	1641	1887
28,000	195	422	681	940	1196	1456	1700	1957
29,000	202	437	706	973	1239	1506	1761	2027
30,000	209	452	729	1006	1282	1558	1821	2096
31,000	216	469	755	1039	1325	1611	1881	2167
32,000	223	482	780	1074	1367	1663	1944	2235
33,000	229	498	804	1107	1411	1714	2004	2307
34,000	238	514	828	1142	1453	1767	2065	2375
35,000	244	528	853	1174	1496	1819	2125	2446
36,000	251	544	877	1208	1540	1871	2187	2518
37,000	257	559	900	1241	1581	1923	2247	2586
38,000	266	573	925	1276	1624	1974	2309	2657
39,000	272	588	949	1308	1666	2026	2367	2725

TABLE 2—BASIC MONTHLY RETIREMENT ANNUITY
FOR CSRS EMPLOYEES (CONT'D)

High-3 Annual Salary	Years of Service							
	5	10	15	20	25	30	35	40
40,000	278	605	974	1342	1708	2079	2429	2796
41,000	285	619	998	1377	1751	2131	2489	2864
42,000	293	633	1023	1410	1795	2182	2550	2936
43,000	300	650	1047	1442	1836	2234	2611	3005
44,000	307	665	1072	1477	1883	2287	2672	3075
45,000	314	678	1096	1509	1923	2338	2732	3145
46,000	321	693	1120	1545	1965	2389	2794	3214
47,000	327	709	1145	1577	2008	2442	2854	3285
48,000	333	724	1168	1611	2051	2494	2915	3354
49,000	342	739	1192	1643	2094	2545	2974	3423
50,000	348	754	1216	1676	2135	2597	3034	3479
51,000	354	767	1239	1709	2177	2648	3095	3562
52,000	362	785	1266	1744	2222	2701	3156	3634
53,000	368	799	1288	1777	2264	2753	3216	3703
54,000	375	813	1313	1812	2306	2805	3277	3772
55,000	383	829	1338	1843	2349	2856	3339	3842
56,000	391	844	1362	1878	2391	2908	3400	3914
57,000	397	860	1386	1911	2434	2961	3461	3983
58,000	403	874	1410	1945	2478	3012	3520	4052
59,000	410	889	1434	1978	2520	3063	3582	4123
60,000	418	905	1461	2013	2564	3117	3643	4193
61,000	425	920	1483	2046	2606	3168	3702	4263
62,000	431	935	1508	2079	2648	3220	3764	4332
63,000	437	949	1533	2112	2690	3273	3824	4402
64,000	446	965	1557	2147	2705	3324	3884	4473

TABLE 2—BASIC MONTHLY RETIREMENT ANNUITY
FOR CSRS EMPLOYEES (CONT'D)

High-3 Annual Salary	Years of Service							
	5	10	15	20	25	30	35	40
65,000	452	980	1583	2181	2776	3377	3947	4543
66,000	461	996	1607	2216	2820	3430	4008	4612
68,000	474	1026	1656	2282	2905	3533	4129	4753
70,000	487	1057	1704	2349	2991	3637	4251	4893
72,000	501	1086	1753	2416	3077	3742	4371	5031
74,000	517	1116	1803	2484	3162	3845	4492	5171
76,000	529	1147	1851	2550	3247	3950	4614	5310
80,000	558	1206	1948	2685	3418	4157	4859	5591
83,000	579	1251	2021	2785	3548	4313	5039	5801
86,000	601	1298	2094	2887	3676	4469	5222	6010
90,000	627	1358	2190	3020	3845	4677	5466	6290
93,000	649	1403	2264	3120	3973	4833	5646	6499
96,000	669	1448	2338	3221	4102	4989	5829	6709
100,000	697	1509	2435	3356	4272	5197	6074	6989
110,000	766	1661	2678	3691	4701	5717	6679	7689

NOTE: According to OPM's recent *Profile of Federal Civilian Non-Postal Employees* only 4% of active federal employees are under the CSRS plan while 96% are in FERS. In 2018, there were 108,000 under CSRS, compared to 2,585,000 under FERS.

The CSRS annuity is computed based on length of civil service including unused sick leave if retiring on an immediate annuity and "high-3" average pay. The high-3 average pay includes locality pay and annual premiums for standby duty and availability if applicable. Other pay such as differentials, overtime, allowances, and others are not included.

Determination of length of CSRS service - add all periods of <u>creditable</u> service, and the period represented by unused sick leave, then eliminate any fractional part of a month. The "high-3" average pay is the highest average basic pay earned during any 3 consecutive - years of service. The basic annuity cannot be more than 80 percent of "high-3" average pay unless the amount over 80 percent is due to crediting unused sick leave.

TABLE 3—BASIC MONTHLY RETIREMENT ANNUITY
FOR FERS EMPLOYEES

High-3 Annual Salary	Years of Service							
	5	10	15	20	25	30	35	40
$15,000	$70	$138	$207	$275	$345	$413	$482	$550
16,000	$74	$146	$220	$293	$365	$440	$514	$587
17,000	$78	$155	$234	$313	$391	$469	$546	$624
18,000	$82	$165	$249	$330	$413	$495	$578	$661
19,000	$86	$175	$263	$349	$436	$524	$611	$697
20,000	$90	$185	$275	$365	$460	$550	$641	$735
22,000	$102	$202	$304	$404	$504	$606	$707	$807
24,000	$112	$220	$330	$441	$550	$662	$771	$881
26,000	$120	$239	$357	$477	$597	$715	$834	$954
28,000	$129	$258	$387	$516	$641	$771	$899	$1,027
30,000	$138	$275	$413	$550	$688	$826	$964	$1,101
32,000	$146	$294	$441	$588	$736	$881	$1,027	$1,175
34,000	$155	$313	$469	$624	$780	$937	$1,093	$1,248
36,000	$164	$330	$495	$662	$826	$990	$1,156	$1,322
38,000	$175	$349	$524	$697	$873	$1,047	$1,220	$1,394
40,000	$185	$366	$550	$736	$917	$1,101	$1,286	$1,467
42,000	$193	$387	$579	$771	$964	$1,156	$1,349	$1,541
44,000	$202	$404	$606	$808	$1,011	$1,212	$1,413	$1,615
46,000	$211	$421	$632	$844	$1,055	$1,265	$1,478	$1,688
48,000	$220	$441	$662	$881	$1,101	$1,322	$1,541	$1,762
50,000	$228	$460	$688	$918	$1,148	$1,377	$1,605	$1,835
53,000	$244	$486	$731	$973	$1,216	$1,459	$1,702	$1,945
55,000	$253	$505	$757	$1,011	$1,261	$1,515	$1,767	$2,017
57,000	$263	$524	$786	$1,047	$1,308	$1,569	$1,832	$2,092
60,000	$275	$550	$826	$1,101	$1,377	$1,652	$1,927	$2,201

TABLE 3—BASIC MONTHLY RETIREMENT ANNUITY
FOR FERS EMPLOYEES (CONT'D)

High-3 Annual Salary	Years of Service							
	5	10	15	20	25	30	35	40
65,000	$299	$597	$895	$1,193	$1,492	$1,790	$2,087	$2,387
66,000	$304	$606	$909	$1,212	$1,515	$1,816	$2,121	$2,421
68,000	$313	$625	$937	$1,248	$1,561	$1,872	$2,185	$2,494
70,000	$322	$642	$964	$1,286	$1,605	$1,927	$2,250	$2,567
72,000	$330	$662	$991	$1,323	$1,652	$1,983	$2,314	$2,642
74,000	$340	$679	$1,019	$1,359	$1,698	$2,038	$2,375	$2,717
76,000	$349	$698	$1,048	$1,395	$1,508	$1,809	$2,111	$2,410
80,000	$366	$736	$1,101	$1,468	$1,836	$2,203	$2,568	$2,937
83,000	$383	$762	$1,144	$1,524	$1,904	$2,284	$2,667	$3,045
86,000	$395	$791	$1,185	$1,578	$1,973	$2,367	$2,761	$3,156
90,000	$413	$827	$1,240	$1,652	$2,065	$2,478	$2,891	$3,302
93,000	$427	$854	$1,282	$1,706	$2,134	$2,560	$2,988	$3,413
96,000	$441	$882	$1,323	$1,763	$2,203	$2,642	$3,083	$3,523
100,000	$460	$918	$1,377	$1,836	$2,293	$2,753	$3,213	$3,670
110,000	$505	$1,012	$1,516	$2,018	$2,525	$3,028	$3,533	$4,037

NOTE: Computation is based on the following:

- 1 percent of high-3 average salary for each year of service if under age 62 at separation for retirement, **OR** age 62 or older with less than 20 years of service

- 1 percent of high-3 average salary for each year of service at age 62 or older at separation with 20 or more years of service.

NOTE: 96.5% of Federal employees are part of the FERS system.

TABLE 4
AMOUNT OF INSURANCE PROTECTION UNDER THE FEDERAL
EMPLOYEES GROUP LIFE INSURANCE ACT OF 1980 (P.L. 96-427)
EFFECTIVE OCTOBER 1, 1981*

Annual Pay		Basic	Amount of Group Life Insurance				
Greater than -	But not greater than -	Insurance Amount	Age 35 and Under	Age 36 (1.9)	Age 37 (1.8)	Age 38 (1.7)	Age 39 (1.6)
$0	$8,000	$10,000	$20,000	$19,000	$ 18,000	$17,000	$16,000
8,000	9,000	11,000	22,000	20,900	19,800	18,700	17,600
9,000	10,000	12,000	24,000	22,800	21,600	20,400	19,200
10,000	11,000	13,000	26,000	24,700	23,400	22,100	20,800
11,000	12,000	14,000	28,000	26,600	25,200	23,800	22,400
12,000	13,000	15,000	30,000	28,500	27,000	25,500	24,000
13,000	14,000	16,000	32,000	30,400	28,800	27,200	25,600
14,000	15,000	17,000	34,000	32,300	30,600	28,900	27,200
15,000	16,000	18,000	36,000	34,200	32,400	30,600	28,800
16,000	17,000	19,000	38,000	36,100	34,200	32,300	30,400
17,000	18,000	20,000	40,000	38,000	36,000	34,000	32,000
18,000	19,000	21,000	42,000	39,900	37,800	35,700	33,600
19,000	20,000	22,000	44,000	41,800	39,600	37,400	35,200
20,000	21,000	23,000	46,000	43,700	41,400	39,100	36,800
21,000	22,000	24,000	48,000	45,600	43,200	40,800	38,400
22,000	23,000	25,000	50,000	47,500	45,000	42,500	40,000
23,000	24,000	26,000	52,000	49,400	46,800	44,200	41,600
24,000	25,000	27,000	54,000	51,300	48,600	45,900	43,200
25,000	26,000	28,000	56,000	53,200	50,400	47,600	44,800
26,000	27,000	29,000	58,000	55,100	52,200	49,300	46,400
27,000	28,000	30,000	60,000	57,000	54,000	51,000	48,000
28,000	29,000	31,000	62,000	58,900	55,800	52,700	49,600
29,000	30,000	32,000	64,000	60,800	57,600	54,400	51,200
30,000	31,000	33,000	66,000	62,700	59,400	56,100	52,800
31,000	32,000	34,000	68,000	64,600	61,200	57,800	54,400
32,000	33,000	35,000	70,000	66,500	63,000	59,500	56,000
33,000	34,000	36,000	72,000	68,400	64,800	61,200	57,600
34,000	35,000	37,000	74,000	70,300	66,600	62,900	59,200
35,000	36,000	38,000	76,000	72,200	68,400	64,600	60,800
36,000	37,000	39,000	78,000	74,100	70,200	63,300	62,400
37,000	38,000	40,000	80,000	76,000	72,000	68,000	64,000
38,000	39,000	41,000	82,000	77,900	73,800	69,700	65,600
39,000	40,000	42,000	84,000	79,800	75,600	71,400	67,200
40,000	41,000	43,000	86,000	81,700	77,400	73,100	68,800
41,000	42,000	44,000	88,000	83,600	79,200	74,800	70,400
42,000	43,000	45,000	90,000	85,500	81,000	76,500	72,000
43,000	44,000	46,000	92,000	87,400	82,800	78,200	73,600
44,000	45,000	47,000	94,000	89,300	84,600	79,900	75,200
45,000	46,000	48,000	96,000	91,200	86,400	81,600	76,800
46,000	47,000	49,000	98,000	93,100	88,200	83,300	78,400
47,000	48,000	50,000	100,000	95,000	90,000	85,000	80,000
48,000	49,000	51,000	102,000	96,900	91,800	86,700	81,600
49,000	50,000	52,000	104,000	98,800	93,600	88,400	83,200
50,000	51,000	53,000	106,000	100,700	95,400	90,100	84,800

**AMOUNT OF INSURANCE PROTECTION UNDER THE FEDERAL
EMPLOYEES GROUP LIFE INSURANCE ACT OF 1980 (P.L. 96-427)
EFFECTIVE OCTOBER 1, 1981***

Amount of Group Life Insurance						Amount of Group Accidental Death and Dismemberment Insurance
Age 40 (1.5)	Age 41 (1.4)	Age 42 (1.3)	Age 43 (1.2)	Age 44 (1.1)	45 and Over (1.0)	
$15,000	$14,000	$13,000	$12,000	$11,000	$10,000	$10,000
16,500	15,400	14,300	13,200	12,100	11,000	11,000
18,000	16,800	15,600	14,400	13,200	12,000	12,000
19,500	18,200	16,900	15,600	14,300	13,000	13,000
21,000	19,600	18,200	16,800	15,400	14,000	14,000
22,500	21,000	19,500	18,000	16,500	15,000	15,000
24,000	22,400	20,800	19,200	17,600	16,000	16,000
25,500	23,800	22,100	20,400	18,700	17,000	17,000
27,000	25,200	23,400	21,600	19,800	18,000	18,000
28,500	26,600	24,700	22,800	20,900	19,000	19,000
30,000	28,000	26,000	24,000	22,000	20,000	20,000
31,500	29,400	27,300	25,200	23,100	21,000	21,000
33,000	30,800	28,600	26,400	24,200	22,000	22,000
34,500	32,200	29,900	27,600	25,300	23,000	23,000
36,000	33,600	31,200	28,800	26,400	24,000	24,000
37,500	35,000	32,500	30,000	27,500	25,000	25,000
39,000	36,400	33,800	31,200	28,600	26,000	26,000
40,500	37,800	35,100	32,400	29,700	27,000	27,000
42,000	39,200	36,400	33,600	30,800	28,000	28,000
43,500	40,600	37,700	34,800	31,900	29,000	29,000
45,000	42,000	39,000	36,000	33,000	30,000	30,000
46,500	43,400	40,300	37,200	34,100	31,000	31,000
48,000	44,800	41,600	38,400	35,200	32,000	32,000
49,500	46,200	42,900	39,600	36,300	33,000	33,000
51,000	47,600	44,200	40,800	37,400	34,000	34,000
52,500	49,000	45,500	42,000	38,500	35,000	35,000
54,000	50,400	46,800	43,200	39,600	36,000	36,000
55,500	51,800	48,100	44,400	40,700	37,000	37,000
57,000	53,200	49,400	45,600	41,800	38,000	38,000
58,500	54,600	50,700	46,800	42,900	39,000	39,000
60,000	56,000	52,000	48,000	44,000	40,000	40,000
61,500	57,400	53,300	49,200	45,100	41,000	41,000
63,000	58,800	54,600	50,400	46,200	42,000	42,000
64,500	60,200	55,900	51,600	47,300	43,000	43,000
66,000	61,600	57,200	52,800	48,400	44,000	44,000
67,500	63,000	58,500	54,000	49,500	45,000	45,000
69,000	64,400	59,800	55,200	50,600	46,000	46,000
70,500	65,800	61,100	56,400	51,700	47,000	47,000
72,000	67,200	62,400	57,600	52,800	48,000	48,000
73,500	68,600	63,700	58,800	53,900	49,000	49,000
75,000	70,000	65,000	60,000	55,000	50,000	50,000
76,500	71,400	66,300	61,200	56,100	51,000	51,000
78,000	72,800	67,600	62,400	57,200	52,000	52,000
79,500	74,200	68,900	63,600	58,300	53,000	53,000

**AMOUNT OF INSURANCE PROTECTION UNDER THE FEDERAL
EMPLOYEES GROUP LIFE INSURANCE ACT OF 1980 (P.L. 96-427)
EFFECTIVE OCTOBER 1, 1981***

Annual Pay		Basic Insurance Amount	Amount of Group Life Insurance				
Greater than -	But not greater than -		Age 35 and Under	Age 36 (1.9)	Age 37 (1.8)	Age 38 (1.7)	Age 39 (1.6)
51,000	52,000	54,000	108,000	102,600	97,200	91,800	86,400
52,000	53,000	55,000	110,000	104,500	99,000	93,500	88,000
53,000	54,000	56,000	112,000	106,400	100,800	95,200	89,600
54,000	55,000	57,000	114,000	108,300	102,600	96,900	91,200
55,000	56,000	58,000	116,000	110,200	104,400	98,600	92,800
56,000	57,000	59,000	118,000	112,100	106,200	100,300	94,400
57,000	58,000	60,000	120,000	114,000	108,000	102,000	96,000
58,000	59,000	61,000	122,000	115,900	109,800	103,700	97,600
59,000	60,000	62,000	124,000	117,800	111,600	105,400	99,200
60,000	61,000	63,000	126,000	119,700	113,400	107,100	100,800
61,000	62,000	64,000	128,000	121,600	115,200	108,800	102,400
62,000	63,000	65,000	130,000	123,500	117,000	110,500	104,000
63,000	64,000	66,000	132,000	125,400	118,800	112,200	105,600
64,000	65,000	67,000	134,000	127,300	120,600	113,900	107,200
65,000	66,000	68,000	136,000	129,200	122,400	115,600	108,800
66,000	67,000	69,000	138,000	131,100	124,200	117,300	110,400
67,000	68,000	70,000	140,000	133,000	126,000	119,000	112,000
68,000	69,000	71,000	142,000	134,900	127,800	120,700	113,600
69,000	70,000	72,000	144,000	136,800	129,600	122,400	115,200
70,000	71,000	73,000	146,000	138,700	131,400	124,100	116,800
71,000	72,000	74,000	148,000	140,600	133,200	125,800	118,400
72,000	73,000	75,000	150,000	142,500	135,000	127,500	120,000
73,000	74,000	76,000	152,000	144,400	136,800	129,200	121,600
74,000	75,000	77,000	154,000	146,300	138,600	130,900	123,200
75,000	76,000	78,000	156,000	148,200	140,400	132,600	124,800
76,000	77,000	79,000	158,000	150,100	142,200	134,300	126,400
77,000	78,000	80,000	160,000	152,000	144,000	136,000	128,000
78,000	79,000	81,000	162,000	153,900	145,800	137,700	129,600
79,000	80,000	82,000	164,000	155,800	147,600	139,400	131,200
80,000	81,000	83,000	166,000	157,700	149,400	141,100	132,800
81,000	82,000	84,000	168,000	159,600	151,200	142,800	134,400
82,000	83,000	85,000	170,000	161,500	153,000	144,500	136,000
83,000	84,000	86,000	172,000	163,400	154,800	146,200	137,600
84,000	85,000	87,000	174,000	165,300	156,600	147,900	139,200
85,000	86,000	88,000	176,000	167,200	158,400	149,600	140,800
86,000	87,000	89,000	178,000	169,100	160,200	151,300	142,400
87,000	88,000	90,000	180,000	171,000	162,000	153,000	144,000
88,000	89,000	91,000	182,000	172,900	163,800	154,700	145,600
89,000	90,000	92,000	184,000	174,800	165,600	156,400	147,200
90,000	91,000	93,000	186,000	176,700	167,400	158,100	148,800

**AMOUNT OF INSURANCE PROTECTION UNDER THE FEDERAL
EMPLOYEES GROUP LIFE INSURANCE ACT OF 1980 (P.L. 96-427)
EFFECTIVE OCTOBER 1, 1981***

Amount of Group Life Insurance						Amount of Group Accidental Death and Dismemberment Insurance
Age 40 (1.5)	Age 41 (1.4)	Age 42 (1.3)	Age 43 (1.2)	Age 44 (1.1)	45 and Over (1.0)	
81,000	75,600	70,200	64,800	59,400	54,000	54,000
82,500	77,000	71,500	66,000	60,500	55,000	55,000
84,000	78,400	72,800	67,200	61,600	56,000	56,000
85,500	79,800	74,100	68,400	62,700	57,000	57,000
87,000	81,200	75,400	69,600	63,800	58,000	58,000
88,500	82,600	76,700	70,800	64,900	59,000	59,000
90,000	84,000	78,000	72,000	66,000	60,000	60,000
91,500	85,400	79,300	73,200	67,100	61,000	61,000
93,000	86,800	80,600	74,400	68,200	62,000	62,000
94,500	88,200	81,900	75,600	69,300	63,000	63,000
96,000	89,600	83,200	76,800	70,400	64,000	64,000
97,500	91,000	84,500	78,000	71,500	65,000	65,000
99,000	92,400	85,800	79,200	72,600	66,000	66,000
100,500	93,800	87,100	80,400	73,700	67,000	67,000
102,000	95,200	88,400	81,600	74,800	68,000	68,000
103,500	96,600	89,700	82,800	75,900	69,000	69,000
105,000	98,000	91,000	84,000	77,000	70,000	70,000
106,500	99,400	92,300	85,200	78,100	71,000	71,000
108,000	100,800	93,600	86,400	79,200	72,000	72,000
109,500	102,200	94,900	87,600	80,300	73,000	73,000
111,000	103,600	96,200	88,800	81,400	74,000	74,000
112,500	105,000	97,500	90,000	82,500	75,000	75,000
114,000	106400	98,800	91,200	83,600	76,000	76,000
115,500	107,800	100,100	92,400	84,700	77,000	77,000
117,000	109,200	101,400	93,600	85,800	78,000	78,000
118,500	110,600	102,700	94,800	86,900	79,000	79,000
120,000	112,000	104,000	96,000	88,000	80,000	80,000
121,500	113,400	105,300	97,200	89,100	81,000	81,000
123,000	114,800	106,600	98,400	90,200	82,000	82,000
124,500	116,200	107,900	99,600	91,300	83,000	83,000
126,000	117,600	109,200	100,800	92,400	84,000	84,000
127,500	119,000	110,500	102,000	93,500	85,000	85,000
129,000	120,400	111,800	103,200	94,600	86,000	86,000
130,500	121,800	113,100	104,400	95,700	87,000	87,000
132,000	123,200	114,400	105,600	96,800	88,000	88,000
133,500	124,600	115,700	106,800	97,900	89,000	89,000
135,000	126,000	117,000	108,000	99,000	90,000	90,000
136,500	127,400	118,300	109,200	100,100	91,000	91,000
138,000	128,800	119,600	110,400	101,200	92,000	92,000
139,500	130,200	120,900	111,600	102,300	93,000	93,000

AMOUNT OF INSURANCE PROTECTION UNDER THE FEDERAL
EMPLOYEES GROUP LIFE INSURANCE ACT OF 1980 (P.L. 96-427)
EFFECTIVE OCTOBER 1, 1981*

Annual Pay		Amount of Group Life Insurance					
Greater than -	But not greater than -	Basic Insurance Amount	Age 35 and Under	Age 36 (1.9)	Age 37 (1.8)	Age 38 (1.7)	Age 39 (1.6)
91,000	92,000	94,000	188,000	178,600	169,200	159,800	150,400
92,000	93,000	95,000	190,000	180,500	171,000	161,500	152,000
93,000	94,000	96,000	192,000	182,400	172,800	163,200	153,600
94,000	95,000	97,000	194,000	184,300	174,600	164,900	155,200
95,000	96,000	98,000	196,000	186,200	176,400	166,600	156,800
96,000	97,000	99,000	198,000	188,100	178,200	168,300	158,400
97,000	98,000	100,000	200,000	190,000	180,000	170,000	160,000
98,000	99,000	101,000	202,000	191,900	181,800	171,700	161,600
99,000	100,000	102,000	204,000	193,800	183,600	173,400	163,200
100,000	101,000	103,000	206,000	195,700	185,400	175,100	164,800
101,000	102,000	104,000	208,000	197,600	187,200	176,800	166,400
102,000	103,000	105,000	210,000	199,500	189,000	178,500	168,000
103,000	104,000	106,000	212,000	201,400	190,800	180,200	169,600
104,000	105,000	107,000	214,000	203,300	192,600	181,900	171,200
105,000	106,000	108,000	216,000	205,200	194,400	183,600	172,800
106,000	107,000	109,000	218,000	207,100	196,200	185,300	174,400
107,000	108,000	110,000	220,000	209,000	198,000	187,000	176,000
108,000	109,000	111,000	222,000	210,900	199,800	188,700	177,600
109,000	110,000	112,000	224,000	212,800	201,600	190,400	179,200
110,000	111,000	113,000	226,000	214,700	203,400	192,100	180,800
111,000	112,000	114,000	228,000	216,600	205,200	193,800	182,400
112,000	113,000	115,000	230,000	218,500	207,000	195,500	184,000
113,000	114,000	116,000	232,000	220,400	208,800	197,200	185,600
114,000	115,000	117,000	234,000	222,300	210,600	198,900	187,200
115,000	116,000	118,000	236,000	224,200	212,400	200,600	188,800
116,000	117,000	119,000	238,000	226,100	214,200	202,300	190,400
117,000	118,000	120,000	240,000	228,000	216,000	204,000	192,000
118,000	119,000	121,000	242,000	229,900	217,800	205,700	193,600
119,000	120,000	122,000	244,000	231,800	219,600	207,400	195,200
120,000	121,000	123,000	246,000	233,700	221,400	209,100	196,800
121,000	122,000	124,000	248,000	235,600	223,200	210,800	198,400
122,000	123,000	125,000	250,000	237,500	225,000	212,500	200,000
123,000	124,000	126,000	252,000	239,400	226,800	214,200	201,600
124,000	125,000	127,000	254,000	241,300	228,600	215,900	203,200
125,000	126,000	128,000	256,000	243,200	230,400	217,600	204,800
126,000	127,000	129,000	258,000	245,100	232,200	219,300	206,400
127,000	128,000	130,000	260,000	247,000	234,000	221,000	208,000
128,000	129,000	131,000	262,000	248,900	235,800	222,700	209,600
129,000	130,000	132,000	264,000	250,800	237,600	224,400	211,200
130,000	131,000	133,000	266,000	252,700	239,400	226,100	212,800
131,000	132,000	134,000	268,000	254,600	241,200	227,800	214,400
132,000	133,000	135,000	270,000	256,500	243,000	229,500	216,000
133,000	134,000	136,000	272,000	258,400	244,800	231,200	217,600
134,000	135,000	137,000	274,000	260,300	246,600	232,900	219,200
135,000	136,000	138,000	276,000	262,200	248,400	234,600	220,800
136,000	137,000	139,000	278,000	264,100	250,200	236,300	222,400
137,000	138,000	140,000	280,000	266,000	252,000	238,000	224,000
138,000	139,000	141,000	282,000	267,900	253,800	239,700	225,600
139,000	140,000	142,000	284,000	269,800	255,600	241,400	227,200
140,000	141,000	143,000	286,000	271,700	257,400	243,100	228,800

AMOUNT OF INSURANCE PROTECTION UNDER THE FEDERAL EMPLOYEES GROUP LIFE INSURANCE ACT OF 1980 (P.L. 96-427) EFFECTIVE OCTOBER 1, 1981*

Amount of Group Life Insurance						Amount of Group Accidental Death and Dismemberment Insurance
Age 40 (1.5)	Age 41 (1.4)	Age 42 (1.3)	Age 43 (1.2)	Age 44 (1.1)	45 and Over (1.0)	
141,000	131,600	122,200	112,800	103,400	94,000	94,000
142,500	133,000	123,500	114,000	104,500	95,000	95,000
144,000	134,400	124,800	115,200	105,600	96,000	96,000
145,500	135,800	126,100	116,400	106,700	97,000	97,000
147,000	137,200	127,400	117,600	107,800	98,000	98,000
148,500	138,600	128,700	118,800	108,900	99,000	99,000
150,000	140,000	130,000	120,000	110,000	100,000	100,000
151,500	141,400	131,300	121,200	111,100	101,000	101,000
153,000	142,800	132,600	122,400	112,200	102,000	102,000
154,500	144,200	133,900	123,600	113,300	103,000	103,000
156,000	145,600	135,200	124,800	114,400	104,000	104,000
157,500	147,000	136,500	126,000	115,500	105,000	105,000
159,000	148,400	137,800	127,200	116,600	106,000	106,000
160,500	149,800	139,100	128,400	117,700	107,000	107,000
162,000	151,200	140,400	129,600	118,800	108,000	108,000
163,500	152,600	141,700	130,800	119,900	109,000	109,000
165,000	154,000	143,000	132,000	121,000	110,000	110,000
166,500	155,400	144,300	133,200	122,100	111,000	111,000
168,000	156,800	145,600	134,400	123,200	112,000	112,000
169,500	158,200	146,900	135,600	124,300	113,000	113,000
171,000	159,600	148,200	136,800	125,400	114,000	114,000
172,500	161,000	149,500	138,000	126,500	115,000	115,000
174,000	162,400	150,800	139,200	127,600	116,000	116,000
175,500	163,800	152,100	140,400	128,700	117,000	117,000
177,000	165,200	153,400	141,600	129,800	118,000	118,000
178,500	166,600	154,700	142,800	130,900	119,000	119,000
180,000	168,000	156,000	144,000	132,000	120,000	120,000
181,500	169,400	157,300	145,200	133,100	121,000	121,000
183,000	170,800	158,600	146,400	134,200	122,000	122,000
184,500	172,200	159,900	147,600	135,300	123,000	123,000
186,000	173,600	161,200	148,800	136,400	124,000	124,000
187,500	175,000	162,500	150,000	137,500	125,000	125,000
189,000	176,400	163,800	151,200	138,600	126,000	126,000
190,500	177,800	165,100	152,400	139,700	127,000	127,000
192,000	179,200	166,400	153,600	140,800	128,000	128,000
193,500	180,600	167,700	154,800	141,900	129,000	129,000
195,000	182,000	169,000	156,000	143,000	130,000	130,000
196,500	183,400	170,300	157,200	144,100	131,000	131,000
198,000	184,800	171,600	158,400	145,200	132,000	132,000
199,500	186,200	172,900	159,600	146,300	133,000	133,000
201,000	187,600	174,200	160,800	147,400	134,000	134,000
202,500	189,000	175,500	162,000	148,500	135,000	135,000
204,000	190,400	176,800	163,200	149,600	136,000	136,000
205,500	191,800	178,100	164,400	150,700	137,000	137,000
207,000	193,200	179,400	165,600	151,800	138,000	138,000
208,500	194,600	180,700	166,800	152,900	139,000	139,000
210,000	196,000	182,000	168,000	154,000	140,000	140,000
211,500	197,400	183,300	169,200	155,100	141,000	141,000
213,000	198,800	184,600	170,400	156,200	142,000	142,000
214,500	200,200	185,900	171,600	157,300	143,000	143,000

* P.L. 96-427 revised the group term life insurance coverage available to civil service employees. The amounts of group term life shown in this table became effective October 1, 1981.

APPENDIX C

SERVICE MEMBERS AND VETERANS TABLES

TABLE 1—COMPARATIVE RANKS
Comparative Officer Ranks

GRADE	ARMY	AIR FORCE	MARINE CORPS	SPACE FORCE	NAVY
COMMISSIONED OFFICERS					
O-10	General	General	General	General	Admiral
O-9	Lieutenant General	Lieutenant General	Lieutenant General	Lieutenant General	Vice Admiral
O-8	Major General	Major General	Major General	Major General	Rear Admiral (Upper Half)
O-7	Brigadier General	Brigadier General	Brigadier General	Brigadier General	Rear Admiral (Lower Half)
O-6	Colonel	Colonel	Colonel	Colonel	Captain
O-5	Lieutenant Colonel	Lieutenant Colonel	Lieutenant Colonel	Lieutenant Colonel	Commander
O-4	Major	Major	Major	Major	Lieutenant Commander
O-3	Captain	Captain	Captain	Captain	Lieutenant
O-2	First Lieutenant	First Lieutenant	First Lieutenant	First Lieutenant	Lieutenant Junior Grade
O-1	Second Lieutenant	Second Lieutenant	Second Lieutenant	Second Lieutenant	Ensign
WARRANT OFFICERS					
W-5	Chief Warrant Officer 5	None	Chief Warrant Officer 5	None	USN Chief Warrant Officer 5
W-4	Chief Warrant Officer 4	None	Chief Warrant Officer 4	None	USN Chief Warrant Officer 4
W-3	Chief Warrant Officer 3	None	Chief Warrant Officer 3	None	USN Chief Warrant Officer 3
W-2	Chief Warrant Officer 2	None	Chief Warrant Officer 2	None	USN Chief Warrant Officer 2
W-1	Warrant Officer 1	None	Warrant Officer 1	None	None

Comparative Ranks—Enlisted Personnel

GRADE	ARMY	AIR FORCE	MARINE CORPS	SPACE FORCE	NAVY
E-9	Sergeant Major/ Command Sergeant Major	Chief Master Sergeant	Sergeant Major & Master Gunnery Sergeant	Chief Master Sergeant	Master Chief Petty Officer
E-8	First Sergeant & Master Sergeant	Senior Master Sergeant	First Sergeant & & Master Sergeant	Senior Master Sergeant	Senior Chief Petty Officer
E-7	Sergeant First Class	Master Sergeant. & Firstt Sergeant	Gunnery Sergeant	Master Sergeant	Chief Petty Officer
E-6	Staff Sergeant	Technical Sergeant	Staff Sergeant	Technical Sergeant	Petty Officer, First Class
E-5	Sergeant	Staff Sergeant	Sergeant	Sergeant	Petty Officer, Second Class
E-4	Corporal	Senior Airman	Corporal	Specialist 4	Petty Officer, Third Class
E-3	Private First Class	Airman, First Class	Lance Corporal	Specialist 3	Seaman
E-2	Private	Airman	Private, First Class	Specialist 2	Seaman Apprentice
E-1	Private	Airman, Basic	Private	Specialist 1	Seaman Recruit

TABLE 2—BASIC MONTHLY PAY RATES†
Effective January 1, 2023 to December 31, 2023 –
(based on 4.6% proposed increase from 2022)

ENLISTED PAY BY YEARS OF SERVICE AND GRADE

GRADE	2 OR LESS	OVER 2	OVER 3	OVER 4	OVER 6	OVER 8
E-9	$-	$-	$-	$-	$-	$-
E-8	$-	$-	$-	$-	$-	$4,957
E-7	$3,446	$3,761	$3,906	$4,095	$4,245	$4,501
E-6	$2,980	$3,280	$3,425	$3,566	$3,712	$4,042
E-5	$2,730	$2,914	$3,055	$3,200	$3,424	$3,659
E-4	$2,503	$2,632	$2,774	$2,915	$3,039	$3,039
E-3	$2,260	$2,403	$2,548	$2,548	$2,548	$2,548
E-2	$2,150	$2,150	$2,150	$2,150	$2,150	$2,150
E-1 > 4 months	$1,917	$1,917	$1,917	$1,917	$1,917	$1,917
E-1 < 4 months		$-	$-	$-	$-	$-

GRADE	OVER 10	OVER 12	OVER 14	OVER 16	OVER 18	OVER 20
E-9	$6,055	$6,192	$6,366	$6,569	$6,775	$7,103
E-8	$5,177	$5,312	$5,475	$5,652	$5,968	$6,130
E-7	$4,645	$4,901	$5,114	$5,258	$5,413	$5,473
E-6	$4,171	$4,420	$4,496	$4,551	$4,616	$4,616
E-5	$3,851	$3,874	$3,874	$3,874	$3,874	$3,874
E-4	$3,039	$3,039	$3,039	$3,039	$3,039	$3,039
E-3	$2,548	$2,548	$2,548	$2,548	$2,548	$2,548
E-2	$2,150	$2,150	$2,150	$2,150	$2,150	$2,150
E-1 > 4 months	$1,917	$1,917	$1,917	$1,917	$1,917	$1,917
E-1 < 4 months	$-	$-	$-	$-	$-	$-

GRADE	OVER 22	OVER 24	OVER 26	OVER 28	OVER 30	OVER 32
E-9	$7,382	$7,673	$8,121	$8,121	$8,527	$8,527
E-8	$6,405	$6,556	$6,931	$6,931	$7,070	$7,070
E-7	$5,675	$5,782	$6,193	$6,193	$6,193	$6,193
E-6	$4,616	$4,616	$4,616	$4,616	$4,616	$4,616
E-5	$3,874	$3,874	$3,874	$3,874	$3,874	$3,874
E-4	$3,039	$3,039	$3,039	$3,039	$3,039	$3,039
E-3	$2,548	$2,548	$2,548	$2,548	$2,548	$2,548
E-2	$2,150	$2,150	$2,150	$2,150	$2,150	$2,150
E-1 > 4 months	$1,917	$1,917	$1,917	$1,917	$1,917	$1,917
E-1 < 4 months	$-	$-	$-	$-	$-	$-

TABLE 2—BASIC MONTHLY PAY RATES† (CONT'D)
Effective January 1, 2023 to December 31, 2023 –
(based on 4.6% proposed increase from 2022)

GRADE	OVER 34	OVER 36	OVER 38	OVER 40
E-9	$8,954	$8,954	$9,402	$9,402
E-8	$7,070	$7,070	$7,070	$7,070
E-7	$6,193	$6,193	$6,193	$6,193
E-6	$4,616	$4,616	$4,616	$4,616
E-5	$3,874	$3,874	$3,874	$3,874
E-4	$3,039	$3,039	$3,039	$3,039
E-3	$2,548	$2,548	$2,548	$2,548
E-2	$2,150	$2,150	$2,150	$2,150
E-1 > 4 months	$1,917	$1,917	$1,917	$1,917
E-1 < 4 months	$-	$-	$-	$-

OFFICERS PAY BY YEARS OF SERVICE AND GRADE

GRADE	2 OR LESS	OVER 2	OVER 3	OVER 4	OVER 6	OVER 8
O-10	$-	$-	$-	$-	$-	$-
O-9	$-	$-	$-	$-	$-	$-
O-8	$12,170	$12,570	$12,834	$12,909	$13,238	$13,789
O-7	$10,113	$10,582	$10,800	$10,974	$11,286	$11,595
O-6	$7,669	$8,426	$8,978	$8,978	$9,012	$9,398
O-5	$6,393	$7,202	$7,701	$7,794	$8,105	$8,292
O-4	$5,517	$6,385	$6,812	$6,907	$7,302	$7,726
O-3	$4,850	$5,498	$5,933	$6,470	$6,780	$7,120
O-2	$4,191	$4,773	$5,497	$5,683	$5,799	$5,799
O-1	$3,637	$3,787	$4,577	$4,577	$4,577	$4,577

GRADE	OVER 10	OVER 12	OVER 14	OVER 16	OVER 18	OVER 20
O-10)	$-	$-	$-	$-	$-	$17,842
O-9	$-	$-	$-	$-	$-	$17,201
O-8	$13,918	$14,442	$14,593	$15,044	$15,696	$16,299
O-7	$11,953	$12,309	$12,667	$13,789	$14,738	$14,738
O-6	$9,450	$9,450	$9,987	$10,936	$11,493	$12,050
O-5	$8,701	$9,002	$9,390	$9,983	$10,265	$10,545
O-4	$8,255	$8,666	$8,951	$9,116	$9,210	$9,210
O-3	$7,340	$7,702	$7,891	$7,891	$7,891	$7,891
O-2	$5,799	$5,799	$5,799	$5,799	$5,799	$5,799
O-1	$4,577	$4,577	$4,577	$4,577	$4,577	$4,577

TABLE 2—BASIC MONTHLY PAY RATES† (CONT'D)
Effective January 1, 2023 to December 31, 2023 –
(based on 4.6% proposed increase from 2022)

GRADE	OVER 22	OVER 24	OVER 26	OVER 28	OVER 30	OVER 32
O-10	$17,842	$17,842	$17,842	$17,842	$17,842	$17,842
O-9	$17,449	$17,807	$17,842	$17,842	$17,842	$17,842
O-8	$16,700	$16,700	$16,700	$16,700	$17,119	$17,119
O-7	$14,738	$14,738	$14,813	$14,813	$15,111	$15,111
O-6	$12,368	$12,689	$13,310	$13,310	$13,577	$13,577
O-5	$10,862	$10,862	$10,862	$10,862	$10,862	$10,862
O-4	$9,210	$9,210	$9,210	$9,210	$9,210	$9,210
O-3	$7,891	$7,891	$7,891	$7,891	$7,891	$7,891
O-2	$5,799	$5,799	$5,799	$5,799	$5,799	$5,799
O-1	$4,577	$4,577	$4,577	$4,577	$4,577	$4,577

GRADE	OVER 34	OVER 36	OVER 38	OVER 40
O-10	$17,842	$17,842	$17,842	$17,842
O-9	$17,842	$17,842	$17,842	$17,842
O-8	$17,546	$17,546	$17,546	$17,546
O-7	$15,111	$15,111	$15,111	$15,111
O-6	$13,577	$13,577	$13,577	$13,577
O-5	$10,862	$10,862	$10,862	$10,862
O-4	$9,210	$9,210	$9,210	$9,210
O-3	$7,891	$7,891	$7,891	$7,891
O-2	$5,799	$5,799	$5,799	$5,799
O-1	$4,577	$4,577	$4,577	$4,577

COMMISSIONED OFFICERS WITH OVER FOUR YEARS OF ACTIVE SERVICE AS A WARRANT OFFICER OR ENLISTED BY YEARS OF SERVICE AND GRADE

GRADE	2 OR LESS	OVER 2	OVER 3	OVER 4	OVER 6	OVER 8
O-3E	$-	$-	$-	$6,470	$6,780	$7,120
O-2E	$-	$-	$-	$5,683	$5,799	$5,984
O-1E	$-	$-	$-	$4,577	$4,887	$5,068

GRADE	OVER 10	OVER 12	OVER 14	OVER 16	OVER 18	OVER 20
O-3E	$7,340	$7,702	$8,007	$8,183	$8,421	$8,421
O-2E	$6,296	$6,536	$6,716	$6,716	$6,716	$6,716
O-1E	$5,253	$5,434	$5,683	$5,683	$5,683	$5,683

TABLE 2—BASIC MONTHLY PAY RATES† (CONT'D)
Effective January 1, 2023 to December 31, 2023 –
(based on 4.6% proposed increase from 2022)

GRADE	OVER 22	OVER 24	OVER 26	OVER 28	OVER 30	OVER 32
O-3E	$8,421	$8,421	$8,421	$8,421	$8,421	$8,421
O-2E	$6,716	$6,716	$6,716	$6,716	$6,716	$6,716
O-1E	$5,683	$5,683	$5,683	$5,683	$5,683	$5,683

GRADE	OVER 34	OVER 36	OVER 38	OVER 40
O-3E	$8,421	$8,421	$8,421	$8,421
O-2E	$6,716	$6,716	$6,716	$6,716
O-1E	$5,683	$5,683	$5,683	$5,683

WARRANT OFFICER BY YEARS OF SERVICE AND GRADE

GRADE	2 OR LESS	OVER 2	OVER 3	OVER 4	OVER 6	OVER 8
W-5	$-	$-	$-	$-	$-	$-
W-4	$5,012	$5,391	$5,546	$5,699	$5,961	$6,221
W-3	$4,577	$4,768	$4,964	$5,028	$5,232	$5,636
W-2	$4,050	$4,434	$4,551	$4,633	$4,894	$5,303
W-1	$3,555	$3,938	$4,041	$4,258	$4,515	$4,894

GRADE	OVER 10	OVER 12	OVER 14	OVER 16	OVER 18	OVER 20
W-5	$-	$-	$-	$-	$-	$8,912
W-4	$6,483	$6,877	$7,225	$7,554	$7,824	$8,088
W-3	$6,056	$6,254	$6,483	$6,718	$7,142	$7,429
W-2	$5,506	$5,705	$5,949	$6,139	$6,311	$6,518
W-1	$5,071	$5,319	$5,562	$5,753	$5,929	$6,143

GRADE	OVER 22	OVER 24	OVER 26	OVER 28	OVER 30	OVER 32
W-5	$9,364	$9,701	$10,073	$10,073	$10,578	$10,578
W-4	$8,474	$8,792	$9,154	$9,154	$9,337	$9,337
W-3	$7,599	$7,781	$8,029	$8,029	$8,029	$8,029
W-2	$6,653	$6,760	$6,760	$6,760	$6,760	$6,760
W-1	$6,143	$6,143	$6,143	$6,143	$6,143	$6,143

GRADE	OVER 34	OVER 36	OVER 38	OVER 40
W-5	$11,106	$11,106	$11,663	$11,663
W-4	$9,337	$9,337	$9,337	$9,337
W-3	$8,029	$8,029	$8,029	$8,029
W-2	$6,760	$6,760	$6,760	$6,760
W-1	$6,143	$6,143	$6,143	$6,143

TABLE 3—CSRS MILITARY MONTHLY RETIREMENT PAY
Effective January 1, 2023 to December 31, 2023

Note that 2023 are based from proposed 2023 pay increases 4.6%.

RETIREES WHO ENTERED SERVICE BEFORE SEPTEMBER 8, 1980

Pay Grade* Over	50.00% 20 Yrs	52.50% 21 Yrs	55.00% 22 Yrs	57.50% 23 Yrs	60.00% 24 Yrs	62.50% 25 Yrs	65.00% 26 Yrs	67.50% 27 Yrs	70.00% 28 Yrs	72.50% 29 Yrs	75.00% 30 Yrs
O-10	$10,193	$10,703	$11,213	$11,723	$12,232	$12,741	$13,252	$13,761	$14,271	$14,780	$15,290
O-9	$8,601	$9,031	$9,461	$9,891	$10,321	$10,751	$11,181	$11,611	$12,042	$12,471	$12,901
O-8	$8,149	$8,557	$8,964	$9,372	$9,779	$10,187	$10,594	$11,002	$11,409	$11,817	$12,225
O-7	$7,369	$7,737	$8,107	$8,475	$8,843	$9,211	$9,580	$9,949	$10,317	$10,685	$11,054
O-6	$6,025	$6,326	$6,627	$6,929	$7,230	$7,531	$7,832	$8,134	$8,435	$8,736	$9,037
O-5	$5,273	$5,536	$5,800	$6,064	$6,327	$6,591	$6,854	$7,118	$7,382	$7,645	$7,909
O-4	$4,606	$4,836	$5,066	$5,296	$5,526	$5,756	$5,986	$6,216	$6,448	$6,678	$6,908
O-3	$3,946	$4,143	$4,340	$4,538	$4,734	$4,932	$5,130	$5,326	$5,524	$5,721	$5,918
O-2	$2,900	$3,045	$3,189	$3,335	$3,479	$3,624	$3,770	$3,914	$4,060	$4,204	$4,349
O-1	$2,289	$2,403	$2,518	$2,632	$2,747	$2,861	$2,975	$3,090	$3,204	$3,319	$3,433
W-5	$4,456	$4,679	$4,902	$5,124	$5,347	$5,570	$5,793	$6,016	$6,238	$6,461	$6,684
W-4	$4,044	$4,246	$4,449	$4,651	$4,852	$5,055	$5,257	$5,459	$5,661	$5,864	$6,066
W-3	$3,714	$3,901	$4,086	$4,272	$4,457	$4,643	$4,828	$5,015	$5,200	$5,386	$5,572
W-2	$3,259	$3,421	$3,585	$3,748	$3,911	$4,073	$4,236	$4,399	$4,563	$4,725	$4,888
W-1	$3,072	$3,225	$3,379	$3,532	$3,686	$3,840	$3,993	$4,146	$4,300	$4,454	$4,608
E-9	$3,552	$3,729	$3,907	$4,085	$4,262	$4,439	$4,617	$4,795	$4,973	$5,149	$5,327
E-8	$3,065	$3,219	$3,371	$3,525	$3,678	$3,831	$3,984	$4,138	$4,291	$4,444	$4,597
E-7	$2,736	$2,873	$3,010	$3,146	$3,283	$3,420	$3,557	$3,694	$3,830	$3,967	$4,105
E-6	$2,309	$2,424	$2,539	$2,654	$2,770	$2,885	$3,000	$3,116	$3,231	$3,346	$3,462
E-5	$1,937	$2,034	$2,131	$2,228	$2,324	$2,421	$2,519	$2,615	$2,712	$2,809	$2,906

* See Table 1, for rank corresponding to pay grade.

TABLE 4—RATES OF DEPENDENCY AND INDEMNITY COMPENSATION— SURVIVING SPOUSE AND CHILDREN OF VETERAN WHO DIED BEFORE JANUARY 1, 1993*
38 USC §1311
Effective December 1, 2022 through December 1, 2023

Pay Grade*	Surviving Spouse** Only	Surviving Spouse** and 1 Child	Surviving Spouse** and 2 Children	Extra Per Child
COMMISSIONED OFFICERS				
O-10	$3,336,41 ***	$3,781.69	$4,137.85	$356.16
O-9	$3,041.87	$3,510.73	$3,866.89	$356.16
O-8	$2,843.80	$3,328.51	$3,684.67	$356.16
O-7	$2,589.11	$3,094.21	$3,450.37	$356.16
O-6	$2,398.78	$2,919.11	$3,275.27	$356.16
O-5	$2,127.39	$2,669.44	$3,025.60	$356.16
O-4	$1,942.36	$2,499.22	$2,855.38	$356.16
O-3	$1,823,83	$2,390.18	$2,746.34	$356.16
O-2	$1,706.81	$2,282.52	$2,638.68	$356.16
O-1	$1,680.22	$2,230.46	$2,586.62	$356.16
WARRANT OFFICERS				
W-4	$1,868.85	$2,431.59	$2,787.75	$356.16
W-3	$1,765.96	$2,336.94	$2,693.10	$356.16
W-2	$1,715.80	$2,290.79	$2,646.95	$356.16
W-1	$11,650.22	$2,230.46	$2,586.62	$356.16
ENLISTED PERSONNEL				
E-9	$1,780.12 ****	$2,349.95	$2,706.11	$356.16
E-8	$1,706.80	$2,282.52	$2,638.68	$356.16
E-7	$1,616,74	$2,199.67	$2,555.83	$356.16
E-6	$1,562.73	$2,149.97	$2,506.13	$356.16
E-5	$1,562.73	$2,149.97	$2,506.13	$356.16
E-4	$1,562.73	$2,149.97	$2,506.13	$356.16
E-3	$1,562.73	$2,149.97	$2,506.13	$356.16
E-2	$1,562.73	$2,149.97	$2,506.13	$356.16
E-1	$1,562.73	$2,149.97	$2,506.13	$356.16

*   See Table 1, for rank corresponding to pay grade. Surviving spouses of veterans who die after January 1, 1994, receive a basic monthly DIC rate of $1,562.73 in 2023. Each child is entitled to $356.16 a month in 2023. Surviving spouses of veterans who die before January 1, 1993, are entitled to the benefits listed above or the new formula, whichever provides the greater benefits.

**   Monthly rate for the surviving spouse is increased by $356.16 if he or she is a patient in a nursing home or is virtually helpless or blind.

*** If the veteran served as Chairman of the Joint Chiefs of Staff or Chief of Staff to one of the services, the surviving spouse's rate shall be $3,580.80

**** The payment to a surviving spouse alone if the veteran was E-9 Special Capacity as Sergeant Major of the Army, Senior Enlisted Advisor of the Navy, Chief Master Sergeant of the Air Force, or Sergeant Major of the Marine Corps, or Master Chief Petty Officer of the Coast Guard is $1,921.60

TABLE 5—RATES OF DEPENDENCY AND INDEMNITY COMPENSATION—PARENTS
Effective December 1, 2021 through November 30, 2022

2023 DIC Payments For Sole Surviving Parent

Yearly Income	Monthly Rate	Amount of Decrease
$800	$774	None
$900	$765	0.08
$1,000	$757	0.08
$1,100	$748	0.08
$1,200	$739	0.08
$1,300	$730	0.08
$1,400	$722	0.08
$1,500	$713	0.08
$1,600	$704	0.08
$1,700	$696	0.08
$1,800	$687	0.08
$1,900	$678	0.08
$2,000	$670	0.08
$2,100	$661	0.08
$2,200	$652	0.08
$2,300	$644	0.08
$2,400	$635	0.08
$2,500	$626	0.08
$2,600	$617	0.08
$2,700	$609	0.08
$2,800	$600	0.08
$2,900	$591	0.08
$3,000	$583	0.08
$3,100	$574	0.08
$3,200	$565	0.08
$3,300	$557	0.08
$3,400	$548	0.08
$3,500	$539	0.08
$3,600	$530	0.08
$3,700	$522	0.08
$3,800	$513	0.08
$3,900	$504	0.08

TABLE 5—RATES OF DEPENDENCY AND INDEMNITY
COMPENSATION—PARENTS
Effective December 1, 2021 through November 30, 2022 (cont'd)

Yearly Income	Monthly Rate	Amount of Decrease
$4,000	$496	0.08
$4,100	$487	0.08
$4,200	$478	0.08
$4,300	$470	0.08
$4,400	$461	0.08
$4,500	$452	0.08
$4,600	$443	0.08
$4,700	$435	0.08
$4,800	$426	0.08
$4,900	$417	0.08
$5,000	$409	0.08
$5,100	$400	0.08
$5,200	$391	0.08
$5,300	$383	0.08
$5,400	$374	0.08
$5,500	$365	0.08
$5,600	$357	0.08
$5,700	$348	0.08
$5,800	$339	0.08
$5,900	$330	0.08
$6,000	$322	0.08
$6,100	$313	0.08
$6,200	$304	0.08
$6,300	$296	0.08
$6,400	$287	0.08
$6,500	$278	0.08
$6,600	$270	0.08
$6,700	$261	0.08
$6,800	$252	0.08
$6,900	$243	0.08
$7,000	$235	0.08
$7,100	$226	0.08
$7,200	$217	0.08

TABLE 5—RATES OF DEPENDENCY AND INDEMNITY COMPENSATION—PARENTS
Effective December 1, 2021 through November 30, 2022 (cont'd)

Yearly Income	Monthly Rate	Amount of Decrease
$7,300	$209	0.08
$7,400	$200	0.08
$7,500	$191	0.08
$7,600	$183	0.08
$7,700	$174	0.08
$7,800	$165	0.08
$7,900	$157	0.08
$8,000	$148	0.08
$8,100	$139	0.08
$8,200	$130	0.08
$8,300	$122	0.08
$8,400	$113	0.08
$8,500	$104	0.08
$8,600	$96	0.08
$8,700	$87	0.08
$8,800	$78	0.08
$8,900	$70	0.08
$9,000	$61	0.08
$9,100	$52	0.08
$9,200	$43	0.08
$9,300	$35	0.08
$9,400	$26	0.08
$9,500	$17	0.08
$9,600	$9	0.08
$9,637	$5	0.08

2023 DIC Payments When One of Two Living Parents Resides Alone

Yearly Income	Monthly Rate	Amount of Decrease
$800	$561	None
$900	$552	0.08
$1,000	$544	0.08
$1,100	$535	0.08
$1,200	$526	0.08

TABLE 5—RATES OF DEPENDENCY AND INDEMNITY COMPENSATION—PARENTS
Effective December 1, 2021 through November 30, 2022 (cont'd)

Yearly Income	Monthly Rate	Amount of Decrease
$1,300	$517	0.08
$1,400	$509	0.08
$1,500	$500	0.08
$1,600	$491	0.08
$1,700	$483	0.08
$1,800	$474	0.08
$1,900	$465	0.08
$2,000	$457	0.08
$2,100	$448	0.08
$2,200	$439	0.08
$2,300	$430	0.08
$2,400	$422	0.08
$2,500	$413	0.08
$2,600	$404	0.08
$2,700	$396	0.08
$2,800	$387	0.08
$2,900	$378	0.08
$3,000	$370	0.08
$3,100	$361	0.08
$3,200	$352	0.08
$3,300	$343	0.08
$3,400	$335	0.08
$3,500	$326	0.08
$3,600	$317	0.08
$3,700	$309	0.08
$3,800	$300	0.08
$3,900	$291	0.08
$4,000	$283	0.08
$4,100	$274	0.08
$4,200	$265	0.08
$4,300	$257	0.08
$4,400	$248	0.08
$4,500	$239	0.08

TABLE 5—RATES OF DEPENDENCY AND INDEMNITY COMPENSATION—PARENTS
Effective December 1, 2021 through November 30, 2022 (cont'd)

Yearly Income	Monthly Rate	Amount of Decrease
$4,600	$230	0.08
$4,700	$222	0.08
$4,800	$213	0.08
$4,900	$204	0.08
$5,000	$196	0.08
$5,100	$187	0.08
$5,200	$178	0.08
$5,300	$170	0.08
$5,400	$161	0.08
$5,500	$152	0.08
$5,600	$143	0.08
$5,700	$135	0.08
$5,800	$126	0.08
$5,900	$117	0.08
$6,000	$109	0.08
$6,100	$100	0.08
$6,200	$91	0.08
$6,300	$83	0.08
$6,400	$74	0.08
$6,500	$65	0.08
$6,600	$57	0.08
$6,700	$48	0.08
$6,800	$39	0.08
$6,900	$30	0.08
$7,000	$22	0.08
$7,100	$13	0.08
$7,187	$5	0.08
7,188 to 16,780	$5	None

2023 DIC Payments When Living Parents Reside Together or With Another Spouse

Yearly Income	Monthly Rate	Amount of Decrease
$1,000	$528	None
$1,100	$525	0.03

TABLE 5—RATES OF DEPENDENCY AND INDEMNITY COMPENSATION—PARENTS
Effective December 1, 2021 through November 30, 2022 (cont'd)

Yearly Income	Monthly Rate	Amount of Decrease
$1,200	$521	0.04
$1,300	$515	0.05
$1,400	$509	0.06
$1,500	$502	0.06
$1,600	$495	0.07
$1,700	$487	0.07
$1,800	$478	0.08
$1,900	$470	0.08
$2,000	$461	0.08
$2,100	$452	0.08
$2,200	$443	0.08
$2,300	$435	0.08
$2,400	$426	0.08
$2,500	$417	0.08
$2,600	$409	0.08
$2,700	$400	0.08
$2,800	$391	0.08
$2,900	$383	0.08
$3,000	$374	0.08
$3,100	$365	0.08
$3,200	$357	0.08
$3,300	$348	0.08
$3,400	$339	0.08
$3,500	$330	0.08
$3,600	$322	0.08
$3,700	$313	0.08
$3,800	$304	(cont'd)
$3,900	$296	0.08
$4,000	$287	0.08
$4,100	$278	0.08
$4,200	$270	0.08
$4,300	$261	0.08
$4,400	$252	0.08

**TABLE 5—RATES OF DEPENDENCY AND INDEMNITY
COMPENSATION—PARENTS**
Effective December 1, 2021 through November 30, 2022 (cont'd)

Yearly Income	Monthly Rate	Amount of Decrease
$4,500	$243	0.08
$4,600	$235	0.08
$4,700	$226	0.08
$4,800	$217	0.08
$4,900	$209	0.08
$5,000	$200	0.08
$5,100	$191	0.08
$5,200	$183	0.08
$5,300	$174	0.08
$5,400	$165	0.08
$5,500	$157	0.08
$5,600	$148	0.08
$5,700	$139	0.08
$5,800	$130	0.08
$5,900	$122	0.08
$6,000	$113	0.08
$6,100	$104	0.08
$6,200	$96	0.08
$6,300	$87	0.08
$6,400	$78	0.08
$6,500	$70	0.08
$6,600	$61	0.08
$6,700	$52	0.08
$6,800	$43	0.08
$6,900	$35	0.08
$7,000	$26	0.08
$7,100	$17	0.08
$7,200	$9	0.08
$7,237	$5	0.08
7,238 to 22,555	$5	None

If entitled to Aid & Attendance allowance add $419 to the monthly rate.

APPENDIX D

MEDICARE TABLES

TABLE OF HOSPITAL INSURANCE (PART A) BENEFITS
Effective January 1, 2023

Service	Benefit	Medicare Pays	A Person Pays
HOSPITALIZATION Semiprivate room and board, general nursing, and other hospital services and supplies.	First 60 days	All but $1,600	$1,600
	61st to 90th day	All but $400 a day	$400 a day
	91st to 150th day[1]	All but $800 a day	$800 a day
	Beyond 150 days	Nothing	All costs
SKILLED NURSING FACILITY CARE Semiprivate room and board, skilled nursing and rehabilitative services and other services and supplies.[2]	First 20 days	100% of approved Amount	Nothing
	Additional 80 days	All but $200 a day	$200 a day
	Beyond 100 days	Nothing	All costs
POST-HOSPITAL HOME HEALTH CARE Part-time or intermittent skilled care, home health aid services, durable medical equipment and supplies and other services.	First 100 days in spell of illness	100% of approved amount; 80% of approved amount for durable medical equipment	Nothing for services; 20% of approved amount for durable medical equipment
HOSPICE CARE Pain relief, symptom management and support services for the terminally ill.	For as long as the doctor certifies need	All but limited costs for outpatient drugs and inpatient respite care	Limited costs for outpatient drugs and inpatient respite care
BLOOD When furnished by a hospital or skilled nursing facility during covered stay.	Unlimited if medically necessary	All but first 3 pints per calendar year	For first 3 pints[3]

1. 60 Reserve days benefit may be used only once in a lifetime.

2. Neither Medicare nor private Medigap insurance will pay for most nursing home care.

3. Blood paid for or replaced under Part B of Medicare during the calendar year does not have to be paid for or replaced under Part A.

TABLE OF MEDICAL INSURANCE (PART B) BENEFITS
Effective January 1, 2023

Service	Benefit	Medicare Pays	Patient Pays
MEDICAL EXPENSE Doctors' services, inpatient and outpatient medical and services surgical services and supplies, physical and speech therapy, diagnostic tests, durable medical equipment and other services.	Unlimited if medically necessary.	80% of approved amount (after $226 deductible). Reduced to 50% for most outpatient mental health services.	$226 deductible,[1] plus 20% of approved amount and limited charges above approved amount.[2]
CLINICAL LABORATORY SERVICES Blood tests, urinalyses, and more.	Unlimited if medically necessary.	Generally 100% of approved amount.	Nothing for services.
HOME HEALTH CARE Part-time or intermittent skilled care, home health aide services, durable medical equipment and supplies and other services.	Unlimited but covers only home health care not covered by Hospital Insurance (Part A).	100% of approved amount; 80% of approved amount for durable medical equipment.	Nothing for services; 20% of approved amount for durable medical equipment.
OUTPATIENT HOSPITAL TREATMENT Services for the diagnosis or treatment of illness or injury.	Unlimited if medically necessary.	Medicare payment to hospital based on hospital cost.	20% of whatever the hospital charges (after $226 deductible).[1]
BLOOD	Unlimited if medically necessary.	80% of approved amount (after $226 deductible and starting with 4th pint).	For first 3 pints plus 20% of approved amount for additional pints (after $226 deductible).[3]
AMBULATORY SURGICAL SERVICES	Unlimited if medically necessary.	80% of predetermined amount (after $226 deductible).	$226 deductible, plus 20% of predetermined amount.

1. Once a person has $226 of expense for covered services in 2023, the Part B deductible does not apply to any further covered services received for the rest of the year.

2. A person pays for charges higher than the amount approved by Medicare unless the doctor or supplier agrees to accept Medicare's approved amount as the total charge for services rendered.

3. Blood paid for or replaced under Part A of Medicare during the calendar year does not have to be paid for or replaced under Part B.

APPENDIX E
WHAT MEDICARE DOES NOT COVER

Some of these items can be covered by Medicare under certain conditions. See text for more detailed information on items covered under special conditions.

- Acupuncture

- Most chiropractic services but does cover

  - manual manipulation of the spine by a chiropractor or other qualified provider if medically necessary to correct a subluxation (when one or more of the bones of your spine move out of position). Medicare doesn't cover other services or tests a chiropractor orders, including X-rays, massage therapy, and acupuncture.

- Cosmetic surgery (except after an accident)

  - Medicare covers breast prostheses for breast reconstruction after mastectomy because of breast cancer.

- Custodial care (Long-term care)

- Concierge care (also called concierge medicine, retainer-based medicine, boutique medicine, platinum practice, or direct care).

- Most dental care

- Dentures

- Most prescription drugs and medicines taken at home (except through Medicare Part D)

- Eyeglasses and eye examinations for prescribing, fitting, or changing eyeglasses

  - Medicare DOES cover cataract surgery that implants an interocular lens.

- First three pints of blood (unless the patient donates it, or someone donates it for them)

- Routine foot care

- Massage therapy

- Coverage received outside of the United States (there ARE exceptions)

- Hearing aids and hearing examinations for prescribing, fitting, or changing hearing aids

- Homemaker services

- Meals delivered to the home

- Naturopaths' services

- Immunizations and vaccinations, except vaccinations against pneumococcal pneumonia, hepatitis B, or influenza virus; and immunizations required because of an injury or immediate risk of infection

- Injections which can be self-administered

- Non-emergency transportation

- Nursing care on full-time basis in the home

- Orthopedic shoes unless they are part of a leg brace and are included in the orthopedist's charge

- Personal convenience items that the patient requests, such as a phone, radio, or television in the room at a hospital or skilled nursing facility

- Physical examinations that are routine and tests directly related to such examinations

- Private nurse care

- Private hospital rooms

- Services performed by immediate relatives or members of the patient's household

- Services that are not reasonable and necessary

- Services for which neither the patient nor another party on his behalf has a legal obligation to pay

- Supportive devices for the feet

- War claims occurring after the effective date of the patient's current Medicare coverage

- Copies of X-Rays

- Services payable by any of the following:

  - Workers' Compensation (including black lung benefits)

  - Liability or no-fault insurance

  - Employer group health plans for employees and their spouses

  - Employer group health plans for people entitled to Medicare solely on the basis of end-stage renal disease

  - Another government program

APPENDIX F

EXAMPLE OF MEDICARE BENEFITS

Mr. Smith is sixty-nine years old, retired, and covered by Hospital Insurance (Part A), Medical Insurance (Part B), and Prescription Drug Insurance (Part D). After suffering a heart attack at his home in January 2023, he is taken to the hospital for surgery. Mr. Smith spends fifteen days in the hospital and seven days in a skilled nursing facility for therapy. When he returns home, he requires the services of a nurse and physical therapist for a short time to continue treatment.

	Total cost:	Mr. Smith pays:	Medicare pays
Hospital bill: *(Patient pays the deductible amount)*	$3,500	$1,600	$1,900
Ambulance to hospital: *(Patient pays 20% plus amount higher than customary charge)*	$200	$40	$160
Surgeon: *(Patient pays $226 deductible and 20% of the remaining bill; Medicare pays 80% of the bill after the deductible)*	$2,000	$580.80	$1,419.20
Anesthesiologist: *(Patient pays 20%; Medicare pays 80%)*	$300	$60	$240
Skilled Nursing Facility: *(Patient pays nothing for first 20 days, then $194.50 a day for 80 days)*	$1,050	$0	$1,050
Home visits by nurse: *(Medicare pays for nurse required for medical reasons)*	$90	$0	$90
Home visits by physical therapist:	$80	$0	$80
Equipment rental (wheelchair): *(Patient pays 20%; Medicare pays 80%)*	$85	$17	$68
Prescription drugs at home: *(Assuming standard $400 deductible).*	$200	$200	$0
Total Cost:	**$7,505**	**2,497.80**	**$5,007.20**

APPENDIX G

MEDICARE ADMINISTRATIVE CONTRACTORS AS OF OCTOBER 2022

MAC Jurisdiction	Processes Part A & Part B Claims for the following states:	MAC
DME A	Connecticut, Delaware, District of Columbia, Maine, Maryland, Massachusetts, New Hampshire, New Jersey, New York, Pennsylvania, Rhode Island, Vermont	Noridian Healthcare Solutions, LLC
DME B	Illinois, Indiana, Kentucky, Michigan, Minnesota, Ohio, Wisconsin	CGS Administrators, LLC
DME C	Alabama, Arkansas, Colorado, Florida, Georgia, Louisiana, Mississippi, New Mexico, North Carolina, Oklahoma, South Carolina, Tennessee, Texas, Virginia, West Virginia, Puerto Rico, U.S. Virgin Islands	CGS Administrators, LLC
DME D	Alaska, Arizona, California, Hawaii, Idaho, Iowa, Kansas, Missouri, Montana, Nebraska, Nevada, North Dakota, Oregon, South Dakota, Utah, Washington, Wyoming, American Samoa, Guam, Northern Marianas Island	Noridian Healthcare Solutions, LLC
5	Iowa, Kansas, Missouri, Nebraska	Noridian Healthcare Solutions, LLC
6	Illinois, Minnesota, Wisconsin **HH + H for the following states: Alaska, American Samoa, Arizona, California, Guam, Hawaii, Idaho, Michigan, Minnesota, Nevada, New Jersey, New York, Northern Mariana Islands, Oregon, Puerto Rico, US Virgin Islands, Wisconsin and Washington	National Government Services, Inc.
8	Indiana, Michigan	Wisconsin Physicians Service Government Health Administrators
15	Kentucky, Ohio **HH + H for the following states: Delaware, District of Columbia, Colorado, Iowa, Kansas, Maryland, Missouri, Montana, Nebraska, North Dakota, Pennsylvania, South Dakota, Utah, Virginia, West Virginia, and Wyoming	CGS Administrators, LLC
E	California, Hawaii, Nevada, American Samoa, Guam, Northern Mariana Islands	Noridian Healthcare Solutions, LLC
F	Alaska, Arizona, Idaho, Montana, North Dakota, Oregon, South Dakota, Utah, Washington, Wyoming	Noridian Healthcare Solutions, LLC
H	Arkansas, Colorado, New Mexico, Oklahoma, Texas, Louisiana, Mississippi	Novitas Solutions, Inc.
J	Alabama, Georgia, Tennessee	Palmetto GBA, LLC

MAC Jurisdiction	Processes Part A & Part B Claims for the following states:	MAC
K	Connecticut, New York, Maine, Massachusetts, New Hampshire, Rhode Island, Vermont **HH + H for the following states: Connecticut, Maine, Massachusetts, New Hampshire, Rhode Island, and Vermont	National Government Services, Inc.
L	Delaware, District of Columbia, Maryland, New Jersey, Pennsylvania (includes Part B for counties of Arlington and Fairfax in Virginia and the city of Alexandria in Virginia)	Novitas Solutions, Inc.
M	North Carolina, South Carolina, Virginia, West Virginia (excludes Part B for the counties of Arlington and Fairfax in Virginia and the city of Alexandria in Virginia) **HH + H for the following states: Alabama, Arkansas, Florida, Georgia, Illinois, Indiana, Kentucky, Louisiana, Mississippi, New Mexico, North Carolina, Ohio, Oklahoma, South Carolina, Tennessee, and Texas	Palmetto GBA, LLC
N	Florida, Puerto Rico, U.S. Virgin Islands	First Coast Service Options, Inc.

** Also Processes Home Health and Hospice claims

APPENDIX H

MEDICARE QUALITY INNOVATION NETWORK (QIN) QUALITY IMPROVEMENT ORGANIZATIONS (QIOs)

The QIO Program is one of the largest federal programs dedicated to improving health quality for Medicare beneficiaries. The program is an integral part of the U.S. Department of Health and Human (HHS) Services' National Quality Strategy for providing better care and better health at lower cost. By law, the mission of the QIO Program is to improve the effectiveness, efficiency, economy, and quality of services delivered to Medicare beneficiaries. Based on this statutory charge, and CMS's program experience, CMS identifies the core functions of the QIO Program as:

- Improving quality of care for beneficiaries;

- Protecting the integrity of the Medicare Trust Fund by ensuring that Medicare pays only for services and goods that are reasonable and necessary and that are provided in the most appropriate setting; and

- Protecting beneficiaries by expeditiously addressing individual complaints, such as beneficiary complaints; provider-based notice appeals; violations of the Emergency Medical Treatment and Labor Act (EMTALA); and other related responsibilities as articulated in QIO-related law.

A Quality Improvement Organization (QIO) is a group of health quality experts, clinicians, and consumers organized to improve the quality of care delivered to people with Medicare.

There are two types of QIOs that work under the direction of the Centers for Medicare & Medicaid Services in support of the QIO Program:

Beneficiary and Family Centered Care (BFCC)-QIOs

BFCC-QIOs help Medicare beneficiaries exercise their right to high-quality health care. They manage all beneficiary complaints and quality of care reviews to ensure consistency in the review process while taking into consideration local factors important to beneficiaries and their families. They also handle cases in which beneficiaries want to appeal a health care provider's decision to discharge them from the hospital or discontinue other types of services. Two designated BFCC-QIOs serve all 50 states and three territories, which are grouped into ten regions.

Quality Innovation Network (QIN)-QIOs

The QIO Program's 14 Quality Innovation Network-QIOs (QIN-QIOs) bring Medicare beneficiaries, providers, and communities together in data-driven initiatives that increase patient safety, make communities healthier, better coordinate post-hospital care, and improve clinical quality. By serving regions of two to six states each, QIN-QIOs are able to help best practices for better care spread more quickly, while still accommodating local conditions and cultural factors.

HOW TO LOCATE A QIN-QIO

Locate a QIO | qioprogram.org

Beneficiary and Family Centered Care (BFCC)-QIOs can be located at the following link when putting in the appropriate state or territory. People with Medicare and their representatives who have a complaint or quality of care concern can get help from their Beneficiary and Family Centered Care (BFCC)-QIO (BFCC-QIO). BFCC-QIOs manage all complaints and quality of care reviews, EMTALA and other types of case review for people with Medicare and their representatives.

https://qioprogram.org/locate-your-bfcc-qio

Locate a Quality Inprovement Network

Quality Innovation Network (QIN)-QIOs are responsible for working with health care providers and the community on data-driven projects to improve patient safety, reduce harm and improve clinical care at the local level. Health care providers, stakeholders or partners interested in learning more about these projects, use the dropdown below to find the QIN-QIO for the appropriate area.

https://qioprogram.org/locate-your-qin-qio

APPENDIX I

Reserved

APPENDIX J

DURABLE MEDICAL EQUIPMENT (DME) MEDICARE ADMINISTRATIVE CONTRACTOR (MAC) JURISDICTIONS

As required by Section 911 of the Medicare Prescription Drug, Improvement and Modernization Act of 2003 (MMA), CMS was required to re-procure the DME MAC contracts every five (5) years. The DME MACs are responsible for processing Medicare Durable Medical Equipment, Orthotics, and Prosthetics (DMEPOS) claims for a defined geographic area or "jurisdiction." CMS has established four DME MAC jurisdictions that perform numerous functions on behalf of Medicare beneficiaries and establish relationships with suppliers of Durable Medical Equipment, Prosthetics, Orthotics and Supplies (DMEPOS).

The table below identifies the four DME MAC Jurisdictions along with their assigned geographic states, territories and districts.

DME MAC TABLE	
Jurisdiction	**States**
DME MAC A	NORIDIAN: Connecticut, Delaware, District of Columbia, Maine, Maryland, Massachusetts, New Hampshire, New Jersey, New York, Pennsylvania, Rhode Island and Vermont
DME MAC B	CGS: Illinois, Indiana, Kentucky, Michigan, Minnesota, Ohio and Wisconsin
DME MAC C	CGS: Alabama, Arkansas, Colorado, Florida, Georgia, Louisiana, Mississippi, New Mexico, North Carolina, Oklahoma, Puerto Rico, South Carolina, Tennessee, Texas, U.S. Virgin Islands, Virginia and West Virginia
DME MAC D	NORIDIAN: Alaska, American Samoa, Arizona, California, Guam, Hawaii, Idaho, Iowa, Kansas, Missouri, Montana, Nebraska, Nevada, North Dakota, Northern Mariana Islands, Oregon, South Dakota, Utah, Washington and Wyoming

APPENDIX K

INSURANCE COUNSELING — GENERAL INFORMATION

In addition to insurance counseling, these state health insurance assistance program offices can answer questions about Medicare bills, Medigap policies, and Medicare plan choices.

State Program	Phone
Alabama SHIP	1-800-243-5463
Alaska SHIP	1-800-478-6065
Arizona SHIP	1-800-432-4040
Arkansas SHIIP	1-800-224-6330
California HICAP	1-800-434-0222
Colorado SHIP	1-888-696-7213
Connecticut CHOICES	1-800-994-9422
Delaware ELDERinfo	1-800-336-9500
District of Columbia HICP	202-739-0668
Florida SHINE	1-800-963-5337
Georgia	1-800-669-8387
Hawaii	1-888-875-9229
Idaho SHIBA	1-800-247-4422
Illinois SHIP	1-800-548-9043
Indiana SHIIP	1-800-452-4800
Iowa SHIIP	1-800-351-4664
Kansas SHICK	1-800-860-5260
Kentucky SHIP	1-877-293-7447
Louisiana SHIIP	1-800-259-5301
Maine SHIP	1-877-353-3771
Maryland SHIP	1-800-243-3425
Massachusetts SHINE	1-800-AGE-INFO (243-4636)
Michigan MMAP	1-800-803-7174
Minnesota SHIP	1-800-333-2433
Mississippi SHIP	1-800-948-3090
Missouri Claim	1-800-390-3330
Montana SHIP	1-800-551-3191
Nebraska SHIIP	1-800-234-7119
Nevada SHIP	1-800-307-4444
New Hampshire SHIP	1-866-634-9412

State Program	Phone
New Jersey SHIP	1-800-792-8820
New Mexico	1-505-476-4799
New York HICAP	1-800-701-0501
North Carolina SHIIP	1-800-443-9354
North Dakota SHIC	1-888-575-6611
Ohio OSHIIP	1-800-686-1578
Oklahoma SHICP	1-800-763-2828
Oregon SHIBA	1-800-722-4134
Pennsylvania APPRISE	1-800-783-7067
Rhode Island SHIP	1-401-462-4444
South Carolina I-CARE	1-800-868-9095
South Dakota SHINE	1-800-536-8197
Tennessee SHIP	1-877-801-0044
Texas HICAP	1-800-252-9240
Utah SHIP	1-800-541-7735
Vermont SHIP	1-800-642-5119
Virginia VICAP	1-800-552-3402
Virgin Islands VI SHIP	1-340-772-7368
Washington SHIBA	1-800-562-6900
West Virginia WV SHIP	1-877-987-4463
Wisconsin SHIP	1-800-242-1060
Wyoming WSHIP	1-800-856-4398

State Program	Website
Alabama SHIP	http://alabamaageline.gov/assets/ship-brochure.pdf
Alaska SHIP	http://dhss.alaska.gov/dsds/Pages/medicare/default.aspx
Arizona SHIP	https://des.az.gov/services/aging-and-adult/state-health-insurance-assistance-program-ship
Arkansas SHIIP	https://insurance.arkansas.gov/pages/consumer-services/senior-health/
California HICAP	https://www.aging.ca.gov/(X(1)S(0rry5ak3zo2fblkjrryyaozx))/hicap/default.aspx?AspxAutoDetectCookieSupport=1
Colorado SHIP	https://www.colorado.gov/dora/division-insurance
Connecticut CHOICES	http://www.ct.gov/agingservices/cwp/view.asp?a=2513&q=313032
Delaware ELDERinfo	http://www.delawareinsurance.gov/DMAB/
District of Columbia HICP	https://dcoa.dc.gov/service/health-insurance-counseling

State Program	Website
Florida SHINE	http://www.floridashine.org/
Georgia	http://aging.dhs.georgia.gov/georgiacares
Hawaii	http://www.hawaiiship.org/
Idaho SHIBA	https://doi.idaho.gov/shiba/
Illinois SHIP	http://www.illinois.gov/aging/ship/Pages/default.aspx
Indiana SHIIP	http://www.in.gov/idoi/2495.htm
Iowa SHIIP	http://www.shiip.state.ia.us/
Kansas SHICK	http://www.kdads.ks.gov/commissions/commission-on-aging/medicare-programs/shick
Kentucky SHIP	http://www.chfs.ky.gov/dail/ship.htm
Louisiana SHIIP	http://www.ldi.la.gov/SHIIP/
Maine SHIP	http://www.maine.gov/dhhs/oads/community-support/ship.html
Maryland SHIP	http://www.aging.maryland.gov/pages/statehealthinsuranceprogram.aspx
Massachusetts SHINE	http://www.mass.gov/elders/healthcare/shine/overview-of-councils-on-aging.html
Michigan MMAP	http://mmapinc.org/
Minnesota SHIP	http://www.mnaging.net/en/Advisor/InsFinBenefits/Health%20Insurance%20Counseling.aspx
Mississippi SHIP	http://www.mdhs.state.ms.us/aging-adult-services/programs-daas/services-for-seniors/
Missouri Claim	http://missouriclaim.org/
Montana SHIP	http://dphhs.mt.gov/sltc/services/aging/SHIP/ship
Nebraska SHIIP	http://www.doi.nebraska.gov/shiip/
Nevada SHIP	http://adsd.nv.gov/Programs/Seniors/SHIP/SHIP_Prog/
New Hampshire SHIP	http://www.servicelink.nh.gov/medicare/index.htm
New Jersey SHIP	http://www.state.nj.us/humanservices/doas/services/ship/
New Mexico	http://www.nmaging.state.nm.us/
New York HICAP	http://www.aging.ny.gov/HealthBenefits/Index.cfm
North Carolina SHIIP	http://www.ncdoi.com/SHIIP/Default.aspx
North Dakota SHIC	http://www.nd.gov/ndins/shic/
Ohio OSHIIP	http://www.insurance.ohio.gov/Consumer/Pages/ConsumerTab2.aspx
Oklahoma SHICP	http://www.ok.gov/oid/Consumers/Information_for_Seniors/SHIP.html
Oregon SHIBA	http://www.oregon.gov/dcbs/insurance/SHIBA/Pages/shiba.aspx
Pennsylvania APPRISE	http://www.aging.pa.gov/aging-services/insurance/Pages/default.aspx
Rhode Island SHIP	http://www.dea.ri.gov/insurance/
South Carolina I-CARE	http://aging.sc.gov/contact/Pages/SHIPContactInformation.aspx
South Dakota SHINE	http://www.shiine.net/

State Program	Website
Tennessee SHIP	http://www.tn.gov/
Texas HICAP	http://www.tdi.texas.gov/consumer/hicap/
Utah SHIP	https://daas.utah.gov/
Vermont SHIP	http://asd.vermont.gov/services/ship
Virginia VICAP	http://www.vda.virginia.gov/vicap2.asp
Virgin Islands VI SHIP	http://ltg.gov.vi/vi-ship-medicare.html
Washington SHIBA	https://www.insurance.wa.gov/contact-shiba
West Virginia WV SHIP	http://www.wvship.org/
Wisconsin SHIP	https://www.dhs.wisconsin.gov/aging/index.htm
Wyoming WSHIP	http://www.wyomingseniors.com/services/wyoming-state-health-insurance-information-program

APPENDIX L

STATE AGENCIES ON AGING

Note: State agencies on aging can provide information and assistance on a variety of Medicare, insurance, and elder care issues.

Alabama
Department of Senior Services
RSA Plaza
201 Monroe Street, Suite 350
Montgomery AL 36104
(877) 425-2242
(334) 242-5743
http://www.alabamaageline.govAgeline@adss.alabama.gov

Alaska
Commission of Aging
Department of Health and Social Services
150 Third Street, No. 103
P.O. Box 110693
Juneau, AK 99811-0693
(907) 465-3250
http://dhss.alaska.gov/acoa/Pages/default.aspx

Arizona
Department of Economic Security
Aging and Adult Administration
1789 West Jefferson Street, #950A
Phoenix, AZ 85007
(602) 542-4446
https://www.azdes.gov/daas/

Arkansas
Division of Aging & Adult Services
P.O. Box 1437, Slot S-530
700 Main Street, 5th Floor, S530
Little Rock, AR 72203-1437
(501) 682-2441
http://www.daas.ar.gov/

California
Department of Aging
1300 National Drive, Number 200
Sacramento, CA 95834-1992
(916) 419-7500
https://www.aging.ca.gov/

Colorado
Division of Aging and Adult Services
Department of Human Services
1575 Sherman Street, 10th Floor
Denver, CO 80203-1714
(303) 866-2800
https://www.agingcare.com/

Connecticut
State Department on Again
55 Farmington Avenue, 12th Floor
Hartford, CT 06105-3730
Phone (860)424-5274
Toll Free (in State) 1-866-218-6631
Fax (860)424-5301
http://www.ct.gov/agingservices

Delaware
Services for Aging & Adults with
Physical Disabilities
Dept. of Health & Social Services
Herman M. Holloway, Sr. Campus
Main Administration Building, First Floor Annex
1901 N. DuPont Highway
New Castle, DE 19720
1-800-223-9074
Fax: (302) 255-4445
http://dhss.delaware.gov/dhss/dsaapd/index.html

District of Columbia
Office on Aging
500 K Street, NE
Washington, DC 20002
(202) 724-5622
http://dcoa.dc.gov/

Florida
Department of Elder Affairs
4040 Esplanade Way, Suite 315
Tallahassee, FL 32399-7000
Phone: 850-414-2000
Fax: 850-414-2004
TDD: 850-414-2001
Email: information@elderaffairs.org
http://elderaffairs.state.fl.us/index.php

Georgia

DHS Division of Aging Services
Two Peachtree Street, NW
33rd Floor
Atlanta, Georgia 30303-3142
Phone: 404.657.5258
Fax: 404.657.5285
Toll Free: 866-55-AGING or 866-552-4464
http://aging.dhs.georgia.gov/

Hawaii

Executive Office on Aging
250 South Hotel Street, Suite 406
Honolulu, HI 96813-2831
(808) 586-0100
http://health.hawaii.gov/eoa/eoa@doh.hawaii.gov

Idaho

Commission on Aging
341 W. Washington
Boise, Idaho 83702
Phone: (208) 334-3833
or 1-800-926-2588
http://www.idahoaging.com

Illinois

Department on Aging
Main Office:
One Natural Resources Way, Suite 100
Springfield, IL 62702-1271
1-800-252-8966
FAX: 217-785-4477
Chicago Office:
Michael A. Bilandic Building (also known as the
State of Illinois Building)
160 North LaSalle St., Suite N-700
Chicago, IL 60601-3117
312-814-2630
FAX: 312-814-2916
Senior HelpLine/Benefit Access Program 1-800-
252-8966
aging.ilsenior@illinois.gov
http://www.state.il.us/aging/2aaa/aaa-main.htm

Indiana

FSSA Division of Aging
402 W. Washington St. W454, P.O. Box 7083,
MS21
Indianapolis, IN 46207-7083
(888) 672-0002
(317) 232-7858
http://www.in.gov/fssa/2329.htm

Iowa

Department of Elder Affairs
Jessie M. Parker Building
510 East 12th St., Suite 2
Des Moines, IA 50319-9025
(515) 725-3333
https://www.iowaaging.gov/

Kansas

Department on Aging
New England Building
503 South Kansas Avenue
Topeka, KS 66603-3404
(785) 296-4986
Toll Free: 800-432-3535 (in Kansas only)
https://www.kdads.ks.gov/contact-us

Kentucky

Department for Aging & Independent Living
Cabinet for Health & Family Services
275 East Main Street, 3W-F
Frankfort, KY 40621
(502) 564-6930
http://chfs.ky.gov/dail/

Louisiana

Governor's Office of Elderly Affairs
Mailing Address: P.O. Box 61, Baton Rouge, LA
70821-0061
Office: 525 Florida Street, Baton Rouge, LA
(225) 342-7100

Maine

Office of Aging and Disability Services
Maine Department of Health and Human Services
SHS 11
Augusta, Maine 04333
Voice: (207) 287-9200 or (800) 262-2232
Fax: (207)287-9229
TTY: Maine relay 711
http://www.maine.gov/dhhs/oads/

Maryland

Department of Aging
301 West Preston Street, Suite 1007
Baltimore, MD 21201-2374
(410) 767-1100
http://www.aging.maryland.gov/

Massachusetts

Executive Office of Elder Affairs
One Ashburton Place, 5th Floor
Boston, MA 02108
617-727-7750
800-243-4636 (nationwide)
800-872-0166 (TTY)
617-727-9368 (FAX)
http://www.mass.gov/elders/

Michigan

Office of Services to the Aging
P.O. Box 30676
300 East Michigan Avenue, Third Floor
Lansing, MI 48909-8176
(517) 373-8230

Minnesota

Board on Aging
Department of Human Services
Minnesota Board on Aging
Mailing Address: P.O. Box 64976, St. Paul, MN
55164-0976 Office: Elmer L. Andersen Human
Services Building, 540 Cedar Street St. Paul, MN
55155
(800) 882-6262
(651) 431-2500
http://www.mnaging.net/
mba@state.mn.us

Mississippi

Council on Aging
Division of Aging & Adult Services
750 N. State Street
Jackson, MS 39202
(800) 948-3090
(601) 359-4929
http://www.mdhs.state.ms.us/aging-adult-
services/

Missouri

Division of Senior & Disability Services
Department of Health & Senior Sciences
P.O. Box 570
Jefferson City, MO 65102-0570
(800) 235-5503
(573) 526-3626
http://www.mdhs.state.ms.us/aging-adult-
services/

Montana

Office on Aging
Senior and Long-Term Care Division
Department of Public Health and Human Services
111 Sanders Street
P.O. Box 4210
Helena, MT 59604
(888) 706-1535 (406) 444-7788
http://dphhs.mt.gov/SLTC

Nebraska

State Unit on Aging
P.O. Box 95026
301 Centennial Mall - South
Lincoln, NE 68509-5026
(800) 942-7830
http://dhhs.ne.gov/medicaid/Aging/pages/
AgingHome.aspx

Nevada

Division for Aging Services
Department of Health & Human Services
3416 Goni Road, Building D-132
Carson City, NV 89706
(775) 687-4210 x226
http://adsd.nv.gov/

New Hampshire

Bureau of Elderly & Adult Services
129 Pleasant Street
Concord, NH 03301-3852
(603) 271-4394
http://www.dhhs.nh.gov/DCBCS/beas/index.
htm

New Jersey
Division of Aging Services
New Jersey Department of Human Services
240 West State Street
P.O. Box 715
Trenton, NJ 08625-0715 (800) 792-8820
(609) 292-4027
http://www.state.nj.us/humanservices/doas/
home/

New Mexico
Aging and Long-Term Services Department
2550 Cerrillos Road
Santa Fe, NM 87505
Mailing Address
P.O. Box 27118
Santa Fe, New Mexico 87502-7118
(800) 432-2080
(505) 476-4799
http://www.nmaging.state.nm.us/

New York
State Office for the Aging
Two Empire State Plaza
Albany, NY 12223-1251
(800) 342-9871
(518) 474-7012
http://www.aging.ny.gov/

North Carolina
Division of Aging & Adult Services
2101 Mail Service Center
101 Blair Drive
Raleigh, NC 27699-2101
(919) 855-4840
http://www.ncdhhs.gov/divisions/daas

North Dakota
Aging Services Division
Department of Human Services
1237 West Divide Avenue #6
Bismarck, ND 58501
(800) 755-8521
(701) 328-4601

Ohio
Ohio Department of Aging
246 N. High St./1st Fl.
Columbus, OH 43215-2406 (800) 266-4346
(614) 466-5500
http://aging.ohio.gov/home/

Oklahoma
Aging Services Division
Department of Human Services
2401 N.W. 23rd St., Suite 40
Oklahoma City, OK 73107-2442
(405) 521-2281
http://www.okdhs.org/programsandservices/
aging/

Oregon
Seniors & People with Disabilities
Department of Human Services
500 Summer Street, N.E., E12
Salem, OR 97301-1073
(800) 282-8096
(503) 945-5811
http://www.oregon.gov/dhs/spwpd/pages/
index.aspx

Pennsylvania
Department of Aging
Forum Place
555 Walnut Street, 5th Floor
Harrisburg, PA 17101-1919
(717) 783-1550
http://www.aging.pa.gov/Pages/default.aspx

Puerto Rico
Governor's Office for Elderly Affairs
P.O. Box 50063
Old San Juan Station
San Juan, PR 00902
(787) 721-6121 (Local)
(787) 725-4300 (Fax)

Rhode Island
Department of Elderly Affairs
Louis Pasteur Building, 2nd Floor
57 Howard Avenue
Cranston, RI 02920 (401) 462-0501
http://www.dea.ri.gov/

South Carolina
Lieutenant Governor's Office on Aging
Bureau of Senior Services
1301 Gervais Street
Suite 350
Columbia, SC 29201
(803) 734-9900
(800) 868=9095
http://aging.sc.gov/Pages/default.aspx

South Dakota
Office of Adult Services & Aging
Department of Social Services
700 Governor's Drive
Pierre, SD 57501-2291
(605) 773-3165
https://dss.sd.gov/asa/

Tennessee
Commission on Aging & Disability
Andrew Jackson Building
500 Deaderick Street, Ninth Floor
Nashville, TN 37243-0860
(615) 741-2056
https://www.tn.gov/aging/

Texas
Department of Aging & Disability Services
John H. Winters Human Services Complex
701 West 51st Street
P.O. Box 149030
Austin, TX 78714-9030
(512) 438-3030
http://www.dads.state.tx.us/

Utah
Division of Aging & Adult Services
Department of Human Services
195 North 1950 West
Salt Lake City, UT 84116
(801) 538-3910
(800) 371-7897
http://www.dads.state.tx.us/

Vermont
Agency of Human Services
Department of Disabilities, Aging &
Independent Living
Weeks Building
103 South Main Street
Waterbury, VT 05671-1601
(802) 241-2401
http://dail.vermont.gov/

Virginia
Department for the Aging and Rehabilitative
Services
1610 Forest Avenue, Suite 100
Henrico, VA 23229
(800) 552-3402
(804) 662-9333
http://www.vda.virginia.gov/

Washington
Aging & Long-Term Support Administration
Department of Social and Health Services
P.O. Box 45600
Olympia, WA 98504-5600 (mailing)
640 Woodland Square Loop SE
Lacey, WA 98503-1045 (physical)
(360) 725-2300
https://www.dshs.wa.gov/altsa

West Virginia
Bureau of Senior Services
1900 Kanawha Boulevard, East
3003 Town Center Mall, Third Level
Charleston, WV 25305-0160
(304) 558-3317
(877) 987-3646
https://www.dshs.wa.gov/altsa

Wisconsin
Bureau of Aging & Disability Resources
Department of Health & Family Services
One West Wilson Street, Room 450
P.O. Box 7851
Madison, WI 53707-7851
(888) 701-1251
(608) 266-1865
https://www.dhs.wisconsin.gov/aging/index.htm

Wyoming
Division on Aging
Department of Health
6101 Yellowstone Road, Suite 259B
Cheyenne, WY 82002-0710
(800) 442-2766
(307) 777-7986
http://www.health.wyo.gov/aging/index.html

APPENDIX M

SOCIAL SECURITY FORMS AVAILABLE ON THE SOCIAL SECURITY WEBSITE

SS-5	Application for a Social Security Card
SSA-827	Authorization to Disclose Information to the Social Security Administration
SSA-3820-BK	Disability Report - Child
IRS W-4V	Voluntary Withholding Request
CMS-40B	Application for Enrollment in Medicare - Part B (Medical Insurance)
CMS-L564	Request for Employment Information
CMS-L564S	Solicitud De Información Sobre El Empleo
HA-85	Request to Withdraw a Hearing Request
HA-86	Discontinue Prior Editions
HA-86-SP	SOLICITUD PARA RETIRAR UNA PETICIÓN PARA REVISIÓN CON EL CONSEJO DE APELACIONES
HA-501-U5	Request for Hearing by Administrative Law Judge
HA-510	Waiver of Timely Written Notice of Hearing
HA-510-SP	Renuncia a la notificación escrita oportuna de la audiencia
HA-520	Request for Review of Hearing Decision/Order
HA-539	Notice Regarding Substitution of Party Upon Death of Claimant
HA-539-SP	Aviso Sobre La Substitución De La Parte Interesada Tras El Fallecimiento Del Reclamante
HA-4608	Waiver of Your Right to Personal Appearance Before an Administrative Law Judge
HA-4631	Claimant's Recent Medical Treatment
HA-4632	Claimant's Medications
HA-4633	Claimant's Work Background
IRS SS-4	Application for Employer Identification Number
Online	Adult Disability Report
Online	Appeal a Recent Medical Decision
Online	Apply for Disability Benefits
Online	Apply for Retirement, Spouse's or Medicare Benefits
Online	Apply Online for Extra Help with Medicare Prescription Drug Plan Costs
Online	Change Address or Telephone Number
Online	Child Disability Report
Online	Get a Replacement Medicare Card
Online	Representative Payee Accounting Report

Online	Request a Form SSA-1099/1042 (Benefit Statement) for tax or other purposes
Online	Request a Proof of Social Security Benefits Letter
Online	Request Special Notices for the Blind or Visually Impaired
Online	Sign Up For or Change Direct Deposit
SS-5-FS	Application for a Social Security Card (Outside of the U.S.)
SS-5-SP	Solicitud para una tarjeta de Seguro Social
SSA-1-BK	Application for Retirement Insurance Benefits
SSA-1-BK-SP	Solicitud Para Beneficios De Seguro Por Jubliación
SSA-2-BK	Application for Wife's or Husband's Insurance Benefits
SSA-2-BK-SP	Solicitud Para Beneficios De Seguro Como Cónyuge
SSA-3	Marriage Certification
SSA-4-BK	Application for Child's Insurance Benefits
SSA-4-BK-SP	Solicitud Para Beneficios De Seguro Para Niños
SSA-4-INST	Reporting Responsibilities for Child's Insurance Benefits
SSA-5-BK	Application for Mother's or Father's Insurance Benefits
SSA-5-BK-SP	Application For Mother's Or Father's Insurance Benefits - Spanish
SSA-5-INST	Reporting Responsibilities for Mother's or Father's Insurance Benefits
SSA-7-F6	Application for Parent's Insurance Benefits
SSA-7-F6-SP	Application for Parent's Insurance Benefits - Spanish
SSA-8	Application for Lump-Sum Death Payment
SSA-8-SP	SOLICITUD DEL PAGO GLOBAL POR DEFUNCIÓN
SSA-10	Application for Widow's or Widower's Insurance Benefits
SSA-10-INST	Reporting Responsibilities for Widow's or Widower's Insurance Benefits
SSA-10-SP	Solicitud Para Beneficios de Seguro como Cónyuge Sobreviviente
SSA-16	Application for Disability Insurance Benefits
SSA-16-SP	Solicitud para beneficios de seguro por incapacidad
SSA-21	Supplement to Claim of Person Outside the United States
SSA-24	Application for Survivors Benefits (Payable Under Title II of the Social Security Act)
SSA-25	Certification of Election for Reduced Spouse's Benefits
SSA-44	Medicare Income-Related Monthly Adjustment Amount - Life-Changing Event
SSA-88	Pre-Approval Form for Consent Based Social Security Number Verification (CBSV)
SSA-89	Authorization for the Social Security Administration To Release Social Security Number (SSN) Verification

SSA-89-SP	Autorización para que la Administración de Seguro Social Divulgue la Verificación de un Número de Seguro Social (SSN)
SSA-131	Employer Report of Special Wage Payments
SSA-150	Modified Benefits Formula Questionnaire
SSA-199	Vocational Rehabilitation Provider Claim
SSA-263	Waiver of Supplemental Security Income Payment Continuation
SSA-308	Modified Benefits Formula Questionnaire, Foreign Pension
SSA-437-BK	Complaint Form for Allegations of Discrimination in Programs or Activities Conducted by the Social Security Administration
SSA-437-BK-SP	Formulario Para Querellas De Alegaciones De Discriminación En Los Programas De La Administración Del Seguro Social
SSA-454-BK	Continuing Disability Review Report
SSA-521	Request for Withdrawal of Application
SSA-521-SP	Solicitud Para Revocar Una Reclamación
SSA-545-BK	Plan for Achieving Self-Support
SSA-546	Worker's Compensation/Public Disability Questionnaire
SSA-561-U2	Request for Reconsideration
SSA-604	Certificate of Incapacity
SSA-632-BK	Request for Waiver of Overpayment Recovery
SSA-632-BK-SP	Solicitud de exoneración de sobrepago
SSA-634	Request for Change in Overpayment Recovery Rate
SSA-634-SP	Solicitud de cambio en la tasa de recuperación de sobrepago
SSA-640	Financial Disclosure for Civil Monetary Penatly (CMP) Debt
SSA-671	Railroad Employment Questionnaire
SSA-711	Request for Deceased Individual's Social Security Record
SSA-714	You can make your payment by Credit Card
SSA-721	Statement of Death by Funeral Director
SSA-731	Notice to Electronic Information Exchange Partners to Provide Contractor List
SSA-753	Statement Regarding Marriage
SSA-754-F5	Statement of Marital Relationship
SSA-769-U4	Request for Change in Time/Place of Disability Hearing
SSA-770-U4	Notice Regarding Substitution of Party Upon Death of Claimant Reconsideration of Disability Cessation
SSA-773-U4	Waiver Of Right To Appear - Disability Hearing
SSA-781	Certificate of Responsibility for Welfare and Care of Child
SSA-783	Statement Regarding Contributions
SSA-788	Statement of Care and Responsibility for Beneficiary

SSA-789-U4	Request for Reconsideration - Disability Cessation
SSA-795	Statement of Claimant or Other Persons
SSA-820-BK	Work Activity Report (Self-Employed Person)
SSA-821-BK	Work Activity Report
SSA-827-INST	Instructions for Completing the SSA-827
SSA-827-INST-SP	Instrucciones para completar el formulario SSA-827
SSA-1020-INST	General Instructions for Completing the Application for Extra Help with Medicare Prescription Drug Plan Costs
SSA-1021	Appeal of Determination for Extra Help with Medicare Prescription Drug Plan Costs
SSA-1021-SP	Apelación de la determinación para recibir el Beneficio Adicional con los gastos del plan de medicamentos recetados de Medicare
SSA-1021-INST	Instructions for Completing the Appeal of Determination for Extra Help with Medicare Prescription Drug Plan Costs
SSA-1021-INST-SP	Instrucciones para llenar la apelación de la determinación para recibir el beneficio adicional con los gastos del plan de medicamentos recetados de Medicare
SSA-1199	International Direct Deposit (IDD)
SSA-1372-BK	Advanced Notice of Termination of Child's Benefits
SSA-1372-BK-FC	Advanced Notice of Termination of Child's Benefits (Foreign Claims)
SSA-1372-BK-FC-SP	Aviso Por Adelantado De Cese De Beneficios Para Niños
SSA-1383	Student Reporting Form
SSA-1383-FC	Reporting to Social Security Administration by Student Outside the United States
SSA-1414	Credit Card Payment Form
SSA-1458	Certification By Religious Group
SSA-1560	Petition For Authorization To Charge And Collect A Fee For Services Before The Social Security Administration
SSA-1691	Eligible Non-Attorney Representative Application
SSA-1693	Fee Agreement for Representation Before the Social Security Administration
SSA-1694	Request for Business Entity Taxpayer Information
SSA-1696	Claimant's Appointment of Representative
SSA-1696-SUP1	Claimant's Revocation of the Appointment of a Representative
SSA-1696-SUP2	Representative's Withdrawal of Acceptance of Appointment
SSA-1699	Registration for Appointed Representative Services and Direct Payment
SSA-1724-F4	Claim for Amounts due in case of a Deceased Beneficiary
SSA-1945	Statement Concerning Your Employment in a Job Not Covered by Social Security

SSA-2010-F6	Statement for Determining Continuing Entitlement for Special Veterans Benefits (SVB)
SSA-2032-BK	Request for Waiver of Special Veterans Benefits (SVB) Overpayment Recovery or Change in Repayment Rate
SSA-2512	Pre-1957 Military Service Federal Benefit Questionnaire
SSA-2519	Child Relationship Statement
SSA-2855	Statement of Funds you Received
SSA-3033	Employee Work Activity Questionnaire
SSA-3105	Important information about your appeal, waiver rights, and repayment options
SSA-3288	Consent for Release of Information
SSA-3288-SP	Consentimiento para divulgar información
SSA-3368-BK	Disability Report - Adult
SSA-3369-BK	Work History Report
SSA-3373-BK	Function Report - Adult
SSA-3375-BK	Function Report - Child Birth to 1st Birthday
SSA-3376-BK	Function Report - Child Age 1 to 3rd Birthday
SSA-3377-BK	Function Report - Child Age 3 to 6th Birthday
SSA-3378-BK	Function Report - Child Age 6 to 12th Birthday
SSA-3379-BK	Function Report - Child Age 12 to 18th Birthday
SSA-3380-BK	Function Report - Adult - Third Party Form
SSA-3441-BK	Disability Report - Appeal
SSA-3881-BK	Questionnaire for Children Claiming SSI Benefits
SSA-3885	Government Pension Questionnaire
SSA-4111	Certification of Election for Reduced Widow(er)'s and Surviving Divorced Spouse's Benefits
SSA-4162	Child Care Dropout Questionnaire
SSA-4814	Medical Report on Adult with Allegation of Human Immunodeficiency Virus (HIV) Infection
SSA-4815	Medical Report on Child with Allegation of Human Immunodeficiency Virus (HIV) Infection
SSA-5062	Claimant's Statement about Loan of Food or Shelter
SSA-5665-BK	Teacher Questionnaire
SSA-5665-BK-SP	Cuestionario para Maestros (Teacher Questionnaire)
SSA-5666	Request for Administrative Information
SSA-7004	Request for Social Security Statement
SSA-7004-SP	Solicitud para un Estado de cuenta del Seguro Social

SSA-7008	Request for Correction of Earnings Record
SSA-7050-F4	Request for Social Security Earnings Information
SSA-7104	Partnership Questionnaire
SSA-7156	Farm Self Employment Questionnaire
SSA-7157-F4	Farm Arrangement Questionnaire
SSA-7160	Employment Relationship Questionnaire
SSA-7163	Questionnaire about Employment or Self Employment
SSA-7163A-F4	Supplemental Statement Regarding Farming Activities
SSA-8240	Authorization for the Social Security Administration to Obtain Wage and Employment Information from Payroll Data Providers
SSA-8510	Authorization for the Social Security Administration to Obtain Personal Information
SSA-L447	Medicare Savings Programs Eligible Letters
SSA-L447-SP	Cartas para saber si tiene derecho al Programa de ahorros de Medicare

These forms are available with live links at: https://www.ssa.gov/forms/ (Current as of October 20, 2022)

INDEX

(All references are to question numbers, unless otherwise noted.)

(All references are to question numbers, unless otherwise noted.)

(All references are to question numbers, unless otherwise noted.)

F

G

(All references are to question numbers, unless otherwise noted.)

(All references are to question numbers, unless otherwise noted.)

M

(All references are to question numbers, unless otherwise noted.)

(All references are to question numbers, unless otherwise noted.)

(All references are to question numbers, unless otherwise noted.)

(All references are to question numbers, unless otherwise noted.)

(All references are to question numbers, unless otherwise noted.)

(All references are to question numbers, unless otherwise noted.)

(All references are to question numbers, unless otherwise noted.)

(All references are to question numbers, unless otherwise noted.)

T

U

V

W